CONTENTS

CONTENTS

Introduction to Career Colleges

State Designation Directory

Financial Advisory Council

Profiles of Allied Members

Profiles of Career Colleges

Indexes

INTRODUCTION TO CAREER COLLEGES

ABOUT THE CAREER COLLEGE ASSOCIATION AND THE CAREER COLLEGE FOUNDATION

CAREER COLLEGE ASSOCIATION

The Career College Association (CCA) is a voluntary membership organization made up of private postsecondary schools, institutes, colleges and universities that comprise the for-profit sector of higher education. CCA's 1,350 members educate, prepare and support nearly 2 million students each year for employment in more than 200 occupational fields.

CCA member institutions cover the full spectrum of postsecondary education: from short-term certificate and diploma programs, to two- and four-year associate and baccalaureate degrees, to master's and doctoral programs. Some of the occupational fields for which CCA institutions provide programs include accounting, allied medical, automotive technology, business administration, commercial art, culinary and hospitality management, information technology, mechanical engineering, and radio and television broadcasting.

Most CCA member institutions participate in federal student financial assistance programs under Title IV of the 1965 Higher Education Act. In order to participate, the institution must be licensed by the state in which it is located, accredited by a recognized national or accrediting body, and approved by the U.S. Department of Education. Many CCA member colleges also participate in other federal, state and local education and workforce-training programs.

Career schools and colleges graduate approximately one-half of the technically trained workers who enter the U.S. workforce each year. They also provide retraining for displaced workers and skills upgrading for a wide variety of public and private employers. For more information, visit www.career.org.

CAREER COLLEGE FOUNDATION

The Career College Foundation (CCF) is a not-for-profit affiliate of the Career College Association established in 1982. CCF is dedicated to providing scholarship programs, conducting research, elevating public awareness, and honoring achievement in career education. The Foundation's bylaws direct its resources to:

- Establish scholarship award and grant programs;
- Demonstrate the value of specialized career education and improve public understanding of the role of career colleges and schools;
- Prepare reports and other up-to-date information on various aspects of career education for the use of schools, educators, researchers, government officials and the public;
- Conduct technical studies and surveys, either directly or by grant, dealing with the technical, legal, administrative, economic aspects of career education; preparing educational materials concerned with careers and career education, and publish the results;
- Present instructional opportunities for career school staff training and development; and
- Recognize individuals and organizations for their outstanding contributions to the field of career education.

Over the past seven years, the Foundation has provided more than $35 million in scholarships and grants through its *Imagine America* scholarship and award programs. CCF currently operates three national scholarship and grant programs, including the *Imagine America* high school scholarship (for graduating high school seniors), *Imagine America* Military Award Program (MAP) (for active duty or honorably discharged U.S. veterans), and the *Imagine America* II adult grant program. The *Imagine America* scholarship and award programs have received several awards from the American Society of Association Executives, including the Award of Excellence and the Summit Award for innovative education and training initiatives.

The Foundation has also continued to release its bi-annual publication, *Fact Book: A Profile of Career Colleges and Universities*. Prepared by leading industry analysts, the *Fact Book* provides important career college statistics and trends, including new information about the postsecondary market. The Foundation has also worked with the Hay Group to conduct the first ever Salary and Benefits survey of CCA members. The Foundation's publications are widely distributed and used by many government and non-government agencies and departments. For more information, visit www.imagine-america.org.

THE *IMAGINE AMERICA* SCHOLARSHIP PROGRAMS

In 1998, the Career College Foundation launched the groundbreaking *Imagine America* scholarship program to help graduating high school seniors attend participating career colleges. Over the past seven years, *Imagine America* has become the premier high school scholarship program of its kind. Each year, every high school in the United States and Puerto Rico may select three graduating high school seniors to receive a $1,000 *Imagine America* scholarship. With more than 35,000 scholarships awarded to high school students in over 10,000 high schools, *Imagine America* has provided more than $35 million in scholarship support. More than 500 career colleges participate in this program. Within the **PROFILES OF CAREER COLLEGES** section of this guide, you will notice that some school profiles contain a (*Imagine America* or Military Award Program) icon. This indicates that the school is a participating institution in one more of our scholarship programs. In addition, the **INDEXES** list participating institutions in boldface.

In 2002, the Foundation established a new adult grant program, *Imagine America* II, which complements the first *Imagine America*. This grant program was created to address the increasing costs of education and the continued lack of scholarship aid specifically designed for enrolled career college students. The *Imagine America* II program is funded through partnerships with key industry leaders, such as Bridgestone/Firestone Trust, Dell Computer Cor-

poration, Lockheed Martin, Mercedes Benz Corporation, Northrop Grumman Litton, the Fields Foundation, the Sallie Mae Fund and EMB Medical Services.

In 2004, the Foundation created the *Imagine America* Military Award Program (MAP). It is a $1,000 career education award that is available to any active duty, honorably discharged or retired veteran of a United States military service branch for attendance at a participating career college. To date, the Foundation has issued more than $1,500,000 in MAP awards. Also in 2004, the Foundation established the *Imagine America* LDRSHIP Award. This award recognizes and honors exceptional career college students. LDRSHIP stands for Loyalty, Duty, Respect, Selfless Service, Honor, Integrity and Personal Courage (LDRSHIP). Honorees are honorably discharged or active duty military personnel attending CCA member institutions. Each recipient receives up to $5,000 toward his or her career education.

HOW DO I APPLY FOR AN *IMAGINE AMERICA* SCHOLARSHIP?

Go online to www.imagine-america.org and follow the instructions listed there. If your school does not have Internet access, you may request a paper application by writing to:

Career College Foundation
Imagine America Scholarships
10 G Street NE, Suite 750
Washington, D.C. 20002

HOW TO USE THIS GUIDE

The *Guide to Career Colleges* profiles more than 1,000 private postsecondary schools, colleges and universities that provide career-specific educational programs. They offer a wide variety of postsecondary education options: from short-term certificate and diploma programs, to two- and four-year associate and baccalaureate degrees, to master's and doctoral programs in the U.S. The programs included are defined as instructional and are designed to prepare individuals with the skills and training required for entry-level employment in a specific trade, occupation or profession. The institutions profiled in this book are all licensed by the state in which they are located, accredited by at least one of the national or regional accrediting agencies recognized by the U.S. Department of Education, and are members of the Career College Association.

WHAT'S INSIDE!

Useful Articles - The first section of this book contains articles covering topics such as accreditation, financing your education and federal tax breaks for education.

State Association Directory - This directory includes a listing of state associations related to career education. Highlighted with the ☉ icon are the associations that offer scholarships to students wishing to pursue a career education.

Financial Advisory Council - Here are members from the financial and investment communities who have an interest in the for-profit career sector of higher education.

Profiles of Allied Members - This listing provides information about organizations that directly serve the career college market. These include financial aid institutions, recruiters, career consultants and other related organizations.

Profiles of Career Colleges - This section provides the main features of the institutions listed in this directory. The *Imagine America* icon represents career schools that offer the *Imagine America* scholarship program. The Military Award Program (MAP) icon represents career schools that offer the *Imagine America* Military Award Program scholarship.

Indexes - Several indexes are offered in this book. The first index is the The "Alphabetical Listing of Allied Members." The next two indexes provide a quick geographical-by-institution and alphabetical glance at who's in this book and on what page. If you know a specific school name or are looking to attend school in a particular state, these two indexes are a good place to start your search. The "Alphabetical Listing of *Imagine America* Scholarship Program Participants" and the Alphabetical Listing of Military Award Program Participants" follow. The last index lists the "Alphabetical Listing of Programs." This index is organized by profession/career objective, allowing you to search by a given discipline to see which career schools offer programs in your field of interest.

In all indexes, you will notice that some career schools appear in boldface while others do not. The boldface type indicates that the school is a participating institution in the *Imagine America* Scholarship Program.

[CD-ROM] In-Depth Descriptions - Additional details on career college offerings are provided by participating institutions. This interactive CD-ROM provides details about each institution that participates in the *Imagine America* scholarship and award programs, their special features, institutional financial aid and scholarship programs available, admissions and graduation requirements, tuition, and any degrees and certificates offered.

DATA COLLECTION PROCEDURES

The data contained in the college indexes and profiles were researched during the fall of 2005. Online surveys were made available to over 1,000 career college member institutions. With minor exceptions, data included in this edition has been submitted by officials (usually admissions officers or headquarters personnel) at the career colleges themselves. All usable information received in time for publication has been included. The omission of any particular item from the profiles or the indexes signifies that the information was either not applicable to that institution, not available, or not provided by the school. Because of our comprehensive editorial review and because all material comes directly from school officials, we believe that the information presented in this guide is accurate. Nonetheless, errors and omissions are possible in a data collection and processing endeavor of this scope. You should check with a specific career college at the time of application to verify pertinent data, which may have changed since publication.

ACCREDITING AGENCIES

Accreditation is a status granted to an institution that meets or exceeds the stated criteria of educational quality. The purposes of accreditation are to assess and enhance the educational quality of an institution, assure consistency in institutional operations, promote institutional improvement, and provide for public accountability. Accreditation functions specifically to:

- evaluate whether an institution meets or exceeds minimum standards of quality;
- assist students in determining acceptable institutions for enrollment;
- assist employers in determining the validity of programs of study and the acceptability of graduate qualifications;
- assist employers in determining eligibility for employee tuition reimbursement programs;
- enable graduates to sit for certification examinations;
- involve staff and faculty members, students, graduates, and advisory boards in institutional evaluation and planning;
- create goals for institutional self-improvement;
- provide a self-regulatory alternative for state oversight functions; and
- provide a basis for determining eligibility for federal student assistance.

Accreditation is a deliberate and thorough process and is entered into voluntarily for purposes of quality assessment and institutional enhancement. Accrediting agencies assess compliance with published administrative and academic standards and seek a continuous pursuit of excellence on the part of the institutions they accredit. As such, the accrediting agencies serve students, society and higher education, as well as their accredited institutions and entities, by striving to ensure academic excellence and ethical standards. Providing appropriate accrediting criteria and offering enhancement services to its membership are key elements in achieving these goals. Accrediting agencies perform peer assessments, pay close attention to educational trends, and maintain a commitment to requiring both ethical business and educational practices at institutions in order to promote qualitative standards, policies and procedures leading to

institutional and organizational effectiveness. The U.S. Department of Education reviews accrediting agencies to determine whether they are reliable authorities regarding educational quality. A list of all such recognized accrediting agencies is available at www.ed.gov/admins/finaid/accred/accreditation_pg6.html.

All of the institutions listed in this publication are accredited by at least one of the national or regional accrediting agencies recognized by the U.S. Department of Education. A listing of these agencies follows.

NATIONAL ACCREDITING AGENCIES

Accrediting Bureau of Health Education Schools (ABHES)
7777 Leesburg Pike, Suite 314 N.
Falls Church, Virginia 22043
Phone: 703-917-9503
Web site: http://www.abhes.org

Accrediting Commission of Career Schools and Colleges of Technology (ACCSCT)
2101 Wilson Boulevard, Suite 302
Arlington, Virginia 22201
Phone: 703-247-4212
Web site: http://www.accsct.org

Accrediting Council for Continuing Education & Training (ACCET)
1722 N Street, NW
Washington, D.C. 20036
Phone: 202-955-1113
Web site: http://www.accet.org

Accrediting Council for Independent Colleges and Schools (ACICS)
750 First Street, NE, Suite 980
Washington, D.C. 20002-4241
Phone: 202-336-6780
Web site: http://www.acics.org

Council on Occupational Education (COE)
41 Perimeter Center East, NE, Suite 640
Atlanta, Georgia 30346

Phone: 770-396-3898 or 800-917-2081
Web site: http://www.council.org

The Distance Education and Training Council (DETC)
1601 18th Street, N.W.
Washington, D.C. 20009
Phone: 202-234-5100
Web site: http://www.detc.org

National Accrediting Commission of Cosmetology Arts & Sciences (NACCAS)
4401 Ford Avenue, Suite 1300
Alexandria, Virginia 22302
Phone: 703-600-7600
Web site: http://www.naccas.org

REGIONAL ACCREDITING AGENCIES

Middle States Commission on Higher Education
3624 Market Street
Philadelphia, Pennsylvania 19104
Phone: 267-284-5000
Web site: http://www.msche.org

New England Association of Schools and Colleges (NEASC)
209 Burlington Road
Bedford, Massachusetts 01730-1433
Phone: 781-271-0022
Web site: http://www.neasc.org

North Central Association of Colleges and Schools (NCACS)
The Higher Learning Commission
30 North LaSalle Street, Suite 2400
Chicago, Illinois 60602-2504
Phone: 312-263-0456 or 800-621-7440
Web site: http://www.ncahigherlearningcommission.org

Northwest Commission on Colleges & Universities (NWCCU)
8060 165th Avenue, NE, Suite 100
Redmond, Washington 98052
Phone: 425-558-4224
Web site: http://www.nwccu.org

Southern Association of Colleges and Schools (SACS)
Commission on Colleges
1866 Southern Lane
Decatur, Georgia 30033
Phone: 404-679-4500
Web site: http://www.sacscoc.org

Western Association of Schools & Colleges (WASC)
985 Atlantic Avenue, Suite 100
Alameda, California 94501
Phone: 510-748-9001
Web site: http://www.wascsenior.org/wasc/

HOW CAREER, INCOME AND EDUCATION RELATE: THE BOTTOM LINE FOR YOUR FUTURE

The relationship between education and work – the fact that the more you invest in your education, the more you will earn – has probably been repeated so often that it has virtually become background noise. At the risk of boring you, here are educational attainment figures from the Census Bureau data:

LEVEL OF EDUCATION ATTAINED	AVERAGE ANNUAL
Bachelor's Degree	$50,623
Associate Degree	$34,744
High School Graduate	$26,795
Not a High School Graduate	$18,793

U.S. Department of Commerce, Bureau of Census Statistical Abstract of United States, 2003, Washington, D.C.

Reliable data on the incomes of career school graduates is not available, but there is other data that might provide some clues as to what these might be. A 1986 study of two-year college graduates showed that Associate degree-earners who took vocational programs had higher incomes than graduates from non-vocational programs. This difference in incomes expanded from 16 percent greater within five years after graduation to 37 percent greater within nine years after graduation. Approximately 59 percent of two-year college graduates in 1992 earned degrees in vocational programs.

FASTEST-GROWING OCCUPATIONS REQUIRE CAREER COLLEGE TRAINING

It is estimated that between 2000 and 2010, positions requiring an Associate degree will increase by 24.1%. Tables 1a, 1b and 1c have the latest projections from the Bureau of Labor Statistics of the fastest-growing occupations in the ten years from 2000 to 2010. Programs for many of these occupations are offered by schools that are represented in this book.

COLLEGE IS NOT FOR EVERYBODY

Thirty years ago, most young people went directly to work. Today, most young people go to school for more training after high school. The figures on income and education demonstrate why this is a good idea. They also demonstrate that earning a Bachelor's degree is a better option than going to vocational-technical school, but we know that a traditional college is not for everybody.

Life events often can interfere with plans to attend college. Responsibilities to a family may materialize that make it impossible to delay earning an income for four years. One may have to work and go to school. In this situation, career training that is measured in months instead of years can be the best choice.

Also, let's be real. College demands certain conventions, behaviors and attitudes that do not fit every kind of person. Whether rooted in personality or upbringing, for some individuals, the intellectual path of traditional college life and years of strict time management and postponed rewards is unsatisfying. On the other hand, the clear structure and demands of working in a real career might be an appealing alternative.

CAREER COLLEGE STUDENTS ACHIEVE THEIR GOALS

A truly positive aspect of career education is that most students who go into it are likely to complete their educational goals. Fifty-five percent of all students working toward an educational certificate (the category defining vo-tech students) complete their educational program. By contrast, only 24 percent of all students working toward an Associate degree complete their degree work, while 54 percent of all students working toward a Bachelor's degree complete their degree work. As the following chart demonstrates, these differences become even more dramatic when such factors as delaying one's education for more than a year after high school, studying part-time, or working while studying are factored in.

For most students, career education programs offer a truer chance of achievement than other alternative paths of education. The careers that can be entered provide the satisfaction of a fulfilling work life with excellent compensation. Vocational-technical education can be a lifesaver for the men and women who choose to refrain from, or postpone, going to a four-year or two-year college.

Table 1a., Industries with the Fastest Wage and Salary Employment Growth, 2000–2010

INDUSTRY DESCRIPTION	2000	2010	2000-2010	RATE OF CHANGE
Computer and Data Processing Services	2,095	3,900	1,805	6.4
Residential Care	806	1,318	512	5.0
Health Services (not elsewhere classified)	1,210	1,900	690	4.6
Cable and Pay Television Services	216	325	109	4.2
Personnel Supply Services	3,887	5,800	1,913	4.1
Warehousing and Storage	206	300	94	3.8
Water Sanitation	214	310	96	3.8
Miscellaneous Business Services	2,301	3,305	1,004	3.7
Miscellaneous Equipment Rental and Leasing	279	397	118	3.6
Management and Public Relations	1,090	1,550	460	3.6

U.S. Department of Labor Statistics. Occupational Employment Projections to 2010

Table 1b., Fastest-Growing Occupations, 2000–2010 • **Number in thousands of jobs**

OCCUPATION	EMPLOYMENT		CHANGE	
	2000	2010	NUMBER	PERCENT
Computer Software Engineers, Applications	380	760	380	100
Computer Support Specialists	506	996	490	97
Computer Software Engineers, System Software	317	601	284	90
Network and Computer Systems Administrators	229	416	187	82
Network Systems and Data Communications Analysts	119	211	92	77
Desktop Publishers	38	63	25	67
Database Administrators	106	176	70	66
Personal and Home Care Aides	414	672	258	62
Computer Systems Analysts	431	689	258	60
Medical Assistants	329	516	187	57

U.S. Department of Labor Statistics. Occupational Employment Projections to 2010

Table 1c., Occupations with the Largest Job Growth, 2000–2010 • **Number in thousands of jobs**

OCCUPATION	EMPLOYMENT		CHANGE	
	2000	2010	NUMBER	PERCENT
Combined Food Preparation and Serving Workers, Including Fast Food	2,206	2,879	673	30
Customer Service Representatives	1,946	2,577	631	32
Registered Nurses	2,194	2,755	561	26
Retail Salespersons	4,109	4,619	510	12
Computer Support Specialists	506	996	490	97
Cashiers, Except Gaming	3,325	3,799	474	14
Office Clerks, General	2,705	3,135	430	16
Security Guards	1,106	1,497	391	35
Computer Software Engineers, Applications	380	760	380	100

U.S. Department of Labor Statistics. Occupational Employment Projections to 2010

Postsecondary Students Who Attained Their Initial Degree Objective

	VOCATIONAL-TECHNICAL CERTIFICATE PROGRAMS	ASSOCIATE DEGREE PROGRAMS	BACHELOR'S DEGREE PROGRAMS
Enrollment More Than a Year After High School	54%	14%	50%
Part-time Student	41%	18%	13%
Also Worked 1- 20 Hours per Week	75%	42%	51%
Also Worked More Than 20 Hours per Week	47%	28%	40%

U.S. Department of Education, National Center for Educational Statistics. 1990 Beginning Postsecondary Students Longitudinal Study (BPS90/94), 1996, Washington, D.C.

PAYING FOR YOUR EDUCATION

The decision to attend a career college is an extremely important one. The specialized education and training will provide you with the necessary tools and knowledge needed to be successful in the career of your choice. You will have the opportunity to grow in many areas, and you will learn the skills needed to prosper in the career of your choice.

Education is an investment in your future. Before you choose your career it is necessary to consider how much time, money and commitment you have to dedicate toward preparing yourself for a career. Remember, your career goals should be reasonable and realistic in terms of your abilities, interests and values. All students are encouraged to think about the amount of financial debt that may be necessary to achieve their educational goals and objectives. In addition, students should look at the effect that student loan indebtedness can have on their future lifestyle. Choosing the right career and paying for college takes planning, forethought, dedication and commitment.

This section is designed to familiarize you with the various kinds of financial aid programs available to help you meet the costs of attending a career college. Understanding the policies and procedures necessary to obtain financial assistance is essential. Although the process may seem confusing and complicated, financial aid helps many students pay for their education. The purpose of financial aid is to assist students with their educational expenses so that financial barriers do not prevent them from achieving their educational goals.

WHAT IS FINANCIAL AID?

Financial aid is the monetary assistance available to help students pay for the costs of attending an educational institution. Such aid is provided by federal, state, institutional or private sources and may consist of grants, loans, work or scholarships. Qualified students may be offered combinations of the various types of aid or aid from a single source. Each year, billions of dollars are given or lent to students, and about half of all students receive some sort of financial aid.

Most financial aid is awarded based on an individual's

financial need, educational costs and the availability of funds. This aid is provided to students because neither they nor their families have all of the necessary resources needed to pay for an education. This kind of aid is referred to as need-based aid.

Merit-based aid is awarded to students who may or may not have financial need. Students are given assistance because they have a special skill or ability, display a particular talent, have a certain grade point average, or are enrolled in a specific program.

TYPES AND SOURCES OF FINANCIAL AID

There are several types of financial aid offered to help pay for educational expenses: grants, loans, student employment (work-study) and scholarships. Grants and scholarships are "gift aid" and do not have to be repaid. Loans are borrowed money that the borrower must pay back over a period of time, usually after the student leaves school. Student employment is normally part-time work arranged for a student during the school year. Wages received by the student are used for specific college expenses.

One main source of aid for students attending a career college is the federal government, which offers both grant and loan financial aid programs. Another source of aid is state assistance. Many states across the country provide some aid for students attending colleges in their own home states. Most state aid programs are grants, although there are a few states that offer special loan and work-study programs. Other sources of aid that award money to students are private foundations, such as corporations, civic associations, unions, fraternal organizations and religious groups. Most of these awards are not based solely on need, although the amount of the award may vary depending on financial need.

In addition, many companies offer tuition reimbursement to their employees and/or their employees' dependents. The human resources department at either your or your parent's place of employment can tell you whether or not the company offers this benefit and who may be eligible. Lastly, there are some colleges that offer awards from their own funds or from money received from various organizations. This type of aid is often referred to as "institutional aid."

GRANTS

Federal Pell Grant

Funded by the federal government, this need-based grant is available for undergraduate students who demonstrate financial need. Award amounts vary according to an eligibility index. The maximum authorized Pell Grant for a full-time student in the 2005-2006 award year is $4,050. This amount may change annually. The financial aid administrator at your institution will be able to tell you what the authorized maximum Pell Grant award is this academic year; if you may be eligible for a Pell Grant; and if so, how much you may be qualified to receive.

Federal Supplemental Educational Opportunity Grant (FSEOG)

Funded by the federal government, this need-based grant is available for undergraduate students who have exceptional financial need. FSEOG awards are determined by the institution and may range from $100 to $4,000 based on student eligibility, the number of students qualifying for FSEOG awards, and the availability of funds.

LOANS

Federal Perkins Loan

The Federal Perkins Loan is awarded on the basis of the student's demonstrated financial need. The interest rate is 5 percent, and the first payment is due nine months after leaving school. The maximum academic year award for a full-time undergraduate student is $4,000, but, like the FSEOG funds, most career colleges have very limited Perkins funding and will award what they can to the neediest students.

Subsidized Federal Stafford Loans

Subsidized Federal Stafford Loans are for students who demonstrate financial need. The interest rate on a Stafford Loan is variable but cannot exceed 8.25 percent. Up to a 4 percent origination fee may be deducted, and loan repayment begins six months after leaving school or dropping below half-time status. The government pays the interest while you are in school and during the six-month grace period. Stafford Loans have a basic ten-year repayment period, but also have several other extended repayment plans available for qualified borrowers.

Unsubsidized Federal Stafford Loans

Unsubsidized Federal Stafford Loans are for students who do not demonstrate financial need. Students may borrow within the same loan limits and at the same interest rates as the Subsidized Stafford Loan program. Up to a 4 percent origination fee may be deducted, and interest payments begin immediately. Most lenders allow students to defer payments while in school but interest continues to accrue and is added to the principal balance. Regular payments begin six months after leaving school or dropping below half-time status.

Some students may borrow additional unsubsidized loan amounts if they meet the federal definition of an independent student or have exceptional circumstances as documented by the financial aid office. (Note: The loan amounts for which you are eligible may be prorated if your program is less than thirty weeks in length.)

Federal Parent Loans for Undergraduate Students (PLUS)

The Federal PLUS Loan program enables parents of dependent students to obtain loans to pay for their child's educational costs. The interest rate for this loan is set once each year with a maximum rate of 9 percent. Parents may borrow up to the cost of attendance minus any other financial aid received by the student.

WORK-STUDY

Federal Work-Study (FWS)

The Federal Work-Study Program provides jobs for students with financial aid eligibility. It gives students a chance to earn money to help pay for educational expenses while also providing valuable work experience. Eligible students are also afforded the opportunity to perform community service work. Many career schools offer FWS, but the number of jobs available tends to be limited.

UNDERSTANDING THE COST OF ATTENDANCE

Every career college establishes an estimate of what it will cost the student to attend the school. The expenses included in the cost of attendance are usually tuition and fees, books and supplies, room and board (including food, rent and utilities), personal expenses, and transportation. The total educational expenses or budgets are referred to as the student's cost of attendance.

DETERMINING FINANCIAL AID ELIGIBILITY AND FINANCIAL NEED

Eligibility for financial aid is determined by subtracting the amount you and your parents can contribute from the cost of attendance. An assessment of your family's ability to contribute toward educational expenses is made based on the information you provide when applying for financial aid. Income, assets, size of family and number of family members in college are some of the factors considered in this calculation. This assessment, referred to as "need analysis," determines your financial need. Financial need is defined as the difference between the total cost of attendance and what you are expected to pay. Need analysis uses a formula mandated by federal legislation. It determines the ability, not the willingness, of the student and parents to finance the cost of attendance. Everyone who applies is treated equally under this analysis. The end result of the need analysis is your Expected Family Contribution (EFC), which represents the amount your family should be able to contribute toward the cost of attendance. The cost of attendance will vary at each college, but the amount your family is expected to contribute should stay the same. Financial need will vary between colleges because of each school's different cost of attendance.

DETERMINING STUDENT STATUS: INDEPENDENT OR DEPENDENT?

If you are considered dependent by federal definition, then your parents' income and assets, as well as yours, will be counted toward the family contribution. If you are considered independent of your parents, only your income (and that of your spouse if you are married) will count in the need analysis formula.

In order to be considered independent for financial aid purposes, you must meet one of the following criteria:
- be at least 24 years old;
- be a veteran of the U.S. armed forces;
- be married at the time of application;
- be an orphan or ward of the court; or, until age 18, were a ward/dependent of the court
- have legal dependents other than a spouse; or
- be a graduate or professional student.

If you can document extraordinary circumstances that might indicate independent status, you will need to show this information to the financial aid administrator at the college you will be attending. Only the financial aid administrator has the authority to make exceptions to the requirements listed above.

APPLYING FOR FINANCIAL AID

To apply for financial aid, it is essential that you properly complete the necessary forms so that your individual financial need can be evaluated. It is important to read all application materials and instructions very carefully. The application process can be a bit confusing, so remember to take it one step at a time. If you run into any problems or have specific questions, contact the financial aid office at the college you will be attending. The financial aid administrator will be happy to provide you with guidance and assistance.

Many career colleges use just one financial aid application – the Free Application for Federal Student Aid (FAFSA). This free form, published by the federal government, is available at your college's financial aid office, your local high school guidance office and state education department offices. Students can apply for federal student aid via the Internet by using FAFSA on the Web (http://www.fafsa.ed.gov). The process is self-paced and interactive with step-by-step guidance. Depending on the availability of information about your income and financial situation, the process can take as little as 20 minutes to complete. The FAFSA that students use to apply for aid for each school year becomes available in the December prior to the year in which aid is awarded. However, do not fill the form out until after January 1. (Note: You should complete the FAFSA as soon as possible after January 1. Although you may apply for aid at any time during the year, many state agencies have early cut-off dates for state aid funding.)

To complete this application you will need to gather specific family information and financial records, such as tax forms, if they are available. If they are not, you can use estimates and make corrections later. Be sure to answer all questions. Omitted information may delay processing of your application. Be sure that you and your parents (if applicable) have signed the form and that you keep a copy of the form for your records. If applying online, you and one parent (if you are dependent) will need to get a Personal Identification Number (PIN) to sign the application. You can get the PIN at www.fafsa.ed.gov. Most students now use the web-based application to apply for financial aid.

The FAFSA processing center will calculate your Expected Family Contribution (EFC) and send the information to the colleges you request. About two to four weeks after you submit your completed FAFSA, you will receive a Student Aid Report (SAR) that shows the information you reported on the FAFSA and your calculated EFC. The colleges you listed on the FAFSA will receive the same information. If you need to make any corrections, you may do so at this time. If you applied online or supplied an e-mail address, you will be notified electronically. It is very important to ensure the e-mail address you supply is accurate and that you notify the FAFSA processor if it changes.

If you are selected for verification by the school you may be asked to submit documentation that will verify the information you reported on the FAFSA. Once the financial aid office is satisfied that all of the information is correct, the college can then determine your financial need and provide you with a financial aid offer for funding your education. If you are eligible to receive aid, most schools will either mail you an award letter or ask you to come into the financial aid office to discuss your financial aid eligibility. (Note: Financial aid is not renewed automatically; you must apply each year. Often, if you are in a program that lasts for more than one year, a renewal application or electronic notification will automatically be mailed to you by the federal processor.)

STUDENT LOANS AND DEBT MANAGEMENT

More than ever before, loans have become an important part of financial assistance. The majority of students find that they must borrow money to finance their education. If you accept a loan, you are incurring a financial obligation. You will have to repay the loan in full along with all of the interest and any additional fees (collection, legal, etc.). Since you will be making loan payments to satisfy the loan obligation, carefully consider the burden your loan amount will impose on you after you leave college. Defaulting on a student loan can jeopardize your financial future. Borrow intelligently.

REPAYMENT OPTIONS

A number of repayment options are available to borrowers of federally guaranteed student loans.

- **The Standard Repayment Plan** requires fixed monthly payments of at least $50 over a fixed period of time, up to ten years. The length of the repayment period depends on the total loan amount. This plan usually results in the lowest total interest paid because the repayment period is shorter than that of other plans.

- **The Extended Repayment Plan** allows loan repayment to be extended over a longer period, generally from twelve to thirty years, depending on the total amount borrowed. Borrowers still pay a fixed amount each month (at least $50), but usually monthly payments will be less than those of the standard repayment plan. This plan may make repayment more manageable, however borrowers will usually pay more interest because the repayment period is longer.

- **The Graduated Repayment Plan** allows payments to start out low and increase every two years. This plan may be helpful to borrowers whose incomes are low initially but will increase steadily. A borrower's monthly payments must be at least half, but may not be more than one-and-a-half times, of what he or she would pay under standard repayment. As in the extended repayment plan, the repayment period will usually vary from twelve to thirty years, depending on the total amount borrowed. Again, monthly payments may be more manageable at first because they are lower, but borrowers will pay more interest because the repayment period is longer.

- **The Income Contingent Repayment Plan** bases monthly payments on adjusted gross income (AGI) and the total amount borrowed. This is currently only available to students who participate in the Direct Loan program, however some FFEL lenders and guaranty agencies provide income-sensitive repayment plans. As income rises or falls each year, monthly payments are adjusted accordingly. The required monthly payment will not exceed 20 percent of the borrower's discretionary income, as calculated under a published formula. Borrowers have up to 25 years to repay; after 25 years, any unpaid amount will be discharged and borrowers must pay taxes on the amount discharged. In other words, if the federal government forgives the balance of a loan, the amount is considered to be part of the borrower's income for that year.

COMMON QUESTIONS ANSWERED

Q: *Are a student's chances of being admitted to a college reduced if the student applies for financial aid?*

A: No. Nearly all colleges have a policy of "need-blind" admissions, which means that a student's financial need is not taken into account in the admission decision. The best advice is to apply for financial aid if the student needs assistance to attend college.

Q: *Are parents penalized for saving money for college?*

A: No. As a matter of fact, families that have made a concerted effort to save money for college are in a much better position than those that have not. For example, a student from a family that has saved money may not have to borrow as much. Furthermore, the "taxing rate" on savings is quite low – only about 5 percent of the parents' assets are assessed, and neither home equity nor retirement savings are included. For example, a single 40-year-old parent who saved $40,000 for college expenses will have about $1,100 counted as part of the parental contribution. Two parents, if the older one is 40 years old (a parent's age factors into the calculation), would have about $150 counted. (Note: The "taxing rate" for student assets is much higher – 35 percent – compared to about 5 percent for parents.)

Q: *How does the financial aid system work in cases of divorce or separation? How are stepparents treated?*

A: In cases of divorce or separation, the financial aid application(s) should be completed by the parent with whom the student lived for the longest period of time in the last twelve months (the custodial parent). If the custodial parent has remarried, the stepparent is considered a family member and must complete the application along with the natural parent. If your family has any special circumstances, you can discuss these directly with the financial aid office. (Note: Colleges that award their own aid may ask the non-custodial natural parent to complete a separate aid application and will then calculate his or her expected contribution.)

Q: *When are students considered independent of parental support in applying for financial aid?*

A: The student must be at least 24 years of age in order to be considered independent. If younger than 24, the student must be married, a graduate or professional student, have legal dependents other than a spouse, be an orphan or ward of the court, or a veteran of the armed forces. However, in very unusual situations, financial aid offices may use their professional judgment to make a student independent for financial aid.

Q: *What can a family do if a job loss occurs?*

A: Financial aid eligibility is based on the previous year's income, so the family's 2004 income would be reported to determine eligibility for the 2005-2006 academic year. In that way, the family's income can be verified with an income tax return. But the previous year's income may not accurately reflect the current financial situation, particularly if a parent loses a job or retires. In these instances, the projected income for the coming year can be used instead. Families should discuss the situation directly with the financial aid office and be prepared to provide appropriate documentation. The financial aid office will determine the most accurate estimate of current income and use this to determine eligibility for aid.

Q: *When my daughter first went to college, we applied for financial aid and were denied because our Expected Family Contribution was too high. Now my son is a high school senior and we will soon have two in college. Will we get the same results?*

A: The results will definitely be different. Both your son and your daughter should apply. As described earlier, need-based financial aid is based on your Expected Family Contribution, or EFC. When you have two children in college the parental portion of the EFC is divided in half for each child. For example, if the parent contribution for a family with one child in college is $6,000, it will be about $3,000 for each when there are two in college. The number of children in college has a big impact on determining the EFC.

Q: *I've heard about the "middle-income squeeze" in regard to financial aid. What is it?*

A: The so-called "middle-income squeeze" is the idea that low-income families qualify for aid, high-income families have adequate resources to pay for post-secondary education, and those in the middle are caught in between, not eligible for aid but also not able to pay full college costs. There is no provision in the Federal Methodology that treats middle-income students differently than others. The Expected Family Contribution (EFC) rises proportionately as income and assets increase. If a middle-income family does not qualify for aid it is because the need analysis formula yields a contribution that exceeds college costs. But keep in mind that if a $60,000-income family does not qualify for aid at a public university with a $10,000 budget, the same family will likely be eligible for aid at a private college with a cost of $25,000 or more. Also, there are now a number of loan programs available to parents and students that are not based on need. Since many of the grant programs funded by federal and state governments are directed at lower-income families, it is likely that a larger share of an aid package for a middle-income student will consist of loans rather than grants.

Q: *Given our financial condition, my daughter will be receiving financial aid. We will help out as much as we can, and in fact, we ourselves will be borrowing. But I am concerned that she will have to take on a lot of loans in order to go to the college of her choice. Does she have any options?*

A: She does. If offered a loan, she can decline all or part of it. One option is for her to ask the financial aid office to have some of the loan changed to a work-study job. If this is not possible, she can find her own part-time work. Often there is an employment office on campus that can help her locate a job. In most cases, the more she works the less she has to borrow. It is important to remember that the educational loans of-fered to students have very attractive terms and conditions with extremely flexible repayment options. Students should look upon these loans as a long-term investment that will reap significant rewards.

Q: *Is it possible to change your financial aid package?*

A: Yes. Most colleges have an appeal process. A request to change a need-based loan to a work-study job could be approved if funds are available. A request to consider special financial circumstances may also be granted. At most colleges, a request for more grant money is rarely approved unless it is based on a change in the information reported. Applicants should speak with the financial aid officer if they have a concern about their financial appeal. Some colleges may even respond to a competitive appeal; that is, a request to match another college's offer.

Q: *My son was awarded a Federal Stafford Loan as part of his financial aid package. His award letter also indicated that we could take out a PLUS Loan. How do we go about choosing our lender? Do we go to our local bank?*

A: Read the material that came with the financial aid award letter. It is likely that the college has a "preferred lender" list for Stafford and PLUS Loans. Although you can borrow from any bank, your loan application will be processed more quickly if you use a lender recommended by the college. Also, some states have programs that offer better terms than the PLUS Loan, so take a few minutes to check out this option with a financial aid officer.

Q: *I'm struggling with the idea that all students should apply to the college of their choice regardless of cost because financial aid will level the playing field. I feel I will be penalized because I have saved for college. My son has been required to save half of his allowance since age six for his college education. Will that count against him when he applies for financial aid? It's difficult to explain to him that his college choices may be limited because of the responsible choices and sacrifices we have made as a family. What can we do to make the most of our situation?*

A: In general, it is always better to have planned ahead for college by saving. Families that have put away sufficient funds to pay for college will quickly realize that they have made the burden easier for themselves and their children. In today's college financing world, schools assume that paying for higher education is a 10-year commitment, similar to a 30-year mortgage on a home or a 4-year loan for a car. By saving when your child is young, you reap significant advantages from compound interest on the assets and reduce the need to borrow as much while in school. This should reduce the number of years after college that you will be burdened with student and parent loans. We advise families to spend the student's assets first since the financial aid formulas count these assets more heavily than parental assets. Then, after the first year, you can explain to the college how you spent these assets and why you might now need additional assistance. When looking at parental information, the income of the family is by far the most important component. Contrary to popular belief, parental assets play a relatively minor role in the calculation of the EFC. With this strategy, you have done the right thing, and in the long run it should prove to be a wise financial plan.

Q: *My son was awarded a $2,500 scholarship. This can be split and used for two years. When filling out the FAFSA, do we have to claim the full amount or just the $1,250 he plans to use the first year?*

A: Congratulations to your son on the scholarship. Nowhere on the FAFSA should you report this scholarship. It is not considered income or an asset. Once you choose a school to attend, you must notify the financial aid office for their advice on how to take the funds. But remember, do NOT report it on the FAFSA.

Q: *I will be receiving a scholarship from my local high school. How will this scholarship be treated in my financial aid award?*

A: Federal student aid regulations specify that all forms of aid must be included within the defined level of need. This means that additional aid, such as outside scholarships, must be combined with any need-based aid you receive; it may not be kept separate and used to reduce your family's contribution. If the college has not filled 100 percent of your need, it will usually allow outside scholarships to close the "unmet need" gap. Once your total need has been met, however, the college must reduce other aid and replace it with the outside award. Most colleges will allow you to use some, if not all, of an outside scholarship to replace self-help aid (loans and Federal Work-Study) rather than grants or other scholarship aid.

Q: *I know we're supposed to apply for financial aid as soon as possible after January 1. What if I don't have my W-2's yet, and my tax return isn't done?*

A: The first financial aid application deadlines usually fall in early February while others are later, usually March 1st or 15th. Chances are you'll have your W-2 forms by then, but you won't have a completed tax return. If that is the case, complete the financial aid application using your best estimates. Then, when you receive the Student Aid Report (SAR), you can use your completed tax return to make corrections. One trick is to use your prior year's tax return and make whatever adjustments you think are applicable, and then complete the FAFSA with this estimated information.

Q: *Is there enough aid available to make it worthwhile for me to consider colleges that are more expensive than I can afford?*

A: Definitely. More than $65 billion in aid is awarded to undergraduates every year. With more than half of all enrolled students qualifying for some type of assistance, this averages out to more than $5,500 per student in available aid. You should view financial aid as a large, national system of tuition discounts, some given according to a student's ability and talent, others based on what a student's family can afford to pay. If you qualify for need-based financial aid, you will essentially pay only your calculated family contribution, regardless of the cost of the college. You will not pay the "sticker price" (the cost of attendance listed in the college catalog) but a lower rate that is reduced by the amount of aid you receive. No college should be ruled out until after financial aid is considered. In addition, when deciding which college to attend, consider that the short-term cost of a college education is only one criterion. If the college meets your educational needs and you are convinced it can launch you on an exciting career, a significant up-front investment may turn out to be a bargain in the long run.

Q: *If I don't qualify for need-based aid, what options are available?*

A: You should try to put together your own aid package to help reduce your parents' share. There are three sources to look into. First is to search for merit scholarships. Second is to seek employment during both the summer and the academic year. The student employment office should be able to help you find a campus job. Third is borrowing. Even if you don't qualify for the need-based loan programs, the unsubsidized Federal Stafford and Direct Loans are available to all students. The terms and conditions are the same as the subsidized loan programs except that interest accrues while you are in college. After you have contributed what you can through scholarships, employment and loans, your parents will be faced with their share of the college bill. Many colleges have monthly payment plans that allow families to spread their payments over the academic year. If these monthly payments turn out to be more than your parents can afford, they can take out a parent loan. By borrowing from the college itself, from a commercial agency or lender, or through PLUS, parents can extend the college payments over a ten-year period or longer. Borrowing reduces the monthly obligation to its lowest level but the total amount paid will be the highest due to principal and interest payments. Contact the financial aid office to discuss the many alternatives that are available.

FAMILIES' GUIDE TO EDUCATION TAX CUTS

Many tax benefits for adults who want to return to school, and for parents who are sending or planning to send their children to college, are now available due to the tax changes signed into law in August 1997. These tax cuts help make the first two years of college more affordable and give many working Americans the financial means to go back to school if they want to choose a new career or upgrade their skills. About 13.1 million students benefit – 5.9 million under the HOPE Scholarship Tax Credit and 7.2 million under the Lifetime Learning Tax Credit. The following is a guide to these tax incentive programs. For more detailed information, refer to IRS Publication 970, "Tax Benefits for Education."

HOPE SCHOLARSHIP TAX CREDIT FOR STUDENTS STARTING COLLEGE

The HOPE Scholarship program helps make the first two years of college or career schooling more affordable by providing up to $1,500 as a non-refundable tax credit. Students receive a 100 percent tax credit for the first $1,000 of tuition and required fees and a 50 percent credit on the second $1,000. This credit is available for tuition and required fees less grants, scholarships and other tax-free educational assistance.

This credit is phased out for filers above a certain income threshold. These limits are adjusted each year for inflation. Check with your financial aid office for the current rate. The credit can be claimed in two years for students who are in their first two years of college or career school and who are enrolled on at least a half-time basis in a degree or certificate program for any portion of the year. The taxpayer can claim a credit for his or her own tuition expense or for the expenses of his or her spouse or dependent children. Students must be enrolled at least half-time for at least one academic period and pursuing an undergraduate or other recognized educational credential. This credit can be claimed for more than one family member since there is no limit on the amount available to be claimed in any one year.

LIFETIME LEARNING TAX CREDIT

This tax credit is targeted at adults who want to go back to school, change careers, or take a course or two to upgrade their skills, and also at college juniors, seniors, and graduate and professional degree students. A family will receive a 20 percent tax credit for the first $10,000 of tuition and required fees paid each year for a maximum non-refundable tax credit of $2,000. Just like the HOPE Scholarship Tax Credit, the Lifetime Learning Tax Credit is available for tuition and required fees less grants, scholarships and other tax-free educational assistance. The maximum credit is determined on a per-taxpayer (family) basis regardless of the number of postsecondary students in the family, and is phased out at the same income levels as the HOPE Scholarship Tax Credit. Families will be able to claim the Lifetime Learning Tax Credit for some members of their family and the HOPE Scholarship Tax Credit for others who qualify in the same year. An eligible taxpayer must file a tax return and owe taxes to claim the credit. The taxpayer must also claim the eligible student as a dependent unless the credit is for the taxpayer or the taxpayer's spouse. Students are not required to pursue a degree or other recognized educational credential and can enroll for as few as one course. The maximum amount that can be claimed in any year is $2,000.

STUDENT LOAN INTEREST DEDUCTION

Those who have paid interest on a student loan in 2004 may be eligible to deduct up to $2,500 of the interest paid on qualified student loans. To qualify, the loan must have been taken out solely to pay qualified educational expenses and cannot be from a related person or made under a qualified employer program. This program phases out for single taxpayers with incomes between $50,000 to $65,000 and joint filers with incomes between $100,000 to $130,000.

TUITION AND FEE DEDUCTION

College students may be able to deduct qualified tuition and related expenses paid during the year for himself or herself, a spouse, or a dependent. The tuition and expenses must be for higher education but cannot include living, personal, family or related expenses. The tuition and fees deduction can reduce the student's income, subject to taxes, by up to $4,000. This tax deduction is currently scheduled to expire after the 2005 tax year.

This program is limited to single taxpayers with incomes up to $65,000 and joint filers with incomes up to $130,000 and generally helps those taxpayers who are often not eligible for the HOPE or Lifetime programs.

INDIVIDUAL RETIREMENT ACCOUNTS/COVERDALE EDUCATION SAVINGS ACCOUNT

Since January 1, 1998, taxpayers have been able to withdraw funds from an IRA without penalty for their own higher education expenses or those of their spouse, child or even grandchild. In addition, for each child under age 18, families may deposit $2,000 per year into an education IRA in the child's name. Earnings in the education IRA will accumulate tax-free, and no taxes are due upon withdrawal if the money is used to pay for postsecondary tuition and required fees, books, equipment, and eligible room and board expenses (less grants, scholarships, and other tax-free educational assistance). Once the child reaches age 30, his or her education IRA must be closed or transferred to a younger member of the family.

A taxpayer's ability to contribute to an education IRA is phased out when the taxpayer is a joint filer with an adjusted gross income between $190,000 and $220,000 or a single filer with an adjusted gross income between $95,000 and $110,000.

STATE TUITION PLANS/QUALIFIED TUITION PROGRAMS (QTPS)

Effective January 2002, withdrawals taken for qualified educational expenses from 529 plans are free from federal income tax through 2010 when a family uses a qualified state-sponsored tuition plan to save for college. Families can now use these plans to save not only for tuition but also for certain room and board expenses for students who attend college on at least a half-time basis. Tuition and required fees paid with withdrawals from a qualified state tuition plan are eligible for the HOPE Scholarship Tax Credit and Lifetime Learning Tax Credit. These benefits became available on January 1, 1998. These programs and other prepayment programs (529 plans) are currently undergoing significant changes. Many states are taking a careful look at how these programs can be modified to ensure their long-term viability. Check with the state agency that is offering the plan for further information.

GOING TO SCHOOL WHILE YOU WORK

Section 127 of the federal tax code allows workers to exclude up to $5,250 of employer-provided education benefits from their income. For courses beginning after January 1, 2002, the payments may be for either undergraduate or graduate-level courses. The payments do not have to be for work-related courses. Expenses include tuition, fees, books, equipment and supplies. Workers may be able to deduct some of the costs related to education as a business expense. This provision enables many Americans to pursue their goals of lifelong learning.

COMMUNITY SERVICE LOAN FORGIVENESS

This provision excludes from income tax student loan amounts forgiven by nonprofit, tax-exempt charitable or educational institutions for borrowers who take community service jobs that address unmet community needs. For example, a recent graduate who takes a low-paying job in a rural school will not owe any additional income tax if, in recognition of this service, her college or another charity forgives a loan it made to her to help pay her college costs. This provision applies to loans forgiven after August 5, 1997.

The AMERICORPS program also offers a number of attractive options to either help finance a college education or pay back federal student loans for students who dedicate a few years to community service. For additional information, call 800-942-2677, or visit their web site at http://www.americorps.org/.

For information on additional student aid programs that will help meet the costs of college and lifelong learning, call 800-4FED-AID.

EARLY IRA DISTRIBUTIONS

Students can take distributions from their IRAs for qualified educational expenses without having to pay the 10 percent additional tax for an early distribution. They may owe income tax on at least part of the amount distributed, but they may not have to pay the 10 percent additional tax. The part not subject to the additional tax is generally the amount of the distribution that is not more than the adjusted qualified expenses for the year. See IRS Publication 970 for more information.

EDUCATIONAL SAVINGS BOND PROGRAM

Students may be able to cash in qualified U.S. savings bonds without having to include in their income some or all of the interest earned on the bonds. A qualified

U.S. savings bond is a series EE bond issued after 1989 or a series I bond. The bond must be issued either in the student's name or in the name of both the student and his or her spouse. The owner must be at least 24 years old before the bond's issue date. The issue date is printed on the front of the savings bond. See IRS Publication 970 for more information.

SUMMARY

There are numerous tax incentives and related programs available to help students who are either planning for college, currently enrolled in higher education, or who have graduated with student loan debt. To get further information, contact the school's financial aid office, the federal government at 800-4FED AID, or an accountant or financial planner. The information presented here is offered as a guide to the many options available but should not be considered as a comprehensive explanation of the specific qualifications of each program. Please check with a qualified tax preparer for current regulations and benefits.

STATE ASSOCIATION DIRECTORY

ALABAMA
Alabama Association of Private Colleges and Schools
5355 Vaughn Road
Montgomery, AL 36116
Phone: 334.395.8800
Fax: 334.395.8859
Contact Person: Victor Biebighauser

ALASKA
Alaska Association of Private Career Educators
1415 E. Tudor Road
Anchorage, AK 99507-1033
Phone: 907.563.7575
Fax: 907.563.8330
Contact Person: Jennifer Deitz
E-mail: jdeitz@careeracademy.net

 ARIZONA
Arizona Private School Association
202 E. McDowell Road, Suite 273
Phoenix, AZ 85004
Phone: 602.254.5199
Fax: 602.254.5073
Web site: www.arizonapsa.org
Contact Person: Frederick Lockhart
E-mail: apas@eschelon.com

CALIFORNIA
California Association of Private Postsecondary Schools
400 Capitol Mall, Suite 1560
Sacramento, CA 95814
Phone: 916.447.5500
Fax: 916.440.8970
Web site: www.cappsonline.org
Contact Person: Robert Johnson, Executive Director
E-mail: Robert@cappsonline.org
Contact Person: Jamie Strong, Assistant to the Executive Director
E-mail: Jamie@cappsoline.org

COLORADO
Colorado Private School Association
1301 Pennsylvania Street, Suite 900
Denver, CO 80203
Phone: 303.863.8367

Fax: 303.860.0175
Web site: www.coloradoprivateschoolassociation.com
Contact: Steven J. Durham
E-mail: comments@coloradoprivateschoolassociation.com

CONNECTICUT
Association of Connecticut Career Schools
342 North Main Street
W. Hartford, CT 06117-2507
Phone: 860.586.7501
Fax: 860.586.7550
Contact Person: Tessa O'Sullivan
E-mail: tosullivan@associationresources.com

FLORIDA
Florida Association of Postsecondary Schools and Colleges
150 South Monroe Street, Suite 303
Tallahassee, FL 32301
Phone: 850.577.3139
Fax: 850.577.3133
Web site: www.fapsc.org
Contact Person: Cecil Kidd
E-mail: mail@FAPSC.org

ILLINOIS
Illinois Career College Association
330 North Green St.
Chicago, IL 60607-1300
Phone: 773.577.8050
Fax: 312.226.3818
Contact Person: Russell Freeman
E-mail: rtf@coyneamerican.edu

INDIANA
Indiana Association of Private Career Schools
7302 Woodland Drive
Indianapolis, IN 46278-1736
Phone: 317.299.6001
Fax: 317.298.6342
Contact Person: Barri Shirk

KENTUCKY
Kentucky Association of Career Colleges and Schools
3880 Priest Lake Drive Box 78

⑤ indicates associations that offer scholarships to students wishing to pursue a career education.

Nashville, TN 37217-4639
Phone: 615.390.7735
Fax: 615.366.9590
Contact Person: Sandy Robert
E-mail: kaccs@comcast.net

LOUISIANA
Louisiana Career College Association
13944 Airline Hwy.
Baton Rouge, Louisiana 70817
Phone: 225.752.4233
Fax: 225.756.0903
Web site: www.lacareer.org
Contact Person: Mark Worthy

$ MARYLAND
Maryland Association of Private Colleges and Career Schools
3100 Dunglow Road
Baltimore, MD 21222
Phone: 410.282.4012
Fax: 410.282.4133
Web site: www.mapccs.org
Contact Person: Diane MacDougall
E-mail: mdapcs@yahoo.com

MASSACHUSETTS
Massachusetts Association of Private Career Schools
P.O. Box 407
North Reading, MA 01864
Phone: 978.664.5146
Fax: 978.664.5154
Web site: www.mapcs.org
Contact Person: Donna Carriker
E-mail: admin@mapcs.org

MICHIGAN
Michigan Association of Career Schools
30821 Barrington
Madison Heights, MI 48071
Phone: 586.214.1475
Fax: 248.585.3774
Web site: www.careerschoolsmi.com
Contact Person: Marea Schobloher
E-mail: mschobloher@dorsey.edu
Contact Person: Joe Belliotti, President
E-mail: jbelliot@cci.edu   Phone: 313-562-4228

MINNESOTA
Minnesota Career College Association
C/O Globe College

7166 10th Street North
Oakdale, MN 55128-5939
Phone: 651.730.5100
Fax: 651.730.5151
Web site: www.mncareercolleges.org
Contact: Jeanne Herrmann

MISSOURI
Missouri Association of Private Career Schools
C/O Metro Business College
10777 Sunset Office Drive, Suite 330
Saint Louis, MO 63127-1019
Phone: 314.966.3000
Fax: 314.966.3414
Contact Person: George Holske

NEBRASKA
Nebraska Council of Private Postsecondary Career Schools
636 Circle Drive
Seward, NE 68434-1031
Phone: 402.643.2639
Fax: 402.643.6236
Contact Person: Ralph Hansen

NEW YORK
Association of Proprietary Colleges
1259 Central Avenue
Albany, NY 12205
Phone: 518.437.1867
Fax: 518.437.1048
Web site: www.apc-colleges.org
Contact Person: Ellen Hollander
E-mail: LNHOL@aol.com

The Coalition of New York State Career Schools
437 Old Albany Post Road
Garrison, NY 10524
Phone: 845.788.5070
Fax: 845.788.5071
Web site: www.coalitionofnewyorkstatecareerschools.com
Contact Person: Terence M. Zaleski
E-mail: tzaleski@sprynet.com

$ NEW JERSEY
Private Career School Association of New Jersey
P.O. Box 11795
New Brunswick, NJ 08906
Phone: 732.545.1399
Fax: 732.545.1527
Web site: www.pcsanj.com

Contact Person: Edith K. Giniger
Contact Person: L. Terry Nighan
Phone: 908.296.0704

(S)OHIO
Ohio Association of Career Colleges and Schools
1857 Northwest Boulevard – Annex
Columbus, Ohio 43212
Phone: 614.487.8180
Fax: 614.487.8190
Web site: www.members.aol.com/oaccs
Contact Person: Max J. Lerner
E-mail: oaccs@aol.com

OKLAHOMA
Oklahoma Private School Association
2620 South Service Road
Moore, Oklahoma 73160
Phone: 405.329.5627
Fax: 405.321.2763
Contact Person: Thorpe A. Mayes
E-mail: tmayes@citycollegeinc.com

OREGON
Oregon Career College Association
16700 NE 79th St., Suite 201
Redmond, WA 98052
Phone: 425.376.0369
Fax: 425.376.1065
Contact Person: Gena Wikstrom
Web site: www.washingtonschools.org
E-mail: exec@washingtonschools.org

PENNSYLVANIA
Pennsylvania Association of Private School Administrators
2090 Wexford Court
Harrisburg, PA 17112
Phone: 717.540.9010
Fax: 717.540.7121
Web site: www.papsa.org
Contact Person: Richard Dumaresq
E-mail: CCDQ@aol.com

TENNESSEE
Tennessee Association of Independent Colleges and Schools
3880 Priest Lake Drive, #78
Nashville, TN 37217-4639
Phone: 615.399.3763
Fax: 615.366.9590
Web site: www.taics.org

Contact Person: Sandy Robert
E-mail: taics@comcast.net

(S)TEXAS
Career Colleges and Schools of Texas
823 Congress St.
Suite 230
Austin, TX 78701
Phone: 512-479-0425
Web site: www.colleges-schools.org
Contact Person: Becky Squires
E-mail: bsquires@aams-texas.com

(S)VIRGINIA
Virginia Career College Association
1108 E. Main Street
Suite 1200
Richmond, VA 23219
Phone: 804.346.2783
Fax: 804.346.8287
Web site: www.va-cca.org
Contact Person: Mark Singer
E-mail: marksinger@va-cca.org

WASHINGTON
Washington Federation of Private Career Schools and Colleges
16700 NE 79th St., Suite 201
Redmond, WA 98052
Phone: 425.376.0369
Fax: 425.376.1065
Web site: www.washingtonschools.org
Contact Person: Gena Wikstrom
E-mail: exec@washingtonschools.org

WEST VIRGINIA
West Virginia Association of Independent Colleges and Schools
144 Willey Street
Morgantown, WV 26505
Phone: 304.296.8284
Fax: 304.296.5612
Contact Person: Michael K. Callen

WISCONSIN
Wisconsin Council for Independent Education
5218 E. Terrace Drive
Madison, WI 53718
Phone: 608.249.6611
Fax: 608.249.8593
Contact Person: Don Madelung
E-mail: dmadelung@msn.herzing.edu

(S) indicates associations that offer scholarships to students wishing to pursue a career education.

FINANCIAL ADVISORY COUNCIL

FINANCIAL ADVISORY COUNCIL

The Financial Advisory Council is comprised of members from the financial and investment communities who have a substantial interest in the for-profit career sector of higher education.

RYAN ALEXANDER
Noonday Asset Management
227 W. Trade St., Suite 2140
Charlotte, NC 28202
(704) 333-9192
ralexander@noonday.com

PAUL BELAND
Citigroup
388 Greenwich St., 28th Floor
New York, NY 10013
(212) 816-1829
paul.m.beland@citigroup.com

GARY BISBEE
Lehman Brothers
745 7th Ave Fl 17
New York, NY 10019-6801
(212) 526-3047
gbisbee@lehman.com

PAUL BLAVIN
Blavin & Company, Inc.
7025 N. Scottsdale Rd., Suite 230
Paradise Valley, AZ 85253
(483) 368-1513
pam@blavin.net

PIETER BOELHOUWER
Matrix Capital
1000 Winter St., Suite 4500
Waltham, MA 2451
(781) 522-4913
pboelhouwer@matrixlp.com

JAMES BURKE, JR.
Stonington Partners
767 5th Ave
New York, NY 10153-0023
(212) 339-8502
jburke@stonington.com

GREGORY CAPPELLI
Credit Suisse First Boston
227 W Monroe St Fl 41
AT&T Corporate Center
Chicago, IL 60606-5055
(312) 750-3138
greg.capelli@csfb.com

PHILLIP CLOUGH
ABS Capital Partners
400 E Pratt St., Suite 910
Baltimore, MD 21202-3116
(410) 246-5613
pclough@abscapital.com

WILL COOK
Ziff Brothers Investments
153 East 53rd Street, 44th Floor
New York, NY 10022
(212) 292-6190
wcook@zbi.com

KEN CORNICK
Arience Capital
745 5th Ave.
New York, NY 10151
(212) 303-3704
ken@ariencecapital.com

JOHN COZZI
AEA Investors LLC
65 E 55th St Fl 27
New York, NY 10022-3362
(212) 702-0504
jcozzi@aeainvestors.com

KIRSTEN EDWARDS, CFA
ThinkEquity Partners
600 Montgomery St., 8th Floor
San Francisco, CA 94111
(415) 249-1362
kedwards@thinkequity.com

KELLY FLYNN
UBS Warburg
1285 Avenue of The Americas
New York, NY 10019-6031
(212) 713-1037
kelly.flynn@ubs.com

DAVID GELOBTER
Tremblant Capital, LP
712 5th Ave, 43rd Floor
New York, NY 10019-4108
(212) 303-7347
dgelobter@tremblantcapital.com

SARA GUBINS
Merrill Lynch
4 World Financial Cener
New York, NY 10080-0001
(212) 449-2943
sara_gubins@ml.com

JAKE HENNEMUTH
Ruane, Cunniff & Co.
767 5th Ave, Suite 4701
New York, NY 10153-0023
(212) 832-5280
jakeh@ruanecunniff.com

SABRINA KAY
Fremont Private Investments, Inc.
137 N. Larchmont Blvd. #533
Los Angeles, CA 90004
(323) 933-5151
sk@sabrinakay.com

LOUIS KENTER
Prospect Partners
200 W Madison St., Suite 2710
Chicago, IL 60606-3414
(312) 782-7400
lkenter@prospect-partners.com

MARK MAROSTICA
U.S. Bancorp Piper Jaffray
800 Nicollet Mall Ste 800
Minneapolis, MN 55402-7020
(612) 303-5572
mark.a.marostica@pjc.com

GERALD ODENING
GRO Capital
151 Library Pl
Princeton, NJ 08540-3019
(609) 921-3758
godening@grocapital.com

ALEXANDER PARIS
Barrington Research
161 N Clark St., Suite 2950
Chicago, IL 60601-3206
(312) 634-6352
aparis@brai.com

DANIEL PIANKO
Ameriquest Capital Group Inc.
461 5th Ave., 8th Floor
New York, NY 10017
(212) 743-9931
dpianko@ameriquestcapital.com

JIM ROWAN
Legg Mason Wood Walker, Inc.
100 Light Street, 34th Floor
Baltimore, MD 21202
(216) 430-1734
jrherman@leggmason.com

JOSEPH SANBERG
Tiger Technology Management
101 Park Ave.
New York, NY 10178
(212) 984-2596
jsanberg@tiger-tech.com

TIM SCHENK
Blue Ridge Capital
122A E Main St
Charlottesville, VA 22902-5220
(434) 923-8901
tim@blueridgelp.com

JOHN SMART
Harris Nesbitt
111 W Monroe St
20th Floor East
Chicago, IL 60603-4096
(312) 461-6022
john.smart@harrisnesbitt.com

TRACE URDAN
Robert W. Baird & Company Inc.
111 Sutter St.
Suite 1800
San Francisco, CA 94111
(415) 733-6728
turdan@rwbaird.com

TOM VANDENBERG
Washington Analysis
1120 Connecticut Ave., NW
Suite 400
Washington, DC 20036
(202) 756-7714
tvandenberg@washingtonanalysis.com

LARA VAUGHAN GORDON
Parchman, Vaughan & Company
717 Light St
Suite 200
Baltimore, MD 21230-3851
(410) 244-8971
lara@parchmanvaughan.com

CLARK WEBB
Select Equity Group
380 Lafayette St
Sixth Floor
New York, NY 10003-6933
(212) 475-3624
ccw@selectequity.com

GREGORY WILSON
CIVC Partners, LLC
191 N. Wacker Dr. Ste. 1100
Chicago, IL 60606
(312) 873-7300
gwilson@civc.com

PROFILES OF ALLIED MEMBERS

CCA's ALIIED AND ALLIED PLUS MEMBERS

provide invaluable services to the career college sector. *denotes all Allied Plus Members

800RESPONSE

200 Church Street
Burlington, VT 05401
Contact: Ms. Laura Noonan, Vice President Marketing
& Corporate Communications
Phone: 800-NEW-SALES
Fax: 802-860-0395
lnoonan@800response.com
www.800response.com

SERVICES: MARKETING

Increase advertising response rates by 30-50% with a custom 800 number. 800response is the premier provider of vanity 800 service and offers the broadest selection of custom 800 numbers available today. Services include counsel on selection of the most appropriate 800 number for businesses, a sophisticated call-routing platform, call recording and extensive real-time, call-tracking reports that provide invaluable demographic information. There are many benefits to using custom 800 numbers as response mechanisms in advertising. They are easy to remember, trackable and recordable. The principals of 800response have over 30 years experience in the industry and are continually developing innovative ways for businesses to market their products and services. For more information, visit our web site or call 1-800-NEW-SALES.

ABACUS MERGERS & ACQUISITIONS

11404 Harbor Blvd., Suite 101
Frisco, Texas 75035
Contact: Mr. Philip Balis, President
Phone: 972-731-7890
Fax: 972-692-8887
PBalis@AbacusMA.com
www.AbacusMA.com

SERVICES: CONSULTING

Abacus Mergers & Acquisitions specializes in school sales, mergers and acquisitions. Our services include valuing schools, preparing marketing packages, find-ing prospective buyers or sellers, advising owners contemplating selling, assisting with negotiations, locating acquisition financing, and assisting with issues arising with due diligence, the definitive agreement and closing. We work with our clients from start to finish - you can count on Abacus.

ACT, INC.

500 ACT Drive
Iowa City, Iowa 52243
Contact: John Roth
Phone: 319-337-1660
Fax: 319-337-1200
John.roth@act.org

SERVICES: TESTING TOOLS AND EQUIPMENT

The Career Programs Assessment Test (CPAT) from ACT (a nonprofit testing organization) is a complete basic skills assessment for career colleges to use as an admissions and advising tool. CPAT was developed specifically to meet the needs of career colleges.

ADx, INC.

23172 Plaza Pointe Dr., Suite 135
Laguna Hills, California 92653
Contact: Judith Munoz, V.P. Marketing
Phone: 949-581-5377 x212
JudyM@adxinc.net
www.adxinc.net

SERVICES: ADVERTISING, MARKETING, RECRUITMENT

ADx is an advertising agency specializing in print materials designed to boost enrollment, enhance recruitment and create dynamic product marketing programs for educational schools and corporations. Our services include ad campaigns, brochures, billboards, stand-alone pieces, public relations, media placement and other related capabilities.

AFFILIATED COMPUTER SERVICES

One World Trade Center, Suite 2200
Long Beach, California 90831
Contact: Ms. Tracy Powell, Director
Phone: 803-329-9067
Tracy.powell@acs-inc.com

www.acs-inc.com/education

SERVICES: ADMINISTRATIVE SERVICES, FINANCIAL AID, IT SOLUTIONS, STUDENT FINANCIAL AID

ACS delivers enrollment optimization and financial aid administration services, which improve student service, financial aid cash flow and cycle times. Career colleges rely on ACS to advise students of their financial aid options, track and move students through the entire process, gather and submit required documents, and ensure they meet all deadlines to start classes on times. ACS handles the burdensome back-office processes associated with delivering financial aid, including student eligibility and certification, award notification and disbursements, and refund processing and reporting. These services are critical for sustaining and growing student enrollments and can help reduce operating costs while helping ensure compliance.

ACS processed financial aid for over 250,000 students across 55 campuses and disbursed $1.5 billion in financial aid in 2004. ACS also provides information technology outsourcing, imaging, student call centers, loan servicing, finance and accounting, and other services to more than 1,000 colleges and universities.

AlaQuest International, Inc.

28 Molasses Hill Road
Lebanon, New Jersey 08833-3206
Contact: Ms. Marsha Magazzu, President
Phone: 908-713-9399
Fax: 908-713-9288
sales@alaquest.com
www.alaquest.com

SERVICES: ADMINISTRATIVE SERVICES, SOFTWARE, ADMISSIONS, ADVERTISING, FINANCIAL AID, IT SOLUTIONS, MANAGEMENT SEARCH, PLACEMENT, RECRUITMENT, RETENTION, SOFTWARE, STUDENT FINANCIAL AID, TUITION FINANCING

AlaQuest International is solely dedicated to the research, development, sales and support of administrative software products for the postsecondary educational marketplace. AlaQuest has products for admissions, scheduling, grades, attendance, student accounts, financial aid, placement, housing, alumni, book sales and more.

Alexander, Kavanagh, Snyder and Lang, P.C.

7935 Perry Highway
Pittsburgh, Pennsylvania 15237

Contact: Mr. John H. Alexander, CPA
Phone: 412-364-6644
Fax: 412-364-8012
jayalex@kavcpa.com

SERVICES: CPA

Certified Public Accountants specializing in trade and technical schools, as well as non-profit educational institutions. Services provided by the firm include, but are not limited to, financial aid audits, consulting, financial statement audits, including OMB 133 audits, and implementation and reporting for retirement plans, including 401k plans.

Almich & Associates

19000 MacArthur Blvd
Suite 610
Irvine, California 92612
Contact: Mr. Robin Almich, Managing Partner
Phone: 949-475-5410
Fax: 949-475-5412
leighann@almichcpa.com
www.almichcpa.com

SERVICES: CPA, CONSULTING, FINANCIAL AID

Almich & Associates is a Certified Public Accounting and Business Services firm that specializes in the education, health care and not-for-profit industries. We offer a variety of valuable accounting and business solutions and have been nationally acknowledged as one of the foremost experts providing professional services in this highly regulated market. Some of our services include Financial Statement Analysis and Financial Statement Audits; Title IV Planning and Audits; Income Tax Planning and Preparation Services; Acquisition, Divestiture and Change of Ownership Planning and Implementation.

AMDG

200 Galleria Parkway, Suite 2000
Atlanta, Georgia 30339
Contact: Mr. Gregory M. Morse, Chairman
Phone: 770-431-5115
Fax: 770-234-5299
gregmorse@amdg.ws
www.amdg.ws

SERVICES: DISTANCE EDUCATION, ELEARNING PROVIDERS, EDUCATIONAL/TRAINING MATERIALS, EDUCATION MANAGEMENT, MISCELLANEOUS, PLACEMENT, RECRUITMENT, TRAINING PROVIDERS

AMDG is one of the nation's most comprehensive education institutions providing student-centered Internet and site-based education programs to learners of all ages. These programs include integrated solutions for accredited online curriculum, high school diplomas, certified training, recruiting, screening and job placement services for government and Fortune 500 organizations. AMDG graduates are better qualified, better trained, more motivated and enjoy a consistent job placement rate of 98%.

AMERICAN EDUCATION CORPORATION

7506 N. Broadway Extension
Oklahoma City, OK 73116
Contact: Mr. Paul Billingsley, V.P. Higher Education
Phone: 405-840-6031
Fax: 405-848-3960
paulb@amered.com
www.advancerlearning.com

SERVICES: ADMISSIONS, ASSESSMENT, DISTANCE EDUCATION, PLACEMENT, RETENTION, SOFTWARE
The publisher of A+dvancer College Readiness Online, a series of prescriptive assessments that identify college entry-level skills deficiencies in Arithmetic, Elementary Algebra, Reading Comprehension and Sentence Skills. A+dvancer can then automatically prescribe and deliver web-based, direct instructional curriculum designed in the universally accepted study, practice, mastery format. The assessment and instructional components may also be deployed independently for separate diagnostic or instructional uses.

AMERICAN MEDICAL TECHNOLOGISTS

710 Higgins Road
Park Ridge, Illinois 60068-5737
Contact: Christopher A. Damon, J.D., Executive Director
Phone: 847-823-5169
Fax: 847-823-0458
mail@amt1.com
www.amt1.com

SERVICES: CERTIFICATION
Established in 1939, AMT has become one of the nation's largest and most established certification agencies for clinical laboratory practitioners and other allied health professionals. AMT provides certification for medical technologists, medical laboratory technicians, office laboratory technicians, laboratory consultants,

phlebotomy technicians, medical and dental assistants and allied health instructors.

BALL & McGRAW, P.C.

351 W. Hatcher
Phoenix, AZ 85021
Contact: Mr. Douglas Ball, Director
Phone: 602-942-3435
Fax: 602-942-8555
ballmcgraw@worldnet.att.net

SERVICES: CPA
Ball & McGraw, P.C., are Certified Public Accountants that provide financial statement audits, Title IV compliance audits, composite score calculation and analysis, change of ownership audits and consulting, file reviews, and internal auditing.

BECKERMEDIA

2633 Telegraph Ave.
Oakland, California 94612
Contact: Mr. Roger Becker, President
Phone: 510-465-6200 x101
Fax: 510-465-6056
roger@beckermedia.net
www.beckermedia.net

SERVICES: ADVERTISING, MARKETING
Becker Media creates full-service advertising campaigns for TV, radio, print and the Web. Becker Media specializes in strategic media selection, strategic planning, and creativity that generates results.

BEELINE WEB SITE PROMOTIONS INC.

Universities, Colleges & Trade Schools
Contact: Ched Gaglardi
Tel: 250.766.2589
Fax: 509.561.2909
E-mail: Ched@beelineweb.com
www.Beelineweb.com
www.Trade-schools.net

SERVICES: MARKETING, LEAD GENERATION
Give your school world-wide exposure through top placement on search engines with Beeline Web Site Promotions. We specialize in pay-per-lead search engine marketing of

colleges and trade schools through organic search engine positioning and other online marketing strategies.

All our sites are owned, operated, and promoted entirely by us, and all leads are generated from these sites, including our high-exposure education portal at www. trade-schools.net. We deliver qualified leads that meet the criteria set by the individual schools. The result is lower cost per enrollment. There are no delays; lead referrals occur in real-time. There are no set-up or administration fees, no long-term commitments, and you can cancel at any time. Our current clients tell us our conversion of inquiries to students is one of the highest they've experienced. Get to the top with Beeline.

BEST ASSOCIATES
2200 Ross Avenue, Suite 3800
Dallas, TX 75201
Contact: Leslie Eisenbraun, Partner
Phone: (214) 438-4100
Fax: (214) 438-4133
leisenbraun@bestassociates.com
www.bestassociates.com

SERVICES: INVESTMENT BANKING
Has a strong commitment to the education industry and a track record of exceptional results. The for-profit education sector will continue to grow rapidly over the next decade. Best Associates is investing in both the K-12 and postsecondary markets here and abroad. The firm acquires companies with proven leadership and a global vision and founds companies in the sector.

*BOAZ PAYMENT SYSTEM
Mr. Matt Tanzy
1000 Holcomb Woods Parkway
Suite 110
Roswell, GA 30076
(800) 358-2763 ext. 1629
smtanzy@boazgroup.com
www.boazgroup.com

SERVICES: CREDIT CARD PAYMENTS

THE BOSTON EDUCATIONAL NETWORK
399 US Highway 4, Suite B
Barrington, NH 03825
Contact: Mr. Paul Zocchi, President
Phone: 603-868-8184

Fax: 603-868-3906
pzocchi@boston-ed.com
www.boston-ed.com

SERVICES: ADMINISTRATIVE SERVICES, CONSULTING, FINANCIAL AID, SOFTWARE
The Boston Educational Network is a consulting/processing/administrative software firm provides unsurpassed personal service to all types of postsecondary educational schools. Our user-friendly, internet-based systems and services - which include financial aid processing, staff training, accreditation assistance and our internet-based administrative software program, Masters - are priced at a very affordable coast. We pride ourselves on delivering value to our clients in the form of quality recommendations and strategies that work. Let former school owners, directors and financial aid officers join your team in maximizing your school's potential.

BOSTON SEARCH GROUP, INC.
224 Clarendon Street
Boston, Massachusetts 02116
Contact: Mr. Ralph Protsik, Managing Director
Phone: 617-266-4333
Fax: 781-735-0562
rprotsik@bostonsearchgroup.com
www.bostonsearchgroup.com

SERVICES: CONSULTING, MANAGEMENT SEARCH
A national leader in retained executive search within the career education and eLearning domains. Specializes in providing leaders for both public and private companies, and it does so with a keen appreciation for the unique requirements of each type of organization. Since 1994, its principals have been engaged to fill more than 100 senior-management positions at the VP level and above.

BRUSTEIN & MANASEVIT
3105 South Street, NW
Washington, DC 20007-4419
Contact: Mr. Leigh Manasevit, Partner
Phone: 202-965-3652
Fax: 202-965-8913
bruman@bruman.com

SERVICES: LEGAL SERVICES
Brustein & Manasevit counsels institutions participating in the Title IV federal financial aid programs. Brustein & Manasevit litigates adverse audits and program reviews;

challenges cohort default rate calculations; and assists with certification and reinstatement applications, accreditation, licensing, and change of ownership issues.

*CAMPUS MANAGEMENT CORPORATION
777 Yamato Rd, Suite 400
Boca Raton, Florida 33431
Contact: Ms. Carol Shear, Director of Sales
Phone: 866-397-2537
Local: 561-999-9904
Fax: 561-999-0096
www.campusmgmt.com

SERVICES: SOFTWARE, ADMISSIONS, ADMINISTRATIVE SERVICES, FINANCIAL AID, DISTANCE EDUCATION, PLACEMENT, EDUCATION MANAGEMENT, ELEARNING PROVIDERS, MARKETING, RECEIVABLES MANAGEMENT, RECRUITMENT, RETENTION, STUDENT FINANCIAL AID

Campus Management Corp. is a leading provider of software and systems technology to the postsecondary education community.

More than 900 colleges across the nation have chosen Campus Management's fully integrated administrative software systems to manage their daily operations.

CCASSURE
901 Dulaney Valley Road
Suite 610
Towson, Maryland 21204
Contact: Mr. Jon Stone Goff
Phone: 800-899-1399
Fax: 410-494-1725
jsgoff@mimsintl.com
www.ccassure.com

SERVICES: INSURANCE

CCAssure Career College Insurance – put your insurance program to the test. Coverages include complete liability, property, automobile, and crime and fiduciary. MIMS International, the programs administrator, has also developed a surety program to meet your needs.

CERTIPORT, INC.
1276 S. 820 E

Suite 200
American Fork, UT 84003-3537
(801) 847-3100
Fax: (801) 492-4118
www.certiport.com

SERVICES: CERTIFICATION, EDUCATIONAL TRAINING, TEST/ TOOL/EQUIPMENT

Certiport provides industry-leading training, assessment and certification solutions that enable individuals to develop the skills necessary to achieve more, distinguish themselves, and advance in today's academic and business environments. These solutions include the Microsoft® Office Specialist Certification and the Internet and Computing Core Certification (IC³ ®), delivered in 20 languages and 128 countries through a channel of more than 9,000 Certiport Centers worldwide. Certiport is a pioneer in using pervasive testing technology and data management systems based on extensive research and professional validation processes.

*CHAMPION COLLEGE SOLUTIONS, FORMERLY HANDS ON, INC.
1201 S. Alma School Rd., Suite 15000
Mesa, Arizona 85210
Contact: Ms. Mary Lyn Hammer
Phone: 480-947-7375 or 800-761-7376
Fax: 480-947-7374
marylyn.hammer@championcollegesolutions.com
www.ChampionCollegeSolutions.com

SERVICES: DEFAULT MANAGEMENT, PLACEMENT, COLLECTION SERVICES, CONSULTING, MISCELLANEOUS, RECRUITMENT MANAGEMENT

Champion College Solutions, established in 1989 as Hands On College Services, is a respected advocate for higher education. By leveraging strategic industry partnerships and integrated knowledge sources, Champion College Solutions delivers unrivaled operating results to institutions; confidence to lenders; and financial and life skills to students. Our portfolio of offerings includes proven-successful Default Prevention, outstanding Skip Tracing, accurate Placement Verification and results-driven Education Debt Recovery.

CISCO SYSTEMS, INC./CISCO NETWORKING ACADEMY PROGRAM
8865 Stanford Blvd. Ste. 201
Columbia, MD 21045

Contact: Ms. Judy Roberts
Phone: 410-309-4818
jurobert@cisco.com
www.cisco.com/go/netacad

SERVICES: IT SOLUTIONS, eLEARNING PROVIDERS
Launched in 1997, the Cisco Networking Academy Program is a comprehensive eLearning program, which provides students with the internet technology skills essential in a global economy. The Networking Academy program delivers web-based content, online assessment, student performance tracking, hands-on-labs, instructor training and support, and preparation for industry standard certifications. For more information, please visit the web site.

CLAIRVEST GROUP, INC.
22 St. Clair Ave. East
Toronto, Ontario M4T 253
Contact: Mr. Mitch Green, Vice President
Phone: 416-925-9270
Fax: 416-925-5753
mitchg@clairvest.com
www.clairvest.com

SERVICES: INVESTMENT BANKING, INVESTMENT MANAGEMENT
Clairvest is a private equity firm that forms investment partnerships with entrepreneurial corporations in a variety of industries. We traditionally invest $10 to $25 million in our partners' businesses and consider both minority and control positions. We seek to be a value-added investor supporting a management team in the education industry that is aggressively growing a business, either organically or through acquisitions.

COLE AND WEBER/RED CELL
308 Occidental Ave. South
Seattle, WA 98104
Contact: Mr. Dave Behn, Director Performance Marketing
Phone: 206-436-3738
Fax: 206-624-7092
dave.behn@cwredcell.com
www.cwredcell.com

SERVICES: ADVERTISING, CONSULTING, IT SOLUTIONS, MARKETING, MEDIA, RECRUITMENT
Cole & Weber/Red Cell is a full-service advertising agency based in Seattle and owned by WPP, one of the world's largest advertising companies. Our general advertising clients include Nike, Microsoft and Gallo, but educators often value our performance-based lead generation programs. We specialize in cost-per-action online advertising and have been active in online education since 1997. Routinely among our clients' top lead performers (volume and matriculation), we currently partner with University of Phoenix, DeVry University, Ellis College and many more.

*THE COLLEGEBOUND NETWORK
1200 South Ave. #207
Staten Island, New York 10314
Contact: Mr. Mario Lupia, Director Online Marketing
Phone: 718-761-3800 ext. 103
Fax: 718-761-1035
MLupia@collegebound.net
www.collegesurfing.com

SERVICES: ADVERTISING, MARKETING, MEDIA, RECRUITMENT
The CollegeBound Network's Lead Generation Division specializes in recruitment lead generation solutions for colleges, universities and career schools. Our services, which include Internet marketing, search marketing, e-marketing, direct marketing, telemarketing, event marketing and print media solutions, are designed to increase education institutions' brands and reach amongst America's leading candidates seeking educational and professional growth.

*COLLEGIATE HOUSING SERVICES
5175 E. 65th St.
Indianapolis, IN 46220-4816
Contact: David Neal
Phone: 317-920-2600
Fax: 317-920-2608
dneal@housingservices.com
www.housingservices.com

SERVICES: HOUSING
Collegiate Housing Services provide career colleges, community colleges and universities a customized housing service, focused on the necessary components of providing an affordable and positive living experience for their students.

With expertise in property development and management, as well as university resident life and student services, we are focused on developing the most comprehensive student housing solutions.

*Comcourse

111 1/2 Cooper Street
Santa Cruz, CA 95060
Contact: Dr. David Grebow
Phone: 1-800-800-1NET
Toll-Free: 831-401-2720
david@comcourse.com
www.comcourse.com

An innovative provider of "end-to-end" online degree and certificate programs for career colleges. Comcourse premier programs are provided under a revenue sharing model, with no other financial commitment to Comcourse. We offer the quickest and best route to delivering online courses to your students. Our course materials have already been successfully presented in accordance with ACCSCT standards, and we have been working carefully to ensure that our materials meet - and exceed - the standards of other accrediting bodies as well. Our programs are all developed and managed by industry leaders. We currently have Allied Health, Business, IT and Criminal Justice programs ready to go.

CONTACT Direct Marketing

2091 E. Murray-Holladay Road, Suite 21
Salt Lake City, Utah 84117
Contact: Mr. Eric Schanz, President
Phone: 1-866-USE-CONTACT (873-2668)
Fax: 801-942-9282
www.contactdm.com

SERVICES: Advertising, marketing

CONTACT Direct Marketing is a full-service direct marketing company. We specialize in eye-catching, innovative direct mail packages. Supercharge your direct marketing efforts with our new Click to CONTACT service. It gives you an online response option that delivers leads to you in real-time. You can count on CONTACT Direct Marketing for expeditious turnaround and superior customer service. For more information, please visit www.contactdm.com.

Corporate Educational Resources, Inc.

225 Gulf Shore Blvd., Ste. 702
Naples, Florida 34103
Contact: Mr. John Huston, President
Phone: 239-263-1200
Toll-Free: 888-861-9001
john@corp-ed.com
www.corp-ed.com

SERVICES: Consulting, miscellaneous, recruitment, admissions, IT solutions, retention

CER was developed to provide colleges with services to improve processes and efficiencies in their admissions, operations and academic departments. Prospect Manager (PMx) was software developed to improve management of leads, conversion rates and electronic target marketing follow-up of leads. Document Retrieval System (DRS) is used to improve management of student information files and bring efficiencies to all departments. DRS produces efficiency in document storage, time of development, retrieval time and reduces chances of lost documents. Classroom Performance System (CPS) is a revolutionary tool that brings ultimate interactivity to the classroom. CPS is a wireless response system that gives faculty immediate feedback from every student in the class for classes of any size. CPS stimulates class discussion with subjective and objective questions using CPS's ad hoc or formal question-authoring capabilities. Research gives evidence of students' learning processes, cognitive engagement and improved desires to attend class. CPS software gives access to easy test development, electronic grading and grade book, leaving the faculty time for other important responsibilities.

Corvus, LLC

53 East North Street
York, Pennsylvania 17403
Phone: 717-845-5600
Fax: 717-845-5620
info@corvusllc.com
Contact: Mr. Loren H. Kroh, President

SERVICES: Retention

Corvus, LLC (http://www.corvusllc.com) is the leader in innovative student success technologies such as GradMax and Campus ToolKit. Campus ToolKit is a holistic approach to improved communications, enhanced student self-understanding, and at-risk student identification and support. Earlier versions of the system have increased student persistence as much as 42 percent and the newest version includes many more features. Best of all, we are now able to provide the system at NO COST to the institution.

*CUnet

445 West Main Street

Wyckoff, New Jersey 07481
Contact: Mr. Tom Ferrara, CEO
Phone: 201-560-1230
Fax: 201-560-1677
Tom@CUnetCorp.com
www.CUnetCorp.com

SERVICES: ADMISSIONS, ADVERTISING, CONSULTING, EM-
PLOYEE ASSESSMENT, MARKETING, SOFTWARE,
PPC MANAGEMENT SERVICES, VENDOR LEAD
MANAGEMENT SYSTEMS, MISCELLANEOUS

CUnet is an established leader and innovator in the education marketing and managed services industry, acting
as a high-quality lead provider and as firm's Agency of
Record in many instances. CUnet currently provides
more than 2,000 schools (online and campus) with
performance-based advertising and lead generations.
In addition, CUnet utilizes industry-leading motivation and career assessments and professional services
to improve their clients "lead to enrollment" conversion rates, as extensive school listing on their flagship
education portal http://www.Collegeand University.net.
CUnet has secured strategic partnerships with leading
media properties across the country, allowing them to
power the education section for over 1,300 geographi-
cally targeted newspapers, network TV stations and radio stations, as well as career and major portal brands
on the web. The networks in partnership with CUnet
are major players in the industry, including ABC, NBC,
CBS, FOX, *Boston Herald*, *The Star Ledger*, Infinity
Radio, Clear Channel, Excite and iWon. CUnet provides schools with highly specific, relevant and targeted
education leads and marketing services. For additional
information, visit http://www.cunetcorp.com or http://
www.CollegeandUniversity.net.

CUSHMAN & WAKEFIELD

601 S. Figueroa St., 47th Floor
Los Angeles, California 90017
Contact: Mr. Jeffery M. Woolf
Phone: 213-955-6467
Fax: 213-955-5120
Jeff_Wolf@cushwake.com
www.cushwake.com

SERVICES: REAL ESTATE INVESTMENT

Cushman and Wakefield is an international commercial
real estate brokerage company with a heavy emphasis
on career college work.

D

*DATAMARK

2305 Presidents Drive
Salt Lake City, Utah 84120
Phone: 800-279-9335
Fax: 801-886-0102
www.datamark.com
E-mail: info@datamark.com
Contact: Mr. Tom Dearden, President and CEO

SERVICES: ADVERTISING/MARKETING/MEDIA/RECRUITING/
RETENTION/ADMISSIONS

Datamark is the nation's leading strategic marketing company exclusively for colleges and proprietary
schools. It provides comprehensive lead generation,
lead conversion, student retention and business growth
solutions that include direct mail, e-marketing, media,
custom research and admissions training.

Since 1987, Datamark's marketing experts have produced unparalleled results through Datamark's hallmark research- and technology-based strategies.

DAVID S. SHEFRIN AND ASSOCIATES, LLC

14301 N. 87th St., Ste. 208
Scottsdale, Arizona 85260
Contact: Mr. David Shefrin
Phone: 480-556-0631
Fax: 480-556-0638
mail@dshefrin.com
www.careerschoolconsulting.com

SERVICES: CONSULTING, RECRUITMENT, MANAGEMENT SEARCH

A private career school consulting group that provides
executive search services, as well as merger and acquisition services to both buyer and seller, primarily to the
career college sector. David Shefrin has over 25 years
of industry experience; previously, he owned one of the
largest computer training school operations in the Northeast. Offices on both West and East coasts allow David S.
Shefrin & Associates to effectively handle clients' needs.
For a list of our most recent schools sold and to whom, as
well as a list of our most recent placements, see our web
site at www.careershoolconsulting.com

DEBORAH JOHN & ASSOCIATES, INC.
108 West Main Street
Mulvane, Kansas 67110-1763
Contact: Ms. Deborah John, President
Phone: 800-242-0977
Fax: 316-777-1703
djainfo@gotodja.com
www.gotodja.com

SERVICES: FINANCIAL AID
Deborah John & Associates (DJA) offers comprehensive financial aid servicing and consulting to Title IV institutions in the postsecondary sector. Since the founding of DJA in 1988, we have seen our clientele increase substantially as a result of our years of experience and commitment to quality. Our growing staff of financial aid professionals is dedicated to providing personalized service with professional results. Additionally, DJA utilized EFAS (Electronic Financial Aid Servicing from DJA), which is a streamlined approach to administering the Title IV programs. The services offered by DJA are both comprehensive and cost-effective, in addition to serving as an invaluable check and balance on your financial aid administration.

*DELL COMPUTER CORPORATION
1 Dell Way
Round Rock, Texas 78682-7000
Contact: Mike Merrill
Phone: 512-728-8718
Fax: 512-283-6590
mike_merrill@dell.com

SERVICES: COMPUTER HARDWARE/CONSULTING/DISTANCE EDUCATION/E-LEARNING PROVIDERS/ EDUCATIONAL TRAINING/INFORMATIONAL TECHNOLOGY SOLUTIONS
The world's leading direct computer systems company, Dell offers an exclusive discount-pricing program to CCA members for institutional and personal purchases. The newest product lines, including switches and projectors; information about the Dell/EMC alliance; and a customized, online catalog are available at http://www.dell.com/hieci/cca or by calling the personal account team at 800-274-7799 (toll-free). Dell works to provide CCA members with high-qualitycomputer equipment and award winning service for the best price.

DIAMOND D, INC.
P.O. Box 235
Kingsburg, California 93631
Contact: Ms. Dianna Atwood, President
Phone: 559-897-7872
Fax: 559-596-1030
dianna@diamondD.biz
www.DiamondD.biz

SERVICES: SOFTWARE
Diamond D, Inc. was founded on the thought that our School Management database system has many facets, like a diamond, that all fit together and become one high quality gem. That gives you the clarity of where your school is going. Among these, we consider the quality of our software, the support provided by our staff, and our setup and end-user training services to be most critical.

DICKSTEIN SHAPIRO MORIN & OSHINSKY, LLP
2101 L Street, N.W.
Washington, DC 20037
Contact: Mr. Neil Lefkowitz, Partner
Phone: 202-828-2260
Fax: 202-887-0689
LefkowitzN@dsmo.com
www.DicksteinShapiro.com

SERVICES: LEGAL
Dickstein Shapiro Morin & Oshinsky LLP, founded in 1953, is a multiservice law firm with more than 325 attorneys in offices in Washington, DC, and New York City. Dickstein Shapiro has significant experience in representing postsecondary proprietary educational companies in merger and acquisition and finance transactions. Dickstein Shapiro also advises postsecondary proprietary educational companies on a full range of legal matters, including insurance coverage; litigation, including securities litigation; employment and employee benefits; tax; and intellectual property.

DOW LOHNES & ALBERTSON, PLLC
1200 New Hampshire Avenue NW, Suite 800
Washington, DC 20036-6802
Contact: Mr. Michael Goldstein, Member
Phone: 202-776-2000
Fax: 202-776-2222
mgoldstein@dowlohnes.com

SERVICES: CONSULTING, DISTANCE EDUCATION, FINANCIAL

AID, LEGAL, STUDENT FINANCIAL AID

Dow, Lohnes & Albertson offers comprehensive legal services to all segments of the education industry. Services for career colleges include advice on student financial aid, accreditation, licensure, acquisitions, finance, telecommunications and information technology.

DRINKER BIDDLE & REATH

1500 K Street NW, Suite 1100
Washington, DC 20005-1209
Contact: Mr. John R. Przypyszny
Phone: 202-842-8858
Fax: 202-842-8465
john.przypyszny@dbr.com

SERVICES: LEGAL

Drinker Biddle & Reath is a full-service law firm founded in 1849 and headquartered in Philadelphia, with offices in Washington, D.C.; New York; Princeton and Florham Park, N.J.; and Berwyn, PA. Drinker Biddle & Reath provides legal services in mergers and acquisitions, joint ventures, and restructuring, as well as advice on institutional eligibility and certification matters and Title IV programs.

DUANE MORRIS

101 West Broadway, Ste. 900
San Diego, CA 92101
Contact: Mr. Keith Zakarin, Partner
Phone: 619-744-2278
Fax: 619-744-2201
kzakarin@duanemorris.com
www.duanemorris.com

SERVICES: LEGAL

We represent California and Florida private postsecondary and vocational schools and colleges in all of the many facets of their complex and specialized businesses. We handle student and employee claims and lawsuits, from simple disputes to large class actions and private attorney general suits. The firm also represents schools before state and federal regulatory and accrediting bodies, as well as in purchase and sale transactions of the schools themselves. We place particular emphasis on the creation and implementation of sound risk management and claim prevention strategies, and work in partnership with our clients to structure their admissions, financial aid and instructor guidelines to maximize profitability while minimizing risk.

E

*eCOLLEGE

4900 South Monaco Street, Suite 200
Denver, Colorado 80237
Contact: Mark Brodsky, Vice President
Phone: 303-873-3866
Fax: 303-873-7449
markb@ecollege.com

SERVICES: DISTANCE EDUCATION, eLEARNING PROVIDERS, TRAINING PROVIDERS

Provides all of the necessary technology and services in an integrated approach to power the profitable growth of online distance programs. The company designs, builds and supports many of the most successful, fully online degree programs in the country; and supports more online degree programs and hosts more student enrollments through its data center than any other eLearning provider. Our outsource solution includes course management system software; program administrative applications; a secure, reliable and scalable hosted environment; and an array of support services for administrator, faculty and student success. Visit our website at www.ecollege.com.

EDFUND

2200 6th Avenue, Ste. 525
Seattle, WA 98121
Contact: Linda Weir
Phone: 206-575-1565
www.edfund.org

SERVICES: FINANCIAL AID

EDFUND, a nonprofit public benefit corporation, is the nation's second largest provider of student loan guarantee services under the Federal Family Education Loan Program. Operating as an auxiliary corporation of the California Student Aid Commission, EDFUND offers students a wide range of financial aid and debt management information, while supporting schools with advanced loan processing solutions and default prevention techniques.

*ED MAP, INC.

296 Harper Street
Nelsonville, Ohio 45764
Contact: Mr. Andrew J. Herd, Director Business De-

velopment
Phone: 740-753-3439 x304
Fax: 740-753-9402
ajherd@edmap.biz
www.edmap.biz

SERVICES: EDUCATIONAL/TRAINING MATERIALS
ED MAP is a company dedicated to providing an array of support services to career colleges in the area of textbook and learning materials distribution. ED MAP has created software and processes that ease the burden of procuring, managing and distributing course materials by bringing together faculty, administrators and students under one virtual roof and allows the institution to generate greater financial rewards and academic control.

EDRECRUIT

P.O. Box 222
Dewittville, New York 14728-0222
Contact: Mr. Brad Jones, President
Phone: 716-386-5415
Fax: 509-271-5313
bjones@cecomet.net

SERVICES: MANAGEMENT SEARCH, RECRUITMENT
EdRecruit is fully dedicated to selective management searches for all levels of management in private postsecondary education. Every effort is made to exercise selectivity, confidentiality and professionalism to achieve a true match. "This is our only business conducted with full-time focus."

EDUCATION CAPITAL GROUP, LLC

113 South Columbus Street
Suite 303
Alexandria, Virginia 22314
Contact: Mr. G. William Bavin, Managing Partner
Phone: 703.684.4600
Fax: 703.997.5660
E-mail: bill.bavin@educationcapital.com
www.educationcapital.com

SERVICES: CONSULTING, INVESTMENT BANKING
A financial and strategic advisory firm providing capital formation, merger and acquisition, and consulting services to K-20 education companies and investors.

EDUCATION SYSTEMS & SOLUTIONS, LLC

5521 Greenville Ave.
Ste. 104-268
Dallas, Texas 75214
Contact: Ms. Jan Friedheim, Strategic Coach
Phone: 214-587-5403
Fax: 214-887-4810
jfriedheim@aol.com

SERVICES: ASSESSMENT, CONSULTING, MISCELLANEOUS, DEVELOPMENT, EDUCATION MANAGEMENT, MANAGEMENT SEARCH, PLACEMENT, RETENTION, TRAINING PROVIDERS
Education Systems & Solutions provides management strategies relating to administration, admissions, accreditation, curriculum development, marketing, retention, placement and public relations. The principals have over 60 years of combined experience on the front lines of career college operations, as well as having served in major national leadership positions. References and proposals provided upon request.

EDUCATIONAL FINANCIAL SERVICES

18757 Burbank Boulevard, Suite 330
P.O. Box 7031
Tarzana, California 91357-7031
Contact: Mr. Philip Rosen, Vice President
Phone: 800-423-5513
Fax: 818-881-2446
info@efs-nlsc.com
www.efs-nlsc.com

SERVICES: TUITION FINANCING, RECEIVABLES MANAGEMENT, STUDENT FINANCIAL AID
Educational Financial Services (EFS) provides financing for students attending colleges and schools throughout the U.S. ... usually at NO COST to the school.

Often students receive insufficient financial aid to cover their entire tuition. Others are simply unable to pay their full course price at the time of enrollment. EFS financing will enable you to enroll these students by offering easy-to-afford payment programs and providing your school up-front money right away. Whether a student needs to make payments over the length of the course (pay-as-you-go) or needs a longer time (extended pay), EFS provides the financing, rather than the school trying to carry the account in-house.

National Loan Servicing Center (NLSC) servicing-only programs are also available for your in-house accounts. NLSC can provide the billing, collection, tracking and reporting to keep your student receivables a valuable, paying portfolio.

EFC financing and NLSC servicing are available to both accredited and non-accredited schools.

EduSearch Network, Inc.

15301 Ventura Blvd.
Sherman Oaks, CA 91403
Contact: Mr. Bryan Hsuan, Business Development
Phone: 818-728-6077
bhsuan@esnmediagroup.com
www.edu-search.com

SERVICES: ADMISSIONS, ADVERTISING, MARKETING, MEDIA RECRUITMENT

EduSearch Network specializes in generating highly targeted prospective student leads through our network of search engine-based web properties. All leads generated for schools featured on EduSearch properties are the product of extensive keyword development based around our client's programs. For more information about EduSearch search engine marketing, please call or visit www.edu-search.com.

Eduventures, Inc.

99 Summer Street, 7th Floor
Boston, Massachusetts 02110
Contact: Ms. Lisa Klett
Phone: 617-426-5622
lklett@eduventures.com
www.eduventures.com

SERVICES: CONSULTING, MISCELLANEOUS

The worldwide authority on the education industry, Eduventures supports the growth of organizations operating in the pre-K-12, postsecondary and corporate learning markets. Eduventures' market forecasts, competitive assessments, analysis of financial transactions and buyer data provide clients with the analysis and insight necessary to develop and execute organizational strategy. Founded in 1993, Eduventures is privately held and headquartered in Boston, Massachusetts.

Elsevier Science

11830 Westline Industrial Drive
St. Louis, Missouri 63146
Contact: Field Support
Phone: 800-222-9570
www.elsevierhealth.com

SERVICES: EDUCATIONAL TRAINING, eLEARNING PROVIDERS, TRAINING PROVIDERS

The world's leading publisher of text and reference products for the health careers. Our imprints of Saunders, Mosby, Churchill Livingstone, and Butterworth Heinemann feature innovative educational solutions in a variety of disciplines, including Medical Assisting, Massage Therapy, Medical Insurance Billing and Coding, Nursing, Pharmacy Technician, Surgical Technology, and more! In addition, the launch of our TEACH (Total Education and Curriculum Help) program has allowed career schools across the nation to easily establish a consistent teaching and learning process. With its customizable series of lesson plans, curriculum guides and instructor development resources that work in conjunction with Elsevier's industry-leading textbooks, TEACH truly is a complete curriculum solution for health career programs.

EMB Medical Services

P.O. Box 20550
Keizer, Oregon 97307
Contact: Mr. Tom Pierson, President
Phone: 888-600-4244
embmedical@aol.com
www.EMBMedical.com

SERVICES: MEDICAL SERVICES

EMB Medical Services is a national occupational health services company serving the career college sector of higher education. We partner with allied health career schools and colleges to design and operate on-campus programs to make student immunizations and health testing convenient and cost-effective. We offer a full menu of immunization services, lab services (blood tests and titers), TB skin tests, health screens and drug tests. We bring the clinic to your campus on a monthly basis, integrating services with your program requirements and start schedules. Our data tracking, reporting and documentations systems greatly reduce your administrative burden and help ensure that your students have their services completed before they enter their externship.

The students we immunize love the convenience of not having to leave school for their shots and blood work. Our clients love having a cost-effective solution that reduces the extra work of managing student compliance with immunization requirements. Call us today to find out how we can help you better manage your student immunizations.

*EMBANET CORPORATION

225 Sparks Avenue
Toronto, Ontario~M2H 2S5~CANADA
Contact: Mr. Jeffrey Feldberg, Chairman and CEO
Phone: 416-494-6622 x 2246
Fax: 416-494-1891
jeffrey@embanet.com
www.embanet.com/cca

SERVICES: eLEARNING PROVIDERS, DISTANCE EDUCATION, TRAINING PROVIDERS

Embanet Corporation provides the most effective solution for online programs to maximize retention rates and profits through its hosting of courses in its Tier 1 Data Center, as well as the industry's best 24/7 live technical support for students and faculty. Embanet offers the industry's only eLearning Insurance™ to safeguard your investment from changing technologies through the total integration of seven leading and non-proprietary learning platforms (ANGEL, Blackboard, FirstClass, IntraLearn, Jones, SAKAI and WebCT).

For over a decade, Embanet Corporation has played a key role with institutions to ensure the success of online programs that scale, are fully automated, have high possible student success and return on investment. Embanet's turn-key solution also includes the industry's best course development, faculty training and systems integrations. This year alone over 48,000 course takers, who otherwise would have dropped their course, will now stay in their course as a direct result of interacting with Embanet's 24/7 live technical support services.

EMC/PARADIGM PUBLISHING, INC.

875 Montreal Way
Saint Paul, Minnesota 55102-4245
Contact: Mr. Robert Galvin, Vice President and National Sales Manager
Phone: 800-535-6865
Fax: 800-328-4564
educate@emcp.com
http://www.emcp.com

SERVICES: EDUCATIONAL TRAINING

EMC/Paradigm Publishing has long been recognized as a leader in creating performance-based learning solutions to prepare postsecondary students for successful careers. For more than 50 years, EMC/Paradigm has been publishing textbook programs and technology tools in the areas of computer technology, distance learning, accounting, allied health, office technology and staff development. Programs include web-based courses, support materials, and training and assessment programs.

ETHICSPOINT

13221 S.W. 68th Pkwy., Ste. 120
Portland, OR 97223
Contact: Ms. Sharene Rekow, Education Channel Director
Phone: 971-250-0075
Fax: 971-250-4125
srekow@ethicspoint.com
www.ethicspoint.com

SERVICES: MISCELLANEOUS

Provides a comprehensive, adaptive suite of services that supports the compliance and governance needs of your institution. Combining code of conduct training, whistle-blower hotline reporting and case management, EthicsPoint delivers the best practice solutions that reduce risk and help educational institutions foster a healthy workplace environment. Our easy-to-use telephone and web-based solutions mean your faculty, staff, students and even visitors can readily report any concerns or issues that could represent tremendous exposure and fiscal risk.

EXECUTIVE SEARCH GROUP

750 Boston Neck Road, Suite 14
Narragansett, Rhode Island 02882
Contact: Mr. Michael Cobb
Phone: 401-788-9373
Fax: 401-788-0707
esearch@att.net
www.esearchgroup.net

SERVICES: CONSULTING, MANAGEMENT SEARCH, MISCELLANEOUS

Executive Search Group (ESG) has 20+ years experience in the education/recruiting fields. The company conducts executive searches for proprietary, college and university positions, such as presidents, COOs, executive directors, corporate management, regional directors, school presidents/directors, directors of admissions, academic deans/directors of education, directors of financial aid and various management and staffing positions. ESG specializes in the brokerage, purchase & sale of career colleges. We will assist owners and buyers in the sale and purchase of their institutions.

FAME

AtlanTech Tower, 6451 N. Federal Hwy, Suite 501
Fort Lauderdale, Florida 33308
Contact: Ms. Julia Brown, Senior Vice President, Marketing and Client Relations
Phone: 800-327-5772
Fax: 954-772-6257
fame@fameinc.com
www.fameinc.com

SERVICES: ADMINISTRATIVE SERVICES, ADMISSIONS, CONSULTING, DEFAULT MANAGEMENT, EDUCATION MANAGEMENT, FINANCIAL AID, IT SOLUTIONS, MISCELLANEOUS, PLACEMENT, RECEIVABLES MANAGEMENT, RECRUITMENT, RETENTION, SOFTWARE, TRAINING PROVIDERS, TUITION FINANCING

FAME is the largest financial aid servicing company in the nation and provides enterprise administrative software solutions to the postsecondary school industry. Since the founding of our company in 1978, FAME has been dedicated to meeting the financial aid regulatory and software needs of career schools and colleges throughout the country. We provide school management software, a full range of federal financial aid services, customized training programs and student loan management for over 1,000 institutions nationwide.
The quality and experience of FAME's staff, when coupled with our impeccable 26-year reputation and dedication to customer service, sets FAME apart from all others.

FINANCIAL AID SERVICES, INC./GENESIS: SMSS

90 Stiles Road
Suite #101
Salem, New Hampshire 03079-4884
Contact: Mr. Albert Gillis, President/CEO
Phone: 603-328-1550
Toll-Free: 800-4-FAS-INC (800-432-7462)
Fax: 603-328-1560
FAS@fasinc.net

www.genesis-smss.com
www.financialaidservices.com
SERVICES: CONSULTING, FINANCIAL AID, SOFTWARE
Founded in 1980, Financial Aid Services, Inc. remains the only nationwide servicing company that provides a customized approach to the personalized consulting and professional management of proprietary institutions' Federal Student Aid programs. We enable schools to completely automate processing using FASLine©, our internet-based software.

FAS can also integrate its financial aid servicing with its own school administrative software, Genesis-SMS©, an entirely Windows-based program that completely automates and generates reports on admissions, academics, attendance, accounting, placement and compliance. Both FAS and Genesis-SMS© have raised the standards in meeting the challenges of school management and Title IV processing.

FIRSTCLASS - OPEN TEXT CORPORATION

38 Leek Crescent
Richmond Hill, ON L4B 4N8
Phone: (905) 762-6022
Fax: (905) 762-6022
www.firstclass.com | www.opentext.com

SERVICES: DISTANCE EDUCATION, ELEARNING PROVIDER, EDUCATION MANAGEMENT, IT SOLUTIONS, SOFTWARE

FirstClass is a feature-rich, independent solution platform that enables academic organizations to create collaborative online communities that connect students, faculty, parents and administrators.

A robust and cost-effective alternative to standard e-mail or groupware solutions, FirstClass delivers a broad range of features and capabilities, including secure e-mail and instant messaging, personal and group calendaring, online testing and reporting, collaboration and document sharing, web publishing, discussion forums, simplified course creation and material sharing, unified messaging, and more. FirstClass is deployed in more than 2,000 academic organizations and has over 8 million users worldwide. For more information on FirstClass solutions, go to www.firstclass.com.

FirstClass is a solution from Open Text™ Corporation, the market leader in providing Enterprise Content Management (ECM) solutions that bring together people, processes and information in global organizations. Today, the company supports almost 20 million seats across 13,000 deployments in 114 countries and 12 languages worldwide. For more information on Open Text, go to www.opentext.com.

FRED W. JURASH & COMPANY, P.C.

175 West Old Marlton Pike
Marlton, New Jersey 08053-2033
Contact: Mr. Fred Jurash, President
Phone: 856-596-9600
Fax: 856-985-9086
jurashcpa@aol.com

SERVICES: CPA

The firm is a full-service tax, audit and consulting firm that specializes in education and not-for-profit industries, including OMP 133 audits. We concentrate on education support services and provide consulting services related to change of ownership, acquisitions, financial analysis, file reviews, internal auditing and year-end planning.

FRIEDMAN, BILLINGS, RAMSEY GROUP, INC.

1001 19th St. North
Arlington, VA 22209
Contact: Mr. David Dunn, Managing Director - Media Investment Bank
Phone: 703-469-1026
Fax: 703-312-1789
ddunn@fbr.com
www.fbrcorp.com

SERVICES: INVESTMENT BANKING

FBR is a top 10 investment bank. The company provides investment banking, institutional brokerage, asset management and private client services through its operating subsidiaries, and invests in mortgage-backed securities and merchant banking opportunities. Investment banking and institutional brokerage provided in the United States by Friedman, Billings, Ramsey & Co., Inc. and in Europe, the Middle East and Asia by Friedman, Billings, Ramsey International, Ltd.

FROEHLE & CO., INC., P.C.

8401 Claude Thomas Road, Suite 45
Franklin, Ohio 45005-1475
Contact: Mr. Jeffery Froehle, President
Phone: 937-746-3999
Fax: 937-746-1556

froehle@froehle.com
www.froehle.com

SERVICES: CPA

CPA firm specializing in services to postsecondary educational institutions, providing audits of Title IV, state financial aid programs, audits of financial statements, consultation and compliance reviews.

THE GAME INSTITUTE

105 Main St.
Cold Spring, NY 10516
Contact: Mr. Thomas F. McKiernan
Phone: 845-265-7895
Fax: 845-265-6319
tom@gameinstitute.com
www.gameinstitute.com

SERVICES: DISTANCE EDUCATION, ELEARNING PROVIDERS, EDUCATIONAL TRAINING MATERIALS

Publishes online courseware in video game programming and graphics. Courses are offered through career colleges and have been approved for undergraduate credit by certain institutions.

GARNET CAPITAL ADVISORS, LLC

383 Madison Avenue, 40th Flr.
New York, NY 10179
Contact: Mr. Michael Chiodo, Vice President
Phone: 212-272-6842
Fax: 212-881-9600
mchiodo@bear.com
www.garnetcapital.com

SERVICES: INVESTMENT BANKING, STUDENT FINANCIAL AID, TUITION FINANCING

Do you want to sell your accounts for the highest possible price?

Garnet Capital Advisors, LLC is a New York-based boutique investment banking firm specializing in monetizing performing and non-performing receivables for credit-granting institutions. In addition, Garnet provides capital raising and M&A advisory services, and business divestitures to a broad spectrum of institutions in the U.S. and in Europe. Garnet Capital also has offices in Warsaw, Poland, and Tokyo, Japan. Bear, Stearns Merchant Banking and Fortress Investment Group are investors in Garnet.

GEMCOR, Inc.

400 Quadrangle Drive
Bolingbrook, IL 60440
Contact: Mr. Donald Grybas, President
Phone: 888-GEMCOR-8 (436-2678)
Fax: 888-9-GEMCOR (943-6267)
info@gemcorinc.com
www.gemcorinc.com

Services: Financial aid

GEMCOR, Inc. is one of the largest third-party servicers in the country, administering federal aid for over 150 institutions. Daily grant and loan processing, cash management, and complete reconciliation and consulting services are available, as is TRAX school administrative software.

GetStarts Inc.

1780 Kettner Blvd., Loft 104
San Diego, CA 92101
Contact: Mr. Sammy James, President
Phone: 619-237-1097
Fax: 619-819-5629
sammy@getstarts.com
www.getstarts.com

Services: Advertising, marketing

A highly creative and innovative advertising agency specializing in private, postsecondary career schools. GetStarts leverages traditional marketing with emerging technologies to enable real-time measurement, reporting and analysis of your marketing expenditures. The result is continuous improvement and efficiencies across all marketing initiatives. To ensure maximum conversion rates from source to start, GetStarts is strategically partnered with Nancy Roger's company, Source for Training. GetStarts - more leads, more starts, more grads.

*Global Financial Aid Services, Inc.

10467 Corporate Drive
Gulfport, Mississippi 39503
Phone: 214-208-0436
Fax: 214-279-0805
mjohnner@globalfas.com
Contact: Mr. Matthew J. Johnner, Vice President, Sales & Marketing

Service: Financial Aid

Special Message: Global Financial Aid Services provides front office and back office financial aid administration for online environment and ground campuses. Our services maximize enrollment, optimize financial aid, improve student services, ensure compliance and reduce costs. We provide proactive financial aid counseling to qualified leads. Global offers online applications and campus kiosk software that automatically packages and awards the student. Global also provides loan certification, disbursement, T4 accounting and compliance servicing. Call today to discuss what results we have achieved in the industry. Additional information is available at the web site (www.globalfas.com).

*Global Compliance Services

13950 Ballantyne Corporate Place
Suite 300
Charlotte, NC 28277
Contact: Mr. Joe Niemann, Vice President, Sales
Toll-Free: 888-475-8270
joe.niemann@globalcompliance.com
www.globalcompliance.com

Services: Governance, risk management and compliance

Global Compliance Services provides colleges and universities with products and services that address risk management, governance and compliance, thus enabling institutions to protect their funding, protect their reputation and increase faculty, staff, student and donor confidence. Our integrated portfolio of products and services includes:
Hotline and Web Reporting – for reporting business misconduct or non-compliance
Information Management – for analysis, trending and case investigation management
Awareness and Training – for program education, communication and promotion
Evaluation and Validation – for measurement of program comprehension and effectiveness
Global Compliance Services has unparalleled expertise and 24 years of experience in ethics and compliance, having introduced the industry's original compliance-reporting hotline. We currently serve colleges and universities throughout the country, along with nearly one-half of the Fortune 100 and one-third of the Fortune 1000.

GORDON, NILES & COMPANY, P.A.
3041 Monument Road, Suite 2
Jacksonville, Florida 32225-1706
Contact: Mr. T. Kipp Gordon, CPA
Phone: 904-642-7456
Fax: 904-642-7974
Kgordon@gordonnilescpa.com

SERVICES: CPA
For more than 20 years, Gordon, Niles & Company has
provided accounting and auditing services, including
financial statement audits and Title IV compliance attestations, for private schools and colleges.

GRAGG ADVERTISING INC.
450 East 4th Street, Suite 100
Kansas City, Missouri 64106
Contact: Mr. Darryl Mattox
Phone: 816-931-0050
Fax: 816-931-0051
E-mail: dmattox@graggadv.com
www.graggadv.com

**SERVICE: INTEGRATED RECRUITMENT, ADVERTISING, CALL
TRACKING, MEDIA BUYING, ADMISSIONS TRAIN-
ING, RETENTION TRAINING, PAY PER LEAD, IN-
TERACTIVE DEVELOPMENT, BROADCAST AND
PRINT PRODUCTION**
Gragg Advertising is the expert in integrated recruitment marketing for the career school sector of higher
education. Their programs focus on lead generation,
admission process management and enrollment retention. Gragg Advertising offers integrated recruitment
campaigns, dedicated phone numbers for call tracking
and recording, media analysis, media buying, research
for site selection and curriculum development, Pay Per
Lead sites and aggregation, Interactive and Web development, admission's training, direct-mail programs,
lead and start goal projection.

GRAYMARK INTERNATIONAL, INC.
P.O. Box 2015
Tustin, California 92781
Contact: Mr. Larry Goddard
Phone: 800-854-7393
Fax: 714-544-2323
lgoddard@graymarkint.com
www.graymarkint.com

SERVICES: EDUCATIONAL TRAINING MATERIALS
Graymark International, Inc., a leading manufacturer of quality courseware and hardware-based IT trainers, electronic
component kits and projects. We proudly celebrate our 40th
anniversary developing trainers that provide a stimulating,
real-world working experience for students, and a simple-to-
complex, success-oriented curriculum for instructors.

HAY GROUP
Suite 1600
303 Peachtree Street NE
Atlanta, Georgia 30308-3267
Contact: Mr. Frank Casagrande, Senior Consultant
Phone: 404-575-8724
Fax: 404-575-8711
Frank_Casagrande@haygroup.com
www.haygroup.com

SERVICES: CONSULTING
Hay Group is a professional services firm that helps organizations worldwide get the most from their people by
creating clarity, capability and commitment. Founded
in 1943 in Philadelphia, today we work from 73 offices
in 39 countries. Our areas of expertise include Organizational Effectiveness, Role Clarity and Work Design
Executive Assessment, Selection and Development;
Compensation, Benefits, and Performance Management; Executive Remuneration and Corporate Governance; and Employee and Customer Attitude Research

HIGH VOLTAGE INTERACTIVE
2658 Bridgeway
Sausalito, California 94965
Contact: Ms. Candise Miller, Business Development
Phone: 415-339-8800 ext. 109
Fax: 415-339-8824
candise@highvoltageinteractive.com
www.highvoltageinteractive.com

**SERVICES: ADMISSIONS, ADVERTISING, CONSULTING, MAR-
KETING, MEDIA, DEVELOPMENT, RECRUITMENT,
SOFTWARE**
The leading online marketing and management solutions company specializing in lead generation services for the education industry. Our performance-based
enrollment marketing services leverage our own user-

based web portal, www.SearchForClasses.com, as well as our vast media network, to generate timely, high-quality and cost-effective leads that convert to active students at unprecedented levels. With a reputation built on strategic direction and precise execution, we deliver an exceptional return on your marketing investment. Also, learn about how we can manage your complete, end-to-end enrollment marketing needs. Contact us today toll free at (866) 383-8161.

HOMERBONNER

1200 Four Seasons Tower
1441 Brickell Avenue
Miami, Florida 33131
Contact: Mr. Kevin Jacobs, Esq.
Phone: 305-350-5188
Fax: 305-982-0068
kjacobs@homerbonner.com
www.homerbonner.com

SERVICES: LEGAL SERVICES

Homer & Bonner, P.A. represents publicly and privately owned postsecondary education companies in connection with student, employee and regulatory disputes, including putative class actions, in federal, state and arbitral forums throughout the nation. The firm has substantial experience in defending student class actions, securities suits, regulatory inquiries and all manner of employee disputes. The firm also represents private education companies in connection with the acquisition of other such companies and on the range of legal matters associated with the operation of such companies.

HORIZON EDUCATIONAL RESOURCES, INC.

P.O. Box 610
Marble, Texas 78715
Contact: Mr. Ron Parker, President
Phone: 830-798-9747
Fax: 830-798-9369
rjparker@horizoned.com
www.horizoned.com

SERVICES: DEFAULT MANAGEMENT

Since 1993, Horizon Educational Resources, Inc. has been offering proactive default prevention services. Horizon has successfully helped schools of all types and sizes reduce student loan defaults, track results, increase internal efficiencies, and improve borrower satisfaction, using default prevention counseling programs it has developed for the FFEL, Direct Loan and Perkins Loan Programs. "For Every Default Prevention Need, We Have a Solution!"

INSIDETRACK

703 Market Street, 20th floor
San Francisco, CA 94103
Contact: Paul Reddy, VP Business Development
Phone: 415-243-4428
Main: 415-243-4440
info@insidetrack.com
www.insidetrack.com

SERVICES: ENROLLMENT MANAGEMENT, RETENTION

InsideTrack helps colleges drive significant revenue increases through improved start rates and increased student retention. The company's results-driven student coaching services eliminate barriers during the start process and provide ongoing, proactive support to each new student to ensure they stay in school and graduate. Highly trained coaches work one-on-one with students to improve motivation, effectiveness and overall success so they can achieve their goals. Working in partnership with InsideTrack, career colleges typically increase starts by 10-15 percent and reduce first-term attrition by 30 percent or more.

INTEGRATED ENROLLMENT SOLUTIONS

422 E. Main, #210
Nacogdoches, Texas 75961
Contact: Susan Backofen, President
Phone: 888-676-5524
susan.backofen@enroll2grad.org
www.enroll2grad.org

SERVICES: ADMISSIONS, CONSULTING, IT SOLUTIONS, RETENTION

Integrated Enrollment Solutions provides consulting services to institutions in designing individualized systems that increase student enrollment. Our team of experts has nearly 100 years combined experience in areas such as enrollment and school management, enrollment forecasting, process automation, admissions, retention, career services, information systems, data integration, report development, data analysis, staff selection, and training and customized software development.

JBL Associates, Inc.
6900 Wisconsin Avenue, Suite 606
Bethesda, Maryland 20815-6114
Contact: Dr. John Lee, President
Phone: 301-654-5154
Fax: 301-654-6242
jbl@jblassoc.com

Services: Consulting
JBL Associates, Inc., a policy research company, has a long history with the private career school industry. JBLA has produced reports on topics including student loan defaults, economic value of private career schools to their community and state, and strategies for improving student persistence.

Jefferson Government Relations
1615 L St NW
Suite 650
Washington, DC 20036-5610
Contact: Tom Netting
Phone: 202-626-8500
tnetting@jeffersongr.com

John Wiley & Sons, Inc.
111 River Street
Hoboken, NJ
Contact: Ms. Jennifer Powers, Market Solutions Manager, Business Solutions Group
Phone: 201-748-5802
Fax: 201-748-6118
jpowers@wiley.com
www.wiley.com

Services: Consulting, eLearning providers, educational training materials, training providers
Creates customized educational solutions for the specialized needs of Wiley's for-profit clients.
We provide university-wide, revenue-enhancement consulting services to assist our clients in achieving their organizational goals of recruitment-retainment-revenue with private-labeled print editions. We provide curricula and content development services, sales of regular titles through a low-returns discount structure, eLearning solutions, and customized textbooks utilizing all of Wiley's rich resources and electronic content.

Wiley is a global publisher of print and electronic products, specializing in scientific, technical and medical books and journals; professional and consumer books and subscription services; and textbooks and other educational materials for undergraduate and graduate students, as well as lifelong learners. Wiley has approximately 22,700 active titles and about 400 journals and publishes about 2,000 new titles in a variety of print and electronic formats each year.

Jones e-global library®
9697 E. Mineral Avenue
Englewood, Colorado 80112
Contact: Dave Willuweit
Phone: 1-800-701-6463
Fax: 303-784-8533
dwilluweit@jonesknowledge.com
www.egloballibrary.com

Services: Library services
Jones e-global library® offers a comprehensive suite of online research tools that provides access to a vast range of academic and business literature. Developed and maintained by professional librarians, elements of this collection can provide an entire online library solution or be selected on an individual basis to complement existing offerings.

Jopling, Inc.
2100 Georgetown Drive, Suite 203
Sewickley, Pennsylvania 15143
Contact: J. Mark Jopling, President
Phone: 724-933-8180
Fax: 724-933-8188
mjopling@joplinginc.com
www.joplinginc.com

Services: Investment banking
Jopling, Inc. is an investment banking firm that specializes in advising owners of private, postsecondary schools.

Jostens, Inc.
26 Cross Point Dr.
Owings, MD 20736
Contact: Marty Murphy, Nat'l. Strategic Accounts Mgr.
Phone: 410-257-6294
marty.murphy@jostens.com
www.jostens.com

SERVICES: MISCELLANEOUS, PROMOTION AND RECOGNITION ITEMS

Minneapolis-based Jostens, founded in 1897, is a leading provider of products, programs and services that help people celebrate important moments, recognize achievements, and build affiliation. The company's products include graduation products, class rings, diplomas, certificates, diploma frames, graduation announcements and achievement awards. Visit www.jostens.com for more information.

JOURNEY EDUCATION MARKETING, INC.

13755 Hutton Drive, Suite 500
Dallas, Texas 75234
Contact: Mr. Greg Lamkin
Phone: 800-874-9001
Fax: 972-481-2100
schoolsales@JourneyEd.com
www.JourneyEd.com

SERVICES: SOFTWARE

Journey Education Marketing is the leading provider of business, digital video, animation, engineering/CAD, web publishing and digital publishing software to educational institutions, faculty members and students nationwide. In addition, Journey also offers eStore solutions to schools, currently operating over 1,900 software eStores. Journey specializes in serving the private, career, postsecondary sector. Visit www.JourneyEd.com for more information.

KESSLER, ORLEAN, SILVER & COMPANY, P.C.

1101 Lake Cook Road, Suite C
Deerfield, IL 60015-5233
Contact: Mr. Sanford Alper, Principal
Phone: 847-580-4100
Fax: 847-580-4199
sfa@koscpa.com
www.koscpa.com

SERVICES: CPA

KESSLER, ORLEAN, SILVER & COMPANY, P.C., (KOS) is a full-service accounting firm located in Deerfield, Illinois. Our firm specializes in different types of institutional audits, year-end planning, consulting, income taxes, 90/10 ratios and other major financial information. KOS is licensed across the United States. We

are large enough to meet your needs and small enough to care. Additional information may be obtained at http://ww.koscpa.com.

KNUTTE & ASSOCIATES, P.C.

7900 South Cass Avenue, Suite 210
Darien, Illinois 60561-5073
Contact: Ms. Kathleen Hays, Marketing Director
Phone: 630-960-3317
Fax: 630-960-9960
kathyh@knutte.com
www.knutte.com

SERVICES: CPA

K&A has been providing career colleges with guidance and solutions for over ten years. The range of services to career colleges includes financial audits, SFA compliance audits and attestations, monthly financial statements, business valuations, regulatory ratio monitoring, tax planning and preparation, and profit sharing and retirement plans. K&A is licensed nationwide and is committed to providing and maintaining service excellence for every client.

LaSALLE BANK NATIONAL ASSOCIATION

135 South LaSalle Street, Suite 1743
Chicago, Illinois 60603
Contact: Mr. Christopher J. O'Brien, Senior Vice President
Phone: 312-904-6570
Fax: 312-606-8423
chris.o'brien@abnamro.com
www.lasallebanks.com/commercial/educational_services.html

SERVICES: CONSULTING, FINANCIAL AID, INVESTMENT BANKING, INVESTMENT MANAGEMENT, STUDENT FINANCIAL AID, TUITION FINANCING

LaSalle Banks is one of the largest middle-market commercial banks in the Midwest. Through its Educational Services Division, we offer financial products and services (e.g. lines of credit, term loans, leasing, cash management services, advisory services, investment services and trust services) tailored to the needs of participants in the postsecondary education industry. Through its Consumer Lending Division, LaSalle Bank makes it easy to finance education costs by offering Stafford and

Plus Loans to students and their parents and should be contacted to discuss borrower benefit options that help students with their financing needs. Additional information is available at the web site http://www.lasalle-banks.com/commercial/educational_services.html

LEAD ADVANTAGE, LLC

1519 S. Bowman Rd., Suite A
Little Rock, Arkansas 72211
Contact: Mr. Phillip Moore, Managing Partner
Phone: 501-687-5323
Fax: 501-225-8163
phillip@leadadvantage.us

SERVICES: ADMISSIONS, ADVERTISING, CONSULTING, MARKETING, TRAINING PROVIDERS

Lead Advantage, L.L.C. is a full-service direct response advertising agency and video production company specializing in lead generation and admission training for the proprietary school industry. Our team of professionals has more than fifty years combined experience in direct response advertising, television production, media placement and admissions training. We offer a unique approach to lead generation and recruiter training.

LIPPINCOTT, WILLIAMS & WILKINS

351 West Camden Street
Baltimore, Maryland 21201-7912
Contact: Ms.Christen DeMarco, Associate Marketing Manager
Phone: 410-528-4000
Fax: 410-528-4305
cdemarco@lww.com

SERVICES: EDUCATIONAL TRAINING MATERIALS

Lippincott, Williams & Wilkins (LWW), a subsidiary of Wolters Kluwer NV, a multi-domestic publishing company, is a global publisher of medical, nursing and allied health information resources in book, journal, newsletter, loose-leaf and electronic media formats.

MAKING YOUR MARK/LDF PUBLISHING, INC.

P.O. Box 45
Port Perry, Ontario CANADA L9L 1A2
Contact: Mr. Don Fraser, Vice President Retention
Phone: 905-985-9990 or 877-492-6845

Fax: 905-985-0713
info@ldfpublishing.com
www.makingyourmark.com

SERVICES: RETENTION

LDF Publishing has been helping colleges develop student success and retention strategies since 1992. Our college success book, *Making Your Mark*, is used in over 1,500 educational institutions across North America and has sold more than 750,000 copies. LDF Publishing also offers faculty training seminars in student retention and student motivation. More than 7,000 college staff members have attended our workshop "The Right Start to College: Student Motivation from Day 1 to Graduation."

MARKETING SOLUTIONS, INC.

1601 Westpark Drive, Suite 3
Little Rock, Arkansas 72204-2432
Contact: Mr. Dewitt Shotts, President
Phone: 501-663-3433
Fax: 501-801-5100
dewitt@msileads.com
sales@msileads.com | www.msileads.com

SERVICES: ADVERTISING, MEDIA, MARKETING

Marketing Solutions specializes in direct response advertising for private career schools. The company assists schools with developing strategic marketing plans and television and direct mail production.

MAXKNOWLEDGE, INC.

3943 Irvine Blvd.
Suite 262
Irvine, CA 92602
Contact: Dr. Amir Moghadam, Executive Director
Phone: (714) 505-0901
Fax: (714) 505-1517
amirm@maxknowledge.com
www.maxknowledge.com

SERVICES: ADMISSIONS, CONSULTING, DISTANCE EDUCATION, EDUCATIONAL TRAINING MATERIALS, ELEARNING PROVIDERS, FINANCIAL AID, MARKETING, PLACEMENT, RETENTION, TRAINING PROVIDERS

In partnership with the Career College Association, MaxKnowledge offers a wide variety of online and blended training programs to enhance the knowledge and skills of career college personnel. Subject areas include: Admissions, Education (Faculty Training), eLearning, Financial Aid, Marketing, Operations, Placement and Retention. Our training courses are facilitated by leading career education experts, and participants receive Continuing Education Units upon completion of training. We also offer a large selection of free courses in soft skills areas, such as communications skills, management, leadership, creativity and innovation. Our ultimate objective is to increase the efficiency, quality and profitability of career college operations through effective training of personnel.

MBS Direct

Mr. Kenneth Rust
2711 West Ash Street
Columbia, MO 65203-4613
Contact: Mr. Kenneth Rust
Phone: 800-325-3249
Fax: 573-446-5242
krust@mbsdirect.net
www.mbsbooks.com/direct

SERVICES: EDUCATIONAL TRAINING, IT SOLUTIONS
MBS Direct provides a virtual bookstore course materials fulfillment program that handles all inventory, receiving student orders, shipping course materials directly to students, a book buyback program, and excellent customer service. College profitability on textbooks is guaranteed. School staff are able to focus on student recruitment and education without the challenges and costs of course material distribution. MBS Direct offers solutions for student financial aid orders and can ship course materials direct to students or classrooms when textbook fees are bundled within tuition.

McClintock & Associates, P.C.

1370 Washington Pike, Suite 201
Bridgeville, Pennsylvania 15017-2839
Contact: Mr. Bruce McClintock, President
Phone: 412-257-5980
Fax: 412-257-2549
bmcclintock@mcclintockcpa.com
www.mcclintockcpa.com

SERVICES: CPA, CONSULTING, FINANCIAL AID
McClintock & Associates is a CPA and consulting firm with a nationwide practice in the education industry, specializing in financial aid audits, financial statement audits, 401(k) audits, mergers and acquisitions, tax consulting and preparation, management consulting, computer consulting, and financial aid consulting.

*McGraw-Hill Career College Group

1285 Fern Ridge Parkway
Suite 200
Saint Louis, Missouri 63141
Contact: Mr. Dennis Spisak, Senior Vice President
Phone: 800- 257-5785
Fax: 314-439-6754
dennis_spisak@mcgraw-hill.com
www.mhhe.com

SERVICES: CONSULTING, DISTANCE EDUCATION, EDUCATIONAL TRAINING MATERIALS, ELEARNING PROVIDER, IT SOLUTIONS, MISCELLANEOUS, RETENTION, SOFTWARE, TRAINING PROVIDERS
McGraw-Hill Career College Group is a full-service publishing company providing a list of products which covers the vast majority of subjects taught and curriculum offered in career colleges. In addition, McGraw-Hill Higher Education offers such services as customized curriculum, textbooks and online programs via our Learning Solutions Group, Faculty Development Programs and Faculty Training for major products.

MDT/Marketing & Design Team

Division of Custom Cuts Printing, Inc.
805 E. Broward Blvd. #301
Fort Lauderdale, Florida 33301
Contact: Mr. Mitch Talenfeld
Phone (800) 424-7397
Fax: (954) 764-5853
mitch@mdtdirect.com

SERVICES: ADMISSIONS, ADVERTISING, CONSULTING, MARKETING, MEDIA, RECRUITMENT, TRAINING
MDT Direct provides its customers with products and services that improve sales efforts and advertising effectiveness. Go to www.mdtdirect.com for details.

Merced Solutions

2400 N. Lincoln Ave.
Altadena, CA 91001
Contact: Jason C. Sickels, Business Development Mgr.
Phone: 310-968-4981
jasons@merced-solutions.com
www.merced-solutions.com

SERVICES: ADMINISTRATIVE SERVICES, ADMISSIONS, ADVERTISING, CONSULTING, DEFAULT MANAGEMENT, DEVELOPMENT, DISTANCE EDUCATION, EDUCATION MANAGEMENT, eLEARNING PROVIDER, FINANCIAL AID, IT SOLUTIONS, PLACEMENT, SOFTWARE

Merced Solutions is the pioneer of Student Lifecycle Management, ranging from recruiting, financial aid, registrar, distance learning and placement. With our end-to-end solutions, you will be able to increase top-line revenue growth with exceptional recruiting tools for better prospect conversion and improve cash flow management and revenue recognition through full financial aid administration and accounting. Merced's workflow approach to student management results in significant gains in productivity and reduction in administrative costs.

MICHAEL BEST & FRIEDRICH, L.L.C.

401 Michigan Avenue, Suite 1900
Chicago, Illinois 60611
Contact: Mr. Daniel Kaufman, Partner
Phone: 312-222-0800
Fax: 312-222-0818
dkaufman@mbf-law.com
www.mbf-law.com

SERVICES: LEGAL

Michael Best & Friedrich represents universities, colleges, technical colleges and school districts on a broad spectrum of issues, ranging from labor and employment issues to intellectual property matters. The organization's attorneys have a thorough understanding of educational systems and the issues affecting them.

*MILITARY ADVANTAGE

799 Market St.
Suite 700
San Francisco, California 94103
Contact: Mr. Josh Brody, Director of Sales
Phone: 415-433-0999 Ext. 233
Josh@MilitaryAdvantage.com
www.Military.com

SERVICES: ADVERTISING, MARKETING, FINANCIAL AID, MEDIA, RECRUITMENT, RETENTION

Military Advantage, the nation's largest military affinity marketing firm, has over 4 million members, 3 million newsletter subscribers and the world's largest online military destination at www.Military.com. Military Advantage connects mature, motivated service members and veterans with GI Bill and tuition assistance benefits to educational institutions through targeted, measurable advertising vehicles, qualified lead generation programs and the Directory of Military-Friendly Schools.

MUNO, SUMMERS & ASSOCIATES

PO Box 882
Oldsmar, FL 34677
Contact: Debbie Muno, Partner
Email: debbie@munosummers.com
Phone: 813-925-8410
1-866-JOB-FITS
www.munosummers.com

SERVICES: ADMINISTRATIVE SERVICES, ADMISSIONS, ASSESSMENT, CONSULTING, EDUCATION MANAGEMENT, TESTING TOOLS AND EQUIPMENT

Muno, Summers & Associates is an employee assessment firm focusing on the employees of career schools. Through the use of our assessment system, career schools have the capability to HIRE MORE TOP TALENT, RETAIN TOP PERFORMERS, COACH and DEVELOP INCUMBENT EMPLOYEES and REDUCE EMPLOYEE TURNOVER. This assessment program utilizes world class assessments that are reliable, valid and compliant. Assessments are online, and results are immediate. Assessments are available in multiple languages. REDUCE YOUR PEOPLE PROBLEMS NOW!

*NATIONAL CENTER FOR COMPETENCY TESTING (NCCT)

7007 College Boulevard, Suite 250
Overland Park, Kansas 66211-1558
Contact: Mr. Bruce Brackett, CEO
Phone: 913-498-1000
Fax: 913-498-1243

SERVICES: ADVERTISING, CERTIFICATION

The National Center for Competency Testing, which offers certification for medical assistants, dental assistants, bookkeepers and CPA assistants, and The Great Incentive Firm (TGIF), which designs lapel pins for incentive programs at proprietary schools.

THE NEW YORK TIMES KNOWLEDGE NETWORK

368 S. McCaslin Blvd. #125
Louisville, CO 80027
Contact: Jan Gilboy
Phone: 888-443-1800
Fax: 303-665-5040
gilboj@nytimes.com
www.nytimes.com/knowledge

SERVICES: EDUCATIONAL TRAINING MATERIALS
A pre-eminent resource for colleges nationwide. It is a comprehensive program that opens up to you an array of content and special services from *The New York Times*. It is also flexible, working with colleges to custom-design programs that provide newspapers at a discounted rate; support faculty in developing active learning strategies that promote student engagement; sponsor events and speaker programs that bring current issues to life; provide discounted rates for advertising; provide discounted rates for rights and permissions site licenses; partner on grants; and provide information about best practices and innovative models of instruction.

NIIT

1050 Crown Pointe Pkwy, Ste. 500
Atlanta, Georgia 30338
Contact: Venkat Srinivasan
Regional Vice President
Phone: 770-290-6056
Email: VenkatS@niit.com
www.niit.com

SERVICES: DISTANCE EDUCATION, EDUCATIONAL TRAINING MATERIALS, eLEARNING PROVIDERS, IT SOLUTIONS AND TRAINING PROVIDERS
NIIT has more than 20 years of experience developing and imparting education to a student body of 500,000 in 31 countries. We can help career colleges secure their competitive advantage with custom solutions that include:
• Custom education material: textbooks, courseware, companion sites, instructor guides, online courses
• Custom program development
• Technology infrastructure for online education
• IT instructors for online and classroom delivery

NORTON NORRIS, INC.

7700 Joliet Dr. So.
Tinley Park, IL 60477
Contact: Mr. Vince Norton, President
Phone: 708-633-6645
Fax: 708-633-7874
vince@nortonnorris.com
www.nortonnorris.com

SERVICES: ADMISSIONS, ADVERTISING, ASSESSMENT, CONSULTING, MARKETING, MEDIA, RECRUITMENT
As specialists in Tactical Enrollment Management, we provide a wide variety of marketing and enrollment management services. This includes admissions training, television, radio and print advertising, developing high school programs, starting and managing telemarketing departments, conducting mystery shopping, and program assessment.

OASIS OUTSOURCING, INC.

2255 Glades Rd. Ste. 305E
Boca Raton, Florida 33431
Contact: Mr. Michael Viola, Senior Vice President
Phone: 561-997-8778
Fax: 561-997-8227
mviola@oasisadvantage.com
www.oasisadvantage.com

SERVICES: ADMINISTRATIVE SERVICES
Oasis is a professional employer organization providing human resource, payroll and benefit services to middle-market companies on an outsourced basis.

ONVEON EDUCATION SEARCH

P.O. Box 1414
Tacoma, WA 98401
Contact: Mr. Alex Rahin, President
Phone: 253-779-0780
Fax: 866-686-4796
info@onveon.com
www.onveon.com

SERVICES: ADMISSIONS, ADVERTISING, CONSULTING, DEVELOPMENT, IT SOLUTIONS, MARKETING, MEDIA, MISCELLANEOUS, PLACEMENT, RECRUITMENT, RETENTION
Onveon is an innovative marketing, advertising and lead generation company, focused on helping the education industry reach and exceed student enrollment goals. Onveon specializes in matching and connecting prospec-

tive students with the schools that meet their education goals using proprietary online technologies and strategies. Onveon's online resources include comprehensive databases of schools and programs specifically targeting prospective students looking for education and career options. Our goal is to provide the most cost-effective recruiting solution to the education industry and build the internet's top destination to help prospective students and professionals achieve their education and career goals.

THE PACIFIC INSTITUTE

1230 South Southlake Drive
Hollywood, Florida 33019-1825
Contact: Dr. Joseph Pace, National/International Director, Education Initiative
Phone: 954-926-5668
Fax: 954-926-5667
drjpace@msn.com

SERVICES: ADMISSIONS, CONSULTING, DEVELOPMENT, DISTANCE EDUCATION, EDUCATION MANAGEMENT, EDUCATIONAL TRAINING MATERIALS, eLEARNING PROVIDER, PLACEMENT, RECRUITMENT, RETENTION, TRAINING PROVIDER

The Pacific Institute, a world leader in high achievement, peak performance and change management training, has designed a process for career schools. The process, Success Strategies for Effective Colleges and Schools, results in greater student success and increased admissions and retention rates.

PARADIGM MEDIA CONSULTANTS

PO Box 6213
Fishers, IN 46038
Contact: Ms. Deb Rishel, President
or Bob Newman
deb@paradigmmedia.net
bob@paradigmmedia.net
Phone 727-214-5038
Fax: 727-214-5038

SERVICES: ADVERTISING, MARKETING, MEDIA, RECRUITMENT, TRAINING PROVIDERS

Paradigm Media Consultants is a full-service, direct response advertising agency that has been helping both privately held and publicly traded schools for over 20

years with all aspects of their marketing, advertising, recruitment and admissions needs. We produce our own creative because we think that is the first step to successful lead generation.

We will be the first to tell you that we are not the biggest advertising agency. We can't throw a bunch of inexperienced college kids at an account. We don't just pull some recycled spot off the shelf and give it a new name and give to our clients. We won't give you canned answers. And we don't believe in "one size fits all" marketing.

If this seems like a refreshing change of pace and your school is interested in results-driven creative, outstanding media buying and excellent client service, then contact us today.

PARAMOUNT CAPITAL GROUP

822 Montgomery Ave
Suite 205
Narberth, Pennsylvania 19072
Contact: Mr. Bruce Bell, Executive Vice President
Phone: 800-924-7492
Fax: 610-664-2768
bbell@paracap.com

SERVICES: TUITION FINANCING

Paramount Capital Group "purchases" and services retail installment for the career and vocational school industry. We also offer a new service to purchase program and portfolio purchase program.

PATH PARTNERS, LLC

609 South Rose Avenue
Bloomington, IN 47401
Contact: David M. Grenat, Managing Director
Phone: 812-335-1966
Fax: 812-335-1967
dmg@pathpartnersllc.com
www.pathpartnersllc.com

SERVICES: CONSULTING, INVESTMENT BANKING

Path Partners provides business valuation and capital formation services to education and training organizations, and our staff has worked with successful postsecondary schools and private equity funds since 1989. Business valuation assignments typically include benchmarking for a sale of a business, evaluating acquisition prospects, pricing management stock option grants, and estate planning. Our complete capital formation services support school owners and investors in funding expansion financings, management buyouts, recapitalizations and strategic acquisitions.

*PEARSON EDUCATION

5 Saddle Brook Rd.
Saratoga Springs, NY 12866
Contact: Mr. Walt Kirby, Director of Career College Sales
Phone: 518-583-2687
walt.kirby@pearsoned.com
www.pearsoned.com

SERVICES: DISTANCE EDUCATION, EDUCATIONAL TRAINING MATERIALS, eLEARNING PROVIDERS, RETENTION, TRAINING PROVIDERS

Pearson Education, the world's largest educational publisher and information services company, is the best source for meeting your total career college needs. Parent company of renowned publishing units such as Prentice-Hall, Addison Wesley, Benjamin Cummings, Allyn & Bacon Longman, Que, SAMS, Peachpit and Cisco Press. Pearson possesses the resources, experience and depth of knowledge no one in the industry can match. Pearson is truly a learning solutions provider for career education by publishing textbooks, developing software, providing online training and assessment materials for students and faculty, and using our sophisticated Custom Publishing services to tailor products to meet the unique needs of your institution.

*PLATTFORM

500 North Rogers Road
Olathe, Kansas 66062
Contact: Mr. Brad Gibbs, Vice President Marketing & Sales
Phone: 913-254-6061
Fax: 913-764-4043
bradg@plattformad.com
www.plattformad.com

SERVICES: ADMISSIONS, ADVERTISING, CONSULTING, MARKETING, MEDIA, RECRUITMENT, TRAINING PROVIDERS

PlattForm is a full-service integrated marketing communications agency specializing in direct-response advertising within the school industry. With its headquarters in Olathe, Kansas, the agency provides all aspects of advertising campaigns in-house. These services include strategic media planning and buying, creative production, web design, full-service web marketing, interactive cost per lead programs and direct mail. PlattForm specializes in the proprietary school market, servicing over 1,000 campus locations across the USA and Canada. For more information, visit www.PlattFormAd.com.

PNC BANK

2600 Greenbriar Dr.
Mansfield, TX 76063
Contact: Mrs. Jennie Hargrove, Campus Relations Manager
Phone: 800-762-1001 ext. 222
Fax: 817-477-0638
jennie.hargrove@pncbank.com
www.eduloans.pncbank.com

SERVICES: FINANCIAL AID

As one of the nation's top education lenders, PNC Bank provides a complete range of financial products and services, from Federal Stafford and PLUS Loans to alternative lending programs, such as our Continuing Education Loan.

POWERS, PYLES, SUTTER & VERVILLE, P.C.

1875 Eye Street, NW, 12th Floor
Washington, DC 20006
Contact: Mr. Stanley Freeman, Attorney-at-Law
Phone: 202-466-6550
Fax: 202-785-1756
sfreeman@ppsv.com
www.ppsv.com

SERVICES: LEGAL

PPS&V is a group of education lawyers representing both privately owned and publicly traded career colleges across the country. The company provides advice on federal regulatory compliance, program review and audit resolution, state licensure, accreditation, acquisitions, and more.

Q

QUAD VENTURES

650 Fifth Avenue, 31st Floor
New York, New York 10019
Contact: Mr. Daniel Neuwirth

Phone: 212-724-2200 x228
Fax: 212-724-4310
dan@quadventures.com
www.quadventures.com

SERVICES: CONSULTING, INVESTMENT MANAGEMENT
Quad Ventures is a private investment firm based in New York that provides growth capital to school owners and acquires career colleges. Quad Ventures has over 12 years of experience in the postsecondary industry and currently has investments in 13 career colleges in the U.S.

*QUINSTREET, INC.
1051 E. Hillsdale Blvd., 8th Floor
Foster City, California 94404-1603
Contact: Ms. Liza Hausman
Phone: 650-578-7837
Fax: 650-578-7604
lhausman@quinstreet.com
www.quinstreet.com

SERVICES: MARKETING
QuinStreet helps companies acquire new customers cost effectively through online lead generation programs that target and qualify customers while they research purchase options online. QuinStreet is one of the few lead generation businesses that operates strictly on a pay-for-performance basis, tests and optimizes lead quality continuously, and delivers lead volumes according to clients' request.

RDASSOCIATES, INC.
257 E. Lancaster Ave. Ste. 200
Wynnewood, PA 19096
Contact: Mr. Richard Douglass, President
Phone: 610-896-6272
Fax: 610-896-6306
info@rdassociates.com
www.rdassociates.com

SERVICES: ADMISSIONS, ASSESSMENT, CONSULTING, DEVELOPMENT, DISTANCE EDUCATION, DEVELOPMENT, EDUCATIONAL TRAINING MATERIALS, MARKETING, MISCELLANEOUS, RECRUITMENT, STUDENT FINANCIAL AID, TUITION FINANCING

RDAssociates, Inc. is a leading business intelligence, market research and consulting firm designed explicitly to help schools identify market opportunities, analyze the competition and impartially assess their own strengths and weaknesses. RDAssociates can help you track your admissions process and staff professionalism, monitor your staff's adherence to compliancy issues, evaluate the overall student experience, profile and benchmark your campuses in relation to competition, and analyze tuition rates and program offerings across the country. We enable our clients to take full advantage of all market opportunities, gain an edge over the competition, and grow their student base.

RECEIVABLE ACQUISITION & MANAGEMENT CORPORATION
2002 Jimmy Durante Blvd. Ste 410
Del Mar, CA 92014
Contact: Max Khan, C.E.O.
gs@ramcoglobal.com
Phone: 858-755-8538
Fax: 858-755-1421
www.ramcoglobal.com

SERVICES: INVESTMENT MANAGEMENT, RECEIVABLES MANAGEMENT
RAMCO is a major purchaser of performing, charged-off, distressed, sub-performing and stressed accounts receivables. RAMCO purchases loans on a national basis and provides account receivable sales opportunities to career colleges throughout the United States and Great Britain. RAMCO can provide quick decision-making and funding backed up with superior customer service.

RESULTS LOAN MANAGEMENT SERVICES
7172 Regional St. #212
Dublin, CA 94568
Contact: Jennifer Gruczelak, Owner
Phone: 925-997-7447
Fax: 925-361-0212
resultslmjg@comcast.net

SERVICES: DEFAULT MANAGEMENT
specializing in default prevention for vocational schools. Our main focus is resolving delinquent borrowers. We accomplish this by continuous contact with the borrowers. This includes skip tracing, phone calls, letters, contact with lenders and state guarantee agencies, and year-round appeals. We would enjoy taking over the

burden of your borrower contact obligations and letting you go back to what you do best - running a profitable, successful school!

RITTENHOUSE CAPITAL PARTNERS

11180 Tattersall Trail
Oakton, VA 22124
Contact: Mr. Edward Meehan
Phone: 703-359-4773
Fax: 703-991-6479
epm@rittenhousecapital.com
www.rittenhousecapital.com

SERVICES: INVESTMENT BANKING, INVESTMENT MANAGEMENT

An advisory firm with a focus on the postsecondary education sector. The principals of the firm have extensive investment banking experience in the sector, having advised more than 30 postsecondary companies on merger and acquisition and financing matters. Representative clients include: Medvance Institute, American Public University, Strayer Education, Whitman Education Group and Capella Education Company.

RITZERT & LEYTON, P.C.

11350 Random Hills Rd., Ste. 400
Fairfax, Virginia 22030-6803
Contact: Mr. Peter Leyton, Attorney-at-Law
Phone: 703-934-2660
Fax: 703-934-9840
pleyton@ritzert-leyton.com

SERVICES: LEGAL

Ritzert & Leyton represents and counsels institutions of higher education in the highly specialized and regulated areas of federal student financial assistance, accreditation and licensure before federal and state agencies, national and regional accrediting agencies and in federal and state court and with respect to mergers and acquisitions and related corporate and tax matters involving private career schools.

*SALLIE MAE, INC.

12061 Bluemont Way
Reston, Virginia 20190
Contact: Ms. Laura Hardman, Manager, Education

Loan Product Management
Phone: 703-984-6211
Fax: 703-810-7132
laura.w.hardman@slma.com

SERVICES: STUDENT FINANCIAL AID

Sallie Mae provides low-cost federal and private education loans for students, whether they attend full-time, half-time or part-time. Sallie Mae's federal loans offer money-saving benefits and flexible repayment options, while the private loans feature low rates, high approvals and extended repayment terms. Visit www.salliemae.com/partners/cca.html for more information.

SALMONBEACH & ASSOCIATES, PLLC

12720 Hillcrest Road, Suite 900
Dallas, Texas 75230-2035
Phone: 972-392-1143 ▪ 888-332-4829
Fax: 972-934-1269
rsalmon@salmonbeach.com
Contact: Mr. Ronald Salmon, President

SERVICES: CERTIFIED PUBLIC ACCOUNTANTS

Headquartered in Dallas, Texas, SalmonBeach & Associates is one of the leading independent accounting firms in North Texas. SalmonBeach provides the support, advice and assurance to help schools manage regulatory risks. The firm has been a recognized leader in compliance management and career school financial consulting for over 25 years.

SalmonBeach's team of career school specialists is dedicated to responsive service and comprehensive tax planning and audit preparation. Other services include: SFA compliance audits and attestations, monthly financial statements, regulatory ratio consulting, and document management strategy. When you need someone you can trust, call SalmonBeach … always focused on your success! For more information, visit www.salmonbeach.com.

SAPIENZA & ASSOCIATES

3020 Annandale Drive
Presto, Pennsylvania 15142
Contact: Mr. Thomas Sapienza
Phone: 412-279-0802
Fax: 412-279-0876
sapienza@aol.com

SERVICES: INVESTMENT MANAGEMENT

Sapienza & Associates is an investment consulting services company.

SchoolDocs, LLC

12720 Hillcrest Road, Suite 918
Dallas, Texas 75230-2035
Contact: Linda Howard, Director of Business Development
Phone: 972-739-1268
Fax: 972-934-1269
lhoward@schooldocsllc.com
http://www.schooldocsllc.com

SERVICES: SOFTWARE

SchoolDocs is the only complete electronic document management software system custom-designed for career schools to manage their many and varied documents. The system provides a simple, efficient, paperless way to capture, manage and distribute student information, dramatically enhancing a school's current student management software. SchoolDocs was designed by a team of financial and technology experts who have been serving the career school profession for more than 25 years.

SECURITY CREDIT SYSTEMS, INC.

Theater Place
622 Main St. Ste. 301
Buffalo, New York 14202
Contact: Mr. Robert Dixon, Vice President of Sales and Marketing
Phone: 716-882-4515
Fax: 716-884-2577
rdixon@securitycreditsystems.com

SERVICES: COLLECTION SERVICES

Security Credit Systems, Inc. is a nationwide college debt recovery service specializing in the recovery of student loan and tuition receivables. Since 1983, SCS has represented colleges and universities across the country and is recognized as an industry leader in higher education receivables.

SHUGART THOMSON & KILROY, P.C.

Twelve Wyandotte Plaza, Suite 1600
120 West 12th St.
Kansas City, Missouri 64105-1929
Contact: Mr. Ronald Holt, Esq.
Phone: 816-421-3355
Fax: 816-374-0509

rholt@stklaw.com
www.stklaw.com

SERVICES: LEGAL

Shughart Thomson & Kilroy is a business law firm with over 170 lawyers in offices in seven cities, including Kansas City, Denver and Phoenix, which provides counsel to institutions of higher learning across the nation on regulatory compliance; representation in lawsuits and agency proceedings concerning accrediting disputes, program reviews, LS&T proceedings and student disputes; labor and employment issues; change of ownership transactional and regulatory work; and tax and corporate members. Information on our education practice can be found at http://www.stklaw.com/practicegroups/education.html.

THE SOURCE FOR TRAINING, INC.

2875 South Delaney Avenue
Orlando, Florida 32806
Contact: Ms. Nancy Rogers, President
Phone: 407-420-1010
Fax: 407-420-9500
sourcetran@aol.com
sourcefortraining.com

SERVICES: ADMISSIONS, ADMINISTRATIVE SERVICES, ADVERTISING, CONSULTING, MARKETING, RECRUITMENT, RETENTION, TRAINING PROVIDERS

For more than 25 years, the Source has worked with private, postsecondary schools in providing support and training throughout the admissions process. Schools can increase productivity and achieve exceptional growth using the Source's highly effective recruiting tools, techniques and proven systems.
Combined, Nancy Rogers and Paul Gordon have 50+ years of experience. Their workshops include topics such as "Admissions - The Basics and Beyond"; "Your Service is Showing"; Retention is Everyone's Job"; "Managing the Entire Admissions Process," etc.

SONNENSCHEIN NATH & ROSENTHAL, LLP

8000 Sears Tower
Chicago, Illinois 60606
Contact: Mr. Eric R. Decator, Partner
Phone: 312-876-2569
Fax: 312-876-7934
edecator@sonnenschein.com
www.sonnenschein.com

SERVICES: LEGAL

Sonnenschein, with 600 attorneys in nine U.S. cities and a global reach throughout Europe, Asia and Latin America, serves the legal needs of many of the world's largest and best-known businesses, nonprofits and individuals. The firm's attorneys have extensive experience representing colleges and universities in all aspects of their operations. We advise clients in both the proprietary and not-for-profit sectors of the higher education industry. In the past few years, we have represented clients in connection with the acquisition and disposition of numerous colleges, universities and other postsecondary schools. Sonnenschein's higher education lawyers routinely collaborate with the firm's lawyers in its corporate, health care, taxation, litigation, antitrust, employment, employee benefits, bankruptcy, environmental and real estate practice groups in Sonnenschein's continuing effort to provide its clients with a broad range of legal expertise.

SPECIALTY BOOKS, INC.

6000 Poston Rd.
Athens, OH 45701
Contact: Ms. Lynne Williams, Director of Business Development
Phone: 858-592-0101
Fax: 858-592-0263

SERVICES: EDUCATIONAL TRAINING MATERIALS, MISCELLANEOUS

Specialty Books provides course materials fulfillment for career colleges across the nation. We create a customized online bookstore for your program and offer a wide range of services to meet your needs, from online student buyback to faculty resources.

As the pioneer in textbook distribution, we have the experience needed to provide you and your students with superior service. We realize that every program has different needs, so we'll treat you like the unique program you are, not just another cookie-cutter account. By handling all inventory management, customer service and shipping, Specialty Books will eliminate your textbook fulfillment headaches, increase your revenue and give you the time to focus on what matters: education.

SPECTRUM INDUSTRIES, INC.

1600 Johnson Street
P.O. Box 400
Chippewa Falls, Wisconsin 54729-1468

Contact: Mr. James Lloyd, National Sales Representative
Phone: 800-235-1262
Fax: 800-335-0473
spectrum@spectrumfurniture.com
www.spectrumfurniture.com

SERVICES: FURNITURE, MISCELLANEOUS

Leaders in modernizing the learning environment, Spectrum Industries offers furniture for computer labs, technology classrooms and multimedia centers. Sold direct from the factory, the furnishings are durable, flexible and ergonomically correct. Using Spectrum's exclusive P'cable-guard wire management system P', their solutions to your furniture needs are economical and look great.

STOUT RISIUS ROSS ADVISORS, LLC

One South Wacker, Ste. 1900
Chicago, IL 60606
Contact: Mr. Jack DiFranco, Managing Director
Phone: 248-432-1230
Fax: 248-208-8822
jdifranco@srr.com

SERVICES: INVESTMENT BANKING

Provides a full range of investment banking services to middle-market business throughout the United States. SRRA draws on relevant transaction experience in the postsecondary space to provide clients with senior-level attention throughout the process. Services include mergers, acquisitions, divestitures, growth and transaction financing, shareholder recapitalizations, and ESOP advisory services.

STUDENT LOAN XPRESS

12680 High Bluff Drive, Suite 400
San Diego, California 92130
Contact: Mr. Gary Rohmann
Phone: 866-759-7737 ext. 6882
Fax: 866-289-7737
gary.rohmann@slxpress.com
www.studentloanxpress.com

SERVICES: FINANCIAL AID, STUDENT FINANCIAL AID

Student Loan Xpress, Inc. offers a new way to look at lending with an experienced and dedicated team providing smart solutions for the financing of educational expenses. We offer Federal Stafford Loans for students and Parent Loans for Undergraduate Students (PLUS Loans) for parents. In addition to Stafford and PLUS Loans,

Student Loan Xpress offers a variety of private Loans to meet any additional funding needs you may have. Student Loan Xpress is here to help, with easy-to-use tools and student loan programs and services for students, parents and schools. Our commitment emphasizes early awareness, debt management and individual financial responsibility for parents and students alike. In cooperation with the Career College Foundation, we also offer the Consolidation Assistance Program (CAP®) to CCA member schools. For more information about FFELP and private loans, students should visit the web at www. studentloanxpress.com or loan consolidation information at http://schools.slxpress.com/ccf.

STUDENT RESOURCE SERVICES, LLC

9338 Olive Boulevard
St. Louis, Missouri 63132
Contact: Janet Mug, MA, LPC, CEAP, President & Owner
Phone: 314-222-4020 x3015
Toll Free: 866-500-2327 x3015
jmug@peopleresourceseap.com
www.peopleresourceseap.com

SERVICES: ADMISSIONS, CONSULTING, eLEARNING PROVIDERS, RETENTION

People Resources, Inc. People Resources has focused over 20 years on developing and delivering customized Student Resource Program (SRP) services for adult students and Employee Assistance Program (EAP) services for employees worldwide. Our Student Resource Program (SRP) is designed for career colleges to enhance student retention and graduation rates. The SRP can support the documentations process for reaccreditation, meet student needs, and provide a better return on student acquisition costs.

Student Resource Program services are delivered through First Clinical Coordination with licensed professionals (24-7), 24 hours a day, seven days a week. Confidential telephone coaching and counseling and face-to-face counseling are provided where the student resides. In addition to the counseling options, extensive web-based services are available. By providing direct access to all available resources, students can have solutions to life's unexpected events and crises. This full-access approach allows students to find around-the-clock solutions for a wide range of personal, housing, financial and family difficulties. This full-access approach will increase the number of students seeking services, thereby addressing the students' personal worries and challenges in a confidential manner and improving the overall success rate of students.

SUNRISE CREDIT SERVICE, INC.

260 Airport Plaza
Farmingdale, NY 11735
Contact: Joseph Vassar, V.P. Sales
Phone: 800-208-8565
Fax: 631-501-8529
jvassar@sunrisecreditservices.com
www.sunrisecreditservices.com

SERVICES: CONSULTING, COLLECTION SERVICES, DEFAULT MANAGEMENT, MARKETING, RECRUITMENT

A full-service nationwide credit and collection agent specializing in all aspects of accounts receivables management. Our programs include: early out, training, skip-trace, traditional third party collections, seminars, etc. It is our goal to provide superior performance while maintaining the highest quality client care.

SUNTRUST EDUCATION LOANS

1001 Semmes Avenue, RVW 7900
Richmond, Virginia 23224
Contact: Sherrye Ward, National Sales Manager
Phone: 804-319-1339
Fax: 804-319-4823
sherrye.ward@suntrust.com
www.SunTrustEducation.com

SERVICES: FINANCIAL AID, STUDENT FINANCIAL AID, TUITION FINANCING

SunTrust is a leading national provider of education loans with a commitment to serving the needs of private career schools and their students. We offer Federal Stafford, PLUS and Consolidation Loans – all with money-saving repayment benefits. SunTrust also offers alternative loan products, including our eCareer® education loan that gives students greater flexibility in paying for school since it is not subject to the lending limits and eligibility requirements of many federal loan programs. Find out more at www.SunTrustEducation.com.

SUSAN F. SCHULZ & ASSOCIATES, INC.

Schools for Sale International, Inc.
2831 NW 23 Court
Boca Raton, Florida 33431
Contact: Dr. Susan F. Schulz, President
Phone: 561-483-9554
Fax: 561-451-4602

susan@susanfschulz.com
www.susanfschulz.com

SERVICES: CONSULTING, DEVELOPMENT, DISTANCE EDUCATION, EDUCATION MANAGEMENT, EDUCATIONAL TRAINING MATERIALS, PLACEMENT, RETENTION

Susan F. Schulz & Associates, Inc. provides consulting services to career schools and colleges in the areas of licensing, accreditation, curriculum development and school development, continuing education, operations assessment, and more. Through our professional and licensed affiliate, Schools for Sale International, Inc., we offer intermediary and consulting services specializing in the purchase and sale of privately held schools and education entities.

TALX CORPORATION - THE WORK NUMBER

1850 Borman Street
St. Louis, MO 63146
Contact: Mr. Charles Krasnicki
Phone: 314-214-7012
Fax: 314-214-7588
ckrasnicki@talx.com
www.theworknumber.com

SERVICES: IT SOLUTIONS, MISCELLANEOUS, PLACEMENT

TALX Corporation, The Work Number®, is the largest source for online employment verifications. Over 1,000 employers outsource their verification workload to The Work Number, which provides online access to over 100 million employment records.

Career placement offices and accrediting agencies have found that instant & accurate online employment data is invaluable to their operations, reducing manual processes required for reporting & auditing placement rates. To learn more about using The Work Number, visit www.theworknumber.com/go or call Steve Dowd at 1-888-577-1999 (or 314-214-7086).

TARGET DIRECT MARKETING

185 Main Street
Gloucester, Massachusetts 01930-1802
Contact: Mr. John Pirroni, President
Phone: 978-281-5967
Fax: 978-282-0311
jpirroni@tdmkt.com

www.targetdirectmarketing.com

SERVICES: ADVERTISING, MARKETING

Target Direct Marketing (TDM) can help clients systematically generate cost-effective quality leads and starts through its proven, directmail programs. TDM does market analysis, campaign planning, list procurement, creative design and copy, mailing, training, and evaluation of results.

TESTOUT CORPORATION

50 S. Main St.
Pleasant Grove, UT 84062
Contact: Mr. David Blakely, Business Development Director
Phone: 801-785-7900
Fax: 801-785-0575
dblakely@testout.com
www.testout.com

SERVICES: CERTIFICATION, DISTANCE EDUCATION, ELEARNING PROVIDER, EDUCATION TRAINING MATERIALS

With more than 11 years experience in technology-based IT training, TestOut Corporation is the leading provider of simulation-based training and testing solutions to higher education and secondary institutions. Its simulation-based training curriculum, consisting of an interactive, simulation-rich LabSim practice environment and ExamSim practice certification exam tools, is used by individuals, academic institutions, publishers and training centers around the globe.

TFC CREDIT CORPORATION

199 Jericho Turnpike, Suite 300
Floral Park, New York 11001-2100
Contact: Mr. Stanley Sobel, President
Phone: 516-358-1900
Fax: 516-358-6357
info@tfccredit.com
www.tfccredit.com

SERVICES: ADMINISTRATIVE SERVICES, COLLECTION SERVICE, FINANCIAL AID, RECEIVABLES MANAGEMENT, STUDENT FINANCIAL AID, TUITION FINANCING

TFC Credit Corporation has been providing tuition financing to students for over 35 years. Our school clients range from the small family-run school to large multistate school organizations. Any portion of tuition that is not covered by financial aid programs may be financed through TFC. We can also finance up to $18,000 of the tuition for courses or students that do not qualify for financial aid. Our extremely competitive interest rates will help enroll and retain more students. Financing is also available to schools not yet accredited.

THOMSON LEARNING
Executive Woods
5 Maxwell Drive
Clifton Park, New York 12065-2919
Contact: Mr. Tom Riendeau, Career College Channel Manager
Phone: 518-348-2300
Fax: 518-881-1250
tom.riendeau@thomson.com
www.anywhereyoulearn.com

SERVICES: EDUCATIONAL TRAINING MATERIALS, eLEARNING PROVIDERS

Thomson Learning is a leading provider of skills-based learning solutions for all areas of study in general education, health care, automotive, computer and information technologies, business, criminal justice, and paralegal studies. Offering a range of solutions from individual products to comprehensive curriculum packages, our wealth of vocational and technical publishers, with proven learning products for all areas of study in general education, allied health, automotive, computer and information technologies, business, criminal justice, and paralegal studies. Our wealth of print, CD-ROM, DVD and online products work individually or together to allow you to choose the best combination for your needs. Thomson/Delmar Learning's ability to bring you knowledge the way you want to receive it makes us the obvious choice for your learning and teaching materials.

TMP WORLDWIDE EDUCATIONAL MARKETING GROUP
205 Hudson Street, 5th Floor
New York, New York 10013
Contact: Mr. Steven Ehrlich, Director
Phone: 646-613-2000
Fax: 646-613-9752
steve.ehrlich@tmp.com
www.tmp.com

SERVICES: MARKETING

TMP Worldwide's Educational Marketing Group is a trusted guide, a thought-provoking partner and a strategic leader. Our goal is to collaborate with our clients to create innovative solutions that traverse the evolving student recruitment landscape. It's a lofty aspiration - one we believe in wholeheartedly. Our desire to form a dynamic relationship with each of our clients compels us to understand their individual challenges, as well as the global dynamics swaying the educational market today. When it comes to selecting a marketing communications & solutions partner, there's really only one word that matters: delivery.

TOP-COLLEGES.COM BY AFFILIATE CREW
6415 S. 3000 E.
Suite 200
Salt Lake City, Utah 84121
Contact: Mr. Ryan Stevenson, Director
Phone: 801-993-2222 ext. 1006
Fax: 801-993-2295
rstevenson@affiliatecrew.com
www.top-colleges.com

SERVICES: ADVERTISING, MARKETING

Top-Colleges.com provides colleges and universities with a cost-effective alternative to traditional offline lead generation. Our online education directory provides a customized experience for each student based on geography and degree type. The result is a highly qualified prospect, matched to the right school in the right location.

TRAINING MASTERS, INC.
2305 Claridge Court
Enola, Pennsylvania 17025
Phone: 877-885-3276
Fax: 800-882-8574
Cell: 717-571-8555
docrita@trainingmasters.com
Contact: Dr. Rita Girondi, President
SERVICES: ADMISSIONS, CONSULTING, EDUCATION MANAGEMENT, EDUCATIONAL TRAINING MATERIALS, INFORMATION TECHNOLOGY SOLUTIONS, PLACEMENT, RETENTION, SOFTWARE, TRAINING PROVIDERS

Special Message:
Training Masters is a training and consulting company offering unique products and services designed for career schools and colleges, as well as other educational institutions and organizations. Training Masters' distinction is its direct experience in successfully operating and owning schools. To improve starts, retention and other key operational areas, Training Masters brings the best practices to schools and keeps compli-

ance and profitability in focus. STARS (Student Tracking, Accounting and Records System) is a comprehensive, integrated administrative software solution that combines information technology tools with internal procedures to create a proven, affordable school operational system. PIE (Pursuing Instructional Excellence) is a computer-based, interactive instructor training program covering topics such as active learning, motivating students, classroom management, building a high retention classroom, the new instructor's guide to career schools and more. Klickerz™ is Training Masters' unique software that utilizes hand-held remotes, creating highly interactive classroom presentations, exciting curriculum support materials and dynamic admissions presentations for the high school market. In-service programs, school retention rallies, new school director training, high-performance team building, personal effectiveness coaching and numerous other services and tools that support schools' goals are available. More information about Training Masters can be found on the Web (http://www.trainingmasters.com).

TUITION MANAGEMENT SYSTEMS

171 Service Avenue, Second Flr.
Warwick, RI 02886
Contact: Mr. Christopher Cimino, National Sales Director
Phone: 800-722-4867
Fax: 401-736-5050
ccimino@afford.com
www.afford.com

SERVICES: ADMISSIONS, FINANCIAL AID, RECRUITMENT MANAGEMENT, RECRUITMENT, STUDENT FINANCIAL AID, TUITION FINANCING

Our mission has remained steadfast: to help families afford education and schools prosper. More than 700 schools have used our proven path to get their bills paid by over 1.5 million students and families. The proven path starts with affordability planning and counseling and moves through bill production, delivery of tailored payment options and loans, and processing of payments. When you work with Tuition Management Systems, any or all parts of a seamless education payment process can be delivered on behalf of your institution's assessments.

USA FUNDS

P.O. Box 6028
Indianapolis, IN 46206
Contact: Denise Feser
Phone: 317-806-1280
Fax: 317-806-1203
dfeser@usafunds.org
www.usafunds.org

SERVICES: FINANCIAL AID

USA Funds® is a nonprofit corporation that works to enhance postsecondary education preparedness, access and success by providing and supporting financial and other valued services. USA Funds links colleges, universities, proprietary schools, private lenders, students and parents to promote financial access to higher learning.

V

*VITAL BUSINESS SUPPLIES, INC.

701 Cooper Road, Suite 12
Voorhees, NJ 08043
Contact: Mr. Frank Phillips, President
Phone: 856-346-1889
Fax: 856-346-8660
vbsinc01@aol.com
www.VitalBusinessSupplies.com

SERVICES: ADMINISTRATIVE SERVICES, COMPUTER HARDWARE, EDUCATIONAL TRAINING, EDUCATION MANAGEMENT, FURNITURE, IT SOLUTIONS, MISCELLANEOUS, SOFTWARE

A national leader in the distribution of educational supplies. Our product lines include textbooks, medical supplies, scrubs, lab coats, office supplies, furniture and computer supplies. Our purchasing power allows us to pass along our deeply discounted prices to you. VBS prides itself on our professional and caring service. We are your one-stop source for all your supply needs. Don't forget to ask about our "Money Back" scholarship program.

W

WEST & COMPANY

2938 N.W. 50th
Oklahoma City, Oklahoma 73112
Contact: Mr. William West, President

Phone: 405-949-9730
Fax: 405-949-9738
westandcompany@aol.com

SERVICES: CPA

West & Company, a Certified Public Accounting firm specializing in the educational industry, provides services in the fields of financial aid audits and attestation engagements, financial statement audits, tax planning and compliance, systems consulting services, and compliance consulting services.

WEWORSKI & ASSOCIATES

4660 La Jolla Village Drive, Suite 880
San Diego, California 92122
Contact: Mr. Michael C. Facer, Partner
Phone: 858-546-1505
Fax: 858-546-1405
mfacer@weworski.com
www.weworski.com

SERVICES: CPA

Weworski & Associates is a Certified Public Accounting firm that was formed specifically to service the proprietary school industry. Our firm has built a solid reputation for providing quality and timely services to our clients. We provide a wide array of services, including financial statement audits, student financial aid audits, income tax planning and preparation, acquisition due to diligence, and other management advisory services to over 100 proprietary schools.

WHITEFORD, TAYLOR & PRESTON

1025 Connecticut Avenue, N.W., Suite 400
Washington, DC 20036
Contact: Mr. Kenneth J. Ingram, Partner
Phone: 202-659-6800
Fax: 202-331-0573
kingram@wtplaw.com

SERVICES: LEGAL

Whiteford, Taylor & Preston represents a number of private, non-profit accrediting agencies, including ACICS, ABHES, ACCET, MEAC and CSWE.

WONDERLIC, INC.

1795 North Butterfield Road
Libertyville, Illinois 60048
Contact: Mr. Justin Long, Director, Educational Relations
Phone: 800-323-3742

Fax: 847-680-9492
justin.long@wonderlic.com
www.wonderlic.com

SERVICES: ADMINISTRATIVE SERVICES, CONSULTING, DISTANCE EDUCATION, RECRUITMENT, RETENTION, TESTING TOOLS AND EQUIPMENT

Wonderlic, Inc. has been a leader in the test publishing, consulting and information gathering business since 1937. Wonderlic is a founding member of the Association of Test Publishers and approved by both the U.S. Department of Education and the American Council of Education. Over 130 million individuals have taken Wonderlic assessments and satisfaction surveys at nearly 60,000 schools, government agencies and businesses worldwide.

WORKFORCE COMMUNICATIONS

627 Bay Shore Dr., Ste 100
Oshkosh, Wisconsin 54901-4975
Contact: Mr. Michael Cooney, Vice President
Phone: 800-558-8250
Fax: 920-231-9977
mcooney@workforce-com.com

SERVICES: ADVERTISING, MARKETING

WorkForce Communications offers fast, responsive and cost-effective production of response-driven career college brochures and TV commercials. High accountability lead generation is provided by our veteran media placement team. Since 1926, the Career Education Review has served as the independent trade publication serving private career colleges.

WRIGHT INTERNATIONAL STUDENT SERVICES

6405 Metcalf Ave., Suite 504
Shawnee Mission, Kansas 66202
Contact: Mr. John Beal, President
Phone: 800-257-4757
Fax: 913-677-0977
john@studentservicesint.com
www.wiss.info

SERVICES: DEFAULT MANAGEMENT

Wright International Student Services (WISS) is the industry leader in default management services. Over 300 institutions, both private and public, utilize WISS for their default reduction needs. The average default rate of WISS' client schools is 4.69 percent.

PROFILES OF CAREER COLLEGES

ALABAMA

CAPPS COLLEGE

200 Vulcan Way
Dothan, AL 36303
Web: http://www.medcareers.net
Programs Offered:
massage therapy; medical/clinical assistant; medical office management; medical transcription; pharmacy technician
Institution Contact:
Phone: 334-677-2832
Fax: 334-677-3756

CAPPS COLLEGE

914 North McKenzie Street
Foley, AL 36535
Web: http://www.medcareers.net
Accreditation: Accrediting Bureau of Health Education Schools
Programs Offered:
medical/clinical assistant
Enrollment: 71 students
Institution Contact: Mrs. Pam Milstead, Director
Phone: 251-970-1460
Fax: 251-970-1660
E-mail: pmilstead@medcareers.net
Admission Contact: Ms. Kimberly Bateman, Admissions Advisor
Phone: 251-970-1460
Fax: 251-970-1660

CAPPS COLLEGE

3590 Pleasant Valley Road
Mobile, AL 36609
Accreditation: Accrediting Bureau of Health Education Schools
Programs Offered:
massage therapy; medical administrative assistant and medical secretary; medical/clinical assistant; pharmacy technician
Enrollment: 201 students
Institution Contact: Ms. Annette Hicks, Campus Director
Phone: 251-344-1203
Fax: 251-344-1299

E-mail: ahicks@medcareers.net
Admission Contact: Mrs. Vicki Green, Admissions Advisor
Phone: 251-344-1203 ext. 12
Fax: 251-344-1299 E-mail: info@medcareers.net

CAPPS COLLEGE

3736 Atlanta Highway
Montgomery, AL 36109
Accreditation: Accrediting Bureau of Health Education Schools
Programs Offered:
medical administrative assistant and medical secretary; medical/clinical assistant; pharmacy technician
Enrollment: 217 students
Institution Contact: Ms. Sheila Brown, Campus Director
Phone: 334-272-3857
Fax: 334-272-3859
E-mail: sbrown@medcareers.net
Admission Contact: Mrs. Sally Gaston, Director of Admissions
Phone: 334-272-3857
Fax: 334-272-3859
E-mail: info@medcareers.net

HERZING COLLEGE

280 West Valley Avenue
Birmingham, AL 35209-4816
Web: http://www.herzing.edu/birmingham
Accreditation: Accrediting Commission of Career Schools and Colleges of Technology; North Central Association of Colleges and Schools
Programs Offered:
business administration and management; communications technology; computer and information systems security; computer engineering technology; computer/information technology administration and management; computer/information technology services administration related; computer programming; computer programming (specific applications); computer programming (vendor/product certification); computer systems analysis; computer systems networking and telecommunications; computer technology/computer systems technology; data processing and data processing technology; e-commerce; electrical, electronic and communications engineering technology; electromechanical technology; health/health care administration; health information/medical records administration;

health information/medical records technology; industrial electronics technology; information technology; medical administrative assistant and medical secretary; medical insurance coding; medical insurance/medical billing; medical office computer specialist; medical office management; system administration; system, networking, and LAN/WAN management; technology management; telecommunications; telecommunications technology; web page, digital/multimedia and information resources design

Enrollment: 445 students
Institution Contact: Mr. Donald Lewis, President
Phone: 205-916-2800
Fax: 205-916-2807
E-mail: donl@bhm.herzing.edu
Admission Contact: Ms. Tess L. Anderson, Director of Admissions
Phone: 205-916-2800
Fax: 205-916-2807
E-mail: info@bhm.herzing.edu

 ITT TECHNICAL INSTITUTE
6270 Park South Drive
Bessemer, AL 35022
Web: http://www.itt-tech.edu
Accreditation: Accrediting Council for Independent Colleges and Schools
Programs Offered:
accounting and business/management; animation, interactive technology, video graphics and special effects; business administration and management; CAD/CADD drafting/design technology; communications technology; computer and information systems security; computer engineering technology; computer software and media applications; computer software engineering; computer systems networking and telecommunications; criminal justice/police science; digital communication and media/multimedia; electrical, electronic and communications engineering technology; technology management; web page, digital/multimedia and information resources design
Institution Contact: Mr. Allen Rice, Director
Phone: 205-497-5700
Fax: 205-497-5799
E-mail: arice@itt-tech.edu
Admission Contact: Mr. Jesse L. Johnson, Director of Recruitment
Phone: 205-497-5700

Fax: 205-497-5799
E-mail: jljohnson@itt-tech.edu

 MEDICAL CAREER CENTER
5901 Airport Blvd
Mobile, AL 36608-3169
Institution contact: Mike Little
Phone: 251-343-7227
Fax: 251-343-7287

REMINGTON COLLEGE - MOBILE CAMPUS
828 Downtowner Loop West
Mobile, AL 36609-5404
Web: http://www.remingtoncollege.edu
Accreditation: Accrediting Commission of Career Schools and Colleges of Technology
Programs Offered:
allied health and medical assisting services related; business administration and management; computer engineering technology; computer installation and repair technology; computer programming; electrical, electronic and communications engineering technology; pharmacy technician
Enrollment: 454 students
Institution Contact: Mr. Micheal Ackerman, Campus President
Phone: 251-343-8200 ext. 209
Fax: 251-343-0577
E-mail: michael.ackerman@remingtoncollege.edu
Admission Contact: Mr. Chris Jones, Director of Recruitment
Phone: 251-343-8200 ext. 221
Fax: 251-343-0577
E-mail: chris.jones@remingtoncollege.com

SOUTH UNIVERSITY
5355 Vaughn Road
Montgomery, AL 36116-1120
Web: http://www.southuniversity.edu/
Accreditation: Southern Association of Colleges and Schools
Programs Offered:
accounting; business administration and management; counselor education/school counseling and guidance; criminal justice/law enforcement administration; health/health care administration; information technol-

ogy; legal assistant/paralegal; medical/clinical assistant; physical therapist assistant; pre-law studies
Enrollment: 400 students
Institution Contact: Mr. Victor K. Biebighauser, President
Phone: 334-395-8800
Fax: 334-395-8859
E-mail: vbiebighauser@southuniversity.edu
Admission Contact: Ms. Anna M. Pearson, Director of Admissions
Phone: 334-395-8800
Fax: 334-395-8859
E-mail: apearson@southuniversity.edu

VC Tech
2790 Pelham Parkway
Pelham, AL 35124
Web: http://www.vc.edu
Accreditation: Accrediting Council for Independent Colleges and Schools
Programs Offered:
autobody/collision and repair technology; automobile/automotive mechanics technology
Enrollment: 240 students
Institution Contact: Ms. Lynne Berg Daigle, Marketing/Advertising Director; Academic Dean
Phone: 205-358-1100 ext. 2937
Fax: 205-358-1124
E-mail: ldaigle@vc.edu
Admission Contact: Mr. Dean Mahaffey, National Director of Admissions
Phone: 205-358-1100 ext. 2920
Fax: 205-358-1124
E-mail: dmahaffey@vc.edu

Virginia College at Birmingham
PO Box 19249
Birmingham, AL 35219-9249
Web: http://www.vc.edu
Accreditation: Accrediting Council for Independent Colleges and Schools
Programs Offered:
accounting; accounting and business/management; accounting related; accounting technology and bookkeeping; administrative assistant and secretarial science; allied health and medical assisting services related; animation, interactive technology, video graphics and special effects; architectural drafting and CAD/CADD; art; autobody/collision and repair technology; automobile/automotive mechanics technology; baking and pastry arts; business administration and management; business automation/technology/data entry; business/corporate communications; business, management, and marketing related; business/managerial economics; business operations support and secretarial services related; CAD/CADD drafting/design technology; commercial and advertising art; computer and information sciences; computer and information sciences and support services related; computer and information sciences related; computer and information systems security; computer graphics; computer/information technology administration and management; computer/information technology services administration related; computer installation and repair technology; computer programming; computer programming related; computer programming (specific applications); computer programming (vendor/product certification); corrections; criminal justice/law enforcement administration; criminal justice/police science; culinary arts; desktop publishing and digital imaging design; diagnostic medical sonography and ultrasound technology; executive assistant/executive secretary; general studies; graphic communications; graphic communications related; health information/medical records administration; health services administration; health services/allied health/health sciences; hospitality administration; human resources management; human resources management and services related; interior design; legal assistant/paralegal; management information systems; management information systems and services related; massage therapy; medical/clinical assistant; medical insurance coding; medical insurance/medical billing; medical office assistant; medical office management; nursing (licensed practical/vocational nurse training); office management; pharmacy technician; physician assistant; surgical technology; system, networking, and LAN/WAN management; telecommunications technology; web/multimedia management and webmaster; web page, digital/multimedia and information resources design; word processing
Enrollment: 2,850 students
Institution Contact: Dr. James Hutton, Chief Executive Officer
Phone: 205-802-1200
Fax: 205-329-7861 E-mail: jdh@vc.edu
Admission Contact: Mrs. Bunty Cantwell, Vice Presi-

dent of Admissions
Phone: 205-802-1200 ext. 1207
Fax: 205-802-7045
E-mail: bcantwell@vc.edu

VIRGINIA COLLEGE AT HUNTSVILLE

2800A Bob Wallace Avenue
Huntsville, AL 35805
Web: http://www.vc.edu
Accreditation: Accrediting Council for Independent Colleges and Schools
Programs Offered:
accounting technology and bookkeeping; administrative assistant and secretarial science; banking and financial support services; business administration and management; CAD/CADD drafting/design technology; computer graphics; computer installation and repair technology; computer systems networking and telecommunications; computer technology/computer systems technology; cosmetology; criminal justice/law enforcement administration; criminal justice/police science; digital communication and media/multimedia; drafting and design technology; graphic communications related; health information/medical records technology; legal administrative assistant/secretary; legal assistant/paralegal; massage therapy; medical administrative assistant and medical secretary; medical/clinical assistant; medical insurance/medical billing; medical office assistant; medical office management; office management; system administration; system, networking, and LAN/WAN management; web/multimedia management and webmaster
Enrollment: 680 students
Institution Contact: Mr. James Foster, Campus President
Phone: 256-533-7387
Fax: 256-533-7785
E-mail: jfoster@vc.edu
Admission Contact: Ms. Pat A. Foster, Vice President of Enrollment
Phone: 256-533-7387
Fax: 256-533-7785
E-mail: pfoster@vc.edu

VIRGINIA COLLEGE AT MOBILE

5901 Airport Boulevard
Mobile, AL 36608

Web: http://www.medcci.com
Accreditation: Accrediting Bureau of Health Education Schools; Accrediting Council for Independent Colleges and Schools
Programs Offered:
accounting technology and bookkeeping; administrative assistant and secretarial science; human resources management; legal administrative assistant/secretary; medical/clinical assistant; medical insurance coding; medical insurance/medical billing; surgical technology
Institution Contact: Mrs. Joy Harden, Campus Administrator
Phone: 251-343-7227 ext. 2405
Fax: 251-343-7287
E-mail: jharden@vc.edu
Admission Contact: Mrs. Tracy McManus, Director of Admissions
Phone: 251-343-7227 ext. 2402
Fax: 251-343-7287
E-mail: tmcmanus@vc.edu

ALASKA

CAREER ACADEMY

1415 East Tudor Road
Anchorage, AK 99507-1033
Web: http://www.careeracademy.edu
Accreditation: Accrediting Commission of Career Schools and Colleges of Technology
Programs Offered:
airline pilot and flight crew; business operations support and secretarial services related; massage therapy; medical/clinical assistant; medical insurance coding; medical insurance/medical billing; office management; phlebotomy; tourism and travel services management
Enrollment: 653 students
Institution Contact: Ms. Jennifer Deitz, President
Phone: 907-563-7575
Fax: 907-563-8330
E-mail: jdeitz@careeracademy.edu
Admission Contact: Ms. Lisa Spencer, Director of Admissions
Phone: 907-563-7575
Fax: 907-563-8330
E-mail: lspencer@careeracademy.edu

CHARTER COLLEGE

2221 East Northern Lights Boulevard, Suite 120
Anchorage, AK 99508-4140
Web: http://www.chartercollege.edu
Accreditation: Accrediting Council for Independent
Colleges and Schools
Programs Offered:
accounting; accounting technology and bookkeeping; administrative assistant and secretarial science; architectural drafting and CAD/CADD; business administration and management; business administration, management and operations related; CAD/CADD drafting/design technology; civil drafting and CAD/CADD; computer engineering related; computer engineering technologies related; computer engineering technology; computer graphics; computer hardware technology; computer/information technology administration and management; computer/information technology services administration related; computer software technology; computer systems networking and telecommunications; computer technology/computer systems technology; health and medical administrative services related; information technology; medical office management; web/multimedia management and webmaster
Enrollment: 489 students
Institution Contact: Dr. Milton Byrd, President
Phone: 907-777-1304
Fax: 907-274-3342
E-mail: mbyrd@chartercollege.edu
Admission Contact: Miss Brenda O'Neill, Associate
Director of Academic Services
Phone: 907-777-1342
Fax: 907-274-3342
E-mail: bo'neill@chartercollege.edu

ARIZONA

ACADEMY OF RADIO BROADCASTING

4914 East McDowell Road, #107
Phoenix, AZ 85008
Web: http://www.arbradio.com
Accreditation: Accrediting Council for Continuing
Education and Training
Programs Offered:
cinematography and film/video production; radio and
television

Institution Contact: Mr. Thomas Gillenwater, President
Phone: 602-267-8001
Fax: 602-273-6411
Admission Contact: Mr. Brian Jewett, Admissions
Director
Phone: 602-267-8001
Fax: 602-273-6411
E-mail: jewettbrianm@aol.com

AMERICAN INSTITUTE OF TECHNOLOGY

440 South 54th Avenue
Phoenix, AZ 85043-4729
Web: http://www.ait-schools.com
Accreditation: Accrediting Commission of Career
Schools and Colleges of Technology
Programs Offered:
truck and bus driver/commercial vehicle operation
Enrollment: 135 students
Institution Contact: Mr. R. Wade Murphree, President
Phone: 602-233-2222
Fax: 602-278-4849
E-mail: wade@ait-schools.com
Admission Contact: Mrs. Julie Wirth, Assistant to the
Vice President
Phone: 602-233-2222
Fax: 602-278-4849
E-mail: admissions@ait-schools.com

ANTHEM COLLEGE ONLINE

2222 W Peoria Ave.
Phoenix, AZ 85029
Institution contact: Mr. David Eby
Phone: 602-889-2700
Fax: 602-889-2799

APOLLO COLLEGE - PHOENIX, INC.

7600 N. 16th St Suite 160
Phoenix, AZ 85020
Web: http://www.apollocollege.edu
Accreditation: Accrediting Bureau of Health Education Schools
Programs Offered:
clinical/medical laboratory technology; dental assisting; medical administrative assistant and medical secretary; medical/clinical assistant; pharmacy technician; veterinary/animal health technology

Institution Contact: Mr. Michael White, JD, Director Of Education
Phone: 602-324-5512
Fax: 602-3245512
E-mail: mwhite@apollocollege.edu
Admission Contact: Mr. Andrew Vaughn, Regional Director of Admissions
Phone: 602-324-5514
Fax: 602-324-5514
E-mail: avaughn@apollocollege.com

Apollo College - Tri-City, Inc.

630 West Southern Avenue
1310 South Country Club Drive
Mesa, AZ 85210
Web: http://www.apollocollege.com
Accreditation: Accrediting Bureau of Health Education Schools
Programs Offered:
dental assisting; massage therapy; medical administrative assistant and medical secretary; medical/clinical assistant; pharmacy technician; respiratory care therapy; veterinary/animal health technology
Institution Contact: Mr. James Norris Miller, Executive Director
Phone: 480-212-1600
Fax: 480-212-1601
E-mail: j.miller@apollocollege.edu
Admission Contact: Mr. James Norris Miller , Executive Director
Phone: 480-212-1600
Fax: 480-212-1600
E-mail: j.miller@apollocollege.edu

Apollo College - Tucson, Inc.

3550 North Oracle Road
Tucson, AZ 85705
Web: http://www.apollocollege.com
Accreditation: Accrediting Bureau of Health Education Schools
Programs Offered:
dental assisting; massage therapy; medical administrative assistant and medical secretary; medical/clinical assistant; medical insurance/medical billing; pharmacy technician; physical therapist assistant; veterinary/animal health technology
Enrollment: 500 students

Institution Contact: Mr. Dennis C. Wilson, Executive Director
Phone: 520-888-5885
Fax: 520-887-3005
E-mail: dwilson@apollocollege.com
Admission Contact: Mr. Stan Basurto, Director of Admissions
Phone: 520-888-5885
Fax: 520-887-3005
E-mail: sbasurto@apollocollege.com

Apollo College - Westside, Inc.

2701 West Bethany Home Road
Phoenix, AZ 85017
Web: http://www.apollocollege.edu
Accreditation: Accrediting Bureau of Health Education Schools
Programs Offered:
computer/information technology services administration related; computer programming; computer software and media applications; computer software engineering; health information/medical records administration; information technology; massage therapy; medical office computer specialist; physical therapist assistant; radiologic technology/science
Enrollment: 421 students
Institution Contact: Mr. Patrick Lydick, Campus Director
Phone: 602-433-1333
Fax: 602-433-1222
E-mail: cnestor@apollocollege.com
Admission Contact: Ms. Roxanne Perkins, Director of Admissions
Phone: 602-433-1333
Fax: 602-433-1414
E-mail: rperkins@apollocollege.edu

Argosy University/Phoenix

2233 West Dunlap Avenue
Phoenix, AZ 85021
Web: http://www.argosyu.edu/
Programs Offered:
counselor education/school counseling and guidance; education
Institution Contact: Admissions
Phone: 866-216-2777

ARIZONA AUTOMOTIVE INSTITUTE

6829 North 46th Avenue
Glendale, AZ 85301
Web: http://www.aai.edu
Accreditation: Accrediting Commission of Career
Schools and Colleges of Technology
Programs Offered:
automobile/automotive mechanics technology; automotive engineering technology; diesel mechanics
technology; heating, air conditioning, ventilation and
refrigeration maintenance technology
Enrollment: 850 students
Institution Contact: Mr. Michael J Zawisky, Executive Director
Phone: 623-934-7273
Fax: 623-937-5000
E-mail: mzawisky@atienterprises.com
Admission Contact: Ms. Cheryl Wilson, Director of
Admissions
Phone: 623-934-7273
Fax: 623-937-5000
E-mail: cwilson@atienterprises.com

ARIZONA COLLEGE OF ALLIED HEALTH

4425 West Olive Avenue, Suite 300
Glendale, AZ 85302
Web: http://www.arizonacollege.edu
Accreditation: Accrediting Bureau of Health Education Schools
Programs Offered:
dental assisting; health information/medical records
technology; legal assistant/paralegal; massage therapy;
medical/clinical assistant; medical insurance/medical
billing; pharmacy technician; phlebotomy
Enrollment: 200 students
Institution Contact: Mr. Larkin Hicks, President
Phone: 602-222-9300
Fax: 623-298-1329
E-mail: lhicks@arizonacollege.edu
Admission Contact: Ms. Donna Pettigrew, Community Relations Director
Phone: 602-222-9300
Fax: 602-200-8726
E-mail: dpettigrew@arizonacollege.edu

ARIZONA SCHOOL OF MASSAGE THERAPY

9201 N. 29th Ave., Suite 35

Phoenix, AZ 85051
Institution Contact: Mr. Joe Price
Phone: 602-331-4325
Fax: 602-331-4120

ARIZONA SCHOOL OF MASSAGE THERAPY - TEMPE

1409 W. Southern Ave., Suite 6
Tempe, AZ 85282
Institution Contact: Ms. CG Funk
Phone: 480-983-2222
Fax: 480-784-9477

THE ART INSTITUTE OF PHOENIX

2233 West Dunlap Avenue
Phoenix, AZ 85021
Web: http://www.aipx.edu
Accreditation: Accrediting Council for Independent
Colleges and Schools
Programs Offered:
advertising; animation, interactive technology, video
graphics and special effects; apparel and accessories
marketing; apparel and textile marketing management;
audiovisual communications technologies related; baking and pastry arts; CAD/CADD drafting/design technology; cinematography and film/video production;
commercial and advertising art; computer graphics;
culinary arts; desktop publishing and digital imaging
design; digital communication and media/multimedia; graphic communications; graphic communications related; interior design; intermedia/multimedia;
photographic and film/video technology; restaurant,
culinary, and catering management; web/multimedia
management and webmaster; web page, digital/multimedia and information resources design
Enrollment: 1,200 students
Institution Contact: Ms. Karen A. Bryant, President
Phone: 800-474-2479 ext. 7501
Fax: 602-331-5300
E-mail: kabryant@aii.edu
Admission Contact: Mr. Jerry Driskill, Director of
Admissions
Phone: 800-474-2479 ext. 7502
Fax: 602-331-5300
E-mail: jdriskill@aii.edu

THE BRYMAN SCHOOL

2250 West Peoria Avenue, Suite A100
Phoenix, AZ 85029
Web: http://www.hightechinstitute.edu
Accreditation: Accrediting Bureau of Health Education Schools; Accrediting Commission of Career Schools and Colleges of Technology
Programs Offered:
dental assisting; health unit coordinator/ward clerk; massage therapy; medical/clinical assistant; medical radiologic technology; pharmacy technician; surgical technology
Enrollment: 1,083 students
Institution Contact: Ms. Cheryl Lynn Edmond, Campus President
Phone: 602-274-4300
Fax: 602-248-9087
E-mail: cedmond@hightechinstitute.edu
Admission Contact: Ms. Teri Garver, Director of Admissions
Phone: 602-274-4300
Fax: 602-248-9087
E-mail: tgarver@hightechinstitue.edu

CHAPARRAL COLLEGE

4585 East Speedway Boulevard, Suite 204
Tucson, AZ 85712
Web: http://www.chap-col.edu
Accreditation: Accrediting Council for Independent Colleges and Schools
Programs Offered:
accounting; accounting technology and bookkeeping; administrative assistant and secretarial science; business administration and management; computer science; computer systems networking and telecommunications; computer technology/computer systems technology; criminal justice/law enforcement administration; emergency medical technology (EMT paramedic); general studies; health information/medical records technology; health/medical claims examination; health professions related; health services/allied health/health sciences; health unit coordinator/ward clerk; information science/studies; medical informatics; medical insurance coding; medical insurance/medical billing; medical transcription
Enrollment: 400 students
Institution Contact: Mr. Todd A. Matthews, Sr., President

Phone: 520-327-6866
Fax: 520-325-0108
E-mail: tmatthews@chap-col.edu
Admission Contact: Ms. Becki Rossini, Director of Admissions
Phone: 520-327-6866
Fax: 520-325-0108
E-mail: becki@chap-col.edu

COLLEGEAMERICA - FLAGSTAFF

1800 South Milton Road
Flagstaff, AZ 86001
Web: http://www.collegeamerica.edu
Accreditation: Accrediting Bureau of Health Education Schools
Programs Offered:
computer technology/computer systems technology; medical/clinical assistant
Enrollment: 230 students
Institution Contact: Mr. Joshua Swayne, Director
Phone: 928-526-0763
Fax: 928-526-3468
E-mail: jswayne@collegeamerica.edu
Admission Contact: Ms. Nicole Dieter, Director of Admissions
Phone: 928-526-0763 ext. 1402
Fax: 928-526-3468
E-mail: ndieter@collegeamerica.edu

COLLINS COLLEGE: A SCHOOL OF DESIGN AND TECHNOLOGY

1140 South Priest Drive
Tempe, AZ 85281-5206
Web: http://www.collinscollege.edu/
Accreditation: Accrediting Commission of Career Schools and Colleges of Technology
Programs Offered:
animation, interactive technology, video graphics and special effects; business administration and management; business administration, management and operations related; cinematography and film/video production; commercial and advertising art; computer programming (specific applications); computer systems networking and telecommunications; computer/technical support; design and visual communications; digital communication and media/multimedia; graphic communications related; information technology;

interior design; system, networking, and LAN/WAN management; web/multimedia management and webmaster; web page, digital/multimedia and information resources design

Enrollment: 2,000 students
Institution Contact: Mr. John Calman, President
Phone: 480-966-3000
Fax: 480-966-2599
E-mail: jcalman@collinscollege.edu
Admission Contact: Ms. Wendy Johnston, Vice President of Marketing and Admissions
Phone: 480-966-3000
Fax: 480-966-2599
E-mail: wjohnston@collinscollege.edu

CONSERVATORY OF RECORDING ARTS AND SCIENCES

2300 East Broadway Road
Tempe, AZ 85282-1707
Web: http://www.audiorecordingschool.com
Accreditation: Accrediting Commission of Career Schools and Colleges of Technology
Programs Offered:
audiovisual communications technologies related; computer software and media applications related; digital communication and media/multimedia; music management and merchandising; recording arts technology
Enrollment: 408 students
Institution Contact: Mr. Kirt R. Hamm, Administrator
Phone: 800-562-6383
Fax: 480-829-1332
E-mail: hamm@cras.org
Admission Contact: Mr. John F. McJunkin, Director of Admissions
Phone: 800-562-6383
Fax: 480-829-1332
E-mail: john@cras.org

EVEREST COLLEGE

10400 North 25th Avenue, Suite 190
Phoenix, AZ 85021-1641
Web: http://everest-college.com/
Accreditation: North Central Association of Colleges and Schools
Programs Offered:
accounting; business administration and manage-

ment; criminal justice/law enforcement administration; criminal justice/police science; forensic science and technology; legal administrative assistant/secretary; legal assistant/paralegal; medical/clinical assistant; medical insurance coding; medical insurance/medical billing; office management; office occupations and clerical services

Enrollment: 648 students
Institution Contact: Ms. Joellyn Engelmann, Academic Dean
Phone: 602-942-4141 ext. 2703
Fax: 602-943-0960
E-mail: jengelmann@cci.edu
Admission Contact: Melissa Agee, Director of Admissions
Phone: 602-942-4141
Fax: 602-943-0960
E-mail: magee@cci.edu

MAP HIGH-TECH INSTITUTE

2250 West Peoria Avenue
Phoenix, AZ 85029
Web: http://www.hightechinstitute.edu
Accreditation: Accrediting Commission of Career Schools and Colleges of Technology
Programs Offered:
CAD/CADD drafting/design technology; computer and information sciences and support services related; computer and information systems security; computer graphics; computer/information technology administration and management; computer/information technology services administration related; computer installation and repair technology; computer software and media applications; computer software and media applications related; computer software technology; computer systems networking and telecommunications; computer/technical support; computer technology/computer systems technology; data processing and data processing technology; design and visual communications; digital communication and media/multimedia; drafting and design technology; electrical/electronics equipment installation and repair; electromechanical technology; industrial radiologic technology; information technology; intermedia/multimedia; medical administrative assistant and medical secretary; medical/clinical assistant; medical insurance coding; robotics technology; telecommunications technology; web/multimedia management and webmaster; web page, digital/multimedia and

information resources design
Enrollment: 1,300 students
Institution Contact: Ms. Carole Miller, Vice President
Phone: 602-328-2800 ext. 2803
Fax: 602-264-8391
E-mail: cmiller@hightechschools.com
Admission Contact: Mr. Todd Rash, Director of
Marketing
Phone: 602-328-2800
Fax: 602-264-8391
E-mail: dkullman@hightechschools.com

INTERNATIONAL IMPORT - EXPORT INSTITUTE

2432 West Peoria, Suite 1026
Phoenix, AZ 85029
Web: http://www.iiei.edu
Accreditation: Distance Education and Training
Council
Programs Offered:
business administration and management; entrepreneurship; international business/trade/commerce;
logistics and materials management; marketing/marketing management
Institution Contact: Barbara Ann Baderman, Executive Director
Phone: 602-648-5750
Fax: 602-648-5755
E-mail: don.burton@expandglobal.com
Admission Contact: Melissa Jensen, Student Services
Coordinator
Phone: 602-648-5750
Fax: 602-648-5755
E-mail: info@expandglobal.com

ITT TECHNICAL INSTITUTE

5005 South Wendler
Tempe, AZ 85282
Web: http://www.itt-tech.edu
Accreditation: Accrediting Council for Independent
Colleges and Schools
Programs Offered:
accounting and business/management; animation,
interactive technology, video graphics and special
effects; business administration and management;
CAD/CADD drafting/design technology; communications technology; computer and information systems
security; computer engineering technology; computer

software and media applications; computer software
engineering; computer systems networking and tele-communications; criminal justice/police science; digital communication and media/multimedia; electrical,
electronic and communications engineering technology; technology management; web page, digital/multi-media and information resources design
Institution Contact: Mr. Chuck Wilson, Director
Phone: 602-437-7500
Fax: 602-437-7505
E-mail: cwilson@itt-tech.edu
Admission Contact: Mr. Gene McWhorter, Director
of Recruitment
Phone: 602-437-7500
Fax: 602-437-7505
E-mail: gmcwhorter@itt-tech.edu

ITT TECHNICAL INSTITUTE

1455 West River Road
Tucson, AZ 85704
Web: http://www.itt-tech.edu
Accreditation: Accrediting Council for Independent
Colleges and Schools
Programs Offered:
accounting and business/management; animation,
interactive technology, video graphics and special
effects; business administration and management;
CAD/CADD drafting/design technology; communications technology; computer and information systems
security; computer engineering technology; computer
software and media applications; computer software
engineering; computer systems networking and tele-communications; criminal justice/police science; digital communication and media/multimedia; electrical,
electronic and communications engineering technology; technology management; web page, digital/multi-media and information resources design
Institution Contact: Mr. Timothy Riordan, Director
Phone: 520-408-7488
Admission Contact: Ms. Linda Lemken, Director of
Recruitment
Phone: 520-408-7488

LAMSON COLLEGE

1126 North Scottsdale Road, Suite 17
Tempe, AZ 85281
Web: http://www.lamsoncollege.com/

Accreditation: Accrediting Council for Independent Colleges and Schools
Programs Offered:
accounting; business administration and management; computer/information technology services administration related; computer systems networking and telecommunications; computer/technical support; computer technology/computer systems technology; executive assistant/executive secretary; legal administrative assistant/secretary; legal assistant/paralegal
Enrollment: 89 students
Institution Contact: Ms. Katherine E. Hopfensperger, Director
Phone: 480-898-7000
Fax: 480-967-6645
E-mail: khopfensperger@yahoo.com
Admission Contact: Ms. Katherine E. Hopfensperger, Director
Phone: 480-898-7000
Fax: 480-967-6645
E-mail: khopfensperger@yahoo.com

LONG TECHNICAL COLLEGE

4646 East Van Buren Street, Suite 350
Phoenix, AZ 85008
Web: http://www.longtechnicalcollege.com
Accreditation: Accrediting Commission of Career Schools and Colleges of Technology
Programs Offered:
legal assistant/paralegal; medical/clinical assistant; pharmacy technician
Enrollment: 173 students
Institution Contact: Mr. Brian K. Dycus, Executive Director
Phone: 602-252-2171
Fax: 602-252-1891
E-mail: bdycus@khec.com
Admission Contact: Mr. Sean McHaney, Director of Admissions
Phone: 602-252-2171
Fax: 602-252-1891
E-mail: smchaney@longtechnicalcollege.com

LONG TECHNICAL COLLEGE-EAST VALLEY

111 West Monroe Street, Suite 800
Phoenix, AZ 85003
Web: http://www.phoenixparalegal.com

Accreditation: Accrediting Council for Independent Colleges and Schools
Programs Offered:
legal assistant/paralegal
Institution Contact: Mr. Dennis Del Valle, Executive Director
Phone: 602-252-2171
Fax: 602-252-1891
E-mail: ddelvalle@phoenixcareercollege.com

MOTORCYCLE MECHANICS INSTITUTE

2844 West Deer Valley Road
Phoenix, AZ 85027-2399
Web: http://www.uticorp.com
Accreditation: Accrediting Commission of Career Schools and Colleges of Technology
Programs Offered:
marine maintenance and ship repair technology; motorcycle maintenance and repair technology
Enrollment: 2,200 students
Institution Contact: Mr. Bryan Fishkind, Campus Director
Phone: 623-869-9644
Fax: 623-581-2871
E-mail: bfishkind@uticorp.com
Admission Contact: Ms. Yolanda Davis, Admissions Office Manager
Phone: 623-869-9644
Fax: 623-516-7660
E-mail: ydavis@uticorp.com

PIMA MEDICAL INSTITUTE

957 South Dobson Road
Mesa, AZ 85202
Web: http://www.pmi.edu
Accreditation: Accrediting Bureau of Health Education Schools
Programs Offered:
dental assisting; massage therapy; medical administrative assistant and medical secretary; medical/clinical assistant; nursing (registered nurse training); pharmacy technician; phlebotomy; physical therapist assistant; radiologic technology/science; respiratory care therapy; veterinary/animal health technology
Enrollment: 592 students
Institution Contact: Mr. Christopher Luebke, Admissions Support Center Director

Phone: 888-898-9048
E-mail: asc@pmi.edu
Admission Contact: Admissions Support Representative
Phone: 888-898-9048

PIMA MEDICAL INSTITUTE

3350 East Grant Road, Suite 200
Tucson, AZ 85716
Web: http://www.pmi.edu
Accreditation: Accrediting Bureau of Health Education Schools
Programs Offered:
dental assisting; health unit coordinator/ward clerk; medical administrative assistant and medical secretary; medical/clinical assistant; pharmacy technician; phlebotomy; physical therapist assistant; radiologic technology/science; respiratory care therapy; veterinary/animal health technology
Enrollment: 567 students
Institution Contact: Mr. Christopher Luebke, Admissions Support Center Director
Phone: 888-898-9048
E-mail: asc@pmi.edu
Admission Contact: Admissions Support Representative
Phone: 888-898-9048
E-mail: asc@pmi.edu

THE REFRIGERATION SCHOOL

4210 East Washington Street
Phoenix, AZ 85034
Web: http://www.refrigerationschool.com/
Accreditation: Accrediting Commission of Career Schools and Colleges of Technology
Programs Offered:
electrician; electromechanical technology; heating, air conditioning and refrigeration technology; heating, air conditioning, ventilation and refrigeration maintenance technology; mechanical engineering/mechanical technology
Enrollment: 329 students
Institution Contact: Ms. Elizabeth Cline, President/Director
Phone: 602-275-7133
Fax: 602-267-4811
E-mail: liz@rsiaz.org
Admission Contact: Ms. Mary Simmons, Admissions Manager

Phone: 602-275-7133
Fax: 602-267-4805
E-mail: mary@rsiaz.org

REMINGTON COLLEGE - TEMPE CAMPUS

875 West Elliot Road, Suite 126
Tempe, AZ 85284
Web: http://www.educationamerica.com/
Accreditation: Accrediting Council for Independent Colleges and Schools
Programs Offered:
computer programming (specific applications); computer systems networking and telecommunications; criminal justice/law enforcement administration; information science/studies; internet information systems
Institution Contact: Mr. Joe Drennen, Campus President
Phone: 480-834-1000
Fax: 480-491-2970
E-mail: jdrennen@edamerica.com
Admission Contact: Mr. Steve Schwartz, Director of Recruitment
Phone: 480-834-1000
Fax: 480-491-2970
E-mail: sschwart@edamerica.com

SCOTTSDALE CULINARY INSTITUTE

8100 East Camelback Road, Suite 1001
Scottsdale, AZ 85251-3940
Web: http://www.chefs.edu/
Accreditation: Accrediting Commission of Career Schools and Colleges of Technology
Programs Offered:
baking and pastry arts; culinary arts; restaurant/food services management
Enrollment: 1,100 students
Institution Contact: Mr. Jon Alberts, President
Phone: 480-990-3773
Fax: 480-990-0351
Admission Contact: Mr. Bruce Trexler, Director of Admissions
Phone: 480-990-3773
Fax: 480-990-0351
E-mail: bruce.trexler@scichefs.com

SONORAN DESERT INSTITUTE

10245 East Via Linda, Suite 102

Scottsdale, AZ 85258
Web: http://www.sonoranlearning.com
Accreditation: Distance Education and Training
Council
Programs Offered:
building/home/construction inspection; gunsmithing
Institution Contact:
Phone: 480-314-2102
Fax: 480-314-2138
E-mail: info@sonoranlearning.com

TUCSON COLLEGE
7310 East 22nd Street
Tucson, AZ 85710
Web: http://www.tucsoncollege.edu
Accreditation: Accrediting Council for Independent
Colleges and Schools
Programs Offered:
administrative assistant and secretarial science;
computer systems networking and telecommunica-
tions; health aide; medical administrative assistant and
medical secretary; medical/clinical assistant; nursing
assistant/aide and patient care assistant; optometric
technician
Enrollment: 176 students
Institution Contact: Mr. George Tesner, Director
Phone: 520-296-3261 ext. 101
Fax: 520-296-3484
E-mail: gtesner@tucsoncollege.edu
Admission Contact: Mrs. Rebecca Montgomery,
Director of Admissions
Phone: 520-296-3261 ext. 107
Fax: 520-296-3484
E-mail: rmontgomery@tucsoncollege.edu

UNIVERSAL TECHNICAL INSTITUTE
10695 West Pierce Street
Avondale, AZ 85323
Web: http://www.uticorp.com
Accreditation: Accrediting Commission of Career
Schools and Colleges of Technology
Programs Offered:
automotive engineering technology; diesel mechanics
technology
Enrollment: 2,200 students
Institution Contact: Mike Klackle, Director
Phone: 623-245-4600

Fax: 623-245-4601
E-mail: mklackle@uticorp.com
Admission Contact: Mr. Rich Brady
Phone: 623-245-4600
Fax: 623-445-9683
E-mail: rbrady@uticorp.com

WESTERN INTERNATIONAL UNIVERSITY
9215 North Black Canyon Highway
Phoenix, AZ 85021
Web: http://www.wintu.edu/
Programs Offered:
accounting; business administration and management;
human resources management; information technol-
ogy; international business/trade/commerce
Institution Contact:
Phone: 602-943-2311
Fax: 602-371-8637
Admission Contact:
Admissions Phone: 602-943-2311
Fax: 602-371-8637

ARKANSAS

EASTERN COLLEGE OF HEALTH VOCATIONS
6423 Forbing Road
Little Rock, AR 72209
Accreditation: Accrediting Bureau of Health Educa-
tion Schools
Programs Offered:
dental assisting; medical/clinical assistant
Institution Contact: Mr. Don E. Enroth, Jr., Director
of Operations
Phone: 228-831-3863
Fax: 228-831-3589
E-mail: denroth@echv.com
Admission Contact: Cyndi Chrisman, Admissions
Officer
Phone: 501-568-0211
Fax: 501-565-4076
E-mail: cchriisman@echv.com

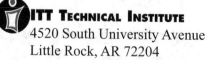

ITT TECHNICAL INSTITUTE
4520 South University Avenue
Little Rock, AR 72204

Web: http://www.itt-tech.edu

Accreditation: Accrediting Council for Independent Colleges and Schools

Programs Offered:

animation, interactive technology, video graphics and special effects; CAD/CADD drafting/design technology; communications technology; computer and information systems security; computer engineering technology; computer software and media applications; computer software engineering; computer systems networking and telecommunications; digital communication and media/multimedia; electrical, electronic and communications engineering technology; technology management; web page, digital/multimedia and information resources design

Institution Contact: Mr. Thomas Crawford, Director

Phone: 501-565-5550

Fax: 501-565-4747

E-mail: tcrawford@itt-tech.edu

Admission Contact: Mr. Reed W. Thompson, Director of Recruitment

Phone: 501-565-5550

Fax: 501-565-4747

E-mail: rthompson@itt-tech.edu

REMINGTON COLLEGE - LITTLE ROCK CAMPUS

19 Remington Drive

Little Rock, AR 72204

Web: http://www.remingtoncollege.edu

Accreditation: Accrediting Commission of Career Schools and Colleges of Technology

Programs Offered:

business operations support and secretarial services related; computer technology/computer systems technology; criminal justice/police science; medical/clinical assistant; pharmacy technician

Enrollment: 459 students

Institution Contact: Mr. David Cunningham, Campus President

Phone: 501-312-0007

Fax: 501-225-3819

E-mail: david.cunningham@remingtoncollege.edu

Admission Contact: Ms. Carla Larson, Director of Recruitment

Phone: 501-312-0007

Fax: 501-225-3819

E-mail: carla.larson@remingtoncollege.edu

BRITISH VIRGIN ISLANDS

NEW ENGLAND CULINARY INSTITUTE AT H. LAVITY STOUTT COMMUNITY COLLEGE

PO Box 3097

Road Town, Tortola, British Virgin Islands

Web: http://www.necibvi.com/

Programs Offered:

baking and pastry arts; culinary arts; food service and dining room management

Institution Contact: Admissions Officer

Phone: 284-494-4994

Fax: 284-494-4996

CALIFORNIA

ACADEMY OF ART UNIVERSITY

79 New Montgomery Street

San Francisco, CA 94105

Web: http://www.academyart.edu

Accreditation: Accrediting Council for Independent Colleges and Schools

Programs Offered:

advertising; animation, interactive technology, video graphics and special effects; architectural drafting and CAD/CADD; ceramic arts and ceramics; cinematography and film/video production; commercial and advertising art; computer graphics; computer software and media applications related; desktop publishing and digital imaging design; English as a second language; fashion/apparel design; fashion merchandising; fiber, textile and weaving arts; fine/studio arts; furniture design and manufacturing; interior design; painting; photography; printmaking; visual and performing arts

Enrollment: 8,400 students

Institution Contact: Mr. Joe Vollaro, Executive Vice President of Financial Aid and Compliance

Phone: 415-274-8688

Fax: 415-296-2098

E-mail: jvollaro@academyart.edu

Admission Contact: Mr. John Meurer, Director of Admissions

Phone: 415-263-5518

Fax: 415-263-4130

E-mail: jmeurer@academyart.edu

ACADEMY OF RADIO BROADCASTING

16052 Beach Boulevard, Suite 263
Huntington Beach, CA 92647
Web: http://www.arbradio.com
Accreditation: Accrediting Council for Continuing
Education and Training
Programs Offered:
cinematography and film/video production; radio and
television
Institution Contact: Mr. Thomas Gillenwater, President
Phone: 714-842-0100
Fax: 714-842-1858
E-mail: arbradio@earthlink.net
Admission Contact: Mr. Mike Kelly, Admissions
Director
Phone: 714-842-0100
Fax: 714-842-1858
E-mail: arbradio@earthlink.net

ACADEMY PACIFIC TRAVEL COLLEGE

1777 North Vine Street
Los Angeles, CA 90028
Web: http://www.academypacific.edu
Accreditation: Accrediting Commission of Career
Schools and Colleges of Technology
Programs Offered:
airline flight attendant; transportation management
Enrollment: 130 students
Institution Contact: Daniel Gilreath, Information
Contact
Phone: 323-462-3211
Fax: 323-462-7755
E-mail: apsws@aol.com

ADVANCED TRAINING ASSOCIATES

1900 Joe Crosson Drive
El Cajon, CA 92020
Web: http://www.advancedtraining.net
Accreditation: Council on Occupational Education
Programs Offered:
aircraft powerplant technology; airframe mechanics
and aircraft maintenance technology; air traffic control; avionics maintenance technology; computer and
information systems security; computer installation
and repair technology; computer systems networking
and telecommunications; customer service support/call
center/teleservice operation; electrical and electronic
engineering technologies related; electrical/electronics
equipment installation and repair; information technology; telecommunications
Institution Contact:
Phone: 619-596-2766
Fax: 619-596-4526
E-mail: edproinc@aol.com

AMERICAN CAREER COLLEGE

1200 North Magnolia Avenue
Anaheim, CA 92801
Web: http://www.americancareer.com
Programs Offered:
health/medical claims examination; medical/clinical
assistant; nursing (licensed practical/vocational nurse
training); optometric technician; pharmacy technician;
surgical technology
Enrollment: 800 students
Institution Contact: Mr. Greg S. Shin, Campus Di-
rector
Phone: 714-784-4622
Fax: 714-484-1546
E-mail: gshin@americancareer.com
Admission Contact: Mr. Robert Woy, Director of
Admissions
Phone: 714-952-9066
E-mail: rwoy@americancareer.com

AMERICAN CAREER COLLEGE, INC.

4021 Rosewood Avenue
Los Angeles, CA 90004
Web: http://www.americancareer.com
Accreditation: Accrediting Bureau of Health Educa-
tion Schools
Programs Offered:
dental assisting; massage therapy; medical/clinical as-
sistant; medical insurance/medical billing; nursing (li-
censed practical/vocational nurse training); opticianry;
pharmacy technician; surgical technology
Enrollment: 1,200 students
Institution Contact: Rita Totten, Executive Director
of Campus Operations
Phone: 323-668-7555
Fax: 323-315-1021

E-mail: rita@americancareer.com
Admission Contact: Tamra Adams, Director of Admissions
Phone: 323-668-7555
Fax: 323-315-1021
E-mail: tamra@americancareer.com

AMERICAN CAREER COLLEGE - NORCO CAMPUS

3299 Horseless Carriage Rd. #C
Norco, CA 92860
Institution Contact: Campus President

AMERICAN INTERCONTINENTAL UNIVERSITY

12655 West Jefferson Boulevard
Los Angeles, CA 90066
Web: http://www.aiula.com
Accreditation: Southern Association of Colleges and Schools
Programs Offered:
business administration and management; commercial and advertising art; criminal justice/law enforcement administration; educational/instructional media design; fashion/apparel design; fashion merchandising; information technology; interior design; international business/trade/commerce; web page, digital/multimedia and information resources design
Enrollment: 1,750 students
Institution Contact: Steven E. Tartaglini, President
Phone: 310-302-2000
Fax: 310-302-2402
E-mail: startaglini@la.aiuniv.edu
Admission Contact: William Level, Director of Admissions
Phone: 888-248-7390
Fax: 310-302-2000
E-mail: wlevel@la.aiuniv.edu

ARGOSY UNIVERSITY/ORANGE COUNTY

3501 West Sunflower Avenue
Santa Ana, CA 92704-9888
Web: http://www.argosyu.edu/
Programs Offered:
education
Institution Contact: Admissions
Phone: 714-338-6200
Fax: 714-437-1697

E-mail: rking@argosyu.edu

ARGOSY UNIVERSITY/SAN FRANCISCO BAY AREA

999-A Canal Blvd
Point Richmond, CA 94804
Web: http://ausfba.com
Enrollment: 595 students
Institution Contact: Dr. Lucille Sansing, President
Phone: 510-2150277
Fax: 510-2150299
E-mail: lsansing@argosyu.edu
Admission Contact: Mr. John Stofan, Director of Admissions
Phone: 866-2152777 ext. 205
Fax: 510-2150299
E-mail: jstofan@argosyu.edu

ARGOSY UNIVERSITY

5126 Ralston St
Ventura, CA 93003-7357
Institution contact: Scott Ables
Phone: 805-676-3030
Fax: 805-676-3033

THE ART INSTITUTE OF CALIFORNIA - LOS ANGELES

2900 31st Street
Santa Monica, CA 90405-3035
Web: http://www.aicala.artinstitutes.edu
Accreditation: Accrediting Council for Independent Colleges and Schools
Programs Offered:
advertising; animation, interactive technology, video graphics and special effects; cinematography and film/video production; commercial and advertising art; culinary arts; interior design; web page, digital/multimedia and information resources design
Enrollment: 2,119 students
Institution Contact: Ms. Laura Soloff, President
Phone: 310-752-4700
Fax: 310-314-6050
E-mail: lsoloff@aii.edu
Admission Contact: Ms. Andrea Sylvester, Director of Admissions
Phone: 310-752-4700
Fax: 310-752-4708
E-mail: asylvester@aii.edu

THE ART INSTITUTE OF CALIFORNIA - ORANGE COUNTY

3601 West Sunflower Avenue
Santa Ana, CA 92704
Web: http://www.aicaoc.artinstitutes.edu
Accreditation: Accrediting Council for Independent Colleges and Schools
Programs Offered:
animation, interactive technology, video graphics and special effects; commercial and advertising art; computer graphics; culinary arts; interior design; web/multimedia management and webmaster; web page, digital/multimedia and information resources design
Institution Contact: Mr. Ken Post, Vice President/Director of Admissions
Phone: 714-830-0200
Fax: 714-556-1923
E-mail: postk@aii.edu
Admission Contact: Mr. Ken Post, Vice President/Director of Admissions
Phone: 888-549-3055
Fax: 714-556-1923
E-mail: postk@aii.edu

THE ART INSTITUTE OF CALIFORNIA - SAN DIEGO

7650 Mission Valley Road
San Diego, CA 92108
Web: http://www.aica.artinstitutes.edu
Accreditation: Accrediting Commission of Career Schools and Colleges of Technology
Programs Offered:
advertising; animation, interactive technology, video graphics and special effects; baking and pastry arts; commercial and advertising art; computer graphics; culinary arts; digital communication and media/multimedia; interior design; web page, digital/multimedia and information resources design
Institution Contact: Ms. Sandy Park, Director of Admissions
Phone: 858-546-0602
Fax: 858-457-0903
E-mail: parks@aii.edu

THE ART INSTITUTE OF CALIFORNIA - SAN FRANCISCO

1170 Market Street
San Francisco, CA 94102

Web: http://www.aicasf.artinstitutes.edu
Accreditation: Accrediting Council for Independent Colleges and Schools
Programs Offered:
animation, interactive technology, video graphics and special effects; commercial and advertising art; computer graphics; computer programming (specific applications); fashion/apparel design; graphic communications; interior design; web/multimedia management and webmaster; web page, digital/multimedia and information resources design
Enrollment: 875 students
Institution Contact: Mr. Charles Nagele, President
Phone: 415-865-0198
Fax: 415-863-5831
E-mail: cnagele@aii.edu
Admission Contact: Mr. Daniel Cardenas, Director of Admissions
Phone: 888-493-3261
Fax: 415-863-6344
E-mail: cardenad@aii.edu

BROOKS COLLEGE

4825 East Pacific Coast Highway
Long Beach, CA 90804
Web: http://www.brookscollege.edu
Accreditation: Western Association of Schools and Colleges
Programs Offered:
commercial and advertising art; computer/information technology administration and management; computer software and media applications; computer systems networking and telecommunications; fashion/apparel design; fashion merchandising; interior design
Enrollment: 800 students
Institution Contact: Mr. Patrick W. Comstock, President
Phone: 800-421-3775
Fax: 562-985-1381
Admission Contact: Ms. Christina Varon, Vice President of Admissions
Phone: 800-421-3775
Fax: 562-597-2591

BROOKS COLLEGE

1120 Kifer Road
Sunnyvale, CA 94086-5303
Web: http://www.brooks-sv.com

Accreditation: Western Association of Schools and Colleges
Programs Offered:
fashion/apparel design; fashion merchandising; graphic communications; system, networking, and LAN/WAN management; web page, digital/multimedia and information resources design
Institution Contact: James H. Mack Nair, Dean of Education
Phone: 408-328-5700
Fax: 408-328-5790
E-mail: jmacknair@brooks-sv.com
Admission Contact: James H. Mack Nair, Dean of Education
Phone: 408-328-5700
Fax: 408-328-5790
E-mail: jmacknair@brooks-sv.com

BROOKS INSTITUTE OF PHOTOGRAPHY
801 Alston Road
Santa Barbara, CA 93108-2399
Web: http://www.brooks.edu
Accreditation: Accrediting Council for Independent Colleges and Schools
Programs Offered:
cinematography and film/video production; photography
Institution Contact: Mr. John Calman, President
Phone: 805-966-3888
Fax: 805-564-1475
E-mail: president@brooks.edu
Admission Contact: Miss Inge Kautzmann, Director of Admissions
Phone: 805-966-3888
Fax: 805-564-1475
E-mail: admissions@brooks.edu

BROWN MACKIE COLLEGE, LOS ANGELES CAMPUS
2900 31st Street
Santa Monica, CA 90405
Programs Offered:
accounting; business administration and management; computer programming; computer software technology; criminal justice/law enforcement administration; legal assistant/paralegal; medical office assistant
Enrollment: 50 students
Institution Contact: Mr. Robert L. Campbell, Campus President

Phone: 310-866-4000 ext. 4030
Fax: 310-452-8720
E-mail: rlcampbell@brownmackie.edu
Admission Contact: Ms. Caroline R. Eckert, Director of Admissions
Phone: 310-866-4000 ext. 4050
Fax: 310-452-8720
E-mail: ceckert@brownmackie.edu

BROWN MACKIE COLLEGE, ORANGE COUNTY CAMPUS
3601 West Sunflower Avenue
Santa Ana, CA 92704
Web: http://www.brownmackie.edu
Programs Offered:
accounting; business, management, and marketing related; computer and information sciences; computer software technology; criminal justice/law enforcement administration; legal assistant/paralegal; medical/clinical assistant
Enrollment: 54 students
Institution Contact: Ms. Lois V. Somohano, Registrar/Business Manager
Phone: 714-338-6304
Fax: 714-338-6350
E-mail: lsomohano@brownmackie.edu
Admission Contact: Ms. Kathy Haston, Second Director of Admissions
Phone: 714-338-6322
Fax: 714-338-6350
E-mail: khaston@brownmackie.edu

BROWN MACKIE COLLEGE, SAN DIEGO CAMPUS
7650 Mission Valley Road
San Diego, CA 92108
Web: http://www.brownmackie.edu/
Programs Offered:
accounting; advertising; business administration and management; CAD/CADD drafting/design technology; computer programming; computer software and media applications; criminal justice/law enforcement administration; graphic communications; legal assistant/paralegal; medical/clinical assistant; medical insurance coding; medical insurance/medical billing; nursing (licensed practical/vocational nurse training); occupational therapy; physical therapy; sales, distribution and marketing

Institution Contact: Admissions
Phone: 866-505-0333
E-mail: bmsdadm@edmc.edu

BRYAN COLLEGE OF COURT REPORTING

2333 Beverly Boulevard, Suite 400
Los Angeles, CA 90057
Web: http://www.bryancollege.edu
Programs Offered:
court reporting
Enrollment: 450 students
Institution Contact: Mr. Adam D. Petersen, President
Phone: 213-484-8850
Fax: 213-483-3936
E-mail: apetersen@bryancollege.edu
Admission Contact: Mr. Glenn M. Allen, Director of Admissions
Phone: 213-484-8850
Fax: 213-483-3936
E-mail: gallen@bryancollege.edu

BRYMAN COLLEGE

2215 West Mission Road
Alhambra, CA 91803
Web: http://www.bryman-college.com
Accreditation: Accrediting Commission of Career Schools and Colleges of Technology
Programs Offered:
business administration and management; dental assisting; massage therapy; medical administrative assistant and medical secretary; medical/clinical assistant; medical insurance coding; medical insurance/medical billing; pharmacy technician
Institution Contact: Mr. Randy Morales, School President
Phone: 626-979-4940
Fax: 626-280-4011
E-mail: rmorales@cci.edu
Admission Contact: Mr. Randy Morales, School President
Phone: 626-979-4940
Fax: 626-280-4011
E-mail: rmorales@cci.edu

BRYMAN COLLEGE

511 North Brookhurst Street, Suite 300

Anaheim, CA 92801
Web: http://www.cci.edu
Accreditation: Accrediting Commission of Career Schools and Colleges of Technology
Programs Offered:
dental assisting; massage therapy; medical administrative assistant and medical secretary; medical/clinical assistant; medical insurance coding; medical insurance/medical billing; pharmacy technician
Institution Contact: Ms. Susie Reed, President
Phone: 714-953-6500
Fax: 714-953-4163
E-mail: sreed@cci.edu
Admission Contact: Mr. Daniel Valdez, Admissions Director
Phone: 714-953-6500
Fax: 714-953-4163
E-mail: dvaldez@cci.edu

BRYMAN COLLEGE

12801 Crossroad Parkway
City of Industry, CA 91746
Web: http://www.bryman-college.com
Accreditation: Accrediting Commission of Career Schools and Colleges of Technology
Programs Offered:
administrative assistant and secretarial science; business administration and management; business/corporate communications; clinical/medical laboratory technology; dental assisting; diagnostic medical sonography and ultrasound technology; massage therapy; medical administrative assistant and medical secretary; medical/clinical assistant; medical insurance/medical billing; medical office management; medical radiologic technology; phlebotomy
Institution Contact: Ms. Lillian Gonzalez, Director of Admissions
Phone: 562-908-2500
Fax: 562-908-7656
E-mail: lilliang@cci.edu

BRYMAN COLLEGE

1045 West Redondo Beach Boulevard, Suite 275
Gardena, CA 90247
Web: http://www.cci.edu
Accreditation: Accrediting Commission of Career Schools and Colleges of Technology

 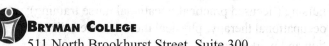 indicates a participating institution in the *Imagine America* Scholarship Program. indicates a participating institution in the Military Award Program.

Programs Offered:
dental assisting; dialysis technology; massage therapy; medical administrative assistant and medical secretary; medical/clinical assistant; medical insurance coding; medical insurance/medical billing
Enrollment: 660 students
Institution Contact: Mrs. Pat Martin, President
Phone: 310-527-7105
Fax: 310-523-3766
E-mail: smartin@cci.edu
Admission Contact: Ms. Hasani Thompson, Director of Admissions
Phone: 310-527-7105
Fax: 310-523-3766
E-mail: hgorden@cci.edu

BRYMAN COLLEGE
22336 Main Street, First Floor
Hayward, CA 94541
Web: http://www.bryman-college.com
Accreditation: Accrediting Commission of Career Schools and Colleges of Technology
Programs Offered:
massage therapy; medical administrative assistant and medical secretary; medical/clinical assistant; medical insurance coding; medical insurance/medical billing; surgical technology
Institution Contact: Mr. Dan Ujueta, Director of Admissions
Phone: 510-582-9500 ext. 124
Fax: 510-582-9645
E-mail: dujueta@cci.edu
Admission Contact: Mr. Dan Ujueta, Director of Admissions
Phone: 510-582-9500 ext. 124
Fax: 510-582-9645
E-mail: dujueta@cci.edu

BRYMAN COLLEGE
3000 South Robertson Boulevard, 3rd Floor
Los Angeles, CA 90034
Web: http://www.bryman-college.com
Accreditation: Accrediting Commission of Career Schools and Colleges of Technology
Programs Offered:
business, management, and marketing related; dental assisting; massage therapy; medical/clinical assistant; medical insurance/medical billing; pharmacy technician

Enrollment: 326 students
Institution Contact: Director of Admissions
Phone: 310-840-5777
Fax: 310-287-2344

BRYMAN COLLEGE
3460 Wilshire Boulevard, Suite 500
Los Angeles, CA 90010
Web: http://www.bryman-college.com
Accreditation: Accrediting Commission of Career Schools and Colleges of Technology
Programs Offered:
dental assisting; medical administrative assistant and medical secretary; medical/clinical assistant; medical insurance coding; medical insurance/medical billing; pharmacy technician
Institution Contact: Marie Guerrero, Director of Admissions
Phone: 213-388-9950
Fax: 313-388-9907
E-mail: mguerrer@cci.edu

BRYMAN COLLEGE
1460 South Milliken Avenue
Ontario, CA 91761
Web: http://bryman-college.com/
Accreditation: Accrediting Commission of Career Schools and Colleges of Technology
Programs Offered:
business administration and management; dental assisting; massage therapy; medical/clinical assistant; medical insurance coding; medical insurance/medical billing; medical radiologic technology
Enrollment: 537 students
Institution Contact: Dan Day, Campus President
Phone: 909-984-5027
Fax: 909-988-9339
E-mail: dday@cci.edu
Admission Contact: Mr. Alfred M. Desrosiers, Director of Admissions
Phone: 909-984-5027
Fax: 909-988-9339
E-mail: adesrosiers@cci.edu

BRYMAN COLLEGE
18040 Sherman Way, Suite 400

Reseda, CA 91335
Web: http://bryman-college.com/
Accreditation: Accrediting Bureau of Health Education Schools; Accrediting Commission of Career Schools and Colleges of Technology
Programs Offered:
dental assisting; massage therapy; medical administrative assistant and medical secretary; medical/clinical assistant; surgical technology
Enrollment: 500 students
Institution Contact: Lani Townsend, President
Phone: 818-774-0550
Fax: 818-774-1577
Admission Contact: Ms. Leslie Greer, Director of Admissions
Phone: 818-774-0550
Fax: 818-774-1577
E-mail: lgreer@cci.edu

 BRYMAN COLLEGE
217 Club Center Drive, Suite A
San Bernardino, CA 92408
Web: http://www.bryman-college.com
Accreditation: Accrediting Council for Independent Colleges and Schools
Programs Offered:
health information/medical records technology; massage therapy; medical administrative assistant and medical secretary; medical/clinical assistant; medical insurance/medical billing; medical office management; office occupations and clerical services
Admission Contact: Mrs. Mary Beth Coutts, Director of Admissions
Phone: 909-777-3300
Fax: 909-777-3313
E-mail: mcook@cci.edu

BRYMAN COLLEGE
814 Mission Street, Suite 500
San Francisco, CA 94103
Web: http://www.cci.edu
Accreditation: Accrediting Commission of Career Schools and Colleges of Technology
Programs Offered:
dental assisting; massage therapy; medical administrative assistant and medical secretary; medical/clinical assistant; pharmacy technician

Enrollment: 500 students
Institution Contact: Mr. David Bent, Director of Admissions
Phone: 415-777-2500
Fax: 415-495-3457
E-mail: dbent@cci.edu
Admission Contact: David Bent, Admissions Director
Phone: 415-777-2500
Fax: 415-495-3457
E-mail: dbent@cci.edu

 **BRYMAN COLLEGE**
1245 South Winchester Boulevard, Suite 102
San Jose, CA 95128
Web: http://www.bryman-college.com
Accreditation: Accrediting Commission of Career Schools and Colleges of Technology
Programs Offered:
dental assisting; massage therapy; medical administrative assistant and medical secretary; medical/clinical assistant; medical insurance coding; pharmacy technician
Institution Contact: George Grayeb, Regional Vice President of Operations
Phone: 408-246-4171
Fax: 408-557-9874
E-mail: ggrayeb@cci.edu
Admission Contact: Ms. Jo Ann Andre, Director of Admissions
Phone: 408-246-4171 ext. 103
Fax: 408-557-9874
E-mail: jandre@cci.edu

BRYMAN COLLEGE
1231 Cabrillo Avenue, Suite 201
Torrance, CA 90501
Accreditation: Accrediting Council for Continuing Education and Training
Programs Offered:
massage therapy; pharmacy technician
Enrollment: 200 students
Institution Contact: Ms. Sandy Ock, College President
Phone: 310-320-3200
Fax: 310-320-3070
E-mail: sock@cci.edu
Admission Contact: Mr. Duemand L. Edwards, Director of Admissions
Phone: 310-320-3200

Fax: 310-320-3070
E-mail: dedwards@cci.edu

CALIFORNIA CULINARY ACADEMY

625 Polk Street
San Francisco, CA 94102
Web: http://www.caculinary.edu
Accreditation: Accrediting Commission of Career
Schools and Colleges of Technology
Programs Offered:
baking and pastry arts; culinary arts; hospitality administration; restaurant/food services management
Enrollment: 1,900 students
Institution Contact: Mr. Greg Martinez, Director of
Admissions
Phone: 415-771-3500
Fax: 415-771-2194
E-mail: admissions@baychef.com

CALIFORNIA DESIGN COLLEGE

3440 Wilshire Boulevard, 10th Floor
Los Angeles, CA 90010
Web: http://www.aicdc.artinstitutes.edu
Accreditation: Accrediting Council for Independent
Colleges and Schools
Programs Offered:
apparel and textile manufacturing; apparel and textile
marketing management; apparel and textiles related;
applied art; art; CAD/CADD drafting/design technology; computer graphics; design and visual communications; drafting and design technology; drawing;
fashion and fabric consulting; fashion/apparel design;
fashion merchandising; fiber, textile and weaving
arts; graphic communications; graphic communications related; interior design; intermedia/multimedia;
marketing/marketing management; merchandising;
merchandising, sales, and marketing operations related (general); retailing; web page, digital/multimedia
and information resources design
Enrollment: 452 students
Institution Contact: William Johnson, President
Phone: 213-251-3636
Fax: 213-385-3545
E-mail: wjohnson@aii.edu
Admission Contact: Melissa Romero, Associate Admissions Director
Phone: 213-251-3636

Fax: 213-385-3545
E-mail: mromero@aii.edu

CALIFORNIA HEALING ARTS COLLEGE

12217 Santa Monica Boulevard, Suite 206
Los Angeles, CA 90025
Web: http://www.chac.edu
Accreditation: Accrediting Commission of Career
Schools and Colleges of Technology
Programs Offered:
massage therapy
Institution Contact: Dr. Paul Schwinghamer, Director
Phone: 310-826-7622
E-mail: drpaul@chac.edu
Admission Contact: Lucinda Chrisman, Director of
Admissions
Phone: 310-826-7622
E-mail: lucinda@chac.edu

CALIFORNIA SCHOOL OF CULINARY ARTS

521 East Green Street
Pasadena, CA 91101
Web: http://www.csca.edu
Accreditation: Accrediting Council for Independent
Colleges and Schools
Programs Offered:
baking and pastry arts; culinary arts; hospitality administration; hotel/motel administration
Enrollment: 1,788 students
Institution Contact: Mr. Tony Bondi, President
Phone: 626-229-1300 ext. 1302
Fax: 626-585-0486
E-mail: tbondi@scsca.com
Admission Contact: Mr. Ed Colon, Vice President of
Admissions
Phone: 626-229-1300 ext. 1374
Fax: 626-403-4835
E-mail: ecolon@scsca.com

CAREER NETWORKS INSTITUTE

3420 Bristol Street, Suite 209
Costa Mesa, CA 92626
Web: http://www.cnicollege.edu
Accreditation: Accrediting Bureau of Health Education Schools
Programs Offered:

criminal justice/law enforcement administration; massage therapy; medical administrative assistant and medical secretary; medical/clinical assistant; medical insurance/medical billing; nursing (licensed practical/vocational nurse training); sport and fitness administration; surgical technology
Institution Contact: Mr. James Buffington, Sr., President
Phone: 714-437-9697
Fax: 714-437-9356
E-mail: jim@cniworks.com
Admission Contact: Patrick O'Hara, Admissions Director
Phone: 714-437-9697
Fax: 714-437-9356
E-mail: patrick@cniworks.com

 CENTRAL COAST COLLEGE
480 South Main Street
Salinas, CA 93901
Web: http://www.centralcoastcollege.edu
Accreditation: Accrediting Council for Continuing Education and Training
Programs Offered:
accounting; accounting technology and bookkeeping; administrative assistant and secretarial science; business machine repair; computer/information technology administration and management; computer installation and repair technology; computer systems networking and telecommunications; computer/technical support; computer technology/computer systems technology; data entry/microcomputer applications; data entry/microcomputer applications related; executive assistant/executive secretary; health information/medical records administration; health unit coordinator/ward clerk; information technology; medical administrative assistant and medical secretary; medical/clinical assistant; medical insurance coding; medical insurance/medical billing; medical office management; medical reception; medical transcription; office occupations and clerical services; pharmacy technician; phlebotomy; receptionist; system administration; word processing
Enrollment: 212 students
Institution Contact: Ms. Elaine M. Giuliano, Compliance Officer/Administrative Coordinator
Phone: 831-753-6660 ext. 17
Fax: 831-753-6485

E-mail: giuel@cccbus.com
Admission Contact: Ms. Cathy Del Fante, Admissions Coordinator
Phone: 831-753-6660 ext. 14
Fax: 831-753-6485
E-mail: delca@cccbus.com

CLARITA CAREER COLLEGE
27125 Sierra Highway, Suite 329
Canyon Country, CA 91351
Web: http://www.claritacareercollege.com/
Accreditation: Accrediting Commission of Career Schools and Colleges of Technology
Programs Offered:
clinical/medical laboratory assistant; dental assisting; legal assistant/paralegal; massage therapy; medical administrative assistant and medical secretary; medical/clinical assistant; pharmacy technician
Enrollment: 160 students
Institution Contact: Julie Ha, President
Phone: 661-252-1864
Fax: 661-252-2153
E-mail: ha_julie@claritacareercollege.com
Admission Contact: Mike Bell, School Director
Phone: 661-252-1864
Fax: 661-252-2153
E-mail: bell_michael@claritacareercollege.com

CLARITA CAREER COLLEGE - LANCASTER CAMPUS
701 West Avenue K, Suite 102
Lancaster, CA 93534
Institution Contact: Campus Director
Fax: 661-252-2153

COLEMAN COLLEGE
7380 Parkway Drive
La Mesa, CA 91942
Web: http://www.coleman.edu
Accreditation: Accrediting Council for Independent Colleges and Schools
Programs Offered:
computer and information sciences; computer and information systems security; computer graphics; computer programming; computer programming related; computer systems analysis; computer systems networking and telecommunications; computer/techni-

cal support; information science/studies; information technology; management information systems; office management; technology management; web page, digital/multimedia and information resources design
Enrollment: 460 students
Institution Contact: Mr. Pritpal S. Panesar, President
Phone: 619-465-3990 ext. 130
Fax: 619-463-0162 E-mail: panesar@coleman.edu
Admission Contact: Stephen Collins, Dean of Academics, Branch Manager
Phone: 619-465-3990 ext. 109
Fax: 619-463-0162
E-mail: scollins@coleman.edu

COLEMAN COLLEGE
1284 West San Marcos Boulevard
San Marcos, CA 92069
Web: http://www.coleman.edu/
Accreditation: Accrediting Council for Independent Colleges and Schools
Programs Offered:
computer and information sciences; computer and information systems security; computer graphics; computer programming; computer systems networking and telecommunications; general studies
Enrollment: 145 students
Institution Contact: Ms. Darlene Ankton, Site Manager
Phone: 760-747-3990
Fax: 760-752-9808
E-mail: dankton@coleman.edu

COMMUNITY BUSINESS COLLEGE
3800 McHenry Avenue, Suite M
Modesto, CA 95356
Web: http: www.communitybusinesscollege.edu
Institution contact: Dan Guerra
Phone: 209-529-3648
Fax: 209-529-0456

EMPIRE COLLEGE
3035 Cleveland Avenue
Santa Rosa, CA 95403
Web: http://www.empcol.edu
Accreditation: Accrediting Council for Independent Colleges and Schools
Programs Offered:

accounting; accounting technology and bookkeeping; administrative assistant and secretarial science; business automation/technology/data entry; clinical/medical laboratory assistant; clinical/medical laboratory technology; computer hardware engineering; computer/information technology administration and management; computer/information technology services administration related; computer systems networking and telecommunications; computer/technical support; computer technology/computer systems technology; data entry/microcomputer applications; data processing and data processing technology; executive assistant/executive secretary; health information/medical records administration; health information/medical records technology; hospitality administration; information technology; legal assistant/paralegal; medical administrative assistant and medical secretary; medical/clinical assistant; medical/health management and clinical assistant; medical insurance coding; medical insurance/medical billing; medical office computer specialist; medical office management; medical reception; medical transcription; office occupations and clerical services; pre-law studies; receptionist; securities services administration; system administration; system, networking, and LAN/WAN management; tourism and travel services management; word processing
Enrollment: 415 students
Institution Contact: Mr. Roy Hurd, President
Phone: 707-546-4000
Fax: 707-546-4058
E-mail: rhurd@empcol.edu
Admission Contact: Ms. Dahnja Straub, Director of Admissions
Phone: 707-546-4000 ext. 238
Fax: 707-546-4058
E-mail: dahnja@empirecollege.com

EVEREST COLLEGE
9616 Archibald Avenue, Suite 100
Rancho Cucamonga, CA 91730
Web: http://www.cci.edu
Accreditation: Accrediting Council for Independent Colleges and Schools
Programs Offered:
accounting; business administration and management; criminal justice/law enforcement administration; legal assistant/paralegal

Enrollment: 1,000 students
Institution Contact: Richard Mallow, President
Phone: 909-484-4311
Fax: 909-484-1162
Admission Contact: Greg Lam, Director of Admissions
Phone: 909-484-4311
Fax: 909-484-1162
E-mail: glam@cci.edu

EX'PRESSION COLLEGE FOR DIGITAL ARTS

6601 Shellmound Street
Emeryville, CA 94608
Web: http://www.expression.edu
Programs Offered:
animation, interactive technology, video graphics and special effects; graphic communications
Enrollment: 680 students
Institution Contact: Mr. Kirk Engel, Chief Executive Officer
Phone: 510-654-2934
E-mail: kengel@expression.edu
Admission Contact: Ms. Catherine Jordan, Director of Admissions
Phone: 510-654-2934
E-mail: cjordan@expression.edu

FOUR-D SUCCESS ACADEMY

1020 East Washington Street
Colton, CA 92324
Web: http://www.4Dcollege.com
Accreditation: Accrediting Bureau of Health Education Schools
Programs Offered:
adult and continuing education; dental assisting; medical/clinical assistant; medical insurance coding; medical insurance/medical billing; nursing assistant/aide and patient care assistant; pharmacy technician
Enrollment: 275 students
Institution Contact: Pebble Thomas, Executive Administrative Assistant
Phone: 909-783-9331
Fax: 909-783-6529
E-mail: 4dadmin.asst@friendsof4d.org
Admission Contact: Paula Herman, Admissions Representative
Phone: 909-783-9331 ext. 254
Fax: 909-783-9334

E-mail: pherman@4dcollege.com

GALEN COLLEGE OF CALIFORNIA, INC.

1325 North Wishon Avenue
Fresno, CA 93728
Accreditation: Accrediting Commission of Career Schools and Colleges of Technology
Programs Offered:
dental assisting; health aide; medical/clinical assistant
Institution Contact: Ms. Stella Mesple, President
Phone: 559-264-9700
E-mail: galencollege@pfny.com
Admission Contact: Mrs. Sandra Marquez, Assistant School Director
Phone: 559-264-9700
E-mail: galencollege@pfny.com

GALEN COLLEGE OF CALIFORNIA, INC.

1604 Ford Avenue
Modesto, CA 95350
Accreditation: Accrediting Commission of Career Schools and Colleges of Technology
Programs Offered:
dental assisting; medical/clinical assistant
Institution Contact: Mrs. Kellie Thornhill, Director
Phone: 559-527-5084
E-mail: galencollege@pfny.com
Admission Contact: Ms. Betsy Johns, Enrollment Officer
Phone: 209-527-5100

GALEN COLLEGE OF CALIFORNIA, INC.

3908 West Caldwell Avenue , Suite A
Visalia, CA 93277
Accreditation: Accrediting Commission of Career Schools and Colleges of Technology
Programs Offered:
dental assisting; medical/clinical assistant
Institution Contact: Mrs. Stella Mesple, President
Phone: 559-732-5200
E-mail: galencollege@pfny.com
Admission Contact: Ms. Beth Esquivel, Admissions
Phone: 559-732-5200
E-mail: galencollege@psnw.com

GEMOLOGICAL INSTITUTE OF AMERICA, INC.

5345 Armada Drive
Carlsbad, CA 92008
Web: http://www.gia.edu
Accreditation: Accrediting Commission of Career Schools and Colleges of Technology; Distance Education and Training Council
Programs Offered:
applied art; business administration and management; metal and jewelry arts
Enrollment: 347 students
Institution Contact: Ms. Christine Galdston, JD, Accreditation and Compliance Officer
Phone: 760-603-4182
Fax: 760-603-4596
E-mail: cgaldsto@gia.edu
Admission Contact: Mr. Jason Drake, Manager, Admissions
Phone: 760-603-4000 ext. 7327
Fax: 760-603-4003
E-mail: jadrake@gia.edu

GEMOLOGICAL INSTITUTE OF AMERICA, INC.

600 Corporate Pointe, Suite 100
Culver City, CA 90230
Web: http://www.gia.edu
Accreditation: Accrediting Commission of Career Schools and Colleges of Technology
Programs Offered:
metal and jewelry arts
Institution Contact: Ms. Veronica Clark-Hudson, Director
Phone: 310-670-2100
Fax: 310-410-4452
E-mail: laedu@gia.edu
Admission Contact: Ms. Lori Geller, Administrator, On Campus Operations
Phone: 310-670-2100
Fax: 310-410-4452
E-mail: laedu@gia.edu

GLENDALE CAREER COLLEGE

1015 Grandview Avenue
Glendale, CA 91201
Web: http://www.success.edu
Accreditation: Accrediting Council for Continuing Education and Training

Programs Offered:
administrative assistant and secretarial science; instrumentation technology; massage therapy; medical/clinical assistant; medical office management; nursing (licensed practical/vocational nurse training); surgical technology
Enrollment: 480 students
Institution Contact: Mr. Tim O'Neil, Campus Director
Phone: 818-243-1131
Fax: 818-243-6028
Admission Contact: Mr. Robert Ramirez, Admissions Director
Phone: 818-243-1131
Fax: 818-243-6028
E-mail: rramirez@success.edu

GLENDALE CAREER COLLEGE - OCEANSIDE

Tri-City Medical Center, 4002 Vista Way
Oceanside, CA 92056
Accreditation: Accrediting Council for Continuing Education and Training
Programs Offered:
surgical technology
Institution Contact: Ms. Cindy Harris, Director
Phone: 760-945-9896
Fax: 760-945-9970

GOLDEN STATE COLLEGE

3356 South Fairway
Visalia, CA 93277
Accreditation: Accrediting Council for Continuing Education and Training
Programs Offered:
accounting; computer and information sciences related; corrections; dental assisting; massage therapy; medical administrative assistant and medical secretary; medical/clinical assistant
Institution Contact: Mr. Dan Serna, Career Services Director
Phone: 800-400-1005
Fax: 559-735-3808
Admission Contact: Ms. Stephanie Farias, Director of Admissions
Phone: 800-400-1005
Fax: 559-735-3808
E-mail: sfarias@goldenstatecollege.com

HIGH-TECH INSTITUTE

1111 Howe Avenue, #250
Sacramento, CA 95825
Web: http://www.hightechschools.com
Accreditation: Accrediting Bureau of Health Education Schools; Accrediting Commission of Career Schools and Colleges of Technology
Programs Offered:
dental assisting; information technology; medical/clinical assistant; surgical technology
Institution Contact: Mr. Richard Dyer, School Director
Phone: 916-929-9700
Fax: 916-929-9703
E-mail: rdyer@hightechschools.com
Admission Contact: Mrs. Sarah Maskovich, Director of Admissions
Phone: 916-929-9700
Fax: 916-929-9703
E-mail: smaskovich@hightechschools.com

INSTITUTE FOR BUSINESS AND TECHNOLOGY

2550 Scott Boulevard
Santa Clara, CA 95050
Web: http://www.ibttech.com
Accreditation: Accrediting Bureau of Health Education Schools; Accrediting Commission of Career Schools and Colleges of Technology; Accrediting Council for Independent Colleges and Schools
Programs Offered:
administrative assistant and secretarial science; clinical/medical laboratory assistant; computer systems networking and telecommunications; electrical, electronic and communications engineering technology; heating, air conditioning and refrigeration technology; medical/clinical assistant
Enrollment: 253 students
Institution Contact: Mr. M. A. Mikhail, President and Chief Executive Officer
Phone: 408-727-1060
Fax: 408-980-9548
E-mail: mikhail@ibttech.com
Admission Contact: Ms. Peggy Quartarola, Director of Admissions
Phone: 408-727-1060
Fax: 408-980-9548
E-mail: peggy@ibttech.com

INSTITUTE OF TECHNOLOGY

1300 E. Shaw Ave., Suite 109
Fresno, CA 93710
Web: www.it-colleges.com
Institution Contact: Mr. Jim Hines
Fax: (559) 229-1865

ITT TECHNICAL INSTITUTE

525 North Muller Street
Anaheim, CA 92801-9938
Web: http://www.itt-tech.edu
Accreditation: Accrediting Council for Independent Colleges and Schools
Programs Offered:
accounting and business/management; animation, interactive technology, video graphics and special effects; business administration and management; CAD/CADD drafting/design technology; communications technology; computer and information systems security; computer engineering technology; computer software and media applications; computer software engineering; computer systems networking and telecommunications; criminal justice/police science; digital communication and media/multimedia; electrical, electronic and communications engineering technology; technology management; web page, digital/multimedia and information resources design
Institution Contact: Mr. Louis Osborn, Director
Phone: 714-535-3700
Admission Contact: Mr. Albert A. Naranjo, Director of Recruitment
Phone: 714-535-3700

ITT TECHNICAL INSTITUTE

16916 South Harlan Road
Lathrop, CA 95330
Web: http://www.itt-tech.edu
Accreditation: Accrediting Council for Independent Colleges and Schools
Programs Offered:
accounting and business/management; animation, interactive technology, video graphics and special effects; business administration and management; CAD/CADD drafting/design technology; communications technology; computer and information systems security; computer engineering technology; computer software and media applications; computer software

engineering; computer systems networking and tele-communications; criminal justice/police science; digital communication and media/multimedia; electrical, electronic and communications engineering technology; technology management; web page, digital/multimedia and information resources design

Institution Contact: Mr. W. Donald Fraser, Director

Phone: 209-858-0077

Admission Contact: Ms. Kathy Paradis, Director of Recruitment

Phone: 209-858-0077

 ITT TECHNICAL INSTITUTE

2051 North Solar Drive, Suite 150

Oxnard, CA 93030

Web: http://www.itt-tech.edu

Accreditation: Accrediting Council for Independent Colleges and Schools

Programs Offered:

accounting and business/management; animation, interactive technology, video graphics and special effects; business administration and management; CAD/CADD drafting/design technology; communications technology; computer and information systems security; computer engineering technology; computer software and media applications; computer software engineering; computer systems networking and tele-communications; criminal justice/police science; digital communication and media/multimedia; electrical, electronic and communications engineering technology; technology management; web page, digital/multimedia and information resources design

Institution Contact: Ms. Lorraine Bunt, Director

Phone: 805-988-0143 ext. 112

Admission Contact: Mr. Dean K. Dunbar, Director of Recruitment

Phone: 805-988-0143

 ITT TECHNICAL INSTITUTE

10863 Gold Center Drive

Rancho Cordova, CA 95670-6034

Web: http://www.itt-tech.edu

Accreditation: Accrediting Council for Independent Colleges and Schools

Programs Offered:

accounting and business/management; animation, interactive technology, video graphics and special

effects; business administration and management; CAD/CADD drafting/design technology; communications technology; computer and information systems security; computer engineering technology; computer software and media applications; computer software engineering; computer systems networking and tele-communications; criminal justice/police science; digital communication and media/multimedia; electrical, electronic and communications engineering technology; technology management; web page, digital/multimedia and information resources design

Institution Contact: Mr. Mark Garland, Director

Phone: 916-851-3900

Admission Contact: Mr. Robert Menszer, Director of Recruitment

Phone: 916-851-3900

 ITT TECHNICAL INSTITUTE

630 East Brier Drive, Suite 150

San Bernardino, CA 92408-2800

Web: http://www.itt-tech.edu

Accreditation: Accrediting Council for Independent Colleges and Schools

Programs Offered:

accounting and business/management; animation, interactive technology, video graphics and special effects; business administration and management; CAD/CADD drafting/design technology; communications technology; computer and information systems security; computer engineering technology; computer software and media applications; computer software engineering; computer systems networking and tele-communications; criminal justice/police science; digital communication and media/multimedia; electrical, electronic and communications engineering technology; technology management; web page, digital/multimedia and information resources design

Institution Contact: Mr. Terry Lorenz, Director

Phone: 909-889-3800 ext. 20

Admission Contact: Mr. Tyron Cooley, Director of Recruitment

Phone: 909-889-3800 ext. 11

 ITT TECHNICAL INSTITUTE

9680 Granite Ridge Drive, Suite 100

San Diego, CA 92123

Web: http://www.itt-tech.edu

Accreditation: Accrediting Council for Independent Colleges and Schools
Programs Offered:
accounting and business/management; animation, interactive technology, video graphics and special effects; business administration and management; CAD/CADD drafting/design technology; communications technology; computer and information systems security; computer engineering technology; computer software and media applications; computer software engineering; computer systems networking and telecommunications; criminal justice/police science; digital communication and media/multimedia; electrical, electronic and communications engineering technology; technology management; web page, digital/multimedia and information resources design
Institution Contact: Mr. David Parker, Director
Phone: 858-571-8500
Admission Contact: Mr. Robert Dutton, Director of Recruitment
Phone: 858-571-8500

ITT TECHNICAL INSTITUTE
12669 Encinitas Avenue
Sylmar, CA 91342-3664
Web: http://www.itt-tech.edu
Accreditation: Accrediting Council for Independent Colleges and Schools
Programs Offered:
accounting and business/management; animation, interactive technology, video graphics and special effects; business administration and management; CAD/CADD drafting/design technology; communications technology; computer and information systems security; computer engineering technology; computer software and media applications; computer software engineering; computer systems networking and telecommunications; computer technology/computer systems technology; criminal justice/police science; digital communication and media/multimedia; electrical, electronic and communications engineering technology; technology management; web page, digital/multimedia and information resources design
Institution Contact: Mr. Nader Mojtabai, Director
Phone: 818-364-5151
Admission Contact: Ms. Kelly Christensen, Director of Recruitment
Phone: 818-364-5151

ITT Technical Institute
20050 South Vermont Avenue
Torrance, CA 90502
Web: http://www.itt-tech.edu
Accreditation: Accrediting Council for Independent Colleges and Schools
Programs Offered:
accounting and business/management; animation, interactive technology, video graphics and special effects; business administration and management; CAD/CADD drafting/design technology; communications technology; computer and information systems security; computer engineering technology; computer software and media applications; computer software engineering; computer systems networking and telecommunications; criminal justice/police science; digital communication and media/multimedia; electrical, electronic and communications engineering technology; technology management; web page, digital/multimedia and information resources design
Institution Contact: Ms. Anne Marie Koerin, Director
Phone: 310-380-1555
Admission Contact: Mr. Freddie Polk, Director of Recruitment
Phone: 310-380-1555

ITT TECHNICAL INSTITUTE
1530 West Cameron Avenue
West Covina, CA 91790-2711
Web: http://www.itt-tech.edu
Accreditation: Accrediting Council for Independent Colleges and Schools
Programs Offered:
accounting and business/management; animation, interactive technology, video graphics and special effects; business administration and management; CAD/CADD drafting/design technology; communications technology; computer and information systems security; computer engineering technology; computer software and media applications; computer software engineering; computer systems networking and telecommunications; criminal justice/police science; digital communication and media/multimedia; electrical, electronic and communications engineering technology; industrial technology; technology management; web page, digital/multimedia and information resources design
Institution Contact: Ms. Maria Alamat, Director

Phone: 626-960-8681
Admission Contact: Ms. JoAnn Meron, Director of Recruitment
Phone: 626-960-8681

KITCHEN ACADEMY
6370 W. Sunset Blvd.
Los Angeles, CA 90028
Web: www.kitchenacademy.com
Institution contact: Mr. Chris Becker

MARIC COLLEGE
1360 South Anaheim Boulevard
Anaheim, CA 92805
Accreditation: Accrediting Council for Independent Colleges and Schools
Programs Offered:
business administration and management; computer and information sciences related; information technology; legal administrative assistant/secretary; legal assistant/paralegal; medical administrative assistant and medical secretary; medical/clinical assistant
Institution Contact: Mr. Gene M. Villarin, Student Services Director
Phone: 714-758-1500 ext. 115
Fax: 714-758-1220
E-mail: gene@mariccollege.com
Admission Contact: Mrs. Dora Tellez, Director of Admissions
Phone: 714-758-1500 ext. 117
Fax: 714-758-1220
E-mail: dora@mariccollege.edu

MARIC COLLEGE - FRESNO
44 Shaw Ave.
Clovis, CA 93612
Institution Contact: Katie Swanger
Phone: 559-325-5100

MARIC COLLEGE
6180 Laurel Canyon Boulevard, #101
North Hollywood, CA 91606
Web: http://www.moderntec.com
Accreditation: Accrediting Commission of Career Schools and Colleges of Technology

Programs Offered:
diagnostic medical sonography and ultrasound technology; electrocardiograph technology; health information/medical records administration; information technology; medical/clinical assistant; medical insurance/medical billing; medical radiologic technology; radiologic technology/science
Institution Contact: Mr. Mark Newman, Executive Director
Phone: 818-763-2563 ext. 240
Fax: 818-763-1623
E-mail: mark@moderntec.com
Admission Contact: Mr. Roger Cranmer, Director of Admissions
Phone: 818-763-2563 ext. 229
Fax: 818-763-1623
E-mail: roger@moderntec.com

MARIC COLLEGE
4330 Watt Avenue, Suite 400
Sacramento, CA 95660
Web: http://www.californiacollegetech.com
Accreditation: Accrediting Council for Independent Colleges and Schools
Programs Offered:
computer systems networking and telecommunications; information technology; interior design; medical/clinical assistant
Institution Contact: Mr. Tapas Ghosh, Executive Director
Phone: 916-649-8168
Fax: 916-649-8344
E-mail: tghosh@californiacollegetech.com
Admission Contact: Mr. Charlie Reese, Director of Admissions
Phone: 916-649-8168
Fax: 916-649-8344
E-mail: creese@californiacollegetech.com

MARIC COLLEGE
5172 Kiernan Court
Salida, CA 95368
Web: http://www.mariccollege.edu
Accreditation: Accrediting Bureau of Health Education Schools; Accrediting Commission of Career Schools and Colleges of Technology
Programs Offered:

allied health and medical assisting services related; medical administrative assistant and medical secretary; medical/clinical assistant

Enrollment: 496 students

Institution Contact: Mrs. MaryAnn Crone, Executive Director

Phone: 209-543-7000

Fax: 209-543-1755

E-mail: mcrone@mariccollege.edu

Admission Contact: Mrs. Linda Stovall, Director of Admissions

Phone: 209-543-7020

Fax: 209-543-1755

E-mail: lstovall@mariccollege.edu

MARIC COLLEGE

9055 Balboa Avenue, Suite 100
San Diego, CA 92123
Web: http://www.mariccollege.edu
Accreditation: Accrediting Bureau of Health Education Schools; Accrediting Commission of Career Schools and Colleges of Technology

Programs Offered:
business administration and management; business administration, management and operations related; business operations support and secretarial services related; criminal justice/law enforcement administration; criminal justice/police science; information technology; legal assistant/paralegal; medical administrative assistant and medical secretary; medical insurance coding; medical insurance/medical billing; medical office assistant; medical office management; medical radiologic technology; nursing assistant/aide and patient care assistant; nursing (licensed practical/vocational nurse training); nursing (registered nurse training)

Enrollment: 1,041 students

Institution Contact: Mr. Michael Seifert, President

Phone: 858-279-4500 ext. 3602

Fax: 858-279-4885

E-mail: mseifert@mariccollege.edu

Admission Contact: Ms. Geraldine Rorrison, Director of Admissions

Phone: 858-279-4500 ext. 3623

Fax: 858-279-4885

E-mail: grorrison@mariccollege.edu

MARIC COLLEGE

2022 University Drive
Vista, CA 92083
Web: http://www.mariccollege.edu
Accreditation: Accrediting Bureau of Health Education Schools; Accrediting Commission of Career Schools and Colleges of Technology

Programs Offered:
computer/information technology administration and management; health aide; legal assistant/paralegal; medical administrative assistant and medical secretary; medical/clinical assistant; medical insurance coding; nursing assistant/aide and patient care assistant; nursing (licensed practical/vocational nurse training); system administration; system, networking, and LAN/WAN management

Institution Contact: Mrs. Jann Mitchell, Campus President

Phone: 760-630-1555

Fax: 760-630-1656

E-mail: jmitchell@mariccollege.edu

Admission Contact: Mrs. Nancie Froning, Director of Admissions

Phone: 760-630-1555

Fax: 760-630-1656

E-mail: nfroning@mariccollege.edu

MARIC COLLEGE

3699 Wilshire Blvd.
Los Angeles, CA 90010
Institution Contact: Mr. Steven Schilling

Phone: 213-351-2000

Fax: 213-351-2004

NATIONAL CAREER EDUCATION

6060 Sunrise Vista Drive
Citrus Heights, CA 95610
Web: http://www.ncecollege.org
Accreditation: Accrediting Bureau of Health Education Schools; Accrediting Commission of Career Schools and Colleges of Technology

Programs Offered:
administrative assistant and secretarial science; clinical/medical laboratory assistant; computer systems networking and telecommunications; medical office management; ophthalmic technology; optometric technician

Enrollment: 150 students
Institution Contact: Mr. J. Paul Langton, Director
Phone: 916-969-4900
Fax: 916-723-7290
E-mail: jplangton@hotmail.com
Admission Contact: Ms. Nora Wilkinson, Director of Admissions
Phone: 916-969-4900
Fax: 916-723-7290

NATIONAL INSTITUTE OF TECHNOLOGY

2161 Technology Place
Long Beach, CA 90810
Web: http://www.nitschools.com
Accreditation: Accrediting Commission of Career Schools and Colleges of Technology
Programs Offered:
automobile/automotive mechanics technology; electrician; heating, air conditioning and refrigeration technology; industrial electronics technology; massage therapy; medical/clinical assistant; plumbing technology
Enrollment: 879 students
Institution Contact: Mr. Dana K. Martin, President
Phone: 562-437-0501
Fax: 562-432-3721
E-mail: dmartin@cci.edu
Admission Contact: Miss Therese El Khoury, Director of Admissions
Phone: 562-437-0501
Fax: 562-432-3721
E-mail: telkhoury@cci.edu

NEWSCHOOL OF ARCHITECTURE & DESIGN

1249 F Street
San Diego, CA 92101-6634
Web: http://www.newschoolarch.edu/
Accreditation: Accrediting Council for Independent Colleges and Schools
Programs Offered:
architectural engineering technology
Enrollment: 402 students
Institution Contact: Dean Gilbert D. Cooke, AIA, President
Phone: 619-235-4100 ext. 108
Fax: 619-235-4651
E-mail: gcooke@newschoolarch.edu
Admission Contact: Ms. Barbara Wingate, Director

of Admissions
Phone: 619-235-4100 ext. 123
Fax: 619-235-4651
E-mail: bvwingate@newschoolarch.edu

PIMA MEDICAL INSTITUTE

780 Bay Boulevard, Suite 101
Chula Vista, CA 91910
Web: http://www.pmi.edu
Accreditation: Accrediting Bureau of Health Education Schools
Programs Offered:
dental assisting; medical administrative assistant and medical secretary; medical/clinical assistant; pharmacy technician; radiologic technology/science; respiratory care therapy; veterinary/animal health technology
Enrollment: 500 students
Institution Contact: Mr. Christopher Luebke, Admissions Support Center Director
Phone: 888-898-9048
E-mail: asc@pmi.edu
Admission Contact: Admissions Support Representative
Phone: 888-898-9048
E-mail: asc@pmi.edu

PLATT COLLEGE

7755 Center Ave, Suite 600
Huntington Beach, CA 92660
Web: http://www.plattcollege.edu
Accreditation: Accrediting Commission of Career Schools and Colleges of Technology
Programs Offered:
animation, interactive technology, video graphics and special effects; commercial and advertising art; computer engineering technology; computer/information technology administration and management; computer/information technology services administration related; computer systems networking and telecommunications; computer technology/computer systems technology; desktop publishing and digital imaging design; information science/studies; information technology; legal assistant/paralegal; system administration; web page, digital/multimedia and information resources design
Enrollment: 215 students
Institution Contact: Ms. Lisa Rhodes, Campus President
Phone: 949-851-4991 ext. 222

Fax: 949-833-0269
E-mail: lrhodes@plattcollege.edu
Admission Contact: Ms. Terrie Taylor, Director of Admissions
Phone: 714-373-3240
Fax: 714-373-3241
E-mail: ttaylor@plattcollege.edu

PLATT COLLEGE

3700 Inland Empire Boulevard
Ontario, CA 91764
Web: http://www.plattcollege.edu
Accreditation: Accrediting Commission of Career Schools and Colleges of Technology
Programs Offered:
animation, interactive technology, video graphics and special effects; commercial and advertising art; computer graphics; computer/information technology administration and management; computer/information technology services administration related; computer/technical support; computer technology/computer systems technology; design and visual communications; information science/studies; information technology; intermedia/multimedia; legal assistant/paralegal; system administration; web page, digital/multimedia and information resources design
Enrollment: 365 students
Institution Contact: Mr. Joe Blackman, Campus Director
Phone: 909-941-9410
Fax: 909-941-9660
E-mail: jblackman@plattcollege.edu
Admission Contact: Ms. Carmen Conceicao, Director of Admissions
Phone: 909-941-9410
Fax: 909-941-9660
E-mail: cconceicao@plattcollege.edu

PLATT COLLEGE - LOS ANGELES, INC

1000 South Fremont A9W
Alhambra, CA 91803
Web: http://www.plattcollege.edu
Accreditation: Accrediting Commission of Career Schools and Colleges of Technology
Programs Offered:
commercial and advertising art; computer graphics; computer/information technology administration and management; computer/information technology services administration related; computer systems networking and telecommunications; graphic communications related; information technology; legal assistant/paralegal; medical/clinical assistant; medical/health management and clinical assistant; medical office assistant; medical office management; web page, digital/multimedia and information resources design
Enrollment: 173 students
Institution Contact: Manfred Rodriguez, Director
Phone: 626-300-5444
Fax: 626-300-3978
E-mail: mrodriguez@plattcollege.edu
Admission Contact: Tyka Burton, Admissions Director
Phone: 626-300-5444
Fax: 626-300-3978
E-mail: tburton@plattcollege.edu

PLATT COLLEGE - SAN DIEGO

6250 El Cajon Boulevard
San Diego, CA 92115-3919
Web: http://www.platt.edu
Accreditation: Accrediting Commission of Career Schools and Colleges of Technology
Programs Offered:
advertising; animation, interactive technology, video graphics and special effects; cinematography and film/video production; commercial and advertising art; computer graphics; computer software and media applications; design and visual communications; desktop publishing and digital imaging design; digital communication and media/multimedia; education; graphic and printing equipment operation/production; graphic communications; graphic communications related; intermedia/multimedia; photographic and film/video technology; visual and performing arts; web/multimedia management and webmaster; web page, digital/multimedia and information resources design
Enrollment: 350 students
Institution Contact: Mr. Steve Gallup, Director of Marketing
Phone: 619-265-0107
Fax: 619-308-0570
E-mail: sgallup@platt.edu
Admission Contact: Ms. Carly Westerfield, Admissions Coordinator
Phone: 619-265-0107
Fax: 619-308-0570

E-mail: cwesterfield@platt.edu

REMINGTON COLLEGE - SAN DIEGO CAMPUS
123 Camino De La Reina, Suite 100 North
San Diego, CA 92108
Web: http://www.remingtoncollege.edu
Accreditation: Accrediting Council for Independent
Colleges and Schools
Programs Offered:
allied health and medical assisting services related;
business administration and management; computer
systems networking and telecommunications; com-
puter/technical support; criminal justice/law enforce-
ment administration; criminal justice/police science;
massage therapy; system, networking, and LAN/WAN
management; word processing
Enrollment: 600 students
Institution Contact: Jose Cisneros, Campus President
Phone: 619-686-8600 ext. 225
Fax: 619-686-8669
E-mail: jose.cisneros@remingtoncollege.edu
Admission Contact: Mr. Lennor Johnson, Director of
Recruitment
Phone: 619-686-8600 ext. 229
Fax: 619-686-8684
E-mail: lennor.johnson@remingtoncollege.edu

SAN JOAQUIN VALLEY COLLEGE
201 New Stine Road
Bakersfield, CA 93309
Web: http://www.sjvc.edu
Accreditation: Western Association of Schools and
Colleges
Programs Offered:
administrative assistant and secretarial science; business
administration and management; computer engineering
technology; computer/information technology services administration related; computer installation and
repair technology; computer systems networking and
telecommunications; computer technology/computer
systems technology; corrections; criminal justice/law
enforcement administration; dental assisting; executive
assistant/executive secretary; health information/medi-
cal records technology; heating, air conditioning and
refrigeration technology; information science/studies;
insurance; medical administrative assistant and medical secretary; medical/clinical assistant; medical office

management; office occupations and clerical services;
receptionist; respiratory care therapy; security and loss
prevention; surgical technology
Institution Contact: Mr. Joseph Holt, Director of
Marketing and Admissions
Phone: 559-651-2500
Fax: 559-651-4864
E-mail: josephh@sjvc.edu
Admission Contact: Mr. David Baker, Campus Director
Phone: 661-834-0126
Fax: 661-834-1021
E-mail: davidb@sjvc.edu

SAN JOAQUIN VALLEY COLLEGE
295 East Sierra Avenue
Fresno, CA 93710
Web: http://www.sjvc.edu
Accreditation: Western Association of Schools and
Colleges
Programs Offered:
business administration and management; computer/
technical support; criminal justice/law enforcement administration; dental assisting; electrical, electronic and
communications engineering technology; health/health
care administration; heating, air conditioning and
refrigeration technology; hospitality administration;
medical administrative assistant and medical secretary;
medical office management; pharmacy technician;
tourism and travel services management
Institution Contact: Director, Fresno Campus
Phone: 559-229-7800
Fax: 559-448-8250
Admission Contact: Admissions Director
Phone: 559-229-7800
Fax: 559-448-8250

SAN JOAQUIN VALLEY COLLEGE

4985 East Anderson Avenue
Fresno, CA 93727
Web: http://www.sjvc.edu
Accreditation: Western Association of Schools and
Colleges
Programs Offered:
airframe mechanics and aircraft maintenance technol-
ogy; avionics maintenance technology
Enrollment: 57 students
Institution Contact: Bob Loogman, Executive Direc-
tor, Aviation Campus

Phone: 559-453-0123
Fax: 559-453-0133
E-mail: bobl@sjvc.edu
Admission Contact: Bob Loogman, Director, Aviation Campus
Phone: 559-453-0123
Fax: 559-453-0133
E-mail: bobl@sjvc.edu

SAN JOAQUIN VALLEY COLLEGE

1700 McHenry Village Way
Modesto, CA 95350
Web: http://www.sjvc.edu
Accreditation: Western Association of Schools and Colleges
Programs Offered:
business administration and management; medical/clinical assistant; medical office management
Phone: 866-808-9387

SAN JOAQUIN VALLEY COLLEGE

10641 Church Street
Rancho Cucamonga, CA 91730
Web: http://www.sjvc.edu
Accreditation: Western Association of Schools and Colleges
Programs Offered:
business administration and management; corrections; dental hygiene; medical administrative assistant and medical secretary; medical/clinical assistant; pharmacy technician; respiratory therapy technician
Enrollment: 600 students
Institution Contact: Mrs. Sherril Hein, Director, Rancho Cucamonga Campus
Phone: 909-948-7582
Fax: 909-945-8400
E-mail: sherrilh@sjvc.edu
Admission Contact: Mr. Ramon Abreu, Enrollment Services Director
Phone: 909-948-7582
Fax: 909-948-3860
E-mail: ramona@sjvc.edu

SAN JOAQUIN VALLEY COLLEGE INC.

11000 Olson Drive, Suite 101
Rancho Cordova, CA 95670

Institution Contact: Ms. Bonita Roznos
Phone: 916-683-7582

SAN JOAQUIN VALLEY COLLEGE

8400 West Mineral King Avenue
Visalia, CA 93291-9283
Web: http://www.sjvc.edu
Accreditation: Western Association of Schools and Colleges
Programs Offered:
accounting; administrative assistant and secretarial science; business administration and management; business automation/technology/data entry; computer installation and repair technology; computer systems networking and telecommunications; computer technology/computer systems technology; corrections; criminal justice/law enforcement administration; data processing and data processing technology; dental assisting; dental hygiene; executive assistant/executive secretary; health information/medical records technology; medical administrative assistant and medical secretary; medical/clinical assistant; medical office management; nursing assistant/aide and patient care assistant; nursing (licensed practical/vocational nurse training); office occupations and clerical services; physician assistant; receptionist; respiratory care therapy
Institution Contact: Mr. Mark Perry, President
Phone: 559-651-2500
Fax: 559-651-0574
E-mail: president@sjvc.edu
Admission Contact: Ms. Wendi Oliviera, Admissions Director
Phone: 559-651-2500
Fax: 559-651-0574
E-mail: wendio@sjvc.edu

SAN JOAQUIN VALLEY COLLEGE INC.

4134 S. Demaree
Visalia, CA 93277
Institution Contact: Cynthia Trent
Phone: 559-734-7582

SANTA BARBARA BUSINESS COLLEGE

211 South Real Road
Bakersfield, CA 93309
Web: http://www.sbbcollege.edu/

Accreditation: Accrediting Bureau of Health Education Schools; Accrediting Council for Independent Colleges and Schools

Programs Offered:
accounting technology and bookkeeping; business administration and management; computer/technical support; criminal justice/law enforcement administration; legal administrative assistant/secretary; legal assistant/paralegal; medical/clinical assistant; medical insurance/medical billing; medical office management; pharmacy technician

Enrollment: 300 students

Institution Contact: Matt Johnston, Vice President

Phone: 805-339-6370 ext. 120

Fax: 805-339-6376

E-mail: mattj@sbbcollege.edu

Admission Contact: Holly Ortiz, Director of Admissions

Phone: 805-339-6370 ext. 131

Fax: 805-339-6376

E-mail: hollyo@sbbcollege.edu

Santa Barbara Business College

5266 Hollister Avenue
Santa Barbara, CA 93111

Accreditation: Accrediting Council for Independent Colleges and Schools

Programs Offered:
accounting; administrative assistant and secretarial science; business administration and management; business administration, management and operations related; criminal justice/law enforcement administration; legal administrative assistant/secretary; legal assistant/paralegal; medical/clinical assistant; medical insurance/medical billing; pharmacy technician

Enrollment: 250 students

Institution Contact: Matt Johnston, Vice President

Phone: 805-339-6370

Fax: 805-339-6374

E-mail: mattj@sbbcollege.edu

Admission Contact: Holly Ortiz, Director of Admissions

Phone: 805-339-6370 ext. 131

Fax: 805-339-6376

E-mail: hollyo@sbbcollege.edu

Santa Barbara Business College

305 East Plaza Drive
Santa Maria, CA 93454
Web: http://www.sbbcollege.com

Accreditation: Accrediting Council for Independent Colleges and Schools

Programs Offered:
accounting; business administration and management; criminal justice/law enforcement administration; legal assistant/paralegal; medical/clinical assistant; medical insurance/medical billing; medical office management; pharmacy technician

Enrollment: 300 students

Institution Contact: Matt Johnston, Vice President

Phone: 805-339-6370

Fax: 805-339-6376

E-mail: mattj@sbbcollege.edu

Admission Contact: Mrs. Holly Ortiz, Director of Admissions

Phone: 805-339-6370 ext. 131

Fax: 805-339-6376

E-mail: hollyo@sbbcollege.edu

Santa Barbara Business College

4839 Market Street
Ventura, CA 93003
Web: http://www.sbbcollege.edu

Programs Offered:
accounting and business/management; business administration and management; criminal justice/law enforcement administration; legal assistant/paralegal; medical/clinical assistant; medical insurance/medical billing; pharmacy technician; phlebotomy

Enrollment: 200 students

Institution Contact: Matt Johnston, Vice President

Phone: 805-339-2999 ext. 120

E-mail: mattj@sbbcollege.edu

Admission Contact: Holly Ortiz, Director of Admissions

Phone: 805-339-2999

E-mail: hollyo@sbbcollege.edu

Silicon Valley College

1400 65th Street, Suite 200
Emeryville, CA 94608
Web: http://www.svcollege.com

Accreditation: Accrediting Commission of Career

Schools and Colleges of Technology
Programs Offered:
commercial and advertising art; drafting and design technology; information technology; medical/clinical assistant
Enrollment: 550 students
Institution Contact: Elvie Engstrom, Executive Director
Phone: 510-601-0133
Fax: 510-601-0793
E-mail: eengstrom@emv.westerncollege.com
Admission Contact: Mr. Robert Zayed, Director of Admissions
Phone: 510-601-0133
Fax: 510-601-0793
E-mail: rzayed@svcollege.com

SILICON VALLEY COLLEGE
41350 Christy Street
Fremont, CA 94538
Web: http://www.siliconvalley.edu
Accreditation: Accrediting Commission of Career Schools and Colleges of Technology
Programs Offered:
commercial and advertising art; computer graphics; computer/information technology administration and management; computer/information technology services administration related; computer systems networking and telecommunications; drafting and design technology; information science/studies; information technology; intermedia/multimedia; massage therapy; medical/clinical assistant; medical office management; pharmacy technician; system administration; system, networking, and LAN/WAN management
Institution Contact: Chuck Ericson, Executive Director
Phone: 510-623-9966
Fax: 510-623-9822
Admission Contact:
Phone: 510-623-9966
Fax: 510-623-9822

SILICON VALLEY COLLEGE
6201 San Ignacio Avenue
San Jose, CA 95119
Web: http://www.siliconvalley.edu
Accreditation: Accrediting Commission of Career Schools and Colleges of Technology

Programs Offered:
CAD/CADD drafting/design technology; commercial and advertising art; computer graphics; computer/information technology administration and management; design and visual communications; drafting and design technology; health information/medical records administration; information science/studies; information technology; internet information systems; massage therapy; medical/clinical assistant; medical office management; pharmacy technician; system administration; system, networking, and LAN/WAN management
Institution Contact: Mr. Steve Ashab, Executive Director
Phone: 408-360-0840
Fax: 408-360-0848
E-mail: sjwebleads@svcollege.com
Admission Contact:
Phone: 408-360-0840
Fax: 408-360-0848

UNITED EDUCATION INSTITUTE
310 3rd Avenue, Suite C6/C7
Chula Vista, CA 91910
Web: http://www.uei-edu.com
Accreditation: Accrediting Council for Continuing Education and Training
Programs Offered:
business administration and management; dental assisting; medical/clinical assistant; system administration; system, networking, and LAN/WAN management
Institution Contact: Ms. Fia Afalava, Executive Director
Phone: 619-409-4111
Fax: 619-409-4114
E-mail: afalavaf@iecglobal.com
Admission Contact: Ms. Nancy Fellciano, Director of Admissions
Phone: 619-409-4111
Fax: 619-409-4114
E-mail: fellcianon@iecglobal.com

UNITED EDUCATION INSTITUTE
3401 Rio Hondo Ave.
El Monte, CA 91731
Institution contact: Campus Director
Phone: 626-927-9000
Fax: 626-927-9350

UNITED EDUCATION INSTITUTE, HUNTINGTON PARK

6812 Pacific Boulevard
Huntington Park, CA 90255
Web: http://www.uei-edu.com
Accreditation: Accrediting Council for Continuing
Education and Training
Programs Offered:
business administration and management; dental assisting; medical/clinical assistant; system administration; system, networking, and LAN/WAN management
Institution Contact: Ms. Myra Hadley, Executive
Director
Phone: 323-277-8000
Fax: 323-588-5484
E-mail: hadleym@iecglobal.com
Admission Contact: Ms. Dora Tellez, Director of
Admissions
Phone: 323-277-8000
Fax: 323-588-5484
E-mail: tellezd@iecglobal.com

UNITED EDUCATION INSTITUTE, LOS ANGELES

3020 Wilshire Boulevard, #250
Los Angeles, CA 90010
Web: http://www.uei-edu.com
Accreditation: Accrediting Council for Continuing
Education and Training
Programs Offered:
business administration and management; computer systems networking and telecommunications; medical/clinical assistant; medical insurance/medical billing; pharmacy technician
Enrollment: 305 students
Institution Contact: Mr. Brian Lahargoue, Executive
Director
Phone: 213-427-3700 ext. 410
Fax: 213-487-1090
E-mail: lahargoueb@ueiglobal.com
Admission Contact: Director of Admissions
Phone: 213-427-3700
Fax: 213-487-1090

UNITED EDUCATION INSTITUTE, ONTARIO CAMPUS

3380 Shelby Street, Suite 150
Ontario, CA 91764
Web: http://www.uei-edu.com
Accreditation: Accrediting Council for Continuing

Education and Training
Programs Offered:
business administration and management; dental assisting; medical/clinical assistant; pharmacy technician; system administration; system, networking, and LAN/WAN management
Institution Contact: Ms. Jacky Ford, Executive
Director
Phone: 909-476-2424
Fax: 909-484-8748
E-mail: fordj@iecglobal.com
Admission Contact: Mr. Juan Tellez, Director of
Admissions
Phone: 909-476-2424
Fax: 909-484-8748
E-mail: tellezj@iecglobal.com

UNITED EDUCATION INSTITUTE, SAN BERNARDINO CAMPUS

295 East Caroline Street, Suite E
San Bernardino, CA 92408
Web: http://www.uei-edu.com
Accreditation: Accrediting Council for Continuing
Education and Training
Programs Offered:
business administration and management; dental assisting; medical/clinical assistant; medical insurance coding; medical insurance/medical billing; pharmacy technician; system, networking, and LAN/WAN management
Institution Contact: Mr. Robert Cios, Executive
Director
Phone: 909-554-1999
Fax: 909-554-1991
E-mail: ciosr@iecglobal.com
Admission Contact: Ms. Elisabeth Miller, Director of
Admissions
Phone: 909-554-1999
Fax: 909-554-1991
E-mail: millere@iecglobal.com

UNITED EDUCATION INSTITUTE, SAN DIEGO CAMPUS

1323 6th Avenue
San Diego, CA 92101
Web: http://www.uei-edu.com
Accreditation: Accrediting Council for Continuing

Education and Training
Programs Offered:
business administration and management; computer/technical support; dental assisting; medical/clinical assistant; pharmacy technician
Institution Contact: Ms. April Bjornsen, Executive Director
Phone: 619-544-9800
Fax: 619-233-3028
E-mail: bjornsena@iecglobal.com
Admission Contact: Ms. Mike Wynn, Director of Admissions
Phone: 619-544-9800
Fax: 619-233-3028
E-mail: wynnm@iecglobal.com

United Education Institute, Van Nuys Campus

7335 Van Nuys Boulevard
Van Nuys, CA 91405
Web: http://www.uei-edu.com
Accreditation: Accrediting Council for Continuing Education and Training
Programs Offered:
business administration and management; dental assisting; medical/clinical assistant; medical insurance/medical billing; pharmacy technician; system administration; system, networking, and LAN/WAN management
Institution Contact: Ms. Carolann Hartmann, Executive Director
Phone: 818-756-1200
Fax: 818-994-2607
E-mail: hartmannc@iecglobal.com
Admission Contact: Ms. Jackie Azizyan, Director of Admissions
Phone: 818-756-1200
Fax: 818-994-2607
E-mail: azizyanj@iecglobal.com

Universal Technical Institute

9494 Haven Avenue
Rancho Cucamonga, CA 91730
Web: http://www.uticorp.com
Accreditation: Accrediting Commission of Career Schools and Colleges of Technology
Programs Offered:
automobile/automotive mechanics technology; automotive engineering technology
Enrollment: 1,950 students
Institution Contact: Mr. Eric Oster, School Director
Phone: 909-484-1929
Fax: 909-510-6406
E-mail: eoster@uticorp.com

Walter Jay M.D. Institute, an Educational Center

1930 Wilshire Blvd., Suite 700
Los Angeles, CA 90057
Institution Contact: Mr. Prasanna Silva
Phone: 213-353-0722
Fax: 213-413-5994

Western Career College

380 Civic Drive, Suite 300
Pleasant Hill, CA 94523
Web: http://www.westerncollege.com
Accreditation: Accrediting Commission of Career Schools and Colleges of Technology; Western Association of Schools and Colleges
Programs Offered:
dental assisting; massage therapy; medical administrative assistant and medical secretary; medical/clinical assistant; medical insurance/medical billing; nursing (licensed practical/vocational nurse training); pharmacy technician; veterinary technology
Institution Contact: LaShawn Wells, Executive Director
Phone: 925-609-6650
Fax: 925-609-6666
E-mail: phwebleads@westerncollege.com

Western Career College

8909 Folsom Boulevard
Sacramento, CA 95826
Web: http://www.westerncollege.com
Accreditation: Accrediting Commission of Career Schools and Colleges of Technology; Western Association of Schools and Colleges
Programs Offered:
dental assisting; dental hygiene; massage therapy; medical administrative assistant and medical secretary; medical/clinical assistant; medical insurance coding;

nursing (licensed practical/vocational nurse training); nursing (registered nurse training); pharmacy technician; veterinary/animal health technology
Enrollment: 1,000 students
Institution Contact: Ms. Sue Smith, Executive Director
Phone: 916-361-1660 ext. 605
Fax: 916-361-6666
E-mail: ssmith@westerncollege.com
Admission Contact: Mr. Laura Lionetti, Director of High School Admissions
Phone: 916-361-1660 ext. 615
Fax: 916-361-6666
E-mail: llionetti@westerncollege.com

WESTERN CAREER COLLEGE
170 Bayfair Mall
San Leandro, CA 94578
Web: http://www.westerncollege.com
Accreditation: Accrediting Commission of Career Schools and Colleges of Technology; Western Association of Schools and Colleges
Programs Offered:
dental assisting; massage therapy; medical administrative assistant and medical secretary; medical/clinical assistant; medical insurance/medical billing; nursing (licensed practical/vocational nurse training); pharmacy technician; veterinary/animal health technology
Institution Contact: Ms. Dawn Matthews, Executive Director
Phone: 510-276-3888
Fax: 510-276-3654
E-mail: slwebleads@westerncollege.com

WESTERN COLLEGE OF SOUTHERN CALIFORNIA
10900 East 183rd Street, Suite 290
Cerritos, CA 90703
Programs Offered:
legal assistant/paralegal; massage therapy
Institution Contact: Admissions
Phone: 562-809-5100
Fax: 562-859-7100

WESTERN STATE UNIVERSITY COLLEGE OF LAW
1111 North State College Boulevard
Fullerton, CA 92831
Web: http://www.wsulaw.edu

Accreditation: Western Association of Schools and Colleges
Programs Offered:
pre-law studies
Enrollment: 490 students
Institution Contact: Mrs. Gloria Switzer, Assistant Dean of Admission
Phone: 714-459-1101
Fax: 714-441-1748
E-mail: gswitzer@wsulaw.edu

WESTWOOD COLLEGE - ANAHEIM
1551 South Douglass Road
Anaheim, CA 92806
Web: http://www.westwood.edu
Accreditation: Accrediting Commission of Career Schools and Colleges of Technology
Programs Offered:
accounting and business/management; animation, interactive technology, video graphics and special effects; business, management, and marketing related; CAD/CADD drafting/design technology; computer engineering technology; computer software engineering; criminal justice/law enforcement administration; information technology; interior design; marketing/marketing management; technology management; web/multimedia management and webmaster; web page, digital/multimedia and information resources design
Enrollment: 832 students
Institution Contact: Mr. Frederick Holland, Executive Director
Phone: 714-704-2721 ext. 200
Fax: 714-939-2011
E-mail: fholland@westwood.edu
Admission Contact: Emily Yost, Director of Admissions
Phone: 714-704-2721 ext. 100
Fax: 714-704-2735
E-mail: eyost@westwood.edu

WESTWOOD COLLEGE - INLAND EMPIRE
20 West 7th Street
Upland, CA 91786
Web: http://www.westwood.edu/
Accreditation: Accrediting Commission of Career Schools and Colleges of Technology
Programs Offered:

accounting; accounting and business/management; animation, interactive technology, video graphics and special effects; business administration and management; CAD/CADD drafting/design technology; commercial and advertising art; computer and information systems security; computer programming; computer software and media applications; computer software engineering; computer software technology; computer systems networking and telecommunications; computer technology/computer systems technology; criminal justice/law enforcement administration; e-commerce; finance; interior design; marketing/marketing management; system, networking, and LAN/WAN management; web page, digital/multimedia and information resources design

Enrollment: 1,100 students

Institution Contact: Ms. Kathy Allin, President

Phone: 909-931-7599 ext. 200

Fax: 909-946-6304

E-mail: kallin@westwood.edu

Admission Contact: Ms. Alma Salazar, Director of Admissions

Phone: 909-931-7550 ext. 104

Fax: 909-931-5962

E-mail: asalazar@westwood.edu

 WESTWOOD COLLEGE - LONG BEACH

19700 South Vermont Avenue, #100

Torrance, CA 90502

Web: http://www.westwood.edu

Accreditation: Accrediting Commission of Career Schools and Colleges of Technology

Programs Offered:

animation, interactive technology, video graphics and special effects; CAD/CADD drafting/design technology; computer/information technology administration and management; computer technology/computer systems technology; criminal justice/law enforcement administration; information technology; interior design; technology management

Enrollment: 410 students

Institution Contact: Ms. Vicki L. Bowles, Executive Director

Phone: 310-965-0877 ext. 200

Fax: 310-965-0244

E-mail: vbowles@westwood.edu

Admission Contact: Mr. Jesse Kamekona, Assistant Director of Admissions

Phone: 310-965-0877 ext. 104

Fax: 310-965-0881

E-mail: jkamekona@westwood.edu

 WESTWOOD COLLEGE - LOS ANGELES

8911 Aviation Boulevard

Inglewood, CA 90301

Web: http://www.westwoodcollege.edu

Accreditation: Council on Occupational Education

Programs Offered:

aircraft powerplant technology; airframe mechanics and aircraft maintenance technology

Enrollment: 632 students

Institution Contact: Mr. Christopher W. Turen, Executive Director

Phone: 310-642-5440 ext. 200

Fax: 310-642-3716

E-mail: cturen@westwood.edu

Admission Contact: Mr. Dewey McGuirk, Director of Admissions

Phone: 310-642-5440 ext. 240

Fax: 310-337-1176

E-mail: dmcguirk@westwood.edu

WESTWOOD COLLEGE - LOS ANGELES

3460 Wilshire Boulevard, Suite 700

Los Angeles, CA 90010

Web: http://www.westwood.edu

Accreditation: Accrediting Council for Independent Colleges and Schools

Programs Offered:

animation, interactive technology, video graphics and special effects; business, management, and marketing related; computer engineering technology; computer graphics; computer/information technology administration and management; computer programming; criminal justice/law enforcement administration; e-commerce; information technology; technology management; web page, digital/multimedia and information resources design

Enrollment: 539 students

Institution Contact: Mr. William Frank, Executive Director

Phone: 213-739-9999 ext. 200

Fax: 213-382-2468

E-mail: bfrank@westwood.edu

Admission Contact: Mr. Ron Milman, Director of

Admissions
Phone: 213-739-9999 ext. 100
Fax: 213-382-2468
E-mail: rmilman@westwood.edu

WyoTech
200 Whitney Place
Fremont, CA 94539-7663
Web: http://www.wyotech.com
Accreditation: Accrediting Commission of Career Schools and Colleges of Technology
Programs Offered:
automobile/automotive mechanics technology; heating, air conditioning and refrigeration technology; plumbing technology
Enrollment: 1,418 students
Institution Contact: Ms. Jan Coble, Interim President
Phone: 510-580-6735
Fax: 510-770-3873
Admission Contact: Mr. Joseph File, Director of Admissions
Phone: 510-580-3507
Fax: 510-490-8599
E-mail: jfile@cci.edu

WyoTech
9636 Earhart Road, Oakland International Airport
Oakland, CA 94621
Web: http://www.wyotech.com
Programs Offered:
aircraft powerplant technology; airframe mechanics and aircraft maintenance technology
Enrollment: 220 students
Institution Contact: Mr. Joseph I. Pappaly, School President
Phone: 510-569-8436
Fax: 510-635-3936
E-mail: ipappaly@cci.edu
Admission Contact: Mr. Joseph File, Regional Director of Admissions
Phone: 510-569-8436
Fax: 510-635-3936
E-mail: jfile@cci.edu

WyoTech
980 Riverside Parkway

West Sacramento, CA 95605
Web: http://www.wyotech.com
Accreditation: Accrediting Commission of Career Schools and Colleges of Technology
Programs Offered:
automobile/automotive mechanics technology
Enrollment: 300 students
Institution Contact: Jeanette M. Prickett, President
Phone: 916-376-8888 ext. 201
Fax: 916-617-2069
E-mail: jprickett@wyotech.edu
Admission Contact: Mr. Steve Coffee, Director of Admissions
Phone: 916-376-8888 ext. 202
Fax: 916-376-8888 ext. 95605
E-mail: scoffee@wyotech.edu

COLORADO

THE ART INSTITUTE OF COLORADO
1200 Lincoln Street
Denver, CO 80203
Web: http://www.aic.artinstitutes.edu
Accreditation: Accrediting Council for Independent Colleges and Schools
Programs Offered:
advertising; art; baking and pastry arts; cinematography and film/video production; commercial and advertising art; commercial photography; computer graphics; culinary arts; hospitality administration; industrial design; interior design; intermedia/multimedia; photography; restaurant, culinary, and catering management; web/multimedia management and webmaster; web page, digital/multimedia and information resources design
Enrollment: 2,259 students
Institution Contact: Mr. Steve Mansdoerfer , Vice President/Director of Administrative and Financial Services
Phone: 303-837-0825
Fax: 303-860-8520
E-mail: smansdoerfer@aii.edu
Admission Contact: Mr. Brian Parker, Director of Admissions
Phone: 800-275-2420
Fax: 303-860-8520
E-mail: baparker@aii.edu

BEL-REA INSTITUTE OF ANIMAL TECHNOLOGY

1681 South Dayton Street
Denver, CO 80247
Web: http://www.bel-rea.com
Accreditation: Accrediting Commission of Career
Schools and Colleges of Technology
Programs Offered:
veterinary/animal health technology; veterinary technology
Enrollment: 700 students
Institution Contact: Mr. Marc Schapiro, Controller
Phone: 303-751-8700
Fax: 303-751-9969
E-mail: schapiro@bel-rea.com
Admission Contact: Ms. Paulette Kaufman, Director
Phone: 800-950-8001
Fax: 303-751-9969
E-mail: kaufman@bel-rea.com

BLAIR COLLEGE

1815 Jetwing Drive
Colorado Springs, CO 80916
Web: http://www.cci.edu
Accreditation: Accrediting Council for Independent
Colleges and Schools
Programs Offered:
accounting; administrative assistant and secretarial
science; business administration and management;
computer programming (specific applications); criminal justice/law enforcement administration; legal assistant/paralegal; medical administrative assistant and
medical secretary; medical/clinical assistant; medical
insurance/medical billing; security and loss prevention; system, networking, and LAN/WAN management
Institution Contact: Mr. Larry M. Jackson, President
Phone: 719-638-6580 ext. 105
Fax: 719-638-6818
E-mail: lajackson@cci.edu
Admission Contact: Ms. Alexandra Fi, Director of
Admissions
Phone: 719-638-6580 ext. 102
Fax: 719-638-6818
E-mail: afi@cci.edu

CAMBRIDGE COLLEGE

350 Blackhawk Street
Aurora, CO 80011

Web: http://www.hightechschools.com/
Accreditation: Accrediting Bureau of Health Education Schools; Accrediting Commission of Career
Schools and Colleges of Technology
Programs Offered:
massage therapy; medical/clinical assistant; medical
insurance/medical billing; medical radiologic technology; surgical technology
Institution Contact: Ms. Deanna West, Campus
President
Phone: 720-859-7900
Fax: 303-344-1376
E-mail: dwest@hightechschools.edu
Admission Contact: Ms. Stacey Keele, Director of
Admissions
Phone: 720-859-7900
Fax: 303-344-1376
E-mail: skeele@hightechschools.edu

COLLEGEAMERICA - COLORADO SPRINGS

3645 Citadel Drive South
Colorado Springs, CO 80909
Web: http://www.CollegeAmerica.com
Accreditation: Accrediting Commission of Career
Schools and Colleges of Technology
Programs Offered:
accounting; business administration and management;
computer and information sciences related; computer
programming; e-commerce; health/health care administration; medical administrative assistant and medical
secretary; medical/clinical assistant; medical insurance
coding; medical insurance/medical billing; medical
office management; pharmacy technician; phlebotomy;
system administration; system, networking, and LAN/
WAN management
Enrollment: 206 students
Institution Contact: Mrs. Rozann R. Kunstle, Executive Director
Phone: 719-637-0600
Fax: 719-637-0806
E-mail: rkunstle@collegeamerica.edu
Admission Contact: Ms. Dawn Collins, Director of
Admissions
Phone: 719-637-0600
Fax: 719-637-0806
E-mail: dcollins@collegeamerica.edu

indicates that the school is a participating institution in the *Imagine America* Scholarship Program.

COLLEGEAMERICA - DENVER

1385 South Colorado Boulevard, 5th Floor
Denver, CO 80222
Web: http://www.collegeamerica.com
Accreditation: Accrediting Commission of Career
Schools and Colleges of Technology
Programs Offered:
accounting; acupuncture; administrative assistant
and secretarial science; business administration and
management; clinical/medical laboratory technology; computer/information technology administration
and management; computer/information technology
services administration related; computer installation
and repair technology; computer programming; computer programming (specific applications); computer
systems networking and telecommunications; com-
puter/technical support; computer technology/com-
puter systems technology; data entry/microcomputer
applications; desktop publishing and digital imaging
design; executive assistant/executive secretary; health
information/medical records administration; market-
ing/marketing management; medical administrative
assistant and medical secretary; medical/clinical assistant; nursing assistant/aide and patient care assistant;
pharmacy technician; system, networking, and LAN/
WAN management; telecommunications; web/multi-
media management and webmaster; web page, digi-
tal/multimedia and information resources design; word
processing
Institution Contact: Ms. Barbara W. Thomas, President
Phone: 303-691-9756
Fax: 303-692-9156
E-mail: collegeamerica@aol.com

COLLEGEAMERICA - FORT COLLINS

4601 South Mason Street
Fort Collins, CO 80525
Web: http://www.collegeamerica.edu
Accreditation: Accrediting Commission of Career
Schools and Colleges of Technology
Programs Offered:
accounting; business administration and management;
commercial and advertising art; computer and informa-
tion sciences related; computer programming; computer
technology/computer systems technology; health/health
care administration; medical/clinical assistant
Enrollment: 314 students
Institution Contact: Ms. Kristy McNear, Assistant

Director of Admission
Phone: 970-223-6060
Fax: 970-225-6059
E-mail: krmcnear@collegeamerica.edu

COLLEGE FOR FINANCIAL PLANNING

6161 South Syracuse Way
Greenwood Village, CO 80111-4707
Web: http://www.fp.edu
Accreditation: North Central Association of Colleges
and Schools
Programs Offered:
finance; finance and financial management services
related; financial planning and services; investments
and securities
Enrollment: 13,200 students
Institution Contact: Mr. John Sears, President
Phone: 303-220-4918
Fax: 303-220-4908
E-mail: john.sears@apollogrp.edu
Admission Contact: Ms. JuliAnna Sanchez, Director
of Enrollment
Phone: 303-220-4992
Fax: 303-220-1810
E-mail: enroll@fp.edu

COLORADO SCHOOL OF TRADES

1575 Hoyt Street
Lakewood, CO 80215-2996
Web: http://schooloftrades.com
Accreditation: Accrediting Commission of Career
Schools and Colleges of Technology
Programs Offered:
gunsmithing; horseshoeing
Enrollment: 120 students
Institution Contact: Mr. Robert Martin, Director
Phone: 303-233-4697 ext. 14
Fax: 303-233-4723
E-mail: robt@schooloftrdades.com
Admission Contact: Admissions
Phone: 303-233-4697 ext. 15
Fax: 303-233-4723
E-mail: info@schooloftrades.com

COLORADO TECHNICAL UNIVERSITY

4435 North Chestnut Street

Colorado Springs, CO 80907
Web: http://www.coloratech.edu
Accreditation: North Central Association of Colleges and Schools
Programs Offered:
accounting; business administration and management; communications technology; computer and information sciences related; computer and information systems security; computer engineering technology; computer software engineering; criminal justice/law enforcement administration; design and visual communications; e-commerce; electrical, electronic and communications engineering technology; entrepreneurship; human resources management; information technology; logistics and materials management; marketing/marketing management; surgical technology; technology management
Enrollment: 1,700 students
Institution Contact: Dr. Scott van Tonningen, Vice President of Academic Affairs
Phone: 719-590-6795
Fax: 719-598-3740
E-mail: svanton@coloradotech.edu
Admission Contact: Mr. Robert Lee, Vice President of Admissions
Phone: 719-590-6710
Fax: 719-598-3740
E-mail: rlee@coloradotech.edu

COLORADO TECHNICAL UNIVERSITY DENVER CAMPUS

5775 Denver Tech Center Boulevard
Greenwood Village , CO 80111-3258
Web: http://www.ctu-denver.com
Accreditation: North Central Association of Colleges and Schools
Programs Offered:
accounting; business administration and management; computer and information sciences related; computer and information systems security; criminal justice/law enforcement administration; electrical, electronic and communications engineering technology; graphic communications related; information technology
Enrollment: 580 students
Institution Contact: Dr. Michael Basham, President
Phone: 303-694-6600
Fax: 303-694-6673
E-mail: mbasham@coloradotech.edu

Admission Contact: Ms. Jennifer Schmidt, Director of Admissions
Phone: 303-694-6600
Fax: 303-694-6673
E-mail: jschmidt@coloradotech.edu

DENVER AUTOMOTIVE AND DIESEL COLLEGE

460 South Lipan Street, PO Box 9366
Denver, CO 80223-9960
Web: http://www.dadc.com
Accreditation: Accrediting Commission of Career Schools and Colleges of Technology
Programs Offered:
automobile/automotive mechanics technology; automotive engineering technology; diesel mechanics technology
Enrollment: 1,248 students
Institution Contact: Ms. Charmaine Wright, Executive Director
Phone: 303-722-5724 ext. 43001
Fax: 303-778-8264
E-mail: cwright@lincolntech.com
Admission Contact: Ms. Charmaine Wright, Director of Admissions
Phone: 303-722-5724
Fax: 303-778-8264
E-mail: cwright@lincolntech.com

DENVER CAREER COLLEGE

500 East 84th Avenue, W-200
Thornton, CO 80229
Web: http://www.denvercareercollege.com
Accreditation: Accrediting Commission of Career Schools and Colleges of Technology
Programs Offered:
business administration and management; criminal justice/law enforcement administration; legal assistant/paralegal; massage therapy; medical/clinical assistant; medical office assistant; pharmacy technician
Enrollment: 210 students
Institution Contact: Mr. Ken Sigmon, Regional Director
Phone: 402-572-8500
Fax: 402-408-1909
E-mail: ksigmon@khec.com
Admission Contact: Ms. Stephanie Parys, Executive Director

Phone: 303-736-0030 ext. 231
Fax: 303-295-0102
E-mail: sparys@denvercareercollege.com

DENVER SCHOOL OF MASSAGE THERAPY - AURORA

14107 E. Exposition Ave.
Aurora, CO 80012
Institution Contact: Mr. Jeff Gauvin
Phone: 303-366-4325
Fax: 303-366-5515

DENVER SCHOOL OF MASSAGE THERAPY - WESTMINSTER

8991 Harlan St., Suite B
Westminster, CO 80031
Institution Contact: Ms. Donna Mannello
Phone: 303-426-5621
Fax: 303-426-6611

HERITAGE COLLEGE

12 Lakeside Lane
Denver, CO 80212
Web: http://www.heritage-education.com
Programs Offered:
aesthetician/esthetician and skin care; allied health and medical assisting services related; massage therapy; medical/clinical assistant; pharmacy technician; rehabilitation and therapeutic professions related
Enrollment: 444 students
Institution Contact: Ms. Jennifer Lynn Sprague, Director
Phone: 303-477-7240 ext. 2633
Fax: 303-477-7276
E-mail: jennifers@heritage-education.com
Admission Contact: Ms. Heidi McDonald, Director of Admissions
Phone: 303-477-7240 ext. 2631
Fax: 303-477-7276
E-mail: heidim@heritage-education.com

ITT TECHNICAL INSTITUTE

500 East 84 Avenue, Suite B12
Thornton, CO 80229
Web: http://www.itt-tech.edu

Accreditation: Accrediting Council for Independent Colleges and Schools
Programs Offered:
accounting and business/management; animation, interactive technology, video graphics and special effects; business administration and management; CAD/CADD drafting/design technology; communications technology; computer and information systems security; computer engineering technology; computer software and media applications; computer software engineering; computer systems networking and telecommunications; criminal justice/police science; digital communication and media/multimedia; electrical, electronic and communications engineering technology; technology management; web page, digital/multimedia and information resources design
Institution Contact: Mr. Fred Hansen, Director
Phone: 303-288-4488
Admission Contact: Ms. Niki Donahue, Director of Recruitment
Phone: 303-288-4488

JONES INTERNATIONAL UNIVERSITY

9697 East Mineral Avenue
Englewood, CO 80112
Web: http://www.jonesinternational.edu
Accreditation: North Central Association of Colleges and Schools
Programs Offered:
business administration and management; business/corporate communications; business, management, and marketing related; communications technology; education; global management
Phone: 303-784-8904
Fax: 303-784-8547
E-mail: info@jonesinternational.edu

NATIONAL AMERICAN UNIVERSITY

5125 North Academy Boulevard
Colorado Springs, CO 80918
Web: http://www.national.edu
Accreditation: North Central Association of Colleges and Schools
Programs Offered:
accounting; allied health and medical assisting services related; business, management, and marketing related; computer/information technology administration and

management; computer programming (specific applications); computer systems networking and telecommunications; hospital and health care facilities administration; information technology
Enrollment: 250 students
Institution Contact: Ms. Audrey DeRubis, Campus Director
Phone: 719-277-0588
Fax: 719-277-0589
E-mail: aderubis@national.edu
Admission Contact: Mrs. Markita McKamie, Director of Admissions
Phone: 719-277-0588
Fax: 719-277-0589
E-mail: mmckamie@national.edu

NATIONAL AMERICAN UNIVERSITY

1325 South Colorado Boulevard
Denver, CO 80222
Web: http://www.national.edu
Accreditation: North Central Association of Colleges and Schools
Programs Offered:
accounting; business administration and management; computer/information technology administration and management; computer programming; computer systems networking and telecommunications; general studies; health/health care administration; information science/studies; information technology; management information systems; medical administrative assistant and medical secretary; medical/clinical assistant
Enrollment: 200 students
Institution Contact: Mr. Nathan M. Larson, Colorado Regional President
Phone: 303-758-6700
Fax: 303-758-6810
E-mail: nlarson@national.edu
Admission Contact: Mr. Nathan M. Larson, Colorado Regional President
Phone: 303-758-6700
Fax: 303-758-6810
E-mail: nlarson@national.edu

PARKS COLLEGE

14280 East Jewell Avenue, Suite 100
Aurora, CO 80012
Web: http://www.parks-college.com

Accreditation: Accrediting Council for Independent Colleges and Schools
Programs Offered:
accounting; assistive/augmentative technology and rehabilitation engineering; business administration and management; computer and information sciences related; criminal justice/law enforcement administration; legal assistant/paralegal; medical/clinical assistant; medical insurance coding; system administration; system, networking, and LAN/WAN management; web/multimedia management and webmaster
Enrollment: 686 students
Institution Contact: Mr. Rick Harding, Director of Admissions
Phone: 303-745-6244
Fax: 303-745-6245
E-mail: rharding@cci.edu

PARKS COLLEGE

9065 Grant Street
Denver, CO 80229
Web: http://www.cci.edu/
Accreditation: Accrediting Council for Independent Colleges and Schools
Programs Offered:
accounting; business administration and management; computer and information sciences related; computer/information technology services administration related; computer technology/computer systems technology; criminal justice/law enforcement administration; legal assistant/paralegal; medical administrative assistant and medical secretary; medical/clinical assistant; medical insurance coding; surgical technology
Enrollment: 827 students
Institution Contact: Mr. Allan Short, President
Phone: 303-457-2757
Fax: 303-457-4030
E-mail: ashort@cci.edu
Admission Contact: Mr. James Henig, Director of Admissions
Phone: 303-457-2757
Fax: 303-457-4030
E-mail: jhenig@cci.edu

PIMA MEDICAL INSTITUTE

370 Printers Parkway
Colorado Springs, CO 80910

indicates a participating institution in the *Imagine America* Scholarship Program. **MAP** indicates a participating institution in the Military Award Program.

Web: http://www.pmi.edu
Accreditation: Accrediting Bureau of Health Education Schools
Programs Offered:
dental assisting; medical administrative assistant and medical secretary; medical/clinical assistant; pharmacy technician; veterinary/animal health technology
Enrollment: 370 students
Institution Contact: Mr. Christopher Luebke, Admissions Support Center Director
Phone: 888-898-9048
E-mail: asc@pmi.edu
Admission Contact: Admissions Support Representative
Phone: 888-898-9048
E-mail: asc@pmi.edu

PIMA MEDICAL INSTITUTE

1701 West 72nd Avenue, Suite 130
Denver, CO 80221
Web: http://www.pmi.edu
Accreditation: Accrediting Bureau of Health Education Schools
Programs Offered:
dental assisting; medical administrative assistant and medical secretary; medical/clinical assistant; ophthalmic technology; pharmacy technician; phlebotomy; physical therapist assistant; radiologic technology/science; respiratory care therapy; veterinary/animal health technology
Enrollment: 724 students
Institution Contact: Mr. Christopher Luebke, Admissions Support Center Director
Phone: 888-898-9048
E-mail: asc@pmi.edu
Admission Contact: Admissions Support Representative
Phone: 888-898-9048
E-mail: asc@pmi.edu

REMINGTON COLLEGE - COLORADO SPRINGS CAMPUS

6050 Erin Park Drive
Colorado Springs, CO 80918-3401
Web: http://www.remingtoncollege.edu
Accreditation: Accrediting Council for Independent Colleges and Schools
Programs Offered:
business administration and management; computer/

technical support; criminal justice/law enforcement administration; medical/clinical assistant; medical insurance coding; pharmacy technician
Enrollment: 195 students
Institution Contact: Ms. Shirley D. McCray, Campus Vice President
Phone: 719-532-1234 ext. 202
Fax: 719-264-1234
E-mail: shirley.mccray@remingtoncollege.edu
Admission Contact: Mr. Larry Schafer, Director of Recruitment
Phone: 719-532-1234 ext. 219
Fax: 719-264-1234
E-mail: larry.schafer@remingtoncollege.edu

REMINGTON COLLEGE - DENVER CAMPUS

11011 West 6th Avenue
Lakewood, CO 80215-5501
Web: http://www.remingtoncollege.edu
Accreditation: Accrediting Council for Independent Colleges and Schools
Programs Offered:
criminal justice/law enforcement administration; medical/clinical assistant; medical insurance coding; operations management
Enrollment: 170 students
Institution Contact: Mrs. Barbara Hiney, Director of Education
Phone: 303-445-0500 ext. 221
Fax: 303-445-0090
E-mail: barbara.hiney@remingtoncollege.edu
Admission Contact: Mr., Director of Recruitment
Phone: 303-445-0500
Fax: 303-445-6839

SAGE TECHNICAL SERVICES

647 4th Avenue
Grand Junction, CO 81501
Web: http://www.sageschools.com
Programs Offered:
driver and safety teacher education; transportation technology; truck and bus driver/commercial vehicle operation
Enrollment: 134 students
Institution Contact: Mr. Jerry Dudley, Director
Phone: 800-523-0492
Fax: 970-257-1593

E-mail: gj@sageschools.com
Admission Contact: Mrs. Lisa Gordon, Staff Assistant
Phone: 970-257-7243
Fax: 970-257-1593

SAGE TECHNICAL SERVICES

9690 Dallas Street, Suite L
Henderson, CO 80640
Web: http://www.sageschools.com
Accreditation: Accrediting Commission of Career Schools and Colleges of Technology
Programs Offered:
ruck and bus driver/commercial vehicle operation
Enrollment: 24 students
Institution Contact: Mr. Robert Lyons, Director
Phone: 800-867-9856
Fax: 303-289-1933
E-mail: rlyons@wcox.com

WESTWOOD COLLEGE - DENVER

10851 West 120th Avenue
Broomfield, CO 80021-3465
Web: http://www.westwood.edu
Accreditation: Accrediting Commission of Career Schools and Colleges of Technology
Programs Offered:
aircraft powerplant technology; airframe mechanics and aircraft maintenance technology; avionics maintenance technology; heating, air conditioning and refrigeration technology
Enrollment: 425 students
Institution Contact: Mr. Kevin Paveglio, Executive Director
Phone: 303-464-2300
Fax: 303-466-2052
E-mail: kpaveglio@westwood.edu
Admission Contact: Mrs. April Chatigny, New Student Advisor
Phone: 303-464-2308
Fax: 303-469-3797
E-mail: achatigny@westwood.edu

WESTWOOD COLLEGE - DENVER NORTH

7350 North Broadway
Denver, CO 80221-3653
Web: http://www.westwood.edu

Accreditation: Accrediting Commission of Career Schools and Colleges of Technology
Programs Offered:
accounting; animation, interactive technology, video graphics and special effects; architectural drafting and CAD/CADD; automobile/automotive mechanics technology; aviation/airway management; business administration and management; business, management, and marketing related; CAD/CADD drafting/design technology; commercial and advertising art; computer engineering technology; computer programming; computer software technology; e-commerce; heating, air conditioning and refrigeration technology; hotel/motel administration; information technology; interior design; marketing/marketing management; medical administrative assistant and medical secretary; medical/clinical assistant; medical transcription; survey technology; system, networking, and LAN/WAN management; technology management; web page, digital/multimedia and information resources design
Enrollment: 1,304 students
Institution Contact: Mr. Anthony Caggiano, Executive Director
Phone: 303-426-7000 ext. 200
Fax: 303-426-4647
E-mail: tcaggiano@westwood.edu
Admission Contact: Mr. Ben Simms, Director of Admissions
Phone: 303-426-7000 ext. 100
Fax: 303-426-1832
E-mail: bsimms@westwood.edu

WESTWOOD COLLEGE - DENVER SOUTH

3150 South Sheridan Boulevard
Denver, CO 80227
Web: http://www.westwood.edu
Accreditation: Accrediting Commission of Career Schools and Colleges of Technology
Programs Offered:
animation, interactive technology, video graphics and special effects; architectural drafting and CAD/CADD; commercial and advertising art; computer and information systems security; computer engineering technology; criminal justice/law enforcement administration; design and visual communications; e-commerce; fashion merchandising; graphic communications related; information technology; interior design; management information systems and services related;

medical/clinical assistant; system, networking, and LAN/WAN management; technology management
Enrollment: 388 students
Institution Contact: Ms. Deb Mahon, Executive Director
Phone: 303-934-1122 ext. 200
Fax: 303-934-2583
E-mail: dmahon@westwood.edu
Admission Contact: Mr. Ron Dejong, Director of Admissions
Phone: 303-934-1122 ext. 100
Fax: 303-934-2583
E-mail: rdejong@westwood.edu

CONNECTICUT

GIBBS COLLEGE
10 Norden Place
Norwalk, CT 06855
Web: http://www.gibbscollege.com/
Accreditation: Accrediting Council for Independent Colleges and Schools
Programs Offered:
administrative assistant and secretarial science; computer graphics; computer/information technology services administration related; computer programming; computer/technical support; digital communication and media/multimedia; e-commerce; fashion/apparel design; fashion merchandising; visual and performing arts
Enrollment: 1,125 students
Institution Contact: Mr. Jim Mellett, President
Phone: 203-663-2314
Fax: 203-854-2936
E-mail: jmellett@gibbsnorwalk.com
Admission Contact: Mr. Ted Havelka, Vice President of Marketing and Admissions
Phone: 203-663-2311
Fax: 203-854-2936
E-mail: thavelka@gibbsnorwalk.com

NEW ENGLAND TECHNICAL INSTITUTE
106 Sebethe Drive
Cromwell, CT 06416
Programs Offered:
automotive engineering technology; culinary arts; heating, air conditioning and refrigeration technology;

medical/clinical assistant; nursing (licensed practical/ vocational nurse training); web page, digital/multimedia and information resources design
Institution Contact: Admissions
Phone: 860-613-3350

NEW ENGLAND TECHNICAL INSTITUTE
109 Sanford Street
Hamden, CT 06514
Web: http://www.newenglandtechnicalinstitute.com/
Programs Offered:
electrician; nursing (licensed practical/vocational nurse training)
Enrollment: 249 students
Institution Contact: Mr. Matthew A. Albano, Campus Director
Phone: 203-287-7300
Fax: 203-287-7305
E-mail: malbano@netiedu.com
Admission Contact: Mr. Bryan Boppert, Senior Admissions Representative
Phone: 203-287-7300
Fax: 203-287-7304
E-mail: bboppert@netiedu.com

NEW ENGLAND TECHNICAL INSTITUTE
8 Progress Drive
Shelton, CT 06848
Programs Offered:
automotive engineering technology; computer systems networking and telecommunications; culinary arts; electrician; heating, air conditioning and refrigeration technology; medical/clinical assistant; nursing (licensed practical/vocational nurse training)
Institution Contact: Admissions
Phone: 203-929-0592
Fax: 203-929-0763

NEW ENGLAND TECHNICAL INSTITUTE OF CONNECTICUT, INC.
200 John Downey Drive
New Britain, CT 06051-0651
Programs Offered:
automotive engineering technology; culinary arts; heating, air conditioning and refrigeration technology; medical/clinical assistant; nursing (licensed practical/

vocational nurse training); web page, digital/multimedia and information resources design
Institution Contact: Admissions
Phone: 800-225-8641

PORTER AND CHESTER INSTITUTE

138 Weymouth Road
Enfield, CT 06082
Web: http://www.porterchester.com
Accreditation: Accrediting Bureau of Health Education Schools; Accrediting Commission of Career Schools and Colleges of Technology
Programs Offered:
automobile/automotive mechanics technology; CAD/CADD drafting/design technology; computer systems networking and telecommunications; computer technology/computer systems technology; dental assisting; electrical and electronic engineering technologies related; heating, air conditioning, ventilation and refrigeration maintenance technology; medical/clinical assistant
Phone: 860-741-2561

PORTER AND CHESTER INSTITUTE

670 Lordship Boulevard
Stratford, CT 06497
Web: http://www.porterchester.com
Accreditation: Accrediting Bureau of Health Education Schools; Accrediting Commission of Career Schools and Colleges of Technology
Programs Offered:
automobile/automotive mechanics technology; CAD/CADD drafting/design technology; computer systems networking and telecommunications; computer technology/computer systems technology; dental assisting; electrical and electronic engineering technologies related; heating, air conditioning, ventilation and refrigeration maintenance technology; medical/clinical assistant
Phone: 203-375-4463

PORTER AND CHESTER INSTITUTE

320 Sylvan Lake Road
Watertown, CT 06779-1400
Web: http://www.porterchester.com
Accreditation: Accrediting Bureau of Health Edu-

cation Schools; Accrediting Commission of Career Schools and Colleges of Technology
Programs Offered:
automobile/automotive mechanics technology; CAD/CADD drafting/design technology; computer systems networking and telecommunications; computer technology/computer systems technology; dental assisting; electrical and electronic engineering technologies related; heating, air conditioning, ventilation and refrigeration maintenance technology; medical/clinical assistant
Phone: 860-274-9294

PORTER AND CHESTER INSTITUTE

125 Silas Deane Highway
Wethersfield, CT 06109
Web: http://www.porterchester.com
Accreditation: Accrediting Bureau of Health Education Schools; Accrediting Commission of Career Schools and Colleges of Technology
Programs Offered:
automobile/automotive mechanics technology; CAD/CADD drafting/design technology; computer systems networking and telecommunications; computer technology/computer systems technology; dental assisting; electrical and electronic engineering technologies related; heating, air conditioning, ventilation and refrigeration maintenance technology; medical/clinical assistant
Institution Contact:
Phone: 860-529-2519

DELAWARE

DAWN TRAINING CENTRE, INC.

3700 Lancaster Pike, Suite 105
Wilmington, DE 19805
Accreditation: Accrediting Commission of Career Schools and Colleges of Technology
Programs Offered:
aesthetician/esthetician and skin care; home health aide/home attendant; legal assistant/paralegal; massage therapy; medical/clinical assistant; medical insurance coding; medical insurance/medical billing; medical office computer specialist; medical transcription; nursing assistant/aide and patient care assistant; pharmacy

technician
Enrollment: 192 students
Institution Contact: Mr. Hollis C. Anglin, President/Director
Phone: 302-633-9075
Fax: 302-633-9077
E-mail: hcanglin@earthlink.net
Admission Contact: Ms. Mary "Fran" Anglin, Director of Admissions/Student Services
Phone: 302-633-9075 ext. 10
Fax: 302-633-9077
E-mail: admissions@dawntrainingcentre.com

HARRISON CAREER INSTITUTE

631 West Newport Pike, Graystone Plaza
Wilmington, DE 19804
Web: http://www.hci.edu
Accreditation: Accrediting Commission of Career Schools and Colleges of Technology
Programs Offered:
cardiovascular technology; dialysis technology; medical/clinical assistant; medical office assistant; pharmacy technician
Enrollment: 200 students
Institution Contact: Mr. Rodney D. Bailey, Director
Phone: 302-999-7827
Fax: 302-999-7983
E-mail: rbailey@hci-inst.net
Admission Contact: Ms. Holly Bott, Career Representative
Phone: 302-999-7827
Fax: 302-999-7983
E-mail: hollyhci@yahoo.com

DISTRICT OF COLUMBIA

POTOMAC COLLEGE

4000 Chesapeake Street, NW
Washington, DC 20016
Web: http://www.potomac.edu/
Accreditation: Accrediting Council for Independent Colleges and Schools; Middle States Association of Colleges and Schools
Programs Offered:

accounting; business administration and management; information science/studies; international business/trade/commerce
Enrollment: 317 students
Institution Contact: Ms. Florence Tate, President
Phone: 202-686-0876
Fax: 202-686-0818
E-mail: ftate@potomac.edu
Admission Contact: Mr. Michael Mella, Vice President
Phone: 202-686-0876
Fax: 202-686-0818
E-mail: mmella@potomac.edu

FLORIDA

ADVANCED CAREER TRAINING

3563 Phillips Highway, Suite 300
Jacksonville, FL 32207
Web: http://www.actglobal.com
Accreditation: Accrediting Commission of Career Schools and Colleges of Technology; Accrediting Council for Continuing Education and Training; Accrediting Council for Independent Colleges and Schools
Programs Offered:
business administration and management; computer technology/computer systems technology; dental assisting; massage therapy; medical/clinical assistant; medical insurance coding; medical insurance/medical billing
Enrollment: 360 students
Institution Contact: Mr. Scott Nelowet, Executive Director
Phone: 904-737-6911
Fax: 904-448-0280
E-mail: nelowets@actglobal.com
Admission Contact: Mr. Montrez Lucas, Director of Admissions
Phone: 904-737-6911
Fax: 904-448-0280
E-mail: lucasm@actglobal.com

AMERICAN INTERCONTINENTAL UNIVERSITY

2250 North Commerce Parkway , Fourth Floor
Weston, FL 33326

Web: http://www.aiufl.edu
Accreditation: Southern Association of Colleges and Schools
Programs Offered:
animation, interactive technology, video graphics and special effects; business administration and management; commercial and advertising art; educational/instructional media design; fashion/apparel design; information technology; interior design; international business/trade/commerce
Institution Contact: Dr. Jim Vernon, President
Phone: 954-446-6100
E-mail: jvernon@aiufl.edu
Admission Contact: Director of Admissions
Phone: 954-446-6100

AMI, INC.
3042 Volusia Ave
Daytona Beach, FL 32124-1010
Institution Contact: Mr. Gaylin Williams
Phone: 904-255-0295

ARGOSY UNIVERSITY/SARASOTA
5250 17th Street
Sarasota, FL 34235
Web: http://www.argosyu.edu
Programs Offered:
accounting
Institution Contact: Ms. Elizabeth Ward, Associate Director of Registration
Phone: 800-331-5995
Fax: 941-379-0404
E-mail: eward@argosyu.edu
Admission Contact: Dr. Linda Volz, Director of Admission
Phone: 800-331-5995
Fax: 941-379-0404
E-mail: lvolz@argosyu.edu

ARGOSY UNIVERSITY/TAMPA PARKSIDE AT TAMPA BAY PARK
4401 North Himes Avenue, Suite 150
Tampa, FL 33614
Programs Offered:
education
Institution Contact: Admissions

Phone: 813-393-5290
Fax: 813-874-1989
E-mail: jgraham@argosyu.edu

THE ART INSTITUTE OF FORT LAUDERDALE
1799 Southeast 17th Street
Fort Lauderdale, FL 33316-3000
Web: http://www.aifl.edu
Accreditation: Accrediting Council for Independent Colleges and Schools
Programs Offered:
advertising; animation, interactive technology, video graphics and special effects; broadcast journalism; communications technology; culinary arts; fashion/apparel design; fashion merchandising; graphic communications related; industrial design; interior design; marine technology; photography; visual and performing arts; web/multimedia management and webmaster; web page, digital/multimedia and information resources design
Enrollment: 3,462 students
Institution Contact: Mrs. Eileen Northrop, Director of Admissions
Phone: 800-275-7603
Fax: 954-728-8637
E-mail: enorthrop@aii.edu

ATI CAREER TRAINING CENTER
2880 Northwest 62nd Street
Fort Lauderdale, FL 33309-9731
Web: http://www.aticareertraining.edu
Accreditation: Accrediting Commission of Career Schools and Colleges of Technology
Programs Offered:
allied health and medical assisting services related; business automation/technology/data entry; CAD/CADD drafting/design technology; civil drafting and CAD/CADD; communications systems installation and repair technology; communications technology; computer and information sciences; computer and information sciences and support services related; computer and information sciences related; computer engineering related; computer engineering technology; computer hardware engineering; computer hardware technology; computer/information technology administration and management; computer/information technology services administration related; computer

installation and repair technology; computer programming; computer programming related; computer programming (specific applications); computer software technology; computer systems analysis; computer systems networking and telecommunications; computer/technical support; computer technology/computer systems technology; drafting and design technology; electrical and electronic engineering technologies related; electrical, electronic and communications engineering technology; electrical/electronics drafting and CAD/CADD; electrical/electronics equipment installation and repair; engineering technology; health/health care administration; health information/medical records administration; health information/medical records technology; hospital and health care facilities administration; information technology; medical administrative assistant and medical secretary; medical/clinical assistant; medical/health management and clinical assistant; medical insurance coding; medical insurance/medical billing; medical office assistant; medical office computer specialist; medical office management; medical reception; medical transcription; office management; telecommunications technology; word processing

Enrollment: 350 students
Institution Contact: Ms. Connie Bailus, Executive Director
Phone: 954-973-4760
Fax: 954-973-6422
E-mail: cbailus@atienterprises.edu

ATI CAREER TRAINING CENTER
1 Northeast 19th Street
Miami, FL 33132
Web: http://www.aticareertraining.com
Accreditation: Accrediting Commission of Career Schools and Colleges of Technology
Programs Offered:
appliance installation and repair technology; automobile/automotive mechanics technology; CAD/CADD drafting/design technology; computer/information technology administration and management; electrical and electronic engineering technologies related; heating, air conditioning and refrigeration technology; information technology
Institution Contact: Errol Stephenson, School Director
Phone: 305-573-1600
Fax: 305-576-8365

E-mail: estephenson@atienterprises.edu

ATI CAREER TRAINING CENTER
3501 Northwest 9th Avenue
Oakland Park, FL 33309-5900
Web: http://www.aticareertraining.com
Accreditation: Accrediting Commission of Career Schools and Colleges of Technology
Programs Offered:
automobile/automotive mechanics technology; heating, air conditioning and refrigeration technology
Enrollment: 300 students
Institution Contact: Ms. Cindy Gordon, Director
Phone: 954-563-5899
Fax: 954-568-0874
E-mail: cgordon@atienterprises.com
Admission Contact: Mr. Donald Robinson, Assistant Director of Admissions
Phone: 954-563-5899
Fax: 954-568-0874
E-mail: cgordon@atienterprises.com

ATI HEALTH EDUCATION CENTER
Plaza Executive Center, 1395 Northwest 167th Street
Building #1
Miami, FL 33169-5745
Web: http://www.aticareertraining.com
Accreditation: Accrediting Commission of Career Schools and Colleges of Technology
Programs Offered:
dental assisting; diagnostic medical sonography and ultrasound technology; medical/clinical assistant; pharmacy technician; respiratory care therapy
Enrollment: 473 students
Institution Contact: Ms. Barbara Woosley, Executive Director
Phone: 305-628-1000
Fax: 305-628-1461
E-mail: bwoosley@atienterprises.edu
Admission Contact: Albert Naranjo, Director of Admissions
Phone: 305-628-1000
Fax: 305-628-1461
E-mail: anaranjo@atienterprises.edu

BARBARA BRENNAN SCHOOL OF HEALING
500 Northeast Spanish River Boulevard, Suite 108
Boca Raton, FL 33431-4559
Web: http://www.barbarabrennan.com
Programs Offered:
alternative and complementary medical support services related; energy and biologically based therapies related
Enrollment: 500 students
Institution Contact: Ms. Linda G. Tarbox, Chief Operating Officer
Phone: 561-620-8767
Fax: 561-620-9028
E-mail: linda.tarbox@barbarabrennan.com
Admission Contact: Ms. Jean Bellegarde, Admissions Representative
Phone: 800-924-2564
Fax: 561-620-9028
E-mail: jean.bellegarde@barbarabrennan.com

BROWN MACKIE COLLEGE, MIAMI CAMPUS
1501 Biscayne Boulevard
Miami, FL 33132
Programs Offered:
accounting; advertising; business administration and management; CAD/CADD drafting/design technology; computer programming; computer software and media applications; criminal justice/law enforcement administration; graphic communications; legal assistant/paralegal; medical/clinical assistant; medical insurance coding; medical insurance/medical billing; nursing (licensed practical/vocational nurse training); occupational therapy; physical therapy; sales, distribution and marketing
Institution Contact: Admissions
Phone: 866-505-0335
E-mail: bmmiadm@edmc.edu

CAPPS COLLEGE
6420 North 9th Avenue
Pensacola, FL 32504
Web: http://www.medcareers.net
Programs Offered:
massage therapy; medical/clinical assistant; medical office management; medical transcription; pharmacy technician
Institution Contact:

Phone: 850-476-7607
Fax: 850-475-5955

CAREER TRAINING INSTITUTE
2463 East Semoran Boulevard
Apopka, FL 32703-5806
Web: http://www.centralfloridacollege.edu
Accreditation: Accrediting Commission of Career Schools and Colleges of Technology
Programs Offered:
barbering; cosmetology; cosmetology, barber/styling, and nail instruction; facial treatment/facialist; nail technician and manicurist
Institution Contact: Ms. Nancy Bradley, Owner/Director
Phone: 407-884-1816
Fax: 407-889-8083
E-mail: nbradley@centralfloridacollege.edu
Admission Contact: Mr. Michael Murray, Director of Admissions
Phone: 407-884-1816
Fax: 407-889-8083
E-mail: mmurray@centralfloridacollege.edu

CENTRAL FLORIDA COLLEGE
1573 West Fairbanks Avenue
Winter Park, FL 32789
Web: http://www.centralfloridacollege.edu
Accreditation: Accrediting Commission of Career Schools and Colleges of Technology
Programs Offered:
accounting; business administration and management; criminal justice/law enforcement administration; health aide; management information systems; medical administrative assistant and medical secretary; medical/clinical assistant; medical insurance coding; pharmacy technician
Enrollment: 450 students
Institution Contact: Ms. Nancy Bradley, Owner/Director
Phone: 407-843-3984
Fax: 407-843-9828
E-mail: nbradley@centralfloridacollege.edu
Admission Contact: Mrs. Gladys Secada, Director of Admissions
Phone: 407-843-3984
Fax: 407-843-9828

E-mail: gsecada@centalfloridacollege.edu

EVERGLADES UNIVERSITY

5002 T-REX Avenue, Suite #100
Boca Raton, FL 33431
Web: http://www.evergladesuniversity.edu
Programs Offered:
alternative and complementary medicine related; aviation/airway management; business administration and management; construction management; information technology
Enrollment: 500 students
Institution Contact: Ms. Kristi Mollis, President
Phone: 561-912-1211
Fax: 561-912-1191
E-mail: kmollis@evergladesuniversity.edu
Admission Contact: Ms. Kathy Wattecamps, Director of Admissions
Phone: 561-912-1211
Fax: 561-912-1191
E-mail: kwattecamps@evergladesuniversity.edu

EVERGLADES UNIVERSITY

5600 Lake Underhill Road , Suite #200
Orlando, FL 32807
Programs Offered:
alternative and complementary medical support services related; aviation/airway management; building/home/construction inspection; building/property maintenance and management; business administration and management; computer/information technology administration and management; management information systems
Enrollment: 32 students
Institution Contact: Shirley A. Long, Vice President
Phone: 407-277-0311
Fax: 407-482-9801
E-mail: slong@evergladesuniversity.edu

EVERGLADES UNIVERSITY

6151 Lake Osprey Drive
Sarasota, FL 34240
Web: http://www.evergladesuniversity.edu
Programs Offered:
alternative and complementary medicine related; aviation/airway management; avionics maintenance

technology; business administration and management; construction management; information technology
Institution Contact: Mr. Brad C. Brewer, Vice President
Phone: 941-907-2262
Fax: 941-907-6634
E-mail: bbrewer@evergladesuniversity.edu
Admission Contact: Ms. Georgia Schmidt, Senior Admissions Coordinator
Phone: 941-907-2262
Fax: 941-907-6634
E-mail: gschmidt@evergladesuniversity.edu

FLORIDA CAREER COLLEGE

3750 W. 18th Ave.
Hialeah, FL 33012
Institution Contact: Ms. Jane Miskell
Phone: 305-825-3231
Fax: 302-825-3436

FLORIDA CAREER COLLEGE

1321 Southwest 107th Avenue, Suite 201B
Miami, FL 33174
Web: http://www.careercollege.edu
Accreditation: Accrediting Council for Independent Colleges and Schools
Programs Offered:
computer engineering technology; computer graphics; computer installation and repair technology; computer programming; computer programming (specific applications); computer software and media applications; computer systems networking and telecommunications; computer technology/computer systems technology; massage therapy; medical/clinical assistant; medical insurance coding; web/multimedia management and webmaster; web page, digital/multimedia and information resources design
Enrollment: 2,224 students
Institution Contact: Mr. David Knobel, Chief Executive Officer
Phone: 954-499-8888
E-mail: dknobel@careercollege.edu
Admission Contact: Mr. Tony Wallace, Director of Admissions
Phone: 305-553-6065
E-mail: twallace@careercollege.edu

FLORIDA CAREER COLLEGE

7891 Pines Blvd.
Pembroke Pines, FL 33024
Institution Contact: Mr. Michael Schwarn
Phone: 954-956-7272
Fax: 954-983-2707

FLORIDA CAREER COLLEGE

6058 Okeechobee Blvd.
West Palm Beach, FL 33417
Institution contact: Mr. David Colozzi
Phone: 561-689-0550
Fax: 561-689-0739

FLORIDA COLLEGE OF NATURAL HEALTH

616 67th Street Circle East
Bradenton, FL 34208
Web: http://steinered.com
Accreditation: Accrediting Commission of Career Schools and Colleges of Technology
Programs Offered:
aesthetician/esthetician and skin care; alternative and complementary medical support services related; Asian bodywork therapy; facial treatment/facialist; massage therapy
Enrollment: 125 students
Institution Contact: Ms. Leonore Barfield, Campus Director
Phone: 941-744-1244
Fax: 941-744-1242
E-mail: lbarfield@fcnh.com
Admission Contact: Admissions Department
Phone: 941-744-1244
Fax: 941-744-1242
E-mail: sarasota@fcnh.com

FLORIDA COLLEGE OF NATURAL HEALTH

2600 Lake Lucien Drive, Suite 140
Maitland, FL 32751
Web: http://steinered.com
Accreditation: Accrediting Commission of Career Schools and Colleges of Technology
Programs Offered:
aesthetician/esthetician and skin care; alternative and complementary medical support services related; Asian bodywork therapy; cosmetology, barber/styling,
and nail instruction; facial treatment/facialist; massage therapy
Enrollment: 389 students
Institution Contact: Mr. Dale Weiberg, Campus Director
Phone: 407-261-0319
Fax: 407-261-0342
E-mail: dweiberg@fcnh.com
Admission Contact: Admissions Department
Phone: 407-261-0319
Fax: 407-261-0342
E-mail: orlando@fcnh.com

FLORIDA COLLEGE OF NATURAL HEALTH

7925 NW 12th Street, Suite 201
Miami, FL 33126
Web: http://steinered.com
Accreditation: Accrediting Commission of Career Schools and Colleges of Technology
Programs Offered:
aesthetician/esthetician and skin care; alternative and complementary medical support services related; Asian bodywork therapy; cosmetology, barber/styling, and nail instruction; facial treatment/facialist; massage therapy
Enrollment: 240 students
Institution Contact: Ms. Debra J. Starr, Campus Director
Phone: 305-597-9599
Fax: 305-597-9110
E-mail: dstarr@fcnh.com
Admission Contact: Admissions Department
Phone: 305-597-9599
Fax: 305-597-9110
E-mail: miami@fcnh.com

FLORIDA COLLEGE OF NATURAL HEALTH

2001 West Sample Road, Suite 100
Pompano Beach, FL 33064
Web: http://steinered.com
Accreditation: Accrediting Commission of Career Schools and Colleges of Technology
Programs Offered:
aesthetician/esthetician and skin care; alternative and complementary medical support services related; Asian bodywork therapy; facial treatment/facialist; massage therapy

indicates a participating institution in the *Imagine America* Scholarship Program. **MAP** indicates a participating institution in the Military Award Program.

Enrollment: 275 students
Institution Contact: Ms. Sherry Parker, Campus Director
Phone: 954-975-6400 ext. 115
Fax: 954-975-9633
E-mail: sparker@fcnh.com
Admission Contact: Admissions Department
Phone: 954-975-6400
Fax: 954-975-9633
E-mail: ftlauderdale@fcnh.com

FLORIDA METROPOLITAN UNIVERSITY - BRANDON CAMPUS

3924 Coconut Palm Drive
Tampa, FL 33619
Web: http://www.fmu.edu
Accreditation: Accrediting Council for Independent Colleges and Schools
Programs Offered:
accounting; business administration and management; computer/information technology services administration related; computer software and media applications; criminal justice/law enforcement administration; legal assistant/paralegal; massage therapy; medical/clinical assistant; medical insurance/medical billing; pharmacy technician; surgical technology
Enrollment: 1,099 students
Institution Contact: Olivia T. Fields, President
Phone: 813-621-0041
Fax: 813-623-5769
E-mail: ofields@cci.edu
Admission Contact: Shandretta Pointer, Director of Admissions
Phone: 813-621-0041 ext. 106
Fax: 813-628-0919
E-mail: spointer@cci.edu

FLORIDA METROPOLITAN UNIVERSITY - JACKSONVILLE CAMPUS

8226 Phillips Highway
Jacksonville, FL 32256
Web: http://www.fmu.edu
Accreditation: Accrediting Council for Independent Colleges and Schools
Programs Offered:
accounting; business administration and management; computer and information sciences related; computer/ information technology administration and management; criminal justice/law enforcement administration; information science/studies; medical/clinical assistant
Enrollment: 900 students
Institution Contact: Peter Neigler, President
Phone: 904-731-4949
Fax: 904-731-0599
E-mail: pneigler@cci.edu
Admission Contact: Admissions
Phone: 904-731-4949
Fax: 904-731-0599

FLORIDA METROPOLITAN UNIVERSITY - LAKELAND CAMPUS

995 East Memorial Boulevard, Suite 110
Lakeland, FL 33801-1919
Web: http://www.cci.edu
Accreditation: Accrediting Council for Independent Colleges and Schools
Programs Offered:
accounting; administrative assistant and secretarial science; business administration and management; business, management, and marketing related; computer and information sciences related; computer programming (vendor/product certification); computer software and media applications; criminal justice/law enforcement administration; executive assistant/executive secretary; health/health care administration; information science/studies; legal assistant/paralegal; marketing/marketing management; massage therapy; medical administrative assistant and medical secretary; medical/clinical assistant; medical insurance coding; office management; pharmacy technician
Enrollment: 760 students
Institution Contact: Ms. Diane Y. Walton, President
Phone: 863-686-1444
Fax: 863-688-9881
E-mail: dwalton@cci.edu
Admission Contact: Ms. Jodi DeLaGarza, Director of Admissions
Phone: 863-686-1444 ext. 101
Fax: 863-688-9881
E-mail: astenbec@cci.edu

FLORIDA METROPOLITAN UNIVERSITY - MELBOURNE CAMPUS

2401 North Harbor City Boulevard

Melbourne, FL 32935
Web: http://www.fmu.edu
Accreditation: Accrediting Council for Independent Colleges and Schools
Programs Offered:
accounting; business administration and management; cinematography and film/video production; computer and information sciences related; criminal justice/law enforcement administration; health and medical administrative services related; health/health care administration; legal assistant/paralegal; medical/clinical assistant; medical insurance/medical billing; pharmacy technician; web page, digital/multimedia and information resources design
Enrollment: 912 students
Institution Contact: Mr. Mark Judge, President
Phone: 321-253-2929 ext. 113
Fax: 321-255-2017
E-mail: mjudge@cci.edu
Admission Contact: Mr. Timothy J. Alexander, Director of Admissions
Phone: 321-253-2929 ext. 121
Fax: 321-255-2017
E-mail: talexand@cci.edu

FLORIDA METROPOLITAN UNIVERSITY - NORTH ORLANDO CAMPUS
5421 Diplomat Circle
Orlando, FL 32810
Web: http://www.cci.edu
Accreditation: Accrediting Council for Independent Colleges and Schools
Programs Offered:
accounting; assistive/augmentative technology and rehabilitation engineering; business administration and management; cinematography and film/video production; commercial and advertising art; computer and information sciences related; criminal justice/law enforcement administration; health/health care administration; information science/studies; legal assistant/paralegal; marketing/marketing management; medical/clinical assistant; pharmacy technician; web page, digital/multimedia and information resources design
Enrollment: 1,481 students
Institution Contact: Ms. Ouida Kirby, President
Phone: 407-628-5870 ext. 101
Fax: 407-628-1344
E-mail: okirby@cci.edu

Admission Contact: Mr. David Ritchie, Director of Admissions
Phone: 407-628-5870 ext. 108
Fax: 407-628-1344
E-mail: okirby@cci.edu

FLORIDA METROPOLITAN UNIVERSITY - ORANGE PARK CAMPUS
805 Wells Road
Orange Park, FL 32073
Accreditation: Accrediting Council for Independent Colleges and Schools
Programs Offered:
business administration and management; criminal justice/law enforcement administration; medical/clinical assistant
Enrollment: 96 students
Institution Contact: Mr. Bruce E. Jones, President
Phone: 904-264-9122 ext. 101
Fax: 904-264-9952
E-mail: brjones@cci.edu
Admission Contact: Mr. Jeff Sherman, Director of Admissions
Phone: 904-264-9122 ext. 108
Fax: 904-264-9952
E-mail: jsherman@cci.edu

FLORIDA METROPOLITAN UNIVERSITY - PINELLAS CAMPUS
2471 McMullen Booth Road
Clearwater, FL 33759
Web: http://www.fmu.edu
Accreditation: Accrediting Council for Independent Colleges and Schools
Programs Offered:
accounting; business administration and management; criminal justice/law enforcement administration; health/health care administration; information science/studies; information technology; legal assistant/paralegal; marketing/marketing management; medical/clinical assistant; medical insurance coding; medical insurance/medical billing
Admission Contact: Ms. Sandra Williams, Director of Admissions
Phone: 727-725-2688
Fax: 727-725-3827

E-mail: sawilliams@cci.edu

FLORIDA METROPOLITAN UNIVERSITY - POMPANO BEACH CAMPUS

225 North Federal Highway
Pompano Beach, FL 33062
Web: http://www.fmu.edu
Accreditation: Accrediting Council for Independent Colleges and Schools
Programs Offered:
accounting; business administration and management; computer and information sciences related; criminal justice/law enforcement administration; English as a second language; hospitality administration; information science/studies; international business/trade/commerce; legal assistant/paralegal; management science; marketing/marketing management; medical/clinical assistant; medical insurance/medical billing
Enrollment: 1,600 students
Institution Contact: Fran Heaston, Director of Admissions
Phone: 954-783-7339
Fax: 954-783-7964
E-mail: fheaston@cci.edu

FLORIDA METROPOLITAN UNIVERSITY - SOUTH ORLANDO CAMPUS

9200 South Park Center Loop
Orlando, FL 32819
Web: http://www.fmu.edu
Accreditation: Accrediting Council for Independent Colleges and Schools
Programs Offered:
accounting; business administration and management; computer and information sciences related; computer engineering related; computer systems networking and telecommunications; criminal justice/law enforcement administration; health/health care administration; legal assistant/paralegal; management science; marketing/marketing management; medical/clinical assistant; medical insurance coding; medical insurance/medical billing
Institution Contact: Mrs. Annette Cloin, Director of Admissions
Phone: 407-851-2525
Fax: 407-354-7946
E-mail: acloin@cci.edu

Admission Contact: Mrs. Annette Cloin, Director of Admissions
Phone: 407-851-2525
Fax: 407-851-7946
E-mail: acloin@cci.edu

FLORIDA METROPOLITAN UNIVERSITY - TAMPA CAMPUS

3319 West Hillsborough Avenue
Tampa, FL 33614
Web: http://www.fmu.edu
Accreditation: Accrediting Council for Independent Colleges and Schools
Programs Offered:
accounting; art; business administration and management; computer systems networking and telecommunications; criminal justice/law enforcement administration; hospital and health care facilities administration; information science/studies; legal assistant/paralegal; marketing/marketing management; massage therapy; medical/clinical assistant; medical insurance coding; medical insurance/medical billing; pharmacy technician
Enrollment: 1,405 students
Institution Contact: Mr. Donnie Broughton, Director of Admissions
Phone: 813-879-6000
Fax: 813-871-2063
E-mail: dbrought@cci.edu

FLORIDA TECHNICAL COLLEGE

298 Havendale Boulevard
Auburndale, FL 33823
Web: http://www.flatech.edu
Accreditation: Accrediting Council for Independent Colleges and Schools
Programs Offered:
business automation/technology/data entry; CAD/CADD drafting/design technology; computer engineering technology; computer programming (vendor/product certification); electrical, electronic and communications engineering technology; health information/medical records technology; medical administrative assistant and medical secretary; medical/clinical assistant; system administration; system, networking, and LAN/WAN management
Enrollment: 165 students
Institution Contact: Chris Georgeti, School Director

Phone: 863-967-8822
Fax: 863-967-4972
Admission Contact: Gregory Pelz, Director of Admissions
Phone: 863-967-8822
Fax: 863-967-4972
E-mail: gpelz@flatech.edu

FLORIDA TECHNICAL COLLEGE
1199 South Woodland Boulevard
DeLand, FL 32720
Web: http://www.flatech.edu
Accreditation: Accrediting Council for Independent Colleges and Schools
Programs Offered:
allied health and medical assisting services related; architectural drafting and CAD/CADD; business administration and management; business administration, management and operations related; business, management, and marketing related; business operations support and secretarial services related; CAD/CADD drafting/design technology; civil drafting and CAD/CADD; computer and information sciences; computer and information sciences and support services related; computer and information sciences related; computer engineering technology; computer graphics; computer hardware technology; computer/information technology administration and management; computer/information technology services administration related; computer installation and repair technology; computer programming; computer programming related; computer programming (specific applications); computer programming (vendor/product certification); computer software and media applications; computer software and media applications related; computer/technical support; computer technology/computer systems technology; design and visual communications; desktop publishing and digital imaging design; drafting and design technology; drafting/design engineering technologies related; electrical and electronic engineering technologies related; electrical/electronics drafting and CAD/CADD; health and medical administrative services related; health services/allied health/health sciences; health unit coordinator/ward clerk; hematology technology; information technology; intermedia/multimedia; management information systems; management information systems and services related; mechanical drafting and CAD/CADD; medical ad-

ministrative assistant and medical secretary; medical/clinical assistant; medical insurance coding; medical insurance/medical billing; medical office assistant; medical office computer specialist; medical office management; medical reception; medical transcription; office management; system administration; system, networking, and LAN/WAN management; web/multimedia management and webmaster; web page, digital/multimedia and information resources design
Enrollment: 304 students
Institution Contact: Mr. Bill Atkinson, Director
Phone: 386-734-3303
Fax: 386-734-5150
E-mail: batkinson@flatech.edu
Admission Contact: Dane Boothe, Director of Admissions
Phone: 386-734-3303
Fax: 386-734-5150
E-mail: dboothe@flatech.edu

FLORIDA TECHNICAL COLLEGE
8711 Lone Star Road
Jacksonville, FL 32211
Web: http://www.flatech.edu
Accreditation: Accrediting Council for Independent Colleges and Schools
Programs Offered:
CAD/CADD drafting/design technology; computer programming; computer technology/computer systems technology; electrical, electronic and communications engineering technology; medical/clinical assistant; system administration; system, networking, and LAN/WAN management
Enrollment: 178 students
Institution Contact: Mr. Barry Durden, Director
Phone: 904-724-2229
Fax: 904-720-0920
E-mail: bdurden@flatech.edu
Admission Contact: Mr. Kelly Hermening, Director of Admissions
Phone: 904-724-2229
Fax: 904-720-0920
E-mail: khermening@flatech.edu

FLORIDA TECHNICAL COLLEGE
12689 Challenger Parkway
Orlando, FL 32826

indicates a participating institution in the *Imagine America* Scholarship Program. **MAP** indicates a participating institution in the Military Award Program.

Web: http://www.flatech.edu
Accreditation: Accrediting Council for Independent Colleges and Schools
Programs Offered:
CAD/CADD drafting/design technology; computer engineering technology; computer programming (vendor/product certification); health information/medical records technology; medical administrative assistant and medical secretary; medical/clinical assistant; medical insurance coding; medical office computer specialist; medical reception; system administration; system, networking, and LAN/WAN management; web page, digital/multimedia and information resources design
Institution Contact: Ann Melone, Director
Phone: 407-447-7300
Fax: 407-447-7301
E-mail: amelone@flatech.edu

FULL SAIL REAL WORLD EDUCATION
3300 University Boulevard
Winter Park, FL 32792-7429
Web: http://www.fullsail.com
Accreditation: Accrediting Commission of Career Schools and Colleges of Technology
Programs Offered:
animation, interactive technology, video graphics and special effects; business, management, and marketing related; cinematography and film/video production; digital communication and media/multimedia; recording arts technology; web page, digital/multimedia and information resources design
Enrollment: 4,720 students
Institution Contact: Mr. Edward Haddock, Jr., Co-Chairman and Chief Executive Officer
Phone: 407-679-0100
Fax: 407-679-8810
E-mail: ehaddock@fullsail.com
Admission Contact: Mary Beth Plank, Vice President of Admissions
Phone: 407-679-0100
Fax: 407-679-8810
E-mail: mbplank@fullsail.com

GULF COAST COLLEGE
3910 US Highway 301 North, Suite 200
Tampa, FL 33619-1259
Web: http://www.webstercollege.com/

Accreditation: Accrediting Council for Independent Colleges and Schools
Programs Offered:
computer/information technology administration and management; computer technology/computer systems technology; medical/clinical assistant; tourism and travel services management
Enrollment: 146 students
Institution Contact: Mr. Todd Matthews, Executive Director
Phone: 813-620-1446
Fax: 813-620-1641
E-mail: tmatthews@webstercollege.com
Admission Contact: Mr. Gregory Bell, Director of Admissions
Phone: 813-620-1446
Fax: 813-620-1641
E-mail: gbell@webstercollege.com

HERITAGE INSTITUTE
6811 Palisades Park Court
Fort Myers, FL 33912
Programs Offered:
massage therapy
Institution Contact: Admissions
Phone: 239-936-5822
Fax: 239-225-9117

HERITAGE INSTITUTE
4130 Salisbury Road, Suite 1100
Jacksonville, FL 32216
Web: http://www.heritage-education.com
Programs Offered:
massage therapy
Enrollment: 280 students
Institution Contact: Mrs. Sonnie Willingham, Director
Phone: 904-332-0910
E-mail: sonniew@heritage-education.com
Admission Contact: Mrs. Tara Wolfe, Director of Admissions
Phone: 904-332-0910
E-mail: taraw@heritage-education.com

 HERZING COLLEGE
1595 South Semoran Boulevard, Suite 1501
Winter Park, FL 32792

Web: http://www.herzing.edu
Accreditation: Accrediting Council for Independent Colleges and Schools; North Central Association of Colleges and Schools
Programs Offered:
business administration and management; computer and information systems security; computer/information technology administration and management; criminal justice/police science; design and visual communications; legal assistant/paralegal; massage therapy; medical/clinical assistant; medical insurance coding; medical office management
Enrollment: 200 students
Institution Contact: Mr. Drew Warren, President
Phone: 407-478-0500
Fax: 407-478-0501
E-mail: dreww@orl.herzing.edu
Admission Contact: Ms. Karen Mohamad, Vice President/Director of Admissions
Phone: 407-478-0500
Fax: 407-478-0501
E-mail: info@orl.herzing.edu

HIGH-TECH INSTITUTE

3710 Maguire Boulevard
Orlando, FL 32803
Web: http://www.hightechinstitute.edu
Accreditation: Accrediting Commission of Career Schools and Colleges of Technology
Programs Offered:
computer and information systems security; dental assisting; massage therapy; medical/clinical assistant; medical insurance/medical billing; medical radiologic technology; pharmacy technician; surgical technology
Institution Contact: Elizabeth Beseke, Campus President
Phone: 407-893-7400
Fax: 407-895-1804 E-mail: ebeseke@hightechinstitute.edu
Admission Contact: Sheryl Ferguson, Director of Admissions
Phone: 407-893-7400
Fax: 407-895-1804
E-mail: sferguson@hightechinstitute.edu

INTERNATIONAL ACADEMY OF DESIGN & TECHNOLOGY

5959 Lake Ellenor Drive
Orlando, FL 32809
Web: http://www.iadt.edu
Accreditation: Accrediting Council for Independent Colleges and Schools
Programs Offered:
advertising; commercial and advertising art; computer graphics; computer/information technology administration and management; computer systems networking and telecommunications; design and visual communications; desktop publishing and digital imaging design; fashion/apparel design; fashion merchandising; graphic communications; interior design; intermedia/multimedia; marketing/marketing management; web page, digital/multimedia and information resources design
Enrollment: 970 students
Institution Contact: Ms. Deborah Lee, Director of Compliance
Phone: 407-857-2300 ext. 5950
Fax: 407-888-5941
E-mail: dlee@iadt.edu
Admission Contact: Dr. John Dietrich, Vice President of Admissions and Marketing
Phone: 877-753-0007 ext. 5934
Fax: 407-251-0465
E-mail: jdietrich@idat.edu

INTERNATIONAL ACADEMY OF DESIGN & TECHNOLOGY

5104 Eisenhower Boulevard
Tampa, FL 33634
Web: http://www.academy.edu
Accreditation: Accrediting Council for Independent Colleges and Schools
Programs Offered:
commercial and advertising art; digital communication and media/multimedia; fashion/apparel design; interior design; marketing/marketing management; merchandising; recording arts technology; web page, digital/multimedia and information resources design
Enrollment: 2,291 students
Institution Contact: Mr. Steve R. Wood, Director of Financial Aid
Phone: 813-880-8056
Fax: 813-885-4695
E-mail: steve@academy.edu

Admission Contact: Mr. Richard Costa, Vice President of Admissions and Marketing
Phone: 813-880-8092
Fax: 813-889-3431
E-mail: rcosta@academy.edu

ITT TECHNICAL INSTITUTE
3401 South University Drive
Fort Lauderdale, FL 33328-2021
Web: http://www.itt-tech.edu
Accreditation: Accrediting Council for Independent Colleges and Schools
Programs Offered:
accounting and business/management; animation, interactive technology, video graphics and special effects; business administration and management; CAD/CADD drafting/design technology; communications technology; computer and information systems security; computer engineering technology; computer software and media applications; computer software engineering; computer systems networking and telecommunications; criminal justice/police science; digital communication and media/multimedia; electrical, electronic and communications engineering technology; technology management; web page, digital/multimedia and information resources design
Institution Contact: Ms. Nanell Lough, Director
Phone: 954-476-9300
Admission Contact: Mr. Robert Bixler, Director of Recruitment
Phone: 954-476-9300

ITT TECHNICAL INSTITUTE
6600 Youngerman Circle, Suite 10
Jacksonville, FL 32244-6630
Web: http://www.itt-tech.edu
Accreditation: Accrediting Council for Independent Colleges and Schools
Programs Offered:
accounting and business/management; animation, interactive technology, video graphics and special effects; business administration and management; CAD/CADD drafting/design technology; communications technology; computer and information systems security; computer engineering technology; computer software and media applications; computer software engineering; computer systems networking and tele-

communications; criminal justice/police science; digital communication and media/multimedia; electrical, electronic and communications engineering technology; technology management; web page, digital/multimedia and information resources design
Institution Contact: Mr. Brian Quirk, Director
Phone: 904-573-9100
Admission Contact: Mr. Jorge Torres, Director of Recruitment
Phone: 904-573-9100

ITT TECHNICAL INSTITUTE
1400 International Parkway South
Lake Mary, FL 32746
Web: http://www.itt-tech.edu
Accreditation: Accrediting Council for Independent Colleges and Schools
Programs Offered:
accounting and business/management; animation, interactive technology, video graphics and special effects; business administration and management; CAD/CADD drafting/design technology; communications technology; computer and information systems security; computer engineering technology; computer software and media applications; computer software engineering; computer systems networking and telecommunications; criminal justice/police science; digital communication and media/multimedia; electrical, electronic and communications engineering technology; technology management; web page, digital/multimedia and information resources design
Institution Contact: Mr. Gary Cosgrove, Director
Phone: 407-660-2900
Admission Contact: Mr. Larry S. Johnson, Director of Recruitment
Phone: 407-660-2900

ITT TECHNICAL INSTITUTE
7955 Northwest 12th Street
Miami, FL 33126
Web: http://www.itt-tech.edu
Accreditation: Accrediting Council for Independent Colleges and Schools
Programs Offered:
accounting and business/management; animation, interactive technology, video graphics and special effects; business administration and management; com-

munications technology; computer and information systems security; computer engineering technology; computer software engineering; computer systems networking and telecommunications; criminal justice/police science; digital communication and media/multimedia; electrical, electronic and communications engineering technology; technology management; web page, digital/multimedia and information resources design

Institution Contact: Mr. Robert T. Hayward, Director
Phone: 305-477-3080
Admission Contact: Mrs. Rosa Sacarello Daratany, Director of Recruitment
Phone: 305-477-3080

ITT TECHNICAL INSTITUTE
4809 Memorial Highway
Tampa, FL 33634-7151
Web: http://www.itt-tech.edu
Accreditation: Accrediting Council for Independent Colleges and Schools
Programs Offered:
animation, interactive technology, video graphics and special effects; business administration and management; CAD/CADD drafting/design technology; communications technology; computer and information systems security; computer engineering technology; computer software and media applications; computer software engineering; computer systems networking and telecommunications; computer technology/computer systems technology; criminal justice/police science; digital communication and media/multimedia; electrical, electronic and communications engineering technology; technology management
Institution Contact: Mr. Dennis Alspaugh, Director
Phone: 813-885-2244
E-mail: dalspaugh@itt-tech.edu
Admission Contact: Mr. Joseph E. Rostkowski, Director of Recruitment
Phone: 813-885-2244
E-mail: jrostkowski@itt-tech.edu

KEISER COLLEGE
1800 Business Park Boulevard
Daytona Beach, FL 32114
Web: http://www.keisercollege.edu
Accreditation: Accrediting Bureau of Health Educa-

tion Schools; Southern Association of Colleges and Schools
Programs Offered:
accounting; business administration and management; computer graphics; computer/information technology administration and management; criminal justice/law enforcement administration; diagnostic medical sonography and ultrasound technology; legal assistant/paralegal; massage therapy; medical/clinical assistant; radiologic technology/science
Institution Contact: Mr. Matt McEnany, Vice President
Phone: 386-274-5060
Fax: 386-274-2745
E-mail: mmcenany@keisercollege.edu
Admission Contact: Ms. Heather Armstrong, Director of Admissions
Phone: 386-274-5060
Fax: 386-274-2725
E-mail: harmstrong@keisercollege.edu

KEISER COLLEGE
1500 Northwest 49th Street
Fort Lauderdale, FL 33309-9722
Web: http://www.keisercollege.edu
Accreditation: Accrediting Bureau of Health Education Schools
Programs Offered:
accounting; business administration and management; clinical/medical laboratory technology; commercial and advertising art; computer engineering technology; computer graphics; computer/information technology administration and management; computer programming; criminal justice/law enforcement administration; diagnostic medical sonography and ultrasound technology; e-commerce; health/health care administration; hospitality administration; legal assistant/paralegal; medical/clinical assistant; nursing (registered nurse training); occupational therapist assistant; physical therapist assistant; radiologic technology/science
Institution Contact: Mr. Todd DeAngelis, Director of Public Relations
Phone: 954-776-4476 ext. 314
Fax: 954-489-2974
E-mail: toddd@keisercollege.edu
Admission Contact: Ms. Linda Ebeling, Admissions Assistant
Phone: 954-776-4456
Fax: 954-351-4043

E-mail: lindae@keisercollege.edu

KEISER COLLEGE

3515 Aviation Drive
Lakeland, FL 33811
Web: http://www.keisercollege.edu
Accreditation: Southern Association of Colleges and Schools
Programs Offered:
accounting; business administration and management; computer graphics; computer/information technology services administration related; criminal justice/law enforcement administration; health/health care administration; legal assistant/paralegal; massage therapy; medical/clinical assistant; radiologic technology/science
Enrollment: 300 students
Institution Contact: Ms. Rebecca Rodgers, Vice President
Phone: 863-701-7789
Fax: 863-701-8758
E-mail: rebeccar@keisercollege.edu
Admission Contact: Mr. Walter Bequette, Director of Admissions
Phone: 863-701-7789
Fax: 863-701-8758
E-mail: wbequette@keisercollege.edu

KEISER COLLEGE

900 South Babcock Street
Melbourne, FL 32901
Web: http://www.keisercollege.cc.fl.us
Accreditation: Accrediting Bureau of Health Education Schools; Southern Association of Colleges and Schools
Programs Offered:
accounting; business administration and management; commercial and advertising art; computer graphics; computer/information technology administration and management; computer programming; e-commerce; hospital and health care facilities administration; hospitality administration; legal assistant/paralegal; medical/clinical assistant; nursing (registered nurse training); occupational therapist assistant; radiologic technology/science
Institution Contact: Ms. Rhonda Fuller, Vice President
Phone: 321-255-2255

Fax: 321-725-3766
E-mail: rhondaf@keisercollege.edu
Admission Contact: Mr. Larry DelVecchio, Director of Admissions
Phone: 321-255-2255
Fax: 321-725-3766
E-mail: larryd@keisercollege.edu

KEISER COLLEGE

8505 Mills Drive
Miami, FL 33183
Web: http://www.keisercollege.edu
Accreditation: Southern Association of Colleges and Schools
Programs Offered:
accounting; business administration and management; computer and information systems security; criminal justice/law enforcement administration; health services administration; legal assistant/paralegal; medical/clinical assistant; nuclear medical technology; nursing (registered nurse training); radiologic technology/science
Enrollment: 750 students
Institution Contact: Mr. Gary Markowitz, Vice President
Phone: 305-596-2226
Fax: 305-596-7077
E-mail: garym@keisercollege.edu
Admission Contact: Mr. Ted Weiner, Director of Admissions
Phone: 305-596-2226
Fax: 305-596-7077
E-mail: tedw@keisercollege.edu

KEISER COLLEGE

5600 Lake Underhill Road
Orlando, FL 32807
Web: http://www.keisercollege.edu
Accreditation: Southern Association of Colleges and Schools
Programs Offered:
accounting; business administration and management; computer and information sciences related; computer graphics; computer systems networking and telecommunications; criminal justice/law enforcement administration; health/health care administration; hospitality administration; legal assistant/paralegal; medical/clinical assistant; radiologic technology/science

Enrollment: 530 students
Institution Contact: Dr. David M. Hubbard, Vice President
Phone: 407-273-5800
Fax: 407-382-2201
E-mail: davidh@keisercollege.edu
Admission Contact: Ms. Vicki Maurer, Director of Admissions
Phone: 407-273-5800
Fax: 407-381-1233
E-mail: vmaurer@keisercollege.edu

KEISER COLLEGE

12520 Pines Boulevard
Pembroke Pines, FL 33027
Web: http://www.keisercareer.com
Accreditation: Accrediting Bureau of Health Education Schools; Council on Occupational Education
Programs Offered:
business administration and management; computer graphics; computer/information technology administration and management; massage therapy; medical/clinical assistant; pharmacy technician
Institution Contact: Mr. Mark Levine, Executive Director
Phone: 954-252-0002
Fax: 954-252-0003
E-mail: markl@keisercollege.cc.fl.us
Admission Contact: Director of Admissions
Phone: 954-252-0002
Fax: 954-252-0003

KEISER COLLEGE

9468 South US Highway 1
Port St. Lucie, FL 34952
Web: http://www.keisercollege.edu
Accreditation: Accrediting Bureau of Health Education Schools; Accrediting Commission of Career Schools and Colleges of Technology; Council on Occupational Education; Southern Association of Colleges and Schools
Programs Offered:
accounting; business administration and management; computer graphics; criminal justice/law enforcement administration; health/health care administration; legal assistant/paralegal; massage therapy; medical/clinical assistant; pharmacy technician; surgical technology

Enrollment: 290 students
Institution Contact: Mr. Jay Lambeth, Vice President
Phone: 772-398-9990 ext. 104
Fax: 772-335-9619
E-mail: jayl@keisercollege.edu
Admission Contact: Mr. Robert Andriola, Director of Admissions
Phone: 772-398-9990 ext. 111
Fax: 772-335-9619
E-mail: randriola@keisercollege.edu

KEISER COLLEGE

6151 Lake Osprey Drive
Sarasota, FL 34240
Web: http://www.keisercollege.edu
Accreditation: Accrediting Bureau of Health Education Schools; Southern Association of Colleges and Schools
Programs Offered:
accounting; business administration and management; computer graphics; computer/information technology administration and management; computer programming; criminal justice/law enforcement administration; emergency medical technology (EMT paramedic); fire science; hospital and health care facilities administration; legal assistant/paralegal; massage therapy; medical/clinical assistant; nursing (registered nurse training); radiologic technology/science; respiratory therapy technician
Institution Contact: Ms. Michele I. Sterner, Vice President
Phone: 941-907-3900
Fax: 941-907-2016
E-mail: micheles@keisercollege.edu
Admission Contact: Ms. Barbara Doran, Director of Admissions
Phone: 941-907-3900
Fax: 941-907-2016
E-mail: bdoran@keisercollege.edu

KEISER COLLEGE

1700 Halstead Boulevard
Tallahassee, FL 32309
Web: http://www.keisercollege.edu
Accreditation: Accrediting Bureau of Health Education Schools; Southern Association of Colleges and Schools

Programs Offered:

accounting; baking and pastry arts; business administration and management; computer and information systems security; computer graphics; computer/information technology administration and management; criminal justice/law enforcement administration; culinary arts; hospital and health care facilities administration; legal assistant/paralegal; medical/clinical assistant; nursing (registered nurse training); radiologic technology/science

Enrollment: 550 students

Institution Contact: Mr. Mark Gutmann, Vice President

Phone: 850-906-9494

Fax: 850-906-9497

E-mail: markg@keisercollege.edu

Admission Contact: Mr. Phil Hooks, Director of Admissions

Phone: 850-906-9494

Fax: 850-906-9497

E-mail: phooks@keisercollege.edu

KEISER COLLEGE

2085 Vista Parkway

West Palm Beach, FL 33411

Web: http://www.keisercareer.com

Accreditation: Accrediting Bureau of Health Education Schools; Accrediting Commission of Career Schools and Colleges of Technology; Council on Occupational Education

Programs Offered:

business administration and management; computer graphics; computer/information technology administration and management; massage therapy; medical/clinical assistant; pharmacy technician

Institution Contact: Ms. Karin I. Cogswell, Vice President

Phone: 561-471-6000

Fax: 561-4717849

E-mail: kcogswell@keisercollege.edu

Admission Contact: Ms. Trudy Suits, Director of Admissions

Phone: 561-471-6000

Fax: 561-471-7849

E-mail: tsuits@keisercollege.edu

KEY COLLEGE

5225 West Broward Boulevard

Fort Lauderdale, FL 33317

Web: http://www.keycollege.edu

Accreditation: Accrediting Council for Independent Colleges and Schools

Programs Offered:

computer programming (specific applications); court reporting; drafting and design technology; legal assistant/paralegal; medical administrative assistant and medical secretary; medical transcription

Institution Contact: Mr. Ronald H. Dooley, President

Phone: 954-923-4440

Fax: 954-583-9458

E-mail: rdooley@keycollege.edu

LA BELLE BEAUTY SCHOOL

775 West 49th Street, Suite #5

Hialeah, FL 33012

Accreditation: Accrediting Commission of Career Schools and Colleges of Technology

Programs Offered:

aesthetician/esthetician and skin care; cosmetology; nail technician and manicurist

Institution Contact: Mr. Humberto Balboa, Director

Phone: 305-558-0562

Fax: 305-362-0665

E-mail: labellehia@beautyacademy.com

Admission Contact: Mrs. Anna Garcia, Admissions

Phone: 305-558-0562

Fax: 305-362-0665

LE CORDON BLEU COLLEGE OF CULINARY ARTS MIAMI

2841 Corporate Way, MPC 15

Miramar, FL 33025

Web: http://www.miamiculinary.com

Programs Offered:

culinary arts

MARINE MECHANICS INSTITUTE

9751 Delegates Drive

Orlando, FL 32837-9835

Web: http://www.uticorp.com

Accreditation: Accrediting Commission of Career Schools and Colleges of Technology

Programs Offered:

marine maintenance and ship repair technology; motorcycle maintenance and repair technology

Enrollment: 1,788 students

Institution Contact: Ms. Dianne Ely, Director

Phone: 407-240-2422 ext. 1610

Fax: 407-240-1318

E-mail: dely@uticorp.com

Admission Contact: Mr. Dwight Berry, Admissions Office Manager

Phone: 407-240-2422 ext. 1128

Fax: 407-240-1318

E-mail: dberry@uticorp.com

MEDVANCE INSTITUTE

170 JFK Drive

Atlantis, FL 33462-6607

Web: http://www.medvance.org

Accreditation: Council on Occupational Education

Programs Offered:

dental assisting; gene therapy; medical/clinical assistant; nursing assistant/aide and patient care assistant; pharmacy technician

Institution Contact: Ms. Brenda P. Cortez, Campus Director

Phone: 561-304-3466

Fax: 561-304-3471

E-mail: bcortez@medvance.org

Admission Contact:

Phone: 561-304-3466

Fax: 561-304-3471

MEDVANCE INSTITUTE

4101 Northwest 3rd Court, Suite 9

Fort Lauderdale, FL 33317-2857

Web: http://www.medvance.edu

Accreditation: Accrediting Bureau of Health Education Schools

Programs Offered:

medical/clinical assistant; medical insurance coding; medical radiologic technology; medical staff services technology; pharmacy technician; surgical technology

Institution Contact:

Phone: 954-587-7100

Fax: 954-587-7704

MEDVANCE INSTITUTE

9035 Sunset Drive, Suite 200

Miami, FL 33173

Web: http://www.medvance.edu

Accreditation: Council on Occupational Education

Programs Offered:

massage therapy; medical administrative assistant and medical secretary; medical/clinical assistant; medical insurance coding; medical radiologic technology; medical staff services technology; nursing (licensed practical/vocational nurse training); pharmacy technician; surgical technology

Institution Contact:

Phone: 305-596-5553

Fax: 305-596-0552

MEDVANCE INSTITUTE

10792 U.S. 1

Port St. Lucie, FL 34592

Web: http://www.medvance.edu

Accreditation: Accrediting Bureau of Health Education Schools

Programs Offered:

massage therapy; medical administrative assistant and medical secretary; medical/clinical assistant; medical insurance coding; medical radiologic technology; medical staff services technology; nursing (licensed practical/vocational nurse training); pharmacy technician; surgical technology

Institution Contact:

Phone: 772-221-9799

Fax: 772-223-0522

MIAMI INTERNATIONAL UNIVERSITY OF ART & DESIGN

1501 Biscayne Boulevard, Suite 100

Miami, FL 33132

Web: http://www.aimiu.aii.edu

Accreditation: Southern Association of Colleges and Schools

Programs Offered:

advertising; apparel and accessories marketing; apparel and textile marketing management; apparel and textiles related; applied art; art; ceramic arts and ceramics; cinematography and film/video production; commercial and advertising art; computer graphics; digital communication and media/multimedia; drawing; fashion/apparel design; fashion merchandising; graphic and printing equipment operation/production;

interior design; photographic and film/video technology; retailing; sculpture; visual and performing arts
Enrollment: 1,400 students
Institution Contact: Ms. Elsia Suarez, Director of Admissions
Phone: 800-225-9023
Fax: 305-374-5933
E-mail: suareze@aii.edu
Admission Contact: Ms. Elisa Suarez, Director of Admissions
Phone: 800-225-9023
Fax: 305-374-5933
E-mail: suareze@aii.edu

 NATIONAL SCHOOL OF TECHNOLOGY, INC.
1040 Bayview Drive
Fort Lauderdale, FL 33304
Web: http://www.nst.cc
Accreditation: Accrediting Bureau of Health Education Schools
Programs Offered:
massage therapy; medical/clinical assistant; medical insurance coding
Institution Contact: Ashly Miller, Director of Admissions
Phone: 954-630-0066
Fax: 954-630-0076
E-mail: amiller@cci.edu

 NATIONAL SCHOOL OF TECHNOLOGY, INC.
4410 West 16th Avenue, Suite 52
Hialeah, FL 33012
Accreditation: Accrediting Bureau of Health Education Schools
Programs Offered:
cardiovascular technology; diagnostic medical sonography and ultrasound technology; massage therapy; medical/clinical assistant; medical insurance coding; pharmacy technician; surgical technology
Enrollment: 846 students
Institution Contact: Dr. Gilbert Delgado, Campus President
Phone: 305-558-9500
Fax: 305-558-4419
E-mail: gdelgado@cci.edu
Admission Contact: Mr. Daniel Alonso, Director of Admission
Phone: 305-558-9500

Fax: 305-558-4419
E-mail: dalonso@cci.edu

 NATIONAL SCHOOL OF TECHNOLOGY, INC.
9020 Southwest 137th Avenue, Suite 200
Miami, FL 33186
Accreditation: Accrediting Bureau of Health Education Schools
Programs Offered:
cardiovascular technology; legal assistant/paralegal; massage therapy; medical/clinical assistant; medical insurance/medical billing; pharmacy technician; surgical technology
Institution Contact: Mr. Randy Kaufman, Academic Dean
Phone: 305-386-9900 ext. 130
Fax: 305-388-1740 E-mail: rkaufman@cci.edu
Admission Contact: Mr. John Rios, Director of Admissions
Phone: 305-386-9900 ext. 109
Fax: 305-388-1740
E-mail: jrios@cci.edu

 NATIONAL SCHOOL OF TECHNOLOGY, INC.
111 Northwest 183rd Street, 2nd Floor
Miami, FL 33169
Web: http://www.nst.cc
Accreditation: Accrediting Bureau of Health Education Schools
Programs Offered:
health aide; massage therapy; medical/clinical assistant; medical insurance coding; pharmacy technician; surgical technology
Enrollment: 830 students
Institution Contact: Dr. Mario Paul Miro, School President
Phone: 305-949-9500
Fax: 305-949-7303
E-mail: mmiro@cci.edu
Admission Contact: Mr. Walter McQuade, Director of Admissions
Phone: 305-949-9500
Fax: 305-956-5758
E-mail: wmcquade@cci.edu

NEW ENGLAND INSTITUTE OF TECHNOLOGY AT PALM BEACH

2410 Metrocentre Boulevard
West Palm Beach, FL 33407
Web: http://www.newenglandtech.com
Accreditation: Accrediting Council for Independent Colleges and Schools; Council on Occupational Education
Programs Offered:
architectural drafting and CAD/CADD; automobile/automotive mechanics technology; baking and pastry arts; business administration and management; CAD/CADD drafting/design technology; computer systems networking and telecommunications; cosmetology; culinary arts; dental assisting; drafting and design technology; electrical, electronic and communications engineering technology; heating, air conditioning, ventilation and refrigeration maintenance technology; legal administrative assistant/secretary; legal assistant/paralegal; medical/clinical assistant; medical insurance coding; medical insurance/medical billing; medical office management; restaurant, culinary, and catering management; sport and fitness administration; system, networking, and LAN/WAN management
Enrollment: 1,400 students
Institution Contact: Mr. Charles H. Halliday, President
Phone: 561-712-5100
Fax: 561-842-9503
E-mail: challiday@newenglandtech.com
Admission Contact: Mr. Kevin Cassidy, Director of Admissions
Phone: 561-688-2001
Fax: 561-842-9503
E-mail: kcassidy@newenglandtech.com

NORTH FLORIDA INSTITUTE

560 Wells Road
Orange Park, FL 32073
Accreditation: Accrediting Council for Independent Colleges and Schools
Programs Offered:
accounting; accounting and business/management; allied health and medical assisting services related; business administration and management; business, management, and marketing related; clinical laboratory science/medical technology; criminal justice/law enforcement administration; criminal justice/police science; health information/medical records adminis-

tration; health information/medical records technology; health professions related; information technology; medical/clinical assistant; medical insurance coding; medical insurance/medical billing; medical office assistant; medical office management; medical staff services technology; nursing assistant/aide and patient care assistant; nursing related; pharmacy technician; phlebotomy; surgical technology
Enrollment: 311 students
Institution Contact: Delaine Wilcott, Campus Director
Phone: 904-269-7086
Fax: 904-269-6664
E-mail: dwilcott@northfloridainstitute.edu
Admission Contact: Ms. Jan Allen, Admissions
Phone: 904-269-7086
Fax: 904-269-6664
E-mail: jallen@northfloridainstitute.edu

ORLANDO CULINARY ACADEMY

8511 Commodity Circle
Orlando, FL 32819
Web: http://www.orlandoculinary.com
Accreditation: Accrediting Council for Independent Colleges and Schools
Programs Offered:
culinary arts
Institution Contact: Mrs. Debbie Taylor, Director of Career Services
Phone: 407-313-8793
Fax: 407-888-4019
E-mail: detaylor@orlandoculinary.com
Admission Contact: Ms. Leigh Hughes, Director of Admissions
Phone: 407-313-8701
Fax: 407-888-4019
E-mail: lhughes@orlandoculinary.com

REMINGTON COLLEGE - JACKSONVILLE CAMPUS

7011 A.C. Skinner Parkway, Suite 140
Jacksonville, FL 32256
Web: http://www.remingtoncollege.edu
Accreditation: Accrediting Commission of Career-Schools and Colleges of Technology
Programs Offered:
allied health and medical assisting services related; business administration, management and operations related; child care and support services management;

computer software and media applications; computer systems networking and telecommunications; computer/technical support; computer technology/computer systems technology; criminal justice/law enforcement administration; data entry/microcomputer applications; massage therapy; medical/clinical assistant; pharmacy technician

Enrollment: 350 students

Institution Contact: Mr. Tony Galang, Campus President

Phone: 904-296-3435

Fax: 904-296-3474

E-mail: tony.galang@remingtoncollege.edu

Admission Contact: Bobby Johns, Director of Recruiter

Phone: 904-296-3435

Fax: 904-296-9097

E-mail: bobby.johns@remingtoncollege.edu

REMINGTON COLLEGE - PINELLAS CAMPUS

8550 Ulmerton Road, Unit 100

Largo, FL 33771

Web: http://www.remingtoncollege.edu

Accreditation: Accrediting Commission of Career Schools and Colleges of Technology

Programs Offered:

business administration and management; business administration, management and operations related; business automation/technology/data entry; business machine repair; business operations support and secretarial services related; computer engineering technology; computer/information technology services administration related; computer installation and repair technology; computer programming; computer programming related; computer programming (specific applications); computer programming (vendor/product certification); computer systems networking and telecommunications; computer technology/computer systems technology; criminal justice/law enforcement administration; data modeling/warehousing and database administration; education; electrical, electronic and communications engineering technology; information science/studies; information technology; internet information systems; massage therapy; medical/clinical assistant; pharmacy technician

Enrollment: 340 students

Institution Contact: Ms. Edna Higgins, Campus President

Phone: 727-532-1999

Fax: 727-530-7710

E-mail: edna.higgins@remingtoncollege.edu

Admission Contact: Ms. Kathy McCabe, Director of Recruitment

Phone: 727-532-1999 ext. 202

Fax: 727-530-7710

E-mail: kathy.mccabe@remingtoncollege.edu

REMINGTON COLLEGE - TAMPA CAMPUS

2410 East Busch Boulevard

Tampa, FL 33612

Web: http://www.remingtoncollege.edu

Accreditation: Accrediting Commission of Career Schools and Colleges of Technology

Programs Offered:

accounting; art; business administration and management; business automation/technology/data entry; commercial and advertising art; commercial photography; computer and information systems security; computer engineering related; computer engineering technology; computer graphics; computer/information technology administration and management; computer/information technology services administration related; computer programming; computer systems networking and telecommunications; desktop publishing and digital imaging design; electrical, electronic and communications engineering technology; engineering technology; information science/studies; information technology; internet information systems; management information systems; operations management; system, networking, and LAN/WAN management; web/multimedia management and webmaster; web page, digital/multimedia and information resources design

Institution Contact: Mr. William D. Polmear, Campus President

Phone: 813-932-0701

Fax: 813-935-7415

E-mail: william.polmear@remingtoncollege.edu

Admission Contact: Ms. Kathleen Miller, Director of Recruitment

Phone: 813-935-5700 ext. 211

Fax: 813-935-7415

E-mail: kathleen.miller@remingtoncollege.edu

ROSS MEDICAL EDUCATION CENTER

6847 Taft Street

Hollywood, FL 33024

Programs Offered:
medical/clinical assistant
Institution Contact: Barbara Franklin, Director
Phone: 954-963-0043
Fax: 954-963-0211

ROSS MEDICAL EDUCATION CENTER
2601 South Military Trail, Suite 29
West Palm Beach, FL 33415-9141
Programs Offered:
medical/clinical assistant
Institution Contact: Ms. Linda Materazzi, Director
Phone: 561-433-1288
Fax: 561-641-8477

SANFORD-BROWN INSTITUTE
10255 Fortune Parkway, Unit 501
Jacksonville, FL 32256
Web: http://www.sbjacksonville.com
Accreditation: Accrediting Bureau of Health Education Schools; Accrediting Council for Independent Colleges and Schools
Programs Offered:
dental assisting; health information/medical records technology; massage therapy; medical/clinical assistant; surgical technology
Enrollment: 350 students
Institution Contact: Mr. Wyman A. Dickey, Campus President
Phone: 904-363-6221
Fax: 904-363-6824
E-mail: wdickey@sbjacksonville.com
Admission Contact: Mr. Sean McHaney, Director of Admissions
Phone: 904-363-6221
Fax: 904-363-6824
E-mail: smchaney@sbjacksonville.com

SANFORD-BROWN INSTITUTE
4780 North State Road 7, #100-E
Lauderdale Lakes, FL 33319-5860
Web: http://www.sbftlaud.com
Accreditation: Accrediting Bureau of Health Education Schools
Programs Offered:
cardiovascular technology; dental assisting; diagnostic medical sonography and ultrasound technology; health information/medical records technology; massage therapy; medical/clinical assistant; surgical technology
Enrollment: 750 students
Institution Contact: Ms. Mary-Jo Greco, President
Phone: 954-733-8900 ext. 2229
Fax: 954-733-8994 E-mail: mgreco@sbftl.com
Admission Contact: Mr. Chris George, Director of Admissions
Phone: 954-733-8900 ext. 2225
Fax: 954-733-8994
E-mail: cgeorge@sbftlaud.com

SANFORD-BROWN INSTITUTE
5701 East Hillsborough Avenue
Tampa, FL 33610
Web: http://www.sbtampa.com/
Accreditation: Accrediting Bureau of Health Education Schools; Accrediting Council for Independent Colleges and Schools
Programs Offered:
cardiovascular technology; dental assisting; diagnostic medical sonography and ultrasound technology; massage therapy; medical/clinical assistant; medical insurance coding; surgical technology
Enrollment: 470 students
Institution Contact: Mrs. Patricia A. Meredith, President
Phone: 813-621-0072 ext. 4255
Fax: 813-626-0392
E-mail: pmeredith@sbtampa.com
Admission Contact: Mr. James Clontz, Director of Admissions
Phone: 813-621-0072 ext. 4271
Fax: 813-626-0392
E-mail: jclontz@sbtampa.com

SOUTH UNIVERSITY
1760 North Congress Avenue
West Palm Beach, FL 33409
Web: http://www.southuniversity.edu/
Accreditation: Southern Association of Colleges and Schools
Programs Offered:
accounting; allied health and medical assisting services related; business administration and management; computer/information technology services administration related; criminal justice/law enforcement admin-

istration; legal administrative assistant/secretary; legal assistant/paralegal; medical/clinical assistant; nursing (registered nurse training); physical therapist assistant; physician assistant

Institution Contact: Mr. Steve Schwab, President
Phone: 561-697-9200
Fax: 561-697-9944
E-mail: sschwab@southuniversity.edu
Admission Contact: Mr. Joe Rogalski, Director of Admissions
Phone: 561-697-9200
Fax: 561-697-9944
E-mail: jrogalski@southuniversity.edu

 SOUTHWEST FLORIDA COLLEGE
3919 Riga Blvd
Tampa, FL 33619
Web: http://www.swfc.edu
Accreditation: Accrediting Council for Independent Colleges and Schools
Programs Offered:
accounting; business administration and management; business, management, and marketing related; CAD/CADD drafting/design technology; child care and support services management; commercial and advertising art; computer graphics; computer/information technology services administration related; computer installation and repair technology; computer programming; computer software and media applications; computer systems networking and telecommunications; computer/technical support; criminal justice/law enforcement administration; drafting and design technology; education (specific levels and methods) related; forensic science and technology; health information/medical records administration; hospitality administration; information technology; interior design; legal assistant/paralegal; massage therapy; medical/clinical assistant; medical office management; medical transcription; pharmacy technician; restaurant, culinary, and catering management; surgical technology
Enrollment: 1,300 students
Institution Contact: Mr. Wayne A. Slater, President
Phone: 813-367-0229
Fax: 813-367-0237
E-mail: wslater@swfc.edu
Admission Contact: Mr. Patrick McDermott, Director of High School Activities
Phone: 813-367-0229

Fax: 813-367-0238
E-mail: pmcdermott@swfc.edu

 SOUTHWEST FLORIDA COLLEGE
3910 Riga Boulevard
Tampa, FL 33619
Web: http://www.swfc.edu/
Accreditation: Accrediting Bureau of Health Education Schools; Accrediting Council for Independent Colleges and Schools
Programs Offered:
accounting; allied health and medical assisting services related; architectural drafting and CAD/CADD; business, management, and marketing related; CAD/CADD drafting/design technology; computer and information sciences; computer and information systems security; computer graphics; computer systems networking and telecommunications; computer/technical support; criminal justice/law enforcement administration; information technology; legal assistant/paralegal; marketing/marketing management; medical administrative assistant and medical secretary; medical/clinical assistant; medical office assistant; medical office management; medical transcription; pharmacy technician; surgical technology; technology management
Enrollment: 550 students
Institution Contact: Mr. Wayne Slater, Chief Operating Officer
Phone: 813-630-4401
Fax: 813-623-8154
E-mail: wslater@sunstate.edu
Admission Contact: Mr. Patrick McDermott, Director of High School Activities
Phone: 813-630-4401
Fax: 813-630-4272
E-mail: pmcdermott@swfc.edu

TULSA WELDING SCHOOL
3500 Southside Boulevard
Jacksonville, FL 32216
Web: http://www.weldingschool.edu
Accreditation: Accrediting Commission of Career Schools and Colleges of Technology
Programs Offered:
welding technology
Enrollment: 181 students
Institution Contact: Mr. Roger Hess, President/Co-

CEO
Phone: 904-646-9353 ext. 222
Fax: 904-646-9467
E-mail: r3h4@aol.com
Admission Contact: Admissions
Phone: 904-646-9353 ext. 221
Fax: 904-646-9956
E-mail: tws@ionet.net

VIRGINIA COLLEGE AT PENSACOLA
19 West Garden Street
Pensacola, FL 32502
Web: http://www.vc.edu
Accreditation: Accrediting Bureau of Health Education Schools; Accrediting Council for Independent Colleges and Schools
Programs Offered:
accounting related; administrative assistant and secretarial science; allied health and medical assisting services related; criminal justice/law enforcement administration; criminal justice/police science; human resources management; legal administrative assistant/ secretary; medical/clinical assistant; medical insurance coding; medical insurance/medical billing; merchandising, sales, and marketing operations related (general); nursing (licensed practical/vocational nurse training); pharmacy technician; surgical technology
Enrollment: 340 students
Institution Contact: Ms. Linda Weldon, President
Phone: 850-436-8444 ext. 2302
Fax: 850-436-8470
E-mail: lweldon@vc.edu
Admission Contact: Mrs. Heather Robbins, Director of Admissions
Phone: 850-436-8444
Fax: 850-436-8470
E-mail: hrobbins@vc.edu

WEBSTER COLLEGE
2127 Grand Boulevard
Holiday, FL 34691
Web: http://www.webstercollege.com
Accreditation: Accrediting Council for Independent Colleges and Schools
Programs Offered:
accounting; business administration and management; computer systems networking and telecommunica-

tions; information technology; management science; medical/clinical assistant
Enrollment: 236 students
Institution Contact: Mrs. Claire Walker, Executive Director
Phone: 727-942-0069
Fax: 727-938-5709
E-mail: cwalker@webstercollege.com

WEBSTER COLLEGE
2221 SW 19th Avenue Road
Ocala, FL 34474
Web: http://www.webstercollege.edu
Accreditation: Accrediting Council for Independent Colleges and Schools
Programs Offered:
accounting; business administration and management; computer/information technology services administration related; medical/clinical assistant
Enrollment: 345 students
Institution Contact: Ms. Greta Ferkel, Campus Director
Phone: 352-629-1941 ext. 102
Fax: 352-629-0926
E-mail: gferkel@webstercollege.edu
Admission Contact: Ms. Rosalina Finelli, Director of Admissions
Phone: 352-629-1941 ext. 105
Fax: 352-629-0926
E-mail: rfinelli@webstercollege.edu

GEORGIA

ADVANCED CAREER TRAINING
2 Executive Park Drive, NW, Building 2, Suite #100
Atlanta, GA 30329
Web: http://www.therightskills.com
Accreditation: Accrediting Council for Continuing Education and Training
Programs Offered:
business administration and management; dental assisting; medical/clinical assistant; technology management
Enrollment: 300 students
Institution Contact: Dr. John A. England, Executive Director
Phone: 404-321-2929 ext. 210
Fax: 404-633-0028

E-mail: englandj@actglobal.com
Admission Contact: Director of Admissions
Phone: 404-321-2929 ext. 220
Fax: 404-633-0028

ADVANCED CAREER TRAINING

7165 Georgia Highway 85
Riverdale, GA 30274
Web: http://www.therightskills.com
Accreditation: Accrediting Council for Continuing
Education and Training
Programs Offered:
business administration and management; dental assist-
ing; medical/clinical assistant; technology management
Institution Contact: Mr. John Mills, Executive Director
Phone: 770-991-9356
Fax: 770-991-2472
E-mail: millsj@actglobal.com
Admission Contact: Mr. John Payton, Director of
Admissions
Phone: 770-991-9356
Fax: 770-991-2472

AMERICAN INTERCONTINENTAL UNIVERSITY

3330 Peachtree Road, NE
Atlanta, GA 30326
Web: http://www.aiubuckhead.com
Accreditation: Southern Association of Colleges and
Schools
Programs Offered:
cinematography and film/video production; commer-
cial and advertising art; criminal justice/police science;
fashion/apparel design; fashion merchandising; interior
design; international business/trade/commerce
Enrollment: 1,476 students
Institution Contact: Mrs. Jo Ann Wilson, President
Phone: 404-965-5782
Fax: 404-965-5997
E-mail: joann.wilson@buckhead.aiuniv.edu
Admission Contact: Mr. Greg Koch, Assistant Vice
President of Admissions and Marketing
Phone: 888-999-4248
Fax: 404-965-5853
E-mail: greg.koch@buckhead.aiuniv.edu

AMERICAN INTERCONTINENTAL UNIVERSITY

6600 Peachtree-Dunwoody Road, 500 Embassy Row
Atlanta, GA 30328
Web: http://www.aiudunwoody.com
Accreditation: Southern Association of Colleges and
Schools
Programs Offered:
business administration and management; commercial
and advertising art; computer and information sciences
and support services related; computer technology/
computer systems technology; criminal justice/law
enforcement administration; health/health care admin-
istration; human resources management; information
technology; intermedia/multimedia; marketing/market-
ing management; marketing related
Enrollment: 1,400 students
Institution Contact: Mr. Peter Buswell, President
Phone: 404-965-6500
Fax: 404-965-6502
E-mail: pbuswell@aiuniv.edu
Admission Contact: Ms. Joy McClure, Vice President
of Admissions
Phone: 800-353-1744
Fax: 404-965-6502
E-mail: jmcclure@aiuniv.edu

AMERICAN PROFESSIONAL INSTITUTE

1990 Riverside
Macon, GA 31211
Institution Contact: Joanne Felton
Phone: 478-314-4444

ARGOSY UNIVERSITY/ATLANTA

980 Hammond Drive, Suite 100
Atlanta, GA 30328
Web: http://www.argosyu.edu/
Programs Offered:
education
Institution Contact: Admissions
Phone: 770-671-1200
Fax: 770-671-0476
E-mail: cholton@argosyu.edu

THE ART INSTITUTE OF ATLANTA

6600 Peachtree-Dunwoody Road, 100 Embassy Row
Atlanta, GA 30328

Web: http://www.aia.artinstitutes.edu

Accreditation: Southern Association of Colleges and Schools

Programs Offered:

advertising; animation, interactive technology, video graphics and special effects; audiovisual communications technologies related; baking and pastry arts; cinematography and film/video production; commercial and advertising art; culinary arts; design and visual communications; drawing; interior design; photography; restaurant, culinary, and catering management; web page, digital/multimedia and information resources design

Enrollment: 2,700 students

Institution Contact: Mrs. Janet S. Day, President

Phone: 770-394-8300

Fax: 770-394-8813

E-mail: aiaadm@aii.edu

Admission Contact: Ms. Donna Scott, Director of Admissions

Phone: 770-394-8300

Fax: 770-394-8813

E-mail: aiaadm@aii.edu

BAUDER COLLEGE

384 Northyards Boulevard, Suite 190
Atlanta, GA 30313
Web: http://www.bauder.edu

Accreditation: Southern Association of Colleges and Schools

Programs Offered:

business administration and management; commercial and advertising art; criminal justice/law enforcement administration; fashion/apparel design; fashion merchandising; fashion modeling; information technology; interior design; marketing/marketing management; medical office assistant

Enrollment: 840 students

Institution Contact: Ms. Kathryn Knox, President and Chief Executive Officer

Phone: 404-237-7573

Fax: 404-237-1619

E-mail: kknox@bauder.edu

Admission Contact: Mr. Victor Tedoff, Director of Admissions

Phone: 404-237-7573

Fax: 404-237-1619

E-mail: vtedoff@bauder.edu

BROWN MACKIE COLLEGE, ATLANTA CAMPUS

4975 Jimmy Carter Boulevard, Suite 600
Norcross, GA 30093

Programs Offered:

accounting technology and bookkeeping; business administration and management; CAD/CADD drafting/design technology; computer and information sciences related; computer programming; computer software technology; criminal justice/law enforcement administration; legal assistant/paralegal; medical/clinical assistant

Institution Contact:

Phone: 888-301-3670

CAREER EDUCATION INSTITUTE

2359 Windy Hill Road
Marietta, GA 30067
Web: http://www.ceitraining.com

Accreditation: Accrediting Council for Independent Colleges and Schools

Programs Offered:

medical administrative assistant and medical secretary; medical/clinical assistant; medical insurance coding; medical insurance/medical billing; system administration

Institution Contact: Executive Director

Phone: 770-226-0056

Fax: 770-226-0084

E-mail: execdirmarietta@lincolntech.com

Admission Contact: Liana Lusson, Executive Director

Phone: 770-226-0056

Fax: 770-226-0084

E-mail: execdirmarietta@lincolntech.com

CAREER EDUCATION INSTITUTE

5675 Jimmy Carter Boulevard, Suite 100
Norcross, GA 30071
Web: http://www.ceitraining.com
Accreditation: Accrediting Council for Independent Colleges and Schools

Programs Offered:

business administration and management; computer systems networking and telecommunications; computer/technical support; massage therapy; medical administrative assistant and medical secretary; medical/clinical assistant; system administration

Enrollment: 400 students

Institution Contact: Mr. Bryan Gulebian, Executive Director

Phone: 678-966-9411
Fax: 678-966-9687
E-mail: bgulebian@ceitraining.com
Admission Contact: Mr. Bryan Gulebian
Phone: 678-966-9411
Fax: 678-966-9687
E-mail: bgulebian@ceitraining.com

THE CHUBB INSTITUTE

4100 Old Milton Parkway
Alpharetta, GA 30005
Web: http://www.chubbinstitute.edu
Accreditation: Accrediting Council for Continuing Education and Training
Programs Offered:
computer programming; data modeling/warehousing and database administration; health information/medical records administration; system administration; system, networking, and LAN/WAN management; web/multimedia management and webmaster
Enrollment: 135 students
Institution Contact: Ms. Julie Jennings, Registrar
Phone: 678-624-4456
Fax: 678-624-4401
E-mail: jjennings@chubbinstitute.edu
Admission Contact: Mr. Jeff Lyons, Director of Admissions
Phone: 678-624-4465
Fax: 678-624-4401
E-mail: jelyons@chubbinstitute.edu

THE CREATIVE CIRCUS, INC.

812 Lambert Drive, NE
Atlanta, GA 30324
Web: http://www.creativecircus.com
Accreditation: Council on Occupational Education
Programs Offered:
advertising; art; design and visual communications; photography
Enrollment: 220 students
Institution Contact: Mr. Bret Johnson, Executive Director
Phone: 800-728-1590
Fax: 404-875-1590
E-mail: bjohnson@creativecircus.com
Admission Contact: Mr. Dan Benner, Senior Admissions Representative, International Admissions

Phone: 800-728-1890
Fax: 404-875-1590
E-mail: dbenner@creativecircus.com

EMPIRE BEAUTY SCHOOL

4719 Ashford-Dunwoody Rd., Suite 205
Dunwoody, GA 30338
Institution Contact: Ms. Vanessa King
Phone: 770-671-1448
Fax: 770-671-1450

EMPIRE BEAUTY SCHOOL

Town Center Plaza
425 Ernest-Barrett Pkwy., Suite H-2
Kennesaw, GA 30144
Institution Contact: Ms. Carla Campbell
Phone: 770-419-2303
Fax: 770-419-9331

EMPIRE BEAUTY SCHOOL

1455 Pleasant Hill Rd., Suite 105
Lawrenceville, GA 30044
Institution Contact: Ms. Michele Grant
Phone: 770-564-0725
Fax: 770-921-3994

GEORGIA MEDICAL INSTITUTE

1750 Beaver Ruin Road, Suite 500
Norcross, GA 30093
Web: http://www.georgia-med.com/
Accreditation: Accrediting Commission of Career Schools and Colleges of Technology
Programs Offered:
dental assisting; massage therapy; medical administrative assistant and medical secretary; medical/clinical assistant
Enrollment: 350 students
Institution Contact: Christine Knouff, School President
Phone: 770-921-1085
Fax: 770-923-4533
E-mail: cknouff@cci.edu
Admission Contact: Sandra Williams, Director of Admissions
Phone: 770-921-1085

Fax: 770-923-4533

GEORGIA MEDICAL INSTITUTE - ATLANTA
101 Marietta Street, Suite 600
Atlanta, GA 30303
Web: http://www.georgia-med.com
Accreditation: Accrediting Bureau of Health Education Schools
Programs Offered:
massage therapy; medical administrative assistant and medical secretary; medical/clinical assistant; medical insurance coding; pharmacy technician
Institution Contact: Mr. Dudley Layfield, Director of Admissions
Phone: 404-525-1111 ext. 116
Fax: 404-588-9406
E-mail: dlayfield@cci.edu
Admission Contact: Mr. Dudley Layfield, Director of Admissions
Phone: 404-525-1111 ext. 116
Fax: 404-588-9406
E-mail: dlayfield@cci.edu

GEORGIA MEDICAL INSTITUTE - DEKALB
1706 Northeast Expressway
Atlanta, GA 30329
Web: http://www.georgia-med.com
Accreditation: Accrediting Commission of Career Schools and Colleges of Technology
Programs Offered:
dialysis technology; massage therapy; medical/clinical assistant; medical insurance coding; medical insurance/medical billing; respiratory care therapy
Enrollment: 476 students
Institution Contact: Mrs. Tira Harney-Clay, School President
Phone: 404-327-8787 ext. 108
Fax: 404-327-8980
E-mail: tharney@cci.edu
Admission Contact: Mr. Miguel Sanchez, Director of Admissions
Phone: 404-327-8787 ext. 102
Fax: 404-327-8980
E-mail: msanchez@cci.edu

GEORGIA MEDICAL INSTITUTE - JONESBORO
6431 Tara Boulevard
Jonesboro, GA 30236
Web: http://www.georgia-med.com
Accreditation: Accrediting Bureau of Health Education Schools
Programs Offered:
dental assisting; health aide; massage therapy; medical administrative assistant and medical secretary; medical/clinical assistant; medical insurance coding; medical insurance/medical billing; pharmacy technician
Admission Contact: Mr. Victor Tedoff, Director of Admissions
Phone: 770-603-0000
Fax: 770-210-3259
E-mail: vtedoff@cci.edu

GEORGIA MEDICAL INSTITUTE - MARIETTA
1600 Terrell Mill Road, Suite G
Marietta, GA 30067
Web: http://www.cci.edu
Accreditation: Accrediting Bureau of Health Education Schools
Programs Offered:
massage therapy; medical administrative assistant and medical secretary; medical/clinical assistant; medical insurance/medical billing; pharmacy technician; surgical technology
Enrollment: 532 students
Institution Contact: Dr. Doris O'Keefe, President
Phone: 770-303-7997
Fax: 770-303-4422
E-mail: dokeefe@cci.edu
Admission Contact: Ms. Lynn M. Jones, Director of Admissions
Phone: 770-303-7997
Fax: 770-303-4422
E-mail: ljones@cci.edu

HERZING COLLEGE
3393 Peachtree Street, NE, Suite 1003
 Atlanta, GA 30326
Web: http://www.herzing.edu
Accreditation: Accrediting Council for Independent Colleges and Schools; North Central Association of Colleges and Schools
Programs Offered:

accounting; accounting and business/management; business administration and management; computer/information technology administration and management; computer installation and repair technology; computer programming; computer programming (specific applications); computer programming (vendor/product certification); computer software and media applications; computer systems analysis; computer systems networking and telecommunications; computer/technical support; computer technology/computer systems technology; health/health care administration; medical administrative assistant and medical secretary; medical insurance coding; medical insurance/medical billing; medical office assistant; system administration; web page, digital/multimedia and information resources design

Enrollment: 320 students

Institution Contact: Mrs. Frank R. Webster, College President

Phone: 404-816-4533

Fax: 404-816-5576

E-mail: fwebster@atl.herzing.edu

Admission Contact: Mrs. Rose White, Director of Admissions

Phone: 404-816-4533

Fax: 404-816-5576

E-mail: rwhite@atl.herzing.edu

High-Tech Institute

1090 Northchase Parkway, Suite 150
Marietta, GA 30067
Web: http://www.hightechinstitute.edu
Accreditation: Accrediting Commission of Career Schools and Colleges of Technology
Programs Offered:
computer and information systems security; digital communication and media/multimedia; massage therapy; medical/clinical assistant; medical insurance coding; medical insurance/medical billing; pharmacy technician; surgical technology
Enrollment: 600 students
Institution Contact: Myra Hadley, Campus President
Phone: 678-279-9000
Fax: 770-988-8824
E-mail: mhadley@hightechinstitute.edu
Admission Contact: Ron Brandt, Director of Admissions
Phone: 678-279-7000

Fax: 770-988-8824

E-mail: rbrandt@hightechinstitute.edu

ITT Technical Institute

10700 Abbotts Bridge Road, Suite 190
Duluth, GA 30097
Web: http://www.itt-tech.edu
Accreditation: Accrediting Council for Independent Colleges and Schools
Programs Offered:
CAD/CADD drafting/design technology; communications technology; computer and information systems security; computer engineering technology; computer software and media applications; computer systems networking and telecommunications; digital communication and media/multimedia; electrical, electronic and communications engineering technology; technology management; web page, digital/multimedia and information resources design
Institution Contact: Ms. Sue Schmith, Director
Phone: 678-957-8510
Admission Contact: Mr. Chip Hinton, Director of Recruitment
Phone: 678-957-8510

ITT Technical Institute

1000 Cobb Place Boulevard, NW
Kennesaw, GA 30144-3685
Web: http://www.itt-tech.edu/
Programs Offered:
business administration and management; CAD/CADD drafting/design technology; computer and information systems security; computer engineering technology; computer software and media applications; computer systems networking and telecommunications; criminal justice/police science; digital communication and media/multimedia; electrical and electronic engineering technologies related; web page, digital/multimedia and information resources design
Phone: 770-426-2300

Le Cordon Bleu College of Culinary Arts, Atlanta

1927 Lakeside Parkway
Tucker, GA 30084
Web: http://www.atlantaculinary.com

Accreditation: Accrediting Commission of Career Schools and Colleges of Technology
Programs Offered:
culinary arts
Enrollment: 729 students
Institution Contact: Mr. Doug Solomon, Director of Education
Phone: 770-723-3575
Fax: 770-938-4571
E-mail: dsolomon@atlantaculinary.com
Admission Contact: Terri Holte, Vice President - Admissions & Marketing
Phone: 770-938-4711
Fax: 770-938-4571
E-mail: tholte@atlantaculinary.com

MEDIX SCHOOL
2108 Cobb Parkway
Smyrna, GA 30080
Web: http://www.medixschool.edu
Accreditation: Accrediting Bureau of Health Education Schools
Programs Offered:
dental assisting; electrocardiograph technology; emergency medical technology (EMT paramedic); massage therapy; medical administrative assistant and medical secretary; medical/clinical assistant; medical insurance/medical billing; nursing assistant/aide and patient care assistant; pharmacy technician; phlebotomy
Enrollment: 487 students
Institution Contact: Mr. Larry Ritchie, Director
Phone: 770-980-0002
Fax: 770-980-0811
E-mail: lritchie@edaff.com

ROFFLER-MOLER HAIRSTYLING COLLEGE
1311 Roswell Road
Marietta, GA 30062
Web: http://www.roffler.net/
Accreditation: Accrediting Commission of Career Schools and Colleges of Technology
Programs Offered:
barbering; cosmetology; cosmetology, barber/styling, and nail instruction
Enrollment: 107 students
Institution Contact: Mr. Dale Sheffield, Director
Phone: 770-565-3285

Fax: 770-477-0136
E-mail: info@roffler.net
Admission Contact: Ms. Becky Sheffield, Administrative Director
Phone: 770-565-3285
Fax: 770-477-0136
E-mail: info@roffler.net

ROSS MEDICAL EDUCATION CENTER
2645 North Decatur Road
Decatur, GA 30033
Programs Offered:
medical/clinical assistant
Institution Contact: Valencia White, Director
Phone: 404-377-5744
Fax: 404-377-6692

ROSS MEDICAL EDUCATION CENTER
2534 Cobb Parkway
Smyrna, GA 30080
Web: http://www.rossmedicaleducation.com
Programs Offered:
medical/clinical assistant
Enrollment: 19 students
Institution Contact: Garrett S. Hall, Director
Phone: 770-951-9255
Fax: 770-951-9722
E-mail: ghall@rosslearning.com

SANFORD-BROWN INSTITUTE
1140 Hammond Drive, Suite 1150-A
Atlanta, GA 30328
Web: http://www.sb-atlanta.com
Accreditation: Accrediting Bureau of Health Education Schools
Programs Offered:
cardiovascular technology; diagnostic medical sonography and ultrasound technology; massage therapy; medical/clinical assistant; medical insurance/medical billing
Enrollment: 650 students
Institution Contact: Mr. Clifton W. Phillips, President
Phone: 770-576-4545
Fax: 770-576-4547
E-mail: cphillips@sb-atlanta.com
Admission Contact: Mrs. Sonya Jabriel, Director of Admissions
Phone: 770-576-3002

Fax: 770-350-0640
E-mail: sjabriel@sb-atlanta.com

SAVANNAH RIVER COLLEGE
2528 Centerwest Parkway, Building A
Augusta, GA 30909
Web: http://www.savannahrivercollege.edu
Accreditation: Accrediting Council for Independent Colleges and Schools
Programs Offered:
accounting; administrative assistant and secretarial science; allied health and medical assisting services related; business administration and management; computer engineering technology; computer/information technology services administration related; computer programming; medical administrative assistant and medical secretary; medical/clinical assistant; medical insurance coding; medical insurance/medical billing; medical office assistant; nursing assistant/aide and patient care assistant; office management; telecommunications technology
Enrollment: 277 students
Institution Contact: Mr. Darryl H. Kerr, President
Phone: 706-738-5046
Fax: 706-736-3599
E-mail: dhkerr@savannahrivercollege.edu
Admission Contact: Mr. Marty Baca , Regional Director of Admissions
Phone: 706-738-5046 ext. 24
Fax: 706-736-3599
E-mail: mbaca@savannahrivercollege.edu

SOUTH UNIVERSITY
709 Mall Boulevard
Savannah, GA 31406
Web: http://www.southuniversity.edu
Accreditation: Southern Association of Colleges and Schools
Programs Offered:
accounting; anesthesiologist assistant; business administration and management; clinical pastoral counseling/patient counseling; computer and information sciences related; computer/information technology administration and management; computer/information technology services administration related; computer programming; computer programming related; computer programming (specific applications); computer software engineering; computer systems analysis; computer systems networking and telecommunications; computer/technical support; computer technology/computer systems technology; criminal justice/law enforcement administration; criminal justice/police science; general studies; health/health care administration; hospital and health care facilities administration; information technology; internet information systems; legal administrative assistant/secretary; legal assistant/paralegal; management information systems; medical administrative assistant and medical secretary; medical/clinical assistant; medical/health management and clinical assistant; medical office management; pharmacy; physical therapist assistant; physician assistant; pre-law studies; system administration; system, networking, and LAN/WAN management; technology management
Enrollment: 756 students
Institution Contact: Mr. John V. Peterson, President
Phone: 912-201-8007
Fax: 912-201-8070
E-mail: jvpeterson@southuniversity.edu
Admission Contact: Mr. Matthew Mills, Director of Admissions
Phone: 912-201-8018
Fax: 912-201-8070

STRAYER UNIVERSITY
3355 Northeast Expressway, Suite 100
Atlanta, GA 30339-3256
Web: http://www.strayer.edu
Programs Offered:
accounting; business administration and management; education; health services administration; information technology
Institution Contact: Ayanna Martin, Campus Manager
Phone: 770-454-9270
Fax: 770-457-6958
E-mail: chamblee@strayer.edu

WESTWOOD COLLEGE - ATLANTA CAMPUS
1100 Spring Street, Suite 101A
Atlanta, GA 30309
Web: http://www.westwood.edu
Accreditation: Accrediting Council for Independent Colleges and Schools
Programs Offered:

accounting; animation, interactive technology, video graphics and special effects; business administration and management; CAD/CADD drafting/design technology; commercial and advertising art; computer engineering related; computer software engineering; graphic communications; interior design; medical/clinical assistant; medical insurance/medical billing; web/multimedia management and webmaster

Enrollment: 160 students

Institution Contact: Mr. Bill Armour, Executive Director

Phone: 404-745-9862 ext. 14200

Fax: 404-892-7253

Admission Contact: Mr. Rory Laney, Director of Admissions

Phone: 404-745-9862 ext. 14100

Fax: 404-892-7253

E-mail: rlaney@westwood.edu

WESTWOOD COLLEGE - ATLANTA NORTHLAKE

2220 Parklake Drive Northeast

Atlanta, GA 30345

Web: http://www.westwoodcollege.net

Accreditation: Accrediting Council for Independent Colleges and Schools

Programs Offered:

animation, interactive technology, video graphics and special effects; business administration and management; business, management, and marketing related; communications technology; computer engineering related; computer/information technology administration and management; computer systems networking and telecommunications; digital communication and media/multimedia

Institution Contact: Admissions Representative

Phone: 877-558-2083

HAWAII

ARGOSY UNIVERSITY/HONOLULU

1001 Bishop Street , ASB Tower, Suite 400

Honolulu, HI 96813

Web: http://www.argosyu.edu/hoh

Programs Offered:

business administration and management; business, management, and marketing related; education; educa-

tional leadership and administration; education (specific levels and methods) related; psychoanalysis and psychotherapy; substance abuse/addiction counseling

Institution Contact: Cherie Andrade, Director of Admissions

Phone: 808-536-5555 ext. 258

Fax: 808-536-5505

E-mail: candrade@argosyu.edu

NEW YORK TECHNICAL INSTITUTE OF HAWAII

1375 Dillingham Boulevard

Honolulu, HI 96817-4415

Accreditation: Accrediting Commission of Career Schools and Colleges of Technology

Programs Offered:

automobile/automotive mechanics technology; heating, air conditioning, ventilation and refrigeration maintenance technology

Institution Contact: Mr. Brian Hamilton, Principal and Second Vice President

Phone: 808-841-5827

Fax: 808-841-5829

E-mail: nytih@gte.net

REMINGTON COLLEGE - HONOLULU CAMPUS

1111 Bishop Street, Suite 400

Honolulu, HI 96813

Web: http://www.remingtoncollege.edu

Accreditation: Accrediting Council for Independent Colleges and Schools

Programs Offered:

computer/technical support; criminal justice/law enforcement administration; hospitality administration related; international business/trade/commerce; massage therapy; medical/clinical assistant; operations management

Enrollment: 550 students

Institution Contact: Mr. Kenneth G. Heinemann, Campus President

Phone: 808-942-1000

Fax: 808-533-3064

E-mail: kenneth.heinemann@remingtoncollege.edu

Admission Contact: Mr. Paul Billington, Director of Recruitment

Phone: 808-942-1000

Fax: 808-550-4802

E-mail: paul.billington@remingtoncollege.edu

IDAHO

APOLLO COLLEGE

1200 North Liberty
Boise, ID 83704
Programs Offered:
dental assisting; dental hygiene; massage therapy; medical administrative assistant and medical secretary; medical/clinical assistant; medical insurance coding; medical insurance/medical billing; nursing (licensed practical/vocational nurse training); pharmacy technician
Enrollment: 540 students
Institution Contact: Mr. Chuck Ericson, Executive Director
Phone: 208-377-8080

ITT TECHNICAL INSTITUTE

12302 West Explorer Drive
Boise, ID 83713
Web: http://www.itt-tech.edu
Accreditation: Accrediting Council for Independent Colleges and Schools
Programs Offered:
accounting and business/management; animation, interactive technology, video graphics and special effects; business administration and management; CAD/CADD drafting/design technology; communications technology; computer and information systems security; computer engineering technology; computer software and media applications; computer software engineering; computer systems networking and telecommunications; criminal justice/police science; digital communication and media/multimedia; electrical, electronic and communications engineering technology; technology management; web page, digital/multimedia and information resources design
Institution Contact: Mrs. Jennifer Kandler, Director
Phone: 208-322-8844
Fax: 208-322-0173
E-mail: jkandler@itt-tech.edu
Admission Contact: Mr. Terry G. Lowder, Director of Recruitment
Phone: 208-322-8844
Fax: 208-322-0173
E-mail: tlowder@itt-tech.edu

SAGE TECHNICAL SERVICES

207 South 34th Avenue
Caldwell, ID 83605
Web: http://www.sageschools.com/
Programs Offered:
truck and bus driver/commercial vehicle operation
Enrollment: 25 students
Institution Contact: Mr. Wayne Rogers, Director
Phone: 800-858-6304
Fax: 208-454-1159
E-mail: caldwell@sageschools.com

SAGE TECHNICAL SERVICES

1420 East 3rd Avenue
Post Falls, ID 83854
Web: http://www.sageschools.com/
Accreditation: Accrediting Commission of Career Schools and Colleges of Technology
Programs Offered:
truck and bus driver/commercial vehicle operation
Institution Contact: Mr. Alan Coldwell, Director
Phone: 800-400-0779
Fax: 208-773-4690
E-mail: postfalls@sageschools.com

STEVENS-HENAGER COLLEGE

730 Americana Boulevard
Boise, ID 83702
Web: http://www.stevenshenager.edu
Accreditation: Accrediting Commission of Career Schools and Colleges of Technology
Programs Offered:
accounting; advertising; business administration and management; cardiovascular technology; commercial and advertising art; computer and information sciences related; computer graphics; computer programming; e-commerce; emergency medical technology (EMT paramedic); health/health care administration; information science/studies; insurance; medical/clinical assistant; medical insurance coding; medical insurance/medical billing; medical transcription; pharmacy technician; system, networking, and LAN/WAN management
Institution Contact: Ms. Vicky Dewsnup, President
Phone: 801-622-1550
Fax: 801-394-1149
E-mail: vdewsnup@stevenshenager.edu

ILLINOIS

ARGOSY UNIVERSITY/CHICAGO

350 North Orleans Street
Chicago, IL 60654
Web: http://www.argosyu.edu
Programs Offered:
accounting; accounting and business/management;
business administration and management; education;
educational leadership and administration; finance;
health/health care administration; health professions
related; health services administration; human resources management and services related; information
technology; international business/trade/commerce;
management science; marketing/marketing manage-
ment; marketing related; mental and social health
services and allied professions related; mental health
counseling
Enrollment: 1,020 students
Institution Contact: Ms. Tyler Shippen, Registrar
Phone: 312-777-7635
Fax: 312-777-7746
E-mail: tshippen@argosyu.edu
Admission Contact: Mrs. Ashley Delaney, Director of
Admissions
Phone: 312-777-7605
Fax: 312-777-7750
E-mail: adelaney@argosyu.edu

ARGOSY UNIVERSITY/SCHAUMBURG

999 Plaza Drive
Schaumburg, IL 60173
Web: http://www.argosyu.edu
Programs Offered:
accounting and business/management; business admin-
istration and management; business, management, and
marketing related; counselor education/school coun-
seling and guidance; education; educational leadership
and administration; international business/trade/com-
merce; organizational behavior; psychoanalysis and
psychotherapy
Enrollment: 498 students
Institution Contact: Dr. Roger H. Widmer, Campus
President
Phone: 847-598-6170
Fax: 847-598-6158

E-mail: rwidmer@argosyu.edu
Admission Contact: Jamal Scott, Director of Admissions
Phone: 847-598-6159
Fax: 847-598-6158
E-mail: jscott@argosyu.edu

BROWN MACKIE COLLEGE, MOLINE CAMPUS

1527 47th Avenue
Moline, IL 61265
Accreditation: Accrediting Council for Independent
Colleges and Schools
Programs Offered:
accounting; business administration and management;
computer and information sciences related; computer
programming; computer software and media applica-
tions; legal assistant/paralegal; medical/clinical assistant
Enrollment: 175 students
Institution Contact: Ms. Ann M. Sandoval, Second
Director of Admissions
Phone: 309-762-2100
Fax: 309-762-2374
E-mail: asandoval@brownmackie.edu

CARDEAN UNIVERSITY

111 North Canal Street, Suite 455
Chicago, IL 60606
Web: http://www.cardean.edu
Programs Offered:
accounting; business administration and management;
e-commerce; economics; finance; global management;
health/health care administration; human resources
management; management information systems; mar-
keting/marketing management; technology management
Enrollment: 87 students
Institution Contact: Dr. Douglas M. Stein
Phone: 312-669-5029
Fax: 312-669-5005
E-mail: dstein@cardean.com
Admission Contact:
Phone: 877-405-4500
Fax: 888-405-5844
E-mail: admissions@cardean.edu

CEC ONLINE EDUCATION GROUP

5550 Prairie Stone Pkwy, Suite #400
Hoffman Estates, IL 60192-3713

Institution Contact: Mr. Steve Fireng
Phone: 847-851-5204
Fax: 847-585-6204

THE CHUBB INSTITUTE
25 East Washington Street
Chicago, IL 60602
Web: http://www.chubbinstitute.com
Accreditation: Accrediting Council for Continuing Education and Training
Programs Offered:
allied health and medical assisting services related; computer and information sciences and support services related; computer and information sciences related; computer and information systems security; computer engineering technologies related; computer graphics; computer programming; computer programming related; computer programming (specific applications); computer programming (vendor/product certification); computer software and media applications; computer systems networking and telecommunications; computer/technical support; desktop publishing and digital imaging design; digital communication and media/multimedia; graphic communications; graphic communications related; health and medical administrative services related; health/health care administration; health information/medical records administration; health information/medical records technology; health professions related; health services/allied health/health sciences; health unit coordinator/ward clerk; massage therapy; medical administrative assistant and medical secretary; medical/clinical assistant; medical/health management and clinical assistant; medical insurance/medical billing; medical office assistant; medical pharmacology and pharmaceutical sciences; medical radiologic technology; medical reception; pharmacy technician; phlebotomy; surgical technology
Enrollment: 230 students
Institution Contact: Ms. Geralyn M. Randich, Campus President
Phone: 312-821-7561
Fax: 312-821-7581
E-mail: grandich@chubbinstitute.edu
Admission Contact: Mr. Todd LaSota, Director of Admissions
Phone: 312-821-7611
Fax: 312-821-7581
E-mail: tlasota@chubbinstitute.edu

THE COOKING AND HOSPITALITY INSTITUTE OF CHICAGO
361 West Chestnut
Chicago, IL 60610-3050
Web: http://www.chicnet.org
Accreditation: Accrediting Commission of Career Schools and Colleges of Technology; North Central Association of Colleges and Schools
Programs Offered:
baking and pastry arts; culinary arts
Enrollment: 1,004 students
Institution Contact: Mr. Lloyd Kirsch, President
Phone: 877-828-7772
Fax: 312-944-8557
E-mail: lkirsch@careered.com
Admission Contact: Mr. Maher Dabbouseh, Vice President of Admissions
Phone: 877-828-7772
Fax: 312-944-8557
E-mail: mdabbouseh@chicnet.org

COYNE AMERICAN INSTITUTE
330 North Green Street
Chicago, IL 60607-1300
Web: http://www.coyneamerican.edu
Accreditation: Accrediting Commission of Career Schools and Colleges of Technology
Programs Offered:
administrative assistant and secretarial science; business automation/technology/data entry; computer installation and repair technology; computer systems networking and telecommunications; computer/technical support; computer technology/computer systems technology; data processing and data processing technology; electrical, electronic and communications engineering technology; electrical/electronics equipment installation and repair; electrician; electromechanical technology; health and medical administrative services related; health/health care administration; health information/medical records administration; health information/medical records technology; health/medical claims examination; health services administration; health services/allied health/health sciences; heating, air conditioning and refrigeration technology; industrial electronics technology; information science/studies; medical administrative assistant and medical secretary; medical insurance coding; medical insurance/medical billing; medical office assistant; medical office man-

agement; medical reception; medical transcription; office occupations and clerical services; receptionist; system, networking, and LAN/WAN management; word processing
Enrollment: 550 students
Institution Contact: Mr. Peter Pauletti, Director of Admissions
Phone: 800-999-5220
Fax: 773-577-8102
E-mail: ppauletti@coyneamerican.edu

COYNE AMERICAN INSTITUTE
230 West Monroe, Suite 400
Chicago, IL 60606
Web: http://www.coyneamerican.com/
Programs Offered:
heating, air conditioning and refrigeration technology; medical administrative assistant and medical secretary; medical/clinical assistant
Institution Contact: Admissions
Phone: 312-334-0900

EMPIRE BEAUTY SCHOOL
1166 West Lake Street
Hanover Park, IL 60133-5421
Institution Contact: Ms. Carla Jones
Phone: 630-830-6560
Fax: 630-830-7981

FOX COLLEGE
4201 West 93rd Street
Oak Lawn, IL 60453
Web: http://www.foxcollege.edu/
Accreditation: Accrediting Council for Independent Colleges and Schools
Programs Offered:
accounting; administrative assistant and secretarial science; computer software and media applications related; computer software technology; executive assistant/executive secretary; medical administrative assistant and medical secretary; medical/clinical assistant; medical office assistant
Enrollment: 210 students
Institution Contact: Mr. Carey Cranston, President
Phone: 708-636-7700
Fax: 708-636-8078

E-mail: ccranston@foxcollege.edu
Admission Contact: Mr. Mark Scheuerell, Admissions Representative
Phone: 708-636-7700
Fax: 708-636-8078
E-mail: mscheuerell@foxcollege.edu

HARRINGTON COLLEGE OF DESIGN
200 West Madison, Suite 200
Chicago, IL 60606
Web: http://www.interiordesign.edu/
Accreditation: Accrediting Council for Independent-Colleges and Schools
Programs Offered:
interior design; photography
Enrollment: 1,555 students
Institution Contact: Mr. Patrick W. Comstock, President
Phone: 312-939-4975
Fax: 312-697-8032
E-mail: pcomstock@interiordesign.edu
Admission Contact: Ms. Wendi Franczyk, Vice President of Admissions
Phone: 312-939-4975
Fax: 312-697-8032
E-mail: wfranczyk@interiordesign.edu

THE ILLINOIS INSTITUTE OF ART - CHICAGO
350 North Orleans, Suite 136
Chicago, IL 60654-1593
Web: http://www.ilia.artinstitutes.edu
Accreditation: Accrediting Commission of Career Schools and Colleges of Technology
Programs Offered:
advertising; animation, interactive technology, video graphics and special effects; apparel and textile manufacturing; apparel and textile marketing management; apparel and textiles related; applied art; art; baking and pastry arts; CAD/CADD drafting/design technology; commercial and advertising art; computer graphics; culinary arts; design and visual communications; digital communication and media/multimedia; fashion and fabric consulting; fashion/apparel design; fashion merchandising; food preparation; interior design; merchandising; retailing; selling skills and sales; visual and performing arts; web page, digital/multimedia and information resources design
Institution Contact: Mr. John C. Becker, Dean of

Education
Phone: 312-280-3500 ext. 6851
Fax: 312-280-8562
E-mail: beckerj@aii.edu
Admission Contact: Ms. Janice Anton, Director of Admissions
Phone: 800-351-3450
Fax: 312-280-8562
E-mail: antonj@aii.edu

THE ILLINOIS INSTITUTE OF ART - SCHAUMBURG

1000 Plaza Drive
Schaumburg, IL 60173
Web: http://www.ilia.aii.edu
Accreditation: Accrediting Commission of Career Schools and Colleges of Technology
Programs Offered:
animation, interactive technology, video graphics and special effects; digital communication and media/multimedia; interior design; web page, digital/multimedia and information resources design
Institution Contact: Mr. Sam T. Hinojosa, Director of Admissions
Phone: 800-314-3450
Fax: 847-619-3064
E-mail: hinojost@aii.edu

ILLINOIS SCHOOL OF HEALTH CAREERS

220 South State Street, Suite 600
Chicago, IL 60604
Web: http://www.ishc.edu
Accreditation: Accrediting Bureau of Health Education Schools
Programs Offered:
dental assisting; massage therapy; medical/clinical assistant; medical insurance coding
Enrollment: 457 students
Institution Contact: Mr. Jeffrey Jarmes, Executive Director
Phone: 312-913-1230
Fax: 312-913-1113
E-mail: jjarmes@ishc.edu
Admission Contact: Mr. Charles Woods, Director of Admissions
Phone: 312-913-1230
Fax: 312-913-1113
E-mail: cwoods@ishc.edu

INTERNATIONAL ACADEMY OF DESIGN & TECHNOLOGY

1 North State Street, Suite 400
Chicago, IL 60602-9736
Web: http://www.iadtchicago.edu
Accreditation: Accrediting Council for Independent Colleges and Schools
Programs Offered:
advertising; CAD/CADD drafting/design technology; commercial and advertising art; computer graphics; computer/information technology administration and management; computer systems analysis; computer/technical support; fashion/apparel design; fashion merchandising; information technology; interior design; intermedia/multimedia; system administration; system, networking, and LAN/WAN management; web/multimedia management and webmaster; web page, digital/multimedia and information resources design
Enrollment: 2,301 students
Institution Contact: Ms. Darlene Ulmer, Director of Compliance
Phone: 312-980-4838
Fax: 312-582-8227
E-mail: dulmer@iadtchicago.com
Admission Contact: Mr. Doug Lochbaum, Associate Vice President of Admissions
Phone: 312-980-9271
Fax: 312-541-3929
E-mail: info@iadtchicago.com

INTERNATIONAL ACADEMY OF DESIGN AND TECHNOLOGY

915 National Parkway
Schaumburg, IL 60173
Web: http://www.iadtschaumburg.com
Accreditation: Accrediting Council for Independent Colleges and Schools
Programs Offered:
digital communication and media/multimedia; fashion/apparel design; interior design; intermedia/multimedia

ITT TECHNICAL INSTITUTE

7040 High Grove Boulevard
Burr Ridge, IL 60521
Web: http://www.itt-tech.edu
Accreditation: Accrediting Council for Independent Colleges and Schools

Programs Offered:
computer and information systems security; computer engineering technology; computer software and media applications; computer systems networking and telecommunications; digital communication and media/multimedia; technology management; web page, digital/multimedia and information resources design
Institution Contact: Ms. Aida Carpenter, Director
Phone: 630-455-6470
Admission Contact: Mr. Andrew Mical, Director of Recruitment
Phone: 630-455-6470

ITT TECHNICAL INSTITUTE
600 Holiday Plaza Drive
Matteson, IL 60443
Web: http://www.itt-tech.edu
Accreditation: Accrediting Council for Independent Colleges and Schools
Programs Offered:
CAD/CADD drafting/design technology; computer engineering technology; computer software and media applications; computer systems networking and telecommunications; digital communication and media/multimedia; technology management; web/multimedia management and webmaster
Institution Contact: Ms. Lillian Williams-McClain, Director
Phone: 708-747-2571
Admission Contact: Ms. Lillian Williams-McClain, Director
Phone: 708-747-2571

ITT TECHNICAL INSTITUTE
1401 Feehanville Drive
Mount Prospect, IL 60056
Web: http://www.itt-tech.edu
Accreditation: Accrediting Council for Independent Colleges and Schools
Programs Offered:
CAD/CADD drafting/design technology; computer and information systems security; computer engineering technology; computer software and media applications; computer systems networking and telecommunications; digital communication and media/multimedia; electrical, electronic and communications engineering technology; technology management; web page, digi-

tal/multimedia and information resources design
Institution Contact: Mr. Elvis Parker, Director
Phone: 847-375-8800
Admission Contact: Mr. Cesar Rodriguez, Jr., Director of Recruitment
Phone: 847-375-8800

LINCOLN TECHNICAL INSTITUTE
8317 West North Avenue
Melrose Park, IL 60160
Web: http://www.lincolntech.com
Accreditation: Accrediting Commission of Career Schools and Colleges of Technology
Programs Offered:
automobile/automotive mechanics technology; electrical/electronics equipment installation and repair; medical/clinical assistant
Enrollment: 1,065 students
Institution Contact: Ms. Helen M. Carver, Executive Director
Phone: 708-344-4700
Fax: 708-345-4065
E-mail: hcarver@lincolntech.com
Admission Contact: Mr. Joseph Painter, Director of Admissions
Phone: 708-344-4700
Fax: 708-345-4065
E-mail: jpainter@lincolntech.com

OLYMPIA COLLEGE
6880 North Frontage Road, Suite 400
Burr Ridge, IL 60527
Web: http://www.olympia-college.com
Accreditation: Accrediting Commission of Career Schools and Colleges of Technology
Programs Offered:
dental assisting; massage therapy; medical administrative assistant and medical secretary; medical/clinical assistant; pharmacy technician
Enrollment: 550 students
Institution Contact: Mr. David Profita, Director of Admissions
Phone: 630-920-1102
Fax: 630-920-9012
E-mail: dprofita@cci.edu

OLYMPIA COLLEGE

247 South State Street , Suite 400
Chicago, IL 60604
Web: http://www.olympia-college.com
Accreditation: Accrediting Commission of Career
Schools and Colleges of Technology
Programs Offered:
massage therapy; medical administrative assistant and
medical secretary; medical/clinical assistant; pharmacy
technician
Institution Contact: Nikee Carnagey, Director of
Admissions
Phone: 312-913-1616
Fax: 312-913-9422
E-mail: ncarnage@cci.edu

OLYMPIA COLLEGE

150 South Lincolnway, Suite 100
North Aurora, IL 60542
Programs Offered:
massage therapy; medical/clinical assistant
Enrollment: 310 students
Institution Contact: Mr. Bob Ernst, President
Phone: 630-896-2140
Fax: 630-896-2144
E-mail: bernst@cci.edu
Admission Contact: Mr. Michael O'Herron, Director
of Admissions
Phone: 630-896-2140
Fax: 630-896-2144
E-mail: moherron@cci.edu

OLYMPIA COLLEGE

9811 Woods Drive, Second Floor
Skokie, IL 60077
Web: http://www.olympia-college.com
Accreditation: Accrediting Commission of Career
Schools and Colleges of Technology
Programs Offered:
massage therapy; medical/clinical assistant; medical
insurance/medical billing; pharmacy technician
Enrollment: 492 students
Institution Contact: Mr. Mark E. Sullivan, President
Phone: 847-470-0277
Fax: 847-470-0266
E-mail: msulliva@cci.edu
Admission Contact: Ms. Jeanette Nowak, Director of

Admissions
Phone: 847-470-0277
Fax: 847-470-0266
E-mail: jnowak@cci.edu

ROCKFORD BUSINESS COLLEGE

730 North Church Street
Rockford, IL 61103
Web: http://www.rockfordbusinesscollege.edu
Accreditation: Accrediting Council for Independent
Colleges and Schools
Programs Offered:
accounting; administrative assistant and secretarial
science; business administration and management;
computer/information technology administration and
management; computer/information technology services
administration related; computer installation and repair
technology; computer programming; computer systems
networking and telecommunications; data processing
and data processing technology; executive assistant/
executive secretary; legal administrative assistant/sec-
retary; legal assistant/paralegal; marketing/marketing
management; medical/clinical assistant; medical office
assistant; office occupations and clerical services
Enrollment: 470 students
Institution Contact: Mr. Guary Bernadelle, President
Phone: 815-965-8616 ext. 223
Fax: 815-965-0360
E-mail: bernadelle@rbcsuccess.com
Admission Contact: Mr. Manuel Carrasquillo, Direc-
tor of Operations
Phone: 815-965-8616 ext. 226
Fax: 815-965-0360
E-mail: cmanuel@rbcsuccess.com

SANFORD-BROWN COLLEGE

1101 Eastport Plaza Drive
Collinsville, IL 62234
Web: http://www.sanford-brown.com
Accreditation: Accrediting Bureau of Health Education Schools; Accrediting Council for Independent
Colleges and Schools
Programs Offered:
accounting and business/management; business administration and management; computer/technical support;
massage therapy; medical/clinical assistant; medical
insurance coding

Enrollment: 512 students
Institution Contact: Ms. Carole Underwood, Executive Director
Phone: 618-344-5600
Fax: 618-421-5256
E-mail: cunderwood@sbc-collinsville.com
Admission Contact: Ms. Connie Frazier, Director of Admissions
Phone: 618-344-5600
Fax: 618-421-5256
E-mail: cfrazier@sbc-collinsville.com

THE SOMA INSTITUTE, THE NATIONAL SCHOOL OF CLINICAL MASSAGE THERAPY

14 East Jackson Boulevard, Suite 1300
Chicago, IL 60604-2232
Web: http://www.thesomainstitute.com
Accreditation: Accrediting Council for Continuing Education and Training
Programs Offered:
massage therapy
Enrollment: 297 students
Institution Contact: Dr. Helen J. Robinson, Vice President, Compliance
Phone: 312-939-2723 ext. 18
Fax: 312-939-0171
E-mail: hjrobinson@thesomainstitute.com
Admission Contact: Mr. David Beverly, Admissions Assistant
Phone: 312-939-2723 ext. 10
Fax: 312-939-0171
E-mail: info@thesomainstitute.com

UNIVERSAL TECHNICAL INSTITUTE, INC.

601 Regency Drive
Glendale Heights, IL 60139
Web: http://www.uticorp.com
Accreditation: Accrediting Commission of Career Schools and Colleges of Technology
Programs Offered:
automobile/automotive mechanics technology; diesel mechanics technology
Enrollment: 2,287 students
Institution Contact: Mr. Karl Lewandowski, Director
Phone: 630-529-2662
Fax: 630-529-7567
E-mail: karllewandowski@uticorp.com

Admission Contact: Mr. Jeremy Conte, Admissions Director
Phone: 800-441-4248
Fax: 630-529-7567
E-mail: jconte@uticorp.com

VATTEROTT COLLEGE

501 North 3rd Street
Quincy, IL 62301
Web: http://www.vatterott-college.edu
Accreditation: Accrediting Commission of Career Schools and Colleges of Technology
Programs Offered:
CAD/CADD drafting/design technology; computer technology/computer systems technology; data entry/microcomputer applications; electrician; heating, air conditioning, ventilation and refrigeration maintenance technology; medical/clinical assistant
Enrollment: 200 students
Institution Contact: Ms. Katrina L. Houser, Director
Phone: 217-224-0600
Fax: 217-223-6771
E-mail: khouser@vatterott-college.edu
Admission Contact: Mr. David A. Stickney, Director of Admissions
Phone: 217-224-0600
Fax: 217-223-6771
E-mail: vattqcy@adams.net

WESTWOOD COLLEGE - CHICAGO DU PAGE

7155 Janes Avenue
Woodridge, IL 60517
Web: http://www.westwood.edu
Accreditation: Accrediting Council for Independent Colleges and Schools
Programs Offered:
animation, interactive technology, video graphics and special effects; CAD/CADD drafting/design technology; commercial and advertising art; computer and information systems security; computer graphics; computer software and media applications; computer software engineering; computer systems networking and telecommunications; criminal justice/law enforcement administration; graphic communications; interior design; web page, digital/multimedia and information resources design
Enrollment: 595 students

Institution Contact: Kelly Thumm Moore, Executive Director
Phone: 630-434-8244 ext. 200
Fax: 630-434-8255
E-mail: kmoore@westwood.edu
Admission Contact: Scott Kawall, Director of Admissions
Phone: 630-434-8244 ext. 100
Fax: 630-434-8255
E-mail: skawall@westwood.edu

WESTWOOD COLLEGE - CHICAGO LOOP CAMPUS

17 North State Street, Suite 300
Chicago, IL 60602
Web: http://www.westwood.edu
Accreditation: Accrediting Council for Independent Colleges and Schools
Programs Offered:
animation, interactive technology, video graphics and special effects; architectural drafting and CAD/CADD; CAD/CADD drafting/design technology; commercial and advertising art; computer/information technology administration and management; computer software engineering; computer systems networking and telecommunications; criminal justice/police science; design and visual communications; e-commerce; interior design; internet information systems; marketing/ marketing management; marketing related; web page, digital/multimedia and information resources design
Enrollment: 590 students
Institution Contact: Ms. Jeanne Glielmi, Executive Assistant
Phone: 312-578-3885
Fax: 312-739-1004
E-mail: jglielmi@westwood.edu
Admission Contact: Mr. Jeff Hill, Director of Admissions
Phone: 312-578-3860
Fax: 312-739-1004
E-mail: jhill@westwood.edu

WESTWOOD COLLEGE - CHICAGO O'HARE AIRPORT

8501 West Higgins Road, Suite 100
Chicago, IL 60631
Web: http://www.westwood.edu
Accreditation: Accrediting Commission of Career Schools and Colleges of Technology; Accrediting

Council for Independent Colleges and Schools
Programs Offered:
advertising; business administration and management; business, management, and marketing related; CAD/CADD drafting/design technology; commercial and advertising art; computer engineering technology; computer programming; computer software technology; corrections; criminal justice/law enforcement administration; criminal justice/police science; drafting and design technology; interior design; intermedia/multimedia; medical administrative assistant and medical secretary; system, networking, and LAN/WAN management; technology management
Enrollment: 472 students
Institution Contact: Mr. Scott Black, Executive Director
Phone: 877-877-8857 ext. 201
E-mail: sblack@westwood.edu
Admission Contact: Mr. David Traub
Phone: 877-877-8857 ext. 100
E-mail: dtraub@westwood.edu

WESTWOOD COLLEGE - CHICAGO RIVER OAKS

80 River Oaks Center, Suite 111
Calumet City, IL 60409
Web: http://www.westwood.edu
Accreditation: Accrediting Council for Independent Colleges and Schools
Programs Offered:
allied health and medical assisting services related; animation, interactive technology, video graphics and special effects; architectural drafting and CAD/CADD; CAD/CADD drafting/design technology; computer and information systems security; computer engineering related; computer engineering technology; criminal justice/law enforcement administration; e-commerce; medical insurance coding; medical insurance/medical billing; system, networking, and LAN/WAN management; technology management
Enrollment: 700 students
Institution Contact: Mr. Bruce McKenzie, Executive Director
Phone: 708-832-1988 ext. 200
Fax: 708-832-6525
E-mail: bmckenzie@westwood.edu
Admission Contact: Mr. Tash Uray, Director of Admissions
Phone: 708-832-1988 ext. 100

Fax: 708-832-9342
E-mail: turay@westwood.edu

INDIANA

BROWN MACKIE COLLEGE, FORT WAYNE CAMPUS

4422 East State Boulevard
Fort Wayne, IN 46815
Web: http://www.michianacollege.com/
Programs Offered:
business administration and management; CAD/CADD drafting/design technology; computer and information sciences related; pre-law studies
Institution Contact:
Phone: 888-300-6802

BROWN MACKIE COLLEGE, MERRILLVILLE CAMPUS

1000 East 80th Place, Suite 101 North
Merrillville, IN 46410
Accreditation: Accrediting Bureau of Health Education Schools; Accrediting Council for Independent Colleges and Schools
Programs Offered:
accounting; CAD/CADD drafting/design technology; computer programming; computer/technical support; criminal justice/law enforcement administration; legal assistant/paralegal; medical/clinical assistant
Institution Contact: Mrs. Sheryl Elston, Director of Admissions
Phone: 219-769-3321
Fax: 219-738-1076
E-mail: selston@amedcts.com

BROWN MACKIE COLLEGE, MICHIGAN CITY CAMPUS

325 East US Highway 20
Michigan City, IN 46360
Accreditation: Accrediting Bureau of Health Education Schools; Accrediting Council for Independent Colleges and Schools
Programs Offered:
accounting; CAD/CADD drafting/design technology; computer programming; computer/technical support; criminal justice/law enforcement administration; legal assistant/paralegal; medical/clinical assistant

Institution Contact: Mrs. Sheryl L. Elston, Director of Admissions
Phone: 219-769-3321
Fax: 219-738-1076
E-mail: selston@amedcts.com

BROWN MACKIE COLLEGE, SOUTH BEND CAMPUS

1030 East Jefferson Boulevard
South Bend, IN 46617
Web: http://www.michianacollege.com
Accreditation: Accrediting Council for Independent Colleges and Schools
Programs Offered:
accounting; business administration and management; CAD/CADD drafting/design technology; computer installation and repair technology; computer programming; computer software technology; computer systems networking and telecommunications; criminal justice/law enforcement administration; legal assistant/paralegal; medical/clinical assistant; occupational therapist assistant; physical therapist assistant
Institution Contact: Ms. Connie S. Adelman, Campus Director
Phone: 574-237-0774
Fax: 574-237-3585
E-mail: cadelman@amedcts.com
Admission Contact: Ms. Laurie Johannesen-Oliver, Director of Admissions
Phone: 574-237-0774
Fax: 574-237-3585
E-mail: ljohannesen@amedcts.com

INDIANA BUSINESS COLLEGE

140 East 53rd Street
Anderson, IN 46013-1717
Web: http://www.ibcschools.edu
Accreditation: Accrediting Council for Independent Colleges and Schools
Programs Offered:
accounting; accounting related; administrative assistant and secretarial science; business administration and management; medical/clinical assistant; medical insurance coding; medical insurance/medical billing
Enrollment: 235 students
Institution Contact: Ms. Charlene Stacy, Executive Director
Phone: 765-644-7514

Fax: 765-644-5724
Admission Contact: Ms. Charlene Stacy , Executive Director
Phone: 765-644-7514
Fax: 765-644-5724

INDIANA BUSINESS COLLEGE
2222 Poshard Drive
Columbus, IN 47203
Web: http://www.ibcschools.edu
Accreditation: Accrediting Council for Independent Colleges and Schools
Programs Offered:
accounting; accounting related; administrative assistant and secretarial science; business administration and management; computer/technical support; information technology; medical/clinical assistant; medical insurance/medical billing
Enrollment: 273 students
Institution Contact: Angela Rentmeesters, Executive Director
Phone: 812-379-9000
Fax: 812-375-0414

INDIANA BUSINESS COLLEGE
4601 Theater Drive
Evansville, IN 47715
Web: http://www.ibcschools.edu
Accreditation: Accrediting Council for Independent Colleges and Schools
Programs Offered:
accounting; administrative assistant and secretarial science; business administration and management; health/medical claims examination; information technology; medical administrative assistant and medical secretary; medical/clinical assistant; medical insurance coding; medical insurance/medical billing; medical office assistant
Enrollment: 295 students
Institution Contact: Mr. Steve Hardin, Regional Director
Phone: 812-476-6000
Fax: 812-471-8576

INDIANA BUSINESS COLLEGE
6413 North Clinton Street

Fort Wayne, IN 46825
Web: http://www.ibcschools.edu
Accreditation: Accrediting Council for Independent Colleges and Schools
Programs Offered:
accounting; accounting related; administrative assistant and secretarial science; business administration and management; health/medical claims examination; health professions related; medical/clinical assistant; medical insurance coding; medical insurance/medical billing; medical office assistant; surgical technology
Enrollment: 384 students
Institution Contact: Ms. Janet Hein, Executive Director
Phone: 260-471-7667
Fax: 260-471-6918

INDIANA BUSINESS COLLEGE

550 East Washington Street
Indianapolis, IN 46204
Web: http://www.ibcschools.edu
Accreditation: Accrediting Council for Independent Colleges and Schools
Programs Offered:
accounting; administrative assistant and secretarial science; business administration and management; communications systems installation and repair technology; computer/information technology services administration related; computer installation and repair technology; computer/technical support; criminal justice/law enforcement administration; fashion merchandising; human resources development; information technology; legal administrative assistant/secretary; medical/clinical assistant; medical office assistant; medical transcription
Enrollment: 670 students
Institution Contact: Pat Mozley, Regional Director
Phone: 317-264-5656
Fax: 317-264-5650
Admission Contact: Pat Mozley, Regional Director
Phone: 317-264-5656
Fax: 317-264-5650

INDIANA BUSINESS COLLEGE
2 Executive Drive
Lafayette, IN 47905-4859
Web: http://www.ibcschools.edu
Accreditation: Accrediting Council for Independent

Colleges and Schools

Programs Offered:
accounting; accounting and business/management; accounting related; administrative assistant and secretarial science; business administration and management; computer and information sciences; health and medical administrative services related; health information/medical records administration; health information/medical records technology; health/medical claims examination; information technology; medical administrative assistant and medical secretary; medical/clinical assistant

Enrollment: 215 students

Institution Contact: Mr. Gregory P. Reger, Executive Director

Phone: 765-447-9550

Fax: 765-447-9550

E-mail: greg.reger@ibcschools.edu

INDIANA BUSINESS COLLEGE

830 North Miller Avenue
Marion, IN 46952
Web: http://www.ibcschools.edu

Accreditation: Accrediting Council for Independent Colleges and Schools

Programs Offered:
accounting; accounting and business/management; accounting related; administrative assistant and secretarial science; business administration and management; health information/medical records technology; medical/clinical assistant; medical insurance coding; medical office assistant

Enrollment: 120 students

Institution Contact: Mr. Richard Herman, Executive-Director

Phone: 765-662-7497

Fax: 765-651-9421

INDIANA BUSINESS COLLEGE

411 West Riggin Road
Muncie, IN 47303-6413
Web: http://www.ibcschools.edu

Accreditation: Accrediting Council for Independent Colleges and Schools

Programs Offered:
accounting; administrative assistant and secretarial science; business administration and management;

computer/technical support; criminal justice/law enforcement administration; health information/medical records technology; information technology; medical/clinical assistant; medical insurance coding; medical office assistant

Enrollment: 310 students

Institution Contact: Mr. Greg Bond, Regional Director

Phone: 765-288-8681

Fax: 765-288-8797

INDIANA BUSINESS COLLEGE

3175 South Third Place
Terre Haute, IN 47802
Web: http://www.ibcschools.edu

Accreditation: Accrediting Council for Independent Colleges and Schools

Programs Offered:
accounting; accounting related; administrative assistant and secretarial science; business administration and management; computer and information sciences related; computer systems networking and telecommunications; health information/medical records technology; medical/clinical assistant; medical insurance coding; medical insurance/medical billing; medical office assistant

Enrollment: 220 students

Institution Contact: Ms. Laura Hale, Executive Director

Phone: 812-232-4458

Fax: 812-234-2361

INDIANA BUSINESS COLLEGE-MEDICAL

8150 Brookville Road
Indianapolis, IN 46239
Web: http://www.ibcschools.edu

Accreditation: Accrediting Council for Independent Colleges and Schools

Programs Offered:
health information/medical records administration; health information/medical records technology; health/medical claims examination; massage therapy; medical administrative assistant and medical secretary; medical/clinical assistant; medical insurance coding; medical insurance/medical billing; medical transcription; surgical technology

Enrollment: 584 students

Institution Contact: Mr. Gary McGee, Senior Re-

gional Director
Phone: 317-375-8000
Fax: 317-351-1871

INTERNATIONAL BUSINESS COLLEGE

5699 Coventry Lane
Fort Wayne, IN 46804
Web: http://www.ibcfortwayne.edu
Accreditation: Accrediting Council for Independent Colleges and Schools
Programs Offered:
accounting; administrative assistant and secretarial science; business administration and management; commercial and advertising art; computer programming; finance; hospitality administration; industrial technology; legal administrative assistant/secretary; legal assistant/paralegal; medical/clinical assistant; retailing; tourism and travel services management
Enrollment: 575 students
Institution Contact: Mr. Jim Zillman, President
Phone: 219-459-4555
Fax: 219-436-1896
E-mail: jzillman@ibcfortwayne.edu
Admission Contact: Mr. Steve M. Kinzer, Director
Phone: 219-459-4513
Fax: 219-436-1896
E-mail: skinzer@ibcfortwayne.edu

INTERNATIONAL BUSINESS COLLEGE

7205 Shadeland Station
Indianapolis, IN 46256
Web: http://www.intlbusinesscollege.com/
Accreditation: Accrediting Council for Independent Colleges and Schools
Programs Offered:
accounting; administrative assistant and secretarial science; commercial and advertising art; computer programming; computer software and media applications related; computer technology/computer systems technology; data entry/microcomputer applications; graphic and printing equipment operation/production; legal administrative assistant/secretary; legal assistant/paralegal; medical/clinical assistant; tourism and travel services management
Enrollment: 332 students
Institution Contact: Ms. Kathy Chivdioni, Director
Phone: 317-813-2300

Fax: 317-841-6419
E-mail: info@ibcindianapolis.edu

ITT TECHNICAL INSTITUTE

4919 Coldwater Road
Fort Wayne, IN 46825-5532
Web: http://www.itt-tech.edu
Accreditation: Accrediting Council for Independent Colleges and Schools
Programs Offered:
accounting and business/management; animation, interactive technology, video graphics and special effects; business administration and management; CAD/CADD drafting/design technology; communications technology; computer and information systems security; computer engineering technology; computer software and media applications; computer software engineering; computer systems networking and telecommunications; criminal justice/police science; digital communication and media/multimedia; electrical, electronic and communications engineering technology; industrial technology; technology management; web page, digital/multimedia and information resources design
Institution Contact: Alois Johnson, Director
Phone: 219-484-4107 ext. 244
Admission Contact: Mr. Michael D. Frantom, Director of Recruitment
Phone: 219-484-4107

ITT TECHNICAL INSTITUTE

9511 Angola Court
Indianapolis, IN 46268-1119
Web: http://www.itt-tech.edu
Accreditation: Accrediting Council for Independent Colleges and Schools
Programs Offered:
accounting and business/management; animation, interactive technology, video graphics and special effects; business administration and management; CAD/CADD drafting/design technology; communications technology; computer and information systems security; computer engineering technology; computer software and media applications; computer software engineering; computer systems networking and telecommunications; criminal justice/police science; digital communication and media/multimedia;

electrical, electronic and communications engineering technology; industrial technology; technology management; web page, digital/multimedia and information resources design

Institution Contact: Mr. James Horner, Director
Phone: 317-875-8640
Fax: 317-875-8641
E-mail: jhorner@itt-tech.edu
Admission Contact: Martha Watson, Director of Recruitment
Phone: 317-875-8640
Fax: 317-875-8641

ITT TECHNICAL INSTITUTE
10999 Stahl Road
Newburgh, IN 47630-7430
Web: http://www.itt-tech.edu
Accreditation: Accrediting Council for Independent Colleges and Schools
Programs Offered:
animation, interactive technology, video graphics and special effects; CAD/CADD drafting/design technology; communications technology; computer and information systems security; computer engineering technology; computer software and media applications; computer software engineering; computer systems networking and telecommunications; digital communication and media/multimedia; electrical, electronic and communications engineering technology; industrial technology; technology management; web page, digital/multimedia and information resources design
Institution Contact: Mr. Ken Butler, Director
Phone: 812-858-1600
Admission Contact: Mr. Tom Campbell, Director of Recruitment
Phone: 812-858-1600

LINCOLN TECHNICAL INSTITUTE

7225 Winton Drive
Indianapolis, IN 46268
Web: http://www.lincolntech.com
Accreditation: Accrediting Commission of Career Schools and Colleges of Technology
Programs Offered:
autobody/collision and repair technology; automobile/automotive mechanics technology; CAD/CADD drafting/design technology; diesel mechanics technology;

electrical/electronics equipment installation and repair
Enrollment: 1,810 students
Institution Contact: Ms. Cindy Ryan, Executive Director
Phone: 317-632-5553
Fax: 317-634-1089
E-mail: cyran@lincolntech.com
Admission Contact: Mr. Alan Schultz, Director of Admissions
Phone: 800-554-4465
Fax: 317-634-1089
E-mail: aschultz@lincolnedu.com

MEDTECH COLLEGE
6612 East 75th Street, Suite 300
Indianapolis, IN 46250
Web: http://www.medtechcollege.com
Accreditation: Accrediting Council for Independent Colleges and Schools
Programs Offered:
massage therapy; medical/clinical assistant; medical insurance coding
Enrollment: 70 students
Institution Contact: Mr. Joe Davis, President
Phone: 317-845-0100 ext. 207
Fax: 317-845-1800
E-mail: jdavis@medtechcollege.com
Admission Contact: Ms. Cindy Andrews, Executive Vice President of Marketing and Recruitment
Phone: 317-845-0100 ext. 202
Fax: 317-845-1800
E-mail: candrews@medtechcollege.com

NATIONAL COLLEGE OF BUSINESS AND TECHNOLOGY
6060 Castleway West Drive
Indianapolis, IN 46250
Web: http://www.ncbt.edu/
Programs Offered:
accounting; administrative assistant and secretarial science; business administration and management; computer and information sciences; health information/medical records technology; medical/clinical assistant; pharmacy technician; surgical technology
Institution Contact: Admissions
Phone: 317-578-7353

OLYMPIA COLLEGE
707 East 80th Place, Suite 200
Merrillville, IN 46410
Web: http://www.olympia-college.com
Accreditation: Accrediting Bureau of Health Education Schools
Programs Offered:
dental assisting; massage therapy; medical administrative assistant and medical secretary; medical/clinical assistant; nursing (licensed practical/vocational nurse training); surgical technology
Enrollment: 550 students
Institution Contact: Ms. Maegan J. Kirby, Director of Admissions
Phone: 219-756-6811
Fax: 219-756-6812
E-mail: mkirby@cci.edu

PROFESSIONAL CAREERS INSTITUTE
7302 Woodland Drive
Indianapolis, IN 46278-1736
Web: http://www.pcicareers.com
Accreditation: Accrediting Commission of Career Schools and Colleges of Technology
Programs Offered:
dental assisting; legal assistant/paralegal; massage therapy; medical administrative assistant and medical secretary; medical/clinical assistant; medical office management
Enrollment: 600 students
Institution Contact: Ms. Barri L. Shirk, Executive Director
Phone: 317-299-6001
Fax: 317-298-6342
E-mail: barri.shirk@pcicareers.com
Admission Contact: Mrs. Paulette Clay, Admissions Director
Phone: 317-299-6001
Fax: 317-298-6342
E-mail: paulette.clay@pcicareers.com

SAWYER COLLEGE
3803 East Lincoln Highway
Merrillville, IN 46410
Accreditation: Accrediting Council for Independent Colleges and Schools
Programs Offered:
accounting; administrative assistant and secretarial science; computer engineering technology; computer hardware engineering; computer programming; computer software and media applications; computer/technical support; data processing and data processing technology; executive assistant/executive secretary; health/health care administration; hospital and health care facilities administration; legal administrative assistant/secretary; massage therapy; medical/clinical assistant; medical office computer specialist
Institution Contact: Mrs. Mary Jo Dixon, President
Phone: 219-736-0436
Fax: 219-942-3762
E-mail: mary.j.dixon@att.net
Admission Contact: Mrs. Linda J. Yednak, Director of Operations
Phone: 219-736-0436
Fax: 219-942-3762
E-mail: lyednak@sawyercollege.edu

IOWA

HAMILTON COLLEGE
3165 Edgewood Parkway, SW
Cedar Rapids, IA 52404
Web: http://www.hamiltonia.edu
Accreditation: North Central Association of Colleges and Schools
Programs Offered:
accounting; administrative assistant and secretarial science; business administration and management; computer systems networking and telecommunications; computer/technical support; criminal justice/law enforcement administration; information science/studies; medical/clinical assistant; medical transcription; multi-/interdisciplinary studies related; tourism and travel services management
Institution Contact: Lori L. Canning, Bookstore Manager
Phone: 319-363-0481
Fax: 319-363-3812
E-mail: canningl@hamiltonia.edu
Admission Contact: Mr. Brad Knudson, Director of Admissions
Phone: 319-363-0481
Fax: 319-363-3812
E-mail: knudsobr@hamiltonia.edu

KAPLAN UNIVERSITY

1801 East Kimberly Road, Suite 1
Davenport, IA 52807
Web: http://www.kucampus.edu
Accreditation: North Central Association of Colleges and Schools
Programs Offered:
accounting; business administration and management; computer programming; computer systems analysis; computer/technical support; criminal justice/law enforcement administration; data modeling/warehousing and database administration; legal assistant/paralegal; medical/clinical assistant; medical transcription; system, networking, and LAN/WAN management; tourism and travel services management; web/multimedia management and webmaster
Enrollment: 800 students
Institution Contact: Ms. Sara J. Campie, Assistant to the Campus President
Phone: 563-355-3500
Fax: 563-355-1320
E-mail: scampie@kucampus.edu
Admission Contact: Mr. Robert Hoffmann, Director of Admissions
Phone: 563-355-3500
Fax: 563-355-1320
E-mail: rhoffmann@kucampus.edu

VATTEROTT COLLEGE

6100 Thornton, Suite 290
Des Moines, IA 50321
Web: http://www.vatterott-college.edu
Accreditation: Accrediting Commission of Career Schools and Colleges of Technology
Programs Offered:
CAD/CADD drafting/design technology; computer systems networking and telecommunications; dental assisting; drafting and design technology; information science/studies; medical office computer specialist
Enrollment: 168 students
Institution Contact: Mr. Henry Franken, Co-Director
Phone: 515-309-9000
Fax: 515-309-0366
E-mail: hfranken@vatterott-college.edu
Admission Contact: Ms. Jodi Clendenen, Co-Director
Phone: 515-309-9000

Fax: 515-309-0336
E-mail: jclendenen@vatterott-college.edu

KANSAS

BROWN MACKIE COLLEGE, LENEXA CAMPUS

9705 Lenexa Drive
Lenexa, KS 66215
Web: http://www.bmcaec.com
Accreditation: North Central Association of Colleges and Schools
Programs Offered:
accounting; accounting technology and bookkeeping; business administration and management; CAD/CADD drafting/design technology; computer engineering technology; computer programming (specific applications); computer software and media applications; computer systems networking and telecommunications; criminal justice/law enforcement administration; criminal justice/police science; data processing and data processing technology; electrical/electronics equipment installation and repair; legal administrative assistant/secretary; legal assistant/paralegal; medical/clinical assistant; medical office management; pre-law studies; system, networking, and LAN/WAN management
Institution Contact: Mr. Richard M. Thome, President
Phone: 913-768-1900
Fax: 913-495-9555
E-mail: rthome@amedcts.com
Admission Contact: Ms. Julia M. Denniston, Director of Admissions
Phone: 913-768-1900
Fax: 913-495-9555
E-mail: jdenniston@amedcts.com

BROWN MACKIE COLLEGE, SALINA CAMPUS

2106 South 9th Street
Salina, KS 67401
Programs Offered:
business administration and management; computer and information sciences related
Institution Contact:
Phone: 888-242-2971

BRYAN COLLEGE

1527 SW Fairlawn Road
Topeka, KS 66604
Accreditation: Accrediting Council for Independent Colleges and Schools
Programs Offered:
business administration and management; computer installation and repair technology; computer programming; medical/clinical assistant; medical office assistant
Enrollment: 176 students
Institution Contact: Mrs. Rebecca A. Cox, Executive Director
Phone: 785-272-0889
Fax: 785-272-4538
E-mail: bcox@bryancc.com
Admission Contact: Mrs. Angela Tyroler, Admissions Representative
Phone: 785-272-0889
Fax: 785-272-4538
E-mail: atyroler@bryancc.com

NATIONAL AMERICAN UNIVERSITY

10310 Mastin
Overland Park, KS 66212
Web: http://www.national.edu
Accreditation: North Central Association of Colleges and Schools
Programs Offered:
accounting; accounting and business/management; business administration and management; business, management, and marketing related; information technology; legal assistant/paralegal; medical administrative assistant and medical secretary; medical/clinical assistant; medical office assistant
Enrollment: 150 students
Institution Contact: Ms. Tunya Carr, Campus Director
Phone: 913-217-2900
Fax: 913-217-2909
E-mail: tcarr@national.edu
Admission Contact: Mr. Marcus Smith, Director of Admissions
Phone: 913-217-2900
Fax: 913-217-2909
E-mail: msmith2@national.edu

PINNACLE CAREER INSTITUTE

1601 West 23rd Street, Suite 200
Lawrence, KS 66046
Web: http://www.pcitraining.edu
Accreditation: Accrediting Council for Independent Colleges and Schools
Programs Offered:
business operations support and secretarial services related; massage therapy; medical/clinical assistant; medical office computer specialist
Enrollment: 121 students
Institution Contact: Angie Kelso, Financial Aid Director
Phone: 785-841-9640 ext. 203
Fax: 785-841-4854
E-mail: akelso@pcitraining.edu
Admission Contact: David Caldwell, Executive Director
Phone: 785-841-9640
Fax: 785-841-4854
E-mail: dcaldwell@pcitraining.edu

VATTEROTT COLLEGE

3639 North Comotara
Wichita, KS 67226
Web: http://www.vatterott-college.edu
Accreditation: Accrediting Commission of Career Schools and Colleges of Technology
Programs Offered:
CAD/CADD drafting/design technology; computer programming; computer technology/computer systems technology; electrician; heating, air conditioning and refrigeration technology; medical/clinical assistant
Institution Contact: Office of Admissions
Phone: 316-634-0066
Fax: 316-634-0002
E-mail: wichita@vatterott-college.edu
Admission Contact: Diana Preston, Office of Admissions
Phone: 316-634-0066
Fax: 316-634-0002
E-mail: dpreston@vatterott-college.edu

WICHITA TECHNICAL INSTITUTE

2051 South Meridian

Wichita, KS 67213-1681
Web: http://www.wti.edu
Accreditation: Accrediting Commission of Career Schools and Colleges of Technology
Programs Offered:

computer technology/computer systems technology; electrical, electronic and communications engineering technology; heating, air conditioning and refrigeration technology

Enrollment: 350 students

Institution Contact: J. Barry Mannion, Director of Administration

Phone: 316-943-2241

Fax: 316-943-5438

E-mail: bmannion@wti.edu

Admission Contact: Christine Bell, Receptionist

Phone: 316-943-2241

Fax: 316-943-5438

E-mail: cbell@wti.edu

WRIGHT BUSINESS SCHOOL

8951 Metcalf Avenue
Overland Park, KS 66212

Programs Offered:

accounting; administrative assistant and secretarial science; information technology; medical/clinical assistant; medical insurance coding; medical transcription; surgical technology

Institution Contact: Admissions

Phone: 800-946-0348

WTI THE ELECTRONIC SCHOOL

3712 SW Burlingame Rd.
Topeka, KS 66609
Web: http://www.wti.edu

Accreditation: Accrediting Commission of Career Schools and Colleges of Technology

Programs Offered:

electrical, electronic and communications engineering technology; electrical/electronics equipment installation and repair

Institution Contact: Mr. Gary Hively, Director

Phone: 785-354-4568

Fax: 785-354-4541

E-mail: ghively@wti.edu

Admission Contact: Mr. Gary Hively, Vice President/Director of Admissions

Phone: 785-354-4568

Fax: 785-354-4541

E-mail: ghively@wti.edu

KENTUCKY

BROWN MACKIE COLLEGE, HOPKINSVILLE CAMPUS

4001 Ft. Campbell Boulevard
Hopkinsville, KY 42240
Web: http://www.retsmbi.com

Accreditation: Accrediting Council for Independent Colleges and Schools

Programs Offered:

accounting; business administration and management; CAD/CADD drafting/design technology; computer programming; computer software technology; computer systems networking and telecommunications; criminal justice/law enforcement administration; legal assistant/paralegal; medical/clinical assistant

Institution Contact:

Phone: 888-296-0262

BROWN MACKIE COLLEGE, LOUISVILLE CAMPUS

300 High Rise Drive
Louisville, KY 40213
Web: http://www.retsaec.com

Programs Offered:

business administration and management; CAD/CADD drafting/design technology; computer and information sciences related; pre-law studies

Institution Contact:

Phone: 888-476-1266

BROWN MACKIE COLLEGE, NORTHERN KENTUCKY CAMPUS

309 Buttermilk Pike
Fort Mitchell, KY 41017
Web: http://socaec.com

Accreditation: Accrediting Council for Independent Colleges and Schools

Programs Offered:

accounting technology and bookkeeping; business administration and management; CAD/CADD drafting/design technology; computer and information sciences related; computer programming; computer software technology; criminal justice/law enforcement administration; legal assistant/paralegal; medical/clinical assistant; nursing (licensed practical/vocational nurse training); pharmacy technician

Enrollment: 476 students
Institution Contact: Mr. Ricky Dean Lemmel, President
Phone: 859-341-5627 ext. 5009
Fax: 859-341-6483
E-mail: rlemmel@edmc.edu
Admission Contact: Ms. Joanne Dellefield, Director of Admissions
Phone: 859-341-5627
Fax: 859-341-6483
E-mail: jdellefield@edmc.edu

 DAYMAR COLLEGE
4400 Breckenridge Lane, Suite 415
Louisville, KY 40218
Web: http://www.daymarcollege.edu
Accreditation: Accrediting Council for Independent Colleges and Schools
Programs Offered:
business administration and management; computer systems networking and telecommunications; criminal justice/police science; health information/medical records administration; health information/medical records technology; legal assistant/paralegal; medical transcription; pharmacy technician
Institution Contact: Miss Shawn McDaniel, Associate Director of Admissions
Phone: 502-495-1040
Fax: 502-495-1518
E-mail: smcdaniel@daymarcollege.edu
Admission Contact: Miss Shawn McDaniel, Associate Director of Admissions
Phone: 502-495-1040
Fax: 502-495-1518
E-mail: smcdaniel@daymarcollege.edu

DAYMAR COLLEGE
76 Carothers Road
Newport, KY 41071
Institution Contact: Robert Tharp
Phone: 859-291-0800
Fax: 859-491-7500

 DAYMAR COLLEGE
3361 Buckland Square
Owensboro, KY 42301
Web: http://www.daymarcollege.edu

Accreditation: Accrediting Council for Independent Colleges and Schools
Programs Offered:
accounting; business administration and management; computer/information technology services administration related; computer software and media applications related; computer systems networking and telecommunications; legal administrative assistant/secretary; legal assistant/paralegal; medical/clinical assistant; medical insurance coding; medical insurance/medical billing; pharmacy technician; phlebotomy
Enrollment: 320 students
Institution Contact: Ms. Vickie McDougal, Director of Admissions
Phone: 270-926-4040
Fax: 270-685-4090

 DRAUGHONS JUNIOR COLLEGE
2421 Fitzgerald Industrial Drive
Bowling Green, KY 42101
Web: http://www.draughons.edu
Accreditation: Accrediting Council for Independent Colleges and Schools
Programs Offered:
accounting; business administration and management; computer/information technology administration and management; computer technology/computer systems technology; criminal justice/law enforcement administration; e-commerce; health/health care administration; legal assistant/paralegal; medical/clinical assistant; pharmacy technician
Enrollment: 450 students
Institution Contact: Mrs. Melva P. Hale, Director
Phone: 270-843-6750
Fax: 270-843-6976
E-mail: mhale@draughons.edu
Admission Contact: Mrs. Traci Henderson, Director of Admissions
Phone: 270-843-6750
Fax: 270-843-6976
E-mail: thenderson@draughons.edu

ITT TECHNICAL INSTITUTE
10509 Timberwood Circle, Suite 100
Louisville, KY 40223-5392
Web: http://www.itt-tech.edu
Accreditation: Accrediting Council for Independent Colleges and Schools

Programs Offered:
accounting and business/management; animation, interactive technology, video graphics and special effects; business administration and management; CAD/CADD drafting/design technology; communications technology; computer and information systems security; computer engineering technology; computer software and media applications; computer software engineering; computer systems networking and telecommunications; criminal justice/police science; digital communication and media/multimedia; electrical, electronic and communications engineering technology; technology management; web page, digital/multimedia and information resources design

Institution Contact: Mr. Alan Crews, Director
Phone: 502-327-7424
Admission Contact: Mr. Steve Allen, Director of Recruitment
Phone: 502-327-7424

MAP LOUISVILLE TECHNICAL INSTITUTE

3901 Atkinson Square Drive
Louisville, KY 40218-4528
Web: http://www.louisvilletech.com
Accreditation: Accrediting Council for Independent Colleges and Schools
Programs Offered:
animation, interactive technology, video graphics and special effects; architectural drafting and CAD/CADD; architectural engineering technology; CAD/CADD drafting/design technology; commercial and advertising art; computer and information systems security; computer engineering related; computer engineering technology; computer graphics; computer/information technology administration and management; computer/information technology services administration related; computer installation and repair technology; computer systems networking and telecommunications; computer/technical support; computer technology/computer systems technology; design and visual communications; desktop publishing and digital imaging design; drafting and design technology; drafting/design engineering technologies related; drawing; electrical and electronic engineering technologies related; electrical/electronics equipment installation and repair; engineering technology; graphic communications; hydraulics and fluid power technology; industrial design; industrial electronics technology;

industrial mechanics and maintenance technology; industrial technology; information technology; instrumentation technology; interior design; intermedia/multimedia; internet information systems; mechanical design technology; mechanical drafting and CAD/CADD; mechanical engineering/mechanical technology; mechanical engineering technologies related; robotics technology; web/multimedia management and webmaster; web page, digital/multimedia and information resources design

Enrollment: 610 students
Institution Contact: Mr. David B. Keene, Executive Director
Phone: 502-456-6509
Fax: 502-456-2341
E-mail: dkeene@louisvilletech.com
Admission Contact: Mr. George Wright, Director of Admissions
Phone: 502-456-6509
Fax: 502-456-2341
E-mail: gwright@louisvilletech.com

NATIONAL COLLEGE OF BUSINESS & TECHNOLOGY

115 East Lexington Avenue
MAP Danville, KY 40422
Web: http://www.ncbt.edu
Accreditation: Accrediting Council for Independent Colleges and Schools
Programs Offered:
accounting; administrative assistant and secretarial science; business administration and management; computer and information sciences related; medical/clinical assistant; medical insurance coding; medical transcription

Institution Contact: Admissions Department
Phone: 859-236-6991
Fax: 859-236-1063

NATIONAL COLLEGE OF BUSINESS & TECHNOLOGY

7627 Ewing Boulevard
MAP Florence, KY 41042
Web: http://www.ncbt.edu
Accreditation: Accrediting Council for Independent Colleges and Schools
Programs Offered:
accounting; administrative assistant and secretarial science; business administration and management;

computer and information sciences related; medical/clinical assistant; medical insurance coding; medical transcription; pharmacy technician
Institution Contact: Admissions Department
Phone: 859-525-6510
Fax: 859-525-8961

 NATIONAL COLLEGE OF BUSINESS & TECHNOLOGY
628 East Main Street
Lexington, KY 40508
Web: http://www.ncbt.edu
Accreditation: Accrediting Council for Independent Colleges and Schools
Programs Offered:
accounting; administrative assistant and secretarial science; business administration and management; computer and information sciences related; executive assistant/executive secretary; legal administrative assistant/secretary; medical administrative assistant and medical secretary; medical/clinical assistant; medical insurance coding; medical transcription; pharmacy technician
Enrollment: 325 students
Institution Contact: Ms. Tracy Harris, Director of Institutional Reporting
Phone: 540-986-1800
Fax: 540-444-4198
E-mail: tharris@ncbt.edu
Admission Contact: Ms. Carolyn Howard
Phone: 859-253-0621
Fax: 859-233-3054
E-mail: choward@educorp.edu

NATIONAL COLLEGE OF BUSINESS & TECHNOLOGY
4205 Dixie Highway
Louisville, KY 40216
Web: http://www.ncbt.edu
Accreditation:
Accrediting Council for Independent Colleges and Schools
Programs Offered:
accounting; business administration and management; computer and information sciences related; health information/medical records technology; medical administrative assistant and medical secretary; medical/clinical assistant; medical insurance coding; medical transcription; pharmacy technician

Institution Contact: Admissions Department
Phone: 502-447-7634
Fax: 502-447-7665

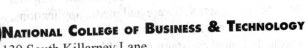 **NATIONAL COLLEGE OF BUSINESS & TECHNOLOGY**
288 South Mayo Trail, Suite 2
Pikeville, KY 41501
Web: http://www.ncbt.edu
Accreditation: Accrediting Council for Independent Colleges and Schools
Programs Offered:
accounting; administrative assistant and secretarial science; business administration and management; computer and information sciences related; medical/clinical assistant; medical insurance coding; medical transcription; pharmacy technician
Enrollment: 225 students
Institution Contact: Ms. Tracy Harris, Director of Institutional Reporting
Phone: 540-986-1800
Fax: 540-444-4198
E-mail: tharris@ncbt.edu
Admission Contact: Mr. Jerry Lafferty, Campus Director
Phone: 606-432-5477
Fax: 606-437-4952
E-mail: lafferty@educorp.edu

NATIONAL COLLEGE OF BUSINESS & TECHNOLOGY
139 South Killarney Lane
Richmond, KY 40475
Web: http://www.ncbt.edu
Accreditation: Accrediting Council for Independent Colleges and Schools
Programs Offered:
accounting; administrative assistant and secretarial science; business administration and management; computer and information sciences related; medical administrative assistant and medical secretary; medical/clinical assistant; medical insurance coding; medical transcription; pharmacy technician
Enrollment: 343 students
Institution Contact: Ms. Tracy Harris, Director of Institutional Reporting
Phone: 540-986-1800 ext. 108
Fax: 540-444-4199
E-mail: tharris@ncbt.edu

Admission Contact: Ms. Keeley Gadd, Campus Director
Phone: 859-623-8956
Fax: 859-624-5544
E-mail: kgadd@educorp.edu

PADUCAH TECHNICAL COLLEGE

509 South 30th Street
Paducah, KY 42001
Programs Offered
administrative assistant and secretarial science; electrical and electronic engineering technologies related; receptionist
Institution Contact: Jesse Adkinson
Phone: 270-444-9676
E-mail: jadkinson@paducahtech.com

SOUTHWESTERN COLLEGE OF BUSINESS

8095 Connector Drive
Florence, KY 41042
Web: http://www.swcollege.net
Accreditation: Accrediting Council for Independent Colleges and Schools
Programs Offered:
accounting; accounting technology and bookkeeping; administrative assistant and secretarial science; business administration and management; computer science; computer software and media applications; medical administrative assistant and medical secretary; medical/clinical assistant; medical insurance coding; medical insurance/medical billing; phlebotomy
Enrollment: 237 students
Institution Contact: Ms. Tina Marie Barnes, Executive Director
Phone: 859-282-9999
Fax: 859-282-7940
E-mail: tbarnes@swcollege.net
Admission Contact: Laura Paletta, Director of Admissions
Phone: 859-282-9999
Fax: 859-282-7940
E-mail: doaflorence@lincolnedu.com

SPENCERIAN COLLEGE

4627 Dixie Highway
Louisville, KY 40216

Accreditation: Accrediting Council for Independent Colleges and Schools
Programs Offered:
accounting; administrative assistant and secretarial science; business administration and management; computer/information technology services administration related; executive assistant/executive secretary; gene therapy; health unit coordinator/ward clerk; medical administrative assistant and medical secretary; medical/clinical assistant; medical insurance coding; medical insurance/medical billing; medical office management; medical radiologic technology; medical transcription; nursing (licensed practical/vocational nurse training); nursing (registered nurse training); surgical technology
Enrollment: 1,327 students
Institution Contact: Ms. Jan M. Gordon, Executive Director
Phone: 502-447-1000 ext. 7802
Fax: 502-447-4574
E-mail: jgordon@spencerian.edu
Admission Contact: Ms. Terri Thomas, Director of Admissions
Phone: 502-447-1000
Fax: 502-447-4574
E-mail: tthomas@spencerian.edu

SPENCERIAN COLLEGE - LEXINGTON

2355 Harrodsburg Road
Lexington, KY 40504
Web: http://www.spencerian.edu
Programs Offered:
computer engineering technology; computer graphics; computer technology/computer systems technology; mechanical design technology
Admission Contact: Ms. Peggy O'Donell, Director of Admissions
Phone: 859-223-9608
Fax: 859-224-7744
E-mail: podonnell@spencerian.edu

SULLIVAN UNIVERSITY

2355 Harrodsburg Road
Lexington, KY 40504
Web: http://www.sullivan.edu
Accreditation: Southern Association of Colleges and Schools

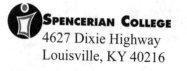

Programs Offered:

accounting; administrative assistant and secretarial science; business administration and management; child care and support services management; computer and information sciences related; computer programming; computer programming (specific applications); computer/technical support; executive assistant/executive secretary; human resources management; information technology; legal administrative assistant/secretary; legal assistant/paralegal; marketing/marketing management; medical administrative assistant and medical secretary; medical/clinical assistant; medical office management; medical radiologic technology; office management; receptionist; tourism and travel services management

Enrollment: 1,219 students

Institution Contact: Mr. David McGuire, Executive Director

Phone: 859-276-4357

Fax: 859-276-1153

E-mail: dmcguire@sullivan.edu

Admission Contact: Ms. Sue Michael, Director of Admissions

Phone: 859-276-4357

Fax: 859-276-1153

E-mail: smichael@sullivan.edu

 SULLIVAN UNIVERSITY

3101 Bardstown Road

Louisville, KY 40205

Web: http://www.sullivan.edu

Accreditation: Southern Association of Colleges and Schools

Programs Offered:

accounting; administrative assistant and secretarial science; baking and pastry arts; business administration and management; child care and support services management; child care provision; computer/information technology administration and management; computer installation and repair technology; computer programming; computer programming (specific applications); computer software engineering; computer systems networking and telecommunications; computer/technical support; culinary arts; executive assistant/executive secretary; finance; food preparation; hospitality administration; hotel/motel administration; information technology; internet information systems; legal administrative assistant/secretary; legal assistant/paralegal;

logistics and materials management; marketing/marketing management; medical administrative assistant and medical secretary; medical office management; restaurant, culinary, and catering management; tourism and travel services management; word processing

Enrollment: 3,264 students

Institution Contact: Mr. Stephen Coppock, EdD, Executive Vice President/CEO

Phone: 502-456-6506 ext. 332

Fax: 502-456-0040

E-mail: gscoppock@sullivan.edu

Admission Contact: Mr. Greg Cawthon , Director of Admissions

Phone: 502-456-6505 ext. 208

Fax: 502-456-0040

E-mail: gcawthon@sullivan.edu

LOUISIANA

AMERICAN COMMERCIAL COLLEGE

3014 Knight Street

Shreveport, LA 71105

Web: http://www.acc-careers.com

Accreditation: Accrediting Council for Independent Colleges and Schools

Programs Offered:

accounting; administrative assistant and secretarial science; allied health and medical assisting services related; business operations support and secretarial services related; data entry/microcomputer applications; medical office computer specialist; medical transcription

Enrollment: 79 students

Institution Contact: Judy Killough, Director

Phone: 318-861-2112

Fax: 318-861-2119

E-mail: jkillough@acc-careers.com

Admission Contact: Jamie Waites, Assistant Director

Phone: 318-861-2112

Fax: 318-261-2119

E-mail: jwaites@acc-careers.com

AYERS INSTITUTE, INC.

PO Box 3941

Shreveport, LA 71133-3941

Accreditation: Council on Occupational Education

Programs Offered:

heating, air conditioning and refrigeration technology; medical/clinical assistant; pharmacy technician
Enrollment: 220 students
Institution Contact: Mr. Bruce Busada, President
Phone: 318-635-0280
Fax: 318-636-9736
E-mail: response@ayersinstitute.com

BLUE CLIFF COLLEGE

3501 Severn Avenue, Suite 20
Metairie, LA 70002
Accreditation: Accrediting Commission of Career Schools and Colleges of Technology
Programs Offered:
massage therapy
Enrollment: 180 students
Institution Contact: Mr. Doug Robertson, Director of Education
Phone: 504-456-3141 ext. 104
Fax: 504-456-7849
E-mail: dougr@bluecliff.com
Admission Contact: Ms. Cathy Goodwin, Director of Admissions
Phone: 504-456-3141 ext. 122
Fax: 504-456-7849
E-mail: cathyg@bluecliffcollege.com

BLUE CLIFF COLLEGE - LAFAYETTE

100 Asma Boulevard, Suite 350
Lafayette, LA 70508
Web: http://www.bluecliffcollege.com
Accreditation: Accrediting Commission of Career Schools and Colleges of Technology
Programs Offered:
information technology; massage therapy
Institution Contact: Admissions
Phone: 337-269-0620
E-mail: admissions_laf@bluecliffcollege.com

BLUE CLIFF COLLEGE - SHREVEPORT

200 North Thomas Drive , Suite A
Shreveport, LA 71107
Accreditation: Accrediting Commission of Career Schools and Colleges of Technology
Programs Offered:
massage therapy; medical/clinical assistant

Enrollment: 61 students
Institution Contact: Jennifer Riffel, Student Services
Phone: 318-425-7941
Fax: 318-425-3740
E-mail: jenniferr@bluecliffcollege.com
Admission Contact: Joey Marange, Admissions Officer
Phone: 318-425-7941
Fax: 318-425-3740
E-mail: joeym@bluecliffcollege.com

BRYMAN COLLEGE

1201 Elmwood Park Boulevard, Suite 600
New Orleans, LA 70123
Web: http://www.bryman-college.com
Accreditation: Accrediting Commission of Career Schools and Colleges of Technology
Programs Offered:
dental assisting; medical administrative assistant and medical secretary; medical/clinical assistant; medical insurance coding; medical insurance/medical billing; pharmacy technician
Enrollment: 545 students
Institution Contact: Mr. Tom Bonesteel, President
Phone: 504-733-7117 ext. 101
Fax: 504-734-1217
E-mail: mbonesteel@cci.edu
Admission Contact: Richard Beard, Director of Admissions
Phone: 504-733-7117
Fax: 504-734-1217
E-mail: rbeard@cci.edu

CAREER TECHNICAL COLLEGE

2319 Louisville Avenue
Monroe, LA 71201
Web: http://www.careertc.com
Accreditation:
Council on Occupational Education
Programs Offered:
business administration and management; computer/information technology services administration related; health and medical administrative services related; health information/medical records technology; massage therapy; medical administrative assistant and medical secretary; medical/clinical assistant; medical insurance coding; phlebotomy; radiologic technology/science; surgical technology

Enrollment: 510 students
Institution Contact: Rick Nail, College Director
Phone: 318-323-2889
Fax: 318-324-9883
E-mail: rnail@careertc.com

CAREER TECHNICAL COLLEGE

1227 Shreveport-Barksdale Hwy.
Shreveport, LA 71105
Institution Contact: Mr. Bret Johnson

DELTA SCHOOL OF BUSINESS & TECHNOLOGY

517 Broad Street
Lake Charles, LA 70601
Web: http://www.deltatech.edu
Accreditation: Accrediting Council for Independent Colleges and Schools
Programs Offered:
accounting; administrative assistant and secretarial science; business administration and management; CAD/CADD drafting/design technology; clinical/medical laboratory technology; computer/information technology administration and management; computer/information technology services administration related; computer software technology; computer systems analysis; computer systems networking and telecommunications; computer/technical support; computer technology/computer systems technology; drafting and design technology; executive assistant/executive secretary; health information/medical records technology; information technology; legal administrative assistant/secretary; medical administrative assistant and medical secretary; medical/clinical assistant; medical office management; medical transcription; nursing assistant/aide and patient care assistant; office occupations and clerical services; physical therapist assistant; receptionist
Enrollment: 420 students
Institution Contact: Mr. Michael Williams, Vice President
Phone: 337-439-5765 ext. 1115
Fax: 337-436-5151
E-mail: mikew@deltatech.edu
Admission Contact: Mrs. Susan Ardoin, Director of Admissions
Phone: 337-439-5765
Fax: 337-436-5151

E-mail: susan@deltatech.edu

EASTERN COLLEGE OF HEALTH VOCATIONS

3321 Hessmer Avenue, Suite 200
Metairie, LA 70002
Institution Contact:
Phone: 504-885-3353
Fax: 504-885-6721

GRANTHAM UNIVERSITY

Two Pershing Square, 2300 Main Street, 9th Floor
Kansas City, MO 64108
Web: http://www.grantham.edu
Accreditation: Distance Education and Training Council
Programs Offered:
business administration and management; computer and information sciences related; computer engineering technology; computer software engineering; criminal justice/law enforcement administration; electrical, electronic and communications engineering technology; engineering technology; general studies; information science/studies; information technology
Enrollment: 8,000 students
Institution Contact: Johanna Altland, Communications Manager
Phone: 703-778-8500 ext. 513
Fax: 703-465-1273
E-mail: jla@granthameducation.com
Admission Contact: Ms. DeAnn Wandler, Director of Admissions
Phone: 816-448-3608
Fax: 816-448-3796
E-mail: deann@grantham.edu

GRETNA CAREER COLLEGE

1415 Whitney Avenue
Gretna, LA 70053
Web: http://www.gretnacareercollege.edu
Accreditation: Accrediting Commission of Career Schools and Colleges of Technology
Programs Offered:
accounting technology and bookkeeping; administrative assistant and secretarial science; adult development and aging; allied health and medical assisting services related; autobody/collision and repair tech-

nology; business automation/technology/data entry; clinical/medical laboratory assistant; computer/information technology services administration related; data entry/microcomputer applications related; e-commerce; executive assistant/executive secretary; health aide; health and medical administrative services related; health information/medical records technology; home health aide/home attendant; medical administrative assistant and medical secretary; medical/clinical assistant; medical insurance coding; medical insurance/medical billing; medical office assistant; medical office computer specialist; medical office management; medical reception; medical transcription; nursing assistant/aide and patient care assistant; office management; office occupations and clerical services; phlebotomy; receptionist; retailing; word processing

Enrollment: 125 students
Institution Contact: Mr. Nick Randazzo, President
Phone: 504-366-5409
Fax: 504-365-1004
E-mail: admissions@gretnacareercollege.com
Admission Contact: Ms. Ava Himes, Admissions Representative
Phone: 504-366-5409
Fax: 504-365-1004
E-mail: admissions@gretnacareercollege.com

HERZING COLLEGE

2400 Veterans Boulevard, Suite 410
Kenner, LA 70062
Web: http://www.herzing.edu
Accreditation: Accrediting Council for Independent Colleges and Schools; North Central Association of Colleges and Schools
Programs Offered:

business administration and management; CAD/CADD drafting/design technology; computer programming; computer systems networking and telecommunications; legal assistant/paralegal; medical insurance coding; pre-law studies; technology management

Enrollment: 279 students
Institution Contact: Ms. Darla Chin, Campus President
Phone: 504-733-0074
Fax: 504-733-0020
E-mail: dchin@nor.herzing.edu
Admission Contact: Ms. Genny Bordelon, Admissions Director
Phone: 504-733-0074

Fax: 504-733-0020
E-mail: genny@nor.herzing.edu

ITI TECHNICAL COLLEGE

13944 Airline Highway
Baton Rouge, LA 70817-5998
Web: http://www.iticollege.edu
Accreditation: Accrediting Commission of Career Schools and Colleges of Technology
Programs Offered:

business automation/technology/data entry; business/corporate communications; business machine repair; CAD/CADD drafting/design technology; civil engineering technology; computer and information systems security; computer engineering technology; computer hardware engineering; computer/information technology administration and management; computer/information technology services administration related; computer installation and repair technology; computer programming; computer programming related; computer programming (specific applications); computer software and media applications; computer software and media applications related; computer software technology; computer systems analysis; computer systems networking and telecommunications; computer/technical support; computer technology/computer systems technology; data entry/microcomputer applications; data entry/microcomputer applications related; data modeling/warehousing and database administration; data processing and data processing technology; desktop publishing and digital imaging design; digital communication and media/multimedia; drafting and design technology; drawing; electrical, electronic and communications engineering technology; electrical/electronics equipment installation and repair; electrician; engineering technology; heating, air conditioning and refrigeration technology; heating, air conditioning, ventilation and refrigeration maintenance technology; hydraulics and fluid power technology; industrial design; industrial electronics technology; industrial mechanics and maintenance technology; industrial radiologic technology; industrial technology; information science/studies; information technology; instrumentation technology; internet information systems; management information systems; mechanical design technology; mechanical engineering/mechanical technology; petroleum technology; system administration; system, networking, and LAN/WAN management;

telecommunications; telecommunications technology; web/multimedia management and webmaster; web page, digital/multimedia and information resources design; word processing

Enrollment: 349 students
Institution Contact: Mr. Mark Worthy, Vice President
Phone: 225-752-4230 ext. 212
Fax: 225-756-0903
E-mail: mworthy@iticollege.edu
Admission Contact: Mr. Joe Martin, III, President
Phone: 225-752-4230 ext. 213
Fax: 225-756-0903
E-mail: jmartin@iticollege.edu

 ITT TECHNICAL INSTITUTE
140 James Drive East
Saint Rose, LA 70087
Web: http://www.itt-tech.edu
Accreditation: Accrediting Council for Independent Colleges and Schools
Programs Offered:
animation, interactive technology, video graphics and special effects; communications technology; computer and information systems security; computer engineering technology; computer software and media applications; computer software engineering; computer systems networking and telecommunications; digital communication and media/multimedia; electrical, electronic and communications engineering technology; technology management; web page, digital/multimedia and information resources design
Institution Contact: Ms. Brenda Nash, Director
Phone: 504-463-0338
Admission Contact: Ms. Heidi Munoz, Director of Recruitment
Phone: 504-463-0338

MEDVANCE INSTITUTE
9255 Interline Avenue
Baton Rouge, LA 70809
Accreditation: Accrediting Bureau of Health Education Schools; Council on Occupational Education
Programs Offered: clinical/medical laboratory technology; medical/clinical assistant; medical insurance coding; medical radiologic technology; pharmacy technician; phlebotomy; radiologic technology/science; surgical technology

Enrollment: 365 students
Institution Contact: Mr. Gene Herman, Campus Director
Phone: 225-248-1015 ext. 207
Fax: 225-248-9517
E-mail: gene.herman@medvance.edu
Admission Contact: Mr. Steve Giddings, Director of Admissions
Phone: 225-248-1015 ext. 203
Fax: 225-248-9517
E-mail: sgiddings@medvance.edu

 REMINGTON COLLEGE - BATON ROUGE CAMPUS
10551 Coursey Boulevard
Baton Rouge, LA 70816
Web: http://www.remingtoncollege.edu
Accreditation: Accrediting Council for Independent Colleges and Schools
Programs Offered:
business administration and management; computer engineering related; computer systems networking and telecommunications; criminal justice/police science; medical/clinical assistant; medical insurance coding; pharmacy technician
Enrollment: 410 students
Institution Contact: Ms. Midge Jacobson, Campus President
Phone: 225-236-3200
Fax: 225-922-9569
E-mail: midge.jacobson@remingtoncollege.edu
Admission Contact: Mrs. Betina Yurkus, Director of Recruitment
Phone: 225-236-3200
Fax: 225-922-9569
E-mail: betina.yurkus@remingtoncollege.edu

REMINGTON COLLEGE - LAFAYETTE CAMPUS
303 Rue Louis XIV
Lafayette, LA 70508
Web: http://www.remingtoncollege.edu
Accreditation: Accrediting Council for Independent Colleges and Schools
Programs Offered:
business administration and management; computer systems networking and telecommunications; criminal justice/police science; electrical, electronic and communications engineering technology; medical/clinical

assistant; medical insurance coding

Enrollment: 427 students

Institution Contact: Mrs. JoAnn Boudreaux, Interim Campus President

Phone: 337-981-4010

Fax: 337-983-7130

E-mail: joann.boudreaux@remingtoncollege.edu

Admission Contact: Mr. Gary Schwartz, Director of Recruitment

Phone: 337-981-4010

Fax: 337-983-7130

E-mail: gary.schwartz@remingtoncollege.edu

REMINGTON COLLEGE - NEW ORLEANS CAMPUS

321 Veterans Memorial Boulevard

Metairie, LA 70005

Web: http://www.remingtoncollege.edu

Accreditation: Accrediting Commission of Career Schools and Colleges of Technology

Programs Offered:

administrative assistant and secretarial science; commercial and advertising art; computer/information technology administration and management; drafting and design technology; electrical, electronic and communications engineering technology; engineering technology; system, networking, and LAN/WAN management

Institution Contact: Mr. Gregg Falcon, Campus President

Phone: 504-831-8889 ext. 246

Fax: 504-831-6803

E-mail: gregg.falcon@remingtoncollege.edu

Admission Contact: Mr. Roy Kimble, Director of Recruitment

Phone: 504-831-8889

Fax: 504-831-6803

E-mail: roy.kimble@remingtoncollege.edu

ANDOVER COLLEGE

901 Washington Avenue

Portland, ME 04103-2791

Web: http://www.andovercollege.com/

Programs Offered:

accounting; business administration and management;

computer technology/computer systems technology; criminal justice/police science; education; legal assistant/paralegal; medical/clinical assistant; tourism and travel services management

Institution Contact: Admissions

Phone: 207-774-6126

NEW ENGLAND SCHOOL OF COMMUNICATIONS

1 College Circle

Bangor, ME 04401-2999

Web: http://www.nescom.edu

Accreditation: Accrediting Commission of Career Schools and Colleges of Technology

Programs Offered:

advertising; broadcast journalism; business/corporate communications; cinematography and film/video production; communications technology; computer software and media applications; desktop publishing and digital imaging design; marketing/marketing management; marketing related; radio and television broadcasting technology; recording arts technology; speech and rhetoric; web/multimedia management and webmaster; web page, digital/multimedia and information resources design

Enrollment: 305 students

Institution Contact: Mr. Benjamin E. Haskell, II, Executive Vice President/Academic Dean

Phone: 207-941-7176 ext. 1094

Fax: 207-947-3987

E-mail: ben@nescom.edu

Admission Contact: Mrs. Louise G. Grant, Director of Admissions

Phone: 207-941-7176 ext. 1093

Fax: 207-947-3987

E-mail: grantl@nescom.edu

BALTIMORE SCHOOL OF MASSAGE

517 Progress Drive, Suite A-L

Linthicum, MD 21090

Web: http://steinered.com

Accreditation: Accrediting Commission of Career Schools and Colleges of Technology

Programs Offered:

alternative and complementary medical support ser-

vices related; Asian bodywork therapy; facial treatment/facialist; massage therapy
Enrollment: 349 students
Institution Contact: Mr. Richard Rynders, Campus Director
Phone: 410-636-7929
Fax: 410-636-7857
E-mail: richardr@steinerleisure.com
Admission Contact: Admissions Department
Phone: 410-636-7929
Fax: 410-636-7857
E-mail: richardr@steinerleisure.com

EMPIRE BEAUTY SCHOOL
9616 Reisterstown Rd., Suite 105
Owings Mills, MD 21117
Institution Contact: Ms. Kia Brown
Phone: 410-581-0317
Fax: 410-581-8675

EVEREST INSTITUTE
8757 Georgia Avenue
Silver Spring, MD 20910
Web: http://www.everest-institute.com/
Programs Offered:
medical/clinical assistant
Institution Contact: Admissions
Phone: 888-741-4270

HAGERSTOWN BUSINESS COLLEGE
18618 Crestwood Drive
Hagerstown, MD 21742
Web: http://www.hagerstownbusinesscol.org
Accreditation: Accrediting Council for Independent Colleges and Schools
Programs Offered:
accounting; administrative assistant and secretarial science; business administration and management; commercial and advertising art; computer graphics; computer/information technology administration and management; computer/information technology services administration related; computer installation and repair technology; computer programming; computer programming related; computer programming (specific applications); computer programming (vendor/product certification); computer software and media applications; computer software and media applications related; computer software technology; computer/technical support; computer technology/computer systems technology; criminal justice/law enforcement administration; customer service management; executive assistant/executive secretary; forensic science and technology; health information/medical records administration; health information/medical records technology; health unit coordinator/ward clerk; information technology; legal administrative assistant/secretary; legal assistant/paralegal; marketing/marketing management; medical administrative assistant and medical secretary; medical/clinical assistant; medical insurance coding; medical insurance/medical billing; medical office management; medical reception; medical transcription; office occupations and clerical services; receptionist; system administration
Enrollment: 950 students
Institution Contact: Mr. W. Christopher Motz, Executive Director
Phone: 301-739-2680 ext. 128
Fax: 301-791-7661
E-mail: cmotz@hagerstownbusinesscol.org
Admission Contact: Ms. Jessica Border, Admissions Representative
Phone: 800-422-2670
Fax: 301-791-7661
E-mail: info@hagerstownbusinesscol.org

HARRISON CAREER INSTITUTE
1040 Park Avenue, Suite 100
Baltimore, MD 21201
Web: http://www.hci.edu
Accreditation: Accrediting Commission of Career Schools and Colleges of Technology
Programs Offered:
cardiovascular technology; electrocardiograph technology; medical/clinical assistant; medical insurance coding; medical insurance/medical billing; medical office computer specialist; medical transcription; phlebotomy
Enrollment: 290 students
Institution Contact: Abdul-Malik Muhammad, Director
Phone: 410-962-0303
E-mail: mmuhammad@hci-inst.net

ITT TECHNICAL INSTITUTE
11301 Red Run Boulevard

Owings Mills, MD 21117
Web: http://www.itt-tech.edu
Programs Offered:
CAD/CADD drafting/design technology; computer and information systems security; computer programming; computer software and media applications; computer systems networking and telecommunications; electrical and electronic engineering technologies related
Phone: 443-394-7115

 LINCOLN TECHNICAL INSTITUTE

9325 Snowden River Parkway
Columbia, MD 21046
Web: http://www.lincolntech.com
Accreditation: Accrediting Commission of Career Schools and Colleges of Technology
Programs Offered:
automobile/automotive mechanics technology; automotive engineering technology; electrical and electronic engineering technologies related; heating, air conditioning and refrigeration technology
Institution Contact: Director of Admissions
Phone: 410-290-7100
Fax: 410-290-7880
E-mail: doacolumbia@lincolnedu.com

MEDIX SCHOOL
700 York Road
Towson, MD 21204-2511
Web: http://www.medixschooltowson.com
Accreditation: Accrediting Bureau of Health Education Schools
Programs Offered:
dental assisting; medical administrative assistant and medical secretary; medical/clinical assistant
Enrollment: 558 students
Institution Contact: Mr. Sean London, Director
Phone: 410-337-5155
Fax: 410-337-5104
E-mail: slondon@edaff.com
Admission Contact: Ms. Lisa Harper, Director of Admissions
Phone: 410-337-5155
Fax: 410-337-5104
E-mail: lharper@edaff.com

 NORTH AMERICAN TRADE SCHOOL
6901 Security Square Boulevard, Suite 16
Gwynn Oak, MD 21244
Programs Offered:
carpentry; diesel mechanics technology; electrical and electronic engineering technologies related
Institution Contact: Admissions
Phone: 410-298-4844
Fax: 410-298-0641

SANFORD-BROWN INSTITUTE
8401 Corporate Drive, Suite 500
Landover, MD 20785
Web: http://www.ultrasounddiagnosticschool.com/default.htm
Accreditation: Accrediting Bureau of Health Education Schools
Programs Offered:
cardiovascular technology; diagnostic medical sonography and ultrasound technology; medical/clinical assistant
Institution Contact: Ms. Janet L. Stanley, Executive Director
Phone: 301-918-8221
Fax: 301-918-8278
E-mail: janet.stanley@wix.net
Admission Contact: Mr. Kerry Haley, Director of Admissions
Phone: 301-918-8221
Fax: 301-918-8278
E-mail: kerry.haley@wix.net

TESST COLLEGE OF TECHNOLOGY
1520 South Caton Avenue
Baltimore, MD 21227-1063
Web: http://www.tesst.com
Accreditation: Accrediting Commission of Career Schools and Colleges of Technology
Programs Offered:
computer/information technology administration and management; computer/information technology services administration related; computer programming related; drafting and design technology; electrical, electronic and communications engineering technology; heating, air conditioning and refrigeration technology; information technology
Institution Contact: Ms. Susan Sherwood, Director

Phone: 410-644-6400
Fax: 410-644-6481
E-mail: ssherwood@tesst.com

TESST COLLEGE OF TECHNOLOGY
4600 Powder Mill Road, Suite 500
Beltsville, MD 20705
Web: http://www.tesst.com
Accreditation: Accrediting Commission of Career
Schools and Colleges of Technology
Programs Offered:
business automation/technology/data entry; business/
corporate communications; CAD/CADD drafting/de-
sign technology; communications technology; computer engineering technology; computer/information
technology services administration related; computer
installation and repair technology; computer software
and media applications; computer software engineering; computer systems networking and telecommunications; computer/technical support; computer technol-
ogy/computer systems technology; criminal justice/law
enforcement administration; data entry/microcomputer
applications; data entry/microcomputer applications
related; data processing and data processing technology; desktop publishing and digital imaging design;
drafting and design technology; electrical, electronic
and communications engineering technology; electrician; engineering technology; information science/
studies; information technology; massage therapy;
medical/clinical assistant; telecommunications; web
page, digital/multimedia and information resources
design; word processing
Enrollment: 611 students
Institution Contact: Mr. Reginald M. Morton, Execu-
tive Director
Phone: 301-937-8448
Fax: 301-937-5327
E-mail: rmorton@tesst.com
Admission Contact: Miss Tina Turk, Director of
Admissions
Phone: 301-937-8448
Fax: 301-937-5327
E-mail: tturk@tesst.com

TESST COLLEGE OF TECHNOLOGY
803 Glen Eagles Court
Towson, MD 21286

Web: http://www.tesst.com
Accreditation: Accrediting Commission of Career
Schools and Colleges of Technology
Programs Offered:
administrative assistant and secretarial science; com-
puter/information technology services administration
related; computer installation and repair technology;
computer systems networking and telecommunications;
computer technology/computer systems technology;
electrical, electronic and communications engineer-
ing technology; information science/studies; massage
therapy; medical/clinical assistant; telecommunications
Institution Contact: Mr. Ray Joll, Executive Director
Phone: 410-296-5350
Fax: 410-296-5356
E-mail: rjoll@tesst.com
Admission Contact: Ms. Alicia Hayman, Director of
Admissions
Phone: 410-296-5350
Fax: 410-296-5356
E-mail: ahayman@tesst.com

MASSACHUSETTS

BAY STATE COLLEGE
122 Commonwealth Avenue
Boston, MA 02116
Web: http://www.baystate.edu
Accreditation: New England Association of Schools
and Colleges
Programs Offered:
accounting; business administration and management;
computer and information sciences related; criminal
justice/law enforcement administration; fashion/ap-
parel design; fashion merchandising; general studies;
medical/clinical assistant; physical therapist assistant;
tourism and travel services management
Enrollment: 750 students
Institution Contact:
Phone: 617-236-8000
Fax: 617-536-1735

BRYMAN INSTITUTE
1505 Commonwealth Avenue
Brighton, MA 02135
Web: http://www.bryman-institute.com

Accreditation: Accrediting Commission of Career Schools and Colleges of Technology
Programs Offered:
dental assisting; massage therapy; medical administrative assistant and medical secretary; medical/clinical assistant
Admission Contact: Mr. Arthur Banaster, Director of Admissions
Phone: 617-783-9955
Fax: 617-783-1166
E-mail: abanaste@cci.edu

BRYMAN INSTITUTE
70 Everett Avenue, 4th Floor
Chelsea, MA 02150
Web: http://www.bryman-institute.com
Accreditation: Accrediting Commission of Career Schools and Colleges of Technology
Programs Offered:
massage therapy; medical/clinical assistant; pharmacy technician
Institution Contact: Kim Villarreal, School President
Phone: 617-889-5999
Fax: 617-889-0340
E-mail: kvillarr@cci.edu
Admission Contact: Mr. Carl Williams, Director of Admissions
Phone: 617-889-5999
Fax: 617-889-0340

CAREER EDUCATION INSTITUTE
375 Westgate Drive
Brockton, MA 02301-1818
Web: http://www.ceitraining.com
Accreditation: Accrediting Council for Independent Colleges and Schools
Programs Offered:
administrative assistant and secretarial science; anatomy; animation, interactive technology, video graphics and special effects; blood bank technology; business automation/technology/data entry; business machine repair; clinical/medical laboratory assistant; clinical/medical laboratory technology; computer and information systems security; computer graphics; computer/information technology administration and management; computer/information technology services administration related; computer installa-

tion and repair technology; computer programming; computer programming (specific applications); computer programming (vendor/product certification); computer software technology; computer systems networking and telecommunications; computer/technical support; computer technology/computer systems technology; data entry/microcomputer applications; data entry/microcomputer applications related; data processing and data processing technology; e-commerce; electrocardiograph technology; electroneurodiagnostic/electroencephalographic technology; executive assistant/executive secretary; gene therapy; health information/medical records administration; health information/medical records technology; hematology technology; hospital and health care facilities administration; information technology; legal administrative assistant/secretary; management information systems; massage therapy; medical administrative assistant and medical secretary; medical/clinical assistant; medical insurance coding; medical insurance/medical billing; medical office computer specialist; medical office management; medical radiologic technology; medical reception; medical transcription; office occupations and clerical services; physician assistant; receptionist; system administration; system, networking, and LAN/WAN management; web/multimedia management and webmaster; web page, digital/multimedia and information resources design; word processing
Enrollment: 300 students
Institution Contact: Mr. Wayne H. Mullin, Executive Director
Phone: 508-941-0730
Fax: 508-587-8436 E-mail: wmullin@ceitraining.com
Admission Contact: Mr. Steve Giddings, Director of Admissions
Phone: 508-941-0730
Fax: 508-587-8436
E-mail: sgiddings@ceitraining.com

CAREER EDUCATION INSTITUTE
211 Plain Street
Lowell, MA 01852
Web: http://www.ceitraining.com
Accreditation: Accrediting Council for Independent Colleges and Schools
Programs Offered:
computer and information sciences and support services related; massage therapy; medical administrative

assistant and medical secretary; medical/clinical assistant; pharmacy technician; system, networking, and LAN/WAN management
Institution Contact: Executive Director
Phone: 978-458-4800
Fax: 978-458-1287
E-mail: execdirlowell@lincontech.com

CATHERINE HINDS INSTITUTE OF ESTHETICS
300 Wildwood Avenue
Woburn, MA 01801
Web: http://www.catherinehinds.edu
Programs Offered:
aesthetician/esthetician and skin care
Enrollment: 150 students
Institution Contact: Kimberly St. Cyr, Director of Marketing and Student Recruitment
Phone: 781-935-3344 ext. 227
Fax: 781-932-6215
E-mail: kstcyr@catherinehinds.edu
Admission Contact: Valerie Sclafani, Admissions Representative
Phone: 781-934-3344 ext. 247
Fax: 781-932-6215
E-mail: vsclafani@catherinehinds.edu

COMPUTER-ED INSTITUTE
5 Middlesex Avenue
Somerville, MA 02145
Web: http://www.ceitraining.com
Accreditation: Accrediting Council for Independent Colleges and Schools
Programs Offered:
computer/technical support; massage therapy; medical administrative assistant and medical secretary; medical/clinical assistant; pharmacy technician; system administration
Institution Contact: Executive Director
Phone: 617-776-3500
Fax: 617-776-1899
E-mail: execdirsomerville@lincolntech.com

EMPIRE BEAUTY SCHOOL
867 Boylston St.
Boston, MA 2199
Institution Contact: Mr. Bill Burns

Phone: 617-424-6565
Fax: 617-266-1884

EMPIRE BEAUTY SCHOOL
384 Main St.
Malden, MA 2148
Institution Contact: Ms. Denise Hickey
Phone: 781-324-3400
Fax: 781-397-8442

GIBBS COLLEGE
126 Newbury Street
Boston, MA 02116
Web: http://www.gibbsboston.com
Accreditation: Accrediting Council for Independent Colleges and Schools
Programs Offered:
accounting; business administration and management; commercial and advertising art; computer/information technology administration and management; digital communication and media/multimedia; legal administrative assistant/secretary; medical administrative assistant and medical secretary
Enrollment: 571 students
Institution Contact: Mr. Stephen Bonkowski, President
Phone: 617-578-7117
Fax: 617-578-7181
E-mail: sbonkowski@gibbsboston.edu
Admission Contact: Ms. Ida N. Zecco, Vice President of Admissions
Phone: 617-578-7716
Fax: 617-578-7163
E-mail: izecco@gibbsboston.edu

HALLMARK INSTITUTE OF PHOTOGRAPHY
PO Box 308
Turners Falls, MA 01376-0308
Web: http://www.hallmark.edu
Accreditation: Accrediting Commission of Career Schools and Colleges of Technology
Programs Offered:
photography
Enrollment: 227 students
Institution Contact: Mr. George Rosa, III, President
Phone: 413-863-2478
Fax: 413-863-4118

E-mail: george@hallmark.edu
Admission Contact: Ms. Shelley Nicholson, Director of Enrollment Services
Phone: 413-863-2478
Fax: 413-863-4118
E-mail: shelley@hallmark.edu

ITT TECHNICAL INSTITUTE
333 Providence Highway
Norwood, MA 02062
Web: http://www.itt-tech.edu
Accreditation: Accrediting Council for Independent Colleges and Schools
Programs Offered:
CAD/CADD drafting/design technology; computer engineering technology; computer software and media applications; computer systems networking and telecommunications; digital communication and media/multimedia; web page, digital/multimedia and information resources design
Institution Contact: Mr. Dennis Saccoia, Director
Phone: 781-278-7200
Admission Contact: Mr. Thomas F. Ryan, Director of *Recruitment Phone:* 781-278-7200

ITT TECHNICAL INSTITUTE
10 Forbes Road
Woburn, MA 01801
Web: http://www.itt-tech.edu
Accreditation: Accrediting Council for Independent Colleges and Schools
Programs Offered:
CAD/CADD drafting/design technology; computer engineering technology; computer software and media applications; computer systems networking and telecommunications; digital communication and media/multimedia; web page, digital/multimedia and information resources design
Institution Contact: Mr. Steve Carter, Director
Phone: 781-937-8324
Admission Contact: Mr. David Lundgren, Director of Recruitment
Phone: 781-937-8324

MILDRED ELLEY
505 East Street, Saint Luke's Square

Pittsfield, MA 01201
Web: http://www.mildred-elley.com
Accreditation: Accrediting Council for Independent Colleges and Schools
Programs Offered:
accounting; administrative assistant and secretarial science; clinical/medical laboratory science and allied professions related; computer software and media applications; digital communication and media/multimedia; legal assistant/paralegal; massage therapy; medical administrative assistant and medical secretary; tourism and travel services management
Enrollment: 200 students
Institution Contact: Ms. Lucille Allarie-Gosselin, Executive Director
Phone: 413-499-8618 ext. 227
Fax: 413-442-2269
E-mail: gosselin@nycap.rr.com
Admission Contact: Ms. Peggy Harrington, Administrative Assistant
Phone: 413-499-8618 ext. 227
Fax: 413-442-2269 ext. 225
E-mail: peggy.harrington@mildred-elley.edu

THE NEW ENGLAND INSTITUTE OF ART
10 Brookline Place, West
Brookline, MA 02445
Web: http://www.neia.aii.edu
Accreditation: New England Association of Schools and Colleges
Programs Offered:
animation, interactive technology, video graphics and special effects; commercial and advertising art; computer graphics; interior design; radio and television; recording arts technology; web/multimedia management and webmaster; web page, digital/multimedia and information resources design
Enrollment: 1,250 students
Institution Contact: Ms. Stacy Sweeney, President
Phone: 617-739-1700
Fax: 617-582-4520
E-mail: sweeneys@aii.edu
Admission Contact: Ms. Deborah Brent, Director of Admissions
Phone: 800-903-4425
Fax: 617-582-4500
E-mail: brentd@aii.edu

PORTER AND CHESTER INSTITUTE
134 Dulong Circle
Chicopee, MA 01022
Web: http://www.porterchester.com
Accreditation: Accrediting Bureau of Health Education Schools; Accrediting Commission of Career Schools and Colleges of Technology
Programs Offered:
automobile/automotive mechanics technology; CAD/CADD drafting/design technology; computer systems networking and telecommunications; computer technology/computer systems technology; dental assisting; electrical and electronic engineering technologies related; heating, air conditioning, ventilation and refrigeration maintenance technology; medical/clinical assistant
Institution Contact:
Phone: 413-593-3339

RETS TECHNICAL CENTER
570 Rutherford Avenue
Charlestown, MA 02129
Web: http://www.retstech.com
Accreditation: Accrediting Commission of Career Schools and Colleges of Technology
Programs Offered:
allied health and medical assisting services related; clinical/medical laboratory assistant; computer hardware technology; electrical/electronics equipment installation and repair; health professions related; health services/allied health/health sciences; heating, air conditioning and refrigeration technology; heating, air conditioning, ventilation and refrigeration maintenance technology; industrial electronics technology; medical administrative assistant and medical secretary; medical/clinical assistant; medical office assistant; medical office computer specialist; medical reception; medical transcription
Enrollment: 291 students
Institution Contact: Mr. Douglas R. Dunn, Executive Director
Phone: 617-580-4010 ext. 4012
Fax: 617-580-4074
E-mail: ddunn@khec.com
Admission Contact: Ms. Julie English, Director of Admissions
Phone: 617-580-4010
Fax: 617-580-4074

E-mail: julie@retstech.com

SANFORD-BROWN INSTITUTE
365 Cadwell Drive, 1st Floor
Springfield, MA 01104-1739
Web: http://www.ultrasounddiagnosticschool.com/default.htm
Accreditation: Accrediting Bureau of Health Education Schools
Programs Offered:
criminal justice/law enforcement administration; massage therapy; medical/clinical assistant; medical insurance coding
Enrollment: 350 students
Institution Contact: Mr. Winn Sanderson, President
Phone: 413-739-4700
Fax: 413-739-4800
E-mail: wsanderson@sbmass.com
Admission Contact: Ms. Susan Dillon, Director of Admissions
Phone: 413-739-4700
Fax: 413-739-4800
E-mail: sdillon@sbmass.com

UNIVERSAL TECHNICAL INSTITUTE
1 Upland Road
Bldg. #200
Norwood, MA 2062
Institution Contact:
Phone: 623-445-9620

WYOTECH
150 Hanscom Drive
Bedford, MA 01730
Web: http://www.wyotech.com
Accreditation: Accrediting Commission of Career Schools and Colleges of Technology
Programs Offered:
aircraft powerplant technology; airframe mechanics and aircraft maintenance technology
Enrollment: 250 students
Institution Contact: Mr. John Buck, School President
Phone: 781-274-8448
Fax: 781-274-8490
E-mail: jbuck@cci.edu
Admission Contact: Mr. John Buck, Jr.

Phone: 781-274-8448
Fax: 781-274-8490
E-mail: jbuck@cci.edu

MICHIGAN

CARNEGIE INSTITUTE
550 Stephenson Highway, Suite 100
Troy, MI 48083-1159
Web: http://www.carnegie-institute.com
Accreditation: Accrediting Commission of Career
Schools and Colleges of Technology
Programs Offered:
cardiovascular technology; electroneurodiagnostic/
electroencephalographic technology; massage therapy;
medical administrative assistant and medical secretary;
medical/clinical assistant; medical insurance/medical
billing; medical transcription
Enrollment: 311 students
Institution Contact: Mr. Robert McEachern
Phone: 248-589-1078
Fax: 248-589-1631
E-mail: carnegie47@aol.com

MAP DORSEY SCHOOLS
30821 Barrington Avenue
Madison Heights, MI 48071
Web: http://www.dorseyschools.com
Accreditation: Accrediting Council for Independent
Colleges and Schools
Programs Offered:
accounting; administrative assistant and secretarial science; computer software and media applications; data
entry/microcomputer applications; executive assistant/
executive secretary; legal administrative assistant/sec-
retary; medical administrative assistant and medical
secretary; medical/clinical assistant; medical/health
management and clinical assistant; medical insurance/
medical billing; medical reception; medical transcription; receptionist; word processing
Enrollment: 147 students
Institution Contact: Ms. Barbara Bubnikovich, Director
Phone: 248-588-9660
Fax: 248-583-4153
E-mail: bbubnikovich@dorsey.edu

Admission Contact: Ms. Patricia Fischer, Director
Phone: 248-588-9660
Fax: 248-583-4153
E-mail: pfischer@dorsey.edu

MAP DORSEY SCHOOLS
31542 Gratiot Avenue
Roseville, MI 48066
Web: http://www.dorseyschools.com
Accreditation: Accrediting Council for Independent
Colleges and Schools
Programs Offered:
accounting; administrative assistant and secretarial science; computer software and media applications; data
entry/microcomputer applications; executive assistant/
executive secretary; legal administrative assistant/secre-
tary; medical administrative assistant and medical secretary; medical/clinical assistant; medical/health manage-
ment and clinical assistant; medical insurance coding;
medical insurance/medical billing; medical reception;
medical transcription; receptionist; word processing
Enrollment: 262 students
Institution Contact: Ms. Kim Peck, Director
Phone: 586-296-3225
Fax: 586-296-6840
E-mail: kpeck@dorsey.edu

MAP DORSEY SCHOOLS
15755 Northline Road
Southgate, MI 48195
Web: http://www.dorseyschools.com
Accreditation: Accrediting Council for Independent
Colleges and Schools
Programs Offered:
accounting; administrative assistant and secretarial science; computer software and media applications; data
entry/microcomputer applications; data entry/micro-
computer applications related; executive assistant/exec-
utive secretary; legal administrative assistant/secretary;
medical administrative assistant and medical secretary;
medical/clinical assistant; medical/health management
and clinical assistant; medical insurance coding; medical insurance/medical billing; medical reception; medical transcription; receptionist; word processing
Enrollment: 124 students
Institution Contact: Ms. Golda Szydlowski, Director
Phone: 734-285-5400

indicates a participating institution in the *Imagine America* Scholarship Program. **MAP** indicates a participating institution in the Military Award Program.

Fax: 734-285-8877
E-mail: gszyd@dorsey.edu

DORSEY SCHOOLS
34841 Veteran's Plaza
Wayne, MI 48184
Web: http://www.dorseyschools.com
Accreditation: Accrediting Council for Independent Colleges and Schools
Programs Offered:
accounting; administrative assistant and secretarial science; computer software and media applications; data entry/microcomputer applications; executive assistant/executive secretary; medical administrative assistant and medical secretary; medical/clinical assistant; medical/health management and clinical assistant; medical insurance/medical billing; medical reception; medical transcription; receptionist; word processing
Enrollment: 187 students
Institution Contact: Ms. Dea Mason, Director
Phone: 734-595-1540
Fax: 734-595-6010
E-mail: dmason@dorsey.edu

FLINT INSTITUTE OF BARBERING
3214 Flushing Road
Flint, MI 48504-4395
Accreditation: Accrediting Commission of Career Schools and Colleges of Technology
Programs Offered:
barbering
Enrollment: 39 students
Institution Contact: Ms. Martha Poulos, Director
Phone: 810-232-4711
Fax: 810-232-3132
E-mail: flintbarbers@sbcglobal.net

INTERNATIONAL ACADEMY OF DESIGN & TECHNOLOGY
1850 Research Drive
Troy, MI 48083
Accreditation: Accrediting Council for Independent Colleges and Schools
Programs Offered:
fashion/apparel design; graphic communications related; interior design

Enrollment: 600 students
Institution Contact: Krista Smith, Marketing and Media Relations
Phone: 248-457-2700 ext. 2728
E-mail: ksmith@iadtdetroit.com
Admission Contact: Mary Durant, Director of Admissions
Phone: 248-457-2700 ext. 2722
Fax: 248-526-1710
E-mail: mdurant@iadtdetroit.com

ITT TECHNICAL INSTITUTE
1905 South Haggerty Road
Canton, MI 48188-2025
Web: http://www.itt-tech.edu
Accreditation: Accrediting Council for Independent Colleges and Schools
Programs Offered:
CAD/CADD drafting/design technology; computer engineering technology; computer software and media applications; computer systems networking and telecommunications; digital communication and media/multimedia; web page, digital/multimedia and information resources design
Institution Contact: Ms. Nadine Palazzolo, Director
Phone: 734-397-7800
Admission Contact: Mr. Dudley Layfield, Director of Recruitment
Phone: 734-397-7800

ITT TECHNICAL INSTITUTE
4020 Sparks Drive, Southeast
Grand Rapids, MI 49546
Web: http://www.itt-tech.edu
Accreditation: Accrediting Council for Independent Colleges and Schools
Programs Offered:
CAD/CADD drafting/design technology; computer engineering technology; computer software and media applications; computer systems networking and telecommunications; digital communication and media/multimedia; web page, digital/multimedia and information resources design
Institution Contact: Mr. Dennis Hormel, Director
Phone: 616-956-1060
Admission Contact: Mr. Todd Peuler, Director of Recruitment
Phone: 616-956-1060

ITT TECHNICAL INSTITUTE
1522 East Big Beaver Road
Troy, MI 48083-1905
Web: http://www.itt-tech.edu
Accreditation: Accrediting Council for Independent
Colleges and Schools
Programs Offered:
CAD/CADD drafting/design technology; computer
engineering technology; computer software and
media applications; computer systems networking
and telecommunications; digital communication and
media/multimedia; web page, digital/multimedia and
information resources design
Institution Contact: Dr. Stephen Goddard, Director
Phone: 248-524-1800
Admission Contact: Ms. Patricia Hyman, Director of
Recruitment
Phone: 248-524-1800

LAWTON SCHOOL
20755 Greenfield Road, Suite 300
Southfield, MI 48075
Accreditation: Accrediting Commission of Career
Schools and Colleges of Technology
Programs Offered:
administrative assistant and secretarial science; com-
puter software and media applications; legal assistant/
paralegal; medical/clinical assistant
Enrollment: 160 students
Institution Contact: Mrs. Tamiko Ogburn, Executive
Director
Phone: 248-569-7787
Fax: 248-569-6974
E-mail: strangetamiko@hotmail.com
Admission Contact: Mr. Oliver Hunter, Jr., Admis-
sion Director
Phone: 248-569-7787
Fax: 248-569-6974

NATIONAL INSTITUTE OF TECHNOLOGY
300 River Place Drive, Suite 1000
Detroit, MI 48207
Web: http://www.nitschools.com
Accreditation: Accrediting Commission of Career
Schools and Colleges of Technology
Programs Offered:
massage therapy; medical/clinical assistant; medical
insurance/medical billing; pharmacy technician

Enrollment: 551 students
Institution Contact: Mr. Joseph M. Egelski, School
President
Phone: 313-567-5350 ext. 101
Fax: 313-567-2095
E-mail: jegelski@cci.edu
Admission Contact: Mr. Mike Draheim, Director of
Admissions
Phone: 313-567-5350 ext. 102
Fax: 313-567-2095
E-mail: mdraheim@cci.edu

NATIONAL INSTITUTE OF TECHNOLOGY
26111 Evergreen Road, Suite 201
Southfield, MI 48076-4491
Web: http://www.cci.edu
Accreditation: Accrediting Commission of Career
Schools and Colleges of Technology
Programs Offered:
computer/information technology services administra-
tion related; computer installation and repair technol-
ogy; computer systems networking and telecommu-
nications; electrical, electronic and communications
engineering technology; massage therapy; medical
administrative assistant and medical secretary; medi-
cal/clinical assistant; medical insurance coding; medi-
cal insurance/medical billing
Enrollment: 762 students
Institution Contact: Mrs. Marchelle Weaver, President
Phone: 248-799-9933
Fax: 248-799-2912
E-mail: mweaver@cci.edu
Admission Contact: Santiago Rocha, Director of
Admissions
Phone: 248-799-9933 ext. 118
Fax: 248-799-2912
E-mail: srocha@cci.edu

NATIONAL INSTITUTE OF TECHNOLOGY - DEARBORN
23400 Michigan Avenue, Suite 200
Dearborn, MI 48124
Web: http://www.nitschools.com
Accreditation: Accrediting Commission of Career
Schools and Colleges of Technology
Programs Offered:

indicates a participating institution in the *Imagine America* Scholarship Program. **MAP** indicates a participating institution in the Military Award Program.

computer/information technology administration and management; computer systems networking and tele-communications; massage therapy; medical/clinical assistant; medical insurance/medical billing; pharmacy technician
Enrollment: 770 students
Institution Contact: Mr. Joseph Belliotti, Jr., President
Phone: 313-562-4228 ext. 102
Fax: 313-562-5774
E-mail: jbelliot@cci.edu
Admission Contact: Mr. Larry Baranski, Director of Admissions
Phone: 313-562-4228 ext. 101
Fax: 313-562-5774
E-mail: lbaranski@cci.edu

OLYMPIA CAREER TRAINING INSTITUTE
1750 Woodworth Street, NE
Grand Rapids, MI 49525
Accreditation: Accrediting Bureau of Health Education Schools
Programs Offered: dental assisting; massage therapy; medical administrative assistant and medical secretary; medical/clinical assistant; medical insurance coding; nursing (licensed practical/vocational nurse training); pharmacy technician
Enrollment: 786 students
Institution Contact: Mrs. Ruth Stewart, President
Phone: 616-364-8464 ext. 110
Fax: 616-364-6404
E-mail: rstewart@cci.edu
Admission Contact: Ms. Bobbi Blok, Director of Admissions
Phone: 616-364-8464 ext. 131
Fax: 616-364-5454
E-mail: rblok@cci.edu

OLYMPIA CAREER TRAINING INSTITUTE
5349 West Main Street
Kalamazoo, MI 49009
Web: http://www.olympia-institute.com
Accreditation: Accrediting Bureau of Health Education Schools
Programs Offered:
dental assisting; massage therapy; medical administrative assistant and medical secretary; medical/clinical assistant; medical insurance coding; pharmacy technician

Enrollment: 450 students
Institution Contact: Ms. Susan Smith, Director of Admissions
Phone: 269-381-9616
Fax: 269-381-2513
E-mail: susans@cci.edu

ROSS MEDICAL EDUCATION CENTER
4741 Washtenaw
Ann Arbor, MI 48108-1411
Programs Offered:
medical/clinical assistant
Enrollment: 70 students
Institution Contact: Pat Sadler, Director
Phone: 734-434-7320
Fax: 734-434-8579

ROSS MEDICAL EDUCATION CENTER
5757 Whitmore Lake Road, Suite 800
Brighton, MI 48116
Programs Offered:
medical/clinical assistant
Institution Contact: Mrs. Sharon J. Tremuth, Director
Phone: 810-227-0160 ext. 2301
Fax: 810-227-9582
E-mail: streumuth@rosslearning.com
Admission Contact:
Phone: 810-227-0160 ext. 2303
Fax: 810-227-09582
E-mail: admissions.brighton@rosslearning.com

ROSS MEDICAL EDUCATION CENTER
2035 28th Street, SE
Grand Rapids, MI 49508
Programs Offered:
medical/clinical assistant
Institution Contact: Brooksie Smith, Director
Phone: 616-243-3070
Fax: 616-243-2937

ROSS MEDICAL EDUCATION CENTER
9327 Telegraph Road
Redford, MI 48239
Programs Offered:
medical/clinical assistant

Institution Contact: Merrideth Perry-Moore, Director
Phone: 313-794-6448
Fax: 313-794-6573

ROSS MEDICAL EDUCATION CENTER

950 Norton Avenue
Roosevelt Park, MI 49441
Programs Offered:
medical/clinical assistant
Institution Contact: Marge Scheneman, Director
Phone: 231-739-1531
Fax: 231-739-7456

ROSS MEDICAL EDUCATION CENTER

27120 Dequindre
Warren, MI 48092
Programs Offered:
medical/clinical assistant
Institution Contact: Terri Charison, Director
Phone: 586-574-0830
Fax: 586-574-0851
E-mail: tcharison@rosslearning.com

ROSS MEDICAL EDUCATION CENTER - SAGINAW CAMPUS

4054 Bay Road
Saginaw, MI 48603
Programs Offered:
medical/clinical assistant
Institution Contact: Kathy Leach, Director
Phone: 989-793-9800
Fax: 989-793-0003
E-mail: kleach@rosslearning.com

SPECS HOWARD SCHOOL OF BROADCAST ARTS

19900 West Nine Mile Road
Southfield, MI 48075-3953
Web: http://www.specshoward.edu
Accreditation: Accrediting Commission of Career Schools and Colleges of Technology
Programs Offered:
radio and television
Enrollment: 535 students
Institution Contact: Mr. Jonathan Liebman, President/CEO
Phone: 248-358-9000

Fax: 248-746-9772
E-mail: jliebman@specshoward.edu
Admission Contact: Ms. Nancy Shiner, Director of Admissions
Phone: 248-358-9000 ext. 226
Fax: 248-746-9772
E-mail: nshiner@specshoward.edu

ACADEMY COLLEGE

1101 East 78th Street, Suite 100
Minneapolis, MN 55420
Web: http://www.academycollege.edu
Accreditation: Accrediting Council for Independent Colleges and Schools
Programs Offered:
accounting; aircraft pilot (private); airline pilot and flight crew; animation, interactive technology, video graphics and special effects; art; aviation/airway management; business administration and management; commercial and advertising art; computer and information systems security; computer graphics; computer installation and repair technology; computer programming; computer programming (specific applications); computer science; computer software and media applications; computer systems networking and telecommunications; computer/technical support; digital communication and media/multimedia; human resources management; legal administrative assistant/secretary; medical administrative assistant and medical secretary; medical/clinical assistant; medical insurance coding; medical office assistant; medical transcription; office management; safety/security technology; system administration; taxation; web/multimedia management and webmaster; web page, digital/multimedia and information resources design
Institution Contact: Ms. Nancy Grazzini-Olson, President
Phone: 952-851-0066
Fax: 952-851-0094
E-mail: ngo@academycollege.edu
Admission Contact: Ms. Char Drechen, Director of Admissions
Phone: 952-851-0066
Fax: 952-851-0094
E-mail: admissions@academycollege.edu

ARGOSY UNIVERSITY/TWIN CITIES

1515 Central Parkway
Eagan, MN 55121
Programs Offered:
business administration and management; education
Institution Contact: Admissions
Phone: 651-846-2882
Fax: 651-994-7956
E-mail: tcadmissions@argosyu.edu

THE ART INSTITUTES INTERNATIONAL MINNESOTA

15 South 9th Street
Minneapolis, MN 55402
Web: http://www.aim.artinstitutes.edu
Accreditation: Accrediting Council for Independent Colleges and Schools
Programs Offered:
advertising; animation, interactive technology, video graphics and special effects; baking and pastry arts; commercial and advertising art; computer graphics; culinary arts; design and visual communications; digital communication and media/multimedia; food service and dining room management; interior design; photography; web/multimedia management and webmaster; web page, digital/multimedia and information resources design
Enrollment: 1,580 students
Institution Contact: Anjila Kozel, Director of Communications
Phone: 800-777-3643 ext. 6862
Fax: 612-338-2417
E-mail: akozel@aii.edu
Admission Contact: Mr. Russ Gill, Director of Admissions
Phone: 800-777-3643 ext. 6820
Fax: 612-332-3934
E-mail: rgill@aii.edu

MAP BROWN COLLEGE

1440 Northland Drive
Mendota Heights, MN 55120-1004
Web: http://www.browncollege.edu
Accreditation: Accrediting Commission of Career Schools and Colleges of Technology
Programs Offered:
broadcast journalism; business administration and management; business/commerce; business/corporate communications; commercial and advertising art; commercial photography; communications technology; computer and information sciences related; computer and information systems security; computer graphics; computer/information technology administration and management; computer/information technology services administration related; computer programming; computer software and media applications; computer systems networking and telecommunications; corrections; desktop publishing and digital imaging design; digital communication and media/multimedia; global management; graphic communications related; information technology; interior design; massage therapy; radio and television; radio and television broadcasting technology; safety/security technology; system administration; system, networking, and LAN/WAN management; web page, digital/multimedia and information resources design
Enrollment: 1,652 students
Institution Contact: Dr. Alan T. Stutts, President/CEO
Phone: 651-905-3400
Fax: 651-905-3510
E-mail: astutts@browncollege.edu
Admission Contact: Mr. Lee Kurimay, Vice President of Admissions
Phone: 651-905-3400
Fax: 651-905-3510
E-mail: lkurimay@browncollege.edu

BRYMAN INSTITUTE

1000 Blue Gentian Road, Suite 250
Spectrum Commerce Center
Eagan, MN 55121
Web: http://www.bryman-institute.com
Accreditation: Accrediting Commission of Career Schools and Colleges of Technology
Programs Offered:
massage therapy; medical/clinical assistant; medical insurance/medical billing
Enrollment: 226 students
Institution Contact: Mr. Kevin L. Sanderson, President
Phone: 651-668-2145 ext. 102
Fax: 651-686-8029
E-mail: ksanderson@cci.edu
Admission Contact: Deborah Peterson, Director of Admissions
Phone: 651-688-2145 ext. 103

Fax: 651-686-8029
E-mail: dpeterson@cci.edu

CAPELLA UNIVERSITY

222 South 9th Street, 20th Floor
Minneapolis, MN 55402
Web: http://www.capellauniversity.edu
Accreditation: North Central Association of Colleges
and Schools
Programs Offered:
adult and continuing education; business administration and management; computer and information systems security; computer graphics; computer/information technology administration and management; computer/information technology services administration related; computer programming; computer programming related; computer programming (specific applications); computer software and media applications; computer software and media applications related; computer software engineering; computer systems analysis; computer systems networking and telecommunications; corrections; counselor education/school counseling and guidance; criminal justice/law enforcement administration; criminal justice/police science; digital communication and media/multimedia; e-commerce; education; educational/instructional media design; educational leadership and administration; education (specific levels and methods) related; elementary education; health/health care administration; human resources development; human resources management; human services; information technology; insurance; management information systems; marketing/marketing management; mental health counseling; quality control technology; secondary education; selling skills and sales; substance abuse/addiction counseling; system, networking, and LAN/WAN management; technology management; web/multimedia management and webmaster; web page, digital/multimedia and information resources design
Enrollment: 10,800 students
Institution Contact: Mr. Gregory Thom, Vice President of Government Affairs
Phone: 612-659-5470
Fax: 612-659-5057
E-mail: greg.thom@capella.edu
Admission Contact: Enrollment Services
Phone: 888-227-3552 ext. 8
Fax: 612-339-8022

E-mail: info@capella.edu

DULUTH BUSINESS UNIVERSITY

4724 Mike Colalillo Drive
Duluth, MN 55807
Web: http://www.dbumn.edu
Accreditation: Accrediting Council for Independent
Colleges and Schools
Programs Offered:
accounting; administrative assistant and secretarial science; business administration and management; graphic communications related; massage therapy; medical/clinical assistant; medical insurance/medical billing; office management; phlebotomy; veterinary/animal health technology; veterinary technology
Enrollment: 335 students
Institution Contact: Ms. Bonnie Kupczynski, Director
Phone: 218-722-4000
Fax: 218-628-2127
E-mail: bonniek@dbumn.edu
Admission Contact: Mr. Mark Truax, Director of
Admissions
Phone: 218-740-4345
Fax: 218-628-2127
E-mail: markt@dbumn.edu

GLOBE COLLEGE

7166 10th Street North
Oakdale, MN 55128
Web: http://www.globecollege.edu
Accreditation: Accrediting Council for Independent
Colleges and Schools
Programs Offered:
accounting; accounting technology and bookkeeping; administrative assistant and secretarial science; advertising; athletic training; business administration and management; business, management, and marketing related; commercial and advertising art; computer engineering technology; computer graphics; computer/information technology administration and management; computer/information technology services administration related; computer software engineering; computer/technical support; information technology; legal administrative assistant/secretary; legal assistant/paralegal; massage therapy; medical administrative assistant and medical secretary; medical/clinical assistant; music management and merchandising;

veterinary technology; web/multimedia management and webmaster

Enrollment: 950 students
Institution Contact: Mr. Mike Hughes, Director
Phone: 651-730-5100 ext. 329
Fax: 651-730-5151
E-mail: mhughes@globecollege.edu
Admission Contact: Miss Christina Hilipipre, Director of Admissions
Phone: 651-730-5100 ext. 331
Fax: 651-730-5151
E-mail: chilipipre@globecollege.edu

HERZING COLLEGE

5700 West Broadway
Minneapolis, MN 55428-3548
Web: http://www.herzing.edu
Accreditation: Accrediting Commission of Career Schools and Colleges of Technology; North Central Association of Colleges and Schools
Programs Offered:
business administration and management; CAD/CADD drafting/design technology; civil drafting and CAD/CADD; computer systems networking and telecommunications; dental assisting; dental hygiene; drafting and design technology; medical/clinical assistant; medical insurance coding; safety/security technology; technology management; web page, digital/multimedia and information resources design
Enrollment: 370 students
Institution Contact: Mr. Thomas Kosel, President
Phone: 763-535-3000 ext. 151
Fax: 763-535-9205
E-mail: tkosel@mpls.herzing.edu
Admission Contact: Mr. James Decker, Director of Admissions
Phone: 763-535-3000 ext. 152
Fax: 763-535-9205
E-mail: jdecker@mpls.herzing.edu

HIGH-TECH INSTITUTE

5100 Gamble Drive
St. Louis Park, MN 55416
Web: http://www.hightechinstitute.edu
Accreditation: Accrediting Bureau of Health Education Schools; Accrediting Commission of Career Schools and Colleges of Technology

Programs Offered:
computer systems networking and telecommunications; massage therapy; medical/clinical assistant; medical insurance coding; medical insurance/medical billing; medical radiologic technology; pharmacy technician; surgical technology
Enrollment: 750 students
Institution Contact: Mr. Todd Brown, Campus President
Phone: 952-417-2200
Fax: 952-545-6149
E-mail: tbrown@hightechinstitute.edu
Admission Contact: Mr. Paul Keprios, Director of Admissions
Phone: 952-417-2200
Fax: 952-545-6149
E-mail: pkeprios@hightechinstitute.edu

THE INSTITUTE OF PRODUCTION AND RECORDING

312 Washington Avenue North
Minneapolis, MN 55401
Web: http://www.iprschool.com
Enrollment: 425 students
Institution Contact: Ms. Stacy Lynn Semler, Admistrative/Human Resources Manager
Phone: 612-375-1900 ext. 135
Fax: 612-375-1919
E-mail: stacysemler@iprschool.com
Admission Contact: Mr. Lance Sabin, Director of Admissions
Phone: 612-375-1900
Fax: 612-375-1919
E-mail: lancesabin@iprschool.com

ITT TECHNICAL INSTITUTE

8911 Columbine Road
Eden Prairie, MN 55347-4143
Web: http://www.itt-tech.edu
Accreditation: Accrediting Council for Independent Colleges and Schools
Programs Offered:
animation, interactive technology, video graphics and special effects; CAD/CADD drafting/design technology; communications technology; computer and information systems security; computer engineering technology; computer software and media applications; computer software engineering; computer systems networking and telecommunications; digital

communication and media/multimedia; electrical, electronic and communications engineering technology; technology management; web page, digital/multimedia and information resources design
Institution Contact: Michele Ernst, Director
Phone: 952-914-5300
Admission Contact: John Nelson , Director of Recruitment
Phone: 952-914-5300

Le Cordon Bleu College of Culinary Arts Minneapolis/St.Paul

1315 Mendota Heights Rd.
Saint Paul, MN 55120
Web: www.twincitiesculinary.com
Institution Contact: Ms. Colleen McDermott
Phone: 651-675-4700
Fax: 651-452-5285

Minneapolis Business College

1711 West County Road B
Roseville, MN 55113
Web: http://www.minneapolisbusinesscollege.edu
Accreditation: Accrediting Council for Independent Colleges and Schools
Programs Offered:
accounting; administrative assistant and secretarial science; commercial and advertising art; computer programming (specific applications); computer systems networking and telecommunications; hotel/motel administration; legal administrative assistant/secretary; medical/clinical assistant; tourism and travel services management
Enrollment: 350 students
Institution Contact: Mr. David Blair Whitman, President
Phone: 651-604-4118
Fax: 651-636-8185
E-mail: dwhitman@minneapolisbusinesscollege.edu

Minnesota School of Business - Brooklyn Center

5910 Shingle Creek Parkway , Suite 200
Brooklyn Center, MN 55430
Web: http://www.msbcollege.edu
Accreditation: Accrediting Council for Independent Colleges and Schools

Programs Offered:
accounting; business administration and management; computer engineering related; computer graphics; computer programming related; design and visual communications; executive assistant/executive secretary; legal administrative assistant/secretary; legal assistant/paralegal; massage therapy; medical administrative assistant and medical secretary; medical/clinical assistant; music management and merchandising; veterinary technology
Enrollment: 875 students
Institution Contact: Ms. Susan Lynne Cooke, Director
Phone: 763-585-5225
Fax: 763-566-7030
E-mail: scooke@msbcollege.edu
Admission Contact: Mr. Jeffrey Lee Georgeson, Director of Admissions
Phone: 763-585-5206
Fax: 763-566-7030
E-mail: jgeorgeson@msbcollege.edu

Minnesota School of Business - Plymouth

1455 County Rd. 101 North
Plymouth, MN 55447
Web: http: www.msbcollege.edu
Institution Contact: Mr. Andrew Hoeveler
Phone: 763-476-2000

Minnesota School of Business - Richfield

1401 West 76th Street
Richfield, MN 55423
Accreditation: Accrediting Council for Independent Colleges and Schools
Programs Offered:
accounting; business administration and management; computer graphics; e-commerce; legal administrative assistant/secretary; legal assistant/paralegal; massage therapy; medical administrative assistant and medical secretary; medical/clinical assistant; veterinary technology
Institution Contact: Mr. George Teagarden, Director
Phone: 612-861-2000
Fax: 612-861-5548
E-mail: gteagarden@msbcollege.edu
Admission Contact: Ms. Patricia Murray, Director of Admissions
Phone: 612-861-2000 ext. 720
Fax: 612-861-5548

E-mail: pmurray@msbcollege.edu

MINNESOTA SCHOOL OF BUSINESS - ROCHESTER

2521 Pennington Dr. NW
Rochester, MN 55901
Web: http: www.msbcollege.edu
Institution Contact: Mr. Dave Tracy
Phone: 507-536-9500
Fax: 507-536-8011

MINNESOTA SCHOOL OF BUSINESS

1200 Shakopee Town Square
Shakopee, MN 55379
Institution Contact: Ms. Lorrie Laurin
Phone: 952-345-1200
Fax: 952-345-1201

MINNESOTA SCHOOL OF BUSINESS - ST. CLOUD

1201 2nd Street South
Waite Park, MN 56387
Institution Contact: Dee Ann Kerr
Phone: 320-257-2000

NATIONAL AMERICAN UNIVERSITY

112 W Market
Minneapolis, MN 55425
Accreditation: North Central Association of Colleges
and Schools
Programs Offered:
accounting; allied health and medical assisting services
related; business administration and management;
health/health care administration; information technol-
ogy; legal assistant/paralegal; massage therapy; medi-
cal administrative assistant and medical secretary
Institution Contact: Ms. Jill Johnson, Campus Director
Phone: 952-883-0439
Fax: 952-883-0106
E-mail: jjohnson@national.edu
Admission Contact: Mr. Matt Mottl, Director of
Admissions
Phone: 952-888-0439
Fax: 952-888-0106
E-mail: mmottl@national..edu

NATIONAL AMERICAN UNIVERSITY

6120 Earle Brown Drive, Suite 100
Brooklyn Center, MN 55430
Web: http://www.national.edu
Accreditation: North Central Association of Colleges
and Schools
Programs Offered:
accounting; business administration and management;
information science/studies; information technology;
legal assistant/paralegal; marketing/marketing man-
agement; pharmacy technician
Enrollment: 200 students
Institution Contact: Dr. Bruce Weiss, Campus Director
Phone: 763-560-8377
Fax: 763-549-9955
E-mail: bweiss@national.edu
Admission Contact: Mr. Matthew Mottl, Director of
Admissions
Phone: 763-560-8377
Fax: 763-549-9955
E-mail: mmottl@national.edu

NATIONAL AMERICAN UNIVERSITY

1550 West Highway 36
Roseville, MN 55113
Web: http://www.national.edu
Accreditation: North Central Association of Colleges
and Schools
Programs Offered:
accounting; allied health and medical assisting services
related; business administration and management;
finance; information technology; legal assistant/para-
legal; management information systems; marketing/
marketing management; massage therapy; medical
administrative assistant and medical secretary; medi-
cal/clinical assistant; medical office assistant; medical
reception; pharmacy technician
Enrollment: 248 students
Institution Contact: Mr. Gene Muilenburg, Campus
Director
Phone: 651-644-1265
Fax: 651-644-0690
E-mail: gmuilenburg@national.edu
Admission Contact: Matthew Mottl, Director of
Admissions
Phone: 651-644-1265
Fax: 651-644-0690
E-mail: mmottl@national.edu

NORTHWEST TECHNICAL INSTITUTE

11995 Singletree Lane
Eden Prairie, MN 55344-5351
Web: http://www.nti.edu
Accreditation: Accrediting Commission of Career Schools and Colleges of Technology
Programs Offered:
architectural drafting and CAD/CADD; CAD/CADD drafting/design technology; drafting and design technology; electrical/electronics drafting and CAD/CADD; engineering technology
Enrollment: 90 students
Institution Contact: Mr. Michael E. Kotchevar, President
Phone: 952-944-0080 ext. 101
Fax: 952-944-9274
E-mail: mkotchevar@nti.edu
Admission Contact: Mr. John K. Hartman, Director of Marketing and Admissions
Phone: 952-944-0080 ext. 103
Fax: 952-944-9274
E-mail: jhartman@nti.edu

RASMUSSEN COLLEGE EAGAN

3500 Federal Drive
Eagan, MN 55122
Web: http://www.rasmussen.edu
Accreditation: Accrediting Council for Independent Colleges and Schools; North Central Association of Colleges and Schools
Programs Offered:
accounting; administrative assistant and secretarial science; banking and financial support services; business administration and management; business/corporate communications; child care and support services management; child care provision; computer and information systems security; computer/information technology administration and management; computer/information technology services administration related; computer systems networking and telecommunications; computer/technical support; data entry/microcomputer applications; data entry/microcomputer applications related; health information/medical records technology; information science/studies; information technology; marketing/marketing management; medical administrative assistant and medical secretary; medical insurance coding; medical office management; medical transcription; restaurant, culinary, and catering management; retailing; selling skills and sales; system,

networking, and LAN/WAN management; web page, digital/multimedia and information resources design; word processing
Institution Contact: Ms. Tawnie L. Cortez, Campus Director
Phone: 651-687-9000
Fax: 651-687-0507
E-mail: tawniec@rasmussen.edu
Admission Contact: Ms. Jacinda Miller, Admission Coordinator
Phone: 651-687-9000
Fax: 651-687-0507
E-mail: jacindam@rasmussen.edu

RASMUSSEN COLLEGE MANKATO

501 Holly Lane
Mankato, MN 56001-6803
Web: http://www.rasmussen.edu/
Accreditation: Accrediting Council for Independent Colleges and Schools; North Central Association of Colleges and Schools
Programs Offered:
accounting; accounting and business/management; administrative assistant and secretarial science; banking and financial support services; business administration and management; business, management, and marketing related; criminal justice/law enforcement administration; health information/medical records technology; health unit coordinator/ward clerk; human resources management; massage therapy; medical administrative assistant and medical secretary; medical/clinical assistant; nursing (licensed practical/vocational nurse training); pharmacy technician; selling skills and sales; surgical technology; system, networking, and LAN/WAN management; web page, digital/multimedia and information resources design
Enrollment: 450 students
Institution Contact: Mr. Douglas Gardner, Director
Phone: 507-625-6556
Fax: 507-625-6557
E-mail: dougg@rasmussen.edu
Admission Contact: Kathy Clifford, Director of Admissions
Phone: 507-625-6556
Fax: 507-625-6557
E-mail: kathyc@rasmussen.edu

RASMUSSEN COLLEGE MINNETONKA
12450 Wayzata Boulevard, Suite 315
Minnetonka, MN 55305-1928
Web: http://www.rasmussen.edu
Accreditation: Accrediting Council for Independent
Colleges and Schools; North Central Association of
Colleges and Schools
Programs Offered:
accounting; accounting technology and bookkeeping;
administrative assistant and secretarial science; banking and financial support services; business administration and management; business/corporate communications; child care and support services management; child care provision; computer and information systems security; computer/information technology administration and management; computer/information technology services administration related; computer software and media applications; computer systems networking and telecommunications; computer/technical support; criminal justice/law enforcement administration; data entry/microcomputer applications; e-commerce; health/health care administration; health information/medical records administration; health information/medical records technology; health unit coordinator/ward clerk; health unit management/ward supervision; human resources management; information science/studies; information technology; legal administrative assistant/secretary; marketing/marketing management; medical administrative assistant and medical secretary; medical/clinical assistant; medical insurance coding; medical office management; medical reception; medical transcription; office management; office occupations and clerical services; receptionist; retailing; selling skills and sales; system, networking, and LAN/WAN management; tourism and travel services management; web page, digital/multimedia and information resources design; word processing
Enrollment: 370 students
Institution Contact: Ms. Kathy P. Howe, Campus
Director
Phone: 952-545-2000
Fax: 952-545-7038
E-mail: kathyh@rasmussen.edu

RASMUSSEN COLLEGE ST. CLOUD
226 Park Avenue, South
St. Cloud, MN 56301-3713
Web: http://www.rasmussen.edu/

Accreditation: Accrediting Council for Independent
Colleges and Schools; North Central Association of
Colleges and Schools
Programs Offered:
accounting; accounting and business/management; accounting and finance; administrative assistant and secretarial science; banking and financial support services; business administration and management; business operations support and secretarial services related; child care and support services management; child care provision; computer hardware technology; computer/information technology services administration related; computer systems networking and telecommunications; computer/technical support; computer technology/computer systems technology; criminal justice/law enforcement administration; criminal justice/police science; desktop publishing and digital imaging design; digital communication and media/multimedia; executive assistant/executive secretary; health information/medical records administration; health information/medical records technology; health unit coordinator/ward clerk; information technology; internet information systems; legal administrative assistant/secretary; marketing/marketing management; massage therapy; medical/clinical assistant; medical insurance coding; medical insurance/medical billing; medical office management; medical pharmacology and pharmaceutical sciences; medical reception; medical transcription; office management; pharmacy technician; receptionist; system, networking, and LAN/WAN management
Enrollment: 589 students
Institution Contact: Mr. Chris Zack, Director
Phone: 320-251-5600
Fax: 320-251-3702
E-mail: chrisz@rasmussen.edu
Admission Contact: Ms. Andrea Peters, Director of
Admissions
Phone: 320-251-5600
Fax: 320-251-3702
E-mail: andreap@rasmussen.edu

MISSISSIPPI

ANTONELLI COLLEGE
1500 North 31st Avenue
Hattiesburg, MS 39401

Programs Offered:
accounting; administrative assistant and secretarial science; allied health and medical assisting services related; computer/technical support; health and medical administrative services related; health unit coordinator/ward clerk; interior design; legal assistant/paralegal; massage therapy; medical insurance coding; medical office assistant; medical transcription; office occupations and clerical services; technology management; web/multimedia management and webmaster

Enrollment: 295 students
Institution Contact: Mrs. Karen Gautreau, Director
Phone: 601-583-4100
Fax: 601-583-0839
E-mail: gautreau@antonellic.com
Admission Contact: Mrs. Karen Gautreau, Director
Phone: 601-583-4100
Fax: 601-583-0839
E-mail: gautreau@antonellic.com

ANTONELLI COLLEGE
2323 Lakeland Drive
Jackson, MS 39322
Programs Offered:
accounting technology and bookkeeping; administrative assistant and secretarial science; allied health and medical assisting services related; business automation/technology/data entry; business operations support and secretarial services related; clinical/medical laboratory assistant; commercial and advertising art; computer hardware technology; computer installation and repair technology; computer/technical support; health information/medical records technology; interior design; legal assistant/paralegal; massage therapy; medical administrative assistant and medical secretary; medical/clinical assistant; medical insurance coding; medical insurance/medical billing; medical office assistant; medical reception; medical transcription

Enrollment: 298 students
Institution Contact: Debra Moore, Director
Phone: 601-362-9991
Fax: 601-362-2333
E-mail: dmoore@antonellic.com

BLUE CLIFF COLLEGE
942 Beach Drive
Gulfport, MS 39507

Web: http://www.bluecliffcollege.com
Accreditation: Accrediting Commission of Career Schools and Colleges of Technology
Programs Offered:
massage therapy
Institution Contact: Admissions
Phone: 228-896-9727
E-mail: admissions_glf@bluecliffcollege.com

VIRGINIA COLLEGE AT JACKSON
5360 I-55 North
Jackson, MS 39211
Web: http://www.vc.edu
Accreditation: Accrediting Council for Independent Colleges and Schools
Programs Offered:
accounting; administrative assistant and secretarial science; aesthetician/esthetician and skin care; biomedical technology; business administration and management; computer engineering related; computer hardware engineering; computer/information technology administration and management; computer installation and repair technology; computer programming related; computer technology/computer systems technology; cosmetology; cosmetology, barber/styling, and nail instruction; criminal justice/law enforcement administration; electrical, electronic and communications engineering technology; human resources management; human resources management and services related; massage therapy; medical/clinical assistant; medical insurance/medical billing; medical office management; nail technician and manicurist; surgical technology

Enrollment: 1,200 students
Institution Contact: Mrs. Madeline Little, President
Phone: 601-977-0960
Fax: 601-956-4325
E-mail: mtlittle@vc.edu
Admission Contact: Mr. Bill Milstead, Director of Admissions
Phone: 601-977-0960
Fax: 601-956-4325
E-mail: bmilstead@vc.edu

MISSOURI

ALLIED COLLEGE

1227 Water Tower Place
Arnold, MO 63010
Web: http://www.alliedcollege.edu
Accreditation: Accrediting Bureau of Health Education Schools
Programs Offered:
dental assisting; massage therapy; medical/clinical assistant; medical insurance coding; medical insurance/medical billing; pharmacy technician
Institution Contact: Admissions
Phone: 866-502-2627

ALLIED COLLEGE

13723 Riverport Drive, Suite 103
Maryland Heights, MO 63043
Accreditation: Accrediting Bureau of Health Education Schools
Programs Offered:
criminal justice/police science; dental assisting; massage therapy; medical/clinical assistant; medical insurance/medical billing; pharmacy technician; surgical technology
Enrollment: 625 students
Institution Contact: Mr. Jeffrey Engh, President
Phone: 314-595-3400
Fax: 314-739-5133
E-mail: jengh@hightechinstitute.edu
Admission Contact: Ms. Erin Cunningham, Director of Admissions
Phone: 314-595-3400
Fax: 314-739-5133
E-mail: ecunningham@hightechinstitute.edu

BRYAN COLLEGE

237 South Florence Avenue
Springfield, MO 65806
Web: http://www.bryancollege.com
Accreditation: Accrediting Council for Independent Colleges and Schools
Programs Offered:
allied health and medical assisting services related; business administration and management; clinical/medical laboratory assistant; computer and information sciences; computer and information sciences and support services related; computer and information sciences related; computer programming related; computer programming (specific applications); computer systems analysis; computer systems networking and telecommunications; computer/technical support; computer technology/computer systems technology; human resources management; information science/studies; information technology; medical/clinical assistant; medical office assistant; sport and fitness administration; system administration; system, networking, and LAN/WAN management; tourism and travel services management
Enrollment: 225 students
Institution Contact: Mr. Brian Stewart, President/CE
Phone: 417-862-5700
Fax: 417-862-9554
E-mail: bstewart@bryancollege.com
Admission Contact: Mrs. Natalie Kyte, Admissions Representative
Phone: 417-862-5700
Fax: 417-865-7144
E-mail: nkyte@bryancollege.com

BRYMAN COLLEGE

3420 Rider Trail South
Earth City, MO 63045
Programs Offered:
medical/clinical assistant; medical insurance/medical billing
Enrollment: 159 students
Institution Contact: Ms. Susan E. Race, School President
Phone: 314-739-7333 ext. 104
Fax: 314-739-6888
E-mail: srace@cci.edu
Admission Contact: Mr. Sandy Kaup, Director of Admissions
Phone: 314-739-7333 ext. 102
Fax: 314-739-6888
E-mail: skaup@cci.edu

HERITAGE COLLEGE

534 East 99th Street
Kansas City, MO 64131-4203
Programs Offered:
massage therapy; medical/clinical assistant; pharmacy technician
Institution Contact: Admissions
Phone: 816-942-5474

Fax: 816-942-5405

HICKEY COLLEGE

940 West Port Plaza
St. Louis, MO 63146
Web: http://www.hickeycollege.edu
Accreditation: Accrediting Council for Independent
Colleges and Schools
Programs Offered:
accounting; administrative assistant and secretarial
science; business administration and management;
business operations support and secretarial services
related; commercial and advertising art; computer
graphics; computer programming; computer programming (specific applications); computer software technology; computer systems networking and telecommunications; computer/technical support; information
resources management; legal administrative assistant/
secretary; legal assistant/paralegal
Enrollment: 450 students
Institution Contact: Mr. Christopher Gearin, President
Phone: 314-434-2212
Fax: 314-434-1974
E-mail: admin@hickeycollege.com

HIGH-TECH INSTITUTE

9001 State Line Road
Kansas City, MO 64114
Web: http://www.hightechinstitute.edu
Accreditation: Accrediting Commission of Career
Schools and Colleges of Technology
Programs Offered:
criminal justice/law enforcement administration; den-
tal assisting; massage therapy; medical/clinical assis-
tant; medical insurance coding; surgical technology
Enrollment: 507 students
Institution Contact: Mrs. Joan Ellison, Campus
President
Phone: 816-444-4300
Fax: 816-444-4494
E-mail: jellison@hightechinstitute.edu
Admission Contact: Ms. Barbette Hatcher, Director
of Admission
Phone: 816-444-4300
Fax: 816-444-4494
E-mail: bhatcher@hightechinstitute.edu

ITT TECHNICAL INSTITUTE

1930 Meyer Drury Drive
Arnold, MO 63010
Web: http://www.itt-tech.edu
Accreditation: Accrediting Council for Independent
Colleges and Schools
Programs Offered:
accounting and business/management; animation,
interactive technology, video graphics and special
effects; business administration and management;
CAD/CADD drafting/design technology; communications technology; computer and information systems
security; computer engineering technology; computer
software and media applications; computer software
engineering; computer systems networking and telecommunications; criminal justice/police science; digital communication and media/multimedia; electrical,
electronic and communications engineering technology; technology management; web page, digital/multi-
media and information resources design
Institution Contact: Ms. Paula Jerden, Director
Phone: 636-464-6600
Admission Contact: Mr. James R. Rowe, Director of
Recruitment
Phone: 636-464-6600

ITT TECHNICAL INSTITUTE

13505 Lakefront Drive
Earth City, MO 63045-1412
Web: http://www.itt-tech.edu
Accreditation: Accrediting Council for Independent
Colleges and Schools
Programs Offered:
accounting and business/management; animation,
interactive technology, video graphics and special
effects; business administration and management;
CAD/CADD drafting/design technology; communications technology; computer and information systems
security; computer engineering technology; computer
software and media applications; computer software
engineering; computer systems networking and telecommunications; criminal justice/police science; digital communication and media/multimedia; electrical,
electronic and communications engineering technology; technology management; web page, digital/multi-
media and information resources design
Institution Contact: Ms. Karen Finkenkeller, Director
Phone: 314-298-7800

Admission Contact: Ms. Karla Milla, Director of Recruitment
Phone: 314-298-7800

ITT Technical Institute
1740 West 92nd Street, Suite 100
Kansas City, MO 64114
Web: http://www.itt-tech.edu/
Programs Offered:
accounting and business/management; business administration and management; computer and information systems security; computer engineering technology; computer systems networking and telecommunications; criminal justice/police science
Institution Contact:
Phone: 816-276-1400

L'Ecole Culinaire
9811 S. Forty Dr.
Saint Louis, MO 63124
Institution Contact: Jim Walsh
Phone: 314-587-2433
Fax: 314-587-2430

Metro Business College
1732 North Kings Highway
Cape Girardeau, MO 63701
Web: http://www.metrobusinesscollege.edu
Accreditation: Accrediting Council for Independent Colleges and Schools
Programs Offered:
administrative assistant and secretarial science; business automation/technology/data entry; computer/information technology administration and management; massage therapy; medical administrative assistant and medical secretary
Enrollment: 149 students
Institution Contact: Ms. Jan Reimann, Director
Phone: 573-334-9181
Fax: 573-334-0617
E-mail: jan@metrobusinesscollege.edu
Admission Contact: Mrs. Denise Acey, Admissions Representative
Phone: 573-334-9181
Fax: 573-334-0617
E-mail: denise@metrobusinesscollege.edu

Metro Business College
1407 Southwest Boulevard
Jefferson City, MO 65109
Web: http://www.metrobusinesscollege.edu
Accreditation: Accrediting Council for Independent Colleges and Schools
Programs Offered:
administrative assistant and secretarial science; business automation/technology/data entry; computer/information technology administration and management; massage therapy; medical administrative assistant and medical secretary; medical reception
Enrollment: 140 students
Institution Contact: Ms. Cheri Chockley, Campus Director
Phone: 573-635-6600
Fax: 573-635-6999
E-mail: cheri@metrobusinesscollege.edu
Admission Contact: Ms. Patti Sander, Admission Representative
Phone: 573-635-6600
Fax: 573-635-6999
E-mail: patti@metrobusinesscollege.edu

Metro Business College
1202 East Highway 72
Rolla, MO 65401
Web: http://www.metrobusinesscollege.edu
Accreditation: Accrediting Council for Independent Colleges and Schools
Programs Offered:
administrative assistant and secretarial science; business automation/technology/data entry; computer/information technology administration and management; massage therapy; medical/health management and clinical assistant; medical office computer specialist; medical reception
Enrollment: 125 students
Institution Contact: Ms. Cristie Barker, Director
Phone: 573-364-8464
Fax: 573-364-8077
E-mail: cbarker@metrobusinesscollege.edu

Missouri College
10121 Manchester Road
St. Louis, MO 63122
Web: http://www.missouricollege.com

Accreditation: Accrediting Commission of Career Schools and Colleges of Technology

Programs Offered:

administrative assistant and secretarial science; computer software engineering; computer systems networking and telecommunications; data entry/microcomputer applications; dental assisting; executive assistant/executive secretary; information technology; massage therapy; medical administrative assistant and medical secretary; medical/clinical assistant; medical office management; selling skills and sales

Institution Contact: Ms. Erin Cunningham, Admissions Director

Phone: 314-821-7700

Fax: 314-821-0891

E-mail: info@missouricollege.com

Admission Contact: Ms. Marina Palmieri, Admissions Director

Phone: 314-821-7700

Fax: 314-821-0891

E-mail: mpalmieri@missouricollege.com

Missouri Tech

1167 Corporate Lake Drive

St. Louis, MO 63132-2907

Web: http://www.motech.edu

Accreditation: Accrediting Commission of Career Schools and Colleges of Technology

Programs Offered:

artificial intelligence and robotics; computer and information sciences related; computer and information systems security; computer engineering related; computer engineering technology; computer graphics; computer hardware engineering; computer/information technology administration and management; computer/information technology services administration related; computer installation and repair technology; computer programming; computer programming related; computer programming (specific applications); computer programming (vendor/product certification); computer software and media applications; computer software and media applications related; computer software engineering; computer software technology; computer systems analysis; computer systems networking and telecommunications; computer/technical support; computer technology/computer systems technology; digital communication and media/multimedia; electrical, electronic and communications engineer-

ing technology; engineering technology; information science/studies; management information systems; system administration; system, networking, and LAN/WAN management; technology management; telecommunications; telecommunications technology

Enrollment: 200 students

Institution Contact: Mr. Paul Dodge, Director

Phone: 314-569-3600

Fax: 314-569-1167

E-mail: pdodge@motech.edu

Admission Contact: Mr. Robert Honaker, Director of Student Affairs

Phone: 314-569-3600

Fax: 314-569-1167

E-mail: bob@motech.edu

National American University

4200 Blue Ridge Boulevard

Kansas City, MO 64133

Accreditation: North Central Association of Colleges and Schools

Programs Offered:

accounting; business administration and management; business, management, and marketing related; computer programming; computer software technology; computer/technical support; e-commerce; general studies; information technology; legal assistant/paralegal; management information systems; nursing related; web/multimedia management and webmaster

Enrollment: 327 students

Institution Contact: Ms. Michelle Holland, Regional President

Phone: 816-353-4554

Fax: 816-353-1176

E-mail: mholland@national.edu

Admission Contact: Mr. Marcus Smith, Director of Admissions

Phone: 816-343-4554

Fax: 816-353-1176

E-mail: msmith2@national.edu

Pinnacle Career Institute

15329 Kensington Avenue

Kansas City, MO 64147

Web: http://www.pcitraining.edu

Programs Offered:

electrical and electronic engineering technologies

related; massage therapy; medical/clinical assistant; telecommunications
Enrollment: 155 students
Institution Contact: Ms. Becky Clothier, Executive Director
Phone: 816-331-5700 ext. 212
Fax: 816-331-2026
E-mail: bc-pvi@swbell.net
Admission Contact: Mr. Spencer Dunlap, Director of Admissions
Phone: 816-331-5700 ext. 206
Fax: 816-331-2026
E-mail: sdunlap@pcitraining.edu

St. Louis College of Health Careers

4044 Butler Hill Road
St. Louis, MO 63129
Web: http://www.slchc.com
Programs Offered:
massage therapy; medical/clinical assistant; medical insurance/medical billing; medical staff services technology; nursing (licensed practical/vocational nurse training); phlebotomy
Institution Contact:
Phone: 314-845-6100
Fax: 314-845-6406

St. Louis College of Health Careers

1297 North Highway Drive
Fenton, MO 63026
Accreditation: Accrediting Bureau of Health Education Schools
Programs Offered:
massage therapy; medical administrative assistant and medical secretary; medical/clinical assistant; medical insurance/medical billing; nursing assistant/aide and patient care assistant; nursing (licensed practical/vocational nurse training); ophthalmic and optometric support services and allied professions related; pharmacy technician; phlebotomy
Enrollment: 250 students
Institution Contact: Dr. Rush L. Robinson, President
Phone: 314-652-0300 ext. 2001
Fax: 314-652-4825
E-mail: rrobinson@slchcmail.com
Admission Contact: Mr. Doug Brinker, Admissions Director

Phone: 636-529-0000 ext. 3100
Fax: 636-529-0430
E-mail: dbrinker@slchcmail.com

Sanford-Brown College

1203 Smizer Mill Road
Fenton, MO 63026
Web: http://www.sanford-brown.edu
Accreditation: Accrediting Council for Independent Colleges and Schools
Programs Offered:
accounting; business administration and management; computer/information technology administration and management; computer systems networking and telecommunications; computer/technical support; criminal justice/law enforcement administration; fashion merchandising; health information/medical records technology; legal assistant/paralegal; massage therapy; medical/clinical assistant; medical insurance coding; medical insurance/medical billing; nursing (licensed practical/vocational nurse training); radiologic technology/science; respiratory care therapy; surgical technology; web page, digital/multimedia and information resources design
Institution Contact: Mr. Franklin Clarkston, Associate Director of Admissions
Phone: 636-349-4900
Fax: 636-349-9317
E-mail: fclarkston@sbc-fenton.com

Sanford-Brown College

75 Village Square
Hazelwood, MO 63042
Web: http://www.sanford-brown.edu
Accreditation: Accrediting Bureau of Health Education Schools; Accrediting Council for Independent Colleges and Schools
Programs Offered:
business administration and management; criminal justice/law enforcement administration; dental assisting; fashion merchandising; legal assistant/paralegal; massage therapy; medical/clinical assistant; occupational therapist assistant; surgical technology
Enrollment: 639 students
Institution Contact: Mr. Clarence Harmon, Campus President
Phone: 314-687-2904

Fax: 314-731-0550
E-mail: charmon@sbc-hazelwood.com
Admission Contact: Ms. Ladon Harris, Director of Admissions
Phone: 314-687-2900
Fax: 314-731-0550
E-mail: lharris@sbc-hazelwood.com

SANFORD-BROWN COLLEGE

520 East 19th Avenue
North Kansas City, MO 64116-3614
Web: http://www.sanford-browncollege.com
Accreditation: Accrediting Bureau of Health Education Schools; Accrediting Council for Independent Colleges and Schools
Programs Offered:
business administration and management; computer/information technology administration and management; criminal justice/law enforcement administration; health/health care administration; marketing/marketing management; massage therapy; medical/clinical assistant; medical insurance/medical billing; nursing (licensed practical/vocational nurse training); radiologic technology/science; surgical technology
Enrollment: 560 students
Institution Contact: Mr. Dennis L. Townsend, Campus President
Phone: 816-472-0275
Fax: 816-472-0688
E-mail: dtownsend@kc.sanfordbrown.com
Admission Contact: Mr. Micheal Murdie, Director of Admissions
Phone: 816-472-0275
Fax: 816-472-0688
E-mail: micheal.murdie@wix.net

SANFORD-BROWN COLLEGE

3555 Franks Drive
St. Charles, MO 63301
Web: http://www.sanford-brown.edu
Accreditation: Accrediting Council for Independent Colleges and Schools
Programs Offered:
accounting; business administration and management; computer systems networking and telecommunications; data entry/microcomputer applications; health/health care administration; intermedia/multimedia; legal assistant/paralegal; nursing (licensed practical/vocational nurse training); nursing (registered nurse training); web page, digital/multimedia and information resources design
Institution Contact: Julia A. Leeman, President
Phone: 636-949-2620
Fax: 636-925-9827
E-mail: jleeman@sbc-stcharles.com
Admission Contact: Mr. Doug Goodwin, Director of Admissions
Phone: 636-949-2620
Fax: 636-949-5081
E-mail: dgoodwin@sbc-stcharles.com

SPRINGFIELD COLLEGE

1010 West Sunshine
Springfield, MO 65807
Web: http://www.Springfield-college.com
Accreditation: Accrediting Council for Independent Colleges and Schools
Programs Offered:
accounting; business administration and management; computer programming (specific applications); dental assisting; legal assistant/paralegal; medical/clinical assistant; medical insurance/medical billing; medical office management; medical transcription
Enrollment: 500 students
Institution Contact: Mr. Gerald F. Terrebrood, President
Phone: 417-864-7220
Fax: 417-864-5697
E-mail: gterrebr@cci.edu
Admission Contact: Mr. Scott Lester, Director of Admissions
Phone: 417-864-7220
Fax: 417-864-5697
E-mail: slester@cci.edu

VATTEROTT COLLEGE

5898 North Main
Joplin, MO 64801
Web: http://www.vatterott-college.edu
Accreditation: Accrediting Commission of Career Schools and Colleges of Technology
Programs Offered:
accounting; CAD/CADD drafting/design technology; computer/information technology administration and management; computer installation and repair technol-

ogy; computer programming; computer software and media applications; cosmetology; medical administrative assistant and medical secretary; nail technician and manicurist

Institution Contact: Office of Admissions
Phone: 417-781-5633
Fax: 417-781-6437
E-mail: joplin@vatterott-college.edu

VATTEROTT COLLEGE

8955 East 38th Terrace
Kansas City, MO 64129
Web: http://www.vatterott-college.edu
Accreditation: Accrediting Commission of Career Schools and Colleges of Technology
Programs Offered:
administrative assistant and secretarial science; business automation/technology/data entry; computer installation and repair technology; computer programming; computer systems networking and telecommunications; drafting and design technology; electrician; heating, air conditioning and refrigeration technology; medical/clinical assistant; pharmacy technician

Institution Contact: Office of Admissions
Phone: 816-861-1000
Fax: 816-861-1400
E-mail: kc@vatterott-college.edu

VATTEROTT COLLEGE

927 East Terra Lane
O'Fallon , MO 63366
Web: http://www.vatterott-college.edu
Accreditation: Accrediting Commission of Career Schools and Colleges of Technology
Programs Offered:
building/property maintenance and management; computer systems networking and telecommunications; computer technology/computer systems technology; electrical/electronics equipment installation and repair; electrician; heating, air conditioning and refrigeration technology; heating, air conditioning, ventilation and refrigeration maintenance technology; medical administrative assistant and medical secretary; medical/clinical assistant; medical office assistant

Enrollment: 150 students
Institution Contact: Mr. Jerry Martin, Director
Phone: 636-978-7488

Fax: 636-978-5121
E-mail: jmartin@vatterott-college.edu
Admission Contact: Jerry Martin, Director of Admissions
Phone: 636-978-7488
Fax: 636-978-5121
E-mail: jmartin@vatterott-college.edu

VATTEROTT COLLEGE

3925 Industrial Drive
St. Ann, MO 63074
Web: http://www.vatterott-college.edu
Accreditation: Accrediting Commission of Career Schools and Colleges of Technology
Programs Offered:
allied health and medical assisting services related; CAD/CADD drafting/design technology; computer engineering technology; computer programming; computer systems analysis; computer systems networking and telecommunications; computer technology/computer systems technology; dental assisting; electrical and electronic engineering technologies related; electrician; electromechanical technology; heating, air conditioning and refrigeration technology; medical office assistant; plumbing technology; web/multimedia management and webmaster; welding technology

Enrollment: 804 students
Institution Contact: Director
Phone: 888-370-7955
Fax: 314-428-5956
Admission Contact: Office of Admissions
Phone: 888-370-7955
Fax: 314-428-5956
E-mail: saintann@vatterott-college.edu

VATTEROTT COLLEGE

3131 Frederick Boulevard
St. Joseph, MO 64506
Web: http://www.vatterott-college.edu
Accreditation: Accrediting Commission of Career Schools and Colleges of Technology
Programs Offered:
administrative assistant and secretarial science; computer programming; computer technology/computer systems technology; cosmetology; drafting and design technology; health information/medical records technology; massage therapy; medical administrative assistant and medical secretary; medical/clinical as-

sistant; medical office management; medical transcription; nail technician and manicurist; office occupations and clerical services

Enrollment: 440 students
Institution Contact: Mr. Wayne Major, Director
Phone: 816-364-5399
Fax: 816-364-1593
E-mail: wmajor@vatterott-college.edu
Admission Contact: Mrs. Sandra Wisdom, Director of Admissions
Phone: 816-364-5399
Fax: 816-364-1593
E-mail: swisdom@vatterott-college.edu

 VATTEROTT COLLEGE
12970 Maurer Industrial Drive
St. Louis, MO 63127
Web: http://www.vatterott-college.edu
Accreditation: Accrediting Commission of Career Schools and Colleges of Technology
Programs Offered:
building/property maintenance and management; CAD/CADD drafting/design technology; computer programming; computer technology/computer systems technology; electrical, electronic and communications engineering technology; heating, air conditioning and refrigeration technology; heating, air conditioning, ventilation and refrigeration maintenance technology; medical/clinical assistant
Institution Contact: Mr. James Rund, Co-Director
Phone: 314-843-4200
Fax: 314-843-1709
E-mail: jrund@vatterott-college.edu
Admission Contact: Mr. Jim Powers, Director of Admissions
Phone: 314-843-4200
Fax: 314-843-1709
E-mail: leeannb@vatterott-college.edu

VATTEROTT COLLEGE
3850 South Campbell
Springfield, MO 65807
Web: http://www.vatterott-college.edu
Accreditation: Accrediting Commission of Career Schools and Colleges of Technology
Programs Offered:
administrative assistant and secretarial science; comput-

er software and media applications; computer technology/computer systems technology; dental assisting; drafting and design technology; legal assistant/paralegal; medical administrative assistant and medical secretary; medical/clinical assistant; pharmacy technician
Enrollment: 229 students
Institution Contact: Mrs. Cheryl Tilley, Director
Phone: 417-831-8116
Fax: 417-831-5099
E-mail: ctilley@vatterott-college.edu
Admission Contact: Admissions
Phone: 417-831-8116
Fax: 417-831-5099
E-mail: springfield@vatterott-college.edu

MONTANA

SAGE TECHNICAL SERVICES
3044 Hesper Road
Billings, MT 59102
Web: http://www.sageschools.com
Accreditation: Accrediting Commission of Career Schools and Colleges of Technology
Programs Offered:
transportation technology; truck and bus driver/commercial vehicle operation
Enrollment: 2 students
Institution Contact: Mr. Lew Grill, Director
Phone: 406-652-3030
Fax: 406-652-3129
E-mail: lew@lewgrill.com

NEBRASKA

COLLEGE OF HAIR DESIGN
304 South 11th Street
Lincoln, NE 68508-2199
Web: http://www.collegeofhairdesign.com
Accreditation: Accrediting Commission of Career Schools and Colleges of Technology
Programs Offered:
barbering; cosmetology; cosmetology, barber/styling, and nail instruction
Enrollment: 125 students
Institution Contact: Mrs. Alyce Howard, President

Phone: 402-477-4040 ext. 118
Fax: 402-474-4075
E-mail: mrsh@collegeofhairdesign.com
Admission Contact: Mr. Chris Hobbs, Director of Admissions
Phone: 402-477-4040 ext. 108
Fax: 402-474-4075
E-mail: chris@collegeofhairdesign.com

ITT TECHNICAL INSTITUTE

9814 M Street
Omaha, NE 68127-2056
Web: http://www.itt-tech.edu
Accreditation: Accrediting Council for Independent Colleges and Schools
Programs Offered:
accounting and business/management; business administration and management; CAD/CADD drafting/design technology; communications technology; computer and information systems security; computer engineering technology; computer software and media applications; computer systems networking and telecommunications; criminal justice/police science; digital communication and media/multimedia; electrical, electronic and communications engineering technology; technology management; web page, digital/multimedia and information resources design
Institution Contact: Mr. Jerome S. Padak, Director
Phone: 402-331-2900
Admission Contact: Ms. Trish Miller, Director of Recruitment
Phone: 402-331-2900

VATTEROTT COLLEGE

11818 "I" Street
Omaha, NE 68137
Web: http://www.vatterott-college.edu
Accreditation: Accrediting Commission of Career Schools and Colleges of Technology
Programs Offered:
accounting technology and bookkeeping; allied health and medical assisting services related; CAD/CADD drafting/design technology; commercial and advertising art; computer engineering technology; computer systems networking and telecommunications; construction management; dental assisting; drafting and design technology; heating, air conditioning, ventila-

tion and refrigeration maintenance technology; pharmacy technician; veterinary technology
Enrollment: 333 students
Institution Contact: Office of Admissions
Phone: 402-891-9411
Fax: 402-891-9413
E-mail: springvalley@vatterott-college.edu

NEVADA

AMERICAN INSTITUTE OF TECHNOLOGY

4610 Vanderberg Drive
North Las Vegas, NV 85043-4729
Web: http://www.ait-schools.com
Accreditation: Accrediting Commission of Career Schools and Colleges of Technology; Accrediting Council for Continuing Education and Training
Programs Offered:
truck and bus driver/commercial vehicle operation
Enrollment: 100 students
Institution Contact: Mr. Chuck Wirth, Vice President
Phone: 702-644-1234
Fax: 702-632-0167
E-mail: cwirth@ait-schools.com
Admission Contact: Ms. Diane Warren, Director of Admissions
Phone: 702-644-1234
Fax: 702-632-0167
E-mail: lvdirector@ait-schools.com

THE ART INSTITUTE OF LAS VEGAS

2350 Corporate Circle
Henderson, NV 89074
Web: http://www.ailv.artinstitutes.edu
Accreditation: Accrediting Commission of Career Schools and Colleges of Technology
Programs Offered:
animation, interactive technology, video graphics and special effects; CAD/CADD drafting/design technology; commercial and advertising art; computer graphics; culinary arts; drafting and design technology; interior design; web/multimedia management and webmaster; web page, digital/multimedia and information resources design
Enrollment: 1,057 students
Institution Contact: Mr. Steve Brooks, President

Phone: 702-369-9944
Fax: 702-992-8555
E-mail: brookss@aii.edu
Admission Contact: Ms. Suzanne Noel, Director of Admissions
Phone: 702-369-9944 ext. 8459
Fax: 702-992-8458
E-mail: snoel@aii.edu

CAREER COLLEGE OF NORTHERN NEVADA

1195-A Corporate Boulevard
Reno, NV 89502
Web: http://www.ccnn4u.com
Accreditation: Accrediting Commission of Career Schools and Colleges of Technology
Programs Offered:
business automation/technology/data entry; computer/information technology administration and management; data processing and data processing technology; electrical, electronic and communications engineering technology; legal administrative assistant/secretary; legal assistant/paralegal; medical/clinical assistant; medical insurance coding; medical insurance/medical billing
Enrollment: 316 students
Institution Contact: Mr. L. Nathan Clark, President
Phone: 775-856-2266
Fax: 775-856-0935
E-mail: nclark@ccnn4u.com
Admission Contact: Laura Goldhammer, Director of Admissions
Phone: 775-856-2266
Fax: 775-856-0935
E-mail: lgoldhammer@ccnn4u.com

CAREER EDUCATION INSTITUTE

2290 Corporate Circle Drive, Suite 100
Henderson, NV 89074
Web: http://www.ceitraining.com
Accreditation: Accrediting Council for Independent Colleges and Schools
Programs Offered:
business administration and management; computer/information technology administration and management; massage therapy; medical administrative assistant and medical secretary; medical/clinical assistant; system, networking, and LAN/WAN management
Enrollment: 250 students

Institution Contact: Mr. David L. Evans, Executive Director
Phone: 702-269-7600 ext. 201
Fax: 702-269-7676
E-mail: devans@lincolntech.com
Admission Contact: Mr. David L. Evans, Admissions Director
Phone: 702-269-7600
Fax: 702-269-7676
E-mail: devans@lincolntech.com

HERITAGE COLLEGE

3305 Spring Mountain Road, Suite 7
Las Vegas, NV 89102
Programs Offered:
business administration and management; legal assistant/paralegal; medical/clinical assistant; pharmacy technician
Institution Contact:
Phone: 702-368-2338
Fax: 702-638-3853

HIGH-TECH INSTITUTE

2320 South Rancho Drive
Las Vegas, NV 89102
Web: http://www.hightechinstitute.edu
Accreditation: Accrediting Commission of Career Schools and Colleges of Technology
Programs Offered:
dental assisting; massage therapy; medical/clinical assistant; medical insurance/medical billing; pharmacy technician; surgical technology
Enrollment: 455 students
Institution Contact: Mr. David Moore, Campus President
Phone: 702-385-6700
Fax: 702-388-4463
E-mail: dmoore@hightechinstitute.edu
Admission Contact: Ms. Amy Tu, Director of Admissions
Phone: 702-385-6700
Fax: 702-388-4463
E-mail: atu@hightechinstitute.edu

INTERNATIONAL ACADEMY OF DESIGN AND TECHNOLOGY

2495 Village View Drive

Henderson, NV 89074
Web: http://www.iadtvegas.com
Accreditation: Accrediting Council for Independent Colleges and Schools
Programs Offered:
design and visual communications; fashion/apparel design; interior design
Enrollment: 405 students
Institution Contact: Mr. Kirt Thompson, President
Phone: 702-990-0150 ext. 5911
Fax: 702-269-1981
E-mail: kirt_thompson@iadtvegas.com
Admission Contact: Ms. Germaine Badar, Vice President of Admissions
Phone: 702-990-0150 ext. 5914
Fax: 702-990-0161
E-mail: gbadar@iadtvegas.com

 ITT TECHNICAL INSTITUTE
168 North Gibson Road
Henderson, NV 89014
Web: http://www.itt-tech.edu
Accreditation: Accrediting Council for Independent Colleges and Schools
Programs Offered:
accounting and business/management; animation, interactive technology, video graphics and special effects; business administration and management; CAD/CADD drafting/design technology; communications technology; computer and information systems security; computer engineering technology; computer software and media applications; computer software engineering; computer systems networking and telecommunications; criminal justice/police science; digital communication and media/multimedia; electrical, electronic and communications engineering technology; technology management; web page, digital/multimedia and information resources design
Institution Contact: Mr. Donn Nimmer, Director
Phone: 702-558-5404
Admission Contact: Ms. Anne Buzak, Director of Recruitment
Phone: 702-558-5404

 LAS VEGAS COLLEGE
170 North Stephanie Street, Suite 145
Henderson, NV 89014

Accreditation: Accrediting Council for Independent Colleges and Schools
Programs Offered:
business administration and management; criminal justice/law enforcement administration; medical/clinical assistant; medical office assistant
Enrollment: 137 students
Institution Contact: Mr. Joel D. Boyd, President
Phone: 702-567-1920
Fax: 702-566-9725
E-mail: jboyd@cci.edu
Admission Contact: Mr. Bart Van Ry, Director of Admissions
Phone: 702-567-1920
Fax: 702-566-9725
E-mail: bvanry@cci.edu

LAS VEGAS COLLEGE
4100 West Flamingo Road, #2100
Las Vegas, NV 89103
Web: http://www.cci.edu
Accreditation: Accrediting Council for Independent Colleges and Schools
Programs Offered:
accounting; administrative assistant and secretarial science; business administration and management; business automation/technology/data entry; court reporting; criminal justice/law enforcement administration; legal assistant/paralegal; medical administrative assistant and medical secretary; medical/clinical assistant; medical insurance coding; medical insurance/medical billing; word processing
Institution Contact: Mr. Sam A. Gentile, President
Phone: 702-368-6200
Fax: 702-368-6464
E-mail: sgentile@cci.edu
Admission Contact: Mr. Shawn Saunders, Admissions Director
Phone: 702-368-6200
Fax: 702-368-6464
E-mail: ssaunder@cci.edu

MAP **LE CORDON BLEU COLLEGE OF CULINARY ARTS, LAS VEGAS**
1451 Center Crossing Road
Las Vegas, NV 89144
Web: http://www.VegasCulinary.com

Accreditation: Accrediting Commission of Career Schools and Colleges of Technology
Programs Offered:
culinary arts
Enrollment: 780 students
Institution Contact: Mr. David Evans, President
Phone: 702-365-7690 ext. 5310
Fax: 702-365-7911
E-mail: devans@vegasculinary.com
Admission Contact: Mr. John Hayet, Vice President, Admissions and Marketing
Phone: 702-365-7690 ext. 5320
Fax: 702-365-7911
E-mail: jhayet@vegasculinary.com

Morrison University

10315 Professional Circle, Suite 201, Reno-Tahoe Tech Center
Reno, NV 89521
Web: http://www.morrison.neumont.edu
Accreditation: Accrediting Council for Independent Colleges and Schools
Programs Offered:
accounting; business administration and management; computer and information sciences related
Enrollment: 110 students
Institution Contact: Mrs. Lisa Kelly, Dean of Academics
Phone: 775-850-0700 ext. 112
Fax: 775-850-0711
E-mail: lisa.kelly@morrison.neumont.edu
Admission Contact: Mrs. Angela Simpson, Director of Enrollment
Phone: 775-850-0700 ext. 113
Fax: 775-850-0711
E-mail: asimpson@morrison.neumont.edu

Nevada Career Academy

950 Industrial Way
Sparks, NV 89431
Web: http://www.nevadacareeracademy.com
Accreditation: Accrediting Council for Continuing Education and Training
Programs Offered:
computer software and media applications; massage therapy; medical/clinical assistant; medical reception; pharmacy technician

Institution Contact: Ms. Cathy Tobin, Vice President of Compliance
Phone: 559-735-3818 ext. 1012
Fax: 559-733-7831
E-mail: ctatcorp@aol.com
Admission Contact: Admissions Representative
Phone: 775-348-7200
Fax: 775-359-7227
E-mail: infonca@nevadacareeracademy.com

Nevada Career Institute

3025 East Desert Inn Road, Suite A
Las Vegas, NV 89121
Web: http://www.nevadacareerinstitute.com
Accreditation: Accrediting Council for Continuing Education and Training
Programs Offered:
massage therapy; medical/clinical assistant; medical office management; surgical technology
Enrollment: 170 students
Institution Contact: Ms. Joanne Q. Leming, Director
Phone: 702-893-3300
Fax: 702-893-3881
E-mail: jqleming@success.edu
Admission Contact: Ms. Alyssa Adelman, Director of Admissions
Phone: 702-893-3300
Fax: 702-893-3881
E-mail: nciinfo@nevadacareerinstitute.com

Nevada Career Institute

3231 N. Decatur Blvd.
Suite 219
Las Vegas, NV 89130
Web: www.nevadacareerinstitute.com
Institution Contact: Arlene Muller
Phone: 702-932-0515
Fax: 702-932-0518

Nevada School of Massage Therapy

2381 E. Windmill Ln., Suite 14
Las Vegas, NV 89123
Institution Contact: Ms. Renee Fabig
Phone: 702-456-4325
Fax: 702-456-9910

PIMA MEDICAL INSTITUTE

3333 East Flamingo Road
Las Vegas, NV 89121
Web: http://www.pmi.edu
Accreditation: Accrediting Bureau of Health Education Schools
Programs Offered:
dental assisting; medical administrative assistant and medical secretary; medical/clinical assistant; pharmacy technician; phlebotomy; radiologic technology/science; respiratory care therapy; veterinary/animal health technology
Enrollment: 303 students
Institution Contact: Mr. Christopher Luebke, Admissions Support Center Director
Phone: 888-898-9048
E-mail: asc@pmi.edu
Admission Contact: Admissions Support Representative
Phone: 888-898-9048
E-mail: asc@pmi.edu

NEW HAMPSHIRE

HESSER COLLEGE

3 Sundial Avenue
Manchester, NH 03103
Web: http://www.hesser.edu/
Accreditation: New England Association of Schools and Colleges
Programs Offered:
accounting; adult and continuing education; allied health and medical assisting services related; business administration and management; business/corporate communications; business, management, and marketing related; clinical/medical laboratory assistant; clinical/medical laboratory science and allied professions related; clinical/medical laboratory technology; commercial and advertising art; communications systems installation and repair technology; computer and information sciences; computer and information sciences and support services related; computer and information sciences related; computer and information systems security; computer engineering technology; computer graphics; computer/information technology administration and management; computer/information technology services administration related; computer installation and repair technology; computer programming; computer programming related; computer programming (specific applications); computer programming (vendor/product certification); computer science; computer systems networking and telecommunications; computer technology/computer systems technology; criminal justice/law enforcement administration; desktop publishing and digital imaging design; general studies; graphic communications; graphic communications related; health and medical administrative services related; health services/allied health/health sciences; information technology; interior design; kindergarten/preschool education; legal assistant/paralegal; marketing/marketing management; massage therapy; medical administrative assistant and medical secretary; medical/clinical assistant; physical therapist assistant; pre-law studies; radio and television; radio and television broadcasting technology; safety/security technology; security and loss prevention; sports medicine; teacher assistant/aide
Institution Contact: Dr. Paul F. Tero, Dean of Academic Affairs
Phone: 603-668-6660 ext. 2154
Fax: 603-666-4722
E-mail: ptero@hesser.edu
Admission Contact: Mrs. Mary Jo Greco, President
Phone: 603-668-6660 ext. 2102
Fax: 603-666-4722
E-mail: mgreco@hesser.edu

McINTOSH COLLEGE

23 Cataract Avenue
Dover, NH 03820-3990
Web: http://www.gomcintosh.com
Accreditation: New England Association of Schools and Colleges
Programs Offered:
accounting; accounting and business/management; accounting and finance; advertising; allied health and medical assisting services related; apparel and accessories marketing; business administration and management; business administration, management and operations related; clinical laboratory science/medical technology; clinical/medical laboratory assistant; clinical/medical laboratory science and allied professions related; clinical/medical laboratory technology; commercial and advertising art; computer graphics; corrections; criminal justice/law enforcement administration;

criminal justice/police science; desktop publishing and digital imaging design; drawing; fashion merchandising; graphic communications; graphic communications related; health/health care administration; health information/medical records administration; health services administration; health services/allied health/health sciences; kinesiotherapy; marketing/marketing management; marketing related; massage therapy; medical/clinical assistant; medical/health management and clinical assistant; medical office assistant; medical office management; merchandising; merchandising, sales, and marketing operations related (general); merchandising, sales, and marketing operations related (specialized); phlebotomy; photography; web/multimedia management and webmaster; web page, digital/multimedia and information resources design; word processing

Enrollment: 1,200 students
Institution Contact: Mrs. Marylin Newell, President
Phone: 800-521-3995
Fax: 603-743-0060
E-mail: mnewell@mcintoshcollege.edu
Admission Contact: Mrs. Jody LaBrie, Director of High School Admissions
Phone: 800-521-3995
Fax: 603-743-0060
E-mail: jlabrie@mcintoshcollege.edu

NEW JERSEY

BERDAN INSTITUTE
265 Route 46 West
Totowa, NJ 07512-1819
Web: http://www.berdaninstitute.com
Accreditation: Accrediting Bureau of Health Education Schools; Accrediting Commission of Career Schools and Colleges of Technology
Programs Offered:
dental assisting; massage therapy; medical administrative assistant and medical secretary; medical/clinical assistant; medical insurance/medical billing; nursing assistant/aide and patient care assistant; pharmacy technician
Enrollment: 345 students
Institution Contact: Mr. E. Lynn Thacker, Director
Phone: 973-256-3444
Fax: 973-256-0816

E-mail: lthacker@berdaninstitute.com
Admission Contact: Mr. Alan Concha, Director of Admissions
Phone: 973-256-3444
Fax: 973-256-0816
E-mail: aconcha@berdaninstitute.com

BERKELEY COLLEGE
64 East Midland Avenue
Paramus, NJ 07652
Web: http://www.BerkeleyCollege.edu
Accreditation: Middle States Association of Colleges and Schools
Programs Offered:
accounting; business administration and management; entrepreneurship; fashion merchandising; human resources management; interior design; international business/trade/commerce; legal assistant/paralegal; management science; marketing/marketing management; system, networking, and LAN/WAN management; web page, digital/multimedia and information resources design
Enrollment: 465 students
Institution Contact: Mr. Timothy D. Luing, Senior Vice President
Phone: 201-967-9667
Fax: 201-265-6446
E-mail: tim@berkeleycollege.edu
Admission Contact: Ms. Maria Fontanetta, Director, High School Admissions
Phone: 201-967-9667
Fax: 201-265-6446
E-mail: bgcampus@berkeleycollege.edu

BERKELEY COLLEGE
44 Rifle Camp Road
West Paterson, NJ 07424
Web: http://www.BerkeleyCollege.edu
Accreditation: Middle States Association of Colleges and Schools
Programs Offered:
accounting; business administration and management; entrepreneurship; fashion merchandising; human resources management; international business/trade/commerce; legal assistant/paralegal; management science; marketing/marketing management; system, networking, and LAN/WAN management; web page,

digital/multimedia and information resources design
Enrollment: 1,387 students
Institution Contact: Dr. Mildred Garcia, President
Phone: 212-986-4343 ext. 4101
Fax: 212-986-8901
E-mail: millieg@berkeleycollege.edu
Admission Contact: Mr. Dave Bertone, Director of High School Admissions
Phone: 973-278-5400
Fax: 973-278-9141
E-mail: info@berkeleycollege.edu

BERKELEY COLLEGE

430 Rahway Avenue
Woodbridge, NJ 07095
Web: http://www.BerkeleyCollege.edu
Accreditation: Middle States Association of Colleges and Schools
Programs Offered:
accounting; business administration and management; entrepreneurship; fashion merchandising; human resources management; international business/trade/commerce; legal assistant/paralegal; management science; marketing/marketing management; system, networking, and LAN/WAN management; web page, digital/multimedia and information resources design
Enrollment: 461 students
Institution Contact: Dr. Mildred Garcia, President
Phone: 212-986-4343 ext. 4101
Fax: 212-986-8901
E-mail: millieg@berkeleycollege.edu
Admission Contact: Ms. Dana Proft, Director, High School Admissions
Phone: 732-750-1800
Fax: 732-750-0652
E-mail: info@berkeleycollege.edu

EMPIRE BEAUTY SCHOOL

2100 State Hwy. #38
Plaza Cherry Hill
Cherry Hill, NJ 8002
Institution Contact: Campus Director
Phone: 856-667-8326
Fax: 856-667-8867

EMPIRE BEAUTY SCHOOL

Commerce Plaza II
1305 Blackwood-Clementon Rd.
Laurel Springs, NJ 08021-5602
Institution Contact: Ms. Evelyn Moriarty
Phone: 856-435-8100
Fax: 856-435-6655

EMPIRE BEAUTY SCHOOL

1719 Brunswick Pike
Lawrenceville, NJ 08648-7631
Institution Contact: Mr. Warren Payton
Phone: 609-392-4545
Fax: 609-392-8224

THE CHUBB INSTITUTE

2100 Route 38 and Mall Drive
Cherry Hill, NJ 08002
Web: http://www.chubbinstitute.edu
Accreditation: Accrediting Council for Independent Colleges and Schools
Programs Offered:
computer and information systems security; computer engineering related; computer engineering technology; computer graphics; computer hardware engineering; computer/information technology administration and management; computer/information technology services administration related; computer installation and repair technology; computer software and media applications; computer systems networking and telecommunications; computer/technical support; computer technology/computer systems technology; massage therapy; medical administrative assistant and medical secretary; medical/clinical assistant; medical insurance coding; medical insurance/medical billing; system, networking, and LAN/WAN management; web page, digital/multimedia and information resources design
Enrollment: 316 students
Institution Contact: Ms. Michelle Bonocore, Executive Director
Phone: 856-755-4800
Fax: 856-755-4801
E-mail: mbonocore@chubbinstitute.edu
Admission Contact: Ms. Dina Gentile, Director of Admissions
Phone: 856-755-4800
Fax: 856-755-4801

E-mail: dgentile@chubbinstitute.edu

THE CHUBB INSTITUTE
40 Journal Square
Jersey City, NJ 07306-4009
Web: http://www.chubbinstitute.com/
Accreditation: Accrediting Commission of Career Schools and Colleges of Technology
Programs Offered:
computer/information technology administration and management; computer programming; computer programming related; computer programming (specific applications); computer software and media applications related; computer systems networking and tele-communications; computer/technical support; computer technology/computer systems technology; design and visual communications; graphic communications related; information technology; medical administrative assistant and medical secretary; medical insurance coding; medical insurance/medical billing; medical office assistant; medical office computer specialist; medical office management; system administration; web page, digital/multimedia and information resources design
Enrollment: 476 students
Institution Contact: Ms. Valeria E. Yancey, Campus President
Phone: 201-876-3800
Fax: 201-656-2091
E-mail: vyancey@chubbinstitute.edu
Admission Contact: Ms. Esther Covington, Admissions Director
Phone: 201-876-3819
Fax: 201-656-2091
E-mail: ecovingtion@chubbinstitute.edu

THE CHUBB INSTITUTE
651 US Route 1 South
North Brunswick, NJ 08902
Web: http://www.chubbinstitute.com/
Accreditation: Accrediting Commission of Career Schools and Colleges of Technology
Programs Offered:
computer and information sciences related; computer engineering technology; computer graphics; computer/information technology administration and management; computer/information technology services administration related; computer installation and repair

technology; computer programming; computer programming related; computer programming (specific applications); computer programming (vendor/product certification); computer software and media applications; computer software and media applications related; computer software engineering; computer systems networking and telecommunications; computer/technical support; computer technology/computer systems technology; data entry/microcomputer applications; data entry/microcomputer applications related; data processing and data processing technology; information technology; medical administrative assistant and medical secretary; medical insurance coding; medical insurance/medical billing; medical office assistant; system administration; system, networking, and LAN/WAN management; web page, digital/multimedia and information resources design
Enrollment: 500 students
Institution Contact: Mr. Dennis Mascali, Campus President
Phone: 732-448-2637
Fax: 732-448-2665
Admission Contact: Mr. Rudolf Rangel, Director of Admissions
Phone: 732-448-2600
Fax: 732-448-2665
E-mail: rthornton@chubbinstitute.com

THE CHUBB INSTITUTE
8 Sylvan Way
Parsippany, NJ 07054-0342
Web: http://www.chubbinstitute.edu/
Accreditation: Accrediting Commission of Career Schools and Colleges of Technology; Accrediting Council for Continuing Education and Training; Accrediting Council for Independent Colleges and Schools
Programs Offered:
allied health and medical assisting services related; computer and information systems security; computer engineering technology; computer graphics; computer hardware engineering; computer installation and repair technology; computer systems networking and tele-communications; computer/technical support; computer technology/computer systems technology; criminal justice/law enforcement administration; design and visual communications; digital communication and media/multimedia; drawing; graphic communications;

health information/medical records administration; information technology; massage therapy; medical administrative assistant and medical secretary; medical/clinical assistant; medical insurance coding; medical insurance/medical billing; medical office assistant; system, networking, and LAN/WAN management; web/multimedia management and webmaster; web page, digital/multimedia and information resources design

Enrollment: 411 students

Institution Contact: Mrs. Diane Gilles, Campus President

Phone: 973-630-4900

Fax: 973-630-4218

E-mail: dgilles@chubbinstitute.edu

Admission Contact: Ms. Stacey Nester, Director of Admissions

Phone: 973-630-4919

Fax: 973-630-4218

E-mail: snester@chubbinstitute.edu

THE CITTONE INSTITUTE

1697 Oak Tree Road

Edison, NJ 08820

Web: http://www.cittone.com/

Accreditation: Accrediting Council for Independent Colleges and Schools

Programs Offered:

business administration and management; massage therapy; medical administrative assistant and medical secretary; medical/clinical assistant; pharmacy technician; system, networking, and LAN/WAN management; web page, digital/multimedia and information resources design

Enrollment: 642 students

Institution Contact: Mr. John Joseph Willie, Executive Director

Phone: 732-548-8798

Fax: 732-548-9682

E-mail: jwillie@cittone.com

Admission Contact: Mr. Ron Barone, Admissions Director

Phone: 732-548-8798

Fax: 732-548-9682

E-mail: rbarone@cittone.com

THE CITTONE INSTITUTE

1000 Howard Boulevard

Mount Laurel, NJ 08054

Web: http://www.cittone.com

Accreditation: Accrediting Council for Independent Colleges and Schools

Programs Offered:

business administration and management; computer systems networking and telecommunications; massage therapy; medical administrative assistant and medical secretary; medical/clinical assistant; pharmacy technician

Enrollment: 444 students

Institution Contact: Ms. Catherine Palmer, Executive Director

Phone: 856-722-9333 ext. 42201

Fax: 856-722-1110

E-mail: catherinepalmer@cittone.com

Admission Contact: Cindy Herbert, Assistant Director, High School Admissions

Phone: 856-722-9333

Fax: 856-722-1110

E-mail: cherbert@cittone.com

THE CITTONE INSTITUTE

160 East Route 4

Paramus, NJ 07652

Web: http://www.cittone.com

Accreditation: Accrediting Council for Independent Colleges and Schools

Programs Offered:

administrative assistant and secretarial science; business administration and management; computer installation and repair technology; computer/technical support; criminal justice/law enforcement administration; criminal justice/police science; massage therapy; medical administrative assistant and medical secretary; medical/clinical assistant; medical insurance coding; medical reception; pharmacy technician; system administration; system, networking, and LAN/WAN management

Enrollment: 500 students

Institution Contact: Mr. Alan Shikowitz, Executive Director

Phone: 201-845-6868

Fax: 201-368-0736

E-mail: ashikowitz@cittone.com

Admission Contact: Mr. Ron Barone, Director of Admissions

Phone: 201-845-6868

Fax: 201-529-3229
E-mail: rbarone@cittone.com

DIVERS ACADEMY INTERNATIONAL

2500 South Broadway
Camden, NJ 08104-2431
Web: http://www.diversacademy.com
Accreditation: Accrediting Commission of Career
Schools and Colleges of Technology
Programs Offered:
diving, professional and instruction
Enrollment: 154 students
Institution Contact: Ms. Tamara Brown, Executive
Director
Phone: 800-238-3483
Fax: 856-541-4355
E-mail: tamara@diversacademy.com
Admission Contact: Ms. Kim Sweeney, Director of
Admissions
Phone: 800-238-3483
Fax: 856-541-4355
E-mail: kim@diversacademy.com

DOVER BUSINESS COLLEGE

East 81, Route 4 West
Paramus, NJ 07652
Web: http://www.doverbusinesscollege.org
Accreditation: Accrediting Council for Independent
Colleges and Schools
Programs Offered:
accounting; accounting and business/management;
business administration and management; computer/
information technology administration and manage-
ment; executive assistant/executive secretary; massage
therapy; medical/clinical assistant; medical insurance
coding; medical insurance/medical billing; medical
office computer specialist; nursing (licensed practi-
cal/vocational nurse training); system, networking, and
LAN/WAN management
Enrollment: 255 students
Institution Contact: Mr. Timothy Luing, Executive
Director
Phone: 201-843-8500
Fax: 201-843-3896
E-mail: tluing@doverbusinesscollege.org
Admission Contact: Mr. Pat Verile, Admissions
Director

Phone: 201-843-8500
Fax: 201-843-3896
E-mail: pverile@doverbusinesscollege.org

GIBBS COLLEGE

630 West Mount Pleasant Avenue
Livingston, NJ 07039
Web: http://www.gibbnj.edu
Programs Offered:
accounting; accounting and business/management;
administrative assistant and secretarial science; allied
health and medical assisting services related; computer
systems networking and telecommunications; crimi-
nal justice/law enforcement administration; executive
assistant/executive secretary; graphic communica-
tions; hospitality administration; marketing/marketing
management; medical/clinical assistant
Enrollment: 1,400 students
Institution Contact: William C Ehrhardt, President
Phone: 973-369-1360
Fax: 973-369-1032
E-mail: behrhardt@gibbsnj.edu
Admission Contact: James Jackson, VP Admissions
Phone: 973-369-1360
Fax: 973-369-1416
E-mail: jjackson@gibbsnj.edu

HARRISON CAREER INSTITUTE

1227-31 Main Avenue
Clifton, NJ 07011
Web: http://www.hci.edu
Accreditation: Accrediting Commission of Career
Schools and Colleges of Technology
Programs Offered:
electrocardiograph technology; medical/clinical
assistant; medical insurance coding; medical insur-
ance/medical billing; medical transcription; pharmacy
technician; phlebotomy
Enrollment: 187 students
Institution Contact: Linda Burke, Director
Phone: 973-253-0444
E-mail: lburke@hci-inst.net

HARRISON CAREER INSTITUTE

4000 Route 130 North, Suite A, 2nd Floor
Delran, NJ 08075

Web: http://www.hci.edu
Accreditation: Accrediting Commission of Career Schools and Colleges of Technology
Programs Offered:
cardiovascular technology; dental assisting; electrocardiograph technology; medical/clinical assistant; medical insurance/medical billing; medical office computer specialist; medical transcription; pharmacy technician; phlebotomy
Enrollment: 100 students
Institution Contact: Mrs. Dawn L. Mack, Director
Phone: 856-764-8933
Fax: 856-764-8829
E-mail: dmack@hci-inst.net

HARRISON CAREER INSTITUTE
The Plaza at Deptford, 1450 Clements Bridge Road
Deptford, NJ 08096
Web: http://www.hci.edu
Accreditation: Accrediting Commission of Career Schools and Colleges of Technology
Programs Offered:
cardiovascular technology; dental assisting; dialysis technology; electrocardiograph technology; gene therapy; medical/clinical assistant; medical insurance/medical billing; medical office computer specialist; nursing (licensed practical/vocational nurse training); pharmacy technician; phlebotomy
Enrollment: 200 students
Institution Contact: Ms. Cheryl L. Papa, Director
Phone: 856-384-2888
Fax: 856-384-1063
E-mail: cpapa@hci-inst.net
Admission Contact: Ms. Keri Krapsho, Admissions Representative
Phone: 856-384-2888
Fax: 856-384-1063

HARRISON CAREER INSTITUTE
1001 Spruce Street
Ewing, NJ 08628
Web: http://www.hci.edu
Accreditation: Accrediting Commission of Career Schools and Colleges of Technology
Programs Offered:
cardiovascular technology; dental assisting; dialysis technology; medical administrative assistant and medi-

cal secretary; medical/clinical assistant; medical office assistant; medical transcription
Enrollment: 182 students
Institution Contact: Ms. Carole M. Heininger, Director
Phone: 609-656-4303
Fax: 609-656-4376
E-mail: cheininger@hci-inst.net
Admission Contact: Ms. Debbie Miller-Moore, Career Advisor
Phone: 609-656-4303
Fax: 609-656-4373
E-mail: dmoore@hci-inst.net

HARRISON CAREER INSTITUTE
600 Pavonia Avenue
Jersey City, NJ 07306
Web: http://www.hci.edu
Accreditation: Accrediting Commission of Career Schools and Colleges of Technology
Programs Offered:
cardiovascular technology; dialysis technology; medical/clinical assistant; medical insurance/medical billing; medical office computer specialist; pharmacy technician
Enrollment: 200 students
Institution Contact: Dr. Robert Feld, Director
Phone: 201-222-1700
Fax: 201-222-9645
E-mail: bfeld@hci-inst.net
Admission Contact: Miss Ysolde Miranda, Career Representative
Phone: 201-222-1700
Fax: 201-222-9645
E-mail: ysolde@hci-inst.net

HARRISON CAREER INSTITUTE
2105 Highway 35
Oakhurst, NJ 07755
Web: http://www.hci.edu
Accreditation: Accrediting Commission of Career Schools and Colleges of Technology
Programs Offered:
allied health and medical assisting services related; clinical/medical laboratory technology; dialysis technology; electrocardiograph technology; health/health care administration; health information/medical records administration; health information/medical re-

cords technology; health/medical claims examination; medical administrative assistant and medical secretary; medical/clinical assistant; medical insurance/medical billing; medical office assistant; medical transcription; phlebotomy; surgical technology

Enrollment: 270 students

Institution Contact: Mr. Scott H. Applegate, Director

Phone: 732-493-1660

Fax: 732-493-2283

E-mail: hcioakh@aol.com

Admission Contact: Mr. Scott Applegate, Director

Phone: 732-493-1660

Fax: 732-493-2283

HARRISON CAREER INSTITUTE

525 South Orange Avenue

South Orange, NJ 07079

Web: http://www.hci.edu

Accreditation: Accrediting Commission of Career Schools and Colleges of Technology

Programs Offered:

cardiovascular technology; dental assisting; electro-cardiograph technology; medical/clinical assistant; medical insurance coding; medical insurance/medical billing; medical office computer specialist; medical transcription; pharmacy technician; phlebotomy

Enrollment: 225 students

Institution Contact: Ms. Lynn M. Lockamy, Director

Phone: 973-763-9484

Fax: 973-763-4645

E-mail: llockamy@hci-inst.net

HARRISON CAREER INSTITUTE

1386 South Delsea Drive

Vineland, NJ 08360-6210

Web: http://www.hci.edu

Accreditation: Accrediting Commission of Career Schools and Colleges of Technology

Programs Offered:

cardiovascular technology; customer service management; dialysis technology; electrocardiograph technology; health professions related; medical administrative assistant and medical secretary; medical/clinical assistant; medical insurance/medical billing; medical office assistant; medical office computer specialist; medical office management; medical transcription; phlebotomy; renal/dialysis technology

Enrollment: 260 students

Institution Contact: Ms. Arline M. Pillows, Director

Phone: 856-696-0500

Fax: 856-691-0701

E-mail: jgmannion@aol.com

Admission Contact: Mrs. Arline M. Pillows, Director

Phone: 856-696-0500

Fax: 856-691-0701

E-mail: hcivineland@aol.com

HOHOKUS HACKENSACK SCHOOL OF BUSINESS AND MEDICAL SCIENCES

66 Moore Street

Hackensack, NJ 07601-7197

Web: http://www.hohokushackensack.com

Accreditation: Accrediting Council for Independent Colleges and Schools

Programs Offered:

accounting technology and bookkeeping; administrative assistant and secretarial science; business administration and management; computer software and media applications related; executive assistant/executive secretary; legal assistant/paralegal; medical/clinical assistant; medical insurance coding; medical office management; nursing (licensed practical/vocational nurse training)

Enrollment: 275 students

Institution Contact: Mrs. Kim Staudt, Director

Phone: 201-488-9400 ext. 23

Fax: 201-488-1007

E-mail: director1@hohokushackensack.com

Admission Contact: Ms. Ruth Zayas, Director of Corporate Admissions

Phone: 201-488-9400 ext. 24

Fax: 201-488-1007

HOHOKUS RETS SCHOOL OF BUSINESS AND MEDICAL TECHNICAL SERVICES

103 Park Avenue

Nutley, NJ 07110-3505

Web: http://www.rets-institute.com

Accreditation: Accrediting Commission of Career Schools and Colleges of Technology

Programs Offered:

administrative assistant and secretarial science; allied health and medical assisting services related; business administration and management; business machine repair; business operations support and secretarial services related; communications technology; computer engineering technology; computer installation and repair technology; computer/technical support; computer technology/computer systems technology; data processing and data processing technology; electrical, electronic and communications engineering technology; health professions related; industrial technology; medical/clinical assistant; medical office assistant; office occupations and clerical services

Enrollment: 300 students

Institution Contact: Mr. Martin Klangasky, Director

Phone: 973-661-0600

Fax: 973-661-2954

E-mail: director@rets-institute.com

Admission Contact: Mr. Dominic Zampella, High School Admissions Director

Phone: 973-661-0600

Fax: 973-661-2954

E-mail: zampella@rets-institute.com

HoHoKus School of Business and Medical Sciences

10 South Franklin Turnpike

Ramsey, NJ 07446

Web: http://www.hohokus.com

Accreditation: Accrediting Council for Independent Colleges and Schools

Programs Offered:

business administration and management; cardiovascular technology; computer and information sciences related; diagnostic medical sonography and ultrasound technology; medical administrative assistant and medical secretary; medical/clinical assistant; medical insurance coding; medical insurance/medical billing; medical office assistant; medical transcription; nursing (licensed practical/vocational nurse training)

Enrollment: 503 students

Institution Contact: Mr. Thomas M. Eastwick, President

Phone: 201-327-8877

Fax: 201-327-9054

E-mail: www.admission2@hohokus.com

Admission Contact: Ms. Ruth I. Zayas, Corporate Director of Admissions

Phone: 201-327-8877 ext. 226

Fax: 201-825-2115

E-mail: www.rzayas@hohokus.com

HoHoKus School of Trade and Technical Services

1118 East Baltimore Avenue

Linden, NJ 07036

Web: http://www.hohokustrades.com

Programs Offered:

building/property maintenance and management; manufacturing technology; welding technology

Enrollment: 50 students

Institution Contact: Mr. Alan E. Concha, Vice President/Director

Phone: 800-646-9353

Fax: 908-486-9321

E-mail: aconcha21@aol.com

Joe Kubert School of Cartoon and Graphic Art Inc.

37 Myrtle Avenue

Dover, NJ 07801-4054

Web: http://www.kubertsworld.com/kubertschool/KubertSchool.htm

Accreditation: Accrediting Commission of Career Schools and Colleges of Technology

Programs Offered:

animation, interactive technology, video graphics and special effects; applied art; commercial and advertising art; computer graphics; computer software and media applications; design and visual communications; drawing

Enrollment: 120 students

Institution Contact: Mrs. Debby Kubert, Director

Phone: 973-361-1327

Fax: 973-361-1844

E-mail: kubert@earthlink.net

Katharine Gibbs School

180 Centennial Avenue

Piscataway, NJ 08854

Web: http://www.gibbseducation.com

Accreditation: Accrediting Council for Independent Colleges and Schools

Programs Offered:

administrative assistant and secretarial science; business administration and management; communications systems installation and repair technology; computer graphics; computer/technical support; executive assistant/executive secretary; fashion merchandising; legal assistant/paralegal; medical/clinical assistant; system

administration; system, networking, and LAN/WAN management; web/multimedia management and webmaster; web page, digital/multimedia and information resources design
Enrollment: 1,200 students
Institution Contact: Mr. Patrick J Conway, Executive Director
Phone: 732-885-1580
Fax: 732-885-0448
E-mail: pconway@gibbsnj.edu
Admission Contact: Ms. Lisa Guzzetta, Vice President of Admissions & Marketing
Phone: 732-885-1580
Fax: 732-885-0448
E-mail: lguzzetta@gibbsnj.edu

LINCOLN TECHNICAL INSTITUTE
70 McKee Drive
Mahwah, NJ 07430
Web: http://www.lincolntech.com
Accreditation: Accrediting Commission of Career Schools and Colleges of Technology
Programs Offered:
automobile/automotive mechanics technology; automotive engineering technology; electrical and electronic engineering technologies related; electrical, electronic and communications engineering technology; electrical/electronics equipment installation and repair; heating, air conditioning and refrigeration technology; industrial electronics technology
Enrollment: 1,005 students
Institution Contact: Mr. Thomas E. Lynch, Executive Director
Phone: 201-529-1414 ext. 106
Fax: 201-529-5295
E-mail: tlynch@lincolntech.com
Admission Contact: Mr. Aldwyn Cook, Director of Admissions
Phone: 201-529-1414
Fax: 201-529-5295
E-mail: acook@lincolntech.com

LINCOLN TECHNICAL INSTITUTE

2299 Vauxhall Road
Union, NJ 07083
Web: http://www.lincolntech.com
Accreditation: Accrediting Commission of Career

Schools and Colleges of Technology
Programs Offered:
automotive engineering technology; electrical, electronic and communications engineering technology; heating, air conditioning and refrigeration technology
Enrollment: 1,291 students
Institution Contact: Mr. Kevin Kirkley, Executive Director
Phone: 908-964-7800
Fax: 908-964-3035
E-mail: kkirkley@lincolntech.com
Admission Contact: Mr. Carl Berne, Admissions Director
Phone: 908-964-7800
Fax: 908-964-3035
E-mail: cberne@lincolntech.com

PENNCO TECH
99 Erial Road, PO Box 1427
Blackwood, NJ 08012-9961
Web: http://www.penncotech.com
Accreditation: Accrediting Commission of Career Schools and Colleges of Technology
Programs Offered:
autobody/collision and repair technology; automobile/automotive mechanics technology; automotive engineering technology; computer installation and repair technology; diesel mechanics technology; drafting and design technology; heating, air conditioning and refrigeration technology; marine technology; medical administrative assistant and medical secretary; system, networking, and LAN/WAN management
Institution Contact: Mr. Doug Johnson, Director
Phone: 856-232-0310
Fax: 856-232-2032
E-mail: dougbristol@yahoo.com

PRISM CAREER INSTITUTE
2 Sindoni Lane
Hammonton, NJ 8037
Web: www.prismcareerinstitute.com
Institution Contact: Judi Sanders
Phone: 609-561-4424
Fax: 609-704-8559

PRISM CAREER INSTITUTE

150 N. Delsea Drive
Sewell, NJ 8080
Institution Contact: Diane Bowler
Phone: 856-881-6555
Fax: 856-232-7112

SOMERSET SCHOOL OF MESSAGE THERAPY

180 Centennial Avenue
Piscataway, NJ 08854
Web: http://www.ssmt.org
Programs Offered:
massage therapy
Enrollment: 250 students
Institution Contact: Rhonda Brunelle, President
Phone: 732-885-3400
Fax: 732-885-0440
E-mail: rbrunelle@cortiva.com
Admission Contact: William Fee, Director of Admissions
Phone: 732-885-3400 ext. 15
Fax: 732-885-0440
E-mail: bfee@cortiva.com

STUART SCHOOL OF BUSINESS ADMINISTRATION

2400 Belmar Boulevard
Wall, NJ 07719
Web: http://www.stuartschool.com
Accreditation: Accrediting Council for Independent Colleges and Schools
Programs Offered:
accounting; administrative assistant and secretarial science; adult and continuing education; business administration and management; computer software and media applications; data entry/microcomputer applications; executive assistant/executive secretary; legal administrative assistant/secretary; medical administrative assistant and medical secretary; medical office management
Enrollment: 90 students
Institution Contact: Mr. Joe Davis, President
Phone: 317-845-0100
Fax: 317-845-1800
E-mail: jdavis@medtechcollege.com
Admission Contact:
Phone: 732-681-7200
Fax: 732-681-7205

TETERBORO SCHOOL OF AERONAUTICS, INC.

Teterboro Airport, 80 Moonachie Avenue
Teterboro, NJ 07608-1083
Web: http://www.teterboroschool.com
Accreditation: Accrediting Commission of Career Schools and Colleges of Technology
Programs Offered:
aircraft powerplant technology; airframe mechanics and aircraft maintenance technology
Enrollment: 135 students
Institution Contact: Mr. Donald Hulse, President
Phone: 201-288-6300
Fax: 201-288-5609
E-mail: tsanj@bellatlantic.net
Admission Contact: Mr. Richard Ciasulli, Director of Admissions
Phone: 201-288-6300
Fax: 201-288-5609
E-mail: tsanj@bellatlantic.net

NEW MEXICO

APOLLO COLLEGE

5301 Central Avenue, Northeast, Suite 101
Albuquerque, NM 87108-1513
Web: http://www.apollocollege.com
Accreditation: Accrediting Bureau of Health Education Schools
Programs Offered:
clinical/medical laboratory technology; dental assisting; health information/medical records administration; massage therapy; medical administrative assistant and medical secretary; medical/clinical assistant; pharmacy technician
Enrollment: 500 students
Institution Contact: Mr. Patrick King, Campus Director
Phone: 505-254-7777
Fax: 505-254-1101
E-mail: pking@apollocollege.com

 ## ITT TECHNICAL INSTITUTE

5100 Masthead Street, NE
Albuquerque, NM 87109-4366
Web: http://www.itt-tech.edu
Accreditation: Accrediting Council for Independent Colleges and Schools

Programs Offered:
accounting and business/management; animation, interactive technology, video graphics and special effects; business administration and management; CAD/CADD drafting/design technology; communications technology; computer and information systems security; computer engineering technology; computer software and media applications; computer software technology; computer systems networking and telecommunications; criminal justice/police science; digital communication and media/multimedia; electrical, electronic and communications engineering technology; technology management; web page, digital/multimedia and information resources design
Institution Contact: Ms. Marianne Rittner, Director
Phone: 505-828-1114
Admission Contact: Mr. John Crooks, Director of Recruitment
Phone: 505-828-1114

NATIONAL AMERICAN UNIVERSITY

4775 Indian School Road, NE, Suite 200
Albuquerque, NM 87110
Web: http://www.national.edu
Accreditation: North Central Association of Colleges and Schools
Programs Offered:
accounting; business administration and management; computer/information technology services administration related; computer programming; computer systems networking and telecommunications; computer technology/computer systems technology; education (specific levels and methods) related; engineering-related technologies; information technology; management information systems; medical/clinical assistant
Enrollment: 532 students
Institution Contact: Mr. J. P. Foley, Regional Vice President
Phone: 505-265-7517
Fax: 505-265-7542
E-mail: jpfoley@national.edu
Admission Contact: Ms. Nancy Pointer, Director of Admissions
Phone: 512-301-4901
Fax: 512-301-4902
E-mail: npointer@national.edu

NATIONAL AMERICAN UNIVERSITY

Highway 528 and Sara Road
Rio Rancho, NM 87124
Accreditation: North Central Association of Colleges and Schools
Programs Offered:
accounting; advertising; allied health and medical assisting services related; business administration and management; business, management, and marketing related; computer and information sciences; engineering/industrial management; engineering-related technologies; engineering technology; general studies; human resources management; information technology; selling skills and sales
Enrollment: 225 students
Institution Contact: Ms. Lisa Knigge, Regional President
Phone: 505-891-1111
Fax: 505-896-2818
E-mail: lknigge@national.edu
Admission Contact: Ms. Wanda Butler, Senior Admissions Representative/Office Manager
Phone: 505-891-1111
E-mail: wbutler@national.edu

PIMA MEDICAL INSTITUTE

2201 San Pedro, NE , Suite 100
Albuquerque , NM 87110
Web: http://www.pmi.edu
Accreditation: Accrediting Bureau of Health Education Schools
Programs Offered:
dental assisting; massage therapy; medical administrative assistant and medical secretary; medical/clinical assistant; ophthalmic technology; pharmacy technician; physical therapist assistant; radiologic technology/science; respiratory care therapy; veterinary/animal health technology
Enrollment: 513 students
Institution Contact: Mr. Christopher Luebke, Admissions Support Center Director
Phone: 888-898-9048
E-mail: asc@pmi.edu
Admission Contact: Admissions Support Representative
Phone: 888-898-9048
E-mail: asc@pmi.edu

SOUTHWEST HEALTH CAREER INSTITUTE

5981 Jefferson Road NE, Suite A
Albuquerque, NM 87109
Web: http://www.swhci.com/
Programs Offered:
dental assisting; massage therapy; medical/clinical assistant; medical insurance coding; medical insurance/medical billing
Institution Contact: Admissions
Phone: 505-345-6800
Fax: 505-345-6868

NEW YORK

APEX TECHNICAL SCHOOL

635 Avenue of the Americas
New York, NY 10011
Web: http://www.ApexTechnicalSchool.com
Accreditation: Accrediting Commission of Career Schools and Colleges of Technology
Programs Offered:
autobody/collision and repair technology; automotive engineering technology; heating, air conditioning and refrigeration technology; welding technology
Enrollment: 1,281 students
Institution Contact: Mr. William Cann, CEO
Phone: 212-989-5656
Fax: 212-463-7510
E-mail: wzc@apexschool.net
Admission Contact: Mr. William Ott, Admissions Director
Phone: 212-645-3300
Fax: 212-645-6985

THE ART INSTITUTE OF NEW YORK CITY

75 Varick Street, 16th Floor
New York, NY 10013
Web: http://www.ainyc.aii.edu
Accreditation: Accrediting Council for Independent Colleges and Schools
Programs Offered:
baking and pastry arts; cinematography and film/video production; culinary arts; design and visual communications; digital communication and media/multimedia; fashion/apparel design; hotel/motel administration; interior design; web page, digital/multimedia and

information resources design
Enrollment: 1,477 students
Institution Contact: Mr. Tim Howard, President
Phone: 212-226-5500 ext. 6003
Fax: 212-625-6094
E-mail: thoward@aii.edu
Admission Contact: Ms. Lauren Malone, Interim Director of Admissions
Phone: 212-226-5500 ext. 6080
Fax: 212-226-5644
E-mail: lmalone@aii.edu

BERKELEY COLLEGE - NEW YORK CITY CAMPUS

3 East 43rd Street
New York, NY 10017
Web: http://www.BerkeleyCollege.edu
Accreditation: Middle States Association of Colleges and Schools
Programs Offered:
accounting; business administration and management; criminal justice/law enforcement administration; fashion merchandising; health information/medical records administration; health services administration; international business/trade/commerce; legal assistant/paralegal; management science; marketing/marketing management
Enrollment: 2,012 students
Institution Contact: Dr. Mildred Garcia, President
Phone: 212-986-4343 ext. 4101
Fax: 212-986-8901
E-mail: millieg@berkeleycollege.edu
Admission Contact: Mr. Stuart Siegman, Director, High School Admissions
Phone: 212-986-4343
Fax: 212-818-1079
E-mail: nycampus@berkeleycollege.edu

BERKELEY COLLEGE - WESTCHESTER CAMPUS

99 Church Street
White Plains, NY 10601
Web: http://www.BerkeleyCollege.edu
Accreditation: Middle States Association of Colleges and Schools
Programs Offered:
accounting; business administration and management; criminal justice/law enforcement administration; fashion merchandising; health information/medical

records administration; health services administration; international business/trade/commerce; legal assistant/paralegal; management science; marketing/marketing management

Enrollment: 658 students

Institution Contact: Dr. Mildred Garcia, President

Phone: 212-986-4343 ext. 4101

Fax: 212-986-8901

E-mail: millieg@berkeleycollege.edu

Admission Contact: Ms. Paige Feinberg, Director of High School Admissions

Phone: 914-694-1122 ext. 3110

Fax: 914-328-9469

E-mail: info@berkeleycollege.edu

BERK TRADE AND BUSINESS SCHOOL

383 Pearl Street, 5th Floor

Brooklyn, NY 11201

Web: http://www.berktradeschool.com

Programs Offered:

automotive engineering technology; electrician; pipefitting and sprinkler fitting; plumbing technology

Institution Contact: Dr. Blanca Burgos, CEO

Phone: 719-625-6037

Fax: 718-725-6299

E-mail: castellanob@aol.com

Admission Contact: Ms. Natylee Santana, Admissions Representative

Phone: 718-625-6037

Fax: 718-625-6299

E-mail: n.santana@berktradeschool.com

BRIARCLIFFE COLLEGE

1055 Stewart Avenue

Bethpage, NY 11714-3545

Web: http://www.Briarcliffe.edu

Accreditation: Middle States Association of Colleges and Schools

Programs Offered:

accounting; accounting related; administrative assistant and secretarial science; art; business administration and management; business administration, management and operations related; business automation/technology/data entry; business, management, and marketing related; business operations support and secretarial services related; commercial and advertising art; communications systems installation and repair technol-

ogy; computer and information sciences; computer and information sciences and support services related; computer and information sciences related; computer and information systems security; computer engineering technology; computer graphics; computer/information technology administration and management; computer/information technology services administration related; computer installation and repair technology; computer programming; computer programming related; computer programming (specific applications); computer software and media applications; computer software and media applications related; computer systems analysis; computer systems networking and telecommunications; computer/technical support; computer technology/computer systems technology; criminal justice/law enforcement administration; criminal justice/police science; data entry/microcomputer applications; data entry/microcomputer applications related; data processing and data processing technology; executive assistant/executive secretary; health and medical administrative services related; health/health care administration; health information/medical records administration; information science/studies; information technology; legal administrative assistant/secretary; legal assistant/paralegal; marketing/marketing management; medical administrative assistant and medical secretary; system administration; system, networking, and LAN/WAN management; telecommunications; web/multimedia management and webmaster; web page, digital/multimedia and information resources design; word processing

Enrollment: 4,310 students

Institution Contact: Ms. Theresa Donohue, Vice President of Marketing and Admissions

Phone: 516-918-3600 ext. 3705

Fax: 516-470-6020

E-mail: tdonohue@bcl.edu

BRIARCLIFFE COLLEGE

10 Lake Street

Patchogue, NY 11772

Web: http://www.briarcliffe.edu

Accreditation: Middle States Association of Colleges and Schools

Programs Offered:

accounting; administrative assistant and secretarial science; applied art; business administration and management; business automation/technology/data entry; commercial and advertising art; communications systems installation and repair technology; computer and information sciences related; computer graphics; computer hardware engineering; computer/information technology administration and management; computer/information technology services administration related; computer installation and repair technology; computer programming; computer programming related; computer programming (specific applications); computer programming (vendor/product certification); computer software and media applications; computer software technology; computer systems analysis; computer systems networking and telecommunications; computer/technical support; computer technology/computer systems technology; criminal justice/law enforcement administration; data entry/microcomputer applications; data entry/microcomputer applications related; data processing and data processing technology; desktop publishing and digital imaging design; drafting and design technology; drawing; executive assistant/executive secretary; graphic and printing equipment operation/production; health information/medical records administration; health information/medical records technology; information science/studies; information technology; intermedia/multimedia; internet information systems; legal administrative assistant/secretary; legal assistant/paralegal; marketing/marketing management; medical reception; medical transcription; office occupations and clerical services; receptionist; retailing; selling skills and sales; system administration; system, networking, and LAN/WAN management; telecommunications; telecommunications technology; visual and performing arts; web/multimedia management and webmaster; web page, digital/multimedia and information resources design; word processing

Institution Contact: Mr. James Swift, Director of High School and National Admissions
Phone: 631-654-5300
Fax: 631-654-5082
E-mail: jswift@bcl.edu
Admission Contact: Ms. Kathy McDermott, Director of Admissions
Phone: 631-730-2010
Fax: 631-730-1244
E-mail: kmcdermott@bcl.edu

CALIBER TRAINING INSTITUTE

500 7th Avenue, 2nd Floor
New York, NY 10018
Web: http://www.caliberny.edu
Accreditation: Accrediting Commission of Career Schools and Colleges of Technology; Accrediting Council for Independent Colleges and Schools
Programs Offered:
banking and financial support services; child care provision; dental assisting; medical administrative assistant and medical secretary; medical/clinical assistant; medical insurance/medical billing; nursing assistant/aide and patient care assistant; securities services administration; tourism and travel services management
Enrollment: 2,500 students
Institution Contact: Mr. Ben Lokos, President
Phone: 212-564-0500
Fax: 212-564-0694
E-mail: caliberny@aol.com
Admission Contact: Mr. John Daniel, Director of Admissions
Phone: 212-564-0500
Fax: 212-564-0694
E-mail: jdaniel@caliberny.edu

CAREER INSTITUTE OF HEALTH AND TECHNOLOGY

340 Flatbush Avenue Extension
Brooklyn, NY 11201
Web: http://www.careerinstitute.edu
Programs Offered:
automobile/automotive mechanics technology; electrician; information technology; medical/clinical assistant; medical insurance/medical billing
Enrollment: 1,115 students
Institution Contact: Monifa Skelton, Campus Director
Phone: 718-4221212 ext. 1402
Fax: 718-422-1131
E-mail: monifas@careerinstitute.edu
Admission Contact: Admissions
Phone: 718-4221212 ext. 1400
Fax: 718-4221222
E-mail: info@careerinstitute.edu

CAREER INSTITUTE OF HEALTH AND TECHNOLOGY

200 Garden City Plaza, Suite 519
Garden City, NY 11530
Web: http://www.ccctraining.edu
Accreditation: Accrediting Council for Independent Colleges and Schools
Programs Offered:

accounting technology and bookkeeping; automobile/automotive mechanics technology; computer and information systems security; computer engineering technology; computer hardware engineering; computer systems networking and telecommunications; computer technology/computer systems technology; customer service management; electrical/electronics equipment installation and repair; electrician; electrocardiograph technology; information technology; internet information systems; medical administrative assistant and medical secretary; medical/clinical assistant; medical insurance coding; medical insurance/medical billing; medical office assistant; system, networking, and LAN/WAN management; web/multimedia management and webmaster

Enrollment: 1,000 students
Institution Contact: Mr. Kenneth G. Barrett, President
Phone: 516-877-1225 ext. 1105
Fax: 516-877-1329
E-mail: kenb@ccctraining.edu
Admission Contact: Ms. Mary Miller, Director of Admissions
Phone: 516-877-1225
Fax: 516-877-1959
E-mail: marym@ccctraining.edu

CAREER INSTITUTE OF HEALTH AND TECHNOLOGY

95-25 Queens Boulevard, Suite 600
Rego Park, NY 11374
Web: http://www.ccctraining.net
Accreditation: Accrediting Council for Independent Colleges and Schools
Programs Offered:
computer and information sciences related; computer engineering technology; medical insurance coding; system, networking, and LAN/WAN management; web/multimedia management and webmaster
Institution Contact: Ms. Barbara Patterson, Director
Phone: 516-877-1225
Fax: 516-877-1959
E-mail: barbarap@ccctraining.net
Admission Contact: Ms. Mary Miller, Admissions Director
Phone: 516-877-1225
Fax: 516-877-1959
E-mail: marym@ccctraining.net

THE CHUBB INSTITUTE

498 Seventh Avenue, 17th Floor
New York, NY 10018
Web: http://www.chubbinstitute.edu
Accreditation: Accrediting Commission of Career Schools and Colleges of Technology; Accrediting Council for Continuing Education and Training
Programs Offered:
computer and information sciences; computer and information sciences related; computer and information systems security; computer graphics; computer installation and repair technology; computer software engineering; computer systems networking and telecommunications; computer technology/computer systems technology; health and medical administrative services related; health/health care administration; health information/medical records administration; health information/medical records technology; health professions related; health services administration; information technology; medical administrative assistant and medical secretary; medical insurance/medical billing; medical office assistant; medical office management; medical reception; system administration; system, networking, and LAN/WAN management; web page, digital/multimedia and information resources design
Enrollment: 439 students
Institution Contact: Mr. Gary E. Duchnowski, Campus President
Phone: 212-659-2116
Fax: 212-659-2175
E-mail: gduchnowski@chubbinstitute.edu
Admission Contact: Mr. Joe Rodriguez, Director of Admissions
Phone: 212-659-2116
Fax: 212-659-2175
E-mail: jrodriguez@chubbinstitute.edu

THE CHUBB INSTITUTE

1400 Old Country Road
Westbury, NY 11590
Web: http://www.chubbinstitute.com
Accreditation: Accrediting Council for Continuing Education and Training
Programs Offered:
computer systems networking and telecommunications; graphic communications; graphic communications related; medical insurance coding; medical insurance/medical billing; medical office assistant; system,

networking, and LAN/WAN management; web page, digital/multimedia and information resources design

Enrollment: 205 students

Institution Contact: Ms. Eileen Jackson, School Director

Phone: 516-997-1400

Fax: 516-997-1496

E-mail: ejackson@chubbinstitute.com

Admission Contact: Mr. Nick Buffardi, Director of Admissions

Phone: 516-997-1400

Fax: 516-997-1496

E-mail: nbuffardi@chubbinstitute.com

EMPIRE BEAUTY SCHOOL

38-15 Broadway

Astoria, NY 11103

Institution Contact: Mr. Anthony Pinnelli

Phone: 212-967-1717

Fax: 212-564-0502

EMPIRE BEAUTY SCHOOL

2384 86th St.

Bensonhurst, NY 11214

Institution Contact: Ms. Mary Lynn Russo

Phone: 718-373-2400

Fax: 718-996-7873

EMPIRE BEAUTY SCHOOL

22 W 34th St.

New York, NY 10001

Institution Contact: Mr. Vince Scala

Phone: 212-967-1717

Fax: 212-564-0502

EMPIRE BEAUTY SCHOOL - THEATRICAL/FILM MAKE-UP

22 W 34th St.

New York, NY 10001

Institution Contact: Vince Scala

Phone: 212-967-1717

Fax: 212-564-0502

THE FRENCH CULINARY INSTITUTE

434 Broadway

New York, NY 10013

Web: http://www.frenchculinary.com

Accreditation: Accrediting Commission of Career Schools and Colleges of Technology

Programs Offered:

baking and pastry arts; culinary arts; restaurant, culinary, and catering management

Enrollment: 600 students

Institution Contact: Mr. Christopher Papagni, PhD, School Director

Phone: 646-254-7510

Fax: 646-254-1210

E-mail: cpapagni@frenchculinary.com

Admission Contact: Mrs. Judy Currie-Hellman, Admission Director

Phone: 212-219-8890

Fax: 212-226-0672

E-mail: admission@frenchculinary.com

GEMOLOGICAL INSTITUTE OF AMERICA, INC.

270 Madison Avenue, 2nd Floor

New York, NY 10016-0601

Web: http://www.gia.edu

Accreditation: Accrediting Commission of Career Schools and Colleges of Technology

Programs Offered:

applied art; metal and jewelry arts

Enrollment: 106 students

Institution Contact: Mr. Daniel Campbell, Director

Phone: 212-944-5900

Fax: 212-719-9563

E-mail: dcampb@gia.edu

INSTITUTE OF AUDIO RESEARCH

64 University Place

New York, NY 10003-4595

Web: http://www.audioschool.com

Accreditation: Accrediting Commission of Career Schools and Colleges of Technology

Programs Offered:

recording arts technology

Enrollment: 500 students

Institution Contact: Ms. Muriel H. Adler, Director

Phone: 212-677-7580

Fax: 212-677-6549

E-mail: murieliar@aol.com
Admission Contact: Mr. Mark L. Kahn, Director of Admissions
Phone: 212-777-8550
Fax: 212-677-6549
E-mail: iarny@aol.com

ISLAND DRAFTING AND TECHNICAL INSTITUTE
128 Broadway
Amityville, NY 11701-2704
Web: http://www.idti.edu
Accreditation: Accrediting Commission of Career Schools and Colleges of Technology
Programs Offered:
architectural drafting and CAD/CADD; CAD/CADD drafting/design technology; civil drafting and CAD/CADD; computer engineering technology; computer/information technology administration and management; computer installation and repair technology; computer systems networking and telecommunications; computer/technical support; computer technology/computer systems technology; data entry/microcomputer applications; drafting and design technology; drafting/design engineering technologies related; electrical, electronic and communications engineering technology; engineering technology; information technology; mechanical design technology; mechanical drafting and CAD/CADD; system, networking, and LAN/WAN management; word processing
Enrollment: 301 students
Institution Contact: Mr. James DiLiberto, President
Phone: 631-691-8733
Fax: 631-691-8738
E-mail: dilibertoj@idti.edu
Admission Contact: Mr. John G. DiLiberto, Vice President
Phone: 631-691-8733
Fax: 631-691-8738
E-mail: johng@idti.edu

ITT TECHNICAL INSTITUTE
13 Airline Drive
Albany, NY 12205
Web: http://www.itt-tech.edu
Accreditation: Accrediting Council for Independent Colleges and Schools
Programs Offered:
computer engineering technology; computer software and media applications; computer systems networking and telecommunications; digital communication and media/multimedia; web page, digital/multimedia and information resources design
Institution Contact: Mr. Christopher Chang, Director
Phone: 518-452-9300
Admission Contact: Mr. John Henebry, Director of Recruitment
Phone: 518-452-9300

ITT TECHNICAL INSTITUTE
2295 Millersport Highway, PO Box 327
Getzville, NY 14068
Web: http://www.itt-tech.edu
Accreditation: Accrediting Council for Independent Colleges and Schools
Programs Offered:
CAD/CADD drafting/design technology; computer engineering technology; computer software and media applications; computer systems networking and telecommunications; digital communication and media/multimedia; web page, digital/multimedia and information resources design
Institution Contact: Mr. Lester Burgess, Director
Phone: 716-689-2200
Admission Contact: Mr. Scott Jaskier, Director of Recruitment
Phone: 716-689-2200

ITT TECHNICAL INSTITUTE
235 Greenfield Parkway
Liverpool, NY 13088
Web: http://www.itt-tech.edu
Accreditation: Accrediting Council for Independent Colleges and Schools
Programs Offered:
computer engineering technology; computer software and media applications; computer systems networking and telecommunications; digital communication and media/multimedia; web page, digital/multimedia and information resources design
Institution Contact: Mr. Terry Riesel , Director of Recruitment
Phone: 315-461-8000
Admission Contact: Mr. Terry Riesel, Director of Recruitment

Phone: 315-461-8000

KATHARINE GIBBS SCHOOL

320 South Service Road
Melville, NY 11747
Web: http://www.gibbsmelville.com
Accreditation: Accrediting Council for Independent Colleges and Schools
Programs Offered:
accounting; administrative assistant and secretarial science; animation, interactive technology, video graphics and special effects; business administration and management; commercial and advertising art; computer graphics; computer/information technology administration and management; computer installation and repair technology; computer software and media applications; computer systems networking and telecommunications; computer/technical support; computer technology/computer systems technology; executive assistant/executive secretary; information technology; marketing/marketing management; medical administrative assistant and medical secretary; medical transcription; receptionist; system, networking, and LAN/WAN management; web page, digital/multimedia and information resources design
Enrollment: 700 students
Institution Contact: Mrs. Tammi D. Palms, Director of Compliance
Phone: 631-370-3300 ext. 3390
Fax: 631-293-4849
E-mail: tpalms@gibbsmelville.com
Admission Contact: Mrs. Patricia Martin, President
Phone: 631-370-3300
Fax: 631-293-2709

KATHARINE GIBBS SCHOOL

50 West 40th Street
New York, NY 10018
Web: http://www.gibbsny.edu
Accreditation: Accrediting Council for Independent Colleges and Schools
Programs Offered:
accounting; administrative assistant and secretarial science; business administration and management; business/corporate communications; commercial and advertising art; computer/information technology administration and management; computer/information technology services administration related; computer/technical support; criminal justice/law enforcement administration; criminal justice/police science; desktop publishing and digital imaging design; digital communication and media/multimedia; executive assistant/executive secretary; fashion/apparel design; fashion merchandising; hospitality administration; hotel/motel administration; legal administrative assistant/secretary; marketing/marketing management; medical administrative assistant and medical secretary; office occupations and clerical services; system, networking, and LAN/WAN management; web page, digital/multimedia and information resources design
Enrollment: 2,000 students
Institution Contact: Ms. Lynn Salvage, President
Phone: 212-867-9300
Fax: 646-218-2550
E-mail: lsalvage@gibbsnewyork.com
Admission Contact: Ms. Mary Ann Grillo, Vice President, Admissions
Phone: 212-867-9300
Fax: 646-218-2459
E-mail: mgrillo@gibbsnewyork.com

MANDL SCHOOL

254 West 54th Street
New York, NY 10019-5516
Web: http://www.mandlschool.com
Accreditation: Accrediting Bureau of Health Education Schools; Accrediting Commission of Career Schools and Colleges of Technology
Programs Offered:
clinical/medical laboratory technology; dental assisting; electrocardiograph technology; gene therapy; home health aide/home attendant; medical/clinical assistant; medical insurance/medical billing; nursing assistant/aide and patient care assistant; ophthalmic technology
Enrollment: 850 students
Institution Contact: Mr. Melvyn Weiner, President
Phone: 212-247-3434
Fax: 212-247-3617
E-mail: melweiner2@aol.com
Admission Contact: Mr. Stuart Weiner, Vice President
Phone: 212-247-3434
Fax: 212-247-3617
E-mail: stu.mandl@prodigy.net

MILDRED ELLEY SCHOOL

Latham Circle Mall
800 New Loudon Road, Suite 5120
Latham, NY 12110
Web: http://www.mildred-elley.edu/
Programs Offered:
accounting; administrative assistant and secretarial
science; business, management, and marketing related; computer/information technology administration
and management; legal assistant/paralegal; massage
therapy; medical/clinical assistant; medical office assistant; tourism and travel services marketing
Institution Contact: Admissions
Phone: 518-786-3171

NEW YORK INSTITUTE OF MASSAGE

PO Box 645
Buffalo, NY 14231
Web: http://www.nyinstituteofmassage.com
Accreditation: Accrediting Commission of Career
Schools and Colleges of Technology
Programs Offered:
adult and continuing education; massage therapy
Enrollment: 180 students
Institution Contact: Ms. Diane Dinsmore, RN, Director
Phone: 716-633-0355
Fax: 716-633-0213
E-mail: nyimdirector@adelphia.net
Admission Contact:
Phone: 716-633-0355

ROCHESTER BUSINESS INSTITUTE

1630 Portland Ave
Rochester, NY 14621-3007
Institution Contact: Mr. Carl Silvio
Phone: 585-266-0430
Fax: 585-266-8243

SANFORD-BROWN INSTITUTE

711 Stewart Avenue
Garden City, NY 11530
Web: http://www.sblongisland.com
Accreditation: Accrediting Bureau of Health Educa-
tion Schools
Programs Offered:
cardiovascular technology; diagnostic medical sonog-
raphy and ultrasound technology; medical/clinical
assistant; medical insurance coding; medical insur-
ance/medical billing
Enrollment: 807 students
Institution Contact: Mr. Steeve Dumerve, President
Phone: 516-247-2900 ext. 2938
Fax: 516-247-2906
E-mail: sdumerve@sblongisland.com
Admission Contact: Mrs. Rosalie Bonavise, Director
of Admissions
Phone: 516-247-2900 ext. 2931
Fax: 516-247-2902
E-mail: rbonavise@sblongisland.com

SANFORD-BROWN INSTITUTE

120 East 16th Street, 2nd Floor
New York, NY 10003
Web: http://www.sbnewyork.com
Accreditation: Accrediting Bureau of Health Educa-
tion Schools
Programs Offered:
cardiovascular technology; diagnostic medical sonog-
raphy and ultrasound technology; health services/allied
health/health sciences; medical/clinical assistant; medi-
cal insurance coding; medical insurance/medical billing
Enrollment: 658 students
Institution Contact: Lynn D. Salvage, President
Phone: 646-313-4556
Fax: 212-253-6507
E-mail: lsalvage@sbnewyork.com
Admission Contact: Mr. Aldwyn Cook, Director of
Admissions
Phone: 646-313-4510
Fax: 212-253-6701

SANFORD-BROWN INSTITUTE

333 Westchester Avenue, West Building
White Plains, NY 10604
Accreditation: Accrediting Bureau of Health Education Schools; Accrediting Council for Independent
Colleges and Schools
Programs Offered:
cardiovascular technology; diagnostic medical sonography and ultrasound technology; medical/clinical
assistant; medical insurance coding; medical insur-
ance/medical billing
Enrollment: 355 students

Institution Contact: Mr. Larry Stieglitz, Campus President
Phone: 914-874-2506
Fax: 914-347-5466
E-mail: lstieglitz@sbwhiteplains.com
Admission Contact: Mr. Emilio Noble, Director of Admissions
Phone: 914-874-2510
Fax: 914-347-5466
E-mail: enoble@sbwhiteplains.com

TAYLOR BUSINESS INSTITUTE

23 West 17th Street, 7th Floor
New York, NY 10011-5501
Web: http://www.tbiglobal.com/
Institution Contact: Admissions
Phone: 800-959-9999
E-mail: admission@tbiglobal.com

TECHNICAL CAREER INSTITUTE

320 West 31st
New York, NY 10001
Web: http://www.tcicollege.com
Accreditation: Middle States Association of Colleges and Schools
Programs Offered:
accounting and business/management; accounting technology and bookkeeping; building/property maintenance and management; computer and information systems security; computer systems networking and telecommunications; computer technology/computer systems technology; digital communication and media/multimedia; electrical and electronic engineering technologies related; health information/medical records technology; heating, air conditioning, ventilation and refrigeration maintenance technology; industrial electronics technology; medical office management; office management; telecommunications technology; transportation technology
Institution Contact: Admissions
Phone: 800-878-8246
E-mail: admissions@tcicollege.edu

WOOD TOBE-COBURN SCHOOL

8 East 40th Street
New York, NY 10016-0190

Web: http://www.woodtobecoburn.com
Programs Offered:
accounting; administrative assistant and secretarial science; clinical/medical laboratory assistant; commercial and advertising art; computer graphics; computer programming; computer programming (specific applications); computer software and media applications; executive assistant/executive secretary; fashion and fabric consulting; fashion/apparel design; fashion merchandising; hospitality administration; medical administrative assistant and medical secretary; medical/clinical assistant; medical office management; medical transcription; retailing; system, networking, and LAN/WAN management; tourism and travel services management; web page, digital/multimedia and information resources design
Institution Contact: Ms. Sandi Gruninger, President
Phone: 212-686-9040
Fax: 212-686-9171
E-mail: info@woodtobecoburn.com
Admission Contact: Ms. Sandra Wendland, Director of Admissions
Phone: 212-686-9040
Fax: 212-686-9171
E-mail: info@woodtobecoburn.com

NORTH CARLOINA

THE ART INSTITUTE OF CHARLOTTE

Three LakePointe Plaza, 2110 Water Ridge Parkway
Charlotte, NC 28217-4536
Web: http://www.aich.artinstitutes.edu
Accreditation: Accrediting Council for Independent Colleges and Schools
Programs Offered:
commercial and advertising art; culinary arts; desktop publishing and digital imaging design; fashion merchandising; interior design; web/multimedia management and webmaster; web page, digital/multimedia and information resources design
Institution Contact: Mrs. Elizabeth Guinan, College President
Phone: 704-357-8020 ext. 2541
Fax: 704-357-1144
E-mail: guinane@aii.edu
Admission Contact: Mr. George Garcia, Director of Admissions

Phone: 800-872-4417 ext. 5872
Fax: 704-357-1133
E-mail: garciag@aii.edu

BROOKSTONE COLLEGE OF BUSINESS

10125 Berkeley Place Drive
Charlotte, NC 28262-1294
Web: http://www.brookstone.edu
Accreditation: Accrediting Council for Independent Colleges and Schools
Programs Offered:
accounting; accounting technology and bookkeeping; administrative assistant and secretarial science; allied health and medical assisting services related; computer installation and repair technology; computer systems networking and telecommunications; medical administrative assistant and medical secretary; medical/clinical assistant; medical insurance coding; medical insurance/medical billing; medical office assistant; medical transcription
Enrollment: 210 students
Institution Contact: Mr. F. Jack Henderson, III, President
Phone: 704-547-8600
Fax: 704-547-8887
E-mail: jhenderson@brookstone.edu
Admission Contact: Admissions Department
Phone: 704-547-8600
Fax: 704-547-8887
E-mail: admissions@brookstone.edu

BROOKSTONE COLLEGE OF BUSINESS

7815 National Service Road, Suite 600
Greensboro, NC 27409-9423
Web: http://www.brookstone.edu
Accreditation: Accrediting Council for Independent Colleges and Schools
Programs Offered:
accounting; accounting and business/management; accounting and finance; accounting related; accounting technology and bookkeeping; administrative assistant and secretarial science; allied health and medical assisting services related; business automation/technology/data entry; computer and information sciences and support services related; computer and information sciences related; computer hardware technology; computer/information technology administration and man-

agement; computer/information technology services administration related; computer installation and repair technology; computer software technology; computer/technical support; computer technology/computer systems technology; data entry/microcomputer applications; data entry/microcomputer applications related; data modeling/warehousing and database administration; data processing and data processing technology; executive assistant/executive secretary; health and medical administrative services related; health information/medical records technology; health services/allied health/health sciences; information technology; medical administrative assistant and medical secretary; medical/clinical assistant; medical insurance coding; medical insurance/medical billing; medical office assistant; medical office computer specialist; medical reception; medical transcription; receptionist; web page, digital/multimedia and information resources design; word processing
Enrollment: 240 students
Institution Contact: Mrs. Bridget Handley, Community Relations Coordinator
Phone: 336-668-2627 ext. 18
Fax: 336-668-2717
E-mail: bhandley@brookstone.edu

ECPI COLLEGE OF TECHNOLOGY

4800 Airport Center Parkway
Charlotte, NC 28208
Web: http://www.ecpi.edu
Accreditation: Southern Association of Colleges and Schools
Programs Offered:
business administration and management; business automation/technology/data entry; computer and information systems security; computer engineering technology; computer installation and repair technology; computer technology/computer systems technology; electrical, electronic and communications engineering technology; health information/medical records administration; health information/medical records technology; information science/studies; medical administrative assistant and medical secretary; medical/clinical assistant; medical transcription; nursing (licensed practical/vocational nurse training); office occupations and clerical services; telecommunications; web page, digital/multimedia and information resources design
Enrollment: 355 students

Institution Contact: Mr. Victor Riley, Provost
Phone: 704-399-1010
Fax: 704-399-9144
E-mail: vriley@ecpi.edu

ECPI COLLEGE OF TECHNOLOGY

7802 Airport Center Drive
Greensboro, NC 27409
Web: http://www.ecpi.edu
Accreditation: Southern Association of Colleges and Schools
Programs Offered:
administrative assistant and secretarial science; business administration and management; business automation/technology/data entry; computer engineering technology; computer installation and repair technology; computer systems networking and telecommunications; computer/technical support; computer technology/computer systems technology; criminal justice/police science; health information/medical records administration; health information/medical records technology; information science/studies; information technology; medical/clinical assistant; medical insurance coding; medical insurance/medical billing; medical office computer specialist; office occupations and clerical services; telecommunications; web page, digital/multimedia and information resources design
Enrollment: 402 students
Institution Contact: Ms. Sue Schmith, Provost
Phone: 336-665-1400
E-mail: ssmith@ecpi.edu

ECPI COLLEGE OF TECHNOLOGY

4101 Doie Cope Road
Raleigh, NC 27613
Web: http://www.ecpi.edu
Accreditation: Accrediting Commission of Career Schools and Colleges of Technology; Southern Association of Colleges and Schools
Programs Offered:
administrative assistant and secretarial science; business administration and management; business automation/technology/data entry; computer engineering technology; computer/information technology administration and management; computer installation and repair technology; computer systems networking and telecommunications; computer/technical support; computer technology/computer systems technology; health information/medical records technology; information science/studies; information technology; office occupations and clerical services; system administration; telecommunications; web page, digital/multimedia and information resources design
Enrollment: 522 students
Institution Contact: Ms. Susan Wells, Provost
Phone: 919-571-0057
Fax: 919-571-0780
E-mail: swells@ecpi.edu

EMPIRE BEAUTY SCHOOL

Shoppes at Kings Grant
10075 Weddington Rd. Ext.
Concord, NC 28027
Institution Contact: Ms. Anila Wali
Phone: 704-979-3500
Fax: 704-979-3434

EMPIRE BEAUTY SCHOOL

11032 E. Independence Blvd.
Matthews, NC 28105
Institution Contact: Ms. Ruth Crumpton
Phone: 704-845-8064
Fax: 704-845-8038

KING'S COLLEGE

322 Lamar Avenue
Charlotte, NC 28204
Web: http://www.kingscollege.org
Accreditation: Accrediting Council for Independent Colleges and Schools
Programs Offered:
accounting; administrative assistant and secretarial science; commercial and advertising art; computer programming; computer/technical support; legal administrative assistant/secretary; legal assistant/paralegal; medical/clinical assistant; tourism and travel services management
Institution Contact: Ms. Barbara Rockecharlie, School Director
Phone: 704-688-3613
Fax: 704-348-2029
E-mail: brockecharlie@kingscollege.org
Admission Contact: Mrs. Diane Ryon, School Director

Phone: 704-372-0266 ext. 3600
Fax: 704-348-2029
E-mail: dryon@kingscollege.org

MILLER-MOTTE TECHNICAL COLLEGE
2205 Walnut St.
Cary, NC 27511
Institution Contact: Shannon Hodge
Phone: 919-532-7171
Fax: 919-532-7151

MILLER-MOTTE TECHNICAL COLLEGE
5000 Market Street
Wilmington, NC 28405
Web: http://www.miller-motte.com
Accreditation: Accrediting Council for Independent Colleges and Schools
Programs Offered:
accounting; administrative assistant and secretarial science; aesthetician/esthetician and skin care; business administration and management; computer software and media applications; computer systems networking and telecommunications; cosmetology; massage therapy; medical/clinical assistant; medical office assistant; nail technician and manicurist; office management; surgical technology
Institution Contact:
Phone: 800-784-2110

NASCAR TECHNICAL INSTITUTE
220 Byers Creek Road
Mooresville, NC 28117
Accreditation: Accrediting Commission of Career Schools and Colleges of Technology
Programs Offered:
automobile/automotive mechanics technology
Enrollment: 1,588 students
Institution Contact: Mr. Mike Fritz, School Director
Phone: 704-658-1950 ext. 17401
Fax: 704-658-1952
E-mail: mfritz@uticorp.com
Admission Contact: Mr. Mike Gavin, Admissions Director
Phone: 704-658-1950 ext. 17417
Fax: 704-658-1952
E-mail: mgavin@uticorp.com

SOUTH COLLEGE - ASHEVILLE
1567 Patton Avenue
Asheville, NC 28806-1748
Accreditation: Accrediting Council for Independent Colleges and Schools
Programs Offered:
accounting; administrative assistant and secretarial science; business administration and management; computer systems networking and telecommunications; criminal justice/law enforcement administration; data entry/microcomputer applications; executive assistant/executive secretary; legal assistant/paralegal; medical/clinical assistant; medical transcription; physical therapist assistant; surgical technology
Enrollment: 117 students
Institution Contact: Mr. Robert A. Davis, Dean of Academic Affairs
Phone: 828-252-2486
Fax: 828-252-8558
E-mail: bdavis@southcollegenc.com
Admission Contact: Mr. Robert Hayden, Director of Admissions
Phone: 828-252-2486
Fax: 828-252-8558
E-mail: rhayden@southcollegenc.com

NORTH DAKOTA

AAKERS BUSINESS COLLEGE
1701 E. Century Ave., Suite 830
Bismarck, ND 58503
Institution Contact: Mr. Jim Ihrke

AAKERS BUSINESS COLLEGE
4012 19th Avenue, SW
Fargo, ND 58103
Accreditation: Accrediting Council for Independent Colleges and Schools
Programs Offered:
accounting; accounting and finance; banking and financial support services; computer/information technology administration and management; computer/technical support; executive assistant/executive secretary; human resources management; legal administrative assistant/secretary; marketing/marketing management; medical administrative assistant and

medical secretary; medical insurance coding; medical office assistant; medical reception; medical transcription; receptionist
Enrollment: 585 students
Institution Contact: Ms. Elizabeth N. Largent, Director
Phone: 701-277-3889
Fax: 701-277-5604
E-mail: blargent@aakers.edu
Admission Contact: Mr. John Wilson, Director of Admissions
Phone: 701-277-3889
Fax: 701-277-5604
E-mail: jwilson@aakers.edu

OHIO

AKRON INSTITUTE
1600 South Arlington Street, Suite 100
Akron, OH 44306
Web: http://www.akroninstitute.com
Accreditation: Accrediting Commission of Career Schools and Colleges of Technology
Programs Offered:
business administration and management; computer technology/computer systems technology; dental assisting; medical/clinical assistant; medical insurance/medical billing
Enrollment: 293 students
Institution Contact: Mr. David L. LaRue, Campus President
Phone: 330-724-1600
Fax: 330-724-9688
E-mail: dlarue@akroninstitute.com
Admission Contact: Ms. Connie Pahls, Director of Admissions
Phone: 330-724-1600
Fax: 330-724-9688
E-mail: cpahls@akroninstitute.com

AMERICAN SCHOOL OF TECHNOLOGY
2100 Morse Road, #4599
Columbus, OH 43229
Accreditation: Accrediting Commission of Career Schools and Colleges of Technology
Programs Offered:
computer and information sciences related; heating,

air conditioning and refrigeration technology; medical/clinical assistant; medical insurance coding
Enrollment: 635 students
Institution Contact: Mrs. Susan Stella, Director and Chief Executive Officer
Phone: 614-436-4820
Admission Contact: Mrs. Tera Wilson, Director of Admissions
Phone: 614-436-4820

ANTONELLI COLLEGE
124 East 7th Street
Cincinnati, OH 45202
Web: http://www.antonellic.com
Programs Offered:
accounting; computer/technical support; graphic communications; interior design; legal administrative assistant/secretary; massage therapy; medical insurance coding; medical office computer specialist; medical transcription; office management; photography
Enrollment: 458 students
Institution Contact: Connie D. Sharp, Director
Phone: 513-2414338
Fax: 513-2419396
E-mail: connie@antonellic.com

THE ART INSTITUTE OF OHIO - CINCINNATI
1011 Glendale Road
Cincinnati, OH 45215
Web: http://www.aioc.artinstitutes.edu/
Programs Offered:
design and visual communications; graphic communications; interior design; marketing related
Institution Contact: Admissions
Phone: 513-771-2821

BRADFORD SCHOOL
2469 Stelzer Road
Columbus, OH 43219
Web: http://www.bradfordschoolcolumbus.edu
Accreditation: Accrediting Council for Independent Colleges and Schools
Programs Offered:
accounting; administrative assistant and secretarial science; commercial and advertising art; computer graphics; computer programming; computer systems

networking and telecommunications; culinary arts; executive assistant/executive secretary; hospitality administration; legal administrative assistant/secretary; legal assistant/paralegal; medical/clinical assistant; tourism and travel services management; veterinary technology

Enrollment: 422 students

Institution Contact: Mr. Dennis Bartels, President

Phone: 614-416-6200

Fax: 614-416-6210

E-mail: dbartels@bradfordschoolcolumbus.edu

Admission Contact: Ms. Raeann Lee, Director of Admissions

Phone: 614-416-6200

Fax: 614-416-6210

E-mail: rlee@bradfordschoolcolumbus.edu

BROWN MACKIE COLLEGE, AKRON CAMPUS

2791 Mogadore Road

Akron, OH 44312

Accreditation: Accrediting Council for Independent Colleges and Schools

Programs Offered:

accounting and business/management; CAD/CADD drafting/design technology; computer programming; computer programming related; computer programming (specific applications); computer programming (vendor/product certification); computer science; computer software and media applications related; computer software technology; computer systems networking and telecommunications; criminal justice/law enforcement administration; electrical and electronic engineering technologies related; electrical, electronic and communications engineering technology; health/health care administration; legal assistant/paralegal; mechanical drafting and CAD/CADD; medical/clinical assistant; pharmacy technician

Enrollment: 521 students

Institution Contact: Ms. Sandra A. Wilk, President

Phone: 330-733-8766

Fax: 330-733-5853

E-mail: swilk@brownmackie.edu

Admission Contact: Mrs. Tanya Foose, Director of Admissions

Phone: 330-733-8766

Fax: 330-733-5853

E-mail: tfoose@brownmackie.edu

BROWN MACKIE COLLEGE, CINCINNATI CAMPUS

1011 Glendale Milford Road

Cincinnati, OH 45215

Web: http://www.brownmackie.edu

Accreditation: Accrediting Council for Independent Colleges and Schools

Programs Offered:

accounting; allied health and medical assisting services related; audiovisual communications technologies related; business, management, and marketing related; CAD/CADD drafting/design technology; computer programming (specific applications); computer software technology; computer systems networking and telecommunications; criminal justice/law enforcement administration; health information/medical records administration; legal assistant/paralegal; medical/clinical assistant; nursing (registered nurse training); opticianry

Enrollment: 1,393 students

Institution Contact: Robin Krout, President

Phone: 513-771-2424 ext. 772

Fax: 513-771-3413

E-mail: rkrout@brownmackie.edu

Admission Contact: Gerry Purcell, Director of Admissions

Phone: 513-771-2424 ext. 730

Fax: 513-771-3413

E-mail: gpurcell@brownmackie.edu

BROWN MACKIE COLLEGE, FINDLAY CAMPUS

1700 Fostoria Avenue, Suite 100

Findlay, OH 45840

Web: http://www.socaec.edu

Accreditation: Accrediting Council for Independent Colleges and Schools

Programs Offered:

accounting; business administration and management; computer software and media applications; criminal justice/law enforcement administration; health services administration; legal assistant/paralegal; medical/clinical assistant; nursing (licensed practical/vocational nurse training); pharmacy technician

Admission Contact: Angelique Walker, Admissions Director

Phone: 419-423-2211

Fax: 419-423-0725

BROWN MACKIE COLLEGE, NORTH CANTON CAMPUS

1320 West Maple Street, NW
North Canton, OH 44720-2854
Web: http://www.ETITech.Com
Accreditation: Accrediting Council for Independent Colleges and Schools
Programs Offered:
accounting; business administration and management; business/corporate communications; CAD/CADD drafting/design technology; computer programming; computer software and media applications related; computer software technology; computer systems networking and telecommunications; computer technology/computer systems technology; criminal justice/law enforcement administration; electrical, electronic and communications engineering technology; legal administrative assistant/secretary; legal assistant/paralegal; medical administrative assistant and medical secretary; medical/clinical assistant
Enrollment: 736 students
Institution Contact: Mr. Peter Perkowski, Director
Phone: 330-494-1214
Fax: 330-494-8112
E-mail: peterp@amedcts.com
Admission Contact: Mr. Greg Laudermilt, Director of Admissions
Phone: 330-494-1214
Fax: 330-494-8112
E-mail: elaudermilt@amedcts.com

BRYMAN INSTITUTE

825 Tech Center Drive
Gahanna, OH 43230-6653
Programs Offered:
medical/clinical assistant; medical insurance coding; medical insurance/medical billing

DAVIS COLLEGE

4747 Monroe Street
Toledo, OH 43623-4307
Web: http://www.daviscollege.edu
Programs Offered:
accounting; administrative assistant and secretarial science; business administration and management; child care and support services management; computer and information sciences; computer/technical support; design and visual communications; fashion merchan-

dising; marketing/marketing management; massage therapy; medical/clinical assistant; medical insurance coding; medical transcription; office management; web/multimedia management and webmaster
Enrollment: 482 students
Institution Contact: Diane Brunner, President
Phone: 419-473-2700
Fax: 419-473-2472
E-mail: dbrunner@daviscollege.edu
Admission Contact: Dana Stern, Admissions Director
Phone: 419-473-2700
Fax: 419-473-2472
E-mail: dstern@daviscollege.edu

EDUTEK COLLEGE

3855 Fishcreek Road
Stow, OH 44224
Web: http://www.edutekcollege.com
Accreditation: Accrediting Council for Independent Colleges and Schools
Programs Offered:
adult and continuing education; computer engineering technology; medical insurance coding; medical insurance/medical billing; medical office assistant; medical office management; medical transcription; office management; pharmacy technician
Institution Contact: Angela J. Daniel, Executive Director
Phone: 330-677-4667
Fax: 330-677-4560
E-mail: adaniel@edutekcollege.com
Admission Contact: Christopher Caraway, Director of Admissions
Phone: 330-677-4667
Fax: 330-677-4560
E-mail: ccaraway@edutekcollege.com

GALLIPOLIS CAREER COLLEGE

1176 Jackson Pike, Suite 312
Gallipolis, OH 45631-2600
Web: http://www.gallipoliscareercollege.com/
Accreditation: Accrediting Council for Independent Colleges and Schools
Programs Offered:
accounting; business administration and management; computer technology/computer systems technology; data entry/microcomputer applications; executive assis-

tant/executive secretary; medical administrative assistant and medical secretary; medical office management

Enrollment: 157 students

Institution Contact: Mr. Robert L. Shirey, President

Phone: 740-446-4367

Fax: 740-446-4124

E-mail: gcc@gallipoliscareercollege.com

Admission Contact: Mr. Jack L. Henson, Director of Admissions

Phone: 740-446-4367

Fax: 740-446-4124

E-mail: admissions@gallipoliscareercollege.com

HONDROS COLLEGE

4140 Executive Parkway

Westerville, OH 43081

Web: http://www.hondros.com

Programs Offered:

financial planning and services; insurance; real estate; sales, distribution and marketing; securities services administration

Institution Contact:

Phone: 614-508-7277

Fax: 614-508-7279

INTERNATIONAL COLLEGE OF BROADCASTING

6 South Smithville Road

Dayton, OH 45431

Web: http://www.icbcollege.com

Accreditation: Accrediting Commission of Career Schools and Colleges of Technology; Accrediting Council for Independent Colleges and Schools

Programs Offered:

broadcast journalism; communications technology; radio and television; recording arts technology

Institution Contact: Mr. J. Michael LeMaster, Director and Vice President of Operations

Phone: 937-258-8251 ext. 201

Fax: 937-258-8714

E-mail: micicb@aol.com

Admission Contact: Mr. Aan McIntosh, Director of Admissions

Phone: 937-258-8251 ext. 202

Fax: 937-258-8714

 ITT TECHNICAL INSTITUTE

3325 Stop Eight Road

Dayton, OH 45414-3425

Web: http://www.itt-tech.edu

Accreditation: Accrediting Council for Independent Colleges and Schools

Programs Offered:

CAD/CADD drafting/design technology; computer engineering technology; computer software and media applications; computer systems networking and telecommunications; digital communication and media/multimedia; web page, digital/multimedia and information resources design

Institution Contact: Mr. Michael S. Shaffer, Director

Phone: 937-454-2267

Admission Contact: Mr. Joe G. Graham, Director of Recruitment

Phone: 937-454-2267

 ITT TECHNICAL INSTITUTE

3781 Park Mill Run Drive

Hilliard, OH 43026

Web: http://www.itt-tech.edu

Accreditation: Accrediting Council for Independent Colleges and Schools

Programs Offered:

accounting and business/management; business administration and management; CAD/CADD drafting/design technology; computer engineering technology; computer software engineering; computer systems networking and telecommunications; criminal justice/police science; digital communication and media/multimedia; web page, digital/multimedia and information resources design

Institution Contact: Mr. James Vaas, Director

Phone: 614-771-4888

Admission Contact: Mr. James Vaas, Director

Phone: 614-771-4888

 ITT TECHNICAL INSTITUTE

4750 Wesley Avenue

Norwood, OH 45212

Web: http://www.itt-tech.edu

Accreditation: Accrediting Council for Independent Colleges and Schools

Programs Offered:

CAD/CADD drafting/design technology; computer

engineering technology; computer software and media applications; computer systems networking and telecommunications; digital communication and media/multimedia; web page, digital/multimedia and information resources design
Institution Contact: Mr. Bill Bradford, Director
Phone: 513-531-8300
Admission Contact: Mr. Greg Hitt, Director of Recruitment
Phone: 513-531-8300

ITT Technical Institute
14955 Sprague Road
Strongsville, OH 44136
Web: http://www.itt-tech.edu
Accreditation: Accrediting Council for Independent Colleges and Schools
Programs Offered:
accounting and business/management; business administration and management; CAD/CADD drafting/design technology; computer engineering technology; computer software and media applications; computer systems networking and telecommunications; criminal justice/police science; digital communication and media/multimedia; web page, digital/multimedia and information resources design
Institution Contact: Mr. Scott Behmer, Director
Phone: 440-234-9091
Admission Contact: Ms. Joanne Dyer, Director of Recruitment
Phone: 440-234-9091

ITT Technical Institute
4700 Richmond Road
Warrensville Heights, OH 44128
Web: http://www.itt-tech.edu
Programs Offered:
business administration and management; CAD/CADD drafting/design technology; computer engineering technology; computer systems networking and telecommunications; criminal justice/law enforcement administration
Institution Contact:
Phone: 216-896-6500

ITT Technical Institute
1030 North Meridian Road
Youngstown, OH 44509-4098
Web: http://www.itt-tech.edu
Accreditation: Accrediting Council for Independent Colleges and Schools
Programs Offered:
CAD/CADD drafting/design technology; computer engineering technology; computer software and media applications; computer systems networking and telecommunications; digital communication and media/multimedia; web page, digital/multimedia and information resources design
Institution Contact: Mr. Frank Quartini, Director
Phone: 330-270-1600
Admission Contact: Mr. Tom Flynn, Director of Recruitment
Phone: 330-270-1600

Miami - Jacobs College
110 North Patterson Boulevard
Dayton, OH 45402
Web: http://www.miamijacobs.edu
Accreditation: Accrediting Council for Independent Colleges and Schools
Programs Offered:
business administration and management; computer systems networking and telecommunications; criminal justice/law enforcement administration; massage therapy; medical/clinical assistant; medical office management; surgical technology
Enrollment: 527 students
Institution Contact: Ms. Darlene R. Waite, President
Phone: 937-461-5174
Fax: 937-461-3384
E-mail: darlene.waite@miamijacobs.edu
Admission Contact: Mr. Sean Kuhn, Director of Admissions
Phone: 937-461-5174 ext. 123
Fax: 937-461-3384
E-mail: sean.kuhn@miamijacobs.edu

National College of Business and Technology
6871 Steger Drive
Cincinnati, OH 45237
Web: http://www.ncbt.edu/

Programs Offered:
accounting; business administration and management; computer and information sciences; medical/clinical assistant; pharmacy technician
Institution Contact: Admissions
Phone: 513-761-1291
Fax: 513-821-1037

NATIONAL COLLEGE OF BUSINESS AND TECHNOLOGY
1837 Woodman Center Drive
Kettering, OH 45420-1157
Programs Offered:
accounting; business administration and management; health information/medical records technology; medical/clinical assistant; pharmacy technician; surgical technology

OHIO INSTITUTE OF PHOTOGRAPHY AND TECHNOLOGY
2029 Edgefield Road
Dayton, OH 45439
Web: http://www.oipt.com
Accreditation: Accrediting Commission of Career Schools and Colleges of Technology
Programs Offered:
medical/clinical assistant; medical office management; pharmacy technician
Institution Contact: Mr. Norman H Dorn, Jr., Director of Admissions
Phone: 800-932-9698
Fax: 937-294-2259
E-mail: ndorn@oipt.com
Admission Contact: Mr. Norman H. Dorn, Jr., Director of Admissions
Phone: 800-932-9698
Fax: 937-294-2259
E-mail: ndorn@oipt.com

OHIO VALLEY COLLEGE OF TECHNOLOGY
16808 St. Clair Avenue, PO Box 7000
East Liverpool, OH 43920
Web: http://www.ovct.edu
Accreditation: Accrediting Council for Independent Colleges and Schools
Programs Offered:

accounting; computer installation and repair technology; computer software and media applications related; dental assisting; medical/clinical assistant; medical office management
Enrollment: 176 students
Institution Contact: Ms. Debra Sanford, Director of Education
Phone: 330-385-1070
Fax: 330-385-4606
E-mail: dsanford@ovct.edu
Admission Contact: Mr. Scott S. Rogers, Director
Phone: 330-385-1070
Fax: 330-385-4606
E-mail: srogers@ovct.edu

REMINGTON COLLEGE - CLEVELAND CAMPUS
14445 Broadway Avenue
Cleveland, OH 44125
Web: http://www.remingtoncollege.edu
Accreditation: Accrediting Commission of Career Schools and Colleges of Technology
Programs Offered:
computer/information technology administration and management; computer programming (specific applications); information science/studies; internet information systems; medical/clinical assistant; medical insurance/medical billing; pharmacy technician; system, networking, and LAN/WAN management
Enrollment: 667 students
Institution Contact: Mrs. Joyce Kucharson, Campus President
Phone: 216-475-7520
Fax: 216-475-6055
E-mail: joyce.kucharson@remingtoncollege.edu
Admission Contact: Mr. William Cassidy, Director of Recruitment
Phone: 216-475-7520
Fax: 216-475-6055
E-mail: william.cassidy@remingtoncollege.edu

REMINGTON COLLEGE - CLEVELAND WEST CAMPUS
26350 Brookpark
North Olmstead, OH 44070
Web: http://www.remingtoncollege.edu
Accreditation: Accrediting Commission of Career Schools and Colleges of Technology
Programs Offered:

computer systems analysis; criminal justice/law enforcement administration; dental assisting; medical/clinical assistant; pharmacy technician
Institution Contact: Mr. Gary Azotea, Vice President
Phone: 440-777-2560
Fax: 440-777-3238
E-mail: gary.azotea@remingtoncollege.edu
Admission Contact: Mr. Vic Hart, Director of Recruitment
Phone: 440-777-2560
Fax: 440-777-3238
E-mail: vic.hart@remingtoncollege.edu

RETS TECH CENTER
555 East Alex Bell Road
Centerville, OH 45459
Web: http://www.retstechcenter.com
Accreditation: Accrediting Commission of Career Schools and Colleges of Technology
Programs Offered:
computer/information technology administration and management; electrical, electronic and communications engineering technology; heating, air conditioning and refrigeration technology; legal assistant/paralegal; medical/clinical assistant; medical insurance coding; nursing (licensed practical/vocational nurse training); tourism and travel services management
Enrollment: 515 students
Institution Contact: Mr. Bill Sero, Campus Director
Phone: 937-433-3410 ext. 220
Fax: 937-435-6516
E-mail: bsero@retstechcenter.com
Admission Contact: Mr. Rich Elkin, Director of Admissions
Phone: 937-433-3410
Fax: 937-435-6516
E-mail: rets@erinet.com

SOUTHEASTERN BUSINESS COLLEGE
1855 Western Avenue
Chillicothe, OH 45601
Web: http://www.southeasternbusinesscollege.com
Accreditation: Accrediting Council for Independent Colleges and Schools
Programs Offered:
accounting; business administration and management; information technology; medical administrative assistant and medical secretary; office management
Enrollment: 98 students
Institution Contact: Connie Pruitt, Director
Phone: 740-774-6300
Fax: 740-774-6317
E-mail: connie_jcorp@yahoo.com
Admission Contact: Elizabeth Scott, Admissions Representative
Phone: 740-774-6300
Fax: 740-774-6317
E-mail: liz_jcorp@yahoo.com

SOUTHEASTERN BUSINESS COLLEGE
504 McCarty Lane
Jackson, OH 45640
Web: http://www.southeasternbusinesscollege.com
Accreditation: Accrediting Council for Independent Colleges and Schools
Programs Offered:
accounting; administrative assistant and secretarial science; business administration and management; computer software and media applications; information technology; medical administrative assistant and medical secretary
Enrollment: 65 students
Institution Contact: Karen Osborne, Director/Director of Education
Phone: 740-286-1554
Fax: 740-286-4476
E-mail: dir_jackson@yahoo.com
Admission Contact: Ronda Smith, Admissions Representative
Phone: 740-286-1554
Fax: 740-286-4476

SOUTHEASTERN BUSINESS COLLEGE
1522 Sheridan Drive
Lancaster, OH 43130-1368
Accreditation: Accrediting Council for Independent Colleges and Schools
Programs Offered:
accounting; administrative assistant and secretarial science; business administration and management; information technology; medical administrative assistant and medical secretary
Enrollment: 74 students
Institution Contact: Ms. Mary Gang, Director

Phone: 740-687-6126
Fax: 740-687-0431
E-mail: dir_lanc@yahoo.com
Admission Contact: Jamie Fauble
Phone: 740-687-6126
Fax: 740-687-0431
E-mail: dir_lanc@yahoo.com

SOUTHEASTERN BUSINESS COLLEGE

3879 Rhodes Avenue
New Boston, OH 45662
Web: http://www.southeasternbusinesscollege.com
Accreditation: Accrediting Council for Independent
Colleges and Schools
Programs Offered:
accounting; administrative assistant and secretarial
science; business administration and management; information technology; medical administrative assistant
and medical secretary
Enrollment: 80 students
Institution Contact: Ms. Betty McAdow, Director/Director of Education
Phone: 740-456-4124
Fax: 740-456-5163
E-mail: dir_nb@yahoo.com
Admission Contact: Mrs. Rebecca Mowery, Admissions Representative
Phone: 740-456-4124
Fax: 740-456-5163
E-mail: admit_nb@yahoo.com

 ## SOUTHWESTERN COLLEGE OF BUSINESS

149 Northland Boulevard
Cincinnati, OH 45246
Web: http://www.swcollege.net
Accreditation: Accrediting Council for Independent
Colleges and Schools
Programs Offered:
accounting; accounting technology and bookkeeping; administrative assistant and secretarial science;
business administration and management; computer
science; computer software and media applications;
medical administrative assistant and medical secretary;
medical/clinical assistant; medical insurance coding;
medical insurance/medical billing; phlebotomy
Admission Contact: Roy Kimble, Director of Admissions

Phone: 513-874-0432
Fax: 513-874-1330
E-mail: doatri-county@lincolnedu.com

 ## SOUTHWESTERN COLLEGE OF BUSINESS

632 Vine Street
Cincinnati, OH 45246
Web: http://www.swcollege.net
Accreditation: Accrediting Council for Independent
Colleges and Schools
Programs Offered:
accounting; administrative assistant and secretarial
science; business administration and management;
computer science; computer software and media applications; medical administrative assistant and medical
secretary; medical/clinical assistant; medical insurance
coding; medical insurance/medical billing; phlebotomy
Admission Contact: Betty Streber, Director of
Admissions
Phone: 513-421-3212
Fax: 513-421-8325
E-mail: doavinestreet@lincolnedu.com

 ## SOUTHWESTERN COLLEGE OF BUSINESS

111 West First Street
Dayton, OH 45402
Web: http://www.swcollege.net
Accreditation: Accrediting Council for Independent
Colleges and Schools
Programs Offered:
accounting; accounting technology and bookkeeping; administrative assistant and secretarial science;
business administration and management; computer
science; computer software and media applications;
medical administrative assistant and medical secretary;
medical/clinical assistant; medical insurance coding;
medical insurance/medical billing; phlebotomy
Admission Contact: Curtis Kirby, Director of
Admissions
Phone: 937-224-0061
Fax: 937-224-0065
E-mail: doadayton@lincolnedu.com

SOUTHWESTERN COLLEGE OF BUSINESS

201 East Second Street
Franklin, OH 45005
Web: http://www.swcollege.net
Accreditation: Accrediting Council for Independent Colleges and Schools
Programs Offered:
accounting; administrative assistant and secretarial science; business administration and management; computer science; computer software and media applications; medical administrative assistant and medical secretary; medical/clinical assistant; medical insurance coding; medical insurance/medical billing; phlebotomy
Enrollment: 222 students
Institution Contact: Mr. Ronald L. Mills, Jr., Executive Director
Phone: 937-746-6633 ext. 45101
Fax: 937-746-6754
E-mail: rmills@swcollege.net
Admission Contact: Lynne Reilly, Director of Admissions
Phone: 937-746-6633
Fax: 937-746-6754
E-mail: doafranklin@lincolnedu.com

TDDS, INC.

1688 North Pricetown Road, SR 534, PO Box 506
Lake Milton, OH 44429
Web: http://www.tdds.edu
Accreditation: Accrediting Commission of Career Schools and Colleges of Technology
Programs Offered:
diesel mechanics technology; truck and bus driver/commercial vehicle operation
Enrollment: 515 students
Institution Contact: Mr. Richard A. Rathburn, Jr., President
Phone: 330-538-2216
Fax: 330-538-2905
E-mail: rick@tdds.edu
Admission Contact: Mr. Michael A. Rouzzo, Admissions Director
Phone: 330-538-2216
Fax: 330-538-2905
E-mail: michael@tdds.edu

TECHNOLOGY EDUCATION COLLEGE

2745 Winchester Pike
Columbus, OH 43232-2087
Web: http://www.teccollege.com
Accreditation: Accrediting Commission of Career Schools and Colleges of Technology
Programs Offered:
accounting; computer programming; computer technology/computer systems technology; criminal justice/law enforcement administration; drafting and design technology; engineering technology; medical/clinical assistant
Institution Contact: Mr. Thomas Greenhouse, Director
Phone: 614-759-7700
Fax: 614-759-7747
E-mail: tgreenhouse@teceducation.com
Admission Contact: Rhonda Frazier
Phone: 614-456-4600
Fax: 800-838-3233
E-mail: rfrazier@teceducation.com

TRUMBULL BUSINESS COLLEGE

3200 Ridge Road
Warren, OH 44484
Web: http://www.tbc-trumbullbusiness.com
Accreditation: Accrediting Council for Independent Colleges and Schools
Programs Offered:
accounting; business administration and management; computer software and media applications; executive assistant/executive secretary; legal administrative assistant/secretary; medical administrative assistant and medical secretary; word processing
Enrollment: 425 students
Institution Contact: Mr. D. J. Griffith, Vice President
Phone: 330-369-3200 ext. 11
Fax: 330-369-6792
E-mail: djgriffith@tbc-trumbullbusiness.com
Admission Contact: Mrs. Amy Gazdik, Admissions Director/High School Coordinator
Phone: 330-369-3200 ext. 14
Fax: 330-369-6792
E-mail: agazdik@tbc-trumbullbusiness.com

VATTEROTT COLLEGE

5025 East Royalton Road
Broadview Heights, OH 44147
Web: http://www.vatterott-college.edu

Accreditation: Accrediting Commission of Career Schools and Colleges of Technology
Programs Offered:
building/property maintenance and management; computer technology/computer systems technology; electrician; heating, air conditioning, ventilation and refrigeration maintenance technology
Enrollment: 240 students
Institution Contact: Mr. Bob Martin, Director
Phone: 440-526-1860
Fax: 440-526-1933
E-mail: bmartin@vatterott-college.edu
Admission Contact: Mr. Kevin Pugely, High School Admissions Coordinator
Phone: 440-526-1860
Fax: 440-526-1933
E-mail: kevin.pugely@vatterott-college.edu

VIRGINIA MARTI COLLEGE OF ART AND DESIGN

11724 Detroit Avenue
Lakewood , OH 44107
Web: http://www.vmcad.edu
Accreditation: Accrediting Commission of Career Schools and Colleges of Technology
Programs Offered:
commercial and advertising art; fashion/apparel design; fashion merchandising; interior design
Enrollment: 300 students
Institution Contact: Mr. Dennis Marti, Assistant Director
Phone: 216-221-8584
Fax: 216-221-2311
E-mail: qmarti@vmcad.edu
Admission Contact: Mr. Quinn E. Marti, Admissions
Phone: 216-221-8584
Fax: 216-221-2311
E-mail: qmarti@vmcad.edu

OKLAHOMA

CAREER POINT INSTITUTE

3138 S Garnett Rd
Tulsa, OK 74146-1933
Institution Contact: Ms. Carol Kendall
Phone: 918-622-4100
Fax: 918-627-4007

CITY COLLEGE, INC.

2620 South Service Road
Moore, OK 73160
Web: http://www.citycollegeinc.com
Accreditation: Accrediting Council for Continuing Education and Training
Programs Offered:
accounting; child care provision; computer technology/computer systems technology; legal administrative assistant/secretary; legal assistant/paralegal; medical insurance coding
Enrollment: 250 students
Institution Contact: Mr. Andrew Moore
Phone: 405-329-5627
Fax: 405-321-2763
E-mail: jmoore@citycollegeinc.com

COMMUNITY CARE COLLEGE

4242 South Sheridan
Tulsa, OK 74145
Web: http://www.communitycarecollege.com
Accreditation: Accrediting Bureau of Health Education Schools
Programs Offered:
dental assisting; massage therapy; medical/clinical assistant; pharmacy technician; phlebotomy; surgical technology; veterinary/animal health technology
Enrollment: 859 students
Institution Contact: Ms. Teresa L. Knox, Chief Executive Officer
Phone: 918-610-0027 ext. 205
Fax: 918-622-9696
E-mail: tknox@communitycarecollege.com
Admission Contact: Ms. Teresa Knox, Chief Executive Officer
Phone: 918-610-0027
Fax: 918-610-0029
E-mail: tknox@communitycarecollege.com

DICKINSON BUSINESS SCHOOL/CAREER POINT BUSINESS SCHOOL

3138 South Garnett Road
Tulsa, OK 74146-1933
Web: http://www.career-point.org
Accreditation: Accrediting Council for Independent Colleges and Schools
Programs Offered:

accounting technology and bookkeeping; administrative assistant and secretarial science; clinical/medical laboratory assistant; computer systems networking and telecommunications; electrocardiograph technology; legal administrative assistant/secretary; medical administrative assistant and medical secretary; medical/clinical assistant; medical insurance coding; medical insurance/medical billing; medical office assistant; medical office computer specialist; office occupations and clerical services

Enrollment: 400 students

Institution Contact: Carol Kendall, School Director

Phone: 918-627-8074

Fax: 918-627-4007

E-mail: tdirector@career-point.org

Admission Contact: James J.D. Endsley, Director of Admissions

Phone: 918-627-8074

Fax: 918-627-4007

E-mail: tadmdir@career-point.org

HERITAGE COLLEGE OF HAIR DESIGN

7100 I-35 Services Road, Suite 7118
Oklahoma City, OK 73149

Programs Offered:

cosmetology

Institution Contact: Admissions

Phone: 405-631-3399

ITT TECHNICAL INSTITUTE

4943 South 78th East Avenue
Tulsa, OK 74145
Web: http://www.itt-tech.edu

Programs Offered:

business administration and management; CAD/CADD drafting/design technology; computer and information systems security; computer engineering technology; criminal justice/law enforcement administration; web/multimedia management and webmaster

Institution Contact:

Phone: 918-619-8700

OKLAHOMA HEALTH ACADEMY

1939 North Moore Avenue
Oklahoma City, OK 73160-3667

Programs Offered:

dental assisting; massage therapy; medical/clinical assistant; surgical technology; veterinary technology

Enrollment: 157 students

Institution Contact: Ms. Kayla Danyeur, Director of Accreditation and Licensing

Phone: 405-912-2777

Fax: 405-912-8039

E-mail: kaylad@oklahomahealthacademy.org

Admission Contact: Ms. Renee Jackson, Director of Admissions

Phone: 405-912-2777

Fax: 405-912-2770

OKLAHOMA HEALTH ACADEMY

2865 East Skelly Drive, Suite 224
Tulsa, OK 74105-6233

Programs Offered:

dental assisting; massage therapy; medical administrative assistant and medical secretary

Enrollment: 118 students

Institution Contact: Mr. Marcus Horn, Director

Phone: 918-748-9900

Fax: 918-748-9937

E-mail: mhorn@oklahomahealthacademy.org

Admission Contact: Mrs. Stephanie Holderman, Admissions

Phone: 918-748-9900

Fax: 918-748-9937

E-mail: stephanieh@oklahomahealthacademy.org

PLATT COLLEGE

112 Southwest 11th Street
Lawton, OK 73501
Web: http://www.plattcollege.org

Accreditation: Accrediting Commission of Career Schools and Colleges of Technology

Programs Offered:

dental assisting; medical/clinical assistant; nursing (licensed practical/vocational nurse training)

Institution Contact: Ms. Kirsten Sellens, Director

Phone: 580-355-4416

Fax: 580-355-4526

E-mail: kirstens@plattcollege.org

Admission Contact: Ms. Lisa Hannah, Admissions Representative

Phone: 580-355-4416

Fax: 580-355-4526

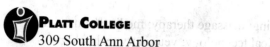

PLATT COLLEGE

309 South Ann Arbor
Oklahoma City, OK 73128
Accreditation: Accrediting Commission of Career Schools and Colleges of Technology
Programs Offered:
dental assisting; medical administrative assistant and medical secretary; medical/clinical assistant; nursing (licensed practical/vocational nurse training); pharmacy technician; surgical technology
Enrollment: 245 students
Institution Contact: Ms. Jane Nowlin, Director
Phone: 405-946-7799
Fax: 405-943-2150
E-mail: janen@plattcollege.org
Admission Contact: Ms. Heather Anson, Director of Admissions
Phone: 405-946-7799
Fax: 405-943-2150
E-mail: heathera@plattcollege.org

PLATT COLLEGE

3801 South Sheridan Road
Tulsa, OK 74145-1132
Web: http://www.plattcollege.org
Accreditation: Accrediting Commission of Career Schools and Colleges of Technology
Programs Offered:
dental assisting; medical/clinical assistant; nursing (licensed practical/vocational nurse training); nursing (registered nurse training); pharmacy technician; surgical technology
Enrollment: 450 students
Institution Contact: Mrs. Gay Pierce, Director
Phone: 918-663-9000
Fax: 918-622-1240
E-mail: gayp@plattcollege.org
Admission Contact: Mrs. Renee Jackson, Director of Admissions
Phone: 918-663-9000
Fax: 918-622-1240
E-mail: reneej@plattcollege.org

STATE BARBER AND HAIR DESIGN COLLEGE INC.

2514 South Agnew
Oklahoma City, OK 73108-6220
Accreditation: Accrediting Commission of Career Schools and Colleges of Technology
Programs Offered:
barbering
Enrollment: 36 students
Institution Contact: Ms. Elaine Gunn, Director
Phone: 405-631-8621
Fax: 405-632-2738
E-mail: statebarber2514@sbcglobal.net

TULSA WELDING SCHOOL

2545 East 11th Street
Tulsa, OK 74104-3909
Web: http://www.weldingschool.edu
Accreditation: Accrediting Commission of Career Schools and Colleges of Technology
Programs Offered:
welding technology
Enrollment: 515 students
Institution Contact: Mr. R. Michael Harter, Chairman and Chief Executive Officer
Phone: 918-587-6789 ext. 223
Fax: 918-295-6821
E-mail: mharter641@aol.com
Admission Contact: Mr. Mike Thurber, Director of Admissions
Phone: 918-587-6789 ext. 240
Fax: 918-587-8170
E-mail: tws@ionet.net

VATTEROTT COLLEGE

4629 Northwest 23rd Street
Oklahoma City, OK 73127
Web: http://www.vatterott-college.edu
Accreditation: Accrediting Commission of Career Schools and Colleges of Technology
Programs Offered:
CAD/CADD drafting/design technology; computer engineering technology; computer programming; computer programming (specific applications); computer technology/computer systems technology; drafting and design technology; electrician; heating, air conditioning, ventilation and refrigeration maintenance technology; medical administrative assistant and medical secretary; medical/clinical assistant; medical insurance coding; medical insurance/medical billing; medical office computer specialist
Institution Contact: Office of Admissions

Phone: 405-945-0088
Fax: 405-945-0788
E-mail: okcity@vatterott-college.edu

VATTEROTT COLLEGE

555 South Memorial Drive
Tulsa, OK 74112
Web: http://www.vatterott-college.edu
Accreditation: Accrediting Commission of Career Schools and Colleges of Technology
Programs Offered:
computer programming; computer technology/computer systems technology; electrician; heating, air conditioning and refrigeration technology; medical office computer specialist; web page, digital/multimedia and information resources design
Institution Contact: Office of Admissions
Phone: 918-835-8288
Fax: 918-836-9698
E-mail: tulsa@vatterott-college.edu

WRIGHT BUSINESS SCHOOL

2219 SW 74th, Suite 124
Oklahoma City, OK 73159
Web: http://www.wrightbusinessschool.com/
Programs Offered:
accounting; administrative assistant and secretarial science; computer/information technology administration and management; medical/clinical assistant; medical insurance coding; medical transcription; surgical technology
Institution Contact: Admissions
Phone: 800-946-0651

WRIGHT BUSINESS SCHOOL

4908 South Sheridan Road
Tulsa, OK 74145
Web: http://www.wrightbusinessschool.com/
Programs Offered:
accounting; administrative assistant and secretarial science; computer/information technology administration and management; information technology; medical administrative assistant and medical secretary; medical/clinical assistant; medical insurance coding; surgical technology
Institution Contact: Admissions

Phone: 800-946-0437

OREGON

APOLLO COLLEGE

2004 Lloyd Center
Portland, OR 97232
Web: http://www.apollocollege.edu
Accreditation: Accrediting Bureau of Health Education Schools
Programs Offered:
clinical/medical laboratory technology; dental assisting; medical administrative assistant and medical secretary; medical/clinical assistant; medical/health management and clinical assistant; medical insurance/medical billing; pharmacy technician; veterinary/animal health technology
Enrollment: 380 students
Institution Contact: Ms. Micaela Sieracki, Campus Director
Phone: 503-761-6100
Fax: 503-761-3351
E-mail: msieracki@apollocollege.edu

THE ART INSTITUTE OF PORTLAND

1122 Northwest Davis Street
Portland, OR 97209
Web: http://www.aipd.artinstitutes.edu
Accreditation: Northwest Association of Schools and Colleges
Programs Offered:
advertising; animation, interactive technology, video graphics and special effects; apparel and accessories marketing; apparel and textile manufacturing; apparel and textile marketing management; apparel and textiles related; applied art; art; CAD/CADD drafting/design technology; cinematography and film/video production; commercial and advertising art; computer graphics; design and visual communications; digital communication and media/multimedia; drawing; fashion and fabric consulting; fashion/apparel design; fashion merchandising; graphic communications; graphic communications related; interior design; web/multimedia management and webmaster; web page, digital/multimedia and information resources design
Enrollment: 1,497 students

Institution Contact: Lori Murray, Director of Admissions
Phone: 503-228-6528
Fax: 503-227-1945
E-mail: murrayl@aii.edu
Admission Contact: Lori Murray, Admissions Office
Phone: 888-228-6528
Fax: 503-227-1945
E-mail: aipdadm@aii.edu

ASHMEAD COLLEGE

9600 Southwest Oak Street, Suite 400
Tigard, OR 97223
Web: http://www.ashmeadcollege.com
Accreditation: Accrediting Council for Continuing
Education and Training
Programs Offered:
massage therapy
Institution Contact: Ms. Siri Sangren McElliott,
Campus President
Phone: 503-892-8100
Fax: 503-892-8871
E-mail: smcelliott@cci.edu
Admission Contact: Ms. Gayle Draney, Director of
Admissions
Phone: 503-892-8100
Fax: 503-892-8871
E-mail: gdraney@cci.edu

CAMBRIDGE COLLEGE

4145 SW Watson Ave. Ste. 300
Beaverton, OR 97005
Programs Offered:
dental assisting; massage therapy; medical/clinical
assistant; medical insurance/medical billing; pharmacy
technician; surgical technology
Enrollment: 328 students
Institution Contact: Ms. Kristin Lynn-Motter, Campus President
Phone: 503-646-6000
Fax: 503-646-6002
E-mail: klynnmotter@hightechinstitute.edu
Admission Contact: Ms. Rebecca Carlson, Director
of Admissions
Phone: 503-646-6000
E-mail: recarlson@hightechinstitute.edu

ITT TECHNICAL INSTITUTE

6035 Northeast 78th Court
Portland, OR 97218-2854
Web: http://www.itt-tech.edu
Accreditation: Accrediting Council for Independent
Colleges and Schools
Programs Offered:
animation, interactive technology, video graphics and
special effects; CAD/CADD drafting/design technology; communications technology; computer and
information systems security; computer software and
media applications; computer software engineering;
computer systems networking and telecommunications; digital communication and media/multimedia;
electrical, electronic and communications engineering
technology; industrial technology; technology management; web page, digital/multimedia and information
resources design
Institution Contact: Mr. Edward Yakimchick, Director
Phone: 503-255-6500
Admission Contact: Mr. Cliff Custer, Director of
Recruitment
Phone: 503-255-6500

PIONEER PACIFIC COLLEGE

8800 SE Sunnyside Road
Clackamas, OR 97015
Web: http://pioneerpacific.edu
Programs Offered:
accounting; business administration and management; criminal justice/law enforcement administration;
health/health care administration; legal assistant/paralegal; marketing/marketing management; medical/clinical assistant; medical insurance/medical billing
Enrollment: 269 students
Institution Contact: Michelle Hanks, Assistant to the
President
Phone: 503-682-3903 ext. 311
Fax: 503-682-1514
E-mail: mhanks@pioneerpacific.edu
Admission Contact: Mary Harris, Vice President of
Marketing
Phone: 503-654—8000
Fax: 503-659-6105
E-mail: mharris@pioneerpacific.edu

PIONEER PACIFIC COLLEGE

27501 Southwest Parkway Avenue
Wilsonville, OR 97070-9296
Web: http://www.pioneerpacific.edu
Accreditation: Accrediting Council for Independent Colleges and Schools
Programs Offered:
accounting; administrative assistant and secretarial science; business administration and management; computer/information technology administration and management; criminal justice/law enforcement administration; health/health care administration; legal assistant/paralegal; marketing/marketing management; massage therapy; medical/clinical assistant; medical insurance/medical billing; nursing (licensed practical/vocational nurse training); pharmacy technician; radiologic technology/science; web/multimedia management and webmaster
Enrollment: 434 students
Institution Contact: Michelle A. Hanks, Assistant to the President
Phone: 503-682-3903 ext. 311
Fax: 503-682-1514
E-mail: mhanks@pioneerpacific.edu
Admission Contact: Mrs. Mary Harris, Vice President of Admissions
Phone: 503-654-8000
Fax: 503-659-6107
E-mail: mharris@pioneerpacific.edu

PIONEER PACIFIC COLLEGE - EUGENE/SPRINGFIELD BRANCH

3800 Sports Way
Springfield, OR 97477
Web: http://pioneerpacific.edu
Accreditation: Accrediting Council for Independent Colleges and Schools
Programs Offered:
accounting; business administration and management; computer systems networking and telecommunications; criminal justice/law enforcement administration; health/health care administration; marketing/marketing management; medical/clinical assistant; medical insurance/medical billing; nursing (licensed practical/vocational nurse training)
Enrollment: 420 students
Institution Contact: Michelle A. Hanks, Assistant to the President
Phone: 503-682-3903 ext. 311
Fax: 503-682-1514
E-mail: mhanks@pioneerpacific.edu
Admission Contact: Debra Marcus, Director
Phone: 541-684-4644
Fax: 541-684-0655
E-mail: inquiries@pioneerpacific.edu

WESTERN BUSINESS COLLEGE

425 Southwest Washington Street
Portland, OR 97204
Web: http://www.cci.edu
Accreditation: Accrediting Council for Independent Colleges and Schools
Programs Offered:
accounting; administrative assistant and secretarial science; computer/information technology administration and management; criminal justice/law enforcement administration; data entry/microcomputer applications; executive assistant/executive secretary; hospitality administration; legal administrative assistant/secretary; legal assistant/paralegal; medical administrative assistant and medical secretary; medical/clinical assistant; medical insurance coding; medical insurance/medical billing; pharmacy technician; receptionist; tourism and travel services management
Enrollment: 662 students
Institution Contact: Mrs. Micaela Sieracki, President
Phone: 503-222-3225
Fax: 503-228-6926
E-mail: msieracki@cci.edu
Admission Contact: Ms. Laurel Coke, Director of Admissions
Phone: 503-222-3225
Fax: 503-228-6926
E-mail: lbuchana@cci.edu

WESTERN CULINARY INSTITUTE

921 SW Morrison Street , Suite 400
Portland, OR 97205
Web: http://www.wci.edu
Accreditation: Accrediting Commission of Career Schools and Colleges of Technology
Programs Offered:
baking and pastry arts; culinary arts; food preparation; food services technology; hospitality administration; hotel/motel administration; restaurant, culinary, and

catering management

Enrollment: 950 students

Institution Contact: Mrs. Joanne Lazo, Director of Marketing

Phone: 503-223-2245 ext. 385

Fax: 503-223-5554

E-mail: jlazo@wci.edu

Admission Contact: Mrs. Janine Carnel, Vice President of Admissions and Marketing

Phone: 503-223-2245 ext. 386

Fax: 503-223-5554

E-mail: jcarnel@wci.edu

PENNSYLVANIA

ACADEMY OF MEDICAL ARTS AND BUSINESS

2301 Academy Drive

Harrisburg, PA 17112-1012

Web: http://www.ACADcampus.com

Accreditation: Accrediting Bureau of Health Education Schools; Accrediting Commission of Career Schools and Colleges of Technology

Programs Offered:

business automation/technology/data entry; child care and support services management; child care provision; computer and information systems security; computer graphics; computer/information technology administration and management; computer/information technology services administration related; computer programming; computer programming (specific applications); computer programming (vendor/product certification); computer software and media applications; computer software and media applications related; computer systems analysis; computer systems networking and telecommunications; computer technology/computer systems technology; culinary arts; data processing and data processing technology; dental assisting; design and visual communications; desktop publishing and digital imaging design; digital communication and media/multimedia; electrocardiograph technology; health information/medical records administration; health information/medical records technology; home health aide/home attendant; information science/studies; information technology; legal administrative assistant/secretary; legal assistant/paralegal; massage therapy; medical administrative assistant and medical secretary; medical/clinical assistant; medi-

cal office management; medical transcription; office occupations and clerical services; receptionist; system administration; system, networking, and LAN/WAN management; web/multimedia management and webmaster; web page, digital/multimedia and information resources design; word processing

Enrollment: 368 students

Institution Contact: Mr. Gary Kay, President

Phone: 717-545-4747

Fax: 717-901-9090

E-mail: info@acadcampus.com

THE ART INSTITUTE OF PHILADELPHIA

1622 Chestnut Street

Philadelphia, PA 19103-5119

Web: http://www.aiph.artinstitutes.edu

Accreditation: Accrediting Council for Independent Colleges and Schools

Programs Offered:

animation, interactive technology, video graphics and special effects; cinematography and film/video production; commercial and advertising art; computer graphics; culinary arts; fashion/apparel design; fashion merchandising; industrial design; interior design; photography; web page, digital/multimedia and information resources design

Enrollment: 3,373 students

Institution Contact: Mr. Larry McHugh, Director of Admissions

Phone: 215-567-7080

Fax: 215-405-6399

E-mail: aiphisr@aii.edu

THE ART INSTITUTE OF PITTSBURGH

420 Boulevard of the Allies

Pittsburgh, PA 15219-1328

Web: http://www.aip.artinstitutes.edu

Accreditation: Accrediting Council for Independent Colleges and Schools; Middle States Association of Colleges and Schools

Programs Offered:

advertising; animation, interactive technology, video graphics and special effects; apparel and textile marketing management; applied art; art; cinematography and film/video production; commercial and advertising art; commercial photography; culinary arts; design and visual communications; desktop publishing and digital

imaging design; fashion merchandising; foodservice systems administration; graphic communications; hotel/motel administration; industrial design; interior design; make-up artist; metal and jewelry arts; photography; restaurant, culinary, and catering management; web/multimedia management and webmaster; web page, digital/multimedia and information resources design
Enrollment: 6,110 students
Institution Contact: Mr. George L. Pry, President
Phone: 412-291-6210
Fax: 412-263-3715
E-mail: gpry@aii.edu
Admission Contact: Mr. Newton Myvett, Director of Admissions
Phone: 800-275-2470
Fax: 412-263-6667
E-mail: nmyvett@aii.edu

AUTOMOTIVE TRAINING CENTER
114 Pickering Way
Exton, PA 19341-1310
Web: http://www.autotraining.edu
Accreditation: Accrediting Commission of Career Schools and Colleges of Technology
Programs Offered:
autobody/collision and repair technology; automobile/automotive mechanics technology; diesel mechanics technology; engine machinist
Enrollment: 600 students
Institution Contact: Mr. Steven C. Hiscox, President
Phone: 610-363-6716
Fax: 610-363-8524
E-mail: shiscox@autotraining.edu
Admission Contact: Mr. Donald S. VanDemark, Jr., Vice President/COO
Phone: 800-411-8031
Fax: 610-363-8524
E-mail: donvan@autotraining.edu

BALTIMORE SCHOOL OF MASSAGE, YORK CAMPUS
170 Red Rock Road
York, PA 17402
Web: http://steinered.com
Accreditation: Accrediting Commission of Career Schools and Colleges of Technology
Programs Offered:
massage therapy

Enrollment: 148 students
Institution Contact: Ms. Anita Perry-Strong, Campus Director
Phone: 717-268-1881
Fax: 717-268-1991
E-mail: anitas@steinerleisure.com
Admission Contact: Admissions Department
Phone: 866-699-1881
Fax: 717-268-1991
E-mail: anitas@steinerleisure.com

BERKS TECHNICAL INSTITUTE
2205 Ridgewood Road
Wyomissing, PA 19610-1168
Web: http://www.berks.edu
Accreditation: Accrediting Commission of Career Schools and Colleges of Technology
Programs Offered:
accounting; accounting and business/management; accounting related; administrative assistant and secretarial science; advertising; allied health and medical assisting services related; animation, interactive technology, video graphics and special effects; business administration and management; business administration, management and operations related; business machine repair; business, management, and marketing related; business operations support and secretarial services related; CAD/CADD drafting/design technology; civil drafting and CAD/CADD; commercial and advertising art; computer and information systems security; computer engineering related; computer engineering technologies related; computer engineering technology; computer graphics; computer hardware technology; computer/information technology administration and management; computer/information technology services administration related; computer installation and repair technology; computer technology/computer systems technology; criminal justice/law enforcement administration; criminal justice/police science; customer service management; customer service support/call center/teleservice operation; data entry/microcomputer applications; data entry/microcomputer applications related; desktop publishing and digital imaging design; drafting and design technology; graphic and printing equipment operation/production; graphic communications; graphic communications related; health aide; health aides/attendants/orderlies related; health and medical administrative services related; health/

health care administration; health information/medical records administration; health information/medical records technology; health/medical claims examination; health services administration; human resources management; human resources management and services related; information technology; legal administrative assistant/secretary; legal assistant/paralegal; massage therapy; medical administrative assistant and medical secretary; medical insurance coding; medical insurance/medical billing; medical office assistant; medical office computer specialist; medical office management; medical reception; medical transcription; nursing assistant/aide and patient care assistant; nursing related; office management; office occupations and clerical services; operations management; phlebotomy; receptionist; Reiki; robotics technology; safety/security technology; securities services administration; selling skills and sales; system administration; system, networking, and LAN/WAN management; web/multimedia management and webmaster; web page, digital/multimedia and information resources design

Enrollment: 550 students
Institution Contact: Mr. Joseph F. Reichard, Executive Director
Phone: 610-372-1722 ext. 119
Fax: 610-376-4684
E-mail: jreichardk@berk.edu
Admission Contact: Ms. Jean Vokes
Phone: 610-372-1722
Fax: 610-376-4684
E-mail: jvokes@berkstech.com

BRADFORD SCHOOL

Gulf Tower, 707 Grant Street
Pittsburgh, PA 15219
Web: http://www.bradfordpittsburgh.edu
Accreditation: Accrediting Council for Independent Colleges and Schools
Programs Offered:
accounting; administrative assistant and secretarial science; business administration and management; business automation/technology/data entry; commercial and advertising art; computer graphics; computer/information technology administration and management; computer programming; computer programming (specific applications); computer software and media applications; computer systems networking and telecommunications; computer/technical support; computer

technology/computer systems technology; data entry/microcomputer applications; data processing and data processing technology; fashion merchandising; health information/medical records administration; health unit management/ward supervision; hospitality administration; hotel/motel administration; legal administrative assistant/secretary; legal assistant/paralegal; medical administrative assistant and medical secretary; medical/clinical assistant; medical office management; medical transcription; office occupations and clerical services; receptionist; restaurant, culinary, and catering management; retailing; selling skills and sales; system, networking, and LAN/WAN management; tourism and travel services management; web/multimedia management and webmaster; web page, digital/multimedia and information resources design

Institution Contact: Mr. Vincent Graziano, President
Phone: 412-391-6710
Fax: 412-471-6714
E-mail: info@bradfordpittsburgh.edu
Admission Contact: Director of Admissions
Phone: 412-391-6710
Fax: 412-471-6714
E-mail: info@bradfordpittsburgh.edu

BRADLEY ACADEMY FOR THE VISUAL ARTS

1409 Williams Road
York, PA 17402-9012
Web: http://www.bradleyacademy.edu
Accreditation: Accrediting Commission of Career Schools and Colleges of Technology
Programs Offered:
animation, interactive technology, video graphics and special effects; apparel and textile marketing management; applied art; art; commercial and advertising art; computer graphics; computer software and media applications; design and visual communications; desktop publishing and digital imaging design; digital communication and media/multimedia; drawing; fashion/apparel design; fashion merchandising; interior design; internet information systems; merchandising; retailing; visual and performing arts; web/multimedia management and webmaster; web page, digital/multimedia and information resources design

Enrollment: 620 students
Institution Contact: Mr. Darin Weeks, Director of Administrative and Financial Services
Phone: 800-864-7725 ext. 2563

Fax: 717-840-1951
E-mail: dweeks@aii.edu
Admission Contact: Mr. James Hannigan, Director of Admissions
Phone: 800-864-7725
Fax: 717-840-1951
E-mail: jhannigan@aii.edu

BUSINESS INSTITUTE OF PENNSYLVANIA

628 Arch Street, Suite B-105
Meadville, PA 16335
Web: http://www.biop.edu
Accreditation: Accrediting Council for Independent Colleges and Schools
Programs Offered:
accounting; administrative assistant and secretarial science; anatomy; business administration, management and operations related; business automation/technology/data entry; business/corporate communications; clinical/medical laboratory assistant; computer/information technology administration and management; computer/information technology services administration related; data entry/microcomputer applications related; data processing and data processing technology; executive assistant/executive secretary; health and medical administrative services related; legal administrative assistant/secretary; medical administrative assistant and medical secretary; medical/health management and clinical assistant; medical insurance coding; medical insurance/medical billing; medical office assistant; medical office computer specialist; medical reception; medical transcription; office occupations and clerical services; receptionist; web page, digital/multimedia and information resources design; word processing
Enrollment: 85 students
Institution Contact: Mrs. Patricia McMahon, President
Phone: 814-724-0700
Fax: 814-724-2777
E-mail: info@biop.edu
Admission Contact: Ms. Anne M. Burger, Acting Director
Phone: 814-724-0700
Fax: 814-724-2777
E-mail: anne3157@hotmail.com

BUSINESS INSTITUTE OF PENNSYLVANIA

335 Boyd Drive
Sharon, PA 16146
Web: http://www.biop.edu
Accreditation: Accrediting Council for Independent Colleges and Schools
Programs Offered:
accounting; administrative assistant and secretarial science; anatomy; business administration and management; business automation/technology/data entry; business/corporate communications; child care provision; clinical/medical laboratory assistant; computer/information technology administration and management; computer/information technology services administration related; data entry/microcomputer applications related; data processing and data processing technology; executive assistant/executive secretary; health/health care administration; health information/medical records technology; legal administrative assistant/secretary; marketing/marketing management; medical administrative assistant and medical secretary; medical/clinical assistant; medical/health management and clinical assistant; medical insurance coding; medical insurance/medical billing; medical reception; medical transcription; office occupations and clerical services; receptionist; web page, digital/multimedia and information resources design; word processing
Enrollment: 100 students
Institution Contact: Mrs. Kathleen McMahon Motolenich, Director
Phone: 724-983-0700
Fax: 724-983-8355
E-mail: kaisim@biop.edu
Admission Contact: Ms. Shannon McNamara, Admission Officer
Phone: 724-983-0711
Fax: 724-983-8355
E-mail: mac2002ten@yahoo.com

CAMTECH

5451 Merwin Ln.
Erie, PA 16510
Institution Contact: Campus Director
Phone: 814-459-5371

CHI Institute

Lawrence Park Shopping Center, 1991 Sproul Road, Suite 42
Broomall, PA 19008
Web: http://www.chi-institute.net/
Accreditation: Accrediting Commission of Career Schools and Colleges of Technology
Programs Offered:
commercial and advertising art; computer installation and repair technology; computer programming; computer programming related; computer programming (vendor/product certification); computer systems networking and telecommunications; computer/technical support; computer technology/computer systems technology; electrician; gene therapy; health information/medical records administration; heating, air conditioning and refrigeration technology; heating, air conditioning, ventilation and refrigeration maintenance technology; information technology; medical administrative assistant and medical secretary; medical/clinical assistant; medical/health management and clinical assistant; surgical technology; system administration; system, networking, and LAN/WAN management
Enrollment: 800 students
Institution Contact: Mr. Robert G. Milot, Executive Director
Phone: 610-353-7630
Fax: 610-359-1370
E-mail: bmilot@chi-institute.net
Admission Contact: Mr. Paul Richardson, Director of Admissions
Phone: 610-353-7630
Fax: 610-359-1370
E-mail: prichardson@chi-institute.net

CHI Institute

520 Street Road
Southampton, PA 18966
Web: http://www.chitraining.com
Accreditation: Accrediting Commission of Career Schools and Colleges of Technology
Programs Offered:
administrative assistant and secretarial science; business automation/technology/data entry; commercial and advertising art; communications systems installation and repair technology; computer engineering technology; computer graphics; computer/information technology services administration related; computer

software and media applications; computer systems networking and telecommunications; computer/technical support; computer technology/computer systems technology; criminal justice/law enforcement administration; data entry/microcomputer applications; electrical/electronics equipment installation and repair; electrician; medical administrative assistant and medical secretary; medical/clinical assistant; medical insurance coding; medical insurance/medical billing; medical office computer specialist; medical office management; medical pharmacology and pharmaceutical sciences; medical reception; office occupations and clerical services; pharmacy; pharmacy technician; phlebotomy; respiratory care therapy; respiratory therapy technician; system administration; system, networking, and LAN/WAN management; telecommunications; telecommunications technology; web/multimedia management and webmaster; web page, digital/multimedia and information resources design; word processing
Enrollment: 677 students
Institution Contact: Ms. Dale Anspach, Executive Director
Phone: 215-357-5100
Fax: 215-357-4212
E-mail: d_anspach@chicareers.com
Admission Contact: Mr. Eric Heller, Director of Admissions
Phone: 215-357-5100
Fax: 215-357-4212
E-mail: eheller@chicareers.com

THE CHUBB INSTITUTE

Marple Crossroads , 400 South State Road
Springfield, PA 19064-3957
Web: http://www.chubbinstitute.edu
Accreditation: Accrediting Council for Independent Colleges and Schools
Programs Offered:
administrative assistant and secretarial science; computer and information sciences related; computer and information systems security; computer graphics; computer/information technology administration and management; computer/information technology services administration related; computer programming; computer programming related; computer programming (specific applications); computer programming (vendor/product certification); computer software and media applications; computer software and media ap-

plications related; computer systems analysis; computer systems networking and telecommunications; computer/technical support; computer technology/computer systems technology; data entry/microcomputer applications; data entry/microcomputer applications related; data processing and data processing technology; information science/studies; information technology; medical administrative assistant and medical secretary; medical insurance coding; medical insurance/medical billing; medical office computer specialist; medical reception; system administration; system, networking, and LAN/WAN management; web page, digital/multimedia and information resources design

Institution Contact: Ms. Judith M. Cole, Campus President

Phone: 610-338-2321

Fax: 610-338-2393

E-mail: jcole@chubbinstitute.edu

Admission Contact: Ms. Kimberly Ewing, Director of Admissions

Phone: 610-338-2305

Fax: 610-338-2399

E-mail: kewing@chubbinstitute.edu

THE CITTONE INSTITUTE

2180 Hornig Road, Building A

Philadelphia, PA 19116

Web: http://www.cittone.com

Accreditation: Accrediting Council for Independent Colleges and Schools

Programs Offered:

allied health and medical assisting services related; computer engineering related; computer engineering technology; computer graphics; computer hardware engineering; computer/information technology administration and management; computer/information technology services administration related; computer software and media applications related; health and medical administrative services related; health information/medical records administration; health information/medical records technology; massage therapy

Enrollment: 443 students

Institution Contact: Mr. James K. Tolbert, Executive Director

Phone: 215-969-0869 ext. 44101

Fax: 215-969-4023

E-mail: jtolbert@cittone.com

Admission Contact: Mr. Thomas A. Driscoll, III,

Director of Admissions

Phone: 215-969-0869 ext. 44103

Fax: 215-969-3457

E-mail: tdriscoll@cittone.com

THE CITTONE INSTITUTE

3600 Market Street

Philadelphia, PA 19104

Web: http://www.cittone.com

Accreditation: Accrediting Council for Independent Colleges and Schools

Programs Offered:

computer systems networking and telecommunications; computer/technical support; medical administrative assistant and medical secretary; medical/clinical assistant; system administration

Institution Contact: Executive Director

Phone: 215-382-1553 ext. 201

Fax: 215-382-3875

E-mail: execdirphilly@lincolntech.com

THE CITTONE INSTITUTE

1 Plymouth Meeting, Suite 300

Plymouth Meeting, PA 19462

Web: http://www.cittone.com

Accreditation: Accrediting Council for Independent Colleges and Schools

Programs Offered:

computer systems networking and telecommunications; massage therapy; medical administrative assistant and medical secretary; medical/clinical assistant; medical/health management and clinical assistant; medical insurance/medical billing; pharmacy technician

Enrollment: 387 students

Institution Contact: Mr. James Hinkel, Executive Director

Phone: 610-941-0319 ext. 156

Fax: 610-941-3367

E-mail: jhinkel@cittone.com

Admission Contact: Mr. Shawn Brady, Director of Admissions

Phone: 610-941-0319 ext. 129

Fax: 610-941-4158

E-mail: sbrady@cittone.com

COMPUTER LEARNING NETWORK

2900 Fairway Drive
Altoona, PA 16602-4457
Web: http://www.cln.edu
Accreditation: Accrediting Commission of Career Schools and Colleges of Technology
Programs Offered:
business automation/technology/data entry; computer installation and repair technology; computer software and media applications; computer systems networking and telecommunications; criminal justice/law enforcement administration; legal administrative assistant/secretary; legal assistant/paralegal; massage therapy; medical office computer specialist; medical office management; medical transcription; office occupations and clerical services; pharmacy technician; receptionist; system, networking, and LAN/WAN management; word processing
Enrollment: 320 students
Institution Contact: Ms. Vickie J. Clements, Director
Phone: 814-944-5643
Fax: 814-944-5309
E-mail: vclements@cln.edu
Admission Contact: Ms. Miriam Kratzer, Admissions Director
Phone: 814-944-5643
Fax: 814-944-5309
E-mail: admissions@cln.edu

COMPUTER LEARNING NETWORK

401 East Winding Hill Road, Suite 101
Mechanicsburg, PA 17055-4989
Web: http://www.clntraining.net
Accreditation: Accrediting Commission of Career Schools and Colleges of Technology
Programs Offered:
administrative assistant and secretarial science; computer and information systems security; computer/information technology administration and management; computer/information technology services administration related; computer installation and repair technology; computer programming; computer programming related; computer programming (specific applications); computer programming (vendor/product certification); computer software and media applications; computer software and media applications related; computer systems networking and telecommunications; computer/technical support; computer technology/computer

systems technology; criminal justice/law enforcement administration; criminal justice/police science; data entry/microcomputer applications; data entry/microcomputer applications related; health information/medical records technology; information science/studies; information technology; massage therapy; medical administrative assistant and medical secretary; medical/clinical assistant; medical transcription; office occupations and clerical services; pharmacy technician; system administration; system, networking, and LAN/WAN management; web/multimedia management and webmaster; web page, digital/multimedia and information resources design; word processing
Enrollment: 417 students
Institution Contact: Mr. Robert J. Grohman, Director
Phone: 717-761-1481
Fax: 717-761-0558
E-mail: rgrohman@clntraining.net
Admission Contact: Mr. Michael R. Wilson, Senior Educational Representative
Phone: 717-761-1481
Fax: 717-761-0558
E-mail: mwilson@clntraining.net

DEAN INSTITUTE OF TECHNOLOGY

1501 West Liberty Avenue
Pittsburgh, PA 15226
Web: http://deantech.edu
Accreditation: Accrediting Commission of Career Schools and Colleges of Technology
Programs Offered:
building/property maintenance and management; electrician; heating, air conditioning and refrigeration technology; welding technology
Enrollment: 225 students
Institution Contact: Mr. James Dean, President
Phone: 412-531-4433
Fax: 412-531-4435
E-mail: deantech@earthlink.net
Admission Contact: Mr. Richard D Ali, Admissions Director
Phone: 412-531-4433
Fax: 412-531-4435
E-mail: info@deantech.edu

DOUGLAS EDUCATION CENTER

130 7th Street
Monessen, PA 15062-1097
Web: http://www.douglas-school.com/
Accreditation: Accrediting Council for Independent Colleges and Schools
Programs Offered:
accounting; accounting related; accounting technology and bookkeeping; administrative assistant and secretarial science; aesthetician/esthetician and skin care; allied health and medical assisting services related; anatomy; animation, interactive technology, video graphics and special effects; banking and financial support services; business administration and management; business automation/technology/data entry; clinical laboratory science/medical technology; clinical/medical laboratory assistant; clinical/medical laboratory science and allied professions related; clinical/medical laboratory technology; commercial and advertising art; computer graphics; cosmetology; cosmetology, barber/styling, and nail instruction; customer service management; data entry/microcomputer applications; data processing and data processing technology; desktop publishing and digital imaging design; digital communication and media/multimedia; executive assistant/executive secretary; facial treatment/facialist; general studies; graphic communications; graphic communications related; health aide; health information/medical records administration; health information/medical records technology; health professions related; health unit coordinator/ward clerk; health unit management/ward supervision; home health aide/home attendant; legal administrative assistant/secretary; make-up artist; medical administrative assistant and medical secretary; medical/clinical assistant; medical/health management and clinical assistant; medical insurance coding; medical insurance/medical billing; medical office assistant; medical office computer specialist; medical office management; medical reception; medical transcription; nail technician and manicurist; nursing assistant/aide and patient care assistant; office management; receptionist; robotics technology; sculpture; web/multimedia management and webmaster; web page, digital/multimedia and information resources design; word processing
Enrollment: 275 students
Institution Contact: Mr. Jeffrey Imbrescia, CPA, President
Phone: 724-684-3684 ext. 113
Fax: 724-684-7463
E-mail: jimbrescia@douglas-school.com
Admission Contact: Ms. Sherry Lee Walters, Director of Enrollment Services
Phone: 724-684-3684 ext. 120
Fax: 724-684-7463
E-mail: swalters@douglas-school.com

DUFF'S BUSINESS INSTITUTE

Kossman Building, Suite 1200
Pittsburgh, PA 15222
Web: http://www.duffs-institute.com
Accreditation: Accrediting Council for Independent Colleges and Schools
Programs Offered:
accounting; administrative assistant and secretarial science; business administration and management; clinical laboratory science/medical technology; computer/information technology administration and management; criminal justice/law enforcement administration; legal administrative assistant/secretary; legal assistant/paralegal; medical administrative assistant and medical secretary; medical/clinical assistant; medical insurance coding; medical staff services technology; pharmacy technician
Institution Contact: James P. Callahan, School President
Phone: 412-261-4520 ext. 224
Fax: 412-261-4546
E-mail: jcallaha@cci.edu
Admission Contact: Lynn Fischer, Director of Admissions
Phone: 412-261-4520 ext. 212
Fax: 412-261-4546
E-mail: lfischer@cci.edu

EMPIRE BEAUTY SCHOOL

Clearview Shopping Center, Carlisle Street
Hanover, PA 17331
Web: http://www.empirebeauty.com/
Programs Offered:
cosmetology; cosmetology, barber/styling, and nail instruction
Institution Contact: Admissions
Phone: 717-429-1800

EMPIRE BEAUTY SCHOOL

3941 Jonestown Road
Harrisburg, PA 17109

Programs Offered:
cosmetology; cosmetology, barber/styling, and nail instruction
Institution Contact: Mr. Larry E. Smith, Jr., School Director
Phone: 717-652-8500

EMPIRE BEAUTY SCHOOL
1801 Columbia Avenue, Wheatland Shopping Center
Lancaster, PA 17603
Web: http://www.empirebeauty.com/
Programs Offered:
cosmetology; cosmetology, barber/styling, and nail instruction
Institution Contact: Admissions
Phone: 717-394-8561

EMPIRE BEAUTY SCHOOL
1776 Quentin Road, Cedar Crest Square
Lebanon, PA 17042
Web: http://www.empirebeauty.com/
Programs Offered:
cosmetology; cosmetology, barber/styling, and nail instruction
Institution Contact: Admissions
Phone: 717-429-1800

EMPIRE BEAUTY SCHOOL
320 Mall Blvd.
The Plaza
Monroeville, PA 15146-2229
Institution Contact: Mr. Darin Martin
Phone: 412-373-7727
Fax: 412-373-9547

EMPIRE BEAUTY SCHOOL
3370 Birney Ave.
Moosic, PA 18507
Institution Contact: Ms. Joan Seaman
Phone: 570-343-4730
Fax: 570-343-4737

EMPIRE BEAUTY SCHOOL
1522 Chestnut St.
Philadelphia, PA 19102-2701
Institution Contact: Ms. Belinda Christian
Phone: 215-568-3980
Fax: 215-568-3745

EMPIRE BEAUTY SCHOOL
Knights Rd. Shopping Ctr.
4026 Woodhaven Rd.
Philadelphia, PA 19154
Institution Contact: Ms. Diane Hengstler
Phone: 215-637-3700
Fax: 215-637-6122

Empire Beauty School
4768 McKnight Rd.
Pittsburgh, PA 15237
Institution Contact: Ms. Ginger Serafini
Phone: 412-367-1765
Fax: 412-367-5077

EMPIRE BEAUTY SCHOOL
141 High Street
Pottstown, PA 19464
Web: http://www.empirebeauty.com/
Programs Offered:
cosmetology; cosmetology, barber/styling, and nail instruction
Institution Contact: Admissions
Phone: 717-429-1800

EMPIRE BEAUTY SCHOOL
324 North Centre Street
Pottsville, PA 17901
Web: http://www.empirebeauty.com/
Programs Offered:
cosmetology; cosmetology, barber/styling, and nail instruction
Institution Contact: Admissions
Phone: 800-223-3271

EMPIRE BEAUTY SCHOOL
2302 North 5th Street
Reading, PA 19605

Web: http://www.empirebeauty.com/
Programs Offered:
cosmetology; cosmetology, barber/styling, and nail instruction
Institution Contact: Admissions
Phone: 610-372-2777

EMPIRE BEAUTY SCHOOL
Orchard Hills Plaza, U.S. Route 11 & 15
Shamokin Dam, PA 17876
Web: http://www.empirebeauty.com/
Programs Offered:
cosmetology; cosmetology, barber/styling, and nail instruction
Institution Contact: Admissions
Phone: 800-223-3271

EMPIRE BEAUTY SCHOOL
206 West Hamilton Avenue
State College, PA 16801
Web: http://www.empirebeauty.com/
Programs Offered:
cosmetology; cosmetology, barber/styling, and nail instruction
Institution Contact: Admissions
Phone: 814-238-1967

EMPIRE BEAUTY SCHOOL
435 York Road
Warminster, PA 18974
Web: http://www.empirebeauty.com/
Programs Offered:
cosmetology; cosmetology, barber/styling, and nail instruction
Institution Contact: Admissions
Phone: 215-443-8446

EMPIRE BEAUTY SCHOOL
313 West Market St.
West Chester, PA 19382
Institution Contact: Ms. Anita Day
Phone: 610-344-7665
Fax: 610-344-9214

EMPIRE BEAUTY SCHOOL
2393 Mountainview Dr.
Century Square Mall
West Mifflin, PA 15122
Institution Contact: Ms. Lisa Long
Phone: 412-653-2870
Fax: 412-653-2874

EMPIRE BEAUTY SCHOOL
1634 MacArthur Road
Whitehall, PA 18052
Web: http://www.empirebeauty.com/
Programs Offered:
cosmetology; cosmetology, barber/styling, and nail instruction
Institution Contact: Admissions
Phone: 610-776-8908

EMPIRE BEAUTY SCHOOL
1808 East Third Street
Williamsport, PA 17701
Web: http://www.empirebeauty.com/
Programs Offered:
cosmetology; cosmetology, barber/styling, and nail instruction
Institution Contact: Admissions
Phone: 570-322-8243

EMPIRE BEAUTY SCHOOL
2592 Eastern Blvd.
York, PA 17402
Programs Offered:
cosmetology; cosmetology, barber/styling, and nail instruction
Enrollment: 92 students
Institution Contact: Ms. Julie A. Clapsaddle, School Director
Phone: 717-600-8111
Fax: 717-600-8404
E-mail: jclapsaddle@empire.edu

ERIE BUSINESS CENTER, MAIN
246 West 9th Street
Erie, PA 16501
Web: http://www.eriebc.edu

Accreditation: Accrediting Council for Independent Colleges and Schools

Programs Offered:

accounting; administrative assistant and secretarial science; computer hardware engineering; computer programming; computer software and media applications related; computer systems networking and telecommunications; computer technology/computer systems technology; executive assistant/executive secretary; health information/medical records technology; insurance; legal administrative assistant/secretary; legal assistant/paralegal; marketing/marketing management; medical administrative assistant and medical secretary; medical/clinical assistant; medical transcription; nursing assistant/aide and patient care assistant; tourism and travel services management; web page, digital/multimedia and information resources design

Enrollment: 400 students

Institution Contact: Mrs. Donna B. Perino, Director

Phone: 814-456-7504 ext. 17

Fax: 814-456-6015

E-mail: perinod@eriebc.edu

ERIE BUSINESS CENTER SOUTH

170 Cascade Galleria
New Castle, PA 16101-3950
Web: http://www.eriebc.edu

Accreditation: Accrediting Council for Independent Colleges and Schools

Programs Offered:

accounting; administrative assistant and secretarial science; business administration and management; computer programming; data entry/microcomputer applications; health information/medical records technology; legal administrative assistant/secretary; medical administrative assistant and medical secretary; medical transcription; tourism and travel services management

Enrollment: 103 students

Institution Contact: Mrs. Irene Marburger, Director

Phone: 800-722-6227

Fax: 724-658-3083

E-mail: marburgeri@eriebcs.com

Admission Contact: Mrs. Rose Hall, Admission Representative

Phone: 800-722-6227

Fax: 724-658-3083

E-mail: hallr@eriebcs.com

GREAT LAKES INSTITUTE OF TECHNOLOGY

5100 Peach Street
Erie, PA 16509
Web: http://www.glit.edu

Accreditation: Accrediting Commission of Career Schools and Colleges of Technology; National Accrediting Commission of Cosmetology Arts and Sciences

Programs Offered:

cosmetology; cosmetology, barber/styling, and nail instruction; dental assisting; diagnostic medical sonography and ultrasound technology; massage therapy; medical administrative assistant and medical secretary; medical/clinical assistant; nail technician and manicurist; pharmacy technician; surgical technology; veterinary/animal health technology

Institution Contact: Mrs. Francine M. Steele, Director of Education

Phone: 814-864-6666 ext. 225

Fax: 814-868-1717

E-mail: fran@glit.edu

Admission Contact: Barbara Bolt, Director of Admissions

Phone: 814-864-6666 ext. 242

Fax: 814-868-1717

E-mail: barbb@glit.edu

HARRISBURG INSTITUTE OF TRADE/TECHNOLOGY

1519 W. Harrisburg Pike
Middletown, PA 17057

Institution Contact: Mr. Roy Hawkins

Phone: 717-944-2731

Fax: 717-944-2542

HARRISON CAREER INSTITUTE

2101 Union Boulevard
Allentown, PA 18109-1633
Web: http://www.hci.edu

Accreditation: Accrediting Commission of Career Schools and Colleges of Technology

Programs Offered:

cardiovascular technology; medical administrative assistant and medical secretary; medical/clinical assistant; surgical technology

Enrollment: 175 students

Institution Contact: Ms. Nancy Seier, Director

Phone: 610-434-9963

Fax: 610-434-8292

E-mail: nseier@hci-inst.net

HARRISON CAREER INSTITUTE

1619 Walnut Street, 3rd Floor
Philadelphia, PA 19103
Web: http://www.hci.edu
Accreditation: Accrediting Commission of Career Schools and Colleges of Technology
Programs Offered:
cardiovascular technology; dental assisting; dialysis technology; medical/clinical assistant; medical office computer specialist; medical transcription; nursing (licensed practical/vocational nurse training); pharmacy technician; phlebotomy; surgical technology
Enrollment: 279 students
Institution Contact: Mr. Michael E. Seeherman, Director
Phone: 215-640-0177
Fax: 215-640-0466
E-mail: mseeherman@hci-inst.net
Admission Contact: Ms. Tammy Potis, Career Representative
Phone: 215-640-0177
Fax: 215-640-0466
E-mail: tpotis@hci-inst.net

HARRISON CAREER INSTITUTE

645 Penn Street, 3rd Floor
Reading, PA 19601
Web: http://www.harrisoncareerinst.com
Accreditation: Accrediting Commission of Career Schools and Colleges of Technology
Programs Offered:
cardiovascular technology; electrocardiograph technology; medical administrative assistant and medical secretary; medical/clinical assistant; medical office computer specialist
Enrollment: 98 students
Institution Contact: Ms. Monica S. Sokoloff, Director
Phone: 610-374-2469
Fax: 610-374-4192
E-mail: msokoloff@hci-inst.net

HUSSIAN SCHOOL OF ART

1118 Market Street
Philadelphia, PA 19107-3679
Web: http://www.hussianart.edu/
Accreditation: Accrediting Commission of Career Schools and Colleges of Technology

Programs Offered:
commercial and advertising art
Enrollment: 150 students
Institution Contact: Lynne D. Wartman, Director of Admissions
Phone: 215-981-0900
Fax: 215-864-9115
E-mail: info@hussianart.edu
Admission Contact: Ms. Lynne D. Wartman, Director of Admissions
Phone: 215-981-0900
Fax: 215-864-9115
E-mail: info@hussianart.edu

ICM SCHOOL OF BUSINESS & MEDICAL CAREERS

10 Wood Street
Pittsburgh, PA 15222
Web: http://www.ICMschool.com
Accreditation: Accrediting Council for Independent Colleges and Schools
Programs Offered:
accounting; business administration and management; computer and information systems security; computer engineering related; computer engineering technology; computer hardware engineering; computer/information technology administration and management; computer/information technology services administration related; computer installation and repair technology; computer programming; computer programming related; computer programming (specific applications); computer programming (vendor/product certification); computer systems networking and telecommunications; computer/technical support; computer technology/computer systems technology; corrections; criminal justice/law enforcement administration; data entry/microcomputer applications related; data modeling/warehousing and database administration; e-commerce; engineering technology; executive assistant/executive secretary; fashion merchandising; health information/medical records technology; legal administrative assistant/secretary; medical administrative assistant and medical secretary; medical/clinical assistant; medical/health management and clinical assistant; medical office management; medical transcription; occupational therapist assistant; office management; pre-law studies; system, networking, and LAN/WAN management; tourism and travel services management; web page, digital/multimedia and information resources design

Enrollment: 1,044 students
Institution Contact: Mr. Bobby Reese, Jr., Executive Director
Phone: 412-261-2647 ext. 302
Fax: 412-261-6491
E-mail: breese@icmschool.com
Admission Contact: Mrs. Marcia Rosenberg, Director of Admissions
Phone: 412-261-2647 ext. 229
Fax: 412-261-0998
E-mail: mrosenberg@icmschool.com

 INTERNATIONAL ACADEMY OF DESIGN & TECHNOLOGY
555 Grant Street, 5th Floor
Pittsburgh, PA 15219
Web: http://www.iadtpitt.com
Accreditation: Accrediting Council for Independent Colleges and Schools
Programs Offered:
business administration and management; commercial and advertising art; computer/information technology administration and management; computer/technical support; criminal justice/law enforcement administration; e-commerce; web page, digital/multimedia and information resources design
Enrollment: 670 students
Institution Contact: Ms. Vicci Essig, Admissions Coordinator
Phone: 800-447-8324 ext. 296
Fax: 412-391-4224
E-mail: vessig@iadt-pitt.com

 ITT TECHNICAL INSTITUTE - BENSALEM
3330 Tillman
Bensalem, PA 19020
Web: http://www.itt-tech.edu

ITT TECHNICAL INSTITUTE
760 Moore Rd.
King of Prussia, PA 19406
Web: http://www.itt-tech.edu

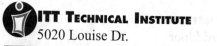  **ITT TECHNICAL INSTITUTE**
5020 Louise Dr.
Mechanicsburg, PA 17055
Web: http://www.itt-tech.edu

ITT TECHNICAL INSTITUTE
105 Mall Blvd., Suite 200E
Monroeville, PA 15146
Web: http://www.itt-tech.edu

ITT TECHNICAL INSTITUTE
10 Parkway Ctr.
Pittsburg, PA 17055
Web: http://www.itt-tech.edu

KATHARINE GIBBS SCHOOL
2501 Monroe Boulevard
Norristown, PA 19403
Web: http://www.pagibbs.com
Accreditation: Accrediting Council for Independent Colleges and Schools
Programs Offered:
business administration and management; commercial and advertising art; computer/information technology administration and management; computer systems networking and telecommunications; criminal justice/ law enforcement administration; fashion merchandising; medical/clinical assistant; system, networking, and LAN/WAN management; web page, digital/multimedia and information resources design
Institution Contact: Dr. David Goodwin, President
Phone: 610-676-0500
Fax: 610-676-0530
E-mail: dgoodwin@pagibbs.com
Admission Contact: Kevin Puls, Director of Admissions
Phone: 866-724-4227
Fax: 610-676-0530
E-mail: kpuls@pagibbs.com

 LANSDALE SCHOOL OF BUSINESS
201 Church Road
North Wales, PA 19454
Web: http://www.LSB.edu
Accreditation: Accrediting Council for Independent

 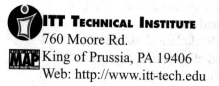 indicates a participating institution in the *Imagine America* Scholarship Program. **MAP** indicates a participating institution in the Military Award Program.

Colleges and Schools

Programs Offered:

accounting; accounting and business/management; administrative assistant and secretarial science; advertising; allied health and medical assisting services related; anatomy; business administration and management; business automation/technology/data entry; business/corporate communications; business, management, and marketing related; business operations support and secretarial services related; clinical/medical laboratory assistant; commercial and advertising art; computer graphics; computer/information technology services administration related; computer software and media applications; computer software and media applications related; corrections; criminal justice/law enforcement administration; desktop publishing and digital imaging design; electrocardiograph technology; executive assistant/executive secretary; health information/medical records technology; insurance; intermedia/multimedia; legal administrative assistant/secretary; legal assistant/paralegal; marketing/marketing management; medical administrative assistant and medical secretary; medical/clinical assistant; medical office management; medical transcription; office occupations and clerical services; operations management; pharmacy technician; phlebotomy; telecommunications; web/multimedia management and webmaster; web page, digital/multimedia and information resources design; word processing

Enrollment: 475 students

Institution Contact: Mr. Marlon D. Keller, President

Phone: 215-699-5700

Fax: 215-699-8770

E-mail: mkeller@lsb.edu

Admission Contact: Mrs. Marianne H. Johnson, Director of Admissions

Phone: 215-699-5700 ext. 112

Fax: 215-699-8770

E-mail: mjohnson@lsb.edu

LAUREL BUSINESS INSTITUTE

11-15 Penn Street, PO Box 877
Uniontown, PA 15401
Web: http://www.laurelbusiness.edu
Accreditation: Accrediting Council for Independent Colleges and Schools
Programs Offered:
accounting; administrative assistant and secretarial

science; aesthetician/esthetician and skin care; allied health and medical assisting services related; child care provision; computer programming; computer software technology; computer technology/computer systems technology; cosmetology; cosmetology, barber/styling, and nail instruction; executive assistant/executive secretary; hospitality administration; information technology; legal administrative assistant/secretary; massage therapy; medical administrative assistant and medical secretary; medical/clinical assistant; medical insurance/medical billing; medical transcription; office management; office occupations and clerical services; small business administration; teacher assistant/aide; tourism and travel services management; web/multimedia management and webmaster

Enrollment: 324 students

Institution Contact: Mrs. Nancy M. Decker, President

Phone: 724-439-4900 ext. 134

Fax: 724-439-3607

E-mail: ndecker@laurelbusiness.edu

Admission Contact: Mrs. Lisa Dolan, Enrollment Supervisor

Phone: 724-439-4900 ext. 158

Fax: 724-439-3607

E-mail: ltressler@laurelbusiness.edu

LEBANON COUNTY CAREER SCHOOL

18 East Weidman Street
Lebanon, PA 17046
Web: http://www.sageschools.com/
Accreditation: Accrediting Commission of Career Schools and Colleges of Technology
Programs Offered:
driver and safety teacher education; transportation technology; truck and bus driver/commercial vehicle operation

Enrollment: 12 students

Institution Contact: Ms. Holly L. Reichert, Director

Phone: 800-694-8804

Fax: 717-274-6036

E-mail: hreichert@sageschools.com

Admission Contact: Mrs. Beth A. Miko, Staff Assistant

Phone: 800-694-8804

Fax: 717-274-6036

E-mail: bmiko@sageschools.com

LEHIGH VALLEY COLLEGE

2809 East Saucon Valley Road
Center Valley, PA 18034
Web: http://www.chooseabs.com/
Accreditation: Accrediting Council for Independent Colleges and Schools
Programs Offered:
accounting; business administration and management; business, management, and marketing related; child care and support services management; commercial and advertising art; commercial photography; computer programming; computer systems networking and telecommunications; criminal justice/law enforcement administration; fashion merchandising; hospitality administration; legal assistant/paralegal; massage therapy; medical administrative assistant and medical secretary; system, networking, and LAN/WAN management; tourism and travel services management; web/multimedia management and webmaster; web page, digital/multimedia and information resources design
Enrollment: 1,450 students
Institution Contact: Mrs. Debra Weninger, Vice President of Academics & Community Relations
Phone: 610-791-5100 ext. 5351
Fax: 610-625-5530
E-mail: dweninger@lehighvalley.edu
Admission Contact: Mrs. Marlyn Kissner, Executive Director of Admissions
Phone: 610-625-5311
Fax: 610-791-7810
E-mail: mkissner@lehighvalley.edu

LINCOLN TECHNICAL INSTITUTE

5151 Tilghman Street
Allentown, PA 18104-3298
Web: http://www.lincolntech.com
Accreditation: Accrediting Commission of Career Schools and Colleges of Technology
Programs Offered:
allied health and medical assisting services related; architectural drafting and CAD/CADD; CAD/CADD drafting/design technology; computer systems networking and telecommunications; drafting and design technology; engineering technology; health information/medical records technology; mechanical drafting and CAD/CADD; medical administrative assistant and medical secretary; medical/clinical assistant; medical insurance coding; medical insurance/medical billing;

pharmacy; pharmacy administration/pharmaceutics; pharmacy technician; phlebotomy; physician assistant
Enrollment: 512 students
Institution Contact: Ms. Lisa Kuntz, Executive Director
Phone: 610-398-5300
Fax: 610-395-2706
E-mail: lkuntz@lincolntech.com
Admission Contact: Mr. Mark Garner, Director of Admissions
Phone: 610-398-5301
Fax: 610-398-5300
E-mail: mgarner@lincolntech.com

LINCOLN TECHNICAL INSTITUTE

9191 Torresdale Avenue
Philadelphia, PA 19136
Web: http://www.lincolntech.com
Accreditation: Accrediting Commission of Career Schools and Colleges of Technology
Programs Offered:
automobile/automotive mechanics technology; automotive engineering technology
Institution Contact: Executive Director
Phone: 215-335-0800
Fax: 215-335-1443
E-mail: execdirphilly@lincolntech.com
Admission Contact: Director of Admissions
Phone: 215-335-0800
Fax: 215-335-1443
E-mail: doaphilly@lincolnedu.com

McCANN SCHOOL OF BUSINESS

14 Maplewood Drive, Humboldt Industrial Park
Hazleton, PA 18202
Accreditation: Accrediting Council for Independent Colleges and Schools
Programs Offered:
accounting; accounting technology and bookkeeping; administrative assistant and secretarial science; anatomy; banking and financial support services; business administration and management; business automation/technology/data entry; business/corporate communications; clinical laboratory science/medical technology; computer and information sciences related; computer hardware engineering; computer/information technology administration and management;

computer/information technology services administration related; computer installation and repair technology; computer programming; computer programming (specific applications); computer software and media applications; computer software technology; computer systems analysis; computer systems networking and telecommunications; computer/technical support; computer technology/computer systems technology; criminal justice/law enforcement administration; criminal justice/police science; data entry/microcomputer applications; data entry/microcomputer applications related; data processing and data processing technology; education (specific levels and methods) related; executive assistant/executive secretary; health information/medical records administration; health information/medical records technology; human resources management; information technology; legal administrative assistant/secretary; legal assistant/paralegal; marketing/marketing management; massage therapy; medical administrative assistant and medical secretary; medical/clinical assistant; medical/health management and clinical assistant; medical insurance coding; medical insurance/medical billing; medical office computer specialist; medical office management; medical reception; medical transcription; office management; office occupations and clerical services; receptionist; surgical technology; system, networking, and LAN/WAN management; web page, digital/multimedia and information resources design; word processing

Enrollment: 250 students

Institution Contact: Mrs. Barbara J. Reese, Director

Phone: 570-454-6172

E-mail: bjr@mccannschool.com

Admission Contact: Mr. Michael S. Mazalusky, Jr., Admissions Representative

Phone: 570-454-6172

E-mail: msm@mccannschool.com

McCANN SCHOOL OF BUSINESS

2650 Woodglen Rd
Pottsville, PA 17901-1335
Institution Contact: Rachel Schoffstall, Campus Director
Website: www.mccannschool.com
Phone: 570-622-7622

McCANN SCHOOL OF BUSINESS

201 Lackawanna Avenue
Scranton, PA 18503
Web: http://www.mccannschool.com
Accreditation: Accrediting Council for Independent Colleges and Schools
Programs Offered:
accounting; administrative assistant and secretarial science; business administration and management; computer and information sciences related; criminal justice/law enforcement administration; kindergarten/preschool education; legal assistant/paralegal; massage therapy; medical/clinical assistant; medical office assistant; surgical technology
Enrollment: 253 students
Institution Contact: Ms. Shelby Deutschle, Campus Director
Phone: 570-969-4330
Fax: 570-969-3139
E-mail: smd@mccannschool.com
Admission Contact: Ms. Karen Stefanski, Director of Education
Phone: 570-969-4330
Fax: 570-969-3139
E-mail: kstefanski@mccannschool.com

McCANN SCHOOL OF BUSINESS

147 North 4th Street
Sunbury, PA 17801
Programs Offered:
accounting; administrative assistant and secretarial science; computer and information sciences related; computer programming; computer software and media applications; computer systems networking and telecommunications; cosmetology; criminal justice/law enforcement administration; health information/medical records technology; legal administrative assistant/secretary; legal assistant/paralegal; marketing/marketing management; massage therapy; medical administrative assistant and medical secretary; medical/clinical assistant; medical office computer specialist; medical office management; surgical technology; word processing
Enrollment: 537 students
Institution Contact: Ms. Susan Harmon, Campus Director
Phone: 570-286-3058
Fax: 570-286-4723
Admission Contact: Mrs. Lisa Davis, Director of

Admissions
Phone: 570-286-3058
Fax: 570-286-4723

NEW CASTLE SCHOOL OF TRADES

4164 Route 422
Pulaski, PA 16143
Web: http://www.ncstrades.com
Accreditation: Accrediting Commission of Career Schools and Colleges of Technology
Programs Offered:
automobile/automotive mechanics technology; construction engineering technology; electrician; heating, air conditioning and refrigeration technology; industrial mechanics and maintenance technology; machine tool technology; truck and bus driver/commercial vehicle operation; welding technology
Enrollment: 405 students
Institution Contact: Mr. Rex Spaulding, Director
Phone: 724-964-8811
Fax: 724-964-8177
E-mail: ncstrades@aol.com
Admission Contact: Mr. James Catheline, Admissions Director
Phone: 724-964-8811
Fax: 724-964-8177
E-mail: ncstrades@aol.com

ORLEANS TECHNICAL INSTITUTE

1330 Rhawn Street
Philadelphia, PA 19111-2899
Web: http://www.orleanstech.edu
Accreditation: Accrediting Commission of Career Schools and Colleges of Technology
Programs Offered:
building/property maintenance and management; carpentry; culinary arts; electrician; heating, air conditioning, ventilation and refrigeration maintenance technology; human services; plumbing technology
Enrollment: 295 students
Institution Contact: Ms. Jayne Siniari, Director
Phone: 215-728-4450
Fax: 215-745-4718
E-mail: trades@jevs.org
Admission Contact: Ms. Deborah M. Bello, Admissions Director
Phone: 215-728-4733

Fax: 215-745-1689
E-mail: bellod@jevs.org

ORLEANS TECHNICAL INSTITUTE - CENTER CITY CAMPUS

1845 Walnut Street, 7th Floor
Philadelphia, PA 19103
Web: http://www.jevs.org
Accreditation: Accrediting Commission of Career Schools and Colleges of Technology
Programs Offered:
court reporting
Enrollment: 166 students
Institution Contact: Ms. Delores Jefferson Swanson, Director
Phone: 215-854-1846
Fax: 215-854-1880
E-mail: swansd@jevs.org
Admission Contact: Ms. Jacqueline Williams, Admissions Representative
Phone: 215-854-1853
Fax: 215-854-1880
E-mail: courtreporting@jevs.org

MAP PEIRCE COLLEGE

1420 Pine Street
Philadelphia, PA 19102
Web: http://www.peirce.edu
Accreditation: Middle States Association of Colleges and Schools
Programs Offered:
accounting and business/management; business administration and management; business, management, and marketing related; computer and information sciences and support services related; computer and information systems security; computer/information technology administration and management; computer/information technology services administration related; computer programming (specific applications); computer programming (vendor/product certification); computer systems networking and telecommunications; computer/technical support; human resources management; information technology; international business/trade/commerce; legal assistant/paralegal; marketing/marketing management; pre-law studies; real estate; system, networking, and LAN/WAN management; technology management

Enrollment: 2,365 students
Institution Contact: Mr. James J. Mergiotti, Executive Vice President and COO
Phone: 215-670-9372
Fax: 215-545-6588
E-mail: jjmergiotti@peirce.edu
Admission Contact: Ms. Nadine M. Maher, Manager, Enrollment Services
Phone: 215-670-9236
Fax: 215-893-4347
E-mail: nmmaher@peirce.edu

PENNCO TECH

3815 Otter Street
Bristol, PA 19007-3696
Web: http://www.penncotech.com
Accreditation: Accrediting Commission of Career Schools and Colleges of Technology
Programs Offered:
accounting; autobody/collision and repair technology; automobile/automotive mechanics technology; computer systems networking and telecommunications; electrician; executive assistant/executive secretary; heating, air conditioning and refrigeration technology; medical/clinical assistant; pharmacy technician
Enrollment: 461 students
Institution Contact: Mr. Alfred W. Parcells, Jr., School Director
Phone: 800-575-9399
Fax: 215-785-1975
E-mail: fparcells@penncotech.com
Admission Contact: Mr. Glenn Slater, Director of Admissions and Marketing
Phone: 215-824-3200
Fax: 215-785-1945
E-mail: admissions@penncotech.com

PENNSYLVANIA CULINARY INSTITUTE

717 Liberty Avenue
Pittsburgh, PA 15222
Web: http://www.paculinary.com
Accreditation: Accrediting Commission of Career Schools and Colleges of Technology
Programs Offered:
baking and pastry arts; culinary arts; restaurant, culinary, and catering management
Enrollment: 1,221 students

Institution Contact: Mrs. Jessica M. Sanders, Compliance Director
Phone: 800-432-2433 ext. 4210
Fax: 412-201-1654
E-mail: jsanders@paculinary.com
Admission Contact: Mr. Chris O'Dell, Vice President of Admissions
Phone: 800-432-2433
Fax: 412-566-2434
E-mail: codell@paculinary.com

PITTSBURGH TECHNICAL INSTITUTE

1111 McKee Road
Oakdale, PA 15071
Web: http://www.pti.edu
Accreditation: Middle States Association of Colleges and Schools
Programs Offered:
accounting; animation, interactive technology, video graphics and special effects; architectural drafting and CAD/CADD; business administration and management; CAD/CADD drafting/design technology; commercial and advertising art; computer and information systems security; computer programming; computer/technical support; criminal justice/law enforcement administration; criminal justice/police science; drafting and design technology; e-commerce; electrical, electronic and communications engineering technology; forensic science and technology; graphic communications; hospitality administration; hotel/motel administration; information technology; marketing/marketing management; mechanical drafting and CAD/CADD; medical administrative assistant and medical secretary; medical/clinical assistant; medical insurance coding; medical office computer specialist; medical office management; safety/security technology; system, networking, and LAN/WAN management; tourism and travel services management; web/multimedia management and webmaster
Enrollment: 1,940 students
Institution Contact: Ms. Cynthia A. Reynolds, President
Phone: 412-809-5100
Fax: 412-809-5320
E-mail: reynolds@pti.edu
Admission Contact: Ms. Marylu Zuk, Vice President of Admissions
Phone: 412-809-5100
Fax: 412-809-5351
E-mail: zuk@pti.edu

The PJA School

7900 West Chester Pike
Upper Darby, PA 19082-1926
Web: http://www.pjaschool.com
Accreditation: Accrediting Commission of Career
Schools and Colleges of Technology
Programs Offered:
accounting; accounting technology and bookkeeping; administrative assistant and secretarial science; business administration and management; computer graphics; computer/information technology administration and management; computer software and media applications; criminal justice/law enforcement administration; data entry/microcomputer applications; executive assistant/executive secretary; finance; legal administrative assistant/secretary; legal assistant/paralegal; real estate; word processing
Enrollment: 300 students
Institution Contact: Mr. David Hudiak, Director
Phone: 610-789-6700
Fax: 610-789-5208
E-mail: pjaschool@dvol.com
Admission Contact: Mr. Daniel A. Alpert, Director of
Institutional Development
Phone: 610-789-6700
Fax: 610-789-5208
E-mail: pjaschool@dvol.com

Prism Career Institute

8040 Roosevelt Boulevard
Philadelphia, PA 19152
Web: www.prismcareerinstitute.com
Institution Contact: Campus Director
Phone: 215-331-4600
Fax: 215-708-0173

The Restaurant School at Walnut Hill College

4207 Walnut Street
Philadelphia, PA 19104
Web: http://www.walnuthillcollege.edu
Accreditation: Accrediting Commission of Career
Schools and Colleges of Technology
Programs Offered:
baking and pastry arts; culinary arts; hotel/motel administration; restaurant, culinary, and catering management; restaurant/food services management
Institution Contact: Office of Admissions

Phone: 215-222-4200
Fax: 215-222-4219

RETS Institute of Technology

777 Penn Center Boulevard
Pittsburgh, PA 15235
Web: http://www.retsaec.com
Accreditation: Accrediting Council for Independent
Colleges and Schools
Programs Offered:
accounting; administrative assistant and secretarial science; computer systems networking and telecommunications; computer/technical support; medical/clinical assistant; medical office management; system administration
Phone: 888-300-4255

Sanford-Brown Institute

3600 Horizon Boulevard, Suite GL 1
Trevose, PA 19053
Web: http://www.careered.com
Accreditation: Accrediting Bureau of Health Education Schools
Programs Offered:
cardiovascular technology; criminal justice/law enforcement administration; dental assisting; diagnostic medical sonography and ultrasound technology; massage therapy; medical/clinical assistant; medical insurance/medical billing
Enrollment: 700 students
Institution Contact: Mr. Joseph E. Nimerfroh, President
Phone: 215-436-6928
Fax: 215-355-4909
E-mail: jnimerfroh@sbphilly.com
Admission Contact: Mr. Douglas Lingo, Director of
Admissions
Phone: 215-436-6921
Fax: 215-355-4909
E-mail: dlingo@sbphilly.com

Schuylkill Institute of Business and Technology

118 South Centre Street, Suite 2
Pottsville, PA 17901
Web: http://www.sibt.edu
Accreditation: Accrediting Council for Independent

Colleges and Schools

Programs Offered:
accounting; accounting and business/management; administrative assistant and secretarial science; architectural drafting and CAD/CADD; business administration, management and operations related; CAD/CADD drafting/design technology; commercial and advertising art; computer and information systems security; computer graphics; computer software and media applications; computer software engineering; computer systems analysis; computer systems networking and telecommunications; computer/technical support; computer technology/computer systems technology; design and visual communications; desktop publishing and digital imaging design; digital communication and media/multimedia; drafting and design technology; executive assistant/executive secretary; health information/medical records technology; legal assistant/paralegal; massage therapy; mechanical drafting and CAD/CADD; medical administrative assistant and medical secretary; medical/clinical assistant; medical/health management and clinical assistant; medical office management; medical reception; office occupations and clerical services

Enrollment: 140 students

Institution Contact: Mr. Anthony H. Dooley, Executive Director

Phone: 570-622-4835

Fax: 570-622-6563

E-mail: tdooley@sibt.edu

Admission Contact: Ms. Gayle Holden, Admissions Representative

Phone: 570-622-4835

Fax: 570-622-6563

E-mail: gholden@sibt.edu

THOMPSON INSTITUTE

2593 Philadelphia Avenue
Chambersburg, PA 17201
Web: http://www.thompson.edu
Accreditation: Accrediting Council for Independent Colleges and Schools
Programs Offered:
accounting; business administration and management; business operations support and secretarial services related; customer service support/call center/teleservice operation; data entry/microcomputer applications; electrical/electronics equipment installation and repair; electrician; electrocardiograph technology; health information/medical records technology; medical administrative assistant and medical secretary; medical/clinical assistant; medical insurance coding; medical insurance/medical billing; medical office assistant; pharmacy technician

Institution Contact: Mrs. Sherry Rosenberg, Executive Director

Phone: 717-709-1311

Fax: 717-709-1332

E-mail: srosenberg@thompson.edu

THOMPSON INSTITUTE

5650 Derry Street
Harrisburg, PA 17111
Web: http://www.thompson.edu
Accreditation: Accrediting Council for Independent Colleges and Schools
Programs Offered:
accounting technology and bookkeeping; business administration and management; CAD/CADD drafting/design technology; computer/information technology administration and management; criminal justice/law enforcement administration; digital communication and media/multimedia; medical/clinical assistant; medical insurance coding

Enrollment: 434 students

Institution Contact: Mr. Roy Hawkins, Executive Director

Phone: 800-272-4632

Fax: 717-564-3779

E-mail: rhawkins@thompson.edu

Admission Contact: Mr. Charles Zimmerman, Director of Admissions

Phone: 717-901-5845

Fax: 717-564-3779

E-mail: czimmerman@thompson.edu

THOMPSON INSTITUTE

3010 Market Street , 2nd Floor
Philadelphia, PA 19104-3325
Web: http://www.thompsoninstitute.org
Accreditation: Accrediting Council for Independent Colleges and Schools
Programs Offered:
medical/clinical assistant; medical office management
Institution Contact: Mr. Scott Dams, Director of

Admissions
Phone: 215-594-4000
Fax: 215-594-4088
E-mail: sdams@thompsoninstitute.org

TRIANGLE TECH, INC. - DUBOIS SCHOOL
PO Box 551
DuBois, PA 15801-0551
Web: http://www.triangle-tech.edu
Accreditation: Accrediting Commission of Career
Schools and Colleges of Technology
Programs Offered:
CAD/CADD drafting/design technology; carpentry;
electrician; welding technology
Enrollment: 251 students
Institution Contact: Mrs. Deborah Hepburn, Director
Phone: 814-371-2090
Fax: 814-371-9227
E-mail: dhepburn@triangle-tech.edu

TRIANGLE TECH, INC. - ERIE SCHOOL
2000 Liberty Street
Erie, PA 16502-9987
Web: http://www.triangle-tech.edu
Accreditation: Accrediting Commission of Career
Schools and Colleges of Technology
Programs Offered:
CAD/CADD drafting/design technology; carpentry;
electrician
Enrollment: 165 students
Institution Contact: Mr. David McMutrie, Director
Phone: 814-453-6016
Fax: 814-454-2818
E-mail: dmcmutrie@triangle-tech.edu

TRIANGLE TECH, INC. - GREENSBURG SCHOOL
222 East Pittsburgh Street
Greensburg, PA 15601-3304
Web: http://www.triangle-tech.edu
Accreditation: Accrediting Commission of Career
Schools and Colleges of Technology
Programs Offered:
CAD/CADD drafting/design technology; carpentry;
electrician; heating, air conditioning and refrigeration
technology
Institution Contact: Mr. Dennis D Frketich, Director

Phone: 724-832-1050
Fax: 724-834-0325
E-mail: dfrketich@triangle-tech.edu

TRIANGLE TECH, INC. - PITTSBURGH SCHOOL
1940 Perrysville Avenue
Pittsburgh, PA 15214-3897
Web: http://www.triangle-tech.edu
Accreditation: Accrediting Commission of Career
Schools and Colleges of Technology
Programs Offered:
architectural drafting and CAD/CADD; carpentry;
electrician; heating, air conditioning and refrigeration
technology; mechanical drafting and CAD/CADD;
welding technology
Enrollment: 325 students
Institution Contact: Mr. Kurt R. Stridinger, Director
Phone: 412-359-1000
Fax: 412-359-1012
E-mail: kstridinger@triangle-tech.edu

TRIANGLE TECH, INC. - SUNBURY SCHOOL
RR 1, Box 51
Sunbury, PA 17801
Web: http://www.triangle-tech.edu
Accreditation: Accrediting Commission of Career
Schools and Colleges of Technology
Programs Offered:
carpentry; electrician
Enrollment: 126 students
Institution Contact: Mr. Jess Null, Director
Phone: 570-988-0700
Fax: 570-988-4641
E-mail: jnull@triangle-tech.edu

TRI-STATE BUSINESS INSTITUTE
5757 West 26th Street
Erie, PA 16506
Web: http://www.tsbi.org
Accreditation: Accrediting Council for Independent
Colleges and Schools
Programs Offered:
accounting; administrative assistant and secretarial science; business administration and management; computer and information systems security; computer installation and repair technology; computer programming;

computer programming (specific applications); computer software and media applications; computer systems networking and telecommunications; computer/technical support; computer technology/computer systems technology; cosmetology; cosmetology, barber/styling, and nail instruction; information technology; legal assistant/paralegal; marketing/marketing management; medical transcription; office occupations and clerical services; system administration; system, networking, and LAN/WAN management; web/multimedia management and webmaster; web page, digital/multimedia and information resources design; word processing
Institution Contact: Mr. Guy Euliano, President
Phone: 814-838-7673
Fax: 814-838-8642
E-mail: geuliano@tsbi.org
Admission Contact: Ms. Karen A. LaPaglia, Enrollment Coordinator
Phone: 814-838-7673
Fax: 814-838-1047
E-mail: klapaglia@tsbi.org

UNIVERSAL TECHNICAL INSTITUTE
750 Pennsylvania Avenue
Exton, PA 19341
Web: http://www.uticorp.com
Accreditation: Accrediting Commission of Career Schools and Colleges of Technology
Programs Offered:
automobile/automotive mechanics technology

WESTERN SCHOOL OF HEALTH AND BUSINESS CAREERS
One Monroeville Center, Suite 125, Route 22
Monroeville, PA 15146-2142
Accreditation: Accrediting Bureau of Health Education Schools; Accrediting Commission of Career Schools and Colleges of Technology
Programs Offered:
business administration and management; criminal justice/law enforcement administration; dental assisting; diagnostic medical sonography and ultrasound technology; legal assistant/paralegal; massage therapy; medical/clinical assistant; medical office computer specialist; pharmacy technician; radiologic technology/science; respiratory care therapy; surgical technology; veterinary technology

Enrollment: 338 students
Institution Contact: Mr. Michael C. Cole, Associate Director of Education
Phone: 412-373-9038 ext. 224
Fax: 412-373-2544
E-mail: mcole@western-school.com
Admission Contact: Mr. Chris Moore, Director of Admissions
Phone: 412-373-9038 ext. 233
E-mail: cmoore@western-school.com

WESTERN SCHOOL OF HEALTH AND BUSINESS CAREERS
421 Seventh Avenue
Pittsburgh, PA 15219-1907
Web: http://www.western-school.com
Programs Offered:
business administration and management; dental assisting; diagnostic medical sonography and ultrasound technology; legal assistant/paralegal; massage therapy; medical/clinical assistant; medical office computer specialist; pharmacy technician; radiologic technology/science; respiratory care therapy; surgical technology; veterinary technology
Enrollment: 540 students
Institution Contact: Mr. Kenneth H. Richards, President
Phone: 412-281-2600 ext. 174
Fax: 412-227-0807
E-mail: krichards@western-school.com
Admission Contact: Mr. Michael Joyce, Director of Admissions
Phone: 412-281-2600 ext. 152
E-mail: mjoyce@western-school.com

WEST VIRGINIA CAREER INSTITUTE
PO Box 278
Mount Braddock, PA 15465
Web: http://www.wvjcmorgantown.edu
Accreditation: Accrediting Council for Independent Colleges and Schools
Programs Offered:
accounting; administrative assistant and secretarial science; computer/information technology administration and management; computer software and media applications; computer/technical support; medical administrative assistant and medical secretary; medical/clinical assistant; medical office management; word processing

Enrollment: 185 students
Institution Contact: Ms. Patricia Callen, Executive Director
Phone: 724-437-4600
Fax: 724-437-6053
Admission Contact: Ms. Amanda Rugg, Admissions Director
Phone: 724-437-4600
Fax: 724-437-6053
E-mail: arugg@wvjcmorgantown.edu

WyoTech
500 Innovation Drive
Blairsville, PA 15717
Web: http://www.wyotech.edu/
Accreditation: Accrediting Commission of Career Schools and Colleges of Technology
Programs Offered:
autobody/collision and repair technology; automobile/automotive mechanics technology; diesel mechanics technology
Enrollment: 1,100 students
Institution Contact: Brenda Heine, Director of Career Services
Phone: 724-459-9500 ext. 281
Fax: 724-459-6499
E-mail: bheine@wyotech.com
Admission Contact: Wendy Hauser, Director of Admissions
Phone: 427-459-9500 ext. 286
Fax: 724-459-6499
E-mail: whauser@wyotech.com

York Technical Institute
3050 Hempland Rd
Lancaster, PA 17601
Institution Contact: Mr. Rick Cunningham
Phone: 717-295-1100
Fax: 717-295-1135

York Technical Institute
1405 Williams Road
York, PA 17402-9017
Web: http://www.yti.edu
Accreditation: Accrediting Commission of Career Schools and Colleges of Technology
Programs Offered:

accounting; baking and pastry arts; business administration and management; CAD/CADD drafting/design technology; computer/technical support; computer technology/computer systems technology; criminal justice/law enforcement administration; culinary arts; drafting and design technology; emergency medical technology (EMT paramedic); heating, air conditioning and refrigeration technology; hospitality administration; hotel/motel administration; industrial technology; information science/studies; marketing/marketing management; mechanical design technology; motorcycle maintenance and repair technology; office management; robotics technology; system, networking, and LAN/WAN management; telecommunications; tourism and travel services management
Institution Contact: Mr. Harold Maley, President
Phone: 717-757-1100
Fax: 717-757-4964
E-mail: hlm@yti.edu
Admission Contact: Ms. Cathi Bost, Executive Vice President
Phone: 717-757-1100
Fax: 717-757-4964
E-mail: bostc@yti.edu

Yorktowne Business Institute
West 7th Avenue
York, PA 17404-9946
Web: http://www.ybi.edu
Accreditation: Accrediting Council for Independent Colleges and Schools
Programs Offered:
accounting; administrative assistant and secretarial science; baking and pastry arts; business administration and management; culinary arts; medical administrative assistant and medical secretary; medical/clinical assistant; medical insurance/medical billing
Enrollment: 330 students
Institution Contact: Ms. Elizabeth Dreibelbis, Executive Director
Phone: 717-846-5000 ext. 125
Fax: 717-848-4584
E-mail: betsyd@ybi.edu
Admission Contact: Ms. Jane Regan, Acting Director
Phone: 717-846-5000 ext. 127
Fax: 717-848-4584
E-mail: jregan@ybi.edu

PUERTO RICO

A-1 BUSINESS AND TECHNICAL COLLEGE
Dr. Rufo Street, #14, PO Box 351
Caguas, PR 00725
Web: http://home.coqui.net/a1colleg/
Accreditation: Accrediting Commission of Career Schools and Colleges of Technology
Programs Offered:
accounting; adult development and aging; computer installation and repair technology; computer programming; cosmetology, barber/styling, and nail instruction; legal administrative assistant/secretary; medical administrative assistant and medical secretary; photography

ANTILLES SCHOOL OF TECHNICAL CAREERS
Avenue Fernandez Juncos, 1851
Santurce, PR 00907
Accreditation: Accrediting Bureau of Health Education Schools
Programs Offered:
dental assisting; funeral service and mortuary science; massage therapy; nursing (licensed practical/vocational nurse training); pharmacy technician; respiratory care therapy; surgical technology
Enrollment: 514 students
Institution Contact: Mr. Alexis R. De Jorge, President
Phone: 787-268-2244
Fax: 787-268-1873
E-mail: antillesexe@aol.com
Admission Contact: Mrs. Lupe Mil·n, Admissions Director
Phone: 787-268-2244
Fax: 787-268-1873
E-mail: antillesexe@aol.com

AUTOMECA TECHNICAL COLLEGE
PO Box 4999
Aguadilla, PR 00605-4999
Web: http://www.automeca.com
Accreditation: Accrediting Council for Continuing Education and Training
Programs Offered:
automobile/automotive mechanics technology; diesel mechanics technology; electromechanical technology; marine technology
Enrollment: 260 students
Institution Contact: Mr. Enrique Caro, Director
Phone: 787-882-2828
Fax: 787-891-5030
E-mail: ecaro@automeca.com
Admission Contact: Miss Jeshika Rodriguez, Admissions Officer
Phone: 787-882-2828
Fax: 787-891-5030
E-mail: aguadilla@automeca.com

AUTOMECA TECHNICAL COLLEGE
PO Box 8569
Bayamon, PR 00960-8569
Web: http://www.automeca.com
Accreditation: Accrediting Council for Continuing Education and Training
Programs Offered:
automobile/automotive mechanics technology; diesel mechanics technology; electromechanical technology; marine technology
Enrollment: 615 students
Institution Contact: Mrs. Carmen Estrada, Director
Phone: 787-779-6161
Fax: 787-779-6100
E-mail: cestrada@automeca.com
Admission Contact: Mrs. Samira Saab, Admissions Officer
Phone: 787-779-6161
Fax: 787-779-6100
E-mail: bayamon@automeca.com

AUTOMECA TECHNICAL COLLEGE
69 Calle Munoz Rivera
Caguas, PR 00725-3642
Web: http://www.automeca.com
Accreditation: Accrediting Council for Continuing Education and Training
Programs Offered:
automobile/automotive mechanics technology; diesel mechanics technology; electromechanical technology; marine technology
Institution Contact: Mrs. Milagros Hernandez, Director
Phone: 787-746-3429
Fax: 787-746-3472
E-mail: mhernandez@automeca.com

Admission Contact: Caipa Santa, Admissions Officer
Phone: 787-746-3429
Fax: 787-746-3472
E-mail: caguas@automeca.com

AUTOMECA TECHNICAL COLLEGE

452 Calle Villa
Ponce, PR 00728-0402
Web: http://www.automeca.com
Accreditation: Accrediting Council for Continuing
Education and Training
Programs Offered:
automobile/automotive mechanics technology; diesel
mechanics technology; electromechanical technology;
marine technology
Institution Contact: Mr. Leo Bagildo Lopez-Saez,
Director
Phone: 787-840-7880
Fax: 787-259-2319
E-mail: aportalatin@automeca.com
Admission Contact: Mr. Juan Tiru, Admissions Of-
ficer
Phone: 787-840-7880
Fax: 787-259-2319
E-mail: ponce@automeca.com

BAYAMON COMMUNITY COLLEGE

PO Box 55176
Bayamon, PR 00960
Accreditation: Accrediting Commission of Career
Schools and Colleges of Technology
Programs Offered:
accounting related; administrative assistant and sec-
retarial science; business administration and manage-
ment; English as a second language; entrepreneurship;
legal assistant/paralegal; medical office assistant; sales,
distribution and marketing
Enrollment: 100 students
Institution Contact: Mr. Tanus J. Saad, President/
CEO
Phone: 787-780-4370
Fax: 787-778-7447
E-mail: saadt@bccpr.org
Admission Contact: Mrs. Nilda Ortiz, Admissions
Director
Phone: 787-780-4370
Fax: 787-778-7447

E-mail: nildaortiz@bccpr.org

CAGUAS INSTITUTE OF MECHANICAL TECHNOLOGY

PO Box 6118, 39-40, B Street, West Industrial Park
Caguas, PR 00726
Accreditation: Accrediting Council for Continuing
Education and Training
Programs Offered:
adult and continuing education; appliance installation and repair technology; artificial intelligence and
robotics; autobody/collision and repair technology;
automobile/automotive mechanics technology; biomedical technology; CAD/CADD drafting/design
technology; computer/information technology services
administration related; computer systems networking
and telecommunications; computer technology/com-
puter systems technology; diesel mechanics technology; electrical/electronics drafting and CAD/CADD;
electrical/electronics equipment installation and repair;
electrician; electromechanical and instrumentation and
maintenance technologies related; electromechanical
technology; heavy equipment maintenance technology;
industrial electronics technology; industrial mechanics
and maintenance technology; marine technology; tool
and die technology; welding technology
Institution Contact: Mr. Edwin J. Colon, President
Phone: 787-744-1060
Fax: 787-744-1035
E-mail: mechtech@caribe.net
Admission Contact: Mrs. Rocio Rosario, Admissions
Director
Phone: 787-744-1060
Fax: 787-744-1035
E-mail: admisiones@mechtechcollege.com

COLEGIO MAYOR DE TECNOLOGIA

PO Box 1490
Arroyo, PR 00714
Accreditation: Accrediting Commission of Career
Schools and Colleges of Technology
Programs Offered:
computer installation and repair technology; computer
programming (specific applications); culinary arts;
data entry/microcomputer applications; dental assisting; electrician; emergency medical technology (EMT
paramedic); hospitality administration; hotel/motel
administration; legal administrative assistant/secre-

tary; nursing assistant/aide and patient care assistant; nursing (licensed practical/vocational nurse training); nursing (registered nurse training)
Institution Contact: Mr. Mancio Vicente, President
Phone: 787-839-5266
Fax: 787-839-0033
E-mail: mvicente@colegiomayortec.com
Admission Contact: Mrs. Julia Melendez, Admission Director
Phone: 787-839-5266
Fax: 787-839-0033
E-mail: estudios@colegiomayortec.com

COLUMBIA COLLEGE

PO Box 8517
Caguas, PR 00726-8517
Web: http://www.columbiaco.edu
Accreditation: Accrediting Council for Independent Colleges and Schools
Programs Offered:
administrative assistant and secretarial science; business administration and management; computer/information technology administration and management; electrical, electronic and communications engineering technology; nursing (registered nurse training)
Enrollment: 780 students
Institution Contact: Ms. Alex De Jorge, President
Phone: 787-258-1501 ext. 212
Fax: 787-746-5616
E-mail: adejorge@columbiaco.edu
Admission Contact: Ms. Ana R. Burgos, Marketing and Admissions Manager
Phone: 787-743-4041 ext. 211
Fax: 787-746-5616
E-mail: arburgos@columbiaco.edu

COLUMBIA COLLEGE

PO Box 3062
Yauco, PR 00698
Accreditation: Accrediting Council for Independent Colleges and Schools
Programs Offered:
administrative assistant and secretarial science; business administration and management; computer/information technology administration and management; nursing (registered nurse training)
Institution Contact: Mr. Alex De Jorge, President

Phone: 787-258-1501 ext. 212
Fax: 787-746-5616
Admission Contact: Mr. Efrain Cruz, Admissions and Recruitment Coordinator
Phone: 787-856-0845
Fax: 787-267-2335

ELECTRONIC DATA PROCESSING COLLEGE OF PUERTO RICO

PO Box 192303
San Juan, PR 00919-2303
Accreditation: Accrediting Council for Independent Colleges and Schools
Programs Offered:
accounting and business/management; administrative assistant and secretarial science; business administration and management; computer programming; desktop publishing and digital imaging design; e-commerce; emergency medical technology (EMT paramedic); management information systems
Enrollment: 905 students
Institution Contact: Ing. Gladys Nieves de Berrìos, President
Phone: 787-765-3560 ext. 240
Fax: 787-777-0025
E-mail: nievglad@edpcollege.edu
Admission Contact: Dr. Juan Varona, Dean of Students
Phone: 787-765-3560 ext. 277
Fax: 787-777-0025
E-mail: jnvarona@edpcollege.edu

ELECTRONIC DATA PROCESSING COLLEGE OF PUERTO RICO - SAN SEBASTIAN

PO Box 1674, Betances #49
San Sebastian, PR 00685
Accreditation: Accrediting Council for Independent Colleges and Schools
Programs Offered:
administrative assistant and secretarial science; business administration and management; computer programming; emergency medical technology (EMT paramedic); nursing (registered nurse training); pharmacy technician
Institution Contact: Mrs. Mayra Rivera, Associate Director/Dean
Phone: 787-896-2252 ext. 234
Fax: 787-896-0066

E-mail: mrivera@edpcollege.edu
Admission Contact: Mrs. Ingrid Gonzalez, Admissions Officer
Phone: 787-896-2252 ext. 290
Fax: 787-896-0066
E-mail: igonzalez@edpcollege.edu

ESCUELA HOTELERA DE SAN JUAN IN PUERTO RICO

Guayama Street, #229, Hato Rey
San Juan, PR 00917
Accreditation: Accrediting Commission of Career Schools and Colleges of Technology
Programs Offered:
baking and pastry arts; bartending; culinary arts; food service and dining room management
Institution Contact: Mrs. Sylvia Cestero , President
Phone: 787-766-0606
Fax: 787-281-6855
E-mail: hotelerasj@prtc.net
Admission Contact: Ms. Devalis Ortiz, Admissions Director
Phone: 787-759-7599
Fax: 787-281-6855
E-mail: hotelerasj@prtc.net

HUERTAS JUNIOR COLLEGE

Box 8429
Caguas, PR 00726
Accreditation: Accrediting Council for Independent Colleges and Schools
Programs Offered:
accounting technology and bookkeeping; administrative assistant and secretarial science; business administration and management; CAD/CADD drafting/design technology; computer installation and repair technology; computer programming; dental assisting; drafting and design technology; electrical, electronic and communications engineering technology; electrician; health information/medical records administration; heating, air conditioning and refrigeration technology; information technology; pharmacy technician; respiratory care therapy; tourism and travel services management
Enrollment: 1,833 students
Institution Contact: Dr. Rafael Ramirez-Rivera, President
Phone: 787-743-0480
Fax: 787-747-0170

E-mail: rrramire@coqui.net
Admission Contact: Mrs. Barbara Hassim, Director of Admissions Office
Phone: 787-743-1242
Fax: 787-743-0203
E-mail: huertas@huertas.org

ICPR JUNIOR COLLEGE - ARECIBO CAMPUS

20 San Patricio Avenue, Box 140067
Arecibo, PR 00614-0067
Web: http://www.icprjc.edu
Accreditation: Middle States Association of Colleges and Schools
Programs Offered:
accounting; administrative assistant and secretarial science; business administration and management; computer installation and repair technology; computer technology/computer systems technology; hospitality administration; information science/studies; marketing/marketing management; medical insurance/medical billing; office occupations and clerical services; tourism and travel services management
Enrollment: 440 students
Institution Contact: Mrs. Elsa N. Banos, Academic Dean
Phone: 787-878-6000
Fax: 787-878-7750
E-mail: ebanos@icprjc.edu
Admission Contact: Mrs. Magdalena Vega, Admissions Director
Phone: 787-878-6000
Fax: 787-878-7750
E-mail: mvega@icprjc.edu

ICPR JUNIOR COLLEGE - HATO REY CAMPUS

558 Munoz Rivera Avenue, PO Box 190304
San Juan, PR 00919-0304
Web: http://www.icprjc.edu
Accreditation: Middle States Association of Colleges and Schools
Programs Offered:
accounting; administrative assistant and secretarial science; business administration and management; computer installation and repair technology; computer technology/computer systems technology; hospitality administration; information science/studies; marketing/marketing management; medical insurance/medi-

cal billing; office occupations and clerical services; tourism and travel services management
Enrollment: 485 students
Institution Contact: Ms. Maria Rivera, Dean/Director
Phone: 787-753-6000
Fax: 787-763-7249
E-mail: mrivera@icprjc.edu
Admission Contact: M. Francisco Mena, Admissions Director
Phone: 787-753-6000
Fax: 787-763-7249
E-mail: fmena@icprjc.edu

ICPR Junior College - Mayaguez Campus
80 West McKinley Street, PO Box 1108
Mayaguez, PR 00681-1108
Web: http://www.icprjc.edu
Accreditation: Middle States Association of Colleges and Schools
Programs Offered:
accounting; administrative assistant and secretarial science; business administration and management; computer installation and repair technology; computer technology/computer systems technology; hospitality administration; information science/studies; marketing/marketing management; medical insurance/medical billing; office occupations and clerical services; tourism and travel services management
Enrollment: 550 students
Institution Contact: Mrs. Dorca Acosta-Ortiz, Dean/Director
Phone: 787-832-6000
Fax: 787-833-2237
E-mail: dacosta@icprjc.edu
Admission Contact: Mr. Jose Ortiz, Admissions Director
Phone: 787-832-6000
Fax: 787-833-2237
E-mail: jortiz@icprjc.edu

Instituto Banca y Comercio
Calle Gautier Benitez #49
Caguas, PR 00725
Web: http://www.ibancapr.com
Accreditation: Accrediting Council for Independent Colleges and Schools
Programs Offered:

baking and pastry arts; banking and financial support services; barbering; computer installation and repair technology; computer programming; cosmetology; culinary arts; data entry/microcomputer applications; dental assisting; drafting and design technology; emergency medical technology (EMT paramedic); nail technician and manicurist; nursing (licensed practical/vocational nurse training); respiratory care therapy; tourism and travel services management
Enrollment: 1,593 students
Institution Contact: Mr. Arcadio Figueroa, Branch Director
Phone: 787-745-9525
Fax: 787-744-4760
E-mail: afigueroa@ibancapr.com
Admission Contact: Ms. Maria Torres, Admission Director
Phone: 787-745-9525
Fax: 787-744-4760
E-mail: atorres@ibancapr.com

Instituto Banca y Comercio
PO Box 37-2710
Cayey, PR 00737
Web: http://www.ibanca.net/
Accreditation: Accrediting Council for Independent Colleges and Schools
Programs Offered:
computer programming; drawing; electrician; emergency medical technology (EMT paramedic); heating, air conditioning, ventilation and refrigeration maintenance technology; nursing (registered nurse training); respiratory care therapy
Institution Contact: Mrs. Lillian Diaz Aponte, Director
Phone: 787-738-7144
Fax: 787-738-7629
E-mail: ibanca@caribe.net
Admission Contact: Mr. Alan Rodriguez Vazquez , Recruiting Director
Phone: 787-738-7144
Fax: 787-738-7629
E-mail: ibanca@caribe.net

Instituto Banca y Comercio
PO Box 822
Fajardo, PR 00738
Web: http://www.ibanca.net/

Accreditation: Accrediting Council for Independent Colleges and Schools
Programs Offered:
banking and financial support services; computer programming related; culinary arts; dental assisting; electrician; heating, air conditioning and refrigeration technology; medical administrative assistant and medical secretary; nursing (licensed practical/vocational nurse training); respiratory therapy technician; tourism and travel services management; word processing
Institution Contact: Ms. Claribel LÛpez, Director
Phone: 787-860-6262
Fax: 787-860-6265
E-mail: ibancafd@coqui.net
Admission Contact: Mr. Luis Rivera, Admissions Director
Phone: 787-860-6262 ext. 24
Fax: 787-860-6265
E-mail: ibancafd@coqui.net

INSTITUTO BANCA Y COMERCIO
Derques Street, #4 Este
Guayama, PR 00784
Web: http://www.ibanca.net/
Accreditation: Accrediting Council for Independent Colleges and Schools
Programs Offered:
banking and financial support services; computer programming; cosmetology, barber/styling, and nail instruction; dental assisting; drafting and design technology; electrician; emergency medical technology (EMT paramedic); medical reception; nursing (registered nurse training); respiratory care therapy; tourism and travel services management; word processing
Institution Contact: Mr. Hector J. Arroyo, Director
Phone: 787-864-8040
Fax: 787-866-3238
E-mail: bancaguayama@prtc.net

INSTITUTO BANCA Y COMERCIO
56 Carretera, #2
Manati, PR 00674
Web: http://www.ibanca.net
Accreditation: Accrediting Council for Independent Colleges and Schools
Programs Offered:
banking and financial support services; barbering;

CAD/CADD drafting/design technology; computer installation and repair technology; computer software technology; cosmetology; culinary arts; electrician; emergency medical technology (EMT paramedic); health information/medical records administration; heating, air conditioning and refrigeration technology; nail technician and manicurist; nursing (registered nurse training); plumbing technology; tourism and travel services management; word processing
Enrollment: 1,125 students
Institution Contact: Mr. Benjamin Padilla, Director
Phone: 787-854-6634
Fax: 787-884-3372
E-mail: bpadilla@ibancapr.com

INSTITUTO BANCA Y COMERCIO
4 Ramos Antonini Street East
Mayaguez, PR 00680-4932
Web: http://www.ibanca.net
Accreditation: Accrediting Council for Independent Colleges and Schools
Programs Offered:
administrative assistant and secretarial science; banking and financial support services; barbering; CAD/CADD drafting/design technology; computer programming; cosmetology; culinary arts; electrician; emergency medical technology (EMT paramedic); heating, air conditioning and refrigeration technology; medical administrative assistant and medical secretary; nursing assistant/aide and patient care assistant
Institution Contact: Angel L. Lopez-Galarza, Director
Phone: 787-833-4647
Fax: 787-833-4746
E-mail: mayaguez@ibanca.net
Admission Contact: Ms. Elizabeth Ramos-Rodriguez, Admissions Director
Phone: 787-833-4647
Fax: 787-833-4746
E-mail: mayaguez@ibanca.net

INSTITUTO BANCA Y COMERCIO
Box 7623
Ponce, PR 00731
Web: http://www.ibanca.net
Accreditation: Accrediting Council for Independent Colleges and Schools
Programs Offered:

administrative assistant and secretarial science; baking and pastry arts; banking and financial support services; barbering; business automation/technology/data entry; CAD/CADD drafting/design technology; computer/information technology services administration related; computer programming; computer programming (specific applications); cosmetology; cosmetology, barber/styling, and nail instruction; electrical, electronic and communications engineering technology; electrical/electronics equipment installation and repair; electrician; emergency medical technology (EMT paramedic); food preparation; health aide; heating, air conditioning and refrigeration technology; heating, air conditioning, ventilation and refrigeration maintenance technology; home health aide/home attendant; hotel/motel administration; machine shop technology; medical administrative assistant and medical secretary; nursing assistant/aide and patient care assistant; respiratory care therapy; respiratory therapy technician; tourism and travel services management

Institution Contact: Mr. Juan A. Orengo, Director
Phone: 787-840-6119
Fax: 787-840-0530
E-mail: orengo_2000@yahoo.com
Admission Contact: Miss Daisy Sigueroa, Admissions Director
Phone: 787-840-6119
Fax: 787-840-0530

INSTITUTO DE BANCA Y COMERCIO

1660 Santa Ana Street
San Juan, PR 00909
Web: http://www.ibanca.net/
Accreditation: Accrediting Council for Independent Colleges and Schools
Programs Offered:
administrative assistant and secretarial science; baking and pastry arts; banking and financial support services; computer programming; cosmetology, barber/styling, and nail instruction; culinary arts; data entry/microcomputer applications; dental assisting; drafting and design technology; electrician; emergency medical technology (EMT paramedic); heating, air conditioning, ventilation and refrigeration maintenance technology; medical administrative assistant and medical secretary; nursing (registered nurse training); respiratory care therapy; tourism and travel services management
Enrollment: 2,000 students

Institution Contact: Mr. Guillermo Nigaglioni, President/CEO
Phone: 787-982-3000
Fax: 787-982-3075
E-mail: gnigaglioni@ibancapr.com
Admission Contact: Mr. Jose Padial, Vice President of Marketing
Phone: 787-982-3000
Fax: 787-982-3003
E-mail: hrivera@ibancapr.com

INSTITUTO VOCATIONAL Y COMMERCIAL EDIC

Urb. Caguas Norte Calle Genova, Num 8, Corner 5, PO Box 9120
Caguas, PR 00726-9120
Web: http://www.ediccollege.com
Accreditation: Accrediting Council for Independent Colleges and Schools
Programs Offered:
cardiovascular technology; diagnostic medical sonography and ultrasound technology; emergency medical technology (EMT paramedic); medical administrative assistant and medical secretary; nursing (licensed practical/vocational nurse training); radiologic technology/science; respiratory care therapy; surgical technology; teacher assistant/aide
Enrollment: 787 students
Institution Contact: Mr. Jose A. Cartagena, President
Phone: 787-746-2730
Fax: 787-743-0855
E-mail: edic@coqui.net
Admission Contact: Mrs. Virginia Cartagena, Admission Director
Phone: 787-744-8519 ext. 231
Fax: 787-258-6300
E-mail: admisiones@ediccollege.com

LICEO DE ARTE Y TECNOLOGIA

405 Ponce De Leon Avenue , 4th Floor
PO Box 192346
San Juan, PR 00919-9955
Web: http://www.liceopr.com
Accreditation: Accrediting Commission of Career Schools and Colleges of Technology
Programs Offered:
automobile/automotive mechanics technology; drafting and design technology; electrician; heating, air

conditioning and refrigeration technology; office management

Enrollment: 987 students
Institution Contact: Mr. Carlos Manzanal, President
Phone: 787-999-2473 ext. 456
Fax: 787-765-7210
E-mail: liceo@liceopr.com
Admission Contact: Ms. Annamalie Manzanal, Admissions Director
Phone: 787-999-2473 ext. 245
Fax: 787-765-7210
E-mail: gmanzanal@liceopr.com

NATIONAL COLLEGE OF BUSINESS AND TECHNOLOGY

PO Box 4035, MSC452
Arecibo, PR 00614
Accreditation: Accrediting Council for Independent Colleges and Schools
Programs Offered:
accounting; administrative assistant and secretarial science; business administration and management; business automation/technology/data entry; computer installation and repair technology; dental assisting; electrical and electronic engineering technologies related; emergency/disaster science; hospitality administration; information science/studies; medical administrative assistant and medical secretary; nursing assistant/aide and patient care assistant; pharmacy technician; tourism and travel services management
Enrollment: 1,412 students
Institution Contact: Mr. Francisco Nunez, Executive Director of Arecibo Campus
Phone: 787-879-5044 ext. 2513
Fax: 787-879-5047
E-mail: fnunez@nationalcollegepr.edu
Admission Contact: Mrs. Mercedes Pagan, Admissions Director
Phone: 787-879-5044 ext. 2504
Fax: 787-879-5047

NATIONAL COLLEGE OF BUSINESS & TECHNOLOGY

PO Box 2036
Bayamon, PR 00960
Accreditation: Accrediting Council for Independent Colleges and Schools
Programs Offered:
accounting; administrative assistant and secretarial

science; business administration and management; computer installation and repair technology; computer programming; data entry/microcomputer applications; dental assisting; educational/instructional media design; emergency/disaster science; engineering technology; information technology; legal administrative assistant/secretary; medical administrative assistant and medical secretary; nursing (licensed practical/vocational nurse training); nursing (registered nurse training); pharmacy technician; tourism and travel services management
Enrollment: 2,098 students
Institution Contact: Mr. Desi Lopez, Vice President of Financial Aid and Compliance
Phone: 787-780-5134 ext. 4400
Fax: 787-786-9093
E-mail: dlopez@nationalcollegepr.edu
Admission Contact: Mr. Ricardo Nieves, Director of Admissions
Phone: 787-780-5134
Fax: 787-740-7360
E-mail: rnieves@nationalcollegepr.edu

NATIONAL COLLEGE OF BUSINESS & TECHNOLOGY

PO Box 3064
Rio Grande, PR 00745
Accreditation: Accrediting Council for Independent Colleges and Schools
Programs Offered:
accounting; entrepreneurship; information technology; nursing (licensed practical/vocational nurse training); office occupations and clerical services; pharmacy technician; tourism and travel services management
Enrollment: 746 students
Institution Contact: Ms. Lourdes Balseiro, Executive Director
Phone: 787-888-8286
Admission Contact: Mr. Miguel Lopez, Admissions Director
Phone: 787-888-8286

PONCE PARAMEDICAL COLLEGE, INC.

PO Box 800106
Coto Laurel, PR 00780-0106
Accreditation: Accrediting Commission of Career Schools and Colleges of Technology
Programs Offered:

child care provision; computer installation and repair technology; culinary arts; dental assisting; emergency medical technology (EMT paramedic); legal assistant/paralegal; massage therapy; medical administrative assistant and medical secretary; medical insurance coding; nursing (registered nurse training); pharmacy technician; respiratory care therapy; sports medicine; surgical technology

Enrollment: 2,390 students
Institution Contact: Angel QuiÒones, President's Assistant
Phone: 787-848-1589 ext. 455
Fax: 787-259-0169
E-mail: ppcadmin@popac.edu
Admission Contact: Mr. Ruth NegrÛn, Admission Director
Phone: 787-848-1589 ext. 413
Fax: 787-259-0169

TRINITY COLLEGE OF PUERTO RICO

834 Hostos Avenue, PO Box 34360
Ponce, PR 00734-4360
Accreditation: Accrediting Council for Independent Colleges and Schools
Programs Offered:
accounting technology and bookkeeping; administrative assistant and secretarial science; computer programming; computer systems networking and telecommunications; data entry/microcomputer applications; health aide; health information/medical records administration; nursing (registered nurse training)
Institution Contact: Mrs. MarÌa Isabel ColÛn, Director
Phone: 787-842-0000 ext. 226
Fax: 787-284-2537
E-mail: dmramos@pucpr.edu
Admission Contact: Mrs. Jenny RÌos, Community Affairs Director
Phone: 787-842-0000 ext. 238
Fax: 787-284-2537
E-mail: dmramos@pucpr.edu

RHODE ISLAND

CAREER EDUCATION INSTITUTE

622 George Washington Highway
Lincoln, RI 02865

Web: http://www.ceitraining.com
Accreditation: Accrediting Council for Independent Colleges and Schools
Programs Offered:
dental assisting; electrical/electronics equipment installation and repair; massage therapy; medical/clinical assistant; medical insurance coding; medical insurance/medical billing; pharmacy technician
Enrollment: 500 students
Institution Contact: Executive Director
Phone: 401-334-2430
Fax: 401-334-5087
E-mail: execdirlincoln@lincolntech.com
Admission Contact: Admissions Director
Phone: 401-334-2430
Fax: 401-334-5087
E-mail: execdirlincoln@lincolntech.com

GIBBS COLLEGE - CRANSTON

85 Garfield Avenue
Cranston, RI 02920
Web: http://www.gibbsri.edu
Accreditation: Accrediting Council for Independent Colleges and Schools
Programs Offered:
administrative assistant and secretarial science; allied health and medical assisting services related; business administration, management and operations related; computer and information sciences and support services related; computer and information systems security; computer graphics; computer hardware technology; computer/information technology administration and management; computer/information technology services administration related; computer installation and repair technology; computer software and media applications; computer/technical support; computer technology/computer systems technology; criminal justice/law enforcement administration; criminal justice/police science; data processing and data processing technology; design and visual communications; desktop publishing and digital imaging design; digital communication and media/multimedia; executive assistant/executive secretary; graphic communications related; health information/medical records administration; health information/medical records technology; hospitality administration; hospitality administration related; information technology; legal administrative assistant/secretary; medical administrative assistant

and medical secretary; medical/clinical assistant; medical insurance coding; medical insurance/medical billing; medical office assistant; medical office management; medical reception; medical transcription; office management; office occupations and clerical services; phlebotomy; receptionist; system administration; system, networking, and LAN/WAN management; web page, digital/multimedia and information resources design; word processing

Enrollment: 550 students

Institution Contact: Mr. Wynn F Blanton, President

Phone: 401-824-5300

Fax: 401-824-5378

E-mail: wblanton@gibbsprovidence..com

Admission Contact: Mr. Ric Jackson, Vice President of Admissions

Phone: 401-824-5300

Fax: 401-824-5378

E-mail: rjackson@gibbsprovidence.com

THE INTERNATIONAL YACHT RESTORATION SCHOOL

449 Thames Street

Newport, RI 02840

Web: http://www.iyrs.org

Accreditation: Accrediting Commission of Career Schools and Colleges of Technology

Programs Offered:

marine maintenance and ship repair technology

Enrollment: 32 students

Institution Contact: Ms. Debra D. Huntington, Coordinator of Academic Services

Phone: 401-848-5777 ext. 205

Fax: 401-842-0669

E-mail: dhuntington@iyrs.org

Admission Contact: Ms. Debra Huntington, Coordinator of Academic Services

Phone: 401-848-5777 ext. 205

Fax: 401-842-0669

E-mail: dhuntington@iyrs.org

 NEW ENGLAND INSTITUTE OF TECHNOLOGY

2500 Post Road

Warwick, RI 02886-2266

Web: http://www.neit.edu

Accreditation: New England Association of Schools and Colleges

Programs Offered:

administrative assistant and secretarial science; architectural drafting and CAD/CADD; architectural engineering technology; autobody/collision and repair technology; automobile/automotive mechanics technology; automotive engineering technology; building/property maintenance and management; business administration and management; cabinetmaking and millwork; CAD/CADD drafting/design technology; carpentry; clinical/medical laboratory assistant; clinical/medical laboratory technology; communications technology; computer and information sciences; computer programming; computer programming (specific applications); computer systems networking and telecommunications; computer/technical support; computer technology/computer systems technology; construction engineering technology; desktop publishing and digital imaging design; digital communication and media/multimedia; drafting and design technology; electrical, electronic and communications engineering technology; electrician; executive assistant/executive secretary; heating, air conditioning and refrigeration technology; information science/studies; information technology; interior design; marine maintenance and ship repair technology; marine technology; mechanical design technology; mechanical engineering/mechanical technology; medical/clinical assistant; occupational therapist assistant; pipefitting and sprinkler fitting; plumbing technology; radio and television; radio and television broadcasting technology; surgical technology; transportation technology; web/multimedia management and webmaster; web page, digital/multimedia and information resources design

Enrollment: 3,162 students

Institution Contact: Mr. Seth Kurn, Executive Vice President

Phone: 401-739-5000 ext. 3323

Fax: 401-738-8990

E-mail: skurn@neit.edu

Admission Contact: Mr. Michael Kwiatkowski, Director of Admissions

Phone: 800-736-7744 ext. 3308

Fax: 401-738-5122

E-mail: mickey_k@neit.edu

SOUTH CAROLINA

ECPI COLLEGE OF TECHNOLOGY
7410 Northside Drive, G101
North Charleston, SC 29420
Web: http://www.ecpi.edu
Accreditation: Southern Association of Colleges and Schools
Programs Offered:
computer and information sciences; computer engineering technology; computer hardware technology; computer/information technology administration and management; computer installation and repair technology; computer science; computer technology/computer systems technology; health and medical administrative services related; information technology; medical/clinical assistant
Enrollment: 148 students
Institution Contact: Mr. James Rund, Provost
Phone: 843-414-0350
Fax: 843-572-8085
E-mail: jrund@ecpi.edu

ECPI COLLEGE OF TECHNOLOGY
15 Brendan Way, Suite 120
Greenville, SC 29615-3514
Web: http://www.ecpi.edu
Accreditation: Southern Association of Colleges and Schools
Programs Offered:
business automation/technology/data entry; computer and information sciences; computer engineering technologies related; computer/information technology administration and management; computer systems networking and telecommunications; computer/technical support; computer technology/computer systems technology; information science/studies; information technology; medical administrative assistant and medical secretary; medical/clinical assistant; medical office assistant; office occupations and clerical services; system, networking, and LAN/WAN management; web page, digital/multimedia and information resources design
Enrollment: 341 students
Institution Contact: Mr. Patrick J. Donivan, Provost
Phone: 864-288-2828
Fax: 864-288-2930
E-mail: pdonivan@ecpi.edu
Admission Contact: Ms. Wendy J. Donivan, Director of Admissions
Phone: 864-288-2828

Fax: 864-288-2930
E-mail: wdonivan@ecpi.edu

ITT TECHNICAL INSTITUTE
6 Independence Pointe
Greenville, SC 29615
Web: http://www.itt-tech.edu
Accreditation: Accrediting Council for Independent Colleges and Schools
Programs Offered:
animation, interactive technology, video graphics and special effects; CAD/CADD drafting/design technology; communications technology; computer and information systems security; computer engineering technology; computer software and media applications; computer software engineering; computer systems networking and telecommunications; digital communication and media/multimedia; electrical, electronic and communications engineering technology; technology management; web page, digital/multimedia and information resources design
Institution Contact: Mr. David Murray, Director
Phone: 864-288-0777 ext. 21
Admission Contact: Mr. Joseph Fisher , Director of Recruitment
Phone: 864-288-0777

MILLER-MOTTE TECHNICAL COLLEGE
8085 Rivers Avenue
North Charleston, SC 29406
Web: http://www.miller-motte.net/
Accreditation: Accrediting Council for Independent Colleges and Schools
Programs Offered:
accounting; business administration and management; computer and information sciences related; computer software and media applications related; criminal justice/police science; data entry/microcomputer applications; international business/trade/commerce; legal assistant/paralegal; massage therapy; medical/clinical assistant; surgical technology
Enrollment: 576 students
Institution Contact: Ms. Julie Corner, Campus Director
Phone: 843-574-0101
Fax: 843-266-3424
E-mail: juliasc@miller-motte.net
Admission Contact: Kerrie Tobias-Roth, Admissions Department Coordinator

Phone: 843-574-0101
Fax: 843-266-3424
E-mail: kerriet@miller-motte.net

South University

3810 North Main Street
Columbia, SC 29203
Web: http://www.southuniversity.edu
Accreditation: Southern Association of Colleges and Schools
Programs Offered:
accounting; business administration and management; computer/information technology administration and management; health/health care administration; health services administration; legal assistant/paralegal; medical/clinical assistant; pre-law studies
Enrollment: 400 students
Institution Contact: Mrs. Anne F. Patton, President
Phone: 803-799-9082
Fax: 803-799-9038
E-mail: apatton@southuniversity.edu
Admission Contact: Ms. Vanessa DeBauche, Associate Director of Admissions
Phone: 803-799-9082
Fax: 803-799-9038
E-mail: vdebauche@southuniversity.edu

SOUTH DAKOTA

Colorado Technical University Sioux Falls Campus

3901 West 59th Street
Sioux Falls, SD 57108
Accreditation: North Central Association of Colleges and Schools
Programs Offered:
accounting; business administration and management; computer science; criminal justice/law enforcement administration; e-commerce; finance; human resources management; information technology; medical/clinical assistant; technology management
Enrollment: 1,250 students
Institution Contact: Mrs. Catherine M. Taplett Allen, Vice President of Admissions
Phone: 605-361-0200 ext. 103
Fax: 605-361-5954

E-mail: callen@sf.coloradotech.edu

National American University

2700 Doolittle Drive
Ellsworth AFB, SD 57706
Accreditation: North Central Association of Colleges and Schools
Programs Offered:
business administration and management; e-commerce; information technology
Institution Contact: Mr. Scott Toothman, Vice President
Phone: 605-923-5856
Fax: 605-923-7674
E-mail: stoothman@national.edu
Admission Contact: Ms. Stephanie Higdon, Admissions Representative
Phone: 605-923-5856
Fax: 605-923-7674
E-mail: shidgon@national.edu

National American University

321 Kansas City Street
Rapid City, SD 57701
Web: http://www.national.edu
Accreditation: North Central Association of Colleges and Schools
Programs Offered:
accounting; athletic training; business administration and management; computer/information technology administration and management; computer programming; computer systems networking and telecommunications; computer/technical support; e-commerce; equestrian studies; finance; general studies; information technology; international business/trade/commerce; legal assistant/paralegal; management information systems; marketing/marketing management; medical/health management and clinical assistant; veterinary/animal health technology; veterinary technology; web/multimedia management and webmaster
Institution Contact: Mr. Richard Buckles, Campus Director
Phone: 605-394-4800
Fax: 605-394-4871
E-mail: rbuckles@national.edu
Admission Contact: Ms. Angela Beck, Director of Admissions
Phone: 605-394-4800

Fax: 605-394-4871
E-mail: abeck@national.edu

NATIONAL AMERICAN UNIVERSITY - SIOUX FALLS BRANCH

2801 South Kiwanis Avenue, Suite 100
Sioux Falls, SD 57105
Web: http://www.national.edu
Accreditation: North Central Association of Colleges and Schools
Programs Offered:
accounting; business administration and management; computer/technical support; general studies; information technology; legal assistant/paralegal; massage therapy; medical/clinical assistant; pre-law studies
Enrollment: 400 students
Institution Contact: Mrs. Patricia Torpey, Campus Vice President
Phone: 605-334-5430
Fax: 605-334-1575
E-mail: ptorpey@national.edu
Admission Contact: Mrs. Lisa L. Houtsma, Director of Admissions
Phone: 605-334-5430
Fax: 605-334-1575
E-mail: lhoutsma@national.edu

TENNESSEE

ARGOSY UNIVERSITY/NASHVILLE

341 Cool Springs Boulevard, Suite 210
Franklin, TN 37067
Web: http://www.argosyu.edu/nashville
Programs Offered:
mental and social health services and allied professions related
Enrollment: 150 students
Institution Contact: Mrs. Marie Q. Neal, Director of Admissions
Phone: 615-369-0616
E-mail: mquinn@argosyu.edu

DRAUGHONS JUNIOR COLLEGE

1860 Wilma Rudolph Boulevard
Clarksville, TN 37040

Web: http://www.draughons.edu
Accreditation: Accrediting Council for Independent Colleges and Schools
Programs Offered:
accounting; business administration and management; computer/information technology administration and management; computer/information technology services administration related; computer programming (specific applications); computer software and media applications; criminal justice/law enforcement administration; dental assisting; e-commerce; health/health care administration; legal assistant/paralegal; medical/clinical assistant; pharmacy technician
Enrollment: 746 students
Institution Contact: Mr. Roger Batson, Student Services Coordinator
Phone: 931-552-7600
Fax: 931-552-3624
E-mail: rbatson@draughons.edu
Admission Contact: Mrs. Christi Nolder, Assistant Admissions Director
Phone: 931-552-7600
Fax: 931-552-3624
E-mail: cnolder@draughons.edu

DRAUGHONS JUNIOR COLLEGE

415 Golden Bear Court
Murfreesboro, TN 37128
Web: http://www.draughons.org
Programs Offered:
accounting technology and bookkeeping; business administration and management; computer/information technology administration and management; computer/technical support; criminal justice/police science; e-commerce; health information/medical records technology; legal assistant/paralegal; medical/clinical assistant; medical insurance coding; medical insurance/medical billing; medical transcription; pharmacy technician
Enrollment: 495 students
Institution Contact: Patrick De Mesa, Campus Director
Phone: 615-217-9347
Fax: 615-217-9348
E-mail: pdemesa@draughons.edu
Admission Contact: Becky Day, Director of Admissions
Phone: 615-217-9347
Fax: 615-217-9348

E-mail: bmiller@draughons.edu

DRAUGHONS JUNIOR COLLEGE

340 Plus Park Boulevard
Nashville, TN 37217
Web: http://www.draughons.edu
Accreditation: Accrediting Council for Independent
Colleges and Schools
Programs Offered:
accounting; allied health and medical assisting services
related; business administration and management;
computer hardware engineering; computer/information
technology administration and management; computer
programming related; computer systems networking
and telecommunications; corrections; criminal jus-
tice/law enforcement administration; dental assisting;
dental hygiene; dental laboratory technology; dental
services and allied professions related; e-commerce;
electrocardiograph technology; information technology; legal assistant/paralegal; medical/clinical assistant;
medical transcription; pharmacy technician
Enrollment: 600 students
Institution Contact: Mr. Darrel E. Hanbury, Regional
Director of Admissions
Phone: 615-361-7555
Fax: 615-367-2736
E-mail: dhanbury@daymargroup.com

FOUNTAINHEAD COLLEGE OF TECHNOLOGY

3203 Tazewell Pike
Knoxville, TN 37918-2530
Web: http://www.fountainheadcollege.edu
Accreditation:
Accrediting Commission of Career Schools and Col-
leges of Technology
Programs Offered:
computer and information systems security; computer
programming; electrical, electronic and communica-
tions engineering technology; forensic science and
technology; information technology; technology man-
agement; web/multimedia management and webmaster
Enrollment: 153 students
Institution Contact: Mr. Richard Rackley, President
Phone: 865-688-9422
Fax: 865-688-2419
E-mail: info@fountainheadcollege.com
Admission Contact: Ms. Casey Rackley, Vice President

Phone: 865-688-9422
Fax: 865-688-2419
E-mail: admissions@fountainheadcollege.com

HIGH-TECH INSTITUTE

5865 Shelby Oaks Circle, Suite 100
Memphis, TN 38134
Accreditation: Accrediting Commission of Career
Schools and Colleges of Technology
Programs Offered:
massage therapy; medical/clinical assistant; medical
insurance/medical billing; surgical technology
Enrollment: 375 students
Institution Contact: Mr. Larry L. Collins, Campus
President
Phone: 901-432-3803
Fax: 901-387-1181
E-mail: cbaird@hightechinstitute.edu
Admission Contact: Ms. Cathy Baird, Director of
Admissions
Phone: 901-432-3803
Fax: 901-387-1181
E-mail: cbaird@hightechinstitute.edu

HIGH-TECH INSTITUTE

2710 Old Lebanon Road, Suite 12
Nashville, TN 37214
Web: http://www.high-techinstitute.com
Accreditation: Accrediting Commission of Career
Schools and Colleges of Technology
Programs Offered:
computer/information technology administration and
management; dental assisting; digital communication
and media/multimedia; massage therapy; medical/clin-
ical assistant; medical radiologic technology; surgical
technology
Institution Contact: Ms. Lisa Bacon, Campus President
Phone: 615-902-9705
Fax: 615-902-9766
E-mail: lbacon@hightechinstitute.edu
Admission Contact: Ms. Leslie Starks, Director of
Admissions
Phone: 615-902-9705
Fax: 615-902-9766
E-mail: lstarks@hightechinstitute.edu

INTERNATIONAL ACADEMY OF DESIGN AND TECHNOLOGY

One Bridgestone Park
Nashville, TN 37214
Web: http://www.iadtnashville.com
Accreditation: Accrediting Council for Independent Colleges and Schools
Programs Offered:
business administration and management; commercial and advertising art; computer graphics; computer systems networking and telecommunications; design and visual communications; fashion/apparel design; interior design
Enrollment: 315 students
Institution Contact: Mr. Richard D. Wechner, President
Phone: 615-232-7384
Fax: 615-883-5285
E-mail: rwechner@iadtnashville.com
Admission Contact: Mr. Kevin McNeil, Vice President of Admissions
Phone: 615-232-7384
Fax: 615-883-5285
E-mail: kmcneil@iadtnashville.com

ITT TECHNICAL INSTITUTE

10208 Technology Drive
Knoxville, TN 37932
Web: http://www.itt-tech.edu
Accreditation: Accrediting Council for Independent Colleges and Schools
Programs Offered:
CAD/CADD drafting/design technology; communications technology; computer and information systems security; computer engineering technology; computer software and media applications; computer systems networking and telecommunications; digital communication and media/multimedia; electrical, electronic and communications engineering technology; technology management; web page, digital/multimedia and information resources design
Institution Contact: Mr. David Reynolds, Director
Phone: 865-671-2800
Admission Contact: Mr. Mike Burke, Director of Recruitment
Phone: 865-671-2800

ITT TECHNICAL INSTITUTE

1255 Lynnfield Road, Suite 192
Memphis, TN 38119
Web: http://www.itt-tech.edu
Accreditation: Accrediting Council for Independent Colleges and Schools
Programs Offered:
accounting and business/management; animation, interactive technology, video graphics and special effects; business administration and management; CAD/CADD drafting/design technology; communications technology; computer and information systems security; computer engineering technology; computer software and media applications; computer software engineering; computer systems networking and telecommunications; criminal justice/police science; digital communication and media/multimedia; electrical, electronic and communications engineering technology; technology management; web page, digital/multimedia and information resources design
Institution Contact: Ms. Melinda Jo Catron, Director
Phone: 901-762-0556 ext. 101
Admission Contact: Mr. James R. Mills, Director of Recruitment
Phone: 901-762-0556

ITT TECHNICAL INSTITUTE

2845 Elm Hill Pike
Nashville, TN 37214-3717
Web: http://www.itt-tech.edu
Accreditation: Accrediting Council for Independent Colleges and Schools
Programs Offered:
accounting and business/management; animation, interactive technology, video graphics and special effects; business administration and management; CAD/CADD drafting/design technology; communications technology; computer and information systems security; computer engineering technology; computer software and media applications; computer software engineering; computer systems networking and telecommunications; criminal justice/police science; digital communication and media/multimedia; electrical, electronic and communications engineering technology; technology management; web page, digital/multimedia and information resources design
Institution Contact: Mr. James Coakley, Director
Phone: 615-889-8700

Admission Contact: Mr. James Royster, Director of Recruitment
Phone: 615-889-8700

MEDVANCE INSTITUTE

1025 Highway 111
Cookeville, TN 38501
Web: http://www.medvance.org
Accreditation: Council on Occupational Education
Programs Offered:
clinical/medical laboratory technology; medical administrative assistant and medical secretary; medical/clinical assistant; medical insurance coding; medical office assistant; pharmacy technician; radiologic technology/science; surgical technology
Enrollment: 242 students
Institution Contact: Mrs. Darla Roberts, Director of Academic Affairs
Phone: 931-526-3660 ext. 238
Fax: 931-526-5415
E-mail: droberts@medvance.org
Admission Contact: Mr. Scotty Woods, Director of Admissions
Phone: 931-526-3660 ext. 223
Fax: 931-372-2603
E-mail: swoods@medvance.org

MILLER-MOTTE TECHNICAL COLLEGE

6020 Shallowford Road
Chattanooga, TN 37421
Web: http://www.miller-motte.com
Accreditation: Accrediting Council for Independent Colleges and Schools
Programs Offered:
business administration and management; cosmetology; criminal justice/law enforcement administration; massage therapy; medical/clinical assistant; surgical technology
Enrollment: 428 students
Institution Contact: Ms. June O. Kearns, Executive Director
Phone: 423-510-9675 ext. 200
Fax: 423-510-9675
E-mail: jkearns@miller-motte.com

MILLER-MOTTE TECHNICAL COLLEGE

1820 Business Park Drive
Clarksville, TN 37040
Web: http://www.miller-motte.com
Accreditation: Accrediting Council for Independent Colleges and Schools
Programs Offered:
administrative assistant and secretarial science; business administration and management; electrician; legal assistant/paralegal; massage therapy; medical/clinical assistant
Phone: 800-558-0071

NASHVILLE AUTO DIESEL COLLEGE

1524 Gallatin Road
Nashville, TN 37206
Web: http://www.nadcedu.com
Accreditation: Accrediting Commission of Career Schools and Colleges of Technology
Programs Offered:
autobody/collision and repair technology; automobile/automotive mechanics technology; diesel mechanics technology
Institution Contact: Executive Director
Phone: 615-226-3990
Fax: 615-262-8466
E-mail: execdirnashville@lincolntech.com

NATIONAL COLLEGE OF BUSINESS & TECHNOLOGY

1328 Hwy 11 W
Bristol, TN 37620
Web: http://www.ncbt.edu
Accreditation: Accrediting Council for Independent Colleges and Schools
Programs Offered:
accounting; administrative assistant and secretarial science; business administration and management; computer/information technology services administration related; medical/clinical assistant; medical insurance coding; medical transcription
Institution Contact: Admissions Department
Phone: 540-669-5333
Fax: 540-669-4793
Admission Contact: Anna Counts, Admissions Department
Phone: 540-669-5333
Fax: 540-669-4793

 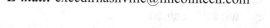

E-mail: acounts@ncbt.edu

NATIONAL COLLEGE OF BUSINESS & TECHNOLOGY

8415 Kingston Pike
Knoxville, TN 37919
Web: http://www.ncbt.edu
Accreditation: Accrediting Council for Independent Colleges and Schools
Programs Offered:
accounting; business administration and management; medical/clinical assistant
Institution Contact: Admissions Department
Phone: 865-539-2011
Fax: 865-824-2778

NATIONAL COLLEGE OF BUSINESS & TECHNOLOGY

3748 Nolensville Pike
Nashville, TN 37211
Web: http://www.ncbt.edu
Accreditation: Accrediting Council for Independent Colleges and Schools
Programs Offered:
business administration and management; computer software and media applications; medical/clinical assistant; office management
Institution Contact: Admissions Department
Phone: 615-333-3344
Fax: 615-333-3429

REMINGTON COLLEGE - MEMPHIS CAMPUS

2731 Nonconnah Boulevard
Memphis, TN 38132-2199
Web: http://www.remingtoncollege.edu
Accreditation: Accrediting Commission of Career Schools and Colleges of Technology
Programs Offered:
computer/information technology administration and management; criminal justice/law enforcement administration; electrical, electronic and communications engineering technology; information technology; medical/clinical assistant; operations management; pharmacy technician; system, networking, and LAN/WAN management
Enrollment: 650 students
Institution Contact: Dr. Lori May, Campus President
Phone: 901-291-4225
Fax: 901-396-8310

E-mail: lori.may@remingtoncollege.edu
Admission Contact: Mr. Preston King, Director of Recruitment
Phone: 901-345-1000
Fax: 901-396-8310
E-mail: preston.king@remingtoncollege.edu

REMINGTON COLLEGE - NASHVILLE CAMPUS

441 Donelson Pike, Suite 150
Nashville, TN 37214
Web: http://www.remingtoncollege.edu
Accreditation: Accrediting Commission of Career Schools and Colleges of Technology
Programs Offered:
computer/information technology services administration related; criminal justice/law enforcement administration; dental assisting; medical administrative assistant and medical secretary; pharmacy technician
Enrollment: 300 students
Institution Contact: Ms. Barbara Holliman, Campus President
Phone: 615-889-5520
Fax: 615-889-5528
E-mail: barbara.holliman@remingtoncollege.edu
Admission Contact: Mr. Ken F. Reynolds, Director of Recruitment
Phone: 615-889-5520
Fax: 615-493-9385
E-mail: ken.reynolds@remingtoncollege.edu

SOUTH COLLEGE

200 Hayfield Road
Knoxville, TN 37922
Web: http://www.southcollegetn.edu
Accreditation: Southern Association of Colleges and Schools
Programs Offered:
accounting; administrative assistant and secretarial science; business administration and management; computer software and media applications related; computer systems networking and telecommunications; criminal justice/law enforcement administration; data entry/microcomputer applications; elementary education; legal administrative assistant/secretary; legal assistant/paralegal; medical/clinical assistant; medical insurance/medical billing; medical transcription; nursing (registered nurse training); occupational

therapist assistant; physical therapist assistant; radiologic technology/science; system, networking, and LAN/WAN management

Enrollment: 625 students

Institution Contact: Mr. Stephen A. South, President

Phone: 865-251-1800

Fax: 865-470-8730

E-mail: ssouth@southcollegetn.edu

Admission Contact: Mr. Walter Hosea, Director of Admissions

Phone: 865-251-1800

Fax: 865-470-8737

E-mail: whosea@southcollegetn.edu

SOUTHEASTERN CAREER COLLEGE

2416 21st Avenue South, Suite 300

Nashville, TN 37212

Web: http://www.southeasterncareercollege.com

Accreditation: Council on Occupational Education

Programs Offered:

criminal justice/law enforcement administration; legal assistant/paralegal; medical/clinical assistant

Enrollment: 275 students

Institution Contact: Ms. Donna M. Clarkin, Executive Director

Phone: 615-269-9900 ext. 14

Fax: 615-297-6678

E-mail: dclarkin@southeasterncareercollege.com

Admission Contact: Ms. Kimberly A. Marino, Director of Admissions

Phone: 615-269-9900 ext. 12

Fax: 615-297-6678

E-mail: kmarino@southeasterncareercollege.com

VATTEROTT COLLEGE

6152 Macon Road

Memphis, TN 38134

Web: http://www.vatterott-college.edu

Accreditation: Accrediting Commission of Career Schools and Colleges of Technology

Programs Offered:

computer technology/computer systems technology; electrician; heating, air conditioning, ventilation and refrigeration maintenance technology; medical/clinical assistant

Enrollment: 225 students

Institution Contact: Ms. Victoria Talley, Director

Phone: 901-761-5730

Fax: 901-763-2897

E-mail: victoria.talley@vatterott-college.edu

Admission Contact: Mr. Ray Hughes, Director of Admissions

Phone: 901-761-5730

Fax: 901-763-2897

E-mail: alphonso.hughes@vatterott-college.edu

WEST TENNESSEE BUSINESS COLLEGE

1186 Highway 45 Bypass

Jackson, TN 38301

Web: http://www.wtbc.com

Accreditation: Accrediting Council for Independent Colleges and Schools

Programs Offered:

administrative assistant and secretarial science; aesthetician/esthetician and skin care; cosmetology; medical administrative assistant and medical secretary; medical/clinical assistant; medical office computer specialist; nail technician and manicurist; office occupations and clerical services

Enrollment: 325 students

Institution Contact: Mrs. Charlotte Burch, President

Phone: 731-668-7240

Fax: 731-668-3824

E-mail: cvburch@wtbc.com

Admission Contact: Miss Ann Record, Director of Admissions

Phone: 731-668-7240

Fax: 731-668-3824

E-mail: arecord@wtbc.com

TEXAS

AMERICAN COMMERCIAL COLLEGE

402 Butternut Street

Abilene, TX 79602

Web: http://www.acc-careers.com

Accreditation: Accrediting Council for Independent Colleges and Schools

Programs Offered:

accounting; administrative assistant and secretarial science; CAD/CADD drafting/design technology; data processing and data processing technology; executive assistant/executive secretary; health information/medi-

cal records administration; medical administrative assistant and medical secretary; medical transcription; office occupations and clerical services; receptionist; word processing
Enrollment: 160 students
Institution Contact: Mr. Tony Delgado, Director
Phone: 325-672-8495
Fax: 325-672-8497
E-mail: tdelgado@acc-careers.com
Admission Contact: Mr. Tony Delgado, Director
Phone: 325-672-8495
Fax: 325-672-8497
E-mail: tdelgado@acc-careers.com

AMERICAN COMMERCIAL COLLEGE

2007 34th Street
Lubbock, TX 79411
Web: http://www.acc-careers.com
Accreditation: Accrediting Council for Independent Colleges and Schools
Programs Offered:
accounting; administrative assistant and secretarial science; business administration and management; computer technology/computer systems technology; data entry/microcomputer applications; electrical/electronics equipment installation and repair; medical administrative assistant and medical secretary; medical/clinical assistant; medical transcription
Enrollment: 125 students
Institution Contact: Mr. Michael J. Otto, Director
Phone: 806-747-4339
Fax: 806-765-9838
E-mail: mjotto@acc-careers.com

AMERICAN COMMERCIAL COLLEGE

2115 East 8th Street
Odessa, TX 76904
Web: http://www.acc-careers.com
Programs Offered:
accounting; administrative assistant and secretarial science; CAD/CADD drafting/design technology; data entry/microcomputer applications; information technology; legal administrative assistant/secretary; medical administrative assistant and medical secretary; medical transcription
Institution Contact:
Phone: 915-332-0768

AMERICAN COMMERCIAL COLLEGE

3177 Executive Drive
San Angelo, TX 76904
Web: http://www.acc-careers.com
Accreditation: Accrediting Council for Independent Colleges and Schools
Programs Offered:
accounting; administrative assistant and secretarial science; business administration and management; business machine repair; computer/information technology services administration related; computer systems networking and telecommunications; drafting and design technology; information technology; legal administrative assistant/secretary; medical administrative assistant and medical secretary; medical office management; medical transcription; office occupations and clerical services; receptionist; system administration; system, networking, and LAN/WAN management
Institution Contact: Mr. B. A. Reed, Director
Phone: 915-942-6797
Fax: 915-949-2330
E-mail: bareed@acc-careers.com

AMERICAN INTERCONTINENTAL UNIVERSITY

9999 Richmond Avenue
Houston, TX 77042
Web: http://www.aiuhouston.com
Accreditation: Southern Association of Colleges and Schools
Programs Offered:
business administration and management; commercial and advertising art; digital communication and media/multimedia; education; information technology
Enrollment: 505 students
Institution Contact: Mr. Randall K. Sheets, President
Phone: 832-201-3626
Fax: 832-201-3633
E-mail: rsheets@aiuhouston.com
Admission Contact: Ms. Maggie Balderas, Vice President of Admissions
Phone: 832-201-3600
Fax: 832-201-3637
E-mail: mbalderas@aiuhouston.com

AMERICAN INTERCONTINENTAL UNIVERSITY

4511 Horizon Hill Blvd
San Antonio, TX 78229-2263

Institution Contact: Mr. Jim Yeaman
Phone: 210-530-9449
Fax: 210-530-9463

AMERICAN SCHOOL OF BUSINESS

4317 Barnett Road
Wichita Falls, TX 76310
Web: http://www.acc-careers.com
Accreditation: Accrediting Council for Independent
Colleges and Schools
Programs Offered:
accounting; administrative assistant and secretarial
science; business automation/technology/data entry;
computer systems networking and telecommunica-
tions; executive assistant/executive secretary; health
information/medical records administration; medical
administrative assistant and medical secretary; medi-
cal/clinical assistant; medical office assistant; medical
reception; medical transcription; word processing
Enrollment: 138 students
Institution Contact: Mr. Don Dobbins, Director
Phone: 940-691-0454
Fax: 940-691-0470
E-mail: ddobbins@acc-careers.com

ARGOSY UNIVERSITY/DALLAS

8080 Park Lane, Suite 400-A
Dallas, TX 75231
Web: http://www.argosyu.edu
Enrollment: 387 students
Institution Contact: Mrs. Kara J. Smith, Director of
Admissions
Phone: 214-890-9900
Fax: 214-378-8555
E-mail: kasmith@argosyu.edu

THE ART INSTITUTE OF DALLAS

2 North Park East, 8080 Park Lane, Suite 100
Dallas, TX 75231-9959
Web: http://www.aid.edu
Accreditation: Southern Association of Colleges and
Schools
Programs Offered:
art; commercial and advertising art; culinary arts;
design and visual communications; fashion/apparel
design; interior design; web page, digital/multimedia

and information resources design
Enrollment: 1,460 students
Institution Contact: Mr. Paul McGuirk, President
Phone: 800-275-4243 ext. 1173
Fax: 214-696-4898
E-mail: mcguirkp@aii.edu
Admission Contact: Mr. Keith Petovello, Director of
Admissions
Phone: 800-275-4243 ext. 1184
Fax: 214-754-9460
E-mail: petovelk@aii.edu

THE ART INSTITUTE OF HOUSTON

1900 Yorktown
Houston, TX 77056
Web: http://www.aih.artinstitutes.edu
Accreditation: Southern Association of Colleges and
Schools
Programs Offered:
applied art; baking and pastry arts; commercial and ad-
vertising art; computer graphics; computer software and
media applications; culinary arts; interior design; res-
taurant, culinary, and catering management; web page,
digital/multimedia and information resources design
Enrollment: 1,568 students
Institution Contact: Mr. Larry Horn, President
Phone: 713-623-2040 ext. 4136
Fax: 713-966-2700
E-mail: lhorn@aii.edu
Admission Contact: Mr. Brian Shumaker, Director of
Admissions
Phone: 800-275-4244
Fax: 713-966-2792
E-mail: bshumaker@aii.edu

ATI CAREER TRAINING CENTER

10003 Technology Boulevard West
Dallas, TX 75220
Web: http://www.aticareertraining.edu
Accreditation: Accrediting Commission of Career
Schools and Colleges of Technology
Programs Offered:
business administration and management; business
automation/technology/data entry; CAD/CADD draft-
ing/design technology; commercial and advertising art;
dental assisting; electrical, electronic and communications engineering technology; information technology;

massage therapy; medical/clinical assistant; respiratory care therapy
Enrollment: 800 students
Institution Contact: Mr. Gerald Parr, Director
Phone: 214-902-8191
Fax: 214-358-7500
E-mail: gparr@atienterprises.edu
Admission Contact: Mr. Stephen brewster, Director of Admissions
Phone: 214-902-8191
Fax: 214-358-7500
E-mail: sbrewster@atienterprises.edu

ATI CAREER TRAINING CENTER
6351 Grapevine Highway, Suite 100
North Richland Hills, TX 76180
Web: http://www.aticareertraining.edu
Accreditation: Accrediting Commission of Career Schools and Colleges of Technology
Programs Offered:
administrative assistant and secretarial science; automobile/automotive mechanics technology; business automation/technology/data entry; commercial and advertising art; computer technology/computer systems technology; dental assisting; electrical, electronic and communications engineering technology; information technology; massage therapy; medical/clinical assistant
Enrollment: 520 students
Institution Contact: Mr. Joe P. Mehlmann, Executive Director
Phone: 817-284-1141
Fax: 817-284-2107
E-mail: jpmehlmann@atienterprises.edu
Admission Contact: Director of Admissions
Phone: 817-284-1141
Fax: 817-284-2107

ATI TECHNICAL TRAINING CENTER
6627 Maple Avenue
Dallas, TX 75235-4623
Web: http://www.aticareertraining.com
Accreditation: Accrediting Commission of Career Schools and Colleges of Technology
Programs Offered:
automobile/automotive mechanics technology; heating, air conditioning and refrigeration technology; welding technology

Enrollment: 550 students
Institution Contact: Mr. Darrell E. Testerman, Executive Director
Phone: 214-352-2222 ext. 107
Fax: 214-350-3951
E-mail: d.testerman@atienterprises.edu
Admission Contact: Mr. Carlo Demanero, Director of Admissions
Phone: 214-352-2222 ext. 104
Fax: 214-350-3951
E-mail: cdemanero@atienterprises.edu

AUSTIN BUSINESS COLLEGE
2101 South IH 35, Suite 300
Austin, TX 78741
Web: http://www.austinbusinesscollege.org
Accreditation: Accrediting Council for Independent Colleges and Schools
Programs Offered:
accounting; accounting technology and bookkeeping; administrative assistant and secretarial science; business automation/technology/data entry; data entry/microcomputer applications; executive assistant/executive secretary; health information/medical records administration; health information/medical records technology; legal administrative assistant/secretary; legal assistant/paralegal; medical administrative assistant and medical secretary; medical office management; medical reception; receptionist; word processing
Institution Contact: Mr. Paul Ellis, President
Phone: 512-447-9415
Fax: 512-447-0194
E-mail: pellis@austinbusinesscollege.org
Admission Contact: Ms. Pam Binns, Director of Admissions
Phone: 512-447-9415
Fax: 512-447-0194
E-mail: pambinns@austinbusinesscollege.org

BRADFORD SCHOOL OF BUSINESS
4669 Southwest Freeway, Suite 300
Houston, TX 77027-7150
Web: http://www.BradfordSchoolHouston.edu
Accreditation: Accrediting Council for Independent Colleges and Schools
Programs Offered:
accounting; administrative assistant and secretarial

science; graphic communications; legal administrative assistant/secretary; medical administrative assistant and medical secretary; medical/clinical assistant
Enrollment: 200 students
Institution Contact: Mr. Robert Puig, Director/Chief Academic Officer
Phone: 713-629-1500
Fax: 713-629-0059
E-mail: rpuig@bradfordschoolhouston.edu
Admission Contact: Mr. Ken Hudspeth, Director of Admissions
Phone: 713-629-1500
Fax: 713-629-0059
E-mail: khudspeth@bradfordschoolhouston.edu

Brown Mackie College, Dallas Campus

1500 Eastgate Drive
Garland, TX 75041
Web: http://www.texasinstitute.com/
Programs Offered:
business administration and management; computer and information sciences related; pre-law studies
Institution Contact:
Phone: 888-300-9346

Brown Mackie College, Fort Worth Campus

301 Northeast Loop 820
Hurst, TX 76053
Accreditation: Accrediting Council for Independent Colleges and Schools
Programs Offered:
accounting and business/management; legal assistant/paralegal; medical/clinical assistant
Institution Contact: Miss Trudy LoMonaco, Campus President
Phone: 817-589-0505
Fax: 817-595-2595
E-mail: tlomonaco@brownmackie.edu
Phone: 817-589-0505
Fax: 817-595-2595

Career Centers of Texas

8360 Burnham Road, Suite 100
El Paso, TX 79907
Web: http://www.careercenters.edu
Accreditation: Accrediting Commission of Career

Schools and Colleges of Technology
Programs Offered:
administrative assistant and secretarial science; dental assisting; electrician; medical/clinical assistant; medical insurance/medical billing; medical office management; pharmacy technician; surgical technology; traffic, customs, and transportation clerk
Enrollment: 725 students
Institution Contact: Ms. Sally Crickard, President
Phone: 915-595-1935 ext. 122
Fax: 915-595-6619
E-mail: scrickard@cct-ep.com
Admission Contact: Ms. Cecy Moreno, Director of Admissions
Phone: 915-595-1935 ext. 124
Fax: 915-595-6619
E-mail: cmoreno@cct-ep.com

Career Point Business School

485 Spencer Lane
San Antonio, TX 78201
Web: http://www.career-point.org
Accreditation: Accrediting Council for Independent Colleges and Schools
Programs Offered:
accounting; administrative assistant and secretarial science; computer systems networking and telecommunications; legal assistant/paralegal; medical administrative assistant and medical secretary; medical/clinical assistant; medical office management; office occupations and clerical services
Enrollment: 875 students
Institution Contact: Ms. Adrienne Divin, Director
Phone: 210-732-3000 ext. 288
Fax: 210-734-9225
E-mail: sdirector@career-point.org
Admission Contact: Mr. David Murguia, Admissions/Marketing
Phone: 210-732-3000 ext. 224
Fax: 210-734-9225

Career Quest

5430 Fredericksburg Road, Suite 310
San Antonio, TX 78229
Institution Contact:
Phone: 210-366-2701

COURT REPORTING INSTITUTE OF DALLAS

8585 North Stemmons Freeway, Suite 200N
Dallas, TX 75247-3821
Web: http://www.crid.com
Accreditation: Accrediting Council for Independent Colleges and Schools
Programs Offered:
court reporting
Enrollment: 700 students
Institution Contact: Mr. Eric S. Juhlin, President
Phone: 214-350-9722
Fax: 214-631-0143
E-mail: ejuhlin@crid.com
Admission Contact: Mrs. Debra Smith-Armstrong, Admissions Director
Phone: 214-350-9722
Fax: 214-631-0143
E-mail: darmstrong@crid.com

COURT REPORTING INSTITUTE OF HOUSTON

13101 Northwest Freeway, Suite 100
Houston, TX 77040
Web: http://www.crid.com
Accreditation: Accrediting Council for Independent Colleges and Schools
Programs Offered:
court reporting
Enrollment: 425 students
Institution Contact: Ms. Cindy Smith, Director
Phone: 713-996-8300
Fax: 713-996-8360
E-mail: csmith@crid.com

EVEREST COLLEGE

2801 East Division Street, Suite 250
Arlington , TX 76011
Web: http://www.everest-college.com
Accreditation: Accrediting Council for Independent Colleges and Schools
Programs Offered:
business administration and management; criminal justice/law enforcement administration; medical/clinical assistant; medical insurance coding; medical insurance/medical billing; pharmacy technician
Enrollment: 500 students
Institution Contact: Bruce J. Schlee, Director of Admissions

Phone: 817-652-7790
Fax: 817-649-6033
E-mail: bschlee@cci.edu

EVEREST COLLEGE

6060 North Central Expressway, Suite 101
Dallas, TX 75206
Web: http://www.everest-college.com
Accreditation: Accrediting Council for Independent Colleges and Schools
Programs Offered:
business administration and management; criminal justice/law enforcement administration; legal assistant/paralegal; medical/clinical assistant; medical insurance/medical billing
Enrollment: 905 students
Institution Contact: Mrs. Darla P Chin, Campus President
Phone: 214-234-4850
Fax: 504-696-6208
E-mail: dchin@cci.edu
Admission Contact: Mr. Brian Bassham, Admissions Manager
Phone: 214-234-4850
Fax: 214-696-6208
E-mail: bbassham@cci.edu

EVEREST COLLEGE

5237 North Riverside Drive, Suite G101
Fort Worth, TX 76137
Programs Offered:
business administration and management; medical/clinical assistant

HALLMARK INSTITUTE OF AERONAUTICS

10401 IH-10 West
San Antonio, TX 78230
Accreditation: Accrediting Commission of Career Schools and Colleges of Technology
Programs Offered:
aircraft powerplant technology; airframe mechanics and aircraft maintenance technology; avionics maintenance technology
Enrollment: 166 students
Institution Contact: Mr. Joe Fisher, President
Phone: 210-690-9000 ext. 244

Fax: 210-697-8225
E-mail: jfisher@hallmarkinstitute.com
Admission Contact: Mrs. Sonia Ross, Vice President of Admissions
Phone: 210-690-9000 ext. 212
Fax: 210-697-8225
E-mail: sross@hallmarkinstitute.com

HALLMARK INSTITUTE OF TECHNOLOGY

10401 IH-10 West
San Antonio, TX 78230
Web: http://www.hallmarkinstitute.com
Accreditation: Accrediting Commission of Career Schools and Colleges of Technology
Programs Offered:
business administration and management; computer technology/computer systems technology; electrical, electronic and communications engineering technology; medical administrative assistant and medical secretary; medical/clinical assistant
Enrollment: 359 students
Institution Contact: Mr. Joe Fisher, President
Phone: 210-690-9000 ext. 244
Fax: 210-697-8225
E-mail: jfisher@hallmarkinstitute.com
Admission Contact: Mrs. Sonia Ross, Vice President of Admissions
Phone: 210-690-9000 ext. 212
Fax: 210-697-8225
E-mail: sross@hallmarkinstitute.com

HIGH-TECH INSTITUTE

4250 North Beltline Road
Irving, TX 75038
Web: http://www.high-techinstitute.com
Accreditation: Accrediting Commission of Career Schools and Colleges of Technology
Programs Offered:
computer systems networking and telecommunications; criminal justice/law enforcement administration; massage therapy; medical/clinical assistant; medical insurance/medical billing; pharmacy technician; surgical technology
Enrollment: 725 students
Institution Contact: Mrs. Claudia A. Stapleton, Campus Director
Phone: 972-871-2824

Fax: 972-871-2860
E-mail: cstapleton@hightechschools.com
Admission Contact: Ms. Juanita Donahue, Director of Admissions
Phone: 972-871-2824
Fax: 972-871-2860
E-mail: jdonahue@hightechschools.com

INTERNATIONAL ACADEMY OF DESIGN AND TECHNOLOGY

4511 Horizon Hill Boulevard
San Antonio, TX 78229
Web: http://www.aiusanantonio.com
Programs Offered:
business, management, and marketing related; fashion/apparel design; graphic communications; health/health care administration; human resources management; information resources management; information technology
Institution Contact: Dr. Alan Stutts, President
Phone: 210-530-9449
Fax: 210-530-9463
E-mail: astutts@aiusanantonio.com
Admission Contact: Mr. Kenneth Thomas, Vice President, Marketing and Admissions
Phone: 210-530-9449
Fax: 210-530-9463
E-mail: kthomas@aiusanantonio.com

INTERNATIONAL BUSINESS COLLEGE

5700 Cromo
El Paso, TX 79912
Web: http://www.ibcelpaso.edu
Accreditation: Accrediting Council for Independent Colleges and Schools
Programs Offered:
accounting; administrative assistant and secretarial science; business administration and management; legal administrative assistant/secretary; medical administrative assistant and medical secretary; medical/clinical assistant; medical insurance/medical billing
Enrollment: 470 students
Institution Contact: Mr. Bob Aguirre, Director
Phone: 915-842-0422
Fax: 915-585-2584
E-mail: bob.aguirre@ibcelpaso.edu
Admission Contact: Mr. Steve Shanabarger, Director of Admissions

Phone: 915-284-0422
Fax: 915-585-2584
E-mail: ateve.shanabarger@ibcelpaso.edu

INTERNATIONAL BUSINESS COLLEGE
1155 North Zaragosa, Suite 100
El Paso, TX 79907-1806
Web: http://www.ibcelpaso.edu
Accreditation: Accrediting Council for Independent
Colleges and Schools
Programs Offered:
accounting; administrative assistant and secretarial
science; business administration, management and op-
erations related; business automation/technology/data
entry; legal administrative assistant/secretary; medical
administrative assistant and medical secretary; medi-
cal/clinical assistant; medical insurance/medical billing
Enrollment: 668 students
Institution Contact: Mr. Don Chittenden, Director
Phone: 915-859-3986
Fax: 915-859-4142
E-mail: donald.chittenden@ibcelpaso.edu
Admission Contact: Mr. Ernest Pettengill, Admis-
sions Representative
Phone: 915-859-3986
Fax: 915-859-4142
E-mail: ernest.pettengill@ibcelpaso.edu

ITT TECHNICAL INSTITUTE
551 Ryan Plaza Drive
Arlington, TX 76011
Web: http://www.itt-tech.edu
Accreditation: Accrediting Council for Independent
Colleges and Schools
Programs Offered:
CAD/CADD drafting/design technology; computer
engineering technology; computer software and
media applications; computer systems networking
and telecommunications; digital communication and
media/multimedia; web page, digital/multimedia and
information resources design
Institution Contact: Ms. Paulette Gallerson, Director
Phone: 817-794-5100
Admission Contact: Mr. Edward Leal, Director of
Recruitment
Phone: 817-794-5100

ITT TECHNICAL INSTITUTE
6330 Highway 290 East, Suite 150
Austin, TX 78723-1061
Web: http://www.itt-tech.edu
Accreditation: Accrediting Council for Independent
Colleges and Schools
Programs Offered:
CAD/CADD drafting/design technology; computer
engineering technology; computer software and
media applications; computer systems networking
and telecommunications; digital communication and
media/multimedia; web page, digital/multimedia and
information resources design
Institution Contact: Ms. Barbara Anthony , Director
Phone: 512-467-6800
Admission Contact: Mr. Jim Branham, Director of
Recruitment
Phone: 512-467-6800

ITT TECHNICAL INSTITUTE
15621 Blue Ash Drive, Suite 160
Houston, TX 77090-5821
Web: http://www.itt-tech.edu
Accreditation: Accrediting Council for Independent
Colleges and Schools
Programs Offered:
CAD/CADD drafting/design technology; computer
engineering technology; computer software and
media applications; computer systems networking
and telecommunications; digital communication and
media/multimedia; web page, digital/multimedia and
information resources design
Institution Contact: Mr. David Champlin, Director
Phone: 281-873-0512
Admission Contact: Mr. Benjamin Moore, Director
of Recruitment
Phone: 281-873-0512

ITT TECHNICAL INSTITUTE
2222 Bay Area Boulevard
Houston, TX 77058
Web: http://www.itt-tech.edu
Accreditation: Accrediting Council for Independent
Colleges and Schools
Programs Offered:
CAD/CADD drafting/design technology; computer
engineering technology; computer software and

media applications; computer systems networking and telecommunications; digital communication and media/multimedia; web page, digital/multimedia and information resources design
Institution Contact: Mr. Robert Jeffords, Director
Phone: 281-486-2630
Admission Contact: Mr. Derrick Sutton, Director of Recruitment
Phone: 281-486-2630

 ITT TECHNICAL INSTITUTE
2950 South Gessner Road
Houston, TX 77063-3751
Web: http://www.itt-tech.edu
Accreditation: Accrediting Council for Independent Colleges and Schools
Programs Offered:
CAD/CADD drafting/design technology; computer engineering technology; computer software and media applications; computer systems networking and telecommunications; digital communication and media/multimedia; web page, digital/multimedia and information resources design
Institution Contact: Mr. Robert Van Elsen, Director
Phone: 713-952-2294
Admission Contact: Mr. Johnny Jackson, Director of Recruitment
Phone: 713-952-2294

ITT TECHNICAL INSTITUTE
2101 Waterview Parkway
Richardson, TX 75080
Web: http://www.itt-tech.edu
Accreditation: Accrediting Council for Independent Colleges and Schools
Programs Offered:
CAD/CADD drafting/design technology; computer engineering technology; computer software and media applications; computer systems networking and tele-communications; digital communication and media/multimedia; electrical, electronic and communications engineering technology; web page, digital/multimedia and information resources design
Institution Contact: Ms. Maureen Clements, Director
Phone: 972-690-9100
Admission Contact: Mr. Nate Wallace, Director of Recruitment

Phone: 972-690-9100

ITT TECHNICAL INSTITUTE
5700 Northwest Parkway
San Antonio, TX 78249-3303
Web: http://www.itt-tech.edu
Accreditation: Accrediting Council for Independent Colleges and Schools
Programs Offered:
CAD/CADD drafting/design technology; computer engineering technology; computer software and media applications; computer systems networking and telecommunications; digital communication and media/multimedia; web page, digital/multimedia and information resources design
Institution Contact: Mr. Stephen Marks, Director
Phone: 210-694-4612
Admission Contact: Mr. Buddy Hoyt, Director of Recruitment
Phone: 210-694-4612

LINCOLN TECHNICAL INSTITUTE
2501 East Arkansas Lane
Grand Prairie, TX 75052
Web: http://www.lincolntech.com
Accreditation: Accrediting Commission of Career Schools and Colleges of Technology
Programs Offered:
automobile/automotive mechanics technology; automotive engineering technology; diesel mechanics technology; heating, air conditioning and refrigeration technology; heating, air conditioning, ventilation and refrigeration maintenance technology
Enrollment: 1,200 students
Institution Contact: Mr. A. Michael Rowan, Executive Director
Phone: 972-660-5701
Fax: 972-660-6148
E-mail: mrowan@lincolntech.com
Admission Contact: Mr. Charles Darling, Director of High School Admission
Phone: 972-660-5701
Fax: 972-660-6148
E-mail: cdarling@lincolntech.com

indicates a participating institution in the *Imagine America* Scholarship Program. **MAP** indicates a participating institution in the Military Award Program.

MEDVANCE INSTITUTE
6220 Westpark, Suite 180
Houston, TX 77057
Web: http://www.medvance.edu
Programs Offered:
medical/clinical assistant; medical insurance/medical billing; pharmacy technician; radiologic technology/science; surgical technology
Institution Contact: Mr. Scott Jay Cotlar, Campus Director
Phone: 713-266-6594
Fax: 713-782-5873
E-mail: scotlar@medvance.org
Admission Contact: Ms. Sonya Sanders, Director of Admissions
Phone: 713-266-6594 ext. 226
Fax: 713-782-5873
E-mail: ssanders@medvance.edu

MTI COLLEGE OF BUSINESS AND TECHNOLOGY
11420 East Freeway
Houston, TX 77029
Web: http://www.mti.edu
Accreditation: Accrediting Commission of Career Schools and Colleges of Technology
Programs Offered:
administrative assistant and secretarial science; business automation/technology/data entry; English as a second language; health information/medical records administration; health information/medical records technology; medical administrative assistant and medical secretary; medical insurance coding; medical office computer specialist; medical reception; office occupations and clerical services; receptionist; word processing
Enrollment: 240 students
Institution Contact: Mr. Ed Kessing, Director
Phone: 713-979-1800
Fax: 713-979-1818
E-mail: ed@mti.edu

MTI COLLEGE OF BUSINESS AND TECHNOLOGY
1275 Space Park Drive, Suite 100
Houston, TX 77058
Web: http://www.mti.edu
Accreditation: Accrediting Commission of Career Schools and Colleges of Technology
Programs Offered:

accounting; accounting technology and bookkeeping; administrative assistant and secretarial science; business administration and management; business automation/technology/data entry; computer and information systems security; computer engineering technology; computer/information technology administration and management; computer/information technology services administration related; computer installation and repair technology; computer systems analysis; computer systems networking and telecommunications; computer/technical support; computer technology/computer systems technology; English as a second language; executive assistant/executive secretary; health information/medical records administration; information science/studies; instrumentation technology; medical administrative assistant and medical secretary; medical insurance coding; medical insurance/medical billing; medical office computer specialist; medical office management; medical reception; medical transcription; office occupations and clerical services; receptionist; system administration; system, networking, and LAN/WAN management; web page, digital/multimedia and information resources design; word processing
Enrollment: 162 students
Institution Contact: Mr. John Springhetti, Director
Phone: 281-333-3363
Fax: 281-333-9281 E-mail: john@mti.edu
Admission Contact: Mr. Raoul Navarro, Admissions Director
Phone: 281-333-3363
Fax: 281-333-4118
E-mail: raouln@mti.edu

MTI COLLEGE OF BUSINESS AND TECHNOLOGY
7277 Regency Square Boulevard
Houston, TX 77036-3163
Web: http://www.mti.edu
Accreditation: Accrediting Commission of Career Schools and Colleges of Technology
Programs Offered:
accounting; administrative assistant and secretarial science; business administration and management; business automation/technology/data entry; computer/information technology services administration related; computer installation and repair technology; computer systems analysis; computer systems networking and telecommunications; computer/technical support;

computer technology/computer systems technology; electrical, electronic and communications engineering technology; English as a second language; health information/medical records administration; information science/studies; instrumentation technology; international business/trade/commerce; medical administrative assistant and medical secretary; medical/clinical assistant; medical insurance coding; medical insurance/medical billing; medical office computer specialist; medical office management; medical transcription; office occupations and clerical services; receptionist; system administration; system, networking, and LAN/WAN management; web/multimedia management and webmaster; web page, digital/multimedia and information resources design; word processing

Enrollment: 741 students

Institution Contact: Mr. Robert Obenhaus, President

Phone: 713-974-7181

Fax: 713-974-2090

E-mail: bob@mti.edu

Admission Contact: Mr. Derrell Beck, Director of Admissions

Phone: 713-974-7181

Fax: 713-974-2090

E-mail: derrell@mti.edu

 NATIONAL INSTITUTE OF TECHNOLOGY

9100 US Highway 290 East, Suite 100

Austin , TX 78754

Web: http://www.nitschools.com

Accreditation: Accrediting Commission of Career Schools and Colleges of Technology

Programs Offered:

dental assisting; heating, air conditioning, ventilation and refrigeration maintenance technology; medical administrative assistant and medical secretary; medical/clinical assistant; pharmacy technician

Enrollment: 643 students

Institution Contact: Mrs. Stacy Pniewski, School President

Phone: 512-928-1933

Fax: 512-927-8587

E-mail: spniewsk@cci.edu

Admission Contact: Ms. Kim Whitehead, Director of Admissions

Phone: 512-928-1933

Fax: 512-927-8587

E-mail: kwhitehe@cci.edu

NATIONAL INSTITUTE OF TECHNOLOGY

4150 Westheimer Road, Suite 200

Houston, TX 77027

Web: http://www.nitschools.com

Accreditation: Accrediting Commission of Career Schools and Colleges of Technology

Programs Offered:

computer engineering technology; electrical, electronic and communications engineering technology; information technology; medical/clinical assistant; medical insurance coding

Enrollment: 457 students

Institution Contact: Mr. Thomas C. Wilson, President

Phone: 713-629-1637

Fax: 713-629-1643

E-mail: twilson@cci.edu

Admission Contact: Mr. Scott Morris, Director of Admissions

Phone: 713-629-1637 ext. 102

Fax: 713-629-1643

E-mail: smorris@cci.edu

NATIONAL INSTITUTE OF TECHNOLOGY

9700 Bissonnet, Suite 1400

Houston, TX 77036

Web: http://www.nitschools.com

Accreditation: Accrediting Commission of Career Schools and Colleges of Technology

Programs Offered:

medical/clinical assistant; medical insurance coding; medical insurance/medical billing; pharmacy technician

Institution Contact: Vanessa Smith, Director of Admissions

Phone: 713-772-4200

Fax: 713-772-4204

E-mail: vasmith@cci.edu

NATIONAL INSTITUTE OF TECHNOLOGY

6550 First Park Ten Boulevard

San Antonio, TX 78213

Web: http://www.cci.edu

Accreditation: Accrediting Commission of Career Schools and Colleges of Technology

Programs Offered:

business automation/technology/data entry; computer technology/computer systems technology; electrical, electronic and communications engineering technology; heating, air conditioning and refrigeration technology; medical administrative assistant and medical secretary; medical/clinical assistant; pharmacy technician; system administration

Enrollment: 626 students
Institution Contact: Mr. James Yeaman, President
Phone: 210-733-6000
Fax: 210-733-3300
E-mail: jyeaman@cci.edu
Admission Contact: Mr. Jimmy Clontz, Director of Admissions
Phone: 210-733-6000
Fax: 210-733-3300
E-mail: jimmyclontz@cci.edu

NATIONAL INSTITUTE OF TECHNOLOGY - GREENSPOINT

255 Northpoint, Suite 100
Houston, TX 77060
Web: http://www.nitschools.com
Accreditation: Accrediting Commission of Career Schools and Colleges of Technology
Programs Offered:
dental assisting; medical/clinical assistant; medical insurance coding; medical insurance/medical billing; pharmacy technician
Enrollment: 700 students
Institution Contact: Mr. Jeff Brown, President
Phone: 281-447-7037
Fax: 281-447-6937
E-mail: jbrown@cci.edu
Admission Contact: Mr. Shawn Washington, Director of Admissions
Phone: 281-447-7037 ext. 101
Fax: 281-447-6937
E-mail: shwashington@cci.edu

NATIONAL INSTITUTE OF TECHNOLOGY - HOBBY

7151 Office City Drive, Suite 100
Houston, TX 77087
Web: http://www.nitschools.com
Accreditation: Accrediting Commission of Career Schools and Colleges of Technology
Programs Offered:
medical/clinical assistant; medical insurance/medical billing; pharmacy technician
Enrollment: 596 students

Institution Contact: Mrs. Barbara Andrews, School President
Phone: 713-645-7404 ext. 101
Fax: 713-645-7346
E-mail: bandrews@cci.edu
Admission Contact: Mr. Greg Lotz, Director of Admissions
Phone: 713-645-7404 ext. 102
Fax: 713-645-7346
E-mail: wlotz@cci.edu

OCEAN CORPORATION

10840 Rockley Road
Houston, TX 77099-3416
Web: http://www.oceancorp.com
Accreditation: Accrediting Commission of Career Schools and Colleges of Technology
Programs Offered:
diving, professional and instruction; quality control technology
Enrollment: 162 students
Institution Contact: Mr. John Wood, President
Phone: 800-321-0298
Fax: 281-530-9143
E-mail: johnswood@worldnet.att.net
Admission Contact: Mr. Bob Browning, Admissions Manager
Phone: 800-321-0298 ext. 127
Fax: 281-530-0202 ext. 127
E-mail: bob.browning@oceancorp.com

PCI HEALTH TRAINING CENTER

8101 John W. Carpenter Freeway
Dallas, TX 75247-4720
Web: http://www.pcihealth.net
Accreditation: Accrediting Commission of Career Schools and Colleges of Technology
Programs Offered:
medical/clinical assistant; medical office computer specialist; nursing assistant/aide and patient care assistant; psychiatric/mental health services technology; substance abuse/addiction counseling
Enrollment: 430 students
Institution Contact: Mr. Don Wood, Director of Compliance and Financial Aid
Phone: 214-630-0568 ext. 323
Fax: 214-630-1002

E-mail: dwood@pcihealth.net
Admission Contact: Kelly Drake, Director of Admissions
Phone: 214-630-0568 ext. 305
Fax: 214-630-1002
E-mail: kdrake@pcihealth.net

PCI HEALTH TRAINING CENTER

1300 International Parkway
Richardson, TX 75081
Programs Offered:
medical/clinical assistant; medical office assistant;
nursing assistant/aide and patient care assistant
Enrollment: 240 students
Institution Contact: Mr. Benjamin Davis, School
Director
Phone: 214-5762600 ext. 101
E-mail: bdavis@pcihealth.net
Admission Contact: Mr. Scott Nixon, Admissions
Representative
Phone: 214-5762600 ext. 115
E-mail: bdavis@pcihealth.net

PLATT COLLEGE - DALLAS

2974 LBJ Freeway, Suite 300
Dallas, TX 75234
Institution Contact: Ms. Susan Rone
Phone: 972-243-0900

REMINGTON COLLEGE

3110 Hayes Road, Suite 380
Houston, TX 77082
Web: http://www.remingtoncollege.edu
Programs Offered:
business administration and management; computer
systems networking and telecommunications; criminal
justice/law enforcement administration; medical/clini-
cal assistant; medical insurance coding; pharmacy
technician
Enrollment: 715 students
Institution Contact: Mr. Christopher Tilley, Campus
President
Phone: 281-899-1240
Fax: 281-597-8466
E-mail: christopher.tilley@remingtoncollege.edu
Admission Contact: Mr. Douglas Dunn, Campus Vice
President

Phone: 281-899-1240
Fax: 281-597-8466
E-mail: douglas.dunn@remingtoncollege.edu

REMINGTON COLLEGE - DALLAS CAMPUS

1800 Eastgate Drive
Garland, TX 75041
Web: http://www.remingtoncollege.edu
Accreditation: Accrediting Council for Independent
Colleges and Schools
Programs Offered:
biomedical technology; business administration and
management; computer systems networking and
telecommunications; culinary arts; medical/clinical
assistant; pharmacy technician
Enrollment: 954 students
Institution Contact: Mr. Skip Walls, Campus President
Phone: 972-686-7878
Fax: 972-686-5116
E-mail: skip.walls@remingtoncollege.edu
Admission Contact: Ms. Shonda Whisenhunt, Direc-
tor of Recruitment
Phone: 972-686-7878
Fax: 972-686-5116
E-mail: shonda.whisenhunt@remingtoncollege.edu

REMINGTON COLLEGE - FORT WORTH CAMPUS

300 East Loop 820
Fort Worth, TX 76112
Web: http://www.remingtoncollege.edu
Accreditation: Accrediting Commission of Career
Schools and Colleges of Technology
Programs Offered:
commercial and advertising art; computer systems
analysis; electrical, electronic and communications
engineering technology; information science/studies;
medical/clinical assistant; system, networking, and
LAN/WAN management
Institution Contact: Ms. Lynn Wey, Campus President
Phone: 817-451-0017
Fax: 817-496-1257
E-mail: lynn.wey@remingtoncollege.edu
Admission Contact: Ms. Annette Latshaw, Director
of Recruitment
Phone: 817-451-0017
Fax: 817-496-1257
E-mail: annette.latshaw@remingtoncollege.edu

REMINGTON COLLEGE - HOUSTON CAMPUS
3110 Hayes Road, Suite 380
Houston, TX 77082
Web: http://www.remingtoncollege.edu
Accreditation: Accrediting Commission of Career
Schools and Colleges of Technology
Programs Offered:
business administration and management; criminal jus-
tice/law enforcement administration; medical/clinical
assistant; medical insurance/medical billing; pharmacy
technician
Enrollment: 454 students
Institution Contact: Ms. Christpher Tilley, Campus
President
Phone: 281-899-1240
Fax: 281-597-8466
E-mail: chris.tilley@remingtoncollege.edu
Admission Contact: Mr. Roger Moore, Director of
Recruitment
Phone: 281-885-4450 ext. 206
Fax: 281-597-8466
E-mail: rogermoore@remingtoncollege.edu

SAN ANTONIO COLLEGE OF MEDICAL AND DENTAL ASSISTANTS
San Pedro Towne Center Phase II, 7142 San Pedro,
Suite 100
San Antonio, TX 78216
Web: http://www.sacmda.com
Accreditation: Accrediting Bureau of Health Edu-
cation Schools; Accrediting Commission of Career
Schools and Colleges of Technology
Programs Offered:
computer software and media applications; computer/
technical support; dental assisting; electrician; heating,
air conditioning, ventilation and refrigeration mainte-
nance technology; medical/clinical assistant; medical
office assistant; pharmacy technician; phlebotomy
Enrollment: 869 students
Institution Contact: Mr. Arthur Rodriguez , President
Phone: 210-733-0777 ext. 5521
Fax: 210-735-2431
E-mail: arodriguez@sac-mda.com
Admission Contact: Mr. Craig Czubati, Admissions
Director
Phone: 210-733-0777 ext. 5561
Fax: 210-735-2431
E-mail: cczubati@sac-mda.com

SANFORD-BROWN INSTITUTE
1250 Mockingbird Lane, Suite 150
Dallas, TX 75247
Web: http://www.sbdallas.com
Accreditation: Accrediting Bureau of Health Educa-
tion Schools
Programs Offered:
business administration and management; cardiovas-
cular technology; computer and information sciences
and support services related; diagnostic medical so-
nography and ultrasound technology; medical/clinical
assistant; medical insurance/medical billing; pharmacy
technician; surgical technology
Enrollment: 440 students
Institution Contact: Mr. Marcus McMellon, CPA,
President
Phone: 214-459-8490
Fax: 214-638-6401
E-mail: mmcmellon@sbdallas.com
Admission Contact: Mr. Todd Sturga, Director of
Admissions
Phone: 214-459-8490
Fax: 214-638-6006
E-mail: tsturga@sbdallas.com

SANFORD-BROWN INSTITUTE
10500 Forum Place Drive , Suite 200
Houston, TX 77036
Web: http://www.sbhouston.com
Accreditation: Accrediting Bureau of Health Educa-
tion Schools
Programs Offered:
business administration and management; cardio-
vascular technology; diagnostic medical sonography
and ultrasound technology; medical/clinical assistant;
medical insurance/medical billing; medicinal and phar-
maceutical chemistry; surgical technology
Enrollment: 1,239 students
Institution Contact: Mr. James C. Garrett, President
Phone: 713-779-1110
Fax: 713-779-2408
E-mail: jgarrett@sbhouston.com
Admission Contact: Mr. Steven Lee, Director of
Admissions
Phone: 713-779-1110
Fax: 713-779-2408
E-mail: slee@sbhouston.com

SANFORD-BROWN INSTITUTE

2627 North Loop West, Suite 100
Houston, TX 77008
Web: http://www.sbnorthloop.com
Institution Contact: Ms. Marilyn Denise Hall, Executive Director
Phone: 713-863-0429
Fax: 713-863-9156
E-mail: m.hall@sbnorthloop.com
Admission Contact: Mr. Rory Laney, Director of Admissions
Phone: 713-863-0429
Fax: 713-863-9156
E-mail: rlaney@sbnorthloop.com

SOUTHEASTERN CAREER INSTITUTE

12005 Ford Rd, #100
Dallas, TX 75234
Web: http://www.southeasterncareerinstitute.com
Accreditation: Council on Occupational Education
Programs Offered:
dental assisting; information technology; legal assistant/paralegal; medical/clinical assistant; medical office management; pharmacy technician
Enrollment: 247 students
Institution Contact: Ms. Cindy M. Lewellen, Executive Director
Phone: 972-385-1446
Fax: 972-385-0641
E-mail: mlewellen@sci-education.com
Admission Contact: Mr. Stan Moffet, Director of Admissions
Phone: 972-385-1446
Fax: 972-385-0641
E-mail: smoffet@sci-dallas.com

TEXAS CAREERS - SAN ANTONIO

1015 Jackson Keller
San Antonio, TX 78213
Web: http://www.texascareers.com
Accreditation: Council on Occupational Education
Programs Offered:
computer/information technology administration and management; legal assistant/paralegal; medical/clinical assistant; medical office computer specialist; nursing assistant/aide and patient care assistant; nursing (registered nurse training)

Enrollment: 579 students
Institution Contact: Ms. Laura M. Bledsoe, President
Phone: 210-308-8584
Fax: 210-308-8985
E-mail: lbledsoe@texascareers.com
Admission Contact: Ms. Tish Hamilton, Director of Admissions
Phone: 210-308-8584
Fax: 210-308-8985
E-mail: thamilton@texascareers.com

TEXAS CULINARY ACADEMY

11400 Burnet Road, Suite 2100
Austin, TX 78758
Web: http://www.tca.edu
Accreditation: Accrediting Council for Independent Colleges and Schools; Council on Occupational Education
Programs Offered:
baking and pastry arts; culinary arts
Institution Contact: Mr. Manuel Ortiz, Director of Admissions
Phone: 512-837-2665
Fax: 512-977-9794
E-mail: mortiz@txca.com

TEXAS SCHOOL OF BUSINESS, INC.

711 Airtex Drive
Houston, TX 77073
Web: http://www.tsb.edu
Accreditation: Accrediting Council for Independent Colleges and Schools
Programs Offered:
accounting; computer science; medical/clinical assistant; office occupations and clerical services
Institution Contact:
Phone: 800-555-8012
E-mail: info@tsb.edu

 ## UNIVERSAL TECHNICAL INSTITUTE

721 Lockhaven Drive
Houston, TX 77073
Web: http://www.uticorp.com
Accreditation: Accrediting Commission of Career Schools and Colleges of Technology
Programs Offered:

autobody/collision and repair technology; automobile/automotive mechanics technology; diesel mechanics technology

Institution Contact: Mr. Ken Golaszewski, School Director

Phone: 281-443-6262 ext. 12202

Fax: 281-443-1866

E-mail: kgolaszewski@uticorp.com

Admission Contact: Mr. Scott Vasko, Admissions Director

Phone: 281-443-6262 ext. 12259

Fax: 281-443-1866

E-mail: svaskoi@uticorp.com

VIRGINIA COLLEGE AT AUSTIN

6301 East Highway 290, Suite 200

Austin, TX 78723

Web: http://www.vc.edu

Accreditation: Accrediting Council for Independent Colleges and Schools

Programs Offered:

accounting technology and bookkeeping; administrative assistant and secretarial science; computer and information systems security; computer systems networking and telecommunications; diagnostic medical sonography and ultrasound technology; legal assistant/paralegal; medical/clinical assistant; medical insurance coding; medical insurance/medical billing; medical office management; office management; surgical technology

Enrollment: 540 students

Institution Contact: Mr. David B. Champlin, Campus President

Phone: 512-371-3500 ext. 2802

Fax: 512-371-3502

E-mail: dchamplin@vc.edu

Admission Contact: Mrs. Charlotte A. Frohnhoefer, Director of Admissions

Phone: 512-371-3500 ext. 2801

Fax: 512-371-3502

E-mail: cfrohnhoefer@vc.edu

WESTERN TECHNICAL COLLEGE

1000 Texas Avenue

El Paso, TX 79901-1536

Web: http://www.wtc-ep.edu

Accreditation: Accrediting Bureau of Health Education Schools; Accrediting Commission of Career Schools and Colleges of Technology

Programs Offered:

automobile/automotive mechanics technology; communications technology; computer/information technology administration and management; computer installation and repair technology; computer systems networking and telecommunications; computer technology/computer systems technology; electrical, electronic and communications engineering technology; health information/medical records administration; health information/medical records technology; heating, air conditioning and refrigeration technology; heating, air conditioning, ventilation and refrigeration maintenance technology; information technology; medical/clinical assistant; medical insurance coding; medical insurance/medical billing; medical transcription; sheet metal technology; telecommunications; telecommunications technology; welding technology

Enrollment: 822 students

Institution Contact: Mr. Bill Terrell, Chief Administrative Officer

Phone: 915-532-3737 ext. 117

Fax: 915-532-6946

E-mail: bterrell@wtc-ep.edu

WESTERN TECHNICAL INSTITUTE

9451 Diana Drive

El Paso, TX 79924

Web: http://www.wtc-ep.edu

Accreditation: Accrediting Bureau of Health Education Schools; Accrediting Commission of Career Schools and Colleges of Technology

Programs Offered:

automobile/automotive mechanics technology; computer/information technology administration and management; computer systems networking and telecommunications; computer technology/computer systems technology; electrical, electronic and communications engineering technology; health/health care administration; health information/medical records administration; heating, air conditioning, ventilation and refrigeration maintenance technology; industrial technology; medical/clinical assistant; telecommunications; welding technology

Enrollment: 960 students

Institution Contact: Mr. Bill Terrell, Chief Administrative Officer

Phone: 915-532-3737 ext. 117
Fax: 915-532-6946
E-mail: bterrell@wtc-ep.edu
Admission Contact: Mr. Jerry Martin, Director, Office of Recruitment & School Relations
Phone: 915-566-9621 ext. 123
Fax: 915-565-9903
E-mail: jmartin@wtc-ep.edu

 WESTWOOD AVIATION INSTITUTE
8880 Telephone Road
Houston, TX 77061
Web: http://www.westwood.edu
Accreditation: Council on Occupational Education; Southern Association of Colleges and Schools
Programs Offered:
aircraft powerplant technology; airframe mechanics and aircraft maintenance technology
Enrollment: 90 students
Institution Contact: Mr. Michael J. Couling, Executive Director
Phone: 713-644-7777
Fax: 713-644-0902
E-mail: mcouling@westwood.edu
Admission Contact: Mr. Glen Feist, Director of Admissions
Phone: 713-644-7777
Fax: 713-644-0902
E-mail: gfeist@westwood.edu

 WESTWOOD COLLEGE - DALLAS
8390 LBJ Freeway, Suite 100
Dallas, TX 75243
Accreditation: Accrediting Council for Independent Colleges and Schools
Programs Offered:
CAD/CADD drafting/design technology; computer engineering technology; graphic and printing equipment operation/production; health information/medical records administration
Enrollment: 568 students
Institution Contact: Mr. Vince Thomae, Executive Director
Phone: 214-570-0100 ext. 200
Fax: 214-570-8502
E-mail: vthomae@westwood.edu
Admission Contact: Mr. Eric Southwell, Director of

Admissions
Phone: 214-570-0100 ext. 100
Fax: 214-570-8502
E-mail: esouthwell@westwood.edu

 WESTWOOD COLLEGE - FORT WORTH
1331 Airport Freeway, Suite 402
Euless, TX 76040
Web: http://www.westwood.edu
Accreditation: Accrediting Council for Independent Colleges and Schools
Programs Offered:
CAD/CADD drafting/design technology; commercial and advertising art; computer systems networking and telecommunications; information technology; medical/clinical assistant
Enrollment: 570 students
Institution Contact: Kelly Coates, Executive Director
Phone: 817-685-9994
Fax: 817-685-8929
E-mail: kcoates@westwood.edu

 WESTWOOD COLLEGE - HOUSTON SOUTH
One Arena Place, 7322 Southwest Freeway, Suite 247
Houston, TX 77074
Web: http://www.westwood.edu
Institution Contact: Sandra Alonzo

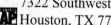 **WESTWOOD COLLEGE - HOUSTON SOUTH CAMPUS**
7322 Southwest Freeway, Suite 110
Houston, TX 77074
Web: http://www.westwood.edu
Accreditation: Accrediting Commission of Career Schools and Colleges of Technology
Programs Offered:
CAD/CADD drafting/design technology; commercial and advertising art; computer engineering related; computer engineering technology; computer systems networking and telecommunications; drafting and design technology; drafting/design engineering technologies related; graphic communications; medical/clinical assistant; medical insurance coding; medical insurance/medical billing
Enrollment: 253 students
Institution Contact: Mr. Rick Skinner, Executive Director

Phone: 713-219-2022
Fax: 713-219-2089
E-mail: rskinner@westwood.edu
Admission Contact: Mr. Ryan Wright, Director of
Admissions
Phone: 713-777-4433
Fax: 713-219-2088
E-mail: rwright@westwood.edu

UTAH

CERTIFIED CAREERS INSTITUTE

775 South 2000 East
Clearfield, UT 84015
Web: http://www.cciutah.edu
Accreditation: Accrediting Commission of Career
Schools and Colleges of Technology
Programs Offered:
massage therapy; medical/clinical assistant; medical
office computer specialist
Enrollment: 77 students
Institution Contact: Mr. Matthew W. Maxwell, Director
Phone: 801-774-9900
Fax: 801-774-0111
E-mail: mmaxwell@cciutah.edu
Admission Contact: Blake Gardner, Admissions
Representative
Phone: 801-774-9900
Fax: 801-774-0111
E-mail: bgardner@cciutah.edu

CERTIFIED CAREERS INSTITUTE

1385 West 2200 South, Suite 100
Salt Lake City, UT 84119
Web: http://www.cciutah.edu
Accreditation: Accrediting Commission of Career
Schools and Colleges of Technology
Programs Offered:
dental assisting; medical/clinical assistant; medical
office management
Enrollment: 60 students
Institution Contact: Mr. Matt Maxwell, School Director
Phone: 801-973-7008
Fax: 801-973-6070
E-mail: mmaxwell@cciutah.edu

EAGLE GATE COLLEGE

5588 South Green Street
Murray, UT 84123
Web: http://www.eaglegatecollege.com
Accreditation: Accrediting Council for Independent
Colleges and Schools
Programs Offered:
accounting; business administration and management;
computer programming; computer systems networking
and telecommunications; dental assisting; digital communication and media/multimedia; medical/clinical
assistant; office management
Institution Contact:
Phone: 801-268-9271

EAGLE GATE COLLEGE - WEBER/DAVIS

915 North 400 West
Layton, UT 84041
Web: http://www.eaglegatecollege.edu
Programs Offered:
accounting; business, management, and marketing
related; criminal justice/law enforcement administration; graphic communications related; health information/medical records administration; medical/clinical
assistant; pharmacy technician
Enrollment: 285 students
Institution Contact: Mr. Mike Townsley
Phone: 801-546-7508
Fax: 801-593-6654
E-mail: miketownsley@eaglegatecollege.edu

EAGLE GATE COLLEGE-WEBER/DAVIS

405 South Main Street
Salt Lake City, UT 84111
Web: http://www.eaglegatecollege.edu
Programs Offered:
design and visual communications; graphic communications; web page, digital/multimedia and information
resources design
Institution Contact: Mr. Mike Townsley
Phone: 801-281-7728
E-mail: miketownsley@eaglegatecollege.edu
Admission Contact: Ms. Rebecca Edwards
E-mail: rebeccaedwards@eaglegatecollege.edu

ITT TECHNICAL INSTITUTE

920 West Levoy Drive
Murray, UT 84123-2500
Web: http://www.itt-tech.edu
Accreditation: Accrediting Council for Independent Colleges and Schools
Programs Offered:
accounting and business/management; animation, interactive technology, video graphics and special effects; business administration and management; CAD/CADD drafting/design technology; communications technology; computer and information systems security; computer engineering technology; computer software and media applications; computer software engineering; computer systems networking and telecommunications; criminal justice/police science; digital communication and media/multimedia; electrical, electronic and communications engineering technology; technology management; web page, digital/multimedia and information resources design
Institution Contact: Dr. P. Michael Linzmaier, Director
Phone: 801-263-3313
Admission Contact: Mr. Gary Wood, Director of Recruitment
Phone: 801-263-3313

MOUNTAIN WEST COLLEGE

3280 West 3500 South
West Valley City, UT 84119
Web: http://www.cci.edu
Accreditation: Accrediting Council for Independent Colleges and Schools
Programs Offered:
accounting; business administration and management; computer programming; computer systems networking and telecommunications; criminal justice/law enforcement administration; legal assistant/paralegal; medical/clinical assistant; medical insurance coding; medical insurance/medical billing; office management; surgical technology; tourism and travel services management
Enrollment: 797 students
Institution Contact: Mr. Larry Banks, PhD, President
Phone: 801-840-4800
Fax: 801-969-0828
E-mail: lbanks@cci.edu
Admission Contact: Mr. Jason Lynn, Director of Admissions
Phone: 801-840-4800

Fax: 801-969-0828
E-mail: jlynn@cci.edu

NEUMONT UNIVERSITY

2755 East Cottonwood Parkway, 6th Floor
Salt Lake City, UT 84121
Web: http://www.northface.edu
Accreditation: Accrediting Council for Independent Colleges and Schools
Programs Offered:
business administration and management; computer and information sciences related; computer software engineering
Institution Contact: Mr. Jamie Wyse, Senior Vice President, Strategic Development
Phone: 801-438-1107
Fax: 801-438-1111
E-mail: jamie.wyse@northface.edu
Admission Contact: Mr. Jeff Marcus, Vice President, Enrollment
Phone: 801-438-1114
Fax: 801-438-1111
E-mail: jeff.marcus@northface.edu

PROVO COLLEGE

1450 West 820 North
Provo, UT 84601
Web: http://www.provocollege.edu
Accreditation: Accrediting Commission of Career Schools and Colleges of Technology
Programs Offered:
accounting; business administration and management; commercial and advertising art; computer programming related; computer systems networking and telecommunications; dental assisting; English as a second language; executive assistant/executive secretary; hospitality administration related; massage therapy; medical/clinical assistant; nursing (registered nurse training); pharmacy technician; physical therapist assistant
Enrollment: 700 students
Institution Contact: Mr. Gordon C. Peters, Campus President
Phone: 801-818-8907
Fax: 801-375-9728
E-mail: gordonp@provocollege.edu
Admission Contact: Mr. Kim T. Miller, Director of Admissions

Phone: 801-375-1861
Fax: 801-375-9728
E-mail: kimm@provocollege.edu

STEVENS-HENAGER COLLEGE

755 South Main Street
Logan, UT 84321
Web: http://www.stevenshenager.edu
Accreditation: Accrediting Commission of Career Schools and Colleges of Technology
Programs Offered:
accounting; administrative assistant and secretarial science; business administration and management; business automation/technology/data entry; clinical/medical laboratory assistant; computer and information sciences related; computer graphics; computer installation and repair technology; computer programming; computer programming related; computer programming (specific applications); computer programming (vendor/product certification); computer systems networking and telecommunications; computer technology/computer systems technology; data entry/microcomputer applications; desktop publishing and digital imaging design; emergency medical technology (EMT paramedic); health/health care administration; health information/medical records administration; health information/medical records technology; marketing/marketing management; medical administrative assistant and medical secretary; medical/clinical assistant; medical office management; medical radiologic technology; medical transcription; nursing assistant/aide and patient care assistant; pharmacy technician; receptionist; respiratory care therapy; surgical technology; system administration; system, networking, and LAN/WAN management; telecommunications; web page, digital/multimedia and information resources design; word processing
Institution Contact: Ms. Vicky Dewsnup, President
Phone: 435-713-4777
Fax: 435-713-4799
E-mail: vdewsnup@stevenshenager.edu
Admission Contact: Katie Curtis, Director of Admissions
Phone: 435-713-4777
Fax: 437-755-7611
E-mail: schclogan@yahoo.com

STEVENS-HENAGER COLLEGE

PO Box 9428
Ogden, UT 84409
Web: http://www.stevenshenager.edu
Accreditation: Accrediting Commission of Career Schools and Colleges of Technology
Programs Offered:
accounting; advertising; business administration and management; cardiovascular technology; commercial and advertising art; computer and information sciences related; computer graphics; computer programming; e-commerce; emergency medical technology (EMT paramedic); health/health care administration; information science/studies; insurance; medical/clinical assistant; medical insurance coding; medical insurance/medical billing; medical transcription; pharmacy technician; surgical technology; system, networking, and LAN/WAN management
Institution Contact: Ms. Vicky Dewsnup, President
Phone: 801-394-7791
E-mail: vdewsnup@yahoo.com
Admission Contact: Ms. Wynn Hurtado, Director of Admissions
Phone: 801-394-7791
E-mail: whurtado@stevenshenager.edu

STEVENS-HENAGER COLLEGE - PROVO

1476 Sandhill Road
Orem, UT 84058
Accreditation: Accrediting Commission of Career Schools and Colleges of Technology
Programs Offered:
accounting; business administration and management; clinical/medical laboratory assistant; clinical/medical laboratory technology; computer and information sciences related; computer graphics; computer hardware engineering; computer/information technology administration and management; computer/information technology services administration related; computer programming; computer programming (specific applications); computer systems networking and telecommunications; finance; gene therapy; health/health care administration; massage therapy; medical/clinical assistant; medical insurance coding; medical insurance/medical billing; medical radiologic technology; medical transcription; physical therapist assistant; physician assistant; real estate; word processing
Enrollment: 325 students

Institution Contact: Ms. Carol Gastiger, President
Phone: 801-375-5455 ext. 2000
Fax: 801-374-9454
E-mail: stevenprovo@aol.com
Admission Contact: Mr. Dan Wright, Director of
Admissions
Phone: 801-375-5455 ext. 2002
Fax: 801-375-9836

STEVENS-HENAGER COLLEGE - SALT LAKE CITY

635 West 5300 South
Salt Lake City, UT 84123
Web: http://www.stevenshenager.edu
Accreditation: Accrediting Commission of Career
Schools and Colleges of Technology; Accrediting
Council for Independent Colleges and Schools
Programs Offered:
accounting; administrative assistant and secretarial
science; business administration and management;
business automation/technology/data entry; clinical/
medical laboratory assistant; computer and information sciences related; computer graphics; computer
installation and repair technology; computer programming; computer programming related; computer programming (specific applications); computer programming (vendor/product certification); computer systems
networking and telecommunications; computer
technology/computer systems technology; data entry/
microcomputer applications; desktop publishing and
digital imaging design; emergency medical technology
(EMT paramedic); health/health care administration;
health information/medical records administration;
health information/medical records technology; mar-
keting/marketing management; medical administrative
assistant and medical secretary; medical/clinical assistant; medical office management; medical radiologic
technology; medical transcription; nursing assistant/
aide and patient care assistant; pharmacy technician;
receptionist; respiratory care therapy; surgical technology; system administration; system, networking, and
LAN/WAN management; telecommunications; web
page, digital/multimedia and information resources
design; word processing
Institution Contact: Mr. Ron Moss, President
Phone: 801-262-7600
Fax: 801-293-9024
E-mail: shcslc@aol.com
Admission Contact: Mr. Scott Sainsbury, Director of

Admissions
Phone: 801-262-7600
Fax: 801-293-9024
E-mail: ssainsbury@stevenshenager.edu

MAP UTAH CAREER COLLEGE

1902 West 7800 South
West Jordan, UT 84088
Accreditation: Accrediting Commission of Career
Schools and Colleges of Technology
Programs Offered:
business administration and management; commercial
and advertising art; legal administrative assistant/sec-
retary; legal assistant/paralegal; massage therapy;
medical/clinical assistant; medical insurance coding;
medical transcription; nursing (registered nurse train-
ing); pharmacy technician; sport and fitness adminis-
tration; veterinary technology
Enrollment: 588 students
Institution Contact: Mr. Nate Herrmann, School
Director
Phone: 801-542-7222
Fax: 801-304-4229
E-mail: nherrmann@utahcollege.edu
Admission Contact: Mrs. Denice Dunker, Director of
Admissions
Phone: 801-542-7201
Fax: 801-304-4229
E-mail: ddunker@utahcollege.edu

UTAH COLLEGE OF MASSAGE THERAPY - UTAH VALLEY CAMPUS

135 S. State St., Suite 12
Lindon, UT 84042
Institution Contact: Ms. Cassandra Cronin
Phone: 801-796-0300
Fax: 801-796-0309

UTAH COLLEGE OF MASSAGE THERAPY - SALT LAKE CITY

25 S. 300 E.
Salt Lake City, UT 84111
Institution Contact: Ms. Heather Hans
Phone: 801-521-3330
Fax: 801-521-3339

VERMONT

NEW ENGLAND CULINARY INSTITUTE
250 Main Street
Montpelier, VT 05602-9720
Web: http://www.neci.edu
Accreditation: Accrediting Commission of Career Schools and Colleges of Technology
Programs Offered:
baking and pastry arts; culinary arts; restaurant, culinary, and catering management
Enrollment: 264 students
Institution Contact: Ms. Dawn Hayward, Director of Admissions
Phone: 802-223-6324
Fax: 802-225-3280
E-mail: dawnh@neci.edu

NEW ENGLAND CULINARY INSTITUTE AT ESSEX
48 1/2 Park Street
Essex Junction, VT 05452
Web: http://www.neci.edu
Accreditation: Accrediting Commission of Career Schools and Colleges of Technology
Programs Offered:
baking and pastry arts; culinary arts; restaurant, culinary, and catering management
Enrollment: 261 students
Institution Contact: Mr. Francis Voigt, Chief Executive Officer
Phone: 802-223-6324
Fax: 802-225-3280
E-mail: emilys@neci.edu
Admission Contact: Ms. Dawn Hayward, Director of Admissions
Phone: 877-223-6324 ext. 3211
Fax: 802-225-3280
E-mail: dawnh@neci.edu

VIRGINIA

ACT COLLEGE
6118 Franconia Road, Suite 200
Alexandria, VA 22310

Web: http://www.actcollege.edu
Accreditation: Accrediting Bureau of Health Education Schools
Programs Offered:
dental assisting; medical/clinical assistant
Enrollment: 142 students
Institution Contact: Mr. Jeffrey S. Moore, President/CEO
Phone: 703-527-6660
Fax: 703-528-4021
E-mail: jeffmoore@actcollege.edu
Admission Contact: Mr. Orlando Moore, Jr., Vice President, Admissions
Phone: 703-719-0700
Fax: 703-719-9700
E-mail: omoore@actcollege.edu

ACT COLLEGE
9302 Lee Highway, Suite 400
Fairfax, VA 22033-3863
Web: http://www.actcollege.edu
Accreditation: Accrediting Bureau of Health Education Schools
Programs Offered:
dental assisting; medical administrative assistant and medical secretary; medical/clinical assistant; pharmacy technician
Enrollment: 377 students
Institution Contact: Mr. Jeffrey S. Moore, President/CEO
Phone: 703-527-6660
Fax: 703-528-4021
E-mail: jeffmoore@actcollege.edu
Admission Contact: Mr. Orlando Moore, Jr., Vice President, Admissions
Phone: 703-527-6660
Fax: 703-527-6688
E-mail: omoore@actcollege.edu

ACT COLLEGE
8870 Rixlew Lane, Suite 201
Manassas, VA 20109-3795
Web: http://www.actcollege.edu
Accreditation: Accrediting Bureau of Health Education Schools
Programs Offered:
medical/clinical assistant; medical radiologic technology

Enrollment: 112 students
Institution Contact: Mr. Jeffrey S. Moore, President/CEO
Phone: 703-527-6660
Fax: 703-528-4021
E-mail: jeffmoore@actcollege.edu
Admission Contact: Mr. Orlando Moore, Jr., Vice President, Admissions
Phone: 703-365-9286
Fax: 703-365-9288
E-mail: omoore@actcollege.edu

ADVANCED TECHNOLOGY INSTITUTE

5700 Southern Boulevard
Virginia Beach, VA 23462
Web: http://www.auto.edu
Accreditation: Accrediting Commission of Career Schools and Colleges of Technology
Programs Offered:
automobile/automotive mechanics technology; automotive engineering technology; diesel mechanics technology; heating, air conditioning and refrigeration technology; heating, air conditioning, ventilation and refrigeration maintenance technology; heavy equipment maintenance technology; truck and bus driver/commercial vehicle operation
Enrollment: 500 students
Institution Contact: Mr. William M. Tomlin, Director
Phone: 757-490-1241
Fax: 757-499-5929
E-mail: btomlin@auto.edu
Admission Contact: Mr. Michael S. Levy, Director of Admissions
Phone: 757-490-1241
Fax: 757-499-5929
E-mail: mlevy@auto.edu

ARGOSY UNIVERSITY/WASHINGTON D.C.

1550 Wilson Blvd., Suite 600
Arlington, VA 22209
Web: http://www.argosyu.edu
Programs Offered:
business administration and management; education; educational leadership and administration
Enrollment: 900 students
Institution Contact: Mrs. Emily Briar Peck, Director of Admissions

Phone: 703-526-5851
Fax: 703-243-8973
E-mail: epeck@argosyu.edu

THE ART INSTITUTE OF WASHINGTON

1820 North Fort Myer Drive
Arlington, VA 22209
Web: http://www.aiw.aii.edu
Accreditation: Southern Association of Colleges and Schools
Programs Offered:
advertising; animation, interactive technology, video graphics and special effects; art; commercial and advertising art; computer graphics; culinary arts; interior design; web/multimedia management and webmaster; web page, digital/multimedia and information resources design
Enrollment: 1,045 students
Institution Contact: Lawrence E. McHugh, Director of Admissions
Phone: 703-247-6850
Fax: 703-358-9759
E-mail: lmchugh@aii.edu
Admission Contact: Mr. Lawrence E. McHugh, Director of Admissions
Phone: 703-247-6850
Fax: 703-358-9759
E-mail: lmchugh@aii.edu

THE CHUBB INSTITUTE

1515 North Courthouse Road, Sixth Floor
Arlington, VA 22201
Web: http://www.chubbinstitute.com
Accreditation: Accrediting Council for Continuing Education and Training
Programs Offered:
administrative assistant and secretarial science; business administration and management; computer and information sciences related; computer and information systems security; computer engineering related; computer engineering technology; computer graphics; computer hardware engineering; computer/information technology administration and management; computer/information technology services administration related; computer installation and repair technology; computer programming; computer programming related; computer programming (specific applications); computer programming (vendor/product certifica-

tion); computer software and media applications; computer software and media applications related; computer software engineering; computer systems analysis; computer systems networking and telecommunications; computer/technical support; computer technology/computer systems technology; data entry/microcomputer applications; data entry/microcomputer applications related; data processing and data processing technology; information science/studies; information technology; system administration; system, networking, and LAN/WAN management; web page, digital/multimedia and information resources design

Enrollment: 125 students

Institution Contact: Mr. Richard G. Rynders, Executive Director

Phone: 703-908-8300

Fax: 703-908-8301

E-mail: rrynders@chubbinstitute.com

Admission Contact: Ms. Tina Turk, Director of Admissions

Phone: 703-908-8300

Fax: 703-908-8301

E-mail: tturk@chubbinstitute.com

ECPI COLLEGE OF TECHNOLOGY

10021 Balls Ford Road, #100
Manassas, VA 20109
Web: http://www.ecpi.edu

Accreditation: Southern Association of Colleges and Schools

Programs Offered:

administrative assistant and secretarial science; biomedical technology; business administration and management; business machine repair; clinical/medical laboratory assistant; computer and information sciences related; computer and information systems security; computer installation and repair technology; computer programming; computer programming (specific applications); computer systems analysis; computer technology/computer systems technology; criminal justice/law enforcement administration; data processing and data processing technology; health information/medical records administration; information science/studies; information technology; management information systems; medical administrative assistant and medical secretary; medical/clinical assistant; medical office computer specialist; nursing (licensed practical/vocational nurse training); receptionist; web/multimedia

management and webmaster; word processing

Enrollment: 434 students

Institution Contact: Mrs. Judith Hughes, Provost

Phone: 703-330-5300

Fax: 703-369-0530

E-mail: jhughes@ecpi.edu

ECPI COLLEGE OF TECHNOLOGY

1001 Omni Boulevard, #100
Newport News, VA 23606
Web: http://www.ecpi.edu

Accreditation: Southern Association of Colleges and Schools

Programs Offered:

accounting; administrative assistant and secretarial science; business administration and management; business automation/technology/data entry; communications technology; computer and information systems security; computer engineering technology; computer/information technology administration and management; computer installation and repair technology; computer programming; computer systems networking and telecommunications; computer/technical support; computer technology/computer systems technology; criminal justice/law enforcement administration; data processing and data processing technology; information science/studies; information technology; medical administrative assistant and medical secretary; medical insurance coding; medical insurance/medical billing; medical office computer specialist; medical reception; medical transcription; security and loss prevention; system, networking, and LAN/WAN management; telecommunications; telecommunications technology; web/multimedia management and webmaster; web page, digital/multimedia and information resources design

Enrollment: 509 students

Institution Contact: Mr. John Olson, Provost

Phone: 757-838-9191

Fax: 757-827-5351

E-mail: jolson@ecpi.edu

Admission Contact: Ms. Cheryl Lokey, Director of Recruitment

Phone: 757-838-9191

Fax: 757-827-5351

E-mail: clokey@ecpi.edu

ECPI COLLEGE OF TECHNOLOGY

5555 Greenwich Road, #300
Virginia Beach, VA 23462-6542
Web: http://www.ecpi.edu
Accreditation: Southern Association of Colleges and Schools
Programs Offered:
accounting; administrative assistant and secretarial science; biomedical technology; business automation/technology/data entry; computer and information systems security; computer engineering technology; computer/information technology administration and management; computer/information technology services administration related; computer installation and repair technology; computer programming; computer programming related; computer programming (specific applications); computer systems networking and tele-communications; computer/technical support; computer technology/computer systems technology; criminal justice/law enforcement administration; data processing and data processing technology; information science/studies; information technology; office occupations and clerical services; system administration; system, networking, and LAN/WAN management; telecommunications; telecommunications technology; web page, digital/multimedia and information resources design
Enrollment: 1,464 students
Institution Contact: Mr. Mark Dreyfus, President
Phone: 757-671-7171 ext. 218
Fax: 757-671-8661
E-mail: president@ecpi.edu
Admission Contact: Ms. Karie Edwards, High School Admissions
Phone: 804-330-5533
Fax: 804-330-5577
E-mail: kedwards@ecpitech.edu

ECPI TECHNICAL COLLEGE

4305 Cox Road
Glen Allen, VA 23060
Web: http://www.ecpitech.edu
Accreditation: Accrediting Commission of Career Schools and Colleges of Technology
Programs Offered:
administrative assistant and secretarial science; business automation/technology/data entry; computer and information systems security; computer engineering technology; computer/information technology adminis-tration and management; computer installation and repair technology; computer programming; computer programming (specific applications); computer/technical support; computer technology/computer systems technology; criminal justice/police science; data processing and data processing technology; information science/studies; information technology; management information systems; office occupations and clerical services; system administration; system, networking, and LAN/WAN management; telecommunications; web page, digital/multimedia and information resources design
Enrollment: 422 students
Institution Contact: Mr. Jacob Pope, Director
Phone: 804-934-0100
Fax: 804-934-0054
E-mail: jpope@ecpitech.edu
Admission Contact: Mr. Ronald Joyner, Director of Admissions
Phone: 804-934-0100
Fax: 804-934-0054
E-mail: rjoyner@ecpitech.edu

ECPI TECHNICAL COLLEGE

800 Moorefield Park Drive
Richmond, VA 23236
Web: http://www.ecpitech.edu
Accreditation: Accrediting Commission of Career Schools and Colleges of Technology
Programs Offered:
administrative assistant and secretarial science; business automation/technology/data entry; computer engineering technology; computer/information technology administration and management; computer installation and repair technology; computer programming; computer programming (specific applications); computer systems networking and telecommunications; computer/technical support; computer technology/computer systems technology; criminal justice/law enforcement administration; data processing and data processing technology; information science/studies; medical administrative assistant and medical secretary; medical insurance coding; medical insurance/medical billing; medical office computer specialist; medical transcription; office occupations and clerical services; system administration; system, networking, and LAN/WAN management; telecommunications; telecommunications technology; web page, digital/multimedia and information resources design

Enrollment: 412 students
Institution Contact: Ms. Ada Gerard, Director
Phone: 804-330-5533
Fax: 804-330-5577
E-mail: agerard@ecpitech.edu
Admission Contact: Ms. Kari Edwards, Admission Coordinator
Phone: 804-330-5533
Fax: 804-330-5577
E-mail: kedward@ecpitech.edu

ECPI TECHNICAL COLLEGE

5234 Airport Road
Roanoke, VA 24012
Web: http://www.ecpitech.edu
Accreditation: Accrediting Commission of Career Schools and Colleges of Technology
Programs Offered:
administrative assistant and secretarial science; business administration and management; clinical laboratory science/medical technology; computer engineering technology; computer/information technology administration and management; computer installation and repair technology; computer systems networking and telecommunications; computer/technical support; computer technology/computer systems technology; information science/studies; medical/clinical assistant; nursing (licensed practical/vocational nurse training); office occupations and clerical services; telecommunications; telecommunications technology; web page, digital/multimedia and information resources design
Enrollment: 315 students
Institution Contact: Mr. Elmer Haas, Director
Phone: 540-563-8080 ext. 205
Fax: 540-362-5400
E-mail: ehaas@ecpitech.edu
Admission Contact: Mr. Brad Kesner, Director of Admissions
Phone: 540-563-8080
Fax: 540-362-5400
E-mail: bkesner@ecpitech.edu

EMPIRE BEAUTY SCHOOL

10807 Hull St. Rd.
Midlothian, VA 23112
Institution Contact: Campus Director
Phone: 804-745-9062
Fax: 804-745-9063

GIBBS SCHOOL

1980 Gallows Road
Vienna, VA 22182
Web: http://www.gibbsva.edu
Accreditation: Accrediting Council for Independent Colleges and Schools
Programs Offered:
business administration and management; computer programming; computer systems networking and telecommunications; criminal justice/law enforcement administration; medical/clinical assistant; visual and performing arts
Institution Contact: Mr. M. Lauck Walton, President
Phone: 703-584-3163
Fax: 703-852-3917
E-mail: lwalton@gibbsva.edu
Admission Contact: Ms. Susan Riggs, Director of Admissions
Phone: 703-584-3151
Fax: 703-559-0953
E-mail: sgriggs@gibbsva.edu

HERITAGE INSTITUTE

350 South Washington Street
Falls Church, VA 22046
Programs Offered:
massage therapy
Institution Contact: Admissions
Phone: 703-532-5050
Fax: 703-534-1142

HERITAGE INSTITUTE

8255 Shopper's Square
Manassas, VA 20111
Web: http://www.heritage-education.com/
Programs Offered:
massage therapy
Institution Contact: Admissions
Phone: 703-361-7775
Fax: 703-335-9987

ITT TECHNICAL INSTITUTE

14420 Albemarle Point Place, Suite 100
Chantilly, VA 20151
Web: http://www.itt-tech.edu
Accreditation: Accrediting Council for Independent

Colleges and Schools
Programs Offered:
accounting and business/management; business administration and management; CAD/CADD drafting/design technology; communications technology; computer and information systems security; computer engineering technology; computer software and media applications; computer systems networking and telecommunications; criminal justice/police science; digital communication and media/multimedia; electrical, electronic and communications engineering technology; technology management; web page, digital/multimedia and information resources design
Institution Contact: Ms. Peggy T. Payne, Director
Phone: 703-263-2541
Admission Contact: Mr. Steve Anderson, Director of Recruitment
Phone: 703-263-2541

ITT TECHNICAL INSTITUTE
863 Glenrock Road, Suite 100
Norfolk, VA 23502-3701
Web: http://www.itt-tech.edu
Accreditation: Accrediting Council for Independent Colleges and Schools
Programs Offered:
accounting and business/management; business administration and management; CAD/CADD drafting/design technology; communications technology; computer and information systems security; computer engineering technology; computer software and media applications; computer software engineering; computer systems networking and telecommunications; criminal justice/police science; digital communication and media/multimedia; electrical, electronic and communications engineering technology; industrial technology; technology management; web page, digital/multimedia and information resources design
Institution Contact: Mr. Calvin Lawrence, Director
Phone: 757-466-1260
Admission Contact: Mr. Jack Keesee, Director of Recruitment
Phone: 757-466-1260

ITT TECHNICAL INSTITUTE
300 Gateway Centre Parkway
Richmond, VA 23235

Web: http://www.itt-tech.edu
Accreditation: Accrediting Commission of Career Schools and Colleges of Technology; Accrediting Council for Independent Colleges and Schools
Programs Offered:
accounting and business/management; animation, interactive technology, video graphics and special effects; business administration and management; CAD/CADD drafting/design technology; communications technology; computer and information systems security; computer engineering technology; computer software and media applications; computer software engineering; computer systems networking and telecommunications; criminal justice/police science; digital communication and media/multimedia; electrical, electronic and communications engineering technology; technology management; web page, digital/multimedia and information resources design
Enrollment: 350 students
Institution Contact: Mr. Doug Howard, Director
Phone: 804-330-4992
Admission Contact: Ms. Elaine Bartoli, Director of Recruitment
Phone: 804-330-4992

 **ITT TECHNICAL INSTITUTE**
7300 Boston Boulevard
Springfield, VA 22153
Web: http://www.itt-tech.edu
Accreditation: Accrediting Council for Independent Colleges and Schools
Programs Offered:
accounting and business/management; business administration and management; CAD/CADD drafting/design technology; communications technology; computer and information systems security; computer engineering technology; computer software and media applications; computer systems networking and telecommunications; criminal justice/police science; digital communication and media/multimedia; electrical, electronic and communications engineering technology; technology management; web page, digital/multimedia and information resources design
Institution Contact: Mr. Paul M. Ochoa, Director of Recruitment
Phone: 703-440-9535
Admission Contact: Mr. Paul M. Ochoa, Director of Recruitment

Phone: 703-440-9535

 KEE BUSINESS COLLEGE

803 Diligence Drive
Newport News, VA 23606
Web: http://www.cci.edu
Accreditation: Accrediting Council for Independent Colleges and Schools
Programs Offered:
accounting; allied health and medical assisting services related; computer/information technology services administration related; computer software and media applications; massage therapy; medical administrative assistant and medical secretary; medical/clinical assistant; medical insurance coding; medical insurance/medical billing; security and loss prevention
Enrollment: 340 students
Institution Contact: Miss Lisa Scott, President
Phone: 757-873-1111
Fax: 757-873-0728
E-mail: lscott@cci.edu
Admission Contact: Mr. Brian Stinson, Sr., Director of Admissions
Phone: 757-873-1111
Fax: 757-873-0728
E-mail: bstinson@cci.edu

 KEE BUSINESS COLLEGE - CHESAPEAKE

825 Greenbrier Circle, Suite 100
Chesapeake, VA 23320-2637
Web: http://kee-business-college.com/
Accreditation: Accrediting Council for Independent Colleges and Schools
Programs Offered:
computer/information technology administration and management; dental assisting; massage therapy; medical administrative assistant and medical secretary; medical/clinical assistant; medical insurance coding; medical insurance/medical billing; safety/security technology
Enrollment: 524 students
Institution Contact: Ms. Lisa S. Scott, President
Phone: 757-361-3900
Fax: 757-361-3917
E-mail: lscott@cci.edu
Admission Contact: Mr. Ed Flores, Director of Admission

Phone: 757-361-3900
Fax: 757-361-3917
E-mail: eflores@cci.edu

MEDICAL CAREERS INSTITUTE
MAP

1001 Omni Boulevard, #200
Newport News, VA 23606-4215
Web: http://www.medical.edu
Accreditation: Council on Occupational Education
Programs Offered:
dental assisting; health and medical administrative services related; massage therapy; medical administrative assistant and medical secretary; medical/clinical assistant; medical office computer specialist; nursing (licensed practical/vocational nurse training); nursing (registered nurse training)
Enrollment: 556 students
Institution Contact: Ms. Barbara Larar, Executive Director
Phone: 757-873-2423
Fax: 757-873-2472
E-mail: blarar@medical.edu

MEDICAL CAREERS INSTITUTE
MAP

800 Moorefield Park Drive, #302
Richmond, VA 23236
Web: http://www.medical.edu
Accreditation: Council on Occupational Education
Programs Offered:
health information/medical records administration; health information/medical records technology; massage therapy; medical/clinical assistant; medical insurance coding; medical insurance/medical billing; medical office computer specialist; medical transcription; nursing (licensed practical/vocational nurse training)
Enrollment: 440 students
Institution Contact: Mr. Jeffrey T. Muroski, Campus Director
Phone: 804-521-0400
Fax: 804-521-0406
E-mail: jmuroski@medical.edu
Admission Contact: Mr. David K. Mayle, Director of Admissions
Phone: 804-521-0400
Fax: 804-521-0406
E-mail: dmayle@medical.edu

MEDICAL CAREERS INSTITUTE

5501 Greenwich Road, #100
Virginia Beach, VA 23462
Web: http://www.medical.edu
Accreditation: Council on Occupational Education
Programs Offered:
health information/medical records administration;
health information/medical records technology;
medical/clinical assistant; medical insurance coding;
medical office computer specialist; medical reception;
medical transcription; nursing (licensed practical/vocational nurse training); nursing (registered nurse training); physical therapist assistant
Enrollment: 555 students
Institution Contact: Mr. Kevin Beaver, Director
Phone: 757-497-8400
Fax: 757-497-8493
E-mail: kbeaver@medical.edu

MILLER-MOTTE TECHNICAL COLLEGE

1011 Creekside Lane
Lynchburg, VA 24502
Web: http://www.miller-motte.com
Accreditation: Accrediting Council for Independent
Colleges and Schools
Programs Offered:
administrative assistant and secretarial science;
aesthetician/esthetician and skin care; business administration and management; criminal justice/law enforcement administration; massage therapy; medical administrative assistant and medical secretary; medical/clinical assistant; pharmacy technician; phlebotomy; surgical technology
Enrollment: 265 students
Institution Contact: Mr. G. David Tipps, Campus
Director
Phone: 434-239-5222
Fax: 434-239-1069
E-mail: dtipps@miller-motte.com

NATIONAL COLLEGE OF BUSINESS & TECHNOLOGY

100 Logan Street
Bluefield, VA 24605
Web: http://www.ncbt.edu
Accreditation: Accrediting Council for Independent
Colleges and Schools
Programs Offered:

accounting; administrative assistant and secretarial
science; business administration and management;
computer software and media applications; medical/
clinical assistant
Institution Contact: Admissions Department
Phone: 276-326-3621
Fax: 276-322-5731

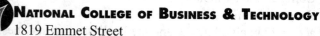

NATIONAL COLLEGE OF BUSINESS & TECHNOLOGY

1819 Emmet Street
Charlottesville, VA 22901
Web: http://www.ncbt.edu
Accreditation: Accrediting Council for Independent
Colleges and Schools
Programs Offered:
accounting; administrative assistant and secretarial science; business administration and management; computer/information technology services administration related; computer software and media applications; medical/clinical assistant; medical insurance coding; medical transcription; pharmacy technician; tourism and travel services management
Enrollment: 168 students
Institution Contact: Mrs. Tracy Harris, Director of
Institutional Reporting
Phone: 540-986-1800
Fax: 540-444-4198
E-mail: tharris@educorp.edu
Admission Contact: Ms. Adrienne D. Granitz, Campus Director
Phone: 434-295-0136
Fax: 434-979-8061
E-mail: agranitz@ncbt.edu

NATIONAL COLLEGE OF BUSINESS & TECHNOLOGY

734 Main Street
Danville, VA 24541
Web: http://www.ncbt.edu
Accreditation: Accrediting Council for Independent
Colleges and Schools
Programs Offered:
accounting; administrative assistant and secretarial science; business administration and management; computer/information technology services administration related; computer software and media applications; medical/clinical assistant; medical insurance coding; medical transcription

Institution Contact: Admissions Department
Phone: 434-793-6822
Fax: 434-793-3634

NATIONAL COLLEGE OF BUSINESS & TECHNOLOGY
51 B Burgess Road
Harrisonburg, VA 22801
Web: http://www.ncbt.edu
Accreditation: Accrediting Council for Independent Colleges and Schools
Programs Offered:
accounting; administrative assistant and secretarial science; business administration and management; computer and information sciences related; medical/clinical assistant; medical insurance coding; medical office assistant; medical transcription; pharmacy technician
Enrollment: 242 students
Institution Contact: Mrs. Tracy Harris, Director of Institutional Reporting
Phone: 540-986-1800
Fax: 540-444-4198
E-mail: tharris@educorp.edu
Admission Contact: Kanika Shipe
Phone: 540-432-0943

NATIONAL COLLEGE OF BUSINESS & TECHNOLOGY
104 Candlewood Court
Lynchburg, VA 24502
Web: http://www.ncbt.edu
Accreditation: Accrediting Council for Independent Colleges and Schools
Programs Offered:
accounting; administrative assistant and secretarial science; business administration and management; computer and information sciences related; medical/clinical assistant; medical insurance coding; medical transcription; pharmacy technician
Institution Contact: Admissions Department
Phone: 434-239-3500
Fax: 434-239-3948

NATIONAL COLLEGE OF BUSINESS & TECHNOLOGY
10 Church Street
Martinsville, VA 24114
Web: http://www.ncbt.edu
Accreditation: Accrediting Council for Independent Colleges and Schools

Programs Offered:
accounting; administrative assistant and secretarial science; business administration and management; computer and information sciences related; medical/clinical assistant; medical insurance coding; medical transcription
Enrollment: 259 students
Institution Contact: Admissions Department
Phone: 276-632-5621
Fax: 276-632-7915

NATIONAL COLLEGE OF BUSINESS & TECHNOLOGY
1813 East Main Street
Salem, VA 24153
Web: http://www.ncbt.edu
Accreditation: Accrediting Council for Independent Colleges and Schools
Programs Offered:
accounting; business administration and management; computer engineering technology; computer software and media applications; hospitality administration; legal assistant/paralegal; medical/clinical assistant; office management; tourism and travel services management
Institution Contact: Admissions Department
Phone: 540-986-1800
Fax: 540-986-1344

PARKS COLLEGE
801 North Quincy Street, Suite 500
Arlington, VA 22203
Web: http://www.parks-college.com
Accreditation: Accrediting Council for Independent Colleges and Schools
Programs Offered:
business administration and management; criminal justice/law enforcement administration; legal assistant/paralegal; securities services administration
Enrollment: 660 students
Institution Contact: Timothy Vogeley, President
Phone: 703-248-8887
Fax: 703-351-2202
E-mail: tvogeley@cci.edu
Admission Contact: Edward Lubin, Director of Admissions
Phone: 703-248-8887
Fax: 703-351-2202
E-mail: elubin@cci.edu

PARKS COLLEGE

1430 Spring Hill Road, Suite 200
McLean, VA 22102
Web: http://www.parks-college.com
Accreditation: Accrediting Council for Independent Colleges and Schools
Programs Offered:
business administration and management; criminal justice/police science; medical/clinical assistant; safety/security technology
Enrollment: 95 students
Institution Contact: Ms. Maxine H. Stine, Campus President
Phone: 703-288-3131
Fax: 703-288-3757
E-mail: mstine@cci.edu

POTOMAC COLLEGE

1029 Herndon Parkway
Herndon, VA 20170
Web: http://www.potomac.edu
Accreditation: Accrediting Council for Independent Colleges and Schools; Middle States Association of Colleges and Schools
Programs Offered:
business administration and management; e-commerce; information science/studies; information technology
Enrollment: 59 students
Institution Contact: Ms. Florence Tate, President
Phone: 202-686-0876
Fax: 202-686-0818
E-mail: ftate@potomac.edu
Admission Contact: Ms. Patricia Rodriguez, Director of Admissions
Phone: 703-709-5875
Fax: 703-709-8972
E-mail: prodriguez@potomac.edu

PROFESSIONAL HEALTHCARE INSTITUTE

PO Box 6400
5385 Mapledale Plaza
Woodbridge, VA 22193
Institution Contact: Ms. Annette Fleming
Phone: 703-580-7951
Fax: 703-580-7183

STRATFORD UNIVERSITY

7777 Leesburg Pike
Falls Church , VA 22043
Web: http://www.stratford.edu
Accreditation: Accrediting Council for Independent Colleges and Schools
Programs Offered:
accounting; baking and pastry arts; business administration and management; computer and information systems security; computer graphics; computer/information technology administration and management; computer/information technology services administration related; computer programming; computer programming (specific applications); computer software and media applications; computer software engineering; computer systems analysis; computer systems networking and telecommunications; computer technology/computer systems technology; culinary arts; digital communication and media/multimedia; e-commerce; engineering technology; finance; food services technology; hotel/motel administration; information science/studies; information technology; international business/trade/commerce; internet information systems; marketing/marketing management; restaurant, culinary, and catering management; technology management; telecommunications; telecommunications technology; web/multimedia management and webmaster; web page, digital/multimedia and information resources design
Enrollment: 500 students
Institution Contact: Ms. Lavona Suppes, Dean of Undergraduate Studies
Phone: 703-734-5321
Fax: 703-734-5335
E-mail: lsuppes@stratford.edu
Admission Contact: Ms. Nicole Kredel, Director of Admissions
Phone: 703-821-8570
Fax: 703-734-5339
E-mail: nkredel@stratford.edu

STRATFORD UNIVERSITY

13576 Minnieville Road
Woodbridge, VA 22192
Web: http://www.stratford.edu
Accreditation: Accrediting Council for Independent Colleges and Schools; Council on Occupational Education
Programs Offered:

business administration and management; computer and information systems security; computer engineering technology; computer/information technology services administration related; computer installation and repair technology; computer programming; computer systems networking and telecommunications; computer/technical support; web page, digital/multimedia and information resources design
Enrollment: 250 students
Institution Contact: Ms. Lavona Suppes, Dean of Undergraduate Studies
Phone: 703-734-5321
Fax: 703-734-5335
E-mail: lsuppes@stratford.edu
Admission Contact: Ted Hart, Director of Admissions
Phone: 703-821-8570
E-mail: admissions@stratford.edu

TESST College of Technology
6315 Bren Mar Drive
Alexandria, VA 22312
Web: http://www.tesst.com
Accreditation: Accrediting Commission of Career Schools and Colleges of Technology
Programs Offered:
business automation/technology/data entry; business machine repair; communications systems installation and repair technology; computer engineering technology; computer hardware engineering; computer/information technology administration and management; computer/information technology services administration related; computer installation and repair technology; computer software and media applications; computer systems networking and telecommunications; computer/technical support; computer technology/computer systems technology; data processing and data processing technology; electrical, electronic and communications engineering technology; electrical/electronics equipment installation and repair; information science/studies; information technology; system administration; system, networking, and LAN/WAN management; telecommunications; web/multimedia management and webmaster; web page, digital/multimedia and information resources design
Institution Contact: Mr. Bob Somers, Director
Phone: 703-548-4800
Fax: 703-683-2765
E-mail: tesstal@erols.com

Admission Contact: Mr. William Scott, Admissions Director
Phone: 703-548-4800
Fax: 703-683-2765
E-mail: alexandriaadmissions@tesst.com

Virginia Career Institute
9210 Arboretum Parkway, Suite 100
Richmond, VA 23236
Web: http://www.virginiacareerinstitute.edu
Accreditation: Accrediting Council for Independent Colleges and Schools
Programs Offered:
massage therapy; medical/clinical assistant; medical office computer specialist
Enrollment: 120 students
Institution Contact: Ms. Danielle M. Rodier, Campus Director
Phone: 804-377-8350 ext. 226
Fax: 804-560-5319
E-mail: drodier@success.edu
Admission Contact: Ms. Janet McGrath, Director of Admissions
Phone: 804-323-1020
Fax: 804-560-5319
E-mail: jmcgrath@success.edu

Virginia Career Institute
100 Constitution Drive, Suite 101
Virginia Beach, VA 23462
Web: http://www.virginiacareerinstitute.edu
Accreditation: Accrediting Council for Independent Colleges and Schools
Programs Offered:
court reporting; massage therapy; medical/clinical assistant; medical office computer specialist; nursing (licensed practical/vocational nurse training)
Institution Contact: Mr. Charles A. Tysinger, School Director
Phone: 757-499-5447
Fax: 757-473-5735
E-mail: atysinger@landmarked.com
Admission Contact: Ms. Katharine Adams, Director of Admissions
Fax: 757-473-5735
E-mail: kadams@success.edu

VIRGINIA SCHOOL OF MASSAGE

2008 Morton Drive
Charlottesville, VA 22903
Web: http://steinered.com
Accreditation: Accrediting Commission of Career Schools and Colleges of Technology
Programs Offered:
alternative and complementary medical support services related; Asian bodywork therapy; facial treatment/facialist; massage therapy
Enrollment: 164 students
Institution Contact: Suzanne Spear, Campus Director
Phone: 434-293-4031
Fax: 434-293-4190
E-mail: suzanne@vasom.com
Admission Contact: Admissions Department
Phone: 434-293-4031
Fax: 434-293-4190
E-mail: suzanne@vasom.com

VIRGINIA SCHOOL OF TECHNOLOGY - RICHMOND CAMPUS

9210 Arboretum Pkwy, Suite 190
Richmond, VA 23236-3472
Institution Contact: Ms. Judy Katzen
Phone: 804-323-1020
Fax: 804-560-5319

VIRGINIA SCHOOL OF TECHNOLOGY

100 Constitution Dr Ste 101
Virginia Beach, VA 23462-6799
Institution Contact: Mr. Charles Tysinger
Phone: 757-499-5447
Fax: 757-473-5735

WASHINGTON

APOLLO COLLEGE

10102 East Knox, Suite 200
Spokane, WA 99206
Web: http://www.apollocollege.com
Accreditation: Accrediting Bureau of Health Education Schools
Programs Offered:
dental assisting; health information/medical records

technology; medical administrative assistant and medical secretary; medical/clinical assistant; medical radiologic technology; pharmacy technician; veterinary/animal health technology
Enrollment: 518 students
Institution Contact: Mr. Walter Leathers, Campus Director
Phone: 509-532-8888
Fax: 509-433-5983
E-mail: wleathers@apollocollege.com
Admission Contact: Mr. Walter Leathers, Campus Director
Phone: 509-532-8888
Fax: 509-433-5983
E-mail: wleathers@apollocollege.com

ARGOSY UNIVERSITY/SEATTLE

1019 Eighth Avenue North
Seattle, WA 98109
Web: http://www.argosyu.edu/
Programs Offered:
education
Institution Contact: Admissions
Phone: 206-283-4500

 THE ART INSTITUTE OF SEATTLE

2323 Elliott Avenue
Seattle, WA 98121
Web: http://www.ais.edu
Accreditation: Northwest Association of Schools and Colleges
Programs Offered:
animation, interactive technology, video graphics and special effects; baking and pastry arts; cinematography and film/video production; commercial and advertising art; computer graphics; culinary arts; design and visual communications; desktop publishing and digital imaging design; digital communication and media/multimedia; fashion/apparel design; fashion merchandising; industrial design; interior design; photography; web/multimedia management and webmaster; web page, digital/multimedia and information resources design
Enrollment: 2,500 students
Institution Contact: Ms. Shelly C. DuBois, President
Phone: 206-239-2314
Fax: 206-448-2501
E-mail: duboiss@aii.edu

Admission Contact: Ms. Karen Shea, Director of Admissions
Phone: 206-239-2242
Fax: 206-448-2501
E-mail: kshea@aii.edu

 ASHMEAD COLLEGE
3019 Colby Avenue
Everett, WA 98201
Web: http://www.ashmeadcollege.com
Accreditation: Accrediting Council for Continuing Education and Training
Programs Offered:
massage therapy
Enrollment: 209 students
Institution Contact: Ms. Meredyth A. Given, College President
Phone: 425-339-2678 ext. 15
Fax: 425-258-2670
E-mail: mgiven@ashmeadcollege.com
Admission Contact: Elizabeth Wade, Director of Admissions
Phone: 425-339-2678
Fax: 425-258-2620
E-mail: ewade@ashmeadcollege.com

ASHMEAD COLLEGE
5005 Pacific Highway East, Suite 20
Fife, WA 98424
Web: http://www.ashmeadcollege.com
Accreditation: Accrediting Council for Continuing Education and Training
Programs Offered:
aromatherapy; athletic training; massage therapy
Enrollment: 400 students
Institution Contact: Lorine Hill, Campus President
Phone: 253-926-1435
Fax: 253-926-0651
E-mail: lhill@cci.edu
Admission Contact: Andrea Niemeyer, Director of Admissions
Phone: 253-926-1435
Fax: 253-926-0651
E-mail: aniemeyer@cci.edu

 ASHMEAD COLLEGE
2111 North Northgate Way, Suite 218
Seattle, WA 98133
Web: http://www.ashmeadcollege.com
Accreditation: Accrediting Council for Continuing Education and Training
Programs Offered:
massage therapy; sport and fitness administration
Institution Contact: Juanita Carpenter, College President
Phone: 206-440-3090
Fax: 206-440-3239
Admission Contact: Juli Lau, Director of Admissions
Phone: 206-440-3090
Fax: 206-440-3239

ASHMEAD COLLEGE SCHOOL OF MASSAGE
120 Northeast 136th Avenue, Suite 220
Vancouver, WA 98684
Web: http://www.ashmeadcollege.com
Accreditation: Accrediting Council for Continuing Education and Training
Programs Offered:
aromatherapy; massage therapy
Institution Contact: Lalitha Pataki, Director of Admissions
Phone: 360-885-3152
Fax: 360-885-3151

BRYMAN COLLEGE
906 Southeast Everett Mall Way, Suite 600
Everett, WA 98208
Web: http://www.bryman-college.com
Accreditation: Accrediting Council for Independent Colleges and Schools
Programs Offered:
dental assisting; medical/clinical assistant; medical insurance/medical billing; pharmacy technician
Institution Contact: School President
Phone: 425-789-7960
Fax: 425-789-7989
Admission Contact: Admissions Representative
Phone: 425-789-7960
Fax: 425-789-7989

BRYMAN COLLEGE
19020 33rd Avenue West, Suite 250
Lynnwood, WA 98036
Web: http://bryman-college.com/about.php?schoolLoc
ation=Lynnwood
Accreditation: Accrediting Commission of Career
Schools and Colleges of Technology
Programs Offered:
dental assisting; medical administrative assistant and
medical secretary; medical/clinical assistant; medical
insurance coding; medical insurance/medical billing
Enrollment: 270 students
Institution Contact: Mr. Frederick L Pressel, President
Phone: 425-778-9894
Fax: 425-778-9794
E-mail: fpressel@cci.edu
Admission Contact: Mr. James Newman, Director of
Admissions
Phone: 425-778-9894
Fax: 425-778-9794
E-mail: jnewman@cci.edu

BRYMAN COLLEGE
3649 Frontage Road
Port Orchard, WA 98367
Web: http://brymancollege.com
Accreditation: Accrediting Council for Independent
Colleges and Schools
Programs Offered:
dental assisting; medical/clinical assistant; medical
insurance/medical billing; pharmacy technician
Institution Contact: Sheila Austin , Director of Ad-
missions
Phone: 360-473-1120
Fax: 360-792-2404
E-mail: saustin@cci.edu
Admission Contact: Sheila Austin, Director of Ad-
missions
Phone: 360-473-1120
Fax: 360-792-2404
E-mail: saustin@cci.edu

BRYMAN COLLEGE
981 Powell Avenue, SW, Suite 200
Renton, WA 98055
Web: http://www.bryman-college.com
Accreditation: Accrediting Commission of Career

Schools and Colleges of Technology
Programs Offered:
dental assisting; medical administrative assistant and
medical secretary; medical/clinical assistant; pharmacy
technician
Admission Contact: Paige Mathis, Director of Admis-
sions
Phone: 425-255-3281
Fax: 425-255-9327
E-mail: pmathis@cci.edu

BRYMAN COLLEGE
2156 Pacific Avenue
Tacoma, WA 98402
Accreditation: Accrediting Council for Independent
Colleges and Schools
Programs Offered:
dental assisting; medical/clinical assistant; medical
insurance/medical billing; pharmacy technician
Enrollment: 426 students
Institution Contact: Mr. Timothy E. Allen, President
Phone: 253-207-4000
Fax: 253-207-4031
E-mail: t.allen@etontech.com
Admission Contact: Mrs. Lynette Rickman, Director
of Admissions
Phone: 253-207-4000
Fax: 253-207-4031
E-mail: l.rickman@etontech.com

CAMBRIDGE COLLEGE
14432 S.E. Eastgate Way Suite 100
Bellevue, WA 98007
Programs Offered:
dental assisting; massage therapy; medical/clinical
assistant; medical insurance coding; medical insur-
ance/medical billing; pharmacy technician; surgical
technology
Institution Contact: Ms. Catherine Jean Weber, Cam-
pus President
Phone: 425-974-7100
Fax: 425-747-0766
E-mail: cweber@hightechinstitute.edu
Admission Contact: Ms. Lori Boe, Director of Ad-
missions
Phone: 425-974-7100
Fax: 425-747-0766

E-mail: lboe@hightechinstitute.edu

GENE JUAREZ ACADEMY – SOUTH SEATTLE CAMPUS

2222 S. 314th St.
Federal Way, WA 98003
Institution Contact: Mr. Jessie Bland
Phone: 253-839-6483
Fax: 253-946-6560

GENE JUAREZ ACADEMY OF BEAUTY

10715 8th Avenue, Northeast
Seattle, WA 98125
Web: http://www.genejuarezacademy.com
Accreditation: National Accrediting Commission of
Cosmetology Arts and Sciences
Programs Offered:
cosmetology; cosmetology, barber/styling, and nail
instruction; nail technician and manicurist
Enrollment: 204 students
Institution Contact: Ms. Linda DeBarros, Vice
President
Phone: 425-748-1404
E-mail: www.lindad@genejuarez.com
Admission Contact: Ms. Kathleeen Mason, Director
of Admissions
Phone: 206-368-0210
E-mail: kathleen@genejuarez.com

INTERNATIONAL ACADEMY OF DESIGN AND TECHNOLOGY

645 Andover Park West
Seattle, WA 98188
Web: http://www.iadtseattle.com
Accreditation: Accrediting Council for Independent
Colleges and Schools
Programs Offered:
fashion/apparel design; graphic communications;
interior design
Enrollment: 370 students
Institution Contact: Mr. Michael Gary Milford,
President
Phone: 206-575-1865
Fax: 206-575-1192
E-mail: mmilford@iadtseattle.com
Admission Contact: Mr. Jack Kempt, Director of

Admissions
Phone: 206-575-1865
Fax: 206-575-1192
E-mail: jkempt@iadtseattle.com

ITT TECHNICAL INSTITUTE

Canyon Park East, 2525 223rd Street, SE
Bothell, WA 98021
Web: http://www.itt-tech.edu
Accreditation: Accrediting Council for Independent
Colleges and Schools
Programs Offered:
accounting and business/management; animation,
interactive technology, video graphics and special
effects; business administration and management;
CAD/CADD drafting/design technology; communications technology; computer and information sciences
related; computer and information systems security;
computer engineering technology; computer software
and media applications; computer software engineering; computer systems networking and telecommunications; criminal justice/police science; digital
communication and media/multimedia; electrical, electronic and communications engineering technology;
technology management; web page, digital/multimedia
and information resources design
Institution Contact: Mr. Mike Milford, Director
Phone: 425-485-0303
Admission Contact: Mr. Jon L. Scherrer, Director of
Recruitment
Phone: 425-485-0303

ITT TECHNICAL INSTITUTE

12720 Gateway Drive, Suite 100
Seattle, WA 98168-3333
Web: http://www.itt-tech.edu
Accreditation: Accrediting Council for Independent
Colleges and Schools
Programs Offered:
accounting and business/management; animation,
interactive technology, video graphics and special
effects; business administration and management;
CAD/CADD drafting/design technology; communications technology; computer and information systems
security; computer engineering technology; computer
software and media applications; computer software
engineering; computer systems networking and tele-

communications; criminal justice/police science; digital communication and media/multimedia; electrical, electronic and communications engineering technology; technology management; web page, digital/multimedia and information resources design
Institution Contact: Mr. Jack Kempt, Director of Recruitment
Phone: 206-244-3300
Admission Contact: Mr. Jack Kempt, Director of Recruitment
Phone: 206-244-3300
E-mail: jkempt@itt-tech.edu

ITT TECHNICAL INSTITUTE
1050 North Argonne Road
Spokane, WA 99212-2682
Web: http://www.itt-tech.edu
Accreditation: Accrediting Council for Independent Colleges and Schools
Programs Offered:
animation, interactive technology, video graphics and special effects; CAD/CADD drafting/design technology; communications technology; computer and information systems security; computer engineering technology; computer software and media applications; computer software engineering; computer systems networking and telecommunications; digital communication and media/multimedia; electrical, electronic and communications engineering technology; technology management; web page, digital/multimedia and information resources design
Institution Contact: Mr. William King, Director
Phone: 509-926-2900
Admission Contact: Mr. Gregory L. Alexander, Director of Recruitment
Phone: 509-926-2900

PIMA MEDICAL INSTITUTE
555 South Renton Village Place, Suite 110
Renton, WA 98055
Web: http://www.pmi.edu
Accreditation: Accrediting Bureau of Health Education Schools
Programs Offered:
dental assisting; medical administrative assistant and medical secretary; medical/clinical assistant; pharmacy technician; phlebotomy; veterinary/animal health

technology
Enrollment: 313 students
Institution Contact: Mr. Christopher Luebke, Admissions Support Center Director
Phone: 888-898-9048
E-mail: asc@pmi.edu
Admission Contact: Admissions Support Representative
Phone: 888-898-9048
E-mail: asc@pmi.edu

PIMA MEDICAL INSTITUTE
1627 Eastlake Avenue East
Seattle, WA 98102
Web: http://www.pmi.edu
Accreditation: Accrediting Bureau of Health Education Schools
Programs Offered:
dental assisting; medical administrative assistant and medical secretary; medical/clinical assistant; pharmacy technician; phlebotomy; radiologic technology/science; veterinary/animal health technology
Enrollment: 314 students
Institution Contact: Mr. Christopher Luebke, Admissions Support Center Director
Phone: 888-898-9048
E-mail: asc@pmi.edu
Admission Contact: Admissions Support Representative
Phone: 888-898-9048
E-mail: asc@pmi.edu

WESTERN BUSINESS COLLEGE
Stonemill Center, 120 Northeast 136th Avenue, Suite 130
Vancouver, WA 98684
Web: http://www.cci.edu
Accreditation: Accrediting Council for Independent Colleges and Schools
Programs Offered:
accounting; administrative assistant and secretarial science; data entry/microcomputer applications; executive assistant/executive secretary; legal administrative assistant/secretary; legal assistant/paralegal; medical administrative assistant and medical secretary; medical/clinical assistant; medical insurance/medical billing; office occupations and clerical services
Enrollment: 350 students
Institution Contact: Mr. Edward Leonard Yakimchick, President

Phone: 360-254-3282
Fax: 360-254-3035
E-mail: eyakimch@cci.edu
Admission Contact: Ms. Renee Schiffhauer, Director of Admissions
Phone: 360-254-3282
Fax: 360-254-3035
E-mail: rschiffhauer@cci.edu

WEST VIRGINIA

AMERICAN PUBLIC EDUCATION, INC.
111 W. Congress
Charles Town, WV 25414
Institution Contact: James Herhusky
Phone: 304-724-3751
Fax: 304-724-3780

 NATIONAL INSTITUTE OF TECHNOLOGY
5514 Big Tyler Road
Cross Lanes, WV 25313
Web: http://www.cci.edu
Accreditation: Accrediting Commission of Career Schools and Colleges of Technology
Programs Offered:
computer engineering technology; computer systems networking and telecommunications; electrical, electronic and communications engineering technology; massage therapy; medical/clinical assistant; pharmacy technician; security and loss prevention
Enrollment: 540 students
Institution Contact: Dr. Robert L. Bliss, President
Phone: 304-776-6290
Fax: 304-776-6262
E-mail: rbliss@cci.edu
Admission Contact: Ms. Karen Wilkinson, Admissions Director
Phone: 304-776-6290
Fax: 304-776-6262
E-mail: kwilkins@cci.edu

WEST VIRGINIA JUNIOR COLLEGE
176 Thompson Drive
Bridgeport, WV 26330
Accreditation: Accrediting Council for Independent

Colleges and Schools
Programs Offered:
administrative assistant and secretarial science; computer/information technology services administration related; computer installation and repair technology; computer software and media applications; computer systems networking and telecommunications; computer/technical support; computer technology/computer systems technology; data entry/microcomputer applications; health information/medical records technology; medical administrative assistant and medical secretary; medical/clinical assistant; medical office management; medical transcription; web/multimedia management and webmaster; web page, digital/multimedia and information resources design; word processing
Enrollment: 216 students
Institution Contact: Ms. Sharron Stephens, Executive Director
Phone: 304-842-4007
Fax: 304-842-8191
E-mail: kstanley@wvjcinfo.net
Admission Contact: Ms. Sharron Stephens, Director of Admissions
Phone: 304-842-4007
Fax: 304-842-8191
E-mail: kstanley@wvjcinfo.net

 WEST VIRGINIA JUNIOR COLLEGE
1000 Virginia Street, East
Charleston, WV 25301
Web: http://www.wvjc.com
Accreditation: Accrediting Council for Independent Colleges and Schools
Programs Offered:
computer/information technology administration and management; legal administrative assistant/secretary; medical administrative assistant and medical secretary; medical/clinical assistant; web page, digital/multimedia and information resources design
Enrollment: 162 students
Institution Contact: Mr. Thomas Crouse, President/Director
Phone: 304-345-2820
Fax: 304-345-1425
E-mail: tacrouse@charter.net
Admission Contact: Mr. Tom Crouse, Director
Phone: 304-345-2820
Fax: 304-345-1425

E-mail: tacrouse@charter.net

WEST VIRGINIA JUNIOR COLLEGE

148 Willey Street
Morgantown, WV 26505
Web: http://www.wvjcmorgantown.edu
Accreditation: Accrediting Council for Independent
Colleges and Schools
Programs Offered:
accounting; administrative assistant and secretarial science; business administration and management; com-
puter/information technology services administration
related; computer installation and repair technology;
computer software and media applications; computer
systems networking and telecommunications; comput-
er/technical support; computer technology/computer
systems technology; data entry/microcomputer applications; legal assistant/paralegal; medical administrative assistant and medical secretary; medical/clinical
assistant; medical office management; medical transcription; receptionist; web/multimedia management
and webmaster; web page, digital/multimedia and
information resources design; word processing
Enrollment: 180 students
Institution Contact: Ms. Patricia Callen, Executive
Director
Phone: 304-296-8282
Fax: 304-296-5612
E-mail: pcallen@wvjc.com
Admission Contact: Ms. Amanda Rugg, Admissions
Director
Phone: 304-296-8282
Fax: 304-296-5612
E-mail: arugg@wvjcmorgantown.edu

WISCONSIN

HERZING COLLEGE

5218 East Terrace Drive
Madison, WI 53718
Web: http://www.herzing.edu
Accreditation: Accrediting Commission of Career
Schools and Colleges of Technology; North Central
Association of Colleges and Schools
Programs Offered:
architectural drafting and CAD/CADD; banking and

financial support services; business administration and
management; business administration, management
and operations related; business/corporate communications; CAD/CADD drafting/design technology; civil
drafting and CAD/CADD; communications technology; computer and information sciences; computer
and information sciences and support services related;
computer and information sciences related; computer
and information systems security; computer engineering technology; computer graphics; computer
hardware technology; computer/information technology administration and management; computer/in-
formation technology services administration related;
computer installation and repair technology; computer
programming; computer programming related; computer programming (specific applications); computer
programming (vendor/product certification); computer
science; computer software technology; computer
systems analysis; computer systems networking and
telecommunications; computer/technical support;
computer technology/computer systems technology;
criminal justice/law enforcement administration;
criminal justice/police science; drafting and design
technology; electrical, electronic and communications
engineering technology; information technology; legal
assistant/paralegal; management information systems;
management information systems and services related;
marketing/marketing management; mechanical design
technology; mechanical drafting and CAD/CADD;
medical administrative assistant and medical secretary;
medical insurance coding; medical insurance/medical
billing; safety/security technology; small business administration; system administration; system, networking, and LAN/WAN management; technology management; telecommunications technology; web page,
digital/multimedia and information resources design
Enrollment: 661 students
Institution Contact: Mr. Donald Madelung, President
Phone: 608-249-6611
Fax: 608-249-8593
E-mail: donmad@msn.herzing.edu
Admission Contact: Ms. Rebecca Abrams, Director
of Admissions
Phone: 608-249-6611
Fax: 608-249-8593
E-mail: rabrams@msn.herzing.edu

ITT TECHNICAL INSTITUTE
470 Security Boulevard
Green Bay, WI 54313
Web: http://www.itt-tech.edu
Accreditation: Accrediting Council for Independent Colleges and Schools
Programs Offered:
accounting and business/management; animation, interactive technology, video graphics and special effects; business administration and management; CAD/CADD drafting/design technology; communications technology; computer and information systems security; computer engineering technology; computer software and media applications; computer software engineering; computer systems networking and telecommunications; criminal justice/police science; digital communication and media/multimedia; electrical, electronic and communications engineering technology; technology management; web page, digital/multimedia and information resources design
Institution Contact: Mr. Raymond Sweetman, Director of Recruitment
Phone: 920-662-9000
Admission Contact: Mr. Raymond Sweetman, Director of Recruitment
Phone: 920-662-9000

ITT TECHNICAL INSTITUTE
6300 West Layton Avenue
Greenfield, WI 53220-4612
Web: http://www.itt-tech.edu
Accreditation: Accrediting Council for Independent Colleges and Schools
Programs Offered:
accounting and business/management; advanced/graduate dentistry and oral sciences related; animation, interactive technology, video graphics and special effects; business administration and management; CAD/CADD drafting/design technology; communications technology; computer and information systems security; computer engineering technology; computer software and media applications; computer software engineering; computer systems networking and telecommunications; criminal justice/police science; digital communication and media/multimedia; electrical, electronic and communications engineering technology; technology management; web page, digital/multimedia and information resources design

Institution Contact: Mr. Jonathan L. Patterson, Director
Phone: 414-282-9494
Admission Contact: Mr. Brian Guenther, Director of Recruitment
Phone: 414-282-9494

MADISON MEDIA INSTITUTE
2702 Agriculture Drive
Madison, WI 53718
Web: http://www.madisonmedia.com
Accreditation: Accrediting Commission of Career Schools and Colleges of Technology
Programs Offered:
animation, interactive technology, video graphics and special effects; digital communication and media/multimedia; radio and television; recording arts technology; web page, digital/multimedia and information resources design
Enrollment: 330 students
Institution Contact: Mr. Chris K. Hutchings, President/Director
Phone: 608-663-2000
Fax: 608-442-0141
E-mail: chutch@madisonmedia.com
Admission Contact: Mr. Steve W. Hutchings, Vice President/Director of Admissions
Phone: 608-663-2000
Fax: 608-442-0141
E-mail: swh@madisonmedia.com

SANFORD-BROWN COLLEGE
6737 W. Washington St., Suite 2355
West Allis, WI 53214
Web: www.sbcmilwaukee.com
Institution Contact: Mr. Sidney Carey
Phone: 414-771-3300
Fax: 414-771-9860

WYOMING

SAGE TECHNICAL SERVICES
2368 Oil Drive
Casper, WY 82604
Web: http://www.sageschools.com
Accreditation: Accrediting Commission of Career

Schools and Colleges of Technology
Programs Offered:
transportation technology; truck and bus driver/commercial vehicle operation
Enrollment: 20 students
Institution Contact: Ms. Lisa Engebretsen, School Director
Phone: 307-234-0242
Fax: 307-234-0552
E-mail: casper@sageschools.com

WYOTECH
4373 North 3rd Street
Laramie, WY 82072-9519
Web: http://www.wyotech.com
Accreditation: Accrediting Commission of Career

Schools and Colleges of Technology
Programs Offered:
autobody/collision and repair technology; automobile/automotive mechanics technology; diesel mechanics technology; engine machinist; sheet metal technology; upholstery; welding technology
Enrollment: 3,224 students
Institution Contact: Ms. Helen Bosler, Director of Licensing and Accreditation, TSi Division
Phone: 307-399-2887
Fax: 307-721-4158
E-mail: hbosler@cci.edu
Admission Contact: Mr. Glenn Halsey, Director of Admissions
Phone: 307-742-3776
Fax: 307-742-4354
E-mail: ghalsey@wyotech.com

indicates a participating institution in the *Imagine America* Scholarship Program. **MAP** indicates a participating institution in the Military Award Program.

ALPHABETICAL LISTING OF ALLIED MEMBERS

GEOGRAPHICAL LISTING OF CAREER COLLEGES

ALABAMA

Capps College, Dothan, AL 70
Capps College, Foley, AL 70
Capps College, Mobile, AL 70
Capps College, Montgomery, AL 70
Herzing College, Birmingham, AL 70
ITT Technical Institute, Bessemer, AL 71
Medical Career Center, Mobile, AL 71
Remington College - Mobile Campus, Mobile, AL 71
South University, Montgomery, AL 71
VC Tech, Pelham, AL 72
Virginia College at Birmingham, Birmingham, AL 72
Virginia College at Huntsville, Huntsville, AL 73
Virginia College at Mobile, Mobile, AL 73

ALASKA

Career Academy, Anchorage, AK 73
Charter College, Anchorage, AK 74

ARIZONA

Academy of Radio Broadcasting, Phoenix, AZ 74
American Institute of Technology, Phoenix, AZ 74
Anthem College Online, Phoenix, AZ 74
Apollo College-Phoenix, Inc., Phoenix, AZ 74
Apollo College-Tri-City, Inc., Mesa, AZ 75
Apollo College-Tucson, Inc., Tucson, AZ 75
Apollo College-Westside, Inc., Phoenix, AZ 75
Argosy University/Phoenix, Phoenix, AZ 75
Arizona Automotive Institute, Glendale, AZ 76
Arizona College of Allied Health, Glendale, AZ 76
Arizona School of Massage Therapy, Phoenix, AZ 76
Arizona School of Massage Therapy - Tempe, Tempe, AZ 76
The Art Institute of Phoenix, Phoenix, AZ 76
The Bryman School, Phoenix, AZ 77
Chaparral College, Tucson, AZ 77
CollegeAmerica-Flagstaff, Flagstaff, AZ 77
Collins College: A School of Design and Technology
Tempe, AZ 77
Conservatory of Recording Arts and Sciences,
Tempe, AZ 78
Everest College, Phoenix, AZ 78
High-Tech Institute, Phoenix, AZ 78
International Import-Export Institute, Phoenix, AZ 79
ITT Technical Institute, Tempe, AZ 79
ITT Technical Institute, Tucson, AZ 79
Lamson College, Tempe, AZ 79
Long Technical College, Phoenix, AZ 80
Long Technical College-East Valley, Phoenix, AZ 80

Motorcycle Mechanics Institute, Phoenix, AZ 80
Pima Medical Institute, Mesa, AZ 80
Pima Medical Institute, Tucson, AZ 81
The Refrigeration School, Phoenix, AZ 81
Remington College - Tempe Campus, Tempe, AZ 81
Scottsdale Culinary Institute, Scottsdale, AZ 81
Sonoran Desert Institute, Scottsdale, AZ 81
Tucson College, Tucson, AZ 82
Universal Technical Institute, Avondale, AZ 82
Western International University, Phoenix, AZ 82

ARKANSAS

Eastern College of Health Vocations, Little Rock, AR 82
ITT Technical Institute, Little Rock, AR 82
Remington College-Little Rock Campus, Little Rock, AR 83

BRITISH VIRGIN ISLANDS

New England Culinary Institute at H. Lavity Stoutt Community College, Road Town, Tortola, British Virgin Islands 83

CALIFORNIA

Academy of Art University, San Francisco, CA 83
Academy of Radio Broadcasting, Huntington Beach, CA 84
Academy Pacific Travel College, Los Angeles, CA 84
Advanced Training Associates, El Cajon, CA 84
American Career College, Anaheim, CA 84
American Career College, Inc., Los Angeles, CA 84
American Career College - Norco Campus, Norco, CA 85
American InterContinental University, Los Angeles, CA 85
Argosy University/Orange County, Santa Ana, CA 85
Argosy University/San Francisco Bay Area, Point Richmond, CA 85
Argosy University, Ventura, CA 85
The Art Institute of California - Los Angeles, Santa Monica, CA 85
The Art Institute of California - Orange County, Santa Ana, CA 86
The Art Institute of California - San Diego, San Diego, CA 86
The Art Institute of California - San Francisco, San Francisco, CA 86
Brooks College, Long Beach, CA 86
Brooks College, Sunnyvale, CA 86
Brooks Institute of Photography, Santa Barbara, CA 87
Brown Mackie College, Los Angeles Campus, Santa Monica, CA 87
Brown Mackie College, Orange County Campus, Santa

Ana, CA 87

Brown Mackie College, San Diego Campus, San Diego, CA 87

Bryan College of Court Reporting, Los Angeles, CA 88

Bryman College, Alhambra, CA 88

Bryman College, Anaheim, CA 88

Bryman College, City of Industry, CA 88

Bryman College, Gardena, CA 88

Bryman College, Hayward, CA 89

Bryman College, Los Angeles, CA 89

Bryman College, Los Angeles, CA 89

Bryman College, Ontario, CA 89

Bryman College, Reseda, CA 89

Bryman College, San Bernardino, CA 90

Bryman College, San Francisco, CA 90

Bryman College, San Jose, CA 90

Bryman College, Torrance, CA 90

California Culinary Academy, San Francisco, CA 91

California Design College, Los Angeles, CA 91

California Healing Arts College, Los Angeles, CA 91

California School of Culinary Arts, Pasadena, CA 91

Career Networks Institute, Costa Mesa, CA 91

Central Coast College, Salinas, CA 92

Clarita Career College, Canyon Country, CA 92

Clarita Career College - Lancaster Campus, Lancaster, CA 92

Coleman College, La Mesa, CA 92

Coleman College, San Marcos, CA 93

Community Business College, Modesto, CA 93

Empire College, Santa Rosa, CA 93

Everest College, Rancho Cucamonga, CA 93

Ex'pression College for Digital Arts, Emeryville, CA 94

Four-D Success Academy, Colton, CA 94

Galen College of California, Inc., Fresno, CA 94

Galen College of California, Inc., Modesto, CA 94

Galen College of California, Inc., Visalia, CA 94

Gemological Institute of America, Inc., Carlsbad, CA 95

Gemological Institute of America, Inc., Culver City, CA 95

Glendale Career College, Glendale, CA 95

Glendale Career College - Oceanside, Oceanside, CA 95

Golden State College, Visalia, CA 95

High-Tech Institute, Sacramento, CA 96

Institute for Business and Technology, Santa Clara, CA 96

Institute of Technology, Fresno, CA 96

ITT Technical Institute, Anaheim, CA 96

ITT Technical Institute, Lathrop, CA 96

ITT Technical Institute, Oxnard, CA 97

ITT Technical Institute, Rancho Cordova, CA 97

ITT Technical Institute, San Bernardino, CA 97

ITT Technical Institute, San Diego, CA 97

ITT Technical Institute, Sylmar, CA 98

ITT Technical Institute, Torrance, CA 98

ITT Technical Institute, West Covina, CA 98

Kitchen Academy, Los Angeles, CA 99

Maric College, Anaheim, CA 99

Maric College - Fresno, Clovis, CA 99

Maric College, North Hollywood, CA 99

Maric College, Sacramento, CA 99

Maric College, Salida, CA 99

Maric College, San Diego, CA 100

Maric College, Vista, CA 100

Maric College, Los Angeles, CA 100

National Career Education, Citrus Heights, CA 100

National Institute of Technology, Long Beach, CA 101

Newschool of Architecture & Design, San Diego, CA 101

Pima Medical Institute, Chula Vista, CA 101

Platt College, Huntington Beach, CA 101

Platt College, Ontario, CA 102

Platt College - Los Angeles, Inc, Alhambra, CA 102

Platt College - San Diego, San Diego, CA 102

Remington College - San Diego Campus, San Diego, CA 103

San Joaquin Valley College, Bakersfield, CA 103

San Joaquin Valley College, Fresno, CA 103

San Joaquin Valley College, Fresno, CA 103

San Joaquin Valley College, Modesto, CA 104

San Joaquin Valley College, Rancho Cucamonga, CA 104

San Joaquin Valley College Inc., Rancho Cordova, CA 104

San Joaquin Valley College, Visalia, CA 104

San Joaquin Valley College Inc., Visalia, CA 104

Santa Barbara Business College, Bakersfield, CA 104

Santa Barbara Business College, Santa Barbara, CA 105

Santa Barbara Business College, Santa Maria, CA 105

Santa Barbara Business College, Ventura, CA 105

Silicon Valley College, Emeryville, CA 105

Silicon Valley College, Fremont, CA 106

Silicon Valley College, San Jose, CA 106

United Education Institute, Chula Vista, CA 106

United Education Institute, El Monte, CA 106

United Education Institute, Huntington Park, Huntington Park, CA 107

United Education Institute, Los Angeles, Los Angeles, CA 107

United Education Institute, Ontario Campus, Ontario, CA 107

United Education Institute, San Bernardino Campus, San Bernardino, CA 107

United Education Institute, San Diego Campus, San Diego, CA 107

United Education Institute, Van Nuys Campus, Van Nuys, CA 108

Universal Technical Institute, Rancho Cucamonga, CA 108

Walter Jay M.D. Institute, an Educational Center, Los Ange-

les, CA 108
Western Career College, Pleasant Hill, CA 108
Western Career College, Sacramento, CA 108
Western Career College, San Leandro, CA 109
Western College of Southern California, Cerritos, CA 109
Western State University College of Law, Fullerton, CA 109
Westwood College - Anaheim, Anaheim, CA 109
Westwood College - Inland Empire, Upland, CA 109
Westwood College - Long Beach, Torrance, CA 110
Westwood College - Los Angeles, Inglewood, CA 110
Westwood College - Los Angeles, Los Angeles, CA 110
WyoTech, Fremont, CA 111
WyoTech, Oakland, CA 111
WyoTech, West Sacramento, CA 111

COLORADO
The Art Institute of Colorado, Denver, CO 111
Bel-Rea Institute of Animal Technology, Denver, CO 112
Blair College, Colorado Springs, CO 112
Cambridge College, Aurora, CO 112
CollegeAmerica - Colorado Springs, Colorado Springs, CO 112
CollegeAmerica - Denver, Denver, CO 113
CollegeAmerica - Fort Collins, Fort Collins, CO 113
College for Financial Planning, Greenwood Village, CO 113
Colorado School of Trades, Lakewood, CO 113
Colorado Technical University, Colorado Springs, CO 113
Colorado Technical University Denver Campus, Greenwood Village, CO 114
Denver Automotive and Diesel College, Denver, CO 114
Denver Career College, Thornton, CO 114
Denver School of Massage Therapy - Aurora, Aurora, CO 115
Denver School of Massage Therapy - Westminster, Westminster, CO 115
Heritage College, Denver, CO 115
ITT Technical Institute, Thornton, CO 115
Jones International University, Englewood, CO 115
National American University, Colorado Springs, CO 115
National American University, Denver, CO 116
Parks College, Aurora, CO 116
Parks College, Denver, CO 116
Pima Medical Institute, Colorado Springs, CO 116
Pima Medical Institute, Denver, CO 117
Remington College - Colorado Springs Campus, Colorado Springs, CO 117
Remington College - Denver Campus, Lakewood, CO 117
Sage Technical Services, Grand Junction, CO 117
Sage Technical Services, Henderson, CO 118
Westwood College - Denver, Broomfield, CO 118
Westwood College - Denver North, Denver, CO 118
Westwood College - Denver South, Denver, CO 118

CONNECTICUT
Gibbs College, Norwalk, CT 119
New England Technical Institute, Cromwell, CT 119
New England Technical Institute, Hamden, CT 119
New England Technical Institute, Shelton, CT 119
New England Technical Institute of Connecticut, Inc., New Britain, CT 119
Porter and Chester Institute, Enfield, CT 120
Porter and Chester Institute, Stratford, CT 120
Porter and Chester Institute, Watertown, CT 120
Porter and Chester Institute, Wethersfield, CT 120

DELEWARE
Dawn Training Centre, Inc., Wilmington, DE 120
Harrison Career Institute, Wilmington, DE 121

DISTRICT OF COLUMBIA
Potomac College, Washington, DC 121

FLORIDA
Advanced Career Training, Jacksonville, FL 121
American InterContinental University, Weston, FL 121
AMI, Inc. , Daytona Beach, FL 122
Argosy University/Sarasota, Sarasota, FL 122
Argosy University/Tampa Parkside at Tampa Bay Park, Tampa, FL 122
The Art Institute of Fort Lauderdale, Fort Lauderdale, FL 122
ATI Career Training Center, Fort Lauderdale, FL 122
ATI Career Training Center, Miami, FL 123
ATI Career Training Center, Oakland Park, FL 123
ATI Health Education Center, Miami, FL 123
Barbara Brennan School of Healing, Boca Raton, FL 124
Brown Mackie College, Miami Campus, Miami, FL 124
Capps College, Pensacola, FL 124
Career Training Institute, Apopka, FL 124
Central Florida College, Winter Park, FL 124
Everglades University, Boca Raton, FL 125
Everglades University, Orlando, FL 125
Everglades University, Sarasota, FL 125
Florida Career College, Hialeah, FL 125
Florida Career College, Miami, FL 125
Florida Career College, Pembroke Pines, FL 126
Florida Career College, West Palm Beach, FL 126
Florida College of Natural Health, Bradenton, FL 126
Florida College of Natural Health, Maitland, FL 126
Florida College of Natural Health, Miami, FL 126
Florida College of Natural Health, Pompano Beach, FL 126
Florida Metropolitan University - Brandon Campus, Tampa, FL 127
Florida Metropolitan University - Jacksonville Campus, Jacksonville, FL 127
Florida Metropolitan University - Lakeland Campus,

Lakeland, FL 127

Florida Metropolitan University-Melbourne Campus, Melbourne, FL 127

Florida Metropolitan University - North Orlando Campus, Orlando, FL 128

Florida Metropolitan University - Orange Park Campus, Orange Park, FL 128

Florida Metropolitan University - Pinellas Campus, Clearwater, FL 128

Florida Metropolitan University - Pompano Beach Campus, Pompano Beach, FL 129

Florida Metropolitan University - South Orlando Campus, Orlando, FL 129

Florida Metropolitan University - Tampa Campus, Tampa, FL 129

Florida Technical College, Auburndale, FL 129

Florida Technical College, DeLand, FL 130

Florida Technical College, Jacksonville, FL 130

Florida Technical College, Orlando, FL 130

Full Sail Real World Education, Winter Park, FL 131

Gulf Coast College, Tampa, FL 131

Heritage Institute, Fort Myers, FL 131

Heritage Institute, Jacksonville, FL 131

Herzing College, Winter Park, FL 131

High-Tech Institute, Orlando, FL 132

International Academy of Design & Technology, Orlando, FL 132

International Academy of Design & Technology, Tampa, FL 132

ITT Technical Institute, Fort Lauderdale, FL 133

ITT Technical Institute, Jacksonville, FL 133

ITT Technical Institute, Lake Mary, FL 133

ITT Technical Institute, Miami, FL 133

ITT Technical Institute, Tampa, FL 134

Keiser College, Daytona Beach, FL 134

Keiser College, Fort Lauderdale, FL 134

Keiser College, Lakeland, FL 135

Keiser College, Melbourne, FL 135

Keiser College, Miami, FL 135

Keiser College, Orlando, FL 135

Keiser College, Pembroke Pines, FL 136

Keiser College, Port St. Lucie, FL 136

Keiser College, Sarasota, FL 136

Keiser College, Tallahassee, FL 136

Keiser College, West Palm Beach, FL 137

Key College, Fort Lauderdale, FL 137

La Belle Beauty School, Hialeah, FL 137

Le Cordon Bleu College of Culinary Arts Miami, Miramar, FL 137

Marine Mechanics Institute, Orlando, FL 137

MedVance Institute, Atlantis, FL 138

MedVance Institute, Fort Lauderdale, FL 138

MedVance Institute, Miami, FL 138

MedVance Institute, Port St. Lucie, FL 138

Miami International University of Art & Design, Miami, FL 138

National School of Technology, Inc., Fort Lauderdale, FL 139

National School of Technology, Inc., Hialeah, FL 139

National School of Technology, Inc., Miami, FL 139

National School of Technology, Inc., Miami, FL 139

New England Institute of Technology at Palm Beach, West Palm Beach, FL 140

North Florida Institute, Orange Park, FL 140

Orlando Culinary Academy, Orlando, FL 140

Remington College - Jacksonville Campus, Jacksonville, FL 140

Remington College - Pinellas Campus, Largo, FL 141

Remington College - Tampa Campus, Tampa, FL 141

Ross Medical Education Center, Hollywood, FL 141

Ross Medical Education Center, West Palm Beach, FL 142

Sanford-Brown Institute, Jacksonville, FL 142

Sanford-Brown Institute, Lauderdale Lakes, FL 142

Sanford-Brown Institute, Tampa, FL 142

South University, West Palm Beach, FL 142

Southwest Florida College, Tampa, FL 143

Southwest Florida College, Tampa, FL 143

Tulsa Welding School, Jacksonville, FL 143

Virginia College at Pensacola, Pensacola, FL 144

Webster College, Holiday, FL 144

Webster College, Ocala, FL 144

GEORGIA

Advanced Career Training, Atlanta, GA 144

Advanced Career Training, Riverdale, GA 145

American InterContinental University, Atlanta, GA 145

American InterContinental University, Atlanta, GA 145

American Professional Institute, Macon, GA 145

Argosy University/Atlanta, Atlanta, GA 145

The Art Institute of Atlanta, Atlanta, GA 145

Bauder College, Atlanta, GA 146

Brown Mackie College, Atlanta Campus, Norcross, GA 146

Career Education Institute, Marietta, GA 146

Career Education Institute, Norcross, GA 146

The Chubb Institute, Alpharetta, GA 147

The Creative Circus, Inc., Atlanta, GA 147

Empire Beauty School, Dunwoody, GA 147

Empire Beauty School, Kennesaw, GA 147

Empire Beauty School, Lawrenceville, GA 147

Georgia Medical Institute, Norcross, GA 147

Georgia Medical Institute - Atlanta, Atlanta, GA 148

Georgia Medical Institute - DeKalb, Atlanta, GA 148

Georgia Medical Institute - Jonesboro, Jonesboro, GA 148

Georgia Medical Institute - Marietta, Marietta, GA 148

Herzing College, Atlanta, GA 148

High-Tech Institute, Marietta, GA 149
ITT Technical Institute, Duluth, GA 149
ITT Technical Institute, Kennesaw, GA 149
Le Cordon Bleu College of Culinary Arts, Atlanta, Tucker, GA 149
Medix School, Smyrna, GA 150
Roffler-Moler Hairstyling College, Marietta, GA 150
Ross Medical Education Center, Decatur, GA 150
Sanford-Brown Institute, Atlanta, GA 150
Savannah River College, Augusta, GA 151
South University, Savannah, GA 151
Strayer University, Atlanta, GA 151
Westwood College - Atlanta Campus, Atlanta, GA 151
Westwood College - Atlanta Northlake, Atlanta, GA 152

HAWAII

Argosy University/Honolulu, Honolulu, HI 152
New York Technical Institute of Hawaii, Honolulu, HI 152
Remington College - Honolulu Campus, Honolulu, HI 152

IDAHO

Apollo College, Boise, ID 153
ITT Technical Institute, Boise, ID 153
Sage Technical Services, Caldwell, ID 153
Sage Technical Services, Post Falls, ID 153
Stevens-Henager College, Boise, ID 153

ILLINOIS

Argosy University/Chicago, Chicago, IL 154
Argosy University/Schaumburg, Schaumburg, IL 154
Brown Mackie College, Moline Campus, Moline, IL 154
Cardean University, Chicago, IL 154
CEC Online Education Group, Hoffman Estates, IL 154
The Chubb Institute, Chicago, IL 155
The Cooking and Hospitality Institute of Chicago, Chicago, IL 155
Coyne American Institute, Chicago, IL 155
Coyne American Institute, Chicago, IL 156
Empire Beauty School, Hanover Park, IL 156
Fox College, Oak Lawn, IL 156
Harrington College of Design, Chicago, IL 156
The Illinois Institute of Art - Chicago, Chicago, IL 156
The Illinois Institute of Art - Schaumburg, Schaumburg, IL 157
Illinois School of Health Careers, Chicago, IL 157
International Academy of Design & Technology, Chicago, IL 157
International Academy of Design and Technology, Schaumburg, IL 157
ITT Technical Institute, Burr Ridge, IL 157
ITT Technical Institute, Matteson, IL 158
ITT Technical Institute, Mount Prospect, IL 158

Lincoln Technical Institute, Melrose Park, IL 158
Olympia College, Burr Ridge, IL 158
Olympia College, Chicago, IL 159
Olympia College, North Aurora, IL 159
Olympia College, Skokie, IL 159
Rockford Business College, Rockford, IL 159
Sanford-Brown College, Collinsville, IL 159
The Soma Institute, The National School of Clinical Massage Therapy, Chicago, IL 160
Universal Technical Institute, Inc., Glendale Heights, IL 160
Vatterott College, Quincy, IL 160
Westwood College - Chicago Du Page, Woodridge, IL 160
Westwood College - Chicago Loop Campus, Chicago, IL 161
Westwood College - Chicago O'Hare Airport, Chicago, IL 161
Westwood College - Chicago River Oaks, Calumet City, IL 161

INDIANA

Brown Mackie College, Fort Wayne Campus, Fort Wayne, IN 162
Brown Mackie College, Merrillville Campus, Merrillville, IN 162
Brown Mackie College, Michigan City Campus, Michigan City, IN 162
Brown Mackie College, South Bend Campus, South Bend, IN 162
Indiana Business College, Anderson, IN 162
Indiana Business College, Columbus, IN 163
Indiana Business College, Evansville, IN 163
Indiana Business College, Fort Wayne, IN 163
Indiana Business College, Indianapolis, IN 163
Indiana Business College, Lafayette, IN 163
Indiana Business College, Marion, IN 164
Indiana Business College, Muncie, IN 164
Indiana Business College, Terre Haute, IN 164
Indiana Business College-Medical, Indianapolis, IN 164
International Business College, Fort Wayne, IN 165
International Business College, Indianapolis, IN 165
ITT Technical Institute, Fort Wayne, IN 165
ITT Technical Institute, Indianapolis, IN 165
ITT Technical Institute, Newburgh, IN 166
Lincoln Technical Institute, Indianapolis, IN 166
MedTech College, Indianapolis, IN 166
National College of Business and Technology, Indianapolis, IN 166
Olympia College, Merrillville, IN 167
Professional Careers Institute, Indianapolis, IN 167
Sawyer College, Merrillville, IN 167

IOWA

Hamilton College, Cedar Rapids, IA 167
Kaplan University, Davenport, IA 168
Vatterott College, Des Moines, IA 168

KANSAS

Brown Mackie College, Lenexa Campus, Lenexa, KS 168
Brown Mackie College, Salina Campus, Salina, KS 168
Bryan College, Topeka, KS 169
National American University, Overland Park, KS 169
Pinnacle Career Institute, Lawrence, KS 169
Vatterott College, Wichita, KS 169
Wichita Technical Institute, Wichita, KS 169
Wright Business School, Overland Park, KS 170
WTI The Electronic School, Topeka, KS 170

KENTUCKY

Brown Mackie College, Hopkinsville Campus, Hopkinsville, KY 170
Brown Mackie College, Louisville Campus, Louisville, KY 170
Brown Mackie College, Northern Kentucky Campus, Fort Mitchell, KY 170
Daymar College, Louisville, KY 171
Daymar College, Newport, KY 171
Daymar College, Owensboro, KY 171
Draughons Junior College, Bowling Green, KY 171
ITT Technical Institute, Louisville, KY 171
Louisville Technical Institute, Louisville, KY 172
National College of Business & Technology, Danville, KY 172
National College of Business & Technology, Florence, KY 172
National College of Business & Technology, Lexington, KY 173
National College of Business & Technology, Louisville, KY 173
National College of Business & Technology, Pikeville, KY 173
National College of Business & Technology, Richmond, KY 173
Paducah Technical College, Paducah, KY 174
Southwestern College of Business, Florence, KY 174
Spencerian College, Louisville, KY 174
Spencerian College-Lexington, Lexington, KY 174
Sullivan University, Lexington, KY 174
Sullivan University, Louisville, KY 175

LOUISIANA

American Commercial College, Shreveport, LA 175
Ayers Institute, Inc., Shreveport, LA 175
Blue Cliff College, Metairie, LA 176
Blue Cliff College - Lafayette, Lafayette, LA 176

Blue Cliff College - Shreveport, Shreveport, LA 176
Bryman College, New Orleans, LA 176
Career Technical College, Monroe, LA 176
Career Technical College, Shreveport, LA 177
Delta School of Business & Technology, Lake Charles, LA 177
Eastern College of Health Vocations, Metairie, LA 177
Grantham University, Kansas City, MO 177
Gretna Career College, Gretna, LA 177
Herzing College, Kenner, LA 178
ITI Technical College, Baton Rouge, LA 178
ITT Technical Institute, Saint Rose, LA 179
MedVance Institute, Baton Rouge, LA 179
Remington College - Baton Rouge Campus, Baton Rouge, LA 179
Remington College - Lafayette Campus, Lafayette, LA 179
Remington College - New Orleans Campus, Metairie, LA 180

MAINE

Andover College, Portland, ME 180
New England School of Communications, Bangor, ME 180

MARYLAND

Baltimore School of Massage, Linthicum, MD 180
Empire Beauty School, Owings Mills, MD 181
Everest Institute, Silver Spring, MD 181
Hagerstown Business College, Hagerstown, MD 181
Harrison Career Institute, Baltimore, MD 181
ITT Technical Institute, Owings Mills, MD 181
Lincoln Technical Institute, Columbia, MD 182
Medix School, Towson, MD 182
North American Trade School, Gwynn Oak, MD 182
Sanford-Brown Institute, Landover, MD 182
TESST College of Technology, Baltimore, MD 182
TESST College of Technology, Beltsville, MD 183
TESST College of Technology, Towson, MD 183

MASSACHUSETTS

Bay State College, Boston, MA 183
Bryman Institute, Brighton, MA 183
Bryman Institute, Chelsea, MA 184
Career Education Institute, Brockton, MA 184
Career Education Institute, Lowell, MA 184
Catherine Hinds Institute of Esthetics, Woburn, MA 185
Computer-Ed Institute, Somerville, MA 185
Empire Beauty School, Boston, MA 185
Empire Beauty School, Malden, MA 185
Gibbs College, Boston, MA 185
Hallmark Institute of Photography, Turners Falls, MA 185
ITT Technical Institute, Norwood, MA 186

ITT Technical Institute, Woburn, MA 186
Mildred Elley, Pittsfield, MA 186
The New England Institute of Art, Brookline, MA 186
Porter and Chester Institute, Chicopee, MA 187
RETS Technical Center, Charlestown, MA 187
Sanford-Brown Institute, Springfield, MA 187
Universal Technical Institute, Norwood, MA 187
WyoTech, Bedford, MA 187

MICHIGAN
Carnegie Institute, Troy, MI 188
Dorsey Schools, Madison Heights, MI 188
Dorsey Schools, Roseville, MI 188
Dorsey Schools, Southgate, MI 188
Dorsey Schools, Wayne, MI 189
Flint Institute of Barbering, Flint, MI 189
International Academy of Design & Technology, Troy, MI 189
ITT Technical Institute, Canton, MI 189
ITT Technical Institute, Grand Rapids, MI 189
ITT Technical Institute, Troy, MI 190
Lawton School, Southfield, MI 190
National Institute of Technology, Detroit, MI 190
National Institute of Technology, Southfield, MI 190
National Institute of Technology - Dearborn, Dearborn, MI 190
Olympia Career Training Institute, Grand Rapids, MI 191
Olympia Career Training Institute, Kalamazoo, MI 191
Ross Medical Education Center, Ann Arbor, MI 191
Ross Medical Education Center, Brighton, MI 191
Ross Medical Education Center, Grand Rapids, MI 191
Ross Medical Education Center, Redford, MI 191
Ross Medical Education Center, Roosevelt Park, MI 192
Ross Medical Education Center, Warren, MI 192
Ross Medical Education Center - Saginaw Campus, Saginaw, MI 192
Specs Howard School of Broadcast Arts Inc., Southfield, MI 192

MINNESOTA
Academy College, Minneapolis, MN 192
Argosy University/Twin Cities, Eagan, MN 193
The Art Institutes International Minnesota, Minneapolis, MN 193
Brown College, Mendota Heights, MN 193
Bryman Institute, Eagan, MN 193
Capella University, Minneapolis, MN 194
Duluth Business University, Duluth, MN 194
Globe College, Oakdale, MN 194
Herzing College, Minneapolis, MN 195
High-Tech Institute, St. Louis Park, MN 195
The Institute of Production and Recording, Minneapolis, MN 195
ITT Technical Institute, Eden Prairie, MN 195
Le Cordon Bleu College of Culinary Arts Minneapolis/St.Paul, Saint Paul, MN 196
Minneapolis Business College, Roseville, MN 196
Minnesota School of Business - Brooklyn Center, Brooklyn Center, MN 196
Minnesota School of Business - Plymouth, Plymouth, MN 196
Minnesota School of Business-Richfield, Richfield, MN 196
Minnesota School of Business - Rochester, Rochester, MN 197
Minnesota School of Business, Shakopee, MN 197
Minnesota School of Business - St. Cloud, Waite Park, MN 197
National American University, Minneapolis, MN 197
National American University, Brooklyn Center, MN 197
National American University, Roseville, MN 197
Northwest Technical Institute, Eden Prairie, MN 198
Rasmussen College Eagan, Eagan, MN 198
Rasmussen College Mankato, Mankato, MN 198
Rasmussen College Minnetonka, Minnetonka, MN 199
Rasmussen College St. Cloud, St. Cloud, MN 199

MISSISSIPPI
Antonelli College, Hattiesburg, MS 199
Antonelli College, Jackson, MS 200
Blue Cliff College, Gulfport, MS 200
Virginia College at Jackson, Jackson, MS 200

MISSOURI
Allied College, Arnold, MO 201
Allied College, Maryland Heights, MO 201
Bryan College, Springfield, MO 201
Bryman College, Earth City, MO 201
Heritage College, Kansas City, MO 201
Hickey College, St. Louis, MO 202
High-Tech Institute, Kansas City, MO 202
ITT Technical Institute, Arnold, MO 202
ITT Technical Institute, Earth City, MO 202
ITT Technical Institute, Kansas City, MO 203
L'Ecole Culinaire, Saint Louis, MO 203
Metro Business College, Cape Girardeau, MO 203
Metro Business College, Jefferson City, MO 203
Metro Business College, Rolla, MO 203
Missouri College, St. Louis, MO 203
Missouri Tech, St. Louis, MO 204
National American University, Kansas City, MO 204
Pinnacle Career Institute, Kansas City, MO 204
St. Louis College of Health Careers, St. Louis, MO 205
St. Louis College of Health Career, Fenton, MO 205
Sanford-Brown College, Fenton, MO 205

Sanford-Brown College, Hazelwood, MO 205
Sanford-Brown College, North Kansas City, MO 206
Sanford-Brown College, St. Charles, MO 206
Springfield College, Springfield, MO 206
Vatterott College, Joplin, MO 206
Vatterott College, Kansas City, MO 207
Vatterott College, O'Fallon , MO 207
Vatterott College, St. Ann, MO 207
Vatterott College, St. Joseph, MO 207
Vatterott College, St. Louis, MO 208
Vatterott College, Springfield, MO 208

MONTANA
Sage Technical Services, Billings, MT 208

NEBRASKA
College of Hair Design, Lincoln, NE 208
ITT Technical Institute, Omaha, NE 209
Vatterott College, Omaha, NE 209

NEVADA
American Institute of Technology, North Las Vegas, NV 209
The Art Institute of Las Vegas, Henderson, NV 209
Career College of Northern Nevada, Reno, NV 210
Career Education Institute, Henderson, NV 210
Heritage College, Las Vegas, NV 210
High-Tech Institute, Las Vegas, NV 210
International Academy of Design and Technology, Henderson, NV 210
ITT Technical Institute, Henderson, NV 211
Las Vegas College, Henderson, NV 211
Las Vegas College, Las Vegas, NV 211
Le Cordon Bleu College of Culinary Arts, Las Vegas, Las Vegas, NV 211
Morrison University, Reno, NV 212
Nevada Career Academy, Sparks, NV 212
Nevada Career Institute, Las Vegas, NV 212
Nevada Career Institute, Las Vegas, NV 212
Nevada School of Massage Therapy, Las Vegas, NV 212
Pima Medical Institute, Las Vegas, NV 213

NEW HAMPSHIRE
Hesser College, Manchester, NH 213
McIntosh College, Dover, NH 213

NEW JERSEY
Berdan Institute, Totowa, NJ 214
Berkeley College, Paramus, NJ 214
Berkeley College, West Paterson, NJ 214
Berkeley College, Woodbridge, NJ 215
Empire Beauty School, Cherry Hill, NJ 215
Empire Beauty School, Laurel Springs, NJ 215
Empire Beauty School, Lawrenceville, NJ 215

The Chubb Institute, Cherry Hill, NJ 215
The Chubb Institute, Jersey City, NJ 216
The Chubb Institute, North Brunswick, NJ 216
The Chubb Institute, Parsippany, NJ 216
The Cittone Institute, Edison, NJ 217
The Cittone Institute, Mount Laurel, NJ 217
The Cittone Institute, Paramus, NJ 217
Divers Academy International, Camden, NJ 218
Dover Business College, Paramus, NJ 218
Gibbs College, Livingston, NJ 218
Harrison Career Institute, Clifton, NJ 218
Harrison Career Institute, Delran, NJ 218
Harrison Career Institute, Deptford, NJ 219
Harrison Career Institute, Ewing, NJ 219
Harrison Career Institute, Jersey City, NJ 219
Harrison Career Institute, Oakhurst, NJ 219
Harrison Career Institute, South Orange, NJ 220
Harrison Career Institute, Vineland, NJ 220
Hohokus Hackensack School of Business and Medical Sciences, Hackensack, NJ 220
HoHoKus RETS School of Business and Medical Technical Services, Nutley, NJ 220
HoHoKus School of Business and Medical Sciences, Ramsey, NJ 221
HoHoKus School of Trade and Technical Services, Linden, NJ 221
Joe Kubert School of Cartoon and Graphic Art Inc., Dover, NJ 221
Katharine Gibbs School, Piscataway, NJ 221
Lincoln Technical Institute, Mahwah, NJ 222
Lincoln Technical Institute, Union, NJ 222
Pennco Tech, Blackwood, NJ 222
Prism Career Institute, Hammonton, NJ 222
Prism Career Institute, Sewell, NJ 223
Somerset School of Message Therapy, Piscataway, NJ 223
Stuart School of Business Administration, Wall, NJ 223
Teterboro School of Aeronautics, Inc., Teterboro, NJ 223

NEW MEXICO
Apollo College, Albuquerque, NM 223
ITT Technical Institute, Albuquerque, NM 223
National American University, Albuquerque, NM 224
National American University, Rio Rancho, NM 224
Pima Medical Institute, Albuquerque, NM 224
Southwest Health Career Institute, Albuquerque, NM 225

NEW YORK
Apex Technical School, New York, NY 225
The Art Institute of New York City, New York, NY 225
Berkeley College - New York City Campus, New York, NY 225
Berkeley College - Westchester Campus, White Plains, NY 225

Boldface type indicates that the school is a participating institution in the 🏛 *Imagine America* Scholarship Program

Berk Trade and Business School, Brooklyn, NY 226
Briarcliffe College, Bethpage, NY 226
Briarcliffe College, Patchogue, NY 226
Caliber Training Institute, New York, NY 227
Career Institute of Health and Technology, Brooklyn, NY 227
Career Institute of Health and Technology, Garden City, NY 227
Career Institute of Health and Technology, Rego Park, NY 228
The Chubb Institute, New York, NY 228
The Chubb Institute, Westbury, NY 228
Empire Beauty School, Astoria, NY 229
Empire Beauty School, Bensonhurst, NY 229
Empire Beauty School, New York, NY 229
Empire Beauty School - Theatrical/Film Make-up, New York, NY 229
The French Culinary Institute, New York, NY 229
Gemological Institute of America, Inc., New York, NY 229
Institute of Audio Research, New York, NY 229
Island Drafting and Technical Institute, Amityville, NY 230
ITT Technical Institute, Albany, NY 230
ITT Technical Institute, Getzville, NY 230
ITT Technical Institute, Liverpool, NY 230
Katharine Gibbs School, Melville, NY 231
Katharine Gibbs School, New York, NY 231
Mandl School, New York, NY 231
Mildred Elley School, Latham, NY 232
New York Institute of Massage, Buffalo, NY 232
Rochester Business Institute, Rochester, NY 232
Sanford-Brown Institute, Garden City, NY 232
Sanford-Brown Institute, New York, NY 232
Sanford-Brown Institute, White Plains, NY 232
Taylor Business Institute, New York, NY 233
Technical Career Institute, New York, NY 233
Wood Tobe-Coburn School, New York, NY 233

NORTH CAROLINA
The Art Institute of Charlotte, Charlotte, NC 233
Brookstone College of Business, Charlotte, NC 234
Brookstone College of Business, Greensboro, NC 234
ECPI College of Technology, Charlotte, NC 234
ECPI College of Technology, Greensboro, NC 235
ECPI College of Technology, Raleigh, NC 235
Empire Beauty School, Concord, NC 235
Empire Beauty School, Matthews, NC 235
King's College, Charlotte, NC 235
Miller-Motte Technical College, Cary, NC 236
Miller-Motte Technical College, Wilmington, NC 236
NASCAR Technical Institute, Mooresville, NC 236
South College - Asheville, Asheville, NC 236

NORTH DAKOTA

Aakers Business College , Bismarck, ND 236
Aakers Business College, Fargo, ND 236

OHIO
Akron Institute, Akron, OH 236
American School of Technology, Columbus, OH 237
Antonelli College, Cincinnati, OH 237
The Art Institute of Ohio - Cincinnati, Cincinnati, OH 237
Bradford School, Columbus, OH 237
Brown Mackie College, Akron Campus, Akron, OH 238
Brown Mackie College, Cincinnati Campus, Cincinnati, OH 238
Brown Mackie College, Findlay Campus, Findlay, OH 238
Brown Mackie College, North Canton Campus, North Canton, OH 239
Bryman Institute, Gahanna, OH 239
Davis College, Toledo, OH 239
EduTek College, Stow, OH 239
Gallipolis Career College, Gallipolis, OH 239
Hondros College, Westerville, OH 240
International College of Broadcasting, Dayton, OH 240
ITT Technical Institute, Dayton, OH 240
ITT Technical Institute, Hilliard, OH 240
ITT Technical Institute, Norwood, OH 240
ITT Technical Institute, Strongsville, OH 241
ITT Technical Institute, Warrensville Heights, OH 241
ITT Technical Institute, Youngstown, OH 241
Miami - Jacobs College, Dayton, OH 241
National College of Business and Technology, Cincinnati, OH 241
National College of Business and Technology, Kettering, OH 242
Ohio Institute of Photography and Technology, Dayton, OH 242
Ohio Valley College of Technology, East Liverpool, OH 242
Remington College - Cleveland Campus, Cleveland, OH 242
Remington College - Cleveland West Campus, North Olmstead, OH 242
RETS Tech Center, Centerville, OH 243
Southeastern Business College, Chillicothe, OH 243
Southeastern Business College, Jackson, OH 243
Southeastern Business College, Lancaster, OH 243
Southeastern Business College, New Boston, OH 244
Southwestern College of Business, Cincinnati, OH 244
Southwestern College of Business, Cincinnati, OH 244
Southwestern College of Business, Dayton, OH 244
Southwestern College of Business, Franklin, OH 245
TDDS, Inc., Lake Milton, OH 245
Technology Education College, Columbus, OH 245
Trumbull Business College, Warren, OH 245
Vatterott College, Broadview Heights, OH 245

Virginia Marti College of Art and Design, Lakewood, OH 246

OKLAHOMA

Career Point Institute, Tulsa, OK 246
City College, Inc., Moore, OK 246
Community Care College, Tulsa, OK 246
Dickinson Business School/Career Point Business School, Tulsa, OK 246
Heritage College of Hair Design, Oklahoma City, OK 247
ITT Technical Institute, Tulsa, OK 247
Oklahoma Health Academy, Oklahoma City, OK 247
Oklahoma Health Academy, Tulsa, OK 247
Platt College, Lawton, OK 247
Platt College, Oklahoma City, OK 248
Platt College, Tulsa, OK 248
State Barber and Hair Design College Inc, Oklahoma City, OK 248
Tulsa Welding School, Tulsa, OK 248
Vatterott College, Oklahoma City, OK 248
Vatterott College, Tulsa, OK 249
Wright Business School, Oklahoma City, OK 249
Wright Business School, Tulsa, OK 249

OREGON

Apollo College, Portland, OR 249
The Art Institute of Portland, Portland, OR 249
Ashmead College, Tigard, OR 250
Cambridge College, Beaverton, OR 250
ITT Technical Institute, Portland, OR 250
Pioneer Pacific College, Clackamas, OR 250
Pioneer Pacific College, Wilsonville, OR 251
Pioneer Pacific College - Eugene/Springfield Branch, Springfield, OR 251
Western Business College, Portland, OR 251
Western Culinary Institute, Portland, OR 251

PENNSYLVANIA

Academy of Medical Arts and Business, Harrisburg, PA 252
The Art Institute of Philadelphia, Philadelphia, PA 252
The Art Institute of Pittsburgh, Pittsburgh, PA 252
Automotive Training Center, Exton, PA 253
Baltimore School of Massage, York Campus, York, PA 253
Berks Technical Institute, Wyomissing, PA 253
Bradford School, Pittsburgh, PA 254
Bradley Academy for the Visual Arts, York, PA 254
Business Institute of Pennsylvania, Meadville, PA 255
Business Institute of Pennsylvania, Sharon, PA 255
Camtech, Erie, PA 255
CHI Institute, Broomall, PA 256
CHI Institute, Southampton, PA 256
The Chubb Institute, Springfield, PA 256

The Cittone Institute, Philadelphia, PA 257
The Cittone Institute, Philadelphia, PA 257
The Cittone Institute, Plymouth Meeting, PA 257
Computer Learning Network, Altoona, PA 258
Computer Learning Network, Mechanicsburg, PA 258
Dean Institute of Technology, Pittsburgh, PA 258
Douglas Education Center, Monessen, PA 259
Duff's Business Institute, Pittsburgh, PA 259
Empire Beauty School, Hanover, PA 259
Empire Beauty School, Harrisburg, PA 259
Empire Beauty School, Lancaster, PA 260
Empire Beauty School, Lebanon, PA 260
Empire Beauty School, Monroeville, PA 260
Empire Beauty School, Moosic, PA 260
Empire Beauty School, Philadelphia, PA 260
Empire Beauty School, Philadelphia, PA 260
Empire Beauty School, Pittsburgh, PA 260
Empire Beauty School, Pottstown, PA 260
Empire Beauty School, Pottsville, PA 260
Empire Beauty School, Reading, PA 260
Empire Beauty School, Shamokin Dam, PA 261
Empire Beauty School, State College, PA 261
Empire Beauty School, Warminster, PA 261
Empire Beauty School, West Chester, PA 261
Empire Beauty School, West Mifflin, PA 261
Empire Beauty School, Whitehall, PA 261
Empire Beauty School, Williamsport, PA 261
Empire Beauty School, York, PA 261
Erie Business Center, Main, Erie, PA 261
Erie Business Center South, New Castle, PA 262
Great Lakes Institute of Technology, Erie, PA 262
Harrisburg Institute of Trade/Technology, Middletown, PA 262
Harrison Career Institute, Allentown, PA 262
Harrison Career Institute, Philadelphia, PA 263
Harrison Career Institute, Reading, PA 263
Hussian School of Art, Philadelphia, PA 263
ICM School of Business & Medical Careers, Pittsburgh, PA 263
International Academy of Design & Technology, Pittsburgh, PA 264
ITT Technical Institute - Bensalem, Bensalem, PA 264
ITT Technical Institute, King of Prussia, PA 264
ITT Technical Institute, Mechanicsburg, PA 264
ITT Technical Institute, Monroeville, PA 264
ITT Technical Institute, Pittsburg, PA 264
Katharine Gibbs School, Norristown, PA 264
Lansdale School of Busines, North Wales, PA 264
Laurel Business Institute, Uniontown, PA 265
Lebanon County Career School, Lebanon, PA 265
Lehigh Valley College, Center Valley, PA 266
Lincoln Technical Institute, Allentown, PA 266
Lincoln Technical Institute, Philadelphia, PA 266

McCann School of Business, Hazleton, PA 266
McCann School of Business, Pottsville, PA267
McCann School of Business, Scranton, PA 267
McCann School of Business, Sunbury, PA 267
New Castle School of Trades, Pulaski, PA 268
Orleans Technical Institute, Philadelphia, PA 268
Orleans Technical Institute - Center City Campus, Philadelphia, PA 268
Peirce College, Philadelphia, PA 268
Pennco Tech, Bristol, PA 269
Pennsylvania Culinary Institute, Pittsburgh, PA 269
Pittsburgh Technical Institute, Oakdale, PA 269
The PJA School, Upper Darby, PA 270
Prism Career Institute, Philadelphia, PA 270
The Restaurant School at Walnut Hill College, Philadelphia, PA 270
RETS Institute of Technology, Pittsburgh, PA 270
Sanford-Brown Institute, Trevose, PA 270
Schuylkill Institute of Business and Technology, Pottsville, PA 270
Thompson Institute, Chambersburg, PA 271
Thompson Institute, Harrisburg, PA 271
Thompson Institute, Philadelphia, PA 271
Triangle Tech, Inc. - DuBois School, DuBois, PA 272
Triangle Tech, Inc. - Erie School, Erie, PA 272
Triangle Tech, Inc. - Greensburg School, Greensburg, PA 272
Triangle Tech, Inc. - Pittsburgh School, Pittsburgh, PA 272
Triangle Tech, Inc. - Sunbury School, Sunbury, PA 272
Tri-State Business Institute, Erie, PA 272
Universal Technical Institute, Exton, PA 273
Western School of Health and Business Careers, Monroeville, PA 273
Western School of Health and Business Careers, Pittsburgh, PA 273
West Virginia Career Institute, Mount Braddock, PA 273
WyoTech, Blairsville, PA 274
York Technical Institute, Lancaster, PA 274
York Technical Institute, York, PA 274
Yorktowne Business Institute, York, PA 274

PUERTO RICO
A-1 Business and Technical College, Caguas, PR 275
Antilles School of Technical Careers, Santurce, PR 275
Automeca Technical College, Aguadilla, PR 275
Automeca Technical College, Bayamon, PR 275
Automeca Technical College, Caguas, PR 275
Automeca Technical College, Ponce, PR 276
Bayamon Community College, Bayamon, PR 276
Caguas Institute of Mechanical Technology, Caguas, PR 276
Colegio Mayor de Tecnologia, Arroyo, PR 276
Columbia College, Caguas, PR 277

Columbia College, Yauco, PR 277
Electronic Data Processing College of Puerto Rico, San Juan, PR 277
Electronic Data Processing College of Puerto Rico - San Sebastian, San Sebastian, PR 277
Escuela Hotelera de San Juan in Puerto Rico, San Juan, PR 278
Huertas Junior College, Caguas, PR 277
ICPR Junior College-Arecibo Campus, Arecibo, PR 278
ICPR Junior College - Hato Rey Campus, San Juan, PR 278
ICPR Junior College - Mayaguez Campus, Mayaguez, PR 279
Instituto Banca y Comercio, Caguas, PR 279
Instituto Banca y Comercio, Cayey, PR 279
Instituto Banca y Comercio, Fajardo, PR 279
Instituto Banca y Comercio, Guayama, PR 280
Instituto Banca y Comercio, Manati, PR 280
Instituto Banca y Comercio, Mayaguez, PR 280
Instituto Banca y Comercio, Ponce, PR 280
Instituto de Banca y Comercio, San Juan, PR 281
Instituto Vocational y Commercial EDIC, Caguas, PR 281
Liceo de Arte y Tecnologia, San Juan, PR 281
National College of Business and Technology, Arecibo, PR 282
National College of Business & Technology, Bayamon, PR 282
National College of Business & Technology, Rio Grande, PR 282
Ponce Paramedical College, Inc., Coto Laurel, PR 282
Trinity College of Puerto Rico, Ponce, PR 283

RHODE ISLAND
Career Education Institute, Lincoln, RI 283
Gibbs College - Cranston, Cranston, RI 283
The International Yacht Restoration School, Newport, RI 284
New England Institute of Technology, Warwick, RI 284

SOUTH CAROLINA
ECPI College of Technology, North Charleston, SC 285
ECPI College of Technology, Greenville, SC 285
ITT Technical Institute, Greenville, SC 285
Miller-Motte Technical College, North Charleston, SC 285
South University, Columbia, SC 286

SOUTH DAKOTA
Colorado Technical University Sioux Falls Campus, Sioux Falls, SD 286
National American University, Ellsworth AFB, SD 286
National American University, Rapid City, SD 286
National American University - Sioux Falls Branch, Sioux Falls, SD 287

TENNESSEE

Argosy University/Nashville, Franklin, TN 287
Draughons Junior College, Clarksville, TN 287
Draughons Junior College, Murfreesboro, TN 287
Draughons Junior College, Nashville, TN 288
Fountainhead College of Technology, Knoxville, TN 288
High-Tech Institute, Memphis, TN 288
High-Tech Institute, Nashville, TN 288
International Academy of Design and Technology, Nashville, TN 289
ITT Technical Institute, Knoxville, TN 289
ITT Technical Institute, Memphis, TN 289
ITT Technical Institute, Nashville, TN 289
MedVance Institute, Cookeville, TN 290
Miller-Motte Technical College, Chattanooga, TN 290
Miller-Motte Technical College, Clarksville, TN 290
Nashville Auto Diesel College, Nashville, TN 290
National College of Business & Technology, Bristol, TN 290
National College of Business & Technology, Knoxville, TN 291
National College of Business & Technology, Nashville, TN 291
Remington College - Memphis Campus, Memphis, TN 291
Remington College - Nashville Campus, Nashville, TN 291
South College, Knoxville, TN 291
Southeastern Career College, Nashville, TN 292
Vatterott College, Memphis, TN 292
West Tennessee Business College, Jackson, TN 292

TEXAS

American Commercial College, Abilene, TX 292
American Commercial College, Lubbock, TX 293
American Commercial College, Odessa, TX 293
American Commercial College, San Angelo, TX 293
American InterContinental University, Houston, TX 293
American InterContinental University, San Antonio, TX 293
American School of Business, Wichita Falls, TX 294
Argosy University/Dallas, Dallas, TX 294
The Art Institute of Dallas, Dallas, TX 294
The Art Institute of Houston, Houston, TX 294
ATI Career Training Center, Dallas, TX 294
ATI Career Training Center, North Richland Hills, TX 295
ATI Technical Training Center, Dallas, TX 295
Austin Business College, Austin, TX 295
Bradford School of Business, Houston, TX 295
Brown Mackie College, Dallas Campus, Garland, TX 296
Brown Mackie College, Fort Worth Campus, Hurst, TX 296

Career Centers of Texas, El Paso, TX 295
Career Point Business School, San Antonio, TX 296
Career Quest, San Antonio, TX 296
Court Reporting Institute of Dallas, Dallas, TX 297
Court Reporting Institute of Houston, Houston, TX 297
Everest College, Arlington , TX 297
Everest College, Dallas, TX 297
Everest College, Fort Worth, TX 297
Hallmark Institute of Aeronautics, San Antonio, TX 297
Hallmark Institute of Technology, San Antonio, TX 298
High-Tech Institute, Irving, TX 298
International Academy of Design and Technology, San Antonio, TX 298
International Business College, El Paso, TX 298
International Business College, El Paso, TX 299
ITT Technical Institute, Arlington, TX 299
ITT Technical Institute, Austin, TX 299
ITT Technical Institute, Houston, TX 299
ITT Technical Institute, Houston, TX 299
ITT Technical Institute, Houston, TX 300
ITT Technical Institute, Richardson, TX 300
ITT Technical Institute, San Antonio, TX 300
Lincoln Technical Institute, Grand Prairie, TX 300
MedVance Institute, Houston, TX 301
MTI College of Business and Technology, Houston, TX 301
MTI College of Business and Technology, Houston, TX 301
MTI College of Business and Technology, Houston, TX 301
National Institute of Technology, Austin , TX 302
National Institute of Technology, Houston, TX 302
National Institute of Technology, Houston, TX 302
National Institute of Technology, San Antonio, TX 302
National Institute of Technology - Greenspoint, Houston, TX 303
National Institute of Technology - Hobby, Houston, TX 303
Ocean Corporation, Houston, TX 303
PCI Health Training Center, Dallas, TX 303
PCI Health Training Center, Richardson, TX 304
Platt College - Dallas, Dallas, TX 304
Remington College, Houston, TX 304
Remington College - Dallas Campus, Garland, TX 304
Remington College - Fort Worth Campus, Fort Worth, TX 304
Remington College - Houston Campus, Houston, TX 305
San Antonio College of Medical and Dental Assistants, San Antonio, TX 305
Sanford-Brown Institute, Dallas, TX 305
Sanford-Brown Institute, Houston, TX 305
Sanford-Brown Institute, Houston, TX 306
Southeastern Career Institute, Dallas, TX 306

Texas Careers - San Antonio, San Antonio, TX 306
Texas Culinary Academy, Austin, TX 306
Texas School of Business, Inc., Houston, TX 306
Universal Technical Institute, Houston, TX 306
Virginia College at Austin, Austin, TX 307
Western Technical College, El Paso, TX 307
Western Technical Institute, El Paso, TX 308
Westwood Aviation Institute, Houston, TX 308
Westwood College - Dallas, Dallas, TX 308
Westwood College - Fort Worth, Euless, TX 308
Westwood College - Houston South, Houston, TX 308
Westwood College - Houston South Campus, Houston, TX 308

UTAH
Certified Careers Institute, Clearfield, UT 309
Certified Careers Institute, Salt Lake City, UT 309
Eagle Gate College, Murray, UT 309
Eagle Gate College - Weber/Davis, Layton, UT 309
Eagle Gate College - Weber/Davis, Salt Lake City, UT 309
ITT Technical Institute, Murray, UT 310
Mountain West College, West Valley City, UT 310
Neumont University, Salt Lake City, UT 310
Provo College, Provo, UT 310
Stevens-Henager College, Logan, UT 311
Stevens-Henager College, Ogden, UT 311
Stevens-Henager College - Provo, Orem, UT 311
Stevens-Henager College - Salt Lake City, Salt Lake City, UT 312
Utah Career College, West Jordan, UT 312
Utah College of Massage Therapy - Utah Valley Campus, Lindon, UT 312
Utah College of Massage Therapy - Salt Lake City, Salt Lake City, UT 312

VERMONT
New England Culinary Institute, Montpelier, VT 313
New England Culinary Institute at Essex, Essex Junction, VT 313

VIRGINIA
ACT College, Alexandria, VA 313
ACT College, Fairfax, VA 313
ACT College, Manassas, VA 313
Advanced Technology Institute, Virginia Beach, VA 314
Argosy University/Washington D.C., Arlington, VA 314
The Art Institute of Washington, Arlington, VA 314
The Chubb Institute, Arlington, VA 314
ECPI College of Technology, Manassas, VA 315
ECPI College of Technology, Newport News, VA 315
ECPI College of Technology, Virginia Beach, VA 316
ECPI Technical College, Glen Allen, VA 316
ECPI Technical College, Richmond, VA 316

ECPI Technical College, Roanoke, VA 317
Empire Beauty School, Midlothian, VA 317
Gibbs School, Vienna, VA 317
Heritage Institute, Falls Church, VA 317
Heritage Institute, Manassas, VA 317
ITT Technical Institute, Chantilly, VA 317
ITT Technical Institute, Norfolk, VA 318
ITT Technical Institute, Richmond, VA 318
ITT Technical Institute, Springfield, VA 318
Kee Business College, Newport News, VA 319
Kee Business College - Chesapeake, Chesapeake, VA 319
Medical Careers Institute, Newport News, VA 319
Medical Careers Institute, Richmond, VA 319
Medical Careers Institute, Virginia Beach, VA 320
Miller-Motte Technical College, Lynchburg, VA 320
National College of Business & Technology, Bluefield, VA 320
National College of Business & Technology, Charlottesville, VA 320
National College of Business & Technology, Danville, VA 320
National College of Business & Technology, Harrisonburg, VA 321
National College of Business & Technology, Lynchburg, VA 321
National College of Business & Technology, Martinsville, VA 321
National College of Business & Technology, Salem, VA 321
Parks College, McLean, VA 321
Potomac College, Herndon, VA 322
Professional Healthcare Institute, Woodbridge, VA 322
Stratford University, Falls Church , VA 322
Stratford University, Woodbridge, VA 322
TESST College of Technology, Alexandria, VA 323
Virginia Career Institute, Richmond, VA 323
Virginia Career Institute, Virginia Beach, VA 323
Virginia School of Massage, Charlottesville, VA 324
Virginia School of Technology - Richmond Campus, Richmond, VA 324
Virginia School of Technology, Virginia Beach, VA 324

WASHINGTON
Apollo College, Spokane, WA 324
Argosy University/Seattle, Seattle, WA 324
The Art Institute of Seattle, Seattle, WA 324
Ashmead College, Everett, WA 325
Ashmead College, Fife, WA 325
Ashmead College, Seattle, WA 325
Ashmead College School of Massage, Vancouver, WA 325
Bryman College, Everett, WA 325
Bryman College, Lynnwood, WA 326
Bryman College, Port Orchard, WA 326

Bryman College, Renton, WA 326
Bryman College, Tacoma, WA 326
Cambridge College, Bellevue, WA 326
Gene Juarez Academy - South Seattle Campus, Federal Way, WA 327
Gene Juarez Academy of Beauty, Seattle, WA 327
International Academy of Design and Technology, Seattle, WA 327
ITT Technical Institute, Bothell, WA 327
ITT Technical Institute, Seattle, WA 327
ITT Technical Institute, Spokane, WA 328
Pima Medical Institute, Renton, WA 328
Pima Medical Institute, Seattle, WA 328
Western Business College, Vancouver, WA 328

WEST VIRGINIA
American Public Education, Inc., Charles Town, WV 329

National Institute of Technology, Cross Lanes, WV 329
West Virginia Junior College, Bridgeport, WV 329
West Virginia Junior College, Charleston, WV 329
West Virginia Junior College, Morgantown, WV 330

WISCONSIN
Herzing College, Madison, WI 330
ITT Technical Institute, Green Bay, WI 331
ITT Technical Institute, Greenfield, WI 331
Madison Media Institute, Madison, WI 331
Sanford-Brown College, West Allis, WI 331

WYOMING
Sage Technical Services, Casper, WY 331
WyoTech, Laramie, WY 332

ALPHABETICAL LISTING OF CAREER COLLEGES

The Art Institute of New York City, New York, NY 225

The Art Institute of Ohio - Cincinnati, Cincinnati, OH 237

The Art Institute of Philadelphia, Philadelphia, PA 252

The Art Institute of Phoenix, Phoenix, AZ 76

The Art Institute of Pittsburgh, Pittsburgh, PA 252

The Art Institute of Portland, Portland, OR 249

The Art Institute of Seattle, Seattle, WA 324

The Art Institute of Washington, Arlington, VA 314

The Art Institutes International Minnesota, Minneapolis, MN 193

Ashmead College School of Massage, Vancouver, WA 325

Ashmead College, Everett, WA 325

Ashmead College, Fife, WA 325

Ashmead College, Seattle, WA 325

Ashmead College, Tigard, OR 250

ATI Career Training Center, Dallas, TX 294

ATI Career Training Center, Fort Lauderdale, FL 122

ATI Career Training Center, Miami, FL 123

ATI Career Training Center, North Richland Hills, TX 295

ATI Career Training Center, Oakland Park, FL 123

ATI Health Education Center, Miami, FL 123

ATI Technical Training Center, Dallas, TX 295

Austin Business College, Austin, TX 295

Automeca Technical College, Aguadilla, PR 275

Automeca Technical College, Bayamon, PR 275

Automeca Technical College, Caguas, PR 275

Automeca Technical College, Ponce, PR 276

Automotive Training Center, Exton, PA 253

Ayers Institute, Inc., Shreveport, LA 175

B

Baltimore School of Massage, Linthicum, MD 180

Baltimore School of Massage, York Campus, York, PA 253

Barbara Brennan School of Healing, Boca Raton, FL 124

Bauder College, Atlanta, GA 146

Bay State College, Boston, MA 183

Bayamon Community College, Bayamon, PR 276

Bel-Rea Institute of Animal Technology, Denver, CO 112

Berdan Institute, Totowa, NJ 214

Berk Trade and Business School, Brooklyn, NY 226

Berkeley College - New York City Campus, New York, NY 225

Berkeley College - Westchester Campus, White Plains, NY 225

Berkeley College, Paramus, NJ 214

Berkeley College, West Paterson, NJ 214

Berkeley College, Woodbridge, NJ 215

Berks Technical Institute, Wyomissing, PA 253

Blair College, Colorado Springs, CO 112

Blue Cliff College - Lafayette, Lafayette, LA 176

Blue Cliff College - Shreveport, Shreveport, LA 176

Blue Cliff College, Gulfport, MS 200

Blue Cliff College, Metairie, LA 176

Bradford School of Business, Houston, TX 295

Bradford School, Columbus, OH 237

Bradford School, Pittsburgh, PA 254

Bradley Academy for the Visual Arts, York, PA 254

Briarcliffe College, Bethpage, NY 226

Briarcliffe College, Patchogue, NY 226

Brooks College, Long Beach, CA 86

Brooks College, Sunnyvale, CA 86

Brooks Institute of Photography, Santa Barbara, CA 87

Brookstone College of Business, Charlotte, NC 234

Brookstone College of Business, Greensboro, NC 234

Brown College, Mendota Heights, MN 193

Brown Mackie College, Akron Campus, Akron, OH 238

Brown Mackie College, Atlanta Campus, Norcross, GA 146

Brown Mackie College, Cincinnati Campus, Cincinnati, OH 238

Brown Mackie College, Dallas Campus, Garland, TX 296

Brown Mackie College, Findlay Campus, Findlay, OH 238

Brown Mackie College, Fort Wayne Campus, Fort Wayne, IN 162

Brown Mackie College, Fort Worth Campus, Hurst, TX 296

Brown Mackie College, Hopkinsville Campus, Hopkinsville, KY 170

Brown Mackie College, Lenexa Campus, Lenexa, KS 168

Brown Mackie College, Los Angeles Campus, Santa Monica, CA 87

Brown Mackie College, Louisville Campus, Louisville, KY 170

Brown Mackie College, Merrillville Campus, Merrillville, IN 162

Brown Mackie College, Miami Campus, Miami, FL 124

Brown Mackie College, Michigan City Campus, Michigan City, IN 162

Brown Mackie College, Moline Campus, Moline, IL 154

Brown Mackie College, North Canton Campus, North Canton, OH 239

Brown Mackie College, Northern Kentucky Campus, Fort Mitchell, KY 170

Brown Mackie College, Orange County Campus, Santa Ana, CA 87

Brown Mackie College, Salina Campus, Salina, KS 168

Brown Mackie College, San Diego Campus, San Diego, CA 87

Brown Mackie College, South Bend Campus, South Bend, IN 162

Bryan College of Court Reporting, Los Angeles, CA 88

Bryan College, Springfield, MO 201

Bryan College, Topeka, KS 169

Bryman College, Alhambra, CA 88

Bryman College, Anaheim, CA 88

Bryman College, City of Industry, CA 88

Bryman College, Earth City, MO 201

Tempe, AZ 77

Colorado School of Trades, Lakewood, CO 113

Colorado Technical University Denver Campus, Greenwood Village, CO 114

Colorado Technical University Sioux Falls Campus, Sioux Falls, SD 286

Colorado Technical University, Colorado Springs, CO 113

Columbia College, Caguas, PR 277

Columbia College, Yauco, PR 277

Community Business College, Modesto, CA 93

Community Care College, Tulsa, OK 246

Computer Learning Network, Altoona, PA 258

Computer Learning Network, Mechanicsburg, PA 258

Computer-Ed Institute, Somerville, MA 185

Conservatory of Recording Arts and Sciences, Tempe, AZ 78

The Cooking and Hospitality Institute of Chicago, Chicago, IL 155

Court Reporting Institute of Dallas, Dallas, TX 297

Court Reporting Institute of Houston, Houston, TX 297

Coyne American Institute, Chicago, IL 155

Coyne American Institute, Chicago, IL 156

The Creative Circus, Inc., Atlanta, GA 147

D

Davis College, Toledo, OH 239

Dawn Training Centre, Inc., Wilmington, DE 120

Daymar College, Louisville, KY 171

Daymar College, Newport, KY 171

Daymar College, Owensboro, KY 171

Dean Institute of Technology, Pittsburgh, PA 258

Delta School of Business & Technology, Lake Charles, LA 177

Denver Automotive and Diesel College, Denver, CO 114

Denver Career College, Thornton, CO 114

Denver School of Massage Therapy - Aurora, Aurora, CO 115

Denver School of Massage Therapy - Westminster, Westminster, CO 115

Dickinson Business School/Career Point Business School, Tulsa, OK 246

Divers Academy International, Camden, NJ 218

Dorsey Schools, Madison Heights, MI 188

Dorsey Schools, Roseville, MI 188

Dorsey Schools, Southgate, MI 188

Dorsey Schools, Wayne, MI 189

Douglas Education Center, Monessen, PA 259

Dover Business College, Paramus, NJ 218

Draughons Junior College, Bowling Green, KY 171

Draughons Junior College, Clarksville, TN 287

Draughons Junior College, Murfreesboro, TN 287

Draughons Junior College, Nashville, TN 288

Duff's Business Institute, Pittsburgh, PA 259

Duluth Business University, Duluth, MN 194

E

Eagle Gate College - Weber/Davis, Layton, UT 309

Eagle Gate College - Weber/Davis, Salt Lake City, UT 309

Eagle Gate College, Murray, UT 309

Eastern College of Health Vocations, Little Rock, AR 82

Eastern College of Health Vocations, Metairie, LA 177

ECPI College of Technology, Charlotte, NC 234

ECPI College of Technology, Greensboro, NC 235

ECPI College of Technology, Greenville, SC 285

ECPI College of Technology, Manassas, VA 315

ECPI College of Technology, Newport News, VA 315

ECPI College of Technology, North Charleston, SC 285

ECPI College of Technology, Raleigh, NC 235

ECPI College of Technology, Virginia Beach, VA 316

ECPI Technical College, Glen Allen, VA 316

ECPI Technical College, Richmond, VA 316

ECPI Technical College, Roanoke, VA 317

EduTek College, Stow, OH 239

Electronic Data Processing College of Puerto Rico - San Sebastian, San Sebastian, PR 277

Electronic Data Processing College of Puerto Rico, San Juan, PR 277

Empire Beauty School - Theatrical/Film Make-up, New York, NY 229

Empire Beauty School, Astoria, NY 229

Empire Beauty School, Bensonhurst, NY 229

Empire Beauty School, Boston, MA 185

Empire Beauty School, Cherry Hill, NJ 215

Empire Beauty School, Concord, NC 235

Empire Beauty School, Dunwoody, GA 147

Empire Beauty School, Hanover Park, IL 156

Empire Beauty School, Hanover, PA 259

Empire Beauty School, Harrisburg, PA 259

Empire Beauty School, Kennesaw, GA 147

Empire Beauty School, Lancaster, PA 260

Empire Beauty School, Laurel Springs, NJ 215

Empire Beauty School, Lawrenceville, GA 147

Empire Beauty School, Lawrenceville, NJ 215

Empire Beauty School, Lebanon, PA 260

Empire Beauty School, Malden, MA 185

Empire Beauty School, Matthews, NC 235

Empire Beauty School, Midlothian, VA 317

Empire Beauty School, Monroeville, PA 260

Empire Beauty School, New York, NY 229

Empire Beauty School, Owings Mills, MD 181

Empire Beauty School, Philadelphia, PA 260

Empire Beauty School, Philadelphia, PA 260

Empire Beauty School, Pittsburgh, PA 260

Empire Beauty School, Pottstown, PA 260

Empire Beauty School, Pottsville, PA 260

Empire Beauty School, Reading, PA 260

Boldface type indicates that the school is a participating institution in the Imagine America Scholarship Program

Keiser College, Fort Lauderdale, FL 134
Keiser College, Lakeland, FL 135
Keiser College, Melbourne, FL 135
Keiser College, Miami, FL 135
Keiser College, Orlando, FL 135
Keiser College, Pembroke Pines, FL 136
Keiser College, Port St. Lucie, FL 136
Keiser College, Sarasota, FL 136
Keiser College, Tallahassee, FL 136
Keiser College, West Palm Beach, FL 137
Key College, Fort Lauderdale, FL 137
King's College, Charlotte, NC 235
Kitchen Academy, Los Angeles, CA 99

L

L'Ecole Culinaire, Saint Louis, MO 203
La Belle Beauty School, Hialeah, FL 137
Lamson College, Tempe, AZ 79
Lansdale School of Busines, North Wales, PA 264
Las Vegas College, Henderson, NV 211
Las Vegas College, Las Vegas, NV 211
Laurel Business Institute, Uniontown, PA 265
Lawton School, Southfield, MI 190
Le Cordon Bleu College of Culinary Arts Miami, Miramar, FL 137
Le Cordon Bleu College of Culinary Arts Minneapolis/ St.Paul, Saint Paul, MN 196
Le Cordon Bleu College of Culinary Arts, Atlanta, Tucker, GA 149
Le Cordon Bleu College of Culinary Arts, Las Vegas, Las Vegas, NV 211
Lebanon County Career School, Lebanon, PA 265
Lehigh Valley College, Center Valley, PA 266
Liceo de Arte y Tecnologia, San Juan, PR 281
Lincoln Technical Institute, Indianapolis, IN 166
Lincoln Technical Institute, Allentown, PA 266
Lincoln Technical Institute, Columbia, MD 182
Lincoln Technical Institute, Grand Prairie, TX 300
Lincoln Technical Institute, Mahwah, NJ 222
Lincoln Technical Institute, Melrose Park, IL 158
Lincoln Technical Institute, Philadelphia, PA 266
Lincoln Technical Institute, Union, NJ 222
Long Technical College, Phoenix, AZ 80
Long Technical College-East Valley, Phoenix, AZ 80
Louisville Technical Institute, Louisville, KY 172

M

Madison Media Institute, Madison, WI 331
Mandl School, New York, NY 231
Maric College - Fresno, Clovis, CA 99
Maric College, Anaheim, CA 99
Maric College, Los Angeles, CA 100
Maric College, North Hollywood, CA 99

Maric College, Sacramento, CA 99
Maric College, Salida, CA 99
Maric College, San Diego, CA 100
Maric College, Vista, CA 100
Marine Mechanics Institute, Orlando, FL 137
McCann School of Business, Hazleton, PA 266
McCann School of Business, Pottsville, PA267
McCann School of Business, Scranton, PA 267
McCann School of Business, Sunbury, PA 267
McIntosh College, Dover, NH 213
Medical Career Center, Mobile, AL 71
Medical Careers Institute, Newport News, VA 319
Medical Careers Institute, Richmond, VA 319
Medical Careers Institute, Virginia Beach, VA 320
Medix School, Smyrna, GA 150
Medix School, Towson, MD 182
MedTech College, Indianapolis, IN 166
MedVance Institute, Atlantis, FL 138
MedVance Institute, Baton Rouge, LA 179
MedVance Institute, Cookeville, TN 290
MedVance Institute, Fort Lauderdale, FL 138
MedVance Institute, Houston, TX 301
MedVance Institute, Miami, FL 138
MedVance Institute, Port St. Lucie, FL 138
Metro Business College, Cape Girardeau, MO 203
Metro Business College, Jefferson City, MO 203
Metro Business College, Rolla, MO 203
Miami - Jacobs College, Dayton, OH 241
Miami International University of Art & Design, Miami, FL 138
Mildred Elley School, Latham, NY 232
Mildred Elley, Pittsfield, MA 186
Miller-Motte Technical College, Cary, NC 236
Miller-Motte Technical College, Chattanooga, TN 290
Miller-Motte Technical College, Clarksville, TN 290
Miller-Motte Technical College, Lynchburg, VA 320
Miller-Motte Technical College, North Charleston, SC 285
Miller-Motte Technical College, Wilmington, NC 236
Minneapolis Business College, Roseville, MN 196
Minnesota School of Business - Brooklyn Center, Brooklyn Center, MN 196
Minnesota School of Business - Plymouth, Plymouth, MN 196
Minnesota School of Business - Rochester, Rochester, MN 197
Minnesota School of Business - St. Cloud, Waite Park, MN 197
Minnesota School of Business, Shakopee, MN 197
Minnesota School of Business-Richfield, Richfield, MN 196
Missouri College, St. Louis, MO 203
Missouri Tech, St. Louis, MO 204
Morrison University, Reno, NV 212
Motorcycle Mechanics Institute, Phoenix, AZ 80

Mountain West College, West Valley City, UT 310

MTI College of Business and Technology, Houston, TX 301

MTI College of Business and Technology, Houston, TX 301

MTI College of Business and Technology, Houston, TX 301

N

NASCAR Technical Institute, Mooresville, NC 236

Nashville Auto Diesel College, Nashville, TN 290

National American University - Sioux Falls Branch, Sioux Falls, SD 287

National American University, Albuquerque, NM 224

National American University, Brooklyn Center, MN 197

National American University, Colorado Springs, CO 115

National American University, Denver, CO 116

National American University, Ellsworth AFB, SD 286

National American University, Kansas City, MO 204

National American University, Minneapolis, MN 197

National American University, Overland Park, KS 169

National American University, Rapid City, SD 286

National American University, Rio Rancho, NM 224

National American University, Roseville, MN 197

National Career Education, Citrus Heights, CA 100

National College of Business & Technology, Bayamon, PR 282

National College of Business & Technology, Bluefield, VA 320

National College of Business & Technology, Bristol, TN 290

National College of Business & Technology, Charlottesville, VA 320

National College of Business & Technology, Danville, KY 172

National College of Business & Technology, Danville, VA 320

National College of Business & Technology, Florence, KY 172

National College of Business & Technology, Harrisonburg, VA 321

National College of Business & Technology, Knoxville, TN 291

National College of Business & Technology, Lexington, KY 173

National College of Business & Technology, Louisville, KY 173

National College of Business & Technology, Lynchburg, VA 321

National College of Business & Technology, Martinsville, VA 321

National College of Business & Technology, Nashville, TN 291

National College of Business & Technology, Pikeville, KY 173

National College of Business & Technology, Richmond, KY 173

National College of Business & Technology, Rio Grande, PR 282

National College of Business & Technology, Salem, VA 321

National College of Business and Technology, Arecibo, PR 282

National College of Business and Technology, Cincinnati, OH 241

National College of Business and Technology, Indianapolis, IN 166

National College of Business and Technology, Kettering, OH 242

National Institute of Technology - Dearborn, Dearborn, MI 190

National Institute of Technology - Greenspoint, Houston, TX 303

National Institute of Technology - Hobby, Houston, TX 303

National Institute of Technology, Austin , TX 302

National Institute of Technology, Cross Lanes, WV 329

National Institute of Technology, Detroit, MI 190

National Institute of Technology, Houston, TX 302

National Institute of Technology, Houston, TX 302

National Institute of Technology, Long Beach, CA 101

National Institute of Technology, San Antonio, TX 302

National Institute of Technology, Southfield, MI 190

National School of Technology, Inc., Fort Lauderdale, FL 139

National School of Technology, Inc., Hialeah, FL 139

National School of Technology, Inc., Miami, FL 139

National School of Technology, Inc., Miami, FL 139

Neumont University, Salt Lake City, UT 310

Nevada Career Academy, Sparks, NV 212

Nevada Career Institute, Las Vegas, NV 212

Nevada Career Institute, Las Vegas, NV 212

Nevada School of Massage Therapy, Las Vegas, NV 212

New Castle School of Trades, Pulaski, PA 268

New England Culinary Institute at Essex, Essex Junction, VT 313

New England Culinary Institute at H. Lavity Stoutt Community College, Road Town, Tortola, British Virgin Islands 83

New England Culinary Institute, Montpelier, VT 313

The New England Institute of Art, Brookline, MA 186

New England Institute of Technology at Palm Beach, West Palm Beach, FL 140

New England Institute of Technology, Warwick, RI 284

New England School of Communications, Bangor, ME 180

New England Technical Institute of Connecticut, Inc., New Britain, CT 119

New England Technical Institute, Cromwell, CT 119
New England Technical Institute, Hamden, CT 119
New England Technical Institute, Shelton, CT 119
New York Institute of Massage, Buffalo, NY 232
New York Technical Institute of Hawaii, Honolulu, HI 152
Newschool of Architecture & Design, San Diego, CA 101
North American Trade School, Gwynn Oak, MD 182
North Florida Institute, Orange Park, FL 140
Northwest Technical Institute, Eden Prairie, MN 198

O

Ocean Corporation, Houston, TX 303
Ohio Institute of Photography and Technology, Dayton, OH 242
Ohio Valley College of Technology, East Liverpool, OH 242
Oklahoma Health Academy, Oklahoma City, OK 247
Oklahoma Health Academy, Tulsa, OK 247
Olympia Career Training Institute, Grand Rapids, MI 191
Olympia Career Training Institute, Kalamazoo, MI 191
Olympia College, Burr Ridge, IL 158
Olympia College, Chicago, IL 159
Olympia College, Merrillville, IN 167
Olympia College, North Aurora, IL 159
Olympia College, Skokie, IL 159
Orlando Culinary Academy, Orlando, FL 140
Orleans Technical Institute - Center City Campus, Philadelphia, PA 268
Orleans Technical Institute, Philadelphia, PA 268

P

Paducah Technical College, Paducah, KY 174
Parks College, Aurora, CO 116
Parks College, Denver, CO 116
Parks College, McLean, VA 321
PCI Health Training Center, Dallas, TX 303
PCI Health Training Center, Richardson, TX 304
Peirce College, Philadelphia, PA 268
Pennco Tech, Bristol, PA 269
Pennco Tech, Blackwood, NJ 222
Pennsylvania Culinary Institute, Pittsburgh, PA 269
Pima Medical Institute, Albuquerque, NM 224
Pima Medical Institute, Chula Vista, CA 101
Pima Medical Institute, Colorado Springs, CO 116
Pima Medical Institute, Denver, CO 117
Pima Medical Institute, Las Vegas, NV 213
Pima Medical Institute, Mesa, AZ 80
Pima Medical Institute, Renton, WA 328
Pima Medical Institute, Seattle, WA 328
Pima Medical Institute, Tucson, AZ 81
Pinnacle Career Institute, Kansas City, MO 204
Pinnacle Career Institute, Lawrence, KS 169

Pioneer Pacific College - Eugene/Springfield Branch, Springfield, OR 251
Pioneer Pacific College, Clackamas, OR 250
Pioneer Pacific College, Wilsonville, OR 251
Pittsburgh Technical Institute, Oakdale, PA 269
The PJA School, Upper Darby, PA 270
Platt College - Dallas, Dallas, TX 304
Platt College - Los Angeles, Inc, Alhambra, CA 102
Platt College - San Diego, San Diego, CA 102
Platt College, Huntington Beach, CA 101
Platt College, Lawton, OK 247
Platt College, Oklahoma City, OK 248
Platt College, Ontario, CA 102
Platt College, Tulsa, OK 248
Ponce Paramedical College, Inc., Coto Laurel, PR 282
Porter and Chester Institute, Chicopee, MA 187
Porter and Chester Institute, Enfield, CT 120
Porter and Chester Institute, Stratford, CT 120
Porter and Chester Institute, Watertown, CT 120
Porter and Chester Institute, Wethersfield, CT 120
Potomac College, Herndon, VA 322
Potomac College, Washington, DC 121
Prism Career Institute, Hammonton, NJ 222
Prism Career Institute, Philadelphia, PA 270
Prism Career Institute, Sewell, NJ 223
Professional Careers Institute, Indianapolis, IN 167
Professional Healthcare Institute, Woodbridge, VA 322
Provo College, Provo, UT 310

R

Rasmussen College Eagan, Eagan, MN 198
Rasmussen College Mankato, Mankato, MN 198
Rasmussen College Minnetonka, Minnetonka, MN 199
Rasmussen College St. Cloud, St. Cloud, MN 199
The Refrigeration School, Phoenix, AZ 81
Remington College - Baton Rouge Campus, Baton Rouge, LA 179
Remington College - Cleveland Campus, Cleveland, OH 242
Remington College - Cleveland West Campus, North Olmstead, OH 242
Remington College - Colorado Springs Campus, Colorado Springs, CO 117
Remington College - Dallas Campus, Garland, TX 304
Remington College - Denver Campus, Lakewood, CO 117
Remington College - Fort Worth Campus, Fort Worth, TX 304
Remington College - Honolulu Campus, Honolulu, HI 152
Remington College - Houston Campus, Houston, TX 305
Remington College - Jacksonville Campus, Jacksonville, FL 140

ALPHABETICAL LISTING OF *IMAGINE AMERICA* SCHOLARSHIP PROGRAM PARTICIPANTS

ITT Technical Institute, Albany, NY 230
ITT Technical Institute, Albuquerque, NM 223
ITT Technical Institute, Anaheim, CA 96
ITT Technical Institute, Arlington, TX 299
ITT Technical Institute, Arnold, MO 202
ITT Technical Institute, Austin, TX 299
ITT Technical Institute, Bessemer, AL 71
ITT Technical Institute, Boise, ID 153
ITT Technical Institute, Bothell, WA 327
ITT Technical Institute, Burr Ridge, IL 157
ITT Technical Institute, Canton, MI 189
ITT Technical Institute, Chantilly, VA 317
ITT Technical Institute, Dayton, OH 240
ITT Technical Institute, Duluth, GA 149
ITT Technical Institute, Earth City, MO 202
ITT Technical Institute, Eden Prairie, MN 195
ITT Technical Institute, Fort Lauderdale, FL 133
ITT Technical Institute, Fort Wayne, IN 165
ITT Technical Institute, Getzville, NY 230
ITT Technical Institute, Grand Rapids, MI 189
ITT Technical Institute, Green Bay, WI 331
ITT Technical Institute, Greenfield, WI 331
ITT Technical Institute, Greenville, SC 285
ITT Technical Institute, Henderson, NV 211
ITT Technical Institute, Hilliard, OH 240
ITT Technical Institute, Houston, TX 299
ITT Technical Institute, Houston, TX 299
ITT Technical Institute, Houston, TX 300
ITT Technical Institute, Indianapolis, IN 165
ITT Technical Institute, Jacksonville, FL 133
ITT Technical Institute, Kansas City, MO 203
ITT Technical Institute, Kennesaw, GA 149
ITT Technical Institute, King of Prussia, PA 264
ITT Technical Institute, Knoxville, TN 289
ITT Technical Institute, Lake Mary, FL 133
ITT Technical Institute, Lathrop, CA 96
ITT Technical Institute, Little Rock, AR 82
ITT Technical Institute, Liverpool, NY 230
ITT Technical Institute, Louisville, KY 171
ITT Technical Institute, Matteson, IL 158
ITT Technical Institute, Mechanicsburg, PA 264
ITT Technical Institute, Memphis, TN 289
ITT Technical Institute, Miami, FL 133
ITT Technical Institute, Monroeville, PA 264
ITT Technical Institute, Mount Prospect, IL 158
ITT Technical Institute, Murray, UT 310
ITT Technical Institute, Nashville, TN 289
ITT Technical Institute, Newburgh, IN 166
ITT Technical Institute, Norfolk, VA 318
ITT Technical Institute, Norwood, MA 186
ITT Technical Institute, Norwood, OH 240
ITT Technical Institute, Omaha, NE 209
ITT Technical Institute, Owings Mills, MD 181

ITT Technical Institute, Oxnard, CA 97
ITT Technical Institute, Pittsburg, PA 264
ITT Technical Institute, Portland, OR 250
ITT Technical Institute, Rancho Cordova, CA 97
ITT Technical Institute, Richardson, TX 300
ITT Technical Institute, Richmond, VA 318
ITT Technical Institute, Saint Rose, LA 179
ITT Technical Institute, San Antonio, TX 300
ITT Technical Institute, San Bernardino, CA 97
ITT Technical Institute, San Diego, CA 97
ITT Technical Institute, Seattle, WA 327
ITT Technical Institute, Spokane, WA 328
ITT Technical Institute, Springfield, VA 318
ITT Technical Institute, Strongsville, OH 241
ITT Technical Institute, Sylmar, CA 98
ITT Technical Institute, Tampa, FL 134
ITT Technical Institute, Tempe, AZ 79
ITT Technical Institute, Thornton, CO 115
ITT Technical Institute, Torrance, CA 98
ITT Technical Institute, Troy, MI 190
ITT Technical Institute, Tucson, AZ 79
ITT Technical Institute, Tulsa, OK 247
ITT Technical Institute, Warrensville Heights, OH 241
ITT Technical Institute, West Covina, CA 98
ITT Technical Institute, Woburn, MA 186
ITT Technical Institute, Youngstown, OH 241

K

Kee Business College - Chesapeake, Chesapeake, VA 319
Kee Business College, Newport News, VA 319

L

L'Ecole Culinaire, Saint Louis, MO 203
Lansdale School of Busines, North Wales, PA 264
Las Vegas College, Henderson, NV 211
Las Vegas College, Las Vegas, NV 211
Le Cordon Bleu College of Culinary Arts Minneapolis/
St.Paul, Saint Paul, MN 196
Lehigh Valley College, Center Valley, PA 266
Lincoln Technical Institute, Indianapolis, IN 166
Lincoln Technical Institute, Allentown, PA 266
Lincoln Technical Institute, Columbia, MD 182
Lincoln Technical Institute, Grand Prairie, TX 300
Lincoln Technical Institute, Mahwah, NJ 222
Lincoln Technical Institute, Melrose Park, IL 158
Lincoln Technical Institute, Philadelphia, PA 266
Lincoln Technical Institute, Union, NJ 222

M

Maric College, San Diego, CA 100
Marine Mechanics Institute, Orlando, FL 137
Medical Careers Institute, Newport News, VA 319
Medical Careers Institute, Richmond, VA 319

PCI Health Training Center, Richardson, TX 304
Pennsylvania Culinary Institute, Pittsburgh, PA 269
Pinnacle Career Institute, Kansas City, MO 204
Pinnacle Career Institute, Lawrence, KS 169
Pioneer Pacific College - Eugene/Springfield Branch, Springfield, OR 251
Pioneer Pacific College, Clackamas, OR 250
Pioneer Pacific College, Wilsonville, OR 251
Platt College - Dallas, Dallas, TX 304
Platt College - Los Angeles, Inc, Alhambra, CA 102
Platt College, Huntington Beach, CA 101
Platt College, Lawton, OK 247
Platt College, Oklahoma City, OK 248
Platt College, Ontario, CA 102
Platt College, Tulsa, OK 248
Professional Healthcare Institute, Woodbridge, VA 322

R

The Refrigeration School, Phoenix, AZ 81
Remington College - Baton Rouge Campus, Baton Rouge, LA 179
Remington College - Cleveland Campus, Cleveland, OH 242
Remington College - Cleveland West Campus, North Olmstead, OH 242
Remington College - Colorado Springs Campus, Colorado Springs, CO 117
Remington College - Dallas Campus, Garland, TX 304
Remington College - Denver Campus, Lakewood, CO 117
Remington College - Fort Worth Campus, Fort Worth, TX 304
Remington College - Honolulu Campus, Honolulu, HI 152
Remington College - Houston Campus, Houston, TX 305
Remington College - Jacksonville Campus, Jacksonville, FL 140
Remington College - Lafayette Campus, Lafayette, LA 179
Remington College - Memphis Campus, Memphis, TN 291
Remington College - Mobile Campus, Mobile, AL 71
Remington College - Nashville Campus, Nashville, TN 291
Remington College - New Orleans Campus, Metairie, LA 180
Remington College - Pinellas Campus, Largo, FL 141
Remington College - San Diego Campus, San Diego, CA 103
Remington College - Tampa Campus, Tampa, FL 141
Remington College - Tempe Campus, Tempe, AZ 81
Remington College, Houston, TX 304
Remington College-Little Rock Campus, Little Rock, AR 83
The Restaurant School at Walnut Hill College, Philadelphia, PA 270
Rochester Business Institute, Rochester, NY 232

S

San Joaquin Valley College Inc., Rancho Cordova, CA 104
San Joaquin Valley College Inc., Visalia, CA 104
San Joaquin Valley College, Bakersfield, CA 103
San Joaquin Valley College, Fresno, CA 103
San Joaquin Valley College, Fresno, CA 103
San Joaquin Valley College, Modesto, CA 104
San Joaquin Valley College, Rancho Cucamonga, CA 104
San Joaquin Valley College, Visalia, CA 104
Savannah River College, Augusta, GA 151
Schuylkill Institute of Business and Technology, Pottsville, PA 270
Southwest Florida College, Tampa, FL 143
Southwest Florida College, Tampa, FL 143
Southwestern College of Business, Cincinnati, OH 244
Southwestern College of Business, Cincinnati, OH 244
Southwestern College of Business, Dayton, OH 244
Southwestern College of Business, Franklin, OH 245
Spencerian College, Louisville, KY 174
Springfield College, Springfield, MO 206
Stratford University, Falls Church , VA 322
Stratford University, Woodbridge, VA 322
Sullivan University, Louisville, KY 175

T

Technology Education College, Columbus, OH 245
Thompson Institute, Chambersburg, PA 271
Triangle Tech, Inc. - DuBois School, DuBois, PA 272
Triangle Tech, Inc. - Erie School, Erie, PA 272
Triangle Tech, Inc. - Greensburg School, Greensburg, PA 272
Triangle Tech, Inc. - Pittsburgh School, Pittsburgh, PA 272
Triangle Tech, Inc. - Sunbury School, Sunbury, PA 272
Trumbull Business College, Warren, OH 245
Tulsa Welding School, Jacksonville, FL 143
Tulsa Welding School, Tulsa, OK 248

U

Universal Technical Institute, Avondale, AZ 82
Universal Technical Institute, Exton, PA 273
Universal Technical Institute, Houston, TX 306
Universal Technical Institute, Inc., Glendale Heights, IL 160
Universal Technical Institute, Norwood, MA 187
Universal Technical Institute, Rancho Cucamonga, CA 108

V

Vatterott College, Broadview Heights, OH 245
Vatterott College, Des Moines, IA 168
Vatterott College, Joplin, MO 206
Vatterott College, Kansas City, MO 207
Vatterott College, Memphis, TN 292
Vatterott College, O'Fallon , MO 207
Vatterott College, Oklahoma City, OK 248

Vatterott College, Omaha, NE 209
Vatterott College, Quincy, IL 160
Vatterott College, Springfield, MO 208
Vatterott College, St. Ann, MO 207
Vatterott College, St. Joseph, MO 207
Vatterott College, St. Louis, MO 208
Vatterott College, Tulsa, OK 249
Vatterott College, Wichita, KS 169
VC Tech, Pelham, AL 72
Virginia College at Austin, Austin, TX 307
Virginia College at Birmingham, Birmingham, AL 72
Virginia College at Huntsville, Huntsville, AL 73
Virginia College at Jackson, Jackson, MS 200
Virginia College at Mobile, Mobile, AL 73
Virginia College at Pensacola, Pensacola, FL 144

W

West Virginia Career Institute, Mount Braddock, PA 273
West Virginia Junior College, Morgantown, WV 330
Western Business College, Portland, OR 251
Western Business College, Vancouver, WA 328
Western Career College, Pleasant Hill, CA 108
Western Career College, Sacramento, CA 108
Western Career College, San Leandro, CA 109
Western Technical Institute, El Paso, TX 308
Westwood Aviation Institute, Houston, TX 308
Westwood College - Anaheim, Anaheim, CA 109
Westwood College - Atlanta Campus, Atlanta, GA 151
Westwood College - Atlanta Northlake, Atlanta, GA 152

Westwood College - Chicago Du Page, Woodridge, IL 160
Westwood College - Chicago Loop Campus, Chicago, IL 161
Westwood College - Chicago O'Hare Airport, Chicago, IL 161
Westwood College - Chicago River Oaks, Calumet City, IL 161
Westwood College - Dallas, Dallas, TX 308
Westwood College - Denver North, Denver, CO 118
Westwood College - Denver South, Denver, CO 118
Westwood College - Denver, Broomfield, CO 118
Westwood College - Fort Worth, Euless, TX 308
Westwood College - Houston South Campus, Houston, TX 308
Westwood College - Houston South, Houston, TX 308
Westwood College - Inland Empire, Upland, CA 109
Westwood College - Long Beach, Torrance, CA 110
Westwood College - Los Angeles, Inglewood, CA 110
Westwood College - Los Angeles, Los Angeles, CA 110
Wichita Technical Institute, Wichita, KS 169
WyoTech, Bedford, MA 187
WyoTech, Blairsville, PA 274
WyoTech, Fremont, CA 111
WyoTech, Laramie, WY 332
WyoTech, Oakland, CA 111
WyoTech, West Sacramento, CA 111

Y

Yorktowne Business Institute, York, PA 274

ALPHABETICAL LISTING OF MILITARY AWARD PROGRAM PARTICIPANTS

A

Academy of Art University, San Francisco, CA 83

Academy of Medical Arts and Business, Harrisburg, PA 252

Advanced Technology Institute, Virginia Beach, VA 314

American InterContinental University, Weston, FL 121

Apex Technical School, New York, NY 225

The Art Institute of Colorado, Denver, CO 111

The Art Institute of Pittsburgh, Pittsburgh, PA 252

ATI Career Training Center, Dallas, TX 294

ATI Career Training Center, Fort Lauderdale, FL 122

ATI Career Training Center, Miami, FL 123

ATI Career Training Center, North Richland Hills, TX 295

ATI Career Training Center, Oakland Park, FL 123

ATI Health Education Center, Miami, FL 123

ATI Technical Training Center, Dallas, TX 295

Austin Business College, Austin, TX 295

Automotive Training Center, Exton, PA 253

B

Bel-Rea Institute of Animal Technology, Denver, CO 112

Berks Technical Institute, Wyomissing, PA 253

Bradford School of Business, Houston, TX 295

Brookstone College of Business, Charlotte, NC 234

Brookstone College of Business, Greensboro, NC 234

Brown College, Mendota Heights, MN 193

Bryman College, Port Orchard, WA 326

C

Career Education Institute, Brockton, MA 184

Career Education Institute, Henderson, NV 210

Career Education Institute, Lincoln, RI 283

Career Education Institute, Lowell, MA 184

Career Education Institute, Marietta, GA 146

Career Education Institute, Norcross, GA 146

CHI Institute, Southampton, PA 256

The Cittone Institute, Edison, NJ 217

The Cittone Institute, Mount Laurel, NJ 217

The Cittone Institute, Paramus, NJ 217

The Cittone Institute, Philadelphia, PA 257

The Cittone Institute, Philadelphia, PA 257

The Cittone Institute, Plymouth Meeting, PA 257

Collins College: A School of Design and Technology, Tempe, AZ 77

Computer Learning Network, Altoona, PA 258

Computer Learning Network, Mechanicsburg, PA 258

Court Reporting Institute of Dallas, Dallas, TX 297

Court Reporting Institute of Houston, Houston, TX 297

Coyne American Institute, Chicago, IL 155

Coyne American Institute, Chicago, IL 156

D

Delta School of Business & Technology, Lake Charles, LA 177

Denver Automotive and Diesel College, Denver, CO 114

Dorsey Schools, Madison Heights, MI 188

Dorsey Schools, Roseville, MI 188

Dorsey Schools, Southgate, MI 188

Dorsey Schools, Wayne, MI 189

Duluth Business University, Duluth, MN 194

E

ECPI College of Technology, Charlotte, NC 234

ECPI College of Technology, Greensboro, NC 235

ECPI College of Technology, Greenville, SC 285

ECPI College of Technology, Manassas, VA 315

ECPI College of Technology, Newport News, VA 315

ECPI College of Technology, North Charleston, SC 285

ECPI College of Technology, Raleigh, NC 235

ECPI College of Technology, Virginia Beach, VA 316

ECPI Technical College, Glen Allen, VA 316

ECPI Technical College, Richmond, VA 316

ECPI Technical College, Roanoke, VA 316

Erie Business Center, Main, Erie, PA 261

F

Florida Metropolitan University - Orange Park Campus, Orange Park, FL 128

Florida Technical College, Auburndale, FL 129

Florida Technical College, DeLand, FL 130

Florida Technical College, Jacksonville, FL 130

Florida Technical College, Orlando, FL 130

The French Culinary Institute, New York, NY 229

H

Hagerstown Business College, Hagerstown, MD 181

Hallmark Institute of Photography, Turners Falls, MA 185

Heritage College, Las Vegas, NV 210

Herzing College, Atlanta, GA 148

Herzing College, Birmingham, AL 70

Herzing College, Madison, WI 330

Herzing College, Minneapolis, MN 195

Herzing College, Winter Park, FL 131

High-Tech Institute, Phoenix, AZ 78

Boldface type indicates that the school is a participating listitution in the *Imagine America* Scholarship Program

Platt College, Oklahoma City, OK 248
Platt College, Ontario, CA 102
Platt College, Tulsa, OK 248

R

The Refrigeration School, Phoenix, AZ 81

S

San Joaquin Valley College Inc., Rancho Cordova, CA 104
San Joaquin Valley College, Bakersfield, CA 103
San Joaquin Valley College, Fresno, CA 103
San Joaquin Valley College, Modesto, CA 104
San Joaquin Valley College, Rancho Cucamonga, CA 104
San Joaquin Valley College, Visalia, CA 104
Schuylkill Institute of Business and Technology, Pottsville, PA 270
The Soma Institute, The National School of Clinical Massage Therapy, Chicago, IL 160
Southwest Florida College, Tampa, FL 143
Southwest Florida College, Tampa, FL 143
Southwestern College of Business, Cincinnati, OH 244
Southwestern College of Business, Cincinnati, OH 244
Southwestern College of Business, Dayton, OH 244
Southwestern College of Business, Florence, KY 174
Southwestern College of Business, Franklin, OH 245
Specs Howard School of Broadcast Arts Inc., Southfield, MI 192
Springfield College, Springfield, MO 206

T

TESST College of Technology, Beltsville, MD 183
Triangle Tech, Inc. - DuBois School, DuBois, PA 272
Triangle Tech, Inc. - Erie School, Erie, PA 272
Triangle Tech, Inc. - Greensburg School, Greensburg, PA 272
Triangle Tech, Inc. - Pittsburgh School, Pittsburgh, PA 272
Triangle Tech, Inc. - Sunbury School, Sunbury, PA 272
Trumbull Business College, Warren, OH 245
Tulsa Welding School, Jacksonville, FL 143
Tulsa Welding School, Tulsa, OK 248

U

Universal Technical Institute, Avondale, AZ 82
Universal Technical Institute, Exton, PA 273
Universal Technical Institute, Houston, TX 306
Universal Technical Institute, Inc., Glendale Heights, IL 160
Universal Technical Institute, Rancho Cucamonga, CA 108

Utah Career College, West Jordan, UT 312

V

Vatterott College, Des Moines, IA 168
Vatterott College, Joplin, MO 206
Vatterott College, Kansas City, MO 207
Vatterott College, Memphis, TN 291
Vatterott College, O'Fallon , MO 207
Vatterott College, Oklahoma City, OK 248
Vatterott College, Omaha, NE 209
Vatterott College, Quincy, IL 160
Vatterott College, Springfield, MO 208
Vatterott College, St. Ann, MO 207
Vatterott College, St. Joseph, MO 207
Vatterott College, Tulsa, OK 249
Vatterott College, Wichita, KS 169
VC Tech, Pelham, AL 72
Virginia College at Pensacola, Pensacola, FL 144

W

Western Technical College, El Paso, TX 308
Westwood Aviation Institute, Houston, TX 308
Westwood College - Anaheim, Anaheim, CA 109
Westwood College - Atlanta Campus, Atlanta, GA 151
Westwood College - Atlanta Northlake, Atlanta, GA 152
Westwood College - Chicago Du Page, Woodridge, IL 160
Westwood College - Chicago Loop Campus, Chicago, IL 161
Westwood College - Chicago O'Hare Airport, Chicago, IL 161
Westwood College - Dallas, Dallas, TX 308
Westwood College - Denver North, Denver, CO 118
Westwood College - Denver South, Denver, CO 118
Westwood College - Fort Worth, Euless, TX 308
Westwood College - Houston South Campus, Houston, TX 308
Westwood College - Houston South, Houston, TX 308
Westwood College - Inland Empire, Upland, CA 109
Westwood College - Long Beach, Torrance, CA 110
Westwood College - Los Angeles, Inglewood, CA 110
Westwood College - Los Angeles, Los Angeles, CA 110
Wichita Technical Institute, Wichita, KS 169
WyoTech, Bedford, MA 187
WyoTech, Blairsville, PA 274
WyoTech, Fremont, CA 111
WyoTech, Laramie, WY 332
WyoTech, Oakland, CA 111
WyoTech, West Sacramento, CA 111

Y

Yorktowne Business Institute, York, PA 274

ALPHABETICAL LISTING OF PROGRAMS

ACCOUNTING

A-1 Business and Technical College, Caguas, PR 275
Aakers Business College , Bismarck, ND 236
Aakers Business College, Fargo, ND 236
Academy College, Minneapolis, MN 192
American Commercial College, Abilene, TX 292
American Commercial College, Lubbock, TX 293
American Commercial College, Odessa, TX 293
American Commercial College, San Angelo, TX 293
American Commercial College, Shreveport, LA 175
American School of Business, Wichita Falls, TX 294
Andover College, Portland, ME 180
Antonelli College, Cincinnati, OH 237
Antonelli College, Hattiesburg, MS 199
Antonelli College, Jackson, MS 200
Argosy University/Chicago, Chicago, IL 154
Argosy University/Sarasota, Sarasota, FL 122
Austin Business College, Austin, TX 295
Bay State College, Boston, MA 183
Berkeley College, Paramus, NJ 214
Berkeley College, West Paterson, NJ 214
Berkeley College, Woodbridge, NJ 215
Berks Technical Institute, Wyomissing, PA 253
Blair College, Colorado Springs, CO 112
Bradford School of Business, Houston, TX 295
Bradford School, Columbus, OH 237
Bradford School, Pittsburgh, PA 254
Briarcliffe College, Bethpage, NY 226
Briarcliffe College, Patchogue, NY 226
Brookstone College of Business, Charlotte, NC 234
Brookstone College of Business, Greensboro, NC 234
Brown Mackie College, Cincinnati Campus, Cincinnati, OH 238
Brown Mackie College, Findlay Campus, Findlay, OH 238
Brown Mackie College, Hopkinsville Campus, Hopkinsville, KY 170
Brown Mackie College, Lenexa Campus, Lenexa, KS 168
Brown Mackie College, Los Angeles Campus, Santa Monica, CA 87
Brown Mackie College, Merrillville Campus, Merrillville, IN 162
Brown Mackie College, Miami Campus, Miami, FL 124
Brown Mackie College, Michigan City Campus, Michigan City, IN 162
Brown Mackie College, Moline Campus, Moline, IL 154
Brown Mackie College, North Canton Campus, North Canton, OH 239
Brown Mackie College, Orange County Campus, Santa Ana, CA 87
Brown Mackie College, San Diego Campus, San Diego, CA 87
Brown Mackie College, South Bend Campus, South Bend, IN 162
Business Institute of Pennsylvania, Meadville, PA 255
Business Institute of Pennsylvania, Sharon, PA 255
Cardean University, Chicago, IL 154
Career Point Business School, San Antonio, TX 296
Central Coast College, Salinas, CA 92
Central Florida College, Winter Park, FL 124
Chaparral College, Tucson, AZ 77
Charter College, Anchorage, AK 74
City College, Inc., Moore, OK 246
CollegeAmerica - Colorado Springs, Colorado Springs, CO 112
CollegeAmerica - Denver, Denver, CO 113
CollegeAmerica - Fort Collins, Fort Collins, CO 113
Colorado Technical University Denver Campus, Greenwood Village, CO 114
Colorado Technical University Sioux Falls Campus, Sioux Falls, SD 286
Colorado Technical University, Colorado Springs, CO 113
Davis College, Toledo, OH 239
Daymar College, Louisville, KY 171
Daymar College, Newport, KY 171
Daymar College, Owensboro, KY 171
Delta School of Business & Technology, Lake Charles, LA 177
Dorsey Schools, Madison Heights, MI 188
Dorsey Schools, Roseville, MI 188
Dorsey Schools, Southgate, MI 188
Dorsey Schools, Wayne, MI 189
Douglas Education Center, Monessen, PA 259
Dover Business College, Paramus, NJ 218
Draughons Junior College, Bowling Green, KY 171
Draughons Junior College, Clarksville, TN 287
Draughons Junior College, Murfreesboro, TN 287
Draughons Junior College, Nashville, TN 288
Duluth Business University, Duluth, MN 194
Eagle Gate College, Murray, UT 309
Eagle Gate College - Weber/Davis, Layton, UT 309
Eagle Gate College - Weber/Davis, Salt Lake City, UT 309
ECPI College of Technology, Charlotte, NC 234
ECPI College of Technology, Greensboro, NC 235
ECPI College of Technology, Greenville, SC 285
ECPI College of Technology, Manassas, VA 315
ECPI College of Technology, Newport News, VA 315

ECPI College of Technology, North Charleston, SC 285
ECPI College of Technology, Raleigh, NC 235
ECPI College of Technology, Virginia Beach, VA 316
Empire College, Santa Rosa, CA 93
Erie Business Center South, New Castle, PA 262
Erie Business Center, Main, Erie, PA 261
Everest College, Arlington , TX 297
Everest College, Dallas, TX 297
Everest College, Fort Worth, TX 297
Everest College, Phoenix, AZ 78
Everest College, Rancho Cucamonga, CA 93
Florida Metropolitan University - Brandon Campus, Tampa, FL 127
Florida Metropolitan University - Jacksonville Campus, Jacksonville, FL 127
Florida Metropolitan University - Lakeland Campus, Lakeland, FL 127
Florida Metropolitan University - North Orlando Campus, Orlando, FL 128
Florida Metropolitan University - Pinellas Campus, Clearwater, FL 128
Florida Metropolitan University - Pompano Beach Campus, Pompano Beach, FL 129
Florida Metropolitan University - South Orlando Campus, Orlando, FL 129
Florida Metropolitan University - Tampa Campus, Tampa, FL 129
Florida Metropolitan University-Melbourne Campus, Melbourne, FL 127
Fox College, Oak Lawn, IL 156
Gallipolis Career College, Gallipolis, OH 239
Gibbs College, Boston, MA 185
Gibbs College, Livingston, NJ 218
Gibbs College, Norwalk, CT 119
Globe College, Oakdale, MN 194
Golden State College, Visalia, CA 95
Hagerstown Business College, Hagerstown, MD 181
Hamilton College, Cedar Rapids, IA 167
Herzing College, Atlanta, GA 148
Herzing College, Birmingham, AL 70
Herzing College, Kenner, LA 178
Herzing College, Madison, WI 330
Herzing College, Minneapolis, MN 195
Herzing College, Winter Park, FL 131
Hesser College, Manchester, NH 213
Hickey College, St. Louis, MO 202
ICM School of Business & Medical Careers, Pittsburgh, PA 263
ICPR Junior College - Hato Rey Campus, San Juan, PR 278
ICPR Junior College - Mayaguez Campus, Mayaguez, PR 279
ICPR Junior College-Arecibo Campus, Arecibo, PR 278

Indiana Business College, Anderson, IN 162
Indiana Business College, Columbus, IN 163
Indiana Business College, Evansville, IN 163
Indiana Business College, Fort Wayne, IN 163
Indiana Business College, Indianapolis, IN 163
Indiana Business College, Lafayette, IN 163
Indiana Business College, Marion, IN 164
Indiana Business College, Muncie, IN 164
Indiana Business College, Terre Haute, IN 164
International Business College, El Paso, TX 298
International Business College, El Paso, TX 299
International Business College, Fort Wayne, IN 165
International Business College, Indianapolis, IN 165
Kaplan University, Davenport, IA 168
Katharine Gibbs School, Melville, NY 231
Katharine Gibbs School, New York, NY 231
Katharine Gibbs School, Norristown, PA 264
Katharine Gibbs School, Piscataway, NJ 221
Kee Business College, Newport News, VA 319
Keiser College, Daytona Beach, FL 134
Keiser College, Fort Lauderdale, FL 134
Keiser College, Lakeland, FL 135
Keiser College, Melbourne, FL 135
Keiser College, Miami, FL 135
Keiser College, Orlando, FL 135
Keiser College, Pembroke Pines, FL 136
Keiser College, Port St. Lucie, FL 136
Keiser College, Sarasota, FL 136
Keiser College, Tallahassee, FL 136
Keiser College, West Palm Beach, FL 137
Lamson College, Tempe, AZ 79
Las Vegas College, Henderson, NV 211
Las Vegas College, Las Vegas, NV 211
Laurel Business Institute, Uniontown, PA 265
Lehigh Valley College, Center Valley, PA 266
McCann School of Business, Hazleton, PA 266
McCann School of Business, Pottsville, PA267
McCann School of Business, Scranton, PA 267
McCann School of Business, Sunbury, PA 267
McIntosh College, Dover, NH 213
Mildred Elley School, Latham, NY 232
Mildred Elley, Pittsfield, MA 186
Miller-Motte Technical College, Cary, NC 236
Miller-Motte Technical College, Chattanooga, TN 290
Miller-Motte Technical College, Clarksville, TN 290
Miller-Motte Technical College, Lynchburg, VA 320
Miller-Motte Technical College, North Charleston, SC 285
Miller-Motte Technical College, Wilmington, NC 236
Minneapolis Business College, Roseville, MN 196
Minnesota School of Business - Brooklyn Center, Brooklyn Center, MN 196
Minnesota School of Business-Richfield, Richfield, MN 196
Morrison University, Reno, NV 212

Mountain West College, West Valley City, UT 310
MTI College of Business and Technology, Houston, TX 301
National American University, Albuquerque, NM 224
National American University, Brooklyn Center, MN 197
National American University, Colorado Springs, CO 115
National American University, Denver, CO 116
National American University, Ellsworth AFB, SD 286
National American University, Kansas City, MO 204
National American University, Minneapolis, MN 197
National American University, Overland Park, KS 169
National American University, Rapid City, SD 286
National American University, Rio Rancho, NM 224
National American University, Roseville, MN 197
National American University - Sioux Falls Branch, Sioux Falls, SD 287
National College of Business & Technology, Bayamon, PR 282
National College of Business & Technology, Bluefield, VA 320
National College of Business & Technology, Bristol, TN 290
National College of Business & Technology, Charlottesville, VA 320
National College of Business & Technology, Danville, KY 172
National College of Business & Technology, Danville, VA 320
National College of Business & Technology, Florence, KY 172
National College of Business & Technology, Harrisonburg, VA 321
National College of Business & Technology, Knoxville, TN 291
National College of Business & Technology, Lexington, KY 173
National College of Business & Technology, Louisville, KY 173
National College of Business & Technology, Lynchburg, VA 321
National College of Business & Technology, Martinsville, VA 321
National College of Business & Technology, Nashville, TN 291
National College of Business & Technology, Pikeville, KY 173
National College of Business & Technology, Richmond, KY 173
National College of Business & Technology, Rio Grande, PR 282
National College of Business & Technology, Salem, VA 321
National College of Business and Technology, Arecibo, PR 282
National College of Business and Technology, Cincinnati, OH 241
National College of Business and Technology, Indianapolis, IN 166
National College of Business and Technology, Kettering, OH 242
North Florida Institute, Orange Park, FL 140
Ohio Valley College of Technology, East Liverpool, OH 242
Parks College, Aurora, CO 116
Parks College, Denver, CO 116
Parks College, McLean, VA 321
Pennco Tech Bristol, PA 269
Pennco Tech, Blackwood, NJ 222
Pioneer Pacific College, Clackamas, OR 250
Pioneer Pacific College, Wilsonville, OR 251
Pittsburgh Technical Institute, Oakdale, PA 269
The PJA School, Upper Darby, PA 270
Potomac College, Herndon, VA 322
Potomac College, Washington, DC 121
Provo College, Provo, UT 310
Rasmussen College Eagan, Eagan, MN 198
Rasmussen College Mankato, Mankato, MN 198
Rasmussen College Minnetonka, Minnetonka, MN 199
Rasmussen College St. Cloud, St. Cloud, MN 199
Remington College - Tampa Campus, Tampa, FL 141
RETS Institute of Technology, Pittsburgh, PA 270
Rockford Business College, Rockford, IL 159
San Joaquin Valley College, Bakersfield, CA 103
San Joaquin Valley College, Fresno, CA 103
San Joaquin Valley College, Modesto, CA 104
San Joaquin Valley College, Rancho Cucamonga, CA 104
San Joaquin Valley College, Visalia, CA 104
Sanford-Brown College, Collinsville, IL 159
Sanford-Brown College, Fenton, MO 205
Sanford-Brown College, Hazelwood, MO 205
Sanford-Brown College, North Kansas City, MO 206
Sanford-Brown College, St. Charles, MO 206
Sanford-Brown College, West Allis, WI 331
Santa Barbara Business College, Bakersfield, CA 104
Santa Barbara Business College, Santa Barbara, CA 105
Santa Barbara Business College, Santa Maria, CA 105
Santa Barbara Business College, Ventura, CA 105
Savannah River College, Augusta, GA 151
Sawyer College, Merrillville, IN 167
Schuylkill Institute of Business and Technology, Pottsville, PA 270
South College, Knoxville, TN 291
South University, Columbia, SC 286
South University, Montgomery, AL 71
South University, Savannah, GA 151

South University, West Palm Beach, FL 142
Southeastern Business College, Chillicothe, OH 243
Southeastern Business College, Jackson, OH 243
Southeastern Business College, Lancaster, OH 243
Southeastern Business College, New Boston, OH 244
Southwest Florida College, Tampa, FL 143
Southwestern College of Business, Cincinnati, OH 244
Southwestern College of Business, Dayton, OH 244
Southwestern College of Business, Florence, KY 174
Southwestern College of Business, Franklin, OH 245
Spencerian College, Louisville, KY 174
Springfield College, Springfield, MO 206
Stevens-Henager College, Boise, ID 153
Stevens-Henager College, Logan, UT 311
Stevens-Henager College, Ogden, UT 311
Stevens-Henager College - Provo, Orem, UT 311
Stevens-Henager College - Salt Lake City, Salt Lake City, UT 312
Stratford University, Falls Church , VA 322
Stratford University, Woodbridge, VA 322
Strayer University, Atlanta, GA 151
Stuart School of Business Administration, Wall, NJ 223
Sullivan University, Lexington, KY 174
Sullivan University, Louisville, KY 175
Technology Education College, Columbus, OH 245
Texas School of Business, Inc., Houston, TX 306
Thompson Institute, Chambersburg, PA 271
Thompson Institute, Harrisburg, PA 271
Thompson Institute, Philadelphia, PA 271
Tri-State Business Institute, Erie, PA 272
Trumbull Business College, Warren, OH 245
Vatterott College, Broadview Heights, OH 245
Vatterott College, Des Moines, IA 168
Vatterott College, Joplin, MO 206
Vatterott College, Kansas City, MO 207
Vatterott College, Memphis, TN 292
Vatterott College, OÆFallon , MO 207
Vatterott College, Oklahoma City, OK 248
Vatterott College, Omaha, NE 209
Vatterott College, Quincy, IL 160
Vatterott College, Springfield, MO 208
Vatterott College, St. Ann, MO 207
Vatterott College, St. Joseph, MO 207
Vatterott College, St. Louis, MO 208
Vatterott College, Tulsa, OK 249
Vatterott College, Wichita, KS 169
Virginia College at Birmingham, Birmingham, AL 72
Virginia College at Jackson, Jackson, MS 200
Webster College, Holiday, FL 144
Webster College, Ocala, FL 144
West Virginia Career Institute, Mount Braddock, PA 273
West Virginia Junior College, Bridgeport, WV 329
West Virginia Junior College, Charleston, WV 329

West Virginia Junior College, Morgantown, WV 330
Western Business College, Portland, OR 251
Western Business College, Vancouver, WA 328
Westwood College - Atlanta Campus, Atlanta, GA 151
Westwood College - Denver North, Denver, CO 118
Westwood College - Inland Empire, Upland, CA 109
Wood Tobe-Coburn School, New York, NY 233
Western International University, Phoenix, AZ 82
Wright Business School, Oklahoma City, OK 249
Wright Business School, Overland Park, KS 170
Wright Business School, Tulsa, OK 249
York Technical Institute, Lancaster, PA 274
York Technical Institute, York, PA 274
Yorktowne Business Institute, York, PA 274

ACCOUNTING AND BUSINESS/ MANAGEMENT

Argosy University/Chicago, Chicago, IL 154
Argosy University/Schaumburg, Schaumburg, IL 154
Berks Technical Institute, Wyomissing, PA 253
Brookstone College of Business, Charlotte, NC 234
Brookstone College of Business, Greensboro, NC 234
Brown Mackie College, Akron Campus, Akron, OH 238
Brown Mackie College, Fort Worth Campus, Hurst, TX 296
Dover Business College, Paramus, NJ 218
Electronic Data Processing College of Puerto Rico, San Juan, PR 277
Gibbs College, Boston, MA 185
Gibbs College, Livingston, NJ 218
Gibbs College, Norwalk, CT 119
Herzing College, Atlanta, GA 148
Herzing College, Birmingham, AL 70
Herzing College, Kenner, LA 178
Herzing College, Madison, WI 330
Herzing College, Minneapolis, MN 195
Herzing College, Winter Park, FL 131
Indiana Business College, Anderson, IN 162
Indiana Business College, Columbus, IN 163
Indiana Business College, Evansville, IN 163
Indiana Business College, Fort Wayne, IN 163
Indiana Business College, Indianapolis, IN 163
Indiana Business College, Lafayette, IN 163
Indiana Business College, Marion, IN 164
Indiana Business College, Muncie, IN 164
Indiana Business College, Terre Haute, IN 164
ITT Technical Institute, Albany, NY 230
ITT Technical Institute, Albuquerque, NM 223
ITT Technical Institute, Anaheim, CA 96
ITT Technical Institute, Arlington, TX 299
ITT Technical Institute, Arnold, MO 202
ITT Technical Institute, Austin, TX 299
ITT Technical Institute, Bessemer, AL 71
ITT Technical Institute, Boise, ID 153

ITT Technical Institute, Bothell, WA 327
ITT Technical Institute, Burr Ridge, IL 157
ITT Technical Institute, Canton, MI 189
ITT Technical Institute, Chantilly, VA 317
ITT Technical Institute, Dayton, OH 240
ITT Technical Institute, Duluth, GA 149
ITT Technical Institute, Earth City, MO 202
ITT Technical Institute, Eden Prairie, MN 195
ITT Technical Institute, Fort Lauderdale, FL 133
ITT Technical Institute, Fort Wayne, IN 165
ITT Technical Institute, Getzville, NY 230
ITT Technical Institute, Grand Rapids, MI 189
ITT Technical Institute, Green Bay, WI 331
ITT Technical Institute, Greenfield, WI 331
ITT Technical Institute, Greenville, SC 285
ITT Technical Institute, Henderson, NV 211
ITT Technical Institute, Hilliard, OH 240
ITT Technical Institute, Houston, TX 299
ITT Technical Institute, Houston, TX 300
ITT Technical Institute, Indianapolis, IN 165
ITT Technical Institute, Jacksonville, FL 133
ITT Technical Institute, Kansas City, MO 203
ITT Technical Institute, Kennesaw, GA 149
ITT Technical Institute, King of Prussia, PA 264
ITT Technical Institute, Knoxville, TN 289
ITT Technical Institute, Lake Mary, FL 133
ITT Technical Institute, Lathrop, CA 96
ITT Technical Institute, Little Rock, AR 82
ITT Technical Institute, Liverpool, NY 230
ITT Technical Institute, Louisville, KY 171
ITT Technical Institute, Matteson, IL 158
ITT Technical Institute, Mechanicsburg, PA 264
ITT Technical Institute, Memphis, TN 289
ITT Technical Institute, Miami, FL 133
ITT Technical Institute, Monroeville, PA 264
ITT Technical Institute, Mount Prospect, IL 158
ITT Technical Institute, Murray, UT 310
ITT Technical Institute, Nashville, TN 289
ITT Technical Institute, Newburgh, IN 166
ITT Technical Institute, Norfolk, VA 318
ITT Technical Institute, Norwood, MA 186
ITT Technical Institute, Norwood, OH 240
ITT Technical Institute, Omaha, NE 209
ITT Technical Institute, Owings Mills, MD 181
ITT Technical Institute, Oxnard, CA 97
ITT Technical Institute, Pittsburg, PA 264
ITT Technical Institute, Portland, OR 250
ITT Technical Institute, Rancho Cordova, CA 97
ITT Technical Institute, Richardson, TX 300
ITT Technical Institute, Richmond, VA 318
ITT Technical Institute, Saint Rose, LA 179
ITT Technical Institute, San Antonio, TX 300
ITT Technical Institute, San Bernardino, CA 97

ITT Technical Institute, San Diego, CA 97
ITT Technical Institute, Seattle, WA 327
ITT Technical Institute, Spokane, WA 328
ITT Technical Institute, Springfield, VA 318
ITT Technical Institute, Strongsville, OH 241
ITT Technical Institute, Sylmar, CA 98
ITT Technical Institute, Tampa, FL 134
ITT Technical Institute, Tempe, AZ 79
ITT Technical Institute, Thornton, CO 115
ITT Technical Institute, Torrance, CA 98
ITT Technical Institute, Troy, MI 190
ITT Technical Institute, Tucson, AZ 79
ITT Technical Institute, Tulsa, OK 247
ITT Technical Institute, Warrensville Heights, OH 241
ITT Technical Institute, West Covina, CA 98
ITT Technical Institute, Woburn, MA 186
ITT Technical Institute, Youngstown, OH 241
McIntosh College, Dover, NH 213
National American University, Albuquerque, NM 224
National American University, Brooklyn Center, MN 197
National American University, Colorado Springs, CO 115
National American University, Denver, CO 116
National American University, Ellsworth AFB, SD 286
National American University, Kansas City, MO 204
National American University, Minneapolis, MN 197
National American University, Overland Park, KS 169
National American University, Rapid City, SD 286
National American University, Rio Rancho, NM 224
National American University, Roseville, MN 197
North Florida Institute, Orange Park, FL 140
Peirce College, Philadelphia, PA 268
Rasmussen College Mankato, Mankato, MN 198
Rasmussen College St. Cloud, St. Cloud, MN 199
Sanford-Brown College, Collinsville, IL 159
Sanford-Brown College, Fenton, MO 205
Sanford-Brown College, Hazelwood, MO 205
Sanford-Brown College, North Kansas City, MO 206
Sanford-Brown College, St. Charles, MO 206
Sanford-Brown College, West Allis, WI 331
Santa Barbara Business College, Bakersfield, CA 104
Santa Barbara Business College, Santa Barbara, CA 105
Santa Barbara Business College, Santa Maria, CA 105
Santa Barbara Business College, Ventura, CA 105
Schuylkill Institute of Business and Technology, Pottsville, PA 270
Technical Career Institute, New York, NY 233
Virginia College at Birmingham, Birmingham, AL 72
Westwood College - Anaheim, Anaheim, CA 109
Westwood College - Inland Empire, Upland, CA 109

ACCOUNTING AND FINANCE
Aakers Business College , Bismarck, ND 236
Aakers Business College, Fargo, ND 236

Brookstone College of Business, Charlotte, NC 234
Brookstone College of Business, Greensboro, NC 234
McIntosh College, Dover, NH 213
Rasmussen College St. Cloud, St. Cloud, MN 199

ACCOUNTING AND RELATED SERVICES, OTHER

Bayamon Community College, Bayamon, PR 276
Berks Technical Institute, Wyomissing, PA 253
Briarcliffe College, Bethpage, NY 226
Briarcliffe College, Patchogue, NY 226
Brookstone College of Business, Charlotte, NC 234
Brookstone College of Business, Greensboro, NC 234
Douglas Education Center, Monessen, PA 259
Indiana Business College, Anderson, IN 162
Indiana Business College, Columbus, IN 163
Indiana Business College, Evansville, IN 163
Indiana Business College, Fort Wayne, IN 163
Indiana Business College, Indianapolis, IN 163
Indiana Business College, Lafayette, IN 163
Indiana Business College, Marion, IN 164
Indiana Business College, Muncie, IN 164
Indiana Business College, Terre Haute, IN 164
Virginia College at Birmingham, Birmingham, AL 72
Virginia College at Pensacola, Pensacola, FL 144

ACCOUNTING TECHNOLOGY/ TECHNICIAN AND BOOKKEEPING

Antonelli College, Cincinnati, OH 237
Antonelli College, Hattiesburg, MS 199
Antonelli College, Jackson, MS 200
Austin Business College, Austin, TX 295
Brookstone College of Business, Charlotte, NC 234
Brookstone College of Business, Greensboro, NC 234
Brown Mackie College, Atlanta Campus, Norcross, GA 146
Brown Mackie College, Lenexa Campus, Lenexa, KS 168
Brown Mackie College, Northern Kentucky Campus, Fort Mitchell, KY 170
Career Institute of Health and Technology, Brooklyn, NY 227
Career Institute of Health and Technology, Garden City, NY 227
Career Institute of Health and Technology, Rego Park, NY 228
Central Coast College, Salinas, CA 92
Chaparral College, Tucson, AZ 77
Charter College, Anchorage, AK 74
Dickinson Business School/Career Point Business School, Tulsa, OK 246
Douglas Education Center, Monessen, PA 259
Draughons Junior College, Bowling Green, KY 171
Draughons Junior College, Clarksville, TN 287
Draughons Junior College, Murfreesboro, TN 287

Draughons Junior College, Nashville, TN 288
Empire College, Santa Rosa, CA 93
Globe College, Oakdale, MN 194
Gretna Career College, Gretna, LA 177
Hohokus Hackensack School of Business and Medical Sciences, Hackensack, NJ 220
Huertas Junior College, Caguas, PR 277
McCann School of Business, Hazleton, PA 266
McCann School of Business, Pottsville, PA 267
McCann School of Business, Scranton, PA 267
McCann School of Business, Sunbury, PA 267
MTI College of Business and Technology, Houston, TX 301
The PJA School, Upper Darby, PA 270
Rasmussen College Minnetonka, Minnetonka, MN 199
Santa Barbara Business College, Bakersfield, CA 104
Santa Barbara Business College, Santa Barbara, CA 105
Santa Barbara Business College, Santa Maria, CA 105
Santa Barbara Business College, Ventura, CA 105
Southwestern College of Business, Cincinnati, OH 244
Southwestern College of Business, Dayton, OH 244
Southwestern College of Business, Florence, KY 174
Southwestern College of Business, Franklin, OH 245
Technical Career Institute, New York, NY 233
Thompson Institute, Chambersburg, PA 271
Thompson Institute, Harrisburg, PA 271
Thompson Institute, Philadelphia, PA 271
Trinity College of Puerto Rico, Ponce, PR 283
Vatterott College, Broadview Heights, OH 245
Vatterott College, Des Moines, IA 168
Vatterott College, Joplin, MO 206
Vatterott College, Kansas City, MO 207
Vatterott College, Memphis, TN 292
Vatterott College, OÆFallon , MO 207
Vatterott College, Oklahoma City, OK 248
Vatterott College, Omaha, NE 209
Vatterott College, Quincy, IL 160
Vatterott College, Springfield, MO 208
Vatterott College, St. Ann, MO 207
Vatterott College, St. Joseph, MO 207
Vatterott College, St. Louis, MO 208
Vatterott College, Tulsa, OK 249
Vatterott College, Wichita, KS 169
Virginia College at Austin, Austin, TX 307
Virginia College at Birmingham, Birmingham, AL 72
Virginia College at Huntsville, Huntsville, AL 73
Virginia College at Mobile, Mobile, AL 73

ADMINISTRATIVE ASSISTANT AND SECRETARIAL SCIENCE, GENERAL

CollegeAmerica - Denver, Denver, CO 113

Boldface type indicates that the school is a participating institution in the 🎓 *Imagine America* Scholarship Program

ADMINISTRATIVE ASSISTANT AND SECRETARIAL SCIENCE, GENERAL

American Commercial College, Abilene, TX 292
American Commercial College, Lubbock, TX 293
American Commercial College, Odessa, TX 293
American Commercial College, San Angelo, TX 293
American Commercial College, Shreveport, LA 175
American School of Business, Wichita Falls, TX 294
Antonelli College, Cincinnati, OH 237
Antonelli College, Hattiesburg, MS 199
Antonelli College, Jackson, MS 200
ATI Career Training Center, Dallas, TX 294
ATI Career Training Center, Fort Lauderdale, FL 122
ATI Career Training Center, Miami, FL 123
ATI Career Training Center, North Richland Hills, TX 295
ATI Career Training Center, Oakland Park, FL 123
Austin Business College, Austin, TX 295
Bayamon Community College, Bayamon, PR 276
Berks Technical Institute, Wyomissing, PA 253
Blair College, Colorado Springs, CO 112
Bradford School of Business, Houston, TX 295
Bradford School, Columbus, OH 237
Bradford School, Pittsburgh, PA 254
Briarcliffe College, Bethpage, NY 226
Briarcliffe College, Patchogue, NY 226
Brookstone College of Business, Charlotte, NC 234
Brookstone College of Business, Greensboro, NC 234
Bryman College, Alhambra, CA 88
Bryman College, Anaheim, CA 88
Bryman College, City of Industry, CA 88
Bryman College, Earth City, MO 201
Bryman College, Everett, WA 325
Bryman College, Gardena, CA 88
Bryman College, Hayward, CA 89
Bryman College, Los Angeles, CA 89
Bryman College, Lynnwood, WA 326
Bryman College, New Orleans, LA 176
Bryman College, Ontario, CA 89
Bryman College, Port Orchard, WA 326
Bryman College, Renton, WA 326
Bryman College, Reseda, CA 89
Bryman College, San Bernardino, CA 90
Bryman College, San Francisco, CA 90
Bryman College, San Jose, CA 90
Bryman College, Tacoma, WA 326
Bryman College, Torrance, CA 90
Business Institute of Pennsylvania, Meadville, PA 255
Business Institute of Pennsylvania, Sharon, PA 255
Career Centers of Texas, El Paso, TX 295
Career Education Institute, Brockton, MA 184
Career Education Institute, Henderson, NV 210
Career Education Institute, Lincoln, RI 283

Career Education Institute, Lowell, MA 184
Career Education Institute, Marietta, GA 146
Career Education Institute, Norcross, GA 146
Career Point Business School, San Antonio, TX 296
Central Coast College, Salinas, CA 92
Chaparral College, Tucson, AZ 77
Charter College, Anchorage, AK 74
CHI Institute, Broomall, PA 256
CHI Institute, Southampton, PA 256
The Chubb Institute, Alpharetta, GA 147
The Chubb Institute, Arlington, VA 314
The Chubb Institute, Cherry Hill, NJ 215
The Chubb Institute, Chicago, IL 155
The Chubb Institute, Jersey City, NJ 216
The Chubb Institute, New York, NY 228
The Chubb Institute, North Brunswick, NJ 216
The Chubb Institute, Parsippany, NJ 216
The Chubb Institute, Springfield, PA 256
The Chubb Institute, Westbury, NY 228
The Cittone Institute, Edison, NJ 217
The Cittone Institute, Mount Laurel, NJ 217
The Cittone Institute, Paramus, NJ 217
The Cittone Institute, Philadelphia, PA 257
The Cittone Institute, Plymouth Meeting, PA 257
CollegeAmerica - Denver, Denver, CO 113
Columbia College, Caguas, PR 277
Columbia College, Yauco, PR 277
Computer Learning Network, Altoona, PA 258
Computer Learning Network, Mechanicsburg, PA 258
Coyne American Institute, Chicago, IL 155
Coyne American Institute, Chicago, IL 156
Davis College, Toledo, OH 239
Delta School of Business & Technology, Lake Charles, LA 177
Dickinson Business School/Career Point Business School, Tulsa, OK 246
Dorsey Schools, Madison Heights, MI 188
Dorsey Schools, Roseville, MI 188
Dorsey Schools, Southgate, MI 188
Dorsey Schools, Wayne, MI 189
Douglas Education Center, Monessen, PA 259
Duluth Business University, Duluth, MN 194
ECPI College of Technology, Charlotte, NC 234
ECPI College of Technology, Greensboro, NC 235
ECPI College of Technology, Greenville, SC 285
ECPI College of Technology, Manassas, VA 315
ECPI College of Technology, Newport News, VA 315
ECPI College of Technology, North Charleston, SC 285
ECPI College of Technology, Raleigh, NC 235
ECPI College of Technology, Virginia Beach, VA 316
ECPI Technical College, Glen Allen, VA 316
ECPI Technical College, Richmond, VA 316
ECPI Technical College, Roanoke, VA 317

ADULT AND CONTINUING EDUCATION AND TEACHING

Caguas Institute of Mechanical Technology, Caguas, PR 276
Capella University, Minneapolis, MN 194
EduTek College, Stow, OH 239
Four-D Success Academy, Colton, CA 94
Hesser College, Manchester, NH 213
New York Institute of Massage, Buffalo, NY 232
Stuart School of Business Administration, Wall, NJ 223

ADULT DEVELOPMENT AND AGING

A-1 Business and Technical College, Caguas, PR 275
Gretna Career College, Gretna, LA 177

ADVANCED/GRADUATE DENTISTRY AND ORAL SCIENCES, OTHER

ITT Technical Institute, Albany, NY 230
ITT Technical Institute, Albuquerque, NM 223
ITT Technical Institute, Anaheim, CA 96
ITT Technical Institute, Arlington, TX 299
ITT Technical Institute, Arnold, MO 202
ITT Technical Institute, Austin, TX 299
ITT Technical Institute, Bessemer, AL 71
ITT Technical Institute, Boise, ID 153
ITT Technical Institute, Bothell, WA 327
ITT Technical Institute, Burr Ridge, IL 157
ITT Technical Institute, Canton, MI 189
ITT Technical Institute, Chantilly, VA 317
ITT Technical Institute, Dayton, OH 240
ITT Technical Institute, Duluth, GA 149
ITT Technical Institute, Earth City, MO 202
ITT Technical Institute, Eden Prairie, MN 195
ITT Technical Institute, Fort Lauderdale, FL 133
ITT Technical Institute, Fort Wayne, IN 165
ITT Technical Institute, Getzville, NY 230
ITT Technical Institute, Grand Rapids, MI 189
ITT Technical Institute, Green Bay, WI 331
ITT Technical Institute, Greenfield, WI 331
ITT Technical Institute, Greenville, SC 285
ITT Technical Institute, Henderson, NV 211
ITT Technical Institute, Hilliard, OH 240
ITT Technical Institute, Houston, TX 299
ITT Technical Institute, Houston, TX 300
ITT Technical Institute, Indianapolis, IN 165
ITT Technical Institute, Jacksonville, FL 133
ITT Technical Institute, Kansas City, MO 203
ITT Technical Institute, Kennesaw, GA 149
ITT Technical Institute, King of Prussia, PA 264
ITT Technical Institute, Knoxville, TN 289
ITT Technical Institute, Lake Mary, FL 133
ITT Technical Institute, Lathrop, CA 96
ITT Technical Institute, Little Rock, AR 82
ITT Technical Institute, Liverpool, NY 230

ITT Technical Institute, Louisville, KY 171
ITT Technical Institute, Matteson, IL 158
ITT Technical Institute, Mechanicsburg, PA 264
ITT Technical Institute, Memphis, TN 289
ITT Technical Institute, Miami, FL 133
ITT Technical Institute, Monroeville, PA 264
ITT Technical Institute, Mount Prospect, IL 158
ITT Technical Institute, Murray, UT 310
ITT Technical Institute, Nashville, TN 289
ITT Technical Institute, Newburgh, IN 166
ITT Technical Institute, Norfolk, VA 318
ITT Technical Institute, Norwood, MA 186
ITT Technical Institute, Norwood, OH 240
ITT Technical Institute, Omaha, NE 209
ITT Technical Institute, Owings Mills, MD 181
ITT Technical Institute, Oxnard, CA 97
ITT Technical Institute, Pittsburg, PA 264
ITT Technical Institute, Portland, OR 250
ITT Technical Institute, Rancho Cordova, CA 97
ITT Technical Institute, Richardson, TX 300
ITT Technical Institute, Richmond, VA 318
ITT Technical Institute, Saint Rose, LA 179
ITT Technical Institute, San Antonio, TX 300
ITT Technical Institute, San Bernardino, CA 97
ITT Technical Institute, San Diego, CA 97
ITT Technical Institute, Seattle, WA 327
ITT Technical Institute, Spokane, WA 328
ITT Technical Institute, Springfield, VA 318
ITT Technical Institute, Strongsville, OH 241
ITT Technical Institute, Sylmar, CA 98
ITT Technical Institute, Tampa, FL 134
ITT Technical Institute, Tempe, AZ 79
ITT Technical Institute, Thornton, CO 115
ITT Technical Institute, Torrance, CA 98
ITT Technical Institute, Troy, MI 190
ITT Technical Institute, Tucson, AZ 79
ITT Technical Institute, Tulsa, OK 247
ITT Technical Institute, Warrensville Heights, OH 241
ITT Technical Institute, West Covina, CA 98
ITT Technical Institute, Woburn, MA 186
ITT Technical Institute, Youngstown, OH 241

ADVERTISING

Academy of Art University, San Francisco, CA 83
The Art Institute of Atlanta, Atlanta, GA 145
The Art Institute of Colorado, Denver, CO 111
The Art Institute of Fort Lauderdale, Fort Lauderdale, FL 122
The Art Institute of California - Los Angeles, Santa Monica, CA 85
The Art Institute of Phoenix, Phoenix, AZ 76
The Art Institute of Pittsburgh, Pittsburgh, PA 252
The Art Institute of Portland, Portland, OR 249

The Art Institute of California - San Diego, San Diego, CA 86

The Art Institute of Washington, Arlington, VA 314

The Art Institutes International Minnesota, Minneapolis, MN 193

Berks Technical Institute, Wyomissing, PA 253

Brown Mackie College, Miami Campus, Miami, FL 124

Brown Mackie College, San Diego Campus, San Diego, CA 87

The Creative Circus, Inc., Atlanta, GA 147

Globe College, Oakdale, MN 194

The Illinois Institute of Art - Chicago, Chicago, IL 156

International Academy of Design & Technology, Chicago, IL 157

International Academy of Design & Technology, Orlando, FL 132

International Academy of Design & Technology, Pittsburgh, PA 264

International Academy of Design & Technology, Tampa, FL 132

International Academy of Design & Technology, Troy, MI 189

McIntosh College, Dover, NH 213

Miami International University of Art & Design, Miami, FL 138

National American University, Albuquerque, NM 224

National American University, Brooklyn Center, MN 197

National American University, Colorado Springs, CO 115

National American University, Denver, CO 116

National American University, Ellsworth AFB, SD 286

National American University, Kansas City, MO 204

National American University, Minneapolis, MN 197

National American University, Overland Park, KS 169

National American University, Rapid City, SD 286

National American University, Rio Rancho, NM 224

National American University, Roseville, MN 197

New England School of Communications, Bangor, ME 180

Stevens-Henager College, Boise, ID 153

Stevens-Henager College, Logan, UT 311

Stevens-Henager College, Ogden, UT 311

Westwood College - Chicago O'Hare Airport, Chicago, IL 161

AESTHETICIAN/ESTHETICIAN AND SKIN CARE SPECIALIST

Catherine Hinds Institute of Esthetics, Woburn, MA 185

Dawn Training Centre, Inc., Wilmington, DE 120

Douglas Education Center, Monessen, PA 259

Florida College of Natural Health, Bradenton, FL 126

Florida College of Natural Health, Maitland, FL 126

Florida College of Natural Health, Miami, FL 126

Florida College of Natural Health, Pompano Beach, FL 126

Heritage College, Denver, CO 115

Heritage College, Kansas City, MO 201

Heritage College, Las Vegas, NV 210

La Belle Beauty School, Hialeah, FL 137

Laurel Business Institute, Uniontown, PA 265

Miller-Motte Technical College, Cary, NC 236

Miller-Motte Technical College, Chattanooga, TN 290

Miller-Motte Technical College, Clarksville, TN 290

Miller-Motte Technical College, Lynchburg, VA 320

Miller-Motte Technical College, North Charleston, SC 285

Miller-Motte Technical College, Wilmington, NC 236

Virginia College at Jackson, Jackson, MS 200

West Tennessee Business College, Jackson, TN 292

AIR TRAFFIC CONTROLLER

Advanced Training Associates, El Cajon, CA 84

AIRCRAFT PILOT (PRIVATE)

Academy College, Minneapolis, MN 192

AIRCRAFT POWERPLANT TECHNOLOGY/TECHNICIAN

Advanced Training Associates, El Cajon, CA 84

Hallmark Institute of Aeronautics, San Antonio, TX 297

Teterboro School of Aeronautics, Inc., Teterboro, NJ 223

Westwood Aviation Institute, Houston, TX 308

Westwood College - Denver, Broomfield, CO 118

Westwood College - Los Angeles, Los Angeles, CA 110

Westwood College - Los Angeles, Inglewood, CA 110

WyoTech, Bedford, MA 187

WyoTech, Blairsville, PA 274

WyoTech, Fremont, CA 111

WyoTech, Laramie, WY 332

WyoTech, Oakland, CA 111

WyoTech, West Sacramento, CA 111

AIRFRAME MECHANICS AND AIRCRAFT MAINTENANCE TECHNOLOGY/TECHNICIAN

Advanced Training Associates, El Cajon, CA 84

Hallmark Institute of Aeronautics, San Antonio, TX 297

San Joaquin Valley College, Bakersfield, CA 103

San Joaquin Valley College, Fresno, CA 103

San Joaquin Valley College, Modesto, CA 104

San Joaquin Valley College, Rancho Cucamonga, CA 104

San Joaquin Valley College, Visalia, CA 104

Teterboro School of Aeronautics, Inc., Teterboro, NJ 223

Westwood Aviation Institute, Houston, TX 308

Westwood College - Denver, Broomfield, CO 118

Westwood College - Los Angeles, Inglewood, CA 110

Westwood College - Los Angeles, Los Angeles, CA 110

WyoTech, Bedford, MA 187

WyoTech, Blairsville, PA 274

WyoTech, Fremont, CA 111
WyoTech, Laramie, WY 332
WyoTech, Oakland, CA 111
WyoTech, West Sacramento, CA 111

AIRLINE FLIGHT ATTENDANT

Academy Pacific Travel College, Los Angeles, CA 84

AIRLINE/COMMERCIAL/ PROFESSIONAL PILOT AND FLIGHT CREW

Academy College, Minneapolis, MN 192
Career Academy, Anchorage, AK 73

ALLIED HEALTH AND MEDICAL ASSISTING SERVICES, OTHER

American Commercial College, Abilene, TX 292
American Commercial College, Lubbock, TX 293
American Commercial College, Odessa, TX 293
American Commercial College, San Angelo, TX 293
American Commercial College, Shreveport, LA 175
Antonelli College, Cincinnati, OH 237
Antonelli College, Hattiesburg, MS 199
Antonelli College, Jackson, MS 200
ATI Career Training Center, Dallas, TX 294
ATI Career Training Center, Fort Lauderdale, FL 122
ATI Career Training Center, Miami, FL 123
ATI Career Training Center, North Richland Hills, TX 295
ATI Career Training Center, Oakland Park, FL 123
Berks Technical Institute, Wyomissing, PA 253
Brookstone College of Business, Charlotte, NC 234
Brookstone College of Business, Greensboro, NC 234
Brown Mackie College, Cincinnati Campus, Cincinnati, OH 238
Bryan College, Springfield, MO 201
Bryan College, Topeka, KS 169
The Chubb Institute, Alpharetta, GA 147
The Chubb Institute, Arlington, VA 314
The Chubb Institute, Cherry Hill, NJ 215
The Chubb Institute, Chicago, IL 155
The Chubb Institute, Jersey City, NJ 216
The Chubb Institute, New York, NY 228
The Chubb Institute, North Brunswick, NJ 216
The Chubb Institute, Parsippany, NJ 216
The Chubb Institute, Springfield, PA 256
The Chubb Institute, Westbury, NY 228
The Cittone Institute, Edison, NJ 217
The Cittone Institute, Mount Laurel, NJ 217
The Cittone Institute, Paramus, NJ 217
The Cittone Institute, Philadelphia, PA 257
The Cittone Institute, Plymouth Meeting, PA 257
Douglas Education Center, Monessen, PA 259

Draughons Junior College, Bowling Green, KY 171
Draughons Junior College, Clarksville, TN 287
Draughons Junior College, Murfreesboro, TN 287
Draughons Junior College, Nashville, TN 288
Florida Technical College, Auburndale, FL 129
Florida Technical College, DeLand, FL 130
Florida Technical College, Jacksonville, FL 130
Florida Technical College, Orlando, FL 130
Gibbs College - Cranston, Cranston, RI 283
Gibbs College, Boston, MA 185
Gibbs College, Livingston, NJ 218
Gibbs College, Norwalk, CT 119
Gretna Career College, Gretna, LA 177
Harrison Career Institute, Allentown, PA 262
Harrison Career Institute, Baltimore, MD 181
Harrison Career Institute, Clifton, NJ 218
Harrison Career Institute, Delran, NJ 218
Harrison Career Institute, Deptford, NJ 219
Harrison Career Institute, Ewing, NJ 219
Harrison Career Institute, Jersey City, NJ 219
Harrison Career Institute, Oakhurst, NJ 219
Harrison Career Institute, Philadelphia, PA 263
Harrison Career Institute, Reading, PA 263
Harrison Career Institute, South Orange, NJ 220
Harrison Career Institute, Vineland, NJ 220
Harrison Career Institute, Wilmington, DE 121
Heritage College, Denver, CO 115
Heritage College, Kansas City, MO 201
Heritage College, Las Vegas, NV 210
Hesser College, Manchester, NH 213
HoHoKus RETS School of Business and Medical Technical Services, Nutley, NJ 220
Kee Business College, Newport News, VA 319
Laurel Business Institute, Uniontown, PA 265
Lincoln Technical Institute Indianapolis, IN 166
Lincoln Technical Institute, Allentown, PA 266
Lincoln Technical Institute, Columbia, MD 182
Lincoln Technical Institute, Grand Prairie, TX 300
Lincoln Technical Institute, Mahwah, NJ 222
Lincoln Technical Institute, Melrose Park, IL 158
Lincoln Technical Institute, Philadelphia, PA 266
Lincoln Technical Institute, Union, NJ 222
Maric College, Anaheim, CA 99
Maric College, Los Angeles, CA 100
Maric College, North Hollywood, CA 99
Maric College, Sacramento, CA 99
Maric College, Salida, CA 99
Maric College, San Diego, CA 100
Maric College, Vista, CA 100
McIntosh College, Dover, NH 213
National American University, Albuquerque, NM 224
National American University, Brooklyn Center, MN 197
National American University, Colorado Springs, CO 115

National American University, Denver, CO 116
National American University, Ellsworth AFB, SD 286
National American University, Kansas City, MO 204
National American University, Minneapolis, MN 197
National American University, Overland Park, KS 169
National American University, Rapid City, SD 286
National American University, Rio Rancho, NM 224
National American University, Roseville, MN 197
North Florida Institute, Orange Park, FL 140
Westwood College - Denver, Broomfield, CO 118
Westwood College - Los Angeles, Inglewood, CA 110
Westwood College - Los Angeles, Los Angeles, CA 110
RETS Technical Center, Charlestown, MA 187
Savannah River College, Augusta, GA 151
South University, Columbia, SC 286
South University, Montgomery, AL 71
South University, Savannah, GA 151
South University, West Palm Beach, FL 142
Southwest Florida College, Tampa, FL 143
Vatterott College, Broadview Heights, OH 245
Vatterott College, Des Moines, IA 168
Vatterott College, Joplin, MO 206
Vatterott College, Kansas City, MO 207
Vatterott College, Memphis, TN 292
Vatterott College, OÆFallon , MO 207
Vatterott College, Oklahoma City, OK 248
Vatterott College, Omaha, NE 209
Vatterott College, Quincy, IL 160
Vatterott College, Springfield, MO 208
Vatterott College, St. Ann, MO 207
Vatterott College, St. Joseph, MO 207
Vatterott College, St. Louis, MO 208
Vatterott College, Tulsa, OK 249
Vatterott College, Wichita, KS 169
Virginia College at Birmingham, Birmingham, AL 72
Virginia College at Pensacola, Pensacola, FL 144
Westwood College - Chicago River Oaks, Calumet City, IL 161

ALTERNATIVE AND COMPLEMENTARY MEDICAL SUPPORT SERVICES, OTHER

Baltimore School of Massage, Linthicum, MD 180
Barbara Brennan School of Healing, Boca Raton, FL 124
Everglades University, Boca Raton, FL 125
Everglades University, Orlando, FL 125
Everglades University, Sarasota, FL 125
Florida College of Natural Health, Bradenton, FL 126
Florida College of Natural Health, Maitland, FL 126
Florida College of Natural Health, Miami, FL 126
Florida College of Natural Health, Pompano Beach, FL 126
Virginia School of Massage, Charlottesville, VA 324

ALTERNATIVE AND COMPLEMENTARY MEDICAL SYSTEMS, OTHER

Everglades University, Boca Raton, FL 125
Everglades University, Orlando, FL 125
Everglades University, Sarasota, FL 125

ANATOMY

Business Institute of Pennsylvania, Meadville, PA 255
Business Institute of Pennsylvania, Sharon, PA 255
Career Education Institute, Brockton, MA 184
Career Education Institute, Henderson, NV 210
Career Education Institute, Lincoln, RI 283
Career Education Institute, Lowell, MA 184
Career Education Institute, Marietta, GA 146
Career Education Institute, Norcross, GA 146
Douglas Education Center, Monessen, PA 259
McCann School of Business, Hazleton, PA 266
McCann School of Business, Pottsville, PA267
McCann School of Business, Scranton, PA 267
McCann School of Business, Sunbury, PA 267

ANESTHESIOLOGIST ASSISTANT

South University, Columbia, SC 286
South University, Montgomery, AL 71
South University, Savannah, GA 151
South University, West Palm Beach, FL 142

ANIMATION, INTERACTIVE TECHNOLOGY, VIDEO GRAPHICS AND SPECIAL EFFECTS

Academy College, Minneapolis, MN 192
Academy of Art University, San Francisco, CA 83
The Art Institute of Atlanta, Atlanta, GA 145
The Art Institute of Fort Lauderdale, Fort Lauderdale, FL 122
The Art Institute of Las Vegas, Henderson, NV 209
The Art Institute of California - Los Angeles, Santa Monica, CA 85
The Art Institute of California - Orange County, Santa Ana, CA 86
The Art Institute of Philadelphia, Philadelphia, PA 252
The Art Institute of Phoenix, Phoenix, AZ 76
The Art Institute of Pittsburgh, Pittsburgh, PA 252
The Art Institute of Portland, Portland, OR 249
The Art Institute of California - San Diego, San Diego, CA 86
The Art Institute of California - San Francisco, San Francisco, CA 86
The Art Institute of Seattle, Seattle, WA 324
The Art Institute of Washington, Arlington, VA 314
The Art Institutes International Minnesota, Minneapolis, MN 193

American InterContinental University, Atlanta, GA 145
American InterContinental University, Houston, TX 293
American InterContinental University, Los Angeles, CA 85
American InterContinental University, San Antonio, TX 293
American InterContinental University, Weston, FL 121
Berks Technical Institute, Wyomissing, PA 253
Bradley Academy for the Visual Arts, York, PA 254
Career Education Institute, Brockton, MA 184
Career Education Institute, Henderson, NV 210
Career Education Institute, Lincoln, RI 283
Career Education Institute, Lowell, MA 184
Career Education Institute, Marietta, GA 146
Career Education Institute, Norcross, GA 146
Collins College: A School of Design and Technology, Tempe, AZ 77
Douglas Education Center, Monessen, PA 259
Full Sail Real World Education, Winter Park, FL 131
ITT Technical Institute, Albany, NY 230
ITT Technical Institute, Albuquerque, NM 223
ITT Technical Institute, Anaheim, CA 96
ITT Technical Institute, Arlington, TX 299
ITT Technical Institute, Arnold, MO 202
ITT Technical Institute, Austin, TX 299
ITT Technical Institute, Bessemer, AL 71
ITT Technical Institute, Boise, ID 153
ITT Technical Institute, Bothell, WA 327
ITT Technical Institute, Burr Ridge, IL 157
ITT Technical Institute, Canton, MI 189
ITT Technical Institute, Chantilly, VA 317
ITT Technical Institute, Dayton, OH 240
ITT Technical Institute, Duluth, GA 149
ITT Technical Institute, Earth City, MO 202
ITT Technical Institute, Eden Prairie, MN 195
ITT Technical Institute, Fort Lauderdale, FL 133
ITT Technical Institute, Fort Wayne, IN 165
ITT Technical Institute, Getzville, NY 230
ITT Technical Institute, Grand Rapids, MI 189
ITT Technical Institute, Green Bay, WI 331
ITT Technical Institute, Greenfield, WI 331
ITT Technical Institute, Greenville, SC 285
ITT Technical Institute, Henderson, NV 211
ITT Technical Institute, Hilliard, OH 240
ITT Technical Institute, Houston, TX 299
ITT Technical Institute, Houston, TX 300
ITT Technical Institute, Indianapolis, IN 165
ITT Technical Institute, Jacksonville, FL 133
ITT Technical Institute, Kansas City, MO 203
ITT Technical Institute, Kennesaw, GA 149
ITT Technical Institute, King of Prussia, PA 264
ITT Technical Institute, Knoxville, TN 289
ITT Technical Institute, Lake Mary, FL 133
ITT Technical Institute, Lathrop, CA 96
ITT Technical Institute, Little Rock, AR 82

ITT Technical Institute, Liverpool, NY 230
ITT Technical Institute, Louisville, KY 171
ITT Technical Institute, Matteson, IL 158
ITT Technical Institute, Mechanicsburg, PA 264
ITT Technical Institute, Memphis, TN 289
ITT Technical Institute, Miami, FL 133
ITT Technical Institute, Monroeville, PA 264
ITT Technical Institute, Mount Prospect, IL 158
ITT Technical Institute, Murray, UT 310
ITT Technical Institute, Nashville, TN 289
ITT Technical Institute, Newburgh, IN 166
ITT Technical Institute, Norfolk, VA 318
ITT Technical Institute, Norwood, MA 186
ITT Technical Institute, Norwood, OH 240
ITT Technical Institute, Omaha, NE 209
ITT Technical Institute, Owings Mills, MD 181
ITT Technical Institute, Oxnard, CA 97
ITT Technical Institute, Pittsburg, PA 264
ITT Technical Institute, Portland, OR 250
ITT Technical Institute, Rancho Cordova, CA 97
ITT Technical Institute, Richardson, TX 300
ITT Technical Institute, Richmond, VA 318
ITT Technical Institute, Saint Rose, LA 179
ITT Technical Institute, San Antonio, TX 300
ITT Technical Institute, San Bernardino, CA 97
ITT Technical Institute, San Diego, CA 97
ITT Technical Institute, Seattle, WA 327
ITT Technical Institute, Spokane, WA 328
ITT Technical Institute, Springfield, VA 318
ITT Technical Institute, Strongsville, OH 241
ITT Technical Institute, Sylmar, CA 98
ITT Technical Institute, Tampa, FL 134
ITT Technical Institute, Tempe, AZ 79
ITT Technical Institute, Thornton, CO 115
ITT Technical Institute, Torrance, CA 98
ITT Technical Institute, Troy, MI 190
ITT Technical Institute, Tucson, AZ 79
ITT Technical Institute, Tulsa, OK 247
ITT Technical Institute, Warrensville Heights, OH 241
ITT Technical Institute, West Covina, CA 98
ITT Technical Institute, Woburn, MA 186
ITT Technical Institute, Youngstown, OH 241
Joe Kubert School of Cartoon and Graphic Art Inc., Dover, NJ 221
Katharine Gibbs School, Melville, NY 231
Katharine Gibbs School, New York, NY 231
Katharine Gibbs School, Norristown, PA 264
Katharine Gibbs School, Piscataway, NJ 221
The Illinois Institute of Art - Chicago, Chicago, IL 156
The Illinois Institute of Art - Schaumburg, Schaumburg, IL 157
Louisville Technical Institute, Louisville, KY 172
Madison Media Institute, Madison, WI 331

The New England Institute of Art, Brookline, MA 186
Pittsburgh Technical Institute, Oakdale, PA 269
Platt College, Huntington Beach, CA 101
Platt College, Lawton, OK 247
Platt College, Oklahoma City, OK 248
Platt College, Ontario, CA 102
Platt College, Tulsa, OK 248
Virginia College at Birmingham, Birmingham, AL 72
Westwood College - Anaheim, Anaheim, CA 109
Westwood College - Atlanta Campus, Atlanta, GA 151
Westwood College - Atlanta Northlake, Atlanta, GA 152
Westwood College - Chicago Du Page, Woodridge, IL 160
Westwood College - Chicago Loop Campus, Chicago, IL 161
Westwood College - Chicago River Oaks, Calumet City, IL 161
Westwood College - Denver North, Denver, CO 118
Westwood College - Denver South, Denver, CO 118
Westwood College - Inland Empire, Upland, CA 109
Westwood College - Long Beach, Torrance, CA 110
Westwood College - Los Angeles, Los Angeles, CA 110
Westwood College - Los Angeles, Inglewood, CA 110

APPAREL AND ACCESSORIES MARKETING OPERATIONS

The Art Institute of Phoenix, Phoenix, AZ 76
The Art Institute of Portland, Portland, OR 249
McIntosh College, Dover, NH 213
Miami International University of Art & Design, Miami, FL 138

APPAREL AND TEXTILE MANUFACTURE

The Art Institute of Portland, Portland, OR 249
California Design College, Los Angeles, CA 91
The Illinois Institute of Art - Chicago, Chicago, IL 156

APPAREL AND TEXTILE MARKETING MANAGEMENT

The Art Institute of Phoenix, Phoenix, AZ 76
The Art Institute of Pittsburgh, Pittsburgh, PA 252
The Art Institute of Portland, Portland, OR 249
Bradley Academy for the Visual Arts, York, PA 254
California Design College, Los Angeles, CA 91
The Illinois Institute of Art - Chicago, Chicago, IL 156
Miami International University of Art & Design, Miami, FL 138

APPAREL AND TEXTILES, OTHER

The Art Institute of Portland, Portland, OR 249
California Design College, Los Angeles, CA 91
The Illinois Institute of Art - Chicago, Chicago, IL 156

Miami International University of Art & Design, Miami, FL 138

APPLIANCE INSTALLATION AND REPAIR TECHNOLOGY/TECHNICIAN

ATI Career Training Center, Dallas, TX 294
ATI Career Training Center, Fort Lauderdale, FL 122
ATI Career Training Center, Miami, FL 123
ATI Career Training Center, North Richland Hills, TX 295
ATI Career Training Center, Oakland Park, FL 123
Caguas Institute of Mechanical Technology, Caguas, PR 276

APPLIED ART

The Art Institute of Houston, Houston, TX 294
The Art Institute of Pittsburgh, Pittsburgh, PA 252
The Art Institute of Portland, Portland, OR 249
Bradley Academy for the Visual Arts, York, PA 254
Briarcliffe College, Bethpage, NY 226
Briarcliffe College, Patchogue, NY 226
California Design College, Los Angeles, CA 91
Gemological Institute of America, Inc., Carlsbad, CA 95
Gemological Institute of America, Inc., Culver City, CA 95
Gemological Institute of America, Inc., New York, NY 229
The Illinois Institute of Art - Chicago, Chicago, IL 156
Joe Kubert School of Cartoon and Graphic Art Inc., Dover, NJ 221
Miami International University of Art & Design, Miami, FL 138

ARCHITECTURAL DRAFTING AND ARCHITECTURAL CAD/CADD

Academy of Art University, San Francisco, CA 83
Charter College, Anchorage, AK 74
Florida Technical College, Auburndale, FL 129
Florida Technical College, DeLand, FL 130
Florida Technical College, Jacksonville, FL 130
Florida Technical College, Orlando, FL 130
Herzing College, Atlanta, GA 148
Herzing College, Birmingham, AL 70
Herzing College, Kenner, LA 178
Herzing College, Madison, WI 330
Herzing College, Minneapolis, MN 195
Herzing College, Winter Park, FL 131
Island Drafting and Technical Institute, Amityville, NY 230
Lincoln Technical Institute Indianapolis, IN 166
Lincoln Technical Institute, Allentown, PA 266
Lincoln Technical Institute, Columbia, MD 182
Lincoln Technical Institute, Grand Prairie, TX 300
Lincoln Technical Institute, Mahwah, NJ 222
Lincoln Technical Institute, Melrose Park, IL 158
Lincoln Technical Institute, Philadelphia, PA 266
Lincoln Technical Institute, Union, NJ 222

Louisville Technical Institute, Louisville, KY 172
New England Institute of Technology at Palm Beach, West Palm Beach, FL 140
New England Institute of Technology, Warwick, RI 284
Northwest Technical Institute, Eden Prairie, MN 198
Pittsburgh Technical Institute, Oakdale, PA 269
Schuylkill Institute of Business and Technology, Pottsville, PA 270
Southwest Florida College, Tampa, FL 143
Triangle Tech, Inc. - Pittsburgh School, Pittsburgh, PA 272
Virginia College at Birmingham, Birmingham, AL 72
Westwood College - Chicago Loop Campus, Chicago, IL 161
Westwood College - Chicago River Oaks, Calumet City, IL 161
Westwood College - Denver North, Denver, CO 118
Westwood College - Denver South, Denver, CO 118

ARCHITECTURAL ENGINEERING TECHNOLOGY/TECHNICIAN

Louisville Technical Institute, Louisville, KY 172
New England Institute of Technology, Warwick, RI 284
Newschool of Architecture & Design, San Diego, CA 101

AROMATHERAPY

Ashmead College School of Massage, Vancouver, WA 325
Ashmead College, Everett, WA 325
Ashmead College, Fife, WA 325
Ashmead College, Seattle, WA 325
Ashmead College, Tigard, OR 250

ART/ART STUDIES, GENERAL

Academy College, Minneapolis, MN 192
The Art Institute of Colorado, Denver, CO 111
The Art Institute of Dallas, Dallas, TX 294
The Art Institute of Pittsburgh, Pittsburgh, PA 252
The Art Institute of Portland, Portland, OR 249
The Art Institute of Washington, Arlington, VA 314
Bradley Academy for the Visual Arts, York, PA 254
Briarcliffe College, Bethpage, NY 226
Briarcliffe College, Patchogue, NY 226
California Design College, Los Angeles, CA 91
The Creative Circus, Inc., Atlanta, GA 147
Florida Metropolitan University - Tampa Campus, Tampa, FL 129
The Illinois Institute of Art - Chicago, Chicago, IL 156
Miami International University of Art & Design, Miami, FL 138
Remington College - Tampa Campus, Tampa, FL 141
Virginia College at Birmingham, Birmingham, AL 72

ARTIFICIAL INTELLIGENCE AND ROBOTICS

Caguas Institute of Mechanical Technology, Caguas, PR 276
Missouri Tech, St. Louis, MO 204

ASIAN BODYWORK THERAPY

Baltimore School of Massage, Linthicum, MD 180
Florida College of Natural Health, Bradenton, FL 126
Florida College of Natural Health, Maitland, FL 126
Florida College of Natural Health, Miami, FL 126
Florida College of Natural Health, Pompano Beach, FL 126
Virginia School of Massage, Charlottesville, VA 324

ASSISTIVE/AUGMENTATIVE TECHNOLOGY AND REHABILITATION ENGINEERING

Florida Metropolitan University - North Orlando Campus, Orlando, FL 128
Parks College, Aurora, CO 116
Parks College, Denver, CO 116
Parks College, McLean, VA 321

ATHLETIC TRAINING/TRAINER

Ashmead College, Everett, WA 325
Ashmead College, Fife, WA 325
Ashmead College, Seattle, WA 325
Ashmead College, Tigard, OR 250
Globe College, Oakdale, MN 194
National American University, Albuquerque, NM 224
National American University, Brooklyn Center, MN 197
National American University, Colorado Springs, CO 115
National American University, Denver, CO 116
National American University, Ellsworth AFB, SD 286
National American University, Kansas City, MO 204
National American University, Minneapolis, MN 197
National American University, Overland Park, KS 169
National American University, Rapid City, SD 286
National American University, Rio Rancho, NM 224
National American University, Roseville, MN 197

AUDIOVISUAL COMMUNICATIONS TECHNOLOGIES/TECHNICIANS, OTHER

The Art Institute of Atlanta, Atlanta, GA 145
The Art Institute of Phoenix, Phoenix, AZ 76
Brown Mackie College, Cincinnati Campus, Cincinnati, OH 238
Conservatory of Recording Arts and Sciences, Tempe, AZ 78

AUTOBODY/COLLISION AND REPAIR TECHNOLOGY/TECHNICIAN

Apex Technical School, New York, NY 225

AUTOMOBILE/AUTOMOTIVE MECHANICS TECHNOLOGY/ TECHNICIAN

AUTOMOTIVE ENGINEERING TECHNOLOGY/TECHNICIAN

Advanced Technology Institute, Virginia Beach, VA 314
Apex Technical School, New York, NY 225
Arizona Automotive Institute, Glendale, AZ 76
Berk Trade and Business School, Brooklyn, NY 226
Denver Automotive and Diesel College, Denver, CO 114
Lincoln Technical Institute Indianapolis, IN 166
Lincoln Technical Institute, Allentown, PA 266
Lincoln Technical Institute, Columbia, MD 182
Lincoln Technical Institute, Grand Prairie, TX 300
Lincoln Technical Institute, Mahwah, NJ 222
Lincoln Technical Institute, Melrose Park, IL 158
Lincoln Technical Institute, Philadelphia, PA 266
Lincoln Technical Institute, Union, NJ 222
New England Institute of Technology, Warwick, RI 284
New England Technical Institute of Connecticut, Inc., New Britain, CT 119
New England Technical Institute, Cromwell, CT 119
New England Technical Institute, Hamden, CT 119
New England Technical Institute, Shelton, CT 119
Pennco Tech Bristol, PA 269
Pennco Tech, Blackwood, NJ 222
Universal Technical Institute, Avondale, AZ 82
Universal Technical Institute, Exton, PA 273
Universal Technical Institute, Houston, TX 306
Universal Technical Institute, Norwood, MA 187
Universal Technical Institute, Rancho Cucamonga, CA 108

AVIATION/AIRWAY MANAGEMENT AND OPERATIONS

Academy College, Minneapolis, MN 192
Everglades University, Boca Raton, FL 125
Everglades University, Orlando, FL 125
Everglades University, Sarasota, FL 125
Westwood College - Denver North, Denver, CO 118

AVIONICS MAINTENANCE TECHNOLOGY/TECHNICIAN

Advanced Training Associates, El Cajon, CA 84
Everglades University, Boca Raton, FL 125
Everglades University, Orlando, FL 125
Everglades University, Sarasota, FL 125
Hallmark Institute of Aeronautics, San Antonio, TX 297
San Joaquin Valley College, Bakersfield, CA 103
San Joaquin Valley College, Fresno, CA 103
San Joaquin Valley College, Modesto, CA 104
San Joaquin Valley College, Rancho Cucamonga, CA 104
San Joaquin Valley College, Visalia, CA 104
Westwood College - Denver, Broomfield, CO 118

BAKING AND PASTRY ARTS/ BAKER/PASTRY CHEF

The Art Institute of Atlanta, Atlanta, GA 145
The Art Institute of Colorado, Denver, CO 111
The Art Institute of Houston, Houston, TX 294
The Art Institute of New York City, New York, NY 225
The Art Institute of Phoenix, Phoenix, AZ 76
The Art Institute of California - San Diego, San Diego, CA 86
The Art Institute of Seattle, Seattle, WA 324
The Art Institutes International Minnesota, Minneapolis, MN 193
California Culinary Academy, San Francisco, CA 91
California School of Culinary Arts, Pasadena, CA 91
The Cooking and Hospitality Institute of Chicago, Chicago, IL 155
Escuela Hotelera de San Juan in Puerto Rico, San Juan, PR 278
The French Culinary Institute, New York, NY 229
The Illinois Institute of Art - Chicago, Chicago, IL 156
Instituto Banca y Comercio, Caguas, PR 279
Instituto Banca y Comercio, Cayey, PR 279
Instituto Banca y Comercio, Fajardo, PR 279
Instituto Banca y Comercio, Guayama, PR 280
Instituto Banca y Comercio, Manati, PR 280
Instituto Banca y Comercio, Mayaguez, PR 280
Instituto Banca y Comercio, Ponce, PR 280
Instituto de Banca y Comercio, San Juan, PR 281
Keiser College, Daytona Beach, FL 134
Keiser College, Fort Lauderdale, FL 134
Keiser College, Lakeland, FL 135
Keiser College, Melbourne, FL 135
Keiser College, Miami, FL 135
Keiser College, Orlando, FL 135
Keiser College, Pembroke Pines, FL 136
Keiser College, Port St. Lucie, FL 136
Keiser College, Sarasota, FL 136
Keiser College, Tallahassee, FL 136
Keiser College, West Palm Beach, FL 137
New England Culinary Institute at Essex, Essex Junction, VT 313
New England Culinary Institute, Montpelier, VT 313
New England Institute of Technology at Palm Beach, West Palm Beach, FL 140
Pennsylvania Culinary Institute, Pittsburgh, PA 269
The Restaurant School at Walnut Hill College, Philadelphia, PA 270
Scottsdale Culinary Institute, Scottsdale, AZ 81
Stratford University, Falls Church , VA 322
Stratford University, Woodbridge, VA 322
Sullivan University, Lexington, KY 174
Sullivan University, Louisville, KY 175
Texas Culinary Academy, Austin, TX 306

Virginia College at Birmingham, Birmingham, AL 72
Western Culinary Institute, Portland, OR 251
York Technical Institute, Lancaster, PA 274
York Technical Institute, York, PA 274
Yorktowne Business Institute, York, PA 274

BANKING AND FINANCIAL SUPPORT SERVICES

Aakers Business College , Bismarck, ND 236
Aakers Business College, Fargo, ND 236
Caliber Training Institute, New York, NY 227
Douglas Education Center, Monessen, PA 259
Herzing College, Atlanta, GA 148
Herzing College, Birmingham, AL 70
Herzing College, Kenner, LA 178
Herzing College, Madison, WI 330
Herzing College, Minneapolis, MN 195
Herzing College, Winter Park, FL 131
Instituto Banca y Comercio, Caguas, PR 279
Instituto Banca y Comercio, Cayey, PR 279
Instituto Banca y Comercio, Fajardo, PR 279
Instituto Banca y Comercio, Guayama, PR 280
Instituto Banca y Comercio, Manati, PR 280
Instituto Banca y Comercio, Mayaguez, PR 280
Instituto Banca y Comercio, Ponce, PR 280
Instituto de Banca y Comercio, San Juan, PR 281
McCann School of Business, Hazleton, PA 266
McCann School of Business, Pottsville, PA267
McCann School of Business, Scranton, PA 267
McCann School of Business, Sunbury, PA 267
Rasmussen College Eagan, Eagan, MN 198
Rasmussen College Mankato, Mankato, MN 198
Rasmussen College Minnetonka, Minnetonka, MN 199
Rasmussen College St. Cloud, St. Cloud, MN 199
Virginia College at Huntsville, Huntsville, AL 73

BARBERING/BARBER

Career Training Institute, Apopka, FL 124
College of Hair Design, Lincoln, NE 208
Flint Institute of Barbering, Flint, MI 189
Instituto Banca y Comercio, Caguas, PR 279
Instituto Banca y Comercio, Cayey, PR 279
Instituto Banca y Comercio, Fajardo, PR 279
Instituto Banca y Comercio, Guayama, PR 280
Instituto Banca y Comercio, Manati, PR 280
Instituto Banca y Comercio, Mayaguez, PR 280
Instituto Banca y Comercio, Ponce, PR 280
Roffler-Moler Hairstyling College, Marietta, GA 150

BARTENDING/BARTENDER

Escuela Hotelera de San Juan in Puerto Rico, San Juan, PR 278

BIOMEDICAL TECHNOLOGY/TECHNICIAN

Caguas Institute of Mechanical Technology, Caguas, PR 276
ECPI College of Technology, Charlotte, NC 234
ECPI College of Technology, Greensboro, NC 235
ECPI College of Technology, Greenville, SC 285
ECPI College of Technology, Manassas, VA 315
ECPI College of Technology, Newport News, VA 315
ECPI College of Technology, North Charleston, SC 285
ECPI College of Technology, Raleigh, NC 235
ECPI College of Technology, Virginia Beach, VA 316
Remington College - Dallas Campus, Garland, TX 304
Virginia College at Jackson, Jackson, MS 200

BLOOD BANK TECHNOLOGY SPECIALIST

Career Education Institute, Brockton, MA 184
Career Education Institute, Henderson, NV 210
Career Education Institute, Lincoln, RI 283
Career Education Institute, Lowell, MA 184
Career Education Institute, Marietta, GA 146
Career Education Institute, Norcross, GA 146

BROADCAST JOURNALISM

The Art Institute of Fort Lauderdale, Fort Lauderdale, FL 122
Brown College, Mendota Heights, MN 193
International College of Broadcasting, Dayton, OH 240
New England School of Communications, Bangor, ME 180

BUILDING/HOME/CONSTRUCTION INSPECTION/INSPECTOR

Everglades University, Boca Raton, FL 125
Everglades University, Orlando, FL 125
Everglades University, Sarasota, FL 125
Sonoran Desert Institute, Scottsdale, AZ 81

BUILDING/PROPERTY MAINTENANCE AND MANAGEMENT

Dean Institute of Technology, Pittsburgh, PA 258
Everglades University, Boca Raton, FL 125
Everglades University, Orlando, FL 125
Everglades University, Sarasota, FL 125
HoHoKus School of Trade and Technical Services, Linden, NJ 221
New England Institute of Technology, Warwick, RI 284
Orleans Technical Institute, Philadelphia, PA 268
Technical Career Institute, New York, NY 233
Vatterott College, Broadview Heights, OH 245
Vatterott College, Des Moines, IA 168
Vatterott College, Joplin, MO 206
Vatterott College, Kansas City, MO 207

Vatterott College, Memphis, TN 292
Vatterott College, O'Fallon , MO 207
Vatterott College, Oklahoma City, OK 248
Vatterott College, Omaha, NE 209
Vatterott College, Quincy, IL 160
Vatterott College, Springfield, MO 208
Vatterott College, St. Ann, MO 207
Vatterott College, St. Joseph, MO 207
Vatterott College, St. Louis, MO 208
Vatterott College, Tulsa, OK 249
Vatterott College, Wichita, KS 169

BUSINESS ADMINISTRATION AND MANAGEMENT, GENERAL

Academy College, Minneapolis, MN 192
Advanced Career Training, Atlanta, GA 144
Advanced Career Training, Jacksonville, FL 121
Advanced Career Training, Riverdale, GA 145
Akron Institute, Akron, OH 236
American Commercial College, Abilene, TX 292
American Commercial College, Lubbock, TX 293
American Commercial College, Odessa, TX 293
American Commercial College, San Angelo, TX 293
American Commercial College, Shreveport, LA 175
American InterContinental University, Atlanta, GA 145
American InterContinental University, Houston, TX 293
American InterContinental University, Los Angeles, CA 85
American InterContinental University, San Antonio, TX 293
American InterContinental University, Weston, FL 121
Andover College, Portland, ME 180
Argosy University/Chicago, Chicago, IL 154
Argosy University/Honolulu, Honolulu, HI 152
Argosy University/Schaumburg, Schaumburg, IL 154
Argosy University/Twin Cities, Eagan, MN 193
Argosy University/Washington D.C., Arlington, VA 314
ATI Career Training Center, Dallas, TX 294
ATI Career Training Center, Fort Lauderdale, FL 122
ATI Career Training Center, Miami, FL 123
ATI Career Training Center, North Richland Hills, TX 295
ATI Career Training Center, Oakland Park, FL 123
Bauder College, Atlanta, GA 146
Bay State College, Boston, MA 183
Bayamon Community College, Bayamon, PR 276
Berkeley College, Paramus, NJ 214
Berkeley College, West Paterson, NJ 214
Berkeley College, Woodbridge, NJ 215
Berks Technical Institute, Wyomissing, PA 253
Blair College, Colorado Springs, CO 112
Bradford School, Columbus, OH 237
Bradford School, Pittsburgh, PA 254
Briarcliffe College, Bethpage, NY 226
Briarcliffe College, Patchogue, NY 226

Brown College, Mendota Heights, MN 193
Brown Mackie College, Atlanta Campus, Norcross, GA 146
Brown Mackie College, Dallas Campus, Garland, TX 296
Brown Mackie College, Findlay Campus, Findlay, OH 238
Brown Mackie College, Fort Wayne Campus, Fort Wayne, IN 162
Brown Mackie College, Hopkinsville Campus, Hopkinsville, KY 170
Brown Mackie College, Lenexa Campus, Lenexa, KS 168
Brown Mackie College, Los Angeles Campus, Santa Monica, CA 87
Brown Mackie College, Louisville Campus, Louisville, KY 170
Brown Mackie College, Miami Campus, Miami, FL 124
Brown Mackie College, Moline Campus, Moline, IL 154
Brown Mackie College, North Canton Campus, North Canton, OH 239
Brown Mackie College, Northern Kentucky Campus, Fort Mitchell, KY 170
Brown Mackie College, Salina Campus, Salina, KS 168
Brown Mackie College, San Diego Campus, San Diego, CA 87
Brown Mackie College, South Bend Campus, South Bend, IN 162
Bryan College, Springfield, MO 201
Bryan College, Topeka, KS 169
Bryman College, Alhambra, CA 88
Bryman College, Anaheim, CA 88
Bryman College, City of Industry, CA 88
Bryman College, Earth City, MO 201
Bryman College, Everett, WA 325
Bryman College, Gardena, CA 88
Bryman College, Hayward, CA 89
Bryman College, Los Angeles, CA 89
Bryman College, Lynnwood, WA 326
Bryman College, New Orleans, LA 176
Bryman College, Ontario, CA 89
Bryman College, Port Orchard, WA 326
Bryman College, Renton, WA 326
Bryman College, Reseda, CA 89
Bryman College, San Bernardino, CA 90
Bryman College, San Francisco, CA 90
Bryman College, San Jose, CA 90
Bryman College, Tacoma, WA 326
Bryman College, Torrance, CA 90
Business Institute of Pennsylvania, Meadville, PA 255
Business Institute of Pennsylvania, Sharon, PA 255
Capella University, Minneapolis, MN 194
Cardean University, Chicago, IL 154
Career Education Institute, Brockton, MA 184
Career Education Institute, Henderson, NV 210
Career Education Institute, Lincoln, RI 283
Career Education Institute, Lowell, MA 184

Boldface type indicates that the school is a participating institution in the *Imagine America* Scholarship Program

Southeastern Business College, New Boston, OH 244
Southwest Florida College, Tampa, FL 143
Southwestern College of Business, Cincinnati, OH 244
Southwestern College of Business, Dayton, OH 244
Southwestern College of Business, Florence, KY 174
Southwestern College of Business, Franklin, OH 245
Spencerian College, Louisville, KY 174
Springfield College, Springfield, MO 206
Stevens-Henager College, Boise, ID 153
Stevens-Henager College, Logan, UT 311
Stevens-Henager College, Ogden, UT 311
Stevens-Henager College - Provo, Orem, UT 311
Stevens-Henager College - Salt Lake City, Salt Lake City, UT 312
Stratford University, Falls Church , VA 322
Stratford University, Woodbridge, VA 322
Strayer University, Atlanta, GA 151
Stuart School of Business Administration, Wall, NJ 223
Sullivan University, Lexington, KY 174
Sullivan University, Louisville, KY 175
Thompson Institute, Chambersburg, PA 271
Thompson Institute, Harrisburg, PA 271
Thompson Institute, Philadelphia, PA 271
Tri-State Business Institute, Erie, PA 272
Trumbull Business College, Warren, OH 245
United Education Institute, Chula Vista, CA 106
United Education Institute, El Monte, CA 106
United Education Institute, Huntington Park, Huntington Park, CA 107
United Education Institute, Los Angeles, Los Angeles, CA 107
United Education Institute, Ontario Campus, Ontario, CA 107
United Education Institute, San Bernardino Campus, San Bernardino, CA 107
United Education Institute, San Diego Campus, San Diego, CA 107
United Education Institute, Van Nuys Campus, Van Nuys, CA 108
Utah Career College, West Jordan, UT 312
Virginia College at Birmingham, Birmingham, AL 72
Virginia College at Huntsville, Huntsville, AL 73
Virginia College at Jackson, Jackson, MS 200
Webster College, Holiday, FL 144
Webster College, Ocala, FL 144
West Virginia Junior College, Bridgeport, WV 329
West Virginia Junior College, Charleston, WV 329
West Virginia Junior College, Morgantown, WV 330
Western International University, Phoenix, AZ 82
Western School of Health and Business Careers, Monroeville, PA 273
Western School of Health and Business Careers, Pittsburgh, PA 273

Westwood College - Atlanta Campus, Atlanta, GA 151
Westwood College - Atlanta Northlake, Atlanta, GA 152
Westwood College - Chicago O'Hare Airport, Chicago, IL 161
Westwood College - Denver North, Denver, CO 118
Westwood College - Inland Empire, Upland, CA 109
York Technical Institute, Lancaster, PA 274
York Technical Institute, York, PA 274
Yorktowne Business Institute, York, PA 274

BUSINESS ADMINISTRATION, MANAGEMENT AND OPERATIONS, OTHER

Berks Technical Institute, Wyomissing, PA 253
Briarcliffe College, Bethpage, NY 226
Briarcliffe College, Patchogue, NY 226
Business Institute of Pennsylvania, Meadville, PA 255
Business Institute of Pennsylvania, Sharon, PA 255
Charter College, Anchorage, AK 74
Collins College: A School of Design and Technology, Tempe, AZ 77
Florida Technical College, Auburndale, FL 129
Florida Technical College, DeLand, FL 130
Florida Technical College, Jacksonville, FL 130
Florida Technical College, Orlando, FL 130
Gibbs College - Cranston, Cranston, RI 283
Herzing College, Atlanta, GA 148
Herzing College, Birmingham, AL 70
Herzing College, Kenner, LA 178
Herzing College, Madison, WI 330
Herzing College, Minneapolis, MN 195
Herzing College, Winter Park, FL 131
International Business College, El Paso, TX 298
International Business College, El Paso, TX 299
International Business College, Fort Wayne, IN 165
International Business College, Indianapolis, IN 165
Maric College, Anaheim, CA 99
Maric College, Los Angeles, CA 100
Maric College, North Hollywood, CA 99
Maric College, Sacramento, CA 99
Maric College, Salida, CA 99
Maric College, San Diego, CA 100
Maric College, Vista, CA 100
McIntosh College, Dover, NH 213
Remington College - Jacksonville Campus, Jacksonville, FL 140
Remington College - Pinellas Campus, Largo, FL 141
Santa Barbara Business College, Bakersfield, CA 104
Santa Barbara Business College, Santa Barbara, CA 105
Santa Barbara Business College, Santa Maria, CA 105
Santa Barbara Business College, Ventura, CA 105
Schuylkill Institute of Business and Technology, Pottsville, PA 270

BUSINESS MACHINE REPAIRER

American Commercial College, Abilene, TX 292
American Commercial College, Lubbock, TX 293
American Commercial College, Odessa, TX 293
American Commercial College, San Angelo, TX 293
American Commercial College, Shreveport, LA 175
Berks Technical Institute, Wyomissing, PA 253
Career Education Institute, Brockton, MA 184
Career Education Institute, Henderson, NV 210
Career Education Institute, Lincoln, RI 283
Career Education Institute, Lowell, MA 184
Career Education Institute, Marietta, GA 146
Career Education Institute, Norcross, GA 146
Central Coast College, Salinas, CA 92
ECPI College of Technology, Charlotte, NC 234
ECPI College of Technology, Greensboro, NC 235
ECPI College of Technology, Greenville, SC 285
ECPI College of Technology, Manassas, VA 315
ECPI College of Technology, Newport News, VA 315
ECPI College of Technology, North Charleston, SC 285
ECPI College of Technology, Raleigh, NC 235
ECPI College of Technology, Virginia Beach, VA 316
HoHoKus RETS School of Business and Medical Technical Services, Nutley, NJ 220
ITI Technical College, Baton Rouge, LA 178
Remington College - Pinellas Campus, Largo, FL 141
TESST College of Technology, Alexandria, VA 323
TESST College of Technology, Baltimore, MD 182
TESST College of Technology, Beltsville, MD 183
TESST College of Technology, Towson, MD 183

BUSINESS OPERATIONS SUPPORT AND SECRETARIAL SERVICES, OTHER

American Commercial College, Abilene, TX 292
American Commercial College, Lubbock, TX 293
American Commercial College, Odessa, TX 293
American Commercial College, San Angelo, TX 293
American Commercial College, Shreveport, LA 175
Antonelli College, Cincinnati, OH 237
Antonelli College, Hattiesburg, MS 199
Antonelli College, Jackson, MS 200
Berks Technical Institute, Wyomissing, PA 253
Briarcliffe College, Bethpage, NY 226
Briarcliffe College, Patchogue, NY 226
Career Academy, Anchorage, AK 73
Florida Technical College, Auburndale, FL 129
Florida Technical College, DeLand, FL 130
Florida Technical College, Jacksonville, FL 130
Florida Technical College, Orlando, FL 130
Hickey College, St. Louis, MO 202
HoHoKus RETS School of Business and Medical Technical Services, Nutley, NJ 220

Maric College, Anaheim, CA 99
Maric College, Los Angeles, CA 100
Maric College, North Hollywood, CA 99
Maric College, Sacramento, CA 99
Maric College, Salida, CA 99
Maric College, San Diego, CA 100
Maric College, Vista, CA 100
Pinnacle Career Institute, Kansas City, MO 204
Pinnacle Career Institute, Lawrence, KS 169
Rasmussen College St. Cloud, St. Cloud, MN 199
Remington College-Little Rock Campus, Little Rock, AR 83
Remington College - Pinellas Campus, Largo, FL 141
Thompson Institute, Chambersburg, PA 271
Thompson Institute, Harrisburg, PA 271
Thompson Institute, Philadelphia, PA 271
Virginia College at Birmingham, Birmingham, AL 72

BUSINESS MANAGEMENT, MARKETING AND RELATED SUPPORT SERVICES, OTHER

Argosy University/Honolulu, Honolulu, HI 152
Argosy University/Schaumburg, Schaumburg, IL 154
Berks Technical Institute, Wyomissing, PA 253
Briarcliffe College, Bethpage, NY 226
Briarcliffe College, Patchogue, NY 226
Brown Mackie College, Cincinnati Campus, Cincinnati, OH 238
Brown Mackie College, Orange County Campus, Santa Ana, CA 87
Bryman College, Alhambra, CA 88
Bryman College, Anaheim, CA 88
Bryman College, City of Industry, CA 88
Bryman College, Earth City, MO 201
Bryman College, Everett, WA 325
Bryman College, Gardena, CA 88
Bryman College, Hayward, CA 89
Bryman College, Los Angeles, CA 89
Bryman College, Lynnwood, WA 326
Bryman College, New Orleans, LA 176
Bryman College, Ontario, CA 89
Bryman College, Port Orchard, WA 326
Bryman College, Renton, WA 326
Bryman College, Reseda, CA 89
Bryman College, San Bernardino, CA 90
Bryman College, San Francisco, CA 90
Bryman College, San Jose, CA 90
Bryman College, Tacoma, WA 326
Bryman College, Torrance, CA 90
Eagle Gate College - Weber/Davis, Layton, UT 309
Eagle Gate College - Weber/Davis, Salt Lake City, UT 309
Florida Metropolitan University - Lakeland Campus, Lakeland, FL 127

Florida Technical College, Auburndale, FL 129
Florida Technical College, DeLand, FL 130
Florida Technical College, Jacksonville, FL 130
Florida Technical College, Orlando, FL 130
Full Sail Real World Education, Winter Park, FL 131
Globe College, Oakdale, MN 194
Hesser College, Manchester, NH 213
International Academy of Design and Technology, Henderson, NV 210
International Academy of Design and Technology, Nashville, TN 289
International Academy of Design and Technology, San Antonio, TX 298
International Academy of Design and Technology, Schaumburg, IL 157
International Academy of Design and Technology, Seattle, WA 327
Jones International University, Englewood, CO 115
Lehigh Valley College, Center Valley, PA 266
Mildred Elley School, Latham, NY 232
National American University, Albuquerque, NM 224
National American University, Brooklyn Center, MN 197
National American University, Colorado Springs, CO 115
National American University, Denver, CO 116
National American University, Ellsworth AFB, SD 286
National American University, Kansas City, MO 204
National American University, Minneapolis, MN 197
National American University, Overland Park, KS 169
National American University, Rapid City, SD 286
National American University, Rio Rancho, NM 224
National American University, Roseville, MN 197
North Florida Institute, Orange Park, FL 140
Peirce College, Philadelphia, PA 268
Rasmussen College Mankato, Mankato, MN 198
Southwest Florida College, Tampa, FL 143
Virginia College at Birmingham, Birmingham, AL 72
Westwood College - Anaheim, Anaheim, CA 109
Westwood College - Atlanta Northlake, Atlanta, GA 152
Westwood College - Chicago O'Hare Airport, Chicago, IL 161
Westwood College - Denver North, Denver, CO 118
Westwood College - Los Angeles, Inglewood, CA 110
Westwood College - Los Angeles, Los Angeles, CA 110

BUSINESS/COMMERCE, GENERAL

Brown College, Mendota Heights, MN 193

BUSINESS/CORPORATE COMMUNICATIONS

Brown College, Mendota Heights, MN 193
Brown Mackie College, North Canton Campus, North Canton, OH 239
Bryman College, Alhambra, CA 88

Bryman College, Anaheim, CA 88
Bryman College, City of Industry, CA 88
Bryman College, Earth City, MO 201
Bryman College, Everett, WA 325
Bryman College, Gardena, CA 88
Bryman College, Hayward, CA 89
Bryman College, Los Angeles, CA 89
Bryman College, Lynnwood, WA 326
Bryman College, New Orleans, LA 176
Bryman College, Ontario, CA 89
Bryman College, Port Orchard, WA 326
Bryman College, Renton, WA 326
Bryman College, Reseda, CA 89
Bryman College, San Bernardino, CA 90
Bryman College, San Francisco, CA 90
Bryman College, San Jose, CA 90
Bryman College, Tacoma, WA 326
Bryman College, Torrance, CA 90
Business Institute of Pennsylvania, Meadville, PA 255
Business Institute of Pennsylvania, Sharon, PA 255
Herzing College, Atlanta, GA 148
Herzing College, Birmingham, AL 70
Herzing College, Kenner, LA 178
Herzing College, Madison, WI 330
Herzing College, Minneapolis, MN 195
Herzing College, Winter Park, FL 131
Hesser College, Manchester, NH 213
ITI Technical College, Baton Rouge, LA 178
Jones International University, Englewood, CO 115
Katharine Gibbs School, Melville, NY 231
Katharine Gibbs School, New York, NY 231
Katharine Gibbs School, Norristown, PA 264
Katharine Gibbs School, Piscataway, NJ 221
McCann School of Business, Hazleton, PA 266
McCann School of Business, Pottsville, PA 267
McCann School of Business, Scranton, PA 267
McCann School of Business, Sunbury, PA 267
New England School of Communications, Bangor, ME 180
Rasmussen College Eagan, Eagan, MN 198
Rasmussen College Minnetonka, Minnetonka, MN 199
TESST College of Technology, Alexandria, VA 323
TESST College of Technology, Baltimore, MD 182
TESST College of Technology, Beltsville, MD 183
TESST College of Technology, Towson, MD 183
Virginia College at Birmingham, Birmingham, AL 72

BUSINESS/MANAGERIAL ECONOMICS

Virginia College at Birmingham, Birmingham, AL 72

BUSINESS/OFFICE AUTOMATION/ TECHNOLOGY/DATA ENTRY

Academy of Medical Arts and Business, Harrisburg, PA 252

American School of Business, Wichita Falls, TX 294

Antonelli College, Cincinnati, OH 237

Antonelli College, Hattiesburg, MS 199

Antonelli College, Jackson, MS 200

ATI Career Training Center, Dallas, TX 294

ATI Career Training Center, Fort Lauderdale, FL 122

ATI Career Training Center, Miami, FL 123

ATI Career Training Center, North Richland Hills, TX 295

ATI Career Training Center, Oakland Park, FL 123

Austin Business College, Austin, TX 295

Bradford School, Columbus, OH 237

Bradford School, Pittsburgh, PA 254

Briarcliffe College, Bethpage, NY 226

Briarcliffe College, Patchogue, NY 226

Brookstone College of Business, Charlotte, NC 234

Brookstone College of Business, Greensboro, NC 234

Business Institute of Pennsylvania, Meadville, PA 255

Business Institute of Pennsylvania, Sharon, PA 255

Career College of Northern Nevada, Reno, NV 210

Career Education Institute, Brockton, MA 184

Career Education Institute, Henderson, NV 210

Career Education Institute, Lincoln, RI 283

Career Education Institute, Lowell, MA 184

Career Education Institute, Marietta, GA 146

Career Education Institute, Norcross, GA 146

CHI Institute, Broomall, PA 256

CHI Institute, Southampton, PA 256

Computer Learning Network, Altoona, PA 258

Computer Learning Network, Mechanicsburg, PA 258

Coyne American Institute, Chicago, IL 155

Coyne American Institute, Chicago, IL 156

Douglas Education Center, Monessen, PA 259

ECPI College of Technology, Charlotte, NC 234

ECPI College of Technology, Greensboro, NC 235

ECPI College of Technology, Greenville, SC 285

ECPI College of Technology, Manassas, VA 315

ECPI College of Technology, Newport News, VA 315

ECPI College of Technology, North Charleston, SC 285

ECPI College of Technology, Raleigh, NC 235

ECPI College of Technology, Virginia Beach, VA 316

ECPI Technical College, Glen Allen, VA 316

ECPI Technical College, Richmond, VA 316

ECPI Technical College, Roanoke, VA 317

Empire College, Santa Rosa, CA 93

Florida Technical College, Auburndale, FL 129

Florida Technical College, DeLand, FL 130

Florida Technical College, Jacksonville, FL 130

Florida Technical College, Orlando, FL 130

Gretna Career College, Gretna, LA 177

Instituto Banca y Comercio, Caguas, PR 279

Instituto Banca y Comercio, Cayey, PR 279

Instituto Banca y Comercio, Fajardo, PR 279

Instituto Banca y Comercio, Guayama, PR 280

Instituto Banca y Comercio, Manati, PR 280

Instituto Banca y Comercio, Mayaguez, PR 280

Instituto Banca y Comercio, Ponce, PR 280

International Business College, El Paso, TX 298

International Business College, El Paso, TX 299

International Business College, Fort Wayne, IN 165

International Business College, Indianapolis, IN 165

ITI Technical College, Baton Rouge, LA 178

Las Vegas College, Henderson, NV 211

Las Vegas College, Las Vegas, NV 211

McCann School of Business, Hazleton, PA 266

McCann School of Business, Pottsville, PA 267

McCann School of Business, Scranton, PA 267

McCann School of Business, Sunbury, PA 267

Metro Business College, Cape Girardeau, MO 203

Metro Business College, Jefferson City, MO 203

Metro Business College, Rolla, MO 203

MTI College of Business and Technology, Houston, TX 301

National College of Business and Technology, Arecibo, PR 282

National College of Business and Technology, Cincinnati, OH 241

National College of Business and Technology, Indianapolis, IN 166

National College of Business and Technology, Kettering, OH 242

National Institute of Technology, Austin , TX 302

National Institute of Technology, Cross Lanes, WV 329

National Institute of Technology, Detroit, MI 190

National Institute of Technology, Houston, TX 302

National Institute of Technology, Long Beach, CA 101

National Institute of Technology, San Antonio, TX 302

National Institute of Technology, Southfield, MI 190

Remington College - Pinellas Campus, Largo, FL 141

Remington College - Tampa Campus, Tampa, FL 141

San Joaquin Valley College, Bakersfield, CA 103

San Joaquin Valley College, Fresno, CA 103

San Joaquin Valley College, Modesto, CA 104

San Joaquin Valley College, Rancho Cucamonga, CA 104

San Joaquin Valley College, Visalia, CA 104

Stevens-Henager College, Boise, ID 153

Stevens-Henager College, Logan, UT 311

Stevens-Henager College, Ogden, UT 311

Stevens-Henager College - Salt Lake City, Salt Lake City, UT 312

TESST College of Technology, Alexandria, VA 323

TESST College of Technology, Baltimore, MD 182
TESST College of Technology, Beltsville, MD 183
TESST College of Technology, Towson, MD 183
Vatterott College, Broadview Heights, OH 245
Vatterott College, Des Moines, IA 168
Vatterott College, Joplin, MO 206
Vatterott College, Kansas City, MO 207
Vatterott College, Memphis, TN 292
Vatterott College, OÆFallon , MO 207
Vatterott College, Oklahoma City, OK 248
Vatterott College, Omaha, NE 209
Vatterott College, Quincy, IL 160
Vatterott College, Springfield, MO 208
Vatterott College, St. Ann, MO 207
Vatterott College, St. Joseph, MO 207
Vatterott College, St. Louis, MO 208
Vatterott College, Tulsa, OK 249
Vatterott College, Wichita, KS 169
Virginia College at Birmingham, Birmingham, AL 72

CABINETMAKING AND MILLWORK/ MILLWRIGHT

New England Institute of Technology, Warwick, RI 284

CAD/CADD AND/OR DESIGN TECHNOLOGY/TECHNICIAN

American Commercial College, Abilene, TX 292
American Commercial College, Lubbock, TX 293
American Commercial College, Odessa, TX 293
American Commercial College, San Angelo, TX 293
American Commercial College, Shreveport, LA 175
The Art Institute of Las Vegas, Henderson, NV 209
The Art Institute of Phoenix, Phoenix, AZ 76
The Art Institute of Portland, Portland, OR 249
ATI Career Training Center, Dallas, TX 294
ATI Career Training Center, Fort Lauderdale, FL 122
ATI Career Training Center, Miami, FL 123
ATI Career Training Center, North Richland Hills, TX 295
ATI Career Training Center, Oakland Park, FL 123
Berks Technical Institute, Wyomissing, PA 253
Brown Mackie College, Akron Campus, Akron, OH 238
Brown Mackie College, Atlanta Campus, Norcross, GA 146
Brown Mackie College, Cincinnati Campus, Cincinnati, OH 238
Brown Mackie College, Fort Wayne Campus, Fort Wayne, IN 162
Brown Mackie College, Hopkinsville Campus, Hopkinsville, KY 170
Brown Mackie College, Lenexa Campus, Lenexa, KS 168
Brown Mackie College, Louisville Campus, Louisville, KY 170
Brown Mackie College, Merrillville Campus, Merrillville, IN 162
Brown Mackie College, Miami Campus, Miami, FL 124
Brown Mackie College, Michigan City Campus, Michigan City, IN 162
Brown Mackie College, North Canton Campus, North Canton, OH 239
Brown Mackie College, Northern Kentucky Campus, Fort Mitchell, KY 170
Brown Mackie College, San Diego Campus, San Diego, CA 87
Brown Mackie College, South Bend Campus, South Bend, IN 162
Caguas Institute of Mechanical Technology, Caguas, PR 276
California Design College, Los Angeles, CA 91
Charter College, Anchorage, AK 74
Delta School of Business & Technology, Lake Charles, LA 177
Florida Technical College, Auburndale, FL 129
Florida Technical College, DeLand, FL 130
Florida Technical College, Jacksonville, FL 130
Florida Technical College, Orlando, FL 130
Herzing College, Atlanta, GA 148
Herzing College, Birmingham, AL 70
Herzing College, Kenner, LA 178
Herzing College, Madison, WI 330
Herzing College, Minneapolis, MN 195
Herzing College, Winter Park, FL 131
High-Tech Institute, Irving, TX 298
High-Tech Institute, Kansas City, MO 202
High-Tech Institute, Las Vegas, NV 210
High-Tech Institute, Marietta, GA 149
High-Tech Institute, Memphis, TN 288
High-Tech Institute, Nashville, TN 288
High-Tech Institute, Orlando, FL 132
High-Tech Institute, Phoenix, AZ 78
High-Tech Institute, Sacramento, CA 96
High-Tech Institute, St. Louis Park, MN 195
Huertas Junior College, Caguas, PR 277
The Illinois Institute of Art - Chicago, Chicago, IL 156
Instituto Banca y Comercio, Caguas, PR 279
Instituto Banca y Comercio, Cayey, PR 279
Instituto Banca y Comercio, Fajardo, PR 279
Instituto Banca y Comercio, Guayama, PR 280
Instituto Banca y Comercio, Manati, PR 280
Instituto Banca y Comercio, Mayaguez, PR 280
Instituto Banca y Comercio, Ponce, PR 280
International Academy of Design & Technology, Chicago, IL 157
International Academy of Design & Technology, Orlando, FL 132
International Academy of Design & Technology, Pittsburgh, PA 264
International Academy of Design & Technology, Tampa, FL

Silicon Valley College, San Jose, CA 106
Southwest Florida College, Tampa, FL 143
TESST College of Technology, Alexandria, VA 323
TESST College of Technology, Baltimore, MD 182
TESST College of Technology, Beltsville, MD 183
TESST College of Technology, Towson, MD 183
Thompson Institute, Chambersburg, PA 271
Thompson Institute, Harrisburg, PA 271
Thompson Institute, Philadelphia, PA 271
Triangle Tech, Inc. - DuBois School, DuBois, PA 272
Triangle Tech, Inc. - Erie School, Erie, PA 272
Triangle Tech, Inc. - Greensburg School, Greensburg, PA 272
Vatterott College, Broadview Heights, OH 245
Vatterott College, Des Moines, IA 168
Vatterott College, Joplin, MO 206
Vatterott College, Kansas City, MO 207
Vatterott College, Memphis, TN 292
Vatterott College, OÆFallon , MO 207
Vatterott College, Oklahoma City, OK 248
Vatterott College, Omaha, NE 209
Vatterott College, Quincy, IL 160
Vatterott College, Springfield, MO 208
Vatterott College, St. Ann, MO 207
Vatterott College, St. Joseph, MO 207
Vatterott College, St. Louis, MO 208
Vatterott College, Tulsa, OK 249
Vatterott College, Wichita, KS 169
Virginia College at Birmingham, Birmingham, AL 72
Virginia College at Huntsville, Huntsville, AL 73
Westwood College - Anaheim, Anaheim, CA 109
Westwood College - Atlanta Campus, Atlanta, GA 151
Westwood College - Chicago Du Page, Woodridge, IL 160
Westwood College - Chicago Loop Campus, Chicago, IL 161
Westwood College - Chicago O'Hare Airport, Chicago, IL 161
Westwood College - Chicago River Oaks, Calumet City, IL 161
Westwood College - Dallas, Dallas, TX 308
Westwood College - Denver North, Denver, CO 118
Westwood College - Fort Worth, Euless, TX 308
Westwood College - Houston South Campus, Houston, TX 308
Westwood College - Inland Empire, Upland, CA 109
Westwood College - Long Beach, Torrance, CA 110
York Technical Institute, Lancaster, PA 274
York Technical Institute, York, PA 274

CARDIOVASCULAR TECHNOLOGY/ TECHNOLOGIST

Carnegie Institute, Troy, MI 188

Harrison Career Institute, Allentown, PA 262
Harrison Career Institute, Baltimore, MD 181
Harrison Career Institute, Clifton, NJ 218
Harrison Career Institute, Delran, NJ 218
Harrison Career Institute, Deptford, NJ 219
Harrison Career Institute, Ewing, NJ 219
Harrison Career Institute, Jersey City, NJ 219
Harrison Career Institute, Oakhurst, NJ 219
Harrison Career Institute, Philadelphia, PA 263
Harrison Career Institute, Reading, PA 263
Harrison Career Institute, South Orange, NJ 220
Harrison Career Institute, Vineland, NJ 220
Harrison Career Institute, Wilmington, DE 121
HoHoKus School of Business and Medical Sciences, Ramsey, NJ 221
Instituto Vocational y Commercial EDIC, Caguas, PR 281
National School of Technology, Inc., Fort Lauderdale, FL 139
National School of Technology, Inc., Hialeah, FL 139
National School of Technology, Inc., Miami, FL 139
Sanford-Brown Institute, Atlanta, GA 150
Sanford-Brown Institute, Dallas, TX 305
Sanford-Brown Institute, Garden City, NY 232
Sanford-Brown Institute, Houston, TX 305
Sanford-Brown Institute, Houston, TX 306
Sanford-Brown Institute, Jacksonville, FL 142
Sanford-Brown Institute, Landover, MD 182
Sanford-Brown Institute, Lauderdale Lakes, FL 142
Sanford-Brown Institute, New York, NY 232
Sanford-Brown Institute, Springfield, MA 187
Sanford-Brown Institute, Tampa, FL 142
Sanford-Brown Institute, Trevose, PA 270
Sanford-Brown Institute, White Plains, NY 232
Stevens-Henager College, Boise, ID 153
Stevens-Henager College, Logan, UT 311
Stevens-Henager College, Ogden, UT 311

CAPENTRY/CARPENTER

New England Institute of Technology, Warwick, RI 284
North American Trade School, Gwynn Oak, MD 182
Orleans Technical Institute, Philadelphia, PA 268
Triangle Tech, Inc. - DuBois School, DuBois, PA 272
Triangle Tech, Inc. - Erie School, Erie, PA 272
Triangle Tech, Inc. - Greensburg School, Greensburg, PA 272
Triangle Tech, Inc. - Pittsburgh School, Pittsburgh, PA 272
Triangle Tech, Inc. - Sunbury School, Sunbury, PA 272

CERAMIC ARTS AND CERAMICS

Academy of Art University, San Francisco, CA 83
Miami International University of Art & Design, Miami, FL 138

CHILD CARE AND SUPPORT SERVICES MANAGEMENT

Academy of Medical Arts and Business, Harrisburg, PA 252

Davis College, Toledo, OH 239

Lehigh Valley College, Center Valley, PA 266

Rasmussen College Eagan, Eagan, MN 198

Rasmussen College Minnetonka, Minnetonka, MN 199

Rasmussen College St. Cloud, St. Cloud, MN 199

Remington College - Jacksonville Campus, Jacksonville, FL 140

Southwest Florida College, Tampa, FL 143

Sullivan University, Lexington, KY 174

Sullivan University, Louisville, KY 175

CHILD CARE PROVIDER/ASSISTANT

Academy of Medical Arts and Business, Harrisburg, PA 252

Business Institute of Pennsylvania, Meadville, PA 255

Business Institute of Pennsylvania, Sharon, PA 255

Caliber Training Institute, New York, NY 227

City College, Inc., Moore, OK 246

Laurel Business Institute, Uniontown, PA 265

Ponce Paramedical College, Inc., Coto Laurel, PR 282

Rasmussen College Eagan, Eagan, MN 198

Rasmussen College Minnetonka, Minnetonka, MN 199

Rasmussen College St. Cloud, St. Cloud, MN 199

Sullivan University, Lexington, KY 174

Sullivan University, Louisville, KY 175

CINEMATOGRAPHY AND FILM/ VIDEO PRODUCTION

Academy of Art University, San Francisco, CA 83

Academy of Radio Broadcasting, Huntington Beach, CA 84

Academy of Radio Broadcasting, Phoenix, AZ 74

American InterContinental University, Atlanta, GA 145

American InterContinental University, Houston, TX 293

American InterContinental University, Los Angeles, CA 85

American InterContinental University, San Antonio, TX 293

American InterContinental University, Weston, FL 121

The Art Institute of Atlanta, Atlanta, GA 145

The Art Institute of California - Los Angeles, Santa Monica, CA 85

The Art Institute of Colorado, Denver, CO 111

The Art Institute of New York City, New York, NY 225

The Art Institute of Philadelphia, Philadelphia, PA 252

The Art Institute of Phoenix, Phoenix, AZ 76

The Art Institute of Pittsburgh, Pittsburgh, PA 252

The Art Institute of Portland, Portland, OR 249

The Art Institute of Seattle, Seattle, WA 324

Brooks Institute of Photography, Santa Barbara, CA 87

Collins College: A School of Design and Technology, Tempe, AZ 77

Florida Metropolitan University-Melbourne Campus, Melbourne, FL 127

Florida Metropolitan University - North Orlando Campus, Orlando, FL 128

Full Sail Real World Education, Winter Park, FL 131

Miami International University of Art & Design, Miami, FL 138

New England School of Communications, Bangor, ME 180

CIVIL DRAFTING AND CIVIL ENGINEERING CAD/CADD

ATI Career Training Center, Dallas, TX 294

ATI Career Training Center, Fort Lauderdale, FL 122

ATI Career Training Center, Miami, FL 123

ATI Career Training Center, North Richland Hills, TX 295

ATI Career Training Center, Oakland Park, FL 123

Berks Technical Institute, Wyomissing, PA 253

Charter College, Anchorage, AK 74

Florida Technical College, Auburndale, FL 129

Florida Technical College, DeLand, FL 130

Florida Technical College, Jacksonville, FL 130

Florida Technical College, Orlando, FL 130

Herzing College, Atlanta, GA 148

Herzing College, Birmingham, AL 70

Herzing College, Kenner, LA 178

Herzing College, Madison, WI 330

Herzing College, Minneapolis, MN 195

Herzing College, Winter Park, FL 131

Island Drafting and Technical Institute, Amityville, NY 230

CIVIL ENGINEERING TECHNOLOGY/ TECHNICIAN

ITI Technical College, Baton Rouge, LA 178

CLINICAL LABORATORY SCIENCE/ MEDICAL TECHNOLOGY/ TECHNOLOGIST

Douglas Education Center, Monessen, PA 259

ECPI Technical College, Glen Allen, VA 316

ECPI Technical College, Richmond, VA 316

ECPI Technical College, Roanoke, VA 317

McCann School of Business, Hazleton, PA 266

McCann School of Business, Pottsville, PA 267

McCann School of Business, Scranton, PA 267

McCann School of Business, Sunbury, PA 267

McIntosh College, Dover, NH 213

North Florida Institute, Orange Park, FL 140

Stevens-Henager College - Provo, Orem, UT 311

Stevens-Henager College - Salt Lake City, Salt Lake City, UT 312

Wood Tobe-Coburn School, New York, NY 233

CLINICAL PASTORAL COUNSELING/ PATIENT COUNSELING

South University, Columbia, SC 286
South University, Montgomery, AL 71
South University, Savannah, GA 151
South University, West Palm Beach, FL 142

CLINICAL/MEDICAL LABORATORY ASSISTANT

Antonelli College, Cincinnati, OH 237
Antonelli College, Hattiesburg, MS 199
Antonelli College, Jackson, MS 200
Bryan College, Springfield, MO 201
Bryan College, Topeka, KS 169
Business Institute of Pennsylvania, Meadville, PA 255
Business Institute of Pennsylvania, Sharon, PA 255
Career Education Institute, Brockton, MA 184
Career Education Institute, Henderson, NV 210
Career Education Institute, Lincoln, RI 283
Career Education Institute, Lowell, MA 184
Career Education Institute, Marietta, GA 146
Career Education Institute, Norcross, GA 146
Clarita Career College, Canyon Country, CA 92
Dickinson Business School/Career Point Business School, Tulsa, OK 246
Douglas Education Center, Monessen, PA 259
ECPI College of Technology, Charlotte, NC 234
ECPI College of Technology, Greensboro, NC 235
ECPI College of Technology, Greenville, SC 285
ECPI College of Technology, Manassas, VA 315
ECPI College of Technology, Newport News, VA 315
ECPI College of Technology, North Charleston, SC 285
ECPI College of Technology, Raleigh, NC 235
ECPI College of Technology, Virginia Beach, VA 316
Empire College, Santa Rosa, CA 93
Gretna Career College, Gretna, LA 177
Hesser College, Manchester, NH 213
Institute for Business and Technology, Santa Clara, CA 96
McIntosh College, Dover, NH 213
National Career Education, Citrus Heights, CA 100
New England Institute of Technology, Warwick, RI 284
RETS Technical Center, Charlestown, MA 187
Stevens-Henager College, Boise, ID 153
Stevens-Henager College, Logan, UT 311
Stevens-Henager College, Ogden, UT 311

CLINICAL/MEDICAL LABORATORY SCIENCES AND ALLIED PROFESSIONS, OTHER

Douglas Education Center, Monessen, PA 259
Hesser College, Manchester, NH 213
McIntosh College, Dover, NH 213
Mildred Elley, Pittsfield, MA 186

CLINICAL/MEDICAL LABORATORY TECHNICIAN

Apollo College, Albuquerque, NM 223
Apollo College, Boise, ID 153
Apollo College-Phoenix, Inc., Phoenix, AZ 74
Apollo College, Portland, OR 249
Apollo College, Spokane, WA 324
Bryman College, Alhambra, CA 88
Bryman College, Anaheim, CA 88
Bryman College, City of Industry, CA 88
Bryman College, Earth City, MO 201
Bryman College, Everett, WA 325
Bryman College, Gardena, CA 88
Bryman College, Hayward, CA 89
Bryman College, Los Angeles, CA 89
Bryman College, Lynnwood, WA 326
Bryman College, New Orleans, LA 176
Bryman College, Ontario, CA 89
Bryman College, Port Orchard, WA 326
Bryman College, Renton, WA 326
Bryman College, Reseda, CA 89
Bryman College, San Bernardino, CA 90
Bryman College, San Francisco, CA 90
Bryman College, San Jose, CA 90
Bryman College, Tacoma, WA 326
Bryman College, Torrance, CA 90
Career Education Institute, Brockton, MA 184
Career Education Institute, Henderson, NV 210
Career Education Institute, Lincoln, RI 283
Career Education Institute, Lowell, MA 184
Career Education Institute, Marietta, GA 146
Career Education Institute, Norcross, GA 146
Delta School of Business & Technology, Lake Charles, LA 177
CollegeAmerica - Denver, Denver, CO 113
Douglas Education Center, Monessen, PA 259
Empire College, Santa Rosa, CA 93
Harrison Career Institute, Allentown, PA 262
Harrison Career Institute, Baltimore, MD 181
Harrison Career Institute, Clifton, NJ 218
Harrison Career Institute, Delran, NJ 218
Harrison Career Institute, Deptford, NJ 219
Harrison Career Institute, Ewing, NJ 219
Harrison Career Institute, Jersey City, NJ 219
Harrison Career Institute, Oakhurst, NJ 219
Harrison Career Institute, Philadelphia, PA 263
Harrison Career Institute, Reading, PA 263
Harrison Career Institute, South Orange, NJ 220
Harrison Career Institute, Vineland, NJ 220
Harrison Career Institute, Wilmington, DE 121
Hesser College, Manchester, NH 213
Keiser College, Daytona Beach, FL 134
Keiser College, Fort Lauderdale, FL 134

Keiser College, Lakeland, FL 135
Keiser College, Melbourne, FL 135
Keiser College, Miami, FL 135
Keiser College, Orlando, FL 135
Keiser College, Pembroke Pines, FL 136
Keiser College, Port St. Lucie, FL 136
Keiser College, Sarasota, FL 136
Keiser College, Tallahassee, FL 136
Keiser College, West Palm Beach, FL 137
Mandl School, New York, NY 231
McIntosh College, Dover, NH 213
MedVance Institute, Atlantis, FL 138
MedVance Institute, Baton Rouge, LA 179
MedVance Institute, Cookeville, TN 290
MedVance Institute, Fort Lauderdale, FL 138
MedVance Institute, Houston, TX 301
MedVance Institute, Miami, FL 138
MedVance Institute, Port St. Lucie, FL 138
New England Institute of Technology, Warwick, RI 284
Stevens-Henager College - Provo, Orem, UT 311

COMMERCIAL AND ADVERTISING ART

Academy College, Minneapolis, MN 192
Academy of Art University, San Francisco, CA 83
American InterContinental University, Atlanta, GA 145
American InterContinental University, Houston, TX 293
American InterContinental University, Los Angeles, CA 85
American InterContinental University, San Antonio, TX 293
American InterContinental University, Weston, FL 121
Antonelli College, Cincinnati, OH 237
Antonelli College, Hattiesburg, MS 199
Antonelli College, Jackson, MS 200
The Art Institute of Atlanta, Atlanta, GA 145
The Art Institute of California - Los Angeles, Santa Monica, CA 85
The Art Institute of California - Orange County, Santa Ana, CA 86
The Art Institute of California - San Diego, San Diego, CA 86
The Art Institute of California - San Francisco, San Francisco, CA 86
The Art Institute of Charlotte, Charlotte, NC 233
The Art Institute of Colorado, Denver, CO 111
The Art Institute of Dallas, Dallas, TX 294
The Art Institute of Houston, Houston, TX 294
The Art Institute of Las Vegas, Henderson, NV 209
The Art Institute of Philadelphia, Philadelphia, PA 252
The Art Institute of Phoenix, Phoenix, AZ 76
The Art Institute of Pittsburgh, Pittsburgh, PA 252
The Art Institute of Portland, Portland, OR 249
The Art Institute of Seattle, Seattle, WA 324
The Art Institute of Washington, Arlington, VA 314

The Art Institutes International Minnesota, Minneapolis, MN 193
ATI Career Training Center, Dallas, TX 294
ATI Career Training Center, Fort Lauderdale, FL 122
ATI Career Training Center, Miami, FL 123
ATI Career Training Center, North Richland Hills, TX 295
ATI Career Training Center, Oakland Park, FL 123
Bauder College, Atlanta, GA 146
Berks Technical Institute, Wyomissing, PA 253
Bradford School, Columbus, OH 237
Bradford School, Pittsburgh, PA 254
Bradley Academy for the Visual Arts, York, PA 254
Briarcliffe College, Bethpage, NY 226
Briarcliffe College, Patchogue, NY 226
Brooks College, Long Beach, CA 86
Brooks College, Sunnyvale, CA 86
Brown College, Mendota Heights, MN 193
CHI Institute, Broomall, PA 256
CHI Institute, Southampton, PA 256
Collins College: A School of Design and Technology, Tempe, AZ 77
CollegeAmerica - Fort Collins, Fort Collins, CO 113
Douglas Education Center, Monessen, PA 259
Florida Metropolitan University - North Orlando Campus, Orlando, FL 128
Gibbs College, Boston, MA 185
Gibbs College, Livingston, NJ 218
Gibbs College, Norwalk, CT 119
Globe College, Oakdale, MN 194
Hagerstown Business College, Hagerstown, MD 181
Hesser College, Manchester, NH 213
Hickey College, St. Louis, MO 202
Hussian School of Art, Philadelphia, PA 263
The Illinois Institute of Art - Chicago, Chicago, IL 156
International Academy of Design & Technology, Chicago, IL 157
International Academy of Design & Technology, Orlando, FL 132
International Academy of Design & Technology, Pittsburgh, PA 264
International Academy of Design & Technology, Tampa, FL 132
International Academy of Design & Technology, Troy, MI 189
International Academy of Design and Technology, Henderson, NV 210
International Academy of Design and Technology, Nashville, TN 289
International Academy of Design and Technology, San Antonio, TX 298
International Academy of Design and Technology, Schaumburg, IL 157

International Academy of Design and Technology, Seattle, WA 327

International Business College, El Paso, TX 298

International Business College, El Paso, TX 299

International Business College, Fort Wayne, IN 165

International Business College, Indianapolis, IN 165

Joe Kubert School of Cartoon and Graphic Art Inc., Dover, NJ 221

Katharine Gibbs School, Melville, NY 231

Katharine Gibbs School, New York, NY 231

Katharine Gibbs School, Norristown, PA 264

Katharine Gibbs School, Piscataway, NJ 221

Keiser College, Daytona Beach, FL 134

Keiser College, Fort Lauderdale, FL 134

Keiser College, Lakeland, FL 135

Keiser College, Melbourne, FL 135

Keiser College, Miami, FL 135

Keiser College, Orlando, FL 135

Keiser College, Pembroke Pines, FL 136

Keiser College, Port St. Lucie, FL 136

Keiser College, Sarasota, FL 136

Keiser College, Tallahassee, FL 136

Keiser College, West Palm Beach, FL 137

Lehigh Valley College, Center Valley, PA 266

Louisville Technical Institute, Louisville, KY 172

McIntosh College, Dover, NH 213

Miami International University of Art & Design, Miami, FL 138

Minneapolis Business College, Roseville, MN 196

Pittsburgh Technical Institute, Oakdale, PA 269

Platt College, Huntington Beach, CA 101

Platt College, Lawton, OK 247

Platt College - Los Angeles, Inc, Alhambra, CA 102

Platt College, Oklahoma City, OK 248

Platt College, Ontario, CA 102

Platt College, Tulsa, OK 248

Provo College, Provo, UT 310

The New England Institute of Art, Brookline, MA 186

Remington College - Fort Worth Campus, Fort Worth, TX 304

Remington College - New Orleans Campus, Metairie, LA 180

Remington College - Tampa Campus, Tampa, FL 141

Schuylkill Institute of Business and Technology, Pottsville, PA 270

Silicon Valley College, Emeryville, CA 105

Silicon Valley College, Fremont, CA 106

Silicon Valley College, San Jose, CA 106

Southwest Florida College, Tampa, FL 143

Stevens-Henager College, Boise, ID 153

Stevens-Henager College, Logan, UT 311

Stevens-Henager College, Ogden, UT 311

Utah Career College, West Jordan, UT 312

Vatterott College, Broadview Heights, OH 245

Vatterott College, Des Moines, IA 168

Vatterott College, Joplin, MO 206

Vatterott College, Kansas City, MO 207

Vatterott College, Memphis, TN 292

Vatterott College, OÆFallon , MO 207

Vatterott College, Oklahoma City, OK 248

Vatterott College, Omaha, NE 209

Vatterott College, Quincy, IL 160

Vatterott College, Springfield, MO 208

Vatterott College, St. Ann, MO 207

Vatterott College, St. Joseph, MO 207

Vatterott College, St. Louis, MO 208

Vatterott College, Tulsa, OK 249

Vatterott College, Wichita, KS 169

Virginia College at Birmingham, Birmingham, AL 72

Virginia Marti College of Art and Design, Lakewood, OH 246

Westwood College - Atlanta Campus, Atlanta, GA 151

Westwood College - Chicago Du Page, Woodridge, IL 160

Westwood College - Chicago Loop Campus, Chicago, IL 161

Westwood College - Chicago O'Hare Airport, Chicago, IL 161

Westwood College - Denver North, Denver, CO 118

Westwood College - Denver South, Denver, CO 118

Westwood College - Fort Worth, Euless, TX 308

Westwood College - Houston South Campus, Houston, TX 308

Westwood College - Inland Empire, Upland, CA 109

Wood Tobe-Coburn School, New York, NY 233

COMMERCIAL PHOTOGRAPHY

The Art Institute of Colorado, Denver, CO 111

The Art Institute of Pittsburgh, Pittsburgh, PA 252

Brown College, Mendota Heights, MN 193

Lehigh Valley College, Center Valley, PA 266

Remington College - Tampa Campus, Tampa, FL 141

COMMUNICATION SYSTEMS INSTALLATION AND REPAIR TECHNOLOGY

ATI Career Training Center, Dallas, TX 294

ATI Career Training Center, Fort Lauderdale, FL 122

ATI Career Training Center, Miami, FL 123

ATI Career Training Center, North Richland Hills, TX 295

ATI Career Training Center, Oakland Park, FL 123

Briarcliffe College, Bethpage, NY 226

Briarcliffe College, Patchogue, NY 226

CHI Institute, Broomall, PA 256

CHI Institute, Southampton, PA 256

Hesser College, Manchester, NH 213

Indiana Business College, Anderson, IN 162

Indiana Business College, Columbus, IN 163

Indiana Business College, Evansville, IN 163

Indiana Business College, Fort Wayne, IN 163

Indiana Business College, Indianapolis, IN 163

Indiana Business College, Lafayette, IN 163

Indiana Business College, Marion, IN 164

Indiana Business College, Muncie, IN 164

Indiana Business College, Terre Haute, IN 164

Katharine Gibbs School, Melville, NY 231

Katharine Gibbs School, New York, NY 231

Katharine Gibbs School, Norristown, PA 264

Katharine Gibbs School, Piscataway, NJ 221

TESST College of Technology, Alexandria, VA 323

TESST College of Technology, Baltimore, MD 182

TESST College of Technology, Beltsville, MD 183

TESST College of Technology, Towson, MD 183

COMMUNICATIONS TECHNOLOGY/ TECHNICIAN

The Art Institute of Fort Lauderdale, Fort Lauderdale, FL 122

ATI Career Training Center, Dallas, TX 294

ATI Career Training Center, Fort Lauderdale, FL 122

ATI Career Training Center, Miami, FL 123

ATI Career Training Center, North Richland Hills, TX 295

ATI Career Training Center, Oakland Park, FL 123

Brown College, Mendota Heights, MN 193

Colorado Technical University, Colorado Springs, CO 113

ECPI College of Technology, Charlotte, NC 234

ECPI College of Technology, Greensboro, NC 235

ECPI College of Technology, Greenville, SC 285

ECPI College of Technology, Manassas, VA 315

ECPI College of Technology, Newport News, VA 315

ECPI College of Technology, North Charleston, SC 285

ECPI College of Technology, Raleigh, NC 235

ECPI College of Technology, Virginia Beach, VA 316

Herzing College, Atlanta, GA 148

Herzing College, Birmingham, AL 70

Herzing College, Kenner, LA 178

Herzing College, Madison, WI 330

Herzing College, Minneapolis, MN 195

Herzing College, Winter Park, FL 131

HoHoKus RETS School of Business and Medical Technical Services, Nutley, NJ 220

International College of Broadcasting, Dayton, OH 240

ITT Technical Institute, Albany, NY 230

ITT Technical Institute, Albuquerque, NM 223

ITT Technical Institute, Anaheim, CA 96

ITT Technical Institute, Arlington, TX 299

ITT Technical Institute, Arnold, MO 202

ITT Technical Institute, Austin, TX 299

ITT Technical Institute, Bessemer, AL 71

ITT Technical Institute, Boise, ID 153

ITT Technical Institute, Bothell, WA 327

ITT Technical Institute, Burr Ridge, IL 157

ITT Technical Institute, Canton, MI 189

ITT Technical Institute, Chantilly, VA 317

ITT Technical Institute, Dayton, OH 240

ITT Technical Institute, Duluth, GA 149

ITT Technical Institute, Earth City, MO 202

ITT Technical Institute, Eden Prairie, MN 195

ITT Technical Institute, Fort Lauderdale, FL 133

ITT Technical Institute, Fort Wayne, IN 165

ITT Technical Institute, Getzville, NY 230

ITT Technical Institute, Grand Rapids, MI 189

ITT Technical Institute, Green Bay, WI 331

ITT Technical Institute, Greenfield, WI 331

ITT Technical Institute, Greenville, SC 285

ITT Technical Institute, Henderson, NV 211

ITT Technical Institute, Hilliard, OH 240

ITT Technical Institute, Houston, TX 299

ITT Technical Institute, Houston, TX 300

ITT Technical Institute, Indianapolis, IN 165

ITT Technical Institute, Jacksonville, FL 133

ITT Technical Institute, Kansas City, MO 203

ITT Technical Institute, Kennesaw, GA 149

ITT Technical Institute, King of Prussia, PA 264

ITT Technical Institute, Knoxville, TN 289

ITT Technical Institute, Lake Mary, FL 133

ITT Technical Institute, Lathrop, CA 96

ITT Technical Institute, Little Rock, AR 82

ITT Technical Institute, Liverpool, NY 230

ITT Technical Institute, Louisville, KY 171

ITT Technical Institute, Matteson, IL 158

ITT Technical Institute, Mechanicsburg, PA 264

ITT Technical Institute, Memphis, TN 289

ITT Technical Institute, Miami, FL 133

ITT Technical Institute, Monroeville, PA 264

ITT Technical Institute, Mount Prospect, IL 158

ITT Technical Institute, Murray, UT 310

ITT Technical Institute, Nashville, TN 289

ITT Technical Institute, Newburgh, IN 166

ITT Technical Institute, Norfolk, VA 318

ITT Technical Institute, Norwood, MA 186

ITT Technical Institute, Norwood, OH 240

ITT Technical Institute, Omaha, NE 209

ITT Technical Institute, Owings Mills, MD 181

ITT Technical Institute, Oxnard, CA 97

ITT Technical Institute, Pittsburg, PA 264

ITT Technical Institute, Portland, OR 250

ITT Technical Institute, Rancho Cordova, CA 97

ITT Technical Institute, Richardson, TX 300

ITT Technical Institute, Richmond, VA 318

ITT Technical Institute, Saint Rose, LA 179
ITT Technical Institute, San Antonio, TX 300
ITT Technical Institute, San Bernardino, CA 97
ITT Technical Institute, San Diego, CA 97
ITT Technical Institute, Seattle, WA 327
ITT Technical Institute, Spokane, WA 328
ITT Technical Institute, Springfield, VA 318
ITT Technical Institute, Strongsville, OH 241
ITT Technical Institute, Sylmar, CA 98
ITT Technical Institute, Tampa, FL 134
ITT Technical Institute, Tempe, AZ 79
ITT Technical Institute, Thornton, CO 115
ITT Technical Institute, Torrance, CA 98
ITT Technical Institute, Troy, MI 190
ITT Technical Institute, Tucson, AZ 79
ITT Technical Institute, Tulsa, OK 247
ITT Technical Institute, Warrensville Heights, OH 241
ITT Technical Institute, West Covina, CA 98
ITT Technical Institute, Woburn, MA 186
ITT Technical Institute, Youngstown, OH 241
Jones International University, Englewood, CO 115
New England Institute of Technology, Warwick, RI 284
New England School of Communications, Bangor, ME 180
TESST College of Technology, Alexandria, VA 323
TESST College of Technology, Baltimore, MD 182
TESST College of Technology, Beltsville, MD 183
TESST College of Technology, Towson, MD 183
Western Technical College, El Paso, TX 307
Westwood College - Atlanta Northlake, Atlanta, GA 152

COMPUTER AND INFORMATION SCIENCES AND SUPPORT SERVICES, OTHER

American InterContinental University, Atlanta, GA 145
American InterContinental University, Houston, TX 293
American InterContinental University, Los Angeles, CA 85
American InterContinental University, San Antonio, TX 293
American InterContinental University, Weston, FL 121
ATI Career Training Center, Dallas, TX 294
ATI Career Training Center, Fort Lauderdale, FL 122
ATI Career Training Center, Miami, FL 123
ATI Career Training Center, North Richland Hills, TX 295
ATI Career Training Center, Oakland Park, FL 123
Briarcliffe College, Bethpage, NY 226
Briarcliffe College, Patchogue, NY 226
Brookstone College of Business, Charlotte, NC 234
Brookstone College of Business, Greensboro, NC 234
Bryan College, Springfield, MO 201
Bryan College, Topeka, KS 169
Career Education Institute, Brockton, MA 184
Career Education Institute, Henderson, NV 210
Career Education Institute, Lincoln, RI 283

Career Education Institute, Lowell, MA 184
Career Education Institute, Marietta, GA 146
Career Education Institute, Norcross, GA 146
The Chubb Institute, Alpharetta, GA 147
The Chubb Institute, Arlington, VA 314
The Chubb Institute, Cherry Hill, NJ 215
The Chubb Institute, Chicago, IL 155
The Chubb Institute, Jersey City, NJ 216
The Chubb Institute, New York, NY 228
The Chubb Institute, North Brunswick, NJ 216
The Chubb Institute, Parsippany, NJ 216
The Chubb Institute, Springfield, PA 256
The Chubb Institute, Westbury, NY 228
Florida Technical College, Auburndale, FL 129
Florida Technical College, DeLand, FL 130
Florida Technical College, Jacksonville, FL 130
Florida Technical College, Orlando, FL 130
Gibbs College - Cranston, Cranston, RI 283
Herzing College, Atlanta, GA 148
Herzing College, Birmingham, AL 70
Herzing College, Kenner, LA 178
Herzing College, Madison, WI 330
Herzing College, Minneapolis, MN 195
Herzing College, Winter Park, FL 131
Hesser College, Manchester, NH 213
High-Tech Institute, Irving, TX 298
High-Tech Institute, Kansas City, MO 202
High-Tech Institute, Las Vegas, NV 210
High-Tech Institute, Marietta, GA 149
High-Tech Institute, Memphis, TN 288
High-Tech Institute, Nashville, TN 288
High-Tech Institute, Orlando, FL 132
High-Tech Institute, Phoenix, AZ 78
High-Tech Institute, Sacramento, CA 96
High-Tech Institute, St. Louis Park, MN 195
Peirce College, Philadelphia, PA 268
Sanford-Brown Institute, Atlanta, GA 150
Sanford-Brown Institute, Dallas, TX 305
Sanford-Brown Institute, Garden City, NY 232
Sanford-Brown Institute, Houston, TX 305
Sanford-Brown Institute, Houston, TX 306
Sanford-Brown Institute, Jacksonville, FL 142
Sanford-Brown Institute, Landover, MD 182
Sanford-Brown Institute, Lauderdale Lakes, FL 142
Sanford-Brown Institute, New York, NY 232
Sanford-Brown Institute, Springfield, MA 187
Sanford-Brown Institute, Tampa, FL 142
Sanford-Brown Institute, Trevose, PA 270
Sanford-Brown Institute, White Plains, NY 232
Virginia College at Birmingham, Birmingham, AL 72

COMPUTER AND INFORMATION SCIENCES, GENERAL

ATI Career Training Center, Dallas, TX 294
ATI Career Training Center, Fort Lauderdale, FL 122
ATI Career Training Center, Miami, FL 123
ATI Career Training Center, North Richland Hills, TX 295
ATI Career Training Center, Oakland Park, FL 123
Briarcliffe College, Bethpage, NY 226
Briarcliffe College, Patchogue, NY 226
Brown Mackie College, Orange County Campus, Santa Ana, CA 87
Bryan College, Springfield, MO 201
Bryan College, Topeka, KS 169
The Chubb Institute, Alpharetta, GA 147
The Chubb Institute, Arlington, VA 314
The Chubb Institute, Cherry Hill, NJ 215
The Chubb Institute, Chicago, IL 155
The Chubb Institute, Jersey City, NJ 216
The Chubb Institute, New York, NY 228
The Chubb Institute, North Brunswick, NJ 216
The Chubb Institute, Parsippany, NJ 216
The Chubb Institute, Springfield, PA 256
The Chubb Institute, Westbury, NY 228
Coleman College, La Mesa, CA 92
Coleman College, San Marcos, CA 93
Davis College, Toledo, OH 239
ECPI College of Technology, Charlotte, NC 234
ECPI College of Technology, Greensboro, NC 235
ECPI College of Technology, Greenville, SC 285
ECPI College of Technology, Manassas, VA 315
ECPI College of Technology, Newport News, VA 315
ECPI College of Technology, North Charleston, SC 285
ECPI College of Technology, Raleigh, NC 235
ECPI College of Technology, Virginia Beach, VA 316
Florida Technical College, Auburndale, FL 129
Florida Technical College, DeLand, FL 130
Florida Technical College, Jacksonville, FL 130
Florida Technical College, Orlando, FL 130
Herzing College, Atlanta, GA 148
Herzing College, Birmingham, AL 70
Herzing College, Kenner, LA 178
Herzing College, Madison, WI 330
Herzing College, Minneapolis, MN 195
Herzing College, Winter Park, FL 131
Hesser College, Manchester, NH 213
Indiana Business College, Anderson, IN 162
Indiana Business College, Columbus, IN 163
Indiana Business College, Evansville, IN 163
Indiana Business College, Fort Wayne, IN 163
Indiana Business College, Indianapolis, IN 163
Indiana Business College, Lafayette, IN 163
Indiana Business College, Marion, IN 164

Indiana Business College, Muncie, IN 164
Indiana Business College, Terre Haute, IN 164
National American University, Albuquerque, NM 224
National American University, Brooklyn Center, MN 197
National American University, Colorado Springs, CO 115
National American University, Denver, CO 116
National American University, Ellsworth AFB, SD 286
National American University, Kansas City, MO 204
National American University, Minneapolis, MN 197
National American University, Overland Park, KS 169
National American University, Rapid City, SD 286
National American University, Rio Rancho, NM 224
National American University, Roseville, MN 197
National College of Business and Technology, Arecibo, PR 282
National College of Business and Technology, Cincinnati, OH 241
National College of Business and Technology, Indianapolis, IN 166
National College of Business and Technology, Kettering, OH 242
New England Institute of Technology, Warwick, RI 284
Southwest Florida College, Tampa, FL 143
Virginia College at Birmingham, Birmingham, AL 72

COMPUTER AND INFORMATION SCIENCES, OTHER

American School of Technology, Columbus, OH 237
ATI Career Training Center, Dallas, TX 294
ATI Career Training Center, Fort Lauderdale, FL 122
ATI Career Training Center, Miami, FL 123
ATI Career Training Center, North Richland Hills, TX 295
ATI Career Training Center, Oakland Park, FL 123
Bay State College, Boston, MA 183
Briarcliffe College, Bethpage, NY 226
Briarcliffe College, Patchogue, NY 226
Brookstone College of Business, Charlotte, NC 234
Brookstone College of Business, Greensboro, NC 234
Brown College, Mendota Heights, MN 193
Brown Mackie College, Atlanta Campus, Norcross, GA 146
Brown Mackie College, Dallas Campus, Garland, TX 296
Brown Mackie College, Fort Wayne Campus, Fort Wayne, IN 162
Brown Mackie College, Louisville Campus, Louisville, KY 170
Brown Mackie College, Moline Campus, Moline, IL 154
Brown Mackie College, Northern Kentucky Campus, Fort Mitchell, KY 170
Brown Mackie College, Salina Campus, Salina, KS 168
Bryan College, Springfield, MO 201
Bryan College, Topeka, KS 169
Career Institute of Health and Technology, Brooklyn, NY

ITT Technical Institute, Miami, FL 133
ITT Technical Institute, Monroeville, PA 264
ITT Technical Institute, Mount Prospect, IL 158
ITT Technical Institute, Murray, UT 310
ITT Technical Institute, Nashville, TN 289
ITT Technical Institute, Newburgh, IN 166
ITT Technical Institute, Norfolk, VA 318
ITT Technical Institute, Norwood, MA 186
ITT Technical Institute, Norwood, OH 240
ITT Technical Institute, Omaha, NE 209
ITT Technical Institute, Owings Mills, MD 181
ITT Technical Institute, Oxnard, CA 97
ITT Technical Institute, Pittsburg, PA 264
ITT Technical Institute, Portland, OR 250
ITT Technical Institute, Rancho Cordova, CA 97
ITT Technical Institute, Richardson, TX 300
ITT Technical Institute, Richmond, VA 318
ITT Technical Institute, Saint Rose, LA 179
ITT Technical Institute, San Antonio, TX 300
ITT Technical Institute, San Bernardino, CA 97
ITT Technical Institute, San Diego, CA 97
ITT Technical Institute, Seattle, WA 327
ITT Technical Institute, Spokane, WA 328
ITT Technical Institute, Springfield, VA 318
ITT Technical Institute, Strongsville, OH 241
ITT Technical Institute, Sylmar, CA 98
ITT Technical Institute, Tampa, FL 134
ITT Technical Institute, Tempe, AZ 79
ITT Technical Institute, Thornton, CO 115
ITT Technical Institute, Torrance, CA 98
ITT Technical Institute, Troy, MI 190
ITT Technical Institute, Tucson, AZ 79
ITT Technical Institute, Tulsa, OK 247
ITT Technical Institute, Warrensville Heights, OH 241
ITT Technical Institute, West Covina, CA 98
ITT Technical Institute, Woburn, MA 186
ITT Technical Institute, Youngstown, OH 241
Keiser College, Daytona Beach, FL 134
Keiser College, Fort Lauderdale, FL 134
Keiser College, Lakeland, FL 135
Keiser College, Melbourne, FL 135
Keiser College, Miami, FL 135
Keiser College, Orlando, FL 135
Keiser College, Pembroke Pines, FL 136
Keiser College, Port St. Lucie, FL 136
Keiser College, Sarasota, FL 136
Keiser College, Tallahassee, FL 136
Keiser College, West Palm Beach, FL 137
Maric College, Anaheim, CA 99
Maric College, Los Angeles, CA 100
Maric College, North Hollywood, CA 99
Maric College, Sacramento, CA 99
Maric College, Salida, CA 99

Maric College, San Diego, CA 100
Maric College, Vista, CA 100
McCann School of Business, Hazleton, PA 266
McCann School of Business, Pottsville, PA267
McCann School of Business, Scranton, PA 267
McCann School of Business, Sunbury, PA 267
Miller-Motte Technical College, Cary, NC 236
Miller-Motte Technical College, Chattanooga, TN 290
Miller-Motte Technical College, Clarksville, TN 290
Miller-Motte Technical College, Lynchburg, VA 320
Miller-Motte Technical College, North Charleston, SC 285
Miller-Motte Technical College, Wilmington, NC 236
Missouri Tech, St. Louis, MO 204
Morrison University, Reno, NV 212
National College of Business & Technology, Bayamon, PR 282
National College of Business & Technology, Bluefield, VA 320
National College of Business & Technology, Bristol, TN 290
National College of Business & Technology, Charlottes-ville, VA 320
National College of Business & Technology, Danville, KY 172
National College of Business & Technology, Danville, VA 320
National College of Business & Technology, Florence, KY 172
National College of Business & Technology, Harrison-burg, VA 321
National College of Business & Technology, Knoxville, TN 291
National College of Business & Technology, Lexington, KY 173
National College of Business & Technology, Louisville, KY 173
National College of Business & Technology, Lynchburg, VA 321
National College of Business & Technology, Martinsville, VA 321
National College of Business & Technology, Nashville, TN 291
National College of Business & Technology, Pikeville, KY 173
National College of Business & Technology, Richmond, KY 173
National College of Business & Technology, Rio Grande, PR 282
National College of Business & Technology, Salem, VA 321
Neumont University, Salt Lake City, UT 310
Parks College, Aurora, CO 116
Parks College, Denver, CO 116

Parks College, McLean, VA 321
South University, Columbia, SC 286
South University, Montgomery, AL 71
South University, Savannah, GA 151
South University, West Palm Beach, FL 142
Stevens-Henager College, Boise, ID 153
Stevens-Henager College, Logan, UT 311
Stevens-Henager College, Ogden, UT 311
Stevens-Henager College - Provo, Orem, UT 311
Stevens-Henager College - Salt Lake City, Salt Lake City, UT 312
Sullivan University, Lexington, KY 174
Sullivan University, Louisville, KY 175
Virginia College at Birmingham, Birmingham, AL 72

COMPUTER AND INFORMATION SYSTEMS SECURITY

Academy College, Minneapolis, MN 192
Academy of Medical Arts and Business, Harrisburg, PA 252
Advanced Training Associates, El Cajon, CA 84
Berks Technical Institute, Wyomissing, PA 253
Briarcliffe College, Bethpage, NY 226
Briarcliffe College, Patchogue, NY 226
Brown College, Mendota Heights, MN 193
Capella University, Minneapolis, MN 194
Career Education Institute, Brockton, MA 184
Career Education Institute, Henderson, NV 210
Career Education Institute, Lincoln, RI 283
Career Education Institute, Lowell, MA 184
Career Education Institute, Marietta, GA 146
Career Education Institute, Norcross, GA 146
Career Institute of Health and Technology, Brooklyn, NY 227
Career Institute of Health and Technology, Garden City, NY 227
Career Institute of Health and Technology, Rego Park, NY 228
The Chubb Institute, Alpharetta, GA 147
The Chubb Institute, Arlington, VA 314
The Chubb Institute, Cherry Hill, NJ 215
The Chubb Institute, Chicago, IL 155
The Chubb Institute, Jersey City, NJ 216
The Chubb Institute, New York, NY 228
The Chubb Institute, North Brunswick, NJ 216
The Chubb Institute, Parsippany, NJ 216
The Chubb Institute, Springfield, PA 256
The Chubb Institute, Westbury, NY 228
Coleman College, La Mesa, CA 92
Coleman College, San Marcos, CA 93
Colorado Technical University Denver Campus, Greenwood Village, CO 114
Colorado Technical University, Colorado Springs, CO 113

Computer Learning Network, Altoona, PA 258
Computer Learning Network, Mechanicsburg, PA 258
ECPI College of Technology, Charlotte, NC 234
ECPI College of Technology, Greensboro, NC 235
ECPI College of Technology, Greenville, SC 285
ECPI College of Technology, Manassas, VA 315
ECPI College of Technology, Newport News, VA 315
ECPI College of Technology, North Charleston, SC 285
ECPI College of Technology, Raleigh, NC 235
ECPI College of Technology, Virginia Beach, VA 316
ECPI Technical College, Glen Allen, VA 316
ECPI Technical College, Richmond, VA 316
ECPI Technical College, Roanoke, VA 317
Fountainhead College of Technology, Knoxville, TN 288
Gibbs College - Cranston, Cranston, RI 283
Herzing College, Atlanta, GA 148
Herzing College, Birmingham, AL 70
Herzing College, Kenner, LA 178
Herzing College, Madison, WI 330
Herzing College, Minneapolis, MN 195
Herzing College, Winter Park, FL 131
Hesser College, Manchester, NH 213
High-Tech Institute, Irving, TX 298
High-Tech Institute, Kansas City, MO 202
High-Tech Institute, Las Vegas, NV 210
High-Tech Institute, Marietta, GA 149
High-Tech Institute, Memphis, TN 288
High-Tech Institute, Nashville, TN 288
High-Tech Institute, Orlando, FL 132
High-Tech Institute, Phoenix, AZ 78
High-Tech Institute, Sacramento, CA 96
High-Tech Institute, St. Louis Park, MN 195
ICM School of Business & Medical Careers, Pittsburgh, PA 263
ITI Technical College, Baton Rouge, LA 178
ITT Technical Institute, Albany, NY 230
ITT Technical Institute, Albuquerque, NM 223
ITT Technical Institute, Anaheim, CA 96
ITT Technical Institute, Arlington, TX 299
ITT Technical Institute, Arnold, MO 202
ITT Technical Institute, Austin, TX 299
ITT Technical Institute, Bessemer, AL 71
ITT Technical Institute, Boise, ID 153
ITT Technical Institute, Bothell, WA 327
ITT Technical Institute, Burr Ridge, IL 157
ITT Technical Institute, Canton, MI 189
ITT Technical Institute, Chantilly, VA 317
ITT Technical Institute, Dayton, OH 240
ITT Technical Institute, Duluth, GA 149
ITT Technical Institute, Earth City, MO 202
ITT Technical Institute, Eden Prairie, MN 195
ITT Technical Institute, Fort Lauderdale, FL 133
ITT Technical Institute, Fort Wayne, IN 165

ITT Technical Institute, Getzville, NY 230
ITT Technical Institute, Grand Rapids, MI 189
ITT Technical Institute, Green Bay, WI 331
ITT Technical Institute, Greenfield, WI 331
ITT Technical Institute, Greenville, SC 285
ITT Technical Institute, Henderson, NV 211
ITT Technical Institute, Hilliard, OH 240
ITT Technical Institute, Houston, TX 299
ITT Technical Institute, Houston, TX 300
ITT Technical Institute, Indianapolis, IN 165
ITT Technical Institute, Jacksonville, FL 133
ITT Technical Institute, Kansas City, MO 203
ITT Technical Institute, Kennesaw, GA 149
ITT Technical Institute, King of Prussia, PA 264
ITT Technical Institute, Knoxville, TN 289
ITT Technical Institute, Lake Mary, FL 133
ITT Technical Institute, Lathrop, CA 96
ITT Technical Institute, Little Rock, AR 82
ITT Technical Institute, Liverpool, NY 230
ITT Technical Institute, Louisville, KY 171
ITT Technical Institute, Matteson, IL 158
ITT Technical Institute, Mechanicsburg, PA 264
ITT Technical Institute, Memphis, TN 289
ITT Technical Institute, Miami, FL 133
ITT Technical Institute, Monroeville, PA 264
ITT Technical Institute, Mount Prospect, IL 158
ITT Technical Institute, Murray, UT 310
ITT Technical Institute, Nashville, TN 289
ITT Technical Institute, Newburgh, IN 166
ITT Technical Institute, Norfolk, VA 318
ITT Technical Institute, Norwood, MA 186
ITT Technical Institute, Norwood, OH 240
ITT Technical Institute, Omaha, NE 209
ITT Technical Institute, Owings Mills, MD 181
ITT Technical Institute, Oxnard, CA 97
ITT Technical Institute, Pittsburg, PA 264
ITT Technical Institute, Portland, OR 250
ITT Technical Institute, Rancho Cordova, CA 97
ITT Technical Institute, Richardson, TX 300
ITT Technical Institute, Richmond, VA 318
ITT Technical Institute, Saint Rose, LA 179
ITT Technical Institute, San Antonio, TX 300
ITT Technical Institute, San Bernardino, CA 97
ITT Technical Institute, San Diego, CA 97
ITT Technical Institute, Seattle, WA 327
ITT Technical Institute, Spokane, WA 328
ITT Technical Institute, Springfield, VA 318
ITT Technical Institute, Strongsville, OH 241
ITT Technical Institute, Sylmar, CA 98
ITT Technical Institute, Tampa, FL 134
ITT Technical Institute, Tempe, AZ 79
ITT Technical Institute, Thornton, CO 115
ITT Technical Institute, Torrance, CA 98

ITT Technical Institute, Troy, MI 190
ITT Technical Institute, Tucson, AZ 79
ITT Technical Institute, Tulsa, OK 247
ITT Technical Institute, Warrensville Heights, OH 241
ITT Technical Institute, West Covina, CA 98
ITT Technical Institute, Woburn, MA 186
ITT Technical Institute, Youngstown, OH 241
Keiser College, Daytona Beach, FL 134
Keiser College, Fort Lauderdale, FL 134
Keiser College, Lakeland, FL 135
Keiser College, Melbourne, FL 135
Keiser College, Miami, FL 135
Keiser College, Orlando, FL 135
Keiser College, Pembroke Pines, FL 136
Keiser College, Port St. Lucie, FL 136
Keiser College, Sarasota, FL 136
Keiser College, Tallahassee, FL 136
Keiser College, West Palm Beach, FL 137
Louisville Technical Institute, Louisville, KY 172
Missouri Tech, St. Louis, MO 204
MTI College of Business and Technology, Houston, TX 301
Peirce College, Philadelphia, PA 268
Pittsburgh Technical Institute, Oakdale, PA 269
Rasmussen College Eagan, Eagan, MN 198
Rasmussen College Minnetonka, Minnetonka, MN 199
Remington College - Tampa Campus, Tampa, FL 141
Schuylkill Institute of Business and Technology, Pottsville, PA 270
Southwest Florida College, Tampa, FL 143
Stratford University, Falls Church , VA 322
Stratford University, Woodbridge, VA 322
Technical Career Institute, New York, NY 233
Tri-State Business Institute, Erie, PA 272
Virginia College at Austin, Austin, TX 307
Virginia College at Birmingham, Birmingham, AL 72
Westwood College - Chicago Du Page, Woodridge, IL 160
Westwood College - Chicago River Oaks, Calumet City, IL 161
Westwood College - Denver South, Denver, CO 118
Westwood College - Inland Empire, Upland, CA 109

COMPUTER ENGINEERING TECHNOLOGIES/TECHNICIANS, OTHER

Berks Technical Institute, Wyomissing, PA 253
Charter College, Anchorage, AK 74
The Chubb Institute, Alpharetta, GA 147
The Chubb Institute, Arlington, VA 314
The Chubb Institute, Cherry Hill, NJ 215
The Chubb Institute, Chicago, IL 155
The Chubb Institute, Jersey City, NJ 216
The Chubb Institute, New York, NY 228

Boldface type indicates that the school is a participating institution in the ⊕ *Imagine America* Scholarship Program

The Chubb Institute, North Brunswick, NJ 216
The Chubb Institute, Parsippany, NJ 216
The Chubb Institute, Springfield, PA 256
The Chubb Institute, Westbury, NY 228
ECPI College of Technology, Charlotte, NC 234
ECPI College of Technology, Greensboro, NC 235
ECPI College of Technology, Greenville, SC 285
ECPI College of Technology, Manassas, VA 315
ECPI College of Technology, Newport News, VA 315
ECPI College of Technology, North Charleston, SC 285
ECPI College of Technology, Raleigh, NC 235
ECPI College of Technology, Virginia Beach, VA 316

COMPUTER ENGINEERING TECHNOLOGY/TECHNICIAN

ATI Career Training Center, Dallas, TX 294
ATI Career Training Center, Fort Lauderdale, FL 122
ATI Career Training Center, Miami, FL 123
ATI Career Training Center, North Richland Hills, TX 295
ATI Career Training Center, Oakland Park, FL 123
Berks Technical Institute, Wyomissing, PA 253
Briarcliffe College, Bethpage, NY 226
Briarcliffe College, Patchogue, NY 226
Brown Mackie College, Lenexa Campus, Lenexa, KS 168
Career Institute of Health and Technology, Brooklyn, NY 227
Career Institute of Health and Technology, Garden City, NY 227
Career Institute of Health and Technology, Rego Park, NY 228
Charter College, Anchorage, AK 74
CHI Institute, Broomall, PA 256
CHI Institute, Southampton, PA 256
The Chubb Institute, Alpharetta, GA 147
The Chubb Institute, Arlington, VA 314
The Chubb Institute, Cherry Hill, NJ 215
The Chubb Institute, Chicago, IL 155
The Chubb Institute, Jersey City, NJ 216
The Chubb Institute, New York, NY 228
The Chubb Institute, North Brunswick, NJ 216
The Chubb Institute, Parsippany, NJ 216
The Chubb Institute, Springfield, PA 256
The Chubb Institute, Westbury, NY 228
The Cittone Institute, Edison, NJ 217
The Cittone Institute, Mount Laurel, NJ 217
The Cittone Institute, Paramus, NJ 217
The Cittone Institute, Philadelphia, PA 257
The Cittone Institute, Plymouth Meeting, PA 257
Colorado Technical University, Colorado Springs, CO 113
ECPI College of Technology, Charlotte, NC 234
ECPI College of Technology, Greensboro, NC 235
ECPI College of Technology, Greenville, SC 285

ECPI College of Technology, Manassas, VA 315
ECPI College of Technology, Newport News, VA 315
ECPI College of Technology, North Charleston, SC 285
ECPI College of Technology, Raleigh, NC 235
ECPI College of Technology, Virginia Beach, VA 316
ECPI Technical College, Glen Allen, VA 316
ECPI Technical College, Richmond, VA 316
ECPI Technical College, Roanoke, VA 317
EduTek College, Stow, OH 239
Florida Career College, Hialeah, FL 125
Florida Career College, Miami, FL 125
Florida Career College, Pembroke Pines, FL 126
Florida Career College, West Palm Beach, FL 126
Florida Technical College, Auburndale, FL 129
Florida Technical College, DeLand, FL 130
Florida Technical College, Jacksonville, FL 130
Florida Technical College, Orlando, FL 130
Globe College, Oakdale, MN 194
Grantham University, Kansas City, MO 177
Herzing College, Atlanta, GA 148
Herzing College, Birmingham, AL 70
Herzing College, Kenner, LA 178
Herzing College, Madison, WI 330
Herzing College, Minneapolis, MN 195
Herzing College, Winter Park, FL 131
Hesser College, Manchester, NH 213
HoHoKus RETS School of Business and Medical Technical Services, Nutley, NJ 220
ICM School of Business & Medical Careers, Pittsburgh, PA 263
Island Drafting and Technical Institute, Amityville, NY 230
ITI Technical College, Baton Rouge, LA 178
ITT Technical Institute, Albany, NY 230
ITT Technical Institute, Albuquerque, NM 223
ITT Technical Institute, Anaheim, CA 96
ITT Technical Institute, Arlington, TX 299
ITT Technical Institute, Arnold, MO 202
ITT Technical Institute, Austin, TX 299
ITT Technical Institute, Bessemer, AL 71
ITT Technical Institute, Boise, ID 153
ITT Technical Institute, Bothell, WA 327
ITT Technical Institute, Burr Ridge, IL 157
ITT Technical Institute, Canton, MI 189
ITT Technical Institute, Chantilly, VA 317
ITT Technical Institute, Dayton, OH 240
ITT Technical Institute, Duluth, GA 149
ITT Technical Institute, Earth City, MO 202
ITT Technical Institute, Eden Prairie, MN 195
ITT Technical Institute, Fort Lauderdale, FL 133
ITT Technical Institute, Fort Wayne, IN 165
ITT Technical Institute, Getzville, NY 230
ITT Technical Institute, Grand Rapids, MI 189
ITT Technical Institute, Green Bay, WI 331

ITT Technical Institute, Greenfield, WI 331
ITT Technical Institute, Greenville, SC 285
ITT Technical Institute, Henderson, NV 211
ITT Technical Institute, Hilliard, OH 240
ITT Technical Institute, Houston, TX 299
ITT Technical Institute, Houston, TX 300
ITT Technical Institute, Indianapolis, IN 165
ITT Technical Institute, Jacksonville, FL 133
ITT Technical Institute, Kansas City, MO 203
ITT Technical Institute, Kennesaw, GA 149
ITT Technical Institute, King of Prussia, PA 264
ITT Technical Institute, Knoxville, TN 289
ITT Technical Institute, Lake Mary, FL 133
ITT Technical Institute, Lathrop, CA 96
ITT Technical Institute, Little Rock, AR 82
ITT Technical Institute, Liverpool, NY 230
ITT Technical Institute, Louisville, KY 171
ITT Technical Institute, Matteson, IL 158
ITT Technical Institute, Mechanicsburg, PA 264
ITT Technical Institute, Memphis, TN 289
ITT Technical Institute, Miami, FL 133
ITT Technical Institute, Monroeville, PA 264
ITT Technical Institute, Mount Prospect, IL 158
ITT Technical Institute, Murray, UT 310
ITT Technical Institute, Nashville, TN 289
ITT Technical Institute, Newburgh, IN 166
ITT Technical Institute, Norfolk, VA 318
ITT Technical Institute, Norwood, MA 186
ITT Technical Institute, Norwood, OH 240
ITT Technical Institute, Omaha, NE 209
ITT Technical Institute, Owings Mills, MD 181
ITT Technical Institute, Oxnard, CA 97
ITT Technical Institute, Pittsburg, PA 264
ITT Technical Institute, Portland, OR 250
ITT Technical Institute, Rancho Cordova, CA 97
ITT Technical Institute, Richardson, TX 300
ITT Technical Institute, Richmond, VA 318
ITT Technical Institute, Saint Rose, LA 179
ITT Technical Institute, San Antonio, TX 300
ITT Technical Institute, San Bernardino, CA 97
ITT Technical Institute, San Diego, CA 97
ITT Technical Institute, Seattle, WA 327
ITT Technical Institute, Spokane, WA 328
ITT Technical Institute, Springfield, VA 318
ITT Technical Institute, Strongsville, OH 241
ITT Technical Institute, Sylmar, CA 98
ITT Technical Institute, Tampa, FL 134
ITT Technical Institute, Tempe, AZ 79
ITT Technical Institute, Thornton, CO 115
ITT Technical Institute, Torrance, CA 98
ITT Technical Institute, Troy, MI 190
ITT Technical Institute, Tucson, AZ 79
ITT Technical Institute, Tulsa, OK 247

ITT Technical Institute, Warrensville Heights, OH 241
ITT Technical Institute, West Covina, CA 98
ITT Technical Institute, Woburn, MA 186
ITT Technical Institute, Youngstown, OH 241
Keiser College, Daytona Beach, FL 134
Keiser College, Fort Lauderdale, FL 134
Keiser College, Lakeland, FL 135
Keiser College, Melbourne, FL 135
Keiser College, Miami, FL 135
Keiser College, Orlando, FL 135
Keiser College, Pembroke Pines, FL 136
Keiser College, Port St. Lucie, FL 136
Keiser College, Sarasota, FL 136
Keiser College, Tallahassee, FL 136
Keiser College, West Palm Beach, FL 137
Louisville Technical Institute, Louisville, KY 172
Missouri Tech, St. Louis, MO 204
MTI College of Business and Technology, Houston, TX 301
National College of Business & Technology, Bayamon, PR 282
National College of Business & Technology, Bluefield, VA 320
National College of Business & Technology, Bristol, TN 290
National College of Business & Technology, Charlottesville, VA 320
National College of Business & Technology, Danville, KY 172
National College of Business & Technology, Danville, VA 320
National College of Business & Technology, Florence, KY 172
National College of Business & Technology, Harrisonburg, VA 321
National College of Business & Technology, Knoxville, TN 291
National College of Business & Technology, Lexington, KY 173
National College of Business & Technology, Louisville, KY 173
National College of Business & Technology, Lynchburg, VA 321
National College of Business & Technology, Martinsville, VA 321
National College of Business & Technology, Nashville, TN 291
National College of Business & Technology, Pikeville, KY 173
National College of Business & Technology, Richmond, KY 173
National College of Business & Technology, Rio Grande, PR 282

National College of Business & Technology, Salem, VA 321

National Institute of Technology, Austin , TX 302

National Institute of Technology, Cross Lanes, WV 329

National Institute of Technology, Detroit, MI 190

National Institute of Technology, Houston, TX 302

National Institute of Technology, Long Beach, CA 101

National Institute of Technology, San Antonio, TX 302

National Institute of Technology, Southfield, MI 190

Platt College, Huntington Beach, CA 101

Platt College, Lawton, OK 247

Platt College, Oklahoma City, OK 248

Platt College, Ontario, CA 102

Platt College, Tulsa, OK 248

Remington College - Mobile Campus, Mobile, AL 71

Remington College - Pinellas Campus, Largo, FL 141

Remington College - Tampa Campus, Tampa, FL 141

San Joaquin Valley College, Bakersfield, CA 103

San Joaquin Valley College, Fresno, CA 103

San Joaquin Valley College, Modesto, CA 104

San Joaquin Valley College, Rancho Cucamonga, CA 104

San Joaquin Valley College, Visalia, CA 104

Savannah River College, Augusta, GA 151

Sawyer College, Merrillville, IN 167

Spencerian College-Lexington, Lexington, KY 174

Stratford University, Falls Church , VA 322

Stratford University, Woodbridge, VA 322

TESST College of Technology, Alexandria, VA 323

TESST College of Technology, Baltimore, MD 182

TESST College of Technology, Beltsville, MD 183

TESST College of Technology, Towson, MD 183

Vatterott College, Broadview Heights, OH 245

Vatterott College, Des Moines, IA 168

Vatterott College, Joplin, MO 206

Vatterott College, Kansas City, MO 207

Vatterott College, Memphis, TN 292

Vatterott College, OÆFallon , MO 207

Vatterott College, Oklahoma City, OK 248

Vatterott College, Omaha, NE 209

Vatterott College, Quincy, IL 160

Vatterott College, Springfield, MO 208

Vatterott College, St. Ann, MO 207

Vatterott College, St. Joseph, MO 207

Vatterott College, St. Louis, MO 208

Vatterott College, Tulsa, OK 249

Vatterott College, Wichita, KS 16

Westwood College - Anaheim, Anaheim, CA 109

Westwood College - Chicago O'Hare Airport, Chicago, IL 161

Westwood College - Chicago River Oaks, Calumet City, IL 161

Westwood College - Dallas, Dallas, TX 308

Westwood College - Denver North, Denver, CO 118

Westwood College - Denver South, Denver, CO 118

Westwood College - Houston South Campus, Houston, TX 308

Westwood College - Los Angeles, Inglewood, CA 110

Westwood College - Los Angeles, Los Angeles, CA 110 9

COMPUTER ENGINEERING, OTHER

ATI Career Training Center, Dallas, TX 294

ATI Career Training Center, Fort Lauderdale, FL 122

ATI Career Training Center, Miami, FL 123

ATI Career Training Center, North Richland Hills, TX 295

ATI Career Training Center, Oakland Park, FL 123

Berks Technical Institute, Wyomissing, PA 253

Charter College, Anchorage, AK 74

The Chubb Institute, Alpharetta, GA 147

The Chubb Institute, Arlington, VA 314

The Chubb Institute, Cherry Hill, NJ 215

The Chubb Institute, Chicago, IL 155

The Chubb Institute, Jersey City, NJ 216

The Chubb Institute, New York, NY 228

The Chubb Institute, North Brunswick, NJ 216

The Chubb Institute, Parsippany, NJ 216

The Chubb Institute, Springfield, PA 256

The Chubb Institute, Westbury, NY 228

The Cittone Institute, Edison, NJ 217

The Cittone Institute, Mount Laurel, NJ 217

The Cittone Institute, Paramus, NJ 217

The Cittone Institute, Philadelphia, PA 257

The Cittone Institute, Plymouth Meeting, PA 257

ICM School of Business & Medical Careers, Pittsburgh, PA 263

Florida Metropolitan University - South Orlando Campus, Orlando, FL 129

Louisville Technical Institute, Louisville, KY 172

Minnesota School of Business - Brooklyn Center, Brooklyn Center, MN 196

Missouri Tech, St. Louis, MO 204

Remington College - Baton Rouge Campus, Baton Rouge, LA 179

Remington College - Tampa Campus, Tampa, FL 141

Virginia College at Jackson, Jackson, MS 200

Westwood College - Atlanta Campus, Atlanta, GA 151

Westwood College - Atlanta Northlake, Atlanta, GA 152

Westwood College - Chicago River Oaks, Calumet City, IL 161

Westwood College - Houston South Campus, Houston, TX 308

COMPUTER GRAPHICS

Academy College, Minneapolis, MN 192

Academy of Art University, San Francisco, CA 83

COMPUTER HARDWARE ENGINEERING

TESST College of Technology, Beltsville, MD 183
TESST College of Technology, Towson, MD 183
Virginia College at Jackson, Jackson, MS 200

COMPUTER HARDWARE TECHNOLOGY/TECHNICIAN

Antonelli College, Cincinnati, OH 237
Antonelli College, Hattiesburg, MS 199
Antonelli College, Jackson, MS 200
ATI Career Training Center, Dallas, TX 294
ATI Career Training Center, Fort Lauderdale, FL 122
ATI Career Training Center, Miami, FL 123
ATI Career Training Center, North Richland Hills, TX 295
ATI Career Training Center, Oakland Park, FL 123
Berks Technical Institute, Wyomissing, PA 253
Brookstone College of Business, Charlotte, NC 234
Brookstone College of Business, Greensboro, NC 234
Charter College, Anchorage, AK 74
ECPI College of Technology, Charlotte, NC 234
ECPI College of Technology, Greensboro, NC 235
ECPI College of Technology, Greenville, SC 285
ECPI College of Technology, Manassas, VA 315
ECPI College of Technology, Newport News, VA 315
ECPI College of Technology, North Charleston, SC 285
ECPI College of Technology, Raleigh, NC 235
ECPI College of Technology, Virginia Beach, VA 316
Florida Technical College, Auburndale, FL 129
Florida Technical College, DeLand, FL 130
Florida Technical College, Jacksonville, FL 130
Florida Technical College, Orlando, FL 130
Gibbs College - Cranston, Cranston, RI 283
Herzing College, Atlanta, GA 148
Herzing College, Birmingham, AL 70
Herzing College, Kenner, LA 178
Herzing College, Madison, WI 330
Herzing College, Minneapolis, MN 195
Herzing College, Winter Park, FL 131
Rasmussen College St. Cloud, St. Cloud, MN 199
RETS Technical Center, Charlestown, MA 187

COMPUTER INSTALLATION AND REPAIR TECHNOLOGY/TECHNICIAN

A-1 Business and Technical College, Caguas, PR 275
Academy College, Minneapolis, MN 192
Advanced Training Associates, El Cajon, CA 84
Antonelli College, Cincinnati, OH 237
Antonelli College, Hattiesburg, MS 199
Antonelli College, Jackson, MS 200
ATI Career Training Center, Dallas, TX 294
ATI Career Training Center, Fort Lauderdale, FL 122
ATI Career Training Center, Miami, FL 123
ATI Career Training Center, North Richland Hills, TX 295

ATI Career Training Center, Oakland Park, FL 123
Berks Technical Institute, Wyomissing, PA 253
Briarcliffe College, Bethpage, NY 226
Briarcliffe College, Patchogue, NY 226
Brookstone College of Business, Charlotte, NC 234
Brookstone College of Business, Greensboro, NC 234
Brown Mackie College, South Bend Campus, South Bend, IN 162
Bryan College, Springfield, MO 201
Bryan College, Topeka, KS 169
Career Education Institute, Brockton, MA 184
Career Education Institute, Henderson, NV 210
Career Education Institute, Lincoln, RI 283
Career Education Institute, Lowell, MA 184
Career Education Institute, Marietta, GA 146
Career Education Institute, Norcross, GA 146
Central Coast College, Salinas, CA 92
CHI Institute, Broomall, PA 256
CHI Institute, Southampton, PA 256
The Chubb Institute, Alpharetta, GA 147
The Chubb Institute, Arlington, VA 314
The Chubb Institute, Cherry Hill, NJ 215
The Chubb Institute, Chicago, IL 155
The Chubb Institute, Jersey City, NJ 216
The Chubb Institute, New York, NY 228
The Chubb Institute, North Brunswick, NJ 216
The Chubb Institute, Parsippany, NJ 216
The Chubb Institute, Springfield, PA 256
The Chubb Institute, Westbury, NY 228
The Cittone Institute, Edison, NJ 217
The Cittone Institute, Mount Laurel, NJ 217
The Cittone Institute, Paramus, NJ 217
The Cittone Institute, Philadelphia, PA 257
The Cittone Institute, Plymouth Meeting, PA 257
Colegio Mayor de Tecnologia, Arroyo, PR 276
CollegeAmerica - Denver, Denver, CO 113
Computer Learning Network, Altoona, PA 258
Computer Learning Network, Mechanicsburg, PA 258
Coyne American Institute, Chicago, IL 155
Coyne American Institute, Chicago, IL 156
ECPI College of Technology, Charlotte, NC 234
ECPI College of Technology, Greensboro, NC 235
ECPI College of Technology, Greenville, SC 285
ECPI College of Technology, Manassas, VA 315
ECPI College of Technology, Newport News, VA 315
ECPI College of Technology, North Charleston, SC 285
ECPI College of Technology, Raleigh, NC 235
ECPI College of Technology, Virginia Beach, VA 316
ECPI Technical College, Glen Allen, VA 316
ECPI Technical College, Richmond, VA 316
ECPI Technical College, Roanoke, VA 317
Florida Career College, Hialeah, FL 125

National College of Business and Technology, Indianapolis, IN 166

National College of Business and Technology, Kettering, OH 242

National Institute of Technology, Austin , TX 302

National Institute of Technology, Cross Lanes, WV 329

National Institute of Technology, Detroit, MI 190

National Institute of Technology, Houston, TX 302

National Institute of Technology, Long Beach, CA 101

National Institute of Technology, San Antonio, TX 302

National Institute of Technology, Southfield, MI 190

Ohio Valley College of Technology, East Liverpool, OH 242

Pennco Tech Bristol, PA 269

Pennco Tech, Blackwood, NJ 222

Ponce Paramedical College, Inc., Coto Laurel, PR 282

Remington College - Mobile Campus, Mobile, AL 71

Remington College - Pinellas Campus, Largo, FL 141

Rockford Business College, Rockford, IL 159

San Joaquin Valley College, Bakersfield, CA 103

San Joaquin Valley College, Fresno, CA 103

San Joaquin Valley College, Modesto, CA 104

San Joaquin Valley College, Rancho Cucamonga, CA 104

San Joaquin Valley College, Visalia, CA 104

Southwest Florida College, Tampa, FL 143

Stevens-Henager College, Boise, ID 153

Stevens-Henager College, Logan, UT 311

Stevens-Henager College, Ogden, UT 311

Stevens-Henager College - Salt Lake City, Salt Lake City, UT 312

Stratford University, Falls Church , VA 322

Stratford University, Woodbridge, VA 322

Sullivan University, Lexington, KY 174

Sullivan University, Louisville, KY 175

TESST College of Technology, Alexandria, VA 323

TESST College of Technology, Baltimore, MD 182

TESST College of Technology, Beltsville, MD 183

TESST College of Technology, Towson, MD 183

Tri-State Business Institute, Erie, PA 272

Vatterott College, Broadview Heights, OH 245

Vatterott College, Des Moines, IA 168

Vatterott College, Joplin, MO 206

Vatterott College, Kansas City, MO 207

Vatterott College, Memphis, TN 292

Vatterott College, OÆFallon , MO 207

Vatterott College, Oklahoma City, OK 248

Vatterott College, Omaha, NE 209

Vatterott College, Quincy, IL 160

Vatterott College, Springfield, MO 208

Vatterott College, St. Ann, MO 207

Vatterott College, St. Joseph, MO 207

Vatterott College, St. Louis, MO 208

Vatterott College, Tulsa, OK 249

Vatterott College, Wichita, KS 169

Virginia College at Birmingham, Birmingham, AL 72

Virginia College at Huntsville, Huntsville, AL 73

Virginia College at Jackson, Jackson, MS 200

West Virginia Junior College, Bridgeport, WV 329

West Virginia Junior College, Charleston, WV 329

West Virginia Junior College, Morgantown, WV 330

Western Technical College, El Paso, TX 307

COMPUTER PROGRAMMING, OTHER

ATI Career Training Center, Dallas, TX 294

ATI Career Training Center, Fort Lauderdale, FL 122

ATI Career Training Center, Miami, FL 123

ATI Career Training Center, North Richland Hills, TX 295

ATI Career Training Center, Oakland Park, FL 123

Briarcliffe College, Bethpage, NY 226

Briarcliffe College, Patchogue, NY 226

Brown Mackie College, Akron Campus, Akron, OH 238

Bryan College, Springfield, MO 201

Bryan College, Topeka, KS 169

Capella University, Minneapolis, MN 194

CHI Institute, Broomall, PA 256

CHI Institute, Southampton, PA 256

The Chubb Institute, Alpharetta, GA 147

The Chubb Institute, Arlington, VA 314

The Chubb Institute, Cherry Hill, NJ 215

The Chubb Institute, Chicago, IL 155

The Chubb Institute, Jersey City, NJ 216

The Chubb Institute, New York, NY 228

The Chubb Institute, North Brunswick, NJ 216

The Chubb Institute, Parsippany, NJ 216

The Chubb Institute, Springfield, PA 256

The Chubb Institute, Westbury, NY 228

Coleman College, La Mesa, CA 92

Coleman College, San Marcos, CA 93

Computer Learning Network, Altoona, PA 258

Computer Learning Network, Mechanicsburg, PA 258

Draughons Junior College, Bowling Green, KY 171

Draughons Junior College, Clarksville, TN 287

Draughons Junior College, Murfreesboro, TN 287

Draughons Junior College, Nashville, TN 288

ECPI College of Technology, Charlotte, NC 234

ECPI College of Technology, Greensboro, NC 235

ECPI College of Technology, Greenville, SC 285

ECPI College of Technology, Manassas, VA 315

ECPI College of Technology, Newport News, VA 315

ECPI College of Technology, North Charleston, SC 285

ECPI College of Technology, Raleigh, NC 235

ECPI College of Technology, Virginia Beach, VA 316

Florida Technical College, Auburndale, FL 129

Florida Technical College, DeLand, FL 130

Florida Technical College, Jacksonville, FL 130
Florida Technical College, Orlando, FL 130
Hagerstown Business College, Hagerstown, MD 181
Herzing College, Atlanta, GA 148
Herzing College, Birmingham, AL 70
Herzing College, Kenner, LA 178
Herzing College, Madison, WI 330
Herzing College, Minneapolis, MN 195
Herzing College, Winter Park, FL 131
Hesser College, Manchester, NH 213
ICM School of Business & Medical Careers, Pittsburgh, PA 263
Instituto Banca y Comercio, Caguas, PR 279
Instituto Banca y Comercio, Cayey, PR 279
Instituto Banca y Comercio, Fajardo, PR 279
Instituto Banca y Comercio, Guayama, PR 280
Instituto Banca y Comercio, Manati, PR 280
Instituto Banca y Comercio, Mayaguez, PR 280
Instituto Banca y Comercio, Ponce, PR 280
ITI Technical College, Baton Rouge, LA 178
Minnesota School of Business - Brooklyn Center, Brooklyn Center, MN 196
Missouri Tech, St. Louis, MO 204
Provo College, Provo, UT 310
Remington College - Pinellas Campus, Largo, FL 141
South University, Columbia, SC 286
South University, Montgomery, AL 71
South University, Savannah, GA 151
South University, West Palm Beach, FL 142
Stevens-Henager College, Boise, ID 153
Stevens-Henager College, Logan, UT 311
Stevens-Henager College, Ogden, UT 311
Stevens-Henager College - Salt Lake City, Salt Lake City, UT 312
TESST College of Technology, Alexandria, VA 323
TESST College of Technology, Baltimore, MD 182
TESST College of Technology, Beltsville, MD 183
TESST College of Technology, Towson, MD 183
Virginia College at Birmingham, Birmingham, AL 72
Virginia College at Jackson, Jackson, MS 200

COMPUTER PROGRAMMING, SPECIFIC APPLICATIONS

Academy College, Minneapolis, MN 192
Academy of Medical Arts and Business, Harrisburg, PA 252
The Art Institute of California - San Francisco, San Francisco, CA 86
ATI Career Training Center, Dallas, TX 294
ATI Career Training Center, Fort Lauderdale, FL 122
ATI Career Training Center, Miami, FL 123
ATI Career Training Center, North Richland Hills, TX 295

ATI Career Training Center, Oakland Park, FL 123
Blair College, Colorado Springs, CO 112
Bradford School, Columbus, OH 237
Bradford School, Pittsburgh, PA 254
Briarcliffe College, Bethpage, NY 226
Briarcliffe College, Patchogue, NY 226
Brown Mackie College, Akron Campus, Akron, OH 238
Brown Mackie College, Cincinnati Campus, Cincinnati, OH 238
Brown Mackie College, Lenexa Campus, Lenexa, KS 168
Bryan College, Springfield, MO 201
Bryan College, Topeka, KS 169
Capella University, Minneapolis, MN 194
Career Education Institute, Brockton, MA 184
Career Education Institute, Henderson, NV 210
Career Education Institute, Lincoln, RI 283
Career Education Institute, Lowell, MA 184
Career Education Institute, Marietta, GA 146
Career Education Institute, Norcross, GA 146
The Chubb Institute, Alpharetta, GA 147
The Chubb Institute, Arlington, VA 314
The Chubb Institute, Cherry Hill, NJ 215
The Chubb Institute, Chicago, IL 155
The Chubb Institute, Jersey City, NJ 216
The Chubb Institute, New York, NY 228
The Chubb Institute, North Brunswick, NJ 216
The Chubb Institute, Parsippany, NJ 216
The Chubb Institute, Springfield, PA 256
The Chubb Institute, Westbury, NY 228
CollegeAmerica - Denver, Denver, CO 113
Colegio Mayor de Tecnologia, Arroyo, PR 276
Collins College: A School of Design and Technology, Tempe, AZ 77
Computer Learning Network, Altoona, PA 258
Computer Learning Network, Mechanicsburg, PA 258
Draughons Junior College, Bowling Green, KY 171
Draughons Junior College, Clarksville, TN 287
Draughons Junior College, Murfreesboro, TN 287
Draughons Junior College, Nashville, TN 288
ECPI College of Technology, Charlotte, NC 234
ECPI College of Technology, Greensboro, NC 235
ECPI College of Technology, Greenville, SC 285
ECPI College of Technology, Manassas, VA 315
ECPI College of Technology, Newport News, VA 315
ECPI College of Technology, North Charleston, SC 285
ECPI College of Technology, Raleigh, NC 235
ECPI College of Technology, Virginia Beach, VA 316
ECPI Technical College, Glen Allen, VA 316
ECPI Technical College, Richmond, VA 316
ECPI Technical College, Roanoke, VA 317
Florida Career College, Hialeah, FL 125
Florida Career College, Miami, FL 125
Florida Career College, Pembroke Pines, FL 126

Florida Career College, West Palm Beach, FL 126
Florida Technical College, Auburndale, FL 129
Florida Technical College, DeLand, FL 130
Florida Technical College, Jacksonville, FL 130
Florida Technical College, Orlando, FL 130
Hagerstown Business College, Hagerstown, MD 181
Herzing College, Atlanta, GA 148
Herzing College, Birmingham, AL 70
Herzing College, Kenner, LA 178
Herzing College, Madison, WI 330
Herzing College, Minneapolis, MN 195
Herzing College, Winter Park, FL 131
Hesser College, Manchester, NH 213
Hickey College, St. Louis, MO 202
ICM School of Business & Medical Careers, Pittsburgh, PA 263
Instituto Banca y Comercio, Caguas, PR 279
Instituto Banca y Comercio, Cayey, PR 279
Instituto Banca y Comercio, Fajardo, PR 279
Instituto Banca y Comercio, Guayama, PR 280
Instituto Banca y Comercio, Manati, PR 280
Instituto Banca y Comercio, Mayaguez, PR 280
Instituto Banca y Comercio, Ponce, PR 280
ITI Technical College, Baton Rouge, LA 178
Key College, Fort Lauderdale, FL 137
McCann School of Business, Hazleton, PA 266
McCann School of Business, Pottsville, PA 267
McCann School of Business, Scranton, PA 267
McCann School of Business, Sunbury, PA 267
Minneapolis Business College, Roseville, MN 196
Missouri Tech, St. Louis, MO 204
National American University, Albuquerque, NM 224
National American University, Brooklyn Center, MN 197
National American University, Colorado Springs, CO 115
National American University, Denver, CO 116
National American University, Ellsworth AFB, SD 286
National American University, Kansas City, MO 204
National American University, Minneapolis, MN 197
National American University, Overland Park, KS 169
National American University, Rapid City, SD 286
National American University, Rio Rancho, NM 224
National American University, Roseville, MN 197
New England Institute of Technology, Warwick, RI 284
Peirce College, Philadelphia, PA 268
Remington College - Cleveland Campus, Cleveland, OH 242
Remington College - Pinellas Campus, Largo, FL 141
Remington College - Tempe Campus, Tempe, AZ 81
South University, Columbia, SC 286
South University, Montgomery, AL 71
South University, Savannah, GA 151
South University, West Palm Beach, FL 142
Springfield College, Springfield, MO 206

Stevens-Henager College, Boise, ID 153
Stevens-Henager College, Logan, UT 311
Stevens-Henager College, Ogden, UT 311
Stevens-Henager College - Provo, Orem, UT 311
Stevens-Henager College - Salt Lake City, Salt Lake City, UT 312
Stratford University, Falls Church , VA 322
Stratford University, Woodbridge, VA 322
Sullivan University, Lexington, KY 174
Sullivan University, Louisville, KY 175
Tri-State Business Institute, Erie, PA 272
Vatterott College, Broadview Heights, OH 245
Vatterott College, Des Moines, IA 168
Vatterott College, Joplin, MO 206
Vatterott College, Kansas City, MO 207
Vatterott College, Memphis, TN 292
Vatterott College, OÆFallon , MO 207
Vatterott College, Oklahoma City, OK 248
Vatterott College, Omaha, NE 209
Vatterott College, Quincy, IL 160
Vatterott College, Springfield, MO 208
Vatterott College, St. Ann, MO 207
Vatterott College, St. Joseph, MO 207
Vatterott College, St. Louis, MO 208
Vatterott College, Tulsa, OK 249
Vatterott College, Wichita, KS 169
Virginia College at Birmingham, Birmingham, AL 72
Wood Tobe-Coburn School, New York, NY 233

COMPUTER PROGRAMMING, VENDOR /PRODUCT CERTIFICATION

Academy of Medical Arts and Business, Harrisburg, PA 252
Briarcliffe College, Bethpage, NY 226
Briarcliffe College, Patchogue, NY 226
Brown Mackie College, Akron Campus, Akron, OH 238
Career Education Institute, Brockton, MA 184
Career Education Institute, Henderson, NV 210
Career Education Institute, Lincoln, RI 283
Career Education Institute, Lowell, MA 184
Career Education Institute, Marietta, GA 146
Career Education Institute, Norcross, GA 146
CHI Institute, Broomall, PA 256
CHI Institute, Southampton, PA 256
The Chubb Institute, Alpharetta, GA 147
The Chubb Institute, Arlington, VA 314
The Chubb Institute, Cherry Hill, NJ 215
The Chubb Institute, Chicago, IL 155
The Chubb Institute, Jersey City, NJ 216
The Chubb Institute, New York, NY 228
The Chubb Institute, North Brunswick, NJ 216
The Chubb Institute, Parsippany, NJ 216
The Chubb Institute, Springfield, PA 256

The Chubb Institute, Westbury, NY 228
Computer Learning Network, Altoona, PA 258
Computer Learning Network, Mechanicsburg, PA 258
Florida Metropolitan University - Lakeland Campus, Lakeland, FL 127
Florida Technical College, Auburndale, FL 129
Florida Technical College, DeLand, FL 130
Florida Technical College, Jacksonville, FL 130
Florida Technical College, Orlando, FL 130
Hagerstown Business College, Hagerstown, MD 181
Herzing College, Atlanta, GA 148
Herzing College, Birmingham, AL 70
Herzing College, Kenner, LA 178
Herzing College, Madison, WI 330
Herzing College, Minneapolis, MN 195
Herzing College, Winter Park, FL 131
Hesser College, Manchester, NH 213
ICM School of Business & Medical Careers, Pittsburgh, PA 263
Missouri Tech, St. Louis, MO 204
Peirce College, Philadelphia, PA 268
Remington College - Pinellas Campus, Largo, FL 141
Stevens-Henager College, Boise, ID 153
Stevens-Henager College, Logan, UT 311
Stevens-Henager College, Ogden, UT 311
Stevens-Henager College - Salt Lake City, Salt Lake City, UT 312
Virginia College at Birmingham, Birmingham, AL 72

COMPUTER PROGRAMMING/ PROGRAMMER, GENERAL

A-1 Business and Technical College, Caguas, PR 275
Academy College, Minneapolis, MN 192
Academy of Medical Arts and Business, Harrisburg, PA 252
Apollo College-Westside, Inc., Phoenix, AZ
ATI Career Training Center, Dallas, TX 294
ATI Career Training Center, Fort Lauderdale, FL 122
ATI Career Training Center, Miami, FL 123
ATI Career Training Center, North Richland Hills, TX 295
ATI Career Training Center, Oakland Park, FL 123
Bradford School, Columbus, OH 237
Bradford School, Pittsburgh, PA 254
Briarcliffe College, Bethpage, NY 226
Briarcliffe College, Patchogue, NY 226
Brown College, Mendota Heights, MN 193
Brown Mackie College, Akron Campus, Akron, OH 238
Brown Mackie College, Atlanta Campus, Norcross, GA 146
Brown Mackie College, Hopkinsville Campus, Hopkinsville, KY 170
Brown Mackie College, Los Angeles Campus, Santa Monica, CA 87

Brown Mackie College, Merrillville Campus, Merrillville, IN 162
Brown Mackie College, Miami Campus, Miami, FL 124
Brown Mackie College, Michigan City Campus, Michigan City, IN 162
Brown Mackie College, Moline Campus, Moline, IL 154
Brown Mackie College, North Canton Campus, North Canton, OH 239
Brown Mackie College, Northern Kentucky Campus, Fort Mitchell, KY 170
Brown Mackie College, San Diego Campus, San Diego, CA 87
Brown Mackie College, South Bend Campus, South Bend, IN 162
Bryan College, Springfield, MO 201
Bryan College, Topeka, KS 169
Capella University, Minneapolis, MN 194
Career Education Institute, Brockton, MA 184
Career Education Institute, Henderson, NV 210
Career Education Institute, Lincoln, RI 283
Career Education Institute, Lowell, MA 184
Career Education Institute, Marietta, GA 146
Career Education Institute, Norcross, GA 146
CHI Institute, Broomall, PA 256
CHI Institute, Southampton, PA 256
The Chubb Institute, Alpharetta, GA 147
The Chubb Institute, Arlington, VA 314
The Chubb Institute, Cherry Hill, NJ 215
The Chubb Institute, Chicago, IL 155
The Chubb Institute, Jersey City, NJ 216
The Chubb Institute, New York, NY 228
The Chubb Institute, North Brunswick, NJ 216
The Chubb Institute, Parsippany, NJ 216
The Chubb Institute, Springfield, PA 256
The Chubb Institute, Westbury, NY 228
Coleman College, La Mesa, CA 92
Coleman College, San Marcos, CA 93
CollegeAmerica - Colorado Springs, Colorado Springs, CO 112
CollegeAmerica - Denver, Denver, CO 113
CollegeAmerica - Fort Collins, Fort Collins, CO 113
Computer Learning Network, Altoona, PA 258
Computer Learning Network, Mechanicsburg, PA 258
Eagle Gate College, Murray, UT 309
Electronic Data Processing College of Puerto Rico - San Sebastian, San Sebastian, PR 277
Electronic Data Processing College of Puerto Rico, San Juan, PR 277
ECPI College of Technology, Charlotte, NC 234
ECPI College of Technology, Greensboro, NC 235
ECPI College of Technology, Greenville, SC 285
ECPI College of Technology, Manassas, VA 315
ECPI College of Technology, Newport News, VA 315

ECPI College of Technology, North Charleston, SC 285
ECPI College of Technology, Raleigh, NC 235
ECPI College of Technology, Virginia Beach, VA 316
ECPI Technical College, Glen Allen, VA 316
ECPI Technical College, Richmond, VA 316
ECPI Technical College, Roanoke, VA 317
Electronic Data Processing College of Puerto Rico, San Juan, PR 277
Erie Business Center South, New Castle, PA 262
Erie Business Center, Main, Erie, PA 261
Florida Career College, Hialeah, FL 125
Florida Career College, Miami, FL 125
Florida Career College, Pembroke Pines, FL 126
Florida Career College, West Palm Beach, FL 126
Florida Technical College, Auburndale, FL 129
Florida Technical College, DeLand, FL 130
Florida Technical College, Jacksonville, FL 130
Florida Technical College, Orlando, FL 130
Fountainhead College of Technology, Knoxville, TN 288
Gibbs College, Boston, MA 185
Gibbs College, Livingston, NJ 218
Gibbs College, Norwalk, CT 119
Gibbs School, Vienna, VA 317
Hagerstown Business College, Hagerstown, MD 181
Herzing College, Atlanta, GA 148
Herzing College, Birmingham, AL 70
Herzing College, Kenner, LA 178
Herzing College, Madison, WI 330
Herzing College, Minneapolis, MN 195
Herzing College, Winter Park, FL 131
Hesser College, Manchester, NH 213
Hickey College, St. Louis, MO 202
Huertas Junior College, Caguas, PR 277
ICM School of Business & Medical Careers, Pittsburgh, PA 263
Instituto Banca y Comercio, Caguas, PR 279
Instituto Banca y Comercio, Cayey, PR 279
Instituto Banca y Comercio, Fajardo, PR 279
Instituto Banca y Comercio, Guayama, PR 280
Instituto Banca y Comercio, Manati, PR 280
Instituto Banca y Comercio, Mayaguez, PR 280
Instituto Banca y Comercio, Ponce, PR 280
Instituto de Banca y Comercio, San Juan, PR 281
International Business College, El Paso, TX 298
International Business College, El Paso, TX 299
International Business College, Fort Wayne, IN 165
International Business College, Indianapolis, IN 165
ITI Technical College, Baton Rouge, LA 178
ITT Technical Institute, Albany, NY 230
ITT Technical Institute, Albuquerque, NM 223
ITT Technical Institute, Anaheim, CA 96
ITT Technical Institute, Arlington, TX 299
ITT Technical Institute, Arnold, MO 202

ITT Technical Institute, Austin, TX 299
ITT Technical Institute, Bessemer, AL 71
ITT Technical Institute, Boise, ID 153
ITT Technical Institute, Bothell, WA 327
ITT Technical Institute, Burr Ridge, IL 157
ITT Technical Institute, Canton, MI 189
ITT Technical Institute, Chantilly, VA 317
ITT Technical Institute, Dayton, OH 240
ITT Technical Institute, Duluth, GA 149
ITT Technical Institute, Earth City, MO 202
ITT Technical Institute, Eden Prairie, MN 195
ITT Technical Institute, Fort Lauderdale, FL 133
ITT Technical Institute, Fort Wayne, IN 165
ITT Technical Institute, Getzville, NY 230
ITT Technical Institute, Grand Rapids, MI 189
ITT Technical Institute, Green Bay, WI 331
ITT Technical Institute, Greenfield, WI 331
ITT Technical Institute, Greenville, SC 285
ITT Technical Institute, Henderson, NV 211
ITT Technical Institute, Hilliard, OH 240
ITT Technical Institute, Houston, TX 299
ITT Technical Institute, Houston, TX 300
ITT Technical Institute, Indianapolis, IN 165
ITT Technical Institute, Jacksonville, FL 133
ITT Technical Institute, Kansas City, MO 203
ITT Technical Institute, Kennesaw, GA 149
ITT Technical Institute, King of Prussia, PA 264
ITT Technical Institute, Knoxville, TN 289
ITT Technical Institute, Lake Mary, FL 133
ITT Technical Institute, Lathrop, CA 96
ITT Technical Institute, Little Rock, AR 82
ITT Technical Institute, Liverpool, NY 230
ITT Technical Institute, Louisville, KY 171
ITT Technical Institute, Matteson, IL 158
ITT Technical Institute, Mechanicsburg, PA 264
ITT Technical Institute, Memphis, TN 289
ITT Technical Institute, Miami, FL 133
ITT Technical Institute, Monroeville, PA 264
ITT Technical Institute, Mount Prospect, IL 158
ITT Technical Institute, Murray, UT 310
ITT Technical Institute, Nashville, TN 289
ITT Technical Institute, Newburgh, IN 166
ITT Technical Institute, Norfolk, VA 318
ITT Technical Institute, Norwood, MA 186
ITT Technical Institute, Norwood, OH 240
ITT Technical Institute, Omaha, NE 209
ITT Technical Institute, Owings Mills, MD 181
ITT Technical Institute, Oxnard, CA 97
ITT Technical Institute, Pittsburg, PA 264
ITT Technical Institute, Portland, OR 250
ITT Technical Institute, Rancho Cordova, CA 97
ITT Technical Institute, Richardson, TX 300
ITT Technical Institute, Richmond, VA 318

Boldface type indicates that the school is a participating institution in the 🎓 *Imagine America* Scholarship Program

Stratford University, Falls Church , VA 322
Stratford University, Woodbridge, VA 322
Sullivan University, Lexington, KY 174
Sullivan University, Louisville, KY 175
Technology Education College, Columbus, OH 245
Trinity College of Puerto Rico, Ponce, PR 283
Tri-State Business Institute, Erie, PA 272
Vatterott College, Broadview Heights, OH 245
Vatterott College, Des Moines, IA 168
Vatterott College, Joplin, MO 206
Vatterott College, Kansas City, MO 207
Vatterott College, Memphis, TN 292
Vatterott College, OÆFallon , MO 207
Vatterott College, Oklahoma City, OK 248
Vatterott College, Omaha, NE 209
Vatterott College, Quincy, IL 160
Vatterott College, Springfield, MO 208
Vatterott College, St. Ann, MO 207
Vatterott College, St. Joseph, MO 207
Vatterott College, St. Louis, MO 208
Vatterott College, Tulsa, OK 249
Vatterott College, Wichita, KS 169
Virginia College at Birmingham, Birmingham, AL 72
Westwood College - Chicago O'Hare Airport, Chicago, IL 161
Westwood College - Denver North, Denver, CO 118
Westwood College - Inland Empire, Upland, CA 109
Westwood College - Los Angeles, Inglewood, CA 110
Westwood College - Los Angeles, Los Angeles, CA 110
Wood Tobe-Coburn School, New York, NY 233

COMPUTER SCIENCE

Academy College, Minneapolis, MN 192
Brown Mackie College, Akron Campus, Akron, OH 238
Chaparral College, Tucson, AZ 77
Colorado Technical University Sioux Falls Campus, Sioux Falls, SD 286
ECPI College of Technology, Charlotte, NC 234
ECPI College of Technology, Greensboro, NC 235
ECPI College of Technology, Greenville, SC 285
ECPI College of Technology, Manassas, VA 315
ECPI College of Technology, Newport News, VA 315
ECPI College of Technology, North Charleston, SC 285
ECPI College of Technology, Raleigh, NC 235
ECPI College of Technology, Virginia Beach, VA 316
Herzing College, Atlanta, GA 148
Herzing College, Birmingham, AL 70
Herzing College, Kenner, LA 178
Herzing College, Madison, WI 330
Herzing College, Minneapolis, MN 195
Herzing College, Winter Park, FL 131
Hesser College, Manchester, NH 213
Southwestern College of Business, Cincinnati, OH 244

Southwestern College of Business, Dayton, OH 244
Southwestern College of Business, Florence, KY 174
Southwestern College of Business, Franklin, OH 245
Texas School of Business, Inc., Houston, TX 306

COMPUTER SOFTWARE AND MEDIA APPLICATIONS

Academy College, Minneapolis, MN 192
Academy of Medical Arts and Business, Harrisburg, PA 252
Apollo College-Westside, Inc., Phoenix, AZ
The Art Institute of Houston, Houston, TX 294
Bradford School, Columbus, OH 237
Bradford School, Pittsburgh, PA 254
Bradley Academy for the Visual Arts, York, PA 254
Briarcliffe College, Bethpage, NY 226
Briarcliffe College, Patchogue, NY 226
Brooks College, Long Beach, CA 86
Brooks College, Sunnyvale, CA 86
Brown College, Mendota Heights, MN 193
Brown Mackie College, Findlay Campus, Findlay, OH 238
Brown Mackie College, Lenexa Campus, Lenexa, KS 168
Brown Mackie College, Miami Campus, Miami, FL 124
Brown Mackie College, Moline Campus, Moline, IL 154
Brown Mackie College, San Diego Campus, San Diego, CA 87
Capella University, Minneapolis, MN 194
CHI Institute, Broomall, PA 256
CHI Institute, Southampton, PA 256
The Chubb Institute, Alpharetta, GA 147
The Chubb Institute, Arlington, VA 314
The Chubb Institute, Cherry Hill, NJ 215
The Chubb Institute, Chicago, IL 155
The Chubb Institute, Jersey City, NJ 216
The Chubb Institute, New York, NY 228
The Chubb Institute, North Brunswick, NJ 216
The Chubb Institute, Parsippany, NJ 216
The Chubb Institute, Springfield, PA 256
The Chubb Institute, Westbury, NY 228
Computer Learning Network, Altoona, PA 258
Computer Learning Network, Mechanicsburg, PA 258
Dorsey Schools, Madison Heights, MI 188
Dorsey Schools, Roseville, MI 188
Dorsey Schools, Southgate, MI 188
Dorsey Schools, Wayne, MI 189
Draughons Junior College, Bowling Green, KY 171
Draughons Junior College, Clarksville, TN 287
Draughons Junior College, Murfreesboro, TN 287
Draughons Junior College, Nashville, TN 288
Florida Career College, Hialeah, FL 125
Florida Career College, Miami, FL 125
Florida Career College, Pembroke Pines, FL 126
Florida Career College, West Palm Beach, FL 126

Boldface type indicates that the school is a participating institution in the 🌐 *Imagine America* Scholarship Program

Wood Tobe-Coburn School, New York, NY 233

COMPUTER SOFTWARE AND MEDIA APPLICATIONS, OTHER

Academy of Art University, San Francisco, CA 83
Academy of Medical Arts and Business, Harrisburg, PA 252
Briarcliffe College, Bethpage, NY 226
Briarcliffe College, Patchogue, NY 226
Brown Mackie College, Akron Campus, Akron, OH 238
Brown Mackie College, North Canton Campus, North Canton, OH 239
Capella University, Minneapolis, MN 194
The Chubb Institute, Alpharetta, GA 147
The Chubb Institute, Arlington, VA 314
The Chubb Institute, Cherry Hill, NJ 215
The Chubb Institute, Chicago, IL 155
The Chubb Institute, Jersey City, NJ 216
The Chubb Institute, New York, NY 228
The Chubb Institute, North Brunswick, NJ 216
The Chubb Institute, Parsippany, NJ 216
The Chubb Institute, Springfield, PA 256
The Chubb Institute, Westbury, NY 228
The Cittone Institute, Edison, NJ 217
The Cittone Institute, Mount Laurel, NJ 217
The Cittone Institute, Paramus, NJ 217
The Cittone Institute, Philadelphia, PA 257
The Cittone Institute, Plymouth Meeting, PA 257
Computer Learning Network, Altoona, PA 258
Computer Learning Network, Mechanicsburg, PA 258
Conservatory of Recording Arts and Sciences, Tempe, AZ 78
Daymar College, Louisville, KY 171
Daymar College, Newport, KY 171
Daymar College, Owensboro, KY 171
Erie Business Center, Main, Erie, PA 261
Florida Technical College, Auburndale, FL 129
Florida Technical College, DeLand, FL 130
Florida Technical College, Jacksonville, FL 130
Florida Technical College, Orlando, FL 130
Fox College, Oak Lawn, IL 156
Hagerstown Business College, Hagerstown, MD 181
High-Tech Institute, Irving, TX 298
High-Tech Institute, Kansas City, MO 202
High-Tech Institute, Las Vegas, NV 210
High-Tech Institute, Marietta, GA 149
High-Tech Institute, Memphis, TN 288
High-Tech Institute, Nashville, TN 288
High-Tech Institute, Orlando, FL 132
High-Tech Institute, Phoenix, AZ 78
High-Tech Institute, Sacramento, CA 96
High-Tech Institute, St. Louis Park, MN 195
Hohokus Hackensack School of Business and Medical Sciences, Hackensack, NJ 220
International Business College, El Paso, TX 298
International Business College, El Paso, TX 299
International Business College, Fort Wayne, IN 165
International Business College, Indianapolis, IN 165
ITI Technical College, Baton Rouge, LA 178
Miller-Motte Technical College, Cary, NC 236
Miller-Motte Technical College, Chattanooga, TN 290
Miller-Motte Technical College, Clarksville, TN 290
Miller-Motte Technical College, Lynchburg, VA 320
Miller-Motte Technical College, North Charleston, SC 285
Miller-Motte Technical College, Wilmington, NC 236
Missouri Tech, St. Louis, MO 204
Ohio Valley College of Technology, East Liverpool, OH 242
South College, Knoxville, TN 291

COMPUTER SOFTWARE ENGINEERING

Apollo College-Westside, Inc., Phoenix, AZ
Capella University, Minneapolis, MN 194
The Chubb Institute, Alpharetta, GA 147
The Chubb Institute, Arlington, VA 314
The Chubb Institute, Cherry Hill, NJ 215
The Chubb Institute, Chicago, IL 155
The Chubb Institute, Jersey City, NJ 216
The Chubb Institute, New York, NY 228
The Chubb Institute, North Brunswick, NJ 216
The Chubb Institute, Parsippany, NJ 216
The Chubb Institute, Springfield, PA 256
The Chubb Institute, Westbury, NY 228
Colorado Technical University, Colorado Springs, CO 113
Globe College, Oakdale, MN 194
Grantham University, Kansas City, MO 177
ITT Technical Institute, Albany, NY 230
ITT Technical Institute, Albuquerque, NM 223
ITT Technical Institute, Anaheim, CA 96
ITT Technical Institute, Arlington, TX 299
ITT Technical Institute, Arnold, MO 202
ITT Technical Institute, Austin, TX 299
ITT Technical Institute, Bessemer, AL 71
ITT Technical Institute, Boise, ID 153
ITT Technical Institute, Bothell, WA 327
ITT Technical Institute, Burr Ridge, IL 157
ITT Technical Institute, Canton, MI 189
ITT Technical Institute, Chantilly, VA 317
ITT Technical Institute, Dayton, OH 240
ITT Technical Institute, Duluth, GA 149
ITT Technical Institute, Earth City, MO 202
ITT Technical Institute, Eden Prairie, MN 195
ITT Technical Institute, Fort Lauderdale, FL 133
ITT Technical Institute, Fort Wayne, IN 165
ITT Technical Institute, Getzville, NY 230
ITT Technical Institute, Grand Rapids, MI 189

ITT Technical Institute, Green Bay, WI 331
ITT Technical Institute, Greenfield, WI 331
ITT Technical Institute, Greenville, SC 285
ITT Technical Institute, Henderson, NV 211
ITT Technical Institute, Hilliard, OH 240
ITT Technical Institute, Houston, TX 299
ITT Technical Institute, Houston, TX 300
ITT Technical Institute, Indianapolis, IN 165
ITT Technical Institute, Jacksonville, FL 133
ITT Technical Institute, Kansas City, MO 203
ITT Technical Institute, Kennesaw, GA 149
ITT Technical Institute, King of Prussia, PA 264
ITT Technical Institute, Knoxville, TN 289
ITT Technical Institute, Lake Mary, FL 133
ITT Technical Institute, Lathrop, CA 96
ITT Technical Institute, Little Rock, AR 82
ITT Technical Institute, Liverpool, NY 230
ITT Technical Institute, Louisville, KY 171
ITT Technical Institute, Matteson, IL 158
ITT Technical Institute, Mechanicsburg, PA 264
ITT Technical Institute, Memphis, TN 289
ITT Technical Institute, Miami, FL 133
ITT Technical Institute, Monroeville, PA 264
ITT Technical Institute, Mount Prospect, IL 158
ITT Technical Institute, Murray, UT 310
ITT Technical Institute, Nashville, TN 289
ITT Technical Institute, Newburgh, IN 166
ITT Technical Institute, Norfolk, VA 318
ITT Technical Institute, Norwood, MA 186
ITT Technical Institute, Norwood, OH 240
ITT Technical Institute, Omaha, NE 209
ITT Technical Institute, Owings Mills, MD 181
ITT Technical Institute, Oxnard, CA 97
ITT Technical Institute, Pittsburg, PA 264
ITT Technical Institute, Portland, OR 250
ITT Technical Institute, Rancho Cordova, CA 97
ITT Technical Institute, Richardson, TX 300
ITT Technical Institute, Richmond, VA 318
ITT Technical Institute, Saint Rose, LA 179
ITT Technical Institute, San Antonio, TX 300
ITT Technical Institute, San Bernardino, CA 97
ITT Technical Institute, San Diego, CA 97
ITT Technical Institute, Seattle, WA 327
ITT Technical Institute, Spokane, WA 328
ITT Technical Institute, Springfield, VA 318
ITT Technical Institute, Strongsville, OH 241
ITT Technical Institute, Sylmar, CA 98
ITT Technical Institute, Tampa, FL 134
ITT Technical Institute, Tempe, AZ 79
ITT Technical Institute, Thornton, CO 115
ITT Technical Institute, Torrance, CA 98
ITT Technical Institute, Troy, MI 190
ITT Technical Institute, Tucson, AZ 79

ITT Technical Institute, Tulsa, OK 247
ITT Technical Institute, Warrensville Heights, OH 241
ITT Technical Institute, West Covina, CA 98
ITT Technical Institute, Woburn, MA 186
ITT Technical Institute, Youngstown, OH 241
Missouri College, St. Louis, MO 203
Missouri Tech, St. Louis, MO 204
Neumont University, Salt Lake City, UT 310
Schuylkill Institute of Business and Technology, Pottsville, PA 270
South University, Columbia, SC 286
South University, Montgomery, AL 71
South University, Savannah, GA 151
South University, West Palm Beach, FL 142
Stratford University, Falls Church , VA 322
Stratford University, Woodbridge, VA 322
Sullivan University, Lexington, KY 174
Sullivan University, Louisville, KY 175
TESST College of Technology, Alexandria, VA 323
TESST College of Technology, Baltimore, MD 182
TESST College of Technology, Beltsville, MD 183
TESST College of Technology, Towson, MD 183
Westwood College - Anaheim, Anaheim, CA 109
Westwood College - Atlanta Campus, Atlanta, GA 151
Westwood College - Chicago Du Page, Woodridge, IL 160
Westwood College - Chicago Loop Campus, Chicago, IL 161
Westwood College - Inland Empire, Upland, CA 109

COMPUTER SOFTWARE TECHNOLOGY/TECHNICIAN

ATI Career Training Center, Dallas, TX 294
ATI Career Training Center, Fort Lauderdale, FL 122
ATI Career Training Center, Miami, FL 123
ATI Career Training Center, North Richland Hills, TX 295
ATI Career Training Center, Oakland Park, FL 123
Briarcliffe College, Bethpage, NY 226
Briarcliffe College, Patchogue, NY 226
Brookstone College of Business, Charlotte, NC 234
Brookstone College of Business, Greensboro, NC 234
Brown Mackie College, Akron Campus, Akron, OH 238
Brown Mackie College, Atlanta Campus, Norcross, GA 146
Brown Mackie College, Cincinnati Campus, Cincinnati, OH 238
Brown Mackie College, Hopkinsville Campus, Hopkinsville, KY 170
Brown Mackie College, Los Angeles Campus, Santa Monica, CA 87
Brown Mackie College, North Canton Campus, North Canton, OH 239
Brown Mackie College, Northern Kentucky Campus, Fort

ITT Technical Institute, Strongsville, OH 241
ITT Technical Institute, Sylmar, CA 98
ITT Technical Institute, Tampa, FL 134
ITT Technical Institute, Tempe, AZ 79
ITT Technical Institute, Thornton, CO 115
ITT Technical Institute, Torrance, CA 98
ITT Technical Institute, Troy, MI 190
ITT Technical Institute, Tucson, AZ 79
ITT Technical Institute, Tulsa, OK 247
ITT Technical Institute, Warrensville Heights, OH 241
ITT Technical Institute, West Covina, CA 98
ITT Technical Institute, Woburn, MA 186
ITT Technical Institute, Youngstown, OH 241
Laurel Business Institute, Uniontown, PA 265
McCann School of Business, Hazleton, PA 266
McCann School of Business, Pottsville, PA267
McCann School of Business, Scranton, PA 267
McCann School of Business, Sunbury, PA 267
Missouri Tech, St. Louis, MO 204
National American University, Albuquerque, NM 224
National American University, Brooklyn Center, MN 197
National American University, Colorado Springs, CO 115
National American University, Denver, CO 116
National American University, Ellsworth AFB, SD 286
National American University, Kansas City, MO 204
National American University, Minneapolis, MN 197
National American University, Overland Park, KS 169
National American University, Rapid City, SD 286
National American University, Rio Rancho, NM 224
National American University, Roseville, MN 197
Westwood College - Chicago O'Hare Airport, Chicago, IL 161
Westwood College - Denver North, Denver, CO 118
Westwood College - Inland Empire, Upland, CA 109

COMPUTER SYSTEMS ANALYSIS/ ANALYST

Academy of Medical Arts and Business, Harrisburg, PA 252
ATI Career Training Center, Dallas, TX 294
ATI Career Training Center, Fort Lauderdale, FL 122
ATI Career Training Center, Miami, FL 123
ATI Career Training Center, North Richland Hills, TX 295
ATI Career Training Center, Oakland Park, FL 123
Briarcliffe College, Bethpage, NY 226
Briarcliffe College, Patchogue, NY 226
Bryan College, Springfield, MO 201
Bryan College, Topeka, KS 169
Capella University, Minneapolis, MN 194
The Chubb Institute, Alpharetta, GA 147
The Chubb Institute, Arlington, VA 314
The Chubb Institute, Cherry Hill, NJ 215

The Chubb Institute, Chicago, IL 155
The Chubb Institute, Jersey City, NJ 216
The Chubb Institute, New York, NY 228
The Chubb Institute, North Brunswick, NJ 216
The Chubb Institute, Parsippany, NJ 216
The Chubb Institute, Springfield, PA 256
The Chubb Institute, Westbury, NY 228
Coleman College, La Mesa, CA 92
Coleman College, San Marcos, CA 93
Delta School of Business & Technology, Lake Charles, LA 177
ECPI College of Technology, Charlotte, NC 234
ECPI College of Technology, Greensboro, NC 235
ECPI College of Technology, Greenville, SC 285
ECPI College of Technology, Manassas, VA 315
ECPI College of Technology, Newport News, VA 315
ECPI College of Technology, North Charleston, SC 285
ECPI College of Technology, Raleigh, NC 235
ECPI College of Technology, Virginia Beach, VA 316
Herzing College, Atlanta, GA 148
Herzing College, Birmingham, AL 70
Herzing College, Kenner, LA 178
Herzing College, Madison, WI 330
Herzing College, Minneapolis, MN 195
Herzing College, Winter Park, FL 131
International Academy of Design & Technology, Chicago, IL 157
International Academy of Design & Technology, Orlando, FL 132
International Academy of Design & Technology, Pittsburgh, PA 264
International Academy of Design & Technology, Tampa, FL 132
International Academy of Design & Technology, Troy, MI 189
ITI Technical College, Baton Rouge, LA 178
Kaplan University, Davenport, IA 168
McCann School of Business, Hazleton, PA 266
McCann School of Business, Pottsville, PA267
McCann School of Business, Scranton, PA 267
McCann School of Business, Sunbury, PA 267
Missouri Tech, St. Louis, MO 204
MTI College of Business and Technology, Houston, TX 301
Remington College - Cleveland West Campus, North Olmstead, OH 242
Remington College - Fort Worth Campus, Fort Worth, TX 304
Schuylkill Institute of Business and Technology, Pottsville, PA 270
South University, Columbia, SC 286
South University, Montgomery, AL 71
South University, Savannah, GA 151

South University, West Palm Beach, FL 142
Stratford University, Falls Church , VA 322
Stratford University, Woodbridge, VA 322
Vatterott College, Broadview Heights, OH 245
Vatterott College, Des Moines, IA 168
Vatterott College, Joplin, MO 206
Vatterott College, Kansas City, MO 207
Vatterott College, Memphis, TN 292
Vatterott College, OÆFallon , MO 207
Vatterott College, Oklahoma City, OK 248
Vatterott College, Omaha, NE 209
Vatterott College, Quincy, IL 160
Vatterott College, Springfield, MO 208
Vatterott College, St. Ann, MO 207
Vatterott College, St. Joseph, MO 207
Vatterott College, St. Louis, MO 208
Vatterott College, Tulsa, OK 249
Vatterott College, Wichita, KS 169

COMPUTER SYSTEMS NETWORKING AND TELECOMMUNICATIONS

Academy College, Minneapolis, MN 192
Academy of Medical Arts and Business, Harrisburg, PA 252
Advanced Training Associates, El Cajon, CA 84
American Commercial College, Abilene, TX 292
American Commercial College, Lubbock, TX 293
American Commercial College, Odessa, TX 293
American Commercial College, San Angelo, TX 293
American Commercial College, Shreveport, LA 175
American School of Business, Wichita Falls, TX 294
ATI Career Training Center, Dallas, TX 294
ATI Career Training Center, Fort Lauderdale, FL 122
ATI Career Training Center, Miami, FL 123
ATI Career Training Center, North Richland Hills, TX 295
ATI Career Training Center, Oakland Park, FL 123
Bradford School, Columbus, OH 237
Bradford School, Pittsburgh, PA 254
Briarcliffe College, Bethpage, NY 226
Briarcliffe College, Patchogue, NY 226
Brooks College, Long Beach, CA 86
Brooks College, Sunnyvale, CA 86
Brookstone College of Business, Charlotte, NC 234
Brookstone College of Business, Greensboro, NC 234
Brown College, Mendota Heights, MN 193
Brown Mackie College, Akron Campus, Akron, OH 238
Brown Mackie College, Cincinnati Campus, Cincinnati, OH 238
Brown Mackie College, Hopkinsville Campus, Hopkinsville, KY 170
Brown Mackie College, Lenexa Campus, Lenexa, KS 168
Brown Mackie College, North Canton Campus, North Can-

ton, OH 239
Brown Mackie College, South Bend Campus, South Bend, IN 162
Bryan College, Springfield, MO 201
Bryan College, Topeka, KS 169
Caguas Institute of Mechanical Technology, Caguas, PR 276
Capella University, Minneapolis, MN 194
Career Education Institute, Brockton, MA 184
Career Education Institute, Henderson, NV 210
Career Education Institute, Lincoln, RI 283
Career Education Institute, Lowell, MA 184
Career Education Institute, Marietta, GA 146
Career Education Institute, Norcross, GA 146
Career Institute of Health and Technology, Brooklyn, NY 227
Career Institute of Health and Technology, Garden City, NY 227
Career Institute of Health and Technology, Rego Park, NY 228
Career Point Business School, San Antonio, TX 296
Central Coast College, Salinas, CA 92
Chaparral College, Tucson, AZ 77
Charter College, Anchorage, AK 74
CHI Institute, Broomall, PA 256
CHI Institute, Southampton, PA 256
The Chubb Institute, Alpharetta, GA 147
The Chubb Institute, Arlington, VA 314
The Chubb Institute, Cherry Hill, NJ 215
The Chubb Institute, Chicago, IL 155
The Chubb Institute, Jersey City, NJ 216
The Chubb Institute, New York, NY 228
The Chubb Institute, North Brunswick, NJ 216
The Chubb Institute, Parsippany, NJ 216
The Chubb Institute, Springfield, PA 256
The Chubb Institute, Westbury, NY 228
The Cittone Institute, Edison, NJ 217
The Cittone Institute, Mount Laurel, NJ 217
The Cittone Institute, Paramus, NJ 217
The Cittone Institute, Philadelphia, PA 257
The Cittone Institute, Plymouth Meeting, PA 257
Coleman College, La Mesa, CA 92
Coleman College, San Marcos, CA 93
CollegeAmerica - Denver, Denver, CO 113
Collins College: A School of Design and Technology, Tempe, AZ 77
Computer Learning Network, Altoona, PA 258
Computer Learning Network, Mechanicsburg, PA 258
Coyne American Institute, Chicago, IL 155
Coyne American Institute, Chicago, IL 156
Daymar College, Louisville, KY 171
Daymar College, Newport, KY 171
Daymar College, Owensboro, KY 171
Delta School of Business & Technology, Lake Charles,

MTI College of Business and Technology, Houston, TX 301

National American University, Albuquerque, NM 224

National American University, Brooklyn Center, MN 197

National American University, Colorado Springs, CO 115

National American University, Denver, CO 116

National American University, Ellsworth AFB, SD 286

National American University, Kansas City, MO 204

National American University, Minneapolis, MN 197

National American University, Overland Park, KS 169

National American University, Rapid City, SD 286

National American University, Rio Rancho, NM 224

National American University, Roseville, MN 197

National Career Education, Citrus Heights, CA 100

National Institute of Technology, Austin , TX 302

National Institute of Technology, Cross Lanes, WV 329

National Institute of Technology - Dearborn, Dearborn, MI 190

National Institute of Technology, Detroit, MI 190

National Institute of Technology, Houston, TX 302

National Institute of Technology, Long Beach, CA 101

National Institute of Technology, San Antonio, TX 302

National Institute of Technology, Southfield, MI 190

New England Institute of Technology at Palm Beach, West Palm Beach, FL 140

New England Institute of Technology, Warwick, RI 284

New England Technical Institute, Cromwell, CT 119

New England Technical Institute, Hamden, CT 119

New England Technical Institute, Shelton, CT 119

Peirce College, Philadelphia, PA 268

Pennco Tech Bristol, PA 269

Pennco Tech, Blackwood, NJ 222

Platt College, Huntington Beach, CA 101

Platt College, Lawton, OK 247

Platt College - Los Angeles, Inc, Alhambra, CA 102

Platt College, Oklahoma City, OK 248

Platt College, Ontario, CA 102

Platt College, Tulsa, OK 248

Porter and Chester Institute, Chicopee, MA 187

Porter and Chester Institute, Enfield, CT 120

Porter and Chester Institute, Stratford, CT 120

Porter and Chester Institute, Watertown, CT 120

Porter and Chester Institute, Wethersfield, CT 120

Provo College, Provo, UT 310

Rasmussen College Eagan, Eagan, MN 198

Rasmussen College Minnetonka, Minnetonka, MN 199

Rasmussen College St. Cloud, St. Cloud, MN 199

Remington College - Baton Rouge Campus, Baton Rouge, LA 179

Remington College - Dallas Campus, Garland, TX 304

Remington College, Houston, TX 304

Remington College - Jacksonville Campus, Jacksonville, FL 140

Remington College - Lafayette Campus, Lafayette, LA 179

Remington College - Pinellas Campus, Largo, FL 141

Remington College - San Diego Campus, San Diego, CA 103

Remington College - Tampa Campus, Tampa, FL 141

Remington College - Tempe Campus, Tempe, AZ 81

RETS Institute of Technology, Pittsburgh, PA 270

Rockford Business College, Rockford, IL 159

San Joaquin Valley College, Bakersfield, CA 103

San Joaquin Valley College, Fresno, CA 103

San Joaquin Valley College, Modesto, CA 104

San Joaquin Valley College, Rancho Cucamonga, CA 104

San Joaquin Valley College, Visalia, CA 104

Sanford-Brown College, Collinsville, IL 159

Sanford-Brown College, Fenton, MO 205

Sanford-Brown College, Hazelwood, MO 205

Sanford-Brown College, North Kansas City, MO 206

Sanford-Brown College, St. Charles, MO 206

Sanford-Brown College, West Allis, WI 331

Schuylkill Institute of Business and Technology, Pottsville, PA 270

Silicon Valley College, Emeryville, CA 105

Silicon Valley College, Fremont, CA 106

Silicon Valley College, San Jose, CA 106

South College, Knoxville, TN 291

South University, Columbia, SC 286

South University, Montgomery, AL 71

South University, Savannah, GA 151

South University, West Palm Beach, FL 142

Southwest Florida College, Tampa, FL 143

Stevens-Henager College, Boise, ID 153

Stevens-Henager College, Logan, UT 311

Stevens-Henager College, Ogden, UT 311

Stevens-Henager College - Provo, Orem, UT 311

Stevens-Henager College - Salt Lake City, Salt Lake City, UT 312

Stratford University, Falls Church , VA 322

Stratford University, Woodbridge, VA 322

Sullivan University, Lexington, KY 174

Sullivan University, Louisville, KY 175

Technical Career Institute, New York, NY 233

TESST College of Technology, Alexandria, VA 323

TESST College of Technology, Baltimore, MD 182

TESST College of Technology, Beltsville, MD 183

TESST College of Technology, Towson, MD 183

Trinity College of Puerto Rico, Ponce, PR 283

Tri-State Business Institute, Erie, PA 272

Tucson College, Tucson, AZ 82

United Education Institute, Los Angeles, Los Angeles, CA 107

Vatterott College, Broadview Heights, OH 245

Vatterott College, Des Moines, IA 168
Vatterott College, Joplin, MO 206
Vatterott College, Kansas City, MO 207
Vatterott College, Memphis, TN 292
Vatterott College, O'Fallon , MO 207
Vatterott College, Oklahoma City, OK 248
Vatterott College, Omaha, NE 209
Vatterott College, Quincy, IL 160
Vatterott College, Springfield, MO 208
Vatterott College, St. Ann, MO 207
Vatterott College, St. Joseph, MO 207
Vatterott College, St. Louis, MO 208
Vatterott College, Tulsa, OK 249
Vatterott College, Wichita, KS 169
Virginia College at Austin, Austin, TX 307
Virginia College at Huntsville, Huntsville, AL 73
Webster College, Holiday, FL 144
Webster College, Ocala, FL 144
West Virginia Junior College, Bridgeport, WV 329
West Virginia Junior College, Charleston, WV 329
West Virginia Junior College, Morgantown, WV 330
Western Technical College, El Paso, TX 307
Western Technical Institute, El Paso, TX 308
Westwood College - Atlanta Northlake, Atlanta, GA 152
Westwood College - Chicago Du Page, Woodridge, IL 160
Westwood College - Chicago Loop Campus, Chicago, IL 161
Westwood College - Fort Worth, Euless, TX 308
Westwood College - Houston South Campus, Houston, TX 308
Westwood College - Inland Empire, Upland, CA 109

COMPUTER TECHNOLOGY/ COMPUTER SYSTEMS TECHNOLOGY

Academy of Medical Arts and Business, Harrisburg, PA 252
Advanced Career Training, Atlanta, GA 144
Advanced Career Training, Jacksonville, FL 121
Advanced Career Training, Riverdale, GA 145
Akron Institute, Akron, OH 236
American Commercial College, Abilene, TX 292
American Commercial College, Lubbock, TX 293
American Commercial College, Odessa, TX 293
American Commercial College, San Angelo, TX 293
American Commercial College, Shreveport, LA 175
American InterContinental University, Atlanta, GA 145
American InterContinental University, Houston, TX 293
American InterContinental University, Los Angeles, CA 85
American InterContinental University, San Antonio, TX 293
American InterContinental University, Weston, FL 121
Andover College, Portland, ME 180
ATI Career Training Center, Dallas, TX 294

ATI Career Training Center, Fort Lauderdale, FL 122
ATI Career Training Center, Miami, FL 123
ATI Career Training Center, North Richland Hills, TX 295
ATI Career Training Center, Oakland Park, FL 123
Berks Technical Institute, Wyomissing, PA 253
Bradford School, Columbus, OH 237
Bradford School, Pittsburgh, PA 254
Briarcliffe College, Bethpage, NY 226
Briarcliffe College, Patchogue, NY 226
Brookstone College of Business, Charlotte, NC 234
Brookstone College of Business, Greensboro, NC 234
Brown Mackie College, North Canton Campus, North Canton, OH 239
Bryan College, Springfield, MO 201
Bryan College, Topeka, KS 169
Caguas Institute of Mechanical Technology, Caguas, PR 276
Career Education Institute, Brockton, MA 184
Career Education Institute, Henderson, NV 210
Career Education Institute, Lincoln, RI 283
Career Education Institute, Lowell, MA 184
Career Education Institute, Marietta, GA 146
Career Education Institute, Norcross, GA 146
Career Institute of Health and Technology, Brooklyn, NY 227
Career Institute of Health and Technology, Garden City, NY 227
Career Institute of Health and Technology, Rego Park, NY 228
Central Coast College, Salinas, CA 92
Chaparral College, Tucson, AZ 77
Charter College, Anchorage, AK 74
CHI Institute, Broomall, PA 256
CHI Institute, Southampton, PA 256
The Chubb Institute, Alpharetta, GA 147
The Chubb Institute, Arlington, VA 314
The Chubb Institute, Cherry Hill, NJ 215
The Chubb Institute, Chicago, IL 155
The Chubb Institute, Jersey City, NJ 216
The Chubb Institute, New York, NY 228
The Chubb Institute, North Brunswick, NJ 216
The Chubb Institute, Parsippany, NJ 216
The Chubb Institute, Springfield, PA 256
The Chubb Institute, Westbury, NY 228
City College, Inc., Moore, OK 246
CollegeAmerica - Denver, Denver, CO 113
CollegeAmerica - Fort Collins, Fort Collins, CO 113
CollegeAmerica-Flagstaff, Flagstaff, AZ 77
Computer Learning Network, Altoona, PA 258
Computer Learning Network, Mechanicsburg, PA 258
Coyne American Institute, Chicago, IL 155
Coyne American Institute, Chicago, IL 156
Delta School of Business & Technology, Lake Charles,

LA 177

Draughons Junior College, Bowling Green, KY 171

Draughons Junior College, Clarksville, TN 287

Draughons Junior College, Murfreesboro, TN 287

Draughons Junior College, Nashville, TN 288

ECPI College of Technology, Charlotte, NC 234

ECPI College of Technology, Greensboro, NC 235

ECPI College of Technology, Greenville, SC 285

ECPI College of Technology, Manassas, VA 315

ECPI College of Technology, Newport News, VA 315

ECPI College of Technology, North Charleston, SC 285

ECPI College of Technology, Raleigh, NC 235

ECPI College of Technology, Virginia Beach, VA 316

ECPI Technical College, Glen Allen, VA 316

ECPI Technical College, Richmond, VA 316

ECPI Technical College, Roanoke, VA 317

Empire College, Santa Rosa, CA 93

Erie Business Center, Main, Erie, PA 261

Florida Career College, Hialeah, FL 125

Florida Career College, Miami, FL 125

Florida Career College, Pembroke Pines, FL 126

Florida Career College, West Palm Beach, FL 126

Florida Technical College, Auburndale, FL 129

Florida Technical College, DeLand, FL 130

Florida Technical College, Jacksonville, FL 130

Florida Technical College, Orlando, FL 130

Gallipolis Career College, Gallipolis, OH 239

Gibbs College - Cranston, Cranston, RI 283

Gulf Coast College, Tampa, FL 131

Hagerstown Business College, Hagerstown, MD 181

Hallmark Institute of Technology, San Antonio, TX 298

Herzing College, Atlanta, GA 148

Herzing College, Birmingham, AL 70

Herzing College, Kenner, LA 178

Herzing College, Madison, WI 330

Herzing College, Minneapolis, MN 195

Herzing College, Winter Park, FL 131

Hesser College, Manchester, NH 213

High-Tech Institute, Irving, TX 298

High-Tech Institute, Kansas City, MO 202

High-Tech Institute, Las Vegas, NV 210

High-Tech Institute, Marietta, GA 149

High-Tech Institute, Memphis, TN 288

High-Tech Institute, Nashville, TN 288

High-Tech Institute, Orlando, FL 132

High-Tech Institute, Phoenix, AZ 78

High-Tech Institute, Sacramento, CA 96

High-Tech Institute, St. Louis Park, MN 195

HoHoKus RETS School of Business and Medical Technical Services, Nutley, NJ 220

ICM School of Business & Medical Careers, Pittsburgh, PA 263

ICPR Junior College - Hato Rey Campus, San Juan, PR 278

ICPR Junior College - Mayaguez Campus, Mayaguez, PR 279

ICPR Junior College-Arecibo Campus, Arecibo, PR 278

International Business College, El Paso, TX 298

International Business College, El Paso, TX 299

International Business College, Fort Wayne, IN 165

International Business College, Indianapolis, IN 165

Island Drafting and Technical Institute, Amityville, NY 230

ITI Technical College, Baton Rouge, LA 178

ITT Technical Institute, Albany, NY 230

ITT Technical Institute, Albuquerque, NM 223

ITT Technical Institute, Anaheim, CA 96

ITT Technical Institute, Arlington, TX 299

ITT Technical Institute, Arnold, MO 202

ITT Technical Institute, Austin, TX 299

ITT Technical Institute, Bessemer, AL 71

ITT Technical Institute, Boise, ID 153

ITT Technical Institute, Bothell, WA 327

ITT Technical Institute, Burr Ridge, IL 157

ITT Technical Institute, Canton, MI 189

ITT Technical Institute, Chantilly, VA 317

ITT Technical Institute, Dayton, OH 240

ITT Technical Institute, Duluth, GA 149

ITT Technical Institute, Earth City, MO 202

ITT Technical Institute, Eden Prairie, MN 195

ITT Technical Institute, Fort Lauderdale, FL 133

ITT Technical Institute, Fort Wayne, IN 165

ITT Technical Institute, Getzville, NY 230

ITT Technical Institute, Grand Rapids, MI 189

ITT Technical Institute, Green Bay, WI 331

ITT Technical Institute, Greenfield, WI 331

ITT Technical Institute, Greenville, SC 285

ITT Technical Institute, Henderson, NV 211

ITT Technical Institute, Hilliard, OH 240

ITT Technical Institute, Houston, TX 299

ITT Technical Institute, Houston, TX 300

ITT Technical Institute, Indianapolis, IN 165

ITT Technical Institute, Jacksonville, FL 133

ITT Technical Institute, Kansas City, MO 203

ITT Technical Institute, Kennesaw, GA 149

ITT Technical Institute, King of Prussia, PA 264

ITT Technical Institute, Knoxville, TN 289

ITT Technical Institute, Lake Mary, FL 133

ITT Technical Institute, Lathrop, CA 96

ITT Technical Institute, Little Rock, AR 82

ITT Technical Institute, Liverpool, NY 230

ITT Technical Institute, Louisville, KY 171

ITT Technical Institute, Matteson, IL 158

ITT Technical Institute, Mechanicsburg, PA 264

ITT Technical Institute, Memphis, TN 289

ITT Technical Institute, Miami, FL 133

ITT Technical Institute, Monroeville, PA 264

Stratford University, Woodbridge, VA 322
Technical Career Institute, New York, NY 233
Technology Education College, Columbus, OH 245
TESST College of Technology, Alexandria, VA 323
TESST College of Technology, Baltimore, MD 182
TESST College of Technology, Beltsville, MD 183
TESST College of Technology, Towson, MD 183
Tri-State Business Institute, Erie, PA 272
Vatterott College, Broadview Heights, OH 245
Vatterott College, Des Moines, IA 168
Vatterott College, Joplin, MO 206
Vatterott College, Kansas City, MO 207
Vatterott College, Memphis, TN 292
Vatterott College, OÆFallon , MO 207
Vatterott College, Oklahoma City, OK 248
Vatterott College, Omaha, NE 209
Vatterott College, Quincy, IL 160
Vatterott College, Springfield, MO 208
Vatterott College, St. Ann, MO 207
Vatterott College, St. Joseph, MO 207
Vatterott College, St. Louis, MO 208
Vatterott College, Tulsa, OK 249
Vatterott College, Wichita, KS 169
Virginia College at Huntsville, Huntsville, AL 73
Virginia College at Jackson, Jackson, MS 200
West Virginia Junior College, Bridgeport, WV 329
West Virginia Junior College, Charleston, WV 329
West Virginia Junior College, Morgantown, WV 330
Western Technical College, El Paso, TX 307
Western Technical Institute, El Paso, TX 308
Wichita Technical Institute, Wichita, KS 169
Westwood College - Inland Empire, Upland, CA 109
Westwood College - Long Beach, Torrance, CA 110
York Technical Institute, Lancaster, PA 274
York Technical Institute, York, PA 274

COMPUTER/INFORMATION TECHNOLOGY ADMINISTRATION AND MANAGEMENT

Aakers Business College , Bismarck, ND 236
Aakers Business College, Fargo, ND 236
Academy of Medical Arts and Business, Harrisburg, PA 252
ATI Career Training Center, Dallas, TX 294
ATI Career Training Center, Fort Lauderdale, FL 122
ATI Career Training Center, Miami, FL 123
ATI Career Training Center, North Richland Hills, TX 295
ATI Career Training Center, Oakland Park, FL 123
Berks Technical Institute, Wyomissing, PA 253
Bradford School, Columbus, OH 237
Bradford School, Pittsburgh, PA 254
Briarcliffe College, Bethpage, NY 226

Briarcliffe College, Patchogue, NY 226
Brooks College, Long Beach, CA 86
Brooks College, Sunnyvale, CA 86
Brookstone College of Business, Charlotte, NC 234
Brookstone College of Business, Greensboro, NC 234
Brown College, Mendota Heights, MN 193
Business Institute of Pennsylvania, Meadville, PA 255
Business Institute of Pennsylvania, Sharon, PA 255
Capella University, Minneapolis, MN 194
Career College of Northern Nevada, Reno, NV 210
Career Education Institute, Brockton, MA 184
Career Education Institute, Henderson, NV 210
Career Education Institute, Lincoln, RI 283
Career Education Institute, Lowell, MA 184
Career Education Institute, Marietta, GA 146
Career Education Institute, Norcross, GA 146
Central Coast College, Salinas, CA 92
Charter College, Anchorage, AK 74
The Chubb Institute, Alpharetta, GA 147
The Chubb Institute, Arlington, VA 314
The Chubb Institute, Cherry Hill, NJ 215
The Chubb Institute, Chicago, IL 155
The Chubb Institute, Jersey City, NJ 216
The Chubb Institute, New York, NY 228
The Chubb Institute, North Brunswick, NJ 216
The Chubb Institute, Parsippany, NJ 216
The Chubb Institute, Springfield, PA 256
The Chubb Institute, Westbury, NY 228
The Cittone Institute, Edison, NJ 217
The Cittone Institute, Mount Laurel, NJ 217
The Cittone Institute, Paramus, NJ 217
The Cittone Institute, Philadelphia, PA 257
The Cittone Institute, Plymouth Meeting, PA 257
CollegeAmerica - Denver, Denver, CO 113
Columbia College, Caguas, PR 277
Columbia College, Yauco, PR 277
Computer Learning Network, Altoona, PA 258
Computer Learning Network, Mechanicsburg, PA 258
Delta School of Business & Technology, Lake Charles, LA 177
Dover Business College, Paramus, NJ 218
Draughons Junior College, Bowling Green, KY 171
Draughons Junior College, Clarksville, TN 287
Draughons Junior College, Murfreesboro, TN 287
Draughons Junior College, Nashville, TN 288
ECPI College of Technology, Charlotte, NC 234
ECPI College of Technology, Greensboro, NC 235
ECPI College of Technology, Greenville, SC 285
ECPI College of Technology, Manassas, VA 315
ECPI College of Technology, Newport News, VA 315
ECPI College of Technology, North Charleston, SC 285
ECPI College of Technology, Raleigh, NC 235
ECPI College of Technology, Virginia Beach, VA 316

ECPI Technical College, Glen Allen, VA 316
ECPI Technical College, Richmond, VA 316
ECPI Technical College, Roanoke, VA 317
Empire College, Santa Rosa, CA 93
Everglades University, Boca Raton, FL 125
Everglades University, Orlando, FL 125
Everglades University, Sarasota, FL 125
Florida Metropolitan University - Jacksonville Campus, Jacksonville, FL 127
Florida Technical College, Auburndale, FL 129
Florida Technical College, DeLand, FL 130
Florida Technical College, Jacksonville, FL 130
Florida Technical College, Orlando, FL 130
Gibbs College - Cranston, Cranston, RI 283
Gibbs College, Boston, MA 185
Gibbs College, Livingston, NJ 218
Gibbs College, Norwalk, CT 119
Globe College, Oakdale, MN 194
Gulf Coast College, Tampa, FL 131
Hagerstown Business College, Hagerstown, MD 181
Herzing College, Atlanta, GA 148
Herzing College, Birmingham, AL 70
Herzing College, Kenner, LA 178
Herzing College, Madison, WI 330
Herzing College, Minneapolis, MN 195
Herzing College, Winter Park, FL 131
Hesser College, Manchester, NH 213
High-Tech Institute, Irving, TX 298
High-Tech Institute, Kansas City, MO 202
High-Tech Institute, Las Vegas, NV 210
High-Tech Institute, Marietta, GA 149
High-Tech Institute, Memphis, TN 288
High-Tech Institute, Nashville, TN 288
High-Tech Institute, Orlando, FL 132
High-Tech Institute, Phoenix, AZ 78
High-Tech Institute, Sacramento, CA 96
High-Tech Institute, St. Louis Park, MN 195
ICM School of Business & Medical Careers, Pittsburgh, PA 263
International Academy of Design & Technology, Chicago, IL 157
International Academy of Design & Technology, Orlando, FL 132
International Academy of Design & Technology, Pittsburgh, PA 264
International Academy of Design & Technology, Tampa, FL 132
International Academy of Design & Technology, Troy, MI 189
Island Drafting and Technical Institute, Amityville, NY 230
ITI Technical College, Baton Rouge, LA 178
Katharine Gibbs School, Melville, NY 231
Katharine Gibbs School, New York, NY 231

Katharine Gibbs School, Norristown, PA 264
Katharine Gibbs School, Piscataway, NJ 221
Kee Business College - Chesapeake, Chesapeake, VA 319
Keiser College, Daytona Beach, FL 134
Keiser College, Fort Lauderdale, FL 134
Keiser College, Lakeland, FL 135
Keiser College, Melbourne, FL 135
Keiser College, Miami, FL 135
Keiser College, Orlando, FL 135
Keiser College, Pembroke Pines, FL 136
Keiser College, Port St. Lucie, FL 136
Keiser College, Sarasota, FL 136
Keiser College, Tallahassee, FL 136
Keiser College, West Palm Beach, FL 137
Louisville Technical Institute, Louisville, KY 172
Maric College, Anaheim, CA 99
Maric College, Los Angeles, CA 100
Maric College, North Hollywood, CA 99
Maric College, Sacramento, CA 99
Maric College, Salida, CA 99
Maric College, San Diego, CA 100
Maric College, Vista, CA 100
McCann School of Business, Hazleton, PA 266
McCann School of Business, Pottsville, PA 267
McCann School of Business, Scranton, PA 267
McCann School of Business, Sunbury, PA 267
Metro Business College, Cape Girardeau, MO 203
Metro Business College, Jefferson City, MO 203
Metro Business College, Rolla, MO 203
Mildred Elley School, Latham, NY 232
Missouri Tech, St. Louis, MO 204
MTI College of Business and Technology, Houston, TX 301
National American University, Albuquerque, NM 224
National American University, Brooklyn Center, MN 197
National American University, Colorado Springs, CO 115
National American University, Denver, CO 116
National American University, Ellsworth AFB, SD 286
National American University, Kansas City, MO 204
National American University, Minneapolis, MN 197
National American University, Overland Park, KS 169
National American University, Rapid City, SD 286
National American University, Rio Rancho, NM 224
National American University, Roseville, MN 197
National Institute of Technology - Dearborn, Dearborn, MI 190
Peirce College, Philadelphia, PA 268
Pioneer Pacific College, Clackamas, OR 250
Pioneer Pacific College, Wilsonville, OR 251
The PJA School, Upper Darby, PA 270
Platt College, Huntington Beach, CA 101
Platt College, Lawton, OK 247
Platt College - Los Angeles, Inc, Alhambra, CA 102

Platt College, Oklahoma City, OK 248
Platt College, Ontario, CA 102
Platt College, Tulsa, OK 248
Rasmussen College Eagan, Eagan, MN 198
Rasmussen College Minnetonka, Minnetonka, MN 199
Remington College - Cleveland Campus, Cleveland, OH 242
Remington College - Memphis Campus, Memphis, TN 291
Remington College - New Orleans Campus, Metairie, LA 180
Remington College - Tampa Campus, Tampa, FL 141
RETS Tech Center, Centerville, OH 243
Rockford Business College, Rockford, IL 159
Sanford-Brown College, Collinsville, IL 159
Sanford-Brown College, Fenton, MO 205
Sanford-Brown College, Hazelwood, MO 205
Sanford-Brown College, North Kansas City, MO 206
Sanford-Brown College, St. Charles, MO 206
Sanford-Brown College, West Allis, WI 331
Silicon Valley College, Emeryville, CA 105
Silicon Valley College, Fremont, CA 106
Silicon Valley College, San Jose, CA 106
South University, Columbia, SC 286
South University, Montgomery, AL 71
South University, Savannah, GA 151
South University, West Palm Beach, FL 142
Stratford University, Falls Church , VA 322
Stratford University, Woodbridge, VA 322
Stevens-Henager College - Provo, Orem, UT 311
Sullivan University, Lexington, KY 174
Sullivan University, Louisville, KY 175
TESST College of Technology, Alexandria, VA 323
TESST College of Technology, Baltimore, MD 182
TESST College of Technology, Beltsville, MD 183
TESST College of Technology, Towson, MD 183
Thompson Institute, Chambersburg, PA 271
Thompson Institute, Harrisburg, PA 271
Thompson Institute, Philadelphia, PA 271
Vatterott College, Broadview Heights, OH 245
Vatterott College, Des Moines, IA 168
Vatterott College, Joplin, MO 206
Vatterott College, Kansas City, MO 207
Vatterott College, Memphis, TN 292
Vatterott College, OÆFallon , MO 207
Vatterott College, Oklahoma City, OK 248
Vatterott College, Omaha, NE 209
Vatterott College, Quincy, IL 160
Vatterott College, Springfield, MO 208
Vatterott College, St. Ann, MO 207
Vatterott College, St. Joseph, MO 207
Vatterott College, St. Louis, MO 208
Vatterott College, Tulsa, OK 249

Vatterott College, Wichita, KS 169
Virginia College at Birmingham, Birmingham, AL 72
Virginia College at Jackson, Jackson, MS 200
West Virginia Career Institute, Mount Braddock, PA 273
West Virginia Junior College, Bridgeport, WV 329
West Virginia Junior College, Charleston, WV 329
West Virginia Junior College, Morgantown, WV 330
Western Business College, Portland, OR 251
Western Business College, Vancouver, WA 328
Western Technical College, El Paso, TX 307
Western Technical Institute, El Paso, TX 308
Westwood College - Atlanta Northlake, Atlanta, GA 152
Westwood College - Chicago Loop Campus, Chicago, IL 161
Westwood College - Long Beach, Torrance, CA 110
Westwood College - Los Angeles, Inglewood, CA 110
Westwood College - Los Angeles, Los Angeles, CA 110
Wright Business School, Oklahoma City, OK 249
Wright Business School, Overland Park, KS 170
Wright Business School, Tulsa, OK 249

COMPUTER/INFORMATION TECHNOLOGY SERVICES/ ADMINISTRATION AND MANAGEMENT, OTHER

Academy of Medical Arts and Business, Harrisburg, PA 252
American Commercial College, Abilene, TX 292
American Commercial College, Lubbock, TX 293
American Commercial College, Odessa, TX 293
American Commercial College, San Angelo, TX 293
American Commercial College, Shreveport, LA 175
Apollo College-Westside, Inc., Phoenix, AZ
ATI Career Training Center, Dallas, TX 294
ATI Career Training Center, Fort Lauderdale, FL 122
ATI Career Training Center, Miami, FL 123
ATI Career Training Center, North Richland Hills, TX 295
ATI Career Training Center, Oakland Park, FL 123
Berks Technical Institute, Wyomissing, PA 253
Briarcliffe College, Bethpage, NY 226
Briarcliffe College, Patchogue, NY 226
Brookstone College of Business, Charlotte, NC 234
Brookstone College of Business, Greensboro, NC 234
Brown College, Mendota Heights, MN 193
Business Institute of Pennsylvania, Meadville, PA 255
Business Institute of Pennsylvania, Sharon, PA 255
Caguas Institute of Mechanical Technology, Caguas, PR 276
Capella University, Minneapolis, MN 194
Career Education Institute, Brockton, MA 184
Career Education Institute, Henderson, NV 210
Career Education Institute, Lincoln, RI 283
Career Education Institute, Lowell, MA 184

Career Education Institute, Marietta, GA 146
Career Education Institute, Norcross, GA 146
Career Technical College, Monroe, LA 176
Career Technical College, Shreveport, LA 177
Charter College, Anchorage, AK 74
CHI Institute, Broomall, PA 256
CHI Institute, Southampton, PA 256
The Chubb Institute, Alpharetta, GA 147
The Chubb Institute, Arlington, VA 314
The Chubb Institute, Cherry Hill, NJ 215
The Chubb Institute, Chicago, IL 155
The Chubb Institute, Jersey City, NJ 216
The Chubb Institute, New York, NY 228
The Chubb Institute, North Brunswick, NJ 216
The Chubb Institute, Parsippany, NJ 216
The Chubb Institute, Springfield, PA 256
The Chubb Institute, Westbury, NY 228
The Cittone Institute, Edison, NJ 217
The Cittone Institute, Mount Laurel, NJ 217
The Cittone Institute, Paramus, NJ 217
The Cittone Institute, Philadelphia, PA 257
The Cittone Institute, Plymouth Meeting, PA 257
CollegeAmerica - Denver, Denver, CO 113
Computer Learning Network, Altoona, PA 258
Computer Learning Network, Mechanicsburg, PA 258
Daymar College, Louisville, KY 171
Daymar College, Newport, KY 171
Daymar College, Owensboro, KY 171
Delta School of Business & Technology, Lake Charles, LA 177
Draughons Junior College, Bowling Green, KY 171
Draughons Junior College, Clarksville, TN 287
Draughons Junior College, Murfreesboro, TN 287
Draughons Junior College, Nashville, TN 288
ECPI College of Technology, Charlotte, NC 234
ECPI College of Technology, Greensboro, NC 235
ECPI College of Technology, Greenville, SC 285
ECPI College of Technology, Manassas, VA 315
ECPI College of Technology, Newport News, VA 315
ECPI College of Technology, North Charleston, SC 285
ECPI College of Technology, Raleigh, NC 235
ECPI College of Technology, Virginia Beach, VA 316
Empire College, Santa Rosa, CA 93
Florida Metropolitan University - Brandon Campus, Tampa, FL 127
Florida Technical College, Auburndale, FL 129
Florida Technical College, DeLand, FL 130
Florida Technical College, Jacksonville, FL 130
Florida Technical College, Orlando, FL 130
Gibbs College - Cranston, Cranston, RI 283
Gibbs College, Boston, MA 185
Gibbs College, Livingston, NJ 218
Gibbs College, Norwalk, CT 119

Globe College, Oakdale, MN 194
Gretna Career College, Gretna, LA 177
Hagerstown Business College, Hagerstown, MD 181
Herzing College, Atlanta, GA 148
Herzing College, Birmingham, AL 70
Herzing College, Kenner, LA 178
Herzing College, Madison, WI 330
Herzing College, Minneapolis, MN 195
Herzing College, Winter Park, FL 131
Hesser College, Manchester, NH 213
High-Tech Institute, Irving, TX 298
High-Tech Institute, Kansas City, MO 202
High-Tech Institute, Las Vegas, NV 210
High-Tech Institute, Marietta, GA 149
High-Tech Institute, Memphis, TN 288
High-Tech Institute, Nashville, TN 288
High-Tech Institute, Orlando, FL 132
High-Tech Institute, Phoenix, AZ 78
High-Tech Institute, Sacramento, CA 96
High-Tech Institute, St. Louis Park, MN 195
ICM School of Business & Medical Careers, Pittsburgh, PA 263
Indiana Business College, Anderson, IN 162
Indiana Business College, Columbus, IN 163
Indiana Business College, Evansville, IN 163
Indiana Business College, Fort Wayne, IN 163
Indiana Business College, Indianapolis, IN 163
Indiana Business College, Lafayette, IN 163
Indiana Business College, Marion, IN 164
Indiana Business College, Muncie, IN 164
Indiana Business College, Terre Haute, IN 164
Instituto Banca y Comercio, Caguas, PR 279
Instituto Banca y Comercio, Cayey, PR 279
Instituto Banca y Comercio, Fajardo, PR 279
Instituto Banca y Comercio, Guayama, PR 280
Instituto Banca y Comercio, Manati, PR 280
Instituto Banca y Comercio, Mayaguez, PR 280
Instituto Banca y Comercio, Ponce, PR 280
ITI Technical College, Baton Rouge, LA 178
Katharine Gibbs School, Melville, NY 231
Katharine Gibbs School, New York, NY 231
Katharine Gibbs School, Norristown, PA 264
Katharine Gibbs School, Piscataway, NJ 221
Kee Business College, Newport News, VA 319
Keiser College, Daytona Beach, FL 134
Keiser College, Fort Lauderdale, FL 134
Keiser College, Lakeland, FL 135
Keiser College, Melbourne, FL 135
Keiser College, Miami, FL 135
Keiser College, Orlando, FL 135
Keiser College, Pembroke Pines, FL 136
Keiser College, Port St. Lucie, FL 136
Keiser College, Sarasota, FL 136

COMPUTER TECHNICAL SUPPORT SPECIALIST

CONSTRUCTION ENGINEERING TECHNOLOGY/TECHNICIAN

CONSTRUCTION MANAGEMENT

CORRECTIONS

COSMETOLOGY, BARBER/STYLING AND NAIL INSTRUCTOR

Florida College of Natural Health, Miami, FL 126
Florida College of Natural Health, Pompano Beach, FL 126
Gene Juarez Academy of Beauty, Seattle, WA 327
Great Lakes Institute of Technology, Erie, PA 262
Instituto Banca y Comercio, Caguas, PR 279
Instituto Banca y Comercio, Cayey, PR 279
Instituto Banca y Comercio, Fajardo, PR 279
Instituto Banca y Comercio, Guayama, PR 280
Instituto Banca y Comercio, Manati, PR 280
Instituto Banca y Comercio, Mayaguez, PR 280
Instituto Banca y Comercio, Ponce, PR 280
Instituto de Banca y Comercio, San Juan, PR 281
Laurel Business Institute, Uniontown, PA 265
Roffler-Moler Hairstyling College, Marietta, GA 150
Tri-State Business Institute, Erie, PA 272
Virginia College at Jackson, Jackson, MS 200

COSMETOLOGY/COSMETOLOGIST, GENERAL

Career Training Institute, Apopka, FL 124
College of Hair Design, Lincoln, NE 208
Douglas Education Center, Monessen, PA 259
Empire Beauty School, Astoria, NY 229
Empire Beauty School, Bensonhurst, NY 229
Empire Beauty School, Boston, MA 185
Empire Beauty School, Cherry Hill, NJ 215
Empire Beauty School, Concord, NC 235
Empire Beauty School, Dunwoody, GA 147
Empire Beauty School, Hanover Park, IL 156
Empire Beauty School, Hanover, PA 259
Empire Beauty School, Harrisburg, PA 259
Empire Beauty School, Kennesaw, GA 147
Empire Beauty School, Lancaster, PA 260
Empire Beauty School, Laurel Springs, NJ 215
Empire Beauty School, Lawrenceville, GA 147
Empire Beauty School, Lawrenceville, NJ 215
Empire Beauty School, Lebanon, PA 260
Empire Beauty School, Malden, MA 185
Empire Beauty School, Matthews, NC 235
Empire Beauty School, Midlothian, VA 317
Empire Beauty School, Monroeville, PA 260
Empire Beauty School, New York, NY 229
Empire Beauty School, Owings Mills, MD 181
Empire Beauty School, Philadelphia, PA 260
Empire Beauty School, Pittsburgh, PA 260
Empire Beauty School, Pottstown, PA 260
Empire Beauty School, Pottsville, PA 260
Empire Beauty School, Reading, PA 260
Empire Beauty School, Shamokin Dam, PA 261
Empire Beauty School, State College, PA 261
Empire Beauty School, Warminster, PA 261
Empire Beauty School, West Chester, PA 261
Empire Beauty School, West Mifflin, PA 261

Empire Beauty School, Whitehall, PA 261
Empire Beauty School, Williamsport, PA 261
Empire Beauty School, York, PA 261
Gene Juarez Academy of Beauty, Seattle, WA 327
Great Lakes Institute of Technology, Erie, PA 262
Heritage College of Hair Design, Oklahoma City, OK 247
Instituto Banca y Comercio, Caguas, PR 279
Instituto Banca y Comercio, Cayey, PR 279
Instituto Banca y Comercio, Fajardo, PR 279
Instituto Banca y Comercio, Guayama, PR 280
Instituto Banca y Comercio, Manati, PR 280
Instituto Banca y Comercio, Mayaguez, PR 280
Instituto Banca y Comercio, Ponce, PR 280
La Belle Beauty School, Hialeah, FL 137
Laurel Business Institute, Uniontown, PA 265
McCann School of Business, Hazleton, PA 266
McCann School of Business, Pottsville, PA 267
McCann School of Business, Scranton, PA 267
McCann School of Business, Sunbury, PA 267
Miller-Motte Technical College, Cary, NC 236
Miller-Motte Technical College, Chattanooga, TN 290
Miller-Motte Technical College, Clarksville, TN 290
Miller-Motte Technical College, Lynchburg, VA 320
Miller-Motte Technical College, North Charleston, SC 285
Miller-Motte Technical College, Wilmington, NC 236
New England Institute of Technology at Palm Beach, West Palm Beach, FL 140
Roffler-Moler Hairstyling College, Marietta, GA 150
Tri-State Business Institute, Erie, PA 272
Vatterott College, Broadview Heights, OH 245
Vatterott College, Des Moines, IA 168
Vatterott College, Joplin, MO 206
Vatterott College, Kansas City, MO 207
Vatterott College, Memphis, TN 292
Vatterott College, O'Fallon , MO 207
Vatterott College, Oklahoma City, OK 248
Vatterott College, Omaha, NE 209
Vatterott College, Quincy, IL 160
Vatterott College, Springfield, MO 208
Vatterott College, St. Ann, MO 207
Vatterott College, St. Joseph, MO 207
Vatterott College, St. Louis, MO 208
Vatterott College, Tulsa, OK 249
Vatterott College, Wichita, KS 169
Virginia College at Huntsville, Huntsville, AL 73
Virginia College at Jackson, Jackson, MS 200
West Tennessee Business College, Jackson, TN 292

COUNSELOR EDUCATION/SCHOOL COUNSELING AND GUIDANCE SERVICES

Argosy University/Phoenix, Phoenix, AZ 75
Argosy University/Schaumburg, Schaumburg, IL 154

Capella University, Minneapolis, MN 194
South University, Columbia, SC 286
South University, Montgomery, AL 71
South University, Savannah, GA 151
South University, West Palm Beach, FL 142

COURT REPORTING/COURT REPORTER

Bryan College of Court Reporting, Los Angeles, CA 88
Court Reporting Institute of Dallas, Dallas, TX 297
Court Reporting Institute of Houston, Houston, TX 297
Key College, Fort Lauderdale, FL 137
Las Vegas College, Henderson, NV 211
Las Vegas College, Las Vegas, NV 211
Virginia Career Institute, Richmond, VA 323
Virginia Career Institute, Virginia Beach, VA 323

CRIMINAL JUSTICE/LAW ENFORCEMENT ADMINISTRATION

American InterContinental University, Atlanta, GA 145
American InterContinental University, Houston, TX 293
American InterContinental University, Los Angeles, CA 85
American InterContinental University, San Antonio, TX 293
American InterContinental University, Weston, FL 121
Bauder College, Atlanta, GA 146
Bay State College, Boston, MA 183
Berks Technical Institute, Wyomissing, PA 253
Blair College, Colorado Springs, CO 112
Briarcliffe College, Bethpage, NY 226
Briarcliffe College, Patchogue, NY 226
Brown Mackie College, Akron Campus, Akron, OH 238
Brown Mackie College, Atlanta Campus, Norcross, GA 146
Brown Mackie College, Cincinnati Campus, Cincinnati, OH 238
Brown Mackie College, Findlay Campus, Findlay, OH 238
Brown Mackie College, Hopkinsville Campus, Hopkinsville, KY 170
Brown Mackie College, Lenexa Campus, Lenexa, KS 168
Brown Mackie College, Los Angeles Campus, Santa Monica, CA 87
Brown Mackie College, Merrillville Campus, Merrillville, IN 162
Brown Mackie College, Miami Campus, Miami, FL 124
Brown Mackie College, Michigan City Campus, Michigan City, IN 162
Brown Mackie College, North Canton Campus, North Canton, OH 239
Brown Mackie College, Northern Kentucky Campus, Fort Mitchell, KY 170
Brown Mackie College, Orange County Campus, Santa Ana, CA 87
Brown Mackie College, San Diego Campus, San Diego, CA 87

Brown Mackie College, South Bend Campus, South Bend, IN 162
Capella University, Minneapolis, MN 194
Career Networks Institute, Costa Mesa, CA 91
Central Florida College, Winter Park, FL 124
Chaparral College, Tucson, AZ 77
CHI Institute, Broomall, PA 256
CHI Institute, Southampton, PA 256
The Chubb Institute, Alpharetta, GA 147
The Chubb Institute, Arlington, VA 314
The Chubb Institute, Cherry Hill, NJ 215
The Chubb Institute, Chicago, IL 155
The Chubb Institute, Jersey City, NJ 216
The Chubb Institute, New York, NY 228
The Chubb Institute, North Brunswick, NJ 216
The Chubb Institute, Parsippany, NJ 216
The Chubb Institute, Springfield, PA 256
The Chubb Institute, Westbury, NY 228
The Cittone Institute, Edison, NJ 217
The Cittone Institute, Mount Laurel, NJ 217
The Cittone Institute, Paramus, NJ 217
The Cittone Institute, Philadelphia, PA 257
The Cittone Institute, Plymouth Meeting, PA 257
Colorado Technical University Denver Campus, Greenwood Village, CO 114
Colorado Technical University Sioux Falls Campus, Sioux Falls, SD 286
Colorado Technical University, Colorado Springs, CO 113
Computer Learning Network, Altoona, PA 258
Computer Learning Network, Mechanicsburg, PA 258
Denver Career College, Thornton, CO 114
Draughons Junior College, Bowling Green, KY 171
Draughons Junior College, Clarksville, TN 287
Draughons Junior College, Murfreesboro, TN 287
Draughons Junior College, Nashville, TN 288
Eagle Gate College - Weber/Davis, Layton, UT 309
Eagle Gate College - Weber/Davis, Salt Lake City, UT 309
ECPI College of Technology, Charlotte, NC 234
ECPI College of Technology, Greensboro, NC 235
ECPI College of Technology, Greenville, SC 285
ECPI College of Technology, Manassas, VA 315
ECPI College of Technology, Newport News, VA 315
ECPI College of Technology, North Charleston, SC 285
ECPI College of Technology, Raleigh, NC 235
ECPI College of Technology, Virginia Beach, VA 316
ECPI Technical College, Glen Allen, VA 316
ECPI Technical College, Richmond, VA 316
ECPI Technical College, Roanoke, VA 317
Everest College, Arlington , TX 297
Everest College, Dallas, TX 297
Everest College, Fort Worth, TX 297
Everest College, Phoenix, AZ 78
Everest College, Rancho Cucamonga, CA 93

Remington College - Tempe Campus, Tempe, AZ 81
San Joaquin Valley College, Bakersfield, CA 103
San Joaquin Valley College, Fresno, CA 103
San Joaquin Valley College, Modesto, CA 104
San Joaquin Valley College, Rancho Cucamonga, CA 104
San Joaquin Valley College, Visalia, CA 104
Sanford-Brown College, Collinsville, IL 159
Sanford-Brown College, Fenton, MO 205
Sanford-Brown College, Hazelwood, MO 205
Sanford-Brown College, North Kansas City, MO 206
Sanford-Brown College, St. Charles, MO 206
Sanford-Brown College, West Allis, WI 331
Sanford-Brown Institute, Atlanta, GA 150
Sanford-Brown Institute, Dallas, TX 305
Sanford-Brown Institute, Garden City, NY 232
Sanford-Brown Institute, Houston, TX 305
Sanford-Brown Institute, Houston, TX 306
Sanford-Brown Institute, Jacksonville, FL 142
Sanford-Brown Institute, Landover, MD 182
Sanford-Brown Institute, Lauderdale Lakes, FL 142
Sanford-Brown Institute, New York, NY 232
Sanford-Brown Institute, Springfield, MA 187
Sanford-Brown Institute, Tampa, FL 142
Sanford-Brown Institute, Trevose, PA 270
Sanford-Brown Institute, White Plains, NY 232
Santa Barbara Business College, Bakersfield, CA 104
Santa Barbara Business College, Santa Barbara, CA 105
Santa Barbara Business College, Santa Maria, CA 105
Santa Barbara Business College, Ventura, CA 105
South College, Knoxville, TN 291
South University, Columbia, SC 286
South University, Montgomery, AL 71
South University, Savannah, GA 151
South University, West Palm Beach, FL 142
Southeastern Career College, Nashville, TN 292
Southwest Florida College, Tampa, FL 143
Technology Education College, Columbus, OH 245
TESST College of Technology, Alexandria, VA 323
TESST College of Technology, Baltimore, MD 182
TESST College of Technology, Beltsville, MD 183
TESST College of Technology, Towson, MD 183
Thompson Institute, Chambersburg, PA 271
Thompson Institute, Harrisburg, PA 271
Thompson Institute, Philadelphia, PA 271
Virginia College at Birmingham, Birmingham, AL 72
Virginia College at Huntsville, Huntsville, AL 73
Virginia College at Jackson, Jackson, MS 200
Virginia College at Pensacola, Pensacola, FL 144
Western Business College, Portland, OR 251
Western Business College, Vancouver, WA 328
Western School of Health and Business Careers, Monroeville, PA 273

Western School of Health and Business Careers, Pittsburgh, PA 273
Westwood College - Anaheim, Anaheim, CA 109
Westwood College - Chicago Du Page, Woodridge, IL 160
Westwood College - Chicago O'Hare Airport, Chicago, IL 161
Westwood College - Chicago River Oaks, Calumet City, IL 161
Westwood College - Denver South, Denver, CO 118
Westwood College - Inland Empire, Upland, CA 109
Westwood College - Long Beach, Torrance, CA 110
Westwood College - Los Angeles, Inglewood, CA 110
Westwood College - Los Angeles, Los Angeles, CA 110
York Technical Institute, Lancaster, PA 274
York Technical Institute, York, PA 274

CRIMINAL JUSTICE/POLICE SCIENCE

Allied College, Arnold, MO 201
Allied College, Maryland Heights, MO 201
American InterContinental University, Atlanta, GA 145
American InterContinental University, Houston, TX 293
American InterContinental University, Los Angeles, CA 85
American InterContinental University, San Antonio, TX 293
American InterContinental University, Weston, FL 121
Andover College, Portland, ME 180
Berks Technical Institute, Wyomissing, PA 253
Briarcliffe College, Bethpage, NY 226
Briarcliffe College, Patchogue, NY 226
Brown Mackie College, Lenexa Campus, Lenexa, KS 168
Capella University, Minneapolis, MN 194
The Cittone Institute, Edison, NJ 217
The Cittone Institute, Mount Laurel, NJ 217
The Cittone Institute, Paramus, NJ 217
The Cittone Institute, Philadelphia, PA 257
The Cittone Institute, Plymouth Meeting, PA 257
Computer Learning Network, Altoona, PA 258
Computer Learning Network, Mechanicsburg, PA 258
Daymar College, Louisville, KY 171
Daymar College, Newport, KY 171
Daymar College, Owensboro, KY 171
Draughons Junior College, Bowling Green, KY 171
Draughons Junior College, Clarksville, TN 287
Draughons Junior College, Murfreesboro, TN 287
Draughons Junior College, Nashville, TN 288
ECPI College of Technology, Charlotte, NC 234
ECPI College of Technology, Greensboro, NC 235
ECPI College of Technology, Greenville, SC 285
ECPI College of Technology, Manassas, VA 315
ECPI College of Technology, Newport News, VA 315
ECPI College of Technology, North Charleston, SC 285
ECPI College of Technology, Raleigh, NC 235
ECPI College of Technology, Virginia Beach, VA 316

McCann School of Business, Scranton, PA 267
McCann School of Business, Sunbury, PA 267
McIntosh College, Dover, NH 213
Miller-Motte Technical College, Cary, NC 236
Miller-Motte Technical College, Chattanooga, TN 290
Miller-Motte Technical College, Clarksville, TN 290
Miller-Motte Technical College, Lynchburg, VA 320
Miller-Motte Technical College, North Charleston, SC 285
Miller-Motte Technical College, Wilmington, NC 236
North Florida Institute, Orange Park, FL 140
Parks College, Aurora, CO 116
Parks College, Denver, CO 116
Parks College, McLean, VA 321
Pittsburgh Technical Institute, Oakdale, PA 269
Rasmussen College St. Cloud, St. Cloud, MN 199
Remington College - Baton Rouge Campus, Baton Rouge, LA 179
Remington College - Lafayette Campus, Lafayette, LA 179
Remington College - San Diego Campus, San Diego, CA 103
Remington College-Little Rock Campus, Little Rock, AR 83
South University, Columbia, SC 286
South University, Montgomery, AL 71
South University, Savannah, GA 151
South University, West Palm Beach, FL 142
Virginia College at Birmingham, Birmingham, AL 72
Virginia College at Huntsville, Huntsville, AL 73
Virginia College at Pensacola, Pensacola, FL 144
Westwood College - Chicago Loop Campus, Chicago, IL 161
Westwood College - Chicago O'Hare Airport, Chicago, IL 161

CULINARY ARTS/CHEF TRAINING

Academy of Medical Arts and Business, Harrisburg, PA 252
The Art Institute of Atlanta, Atlanta, GA 145
The Art Institute of California - Los Angeles, Santa Monica, CA 85
The Art Institute of California - Orange County, Santa Ana, CA 86
The Art Institute of California - San Diego, San Diego, CA 86
The Art Institute of Charlotte, Charlotte, NC 233
The Art Institute of Colorado, Denver, CO 111
The Art Institute of Dallas, Dallas, TX 294
The Art Institute of Fort Lauderdale, Fort Lauderdale, FL 122
The Art Institute of Houston, Houston, TX 294
The Art Institute of Las Vegas, Henderson, NV 209
The Art Institute of New York City, New York, NY 225

The Art Institute of Philadelphia, Philadelphia, PA 252
The Art Institute of Phoenix, Phoenix, AZ 76
The Art Institute of Pittsburgh, Pittsburgh, PA 252
The Art Institute of Seattle, Seattle, WA 324
The Art Institute of Washington, Arlington, VA 314
The Art Institutes International Minnesota, Minneapolis, MN 193
Bradford School, Columbus, OH 237
Bradford School, Pittsburgh, PA 254
California Culinary Academy, San Francisco, CA 91
California School of Culinary Arts, Pasadena, CA 91
Colegio Mayor de Tecnologia, Arroyo, PR 276
The Cooking and Hospitality Institute of Chicago, Chicago, IL 155
Escuela Hotelera de San Juan in Puerto Rico, San Juan, PR 278
The French Culinary Institute, New York, NY 229
The Illinois Institute of Art - Chicago, Chicago, IL 156
Instituto Banca y Comercio, Caguas, PR 279
Instituto Banca y Comercio, Cayey, PR 279
Instituto Banca y Comercio, Fajardo, PR 279
Instituto Banca y Comercio, Guayama, PR 280
Instituto Banca y Comercio, Manati, PR 280
Instituto Banca y Comercio, Mayaguez, PR 280
Instituto Banca y Comercio, Ponce, PR 280
Instituto de Banca y Comercio, San Juan, PR 281
Keiser College, Daytona Beach, FL 134
Keiser College, Fort Lauderdale, FL 134
Keiser College, Lakeland, FL 135
Keiser College, Melbourne, FL 135
Keiser College, Miami, FL 135
Keiser College, Orlando, FL 135
Keiser College, Pembroke Pines, FL 136
Keiser College, Port St. Lucie, FL 136
Keiser College, Sarasota, FL 136
Keiser College, Tallahassee, FL 136
Keiser College, West Palm Beach, FL 137
Le Cordon Bleu College of Culinary Arts Miami, Miramar, FL 137
Le Cordon Bleu College of Culinary Arts, Atlanta, Tucker, GA 149
Le Cordon Bleu College of Culinary Arts, Las Vegas, Las Vegas, NV 211
New England Culinary Institute at Essex, Essex Junction, VT 313
New England Culinary Institute, Montpelier, VT 313
New England Institute of Technology at Palm Beach, West Palm Beach, FL 140
New England Technical Institute of Connecticut, Inc., New Britain, CT 119
New England Technical Institute, Cromwell, CT 119
New England Technical Institute, Hamden, CT 119
New England Technical Institute, Shelton, CT 119

Orlando Culinary Academy, Orlando, FL 140
Orleans Technical Institute, Philadelphia, PA 268
Pennsylvania Culinary Institute, Pittsburgh, PA 269
Ponce Paramedical College, Inc., Coto Laurel, PR 282
Remington College - Dallas Campus, Garland, TX 304
The Restaurant School at Walnut Hill College, Philadelphia, PA 270
Scottsdale Culinary Institute, Scottsdale, AZ 81
Stratford University, Falls Church , VA 322
Stratford University, Woodbridge, VA 322
Sullivan University, Lexington, KY 174
Sullivan University, Louisville, KY 175
Texas Culinary Academy, Austin, TX 306
Virginia College at Birmingham, Birmingham, AL 72
Western Culinary Institute, Portland, OR 251
York Technical Institute, Lancaster, PA 274
York Technical Institute, York, PA 274
Yorktowne Business Institute, York, PA 274

CUSTOMER SERVICE MANAGEMENT

Berks Technical Institute, Wyomissing, PA 253
Career Institute of Health and Technology, Brooklyn, NY 227
Career Institute of Health and Technology, Garden City, NY 227
Career Institute of Health and Technology, Rego Park, NY 228
Douglas Education Center, Monessen, PA 259
Hagerstown Business College, Hagerstown, MD 181
Harrison Career Institute, Allentown, PA 262
Harrison Career Institute, Baltimore, MD 181
Harrison Career Institute, Clifton, NJ 218
Harrison Career Institute, Delran, NJ 218
Harrison Career Institute, Deptford, NJ 219
Harrison Career Institute, Ewing, NJ 219
Harrison Career Institute, Jersey City, NJ 219
Harrison Career Institute, Oakhurst, NJ 219
Harrison Career Institute, Philadelphia, PA 263
Harrison Career Institute, Reading, PA 263
Harrison Career Institute, South Orange, NJ 220
Harrison Career Institute, Vineland, NJ 220
Harrison Career Institute, Wilmington, DE 121

CUSTOMER SERVICE SUPPORT/CALL CENTER/TELESERVICE OPERATION

Advanced Training Associates, El Cajon, CA 84
Berks Technical Institute, Wyomissing, PA 253
Thompson Institute, Chambersburg, PA 271
Thompson Institute, Harrisburg, PA 271
Thompson Institute, Philadelphia, PA 271

DATAENTRY/MICROCOMPUTER APPLICATIONS, GENERAL

American Commercial College, Abilene, TX 292
American Commercial College, Lubbock, TX 293
American Commercial College, Odessa, TX 293
American Commercial College, San Angelo, TX 293
American Commercial College, Shreveport, LA 175
Austin Business College, Austin, TX 295
Berks Technical Institute, Wyomissing, PA 253
Bradford School, Columbus, OH 237
Bradford School, Pittsburgh, PA 254
Briarcliffe College, Bethpage, NY 226
Briarcliffe College, Patchogue, NY 226
Brookstone College of Business, Charlotte, NC 234
Brookstone College of Business, Greensboro, NC 234
Career Education Institute, Brockton, MA 184
Career Education Institute, Henderson, NV 210
Career Education Institute, Lincoln, RI 283
Career Education Institute, Lowell, MA 184
Career Education Institute, Marietta, GA 146
Career Education Institute, Norcross, GA 146
Central Coast College, Salinas, CA 92
CHI Institute, Broomall, PA 256
CHI Institute, Southampton, PA 256
The Chubb Institute, Alpharetta, GA 147
The Chubb Institute, Arlington, VA 314
The Chubb Institute, Cherry Hill, NJ 215
The Chubb Institute, Chicago, IL 155
The Chubb Institute, Jersey City, NJ 216
The Chubb Institute, New York, NY 228
The Chubb Institute, North Brunswick, NJ 216
The Chubb Institute, Parsippany, NJ 216
The Chubb Institute, Springfield, PA 256
The Chubb Institute, Westbury, NY 228
Colegio Mayor de Tecnologia, Arroyo, PR 276
CollegeAmerica - Denver, Denver, CO 113
Computer Learning Network, Altoona, PA 258
Computer Learning Network, Mechanicsburg, PA 258
Dorsey Schools, Madison Heights, MI 188
Dorsey Schools, Roseville, MI 188
Dorsey Schools, Southgate, MI 188
Dorsey Schools, Wayne, MI 189
Douglas Education Center, Monessen, PA 259
Empire College, Santa Rosa, CA 93
Erie Business Center South, New Castle, PA 262
Gallipolis Career College, Gallipolis, OH 239
Instituto Banca y Comercio, Caguas, PR 279
Instituto Banca y Comercio, Cayey, PR 279
Instituto Banca y Comercio, Fajardo, PR 279
Instituto Banca y Comercio, Guayama, PR 280
Instituto Banca y Comercio, Manati, PR 280
Instituto Banca y Comercio, Mayaguez, PR 280
Instituto Banca y Comercio, Ponce, PR 280

Instituto de Banca y Comercio, San Juan, PR 281
International Business College, El Paso, TX 298
International Business College, El Paso, TX 299
International Business College, Fort Wayne, IN 165
International Business College, Indianapolis, IN 165
Island Drafting and Technical Institute, Amityville, NY 230
ITI Technical College, Baton Rouge, LA 178
McCann School of Business, Hazleton, PA 266
McCann School of Business, Pottsville, PA 267
McCann School of Business, Scranton, PA 267
McCann School of Business, Sunbury, PA 267
Miller-Motte Technical College, Cary, NC 236
Miller-Motte Technical College, Chattanooga, TN 290
Miller-Motte Technical College, Clarksville, TN 290
Miller-Motte Technical College, Lynchburg, VA 320
Miller-Motte Technical College, North Charleston, SC 285
Miller-Motte Technical College, Wilmington, NC 236
Missouri College, St. Louis, MO 203
National College of Business & Technology, Bayamon, PR 282
National College of Business & Technology, Bluefield, VA 320
National College of Business & Technology, Bristol, TN 290
National College of Business & Technology, Charlottesville, VA 320
National College of Business & Technology, Danville, KY 172
National College of Business & Technology, Danville, VA 320
National College of Business & Technology, Florence, KY 172
National College of Business & Technology, Harrisonburg, VA 321
National College of Business & Technology, Knoxville, TN 291
National College of Business & Technology, Lexington, KY 173
National College of Business & Technology, Louisville, KY 173
National College of Business & Technology, Lynchburg, VA 321
National College of Business & Technology, Martinsville, VA 321
National College of Business & Technology, Nashville, TN 291
National College of Business & Technology, Pikeville, KY 173
National College of Business & Technology, Richmond, KY 173
National College of Business & Technology, Rio Grande, PR 282
National College of Business & Technology, Salem, VA 321

The PJA School, Upper Darby, PA 270
Rasmussen College Eagan, Eagan, MN 198
Rasmussen College Minnetonka, Minnetonka, MN 199
Remington College - Jacksonville Campus, Jacksonville, FL 140
Sanford-Brown College, Collinsville, IL 159
Sanford-Brown College, Fenton, MO 205
Sanford-Brown College, Hazelwood, MO 205
Sanford-Brown College, North Kansas City, MO 206
Sanford-Brown College, St. Charles, MO 206
Sanford-Brown College, West Allis, WI 331
South College, Knoxville, TN 291
Stevens-Henager College, Boise, ID 153
Stevens-Henager College, Logan, UT 311
Stevens-Henager College, Ogden, UT 311
Stevens-Henager College - Salt Lake City, Salt Lake City, UT 312
Stuart School of Business Administration, Wall, NJ 223
TESST College of Technology, Alexandria, VA 323
TESST College of Technology, Baltimore, MD 182
TESST College of Technology, Beltsville, MD 183
TESST College of Technology, Towson, MD 183
Thompson Institute, Chambersburg, PA 271
Thompson Institute, Harrisburg, PA 271
Thompson Institute, Philadelphia, PA 271
Trinity College of Puerto Rico, Ponce, PR 283
Vatterott College, Broadview Heights, OH 245
Vatterott College, Des Moines, IA 168
Vatterott College, Joplin, MO 206
Vatterott College, Kansas City, MO 207
Vatterott College, Memphis, TN 292
Vatterott College, OÆFallon , MO 207
Vatterott College, Oklahoma City, OK 248
Vatterott College, Omaha, NE 209
Vatterott College, Quincy, IL 160
Vatterott College, Springfield, MO 208
Vatterott College, St. Ann, MO 207
Vatterott College, St. Joseph, MO 207
Vatterott College, St. Louis, MO 208
Vatterott College, Tulsa, OK 249
Vatterott College, Wichita, KS 169
West Virginia Junior College, Bridgeport, WV 329
West Virginia Junior College, Charleston, WV 329
West Virginia Junior College, Morgantown, WV 330
Western Business College, Portland, OR 251
Western Business College, Vancouver, WA 328

DATAENTRY/MICROCOMPUTER APPLICATIONS, OTHER

Berks Technical Institute, Wyomissing, PA 253
Briarcliffe College, Bethpage, NY 226
Briarcliffe College, Patchogue, NY 226

Brookstone College of Business, Charlotte, NC 234
Brookstone College of Business, Greensboro, NC 234
Business Institute of Pennsylvania, Meadville, PA 255
Business Institute of Pennsylvania, Sharon, PA 255
Career Education Institute, Brockton, MA 184
Career Education Institute, Henderson, NV 210
Career Education Institute, Lincoln, RI 283
Career Education Institute, Lowell, MA 184
Career Education Institute, Marietta, GA 146
Career Education Institute, Norcross, GA 146
Central Coast College, Salinas, CA 92
The Chubb Institute, Alpharetta, GA 147
The Chubb Institute, Arlington, VA 314
The Chubb Institute, Cherry Hill, NJ 215
The Chubb Institute, Chicago, IL 155
The Chubb Institute, Jersey City, NJ 216
The Chubb Institute, New York, NY 228
The Chubb Institute, North Brunswick, NJ 216
The Chubb Institute, Parsippany, NJ 216
The Chubb Institute, Springfield, PA 256
The Chubb Institute, Westbury, NY 228
Computer Learning Network, Altoona, PA 258
Computer Learning Network, Mechanicsburg, PA 258
Dorsey Schools, Madison Heights, MI 188
Dorsey Schools, Roseville, MI 188
Dorsey Schools, Southgate, MI 188
Dorsey Schools, Wayne, MI 189
Gretna Career College, Gretna, LA 177
ICM School of Business & Medical Careers, Pittsburgh, PA 263
ITI Technical College, Baton Rouge, LA 178
McCann School of Business, Hazleton, PA 266
McCann School of Business, Pottsville, PA 267
McCann School of Business, Scranton, PA 267
McCann School of Business, Sunbury, PA 267
Rasmussen College Eagan, Eagan, MN 198
TESST College of Technology, Alexandria, VA 323
TESST College of Technology, Baltimore, MD 182
TESST College of Technology, Beltsville, MD 183
TESST College of Technology, Towson, MD 183

DATA MODELING/WAREHOUSING AND DATABASE ADMINISTRATION

Brookstone College of Business, Charlotte, NC 234
Brookstone College of Business, Greensboro, NC 234
The Chubb Institute, Alpharetta, GA 147
The Chubb Institute, Arlington, VA 314
The Chubb Institute, Cherry Hill, NJ 215
The Chubb Institute, Chicago, IL 155
The Chubb Institute, Jersey City, NJ 216
The Chubb Institute, New York, NY 228
The Chubb Institute, North Brunswick, NJ 216
The Chubb Institute, Parsippany, NJ 216

The Chubb Institute, Springfield, PA 256
The Chubb Institute, Westbury, NY 228
ICM School of Business & Medical Careers, Pittsburgh, PA 263
ITI Technical College, Baton Rouge, LA 178
Kaplan University, Davenport, IA 168
Remington College - Pinellas Campus, Largo, FL 141

DATA PROCESSING AND DATA PROCESSING TECHNOLOGY/ TECHNICIAN

Academy of Medical Arts and Business, Harrisburg, PA 252
American Commercial College, Abilene, TX 292
American Commercial College, Lubbock, TX 293
American Commercial College, Odessa, TX 293
American Commercial College, San Angelo, TX 293
American Commercial College, Shreveport, LA 175
Bradford School, Columbus, OH 237
Bradford School, Pittsburgh, PA 254
Briarcliffe College, Bethpage, NY 226
Briarcliffe College, Patchogue, NY 226
Brookstone College of Business, Charlotte, NC 234
Brookstone College of Business, Greensboro, NC 234
Brown Mackie College, Lenexa Campus, Lenexa, KS 168
Business Institute of Pennsylvania, Meadville, PA 255
Business Institute of Pennsylvania, Sharon, PA 255
Career College of Northern Nevada, Reno, NV 210
Career Education Institute, Brockton, MA 184
Career Education Institute, Henderson, NV 210
Career Education Institute, Lincoln, RI 283
Career Education Institute, Lowell, MA 184
Career Education Institute, Marietta, GA 146
Career Education Institute, Norcross, GA 146
The Chubb Institute, Alpharetta, GA 147
The Chubb Institute, Arlington, VA 314
The Chubb Institute, Cherry Hill, NJ 215
The Chubb Institute, Chicago, IL 155
The Chubb Institute, Jersey City, NJ 216
The Chubb Institute, New York, NY 228
The Chubb Institute, North Brunswick, NJ 216
The Chubb Institute, Parsippany, NJ 216
The Chubb Institute, Springfield, PA 256
The Chubb Institute, Westbury, NY 228
Coyne American Institute, Chicago, IL 155
Coyne American Institute, Chicago, IL 156
Douglas Education Center, Monessen, PA 259
ECPI College of Technology, Charlotte, NC 234
ECPI College of Technology, Greensboro, NC 235
ECPI College of Technology, Greenville, SC 285
ECPI College of Technology, Manassas, VA 315
ECPI College of Technology, Newport News, VA 315
ECPI College of Technology, North Charleston, SC 285

ECPI College of Technology, Raleigh, NC 235
ECPI College of Technology, Virginia Beach, VA 316
ECPI Technical College, Glen Allen, VA 316
ECPI Technical College, Richmond, VA 316
ECPI Technical College, Roanoke, VA 317
Empire College, Santa Rosa, CA 93
Gibbs College - Cranston, Cranston, RI 283
Herzing College, Atlanta, GA 148
Herzing College, Birmingham, AL 70
Herzing College, Kenner, LA 178
Herzing College, Madison, WI 330
Herzing College, Minneapolis, MN 195
Herzing College, Winter Park, FL 131
High-Tech Institute, Irving, TX 298
High-Tech Institute, Kansas City, MO 202
High-Tech Institute, Las Vegas, NV 210
High-Tech Institute, Marietta, GA 149
High-Tech Institute, Memphis, TN 288
High-Tech Institute, Nashville, TN 288
High-Tech Institute, Orlando, FL 132
High-Tech Institute, Phoenix, AZ 78
High-Tech Institute, Sacramento, CA 96
High-Tech Institute, St. Louis Park, MN 195
HoHoKus RETS School of Business and Medical Technical
Services, Nutley, NJ 220
ITI Technical College, Baton Rouge, LA 178
McCann School of Business, Hazleton, PA 266
McCann School of Business, Pottsville, PA267
McCann School of Business, Scranton, PA 267
McCann School of Business, Sunbury, PA 267
Rockford Business College, Rockford, IL 159
San Joaquin Valley College, Bakersfield, CA 103
San Joaquin Valley College, Fresno, CA 103
San Joaquin Valley College, Modesto, CA 104
**San Joaquin Valley College, Rancho Cucamonga, CA
104**
San Joaquin Valley College, Visalia, CA 104
Sawyer College, Merrillville, IN 167
TESST College of Technology, Alexandria, VA 323
TESST College of Technology, Baltimore, MD 182
TESST College of Technology, Beltsville, MD 183
TESST College of Technology, Towson, MD 183

DENTAL ASSISTING/ASSISTANT

**Academy of Medical Arts and Business, Harrisburg, PA
252**
ACT College, Alexandria, VA 313
ACT College, Fairfax, VA 313
ACT College, Manassas, VA 313
Advanced Career Training, Atlanta, GA 144
Advanced Career Training, Jacksonville, FL 121
Advanced Career Training, Riverdale, GA 145
Akron Institute, Akron, OH 236

Allied College, Arnold, MO 201
Allied College, Maryland Heights, MO 201
Antilles School of Technical Careers, Santurce, PR 275
Apollo College, Albuquerque, NM 223
Apollo College, Boise, ID 153
Apollo College-Phoenix, Inc., Phoenix, AZ 74
Apollo College, Portland, OR 249
Apollo College, Spokane, WA 324
Apollo College-Tri-City, Inc., Mesa, AZ 75
Apollo College-Tucson, Inc., Tucson, AZ 75
Arizona College of Allied Health, Glendale, AZ 76
ATI Career Training Center, Dallas, TX 294
ATI Career Training Center, Fort Lauderdale, FL 122
ATI Career Training Center, Miami, FL 123
**ATI Career Training Center, North Richland Hills, TX
295**
ATI Career Training Center, Oakland Park, FL 123
ATI Health Education Center, Miami, FL 123
Berdan Institute, Totowa, NJ 214
Bryman College, Alhambra, CA 88
Bryman College, Anaheim, CA 88
Bryman College, City of Industry, CA 88
Bryman College, Earth City, MO 201
Bryman College, Everett, WA 325
Bryman College, Gardena, CA 88
Bryman College, Hayward, CA 89
Bryman College, Los Angeles, CA 89
Bryman College, Lynnwood, WA 326
Bryman College, New Orleans, LA 176
Bryman College, Ontario, CA 89
Bryman College, Port Orchard, WA 326
Bryman College, Renton, WA 326
Bryman College, Reseda, CA 89
Bryman College, San Bernardino, CA 90
Bryman College, San Francisco, CA 90
Bryman College, San Jose, CA 90
Bryman College, Tacoma, WA 326
Bryman College, Torrance, CA 90
Bryman Institute, Brighton, MA 183
Bryman Institute, Chelsea, MA 184
Bryman Institute, Eagan, MN 193
Bryman Institute, Gahanna, OH 239
The Bryman School, Phoenix, AZ 77
Caliber Training Institute, New York, NY 227
Cambridge College, Aurora, CO 112
Cambridge College, Beaverton, OR 250
Cambridge College, Bellevue, WA 326
Career Centers of Texas, El Paso, TX 295
Career Education Institute, Brockton, MA 184
Career Education Institute, Henderson, NV 210
Career Education Institute, Lincoln, RI 283
Career Education Institute, Lowell, MA 184
Career Education Institute, Marietta, GA 146

Vatterott College, Joplin, MO 206
Vatterott College, Kansas City, MO 207
Vatterott College, Memphis, TN 292
Vatterott College, OÆFallon , MO 207
Vatterott College, Oklahoma City, OK 248
Vatterott College, Omaha, NE 209
Vatterott College, Quincy, IL 160
Vatterott College, Springfield, MO 208
Vatterott College, St. Ann, MO 207
Vatterott College, St. Joseph, MO 207
Vatterott College, St. Louis, MO 208
Vatterott College, Tulsa, OK 249
Vatterott College, Wichita, KS 169
Western Career College, Pleasant Hill, CA 108
Western Career College, Sacramento, CA 108
Western Career College, San Leandro, CA 109
Western School of Health and Business Careers, Monroe-eville, PA 273
Western School of Health and Business Careers, Pittsburgh, PA 273

DENTAL HYGIENE/HYGIENIST

Apollo College, Albuquerque, NM 223
Apollo College, Boise, ID 153
Apollo College, Portland, OR 249
Apollo College, Spokane, WA 324
Draughons Junior College, Bowling Green, KY 171
Draughons Junior College, Clarksville, TN 287
Draughons Junior College, Murfreesboro, TN 287
Draughons Junior College, Nashville, TN 288
Herzing College, Atlanta, GA 148
Herzing College, Birmingham, AL 70
Herzing College, Kenner, LA 178
Herzing College, Madison, WI 330
Herzing College, Minneapolis, MN 195
Herzing College, Winter Park, FL 131
San Joaquin Valley College, Bakersfield, CA 103
San Joaquin Valley College, Fresno, CA 103
San Joaquin Valley College, Modesto, CA 104
San Joaquin Valley College, Rancho Cucamonga, CA 104
San Joaquin Valley College, Visalia, CA 104
Western Career College, Pleasant Hill, CA 108
Western Career College, Sacramento, CA 108
Western Career College, San Leandro, CA 109

DENTAL LABORATORY TECHNOLOGY/TECHNICIAN

Draughons Junior College, Bowling Green, KY 171
Draughons Junior College, Clarksville, TN 287
Draughons Junior College, Murfreesboro, TN 287
Draughons Junior College, Nashville, TN 288

DENTAL SERVICES AND ALLIED PROFESSIONS, OTHER

Draughons Junior College, Bowling Green, KY 171
Draughons Junior College, Clarksville, TN 287
Draughons Junior College, Murfreesboro, TN 287
Draughons Junior College, Nashville, TN 288

DESIGN AND VISUAL COMMUNICATIONS, GENERAL

Academy of Medical Arts and Business, Harrisburg, PA 252
The Art Institute of Atlanta, Atlanta, GA 145
The Art Institute of Dallas, Dallas, TX 294
The Art Institute of New York City, New York, NY 225
The Art Institute of Ohio - Cincinnati, Cincinnati, OH 237
The Art Institute of Pittsburgh, Pittsburgh, PA 252
The Art Institute of Portland, Portland, OR 249
The Art Institute of Seattle, Seattle, WA 324
The Art Institutes International Minnesota, Minneapolis, MN 193
Bradley Academy for the Visual Arts, York, PA 254
California Design College, Los Angeles, CA 91
The Chubb Institute, Alpharetta, GA 147
The Chubb Institute, Arlington, VA 314
The Chubb Institute, Cherry Hill, NJ 215
The Chubb Institute, Chicago, IL 155
The Chubb Institute, Jersey City, NJ 216
The Chubb Institute, New York, NY 228
The Chubb Institute, North Brunswick, NJ 216
The Chubb Institute, Parsippany, NJ 216
The Chubb Institute, Springfield, PA 256
The Chubb Institute, Westbury, NY 228
Collins College: A School of Design and Technology, Tempe, AZ 77
Colorado Technical University, Colorado Springs, CO 113
The Creative Circus, Inc., Atlanta, GA 147
Davis College, Toledo, OH 239
Eagle Gate College - Weber/Davis, Layton, UT 309
Eagle Gate College - Weber/Davis, Salt Lake City, UT 309
Florida Technical College, Auburndale, FL 129
Florida Technical College, DeLand, FL 130
Florida Technical College, Jacksonville, FL 130
Florida Technical College, Orlando, FL 130
Gibbs College - Cranston, Cranston, RI 283
Herzing College, Atlanta, GA 148
Herzing College, Birmingham, AL 70
Herzing College, Kenner, LA 178
Herzing College, Madison, WI 330
Herzing College, Minneapolis, MN 195
Herzing College, Winter Park, FL 131
High-Tech Institute, Irving, TX 298
High-Tech Institute, Kansas City, MO 202
High-Tech Institute, Las Vegas, NV 210

High-Tech Institute, Marietta, GA 149
High-Tech Institute, Memphis, TN 288
High-Tech Institute, Nashville, TN 288
High-Tech Institute, Orlando, FL 132
High-Tech Institute, Phoenix, AZ 78
High-Tech Institute, Sacramento, CA 96
High-Tech Institute, St. Louis Park, MN 195
The Illinois Institute of Art - Chicago, Chicago, IL 156
International Academy of Design & Technology, Chicago, IL 157
International Academy of Design & Technology, Orlando, FL 132
International Academy of Design & Technology, Pittsburgh, PA 264
International Academy of Design & Technology, Tampa, FL 132
International Academy of Design & Technology, Troy, MI 189
International Academy of Design and Technology, Henderson, NV 210
International Academy of Design and Technology, Nashville, TN 289
International Academy of Design and Technology, San Antonio, TX 298
International Academy of Design and Technology, Schaumburg, IL 157
International Academy of Design and Technology, Seattle, WA 327
Joe Kubert School of Cartoon and Graphic Art Inc., Dover, NJ 221
Louisville Technical Institute, Louisville, KY 172
Minnesota School of Business - Brooklyn Center, Brooklyn Center, MN 196
Platt College, Huntington Beach, CA 101
Platt College, Lawton, OK 247
Platt College, Oklahoma City, OK 248
Platt College, Ontario, CA 102
Platt College, Tulsa, OK 248
Schuylkill Institute of Business and Technology, Pottsville, PA 270
Silicon Valley College, Emeryville, CA 105
Silicon Valley College, Fremont, CA 106
Silicon Valley College, San Jose, CA 106

DIAGNOSTIC MEDICAL SONOGRAPHY/SONOGRAPHER AND ULTRASOUND TECHNICIAN

ATI Health Education Center, Miami, FL 123
Bryman College, Alhambra, CA 88
Bryman College, Anaheim, CA 88
Bryman College, City of Industry, CA 88
Bryman College, Earth City, MO 201
Bryman College, Everett, WA 325

Bryman College, Gardena, CA 88
Bryman College, Hayward, CA 89
Bryman College, Los Angeles, CA 89
Bryman College, Lynnwood, WA 326
Bryman College, New Orleans, LA 176
Bryman College, Ontario, CA 89
Bryman College, Port Orchard, WA 326
Bryman College, Renton, WA 326
Bryman College, Reseda, CA 89
Bryman College, San Bernardino, CA 90
Bryman College, San Francisco, CA 90
Bryman College, San Jose, CA 90
Bryman College, Tacoma, WA 326
Bryman College, Torrance, CA 90
Great Lakes Institute of Technology, Erie, PA 262
HoHoKus School of Business and Medical Sciences, Ramsey, NJ 221
Instituto Vocational y Commercial EDIC, Caguas, PR 281
Keiser College, Daytona Beach, FL 134
Keiser College, Fort Lauderdale, FL 134
Keiser College, Lakeland, FL 135
Keiser College, Melbourne, FL 135
Keiser College, Miami, FL 135
Keiser College, Orlando, FL 135
Keiser College, Pembroke Pines, FL 136
Keiser College, Port St. Lucie, FL 136
Keiser College, Sarasota, FL 136
Keiser College, Tallahassee, FL 136
Keiser College, West Palm Beach, FL 137
Maric College, Anaheim, CA 99
Maric College, Los Angeles, CA 100
Maric College, North Hollywood, CA 99
Maric College, Sacramento, CA 99
Maric College, Salida, CA 99
Maric College, San Diego, CA 100
Maric College, Vista, CA 100
National School of Technology, Inc., Fort Lauderdale, FL 139
National School of Technology, Inc., Hialeah, FL 139
National School of Technology, Inc., Miami, FL 139
Sanford-Brown Institute, Atlanta, GA 150
Sanford-Brown Institute, Dallas, TX 305
Sanford-Brown Institute, Garden City, NY 232
Sanford-Brown Institute, Houston, TX 305
Sanford-Brown Institute, Houston, TX 306
Sanford-Brown Institute, Jacksonville, FL 142
Sanford-Brown Institute, Landover, MD 182
Sanford-Brown Institute, Lauderdale Lakes, FL 142
Sanford-Brown Institute, New York, NY 232
Sanford-Brown Institute, Springfield, MA 187
Sanford-Brown Institute, Tampa, FL 142
Sanford-Brown Institute, Trevose, PA 270
Sanford-Brown Institute, White Plains, NY 232

Virginia College at Austin, Austin, TX 307
Virginia College at Birmingham, Birmingham, AL 72
Western School of Health and Business Careers, Monroeville, PA 273
Western School of Health and Business Careers, Pittsburgh, PA 273
Westwood College - Chicago Loop Campus, Chicago, IL 161
Westwood College - Denver South, Denver, CO 118

DIALYSIS TECHNOLOGY

Bryman College, Alhambra, CA 88
Bryman College, Anaheim, CA 88
Bryman College, City of Industry, CA 88
Bryman College, Earth City, MO 201
Bryman College, Everett, WA 325
Bryman College, Gardena, CA 88
Bryman College, Hayward, CA 89
Bryman College, Los Angeles, CA 89
Bryman College, Lynnwood, WA 326
Bryman College, New Orleans, LA 176
Bryman College, Ontario, CA 89
Bryman College, Port Orchard, WA 326
Bryman College, Renton, WA 326
Bryman College, Reseda, CA 89
Bryman College, San Bernardino, CA 90
Bryman College, San Francisco, CA 90
Bryman College, San Jose, CA 90
Bryman College, Tacoma, WA 326
Bryman College, Torrance, CA 90
Georgia Medical Institute - DeKalb, Atlanta, GA 148
Harrison Career Institute, Allentown, PA 262
Harrison Career Institute, Baltimore, MD 181
Harrison Career Institute, Clifton, NJ 218
Harrison Career Institute, Delran, NJ 218
Harrison Career Institute, Deptford, NJ 219
Harrison Career Institute, Ewing, NJ 219
Harrison Career Institute, Jersey City, NJ 219
Harrison Career Institute, Oakhurst, NJ 219
Harrison Career Institute, Philadelphia, PA 263
Harrison Career Institute, Reading, PA 263
Harrison Career Institute, South Orange, NJ 220
Harrison Career Institute, Vineland, NJ 220
Harrison Career Institute, Wilmington, DE 121

DIESEL MECHANICS TECHNOLOGY/ TECHNICIAN

Advanced Technology Institute, Virginia Beach, VA 314
Arizona Automotive Institute, Glendale, AZ 76
Automeca Technical College, Aguadilla, PR 275
Automeca Technical College, Bayamon, PR 275
Automeca Technical College, Caguas, PR 275
Automeca Technical College, Ponce, PR 276

Automotive Training Center, Exton, PA 253
Caguas Institute of Mechanical Technology, Caguas, PR 276
Denver Automotive and Diesel College, Denver, CO 114
Lincoln Technical Institute Indianapolis, IN 166
Lincoln Technical Institute, Allentown, PA 266
Lincoln Technical Institute, Columbia, MD 182
Lincoln Technical Institute, Grand Prairie, TX 300
Lincoln Technical Institute, Mahwah, NJ 222
Lincoln Technical Institute, Melrose Park, IL 158
Lincoln Technical Institute, Philadelphia, PA 266
Lincoln Technical Institute, Union, NJ 222
Nashville Auto Diesel College, Nashville, TN 290
North American Trade School, Gwynn Oak, MD 182
Pennco Tech Bristol, PA 269
Pennco Tech, Blackwood, NJ 222
TDDS, Inc., Lake Milton, OH 245
Universal Technical Institute, Avondale, AZ 82
Universal Technical Institute, Exton, PA 273
Universal Technical Institute, Houston, TX 306
Universal Technical Institute, Inc., Glendale Heights, IL 160
Universal Technical Institute, Norwood, MA 187
Universal Technical Institute, Rancho Cucamonga, CA 108
WyoTech, Bedford, MA 187
WyoTech, Blairsville, PA 274
WyoTech, Fremont, CA 111
WyoTech, Laramie, WY 332
WyoTech, Oakland, CA 111
WyoTech, West Sacramento, CA 111

DIGITAL COMMUNICATIONS AND MEDIA/MULTIMEDIA

Academy College, Minneapolis, MN 192
Academy of Medical Arts and Business, Harrisburg, PA 252
American InterContinental University, Atlanta, GA 145
American InterContinental University, Houston, TX 293
American InterContinental University, Los Angeles, CA 85
American InterContinental University, San Antonio, TX 293
American InterContinental University, Weston, FL 121
The Art Institute of California - San Diego, San Diego, CA 86
The Art Institute of New York City, New York, NY 225
The Art Institute of Phoenix, Phoenix, AZ 76
The Art Institute of Portland, Portland, OR 249
The Art Institute of Seattle, Seattle, WA 324
The Art Institutes International Minnesota, Minneapolis, MN 193
Bradley Academy for the Visual Arts, York, PA 254
Brown College, Mendota Heights, MN 193
Capella University, Minneapolis, MN 194
The Chubb Institute, Alpharetta, GA 147
The Chubb Institute, Arlington, VA 314

The Chubb Institute, Cherry Hill, NJ 215
The Chubb Institute, Chicago, IL 155
The Chubb Institute, Jersey City, NJ 216
The Chubb Institute, New York, NY 228
The Chubb Institute, North Brunswick, NJ 216
The Chubb Institute, Parsippany, NJ 216
The Chubb Institute, Springfield, PA 256
The Chubb Institute, Westbury, NY 228
Collins College: A School of Design and Technology, Tempe, AZ 77
Conservatory of Recording Arts and Sciences, Tempe, AZ 78
Douglas Education Center, Monessen, PA 259
Eagle Gate College, Murray, UT 309
Full Sail Real World Education, Winter Park, FL 131
Gibbs College - Cranston, Cranston, RI 283
Gibbs College, Boston, MA 185
Gibbs College, Livingston, NJ 218
Gibbs College, Norwalk, CT 119
High-Tech Institute, Irving, TX 298
High-Tech Institute, Kansas City, MO 202
High-Tech Institute, Las Vegas, NV 210
High-Tech Institute, Marietta, GA 149
High-Tech Institute, Memphis, TN 288
High-Tech Institute, Nashville, TN 288
High-Tech Institute, Orlando, FL 132
High-Tech Institute, Phoenix, AZ 78
High-Tech Institute, Sacramento, CA 96
High-Tech Institute, St. Louis Park, MN 195
The Illinois Institute of Art - Chicago, Chicago, IL 156
The Illinois Institute of Art - Schaumburg, Schaumburg, IL 157
International Academy of Design & Technology, Chicago, IL 157
International Academy of Design & Technology, Orlando, FL 132
International Academy of Design & Technology, Pittsburgh, PA 264
International Academy of Design & Technology, Tampa, FL 132
International Academy of Design & Technology, Troy, MI 189
International Academy of Design and Technology, Henderson, NV 210
International Academy of Design and Technology, Nashville, TN 289
International Academy of Design and Technology, San Antonio, TX 298
International Academy of Design and Technology, Schaumburg, IL 157
International Academy of Design and Technology, Seattle, WA 327
ITI Technical College, Baton Rouge, LA 178

ITT Technical Institute, Albany, NY 230
ITT Technical Institute, Albuquerque, NM 223
ITT Technical Institute, Anaheim, CA 96
ITT Technical Institute, Arlington, TX 299
ITT Technical Institute, Arnold, MO 202
ITT Technical Institute, Austin, TX 299
ITT Technical Institute, Bessemer, AL 71
ITT Technical Institute, Boise, ID 153
ITT Technical Institute, Bothell, WA 327
ITT Technical Institute, Burr Ridge, IL 157
ITT Technical Institute, Canton, MI 189
ITT Technical Institute, Chantilly, VA 317
ITT Technical Institute, Dayton, OH 240
ITT Technical Institute, Duluth, GA 149
ITT Technical Institute, Earth City, MO 202
ITT Technical Institute, Eden Prairie, MN 195
ITT Technical Institute, Fort Lauderdale, FL 133
ITT Technical Institute, Fort Wayne, IN 165
ITT Technical Institute, Getzville, NY 230
ITT Technical Institute, Grand Rapids, MI 189
ITT Technical Institute, Green Bay, WI 331
ITT Technical Institute, Greenfield, WI 331
ITT Technical Institute, Greenville, SC 285
ITT Technical Institute, Henderson, NV 211
ITT Technical Institute, Hilliard, OH 240
ITT Technical Institute, Houston, TX 299
ITT Technical Institute, Houston, TX 300
ITT Technical Institute, Indianapolis, IN 165
ITT Technical Institute, Jacksonville, FL 133
ITT Technical Institute, Kansas City, MO 203
ITT Technical Institute, Kennesaw, GA 149
ITT Technical Institute, King of Prussia, PA 264
ITT Technical Institute, Knoxville, TN 289
ITT Technical Institute, Lake Mary, FL 133
ITT Technical Institute, Lathrop, CA 96
ITT Technical Institute, Little Rock, AR 82
ITT Technical Institute, Liverpool, NY 230
ITT Technical Institute, Louisville, KY 171
ITT Technical Institute, Matteson, IL 158
ITT Technical Institute, Mechanicsburg, PA 264
ITT Technical Institute, Memphis, TN 289
ITT Technical Institute, Miami, FL 133
ITT Technical Institute, Monroeville, PA 264
ITT Technical Institute, Mount Prospect, IL 158
ITT Technical Institute, Murray, UT 310
ITT Technical Institute, Nashville, TN 289
ITT Technical Institute, Newburgh, IN 166
ITT Technical Institute, Norfolk, VA 318
ITT Technical Institute, Norwood, MA 186
ITT Technical Institute, Norwood, OH 240
ITT Technical Institute, Omaha, NE 209
ITT Technical Institute, Owings Mills, MD 181
ITT Technical Institute, Oxnard, CA 97

ITT Technical Institute, Pittsburg, PA 264
ITT Technical Institute, Portland, OR 250
ITT Technical Institute, Rancho Cordova, CA 97
ITT Technical Institute, Richardson, TX 300
ITT Technical Institute, Richmond, VA 318
ITT Technical Institute, Saint Rose, LA 179
ITT Technical Institute, San Antonio, TX 300
ITT Technical Institute, San Bernardino, CA 97
ITT Technical Institute, San Diego, CA 97
ITT Technical Institute, Seattle, WA 327
ITT Technical Institute, Spokane, WA 328
ITT Technical Institute, Springfield, VA 318
ITT Technical Institute, Strongsville, OH 241
ITT Technical Institute, Sylmar, CA 98
ITT Technical Institute, Tampa, FL 134
ITT Technical Institute, Tempe, AZ 79
ITT Technical Institute, Thornton, CO 115
ITT Technical Institute, Torrance, CA 98
ITT Technical Institute, Troy, MI 190
ITT Technical Institute, Tucson, AZ 79
ITT Technical Institute, Tulsa, OK 247
ITT Technical Institute, Warrensville Heights, OH 241
ITT Technical Institute, West Covina, CA 98
ITT Technical Institute, Woburn, MA 186
ITT Technical Institute, Youngstown, OH 241
Katharine Gibbs School, Melville, NY 231
Katharine Gibbs School, New York, NY 231
Katharine Gibbs School, Norristown, PA 264
Katharine Gibbs School, Piscataway, NJ 221
Madison Media Institute, Madison, WI 331
Miami International University of Art & Design, Miami, FL 138
Mildred Elley, Pittsfield, MA 186
Missouri Tech, St. Louis, MO 204
New England Institute of Technology, Warwick, RI 284
Rasmussen College St. Cloud, St. Cloud, MN 199
Schuylkill Institute of Business and Technology, Pottsville, PA 270
Stratford University, Falls Church , VA 322
Stratford University, Woodbridge, VA 322
Technical Career Institute, New York, NY 233
Thompson Institute, Chambersburg, PA 271
Thompson Institute, Harrisburg, PA 271
Thompson Institute, Philadelphia, PA 271
Virginia College at Huntsville, Huntsville, AL 73
Westwood College - Atlanta Northlake, Atlanta, GA 152

DRIVER, PROFESSIONAL AND INSTRUCTOR

Divers Academy International, Camden, NJ 218
Ocean Corporation, Houston, TX 303

DRAFTING AND DESIGN TECHNOLOGY/TECHNICIAN, GENERAL

American Commercial College, Abilene, TX 292
American Commercial College, Lubbock, TX 293
American Commercial College, Odessa, TX 293
American Commercial College, San Angelo, TX 293
American Commercial College, Shreveport, LA 175
The Art Institute of Las Vegas, Henderson, NV 209
ATI Career Training Center, Dallas, TX 294
ATI Career Training Center, Fort Lauderdale, FL 122
ATI Career Training Center, Miami, FL 123
ATI Career Training Center, North Richland Hills, TX 295
ATI Career Training Center, Oakland Park, FL 123
Berks Technical Institute, Wyomissing, PA 253
Briarcliffe College, Bethpage, NY 226
Briarcliffe College, Patchogue, NY 226
California Design College, Los Angeles, CA 91
Delta School of Business & Technology, Lake Charles, LA 177
Florida Technical College, Auburndale, FL 129
Florida Technical College, DeLand, FL 130
Florida Technical College, Jacksonville, FL 130
Florida Technical College, Orlando, FL 130
Herzing College, Atlanta, GA 148
Herzing College, Birmingham, AL 70
Herzing College, Kenner, LA 178
Herzing College, Madison, WI 330
Herzing College, Minneapolis, MN 195
Herzing College, Winter Park, FL 131
High-Tech Institute, Irving, TX 298
High-Tech Institute, Kansas City, MO 202
High-Tech Institute, Las Vegas, NV 210
High-Tech Institute, Marietta, GA 149
High-Tech Institute, Memphis, TN 288
High-Tech Institute, Nashville, TN 288
High-Tech Institute, Orlando, FL 132
High-Tech Institute, Phoenix, AZ 78
High-Tech Institute, Sacramento, CA 96
High-Tech Institute, St. Louis Park, MN 195
Huertas Junior College, Caguas, PR 277
Instituto Banca y Comercio, Caguas, PR 279
Instituto Banca y Comercio, Cayey, PR 279
Instituto Banca y Comercio, Fajardo, PR 279
Instituto Banca y Comercio, Guayama, PR 280
Instituto Banca y Comercio, Manati, PR 280
Instituto Banca y Comercio, Mayaguez, PR 280
Instituto Banca y Comercio, Ponce, PR 280
Instituto de Banca y Comercio, San Juan, PR 281
Island Drafting and Technical Institute, Amityville, NY 230
ITI Technical College, Baton Rouge, LA 178
Key College, Fort Lauderdale, FL 137

DRAFTING/DESIGN ENGINEERING TECHNOLOGIES/TECHNICIANS, OTHER

DRAWING

DRIVER AND SAFETY TEACHER EDUCATION

E-COMMERCE/ELECTRONIC COMMERCE

Capella University, Minneapolis, MN 194
Cardean University, Chicago, IL 154
Career Education Institute, Brockton, MA 184
Career Education Institute, Henderson, NV 210
Career Education Institute, Lincoln, RI 283
Career Education Institute, Lowell, MA 184
Career Education Institute, Marietta, GA 146
Career Education Institute, Norcross, GA 146
CollegeAmerica - Colorado Springs, Colorado Springs, CO 112
Colorado Technical University Sioux Falls Campus, Sioux Falls, SD 286
Colorado Technical University, Colorado Springs, CO 113
Draughons Junior College, Bowling Green, KY 171
Draughons Junior College, Clarksville, TN 287
Draughons Junior College, Murfreesboro, TN 287
Draughons Junior College, Nashville, TN 288
Electronic Data Processing College of Puerto Rico, San Juan, PR 277
Gibbs College, Boston, MA 185
Gibbs College, Livingston, NJ 218
Gibbs College, Norwalk, CT 119
Gretna Career College, Gretna, LA 177
Herzing College, Atlanta, GA 148
Herzing College, Birmingham, AL 70
Herzing College, Kenner, LA 178
Herzing College, Madison, WI 330
Herzing College, Minneapolis, MN 195
Herzing College, Winter Park, FL 131
ICM School of Business & Medical Careers, Pittsburgh, PA 263
International Academy of Design & Technology, Chicago, IL 157
International Academy of Design & Technology, Orlando, FL 132
International Academy of Design & Technology, Pittsburgh, PA 264
International Academy of Design & Technology, Tampa, FL 132
International Academy of Design & Technology, Troy, MI 189
Keiser College, Daytona Beach, FL 134
Keiser College, Fort Lauderdale, FL 134
Keiser College, Lakeland, FL 135
Keiser College, Melbourne, FL 135
Keiser College, Miami, FL 135
Keiser College, Orlando, FL 135
Keiser College, Pembroke Pines, FL 136
Keiser College, Port St. Lucie, FL 136
Keiser College, Sarasota, FL 136
Keiser College, Tallahassee, FL 136
Keiser College, West Palm Beach, FL 137
Minnesota School of Business-Richfield, Richfield, MN 196
National American University, Albuquerque, NM 224
National American University, Brooklyn Center, MN 197
National American University, Colorado Springs, CO 115
National American University, Denver, CO 116
National American University, Ellsworth AFB, SD 286
National American University, Kansas City, MO 204
National American University, Minneapolis, MN 197
National American University, Overland Park, KS 169
National American University, Rapid City, SD 286
National American University, Rio Rancho, NM 224
National American University, Roseville, MN 197
Pittsburgh Technical Institute, Oakdale, PA 269
Potomac College, Herndon, VA 322
Potomac College, Washington, DC 121
Rasmussen College Minnetonka, Minnetonka, MN 199
Stevens-Henager College, Boise, ID 153
Stevens-Henager College, Logan, UT 311
Stevens-Henager College, Ogden, UT 311
Stratford University, Falls Church , VA 322
Stratford University, Woodbridge, VA 322
Westwood College - Chicago Loop Campus, Chicago, IL 161
Westwood College - Chicago River Oaks, Calumet City, IL 161
Westwood College - Denver North, Denver, CO 118
Westwood College - Denver South, Denver, CO 118
Westwood College - Inland Empire, Upland, CA 109
Westwood College - Los Angeles, Inglewood, CA 110
Westwood College - Los Angeles, Los Angeles, CA 110

ECONOMICS, GENERAL

Cardean University, Chicago, IL 154

EDUCATION, GENERAL

American InterContinental University, Atlanta, GA 145
American InterContinental University, Houston, TX 293
American InterContinental University, Los Angeles, CA 85
American InterContinental University, San Antonio, TX 293
American InterContinental University, Weston, FL 121
Andover College, Portland, ME 180
Argosy University/Atlanta, Atlanta, GA 145
Argosy University/Chicago, Chicago, IL 154
Argosy University/Honolulu, Honolulu, HI 152
Argosy University/Orange County, Santa Ana, CA 85
Argosy University/Phoenix, Phoenix, AZ 75
Argosy University/Schaumburg, Schaumburg, IL 154
Argosy University/Seattle, Seattle, WA 324
Argosy University/Twin Cities, Eagan, MN 193
Argosy University/Washington D.C., Arlington, VA 314
Capella University, Minneapolis, MN 194
Jones International University, Englewood, CO 115

Remington College - Pinellas Campus, Largo, FL 141
Strayer University, Atlanta, GA 151

EDUCATION LEADERSHIP AND ADMINISTRATION, GENERAL

Argosy University/Chicago, Chicago, IL 154
Argosy University/Honolulu, Honolulu, HI 152
Argosy University/Schaumburg, Schaumburg, IL 154
Argosy University/Washington D.C., Arlington, VA 314
Capella University, Minneapolis, MN 194

EDUCATION/INSTRUCTIONAL MEDIA DESIGN

American InterContinental University, Atlanta, GA 145
American InterContinental University, Houston, TX 293
American InterContinental University, Los Angeles, CA 85
American InterContinental University, San Antonio, TX 293
American InterContinental University, Weston, FL 121
Capella University, Minneapolis, MN 194
National College of Business & Technology, Bayamon, PR 282
National College of Business & Technology, Bluefield, VA 320
National College of Business & Technology, Bristol, TN 290
National College of Business & Technology, Charlottesville, VA 320
National College of Business & Technology, Danville, KY 172
National College of Business & Technology, Danville, VA 320
National College of Business & Technology, Florence, KY 172
National College of Business & Technology, Harrisonburg, VA 321
National College of Business & Technology, Knoxville, TN 291
National College of Business & Technology, Lexington, KY 173
National College of Business & Technology, Louisville, KY 173
National College of Business & Technology, Lynchburg, VA 321
National College of Business & Technology, Martinsville, VA 321
National College of Business & Technology, Nashville, TN 291
National College of Business & Technology, Pikeville, KY 173
National College of Business & Technology, Richmond, KY 173
National College of Business & Technology, Rio Grande, PR 282

National College of Business & Technology, Salem, VA 321

ELECTRICAL AND ELECTRONIC ENGINEERING TECHNOLOGIES/ TECHNICIANS, OTHER

Advanced Training Associates, El Cajon, CA 84
ATI Career Training Center, Dallas, TX 294
ATI Career Training Center, Fort Lauderdale, FL 122
ATI Career Training Center, Miami, FL 123
ATI Career Training Center, North Richland Hills, TX 295
ATI Career Training Center, Oakland Park, FL 123
Brown Mackie College, Akron Campus, Akron, OH 238
Florida Technical College, Auburndale, FL 129
Florida Technical College, DeLand, FL 130
Florida Technical College, Jacksonville, FL 130
Florida Technical College, Orlando, FL 130
ITT Technical Institute, Albany, NY 230
ITT Technical Institute, Albuquerque, NM 223
ITT Technical Institute, Anaheim, CA 96
ITT Technical Institute, Arlington, TX 299
ITT Technical Institute, Arnold, MO 202
ITT Technical Institute, Austin, TX 299
ITT Technical Institute, Bessemer, AL 71
ITT Technical Institute, Boise, ID 153
ITT Technical Institute, Bothell, WA 327
ITT Technical Institute, Burr Ridge, IL 157
ITT Technical Institute, Canton, MI 189
ITT Technical Institute, Chantilly, VA 317
ITT Technical Institute, Dayton, OH 240
ITT Technical Institute, Duluth, GA 149
ITT Technical Institute, Earth City, MO 202
ITT Technical Institute, Eden Prairie, MN 195
ITT Technical Institute, Fort Lauderdale, FL 133
ITT Technical Institute, Fort Wayne, IN 165
ITT Technical Institute, Getzville, NY 230
ITT Technical Institute, Grand Rapids, MI 189
ITT Technical Institute, Green Bay, WI 331
ITT Technical Institute, Greenfield, WI 331
ITT Technical Institute, Greenville, SC 285
ITT Technical Institute, Henderson, NV 211
ITT Technical Institute, Hilliard, OH 240
ITT Technical Institute, Houston, TX 299
ITT Technical Institute, Houston, TX 300
ITT Technical Institute, Indianapolis, IN 165
ITT Technical Institute, Jacksonville, FL 133
ITT Technical Institute, Kansas City, MO 203
ITT Technical Institute, Kennesaw, GA 149
ITT Technical Institute, King of Prussia, PA 264
ITT Technical Institute, Knoxville, TN 289
ITT Technical Institute, Lake Mary, FL 133
ITT Technical Institute, Lathrop, CA 96

ITT Technical Institute, Little Rock, AR 82
ITT Technical Institute, Liverpool, NY 230
ITT Technical Institute, Louisville, KY 171
ITT Technical Institute, Matteson, IL 158
ITT Technical Institute, Mechanicsburg, PA 264
ITT Technical Institute, Memphis, TN 289
ITT Technical Institute, Miami, FL 133
ITT Technical Institute, Monroeville, PA 264
ITT Technical Institute, Mount Prospect, IL 158
ITT Technical Institute, Murray, UT 310
ITT Technical Institute, Nashville, TN 289
ITT Technical Institute, Newburgh, IN 166
ITT Technical Institute, Norfolk, VA 318
ITT Technical Institute, Norwood, MA 186
ITT Technical Institute, Norwood, OH 240
ITT Technical Institute, Omaha, NE 209
ITT Technical Institute, Owings Mills, MD 181
ITT Technical Institute, Oxnard, CA 97
ITT Technical Institute, Pittsburg, PA 264
ITT Technical Institute, Portland, OR 250
ITT Technical Institute, Rancho Cordova, CA 97
ITT Technical Institute, Richardson, TX 300
ITT Technical Institute, Richmond, VA 318
ITT Technical Institute, Saint Rose, LA 179
ITT Technical Institute, San Antonio, TX 300
ITT Technical Institute, San Bernardino, CA 97
ITT Technical Institute, San Diego, CA 97
ITT Technical Institute, Seattle, WA 327
ITT Technical Institute, Spokane, WA 328
ITT Technical Institute, Springfield, VA 318
ITT Technical Institute, Strongsville, OH 241
ITT Technical Institute, Sylmar, CA 98
ITT Technical Institute, Tampa, FL 134
ITT Technical Institute, Tempe, AZ 79
ITT Technical Institute, Thornton, CO 115
ITT Technical Institute, Torrance, CA 98
ITT Technical Institute, Troy, MI 190
ITT Technical Institute, Tucson, AZ 79
ITT Technical Institute, Tulsa, OK 247
ITT Technical Institute, Warrensville Heights, OH 241
ITT Technical Institute, West Covina, CA 98
ITT Technical Institute, Woburn, MA 186
ITT Technical Institute, Youngstown, OH 241
Lincoln Technical Institute Indianapolis, IN 166
Lincoln Technical Institute, Allentown, PA 266
Lincoln Technical Institute, Columbia, MD 182
Lincoln Technical Institute, Grand Prairie, TX 300
Lincoln Technical Institute, Mahwah, NJ 222
Lincoln Technical Institute, Melrose Park, IL 158
Lincoln Technical Institute, Philadelphia, PA 266
Lincoln Technical Institute, Union, NJ 222
Louisville Technical Institute, Louisville, KY 172
National College of Business and Technology, Arecibo, PR 282
National College of Business and Technology, Cincinnati, OH 241
National College of Business and Technology, Indianapolis, IN 166
National College of Business and Technology, Kettering, OH 242
North American Trade School, Gwynn Oak, MD 182
Paducah Technical College, Paducah, KY 174
Pinnacle Career Institute, Kansas City, MO 204
Pinnacle Career Institute, Lawrence, KS 169
Porter and Chester Institute, Chicopee, MA 187
Porter and Chester Institute, Enfield, CT 120
Porter and Chester Institute, Stratford, CT 120
Porter and Chester Institute, Watertown, CT 120
Porter and Chester Institute, Wethersfield, CT 120
Technical Career Institute, New York, NY 233
Vatterott College, Broadview Heights, OH 245
Vatterott College, Des Moines, IA 168
Vatterott College, Joplin, MO 206
Vatterott College, Kansas City, MO 207
Vatterott College, Memphis, TN 292
Vatterott College, OÆFallon , MO 207
Vatterott College, Oklahoma City, OK 248
Vatterott College, Omaha, NE 209
Vatterott College, Quincy, IL 160
Vatterott College, Springfield, MO 208
Vatterott College, St. Ann, MO 207
Vatterott College, St. Joseph, MO 207
Vatterott College, St. Louis, MO 208
Vatterott College, Tulsa, OK 249
Vatterott College, Wichita, KS 169

ELECTRICAL, ELECTRONIC AND COMMUNICATIONS ENGINEERING TECHNOLOGY/TECHNICIAN

ATI Career Training Center, Dallas, TX 294
ATI Career Training Center, Fort Lauderdale, FL 122
ATI Career Training Center, Miami, FL 123
ATI Career Training Center, North Richland Hills, TX 295
ATI Career Training Center, Oakland Park, FL 123
Brown Mackie College, Akron Campus, Akron, OH 238
Brown Mackie College, North Canton Campus, North Canton, OH 239
Career College of Northern Nevada, Reno, NV 210
Colorado Technical University Denver Campus, Greenwood Village, CO 114
Colorado Technical University, Colorado Springs, CO 113
Columbia College, Caguas, PR 277
Columbia College, Yauco, PR 277
Coyne American Institute, Chicago, IL 155
Coyne American Institute, Chicago, IL 156

ECPI College of Technology, Charlotte, NC 234
ECPI College of Technology, Greensboro, NC 235
ECPI College of Technology, Greenville, SC 285
ECPI College of Technology, Manassas, VA 315
ECPI College of Technology, Newport News, VA 315
ECPI College of Technology, North Charleston, SC 285
ECPI College of Technology, Raleigh, NC 235
ECPI College of Technology, Virginia Beach, VA 316
Florida Technical College, Auburndale, FL 129
Florida Technical College, DeLand, FL 130
Florida Technical College, Jacksonville, FL 130
Florida Technical College, Orlando, FL 130
Fountainhead College of Technology, Knoxville, TN 288
Grantham University, Kansas City, MO 177
Hallmark Institute of Technology, San Antonio, TX 298
Herzing College, Atlanta, GA 148
Herzing College, Birmingham, AL 70
Herzing College, Kenner, LA 178
Herzing College, Madison, WI 330
Herzing College, Minneapolis, MN 195
Herzing College, Winter Park, FL 131
HoHoKus RETS School of Business and Medical Technical Services, Nutley, NJ 220
Huertas Junior College, Caguas, PR 277
Institute for Business and Technology, Santa Clara, CA 96
Instituto Banca y Comercio, Caguas, PR 279
Instituto Banca y Comercio, Cayey, PR 279
Instituto Banca y Comercio, Fajardo, PR 279
Instituto Banca y Comercio, Guayama, PR 280
Instituto Banca y Comercio, Manati, PR 280
Instituto Banca y Comercio, Mayaguez, PR 280
Instituto Banca y Comercio, Ponce, PR 280
Island Drafting and Technical Institute, Amityville, NY 230
ITI Technical College, Baton Rouge, LA 178
ITT Technical Institute, Albany, NY 230
ITT Technical Institute, Albuquerque, NM 223
ITT Technical Institute, Anaheim, CA 96
ITT Technical Institute, Arlington, TX 299
ITT Technical Institute, Arnold, MO 202
ITT Technical Institute, Austin, TX 299
ITT Technical Institute, Bessemer, AL 71
ITT Technical Institute, Boise, ID 153
ITT Technical Institute, Bothell, WA 327
ITT Technical Institute, Burr Ridge, IL 157
ITT Technical Institute, Canton, MI 189
ITT Technical Institute, Chantilly, VA 317
ITT Technical Institute, Dayton, OH 240
ITT Technical Institute, Duluth, GA 149
ITT Technical Institute, Earth City, MO 202
ITT Technical Institute, Eden Prairie, MN 195
ITT Technical Institute, Fort Lauderdale, FL 133
ITT Technical Institute, Fort Wayne, IN 165
ITT Technical Institute, Getzville, NY 230

ITT Technical Institute, Grand Rapids, MI 189
ITT Technical Institute, Green Bay, WI 331
ITT Technical Institute, Greenfield, WI 331
ITT Technical Institute, Greenville, SC 285
ITT Technical Institute, Henderson, NV 211
ITT Technical Institute, Hilliard, OH 240
ITT Technical Institute, Houston, TX 299
ITT Technical Institute, Houston, TX 300
ITT Technical Institute, Indianapolis, IN 165
ITT Technical Institute, Jacksonville, FL 133
ITT Technical Institute, Kansas City, MO 203
ITT Technical Institute, Kennesaw, GA 149
ITT Technical Institute, King of Prussia, PA 264
ITT Technical Institute, Knoxville, TN 289
ITT Technical Institute, Lake Mary, FL 133
ITT Technical Institute, Lathrop, CA 96
ITT Technical Institute, Little Rock, AR 82
ITT Technical Institute, Liverpool, NY 230
ITT Technical Institute, Louisville, KY 171
ITT Technical Institute, Matteson, IL 158
ITT Technical Institute, Mechanicsburg, PA 264
ITT Technical Institute, Memphis, TN 289
ITT Technical Institute, Miami, FL 133
ITT Technical Institute, Monroeville, PA 264
ITT Technical Institute, Mount Prospect, IL 158
ITT Technical Institute, Murray, UT 310
ITT Technical Institute, Nashville, TN 289
ITT Technical Institute, Newburgh, IN 166
ITT Technical Institute, Norfolk, VA 318
ITT Technical Institute, Norwood, MA 186
ITT Technical Institute, Norwood, OH 240
ITT Technical Institute, Omaha, NE 209
ITT Technical Institute, Owings Mills, MD 181
ITT Technical Institute, Oxnard, CA 97
ITT Technical Institute, Pittsburg, PA 264
ITT Technical Institute, Portland, OR 250
ITT Technical Institute, Rancho Cordova, CA 97
ITT Technical Institute, Richardson, TX 300
ITT Technical Institute, Richmond, VA 318
ITT Technical Institute, Saint Rose, LA 179
ITT Technical Institute, San Antonio, TX 300
ITT Technical Institute, San Bernardino, CA 97
ITT Technical Institute, San Diego, CA 97
ITT Technical Institute, Seattle, WA 327
ITT Technical Institute, Spokane, WA 328
ITT Technical Institute, Springfield, VA 318
ITT Technical Institute, Strongsville, OH 241
ITT Technical Institute, Sylmar, CA 98
ITT Technical Institute, Tampa, FL 134
ITT Technical Institute, Tempe, AZ 79
ITT Technical Institute, Thornton, CO 115
ITT Technical Institute, Torrance, CA 98
ITT Technical Institute, Troy, MI 190

Boldface type indicates that the school is a participating institution in the *Imagine America* Scholarship Program

ITT Technical Institute, Tucson, AZ 79
ITT Technical Institute, Tulsa, OK 247
ITT Technical Institute, Warrensville Heights, OH 241
ITT Technical Institute, West Covina, CA 98
ITT Technical Institute, Woburn, MA 186
ITT Technical Institute, Youngstown, OH 241
Lincoln Technical Institute Indianapolis, IN 166
Lincoln Technical Institute, Allentown, PA 266
Lincoln Technical Institute, Columbia, MD 182
Lincoln Technical Institute, Grand Prairie, TX 300
Lincoln Technical Institute, Mahwah, NJ 222
Lincoln Technical Institute, Melrose Park, IL 158
Lincoln Technical Institute, Philadelphia, PA 266
Lincoln Technical Institute, Union, NJ 222
Missouri Tech, St. Louis, MO 204
MTI College of Business and Technology, Houston, TX 301
National Institute of Technology, Austin , TX 302
National Institute of Technology, Cross Lanes, WV 329
National Institute of Technology, Detroit, MI 190
National Institute of Technology, Houston, TX 302
National Institute of Technology, Long Beach, CA 101
National Institute of Technology, San Antonio, TX 302
National Institute of Technology, Southfield, MI 190
New England Institute of Technology at Palm Beach, West Palm Beach, FL 140
New England Institute of Technology, Warwick, RI 284
Pittsburgh Technical Institute, Oakdale, PA 269
Remington College - Fort Worth Campus, Fort Worth, TX 304
Remington College - Lafayette Campus, Lafayette, LA 179
Remington College - Memphis Campus, Memphis, TN 291
Remington College - Mobile Campus, Mobile, AL 71
Remington College - New Orleans Campus, Metairie, LA 180
Remington College - Pinellas Campus, Largo, FL 141
Remington College - Tampa Campus, Tampa, FL 141
RETS Tech Center, Centerville, OH 243
San Joaquin Valley College, Bakersfield, CA 103
San Joaquin Valley College, Fresno, CA 103
San Joaquin Valley College, Modesto, CA 104
San Joaquin Valley College, Rancho Cucamonga, CA 104
San Joaquin Valley College, Visalia, CA 104
TESST College of Technology, Alexandria, VA 323
TESST College of Technology, Baltimore, MD 182
TESST College of Technology, Beltsville, MD 183
TESST College of Technology, Towson, MD 183
Vatterott College, Broadview Heights, OH 245
Vatterott College, Des Moines, IA 168
Vatterott College, Joplin, MO 206

Vatterott College, Kansas City, MO 207
Vatterott College, Memphis, TN 292
Vatterott College, OÆFallon , MO 207
Vatterott College, Oklahoma City, OK 248
Vatterott College, Omaha, NE 209
Vatterott College, Quincy, IL 160
Vatterott College, Springfield, MO 208
Vatterott College, St. Ann, MO 207
Vatterott College, St. Joseph, MO 207
Vatterott College, St. Louis, MO 208
Vatterott College, Tulsa, OK 249
Vatterott College, Wichita, KS 169
Virginia College at Jackson, Jackson, MS 200
Western Technical College, El Paso, TX 307
Western Technical Institute, El Paso, TX 308
Wichita Technical Institute, Wichita, KS 169
WTI The Electronic School, Topeka, KS 170

ELECTRICAL, ELECTRONIC DRAFTING AND ELECTRICAL/ELECTRONICS CAD/CADD

ATI Career Training Center, Dallas, TX 294
ATI Career Training Center, Fort Lauderdale, FL 122
ATI Career Training Center, Miami, FL 123
ATI Career Training Center, North Richland Hills, TX 295
ATI Career Training Center, Oakland Park, FL 123
Caguas Institute of Mechanical Technology, Caguas, PR 276
Florida Technical College, Auburndale, FL 129
Florida Technical College, DeLand, FL 130
Florida Technical College, Jacksonville, FL 130
Florida Technical College, Orlando, FL 130
Northwest Technical Institute, Eden Prairie, MN 198

ELECTRICAL/ELECTRONIC EQUIPMENT INSTALLATION AND REPAIR, GENERAL

Advanced Training Associates, El Cajon, CA 84
American Commercial College, Abilene, TX 292
American Commercial College, Lubbock, TX 293
American Commercial College, Odessa, TX 293
American Commercial College, San Angelo, TX 293
American Commercial College, Shreveport, LA 175
ATI Career Training Center, Dallas, TX 294
ATI Career Training Center, Fort Lauderdale, FL 122
ATI Career Training Center, Miami, FL 123
ATI Career Training Center, North Richland Hills, TX 295
ATI Career Training Center, Oakland Park, FL 123
Brown Mackie College, Lenexa Campus, Lenexa, KS 168
Caguas Institute of Mechanical Technology, Caguas, PR 276
Career Education Institute, Brockton, MA 184
Career Education Institute, Henderson, NV 210

Career Education Institute, Lincoln, RI 283
Career Education Institute, Lowell, MA 184
Career Education Institute, Marietta, GA 146
Career Education Institute, Norcross, GA 146
Career Institute of Health and Technology, Brooklyn, NY 227
Career Institute of Health and Technology, Garden City, NY 227
Career Institute of Health and Technology, Rego Park, NY 228
CHI Institute, Broomall, PA 256
CHI Institute, Southampton, PA 256
Coyne American Institute, Chicago, IL 155
Coyne American Institute, Chicago, IL 156
High-Tech Institute, Irving, TX 298
High-Tech Institute, Kansas City, MO 202
High-Tech Institute, Las Vegas, NV 210
High-Tech Institute, Marietta, GA 149
High-Tech Institute, Memphis, TN 288
High-Tech Institute, Nashville, TN 288
High-Tech Institute, Orlando, FL 132
High-Tech Institute, Phoenix, AZ 78
High-Tech Institute, Sacramento, CA 96
High-Tech Institute, St. Louis Park, MN 195
Instituto Banca y Comercio, Caguas, PR 279
Instituto Banca y Comercio, Cayey, PR 279
Instituto Banca y Comercio, Fajardo, PR 279
Instituto Banca y Comercio, Guayama, PR 280
Instituto Banca y Comercio, Manati, PR 280
Instituto Banca y Comercio, Mayaguez, PR 280
Instituto Banca y Comercio, Ponce, PR 280
ITI Technical College, Baton Rouge, LA 178
Lincoln Technical Institute Indianapolis, IN 166
Lincoln Technical Institute, Allentown, PA 266
Lincoln Technical Institute, Columbia, MD 182
Lincoln Technical Institute, Grand Prairie, TX 300
Lincoln Technical Institute, Mahwah, NJ 222
Lincoln Technical Institute, Melrose Park, IL 158
Lincoln Technical Institute, Philadelphia, PA 266
Lincoln Technical Institute, Union, NJ 222
Louisville Technical Institute, Louisville, KY 172
RETS Technical Center, Charlestown, MA 187
TESST College of Technology, Alexandria, VA 323
TESST College of Technology, Baltimore, MD 182
TESST College of Technology, Beltsville, MD 183
TESST College of Technology, Towson, MD 183
Thompson Institute, Chambersburg, PA 271
Thompson Institute, Harrisburg, PA 271
Thompson Institute, Philadelphia, PA 271
Vatterott College, Broadview Heights, OH 245
Vatterott College, Des Moines, IA 168
Vatterott College, Joplin, MO 206
Vatterott College, Kansas City, MO 207

Vatterott College, Memphis, TN 292
Vatterott College, OÆFallon , MO 207
Vatterott College, Oklahoma City, OK 248
Vatterott College, Omaha, NE 209
Vatterott College, Quincy, IL 160
Vatterott College, Springfield, MO 208
Vatterott College, St. Ann, MO 207
Vatterott College, St. Joseph, MO 207
Vatterott College, St. Louis, MO 208
Vatterott College, Tulsa, OK 249
Vatterott College, Wichita, KS 169
WTI The Electronic School, Topeka, KS 170

ELECTRICIAN

Berk Trade and Business School, Brooklyn, NY 226
Caguas Institute of Mechanical Technology, Caguas, PR 276
Career Centers of Texas, El Paso, TX 295
Career Institute of Health and Technology, Brooklyn, NY 227
Career Institute of Health and Technology, Garden City, NY 227
Career Institute of Health and Technology, Rego Park, NY 228
CHI Institute, Broomall, PA 256
CHI Institute, Southampton, PA 256
Colegio Mayor de Tecnologia, Arroyo, PR 276
Coyne American Institute, Chicago, IL 155
Coyne American Institute, Chicago, IL 156
Dean Institute of Technology, Pittsburgh, PA 258
Huertas Junior College, Caguas, PR 277
Instituto Banca y Comercio, Caguas, PR 279
Instituto Banca y Comercio, Cayey, PR 279
Instituto Banca y Comercio, Fajardo, PR 279
Instituto Banca y Comercio, Guayama, PR 280
Instituto Banca y Comercio, Manati, PR 280
Instituto Banca y Comercio, Mayaguez, PR 280
Instituto Banca y Comercio, Ponce, PR 280
Instituto de Banca y Comercio, San Juan, PR 281
ITI Technical College, Baton Rouge, LA 178
Liceo de Arte y Tecnologia, San Juan, PR 281
Miller-Motte Technical College, Cary, NC 236
Miller-Motte Technical College, Chattanooga, TN 290
Miller-Motte Technical College, Clarksville, TN 290
Miller-Motte Technical College, Lynchburg, VA 320
Miller-Motte Technical College, North Charleston, SC 285
Miller-Motte Technical College, Wilmington, NC 236
National Institute of Technology, Austin , TX 302
National Institute of Technology, Cross Lanes, WV 329
National Institute of Technology, Detroit, MI 190
National Institute of Technology, Houston, TX 302
National Institute of Technology, Long Beach, CA 101
National Institute of Technology, San Antonio, TX 302
National Institute of Technology, Southfield, MI 190

Boldface type indicates that the school is a participating institution in the *Imagine America* Scholarship Program

New Castle School of Trades, Pulaski, PA 268
New England Institute of Technology, Warwick, RI 284
New England Technical Institute, Cromwell, CT 119
New England Technical Institute, Hamden, CT 119
New England Technical Institute, Shelton, CT 119
Orleans Technical Institute, Philadelphia, PA 268
Pennco Tech Bristol, PA 269
Pennco Tech, Blackwood, NJ 222
The Refrigeration School, Phoenix, AZ 81
San Antonio College of Medical and Dental Assistants, San Antonio, TX 305
TESST College of Technology, Alexandria, VA 323
TESST College of Technology, Baltimore, MD 182
TESST College of Technology, Beltsville, MD 183
TESST College of Technology, Towson, MD 183
Thompson Institute, Chambersburg, PA 271
Thompson Institute, Harrisburg, PA 271
Thompson Institute, Philadelphia, PA 271
Triangle Tech, Inc. - DuBois School, DuBois, PA 272
Triangle Tech, Inc. - Erie School, Erie, PA 272
Triangle Tech, Inc. - Greensburg School, Greensburg, PA 272
Triangle Tech, Inc. - Pittsburgh School, Pittsburgh, PA 272
Triangle Tech, Inc. - Sunbury School, Sunbury, PA 272
Vatterott College, Broadview Heights, OH 245
Vatterott College, Des Moines, IA 168
Vatterott College, Joplin, MO 206
Vatterott College, Kansas City, MO 207
Vatterott College, Memphis, TN 292
Vatterott College, OÆFallon , MO 207
Vatterott College, Oklahoma City, OK 248
Vatterott College, Omaha, NE 209
Vatterott College, Quincy, IL 160
Vatterott College, Springfield, MO 208
Vatterott College, St. Ann, MO 207
Vatterott College, St. Joseph, MO 207
Vatterott College, St. Louis, MO 208
Vatterott College, Tulsa, OK 249
Vatterott College, Wichita, KS 169

ELECTROCARDIOGRAPH TECHNOLOGY/TECHNICIAN

Academy of Medical Arts and Business, Harrisburg, PA 252
Career Education Institute, Brockton, MA 184
Career Education Institute, Henderson, NV 210
Career Education Institute, Lincoln, RI 283
Career Education Institute, Lowell, MA 184
Career Education Institute, Marietta, GA 146
Career Education Institute, Norcross, GA 146
Career Institute of Health and Technology, Brooklyn, NY 227

Career Institute of Health and Technology, Garden City, NY 227
Career Institute of Health and Technology, Rego Park, NY 228
Dickinson Business School/Career Point Business School, Tulsa, OK 246
Draughons Junior College, Bowling Green, KY 171
Draughons Junior College, Clarksville, TN 287
Draughons Junior College, Murfreesboro, TN 287
Draughons Junior College, Nashville, TN 288
Harrison Career Institute, Allentown, PA 262
Harrison Career Institute, Baltimore, MD 181
Harrison Career Institute, Clifton, NJ 218
Harrison Career Institute, Delran, NJ 218
Harrison Career Institute, Deptford, NJ 219
Harrison Career Institute, Ewing, NJ 219
Harrison Career Institute, Jersey City, NJ 219
Harrison Career Institute, Oakhurst, NJ 219
Harrison Career Institute, Philadelphia, PA 263
Harrison Career Institute, Reading, PA 263
Harrison Career Institute, South Orange, NJ 220
Harrison Career Institute, Vineland, NJ 220
Harrison Career Institute, Wilmington, DE 121
Mandl School, New York, NY 231
Maric College, Anaheim, CA 99
Maric College, Los Angeles, CA 100
Maric College, North Hollywood, CA 99
Maric College, Sacramento, CA 99
Maric College, Salida, CA 99
Maric College, San Diego, CA 100
Maric College, Vista, CA 100
Medix School, Smyrna, GA 150
Medix School, Towson, MD 182
Thompson Institute, Chambersburg, PA 271
Thompson Institute, Harrisburg, PA 271
Thompson Institute, Philadelphia, PA 271

ELECTROMECHANICAL AND INSTRUMENTATION AND MAINTENANCE TECHNOLOGIES/ TECHNICIANS, OTHER

Caguas Institute of Mechanical Technology, Caguas, PR 276

ELECTROMECHANICAL TECHNOLOGY/ ELECTROMECHANICAL ENGINEERING TECHNOLOGY

Automeca Technical College, Aguadilla, PR 275
Automeca Technical College, Bayamon, PR 275
Automeca Technical College, Caguas, PR 275
Automeca Technical College, Ponce, PR 276
Caguas Institute of Mechanical Technology, Caguas, PR 276
Coyne American Institute, Chicago, IL 155

Coyne American Institute, Chicago, IL 156
Herzing College, Atlanta, GA 148
Herzing College, Birmingham, AL 70
Herzing College, Kenner, LA 178
Herzing College, Madison, WI 330
Herzing College, Minneapolis, MN 195
Herzing College, Winter Park, FL 131
High-Tech Institute, Irving, TX 298
High-Tech Institute, Kansas City, MO 202
High-Tech Institute, Las Vegas, NV 210
High-Tech Institute, Marietta, GA 149
High-Tech Institute, Memphis, TN 288
High-Tech Institute, Nashville, TN 288
High-Tech Institute, Orlando, FL 132
High-Tech Institute, Phoenix, AZ 78
High-Tech Institute, Sacramento, CA 96
High-Tech Institute, St. Louis Park, MN 195
The Refrigeration School, Phoenix, AZ 81
Vatterott College, Broadview Heights, OH 245
Vatterott College, Des Moines, IA 168
Vatterott College, Joplin, MO 206
Vatterott College, Kansas City, MO 207
Vatterott College, Memphis, TN 292
Vatterott College, OÆFallon , MO 207
Vatterott College, Oklahoma City, OK 248
Vatterott College, Omaha, NE 209
Vatterott College, Quincy, IL 160
Vatterott College, Springfield, MO 208
Vatterott College, St. Ann, MO 207
Vatterott College, St. Joseph, MO 207
Vatterott College, St. Louis, MO 208
Vatterott College, Tulsa, OK 249
Vatterott College, Wichita, KS 169

ELECTRONEURODIAGNOSTIC/ ELECTROENCEPHALOGRAPHIC TECHNOLOGY/TECHNOLOGIST

Career Education Institute, Brockton, MA 184
Career Education Institute, Henderson, NV 210
Career Education Institute, Lincoln, RI 283
Career Education Institute, Lowell, MA 184
Career Education Institute, Marietta, GA 146
Career Education Institute, Norcross, GA 146
Carnegie Institute, Troy, MI 188

ELEMENTARY EDUCATION AND TEACHING

Capella University, Minneapolis, MN 194
South College, Knoxville, TN 291

EMERGENCY MEDICAL TECHNOLOGY/TECHNICIAN (EMT PARAMEDIC)

Chaparral College, Tucson, AZ 77
Colegio Mayor de Tecnologia, Arroyo, PR 276
Electronic Data Processing College of Puerto Rico, San Juan, PR 277
Electronic Data Processing College of Puerto Rico - San Sebastian, San Sebastian, PR 277
Instituto Banca y Comercio, Caguas, PR 279
Instituto Banca y Comercio, Cayey, PR 279
Instituto Banca y Comercio, Fajardo, PR 279
Instituto Banca y Comercio, Guayama, PR 280
Instituto Banca y Comercio, Manati, PR 280
Instituto Banca y Comercio, Mayaguez, PR 280
Instituto Banca y Comercio, Ponce, PR 280
Instituto de Banca y Comercio, San Juan, PR 281
Instituto Vocational y Commercial EDIC, Caguas, PR 281
Keiser College, Daytona Beach, FL 134
Keiser College, Fort Lauderdale, FL 134
Keiser College, Lakeland, FL 135
Keiser College, Melbourne, FL 135
Keiser College, Miami, FL 135
Keiser College, Orlando, FL 135
Keiser College, Pembroke Pines, FL 136
Keiser College, Port St. Lucie, FL 136
Keiser College, Sarasota, FL 136
Keiser College, Tallahassee, FL 136
Keiser College, West Palm Beach, FL 137
Medix School, Smyrna, GA 150
Medix School, Towson, MD 182
Ponce Paramedical College, Inc., Coto Laurel, PR 282
Stevens-Henager College, Boise, ID 153
Stevens-Henager College, Logan, UT 311
Stevens-Henager College, Ogden, UT 311
Stevens-Henager College - Salt Lake City, Salt Lake City, UT 312
York Technical Institute, Lancaster, PA 274
York Technical Institute, York, PA 274

EMERGENCY/DISASTER SCIENCE

National College of Business & Technology, Bayamon, PR 282
National College of Business & Technology, Bluefield, VA 320
National College of Business & Technology, Bristol, TN 290
National College of Business & Technology, Charlottesville, VA 320
National College of Business & Technology, Danville, KY 172
National College of Business & Technology, Danville, VA 320

Boldface type indicates that the school is a participating institution in the ⊕ *Imagine America* Scholarship Program

National College of Business & Technology, Florence, KY 172

National College of Business & Technology, Harrisonburg, VA 321

National College of Business & Technology, Knoxville, TN 291

National College of Business & Technology, Lexington, KY 173

National College of Business & Technology, Louisville, KY 173

National College of Business & Technology, Lynchburg, VA 321

National College of Business & Technology, Martinsville, VA 321

National College of Business & Technology, Nashville, TN 291

National College of Business & Technology, Pikeville, KY 173

National College of Business & Technology, Richmond, KY 173

National College of Business & Technology, Rio Grande, PR 282

National College of Business & Technology, Salem, VA 321

National College of Business and Technology, Arecibo, PR 282

National College of Business and Technology, Cincinnati, OH 241

National College of Business and Technology, Indianapolis, IN 166

National College of Business and Technology, Kettering, OH 242

ENERGY AND BIOLOGICALLY BASED\THERAPIES, OTHER

Barbara Brennan School of Healing, Boca Raton, FL 124

ENGINE MACHINIST

Automotive Training Center, Exton, PA 253
WyoTech, Bedford, MA 187
WyoTech, Blairsville, PA 274
WyoTech, Fremont, CA 111
WyoTech, Laramie, WY 332
WyoTech, Oakland, CA 111
WyoTech, West Sacramento, CA 111

ENGINEERING TECHNOLOGY, GENERAL

ATI Career Training Center, Dallas, TX 294
ATI Career Training Center, Fort Lauderdale, FL 122
ATI Career Training Center, Miami, FL 123
ATI Career Training Center, North Richland Hills, TX 295

ATI Career Training Center, Oakland Park, FL 123
Grantham University, Kansas City, MO 177
ICM School of Business & Medical Careers, Pittsburgh, PA 263
Island Drafting and Technical Institute, Amityville, NY 230
ITI Technical College, Baton Rouge, LA 178
Lincoln Technical Institute Indianapolis, IN 166
Lincoln Technical Institute, Allentown, PA 266
Lincoln Technical Institute, Columbia, MD 182
Lincoln Technical Institute, Grand Prairie, TX 300
Lincoln Technical Institute, Mahwah, NJ 222
Lincoln Technical Institute, Melrose Park, IL 158
Lincoln Technical Institute, Philadelphia, PA 266
Lincoln Technical Institute, Union, NJ 222
Louisville Technical Institute, Louisville, KY 172
Missouri Tech, St. Louis, MO 204
National American University, Albuquerque, NM 224
National American University, Brooklyn Center, MN 197
National American University, Colorado Springs, CO 115
National American University, Denver, CO 116
National American University, Ellsworth AFB, SD 286
National American University, Kansas City, MO 204
National American University, Minneapolis, MN 197
National American University, Overland Park, KS 169
National American University, Rapid City, SD 286
National American University, Rio Rancho, NM 224
National American University, Roseville, MN 197

National College of Business & Technology, Bayamon, PR 282

National College of Business & Technology, Bluefield, VA 320

National College of Business & Technology, Bristol, TN 290

National College of Business & Technology, Charlottesville, VA 320

National College of Business & Technology, Danville, KY 172

National College of Business & Technology, Danville, VA 320

National College of Business & Technology, Florence, KY 172

National College of Business & Technology, Harrisonburg, VA 321

National College of Business & Technology, Knoxville, TN 291

National College of Business & Technology, Lexington, KY 173

National College of Business & Technology, Louisville, KY 173

National College of Business & Technology, Lynchburg, VA 321

National College of Business & Technology, Martinsville, VA 321

National College of Business & Technology, Nashville, TN 291

National College of Business & Technology, Pikeville, KY 173

National College of Business & Technology, Richmond, KY 173

National College of Business & Technology, Rio Grande, PR 282

National College of Business & Technology, Salem, VA 321

Northwest Technical Institute, Eden Prairie, MN 198

Remington College - New Orleans Campus, Metairie, LA 180

Remington College - Tampa Campus, Tampa, FL 141

Stratford University, Falls Church , VA 322

Stratford University, Woodbridge, VA 322

Technology Education College, Columbus, OH 245

TESST College of Technology, Alexandria, VA 323

TESST College of Technology, Baltimore, MD 182

TESST College of Technology, Beltsville, MD 183

TESST College of Technology, Towson, MD 183

ENGINEERING/INDUSTRIAL MANAGEMENT

National American University, Albuquerque, NM 224

National American University, Brooklyn Center, MN 197

National American University, Colorado Springs, CO 115

National American University, Denver, CO 116

National American University, Ellsworth AFB, SD 286

National American University, Kansas City, MO 204

National American University, Minneapolis, MN 197

National American University, Overland Park, KS 169

National American University, Rapid City, SD 286

National American University, Rio Rancho, NM 224

National American University, Roseville, MN 197

ENGINEERING-RELATED TECHNOLOGIES, OTHER

National American University, Albuquerque, NM 224

National American University, Brooklyn Center, MN 197

National American University, Colorado Springs, CO 115

National American University, Denver, CO 116

National American University, Ellsworth AFB, SD 286

National American University, Kansas City, MO 204

National American University, Minneapolis, MN 197

National American University, Overland Park, KS 169

National American University, Rapid City, SD 286

National American University, Rio Rancho, NM 224

National American University, Roseville, MN 197

ENGLISH AS A SECOND LANGUAGE

Academy of Art University, San Francisco, CA 83

Bayamon Community College, Bayamon, PR 276

Florida Metropolitan University - Pompano Beach Campus, Pompano Beach, FL 129

MTI College of Business and Technology, Houston, TX 301

Provo College, Provo, UT 310

ENTREPRENEURSHIP/ ENTREPRENEURIAL STUDIES

Bayamon Community College, Bayamon, PR 276

Berkeley College, Paramus, NJ 214

Berkeley College, West Paterson, NJ 214

Berkeley College, Woodbridge, NJ 215

Colorado Technical University, Colorado Springs, CO 113

International Import-Export Institute, Phoenix, AZ 79

National College of Business & Technology, Bayamon, PR 282

National College of Business & Technology, Bluefield, VA 320

National College of Business & Technology, Bristol, TN 290

National College of Business & Technology, Charlottesville, VA 320

National College of Business & Technology, Danville, KY 172

National College of Business & Technology, Danville, VA 320

National College of Business & Technology, Florence, KY 172

National College of Business & Technology, Harrisonburg, VA 321

National College of Business & Technology, Knoxville, TN 291

National College of Business & Technology, Lexington, KY 173

National College of Business & Technology, Louisville, KY 173

National College of Business & Technology, Lynchburg, VA 321

National College of Business & Technology, Martinsville, VA 321

National College of Business & Technology, Nashville, TN 291

National College of Business & Technology, Pikeville, KY 173

National College of Business & Technology, Richmond, KY 173

National College of Business & Technology, Rio Grande, PR 282

National College of Business & Technology, Salem, VA 321

EQUESTRIAN/EQUINE STUDIES

National American University, Albuquerque, NM 224

National American University, Brooklyn Center, MN 197
National American University, Colorado Springs, CO 115
National American University, Denver, CO 116
National American University, Ellsworth AFB, SD 286
National American University, Kansas City, MO 204
National American University, Minneapolis, MN 197
National American University, Overland Park, KS 169
National American University, Rapid City, SD 286
National American University, Rio Rancho, NM 224
National American University, Roseville, MN 197

EXECUTIVE ASSISTANT/EXECUTIVE SECRETARY

Aakers Business College , Bismarck, ND 236
Aakers Business College, Fargo, ND 236
American Commercial College, Abilene, TX 292
American Commercial College, Lubbock, TX 293
American Commercial College, Odessa, TX 293
American Commercial College, San Angelo, TX 293
American Commercial College, Shreveport, LA 175
American School of Business, Wichita Falls, TX 294
Austin Business College, Austin, TX 295
Bradford School, Columbus, OH 237
Bradford School, Pittsburgh, PA 254
Briarcliffe College, Bethpage, NY 226
Briarcliffe College, Patchogue, NY 226
Brookstone College of Business, Charlotte, NC 234
Brookstone College of Business, Greensboro, NC 234
Business Institute of Pennsylvania, Meadville, PA 255
Business Institute of Pennsylvania, Sharon, PA 255
Career Education Institute, Brockton, MA 184
Career Education Institute, Henderson, NV 210
Career Education Institute, Lincoln, RI 283
Career Education Institute, Lowell, MA 184
Career Education Institute, Marietta, GA 146
Career Education Institute, Norcross, GA 146
Central Coast College, Salinas, CA 92
CollegeAmerica - Denver, Denver, CO 113
Delta School of Business & Technology, Lake Charles, LA 177
Dorsey Schools, Madison Heights, MI 188
Dorsey Schools, Roseville, MI 188
Dorsey Schools, Southgate, MI 188
Dorsey Schools, Wayne, MI 189
Douglas Education Center, Monessen, PA 259
Dover Business College, Paramus, NJ 218
Empire College, Santa Rosa, CA 93
Erie Business Center, Main, Erie, PA 261
Florida Metropolitan University - Lakeland Campus, Lakeland, FL 127
Fox College, Oak Lawn, IL 156
Gallipolis Career College, Gallipolis, OH 239
Gibbs College - Cranston, Cranston, RI 283

Gibbs College, Boston, MA 185
Gibbs College, Livingston, NJ 218
Gibbs College, Norwalk, CT 119
Gretna Career College, Gretna, LA 177
Hagerstown Business College, Hagerstown, MD 181
Hohokus Hackensack School of Business and Medical Sciences, Hackensack, NJ 220
ICM School of Business & Medical Careers, Pittsburgh, PA 263
Katharine Gibbs School, Melville, NY 231
Katharine Gibbs School, New York, NY 231
Katharine Gibbs School, Norristown, PA 264
Katharine Gibbs School, Piscataway, NJ 221
Lamson College, Tempe, AZ 79
Laurel Business Institute, Uniontown, PA 265
McCann School of Business, Hazleton, PA 266
McCann School of Business, Pottsville, PA 267
McCann School of Business, Scranton, PA 267
McCann School of Business, Sunbury, PA 267
Minnesota School of Business - Brooklyn Center, Brooklyn Center, MN 196
Missouri College, St. Louis, MO 203
MTI College of Business and Technology, Houston, TX 301
National College of Business & Technology, Bayamon, PR 282
National College of Business & Technology, Bluefield, VA 320
National College of Business & Technology, Bristol, TN 290
National College of Business & Technology, Charlottesville, VA 320
National College of Business & Technology, Danville, KY 172
National College of Business & Technology, Danville, VA 320
National College of Business & Technology, Florence, KY 172
National College of Business & Technology, Harrisonburg, VA 321
National College of Business & Technology, Knoxville, TN 291
National College of Business & Technology, Lexington, KY 173
National College of Business & Technology, Louisville, KY 173
National College of Business & Technology, Lynchburg, VA 321
National College of Business & Technology, Martinsville, VA 321
National College of Business & Technology, Nashville, TN 291
National College of Business & Technology, Pikeville,

KY 173

National College of Business & Technology, Richmond, KY 173

National College of Business & Technology, Rio Grande, PR 282

National College of Business & Technology, Salem, VA 321

New England Institute of Technology, Warwick, RI 284

Pennco Tech Bristol, PA 269

Pennco Tech, Blackwood, NJ 222

The PJA School, Upper Darby, PA 270

Provo College, Provo, UT 310

Rasmussen College St. Cloud, St. Cloud, MN 199

Rockford Business College, Rockford, IL 159

San Joaquin Valley College, Bakersfield, CA 103

San Joaquin Valley College, Fresno, CA 103

San Joaquin Valley College, Modesto, CA 104

San Joaquin Valley College, Rancho Cucamonga, CA 104

San Joaquin Valley College, Visalia, CA 104

Sawyer College, Merrillville, IN 167

Schuylkill Institute of Business and Technology, Pottsville, PA 270

Spencerian College, Louisville, KY 174

Stuart School of Business Administration, Wall, NJ 223

Sullivan University, Lexington, KY 174

Sullivan University, Louisville, KY 175

Trumbull Business College, Warren, OH 245

Virginia College at Birmingham, Birmingham, AL 72

Western Business College, Portland, OR 251

Western Business College, Vancouver, WA 328

Wood Tobe-Coburn School, New York, NY 233

FACIAL TREATMENT SPECIALIST/ FACIALIST

Baltimore School of Massage, Linthicum, MD 180

Career Training Institute, Apopka, FL 124

Douglas Education Center, Monessen, PA 259

Florida College of Natural Health, Bradenton, FL 126

Florida College of Natural Health, Maitland, FL 126

Florida College of Natural Health, Miami, FL 126

Florida College of Natural Health, Pompano Beach, FL 126

Virginia School of Massage, Charlottesville, VA 324

FASHION AND FABRIC CONSULTANT

The Art Institute of Portland, Portland, OR 249

California Design College, Los Angeles, CA 91

The Illinois Institute of Art - Chicago, Chicago, IL 156

Wood Tobe-Coburn School, New York, NY 233

FASHION MERCHANDISING

Academy of Art University, San Francisco, CA 83

American InterContinental University, Atlanta, GA 145

American InterContinental University, Houston, TX 293

American InterContinental University, Los Angeles, CA 85

American InterContinental University, San Antonio, TX 293

American InterContinental University, Weston, FL 121

The Art Institute of Charlotte, Charlotte, NC 233

The Art Institute of Fort Lauderdale, Fort Lauderdale, FL 122

The Art Institute of Philadelphia, Philadelphia, PA 252

The Art Institute of Pittsburgh, Pittsburgh, PA 252

The Art Institute of Portland, Portland, OR 249

The Art Institute of Seattle, Seattle, WA 324

Bauder College, Atlanta, GA 146

Bay State College, Boston, MA 183

Berkeley College, Paramus, NJ 214

Berkeley College, West Paterson, NJ 214

Berkeley College, Woodbridge, NJ 215

Bradford School, Columbus, OH 237

Bradford School, Pittsburgh, PA 254

Bradley Academy for the Visual Arts, York, PA 254

Brooks College, Long Beach, CA 86

Brooks College, Sunnyvale, CA 86

California Design College, Los Angeles, CA 91

Davis College, Toledo, OH 239

Gibbs College, Boston, MA 185

Gibbs College, Livingston, NJ 218

Gibbs College, Norwalk, CT 119

ICM School of Business & Medical Careers, Pittsburgh, PA 263

The Illinois Institute of Art - Chicago, Chicago, IL 156

Indiana Business College, Anderson, IN 162

Indiana Business College, Columbus, IN 163

Indiana Business College, Evansville, IN 163

Indiana Business College, Fort Wayne, IN 163

Indiana Business College, Indianapolis, IN 163

Indiana Business College, Lafayette, IN 163

Indiana Business College, Marion, IN 164

Indiana Business College, Muncie, IN 164

Indiana Business College, Terre Haute, IN 164

International Academy of Design & Technology, Chicago, IL 157

International Academy of Design & Technology, Orlando, FL 132

International Academy of Design & Technology, Pittsburgh, PA 264

International Academy of Design & Technology, Tampa, FL 132

International Academy of Design & Technology, Troy, MI 189

Katharine Gibbs School, Melville, NY 231

Katharine Gibbs School, New York, NY 231

Katharine Gibbs School, Norristown, PA 264

Katharine Gibbs School, Piscataway, NJ 221

Lehigh Valley College, Center Valley, PA 266

McIntosh College, Dover, NH 213

Miami International University of Art & Design, Miami, FL 138

Sanford-Brown College, Collinsville, IL 159

Sanford-Brown College, Fenton, MO 205

Sanford-Brown College, Hazelwood, MO 205

Sanford-Brown College, North Kansas City, MO 206

Sanford-Brown College, St. Charles, MO 206

Sanford-Brown College, West Allis, WI 331

Virginia Marti College of Art and Design, Lakewood, OH 246

Westwood College - Denver South, Denver, CO 118

Wood Tobe-Coburn School, New York, NY 233

FASHION MODELING

Bauder College, Atlanta, GA 146

FASHION/APPAREL DESIGN

Academy of Art University, San Francisco, CA 83

American InterContinental University, Atlanta, GA 145

American InterContinental University, Houston, TX 293

American InterContinental University, Los Angeles, CA 85

American InterContinental University, San Antonio, TX 293

American InterContinental University, Weston, FL 121

The Art Institute of California - San Francisco, San Francisco, CA 86

The Art Institute of Dallas, Dallas, TX 294

The Art Institute of Fort Lauderdale, Fort Lauderdale, FL 122

The Art Institute of New York City, New York, NY 225

The Art Institute of Philadelphia, Philadelphia, PA 252

The Art Institute of Portland, Portland, OR 249

The Art Institute of Seattle, Seattle, WA 324

Bauder College, Atlanta, GA 146

Bay State College, Boston, MA 183

Bradley Academy for the Visual Arts, York, PA 254

Brooks College, Long Beach, CA 86

Brooks College, Sunnyvale, CA 86

California Design College, Los Angeles, CA 91

Gibbs College, Boston, MA 185

Gibbs College, Livingston, NJ 218

Gibbs College, Norwalk, CT 119

The Illinois Institute of Art - Chicago, Chicago, IL 156

International Academy of Design & Technology, Chicago, IL 157

International Academy of Design & Technology, Orlando, FL 132

International Academy of Design & Technology, Pittsburgh, PA 264

International Academy of Design & Technology, Tampa, FL 132

International Academy of Design & Technology, Troy, MI 189

International Academy of Design and Technology, Henderson, NV 210

International Academy of Design and Technology, Nashville, TN 289

International Academy of Design and Technology, San Antonio, TX 298

International Academy of Design and Technology, Schaumburg, IL 157

International Academy of Design and Technology, Seattle, WA 327

Katharine Gibbs School, Melville, NY 231

Katharine Gibbs School, New York, NY 231

Katharine Gibbs School, Norristown, PA 264

Katharine Gibbs School, Piscataway, NJ 221

Miami International University of Art & Design, Miami, FL 138

Virginia Marti College of Art and Design, Lakewood, OH 246

Wood Tobe-Coburn School, New York, NY 233

FIBER, TEXTILE AND WEAVING ARTS

Academy of Art University, San Francisco, CA 83

California Design College, Los Angeles, CA 91

FINANCE AND FINANCIAL MANAGEMENT SERVICES, OTHER

College for Financial Planning, Greenwood Village, CO 113

FINANCE, GENERAL

Argosy University/Chicago, Chicago, IL 154

Cardean University, Chicago, IL 154

College for Financial Planning, Greenwood Village, CO 113

Colorado Technical University Sioux Falls Campus, Sioux Falls, SD 286

International Business College, El Paso, TX 298

International Business College, El Paso, TX 299

International Business College, Fort Wayne, IN 165

International Business College, Indianapolis, IN 165

National American University, Albuquerque, NM 224

National American University, Brooklyn Center, MN 197

National American University, Colorado Springs, CO 115

National American University, Denver, CO 116

National American University, Ellsworth AFB, SD 286

National American University, Kansas City, MO 204

National American University, Minneapolis, MN 197

National American University, Overland Park, KS 169

National American University, Rapid City, SD 286

National American University, Rio Rancho, NM 224

National American University, Roseville, MN 197

The PJA School, Upper Darby, PA 270

Stevens-Henager College - Provo, Orem, UT 311

Stratford University, Falls Church , VA 322

Stratford University, Woodbridge, VA 322
Sullivan University, Lexington, KY 174
Sullivan University, Louisville, KY 175
Westwood College - Inland Empire, Upland, CA 109

FINANCIAL PLANNING AND SERVICES

College for Financial Planning, Greenwood Village, CO 113
Hondros College, Westerville, OH 240

FINE/STUDIO ARTS, GENERAL

Academy of Art University, San Francisco, CA 83

FIRE SCIENCE/FIREFIGHTING

Keiser College, Daytona Beach, FL 134
Keiser College, Fort Lauderdale, FL 134
Keiser College, Lakeland, FL 135
Keiser College, Melbourne, FL 135
Keiser College, Miami, FL 135
Keiser College, Orlando, FL 135
Keiser College, Pembroke Pines, FL 136
Keiser College, Port St. Lucie, FL 136
Keiser College, Sarasota, FL 136
Keiser College, Tallahassee, FL 136
Keiser College, West Palm Beach, FL 137

FOOD PREPARATION/ PROFESSIONAL COOKING/KITCHEN ASSISTANT

Instituto Banca y Comercio, Caguas, PR 279
Instituto Banca y Comercio, Cayey, PR 279
Instituto Banca y Comercio, Fajardo, PR 279
Instituto Banca y Comercio, Guayama, PR 280
Instituto Banca y Comercio, Manati, PR 280
Instituto Banca y Comercio, Mayaguez, PR 280
Instituto Banca y Comercio, Ponce, PR 280
Sullivan University, Lexington, KY 174
Sullivan University, Louisville, KY 175
Western Culinary Institute, Portland, OR 251

FOOD SERVICE, WAITER/WAITRESS, AND DINING ROOM MANAGEMENT/MANAGER

The Art Institutes International Minnesota, Minneapolis, MN 193
Escuela Hotelera de San Juan in Puerto Rico, San Juan, PR 278

FOOD SERVICES TECHNOLOGY

Stratford University, Falls Church , VA 322
Stratford University, Woodbridge, VA 322
Western Culinary Institute, Portland, OR 251

FOODSERVICE SYSTEMS ADMINISTRATION/MANAGEMENT

The Art Institute of Pittsburgh, Pittsburgh, PA 252
The Illinois Institute of Art - Chicago, Chicago, IL 156

FORENSIC SCIENCE AND TECHNOLOGY

Everest College, Arlington , TX 297
Everest College, Dallas, TX 297
Everest College, Fort Worth, TX 297
Everest College, Phoenix, AZ 78
Everest College, Rancho Cucamonga, CA 93
Fountainhead College of Technology, Knoxville, TN 288
Hagerstown Business College, Hagerstown, MD 181
Pittsburgh Technical Institute, Oakdale, PA 269
Southwest Florida College, Tampa, FL 143

FUNERAL SERVICE AND MORTUARY SCIENCE, GENERAL

Antilles School of Technical Careers, Santurce, PR 275

FURNITURE DESIGN AND MANUFACTURING

Academy of Art University, San Francisco, CA 83

GENE/GENETIC THERAPY

Career Education Institute, Brockton, MA 184
Career Education Institute, Henderson, NV 210
Career Education Institute, Lincoln, RI 283
Career Education Institute, Lowell, MA 184
Career Education Institute, Marietta, GA 146
Career Education Institute, Norcross, GA 146
CHI Institute, Broomall, PA 256
CHI Institute, Southampton, PA 256
Harrison Career Institute, Allentown, PA 262
Harrison Career Institute, Baltimore, MD 181
Harrison Career Institute, Clifton, NJ 218
Harrison Career Institute, Delran, NJ 218
Harrison Career Institute, Deptford, NJ 219
Harrison Career Institute, Ewing, NJ 219
Harrison Career Institute, Jersey City, NJ 219
Harrison Career Institute, Oakhurst, NJ 219
Harrison Career Institute, Philadelphia, PA 263
Harrison Career Institute, Reading, PA 263
Harrison Career Institute, South Orange, NJ 220
Harrison Career Institute, Vineland, NJ 220
Harrison Career Institute, Wilmington, DE 121
Mandl School, New York, NY 231
MedVance Institute, Atlantis, FL 138
MedVance Institute, Baton Rouge, LA 179
MedVance Institute, Cookeville, TN 290
MedVance Institute, Fort Lauderdale, FL 138
MedVance Institute, Houston, TX 301

Boldface type indicates that the school is a participating institution in the ⬤ *Imagine America* Scholarship Program

MedVance Institute, Miami, FL 138
MedVance Institute, Port St. Lucie, FL 138
Spencerian College, Louisville, KY 174
Stevens-Henager College - Provo, Orem, UT 311

GENERAL MERCHANDISING, SALES, AND RELATED MARKETING OPERATIONS, OTHER

California Design College, Los Angeles, CA 91
McIntosh College, Dover, NH 213
Virginia College at Pensacola, Pensacola, FL 144

GENERAL OFFICE OCCUPATIONS AND CLERICAL SERVICES

Academy of Medical Arts and Business, Harrisburg, PA 252
American Commercial College, Abilene, TX 292
American Commercial College, Lubbock, TX 293
American Commercial College, Odessa, TX 293
American Commercial College, San Angelo, TX 293
American Commercial College, Shreveport, LA 175
Antonelli College, Cincinnati, OH 237
Antonelli College, Hattiesburg, MS 199
Antonelli College, Jackson, MS 200
Berks Technical Institute, Wyomissing, PA 253
Bradford School, Columbus, OH 237
Bradford School, Pittsburgh, PA 254
Briarcliffe College, Bethpage, NY 226
Briarcliffe College, Patchogue, NY 226
Bryman College, Alhambra, CA 88
Bryman College, Anaheim, CA 88
Bryman College, City of Industry, CA 88
Bryman College, Earth City, MO 201
Bryman College, Everett, WA 325
Bryman College, Gardena, CA 88
Bryman College, Hayward, CA 89
Bryman College, Los Angeles, CA 89
Bryman College, Lynnwood, WA 326
Bryman College, New Orleans, LA 176
Bryman College, Ontario, CA 89
Bryman College, Port Orchard, WA 326
Bryman College, Renton, WA 326
Bryman College, Reseda, CA 89
Bryman College, San Bernardino, CA 90
Bryman College, San Francisco, CA 90
Bryman College, San Jose, CA 90
Bryman College, Tacoma, WA 326
Bryman College, Torrance, CA 90
Business Institute of Pennsylvania, Meadville, PA 255
Business Institute of Pennsylvania, Sharon, PA 255
Career Education Institute, Brockton, MA 184
Career Education Institute, Henderson, NV 210
Career Education Institute, Lincoln, RI 283

Career Education Institute, Lowell, MA 184
Career Education Institute, Marietta, GA 146
Career Education Institute, Norcross, GA 146
Career Point Business School, San Antonio, TX 296
Central Coast College, Salinas, CA 92
CHI Institute, Broomall, PA 256
CHI Institute, Southampton, PA 256
Computer Learning Network, Altoona, PA 258
Computer Learning Network, Mechanicsburg, PA 258
Coyne American Institute, Chicago, IL 155
Coyne American Institute, Chicago, IL 156
Delta School of Business & Technology, Lake Charles, LA 177
Dickinson Business School/Career Point Business School, Tulsa, OK 246
ECPI College of Technology, Charlotte, NC 234
ECPI College of Technology, Greensboro, NC 235
ECPI College of Technology, Greenville, SC 285
ECPI College of Technology, Manassas, VA 315
ECPI College of Technology, Newport News, VA 315
ECPI College of Technology, North Charleston, SC 285
ECPI College of Technology, Raleigh, NC 235
ECPI College of Technology, Virginia Beach, VA 316
ECPI Technical College, Glen Allen, VA 316
ECPI Technical College, Richmond, VA 316
ECPI Technical College, Roanoke, VA 317
Empire College, Santa Rosa, CA 93
Everest College, Arlington , TX 297
Everest College, Dallas, TX 297
Everest College, Fort Worth, TX 297
Everest College, Phoenix, AZ 78
Everest College, Rancho Cucamonga, CA 93
Gibbs College - Cranston, Cranston, RI 283
Gretna Career College, Gretna, LA 177
Hagerstown Business College, Hagerstown, MD 181
HoHoKus RETS School of Business and Medical Technical Services, Nutley, NJ 220
ICPR Junior College-Arecibo Campus, Arecibo, PR 278
ICPR Junior College - Hato Rey Campus, San Juan, PR 278
ICPR Junior College - Mayaguez Campus, Mayaguez, PR 279
Katharine Gibbs School, Melville, NY 231
Katharine Gibbs School, New York, NY 231
Katharine Gibbs School, Norristown, PA 264
Katharine Gibbs School, Piscataway, NJ 221
Laurel Business Institute, Uniontown, PA 265
McCann School of Business, Hazleton, PA 266
McCann School of Business, Pottsville, PA 267
McCann School of Business, Scranton, PA 267
McCann School of Business, Sunbury, PA 267
MTI College of Business and Technology, Houston, TX 301

National College of Business & Technology, Bayamon, PR 282

National College of Business & Technology, Bluefield, VA 320

National College of Business & Technology, Bristol, TN 290

National College of Business & Technology, Charlottesville, VA 320

National College of Business & Technology, Danville, KY 172

National College of Business & Technology, Danville, VA 320

National College of Business & Technology, Florence, KY 172

National College of Business & Technology, Harrisonburg, VA 321

National College of Business & Technology, Knoxville, TN 291

National College of Business & Technology, Lexington, KY 173

National College of Business & Technology, Louisville, KY 173

National College of Business & Technology, Lynchburg, VA 321

National College of Business & Technology, Martinsville, VA 321

National College of Business & Technology, Nashville, TN 291

National College of Business & Technology, Pikeville, KY 173

National College of Business & Technology, Richmond, KY 173

National College of Business & Technology, Rio Grande, PR 282

National College of Business & Technology, Salem, VA 321

Rasmussen College Minnetonka, Minnetonka, MN 199

Rockford Business College, Rockford, IL 159

San Joaquin Valley College, Bakersfield, CA 103

San Joaquin Valley College, Fresno, CA 103

San Joaquin Valley College, Modesto, CA 104

San Joaquin Valley College, Rancho Cucamonga, CA 104

San Joaquin Valley College, Visalia, CA 104

Schuylkill Institute of Business and Technology, Pottsville, PA 270

Texas School of Business, Inc., Houston, TX 306

Tri-State Business Institute, Erie, PA 272

Vatterott College, Broadview Heights, OH 245

Vatterott College, Des Moines, IA 168

Vatterott College, Joplin, MO 206

Vatterott College, Kansas City, MO 207

Vatterott College, Memphis, TN 292

Vatterott College, OÆFallon , MO 207

Vatterott College, Oklahoma City, OK 248

Vatterott College, Omaha, NE 209

Vatterott College, Quincy, IL 160

Vatterott College, Springfield, MO 208

Vatterott College, St. Ann, MO 207

Vatterott College, St. Joseph, MO 207

Vatterott College, St. Louis, MO 208

Vatterott College, Tulsa, OK 249

Vatterott College, Wichita, KS 169

West Tennessee Business College, Jackson, TN 292

Western Business College, Portland, OR 251

Western Business College, Vancouver, WA 328

GENERAL STUDIES

Bay State College, Boston, MA 183

Chaparral College, Tucson, AZ 77

Coleman College, La Mesa, CA 92

Coleman College, San Marcos, CA 93

Douglas Education Center, Monessen, PA 259

Grantham University, Kansas City, MO 177

Hesser College, Manchester, NH 213

National American University, Albuquerque, NM 224

National American University, Brooklyn Center, MN 197

National American University, Colorado Springs, CO 115

National American University, Denver, CO 116

National American University, Ellsworth AFB, SD 286

National American University, Kansas City, MO 204

National American University, Minneapolis, MN 197

National American University, Overland Park, KS 169

National American University, Rapid City, SD 286

National American University, Rio Rancho, NM 224

National American University, Roseville, MN 197

National American University - Sioux Falls Branch, Sioux Falls, SD 287

South University, Columbia, SC 286

South University, Montgomery, AL 71

South University, Savannah, GA 151

South University, West Palm Beach, FL 142

Virginia College at Birmingham, Birmingham, AL 72

GLOBAL MANAGEMENT

Brown College, Mendota Heights, MN 193

Cardean University, Chicago, IL 154

Jones International University, Englewood, CO 115

GRAPHIC AND PRINTING EQUIPMENT OPERATOR, GENERAL PRODUCTION

Berks Technical Institute, Wyomissing, PA 253

Briarcliffe College, Bethpage, NY 226

Briarcliffe College, Patchogue, NY 226

International Business College, El Paso, TX 298

International Business College, El Paso, TX 299
International Business College, Fort Wayne, IN 165
International Business College, Indianapolis, IN 165
Miami International University of Art & Design, Miami, FL 138
Westwood College - Dallas, Dallas, TX 308

GRAPHIC COMMUNICATIONS, GENERAL

Antonelli College, Cincinnati, OH 237
Antonelli College, Hattiesburg, MS 199
Antonelli College, Jackson, MS 200
The Art Institute of California - San Francisco, San Francisco, CA 86
The Art Institute of Ohio - Cincinnati, Cincinnati, OH 237
The Art Institute of Phoenix, Phoenix, AZ 76
The Art Institute of Pittsburgh, Pittsburgh, PA 252
The Art Institute of Portland, Portland, OR 249
Berks Technical Institute, Wyomissing, PA 253
Bradford School of Business, Houston, TX 295
Brooks College, Long Beach, CA 86
Brooks College, Sunnyvale, CA 86
Brown Mackie College, Miami Campus, Miami, FL 124
Brown Mackie College, San Diego Campus, San Diego, CA 87
California Design College, Los Angeles, CA 91
The Chubb Institute, Alpharetta, GA 147
The Chubb Institute, Arlington, VA 314
The Chubb Institute, Cherry Hill, NJ 215
The Chubb Institute, Chicago, IL 155
The Chubb Institute, Jersey City, NJ 216
The Chubb Institute, New York, NY 228
The Chubb Institute, North Brunswick, NJ 216
The Chubb Institute, Parsippany, NJ 216
The Chubb Institute, Springfield, PA 256
The Chubb Institute, Westbury, NY 228
Douglas Education Center, Monessen, PA 259
Eagle Gate College - Weber/Davis, Layton, UT 309
Eagle Gate College - Weber/Davis, Salt Lake City, UT 309
Gibbs College, Boston, MA 185
Gibbs College, Livingston, NJ 218
Gibbs College, Norwalk, CT 119
Hesser College, Manchester, NH 213
International Academy of Design & Technology, Chicago, IL 157
International Academy of Design & Technology, Orlando, FL 132
International Academy of Design & Technology, Pittsburgh, PA 264
International Academy of Design & Technology, Tampa, FL 132
International Academy of Design & Technology, Troy, MI 189

International Academy of Design and Technology, Henderson, NV 210
International Academy of Design and Technology, Nashville, TN 289
International Academy of Design and Technology, San Antonio, TX 298
International Academy of Design and Technology, Schaumburg, IL 157
International Academy of Design and Technology, Seattle, WA 327
Louisville Technical Institute, Louisville, KY 172
McIntosh College, Dover, NH 213
Pittsburgh Technical Institute, Oakdale, PA 269
Virginia College at Birmingham, Birmingham, AL 72
Westwood College - Atlanta Campus, Atlanta, GA 151
Westwood College - Chicago Du Page, Woodridge, IL 160
Westwood College - Houston South Campus, Houston, TX 308

GRAPHIC COMMUNICATIONS, OTHER

The Art Institute of Fort Lauderdale, Fort Lauderdale, FL 122
The Art Institute of Phoenix, Phoenix, AZ 76
The Art Institute of Portland, Portland, OR 249
Berks Technical Institute, Wyomissing, PA 253
Brown College, Mendota Heights, MN 193
California Design College, Los Angeles, CA 91
The Chubb Institute, Alpharetta, GA 147
The Chubb Institute, Arlington, VA 314
The Chubb Institute, Cherry Hill, NJ 215
The Chubb Institute, Chicago, IL 155
The Chubb Institute, Jersey City, NJ 216
The Chubb Institute, New York, NY 228
The Chubb Institute, North Brunswick, NJ 216
The Chubb Institute, Parsippany, NJ 216
The Chubb Institute, Springfield, PA 256
The Chubb Institute, Westbury, NY 228
Collins College: A School of Design and Technology, Tempe, AZ 77
Colorado Technical University Denver Campus, Greenwood Village, CO 114
Douglas Education Center, Monessen, PA 259
Duluth Business University, Duluth, MN 194
Eagle Gate College - Weber/Davis, Layton, UT 309
Eagle Gate College - Weber/Davis, Salt Lake City, UT 309
Gibbs College - Cranston, Cranston, RI 283
Hesser College, Manchester, NH 213
International Academy of Design & Technology, Chicago, IL 157
International Academy of Design & Technology, Orlando, FL 132

International Academy of Design & Technology, Pittsburgh, PA 264

International Academy of Design & Technology, Tampa, FL 132

International Academy of Design & Technology, Troy, MI 189

McIntosh College, Dover, NH 213

Platt College - Los Angeles, Inc, Alhambra, CA 102

Virginia College at Birmingham, Birmingham, AL 72

Virginia College at Huntsville, Huntsville, AL 73

Westwood College - Denver South, Denver, CO 118

GUNSMITHING/GUNSMITH

Colorado School of Trades, Lakewood, CO 113

Sonoran Desert Institute, Scottsdale, AZ 81

HEALTH AIDE

Berks Technical Institute, Wyomissing, PA 253

Central Florida College, Winter Park, FL 124

Douglas Education Center, Monessen, PA 259

Galen College of California, Inc., Fresno, CA 94

Galen College of California, Inc., Modesto, CA 94

Galen College of California, Inc., Visalia, CA 94

Georgia Medical Institute - Jonesboro, Jonesboro, GA 148

Gretna Career College, Gretna, LA 177

Instituto Banca y Comercio, Caguas, PR 279

Instituto Banca y Comercio, Cayey, PR 279

Instituto Banca y Comercio, Fajardo, PR 279

Instituto Banca y Comercio, Guayama, PR 280

Instituto Banca y Comercio, Manati, PR 280

Instituto Banca y Comercio, Mayaguez, PR 280

Instituto Banca y Comercio, Ponce, PR 280

Maric College, Anaheim, CA 99

Maric College, Los Angeles, CA 100

Maric College, North Hollywood, CA 99

Maric College, Sacramento, CA 99

Maric College, Salida, CA 99

Maric College, San Diego, CA 100

Maric College, Vista, CA 100

National School of Technology, Inc., Fort Lauderdale, FL 139

National School of Technology, Inc., Hialeah, FL 139

National School of Technology, Inc., Miami, FL 139

Trinity College of Puerto Rico, Ponce, PR 283

Tucson College, Tucson, AZ 82

HEALTH AIDES/ATTENDANTS/ ORDERLIES, OTHER

Berks Technical Institute, Wyomissing, PA 253

HEALTH AND MEDICAL ADMINISTRATIVE SERVICES, OTHER

Antonelli College, Cincinnati, OH 237

Antonelli College, Hattiesburg, MS 199

Antonelli College, Jackson, MS 200

Berks Technical Institute, Wyomissing, PA 253

Briarcliffe College, Bethpage, NY 226

Briarcliffe College, Patchogue, NY 226

Brookstone College of Business, Charlotte, NC 234

Brookstone College of Business, Greensboro, NC 234

Business Institute of Pennsylvania, Meadville, PA 255

Business Institute of Pennsylvania, Sharon, PA 255

Career Technical College, Monroe, LA 176

Career Technical College, Shreveport, LA 177

Charter College, Anchorage, AK 74

The Chubb Institute, Alpharetta, GA 147

The Chubb Institute, Arlington, VA 314

The Chubb Institute, Cherry Hill, NJ 215

The Chubb Institute, Chicago, IL 155

The Chubb Institute, Jersey City, NJ 216

The Chubb Institute, New York, NY 228

The Chubb Institute, North Brunswick, NJ 216

The Chubb Institute, Parsippany, NJ 216

The Chubb Institute, Springfield, PA 256

The Chubb Institute, Westbury, NY 228

The Cittone Institute, Edison, NJ 217

The Cittone Institute, Mount Laurel, NJ 217

The Cittone Institute, Paramus, NJ 217

The Cittone Institute, Philadelphia, PA 257

The Cittone Institute, Plymouth Meeting, PA 257

Coyne American Institute, Chicago, IL 155

Coyne American Institute, Chicago, IL 156

ECPI College of Technology, Charlotte, NC 234

ECPI College of Technology, Greensboro, NC 235

ECPI College of Technology, Greenville, SC 285

ECPI College of Technology, Manassas, VA 315

ECPI College of Technology, Newport News, VA 315

ECPI College of Technology, North Charleston, SC 285

ECPI College of Technology, Raleigh, NC 235

ECPI College of Technology, Virginia Beach, VA 316

Florida Metropolitan University-Melbourne Campus, Melbourne, FL 127

Florida Technical College, Auburndale, FL 129

Florida Technical College, DeLand, FL 130

Florida Technical College, Jacksonville, FL 130

Florida Technical College, Orlando, FL 130

Gretna Career College, Gretna, LA 177

Hesser College, Manchester, NH 213

Indiana Business College, Anderson, IN 162

Indiana Business College, Columbus, IN 163

Indiana Business College, Evansville, IN 163

Indiana Business College, Fort Wayne, IN 163

Indiana Business College, Indianapolis, IN 163

National College of Business & Technology, Harrisonburg, VA 321

National College of Business & Technology, Knoxville, TN 291

National College of Business & Technology, Lexington, KY 173

National College of Business & Technology, Louisville, KY 173

National College of Business & Technology, Lynchburg, VA 321

National College of Business & Technology, Martinsville, VA 321

National College of Business & Technology, Nashville, TN 291

National College of Business & Technology, Pikeville, KY 173

National College of Business & Technology, Richmond, KY 173

National College of Business & Technology, Rio Grande, PR 282

National College of Business & Technology, Salem, VA 321

National College of Business and Technology, Arecibo, PR 282

National College of Business and Technology, Cincinnati, OH 241

National College of Business and Technology, Indianapolis, IN 166

National College of Business and Technology, Kettering, OH 242

North Florida Institute, Orange Park, FL 140

Rasmussen College Eagan, Eagan, MN 198

Rasmussen College Mankato, Mankato, MN 198

Rasmussen College Minnetonka, Minnetonka, MN 199

Rasmussen College St. Cloud, St. Cloud, MN 199

San Joaquin Valley College, Bakersfield, CA 103

San Joaquin Valley College, Fresno, CA 103

San Joaquin Valley College, Modesto, CA 104

San Joaquin Valley College, Rancho Cucamonga, CA 104

San Joaquin Valley College, Visalia, CA 104

Sanford-Brown College, Collinsville, IL 159

Sanford-Brown College, Fenton, MO 205

Sanford-Brown College, Hazelwood, MO 205

Sanford-Brown College, North Kansas City, MO 206

Sanford-Brown College, St. Charles, MO 206

Sanford-Brown College, West Allis, WI 331

Sanford-Brown Institute, Atlanta, GA 150

Sanford-Brown Institute, Dallas, TX 305

Sanford-Brown Institute, Garden City, NY 232

Sanford-Brown Institute, Houston, TX 305

Sanford-Brown Institute, Houston, TX 306

Sanford-Brown Institute, Jacksonville, FL 142

Sanford-Brown Institute, Landover, MD 182

Sanford-Brown Institute, Lauderdale Lakes, FL 142

Sanford-Brown Institute, New York, NY 232

Sanford-Brown Institute, Springfield, MA 187

Sanford-Brown Institute, Tampa, FL 142

Sanford-Brown Institute, Trevose, PA 270

Sanford-Brown Institute, White Plains, NY 232

Schuylkill Institute of Business and Technology, Pottsville, PA 270

Stevens-Henager College, Boise, ID 153

Stevens-Henager College, Logan, UT 311

Stevens-Henager College, Ogden, UT 311

Stevens-Henager College - Salt Lake City, Salt Lake City, UT 312

Technical Career Institute, New York, NY 233

Thompson Institute, Chambersburg, PA 271

Thompson Institute, Harrisburg, PA 271

Thompson Institute, Philadelphia, PA 271

Vatterott College, Broadview Heights, OH 245

Vatterott College, Des Moines, IA 168

Vatterott College, Joplin, MO 206

Vatterott College, Kansas City, MO 207

Vatterott College, Memphis, TN 292

Vatterott College, OÆFallon , MO 207

Vatterott College, Oklahoma City, OK 248

Vatterott College, Omaha, NE 209

Vatterott College, Quincy, IL 160

Vatterott College, Springfield, MO 208

Vatterott College, St. Ann, MO 207

Vatterott College, St. Joseph, MO 207

Vatterott College, St. Louis, MO 208

Vatterott College, Tulsa, OK 249

Vatterott College, Wichita, KS 169

Virginia College at Huntsville, Huntsville, AL 73

West Virginia Junior College, Bridgeport, WV 329

West Virginia Junior College, Charleston, WV 329

West Virginia Junior College, Morgantown, WV 330

Western Technical College, El Paso, TX 307

HEALTH PROFESSIONS AND RELATED CLINICAL SCIENCES, OTHER

Argosy University/Chicago, Chicago, IL 154

Chaparral College, Tucson, AZ 77

The Chubb Institute, Alpharetta, GA 147

The Chubb Institute, Arlington, VA 314

The Chubb Institute, Cherry Hill, NJ 215

The Chubb Institute, Chicago, IL 155

The Chubb Institute, Jersey City, NJ 216

The Chubb Institute, New York, NY 228

The Chubb Institute, North Brunswick, NJ 216

The Chubb Institute, Parsippany, NJ 216

The Chubb Institute, Springfield, PA 256

The Chubb Institute, Westbury, NY 228

Douglas Education Center, Monessen, PA 259
Harrison Career Institute, Allentown, PA 262
Harrison Career Institute, Baltimore, MD 181
Harrison Career Institute, Clifton, NJ 218
Harrison Career Institute, Delran, NJ 218
Harrison Career Institute, Deptford, NJ 219
Harrison Career Institute, Ewing, NJ 219
Harrison Career Institute, Jersey City, NJ 219
Harrison Career Institute, Oakhurst, NJ 219
Harrison Career Institute, Philadelphia, PA 263
Harrison Career Institute, Reading, PA 263
Harrison Career Institute, South Orange, NJ 220
Harrison Career Institute, Vineland, NJ 220
Harrison Career Institute, Wilmington, DE 121
HoHoKus RETS School of Business and Medical Technical Services, Nutley, NJ 220
Indiana Business College, Anderson, IN 162
Indiana Business College, Columbus, IN 163
Indiana Business College, Evansville, IN 163
Indiana Business College, Fort Wayne, IN 163
Indiana Business College, Indianapolis, IN 163
Indiana Business College, Lafayette, IN 163
Indiana Business College, Marion, IN 164
Indiana Business College, Muncie, IN 164
Indiana Business College, Terre Haute, IN 164
North Florida Institute, Orange Park, FL 140
RETS Technical Center, Charlestown, MA 187

HEALTH SERVICES ADMINISTRATION

Argosy University/Chicago, Chicago, IL 154
Berks Technical Institute, Wyomissing, PA 253
Brown Mackie College, Findlay Campus, Findlay, OH 238
The Chubb Institute, Alpharetta, GA 147
The Chubb Institute, Arlington, VA 314
The Chubb Institute, Cherry Hill, NJ 215
The Chubb Institute, Chicago, IL 155
The Chubb Institute, Jersey City, NJ 216
The Chubb Institute, New York, NY 228
The Chubb Institute, North Brunswick, NJ 216
The Chubb Institute, Parsippany, NJ 216
The Chubb Institute, Springfield, PA 256
The Chubb Institute, Westbury, NY 228
Coyne American Institute, Chicago, IL 155
Coyne American Institute, Chicago, IL 156
Keiser College, Daytona Beach, FL 134
Keiser College, Fort Lauderdale, FL 134
Keiser College, Lakeland, FL 135
Keiser College, Melbourne, FL 135
Keiser College, Miami, FL 135
Keiser College, Orlando, FL 135
Keiser College, Pembroke Pines, FL 136
Keiser College, Port St. Lucie, FL 136
Keiser College, Sarasota, FL 136

Keiser College, Tallahassee, FL 136
Keiser College, West Palm Beach, FL 137
McIntosh College, Dover, NH 213
South University, Columbia, SC 286
South University, Montgomery, AL 71
South University, Savannah, GA 151
South University, West Palm Beach, FL 142
Strayer University, Atlanta, GA 151
Virginia College at Birmingham, Birmingham, AL 72

HEALTH SERVICES/ALLIED HEALTH/ HEALTH SCIENCES, GENERAL

Brookstone College of Business, Charlotte, NC 234
Brookstone College of Business, Greensboro, NC 234
Chaparral College, Tucson, AZ 77
The Chubb Institute, Alpharetta, GA 147
The Chubb Institute, Arlington, VA 314
The Chubb Institute, Cherry Hill, NJ 215
The Chubb Institute, Chicago, IL 155
The Chubb Institute, Jersey City, NJ 216
The Chubb Institute, New York, NY 228
The Chubb Institute, North Brunswick, NJ 216
The Chubb Institute, Parsippany, NJ 216
The Chubb Institute, Springfield, PA 256
The Chubb Institute, Westbury, NY 228
Coyne American Institute, Chicago, IL 155
Coyne American Institute, Chicago, IL 156
Florida Technical College, Auburndale, FL 129
Florida Technical College, DeLand, FL 130
Florida Technical College, Jacksonville, FL 130
Florida Technical College, Orlando, FL 130
Hesser College, Manchester, NH 213
McIntosh College, Dover, NH 213
RETS Technical Center, Charlestown, MA 187
Sanford-Brown Institute, Atlanta, GA 150
Sanford-Brown Institute, Dallas, TX 305
Sanford-Brown Institute, Garden City, NY 232
Sanford-Brown Institute, Houston, TX 305
Sanford-Brown Institute, Houston, TX 306
Sanford-Brown Institute, Jacksonville, FL 142
Sanford-Brown Institute, Landover, MD 182
Sanford-Brown Institute, Lauderdale Lakes, FL 142
Sanford-Brown Institute, New York, NY 232
Sanford-Brown Institute, Springfield, MA 187
Sanford-Brown Institute, Tampa, FL 142
Sanford-Brown Institute, Trevose, PA 270
Sanford-Brown Institute, White Plains, NY 232
Virginia College at Birmingham, Birmingham, AL 72

HEALTH UNIT COORDINATOR/ WARD CLERK

Antonelli College, Cincinnati, OH 237
Antonelli College, Hattiesburg, MS 199

Antonelli College, Jackson, MS 200
The Bryman School, Phoenix, AZ 77
Central Coast College, Salinas, CA 92
Chaparral College, Tucson, AZ 77
The Chubb Institute, Alpharetta, GA 147
The Chubb Institute, Arlington, VA 314
The Chubb Institute, Cherry Hill, NJ 215
The Chubb Institute, Chicago, IL 155
The Chubb Institute, Jersey City, NJ 216
The Chubb Institute, New York, NY 228
The Chubb Institute, North Brunswick, NJ 216
The Chubb Institute, Parsippany, NJ 216
The Chubb Institute, Springfield, PA 256
The Chubb Institute, Westbury, NY 228
Douglas Education Center, Monessen, PA 259
Florida Technical College, Auburndale, FL 129
Florida Technical College, DeLand, FL 130
Florida Technical College, Jacksonville, FL 130
Florida Technical College, Orlando, FL 130
Hagerstown Business College, Hagerstown, MD 181
Pima Medical Institute, Albuquerque, NM 224
Pima Medical Institute, Chula Vista, CA 101
Pima Medical Institute, Colorado Springs, CO 116
Pima Medical Institute, Denver, CO 117
Pima Medical Institute, Las Vegas, NV 213
Pima Medical Institute, Mesa, AZ 80
Pima Medical Institute, Renton, WA 328
Pima Medical Institute, Seattle, WA 328
Pima Medical Institute, Tucson, AZ 81
Rasmussen College Mankato, Mankato, MN 198
Rasmussen College Minnetonka, Minnetonka, MN 199
Rasmussen College St. Cloud, St. Cloud, MN 199
Spencerian College, Louisville, KY 174

HEALTH UNIT MANAGER/WARD SUPERVISOR

Bradford School, Columbus, OH 237
Bradford School, Pittsburgh, PA 254
Douglas Education Center, Monessen, PA 259
Rasmussen College Minnetonka, Minnetonka, MN 199

HEALTH/HEALTH CARE ADMINISTRATION/MANAGEMENT

American InterContinental University, Atlanta, GA 145
American InterContinental University, Houston, TX 293
American InterContinental University, Los Angeles, CA 85
American InterContinental University, San Antonio, TX 293
American InterContinental University, Weston, FL 121
Argosy University/Chicago, Chicago, IL 154
ATI Career Training Center, Dallas, TX 294
ATI Career Training Center, Fort Lauderdale, FL 122
ATI Career Training Center, Miami, FL 123
ATI Career Training Center, North Richland Hills, TX
295
ATI Career Training Center, Oakland Park, FL 123
Berks Technical Institute, Wyomissing, PA 253
Briarcliffe College, Bethpage, NY 226
Briarcliffe College, Patchogue, NY 226
Brown Mackie College, Akron Campus, Akron, OH 238
Business Institute of Pennsylvania, Meadville, PA 255
Business Institute of Pennsylvania, Sharon, PA 255
Capella University, Minneapolis, MN 194
Cardean University, Chicago, IL 154
The Chubb Institute, Alpharetta, GA 147
The Chubb Institute, Arlington, VA 314
The Chubb Institute, Cherry Hill, NJ 215
The Chubb Institute, Chicago, IL 155
The Chubb Institute, Jersey City, NJ 216
The Chubb Institute, New York, NY 228
The Chubb Institute, North Brunswick, NJ 216
The Chubb Institute, Parsippany, NJ 216
The Chubb Institute, Springfield, PA 256
The Chubb Institute, Westbury, NY 228
CollegeAmerica - Colorado Springs, Colorado Springs, CO 112
CollegeAmerica - Fort Collins, Fort Collins, CO 113
Coyne American Institute, Chicago, IL 155
Coyne American Institute, Chicago, IL 156
Draughons Junior College, Bowling Green, KY 171
Draughons Junior College, Clarksville, TN 287
Draughons Junior College, Murfreesboro, TN 287
Draughons Junior College, Nashville, TN 288
Florida Metropolitan University - Lakeland Campus, Lakeland, FL 127
Florida Metropolitan University - North Orlando Campus, Orlando, FL 128
Florida Metropolitan University - Pinellas Campus, Clearwater, FL 128
Florida Metropolitan University - South Orlando Campus, Orlando, FL 129
Florida Metropolitan University-Melbourne Campus, Melbourne, FL 127
Harrison Career Institute, Allentown, PA 262
Harrison Career Institute, Baltimore, MD 181
Harrison Career Institute, Clifton, NJ 218
Harrison Career Institute, Delran, NJ 218
Harrison Career Institute, Deptford, NJ 219
Harrison Career Institute, Ewing, NJ 219
Harrison Career Institute, Jersey City, NJ 219
Harrison Career Institute, Oakhurst, NJ 219
Harrison Career Institute, Philadelphia, PA 263
Harrison Career Institute, Reading, PA 263
Harrison Career Institute, South Orange, NJ 220
Harrison Career Institute, Vineland, NJ 220
Harrison Career Institute, Wilmington, DE 121
Herzing College, Atlanta, GA 148

Herzing College, Birmingham, AL 70
Herzing College, Kenner, LA 178
Herzing College, Madison, WI 330
Herzing College, Minneapolis, MN 195
Herzing College, Winter Park, FL 131
International Academy of Design and Technology, Henderson, NV 210
International Academy of Design and Technology, Nashville, TN 289
International Academy of Design and Technology, San Antonio, TX 298
International Academy of Design and Technology, Schaumburg, IL 157
International Academy of Design and Technology, Seattle, WA 327
Keiser College, Daytona Beach, FL 134
Keiser College, Fort Lauderdale, FL 134
Keiser College, Lakeland, FL 135
Keiser College, Melbourne, FL 135
Keiser College, Miami, FL 135
Keiser College, Orlando, FL 135
Keiser College, Pembroke Pines, FL 136
Keiser College, Port St. Lucie, FL 136
Keiser College, Sarasota, FL 136
Keiser College, Tallahassee, FL 136
Keiser College, West Palm Beach, FL 137
McIntosh College, Dover, NH 213
National American University, Albuquerque, NM 224
National American University, Brooklyn Center, MN 197
National American University, Colorado Springs, CO 115
National American University, Denver, CO 116
National American University, Ellsworth AFB, SD 286
National American University, Kansas City, MO 204
National American University, Minneapolis, MN 197
National American University, Overland Park, KS 169
National American University, Rapid City, SD 286
National American University, Rio Rancho, NM 224
National American University, Roseville, MN 197
Pioneer Pacific College, Clackamas, OR 250
Pioneer Pacific College, Wilsonville, OR 251
Rasmussen College Minnetonka, Minnetonka, MN 199
San Joaquin Valley College, Bakersfield, CA 103
San Joaquin Valley College, Fresno, CA 103
San Joaquin Valley College, Modesto, CA 104
San Joaquin Valley College, Rancho Cucamonga, CA 104
San Joaquin Valley College, Visalia, CA 104
Sanford-Brown College, Collinsville, IL 159
Sanford-Brown College, Fenton, MO 205
Sanford-Brown College, Hazelwood, MO 205
Sanford-Brown College, North Kansas City, MO 206
Sanford-Brown College, St. Charles, MO 206
Sanford-Brown College, West Allis, WI 331

Sawyer College, Merrillville, IN 167
South University, Columbia, SC 286
South University, Montgomery, AL 71
South University, Savannah, GA 151
South University, West Palm Beach, FL 142
Stevens-Henager College, Boise, ID 153
Stevens-Henager College, Logan, UT 311
Stevens-Henager College, Ogden, UT 311
Stevens-Henager College - Provo, Orem, UT 311
Stevens-Henager College - Salt Lake City, Salt Lake City, UT 312
Western Technical Institute, El Paso, TX 308

HEALTH/MEDICAL CLAIMS EXAMINER

American Career College, Anaheim, CA 84
Berks Technical Institute, Wyomissing, PA 253
Chaparral College, Tucson, AZ 77
Coyne American Institute, Chicago, IL 155
Coyne American Institute, Chicago, IL 156
Harrison Career Institute, Allentown, PA 262
Harrison Career Institute, Baltimore, MD 181
Harrison Career Institute, Clifton, NJ 218
Harrison Career Institute, Delran, NJ 218
Harrison Career Institute, Deptford, NJ 219
Harrison Career Institute, Ewing, NJ 219
Harrison Career Institute, Jersey City, NJ 219
Harrison Career Institute, Oakhurst, NJ 219
Harrison Career Institute, Philadelphia, PA 263
Harrison Career Institute, Reading, PA 263
Harrison Career Institute, South Orange, NJ 220
Harrison Career Institute, Vineland, NJ 220
Harrison Career Institute, Wilmington, DE 121
Indiana Business College, Anderson, IN 162
Indiana Business College, Columbus, IN 163
Indiana Business College, Evansville, IN 163
Indiana Business College, Fort Wayne, IN 163
Indiana Business College, Indianapolis, IN 163
Indiana Business College, Lafayette, IN 163
Indiana Business College, Marion, IN 164
Indiana Business College, Muncie, IN 164
Indiana Business College, Terre Haute, IN 164
Indiana Business College-Medical, Indianapolis, IN 164

HEATING, AIR CONDITIONING AND REFRIGERATION TECHNOLOGY/ TECHNICIAN (ACH/ACR/ACHR/ HRAC/HVAC/AC TECHNOLOGY)

Advanced Technology Institute, Virginia Beach, VA 314
American School of Technology, Columbus, OH 237
Apex Technical School, New York, NY 225
ATI Career Training Center, Dallas, TX 294
ATI Career Training Center, Fort Lauderdale, FL 122

ATI Career Training Center, Miami, FL 123
ATI Career Training Center, North Richland Hills, TX 295
ATI Career Training Center, Oakland Park, FL 123
ATI Technical Training Center, Dallas, TX 295
Ayers Institute, Inc., Shreveport, LA 175
CHI Institute, Broomall, PA 256
CHI Institute, Southampton, PA 256
Coyne American Institute, Chicago, IL 155
Coyne American Institute, Chicago, IL 156
Dean Institute of Technology, Pittsburgh, PA 258
Huertas Junior College, Caguas, PR 277
Institute for Business and Technology, Santa Clara, CA 96
Instituto Banca y Comercio, Caguas, PR 279
Instituto Banca y Comercio, Cayey, PR 279
Instituto Banca y Comercio, Fajardo, PR 279
Instituto Banca y Comercio, Guayama, PR 280
Instituto Banca y Comercio, Manati, PR 280
Instituto Banca y Comercio, Mayaguez, PR 280
Instituto Banca y Comercio, Ponce, PR 280
ITI Technical College, Baton Rouge, LA 178
Liceo de Arte y Tecnologia, San Juan, PR 281
Lincoln Technical Institute Indianapolis, IN 166
Lincoln Technical Institute, Allentown, PA 266
Lincoln Technical Institute, Columbia, MD 182
Lincoln Technical Institute, Grand Prairie, TX 300
Lincoln Technical Institute, Mahwah, NJ 222
Lincoln Technical Institute, Melrose Park, IL 158
Lincoln Technical Institute, Philadelphia, PA 266
Lincoln Technical Institute, Union, NJ 222
National Institute of Technology, Austin , TX 302
National Institute of Technology, Cross Lanes, WV 329
National Institute of Technology, Detroit, MI 190
National Institute of Technology, Houston, TX 302
National Institute of Technology, Long Beach, CA 101
National Institute of Technology, San Antonio, TX 302
National Institute of Technology, Southfield, MI 190
New Castle School of Trades, Pulaski, PA 268
New England Institute of Technology, Warwick, RI 284
New England Technical Institute of Connecticut, Inc., New Britain, CT 119
New England Technical Institute, Cromwell, CT 119
New England Technical Institute, Hamden, CT 119
New England Technical Institute, Shelton, CT 119
Pennco Tech Bristol, PA 269
Pennco Tech, Blackwood, NJ 222
RETS Tech Center, Centerville, OH 243
RETS Technical Center, Charlestown, MA 187
San Joaquin Valley College, Bakersfield, CA 103
San Joaquin Valley College, Fresno, CA 103
San Joaquin Valley College, Modesto, CA 104
San Joaquin Valley College, Rancho Cucamonga, CA 104

San Joaquin Valley College, Visalia, CA 104
TESST College of Technology, Alexandria, VA 323
TESST College of Technology, Baltimore, MD 182
TESST College of Technology, Beltsville, MD 183
TESST College of Technology, Towson, MD 183
Triangle Tech, Inc. - Greensburg School, Greensburg, PA 272
Triangle Tech, Inc. - Pittsburgh School, Pittsburgh, PA 272
The Refrigeration School, Phoenix, AZ 81
Vatterott College, Broadview Heights, OH 245
Vatterott College, Des Moines, IA 168
Vatterott College, Joplin, MO 206
Vatterott College, Kansas City, MO 207
Vatterott College, Memphis, TN 292
Vatterott College, OÆFallon , MO 207
Vatterott College, Oklahoma City, OK 248
Vatterott College, Omaha, NE 209
Vatterott College, Quincy, IL 160
Vatterott College, Springfield, MO 208
Vatterott College, St. Ann, MO 207
Vatterott College, St. Joseph, MO 207
Vatterott College, St. Louis, MO 208
Vatterott College, Tulsa, OK 249
Vatterott College, Wichita, KS 169
Western Technical College, El Paso, TX 307
Westwood College - Denver, Broomfield, CO 118
Westwood College - Denver North, Denver, CO 118
Wichita Technical Institute, Wichita, KS 169
WyoTech, Bedford, MA 187
WyoTech, Blairsville, PA 274
WyoTech, Fremont, CA 111
WyoTech, Laramie, WY 332
WyoTech, Oakland, CA 111
WyoTech, West Sacramento, CA 111
York Technical Institute, Lancaster, PA 274
York Technical Institute, York, PA 274

HEATING, AIR CONDITIONING, VENTILATION AND REFRIGERATION MAINTENANCE TECHNOLOGY/ TECHNICIAN (HAC, HACR, HVAC, HVACR)

Advanced Technology Institute, Virginia Beach, VA 314
Arizona Automotive Institute, Glendale, AZ 76
CHI Institute, Broomall, PA 256
CHI Institute, Southampton, PA 256
Instituto Banca y Comercio, Caguas, PR 279
Instituto Banca y Comercio, Cayey, PR 279
Instituto Banca y Comercio, Fajardo, PR 279
Instituto Banca y Comercio, Guayama, PR 280
Instituto Banca y Comercio, Manati, PR 280
Instituto Banca y Comercio, Mayaguez, PR 280

Instituto Banca y Comercio, Ponce, PR 280
Instituto de Banca y Comercio, San Juan, PR 281
ITI Technical College, Baton Rouge, LA 178
Lincoln Technical Institute Indianapolis, IN 166
Lincoln Technical Institute, Allentown, PA 266
Lincoln Technical Institute, Columbia, MD 182
Lincoln Technical Institute, Grand Prairie, TX 300
Lincoln Technical Institute, Mahwah, NJ 222
Lincoln Technical Institute, Melrose Park, IL 158
Lincoln Technical Institute, Philadelphia, PA 266
Lincoln Technical Institute, Union, NJ 222
National Institute of Technology, Austin , TX 302
National Institute of Technology, Cross Lanes, WV 329
National Institute of Technology, Detroit, MI 190
National Institute of Technology, Houston, TX 302
National Institute of Technology, Long Beach, CA 101
National Institute of Technology, San Antonio, TX 302
National Institute of Technology, Southfield, MI 190
New England Institute of Technology at Palm Beach, West Palm Beach, FL 140
New York Technical Institute of Hawaii, Honolulu, HI 152
Orleans Technical Institute, Philadelphia, PA 268
Porter and Chester Institute, Chicopee, MA 187
Porter and Chester Institute, Enfield, CT 120
Porter and Chester Institute, Stratford, CT 120
Porter and Chester Institute, Watertown, CT 120
Porter and Chester Institute, Wethersfield, CT 120
The Refrigeration School, Phoenix, AZ 81
RETS Technical Center, Charlestown, MA 187
San Antonio College of Medical and Dental Assistants, San Antonio, TX 305
Technical Career Institute, New York, NY 233
Vatterott College, Broadview Heights, OH 245
Vatterott College, Des Moines, IA 168
Vatterott College, Joplin, MO 206
Vatterott College, Kansas City, MO 207
Vatterott College, Memphis, TN 292
Vatterott College, OÆFallon , MO 207
Vatterott College, Oklahoma City, OK 248
Vatterott College, Omaha, NE 209
Vatterott College, Quincy, IL 160
Vatterott College, Springfield, MO 208
Vatterott College, St. Ann, MO 207
Vatterott College, St. Joseph, MO 207
Vatterott College, St. Louis, MO 208
Vatterott College, Tulsa, OK 249
Vatterott College, Wichita, KS 169
Western Technical College, El Paso, TX 307
Western Technical Institute, El Paso, TX 308

HEAVY EQUIPMENT MAINTENANCE TECHNOLOGY/TECHNICIAN
Advanced Technology Institute, Virginia Beach, VA 314

Caguas Institute of Mechanical Technology, Caguas, PR 276

HEMATOLOGY TECHNOLOGY/ TECHNICIAN
Career Education Institute, Brockton, MA 184
Career Education Institute, Henderson, NV 210
Career Education Institute, Lincoln, RI 283
Career Education Institute, Lowell, MA 184
Career Education Institute, Marietta, GA 146
Career Education Institute, Norcross, GA 146
Florida Technical College, Auburndale, FL 129
Florida Technical College, DeLand, FL 130
Florida Technical College, Jacksonville, FL 130
Florida Technical College, Orlando, FL 130

HOME HEALTH AIDE/HOME ATTENDANT
Academy of Medical Arts and Business, Harrisburg, PA 252
Dawn Training Centre, Inc., Wilmington, DE 120
Douglas Education Center, Monessen, PA 259
Gretna Career College, Gretna, LA 177
Instituto Banca y Comercio, Caguas, PR 279
Instituto Banca y Comercio, Cayey, PR 279
Instituto Banca y Comercio, Fajardo, PR 279
Instituto Banca y Comercio, Guayama, PR 280
Instituto Banca y Comercio, Manati, PR 280
Instituto Banca y Comercio, Mayaguez, PR 280
Instituto Banca y Comercio, Ponce, PR 280
Mandl School, New York, NY 231

HORSESHOEING
Colorado School of Trades, Lakewood, CO 113

HOSPITAL AND HEALTH CARE FACILITIES ADMINISTRATION/ MANAGEMENT
ATI Career Training Center, Dallas, TX 294
ATI Career Training Center, Fort Lauderdale, FL 122
ATI Career Training Center, Miami, FL 123
ATI Career Training Center, North Richland Hills, TX 295
ATI Career Training Center, Oakland Park, FL 123
Career Education Institute, Brockton, MA 184
Career Education Institute, Henderson, NV 210
Career Education Institute, Lincoln, RI 283
Career Education Institute, Lowell, MA 184
Career Education Institute, Marietta, GA 146
Career Education Institute, Norcross, GA 146
Florida Metropolitan University - Tampa Campus, Tampa, FL 129
Keiser College, Daytona Beach, FL 134
Keiser College, Fort Lauderdale, FL 134

Keiser College, Lakeland, FL 135
Keiser College, Melbourne, FL 135
Keiser College, Miami, FL 135
Keiser College, Orlando, FL 135
Keiser College, Pembroke Pines, FL 136
Keiser College, Port St. Lucie, FL 136
Keiser College, Sarasota, FL 136
Keiser College, Tallahassee, FL 136
Keiser College, West Palm Beach, FL 137
National American University, Albuquerque, NM 224
National American University, Brooklyn Center, MN 197
National American University, Colorado Springs, CO 115
National American University, Denver, CO 116
National American University, Ellsworth AFB, SD 286
National American University, Kansas City, MO 204
National American University, Minneapolis, MN 197
National American University, Overland Park, KS 169
National American University, Rapid City, SD 286
National American University, Rio Rancho, NM 224
National American University, Roseville, MN 197
Sawyer College, Merrillville, IN 167
South University, Columbia, SC 286
South University, Montgomery, AL 71
South University, Savannah, GA 151
South University, West Palm Beach, FL 142

HOSPITALITY ADMINISTRATION/ MANAGEMENT, GENERAL

The Art Institute of Colorado, Denver, CO 111
Bradford School, Columbus, OH 237
Bradford School, Pittsburgh, PA 254
California Culinary Academy, San Francisco, CA 91
California School of Culinary Arts, Pasadena, CA 91
Colegio Mayor de Tecnologia, Arroyo, PR 276
Empire College, Santa Rosa, CA 93
Florida Metropolitan University - Pompano Beach Campus, Pompano Beach, FL 129
Gibbs College - Cranston, Cranston, RI 283
Gibbs College, Boston, MA 185
Gibbs College, Livingston, NJ 218
Gibbs College, Norwalk, CT 119
ICPR Junior College - Hato Rey Campus, San Juan, PR 278
ICPR Junior College - Mayaguez Campus, Mayaguez, PR 279
ICPR Junior College-Arecibo Campus, Arecibo, PR 278
International Business College, El Paso, TX 298
International Business College, El Paso, TX 299
International Business College, Fort Wayne, IN 165
International Business College, Indianapolis, IN 165
Katharine Gibbs School, Melville, NY 231
Katharine Gibbs School, New York, NY 231
Katharine Gibbs School, Norristown, PA 264

Katharine Gibbs School, Piscataway, NJ 221
Keiser College, Daytona Beach, FL 134
Keiser College, Fort Lauderdale, FL 134
Keiser College, Lakeland, FL 135
Keiser College, Melbourne, FL 135
Keiser College, Miami, FL 135
Keiser College, Orlando, FL 135
Keiser College, Pembroke Pines, FL 136
Keiser College, Port St. Lucie, FL 136
Keiser College, Sarasota, FL 136
Keiser College, Tallahassee, FL 136
Keiser College, West Palm Beach, FL 137
Laurel Business Institute, Uniontown, PA 265
Lehigh Valley College, Center Valley, PA 266
National College of Business & Technology, Bayamon, PR 282
National College of Business & Technology, Bluefield, VA 320
National College of Business & Technology, Bristol, TN 290
National College of Business & Technology, Charlottesville, VA 320
National College of Business & Technology, Danville, KY 172
National College of Business & Technology, Danville, VA 320
National College of Business & Technology, Florence, KY 172
National College of Business & Technology, Harrisonburg, VA 321
National College of Business & Technology, Knoxville, TN 291
National College of Business & Technology, Lexington, KY 173
National College of Business & Technology, Louisville, KY 173
National College of Business & Technology, Lynchburg, VA 321
National College of Business & Technology, Martinsville, VA 321
National College of Business & Technology, Nashville, TN 291
National College of Business & Technology, Pikeville, KY 173
National College of Business & Technology, Richmond, KY 173
National College of Business & Technology, Rio Grande, PR 282
National College of Business & Technology, Salem, VA 321
National College of Business and Technology, Arecibo, PR 282
National College of Business and Technology, Cincinnati,

Boldface type indicates that the school is a participating institution in the *Imagine America* Scholarship Program

OH 241

National College of Business and Technology, Indianapolis, IN 166

National College of Business and Technology, Kettering, OH 242

Pittsburgh Technical Institute, Oakdale, PA 269

San Joaquin Valley College, Bakersfield, CA 103

San Joaquin Valley College, Fresno, CA 103

San Joaquin Valley College, Modesto, CA 104

San Joaquin Valley College, Rancho Cucamonga, CA 104

San Joaquin Valley College, Visalia, CA 104

Southwest Florida College, Tampa, FL 143

Sullivan University, Lexington, KY 174

Sullivan University, Louisville, KY 175

Virginia College at Birmingham, Birmingham, AL 72

Western Business College, Portland, OR 251

Western Business College, Vancouver, WA 328

Western Culinary Institute, Portland, OR 251

Wood Tobe-Coburn School, New York, NY 233

York Technical Institute, Lancaster, PA 274

York Technical Institute, York, PA 274

HOSPITALITY ADMINISTRATION/ MANAGEMENT, OTHER

Gibbs College - Cranston, Cranston, RI 283

Provo College, Provo, UT 310

Remington College - Honolulu Campus, Honolulu, HI 152

HOTEL/MOTEL ADMINISTRATION/ MANAGEMENT

The Art Institute of New York City, New York, NY 225

The Art Institute of Pittsburgh, Pittsburgh, PA 252

Bradford School, Columbus, OH 237

Bradford School, Pittsburgh, PA 254

California School of Culinary Arts, Pasadena, CA 91

Colegio Mayor de Tecnologia, Arroyo, PR 276

Instituto Banca y Comercio, Caguas, PR 279

Instituto Banca y Comercio, Cayey, PR 279

Instituto Banca y Comercio, Fajardo, PR 279

Instituto Banca y Comercio, Guayama, PR 280

Instituto Banca y Comercio, Manati, PR 280

Instituto Banca y Comercio, Mayaguez, PR 280

Instituto Banca y Comercio, Ponce, PR 280

Katharine Gibbs School, Melville, NY 231

Katharine Gibbs School, New York, NY 231

Katharine Gibbs School, Norristown, PA 264

Katharine Gibbs School, Piscataway, NJ 221

Minneapolis Business College, Roseville, MN 196

Pittsburgh Technical Institute, Oakdale, PA 269

The Restaurant School at Walnut Hill College, Philadelphia, PA 270

Stratford University, Falls Church , VA 322

Stratford University, Woodbridge, VA 322

Sullivan University, Lexington, KY 174

Sullivan University, Louisville, KY 175

Western Culinary Institute, Portland, OR 251

Westwood College - Denver North, Denver, CO 118

York Technical Institute, Lancaster, PA 274

York Technical Institute, York, PA 274

HUMAN RESOURCES DEVELOPMENT

Capella University, Minneapolis, MN 194

Indiana Business College, Anderson, IN 162

Indiana Business College, Columbus, IN 163

Indiana Business College, Evansville, IN 163

Indiana Business College, Fort Wayne, IN 163

Indiana Business College, Indianapolis, IN 163

Indiana Business College, Lafayette, IN 163

Indiana Business College, Marion, IN 164

Indiana Business College, Muncie, IN 164

Indiana Business College, Terre Haute, IN 164

HUMAN RESOURCES MANAGEMENT AND SERVICES, OTHER

Argosy University/Chicago, Chicago, IL 154

Berks Technical Institute, Wyomissing, PA 253

Virginia College at Birmingham, Birmingham, AL 72

Virginia College at Jackson, Jackson, MS 200

HUMAN RESOURCES MANAGEMENT/PERSONNEL ADMINISTRATION, GENERAL

Aakers Business College , Bismarck, ND 236

Aakers Business College, Fargo, ND 236

Academy College, Minneapolis, MN 192

American InterContinental University, Atlanta, GA 145

American InterContinental University, Houston, TX 293

American InterContinental University, Los Angeles, CA 85

American InterContinental University, San Antonio, TX 293

American InterContinental University, Weston, FL 121

Berkeley College, Paramus, NJ 214

Berkeley College, West Paterson, NJ 214

Berkeley College, Woodbridge, NJ 215

Berks Technical Institute, Wyomissing, PA 253

Bryan College, Springfield, MO 201

Bryan College, Topeka, KS 169

Capella University, Minneapolis, MN 194

Cardean University, Chicago, IL 154

Colorado Technical University Sioux Falls Campus, Sioux Falls, SD 286

Colorado Technical University, Colorado Springs, CO 113

International Academy of Design and Technology, Henderson, NV 210

International Academy of Design and Technology, Nash-

ville, TN 289
International Academy of Design and Technology, San Antonio, TX 298
International Academy of Design and Technology, Schaumburg, IL 157
International Academy of Design and Technology, Seattle, WA 327
McCann School of Business, Hazleton, PA 266
McCann School of Business, Pottsville, PA267
McCann School of Business, Scranton, PA 267
McCann School of Business, Sunbury, PA 267
National American University, Albuquerque, NM 224
National American University, Brooklyn Center, MN 197
National American University, Colorado Springs, CO 115
National American University, Denver, CO 116
National American University, Ellsworth AFB, SD 286
National American University, Kansas City, MO 204
National American University, Minneapolis, MN 197
National American University, Overland Park, KS 169
National American University, Rapid City, SD 286
National American University, Rio Rancho, NM 224
National American University, Roseville, MN 197
Peirce College, Philadelphia, PA 268
Rasmussen College Mankato, Mankato, MN 198
Rasmussen College Minnetonka, Minnetonka, MN 199
Sullivan University, Lexington, KY 174
Sullivan University, Louisville, KY 175
Virginia College at Birmingham, Birmingham, AL 72
Virginia College at Jackson, Jackson, MS 200
Virginia College at Mobile, Mobile, AL 73
Virginia College at Pensacola, Pensacola, FL 144
Western International University, Phoenix, AZ 82

HUMAN SERVICES, GENERAL

Capella University, Minneapolis, MN 194
Orleans Technical Institute, Philadelphia, PA 268

HYDRAULICS AND FLUID POWER TECHNOLOGY/TECHNICIAN

ITI Technical College, Baton Rouge, LA 178
Louisville Technical Institute, Louisville, KY 172

INDUSTRIAL DESIGN

The Art Institute of Colorado, Denver, CO 111
The Art Institute of Fort Lauderdale, Fort Lauderdale, FL 122
The Art Institute of Philadelphia, Philadelphia, PA 252
The Art Institute of Pittsburgh, Pittsburgh, PA 252
The Art Institute of Seattle, Seattle, WA 324
ITI Technical College, Baton Rouge, LA 178
Louisville Technical Institute, Louisville, KY 172

INDUSTRIAL ELECTRONICS TECHNOLOGY/TECHNICIAN

Caguas Institute of Mechanical Technology, Caguas, PR 276
Coyne American Institute, Chicago, IL 155
Coyne American Institute, Chicago, IL 156
Herzing College, Atlanta, GA 148
Herzing College, Birmingham, AL 70
Herzing College, Kenner, LA 178
Herzing College, Madison, WI 330
Herzing College, Minneapolis, MN 195
Herzing College, Winter Park, FL 131
ITI Technical College, Baton Rouge, LA 178
Lincoln Technical Institute Indianapolis, IN 166
Lincoln Technical Institute, Allentown, PA 266
Lincoln Technical Institute, Columbia, MD 182
Lincoln Technical Institute, Grand Prairie, TX 300
Lincoln Technical Institute, Mahwah, NJ 222
Lincoln Technical Institute, Melrose Park, IL 158
Lincoln Technical Institute, Philadelphia, PA 266
Lincoln Technical Institute, Union, NJ 222
Louisville Technical Institute, Louisville, KY 172
National Institute of Technology, Austin , TX 302
National Institute of Technology, Cross Lanes, WV 329
National Institute of Technology, Detroit, MI 190
National Institute of Technology, Houston, TX 302
National Institute of Technology, Long Beach, CA 101
National Institute of Technology, San Antonio, TX 302
National Institute of Technology, Southfield, MI 190
RETS Technical Center, Charlestown, MA 187
Technical Career Institute, New York, NY 233

INDUSTRIAL MECHANICS AND MAINTENANCE TECHNOLOGY

Caguas Institute of Mechanical Technology, Caguas, PR 276
ITI Technical College, Baton Rouge, LA 178
Louisville Technical Institute, Louisville, KY 172
New Castle School of Trades, Pulaski, PA 268

INDUSTRIAL RADIOLOGIC TECHNOLOGY/TECHNICIAN

High-Tech Institute, Irving, TX 298
High-Tech Institute, Kansas City, MO 202
High-Tech Institute, Las Vegas, NV 210
High-Tech Institute, Marietta, GA 149
High-Tech Institute, Memphis, TN 288
High-Tech Institute, Nashville, TN 288
High-Tech Institute, Orlando, FL 132
High-Tech Institute, Phoenix, AZ 78
High-Tech Institute, Sacramento, CA 96
High-Tech Institute, St. Louis Park, MN 195
ITI Technical College, Baton Rouge, LA 178

INDUSTRIAL TECHNOLOGY/ TECHNICIAN

HoHoKus RETS School of Business and Medical Technical Services, Nutley, NJ 220

International Business College, El Paso, TX 298

International Business College, El Paso, TX 299

International Business College, Fort Wayne, IN 165

International Business College, Indianapolis, IN 165

ITI Technical College, Baton Rouge, LA 178

ITT Technical Institute, Albany, NY 230

ITT Technical Institute, Albuquerque, NM 223

ITT Technical Institute, Anaheim, CA 96

ITT Technical Institute, Arlington, TX 299

ITT Technical Institute, Arnold, MO 202

ITT Technical Institute, Austin, TX 299

ITT Technical Institute, Bessemer, AL 71

ITT Technical Institute, Boise, ID 153

ITT Technical Institute, Bothell, WA 327

ITT Technical Institute, Burr Ridge, IL 157

ITT Technical Institute, Canton, MI 189

ITT Technical Institute, Chantilly, VA 317

ITT Technical Institute, Dayton, OH 240

ITT Technical Institute, Duluth, GA 149

ITT Technical Institute, Earth City, MO 202

ITT Technical Institute, Eden Prairie, MN 195

ITT Technical Institute, Fort Lauderdale, FL 133

ITT Technical Institute, Fort Wayne, IN 165

ITT Technical Institute, Getzville, NY 230

ITT Technical Institute, Grand Rapids, MI 189

ITT Technical Institute, Green Bay, WI 331

ITT Technical Institute, Greenfield, WI 331

ITT Technical Institute, Greenville, SC 285

ITT Technical Institute, Henderson, NV 211

ITT Technical Institute, Hilliard, OH 240

ITT Technical Institute, Houston, TX 299

ITT Technical Institute, Houston, TX 300

ITT Technical Institute, Indianapolis, IN 165

ITT Technical Institute, Jacksonville, FL 133

ITT Technical Institute, Kansas City, MO 203

ITT Technical Institute, Kennesaw, GA 149

ITT Technical Institute, King of Prussia, PA 264

ITT Technical Institute, Knoxville, TN 289

ITT Technical Institute, Lake Mary, FL 133

ITT Technical Institute, Lathrop, CA 96

ITT Technical Institute, Little Rock, AR 82

ITT Technical Institute, Liverpool, NY 230

ITT Technical Institute, Louisville, KY 171

ITT Technical Institute, Matteson, IL 158

ITT Technical Institute, Mechanicsburg, PA 264

ITT Technical Institute, Memphis, TN 289

ITT Technical Institute, Miami, FL 133

ITT Technical Institute, Monroeville, PA 264

ITT Technical Institute, Mount Prospect, IL 158

ITT Technical Institute, Murray, UT 310

ITT Technical Institute, Nashville, TN 289

ITT Technical Institute, Newburgh, IN 166

ITT Technical Institute, Norfolk, VA 318

ITT Technical Institute, Norwood, MA 186

ITT Technical Institute, Norwood, OH 240

ITT Technical Institute, Omaha, NE 209

ITT Technical Institute, Owings Mills, MD 181

ITT Technical Institute, Oxnard, CA 97

ITT Technical Institute, Pittsburg, PA 264

ITT Technical Institute, Portland, OR 250

ITT Technical Institute, Rancho Cordova, CA 97

ITT Technical Institute, Richardson, TX 300

ITT Technical Institute, Richmond, VA 318

ITT Technical Institute, Saint Rose, LA 179

ITT Technical Institute, San Antonio, TX 300

ITT Technical Institute, San Bernardino, CA 97

ITT Technical Institute, San Diego, CA 97

ITT Technical Institute, Seattle, WA 327

ITT Technical Institute, Spokane, WA 328

ITT Technical Institute, Springfield, VA 318

ITT Technical Institute, Strongsville, OH 241

ITT Technical Institute, Sylmar, CA 98

ITT Technical Institute, Tampa, FL 134

ITT Technical Institute, Tempe, AZ 79

ITT Technical Institute, Thornton, CO 115

ITT Technical Institute, Torrance, CA 98

ITT Technical Institute, Troy, MI 190

ITT Technical Institute, Tucson, AZ 79

ITT Technical Institute, Tulsa, OK 247

ITT Technical Institute, Warrensville Heights, OH 241

ITT Technical Institute, West Covina, CA 98

ITT Technical Institute, Woburn, MA 186

ITT Technical Institute, Youngstown, OH 241

Louisville Technical Institute, Louisville, KY 172

Western Technical Institute, El Paso, TX 308

York Technical Institute, Lancaster, PA 274

York Technical Institute, York, PA 274

INFORMATION RESOURCES MANAGEMENT/CIO TRAINING

Hickey College, St. Louis, MO 202

International Academy of Design and Technology, Henderson, NV 210

International Academy of Design and Technology, Nashville, TN 289

International Academy of Design and Technology, San Antonio, TX 298

International Academy of Design and Technology, Schaumburg, IL 157

International Academy of Design and Technology, Seattle, WA 327

INFORMATION SCIENCE/STUDIES

Academy of Medical Arts and Business, Harrisburg, PA 252

Briarcliffe College, Bethpage, NY 226

Briarcliffe College, Patchogue, NY 226

Bryan College, Springfield, MO 201

Bryan College, Topeka, KS 169

Chaparral College, Tucson, AZ 77

The Chubb Institute, Alpharetta, GA 147

The Chubb Institute, Arlington, VA 314

The Chubb Institute, Cherry Hill, NJ 215

The Chubb Institute, Chicago, IL 155

The Chubb Institute, Jersey City, NJ 216

The Chubb Institute, New York, NY 228

The Chubb Institute, North Brunswick, NJ 216

The Chubb Institute, Parsippany, NJ 216

The Chubb Institute, Springfield, PA 256

The Chubb Institute, Westbury, NY 228

Coleman College, La Mesa, CA 92

Coleman College, San Marcos, CA 93

Computer Learning Network, Altoona, PA 258

Computer Learning Network, Mechanicsburg, PA 258

Coyne American Institute, Chicago, IL 155

Coyne American Institute, Chicago, IL 156

ECPI College of Technology, Charlotte, NC 234

ECPI College of Technology, Greensboro, NC 235

ECPI College of Technology, Greenville, SC 285

ECPI College of Technology, Manassas, VA 315

ECPI College of Technology, Newport News, VA 315

ECPI College of Technology, North Charleston, SC 285

ECPI College of Technology, Raleigh, NC 235

ECPI College of Technology, Virginia Beach, VA 316

ECPI Technical College, Glen Allen, VA 316

ECPI Technical College, Richmond, VA 316

ECPI Technical College, Roanoke, VA 317

Florida Metropolitan University - Jacksonville Campus, Jacksonville, FL 127

Florida Metropolitan University - Lakeland Campus, Lakeland, FL 127

Florida Metropolitan University - North Orlando Campus, Orlando, FL 128

Florida Metropolitan University - Pinellas Campus, Clearwater, FL 128

Florida Metropolitan University - Pompano Beach Campus, Pompano Beach, FL 129

Florida Metropolitan University - Tampa Campus, Tampa, FL 129

Grantham University, Kansas City, MO 177

Hamilton College, Cedar Rapids, IA 167

ICPR Junior College - Hato Rey Campus, San Juan, PR 278

ICPR Junior College - Mayaguez Campus, Mayaguez, PR 279

ICPR Junior College-Arecibo Campus, Arecibo, PR 278

ITI Technical College, Baton Rouge, LA 178

Missouri Tech, St. Louis, MO 204

MTI College of Business and Technology, Houston, TX 301

National American University, Albuquerque, NM 224

National American University, Brooklyn Center, MN 197

National American University, Colorado Springs, CO 115

National American University, Denver, CO 116

National American University, Ellsworth AFB, SD 286

National American University, Kansas City, MO 204

National American University, Minneapolis, MN 197

National American University, Overland Park, KS 169

National American University, Rapid City, SD 286

National American University, Rio Rancho, NM 224

National American University, Roseville, MN 197

National College of Business and Technology, Arecibo, PR 282

National College of Business and Technology, Cincinnati, OH 241

National College of Business and Technology, Indianapolis, IN 166

National College of Business and Technology, Kettering, OH 242

New England Institute of Technology, Warwick, RI 284

Platt College, Huntington Beach, CA 101

Platt College, Lawton, OK 247

Platt College, Oklahoma City, OK 248

Platt College, Ontario, CA 102

Platt College, Tulsa, OK 248

Potomac College, Herndon, VA 322

Potomac College, Washington, DC 121

Rasmussen College Eagan, Eagan, MN 198

Rasmussen College Minnetonka, Minnetonka, MN 199

Remington College - Cleveland Campus, Cleveland, OH 242

Remington College - Fort Worth Campus, Fort Worth, TX 304

Remington College - Pinellas Campus, Largo, FL 141

Remington College - Tampa Campus, Tampa, FL 141

Remington College - Tempe Campus, Tempe, AZ 81

San Joaquin Valley College, Bakersfield, CA 103

San Joaquin Valley College, Fresno, CA 103

San Joaquin Valley College, Modesto, CA 104

San Joaquin Valley College, Rancho Cucamonga, CA 104

San Joaquin Valley College, Visalia, CA 104

Silicon Valley College, Emeryville, CA 105

Silicon Valley College, Fremont, CA 106

Silicon Valley College, San Jose, CA 106

Stevens-Henager College, Boise, ID 153

Stevens-Henager College, Logan, UT 311

Stevens-Henager College, Ogden, UT 311

Stratford University, Falls Church , VA 322
Stratford University, Woodbridge, VA 322
TESST College of Technology, Alexandria, VA 323
TESST College of Technology, Baltimore, MD 182
TESST College of Technology, Beltsville, MD 183
TESST College of Technology, Towson, MD 183
Vatterott College, Broadview Heights, OH 245
Vatterott College, Des Moines, IA 168
Vatterott College, Joplin, MO 206
Vatterott College, Kansas City, MO 207
Vatterott College, Memphis, TN 292
Vatterott College, OÆFallon , MO 207
Vatterott College, Oklahoma City, OK 248
Vatterott College, Omaha, NE 209
Vatterott College, Quincy, IL 160
Vatterott College, Springfield, MO 208
Vatterott College, St. Ann, MO 207
Vatterott College, St. Joseph, MO 207
Vatterott College, St. Louis, MO 208
Vatterott College, Tulsa, OK 249
Vatterott College, Wichita, KS 169
York Technical Institute, Lancaster, PA 274
York Technical Institute, York, PA 274

INFORMATION TECHNOLOGY

Academy of Medical Arts and Business, Harrisburg, PA 252
Advanced Training Associates, El Cajon, CA 84
American Commercial College, Abilene, TX 292
American Commercial College, Lubbock, TX 293
American Commercial College, Odessa, TX 293
American Commercial College, San Angelo, TX 293
American Commercial College, Shreveport, LA 175
American InterContinental University, Atlanta, GA 145
American InterContinental University, Houston, TX 293
American InterContinental University, Los Angeles, CA 85
American InterContinental University, San Antonio, TX 293
American InterContinental University, Weston, FL 121
Apollo College-Westside, Inc., Phoenix, AZ
Argosy University/Chicago, Chicago, IL 154
ATI Career Training Center, Dallas, TX 294
ATI Career Training Center, Fort Lauderdale, FL 122
ATI Career Training Center, Miami, FL 123
ATI Career Training Center, North Richland Hills, TX 295
ATI Career Training Center, Oakland Park, FL 123
Bauder College, Atlanta, GA 146
Berks Technical Institute, Wyomissing, PA 253
Briarcliffe College, Bethpage, NY 226
Briarcliffe College, Patchogue, NY 226
Brookstone College of Business, Charlotte, NC 234
Brookstone College of Business, Greensboro, NC 234
Brown College, Mendota Heights, MN 193

Bryan College, Springfield, MO 201
Bryan College, Topeka, KS 169
Capella University, Minneapolis, MN 194
Career Education Institute, Brockton, MA 184
Career Education Institute, Henderson, NV 210
Career Education Institute, Lincoln, RI 283
Career Education Institute, Lowell, MA 184
Career Education Institute, Marietta, GA 146
Career Education Institute, Norcross, GA 146
Career Institute of Health and Technology, Brooklyn, NY 227
Career Institute of Health and Technology, Garden City, NY 227
Career Institute of Health and Technology, Rego Park, NY 228
Central Coast College, Salinas, CA 92
Charter College, Anchorage, AK 74
CHI Institute, Broomall, PA 256
CHI Institute, Southampton, PA 256
The Chubb Institute, Alpharetta, GA 147
The Chubb Institute, Arlington, VA 314
The Chubb Institute, Cherry Hill, NJ 215
The Chubb Institute, Chicago, IL 155
The Chubb Institute, Jersey City, NJ 216
The Chubb Institute, New York, NY 228
The Chubb Institute, North Brunswick, NJ 216
The Chubb Institute, Parsippany, NJ 216
The Chubb Institute, Springfield, PA 256
The Chubb Institute, Westbury, NY 228
Coleman College, La Mesa, CA 92
Coleman College, San Marcos, CA 93
Collins College: A School of Design and Technology, Tempe, AZ 77
Colorado Technical University Denver Campus, Greenwood Village, CO 114
Colorado Technical University Sioux Falls Campus, Sioux Falls, SD 286
Colorado Technical University, Colorado Springs, CO 113
Computer Learning Network, Altoona, PA 258
Computer Learning Network, Mechanicsburg, PA 258
Delta School of Business & Technology, Lake Charles, LA 177
Draughons Junior College, Bowling Green, KY 171
Draughons Junior College, Clarksville, TN 287
Draughons Junior College, Murfreesboro, TN 287
Draughons Junior College, Nashville, TN 288
ECPI College of Technology, Charlotte, NC 234
ECPI College of Technology, Greensboro, NC 235
ECPI College of Technology, Greenville, SC 285
ECPI College of Technology, Manassas, VA 315
ECPI College of Technology, Newport News, VA 315
ECPI College of Technology, North Charleston, SC 285
ECPI College of Technology, Raleigh, NC 235

Boldface type indicates that the school is a participating institution in the 🎓 *Imagine America* Scholarship Program

ville, VA 320

National College of Business & Technology, Danville, KY 172

National College of Business & Technology, Danville, VA 320

National College of Business & Technology, Florence, KY 172

National College of Business & Technology, Harrisonburg, VA 321

National College of Business & Technology, Knoxville, TN 291

National College of Business & Technology, Lexington, KY 173

National College of Business & Technology, Louisville, KY 173

National College of Business & Technology, Lynchburg, VA 321

National College of Business & Technology, Martinsville, VA 321

National College of Business & Technology, Nashville, TN 291

National College of Business & Technology, Pikeville, KY 173

National College of Business & Technology, Richmond, KY 173

National College of Business & Technology, Rio Grande, PR 282

National College of Business & Technology, Salem, VA 321

National Institute of Technology, Austin , TX 302

National Institute of Technology, Cross Lanes, WV 329

National Institute of Technology, Detroit, MI 190

National Institute of Technology, Houston, TX 302

National Institute of Technology, Long Beach, CA 101

National Institute of Technology, San Antonio, TX 302

National Institute of Technology, Southfield, MI 190

New England Institute of Technology, Warwick, RI 284

North Florida Institute, Orange Park, FL 140

Peirce College, Philadelphia, PA 268

Pittsburgh Technical Institute, Oakdale, PA 269

Platt College, Huntington Beach, CA 101

Platt College, Lawton, OK 247

Platt College - Los Angeles, Inc, Alhambra, CA 102

Platt College, Oklahoma City, OK 248

Platt College, Ontario, CA 102

Platt College, Tulsa, OK 248

Potomac College, Herndon, VA 322

Potomac College, Washington, DC 121

Rasmussen College Eagan, Eagan, MN 198

Rasmussen College Minnetonka, Minnetonka, MN 199

Rasmussen College St. Cloud, St. Cloud, MN 199

Remington College - Memphis Campus, Memphis, TN 291

Remington College - Pinellas Campus, Largo, FL 141

Remington College - Tampa Campus, Tampa, FL 141

Silicon Valley College, Emeryville, CA 105

Silicon Valley College, Fremont, CA 106

Silicon Valley College, San Jose, CA 106

South University, Columbia, SC 286

South University, Montgomery, AL 71

South University, Savannah, GA 151

South University, West Palm Beach, FL 142

Southeastern Business College, Chillicothe, OH 243

Southeastern Business College, Jackson, OH 243

Southeastern Business College, Lancaster, OH 243

Southeastern Business College, New Boston, OH 244

Southeastern Career Institute, Dallas, TX 306

Southwest Florida College, Tampa, FL 143

Stratford University, Falls Church , VA 322

Stratford University, Woodbridge, VA 322

Strayer University, Atlanta, GA 151

Sullivan University, Lexington, KY 174

Sullivan University, Louisville, KY 175

TESST College of Technology, Alexandria, VA 323

TESST College of Technology, Baltimore, MD 182

TESST College of Technology, Beltsville, MD 183

TESST College of Technology, Towson, MD 183

Tri-State Business Institute, Erie, PA 272

Webster College, Holiday, FL 144

Webster College, Ocala, FL 144

Western International University, Phoenix, AZ 82

Western Technical College, El Paso, TX 307

Westwood College - Anaheim, Anaheim, CA 109

Westwood College - Denver North, Denver, CO 118

Westwood College - Denver South, Denver, CO 118

Westwood College - Fort Worth, Euless, TX 308

Westwood College - Long Beach, Torrance, CA 110

Westwood College - Los Angeles, Inglewood, CA 110

Westwood College - Los Angeles, Los Angeles, CA 110

Wright Business School, Oklahoma City, OK 249

Wright Business School, Overland Park, KS 170

Wright Business School, Tulsa, OK 249

INSTRUMENTATION TECHNOLOGY/ TECHNICIAN

Glendale Career College, Glendale, CA 95

ITI Technical College, Baton Rouge, LA 178

Louisville Technical Institute, Louisville, KY 172

MTI College of Business and Technology, Houston, TX 301

INSURANCE

Capella University, Minneapolis, MN 194

Erie Business Center, Main, Erie, PA 261

Hondros College, Westerville, OH 240

San Joaquin Valley College, Bakersfield, CA 103

San Joaquin Valley College, Fresno, CA 103
San Joaquin Valley College, Modesto, CA 104
San Joaquin Valley College, Rancho Cucamonga, CA 104
San Joaquin Valley College, Visalia, CA 104
Stevens-Henager College, Boise, ID 153
Stevens-Henager College, Logan, UT 311
Stevens-Henager College, Ogden, UT 311

INTERIOR DESIGN

Academy of Art University, San Francisco, CA 83
American InterContinental University, Atlanta, GA 145
American InterContinental University, Houston, TX 293
American InterContinental University, Los Angeles, CA 85
American InterContinental University, San Antonio, TX 293
American InterContinental University, Weston, FL 121
Antonelli College, Cincinnati, OH 237
Antonelli College, Hattiesburg, MS 199
Antonelli College, Jackson, MS 200
The Art Institute of Atlanta, Atlanta, GA 145
The Art Institute of California - Los Angeles, Santa Monica, CA 85
The Art Institute of California - Orange County, Santa Ana, CA 86
The Art Institute of California - San Diego, San Diego, CA 86
The Art Institute of California - San Francisco, San Francisco, CA 86
The Art Institute of Charlotte, Charlotte, NC 233
The Art Institute of Colorado, Denver, CO 111
The Art Institute of Dallas, Dallas, TX 294
The Art Institute of Fort Lauderdale, Fort Lauderdale, FL 122
The Art Institute of Houston, Houston, TX 294
The Art Institute of Las Vegas, Henderson, NV 209
The Art Institute of New York City, New York, NY 225
The Art Institute of Ohio - Cincinnati, Cincinnati, OH 237
The Art Institute of Philadelphia, Philadelphia, PA 252
The Art Institute of Phoenix, Phoenix, AZ 76
The Art Institute of Pittsburgh, Pittsburgh, PA 252
The Art Institute of Portland, Portland, OR 249
The Art Institute of Seattle, Seattle, WA 324
The Art Institute of Washington, Arlington, VA 314
The Art Institutes International Minnesota, Minneapolis, MN 193
Bauder College, Atlanta, GA 146
Berkeley College, Paramus, NJ 214
Berkeley College, West Paterson, NJ 214
Berkeley College, Woodbridge, NJ 215
Bradley Academy for the Visual Arts, York, PA 254
Brooks College, Long Beach, CA 86
Brooks College, Sunnyvale, CA 86
Brown College, Mendota Heights, MN 193

California Design College, Los Angeles, CA 91
Collins College: A School of Design and Technology, Tempe, AZ 77
Harrington College of Design, Chicago, IL 156
Hesser College, Manchester, NH 213
The Illinois Institute of Art - Chicago, Chicago, IL 156
The Illinois Institute of Art - Schaumburg, Schaumburg, IL 157
International Academy of Design & Technology, Chicago, IL 157
International Academy of Design & Technology, Orlando, FL 132
International Academy of Design & Technology, Pittsburgh, PA 264
International Academy of Design & Technology, Tampa, FL 132
International Academy of Design & Technology, Troy, MI 189
International Academy of Design and Technology, Henderson, NV 210
International Academy of Design and Technology, Nashville, TN 289
International Academy of Design and Technology, San Antonio, TX 298
International Academy of Design and Technology, Schaumburg, IL 157
International Academy of Design and Technology, Seattle, WA 327
Louisville Technical Institute, Louisville, KY 172
Maric College, Anaheim, CA 99
Maric College, Los Angeles, CA 100
Maric College, North Hollywood, CA 99
Maric College, Sacramento, CA 99
Maric College, Salida, CA 99
Maric College, San Diego, CA 100
Maric College, Vista, CA 100
Miami International University of Art & Design, Miami, FL 138
The New England Institute of Art, Brookline, MA 186
New England Institute of Technology, Warwick, RI 284
Southwest Florida College, Tampa, FL 143
Virginia College at Birmingham, Birmingham, AL 72
Virginia Marti College of Art and Design, Lakewood, OH 246
Westwood College - Anaheim, Anaheim, CA 109
Westwood College - Atlanta Campus, Atlanta, GA 151
Westwood College - Chicago Du Page, Woodridge, IL 160
Westwood College - Chicago Loop Campus, Chicago, IL 161
Westwood College - Chicago O'Hare Airport, Chicago, IL 161
Westwood College - Denver North, Denver, CO 118

Westwood College - Denver South, Denver, CO 118
Westwood College - Inland Empire, Upland, CA 109
Westwood College - Long Beach, Torrance, CA 110

INTERMEDIA/MULTIMEDIA

American InterContinental University, Atlanta, GA 145
American InterContinental University, Houston, TX 293
American InterContinental University, Los Angeles, CA 85
American InterContinental University, San Antonio, TX 293
American InterContinental University, Weston, FL 121
The Art Institute of Colorado, Denver, CO 111
The Art Institute of Phoenix, Phoenix, AZ 76
Briarcliffe College, Bethpage, NY 226
Briarcliffe College, Patchogue, NY 226
California Design College, Los Angeles, CA 91
Florida Technical College, Auburndale, FL 129
Florida Technical College, DeLand, FL 130
Florida Technical College, Jacksonville, FL 130
Florida Technical College, Orlando, FL 130
High-Tech Institute, Irving, TX 298
High-Tech Institute, Kansas City, MO 202
High-Tech Institute, Las Vegas, NV 210
High-Tech Institute, Marietta, GA 149
High-Tech Institute, Memphis, TN 288
High-Tech Institute, Nashville, TN 288
High-Tech Institute, Orlando, FL 132
High-Tech Institute, Phoenix, AZ 78
High-Tech Institute, Sacramento, CA 96
High-Tech Institute, St. Louis Park, MN 195
International Academy of Design & Technology, Chicago, IL 157
International Academy of Design & Technology, Orlando, FL 132
International Academy of Design & Technology, Pittsburgh, PA 264
International Academy of Design & Technology, Tampa, FL 132
International Academy of Design & Technology, Troy, MI 189
International Academy of Design and Technology, Henderson, NV 210
International Academy of Design and Technology, Nashville, TN 289
International Academy of Design and Technology, San Antonio, TX 298
International Academy of Design and Technology, Schaumburg, IL 157
International Academy of Design and Technology, Seattle, WA 327
Louisville Technical Institute, Louisville, KY 172
Platt College, Huntington Beach, CA 101
Platt College, Lawton, OK 247
Platt College, Oklahoma City, OK 248

Platt College, Ontario, CA 102
Platt College, Tulsa, OK 248
Sanford-Brown College, Collinsville, IL 159
Sanford-Brown College, Fenton, MO 205
Sanford-Brown College, Hazelwood, MO 205
Sanford-Brown College, North Kansas City, MO 206
Sanford-Brown College, St. Charles, MO 206
Sanford-Brown College, West Allis, WI 331
Silicon Valley College, Emeryville, CA 105
Silicon Valley College, Fremont, CA 106
Silicon Valley College, San Jose, CA 106
Westwood College - Chicago O'Hare Airport, Chicago, IL 161

INTERNATIONAL BUSINESS/TRADE/COMMERCE

American InterContinental University, Atlanta, GA 145
American InterContinental University, Houston, TX 293
American InterContinental University, Los Angeles, CA 85
American InterContinental University, San Antonio, TX 293
American InterContinental University, Weston, FL 121
Argosy University/Chicago, Chicago, IL 154
Argosy University/Schaumburg, Schaumburg, IL 154
Berkeley College, Paramus, NJ 214
Berkeley College, West Paterson, NJ 214
Berkeley College, Woodbridge, NJ 215
Florida Metropolitan University - Pompano Beach Campus, Pompano Beach, FL 129
International Import-Export Institute, Phoenix, AZ 79
Miller-Motte Technical College, Cary, NC 236
Miller-Motte Technical College, Chattanooga, TN 290
Miller-Motte Technical College, Clarksville, TN 290
Miller-Motte Technical College, Lynchburg, VA 320
Miller-Motte Technical College, North Charleston, SC 285
Miller-Motte Technical College, Wilmington, NC 236
MTI College of Business and Technology, Houston, TX 301
National American University, Albuquerque, NM 224
National American University, Brooklyn Center, MN 197
National American University, Colorado Springs, CO 115
National American University, Denver, CO 116
National American University, Ellsworth AFB, SD 286
National American University, Kansas City, MO 204
National American University, Minneapolis, MN 197
National American University, Overland Park, KS 169
National American University, Rapid City, SD 286
National American University, Rio Rancho, NM 224
National American University, Roseville, MN 197
Peirce College, Philadelphia, PA 268
Potomac College, Herndon, VA 322
Potomac College, Washington, DC 121
Remington College - Honolulu Campus, Honolulu, HI 152
Stratford University, Falls Church , VA 322

Stratford University, Woodbridge, VA 322
Western International University, Phoenix, AZ 82

INTERNET INFORMATION SYSTEMS

Bradley Academy for the Visual Arts, York, PA 254
Briarcliffe College, Bethpage, NY 226
Briarcliffe College, Patchogue, NY 226
Career Institute of Health and Technology, Brooklyn, NY 227
Career Institute of Health and Technology, Garden City, NY 227
Career Institute of Health and Technology, Rego Park, NY 228
ITI Technical College, Baton Rouge, LA 178
Louisville Technical Institute, Louisville, KY 172
Rasmussen College St. Cloud, St. Cloud, MN 199
Remington College - Cleveland Campus, Cleveland, OH 242
Remington College - Pinellas Campus, Largo, FL 141
Remington College - Tampa Campus, Tampa, FL 141
Remington College - Tempe Campus, Tempe, AZ 81
Silicon Valley College, Emeryville, CA 105
Silicon Valley College, Fremont, CA 106
Silicon Valley College, San Jose, CA 106
South University, Columbia, SC 286
South University, Montgomery, AL 71
South University, Savannah, GA 151
South University, West Palm Beach, FL 142
Stratford University, Falls Church , VA 322
Stratford University, Woodbridge, VA 322
Sullivan University, Lexington, KY 174
Sullivan University, Louisville, KY 175
Westwood College - Chicago Loop Campus, Chicago, IL 161

INVESTMENTS AND SECURITIES

College for Financial Planning, Greenwood Village, CO 113

KINDERGARTEN/PRESCHOOL EDUCATION AND TEACHING

Hesser College, Manchester, NH 213
McCann School of Business, Hazleton, PA 266
McCann School of Business, Pottsville, PA 267
McCann School of Business, Scranton, PA 267
McCann School of Business, Sunbury, PA 267

KINESIOTHERAPY/ KINESIOTHERAPIST

McIntosh College, Dover, NH 213

LEGAL ADMINISTRATIVE ASSISTANT/SECRETARY

A-1 Business and Technical College, Caguas, PR 275

Aakers Business College , Bismarck, ND 236
Aakers Business College, Fargo, ND 236
Academy College, Minneapolis, MN 192
Academy of Medical Arts and Business, Harrisburg, PA 252
American Commercial College, Abilene, TX 292
American Commercial College, Lubbock, TX 293
American Commercial College, Odessa, TX 293
American Commercial College, San Angelo, TX 293
American Commercial College, Shreveport, LA 175
Antonelli College, Cincinnati, OH 237
Antonelli College, Hattiesburg, MS 199
Antonelli College, Jackson, MS 200
Austin Business College, Austin, TX 295
Berks Technical Institute, Wyomissing, PA 253
Bradford School of Business, Houston, TX 295
Bradford School, Columbus, OH 237
Bradford School, Pittsburgh, PA 254
Briarcliffe College, Bethpage, NY 226
Briarcliffe College, Patchogue, NY 226
Brown Mackie College, Lenexa Campus, Lenexa, KS 168
Brown Mackie College, North Canton Campus, North Canton, OH 239
Business Institute of Pennsylvania, Meadville, PA 255
Business Institute of Pennsylvania, Sharon, PA 255
Career College of Northern Nevada, Reno, NV 210
Career Education Institute, Brockton, MA 184
Career Education Institute, Henderson, NV 210
Career Education Institute, Lincoln, RI 283
Career Education Institute, Lowell, MA 184
Career Education Institute, Marietta, GA 146
Career Education Institute, Norcross, GA 146
City College, Inc., Moore, OK 246
Colegio Mayor de Tecnologia, Arroyo, PR 276
Computer Learning Network, Altoona, PA 258
Computer Learning Network, Mechanicsburg, PA 258
Daymar College, Louisville, KY 171
Daymar College, Newport, KY 171
Daymar College, Owensboro, KY 171
Delta School of Business & Technology, Lake Charles, LA 177
Dickinson Business School/Career Point Business School, Tulsa, OK 246
Dorsey Schools, Madison Heights, MI 188
Dorsey Schools, Roseville, MI 188
Dorsey Schools, Southgate, MI 188
Dorsey Schools, Wayne, MI 189
Douglas Education Center, Monessen, PA 259
Erie Business Center South, New Castle, PA 262
Erie Business Center, Main, Erie, PA 261
Everest College, Arlington , TX 297
Everest College, Dallas, TX 297
Everest College, Fort Worth, TX 297

West Virginia Junior College, Charleston, WV 329
West Virginia Junior College, Morgantown, WV 330
Western Business College, Portland, OR 251
Western Business College, Vancouver, WA 328

LEGAL ASSISTANT/PARALEGAL

Academy of Medical Arts and Business, Harrisburg, PA 252
Andover College, Portland, ME 180
Antonelli College, Cincinnati, OH 237
Antonelli College, Hattiesburg, MS 199
Antonelli College, Jackson, MS 200
Arizona College of Allied Health, Glendale, AZ 76
Austin Business College, Austin, TX 295
Bayamon Community College, Bayamon, PR 276
Berkeley College, Paramus, NJ 214
Berkeley College, West Paterson, NJ 214
Berkeley College, Woodbridge, NJ 215
Berks Technical Institute, Wyomissing, PA 253
Blair College, Colorado Springs, CO 112
Bradford School, Columbus, OH 237
Bradford School, Pittsburgh, PA 254
Briarcliffe College, Bethpage, NY 226
Briarcliffe College, Patchogue, NY 226
Brown Mackie College, Akron Campus, Akron, OH 238
Brown Mackie College, Atlanta Campus, Norcross, GA 146
Brown Mackie College, Cincinnati Campus, Cincinnati, OH 238
Brown Mackie College, Findlay Campus, Findlay, OH 238
Brown Mackie College, Fort Worth Campus, Hurst, TX 296
Brown Mackie College, Hopkinsville Campus, Hopkinsville, KY 170
Brown Mackie College, Lenexa Campus, Lenexa, KS 168
Brown Mackie College, Los Angeles Campus, Santa Monica, CA 87
Brown Mackie College, Merrillville Campus, Merrillville, IN 162
Brown Mackie College, Miami Campus, Miami, FL 124
Brown Mackie College, Michigan City Campus, Michigan City, IN 162
Brown Mackie College, Moline Campus, Moline, IL 154
Brown Mackie College, North Canton Campus, North Canton, OH 239
Brown Mackie College, Northern Kentucky Campus, Fort Mitchell, KY 170
Brown Mackie College, Orange County Campus, Santa Ana, CA 87
Brown Mackie College, San Diego Campus, San Diego, CA 87
Brown Mackie College, South Bend Campus, South Bend, IN 162
Career College of Northern Nevada, Reno, NV 210
Career Point Business School, San Antonio, TX 296

City College, Inc., Moore, OK 246
Clarita Career College, Canyon Country, CA 92
Computer Learning Network, Altoona, PA 258
Computer Learning Network, Mechanicsburg, PA 258
Dawn Training Centre, Inc., Wilmington, DE 120
Daymar College, Louisville, KY 171
Daymar College, Newport, KY 171
Daymar College, Owensboro, KY 171
Denver Career College, Thornton, CO 114
Draughons Junior College, Bowling Green, KY 171
Draughons Junior College, Clarksville, TN 287
Draughons Junior College, Murfreesboro, TN 287
Draughons Junior College, Nashville, TN 288
Empire College, Santa Rosa, CA 93
Erie Business Center, Main, Erie, PA 261
Everest College, Arlington , TX 297
Everest College, Dallas, TX 297
Everest College, Fort Worth, TX 297
Everest College, Phoenix, AZ 78
Everest College, Rancho Cucamonga, CA 93
Florida Metropolitan University - Brandon Campus, Tampa, FL 127
Florida Metropolitan University - Lakeland Campus, Lakeland, FL 127
Florida Metropolitan University - North Orlando Campus, Orlando, FL 128
Florida Metropolitan University - Pinellas Campus, Clearwater, FL 128
Florida Metropolitan University - Pompano Beach Campus, Pompano Beach, FL 129
Florida Metropolitan University - South Orlando Campus, Orlando, FL 129
Florida Metropolitan University - Tampa Campus, Tampa, FL 129
Florida Metropolitan University-Melbourne Campus, Melbourne, FL 127
Globe College, Oakdale, MN 194
Hagerstown Business College, Hagerstown, MD 181
Heritage College, Denver, CO 115
Heritage College, Kansas City, MO 201
Heritage College, Las Vegas, NV 210
Herzing College, Atlanta, GA 148
Herzing College, Birmingham, AL 70
Herzing College, Kenner, LA 178
Herzing College, Madison, WI 330
Herzing College, Minneapolis, MN 195
Herzing College, Winter Park, FL 131
Hesser College, Manchester, NH 213
Hickey College, St. Louis, MO 202
Hohokus Hackensack School of Business and Medical Sciences, Hackensack, NJ 220
International Business College, El Paso, TX 298
International Business College, El Paso, TX 299

Peirce College, Philadelphia, PA 268
Pioneer Pacific College, Clackamas, OR 250
Pioneer Pacific College, Wilsonville, OR 251
The PJA School, Upper Darby, PA 270
Platt College, Huntington Beach, CA 101
Platt College, Lawton, OK 247
Platt College - Los Angeles, Inc, Alhambra, CA 102
Platt College, Oklahoma City, OK 248
Platt College, Ontario, CA 102
Platt College, Tulsa, OK 248
Ponce Paramedical College, Inc., Coto Laurel, PR 282
Professional Careers Institute, Indianapolis, IN 167
RETS Tech Center, Centerville, OH 243
Rockford Business College, Rockford, IL 159
Sanford-Brown College, Collinsville, IL 159
Sanford-Brown College, Fenton, MO 205
Sanford-Brown College, Hazelwood, MO 205
Sanford-Brown College, North Kansas City, MO 206
Sanford-Brown College, St. Charles, MO 206
Sanford-Brown College, West Allis, WI 331
Santa Barbara Business College, Bakersfield, CA 104
Santa Barbara Business College, Santa Barbara, CA 105
Santa Barbara Business College, Santa Maria, CA 105
Santa Barbara Business College, Ventura, CA 105
Schuylkill Institute of Business and Technology, Potts-ville, PA 270
South College, Knoxville, TN 291
South University, Columbia, SC 286
South University, Montgomery, AL 71
South University, Savannah, GA 151
South University, West Palm Beach, FL 142
Southeastern Career College, Nashville, TN 292
Southeastern Career Institute, Dallas, TX 306
Southwest Florida College, Tampa, FL 143
Springfield College, Springfield, MO 206
Sullivan University, Lexington, KY 174
Sullivan University, Louisville, KY 175
Tri-State Business Institute, Erie, PA 272
Utah Career College, West Jordan, UT 312
Vatterott College, Broadview Heights, OH 245
Vatterott College, Des Moines, IA 168
Vatterott College, Joplin, MO 206
Vatterott College, Kansas City, MO 207
Vatterott College, Memphis, TN 292
Vatterott College, OÆFallon , MO 207
Vatterott College, Oklahoma City, OK 248
Vatterott College, Omaha, NE 209
Vatterott College, Quincy, IL 160
Vatterott College, Springfield, MO 208
Vatterott College, St. Ann, MO 207
Vatterott College, St. Joseph, MO 207
Vatterott College, St. Louis, MO 208
Vatterott College, Tulsa, OK 249

Vatterott College, Wichita, KS 169
Virginia College at Austin, Austin, TX 307
Virginia College at Birmingham, Birmingham, AL 72
Virginia College at Huntsville, Huntsville, AL 73
West Virginia Junior College, Bridgeport, WV 329
West Virginia Junior College, Charleston, WV 329
West Virginia Junior College, Morgantown, WV 330
Western Business College, Portland, OR 251
Western Business College, Vancouver, WA 328
Western College of Southern California, Cerritos, CA 109
Western School of Health and Business Careers, Monroe-ville, PA 273
Western School of Health and Business Careers, Pittsburgh, PA 273

LICENSED PRACTICAL/VOCATIONAL NURSE TRAINING (LPN, LVN, CERT, DIPL, AAS)

American Career College, Anaheim, CA 84
Antilles School of Technical Careers, Santurce, PR 275
Apollo College, Albuquerque, NM 223
Apollo College, Boise, ID 153
Apollo College, Portland, OR 249
Apollo College, Spokane, WA 324
Brown Mackie College, Findlay Campus, Findlay, OH 238
Brown Mackie College, Miami Campus, Miami, FL 124
Brown Mackie College, Northern Kentucky Campus, Fort Mitchell, KY 170
Brown Mackie College, San Diego Campus, San Diego, CA 87
Career Networks Institute, Costa Mesa, CA 91
Colegio Mayor de Tecnologia, Arroyo, PR 276
Dover Business College, Paramus, NJ 218
ECPI College of Technology, Charlotte, NC 234
ECPI College of Technology, Greensboro, NC 235
ECPI College of Technology, Greenville, SC 285
ECPI College of Technology, Manassas, VA 315
ECPI College of Technology, Newport News, VA 315
ECPI College of Technology, North Charleston, SC 285
ECPI College of Technology, Raleigh, NC 235
ECPI College of Technology, Virginia Beach, VA 316
ECPI Technical College, Glen Allen, VA 316
ECPI Technical College, Richmond, VA 316
ECPI Technical College, Roanoke, VA 317
Glendale Career College, Glendale, CA 95
Harrison Career Institute, Allentown, PA 262
Harrison Career Institute, Baltimore, MD 181
Harrison Career Institute, Clifton, NJ 218
Harrison Career Institute, Delran, NJ 218
Harrison Career Institute, Deptford, NJ 219
Harrison Career Institute, Ewing, NJ 219
Harrison Career Institute, Jersey City, NJ 219
Harrison Career Institute, Oakhurst, NJ 219

Virginia Career Institute, Richmond, VA 323
Virginia Career Institute, Virginia Beach, VA 323
Virginia College at Birmingham, Birmingham, AL 72
Virginia College at Pensacola, Pensacola, FL 144
Western Career College, Pleasant Hill, CA 108
Western Career College, Sacramento, CA 108
Western Career College, San Leandro, CA 109

LOGISTICS AND MATERIALS MANAGEMENT

Colorado Technical University, Colorado Springs, CO 113
International Import-Export Institute, Phoenix, AZ 79
Sullivan University, Lexington, KY 174
Sullivan University, Louisville, KY 175

MACHINE SHOP TECHNOLOGY/ ASSISTANT

Instituto Banca y Comercio, Caguas, PR 279
Instituto Banca y Comercio, Cayey, PR 279
Instituto Banca y Comercio, Fajardo, PR 279
Instituto Banca y Comercio, Guayama, PR 280
Instituto Banca y Comercio, Manati, PR 280
Instituto Banca y Comercio, Mayaguez, PR 280
Instituto Banca y Comercio, Ponce, PR 280

MACHINE TOOL TECHNOLOGY/ MACHINIST

New Castle School of Trades, Pulaski, PA 268

MAKE-UP ARTIST/SPECIALIST

The Art Institute of Pittsburgh, Pittsburgh, PA 252
Douglas Education Center, Monessen, PA 259

MANAGEMENT INFORMATION SYSTEMS AND SERVICES, OTHER

Florida Technical College, Auburndale, FL 129
Florida Technical College, DeLand, FL 130
Florida Technical College, Jacksonville, FL 130
Florida Technical College, Orlando, FL 130
Herzing College, Atlanta, GA 148
Herzing College, Birmingham, AL 70
Herzing College, Kenner, LA 178
Herzing College, Madison, WI 330
Herzing College, Minneapolis, MN 195
Herzing College, Winter Park, FL 131
Virginia College at Birmingham, Birmingham, AL 72
Westwood College - Denver South, Denver, CO 118

MANAGEMENT INFORMATION SYSTEMS, GENERAL

Capella University, Minneapolis, MN 194
Cardean University, Chicago, IL 154
Career Education Institute, Brockton, MA 184

Career Education Institute, Henderson, NV 210
Career Education Institute, Lincoln, RI 283
Career Education Institute, Lowell, MA 184
Career Education Institute, Marietta, GA 146
Career Education Institute, Norcross, GA 146
Central Florida College, Winter Park, FL 124
Coleman College, La Mesa, CA 92
Coleman College, San Marcos, CA 93
ECPI College of Technology, Charlotte, NC 234
ECPI College of Technology, Greensboro, NC 235
ECPI College of Technology, Greenville, SC 285
ECPI College of Technology, Manassas, VA 315
ECPI College of Technology, Newport News, VA 315
ECPI College of Technology, North Charleston, SC 285
ECPI College of Technology, Raleigh, NC 235
ECPI College of Technology, Virginia Beach, VA 316
ECPI Technical College, Glen Allen, VA 316
ECPI Technical College, Richmond, VA 316
ECPI Technical College, Roanoke, VA 317
Electronic Data Processing College of Puerto Rico, San Juan, PR 277
Everglades University, Boca Raton, FL 125
Everglades University, Orlando, FL 125
Everglades University, Sarasota, FL 125
Florida Technical College, Auburndale, FL 129
Florida Technical College, DeLand, FL 130
Florida Technical College, Jacksonville, FL 130
Florida Technical College, Orlando, FL 130
Herzing College, Atlanta, GA 148
Herzing College, Birmingham, AL 70
Herzing College, Kenner, LA 178
Herzing College, Madison, WI 330
Herzing College, Minneapolis, MN 195
Herzing College, Winter Park, FL 131
ITI Technical College, Baton Rouge, LA 178
Missouri Tech, St. Louis, MO 204
National American University, Albuquerque, NM 224
National American University, Brooklyn Center, MN 197
National American University, Colorado Springs, CO 115
National American University, Denver, CO 116
National American University, Ellsworth AFB, SD 286
National American University, Kansas City, MO 204
National American University, Minneapolis, MN 197
National American University, Overland Park, KS 169
National American University, Rapid City, SD 286
National American University, Rio Rancho, NM 224
National American University, Roseville, MN 197
Remington College - Tampa Campus, Tampa, FL 141
South University, Columbia, SC 286
South University, Montgomery, AL 71
South University, Savannah, GA 151
South University, West Palm Beach, FL 142
Virginia College at Birmingham, Birmingham, AL 72

MANAGEMENT SCIENCE, GENERAL

Argosy University/Chicago, Chicago, IL 154
Berkeley College, Paramus, NJ 214
Berkeley College, West Paterson, NJ 214
Berkeley College, Woodbridge, NJ 215
Florida Metropolitan University - Pompano Beach Campus, Pompano Beach, FL 129
Florida Metropolitan University - South Orlando Campus, Orlando, FL 129
Webster College, Holiday, FL 144
Webster College, Ocala, FL 144

MANUFACTURING TECHNOLOGY/ TECHNICIAN

HoHoKus School of Trade and Technical Services, Linden, NJ 221

MARINE MAINTENANCE/FITTER AND SHIP REPAIR TECHNOLOGY/ TECHNICIAN

Marine Mechanics Institute, Orlando, FL 137
Motorcycle Mechanics Institute, Phoenix, AZ 80
New England Institute of Technology, Warwick, RI 284
The International Yacht Restoration School, Newport, RI 284

MARINE TECHNOLOGY

The Art Institute of Fort Lauderdale, Fort Lauderdale, FL 122
Automeca Technical College, Aguadilla, PR 275
Automeca Technical College, Bayamon, PR 275
Automeca Technical College, Caguas, PR 275
Automeca Technical College, Ponce, PR 276
Caguas Institute of Mechanical Technology, Caguas, PR 276
New England Institute of Technology, Warwick, RI 284
Pennco Tech Bristol, PA 269
Pennco Tech, Blackwood, NJ 222

MARKETING, OTHER

American InterContinental University, Atlanta, GA 145
American InterContinental University, Houston, TX 293
American InterContinental University, Los Angeles, CA 85
American InterContinental University, San Antonio, TX 293
American InterContinental University, Weston, FL 121
Argosy University/Chicago, Chicago, IL 154
The Art Institute of Ohio - Cincinnati, Cincinnati, OH 237
McIntosh College, Dover, NH 213
New England School of Communications, Bangor, ME 180
Westwood College - Chicago Loop Campus, Chicago, IL 161

MARKETING/MARKETING MANAGEMENT, GENERAL

Aakers Business College , Bismarck, ND 236
Aakers Business College, Fargo, ND 236
American InterContinental University, Atlanta, GA 145
American InterContinental University, Houston, TX 293
American InterContinental University, Los Angeles, CA 85
American InterContinental University, San Antonio, TX 293
American InterContinental University, Weston, FL 121
Argosy University/Chicago, Chicago, IL 154
Bauder College, Atlanta, GA 146
Berkeley College, Paramus, NJ 214
Berkeley College, West Paterson, NJ 214
Berkeley College, Woodbridge, NJ 215
Briarcliffe College, Bethpage, NY 226
Briarcliffe College, Patchogue, NY 226
Business Institute of Pennsylvania, Meadville, PA 255
Business Institute of Pennsylvania, Sharon, PA 255
California Design College, Los Angeles, CA 91
Capella University, Minneapolis, MN 194
Cardean University, Chicago, IL 154
CollegeAmerica - Denver, Denver, CO 113
Colorado Technical University, Colorado Springs, CO 113
Davis College, Toledo, OH 239
Erie Business Center, Main, Erie, PA 261
Florida Metropolitan University - Lakeland Campus, Lakeland, FL 127
Florida Metropolitan University - North Orlando Campus, Orlando, FL 128
Florida Metropolitan University - Pinellas Campus, Clearwater, FL 128
Florida Metropolitan University - Pompano Beach Campus, Pompano Beach, FL 129
Florida Metropolitan University - South Orlando Campus, Orlando, FL 129
Florida Metropolitan University - Tampa Campus, Tampa, FL 129
Gibbs College, Boston, MA 185
Gibbs College, Livingston, NJ 218
Gibbs College, Norwalk, CT 119
Hagerstown Business College, Hagerstown, MD 181
Herzing College, Atlanta, GA 148
Herzing College, Birmingham, AL 70
Herzing College, Kenner, LA 178
Herzing College, Madison, WI 330
Herzing College, Minneapolis, MN 195
Herzing College, Winter Park, FL 131
Hesser College, Manchester, NH 213
ICPR Junior College - Hato Rey Campus, San Juan, PR 278
ICPR Junior College - Mayaguez Campus, Mayaguez, PR 279
ICPR Junior College-Arecibo Campus, Arecibo, PR 278

International Academy of Design & Technology, Chicago, IL 157

International Academy of Design & Technology, Orlando, FL 132

International Academy of Design & Technology, Pittsburgh, PA 264

International Academy of Design & Technology, Tampa, FL 132

International Academy of Design & Technology, Troy, MI 189

International Import-Export Institute, Phoenix, AZ 79

Katharine Gibbs School, Melville, NY 231

Katharine Gibbs School, New York, NY 231

Katharine Gibbs School, Norristown, PA 264

Katharine Gibbs School, Piscataway, NJ 221

McCann School of Business, Hazleton, PA 266

McCann School of Business, Pottsville, PA 267

McCann School of Business, Scranton, PA 267

McCann School of Business, Sunbury, PA 267

McIntosh College, Dover, NH 213

National American University, Albuquerque, NM 224

National American University, Brooklyn Center, MN 197

National American University, Colorado Springs, CO 115

National American University, Denver, CO 116

National American University, Ellsworth AFB, SD 286

National American University, Kansas City, MO 204

National American University, Minneapolis, MN 197

National American University, Overland Park, KS 169

National American University, Rapid City, SD 286

National American University, Rio Rancho, NM 224

National American University, Roseville, MN 197

New England School of Communications, Bangor, ME 180

Peirce College, Philadelphia, PA 268

Pioneer Pacific College, Clackamas, OR 250

Pioneer Pacific College, Wilsonville, OR 251

Pittsburgh Technical Institute, Oakdale, PA 269

Rasmussen College Eagan, Eagan, MN 198

Rasmussen College Minnetonka, Minnetonka, MN 199

Rasmussen College St. Cloud, St. Cloud, MN 199

Rockford Business College, Rockford, IL 159

Sanford-Brown College, Collinsville, IL 159

Sanford-Brown College, Fenton, MO 205

Sanford-Brown College, Hazelwood, MO 205

Sanford-Brown College, North Kansas City, MO 206

Sanford-Brown College, St. Charles, MO 206

Sanford-Brown College, West Allis, WI 331

Southwest Florida College, Tampa, FL 143

Stevens-Henager College, Boise, ID 153

Stevens-Henager College, Logan, UT 311

Stevens-Henager College, Ogden, UT 311

Stevens-Henager College - Salt Lake City, Salt Lake City, UT 312

Stratford University, Falls Church , VA 322

Stratford University, Woodbridge, VA 322

Sullivan University, Lexington, KY 174

Sullivan University, Louisville, KY 175

Tri-State Business Institute, Erie, PA 272

Westwood College - Anaheim, Anaheim, CA 109

Westwood College - Chicago Loop Campus, Chicago, IL 161

Westwood College - Denver North, Denver, CO 118

Westwood College - Inland Empire, Upland, CA 109

York Technical Institute, Lancaster, PA 274

York Technical Institute, York, PA 274

MASSAGE THERAPY/THERAPEUTIC MASSAGE

Academy of Medical Arts and Business, Harrisburg, PA 252

Advanced Career Training, Atlanta, GA 144

Advanced Career Training, Jacksonville, FL 121

Advanced Career Training, Riverdale, GA 145

Allied College, Arnold, MO 201

Allied College, Maryland Heights, MO 201

Antilles School of Technical Careers, Santurce, PR 275

Antonelli College, Cincinnati, OH 237

Antonelli College, Hattiesburg, MS 199

Antonelli College, Jackson, MS 200

Apollo College, Albuquerque, NM 223

Apollo College, Boise, ID 153

Apollo College, Portland, OR 249

Apollo College, Spokane, WA 324

Apollo College-Tri-City, Inc., Mesa, AZ 75

Apollo College-Tucson, Inc., Tucson, AZ 75

Apollo College-Westside, Inc., Phoenix, AZ

Arizona College of Allied Health, Glendale, AZ 76

Ashmead College School of Massage, Vancouver, WA 325

Ashmead College, Everett, WA 325

Ashmead College, Fife, WA 325

Ashmead College, Seattle, WA 325

Ashmead College, Tigard, OR 250

ATI Career Training Center, Dallas, TX 294

ATI Career Training Center, Fort Lauderdale, FL 122

ATI Career Training Center, Miami, FL 123

ATI Career Training Center, North Richland Hills, TX 295

ATI Career Training Center, Oakland Park, FL 123

Baltimore School of Massage, Linthicum, MD 180

Baltimore School of Massage, York Campus, York, PA 253

Berdan Institute, Totowa, NJ 214

Berks Technical Institute, Wyomissing, PA 253

Blue Cliff College, Gulfport, MS 200

Blue Cliff College, Metairie, LA 176

Brown College, Mendota Heights, MN 193

Bryman College, Alhambra, CA 88

Bryman College, Anaheim, CA 88

Boldface type indicates that the school is a participating institution in the *Imagine America* Scholarship Program

MECHANICAL DESIGN TECHNOLOGY

MECHANICAL DRAFTING AND MECHANICAL DRAFTING CAD/CADD

Florida Technical College, DeLand, FL 130
Florida Technical College, Jacksonville, FL 130
Florida Technical College, Orlando, FL 130
Herzing College, Atlanta, GA 148
Herzing College, Birmingham, AL 70
Herzing College, Kenner, LA 178
Herzing College, Madison, WI 330
Herzing College, Minneapolis, MN 195
Herzing College, Winter Park, FL 131
Island Drafting and Technical Institute, Amityville, NY 230
Lincoln Technical Institute Indianapolis, IN 166
Lincoln Technical Institute, Allentown, PA 266
Lincoln Technical Institute, Columbia, MD 182
Lincoln Technical Institute, Grand Prairie, TX 300
Lincoln Technical Institute, Mahwah, NJ 222
Lincoln Technical Institute, Melrose Park, IL 158
Lincoln Technical Institute, Philadelphia, PA 266
Lincoln Technical Institute, Union, NJ 222
Louisville Technical Institute, Louisville, KY 172
Pittsburgh Technical Institute, Oakdale, PA 269
Schuylkill Institute of Business and Technology, Pottsville, PA 270
Triangle Tech, Inc. - Pittsburgh School, Pittsburgh, PA 272

MECHANICAL ENGINEERING RELATED TECHNOLOGIES/TECHNICIANS, OTHER

Louisville Technical Institute, Louisville, KY 172

MECHANICAL ENGINEERING/MECHANICAL TECHNOLOGY/TECHNICIAN

ITI Technical College, Baton Rouge, LA 178
Louisville Technical Institute, Louisville, KY 172
New England Institute of Technology, Warwick, RI 284
The Refrigeration School, Phoenix, AZ 81

MEDICAL ADMINISTRATIVE/EXECUTIVE ASSISTANT AND MEDICAL SECRETARY

A-1 Business and Technical College, Caguas, PR 275
Aakers Business College , Bismarck, ND 236
Aakers Business College, Fargo, ND 236
Academy College, Minneapolis, MN 192
Academy of Medical Arts and Business, Harrisburg, PA 252
ACT College, Alexandria, VA 313
ACT College, Fairfax, VA 313
ACT College, Manassas, VA 313
American Commercial College, Abilene, TX 292
American Commercial College, Lubbock, TX 293
American Commercial College, Odessa, TX 293
American Commercial College, San Angelo, TX 293

American Commercial College, Shreveport, LA 175
American School of Business, Wichita Falls, TX 294
Antonelli College, Cincinnati, OH 237
Antonelli College, Hattiesburg, MS 199
Antonelli College, Jackson, MS 200
Apollo College, Albuquerque, NM 223
Apollo College, Boise, ID 153
Apollo College-Phoenix, Inc., Phoenix, AZ 74
Apollo College, Portland, OR 249
Apollo College, Spokane, WA 324
Apollo College-Tri-City, Inc., Mesa, AZ 75
Apollo College-Tucson, Inc., Tucson, AZ 75
ATI Career Training Center, Dallas, TX 294
ATI Career Training Center, Fort Lauderdale, FL 122
ATI Career Training Center, Miami, FL 123
ATI Career Training Center, North Richland Hills, TX 295
ATI Career Training Center, Oakland Park, FL 123
Austin Business College, Austin, TX 295
Berdan Institute, Totowa, NJ 214
Berks Technical Institute, Wyomissing, PA 253
Blair College, Colorado Springs, CO 112
Bradford School of Business, Houston, TX 295
Bradford School, Columbus, OH 237
Bradford School, Pittsburgh, PA 254
Briarcliffe College, Bethpage, NY 226
Briarcliffe College, Patchogue, NY 226
Brookstone College of Business, Charlotte, NC 234
Brookstone College of Business, Greensboro, NC 234
Brown Mackie College, North Canton Campus, North Canton, OH 239
Bryman College, Alhambra, CA 88
Bryman College, Anaheim, CA 88
Bryman College, City of Industry, CA 88
Bryman College, Earth City, MO 201
Bryman College, Everett, WA 325
Bryman College, Gardena, CA 88
Bryman College, Hayward, CA 89
Bryman College, Los Angeles, CA 89
Bryman College, Lynnwood, WA 326
Bryman College, New Orleans, LA 176
Bryman College, Ontario, CA 89
Bryman College, Port Orchard, WA 326
Bryman College, Renton, WA 326
Bryman College, Reseda, CA 89
Bryman College, San Bernardino, CA 90
Bryman College, San Francisco, CA 90
Bryman College, San Jose, CA 90
Bryman College, Tacoma, WA 326
Bryman College, Torrance, CA 90
Bryman Institute, Brighton, MA 183
Bryman Institute, Chelsea, MA 184
Bryman Institute, Eagan, MN 193

Boldface type indicates that the school is a participating institution in the ⊕ *Imagine America* Scholarship Program

Boldface type indicates that the school is a participating institution in the 🏛 *Imagine America* Scholarship Program

San Joaquin Valley College, Rancho Cucamonga, CA 104

San Joaquin Valley College, Visalia, CA 104

Savannah River College, Augusta, GA 151

Schuylkill Institute of Business and Technology, Pottsville, PA 270

South University, Columbia, SC 286

South University, Montgomery, AL 71

South University, Savannah, GA 151

South University, West Palm Beach, FL 142

Southeastern Business College, Chillicothe, OH 243

Southeastern Business College, Jackson, OH 243

Southeastern Business College, Lancaster, OH 243

Southeastern Business College, New Boston, OH 244

Southwest Florida College, Tampa, FL 143

Southwestern College of Business, Cincinnati, OH 244

Southwestern College of Business, Dayton, OH 244

Southwestern College of Business, Florence, KY 174

Southwestern College of Business, Franklin, OH 245

Spencerian College, Louisville, KY 174

St. Louis College of Health Careers, St. Louis, MO 205

Stevens-Henager College, Boise, ID 153

Stevens-Henager College, Logan, UT 311

Stevens-Henager College, Ogden, UT 311

Stevens-Henager College - Salt Lake City, Salt Lake City, UT 312

Stuart School of Business Administration, Wall, NJ 223

Sullivan University, Lexington, KY 174

Sullivan University, Louisville, KY 175

Thompson Institute, Chambersburg, PA 271

Thompson Institute, Harrisburg, PA 271

Thompson Institute, Philadelphia, PA 271

Trumbull Business College, Warren, OH 245

Tucson College, Tucson, AZ 82

Vatterott College, Broadview Heights, OH 245

Vatterott College, Des Moines, IA 168

Vatterott College, Joplin, MO 206

Vatterott College, Kansas City, MO 207

Vatterott College, Memphis, TN 292

Vatterott College, OÆFallon , MO 207

Vatterott College, Oklahoma City, OK 248

Vatterott College, Omaha, NE 209

Vatterott College, Quincy, IL 160

Vatterott College, Springfield, MO 208

Vatterott College, St. Ann, MO 207

Vatterott College, St. Joseph, MO 207

Vatterott College, St. Louis, MO 208

Vatterott College, Tulsa, OK 249

Vatterott College, Wichita, KS 169

Virginia College at Huntsville, Huntsville, AL 73

West Tennessee Business College, Jackson, TN 292

West Virginia Career Institute, Mount Braddock, PA 273

West Virginia Junior College, Bridgeport, WV 329

West Virginia Junior College, Charleston, WV 329

West Virginia Junior College, Morgantown, WV 330

Western Business College, Portland, OR 251

Western Business College, Vancouver, WA 328

Western Career College, Pleasant Hill, CA 108

Western Career College, Sacramento, CA 108

Western Career College, San Leandro, CA 109

Westwood College - Chicago O'Hare Airport, Chicago, IL 161

Westwood College - Denver North, Denver, CO 118

Wood Tobe-Coburn School, New York, NY 233

Wright Business School, Oklahoma City, OK 249

Wright Business School, Overland Park, KS 170

Wright Business School, Tulsa, OK 249

Yorktowne Business Institute, York, PA 274

MEDICAL INFORMATICS
Chaparral College, Tucson, AZ 77

MEDICAL INSURANCE CODING SPECIALIST/CODER
Aakers Business College , Bismarck, ND 236

Aakers Business College, Fargo, ND 236

Academy College, Minneapolis, MN 192

Advanced Career Training, Atlanta, GA 144

Advanced Career Training, Jacksonville, FL 121

Advanced Career Training, Riverdale, GA 145

Allied College, Arnold, MO 201

Allied College, Maryland Heights, MO 201

American School of Technology, Columbus, OH 237

Antonelli College, Cincinnati, OH 237

Antonelli College, Hattiesburg, MS 199

Antonelli College, Jackson, MS 200

Apollo College, Albuquerque, NM 223

Apollo College, Boise, ID 153

Apollo College, Portland, OR 249

Apollo College, Spokane, WA 324

ATI Career Training Center, Dallas, TX 294

ATI Career Training Center, Fort Lauderdale, FL 122

ATI Career Training Center, Miami, FL 123

ATI Career Training Center, North Richland Hills, TX 295

ATI Career Training Center, Oakland Park, FL 123

Berks Technical Institute, Wyomissing, PA 253

Brookstone College of Business, Charlotte, NC 234

Brookstone College of Business, Greensboro, NC 234

Brown Mackie College, Miami Campus, Miami, FL 124

Brown Mackie College, San Diego Campus, San Diego, CA 87

Bryman College, Alhambra, CA 88

Bryman College, Anaheim, CA 88

Bryman College, City of Industry, CA 88

Bryman College, Earth City, MO 201

Boldface type indicates that the school is a participating institution in the 🎓 *Imagine America* Scholarship Program

Vatterott College, Memphis, TN 292
Vatterott College, OÆFallon , MO 207
Vatterott College, Oklahoma City, OK 248
Vatterott College, Omaha, NE 209
Vatterott College, Quincy, IL 160
Vatterott College, Springfield, MO 208
Vatterott College, St. Ann, MO 207
Vatterott College, St. Joseph, MO 207
Vatterott College, St. Louis, MO 208
Vatterott College, Tulsa, OK 249
Vatterott College, Wichita, KS 169
Virginia College at Austin, Austin, TX 307
Virginia College at Birmingham, Birmingham, AL 72
Virginia College at Mobile, Mobile, AL 73
Virginia College at Pensacola, Pensacola, FL 144
Western Business College, Portland, OR 251
Western Business College, Vancouver, WA 328
Western Career College, Pleasant Hill, CA 108
Western Career College, Sacramento, CA 108
Western Career College, San Leandro, CA 109
Western Technical College, El Paso, TX 307
Western Technical College, El Paso, TX 307
Westwood College - Chicago River Oaks, Calumet City, IL 161
Westwood College - Houston South Campus, Houston, TX 308
Wright Business School, Oklahoma City, OK 249
Wright Business School, Overland Park, KS 170
Wright Business School, Tulsa, OK 249

MEDICAL INSURANCE SPECIALIST/ MEDICAL BILLER

Advanced Career Training, Atlanta, GA 144
Advanced Career Training, Jacksonville, FL 121
Advanced Career Training, Riverdale, GA 145
Akron Institute, Akron, OH 236
Allied College, Arnold, MO 201
Allied College, Maryland Heights, MO 201
Antonelli College, Cincinnati, OH 237
Antonelli College, Hattiesburg, MS 199
Antonelli College, Jackson, MS 200
Apollo College, Albuquerque, NM 223
Apollo College, Boise, ID 153
Apollo College, Portland, OR 249
Apollo College, Spokane, WA 324
Apollo College-Tucson, Inc., Tucson, AZ 75
Arizona College of Allied Health, Glendale, AZ 76
ATI Career Training Center, Dallas, TX 294
ATI Career Training Center, Fort Lauderdale, FL 122
ATI Career Training Center, Miami, FL 123
ATI Career Training Center, North Richland Hills, TX 295
ATI Career Training Center, Oakland Park, FL 123
Berdan Institute, Totowa, NJ 214

Berks Technical Institute, Wyomissing, PA 253
Blair College, Colorado Springs, CO 112
Brookstone College of Business, Charlotte, NC 234
Brookstone College of Business, Greensboro, NC 234
Brown Mackie College, Miami Campus, Miami, FL 124
Brown Mackie College, San Diego Campus, San Diego, CA 87
Bryman College, Alhambra, CA 88
Bryman College, Anaheim, CA 88
Bryman College, City of Industry, CA 88
Bryman College, Earth City, MO 201
Bryman College, Everett, WA 325
Bryman College, Gardena, CA 88
Bryman College, Hayward, CA 89
Bryman College, Los Angeles, CA 89
Bryman College, Lynnwood, WA 326
Bryman College, New Orleans, LA 176
Bryman College, Ontario, CA 89
Bryman College, Port Orchard, WA 326
Bryman College, Renton, WA 326
Bryman College, Reseda, CA 89
Bryman College, San Bernardino, CA 90
Bryman College, San Francisco, CA 90
Bryman College, San Jose, CA 90
Bryman College, Tacoma, WA 326
Bryman College, Torrance, CA 90
Bryman Institute, Brighton, MA 183
Bryman Institute, Chelsea, MA 184
Bryman Institute, Eagan, MN 193
Bryman Institute, Gahanna, OH 239
Business Institute of Pennsylvania, Meadville, PA 255
Business Institute of Pennsylvania, Sharon, PA 255
Caliber Training Institute, New York, NY 227
Cambridge College, Aurora, CO 112
Cambridge College, Beaverton, OR 250
Cambridge College, Bellevue, WA 326
Career Academy, Anchorage, AK 73
Career Centers of Texas, El Paso, TX 295
Career College of Northern Nevada, Reno, NV 210
Career Education Institute, Brockton, MA 184
Career Education Institute, Henderson, NV 210
Career Education Institute, Lincoln, RI 283
Career Education Institute, Lowell, MA 184
Career Education Institute, Marietta, GA 146
Career Education Institute, Norcross, GA 146
Career Institute of Health and Technology, Brooklyn, NY 227
Career Institute of Health and Technology, Garden City, NY 227
Career Institute of Health and Technology, Rego Park, NY 228
Career Networks Institute, Costa Mesa, CA 91
Carnegie Institute, Troy, MI 188

Boldface type indicates that the school is a participating institution in the 🎓 *Imagine America* Scholarship Program

MEDICAL OFFICE ASSISTANT/ SPECIALIST

National College of Business & Technology, Charlottesville, VA 320

National College of Business & Technology, Danville, KY 172

National College of Business & Technology, Danville, VA 320

National College of Business & Technology, Florence, KY 172

National College of Business & Technology, Harrisonburg, VA 321

National College of Business & Technology, Knoxville, TN 291

National College of Business & Technology, Lexington, KY 173

National College of Business & Technology, Louisville, KY 173

National College of Business & Technology, Lynchburg, VA 321

National College of Business & Technology, Martinsville, VA 321

National College of Business & Technology, Nashville, TN 291

National College of Business & Technology, Pikeville, KY 173

National College of Business & Technology, Richmond, KY 173

National College of Business & Technology, Rio Grande, PR 282

National College of Business & Technology, Salem, VA 321

North Florida Institute, Orange Park, FL 140

PCI Health Training Center, Dallas, TX 303

PCI Health Training Center, Richardson, TX 304

Platt College - Los Angeles, Inc, Alhambra, CA 102

RETS Technical Center, Charlestown, MA 187

Rockford Business College, Rockford, IL 159

San Antonio College of Medical and Dental Assistants, San Antonio, TX 305

Savannah River College, Augusta, GA 151

Southwest Florida College, Tampa, FL 143

Thompson Institute, Chambersburg, PA 271

Thompson Institute, Harrisburg, PA 271

Thompson Institute, Philadelphia, PA 271

Vatterott College, Broadview Heights, OH 245

Vatterott College, Des Moines, IA 168

Vatterott College, Joplin, MO 206

Vatterott College, Kansas City, MO 207

Vatterott College, Memphis, TN 292

Vatterott College, OÆFallon, MO 207

Vatterott College, Oklahoma City, OK 248

Vatterott College, Omaha, NE 209

Vatterott College, Quincy, IL 160

Vatterott College, Springfield, MO 208

Vatterott College, St. Ann, MO 207

Vatterott College, St. Joseph, MO 207

Vatterott College, St. Louis, MO 208

Vatterott College, Tulsa, OK 249

Vatterott College, Wichita, KS 169

Virginia College at Birmingham, Birmingham, AL 72

Virginia College at Huntsville, Huntsville, AL 73

MEDICAL OFFICE COMPUTER SPECIALIST/ASSISTANT

American Commercial College, Abilene, TX 292

American Commercial College, Lubbock, TX 293

American Commercial College, Odessa, TX 293

American Commercial College, San Angelo, TX 293

American Commercial College, Shreveport, LA 175

Antonelli College, Cincinnati, OH 237

Antonelli College, Hattiesburg, MS 199

Antonelli College, Jackson, MS 200

Apollo College-Westside, Inc., Phoenix, AZ

ATI Career Training Center, Dallas, TX 294

ATI Career Training Center, Fort Lauderdale, FL 122

ATI Career Training Center, Miami, FL 123

ATI Career Training Center, North Richland Hills, TX 295

ATI Career Training Center, Oakland Park, FL 123

Berks Technical Institute, Wyomissing, PA 253

Brookstone College of Business, Charlotte, NC 234

Brookstone College of Business, Greensboro, NC 234

Business Institute of Pennsylvania, Meadville, PA 255

Business Institute of Pennsylvania, Sharon, PA 255

Career Education Institute, Brockton, MA 184

Career Education Institute, Henderson, NV 210

Career Education Institute, Lincoln, RI 283

Career Education Institute, Lowell, MA 184

Career Education Institute, Marietta, GA 146

Career Education Institute, Norcross, GA 146

Certified Careers Institute, Clearfield, UT 309

Certified Careers Institute, Salt Lake City, UT 309

CHI Institute, Broomall, PA 256

CHI Institute, Southampton, PA 256

The Chubb Institute, Alpharetta, GA 147

The Chubb Institute, Arlington, VA 314

The Chubb Institute, Cherry Hill, NJ 215

The Chubb Institute, Chicago, IL 155

The Chubb Institute, Jersey City, NJ 216

The Chubb Institute, New York, NY 228

The Chubb Institute, North Brunswick, NJ 216

The Chubb Institute, Parsippany, NJ 216

The Chubb Institute, Springfield, PA 256

The Chubb Institute, Westbury, NY 228

Computer Learning Network, Altoona, PA 258

Computer Learning Network, Mechanicsburg, PA 258

Dawn Training Centre, Inc., Wilmington, DE 120

Dickinson Business School/Career Point Business School, Tulsa, OK 246

Douglas Education Center, Monessen, PA 259

Dover Business College, Paramus, NJ 218

ECPI College of Technology, Charlotte, NC 234

ECPI College of Technology, Greensboro, NC 235

ECPI College of Technology, Greenville, SC 285

ECPI College of Technology, Manassas, VA 315

ECPI College of Technology, Newport News, VA 315

ECPI College of Technology, North Charleston, SC 285

ECPI College of Technology, Raleigh, NC 235

ECPI College of Technology, Virginia Beach, VA 316

ECPI Technical College, Glen Allen, VA 316

ECPI Technical College, Richmond, VA 316

ECPI Technical College, Roanoke, VA 317

Empire College, Santa Rosa, CA 93

Florida Technical College, Auburndale, FL 129

Florida Technical College, DeLand, FL 130

Florida Technical College, Jacksonville, FL 130

Florida Technical College, Orlando, FL 130

Gretna Career College, Gretna, LA 177

Harrison Career Institute, Allentown, PA 262

Harrison Career Institute, Baltimore, MD 181

Harrison Career Institute, Clifton, NJ 218

Harrison Career Institute, Delran, NJ 218

Harrison Career Institute, Deptford, NJ 219

Harrison Career Institute, Ewing, NJ 219

Harrison Career Institute, Jersey City, NJ 219

Harrison Career Institute, Oakhurst, NJ 219

Harrison Career Institute, Philadelphia, PA 263

Harrison Career Institute, Reading, PA 263

Harrison Career Institute, South Orange, NJ 220

Harrison Career Institute, Vineland, NJ 220

Harrison Career Institute, Wilmington, DE 121

Herzing College, Atlanta, GA 148

Herzing College, Birmingham, AL 70

Herzing College, Kenner, LA 178

Herzing College, Madison, WI 330

Herzing College, Minneapolis, MN 195

Herzing College, Winter Park, FL 131

McCann School of Business, Hazleton, PA 266

McCann School of Business, Pottsville, PA 267

McCann School of Business, Scranton, PA 267

McCann School of Business, Sunbury, PA 267

Medical Careers Institute, Newport News, VA 319

Medical Careers Institute, Richmond, VA 319

Medical Careers Institute, Virginia Beach, VA 320

Metro Business College, Cape Girardeau, MO 203

Metro Business College, Jefferson City, MO 203

Metro Business College, Rolla, MO 203

MTI College of Business and Technology, Houston, TX 301

PCI Health Training Center, Dallas, TX 303

PCI Health Training Center, Richardson, TX 304

Pinnacle Career Institute, Kansas City, MO 204

Pinnacle Career Institute, Lawrence, KS 169

Pittsburgh Technical Institute, Oakdale, PA 269

RETS Technical Center, Charlestown, MA 187

Sawyer College, Merrillville, IN 167

Vatterott College, Broadview Heights, OH 245

Vatterott College, Des Moines, IA 168

Vatterott College, Joplin, MO 206

Vatterott College, Kansas City, MO 207

Vatterott College, Memphis, TN 292

Vatterott College, OÆFallon , MO 207

Vatterott College, Oklahoma City, OK 248

Vatterott College, Omaha, NE 209

Vatterott College, Quincy, IL 160

Vatterott College, Springfield, MO 208

Vatterott College, St. Ann, MO 207

Vatterott College, St. Joseph, MO 207

Vatterott College, St. Louis, MO 208

Vatterott College, Tulsa, OK 249

Vatterott College, Wichita, KS 169

Virginia Career Institute, Richmond, VA 323

Virginia Career Institute, Virginia Beach, VA 323

West Tennessee Business College, Jackson, TN 292

Western School of Health and Business Careers, Monroeville, PA 273

Western School of Health and Business Careers, Pittsburgh, PA 273

MEDICAL OFFICE MANAGEMENT/ ADMINISTRATION

Academy of Medical Arts and Business, Harrisburg, PA 252

American Commercial College, Abilene, TX 292

American Commercial College, Lubbock, TX 293

American Commercial College, Odessa, TX 293

American Commercial College, San Angelo, TX 293

American Commercial College, Shreveport, LA 175

ATI Career Training Center, Dallas, TX 294

ATI Career Training Center, Fort Lauderdale, FL 122

ATI Career Training Center, Miami, FL 123

ATI Career Training Center, North Richland Hills, TX 295

ATI Career Training Center, Oakland Park, FL 123

Austin Business College, Austin, TX 295

Berks Technical Institute, Wyomissing, PA 253

Bradford School, Columbus, OH 237

Bradford School, Pittsburgh, PA 254

Brown Mackie College, Lenexa Campus, Lenexa, KS 168

Bryman College, Alhambra, CA 88

Bryman College, Anaheim, CA 88

Bryman College, City of Industry, CA 88

Bryman College, Earth City, MO 201

MEDICAL RADIOLOGIC TECHNOLOGY/SCIENCE - RADIATION THERAPIST

Career Education Institute, Henderson, NV 210
Career Education Institute, Lincoln, RI 283
Career Education Institute, Lowell, MA 184
Career Education Institute, Marietta, GA 146
Career Education Institute, Norcross, GA 146
The Chubb Institute, Alpharetta, GA 147
The Chubb Institute, Arlington, VA 314
The Chubb Institute, Cherry Hill, NJ 215
The Chubb Institute, Chicago, IL 155
The Chubb Institute, Jersey City, NJ 216
The Chubb Institute, New York, NY 228
The Chubb Institute, North Brunswick, NJ 216
The Chubb Institute, Parsippany, NJ 216
The Chubb Institute, Springfield, PA 256
The Chubb Institute, Westbury, NY 228
High-Tech Institute, Irving, TX 298
High-Tech Institute, Kansas City, MO 202
High-Tech Institute, Las Vegas, NV 210
High-Tech Institute, Marietta, GA 149
High-Tech Institute, Memphis, TN 288
High-Tech Institute, Nashville, TN 288
High-Tech Institute, Orlando, FL 132
High-Tech Institute, Phoenix, AZ 78
High-Tech Institute, Sacramento, CA 96
High-Tech Institute, St. Louis Park, MN 195
Maric College, Anaheim, CA 99
Maric College, Los Angeles, CA 100
Maric College, North Hollywood, CA 99
Maric College, Sacramento, CA 99
Maric College, Salida, CA 99
Maric College, San Diego, CA 100
Maric College, Vista, CA 100
MedVance Institute, Atlantis, FL 138
MedVance Institute, Baton Rouge, LA 179
MedVance Institute, Cookeville, TN 290
MedVance Institute, Fort Lauderdale, FL 138
MedVance Institute, Houston, TX 301
MedVance Institute, Miami, FL 138
MedVance Institute, Port St. Lucie, FL 138
Spencerian College, Louisville, KY 174
Stevens-Henager College, Boise, ID 153
Stevens-Henager College, Logan, UT 311
Stevens-Henager College, Ogden, UT 311
Stevens-Henager College - Provo, Orem, UT 311
Stevens-Henager College - Salt Lake City, Salt Lake City, UT 312
Sullivan University, Lexington, KY 174
Sullivan University, Louisville, KY 175

MEDICAL RECEPTION/RECEPTIONIST

Aakers Business College , Bismarck, ND 236
Aakers Business College, Fargo, ND 236
American School of Business, Wichita Falls, TX 294

Antonelli College, Cincinnati, OH 237
Antonelli College, Hattiesburg, MS 199
Antonelli College, Jackson, MS 200
ATI Career Training Center, Dallas, TX 294
ATI Career Training Center, Fort Lauderdale, FL 122
ATI Career Training Center, Miami, FL 123
ATI Career Training Center, North Richland Hills, TX 295
ATI Career Training Center, Oakland Park, FL 123
Austin Business College, Austin, TX 295
Berks Technical Institute, Wyomissing, PA 253
Briarcliffe College, Bethpage, NY 226
Briarcliffe College, Patchogue, NY 226
Brookstone College of Business, Charlotte, NC 234
Brookstone College of Business, Greensboro, NC 234
Business Institute of Pennsylvania, Meadville, PA 255
Business Institute of Pennsylvania, Sharon, PA 255
Career Education Institute, Brockton, MA 184
Career Education Institute, Henderson, NV 210
Career Education Institute, Lincoln, RI 283
Career Education Institute, Lowell, MA 184
Career Education Institute, Marietta, GA 146
Career Education Institute, Norcross, GA 146
Central Coast College, Salinas, CA 92
CHI Institute, Broomall, PA 256
CHI Institute, Southampton, PA 256
The Chubb Institute, Alpharetta, GA 147
The Chubb Institute, Arlington, VA 314
The Chubb Institute, Cherry Hill, NJ 215
The Chubb Institute, Chicago, IL 155
The Chubb Institute, Jersey City, NJ 216
The Chubb Institute, New York, NY 228
The Chubb Institute, North Brunswick, NJ 216
The Chubb Institute, Parsippany, NJ 216
The Chubb Institute, Springfield, PA 256
The Chubb Institute, Westbury, NY 228
The Cittone Institute, Edison, NJ 217
The Cittone Institute, Mount Laurel, NJ 217
The Cittone Institute, Paramus, NJ 217
The Cittone Institute, Philadelphia, PA 257
The Cittone Institute, Plymouth Meeting, PA 257
Coyne American Institute, Chicago, IL 155
Coyne American Institute, Chicago, IL 156
Dorsey Schools, Madison Heights, MI 188
Dorsey Schools, Roseville, MI 188
Dorsey Schools, Southgate, MI 188
Dorsey Schools, Wayne, MI 189
Douglas Education Center, Monessen, PA 259
ECPI College of Technology, Charlotte, NC 234
ECPI College of Technology, Greensboro, NC 235
ECPI College of Technology, Greenville, SC 285
ECPI College of Technology, Manassas, VA 315
ECPI College of Technology, Newport News, VA 315

ECPI College of Technology, North Charleston, SC 285
ECPI College of Technology, Raleigh, NC 235
ECPI College of Technology, Virginia Beach, VA 316
Empire College, Santa Rosa, CA 93
Florida Technical College, Auburndale, FL 129
Florida Technical College, DeLand, FL 130
Florida Technical College, Jacksonville, FL 130
Florida Technical College, Orlando, FL 130
Gibbs College - Cranston, Cranston, RI 283
Gretna Career College, Gretna, LA 177
Hagerstown Business College, Hagerstown, MD 181
Instituto Banca y Comercio, Caguas, PR 279
Instituto Banca y Comercio, Cayey, PR 279
Instituto Banca y Comercio, Fajardo, PR 279
Instituto Banca y Comercio, Guayama, PR 280
Instituto Banca y Comercio, Manati, PR 280
Instituto Banca y Comercio, Mayaguez, PR 280
Instituto Banca y Comercio, Ponce, PR 280
McCann School of Business, Hazleton, PA 266
McCann School of Business, Pottsville, PA 267
McCann School of Business, Scranton, PA 267
McCann School of Business, Sunbury, PA 267
Medical Careers Institute, Newport News, VA 319
Medical Careers Institute, Richmond, VA 319
Medical Careers Institute, Virginia Beach, VA 320
Metro Business College, Cape Girardeau, MO 203
Metro Business College, Jefferson City, MO 203
Metro Business College, Rolla, MO 203
MTI College of Business and Technology, Houston, TX 301
National American University, Albuquerque, NM 224
National American University, Brooklyn Center, MN 197
National American University, Colorado Springs, CO 115
National American University, Denver, CO 116
National American University, Ellsworth AFB, SD 286
National American University, Kansas City, MO 204
National American University, Minneapolis, MN 197
National American University, Overland Park, KS 169
National American University, Rapid City, SD 286
National American University, Rio Rancho, NM 224
National American University, Roseville, MN 197
Nevada Career Academy, Sparks, NV 212
Rasmussen College Minnetonka, Minnetonka, MN 199
Rasmussen College St. Cloud, St. Cloud, MN 199
RETS Technical Center, Charlestown, MA 187
Schuylkill Institute of Business and Technology, Pottsville, PA 270

MEDICAL STAFF SERVICES TECHNOLOGY/TECHNICIAN

MedVance Institute, Atlantis, FL 138
MedVance Institute, Baton Rouge, LA 179
MedVance Institute, Cookeville, TN 290

MedVance Institute, Fort Lauderdale, FL 138
MedVance Institute, Houston, TX 301
MedVance Institute, Miami, FL 138
MedVance Institute, Port St. Lucie, FL 138
North Florida Institute, Orange Park, FL 140
St. Louis College of Health Careers, St. Louis, MO 205

MEDICAL TRANSCRIPTION/ TRANSCRIPTIONIST

Aakers Business College , Bismarck, ND 236
Aakers Business College , Fargo, ND 236
Academy College, Minneapolis, MN 192
Academy of Medical Arts and Business, Harrisburg, PA 252
American Commercial College, Abilene, TX 292
American Commercial College, Lubbock, TX 293
American Commercial College, Odessa, TX 293
American Commercial College, San Angelo, TX 293
American Commercial College, Shreveport, LA 175
American School of Business, Wichita Falls, TX 294
Antonelli College, Cincinnati, OH 237
Antonelli College, Hattiesburg, MS 199
Antonelli College, Jackson, MS 200
ATI Career Training Center, Dallas, TX 294
ATI Career Training Center, Fort Lauderdale, FL 122
ATI Career Training Center, Miami, FL 123
ATI Career Training Center, North Richland Hills, TX 295
ATI Career Training Center, Oakland Park, FL 123
Berks Technical Institute, Wyomissing, PA 253
Bradford School, Columbus, OH 237
Bradford School, Pittsburgh, PA 254
Briarcliffe College, Bethpage, NY 226
Briarcliffe College, Patchogue, NY 226
Brookstone College of Business, Charlotte, NC 234
Brookstone College of Business, Greensboro, NC 234
Business Institute of Pennsylvania, Meadville, PA 255
Business Institute of Pennsylvania, Sharon, PA 255
Capps College, Dothan, AL 70
Capps College, Foley, AL 70
Capps College, Mobile, AL 70
Capps College, Montgomery, AL 70
Capps College, Pensacola, FL 124
Career Education Institute, Brockton, MA 184
Career Education Institute, Henderson, NV 210
Career Education Institute, Lincoln, RI 283
Career Education Institute, Lowell, MA 184
Career Education Institute, Marietta, GA 146
Career Education Institute, Norcross, GA 146
Carnegie Institute, Troy, MI 188
Central Coast College, Salinas, CA 92
Chaparral College, Tucson, AZ 77
Computer Learning Network, Altoona, PA 258
Computer Learning Network, Mechanicsburg, PA 258

National College of Business & Technology, Lynchburg, VA 321

National College of Business & Technology, Martinsville, VA 321

National College of Business & Technology, Nashville, TN 291

National College of Business & Technology, Pikeville, KY 173

National College of Business & Technology, Richmond, KY 173

National College of Business & Technology, Rio Grande, PR 282

National College of Business & Technology, Salem, VA 321

Rasmussen College Eagan, Eagan, MN 198

Rasmussen College Minnetonka, Minnetonka, MN 199

Rasmussen College St. Cloud, St. Cloud, MN 199

RETS Technical Center, Charlestown, MA 187

South College, Knoxville, TN 291

Southwest Florida College, Tampa, FL 143

Spencerian College, Louisville, KY 174

Springfield College, Springfield, MO 206

Stevens-Henager College, Boise, ID 153

Stevens-Henager College, Logan, UT 311

Stevens-Henager College, Ogden, UT 311

Stevens-Henager College - Provo, Orem, UT 311

Stevens-Henager College - Salt Lake City, Salt Lake City, UT 312

Tri-State Business Institute, Erie, PA 272

Utah Career College, West Jordan, UT 312

Vatterott College, Broadview Heights, OH 245

Vatterott College, Des Moines, IA 168

Vatterott College, Joplin, MO 206

Vatterott College, Kansas City, MO 207

Vatterott College, Memphis, TN 292

Vatterott College, OÆFallon , MO 207

Vatterott College, Oklahoma City, OK 248

Vatterott College, Omaha, NE 209

Vatterott College, Quincy, IL 160

Vatterott College, Springfield, MO 208

Vatterott College, St. Ann, MO 207

Vatterott College, St. Joseph, MO 207

Vatterott College, St. Louis, MO 208

Vatterott College, Tulsa, OK 249

Vatterott College, Wichita, KS 169

West Virginia Junior College, Bridgeport, WV 329

West Virginia Junior College, Charleston, WV 329

West Virginia Junior College, Morgantown, WV 330

Western Technical College, El Paso, TX 307

Westwood College - Denver North, Denver, CO 118

Wood Tobe-Coburn School, New York, NY 233

Wright Business School, Oklahoma City, OK 249

Wright Business School, Overland Park, KS 170

Wright Business School, Tulsa, OK 249

MEDICAL/CLINICAL ASSISTANT

Academy College, Minneapolis, MN 192

Academy of Medical Arts and Business, Harrisburg, PA 252

ACT College, Alexandria, VA 313

ACT College, Fairfax, VA 313

ACT College, Manassas, VA 313

Advanced Career Training, Atlanta, GA 144

Advanced Career Training, Jacksonville, FL 121

Advanced Career Training, Riverdale, GA 145

Akron Institute, Akron, OH 236

Allied College, Arnold, MO 201

Allied College, Maryland Heights, MO 201

American Career College, Anaheim, CA 84

American Commercial College, Abilene, TX 292

American Commercial College, Lubbock, TX 293

American Commercial College, Odessa, TX 293

American Commercial College, San Angelo, TX 293

American Commercial College, Shreveport, LA 175

American School of Business, Wichita Falls, TX 294

American School of Technology, Columbus, OH 237

Andover College, Portland, ME 180

Antonelli College, Cincinnati, OH 237

Antonelli College, Hattiesburg, MS 199

Antonelli College, Jackson, MS 200

Apollo College, Albuquerque, NM 223

Apollo College, Boise, ID 153

Apollo College-Phoenix, Inc., Phoenix, AZ 74

Apollo College, Portland, OR 249

Apollo College, Spokane, WA 324

Apollo College-Tri-City, Inc., Mesa, AZ 75

Apollo College-Tucson, Inc., Tucson, AZ 75

Arizona College of Allied Health, Glendale, AZ 76

ATI Career Training Center, Dallas, TX 294

ATI Career Training Center, Fort Lauderdale, FL 122

ATI Career Training Center, Miami, FL 123

ATI Career Training Center, North Richland Hills, TX 295

ATI Career Training Center, Oakland Park, FL 123

ATI Health Education Center, Miami, FL 123

Ayers Institute, Inc., Shreveport, LA 175

Bay State College, Boston, MA 183

Berdan Institute, Totowa, NJ 214

Blair College, Colorado Springs, CO 112

Bradford School of Business, Houston, TX 295

Bradford School, Columbus, OH 237

Bradford School, Pittsburgh, PA 254

Brookstone College of Business, Charlotte, NC 234

Brookstone College of Business, Greensboro, NC 234

Brown Mackie College, Akron Campus, Akron, OH 238

Brown Mackie College, Atlanta Campus, Norcross, GA 146

Boldface type indicates that the school is a participating institution in the *Imagine America* Scholarship Program

Medix School, Towson, MD 182
MedTech College, Indianapolis, IN 166
MedVance Institute, Atlantis, FL 138
MedVance Institute, Baton Rouge, LA 179
MedVance Institute, Cookeville, TN 290
MedVance Institute, Fort Lauderdale, FL 138
MedVance Institute, Houston, TX 301
MedVance Institute, Miami, FL 138
MedVance Institute, Port St. Lucie, FL 138
Miami - Jacobs College, Dayton, OH 241
Mildred Elley School, Latham, NY 232
Miller-Motte Technical College, Cary, NC 236
Miller-Motte Technical College, Chattanooga, TN 290
Miller-Motte Technical College, Clarksville, TN 290
Miller-Motte Technical College, Lynchburg, VA 320
Miller-Motte Technical College, North Charleston, SC 285
Miller-Motte Technical College, Wilmington, NC 236
Minneapolis Business College, Roseville, MN 196
Minnesota School of Business - Brooklyn Center, Brooklyn Center, MN 196
Minnesota School of Business-Richfield, Richfield, MN 196
Missouri College, St. Louis, MO 203
Mountain West College, West Valley City, UT 310
MTI College of Business and Technology, Houston, TX 301
National American University, Albuquerque, NM 224
National American University, Brooklyn Center, MN 197
National American University, Colorado Springs, CO 115
National American University, Denver, CO 116
National American University, Ellsworth AFB, SD 286
National American University, Kansas City, MO 204
National American University, Minneapolis, MN 197
National American University, Overland Park, KS 169
National American University, Rapid City, SD 286
National American University, Rio Rancho, NM 224
National American University, Roseville, MN 197
National American University - Sioux Falls Branch, Sioux Falls, SD 287
National College of Business & Technology, Bayamon, PR 282
National College of Business & Technology, Bluefield, VA 320
National College of Business & Technology, Bristol, TN 290
National College of Business & Technology, Charlottesville, VA 320
National College of Business & Technology, Danville, KY 172
National College of Business & Technology, Danville, VA 320
National College of Business & Technology, Florence, KY 172
National College of Business & Technology, Harrison-

burg, VA 321
National College of Business & Technology, Knoxville, TN 291
National College of Business & Technology, Lexington, KY 173
National College of Business & Technology, Louisville, KY 173
National College of Business & Technology, Lynchburg, VA 321
National College of Business & Technology, Martinsville, VA 321
National College of Business & Technology, Nashville, TN 291
National College of Business & Technology, Pikeville, KY 173
National College of Business & Technology, Richmond, KY 173
National College of Business & Technology, Rio Grande, PR 282
National College of Business & Technology, Salem, VA 321
National College of Business and Technology, Arecibo, PR 282
National College of Business and Technology, Cincinnati, OH 241
National College of Business and Technology, Indianapolis, IN 166
National College of Business and Technology, Kettering, OH 242
National Institute of Technology, Austin , TX 302
National Institute of Technology, Cross Lanes, WV 329
National Institute of Technology - Dearborn, Dearborn, MI 190
National Institute of Technology, Detroit, MI 190
National Institute of Technology - Greenspoint, Houston, TX 303
National Institute of Technology - Hobby, Houston, TX 303
National Institute of Technology, Houston, TX 302
National Institute of Technology, Long Beach, CA 101
National Institute of Technology, San Antonio, TX 302
National Institute of Technology, Southfield, MI 190
National School of Technology, Inc., Fort Lauderdale, FL 139
National School of Technology, Inc., Hialeah, FL 139
National School of Technology, Inc., Miami, FL 139
Nevada Career Academy, Sparks, NV 212
Nevada Career Institute, Las Vegas, NV 212
New England Institute of Technology at Palm Beach, West Palm Beach, FL 140
New England Institute of Technology, Warwick, RI 284
New England Technical Institute of Connecticut, Inc., New Britain, CT 119

Boldface type indicates that the school is a participating institution in the ⬤ *Imagine America* Scholarship Program

Western Business College, Portland, OR 251
Western Business College, Vancouver, WA 328
Western Career College, Pleasant Hill, CA 108
Western Career College, Sacramento, CA 108
Western Career College, San Leandro, CA 109
Western School of Health and Business Careers, Monroeville, PA 273
Western School of Health and Business Careers, Pittsburgh, PA 273
Western Technical College, El Paso, TX 307
Western Technical Institute, El Paso, TX 308 Westwood College - Atlanta Campus, Atlanta, GA 151
Westwood College - Denver North, Denver, CO 118
Westwood College - Denver South, Denver, CO 118
Westwood College - Fort Worth, Euless, TX 308
Westwood College - Houston South Campus, Houston, TX 308
Wood Tobe-Coburn School, New York, NY 233
Wright Business School, Oklahoma City, OK 249
Wright Business School, Overland Park, KS 170
Wright Business School, Tulsa, OK 249
Yorktowne Business Institute, York, PA 274

MEDICAL/HEALTH MANAGEMENT AND CLINICAL ASSISTANT/ SPECIALIST

Apollo College, Albuquerque, NM 223
Apollo College, Boise, ID 153
Apollo College, Portland, OR 249
Apollo College, Spokane, WA 324
ATI Career Training Center, Dallas, TX 294
ATI Career Training Center, Fort Lauderdale, FL 122
ATI Career Training Center, Miami, FL 123
ATI Career Training Center, North Richland Hills, TX 295
ATI Career Training Center, Oakland Park, FL 123
Business Institute of Pennsylvania, Meadville, PA 255
Business Institute of Pennsylvania, Sharon, PA 255
CHI Institute, Broomall, PA 256
CHI Institute, Southampton, PA 256
The Chubb Institute, Alpharetta, GA 147
The Chubb Institute, Arlington, VA 314
The Chubb Institute, Cherry Hill, NJ 215
The Chubb Institute, Chicago, IL 155
The Chubb Institute, Jersey City, NJ 216
The Chubb Institute, New York, NY 228
The Chubb Institute, North Brunswick, NJ 216
The Chubb Institute, Parsippany, NJ 216
The Chubb Institute, Springfield, PA 256
The Chubb Institute, Westbury, NY 228
The Cittone Institute, Edison, NJ 217
The Cittone Institute, Mount Laurel, NJ 217
The Cittone Institute, Paramus, NJ 217

The Cittone Institute, Philadelphia, PA 257
The Cittone Institute, Plymouth Meeting, PA 257
Dorsey Schools, Madison Heights, MI 188
Dorsey Schools, Roseville, MI 188
Dorsey Schools, Southgate, MI 188
Dorsey Schools, Wayne, MI 189
Douglas Education Center, Monessen, PA 259
Empire College, Santa Rosa, CA 93
ICM School of Business & Medical Careers, Pittsburgh, PA 263
McCann School of Business, Hazleton, PA 266
McCann School of Business, Pottsville, PA 267
McCann School of Business, Scranton, PA 267
McCann School of Business, Sunbury, PA 267
McIntosh College, Dover, NH 213
Metro Business College, Cape Girardeau, MO 203
Metro Business College, Jefferson City, MO 203
Metro Business College, Rolla, MO 203
National American University, Albuquerque, NM 224
National American University, Brooklyn Center, MN 197
National American University, Colorado Springs, CO 115
National American University, Denver, CO 116
National American University, Ellsworth AFB, SD 286
National American University, Kansas City, MO 204
National American University, Minneapolis, MN 197
National American University, Overland Park, KS 169
National American University, Rapid City, SD 286
National American University, Rio Rancho, NM 224
National American University, Roseville, MN 197
Platt College - Los Angeles, Inc, Alhambra, CA 102
Schuylkill Institute of Business and Technology, Pottsville, PA 270
South University, Columbia, SC 286
South University, Montgomery, AL 71
South University, Savannah, GA 151
South University, West Palm Beach, FL 142

MEDICINAL AND PHARMACEUTICAL CHEMISTRY

Sanford-Brown Institute, Atlanta, GA 150
Sanford-Brown Institute, Dallas, TX 305
Sanford-Brown Institute, Garden City, NY 232
Sanford-Brown Institute, Houston, TX 305
Sanford-Brown Institute, Houston, TX 306
Sanford-Brown Institute, Jacksonville, FL 142
Sanford-Brown Institute, Landover, MD 182
Sanford-Brown Institute, Lauderdale Lakes, FL 142
Sanford-Brown Institute, New York, NY 232
Sanford-Brown Institute, Springfield, MA 187
Sanford-Brown Institute, Tampa, FL 142
Sanford-Brown Institute, Trevose, PA 270
Sanford-Brown Institute, White Plains, NY 232

MENTAL AND SOCIAL HEALTH SERVICES AND ALLIED PROFESSIONS, OTHER

Argosy University/Chicago, Chicago, IL 154
Argosy University/Nashville, Franklin, TN 287

MENTAL HEALTH COUNSELING/ COUNSELOR

Argosy University/Chicago, Chicago, IL 154
Capella University, Minneapolis, MN 194

MERCHANDISING AND BUYING OPERATIONS

Bradley Academy for the Visual Arts, York, PA 254
California Design College, Los Angeles, CA 91
The Illinois Institute of Art - Chicago, Chicago, IL 156
International Academy of Design & Technology, Chicago, IL 157
International Academy of Design & Technology, Orlando, FL 132
International Academy of Design & Technology, Pittsburgh, PA 264
International Academy of Design & Technology, Tampa, FL 132
International Academy of Design & Technology, Troy, MI 189
McIntosh College, Dover, NH 213

METAL AND JEWELRY ARTS

The Art Institute of Pittsburgh, Pittsburgh, PA 252
Gemological Institute of America, Inc., Carlsbad, CA 95
Gemological Institute of America, Inc., Culver City, CA 95
Gemological Institute of America, Inc., New York, NY 229

MOTORCYCLE MAINTENANCE AND REPAIR TECHNOLOGY/TECHNICIAN

Marine Mechanics Institute, Orlando, FL 137
Motorcycle Mechanics Institute, Phoenix, AZ 80
York Technical Institute, Lancaster, PA 274
York Technical Institute, York, PA 274

MULTI-/INTERDISCIPLINARY STUDIES, OTHER

Hamilton College, Cedar Rapids, IA 167

MUSIC MANAGEMENT AND MERCHANDISING

Conservatory of Recording Arts and Sciences, Tempe, AZ 78
Globe College, Oakdale, MN 194
Minnesota School of Business - Brooklyn Center, Brooklyn Center, MN 196

NAIL TECHNICIAN/SPECIALIST AND MANICURIST

Career Training Institute, Apopka, FL 124
Douglas Education Center, Monessen, PA 259
Gene Juarez Academy of Beauty, Seattle, WA 327
Great Lakes Institute of Technology, Erie, PA 262
Instituto Banca y Comercio, Caguas, PR 279
Instituto Banca y Comercio, Cayey, PR 279
Instituto Banca y Comercio, Fajardo, PR 279
Instituto Banca y Comercio, Guayama, PR 280
Instituto Banca y Comercio, Manati, PR 280
Instituto Banca y Comercio, Mayaguez, PR 280
Instituto Banca y Comercio, Ponce, PR 280
La Belle Beauty School, Hialeah, FL 137
Miller-Motte Technical College, Cary, NC 236
Miller-Motte Technical College, Chattanooga, TN 290
Miller-Motte Technical College, Clarksville, TN 290
Miller-Motte Technical College, Lynchburg, VA 320
Miller-Motte Technical College, North Charleston, SC 285
Miller-Motte Technical College, Wilmington, NC 236
Vatterott College, Broadview Heights, OH 245
Vatterott College, Des Moines, IA 168
Vatterott College, Joplin, MO 206
Vatterott College, Kansas City, MO 207
Vatterott College, Memphis, TN 292
Vatterott College, OÆFallon , MO 207
Vatterott College, Oklahoma City, OK 248
Vatterott College, Omaha, NE 209
Vatterott College, Quincy, IL 160
Vatterott College, Springfield, MO 208
Vatterott College, St. Ann, MO 207
Vatterott College, St. Joseph, MO 207
Vatterott College, St. Louis, MO 208
Vatterott College, Tulsa, OK 249
Vatterott College, Wichita, KS 169
Virginia College at Jackson, Jackson, MS 200
West Tennessee Business College, Jackson, TN 292

NUCLEAR MEDICAL TECHNOLOGY/ TECHNOLOGIST

Keiser College, Daytona Beach, FL 134
Keiser College, Fort Lauderdale, FL 134
Keiser College, Lakeland, FL 135
Keiser College, Melbourne, FL 135
Keiser College, Miami, FL 135
Keiser College, Orlando, FL 135
Keiser College, Pembroke Pines, FL 136
Keiser College, Port St. Lucie, FL 136
Keiser College, Sarasota, FL 136
Keiser College, Tallahassee, FL 136
Keiser College, West Palm Beach, FL 137

NURSE/NURSING ASSISTANT/AIDE AND PATIENT CARE ASSISTANT

Berdan Institute, Totowa, NJ 214

Berks Technical Institute, Wyomissing, PA 253

Caliber Training Institute, New York, NY 227

Colegio Mayor de Tecnologia, Arroyo, PR 276

CollegeAmerica - Denver, Denver, CO 113

Dawn Training Centre, Inc., Wilmington, DE 120

Delta School of Business & Technology, Lake Charles, LA 177

Douglas Education Center, Monessen, PA 259

Erie Business Center, Main, Erie, PA 261

Four-D Success Academy, Colton, CA 94

Gretna Career College, Gretna, LA 177

Instituto Banca y Comercio, Caguas, PR 279

Instituto Banca y Comercio, Cayey, PR 279

Instituto Banca y Comercio, Fajardo, PR 279

Instituto Banca y Comercio, Guayama, PR 280

Instituto Banca y Comercio, Manati, PR 280

Instituto Banca y Comercio, Mayaguez, PR 280

Instituto Banca y Comercio, Ponce, PR 280

Mandl School, New York, NY 231

Maric College, Anaheim, CA 99

Maric College, Los Angeles, CA 100

Maric College, North Hollywood, CA 99

Maric College, Sacramento, CA 99

Maric College, Salida, CA 99

Maric College, San Diego, CA 100

Maric College, Vista, CA 100

Medix School, Smyrna, GA 150

Medix School, Towson, MD 182

MedVance Institute, Atlantis, FL 138

MedVance Institute, Baton Rouge, LA 179

MedVance Institute, Cookeville, TN 290

MedVance Institute, Fort Lauderdale, FL 138

MedVance Institute, Houston, TX 301

MedVance Institute, Miami, FL 138

MedVance Institute, Port St. Lucie, FL 138

National College of Business and Technology, Arecibo, PR 282

National College of Business and Technology, Cincinnati, OH 241

National College of Business and Technology, Indianapolis, IN 166

National College of Business and Technology, Kettering, OH 242

North Florida Institute, Orange Park, FL 140

PCI Health Training Center, Dallas, TX 303

PCI Health Training Center, Richardson, TX 304

San Joaquin Valley College, Bakersfield, CA 103

San Joaquin Valley College, Fresno, CA 103

San Joaquin Valley College, Modesto, CA 104

San Joaquin Valley College, Rancho Cucamonga, CA 104

San Joaquin Valley College, Visalia, CA 104

Savannah River College, Augusta, GA 151

St. Louis College of Health Careers, St. Louis, MO 205

Stevens-Henager College, Boise, ID 153

Stevens-Henager College, Logan, UT 311

Stevens-Henager College, Ogden, UT 311

Stevens-Henager College - Salt Lake City, Salt Lake City, UT 312

Tucson College, Tucson, AZ 82

NURSING - REGISTERED NURSE TRAINING (RN, ASN, BSN, MSN)

Brown Mackie College, Cincinnati Campus, Cincinnati, OH 238

Colegio Mayor de Tecnologia, Arroyo, PR 276

Columbia College, Caguas, PR 277

Columbia College, Yauco, PR 277

Electronic Data Processing College of Puerto Rico - San Sebastian, San Sebastian, PR 277

Instituto Banca y Comercio, Caguas, PR 279

Instituto Banca y Comercio, Cayey, PR 279

Instituto Banca y Comercio, Fajardo, PR 279

Instituto Banca y Comercio, Guayama, PR 280

Instituto Banca y Comercio, Manati, PR 280

Instituto Banca y Comercio, Mayaguez, PR 280

Instituto Banca y Comercio, Ponce, PR 280

Instituto de Banca y Comercio, San Juan, PR 281

Keiser College, Daytona Beach, FL 134

Keiser College, Fort Lauderdale, FL 134

Keiser College, Lakeland, FL 135

Keiser College, Melbourne, FL 135

Keiser College, Miami, FL 135

Keiser College, Orlando, FL 135

Keiser College, Pembroke Pines, FL 136

Keiser College, Port St. Lucie, FL 136

Keiser College, Sarasota, FL 136

Keiser College, Tallahassee, FL 136

Keiser College, West Palm Beach, FL 137

Maric College, Anaheim, CA 99

Maric College, Los Angeles, CA 100

Maric College, North Hollywood, CA 99

Maric College, Sacramento, CA 99

Maric College, Salida, CA 99

Maric College, San Diego, CA 100

Maric College, Vista, CA 100

Medical Careers Institute, Newport News, VA 319

Medical Careers Institute, Richmond, VA 319

Medical Careers Institute, Virginia Beach, VA 320

National College of Business & Technology, Bayamon, PR 282

National College of Business & Technology, Bluefield, VA 320

National College of Business & Technology, Bristol, TN 290

National College of Business & Technology, Charlottesville, VA 320

National College of Business & Technology, Danville, KY 172

National College of Business & Technology, Danville, VA 320

National College of Business & Technology, Florence, KY 172

National College of Business & Technology, Harrisonburg, VA 321

National College of Business & Technology, Knoxville, TN 291

National College of Business & Technology, Lexington, KY 173

National College of Business & Technology, Louisville, KY 173

National College of Business & Technology, Lynchburg, VA 321

National College of Business & Technology, Martinsville, VA 321

National College of Business & Technology, Nashville, TN 291

National College of Business & Technology, Pikeville, KY 173

National College of Business & Technology, Richmond, KY 173

National College of Business & Technology, Rio Grande, PR 282

National College of Business & Technology, Salem, VA 321

Pima Medical Institute, Albuquerque, NM 224
Pima Medical Institute, Chula Vista, CA 101
Pima Medical Institute, Colorado Springs, CO 116
Pima Medical Institute, Denver, CO 117
Pima Medical Institute, Las Vegas, NV 213
Pima Medical Institute, Mesa, AZ 80
Pima Medical Institute, Renton, WA 328
Pima Medical Institute, Seattle, WA 328
Pima Medical Institute, Tucson, AZ 81
Platt College, Huntington Beach, CA 101
Platt College, Lawton, OK 247
Platt College, Oklahoma City, OK 248
Platt College, Ontario, CA 102
Platt College, Tulsa, OK 248
Ponce Paramedical College, Inc., Coto Laurel, PR 282
Provo College, Provo, UT 310
Sanford-Brown College, Collinsville, IL 159
Sanford-Brown College, Fenton, MO 205
Sanford-Brown College, Hazelwood, MO 205
Sanford-Brown College, North Kansas City, MO 206
Sanford-Brown College, St. Charles, MO 206

Sanford-Brown College, West Allis, WI 331
South College, Knoxville, TN 291
South University, Columbia, SC 286
South University, Montgomery, AL 71
South University, Savannah, GA 151
South University, West Palm Beach, FL 142
Spencerian College, Louisville, KY 174
Trinity College of Puerto Rico, Ponce, PR 283
Utah Career College, West Jordan, UT 312
Western Career College, Pleasant Hill, CA 108
Western Career College, Sacramento, CA 108
Western Career College, San Leandro, CA 109

NURSING, OTHER

Berks Technical Institute, Wyomissing, PA 253
National American University, Albuquerque, NM 224
National American University, Brooklyn Center, MN 197
National American University, Colorado Springs, CO 115
National American University, Denver, CO 116
National American University, Ellsworth AFB, SD 286
National American University, Kansas City, MO 204
National American University, Minneapolis, MN 197
National American University, Overland Park, KS 169
National American University, Rapid City, SD 286
National American University, Rio Rancho, NM 224
National American University, Roseville, MN 197
North Florida Institute, Orange Park, FL 140

OCCUPATIONAL THERAPIST ASSISTANT

Brown Mackie College, South Bend Campus, South Bend, IN 162
ICM School of Business & Medical Careers, Pittsburgh, PA 263
Keiser College, Daytona Beach, FL 134
Keiser College, Fort Lauderdale, FL 134
Keiser College, Lakeland, FL 135
Keiser College, Melbourne, FL 135
Keiser College, Miami, FL 135
Keiser College, Orlando, FL 135
Keiser College, Pembroke Pines, FL 136
Keiser College, Port St. Lucie, FL 136
Keiser College, Sarasota, FL 136
Keiser College, Tallahassee, FL 136
Keiser College, West Palm Beach, FL 137
New England Institute of Technology, Warwick, RI 284
Sanford-Brown College, Collinsville, IL 159
Sanford-Brown College, Fenton, MO 205
Sanford-Brown College, Hazelwood, MO 205
Sanford-Brown College, North Kansas City, MO 206
Sanford-Brown College, St. Charles, MO 206
Sanford-Brown College, West Allis, WI 331
South College, Knoxville, TN 291

OCCUPATIONAL THERAPY/ THERAPIST

Brown Mackie College, Miami Campus, Miami, FL 124
Brown Mackie College, San Diego Campus, San Diego, CA 87

OFFICE MANAGEMENT AND SUPERVISION

Academy College, Minneapolis, MN 192
Antonelli College, Cincinnati, OH 237
Antonelli College, Hattiesburg, MS 199
Antonelli College, Jackson, MS 200
ATI Career Training Center, Dallas, TX 294
ATI Career Training Center, Fort Lauderdale, FL 122
ATI Career Training Center, Miami, FL 123
ATI Career Training Center, North Richland Hills, TX 295
ATI Career Training Center, Oakland Park, FL 123
Berks Technical Institute, Wyomissing, PA 253
Career Academy, Anchorage, AK 73
Coleman College, La Mesa, CA 92
Coleman College, San Marcos, CA 93
Davis College, Toledo, OH 239
Douglas Education Center, Monessen, PA 259
Duluth Business University, Duluth, MN 194
Eagle Gate College, Murray, UT 309
EduTek College, Stow, OH 239
Everest College, Arlington , TX 297
Everest College, Dallas, TX 297
Everest College, Fort Worth, TX 297
Everest College, Phoenix, AZ 78
Everest College, Rancho Cucamonga, CA 93
Florida Metropolitan University - Lakeland Campus, Lakeland, FL 127
Florida Technical College, Auburndale, FL 129
Florida Technical College, DeLand, FL 130
Florida Technical College, Jacksonville, FL 130
Florida Technical College, Orlando, FL 130
Gibbs College - Cranston, Cranston, RI 283
Gretna Career College, Gretna, LA 177
ICM School of Business & Medical Careers, Pittsburgh, PA 263
Laurel Business Institute, Uniontown, PA 265
Liceo de Arte y Tecnologia, San Juan, PR 281
McCann School of Business, Hazleton, PA 266
McCann School of Business, Pottsville, PA267
McCann School of Business, Scranton, PA 267
McCann School of Business, Sunbury, PA 267
Miller-Motte Technical College, Cary, NC 236
Miller-Motte Technical College, Chattanooga, TN 290
Miller-Motte Technical College, Clarksville, TN 290
Miller-Motte Technical College, Lynchburg, VA 320
Miller-Motte Technical College, North Charleston, SC 285
Miller-Motte Technical College, Wilmington, NC 236
Mountain West College, West Valley City, UT 310
National College of Business & Technology, Bayamon, PR 282
National College of Business & Technology, Bluefield, VA 320
National College of Business & Technology, Bristol, TN 290
National College of Business & Technology, Charlottesville, VA 320
National College of Business & Technology, Danville, KY 172
National College of Business & Technology, Danville, VA 320
National College of Business & Technology, Florence, KY 172
National College of Business & Technology, Harrisonburg, VA 321
National College of Business & Technology, Knoxville, TN 291
National College of Business & Technology, Lexington, KY 173
National College of Business & Technology, Louisville, KY 173
National College of Business & Technology, Lynchburg, VA 321
National College of Business & Technology, Martinsville, VA 321
National College of Business & Technology, Nashville, TN 291
National College of Business & Technology, Pikeville, KY 173
National College of Business & Technology, Richmond, KY 173
National College of Business & Technology, Rio Grande, PR 282
National College of Business & Technology, Salem, VA 321
Rasmussen College Minnetonka, Minnetonka, MN 199
Rasmussen College St. Cloud, St. Cloud, MN 199
Savannah River College, Augusta, GA 151
Southeastern Business College, Chillicothe, OH 243
Southeastern Business College, Jackson, OH 243
Southeastern Business College, Lancaster, OH 243
Southeastern Business College, New Boston, OH 244
Sullivan University, Lexington, KY 174
Sullivan University, Louisville, KY 175
Technical Career Institute, New York, NY 233
Virginia College at Austin, Austin, TX 307
Virginia College at Birmingham, Birmingham, AL 72
Virginia College at Huntsville, Huntsville, AL 73
York Technical Institute, Lancaster, PA 274
York Technical Institute, York, PA 274

OPERATIONS MANAGEMENT AND SUPERVISION

Berks Technical Institute, Wyomissing, PA 253

Remington College - Denver Campus, Lakewood, CO 117

Remington College - Honolulu Campus, Honolulu, HI 152

Remington College - Memphis Campus, Memphis, TN 291

Remington College - Tampa Campus, Tampa, FL 141

OPHTHALMIC AND OPTOMETRIC SUPPORT SERVICES AND ALLIED PROFESSIONS, OTHER

St. Louis College of Health Careers, St. Louis, MO 205

OPHTHALMIC TECHNICIAN/ TECHNOLOGIST

Mandl School, New York, NY 231

National Career Education, Citrus Heights, CA 100

Pima Medical Institute, Albuquerque, NM 224

Pima Medical Institute, Chula Vista, CA 101

Pima Medical Institute, Colorado Springs, CO 116

Pima Medical Institute, Denver, CO 117

Pima Medical Institute, Las Vegas, NV 213

Pima Medical Institute, Mesa, AZ 80

Pima Medical Institute, Renton, WA 328

Pima Medical Institute, Seattle, WA 328

Pima Medical Institute, Tucson, AZ 81

OPTICIANRY/OPHTHALMIC DISPENSING OPTICIAN

Brown Mackie College, Cincinnati Campus, Cincinnati, OH 238

OPTOMETRIC TECHNICIAN/ ASSISTANT

American Career College, Anaheim, CA 84

National Career Education, Citrus Heights, CA 100

Tucson College, Tucson, AZ 82

ORGANIZATIONAL BEHAVIOR STUDIES

Argosy University/Schaumburg, Schaumburg, IL 154

PAINTING

Academy of Art University, San Francisco, CA 83

PETROLEUM TECHNOLOGY/ TECHNICIAN

ITI Technical College, Baton Rouge, LA 178

PHARMACEUTICS AND DRUG DESIGN (MS, PHD)

CHI Institute, Broomall, PA 256

CHI Institute, Southampton, PA 256

The Chubb Institute, Alpharetta, GA 147

The Chubb Institute, Arlington, VA 314

The Chubb Institute, Cherry Hill, NJ 215

The Chubb Institute, Chicago, IL 155

The Chubb Institute, Jersey City, NJ 216

The Chubb Institute, New York, NY 228

The Chubb Institute, North Brunswick, NJ 216

The Chubb Institute, Parsippany, NJ 216

The Chubb Institute, Springfield, PA 256

The Chubb Institute, Westbury, NY 228

Rasmussen College St. Cloud, St. Cloud, MN 199

PHARMACY (PHARMD [USA] PHARMD, BS/BPHARM [CANADA])

CHI Institute, Broomall, PA 256

CHI Institute, Southampton, PA 256

Lincoln Technical Institute Indianapolis, IN 166

Lincoln Technical Institute, Allentown, PA 266

Lincoln Technical Institute, Columbia, MD 182

Lincoln Technical Institute, Grand Prairie, TX 300

Lincoln Technical Institute, Mahwah, NJ 222

Lincoln Technical Institute, Melrose Park, IL 158

Lincoln Technical Institute, Philadelphia, PA 266

Lincoln Technical Institute, Union, NJ 222

South University, Columbia, SC 286

South University, Montgomery, AL 71

South University, Savannah, GA 151

South University, West Palm Beach, FL 142

PHARMACY ADMINISTRATION AND PHARMACY POLICY AND REGULATORY AFFAIRS (MS, PHD)

Lincoln Technical Institute Indianapolis, IN 166

Lincoln Technical Institute, Allentown, PA 266

Lincoln Technical Institute, Columbia, MD 182

Lincoln Technical Institute, Grand Prairie, TX 300

Lincoln Technical Institute, Mahwah, NJ 222

Lincoln Technical Institute, Melrose Park, IL 158

Lincoln Technical Institute, Philadelphia, PA 266

Lincoln Technical Institute, Union, NJ 222

PHARMACY TECHNICIAN/ ASSISTANT

ACT College, Alexandria, VA 313

ACT College, Fairfax, VA 313

ACT College, Manassas, VA 313

Allied College, Arnold, MO 201

Allied College, Maryland Heights, MO 201

American Career College, Anaheim, CA 84

Boldface type indicates that the school is a participating institution in the Imagine America Scholarship Program

pus, Orlando, FL 128

Florida Metropolitan University - Tampa Campus, Tampa, FL 129

Florida Metropolitan University-Melbourne Campus, Melbourne, FL 127

Four-D Success Academy, Colton, CA 94

Great Lakes Institute of Technology, Erie, PA 262

Georgia Medical Institute - Atlanta, Atlanta, GA 148

Georgia Medical Institute - Jonesboro, Jonesboro, GA 148

Georgia Medical Institute - Marietta, Marietta, GA 148

Harrison Career Institute, Allentown, PA 262

Harrison Career Institute, Baltimore, MD 181

Harrison Career Institute, Clifton, NJ 218

Harrison Career Institute, Delran, NJ 218

Harrison Career Institute, Deptford, NJ 219

Harrison Career Institute, Ewing, NJ 219

Harrison Career Institute, Jersey City, NJ 219

Harrison Career Institute, Oakhurst, NJ 219

Harrison Career Institute, Philadelphia, PA 263

Harrison Career Institute, Reading, PA 263

Harrison Career Institute, South Orange, NJ 220

Harrison Career Institute, Vineland, NJ 220

Harrison Career Institute, Wilmington, DE 121

Heritage College, Denver, CO 115

Heritage College, Kansas City, MO 201

Heritage College, Las Vegas, NV 210

High-Tech Institute, Irving, TX 298

High-Tech Institute, Kansas City, MO 202

High-Tech Institute, Las Vegas, NV 210

High-Tech Institute, Marietta, GA 149

High-Tech Institute, Memphis, TN 288

High-Tech Institute, Nashville, TN 288

High-Tech Institute, Orlando, FL 132

High-Tech Institute, Phoenix, AZ 78

High-Tech Institute, Sacramento, CA 96

High-Tech Institute, St. Louis Park, MN 195

Huertas Junior College, Caguas, PR 277

Keiser College, Daytona Beach, FL 134

Keiser College, Fort Lauderdale, FL 134

Keiser College, Lakeland, FL 135

Keiser College, Melbourne, FL 135

Keiser College, Miami, FL 135

Keiser College, Orlando, FL 135

Keiser College, Pembroke Pines, FL 136

Keiser College, Port St. Lucie, FL 136

Keiser College, Sarasota, FL 136

Keiser College, Tallahassee, FL 136

Keiser College, West Palm Beach, FL 137

Lincoln Technical Institute Indianapolis, IN 166

Lincoln Technical Institute, Allentown, PA 266

Lincoln Technical Institute, Columbia, MD 182

Lincoln Technical Institute, Grand Prairie, TX 300

Lincoln Technical Institute, Mahwah, NJ 222

Lincoln Technical Institute, Melrose Park, IL 158

Lincoln Technical Institute, Philadelphia, PA 266

Lincoln Technical Institute, Union, NJ 222

Long Technical College, Phoenix, AZ 80

Medix School, Smyrna, GA 150

Medix School, Towson, MD 182

MedVance Institute, Atlantis, FL 138

MedVance Institute, Baton Rouge, LA 179

MedVance Institute, Cookeville, TN 290

MedVance Institute, Fort Lauderdale, FL 138

MedVance Institute, Houston, TX 301

MedVance Institute, Miami, FL 138

MedVance Institute, Port St. Lucie, FL 138

Miller-Motte Technical College, Cary, NC 236

Miller-Motte Technical College, Chattanooga, TN 290

Miller-Motte Technical College, Clarksville, TN 290

Miller-Motte Technical College, Lynchburg, VA 320

Miller-Motte Technical College, North Charleston, SC 285

Miller-Motte Technical College, Wilmington, NC 236

National American University, Albuquerque, NM 224

National American University, Brooklyn Center, MN 197

National American University, Colorado Springs, CO 115

National American University, Denver, CO 116

National American University, Ellsworth AFB, SD 286

National American University, Kansas City, MO 204

National American University, Minneapolis, MN 197

National American University, Overland Park, KS 169

National American University, Rapid City, SD 286

National American University, Rio Rancho, NM 224

National American University, Roseville, MN 197

National College of Business & Technology, Bayamon, PR 282

National College of Business & Technology, Bluefield, VA 320

National College of Business & Technology, Bristol, TN 290

National College of Business & Technology, Charlottesville, VA 320

National College of Business & Technology, Danville, KY 172

National College of Business & Technology, Danville, VA 320

National College of Business & Technology, Florence, KY 172

National College of Business & Technology, Harrisonburg, VA 321

National College of Business & Technology, Knoxville, TN 291

National College of Business & Technology, Lexington, KY 173

National College of Business & Technology, Louisville, KY 173

PHLEBOTOMY/PHLEBOTOMIST

Daymar College, Louisville, KY 171
Daymar College, Newport, KY 171
Daymar College, Owensboro, KY 171
Duluth Business University, Duluth, MN 194
Gibbs College - Cranston, Cranston, RI 283
Gretna Career College, Gretna, LA 177
Harrison Career Institute, Allentown, PA 262
Harrison Career Institute, Baltimore, MD 181
Harrison Career Institute, Clifton, NJ 218
Harrison Career Institute, Delran, NJ 218
Harrison Career Institute, Deptford, NJ 219
Harrison Career Institute, Ewing, NJ 219
Harrison Career Institute, Jersey City, NJ 219
Harrison Career Institute, Oakhurst, NJ 219
Harrison Career Institute, Philadelphia, PA 263
Harrison Career Institute, Reading, PA 263
Harrison Career Institute, South Orange, NJ 220
Harrison Career Institute, Vineland, NJ 220
Harrison Career Institute, Wilmington, DE 121
Lincoln Technical Institute Indianapolis, IN 166
Lincoln Technical Institute, Allentown, PA 266
Lincoln Technical Institute, Columbia, MD 182
Lincoln Technical Institute, Grand Prairie, TX 300
Lincoln Technical Institute, Mahwah, NJ 222
Lincoln Technical Institute, Melrose Park, IL 158
Lincoln Technical Institute, Philadelphia, PA 266
Lincoln Technical Institute, Union, NJ 222
McIntosh College, Dover, NH 213
Medix School, Smyrna, GA 150
Medix School, Towson, MD 182
MedVance Institute, Atlantis, FL 138
MedVance Institute, Baton Rouge, LA 179
MedVance Institute, Cookeville, TN 290
MedVance Institute, Fort Lauderdale, FL 138
MedVance Institute, Houston, TX 301
MedVance Institute, Miami, FL 138
MedVance Institute, Port St. Lucie, FL 138
Miller-Motte Technical College, Cary, NC 236
Miller-Motte Technical College, Chattanooga, TN 290
Miller-Motte Technical College, Clarksville, TN 290
Miller-Motte Technical College, Lynchburg, VA 320
Miller-Motte Technical College, North Charleston, SC 285
Miller-Motte Technical College, Wilmington, NC 236
North Florida Institute, Orange Park, FL 140
Pima Medical Institute, Albuquerque, NM 224
Pima Medical Institute, Chula Vista, CA 101
Pima Medical Institute, Colorado Springs, CO 116
Pima Medical Institute, Denver, CO 117
Pima Medical Institute, Las Vegas, NV 213
Pima Medical Institute, Mesa, AZ 80
Pima Medical Institute, Renton, WA 328
Pima Medical Institute, Seattle, WA 328
Pima Medical Institute, Tucson, AZ 81

San Antonio College of Medical and Dental Assistants, San Antonio, TX 305
Santa Barbara Business College, Bakersfield, CA 104
Santa Barbara Business College, Santa Barbara, CA 105
Santa Barbara Business College, Santa Maria, CA 105
Santa Barbara Business College, Ventura, CA 105
Southwestern College of Business, Cincinnati, OH 244
Southwestern College of Business, Dayton, OH 244
Southwestern College of Business, Florence, KY 174
Southwestern College of Business, Franklin, OH 245
St. Louis College of Health Careers, St. Louis, MO 205

PHOTOGRAPHIC AND FILM/VIDEO TECHNOLOGY/TECHNICIAN AND ASSISTANT

The Art Institute of Phoenix, Phoenix, AZ 76
Miami International University of Art & Design, Miami, FL 138

PHOTOGRAPHY

A-1 Business and Technical College, Caguas, PR 275
Academy of Art University, San Francisco, CA 83
Antonelli College, Cincinnati, OH 237
Antonelli College, Hattiesburg, MS 199
Antonelli College, Jackson, MS 200
The Art Institute of Atlanta, Atlanta, GA 145
The Art Institute of Colorado, Denver, CO 111
The Art Institute of Fort Lauderdale, Fort Lauderdale, FL 122
The Art Institute of Philadelphia, Philadelphia, PA 252
The Art Institute of Pittsburgh, Pittsburgh, PA 252
The Art Institute of Seattle, Seattle, WA 324
The Art Institutes International Minnesota, Minneapolis, MN 193
Brooks Institute of Photography, Santa Barbara, CA 87
The Creative Circus, Inc., Atlanta, GA 147
Hallmark Institute of Photography, Turners Falls, MA 185
Harrington College of Design, Chicago, IL 156
McIntosh College, Dover, NH 213

PHYSICAL THERAPIST ASSISTANT

Apollo College-Tucson, Inc., Tucson, AZ 75
Apollo College-Westside, Inc., Phoenix, AZ
Bay State College, Boston, MA 183
Brown Mackie College, South Bend Campus, South Bend, IN 162
Delta School of Business & Technology, Lake Charles, LA 177
Hesser College, Manchester, NH 213
Keiser College, Daytona Beach, FL 134
Keiser College, Fort Lauderdale, FL 134
Keiser College, Lakeland, FL 135

Keiser College, Melbourne, FL 135
Keiser College, Miami, FL 135
Keiser College, Orlando, FL 135
Keiser College, Pembroke Pines, FL 136
Keiser College, Port St. Lucie, FL 136
Keiser College, Sarasota, FL 136
Keiser College, Tallahassee, FL 136
Keiser College, West Palm Beach, FL 137
Medical Careers Institute, Newport News, VA 319
Medical Careers Institute, Richmond, VA 319
Medical Careers Institute, Virginia Beach, VA 320
Pima Medical Institute, Albuquerque, NM 224
Pima Medical Institute, Chula Vista, CA 101
Pima Medical Institute, Colorado Springs, CO 116
Pima Medical Institute, Denver, CO 117
Pima Medical Institute, Las Vegas, NV 213
Pima Medical Institute, Mesa, AZ 80
Pima Medical Institute, Renton, WA 328
Pima Medical Institute, Seattle, WA 328
Pima Medical Institute, Tucson, AZ 81
Provo College, Provo, UT 310
South College, Knoxville, TN 291
South University, Columbia, SC 286
South University, Montgomery, AL 71
South University, Savannah, GA 151
South University, West Palm Beach, FL 142
Stevens-Henager College - Provo, Orem, UT 311

PHYSICAL THERAPY/THERAPIST

Brown Mackie College, Miami Campus, Miami, FL 124
Brown Mackie College, San Diego Campus, San Diego, CA 87

PHYSICIAN ASSISTANT

Career Education Institute, Brockton, MA 184
Career Education Institute, Henderson, NV 210
Career Education Institute, Lincoln, RI 283
Career Education Institute, Lowell, MA 184
Career Education Institute, Marietta, GA 146
Career Education Institute, Norcross, GA 146
Lincoln Technical Institute Indianapolis, IN 166
Lincoln Technical Institute, Allentown, PA 266
Lincoln Technical Institute, Columbia, MD 182
Lincoln Technical Institute, Grand Prairie, TX 300
Lincoln Technical Institute, Mahwah, NJ 222
Lincoln Technical Institute, Melrose Park, IL 158
Lincoln Technical Institute, Philadelphia, PA 266
Lincoln Technical Institute, Union, NJ 222
San Joaquin Valley College, Bakersfield, CA 103
San Joaquin Valley College, Fresno, CA 103
San Joaquin Valley College, Modesto, CA 104
San Joaquin Valley College, Rancho Cucamonga, CA 104

San Joaquin Valley College, Visalia, CA 104
South University, Columbia, SC 286
South University, Montgomery, AL 71
South University, Savannah, GA 151
South University, West Palm Beach, FL 142
Stevens-Henager College - Provo, Orem, UT 311
Virginia College at Birmingham, Birmingham, AL 72

PIPEFITTING/PIPEFITTER AND SPRINKLER FITTER

Berk Trade and Business School, Brooklyn, NY 226
New England Institute of Technology, Warwick, RI 284

PLUMBING TECHNOLOGY/PLUMBER

Berk Trade and Business School, Brooklyn, NY 226
Instituto Banca y Comercio, Caguas, PR 279
Instituto Banca y Comercio, Cayey, PR 279
Instituto Banca y Comercio, Fajardo, PR 279
Instituto Banca y Comercio, Guayama, PR 280
Instituto Banca y Comercio, Manati, PR 280
Instituto Banca y Comercio, Mayaguez, PR 280
Instituto Banca y Comercio, Ponce, PR 280
National Institute of Technology, Austin , TX 302
National Institute of Technology, Cross Lanes, WV 329
National Institute of Technology, Detroit, MI 190
National Institute of Technology, Houston, TX 302
National Institute of Technology, Long Beach, CA 101
National Institute of Technology, San Antonio, TX 302
National Institute of Technology, Southfield, MI 190
New England Institute of Technology, Warwick, RI 284
Orleans Technical Institute, Philadelphia, PA 268
Vatterott College, Broadview Heights, OH 245
Vatterott College, Des Moines, IA 168
Vatterott College, Joplin, MO 206
Vatterott College, Kansas City, MO 207
Vatterott College, Memphis, TN 292
Vatterott College, OÆFallon , MO 207
Vatterott College, Oklahoma City, OK 248
Vatterott College, Omaha, NE 209
Vatterott College, Quincy, IL 160
Vatterott College, Springfield, MO 208
Vatterott College, St. Ann, MO 207
Vatterott College, St. Joseph, MO 207
Vatterott College, St. Louis, MO 208
Vatterott College, Tulsa, OK 249
Vatterott College, Wichita, KS 169
WyoTech, Bedford, MA 187
WyoTech, Blairsville, PA 274
WyoTech, Fremont, CA 111
WyoTech, Laramie, WY 332
WyoTech, Oakland, CA 111
WyoTech, West Sacramento, CA 111

PRE-LAW STUDIES

Brown Mackie College, Dallas Campus, Garland, TX 296
Brown Mackie College, Fort Wayne Campus, Fort Wayne, IN 162
Brown Mackie College, Lenexa Campus, Lenexa, KS 168
Brown Mackie College, Louisville Campus, Louisville, KY 170
Empire College, Santa Rosa, CA 93
Herzing College, Atlanta, GA 148
Herzing College, Birmingham, AL 70
Herzing College, Kenner, LA 178
Herzing College, Madison, WI 330
Herzing College, Minneapolis, MN 195
Herzing College, Winter Park, FL 131
Hesser College, Manchester, NH 213
ICM School of Business & Medical Careers, Pittsburgh, PA 263
National American University - Sioux Falls Branch, Sioux Falls, SD 287
Peirce College, Philadelphia, PA 268
South University, Columbia, SC 286
South University, Montgomery, AL 71
South University, Savannah, GA 151
South University, West Palm Beach, FL 142
Western State University College of Law, Fullerton, CA 109

PREPRESS/DESKTOP PUBLISHING AND DIGITAL IMAGING DESIGN

Academy of Art University, San Francisco, CA 83
Academy of Medical Arts and Business, Harrisburg, PA 252
The Art Institute of Charlotte, Charlotte, NC 233
The Art Institute of Phoenix, Phoenix, AZ 76
The Art Institute of Pittsburgh, Pittsburgh, PA 252
The Art Institute of Seattle, Seattle, WA 324
Berks Technical Institute, Wyomissing, PA 253
Bradley Academy for the Visual Arts, York, PA 254
Briarcliffe College, Bethpage, NY 226
Briarcliffe College, Patchogue, NY 226
Brown College, Mendota Heights, MN 193
The Chubb Institute, Alpharetta, GA 147
The Chubb Institute, Arlington, VA 314
The Chubb Institute, Cherry Hill, NJ 215
The Chubb Institute, Chicago, IL 155
The Chubb Institute, Jersey City, NJ 216
The Chubb Institute, New York, NY 228
The Chubb Institute, North Brunswick, NJ 216
The Chubb Institute, Parsippany, NJ 216
The Chubb Institute, Springfield, PA 256
The Chubb Institute, Westbury, NY 228
CollegeAmerica - Denver, Denver, CO 113
Douglas Education Center, Monessen, PA 259
Electronic Data Processing College of Puerto Rico, San Juan, PR 277
Florida Technical College, Auburndale, FL 129
Florida Technical College, DeLand, FL 130
Florida Technical College, Jacksonville, FL 130
Florida Technical College, Orlando, FL 130
Gibbs College - Cranston, Cranston, RI 283
Hesser College, Manchester, NH 213
International Academy of Design & Technology, Chicago, IL 157
International Academy of Design & Technology, Orlando, FL 132
International Academy of Design & Technology, Pittsburgh, PA 264
International Academy of Design & Technology, Tampa, FL 132
International Academy of Design & Technology, Troy, MI 189
ITI Technical College, Baton Rouge, LA 178
Katharine Gibbs School, Melville, NY 231
Katharine Gibbs School, New York, NY 231
Katharine Gibbs School, Norristown, PA 264
Katharine Gibbs School, Piscataway, NJ 221
Louisville Technical Institute, Louisville, KY 172
McIntosh College, Dover, NH 213
New England Institute of Technology, Warwick, RI 284
New England School of Communications, Bangor, ME 180
Platt College, Huntington Beach, CA 101
Platt College, Lawton, OK 247
Platt College, Oklahoma City, OK 248
Platt College, Ontario, CA 102
Platt College, Tulsa, OK 248
Rasmussen College St. Cloud, St. Cloud, MN 199
Remington College - Tampa Campus, Tampa, FL 141
Schuylkill Institute of Business and Technology, Pottsville, PA 270
Stevens-Henager College, Boise, ID 153
Stevens-Henager College, Logan, UT 311
Stevens-Henager College, Ogden, UT 311
Stevens-Henager College - Salt Lake City, Salt Lake City, UT 312
TESST College of Technology, Alexandria, VA 323
TESST College of Technology, Baltimore, MD 182
TESST College of Technology, Beltsville, MD 183
TESST College of Technology, Towson, MD 183
Virginia College at Birmingham, Birmingham, AL 72

PRINTMAKING

Academy of Art University, San Francisco, CA 83

PSYCHIATRIC/MENTAL HEALTH SERVICES TECHNICIAN

PCI Health Training Center, Dallas, TX 303
PCI Health Training Center, Richardson, TX 304

PSYCHOANALYSIS AND PSYCHOTHERAPY

Argosy University/Honolulu, Honolulu, HI 152
Argosy University/Schaumburg, Schaumburg, IL 154

QUALITY CONTROL TECHNOLOGY/ TECHNICIAN

Capella University, Minneapolis, MN 194
Ocean Corporation, Houston, TX 303

RADIO AND TELEVISION

Academy of Radio Broadcasting, Huntington Beach, CA 84
Academy of Radio Broadcasting, Phoenix, AZ 74
Brown College, Mendota Heights, MN 193
Hesser College, Manchester, NH 213
International College of Broadcasting, Dayton, OH 240
Madison Media Institute, Madison, WI 331
The New England Institute of Art, Brookline, MA 186
New England Institute of Technology, Warwick, RI 284
Specs Howard School of Broadcast Arts Inc., Southfield, MI 192

RADIO AND TELEVISION BROADCASTING TECHNOLOGY/ TECHNICIAN

Brown College, Mendota Heights, MN 193
Hesser College, Manchester, NH 213
New England Institute of Technology, Warwick, RI 284
New England School of Communications, Bangor, ME 180

RADIOLOGIC TECHNOLOGY/ SCIENCE - RADIOGRAPHER

Apollo College-Westside, Inc., Phoenix, AZ
Career Technical College, Monroe, LA 176
Career Technical College, Shreveport, LA 177
Instituto Vocational y Commercial EDIC, Caguas, PR 281
Keiser College, Daytona Beach, FL 134
Keiser College, Fort Lauderdale, FL 134
Keiser College, Lakeland, FL 135
Keiser College, Melbourne, FL 135
Keiser College, Miami, FL 135
Keiser College, Orlando, FL 135
Keiser College, Pembroke Pines, FL 136
Keiser College, Port St. Lucie, FL 136
Keiser College, Sarasota, FL 136
Keiser College, Tallahassee, FL 136
Keiser College, West Palm Beach, FL 137
Maric College, Anaheim, CA 99
Maric College, Los Angeles, CA 100
Maric College, North Hollywood, CA 99
Maric College, Sacramento, CA 99
Maric College, Salida, CA 99
Maric College, San Diego, CA 100

Maric College, Vista, CA 100
MedVance Institute, Atlantis, FL 138
MedVance Institute, Baton Rouge, LA 179
MedVance Institute, Cookeville, TN 290
MedVance Institute, Fort Lauderdale, FL 138
MedVance Institute, Houston, TX 301
MedVance Institute, Miami, FL 138
MedVance Institute, Port St. Lucie, FL 138
Pima Medical Institute, Albuquerque, NM 224
Pima Medical Institute, Chula Vista, CA 101
Pima Medical Institute, Colorado Springs, CO 116
Pima Medical Institute, Denver, CO 117
Pima Medical Institute, Las Vegas, NV 213
Pima Medical Institute, Mesa, AZ 80
Pima Medical Institute, Renton, WA 328
Pima Medical Institute, Seattle, WA 328
Pima Medical Institute, Tucson, AZ 81
Pioneer Pacific College, Clackamas, OR 250
Pioneer Pacific College, Wilsonville, OR 251
Sanford-Brown College, Collinsville, IL 159
Sanford-Brown College, Fenton, MO 205
Sanford-Brown College, Hazelwood, MO 205
Sanford-Brown College, North Kansas City, MO 206
Sanford-Brown College, St. Charles, MO 206
Sanford-Brown College, West Allis, WI 331
South College, Knoxville, TN 291
Western School of Health and Business Careers, Monroeville, PA 273
Western School of Health and Business Careers, Pittsburgh, PA 273

REAL ESTATE

Hondros College, Westerville, OH 240
Peirce College, Philadelphia, PA 268
The PJA School, Upper Darby, PA 270
Stevens-Henager College - Provo, Orem, UT 311

RECEPTIONIST

Aakers Business College , Bismarck, ND 236
Aakers Business College, Fargo, ND 236
Academy of Medical Arts and Business, Harrisburg, PA 252
American Commercial College, Abilene, TX 292
American Commercial College, Lubbock, TX 293
American Commercial College, Odessa, TX 293
American Commercial College, San Angelo, TX 293
American Commercial College, Shreveport, LA 175
Austin Business College, Austin, TX 295
Berks Technical Institute, Wyomissing, PA 253
Bradford School, Columbus, OH 237
Bradford School, Pittsburgh, PA 254
Briarcliffe College, Bethpage, NY 226
Briarcliffe College, Patchogue, NY 226
Brookstone College of Business, Charlotte, NC 234

Brookstone College of Business, Greensboro, NC 234
Business Institute of Pennsylvania, Meadville, PA 255
Business Institute of Pennsylvania, Sharon, PA 255
Career Education Institute, Brockton, MA 184
Career Education Institute, Henderson, NV 210
Career Education Institute, Lincoln, RI 283
Career Education Institute, Lowell, MA 184
Career Education Institute, Marietta, GA 146
Career Education Institute, Norcross, GA 146
Central Coast College, Salinas, CA 92
Computer Learning Network, Altoona, PA 258
Computer Learning Network, Mechanicsburg, PA 258
Coyne American Institute, Chicago, IL 155
Coyne American Institute, Chicago, IL 156
Delta School of Business & Technology, Lake Charles, LA 177
Dorsey Schools, Madison Heights, MI 188
Dorsey Schools, Roseville, MI 188
Dorsey Schools, Southgate, MI 188
Dorsey Schools, Wayne, MI 189
Douglas Education Center, Monessen, PA 259
ECPI College of Technology, Charlotte, NC 234
ECPI College of Technology, Greensboro, NC 235
ECPI College of Technology, Greenville, SC 285
ECPI College of Technology, Manassas, VA 315
ECPI College of Technology, Newport News, VA 315
ECPI College of Technology, North Charleston, SC 285
ECPI College of Technology, Raleigh, NC 235
ECPI College of Technology, Virginia Beach, VA 316
Empire College, Santa Rosa, CA 93
Gibbs College - Cranston, Cranston, RI 283
Gretna Career College, Gretna, LA 177
Hagerstown Business College, Hagerstown, MD 181
Katharine Gibbs School, Melville, NY 231
Katharine Gibbs School, New York, NY 231
Katharine Gibbs School, Norristown, PA 264
Katharine Gibbs School, Piscataway, NJ 221
McCann School of Business, Hazleton, PA 266
McCann School of Business, Pottsville, PA 267
McCann School of Business, Scranton, PA 267
McCann School of Business, Sunbury, PA 267
MTI College of Business and Technology, Houston, TX 301
Paducah Technical College, Paducah, KY 174
Rasmussen College Minnetonka, Minnetonka, MN 199
Rasmussen College St. Cloud, St. Cloud, MN 199
San Joaquin Valley College, Bakersfield, CA 103
San Joaquin Valley College, Fresno, CA 103
San Joaquin Valley College, Modesto, CA 104
San Joaquin Valley College, Rancho Cucamonga, CA 104
San Joaquin Valley College, Visalia, CA 104
Stevens-Henager College, Boise, ID 153
Stevens-Henager College, Logan, UT 311
Stevens-Henager College, Ogden, UT 311
Stevens-Henager College - Salt Lake City, Salt Lake City, UT 312
Sullivan University, Lexington, KY 174
Sullivan University, Louisville, KY 175
West Virginia Junior College, Bridgeport, WV 329
West Virginia Junior College, Charleston, WV 329
West Virginia Junior College, Morgantown, WV 330
Western Business College, Portland, OR 251
Western Business College, Vancouver, WA 328

RECORDING ARTS TECHNOLOGY/ TECHNICIAN

Conservatory of Recording Arts and Sciences, Tempe, AZ 78
Full Sail Real World Education, Winter Park, FL 131
Institute of Audio Research, New York, NY 229
International Academy of Design & Technology, Chicago, IL 157
International Academy of Design & Technology, Orlando, FL 132
International Academy of Design & Technology, Pittsburgh, PA 264
International Academy of Design & Technology, Tampa, FL 132
International Academy of Design & Technology, Troy, MI 189
International College of Broadcasting, Dayton, OH 240
Madison Media Institute, Madison, WI 331
The New England Institute of Art, Brookline, MA 186
New England School of Communications, Bangor, ME 180

REHABILITATION AND THERAPEUTIC PROFESSIONS, OTHER

Heritage College, Denver, CO 115
Heritage College, Kansas City, MO 201
Heritage College, Las Vegas, NV 210

REIKI
Berks Technical Institute, Wyomissing, PA 253

RENAL/DIALYSIS TECHNOLOGIST/ TECHNICIAN

Harrison Career Institute, Allentown, PA 262
Harrison Career Institute, Baltimore, MD 181
Harrison Career Institute, Clifton, NJ 218
Harrison Career Institute, Delran, NJ 218
Harrison Career Institute, Deptford, NJ 219
Harrison Career Institute, Ewing, NJ 219
Harrison Career Institute, Jersey City, NJ 219
Harrison Career Institute, Oakhurst, NJ 219
Harrison Career Institute, Philadelphia, PA 263

Harrison Career Institute, Reading, PA 263
Harrison Career Institute, South Orange, NJ 220
Harrison Career Institute, Vineland, NJ 220
Harrison Career Institute, Wilmington, DE 121

RESPIRATORY CARE THERAPY/ THERAPIST

Antilles School of Technical Careers, Santurce, PR 275
Apollo College-Tri-City, Inc., Mesa, AZ 75
ATI Career Training Center, Dallas, TX 294
ATI Career Training Center, Fort Lauderdale, FL 122
ATI Career Training Center, Miami, FL 123
ATI Career Training Center, North Richland Hills, TX 295
ATI Career Training Center, Oakland Park, FL 123
ATI Health Education Center, Miami, FL 123
CHI Institute, Broomall, PA 256
CHI Institute, Southampton, PA 256
Georgia Medical Institute - DeKalb, Atlanta, GA 148
Huertas Junior College, Caguas, PR 277
Instituto Banca y Comercio, Caguas, PR 279
Instituto Banca y Comercio, Cayey, PR 279
Instituto Banca y Comercio, Fajardo, PR 279
Instituto Banca y Comercio, Guayama, PR 280
Instituto Banca y Comercio, Manati, PR 280
Instituto Banca y Comercio, Mayaguez, PR 280
Instituto Banca y Comercio, Ponce, PR 280
Instituto de Banca y Comercio, San Juan, PR 281
Instituto Vocational y Commercial EDIC, Caguas, PR 281
Pima Medical Institute, Albuquerque, NM 224
Pima Medical Institute, Chula Vista, CA 101
Pima Medical Institute, Colorado Springs, CO 116
Pima Medical Institute, Denver, CO 117
Pima Medical Institute, Las Vegas, NV 213
Pima Medical Institute, Mesa, AZ 80
Pima Medical Institute, Renton, WA 328
Pima Medical Institute, Seattle, WA 328
Pima Medical Institute, Tucson, AZ 81
Ponce Paramedical College, Inc., Coto Laurel, PR 282
San Joaquin Valley College, Bakersfield, CA 103
San Joaquin Valley College, Fresno, CA 103
San Joaquin Valley College, Modesto, CA 104
San Joaquin Valley College, Rancho Cucamonga, CA 104
San Joaquin Valley College, Visalia, CA 104
Sanford-Brown College, Collinsville, IL 159
Sanford-Brown College, Fenton, MO 205
Sanford-Brown College, Hazelwood, MO 205
Sanford-Brown College, North Kansas City, MO 206
Sanford-Brown College, St. Charles, MO 206
Sanford-Brown College, West Allis, WI 331
Stevens-Henager College, Boise, ID 153
Stevens-Henager College, Logan, UT 311

Stevens-Henager College, Ogden, UT 311
Stevens-Henager College - Salt Lake City, Salt Lake City, UT 312
Western School of Health and Business Careers, Monroeville, PA 273
Western School of Health and Business Careers, Pittsburgh, PA 273

RESPIRATORY THERAPY TECHNICIAN/ASSISTANT

CHI Institute, Broomall, PA 256
CHI Institute, Southampton, PA 256
Instituto Banca y Comercio, Caguas, PR 279
Instituto Banca y Comercio, Cayey, PR 279
Instituto Banca y Comercio, Fajardo, PR 279
Instituto Banca y Comercio, Guayama, PR 280
Instituto Banca y Comercio, Manati, PR 280
Instituto Banca y Comercio, Mayaguez, PR 280
Instituto Banca y Comercio, Ponce, PR 280
Keiser College, Daytona Beach, FL 134
Keiser College, Fort Lauderdale, FL 134
Keiser College, Lakeland, FL 135
Keiser College, Melbourne, FL 135
Keiser College, Miami, FL 135
Keiser College, Orlando, FL 135
Keiser College, Pembroke Pines, FL 136
Keiser College, Port St. Lucie, FL 136
Keiser College, Sarasota, FL 136
Keiser College, Tallahassee, FL 136
Keiser College, West Palm Beach, FL 137
San Joaquin Valley College, Bakersfield, CA 103
San Joaquin Valley College, Fresno, CA 103
San Joaquin Valley College, Modesto, CA 104
San Joaquin Valley College, Rancho Cucamonga, CA 104
San Joaquin Valley College, Visalia, CA 104

RESTAURANT, CULINARY, AND CATERING MANAGEMENT/ MANAGER

The Art Institute of Atlanta, Atlanta, GA 145
The Art Institute of Colorado, Denver, CO 111
The Art Institute of Houston, Houston, TX 294
The Art Institute of Phoenix, Phoenix, AZ 76
The Art Institute of Pittsburgh, Pittsburgh, PA 252
Bradford School, Columbus, OH 237
Bradford School, Pittsburgh, PA 254
The French Culinary Institute, New York, NY 229
New England Culinary Institute at Essex, Essex Junction, VT 313
New England Culinary Institute, Montpelier, VT 313
New England Institute of Technology at Palm Beach, West Palm Beach, FL 140

Pennsylvania Culinary Institute, Pittsburgh, PA 269
Rasmussen College Eagan, Eagan, MN 198
The Restaurant School at Walnut Hill College, Philadelphia, PA 270
Southwest Florida College, Tampa, FL 143
Stratford University, Falls Church , VA 322
Stratford University, Woodbridge, VA 322
Sullivan University, Lexington, KY 174
Sullivan University, Louisville, KY 175
Western Culinary Institute, Portland, OR 251

RESTAURANT/FOOD SERVICES MANAGEMENT

California Culinary Academy, San Francisco, CA 91
The Restaurant School at Walnut Hill College, Philadelphia, PA 270
Scottsdale Culinary Institute, Scottsdale, AZ 81

RETAILING AND RETAIL OPERATIONS

Bradford School, Columbus, OH 237
Bradford School, Pittsburgh, PA 254
Bradley Academy for the Visual Arts, York, PA 254
Briarcliffe College, Bethpage, NY 226
Briarcliffe College, Patchogue, NY 226
California Design College, Los Angeles, CA 91
Gretna Career College, Gretna, LA 177
The Illinois Institute of Art - Chicago, Chicago, IL 156
International Business College, El Paso, TX 298
International Business College, El Paso, TX 299
International Business College, Fort Wayne, IN 165
International Business College, Indianapolis, IN 165
Miami International University of Art & Design, Miami, FL 138
Rasmussen College Eagan, Eagan, MN 198
Rasmussen College Minnetonka, Minnetonka, MN 199
Wood Tobe-Coburn School, New York, NY 233

ROBOTICS TECHNOLOGY/ TECHNICIAN

Berks Technical Institute, Wyomissing, PA 253
Douglas Education Center, Monessen, PA 259
High-Tech Institute, Irving, TX 298
High-Tech Institute, Kansas City, MO 202
High-Tech Institute, Las Vegas, NV 210
High-Tech Institute, Marietta, GA 149
High-Tech Institute, Memphis, TN 288
High-Tech Institute, Nashville, TN 288
High-Tech Institute, Orlando, FL 132
High-Tech Institute, Phoenix, AZ 78
High-Tech Institute, Sacramento, CA 96
High-Tech Institute, St. Louis Park, MN 195
Louisville Technical Institute, Louisville, KY 172

York Technical Institute, Lancaster, PA 274
York Technical Institute, York, PA 274

SAFETY AND SECURITY TECHNOLOGY

Academy College, Minneapolis, MN 192
Berks Technical Institute, Wyomissing, PA 253
Brown College, Mendota Heights, MN 193
Herzing College, Atlanta, GA 148
Herzing College, Birmingham, AL 70
Herzing College, Kenner, LA 178
Herzing College, Madison, WI 330
Herzing College, Minneapolis, MN 195
Herzing College, Winter Park, FL 131
Hesser College, Manchester, NH 213
Kee Business College - Chesapeake, Chesapeake, VA 319
Parks College, Aurora, CO 116
Parks College, Denver, CO 116
Parks College, McLean, VA 321
Pittsburgh Technical Institute, Oakdale, PA 269

SALES, DISTRIBUTION AND MARKETING OPERATIONS, GENERAL

Bayamon Community College, Bayamon, PR 276
Brown Mackie College, Miami Campus, Miami, FL 124
Brown Mackie College, San Diego Campus, San Diego, CA 87
Hondros College, Westerville, OH 240

SCULPTURE

Douglas Education Center, Monessen, PA 259
Miami International University of Art & Design, Miami, FL 138

SECONDARY EDUCATION AND TEACHING

Capella University, Minneapolis, MN 194

SECURITIES SERVICES ADMINISTRATION/MANAGEMENT

Berks Technical Institute, Wyomissing, PA 253
Caliber Training Institute, New York, NY 227
Empire College, Santa Rosa, CA 93
Hondros College, Westerville, OH 240
Parks College, Aurora, CO 116
Parks College, Denver, CO 116
Parks College, McLean, VA 321

SECURITY AND LOSS PREVENTION SERVICES

Blair College, Colorado Springs, CO 112
ECPI College of Technology, Charlotte, NC 234

ECPI College of Technology, Greensboro, NC 235
ECPI College of Technology, Greenville, SC 285
ECPI College of Technology, Manassas, VA 315
ECPI College of Technology, Newport News, VA 315
ECPI College of Technology, North Charleston, SC 285
ECPI College of Technology, Raleigh, NC 235
ECPI College of Technology, Virginia Beach, VA 316
Hesser College, Manchester, NH 213
Kee Business College, Newport News, VA 319
National Institute of Technology, Austin , TX 302
National Institute of Technology, Cross Lanes, WV 329
National Institute of Technology, Detroit, MI 190
National Institute of Technology, Houston, TX 302
National Institute of Technology, Long Beach, CA 101
National Institute of Technology, San Antonio, TX 302
National Institute of Technology, Southfield, MI 190
San Joaquin Valley College, Bakersfield, CA 103
San Joaquin Valley College, Fresno, CA 103
San Joaquin Valley College, Modesto, CA 104
San Joaquin Valley College, Rancho Cucamonga, CA 104
San Joaquin Valley College, Visalia, CA 104

SELLING SKILLS AND SALES OPERATIONS

Berks Technical Institute, Wyomissing, PA 253
Bradford School, Columbus, OH 237
Bradford School, Pittsburgh, PA 254
Briarcliffe College, Bethpage, NY 226
Briarcliffe College, Patchogue, NY 226
Capella University, Minneapolis, MN 194
The Illinois Institute of Art - Chicago, Chicago, IL 156
Missouri College, St. Louis, MO 203
National American University, Albuquerque, NM 224
National American University, Brooklyn Center, MN 197
National American University, Colorado Springs, CO 115
National American University, Denver, CO 116
National American University, Ellsworth AFB, SD 286
National American University, Kansas City, MO 204
National American University, Minneapolis, MN 197
National American University, Overland Park, KS 169
National American University, Rapid City, SD 286
National American University, Rio Rancho, NM 224
National American University, Roseville, MN 197
Rasmussen College Eagan, Eagan, MN 198
Rasmussen College Mankato, Mankato, MN 198
Rasmussen College Minnetonka, Minnetonka, MN 199

SHEET METAL TECHNOLOGY/ SHEETWORKING

Western Technical College, El Paso, TX 307
WyoTech, Bedford, MA 187
WyoTech, Blairsville, PA 274

WyoTech, Fremont, CA 111
WyoTech, Laramie, WY 332
WyoTech, Oakland, CA 111
WyoTech, West Sacramento, CA 111

SMALL BUSINESS ADMINISTRATION/MANAGEMENT

Herzing College, Atlanta, GA 148
Herzing College, Birmingham, AL 70
Herzing College, Kenner, LA 178
Herzing College, Madison, WI 330
Herzing College, Minneapolis, MN 195
Herzing College, Winter Park, FL 131
Laurel Business Institute, Uniontown, PA 265

SPECIALIZED MERCHANDISING, SALES, AND MARKETING OPERATIONS, OTHER

McIntosh College, Dover, NH 213

SPEECH AND RHETORICAL STUDIES

New England School of Communications, Bangor, ME 180

SPORT AND FITNESS ADMINISTRATION/MANAGEMENT

Ashmead College, Everett, WA 325
Ashmead College, Fife, WA 325
Ashmead College, Seattle, WA 325
Ashmead College, Tigard, OR 250
Bryan College, Springfield, MO 201
Bryan College, Topeka, KS 169
Career Networks Institute, Costa Mesa, CA 91
New England Institute of Technology at Palm Beach, West Palm Beach, FL 140
Utah Career College, West Jordan, UT 312

SPORTS MEDICINE

Hesser College, Manchester, NH 213
Ponce Paramedical College, Inc., Coto Laurel, PR 282

SUBSTANCE ABUSE/ADDICTION COUNSELING

Argosy University/Honolulu, Honolulu, HI 152
Capella University, Minneapolis, MN 194
PCI Health Training Center, Dallas, TX 303
PCI Health Training Center, Richardson, TX 304

SURGICAL TECHNOLOGY/ TECHNOLOGIST

Allied College, Arnold, MO 201
Allied College, Maryland Heights, MO 201
American Career College, Anaheim, CA 84
Antilles School of Technical Careers, Santurce, PR 275

Miller-Motte Technical College, Clarksville, TN 290
Miller-Motte Technical College, Lynchburg, VA 320
Miller-Motte Technical College, North Charleston, SC 285
Miller-Motte Technical College, Wilmington, NC 236
Mountain West College, West Valley City, UT 310
National College of Business and Technology, Arecibo, PR 282
National College of Business and Technology, Cincinnati, OH 241
National College of Business and Technology, Indianapolis, IN 166
National College of Business and Technology, Kettering, OH 242
National School of Technology, Inc., Fort Lauderdale, FL 139
National School of Technology, Inc., Hialeah, FL 139
National School of Technology, Inc., Miami, FL 139
Nevada Career Institute, Las Vegas, NV 212
New England Institute of Technology, Warwick, RI 284
North Florida Institute, Orange Park, FL 140
Oklahoma Health Academy, Oklahoma City, OK 247
Oklahoma Health Academy, Tulsa, OK 247
Olympia College, Burr Ridge, IL 158
Olympia College, Chicago, IL 159
Olympia College, Merrillville, IN 167
Olympia College, North Aurora, IL 159
Olympia College, Skokie, IL 159
Parks College, Aurora, CO 116
Parks College, Denver, CO 116
Parks College, McLean, VA 321
Platt College, Huntington Beach, CA 101
Platt College, Lawton, OK 247
Platt College, Oklahoma City, OK 248
Platt College, Ontario, CA 102
Platt College, Tulsa, OK 248
Ponce Paramedical College, Inc., Coto Laurel, PR 282
Rasmussen College Mankato, Mankato, MN 198
San Joaquin Valley College, Bakersfield, CA 103
San Joaquin Valley College, Fresno, CA 103
San Joaquin Valley College, Modesto, CA 104
San Joaquin Valley College, Rancho Cucamonga, CA 104
San Joaquin Valley College, Visalia, CA 104
Sanford-Brown College, Collinsville, IL 159
Sanford-Brown College, Fenton, MO 205
Sanford-Brown College, Hazelwood, MO 205
Sanford-Brown College, North Kansas City, MO 206
Sanford-Brown College, St. Charles, MO 206
Sanford-Brown College, West Allis, WI 331
Sanford-Brown Institute, Atlanta, GA 150
Sanford-Brown Institute, Dallas, TX 305
Sanford-Brown Institute, Garden City, NY 232
Sanford-Brown Institute, Houston, TX 305

Sanford-Brown Institute, Houston, TX 306
Sanford-Brown Institute, Jacksonville, FL 142
Sanford-Brown Institute, Landover, MD 182
Sanford-Brown Institute, Lauderdale Lakes, FL 142
Sanford-Brown Institute, New York, NY 232
Sanford-Brown Institute, Springfield, MA 187
Sanford-Brown Institute, Tampa, FL 142
Sanford-Brown Institute, Trevose, PA 270
Sanford-Brown Institute, White Plains, NY 232
Southwest Florida College, Tampa, FL 143
Spencerian College, Louisville, KY 174
Stevens-Henager College, Boise, ID 153
Stevens-Henager College, Logan, UT 311
Stevens-Henager College, Ogden, UT 311
Stevens-Henager College - Salt Lake City, Salt Lake City, UT 312
Virginia College at Austin, Austin, TX 307
Virginia College at Birmingham, Birmingham, AL 72
Virginia College at Jackson, Jackson, MS 200
Virginia College at Mobile, Mobile, AL 73
Virginia College at Pensacola, Pensacola, FL 144
Western School of Health and Business Careers, Monroeville, PA 273
Western School of Health and Business Careers, Pittsburgh, PA 273
Wright Business School, Oklahoma City, OK 249
Wright Business School, Overland Park, KS 170
Wright Business School, Tulsa, OK 249

SURVEY TECHNOLOGY/SURVEYING
Westwood College - Denver North, Denver, CO 118

SYSTEM ADMINISTRATION/ADMINISTRATOR
Academy College, Minneapolis, MN 192
Academy of Medical Arts and Business, Harrisburg, PA 252
American Commercial College, Abilene, TX 292
American Commercial College, Lubbock, TX 293
American Commercial College, Odessa, TX 293
American Commercial College, San Angelo, TX 293
American Commercial College, Shreveport, LA 175
Berks Technical Institute, Wyomissing, PA 253
Briarcliffe College, Bethpage, NY 226
Briarcliffe College, Patchogue, NY 226
Brown College, Mendota Heights, MN 193
Bryan College, Springfield, MO 201
Bryan College, Topeka, KS 169
Career Education Institute, Brockton, MA 184
Career Education Institute, Henderson, NV 210
Career Education Institute, Lincoln, RI 283
Career Education Institute, Lowell, MA 184
Career Education Institute, Marietta, GA 146
Career Education Institute, Norcross, GA 146

United Education Institute, El Monte, CA 106

United Education Institute, Huntington Park, Huntington Park, CA 107

United Education Institute, Ontario Campus, Ontario, CA 107

United Education Institute, Van Nuys Campus, Van Nuys, CA 108

Virginia College at Huntsville, Huntsville, AL 73

SYSTEM, NETWORKING, AND LAN/WAN MANAGEMENT/MANAGER

Academy of Medical Arts and Business, Harrisburg, PA 252

American Commercial College, Abilene, TX 292

American Commercial College, Lubbock, TX 293

American Commercial College, Odessa, TX 293

American Commercial College, San Angelo, TX 293

American Commercial College, Shreveport, LA 175

Berkeley College, Paramus, NJ 214

Berkeley College, West Paterson, NJ 214

Berkeley College, Woodbridge, NJ 215

Berks Technical Institute, Wyomissing, PA 253

Blair College, Colorado Springs, CO 112

Bradford School, Columbus, OH 237

Bradford School, Pittsburgh, PA 254

Briarcliffe College, Bethpage, NY 226

Briarcliffe College, Patchogue, NY 226

Brooks College, Long Beach, CA 86

Brooks College, Sunnyvale, CA 86

Brown College, Mendota Heights, MN 193

Brown Mackie College, Lenexa Campus, Lenexa, KS 168

Bryan College, Springfield, MO 201

Bryan College, Topeka, KS 169

Capella University, Minneapolis, MN 194

Career Education Institute, Brockton, MA 184

Career Education Institute, Henderson, NV 210

Career Education Institute, Lincoln, RI 283

Career Education Institute, Lowell, MA 184

Career Education Institute, Marietta, GA 146

Career Education Institute, Norcross, GA 146

Career Institute of Health and Technology, Brooklyn, NY 227

Career Institute of Health and Technology, Garden City, NY 227

Career Institute of Health and Technology, Rego Park, NY 228

CHI Institute, Broomall, PA 256

CHI Institute, Southampton, PA 256

The Chubb Institute, Alpharetta, GA 147

The Chubb Institute, Arlington, VA 314

The Chubb Institute, Cherry Hill, NJ 215

The Chubb Institute, Chicago, IL 155

The Chubb Institute, Jersey City, NJ 216

The Chubb Institute, New York, NY 228

The Chubb Institute, North Brunswick, NJ 216

The Chubb Institute, Parsippany, NJ 216

The Chubb Institute, Springfield, PA 256

The Chubb Institute, Westbury, NY 228

The Cittone Institute, Edison, NJ 217

The Cittone Institute, Mount Laurel, NJ 217

The Cittone Institute, Paramus, NJ 217

The Cittone Institute, Philadelphia, PA 257

The Cittone Institute, Plymouth Meeting, PA 257

CollegeAmerica - Colorado Springs, Colorado Springs, CO 112

CollegeAmerica - Denver, Denver, CO 113

Collins College: A School of Design and Technology, Tempe, AZ 77

Computer Learning Network, Altoona, PA 258

Computer Learning Network, Mechanicsburg, PA 258

Coyne American Institute, Chicago, IL 155

Coyne American Institute, Chicago, IL 156

Dover Business College, Paramus, NJ 218

ECPI College of Technology, Charlotte, NC 234

ECPI College of Technology, Greensboro, NC 235

ECPI College of Technology, Greenville, SC 285

ECPI College of Technology, Manassas, VA 315

ECPI College of Technology, Newport News, VA 315

ECPI College of Technology, North Charleston, SC 285

ECPI College of Technology, Raleigh, NC 235

ECPI College of Technology, Virginia Beach, VA 316

ECPI Technical College, Glen Allen, VA 316

ECPI Technical College, Richmond, VA 316

ECPI Technical College, Roanoke, VA 317

Empire College, Santa Rosa, CA 93

Florida Technical College, Auburndale, FL 129

Florida Technical College, DeLand, FL 130

Florida Technical College, Jacksonville, FL 130

Florida Technical College, Orlando, FL 130

Gibbs College - Cranston, Cranston, RI 283

Herzing College, Atlanta, GA 148

Herzing College, Birmingham, AL 70

Herzing College, Kenner, LA 178

Herzing College, Madison, WI 330

Herzing College, Minneapolis, MN 195

Herzing College, Winter Park, FL 131

ICM School of Business & Medical Careers, Pittsburgh, PA 263

International Academy of Design & Technology, Chicago, IL 157

International Academy of Design & Technology, Orlando, FL 132

International Academy of Design & Technology, Pittsburgh, PA 264

International Academy of Design & Technology, Tampa, FL 132

TAXATION

TEACHER ASSISTANT/AIDE

TEACHER EDUCATION AND PROFESSIONAL DEVELOPMENT, SPECIFIC LEVELS AND METHODS, OTHER

McCann School of Business, Sunbury, PA 267
National American University, Albuquerque, NM 224
National American University, Brooklyn Center, MN 197
National American University, Colorado Springs, CO 115
National American University, Denver, CO 116
National American University, Ellsworth AFB, SD 286
National American University, Kansas City, MO 204
National American University, Minneapolis, MN 197
National American University, Overland Park, KS 169
National American University, Rapid City, SD 286
National American University, Rio Rancho, NM 224
National American University, Roseville, MN 197
Southwest Florida College, Tampa, FL 143

TECHNOLOGY MANAGEMENT

Advanced Career Training, Atlanta, GA 144
Advanced Career Training, Jacksonville, FL 121
Advanced Career Training, Riverdale, GA 145
Antonelli College, Cincinnati, OH 237
Antonelli College, Hattiesburg, MS 199
Antonelli College, Jackson, MS 200
Capella University, Minneapolis, MN 194
Cardean University, Chicago, IL 154
Coleman College, La Mesa, CA 92
Coleman College, San Marcos, CA 93
Colorado Technical University Sioux Falls Campus, Sioux Falls, SD 286
Colorado Technical University, Colorado Springs, CO 113
Fountainhead College of Technology, Knoxville, TN 288
Herzing College, Atlanta, GA 148
Herzing College, Birmingham, AL 70
Herzing College, Kenner, LA 178
Herzing College, Madison, WI 330
Herzing College, Minneapolis, MN 195
Herzing College, Winter Park, FL 131
ITT Technical Institute, Albany, NY 230
ITT Technical Institute, Albuquerque, NM 223
ITT Technical Institute, Anaheim, CA 96
ITT Technical Institute, Arlington, TX 299
ITT Technical Institute, Arnold, MO 202
ITT Technical Institute, Austin, TX 299
ITT Technical Institute, Bessemer, AL 71
ITT Technical Institute, Boise, ID 153
ITT Technical Institute, Bothell, WA 327
ITT Technical Institute, Burr Ridge, IL 157
ITT Technical Institute, Canton, MI 189
ITT Technical Institute, Chantilly, VA 317
ITT Technical Institute, Dayton, OH 240
ITT Technical Institute, Duluth, GA 149
ITT Technical Institute, Earth City, MO 202
ITT Technical Institute, Eden Prairie, MN 195
ITT Technical Institute, Fort Lauderdale, FL 133
ITT Technical Institute, Fort Wayne, IN 165

ITT Technical Institute, Getzville, NY 230
ITT Technical Institute, Grand Rapids, MI 189
ITT Technical Institute, Green Bay, WI 331
ITT Technical Institute, Greenfield, WI 331
ITT Technical Institute, Greenville, SC 285
ITT Technical Institute, Henderson, NV 211
ITT Technical Institute, Hilliard, OH 240
ITT Technical Institute, Houston, TX 299
ITT Technical Institute, Houston, TX 300
ITT Technical Institute, Indianapolis, IN 165
ITT Technical Institute, Jacksonville, FL 133
ITT Technical Institute, Kansas City, MO 203
ITT Technical Institute, Kennesaw, GA 149
ITT Technical Institute, King of Prussia, PA 264
ITT Technical Institute, Knoxville, TN 289
ITT Technical Institute, Lake Mary, FL 133
ITT Technical Institute, Lathrop, CA 96
ITT Technical Institute, Little Rock, AR 82
ITT Technical Institute, Liverpool, NY 230
ITT Technical Institute, Louisville, KY 171
ITT Technical Institute, Matteson, IL 158
ITT Technical Institute, Mechanicsburg, PA 264
ITT Technical Institute, Memphis, TN 289
ITT Technical Institute, Miami, FL 133
ITT Technical Institute, Monroeville, PA 264
ITT Technical Institute, Mount Prospect, IL 158
ITT Technical Institute, Murray, UT 310
ITT Technical Institute, Nashville, TN 289
ITT Technical Institute, Newburgh, IN 166
ITT Technical Institute, Norfolk, VA 318
ITT Technical Institute, Norwood, MA 186
ITT Technical Institute, Norwood, OH 240
ITT Technical Institute, Omaha, NE 209
ITT Technical Institute, Owings Mills, MD 181
ITT Technical Institute, Oxnard, CA 97
ITT Technical Institute, Pittsburg, PA 264
ITT Technical Institute, Portland, OR 250
ITT Technical Institute, Rancho Cordova, CA 97
ITT Technical Institute, Richardson, TX 300
ITT Technical Institute, Richmond, VA 318
ITT Technical Institute, Saint Rose, LA 179
ITT Technical Institute, San Antonio, TX 300
ITT Technical Institute, San Bernardino, CA 97
ITT Technical Institute, San Diego, CA 97
ITT Technical Institute, Seattle, WA 327
ITT Technical Institute, Spokane, WA 328
ITT Technical Institute, Springfield, VA 318
ITT Technical Institute, Strongsville, OH 241
ITT Technical Institute, Sylmar, CA 98
ITT Technical Institute, Tampa, FL 134
ITT Technical Institute, Tempe, AZ 79
ITT Technical Institute, Thornton, CO 115
ITT Technical Institute, Torrance, CA 98

ITT Technical Institute, Troy, MI 190
ITT Technical Institute, Tucson, AZ 79
ITT Technical Institute, Tulsa, OK 247
ITT Technical Institute, Warrensville Heights, OH 241
ITT Technical Institute, West Covina, CA 98
ITT Technical Institute, Woburn, MA 186
ITT Technical Institute, Youngstown, OH 241
Missouri Tech, St. Louis, MO 204
Peirce College, Philadelphia, PA 268
South University, Columbia, SC 286
South University, Montgomery, AL 71
South University, Savannah, GA 151
South University, West Palm Beach, FL 142
Southwest Florida College, Tampa, FL 143
Stratford University, Falls Church , VA 322
Stratford University, Woodbridge, VA 322
Westwood College - Chicago O'Hare Airport, Chicago, IL 161
Westwood College - Anaheim, Anaheim, CA 109
Westwood College - Chicago River Oaks, Calumet City, IL 161
Westwood College - Denver North, Denver, CO 118
Westwood College - Denver South, Denver, CO 118
Westwood College - Long Beach, Torrance, CA 110
Westwood College - Los Angeles, Inglewood, CA 110
Westwood College - Los Angeles, Los Angeles, CA 110

TELECOMMUNICATIONS

Advanced Training Associates, El Cajon, CA 84
Briarcliffe College, Bethpage, NY 226
Briarcliffe College, Patchogue, NY 226
CHI Institute, Broomall, PA 256
CHI Institute, Southampton, PA 256
CollegeAmerica - Denver, Denver, CO 113
ECPI College of Technology, Charlotte, NC 234
ECPI College of Technology, Greensboro, NC 235
ECPI College of Technology, Greenville, SC 285
ECPI College of Technology, Manassas, VA 315
ECPI College of Technology, Newport News, VA 315
ECPI College of Technology, North Charleston, SC 285
ECPI College of Technology, Raleigh, NC 235
ECPI College of Technology, Virginia Beach, VA 316
ECPI Technical College, Glen Allen, VA 316
ECPI Technical College, Richmond, VA 316
ECPI Technical College, Roanoke, VA 317
Herzing College, Atlanta, GA 148
Herzing College, Birmingham, AL 70
Herzing College, Kenner, LA 178
Herzing College, Madison, WI 330
Herzing College, Minneapolis, MN 195
Herzing College, Winter Park, FL 131
ITI Technical College, Baton Rouge, LA 178
Missouri Tech, St. Louis, MO 204

Pinnacle Career Institute, Kansas City, MO 204
Pinnacle Career Institute, Lawrence, KS 169
Stevens-Henager College, Boise, ID 153
Stevens-Henager College, Logan, UT 311
Stevens-Henager College, Ogden, UT 311
Stevens-Henager College - Salt Lake City, Salt Lake City, UT 312
Stratford University, Falls Church , VA 322
Stratford University, Woodbridge, VA 322
TESST College of Technology, Alexandria, VA 323
TESST College of Technology, Baltimore, MD 182
TESST College of Technology, Beltsville, MD 183
TESST College of Technology, Towson, MD 183
Western Technical College, El Paso, TX 307
Western Technical Institute, El Paso, TX 308
York Technical Institute, Lancaster, PA 274
York Technical Institute, York, PA 274

TELECOMMUNICATIONS TECHNOLOGY/TECHNICIAN

ATI Career Training Center, Dallas, TX 294
ATI Career Training Center, Fort Lauderdale, FL 122
ATI Career Training Center, Miami, FL 123
ATI Career Training Center, North Richland Hills, TX 295
ATI Career Training Center, Oakland Park, FL 123
Briarcliffe College, Bethpage, NY 226
Briarcliffe College, Patchogue, NY 226
CHI Institute, Broomall, PA 256
CHI Institute, Southampton, PA 256
ECPI College of Technology, Charlotte, NC 234
ECPI College of Technology, Greensboro, NC 235
ECPI College of Technology, Greenville, SC 285
ECPI College of Technology, Manassas, VA 315
ECPI College of Technology, Newport News, VA 315
ECPI College of Technology, North Charleston, SC 285
ECPI College of Technology, Raleigh, NC 235
ECPI College of Technology, Virginia Beach, VA 316
ECPI Technical College, Glen Allen, VA 316
ECPI Technical College, Richmond, VA 316
ECPI Technical College, Roanoke, VA 317
Herzing College, Atlanta, GA 148
Herzing College, Birmingham, AL 70
Herzing College, Kenner, LA 178
Herzing College, Madison, WI 330
Herzing College, Minneapolis, MN 195
Herzing College, Winter Park, FL 131
High-Tech Institute, Irving, TX 298
High-Tech Institute, Kansas City, MO 202
High-Tech Institute, Las Vegas, NV 210
High-Tech Institute, Marietta, GA 149
High-Tech Institute, Memphis, TN 288
High-Tech Institute, Nashville, TN 288

High-Tech Institute, Orlando, FL 132
High-Tech Institute, Phoenix, AZ 78
High-Tech Institute, Sacramento, CA 96
High-Tech Institute, St. Louis Park, MN 195
ITI Technical College, Baton Rouge, LA 178
Missouri Tech, St. Louis, MO 204
Savannah River College, Augusta, GA 151
Stratford University, Falls Church , VA 322
Stratford University, Woodbridge, VA 322
Technical Career Institute, New York, NY 233
Virginia College at Birmingham, Birmingham, AL 72
Western Technical College, El Paso, TX 307

TOOL AND DIE TECHNOLOGY/ TECHNICIAN

Caguas Institute of Mechanical Technology, Caguas, PR 276

TOURISM AND TRAVEL SERVICES MANAGEMENT

Andover College, Portland, ME 180
Bay State College, Boston, MA 183
Bradford School, Columbus, OH 237
Bradford School, Pittsburgh, PA 254
Bryan College, Springfield, MO 201
Bryan College, Topeka, KS 169
Caliber Training Institute, New York, NY 227
Career Academy, Anchorage, AK 73
Empire College, Santa Rosa, CA 93
Erie Business Center South, New Castle, PA 262
Erie Business Center, Main, Erie, PA 261
Gulf Coast College, Tampa, FL 131
Hamilton College, Cedar Rapids, IA 167
Huertas Junior College, Caguas, PR 277
ICM School of Business & Medical Careers, Pittsburgh, PA 263
ICPR Junior College - Hato Rey Campus, San Juan, PR 278
ICPR Junior College - Mayaguez Campus, Mayaguez, PR 279
ICPR Junior College-Arecibo Campus, Arecibo, PR 278
Instituto Banca y Comercio, Caguas, PR 279
Instituto Banca y Comercio, Cayey, PR 279
Instituto Banca y Comercio, Fajardo, PR 279
Instituto Banca y Comercio, Guayama, PR 280
Instituto Banca y Comercio, Manati, PR 280
Instituto Banca y Comercio, Mayaguez, PR 280
Instituto Banca y Comercio, Ponce, PR 280
Instituto de Banca y Comercio, San Juan, PR 281
International Business College, El Paso, TX 298
International Business College, El Paso, TX 299
International Business College, Fort Wayne, IN 165
International Business College, Indianapolis, IN 165
Kaplan University, Davenport, IA 168

Laurel Business Institute, Uniontown, PA 265
Lehigh Valley College, Center Valley, PA 266
Mildred Elley, Pittsfield, MA 186
Minneapolis Business College, Roseville, MN 196
Mountain West College, West Valley City, UT 310
National College of Business & Technology, Bayamon, PR 282
National College of Business & Technology, Bluefield, VA 320
National College of Business & Technology, Bristol, TN 290
National College of Business & Technology, Charlottes- ville, VA 320
National College of Business & Technology, Danville, KY 172
National College of Business & Technology, Danville, VA 320
National College of Business & Technology, Florence, KY 172
National College of Business & Technology, Harrison- burg, VA 321
National College of Business & Technology, Knoxville, TN 291
National College of Business & Technology, Lexington, KY 173
National College of Business & Technology, Louisville, KY 173
National College of Business & Technology, Lynchburg, VA 321
National College of Business & Technology, Martinsville, VA 321
National College of Business & Technology, Nashville, TN 291
National College of Business & Technology, Pikeville, KY 173
National College of Business & Technology, Richmond, KY 173
National College of Business & Technology, Rio Grande, PR 282
National College of Business & Technology, Salem, VA 321
National College of Business and Technology, Arecibo, PR 282
National College of Business and Technology, Cincinnati, OH 241
National College of Business and Technology, Indianapo- lis, IN 166
National College of Business and Technology, Kettering, OH 242
Pittsburgh Technical Institute, Oakdale, PA 269
Rasmussen College Minnetonka, Minnetonka, MN 199
RETS Tech Center, Centerville, OH 243
San Joaquin Valley College, Bakersfield, CA 103

San Joaquin Valley College, Fresno, CA 103
San Joaquin Valley College, Modesto, CA 104
San Joaquin Valley College, Rancho Cucamonga, CA 104
San Joaquin Valley College, Visalia, CA 104
Sullivan University, Lexington, KY 174
Sullivan University, Louisville, KY 175
Western Business College, Portland, OR 251
Western Business College, Vancouver, WA 328
York Technical Institute, Lancaster, PA 274
York Technical Institute, York, PA 274
Wood Tobe-Coburn School, New York, NY 233

TOURISM AND TRAVEL SERVICES MARKETING OPERATIONS

Mildred Elley School, Latham, NY 232

TRAFFIC, CUSTOMS, AND TRANSPORTATION CLERK/ TECHNICIAN

Career Centers of Texas, El Paso, TX 295

TRANSPORTATION TECHNOLOGIES

Lebanon County Career School, Lebanon, PA 265
New England Institute of Technology, Warwick, RI 284
Sage Technical Services, Billings, MT 208
Sage Technical Services, Caldwell, ID 153
Sage Technical Services, Casper, WY 331
Sage Technical Services, Grand Junction, CO 117
Sage Technical Services, Henderson, CO 118
Sage Technical Services, Post Falls, ID 153
Technical Career Institute, New York, NY 233

TRANSPORTATION/ TRANSPORTATION MANAGEMENT

Academy Pacific Travel College, Los Angeles, CA 84

TRUCK AND BUS DRIVER/ COMMERCIAL VEHICLE OPERATION

Advanced Technology Institute, Virginia Beach, VA 314
American Institute of Technology, North Las Vegas, NV 209
American Institute of Technology, Phoenix, AZ 74
Lebanon County Career School, Lebanon, PA 265
New Castle School of Trades, Pulaski, PA 268
Sage Technical Services, Billings, MT 208
Sage Technical Services, Caldwell, ID 153
Sage Technical Services, Casper, WY 331
Sage Technical Services, Grand Junction, CO 117
Sage Technical Services, Henderson, CO 118
Sage Technical Services, Post Falls, ID 153
TDDS, Inc., Lake Milton, OH 245

UPHOLSTERY/UPHOLSTERER

WyoTech, Bedford, MA 187
WyoTech, Blairsville, PA 274
WyoTech, Fremont, CA 111
WyoTech, Laramie, WY 332
WyoTech, Oakland, CA 111
WyoTech, West Sacramento, CA 111

VETERINARY TECHNOLOGY

Bel-Rea Institute of Animal Technology, Denver, CO 112
Bradford School, Columbus, OH 237
Bradford School, Pittsburgh, PA 254
Duluth Business University, Duluth, MN 194
Globe College, Oakdale, MN 194
Minnesota School of Business-Richfield, Richfield, MN 196
Minnesota School of Business - Brooklyn Center, Brooklyn Center, MN 196
National American University, Albuquerque, NM 224
National American University, Brooklyn Center, MN 197
National American University, Colorado Springs, CO 115
National American University, Denver, CO 116
National American University, Ellsworth AFB, SD 286
National American University, Kansas City, MO 204
National American University, Minneapolis, MN 197
National American University, Overland Park, KS 169
National American University, Rapid City, SD 286
National American University, Rio Rancho, NM 224
National American University, Roseville, MN 197
Oklahoma Health Academy, Oklahoma City, OK 247
Oklahoma Health Academy, Tulsa, OK 247
Utah Career College, West Jordan, UT 312
Vatterott College, Broadview Heights, OH 245
Vatterott College, Des Moines, IA 168
Vatterott College, Joplin, MO 206
Vatterott College, Kansas City, MO 207
Vatterott College, Memphis, TN 292
Vatterott College, OÆFallon , MO 207
Vatterott College, Oklahoma City, OK 248
Vatterott College, Omaha, NE 209
Vatterott College, Quincy, IL 160
Vatterott College, Springfield, MO 208
Vatterott College, St. Ann, MO 207
Vatterott College, St. Joseph, MO 207
Vatterott College, St. Louis, MO 208
Vatterott College, Tulsa, OK 249
Vatterott College, Wichita, KS 169
Western Career College, Pleasant Hill, CA 108
Western Career College, Sacramento, CA 108
Western Career College, San Leandro, CA 109
Western School of Health and Business Careers, Monroeville, PA 273
Western School of Health and Business Careers, Pittsburgh, PA 273

VETERINARY/ANIMAL HEALTH TECHNOLOGY/TECHNICIAN AND VETERINARY ASSISTANT

Apollo College, Albuquerque, NM 223
Apollo College, Boise, ID 153
Apollo College-Phoenix, Inc., Phoenix, AZ 74
Apollo College, Portland, OR 249
Apollo College, Spokane, WA 324
Apollo College-Tri-City, Inc., Mesa, AZ 75
Apollo College-Tucson, Inc., Tucson, AZ 75
Bel-Rea Institute of Animal Technology, Denver, CO 112
Community Care College, Tulsa, OK 246
Duluth Business University, Duluth, MN 194
Great Lakes Institute of Technology, Erie, PA 262
National American University, Albuquerque, NM 224
National American University, Brooklyn Center, MN 197
National American University, Colorado Springs, CO 115
National American University, Denver, CO 116
National American University, Ellsworth AFB, SD 286
National American University, Kansas City, MO 204
National American University, Minneapolis, MN 197
National American University, Overland Park, KS 169
National American University, Rapid City, SD 286
National American University, Rio Rancho, NM 224
National American University, Roseville, MN 197
Pima Medical Institute, Albuquerque, NM 224
Pima Medical Institute, Chula Vista, CA 101
Pima Medical Institute, Colorado Springs, CO 116
Pima Medical Institute, Denver, CO 117
Pima Medical Institute, Las Vegas, NV 213
Pima Medical Institute, Mesa, AZ 80
Pima Medical Institute, Renton, WA 328
Pima Medical Institute, Seattle, WA 328
Pima Medical Institute, Tucson, AZ 81
Western Career College, Pleasant Hill, CA 108
Western Career College, Sacramento, CA 108
Western Career College, San Leandro, CA 109

VISUAL AND PERFORMING ARTS, GENERAL

Academy of Art University, San Francisco, CA 83
The Art Institute of Fort Lauderdale, Fort Lauderdale, FL 122
Bradley Academy for the Visual Arts, York, PA 254
Briarcliffe College, Bethpage, NY 226
Briarcliffe College, Patchogue, NY 226
Gibbs College, Boston, MA 185
Gibbs College, Livingston, NJ 218
Gibbs College, Norwalk, CT 119
Gibbs School, Vienna, VA 317
The Illinois Institute of Art - Chicago, Chicago, IL 156
Miami International University of Art & Design, Miami, FL 138

WEB PAGE, DIGITAL/MULTIMEDIA AND INFORMATION RESOURCES DESIGN

Academy College, Minneapolis, MN 192
Academy of Medical Arts and Business, Harrisburg, PA 252
American InterContinental University, Atlanta, GA 145
American InterContinental University, Houston, TX 293
American InterContinental University, Los Angeles, CA 85
American InterContinental University, San Antonio, TX 293
American InterContinental University, Weston, FL 121
The Art Institute of Atlanta, Atlanta, GA 145
The Art Institute of California - Los Angeles, Santa Monica, CA 85
The Art Institute of California - Orange County, Santa Ana, CA 86
The Art Institute of California - San Diego, San Diego, CA 86
The Art Institute of California - San Francisco, San Francisco, CA 86
The Art Institute of Charlotte, Charlotte, NC 233
The Art Institute of Colorado, Denver, CO 111
The Art Institute of Dallas, Dallas, TX 294
The Art Institute of Fort Lauderdale, Fort Lauderdale, FL 122
The Art Institute of Houston, Houston, TX 294
The Art Institute of Las Vegas, Henderson, NV 209
The Art Institute of New York City, New York, NY 225
The Art Institute of Philadelphia, Philadelphia, PA 252
The Art Institute of Phoenix, Phoenix, AZ 76
The Art Institute of Pittsburgh, Pittsburgh, PA 252
The Art Institute of Portland, Portland, OR 249
The Art Institute of Seattle, Seattle, WA 324
The Art Institute of Washington, Arlington, VA 314
The Art Institutes International Minnesota, Minneapolis, MN 193
Berkeley College, Paramus, NJ 214
Berkeley College, West Paterson, NJ 214
Berkeley College, Woodbridge, NJ 215
Berks Technical Institute, Wyomissing, PA 253
Bradford School, Columbus, OH 237
Bradford School, Pittsburgh, PA 254
Bradley Academy for the Visual Arts, York, PA 254
Briarcliffe College, Bethpage, NY 226
Briarcliffe College, Patchogue, NY 226
Brooks College, Long Beach, CA 86
Brooks College, Sunnyvale, CA 86
Brookstone College of Business, Charlotte, NC 234
Brookstone College of Business, Greensboro, NC 234
Brown College, Mendota Heights, MN 193
Business Institute of Pennsylvania, Meadville, PA 255
Business Institute of Pennsylvania, Sharon, PA 255
California Design College, Los Angeles, CA 91
Capella University, Minneapolis, MN 194

Boldface type indicates that the school is a participating institution in the *Imagine America* Scholarship Program

WEB/MULTIMEDIA MANAGEMENT AND WEBMASTER

Boldface type indicates that the school is a participating institution in the *Imagine America* Scholarship Program

WELDING TECHNOLOGY/WELDER

WORD PROCESSING

Boldface type indicates that the school is a participating institution in the *Imagine America* Scholarship Program

NOTES

NOTES

NOTES